I'd like to thank my wife, Ali, and my four children, Kyle, Cameron, Gillian, and Curtis, for their love and support. While they might not have written any of the words directly, they certainly helped create an environment where I could get my ideas out my head and into the computer.

—Bruce Johnson

CREDITS

ACQUISITIONS EDITOR
Mary James

PROJECT EDITOR
Kelly Talbot

TECHNICAL EDITORS
Joe Bennett
Andrew Moore

PRODUCTION EDITOR
Christine Mugnolo

COPY EDITOR
San Dee Phillips

EDITORIAL MANAGER
Mary Beth Wakefield

FREELANCER EDITORIAL MANAGER
Rosemarie Graham

ASSOCIATE DIRECTOR OF MARKETING
David Mayhew

MARKETING MANAGER
Ashley Zurcher

BUSINESS MANAGER
Amy Knies

PRODUCTION MANAGER
Tim Tate

VICE PRESIDENT AND EXECUTIVE GROUP PUBLISHER
Richard Swadley

VICE PRESIDENT AND EXECUTIVE PUBLISHER
Neil Edde

ASSOCIATE PUBLISHER
Jim Minatel

PROJECT COORDINATOR, COVER
Katie Crocker

PROOFREADERS
Jennifer Bennett, Word One New York
Scott Klemp, Word One New York
James Saturnio, Word One New York

INDEXER
Johnna VanHoose Dinse

COVER DESIGNER
LeAndra Young

COVER IMAGE
© Eric Delmar / iStockPhoto

ABOUT THE AUTHOR

BRUCE JOHNSON is a partner at ObjectSharp Consulting and a 30-year veteran of the computer industry. The first third of his career was spent doing "real work," otherwise known as coding in the UNIX world. But for almost 20 years, he has been working on projects that are at the leading edge of Windows technology, from C++ through Visual Basic to C#, and from thick client applications to websites to services.

As well as having fun with building systems, Bruce has spoken hundreds of times at conferences and user groups throughout North America. He has been a Microsoft Certified Trainer (MCT) for the past three years and he is a co-president of the Metro Toronto .NET User Group. He has also written columns and articles for numerous magazines. While the quantity of the posts on his blog (`http://blogs.objectsharp.com/author/bruce.aspx`) has decreased recently, the activity on his Twitter account (`http://www.twitter.com/lacanuck`) has shown a corresponding increase. For all of this activity (or, perhaps, in spite of it), Bruce has been privileged to be recognized as a Microsoft MVP for the past six years.

ACKNOWLEDGMENTS

TO THE OUTSIDE, it might look like the writing of a book is an individual effort. Having gone through this act of creation a number of times, I can tell you that nothing is further from the truth. Yes, there is a lot of effort on the part of the author (and the feeling of joy you get as you hand in your last rewrite is quite palpable). But I can also tell you that without the rarely acknowledged efforts of the others involved in the editorial process, the book would never have made it to completion. And if you, as the reader, take something useful from this book, odds are that my editor, my technical reviewer, and the project editor are the reason why.

I would especially like to thank everyone at Wrox who has helped me through this process. In particular, thanks go out to Kelly Talbot, whose patience and attention to detail are quite impressive. Thanks also go to Andrew Moore and Joe Bennett, who did a great job making sure that the technical details of the book were accurate. Finally, thanks to San Dee Phillips, who had the unenviable chore of ensuring that I wasn't writing in the passive voice and fixed it when I stopped writing so well. The efforts of all of these individuals are what make the book possible and, hopefully, a success. Thanks also to Mary James, who was kind enough to take a chance on my ability to write.

Lastly, I would like to thank all of my associates at ObjectSharp and the people at Microsoft who, although they might not have realized it, were keeping the writing process going by answering any questions I had.

—BRUCE JOHNSON

CONTENTS

PART III: DIGGING DEEPER

PART VI: DATA

PART X: BUILD AND DEPLOYMENT

INTRODUCTION

THROUGHOUT ITS HISTORY, Visual Studio has incorporated the latest advances in Microsoft's premier programming languages (Visual Basic and C#) and this version is no different. But alongside support for language features, is also continuing support for developers. In theory, it is possible to create any .NET application using tools as simple as Notepad and a command-line window. But the typical developer would never think to do so. The tools and utilities that come with Visual Studio do more to increase the productivity of developers than any other single piece of software currently available. Visual Studio 2012 is no different from previous versions in this respect. It includes a host of improvements and new features that are aimed at making the life of a developer easier.

Visual Studio 2012 is an enormous product no matter which way you look at it. It can be intimidating to newcomers and difficult for even experienced .NET developers to find what they need. And that's where this book comes in. *Professional Visual Studio 2012* looks at every major aspect of this developer tool, showing you how to harness each feature and offering advice about how best to utilize the various components effectively. It shows you the building blocks that make up Visual Studio 2012, breaking the user interface down into manageable chunks for you to understand. It then expands on each of these components with additional details about exactly how they work both in isolation and in conjunction with other parts of Visual Studio 2012, along with tools that are not included in the out-of-the-box product, to make your development efforts even more efficient.

WHO THIS BOOK IS FOR

Professional Visual Studio 2012 is for developers who are new to Visual Studio as well as those programmers who have some experience but want to learn about features they may have previously overlooked.

Even if you are familiar with the way previous versions of Visual Studio worked, you may want to at least skim over Part I. These chapters deal with the basic constructs that make up the user interface. In the past, the basic interface didn't change much from version to version. But as soon as you launch Visual Studio 2012 for the first time, you'll notice that the user interface has gone through some significant changes. While you can get by without Part I, some of the changes in Visual Studio 2012 can make you a more efficient developer. And, after all, that's what you're looking to get out of this book.

If you're just starting out, you'll greatly benefit from the first part, where basic concepts are explained and you're introduced to the user interface and how to customize it to suit your own style.

WHAT THIS BOOK COVERS

Microsoft Visual Studio 2012 is arguably the most advanced integrated development environment (IDE) available for programmers today. It is based on a long history of programming languages and interfaces and has been influenced by many different variations on the theme of development environments.

With Visual Studio 2012, Microsoft took a chance (and received some pushback) for its decision to revamp the user interface. Existing developers will find it off-putting at first (although you do get used to it quickly and will rarely miss what is no longer visible by default). But newcomers to Visual Studio will find it much easier to work with. This book covers the breadth of Visual Studio 2012. Along the way, you will become more familiar and comfortable with the new interface.

Visual Studio 2012 comes in several versions: Express, Professional, Premium, and Ultimate. The majority of this book deals with the Professional Edition of Visual Studio 2012, but some parts utilize features found only in the Premium and Ultimate editions. If you haven't used these editions before, read through Chapters 54 to 57 for an overview of the features they offer over and above the Professional Edition.

HOW THIS BOOK IS STRUCTURED

This book's first section is dedicated to familiarizing you with the core aspects of Visual Studio 2012. Everything you need is contained in the first five chapters, from the IDE structure and layout to the various options and settings you can change to make the user interface synchronize with your own way of doing things.

From there, the remainder of the book is broken into 11 parts:

- **Getting Started:** In this part, you learn how to take control of your projects and how to organize them in ways that work with your own style.
- **Digging Deeper:** Though the many graphical components of Visual Studio that make a programmer's job easier are discussed in many places throughout this book, you often need help when you're in the process of actually writing code. This part deals with features that support the coding of applications such as IntelliSense, code refactoring, and creating and running unit tests The .NET Framework supports dynamic languages and strengthens feature parity between the two primary .NET languages, C# and VB. This part covers these languages, as well as looking at a range of features that will help you write better and more consistent code.
- **Rich Client Applications** and **Web Applications:** For support with building everything from Office add-ins to cloud applications, Visual Studio enables you to develop applications for a wide range of platforms. These two parts cover the application platforms that are supported within Visual Studio 2012, including ASP.NET and Office, WPF, Silverlight 5, and ASP.NET MVC. Also, Chapter 20 takes a look into the support provided for the new Windows Store applications.
- **Data:** A large proportion of applications use some form of data storage. Visual Studio 2012 and the .NET Framework include strong support for working with databases and other data sources. This part examines how to use DataSets, the Visual Database Tools, LINQ, Synchronization Services, and ADO.NET Entity Framework to build applications that work with data. It also shows you how you can then present this data using Reporting.
- **Application Services:** Through the course of building an application, you are likely to require access to services that may or may not reside within your organization. This part covers core technologies such as WCF, WF, Synchronization Services, and WCF RIA services that you can use to connect to these services.
- **Configuration and Resources:** The built-in support for configuration files allows you to adjust the way an application functions on the fly without having to rebuild it. Furthermore, resource files can be used to both access static data and easily localize an application into foreign languages and cultures. This part of the book shows how to use .NET configuration and resource files.
- **Debugging:** Application debugging is one of the more challenging tasks developers have to tackle, but correct use of the Visual Studio 2012 debugging features will help you analyze the state of the application and determine the cause of any bugs. This part examines the debugging support provided by the IDE.
- **Build and Deployment:** In addition to discussing how to build your solutions effectively and getting applications into the hands of your end users, this part also deals with the process of upgrading your projects from previous versions.

- **Customizing and Extending Visual Studio:** If the functionality found in the previous part isn't enough to help you in your coding efforts, Visual Studio 2012 is even more extensible. This part covers the automation model, how to write add-ins, and then how to use the Microsoft Extensibility Framework (MEF) to extend Visual Studio 2012.
- **Visual Studio Ultimate:** The final part of the book examines the additional features only available in the Premium and Ultimate versions of Visual Studio 2012. In addition, you'll also learn how the Team Foundation Server provides an essential tool for managing software projects.

Though this breakdown of the Visual Studio feature set provides the most logical and easily understood set of topics, you may need to look for specific functions that will aid you in a particular activity. To address this need, references to appropriate chapters are provided whenever a feature is covered in more detail elsewhere in the book.

WHAT YOU NEED TO USE THIS BOOK

To use this book effectively, you'll need only one additional item — Microsoft Visual Studio 2012 Professional Edition. With this software installed and the information found in this book, you'll be able to get a handle on how to use Visual Studio 2012 effectively in a very short period of time.

This book assumes that you are familiar with the traditional programming model, and it uses both the C# and Visual Basic (VB) languages to illustrate features within Visual Studio 2012. In addition, it is assumed that you can understand the code listings without an explanation of basic programming concepts in either language. If you're new to programming and want to learn Visual Basic, please take a look at *Beginning Visual Basic 2012* by Bryan Newsome. Similarly, if you are after a great book on C#, track down *Beginning Visual C# 2012*, written collaboratively by a host of authors.

Some chapters discuss additional products and tools that work in conjunction with Visual Studio. The following are all available to download either on a trial basis or for free:

- **Code Snippet Editor:** This is a third-party tool developed for creating code snippets in VB. The Snippet Editor tool is discussed in Chapter 8.
- **Sandcastle:** Using Sandcastle, you can generate comprehensive documentation for every member and class within your solutions from the XML comments in your code. XML comments and Sandcastle are discussed in Chapter 12.
- **SQL Server 2012:** The installation of Visual Studio 2012 includes an install of SQL Server 2012 Express, enabling you to build applications that use database files. However, for more comprehensive enterprise solutions, you can use SQL Server 2012 instead. Database connectivity is covered in Chapter 27.
- **Visual Studio 2012 Premium or Ultimate Edition:** These more advanced versions of Visual Studio introduce tools for other parts of the development process such as testing and design. They are discussed in Chapters 54–57.
- **Team Foundation Server:** The server product that provides application lifecycle management throughout Visual Studio 2012. This is covered in Chapter 57.
- **Windows 7 or Windows 8:** Visual Studio 2012 is compatible with Windows 7 and 8, and it can produce applications that run on Windows XP, Windows Vista, Windows 7, and Windows 8.

CONVENTIONS

To help you get the most from the text and keep track of what's happening, we've used a number of conventions throughout the book.

> **WARNING** *Boxes like this one hold important, not-to-be forgotten information that is directly relevant to the surrounding text.*

> **NOTE** *Notes, tips, hints, tricks, and asides to the current discussion are offset and placed in italics like this.*

As for styles in the text:

- We *highlight* new terms and important words when we introduce them.
- We show URLs and code within the text like so: `persistence.properties`.
- We present code in the following way:

```
We use a monofont type for code examples.

We use bold to emphasize code that is particularly important in the present context or to show
changes from a previous code snippet.
```

ERRATA

We make every effort to ensure that there are no errors in the text or in the code. However, no one is perfect, and mistakes do occur. If you find an error in one of our books, like a spelling mistake or faulty piece of code, we would be very grateful for your feedback. By sending in errata you may save another reader hours of frustration and at the same time you will be helping us provide even higher quality information.

To find the errata page for this book, go to `www.wrox.com` and locate the title using the Search box or one of the title lists. Then, on the Book Search Results page, click the Errata link. On this page you can view all errata that has been submitted for this book and posted by Wrox editors.

> **NOTE** *A complete book list including links to errata is also available at* `www.wrox.com/misc-pages/booklist.shtml`.

If you don't spot "your" error on the Errata page, click the Errata Form link and complete the form to send us the error you have found. We'll check the information and, if appropriate, post a message to the book's errata page and fix the problem in subsequent editions of the book.

P2P.WROX.COM

For author and peer discussion, join the P2P forums at `p2p.wrox.com`. The forums are a Web-based system for you to post messages relating to Wrox books and related technologies and interact with other readers and technology users. The forums offer a subscription feature to e-mail you topics of interest of your choosing when new posts are made to the forums. Wrox authors, editors, other industry experts, and your fellow readers are present on these forums.

At `http://p2p.wrox.com` you will find a number of different forums that will help you not only as you read this book, but also as you develop your own applications. To join the forums, just follow these steps:

1. Go to `p2p.wrox.com` and click the Register link.
2. Read the terms of use and click Agree.
3. Complete the required information to join as well as any optional information you wish to provide and click Submit.
4. You will receive an e-mail with information describing how to verify your account and complete the joining process.

> **NOTE** *You can read messages in the forums without joining P2P but in order to post your own messages, you must join.*

Once you join, you can post new messages and respond to messages other users post. You can read messages at any time on the Web. If you would like to have new messages from a particular forum e-mailed to you, click the Subscribe to this Forum icon by the forum name in the forum listing.

For more information about how to use the Wrox P2P, be sure to read the P2P FAQs for answers to questions about how the forum software works as well as many common questions specific to P2P and Wrox books. To read the FAQs, click the FAQ link on any P2P page.

PART I
Integrated Development Environment

1

A Quick Tour

WHAT'S IN THIS CHAPTER?

- Installing and getting started with Visual Studio 2012
- Creating and running your first application
- Debugging and deploying an application

Ever since software has been developed, there has been a need for tools to help write, compile, debug, and deploy applications. Microsoft Visual Studio 2012 is the next iteration in the continual evolution of a best-of-breed integrated development environment (IDE).

This chapter introduces the Visual Studio 2012 user experience and shows you how to work with the various menus, toolbars, and windows. It serves as a quick tour of the IDE, and as such it doesn't go into detail about what settings can be changed or how to go about customizing the layout because these topics are explored in the following chapters.

GETTING STARTED

With each iteration of the Visual Studio product, the installation process has been incrementally improved, meaning that you can get up and running with Visual Studio 2012 with minimal fuss. This section walks you through the installation process and getting started with the IDE.

Installing Visual Studio 2012

When you launch Visual Studio 2012 setup, you'll see the dialog in Figure 1-1 enabling you to specify the location for the installation. After you have read the licensing information (in great detail, of course), you can click the check box to accept the terms and

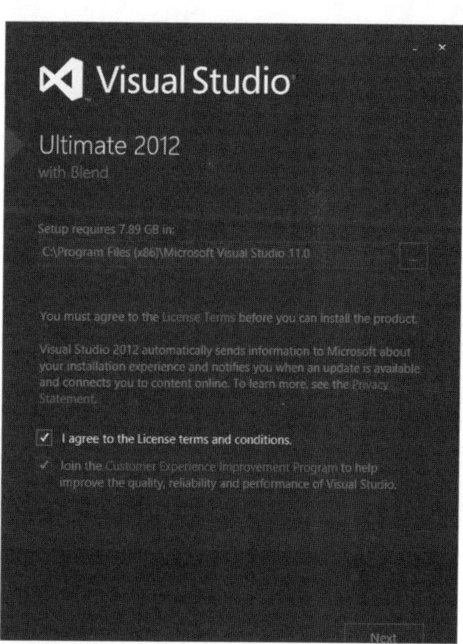

FIGURE 1-1

move to the next screen in the installation sequence. You'll also notice an option to join the Customer Experience Improvement program. If you do so, anonymous information about how you use the product will be sent to Microsoft occasionally. And just so you have a sense of how that information is used, realize that many of the user interface changes that you're about to see were determined based on this feedback.

Visual Studio 2012 naturally has a number of mandatory features. Because these features are built in, the installation process doesn't bother mentioning them. However, you can select from a number of optional features, as shown in Figure 1-2. Choose the features you believe you need (keeping in mind that you can always add or remove them later) and click Install to begin the process.

At this point, you'll see the updated progress dialog, as shown in Figure 1-3. Depending on which components you already have installed on your computer, you may be prompted to restart your computer midway through the installation process. When all the components have been successfully installed, a Setup Summary dialog indicates that there were no problems with the installation process.

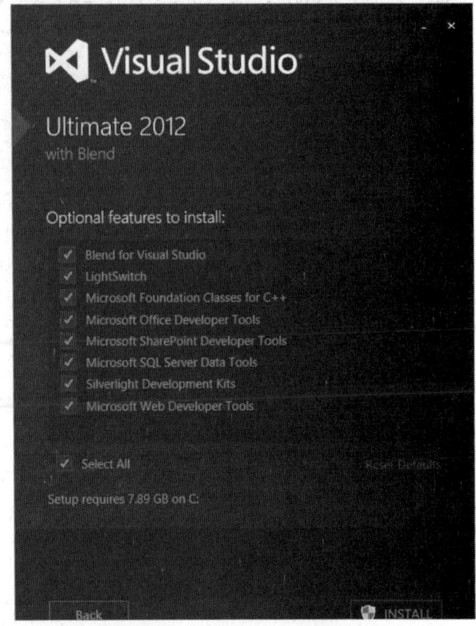

FIGURE 1-2

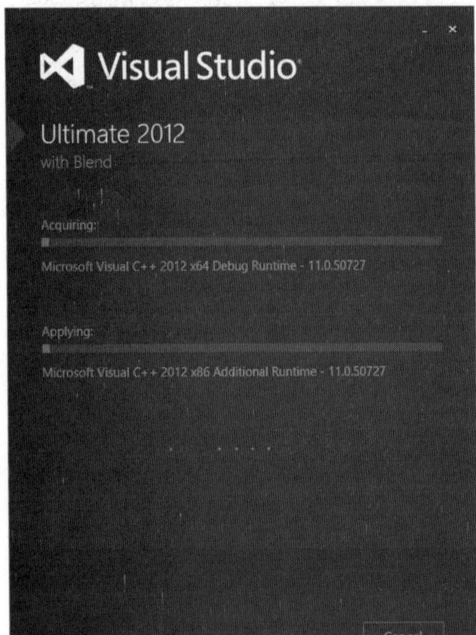

FIGURE 1-3

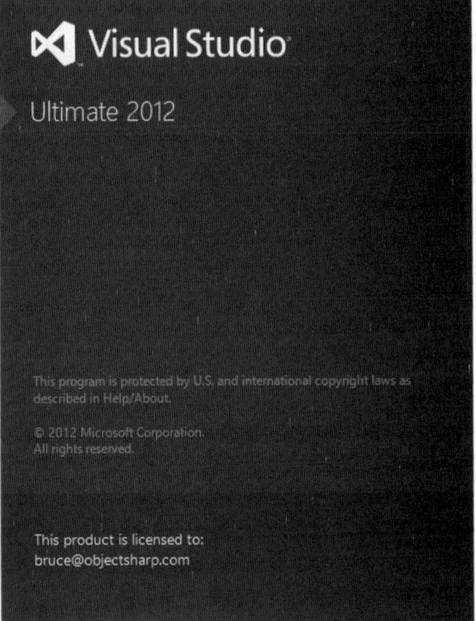

FIGURE 1-4

Running Visual Studio 2012

When you launch Visual Studio, the Microsoft Visual Studio 2012 splash screen appears. Like a lot of splash screens, it provides information about the version of the product and to whom it has been licensed, as shown in Figure 1-4.

> **NOTE** *An interesting fact about the splash screen is that although a large portion of Visual Studio uses WPF to display its content, the splash screen in Visual Studio 2012 is still done in native code so that it displays as soon as possible after you start Visual Studio. A significant amount of time went into hand-crafting the wave at the bottom of the splash screen, so make sure you marvel at it whenever you sit there patiently waiting for Visual Studio to load.*

The first time you run Visual Studio 2012, you'll see the splash screen only for a short period before you are prompted to select the default environment settings. It may seem unusual to ask those who haven't used a product before how they imagine themselves using it. Because Microsoft has consolidated a number of languages and technologies into a single IDE, that IDE must account for the subtle (and sometimes not so subtle) differences in the way developers work.

Take a moment to review the various options in this list, as shown in Figure 1-5. The differences between them as reflected in the IDE vary. You'll find that the environment settings affect the position and visibility of various windows, menus, toolbars, and even keyboard shortcuts. You can't see the differences while you're in this list (naturally). But if you select a particular option, such as General Development Settings, a description of the changes that will be applied appears to the right. Chapter 3, "Options and Customizations," covers how you can change your default environment settings at a later stage.

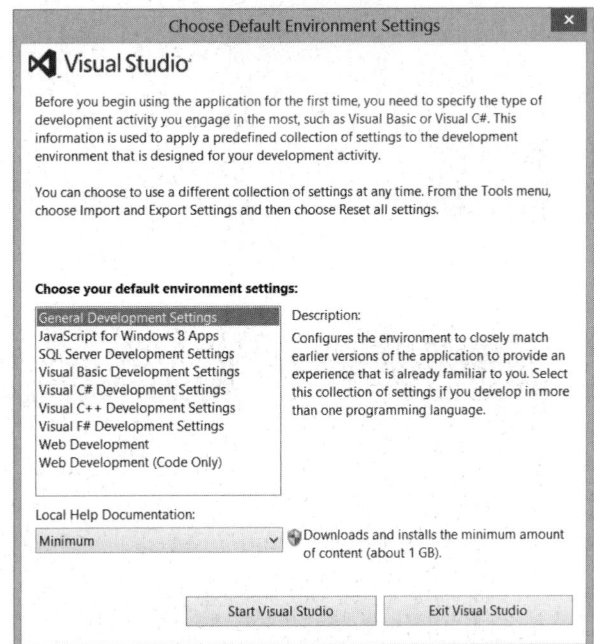

FIGURE 1-5

> **NOTE** *The name "Visual Basic Development Settings" makes it sound like it's a natural fit for Visual Basic .NET developers. However, it's not. These settings have been configured for VB6 developers and will infuriate Visual Basic .NET developers who are not familiar with VB6 because they will be used for different shortcut key mappings. Visual Basic .NET developers should use the general development settings because these use the standard keyboard mappings without being geared toward another development language.*

THE VISUAL STUDIO IDE

Depending on which set of environment settings you select, when you click the Start Visual Studio button, you will most likely see a dialog indicating that Visual Studio is configuring the development environment. When this process is complete, Visual Studio 2012 opens, ready for you to start working, as shown in Figure 1-6.

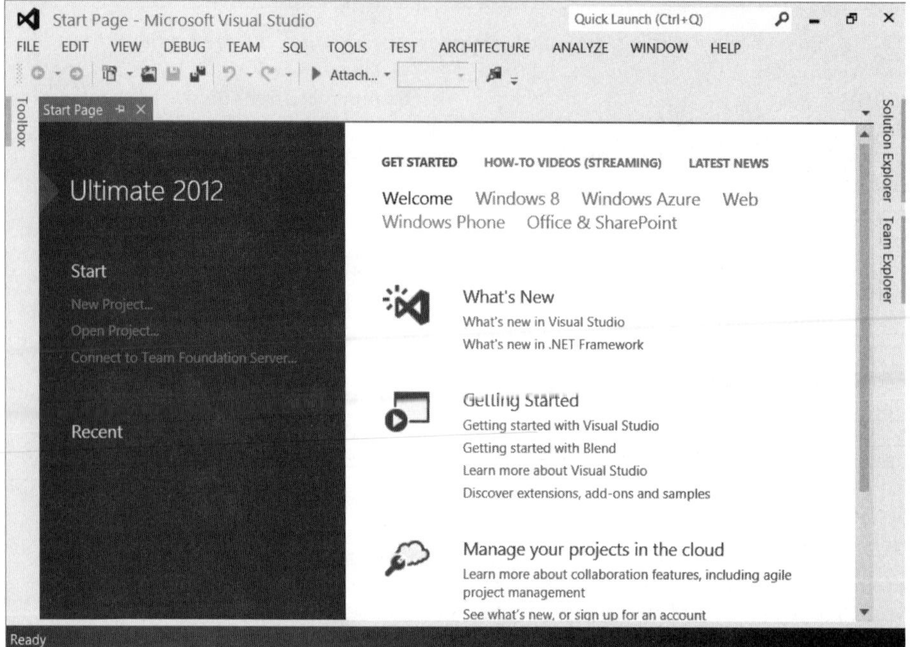

FIGURE 1-6

Regardless of the environment settings you select, you'll see the Start Page in the center of the screen. However, the contents of the Start Page and the surrounding toolbars and tool windows can vary.

> **NOTE** *If you click the Latest News, this opens a screen that enables you to set up an RSS feed containing news related to Visual Studio and .NET development. Clicking the button labeled Enable RSS Feed enables an RSS feed determined by the environment settings you specified. Each item displays with a title and summary, enabling you to click through to the full article. You can customize this feed by changing the Start Page News Channel property on the Environment ⇨ Startup node of the Options dialog, accessible via the Options item on the Tools menu.*

Before you launch into building your first application, you must take a step back to look at the components that make up the Visual Studio 2012 IDE. Menus and toolbars are positioned along the top of the environment, and a selection of subwindows, or panes, appears on the left, right, and bottom of the main window area. In the center is the main editor space. Whenever you open a code file, an XML document, a form, or some other file, it appears in this space for editing. With each file you open, a tab is created so that you can easily switch between opened files.

On either side of the editor space is a set of tool windows. These areas provide additional contextual information and functionality. For the general developer settings, the default layout includes the Solution Explorer and Class View on the right, and the Server Explorer and Toolbox on the left. The tool windows on the left are in their collapsed, or *unpinned*, state. If you click a tool window's title, it expands; it collapses again when it no longer has focus or you move the cursor to another area of the screen. When a tool window is expanded, you see a series of three icons at the top right of the window, similar to those shown in the left image of Figure 1-7.

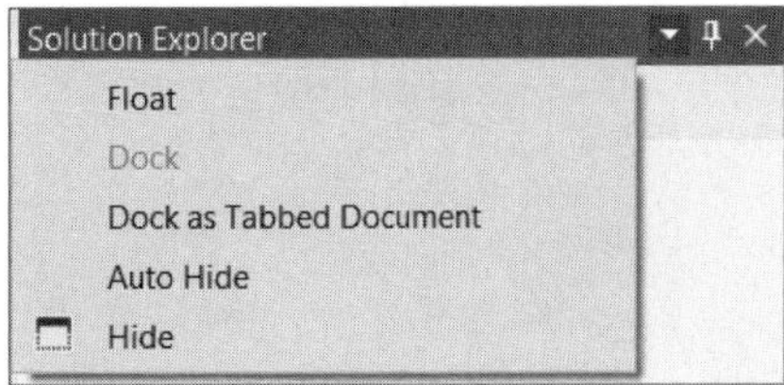

FIGURE 1-7

If you want the tool window to remain in its expanded, or *pinned*, state, you can click the middle icon, which looks like a pin. The pin rotates 90 degrees to indicate that the window is now pinned. Clicking the third icon, the X, closes the window. If later you want to reopen this or another tool window, you can select it from the View menu.

> **NOTE** *Some tool windows are not accessible via the View menu; for example, those having to do with debugging, such as threads and watch windows. In most cases these windows are available via an alternative menu item; for the debugging windows, it is the Debug menu.*

The right image in Figure 1-7 shows the context menu that appears when the first icon, the down arrow, is clicked. Each item in this list represents a different way to arrange the tool window. As you would imagine, the Float option enables the tool window to be placed anywhere on the screen, independent of the main IDE window. This is useful if you have multiple screens because you can move the various tool windows onto the additional screen, allowing the editor space to use the maximum screen real estate. Selecting the Dock as Tabbed Document option makes the tool window into an additional tab in the editor space. In Chapter 4, "The Visual Studio Workspace," you'll learn how to effectively manage the workspace by docking and pinning tool windows.

Developing, Building, Debugging, and Deploying Your First Application

Now that you have seen an overview of the Visual Studio 2012 IDE, this section walks you through creating a simple application that demonstrates working with some of these components. This is, of course, the mandatory "Hello World" sample that every developer needs to know, and it can be done in either Visual Basic .NET or C#, depending on what you feel more comfortable with.

1. Start by selecting File ⇨ New ⇨ Project. This opens the New Project dialog, as shown in Figure 1-8. If you have worked with earlier versions of Visual Studio (prior to 2010) you'll notice that this dialog has had a significant facelift. There is a tree on the left side of the dialog for grouping templates based on language and technology. And there is also a search box in the top-right corner. The right pane of this dialog displays additional information about the project template you have selected. Lastly, you can select the version of the .NET Framework that the application will target using the drop-down at the top of the dialog.

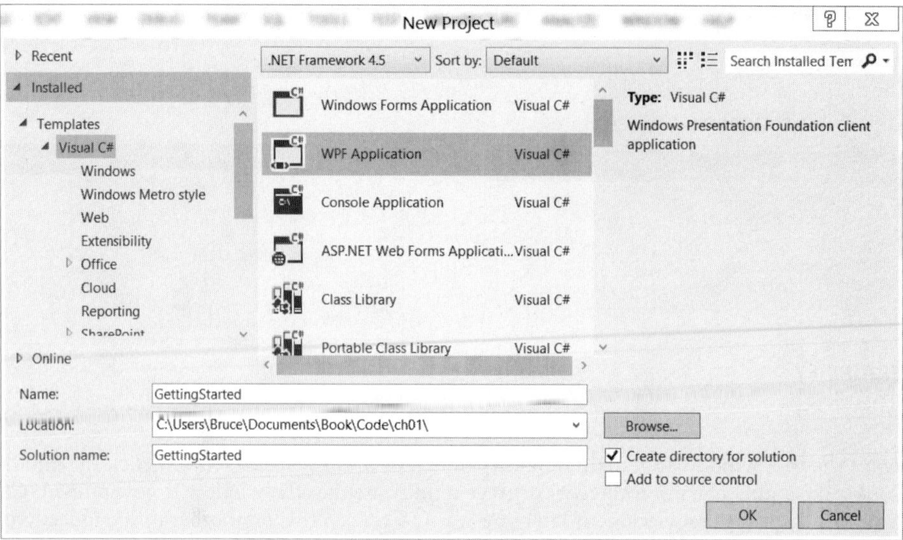

FIGURE 1-8

Select the WPF Application from the Templates area (this item exists under the root Visual Basic and Visual C# nodes, or under the subnode Windows) and set the Name to **GettingStarted** before selecting OK. This creates a new WPF application project, which includes a single startup window and is contained within a GettingStarted solution, as shown in the Solution Explorer window of Figure 1-9. This startup window has automatically opened in the visual designer, giving you a graphical representation of what the window will look like when you run the application. The Properties tool window is collapsed and sits on the right-side of the windows.

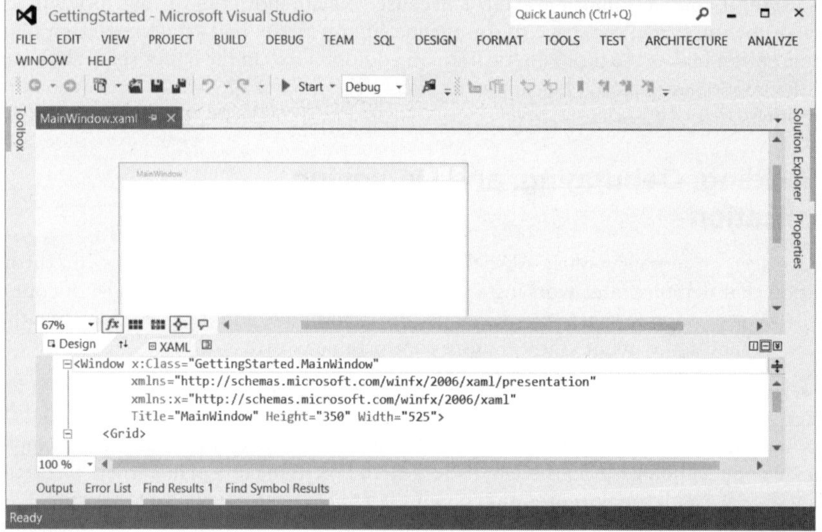

FIGURE 1-9

2. Click the collapsed Toolbox window, which appears on the left side of the screen. This causes the Toolbox to expand. Then click on the pin icon, which keeps the tool window open. To add controls to the window in the GettingStarted project, select the appropriate items from the Toolbox and drag them onto the form. Alternatively, you can double-click the item, and Visual Studio automatically adds them to the window.
3. Add a button and textbox to the form so that the layout looks similar to the one shown in Figure 1-10. Select the textbox, and select the Properties tool window. (You can press F4 to automatically open the Properties tool window.) Change the name of the control (found at the top of the Properties tool window) to **txtSayHello**. Repeat for the Button control, naming it **btnSayHello** and setting the `Content` property to **Say Hello!**

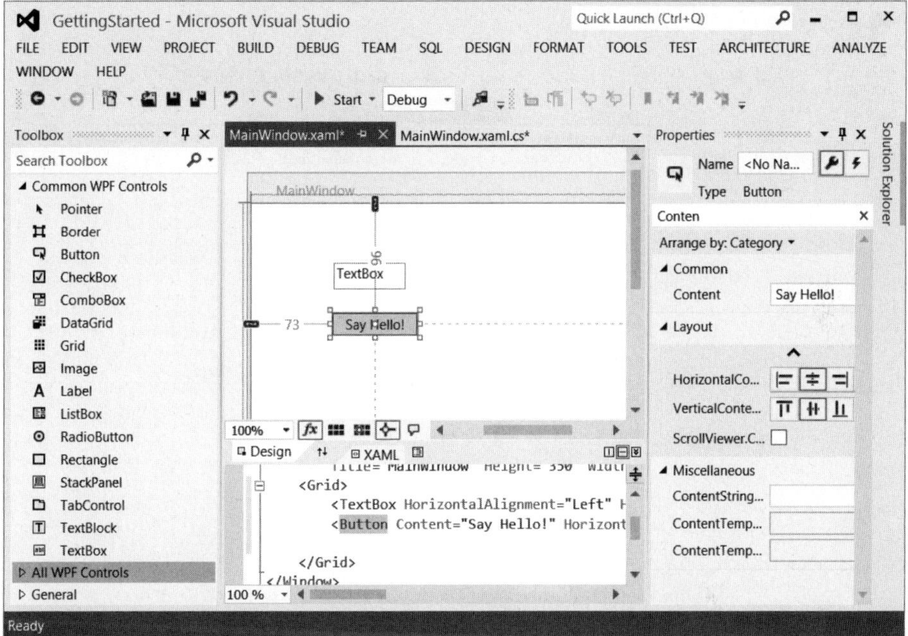

FIGURE 1-10

You can quickly locate a property by typing its name into the search field located beneath the Name field. In Figure 1-10 **Conten** has been entered to reduce the list of Properties so that it's easier to locate the Content property.

After you add controls to the window, the tab is updated with an asterisk (*) after the text to indicate that there are unsaved changes to that particular item. If you attempt to close this item while changes are pending, you are asked if you want to save the changes. When you build the application, any unsaved files are automatically saved as part of the build process.

> **NOTE** *One thing to be aware of is that some files, such as the solution file, are modified when you make changes within Visual Studio 2012 without your being given any indication that they have changed. If you try to exit the application or close the solution, you are still prompted to save these changes.*

4. Deselect all controls (you can click an empty spot on the screen to do this), and then double-click the button. This not only opens the code editor with the code-behind file for this form, it also creates and wires up an event handler for the click event on the button. Figure 1-11 shows the code window after a single line has been added to echo the message to the user.

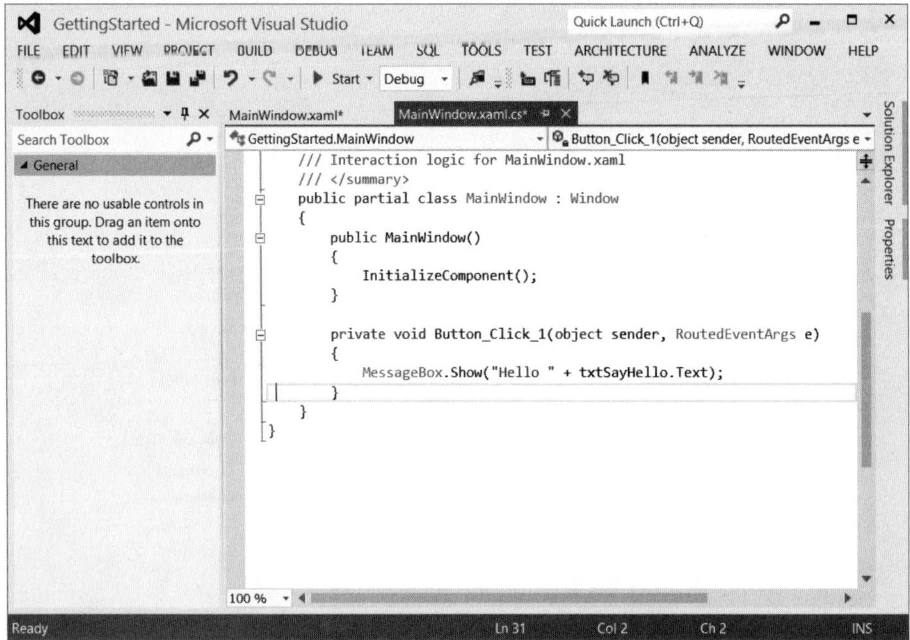

FIGURE 1-11

5. Before you build and execute your application, place the cursor somewhere on the line containing `MessageBox.Show` and press F9. This sets a breakpoint; when you run the application by pressing F5 and then click the "Say Hello!" button, the execution halts at this line. Figure 1-12 illustrates this breakpoint being reached. The data tip, which appears when the mouse hovers over the line, shows the contents of the `txtSayHello.Text` property.

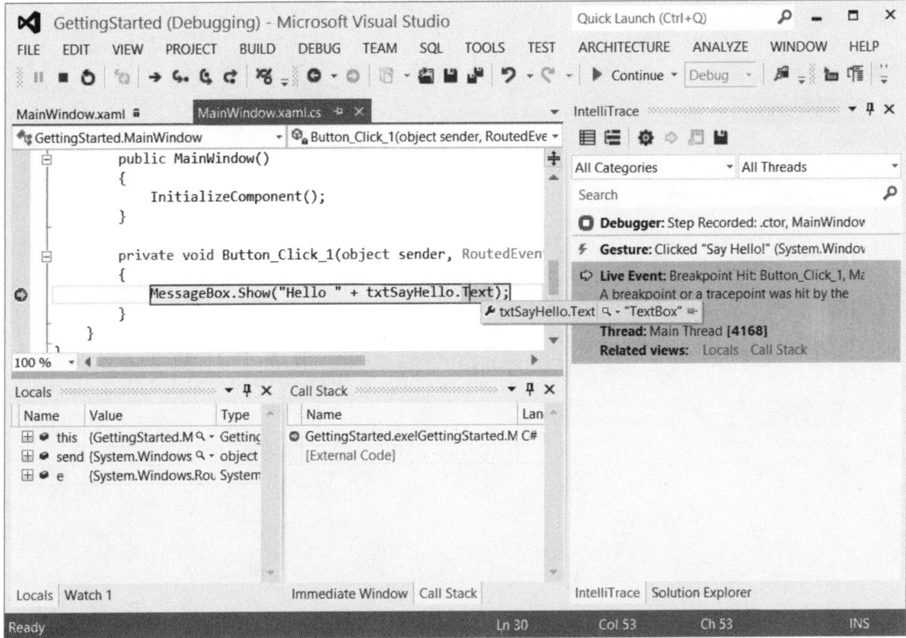

FIGURE 1-12

The layout of Visual Studio in Figure 1-12 is significantly different from the previous screenshots because a number of new tool windows are visible in the lower half of the screen, and new command bars are visible at the top. Also, as a significant change from previous versions of Visual Studio, the status bar at the bottom of the IDE is a different color (orange versus the blue that appears when in design mode). When you stop running or debugging your application, Visual Studio returns to the previous layout. Visual Studio 2012 maintains two separate layouts: design time and run time. Menus, toolbars, and various windows have default layouts for when you edit a project, whereas a different setup is defined for when a project is executed and debugged. You can modify each of these layouts to suit your own style, and Visual Studio 2012 remembers them.

6. You need to deploy your application. Whether you build a rich client application using Windows Forms or WPF, or a web application, Visual Studio 2012 has the capability to publish your application. Double-click the Properties node in Solution Explorer, and select the Publish node to display the options for publishing your application, as shown in Figure 1-13.

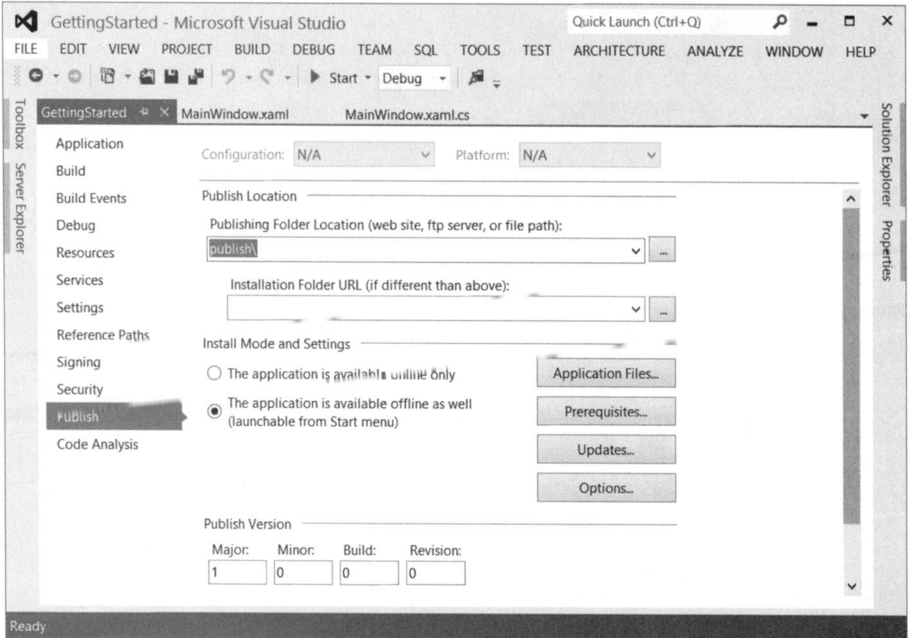

FIGURE 1-13

In Figure 1-13, the publishing folder has been set to a local path (by default, the path is relative to the directory in which the project is found), but you can specify a network folder, an IIS folder, or an FTP site instead. After you specify where you want to publish to, clicking Publish Now publishes your application to that location.

SUMMARY

You've now seen how the various components of Visual Studio 2012 work together to build an application. The following list outlines the typical process of creating a solution:

1. Use the File menu to create a solution.
2. Use the Solution Explorer to locate the window that needs editing, and double-click the item to show it in the main workspace area.
3. Drag the necessary components onto the window from the Toolbox.
4. Select the window and each component in turn, and edit the properties in the Properties window.
5. Double-click the window or a control to access the code behind the component's graphical interface.
6. Use the main workspace area to write code and design the graphical interface, switching between the two via the tabs at the top of the area.
7. Use the toolbars to start the program.
8. If errors occur, review them in the Error List and Output windows.
9. Save the project using either toolbar or menu commands, and exit Visual Studio 2012.

In subsequent chapters, you'll learn how to customize the IDE to more closely fit your own working style, and how Visual Studio 2012 takes a lot of the guesswork out of the application development process. You'll also see a number of best practices for working with Visual Studio 2012 that you can reuse as a developer.

2 The Solution Explorer, Toolbox, and Properties

WHAT'S IN THIS CHAPTER?

- Arranging files with the Solution Explorer
- Adding projects, items, and references to your solution
- Working with the Properties tool window
- Include your own properties in the Properties tool window

In Chapter 1, "A Quick Tour," you briefly saw and interacted with a number of the components that make up the Visual Studio 2012 IDE. Now you get an opportunity to work with three of the most commonly used tool windows: the Solution Explorer, the Toolbox, and Properties.

Throughout this and other chapters you see references to keyboard shortcuts, such as Ctrl+S. In these cases, we assume the use of the general development settings, as shown in Chapter 1. Other profiles may have different key combinations. And, as you will see in upcoming chapters, you can use the Quick Launch area to get to commands regardless of the development settings that you use.

THE SOLUTION EXPLORER

Whenever you create or open an application, or for that matter just a single file, Visual Studio 2012 uses the concept of a solution to tie everything together. Typically, a solution is made up of one or more projects, each of which can have multiple items associated with it. In the past these items were typically just files, but increasingly projects are made up of items that may consist of multiple files, or in some cases no files at all. Chapter 6, "Solutions, Projects, and Items," goes into more detail about projects, the structure of solutions, and how items are related.

The Solution Explorer tool window (Ctrl+Alt+L) provides a convenient visual representation of the solution, projects, and items, as shown in Figure 2-1. In this figure you can see three projects presented in a tree: a C# WPF application, a C# WCF service library, and a VB class library.

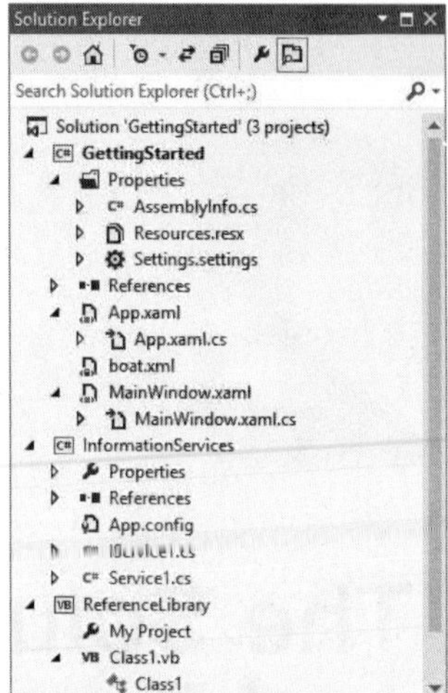

FIGURE 2-1

Each project has an icon associated with it that typically indicates the type of project and the language it is written in. There are some exceptions to this rule: Some projects, such as SQL Server or Modeling projects, aren't tied to a specific language.

One node is particularly noticeable because the font is boldfaced. This indicates that this project is the startup project — in other words, the project that is launched when you select Debug ➪ Start Debugging or press F5. To change the startup project, right-click the project you want to nominate and select Set as StartUp Project. You can also nominate multiple projects as startup projects via the Solution Properties dialog, which you can reach by selecting Properties from the right-click menu of the Solution node.

> **NOTE** *With certain environment settings (see "Getting Started" in Chapter 1), the Solution node is not visible when only a single project exists. A problem with this setting is that it becomes difficult to access the Solution Properties window. To get the Solution node to appear, you can either add another project to the solution or check the Always Show Solution item from the Projects and Solutions node in the Options dialog, accessible via Tools ➪ Options.*

The toolbar across the top of the Solution Explorer gives access to a number of different functions related to the solution, from the ability to collapse all the files in the tree to creating a new instance of the Solution Explorer. For example, the Show All Files button (see Figure 2-2) expands the solution listing to display the additional files and folders.

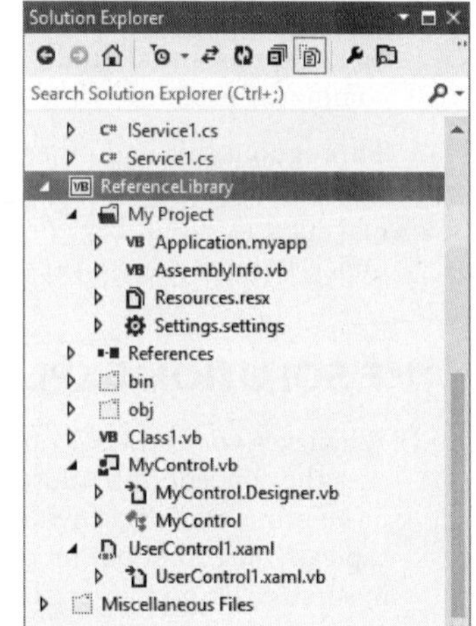

FIGURE 2-2

In this expanded view you can see all the files and folders contained under the project structure. Unfortunately, if the Filesystem changes, the Solution Explorer does not automatically update to reflect these changes. Use the Refresh button to make sure you see the current list of files and folders.

The Solution Explorer toolbar is contextually aware, with different buttons displayed depending on the type of node selected. This is shown in Figure 2-2, where there are two folders that are not part of the project (as indicated by the faded icon color) and the remaining buttons from Figure 2-1 are not visible.

> **NOTE** *If you don't already have a class diagram in your project, clicking the View Class Diagram button inserts one and automatically adds all the classes. For a project with a lot of classes, this can be quite time-consuming and can result in a large and unwieldy class diagram. It is generally a better idea to manually add one or more class diagrams, which gives you total control.*

There is another, relatively unusual, mechanism for navigating through the projects and files in a solution. To the left of each item in the tree is an icon, which when clicked shows a different context menu. One of the changes that appear in Visual Studio 2012 is the addition of a new option in the context menu called Scope to This. When the Scope to This option is clicked, the contents of the Solution Explorer change so that the selected node in the solution becomes the top level of the tree view. Figure 2-3 shows the view when Scope to This has been clicked for the GettingStarted project.

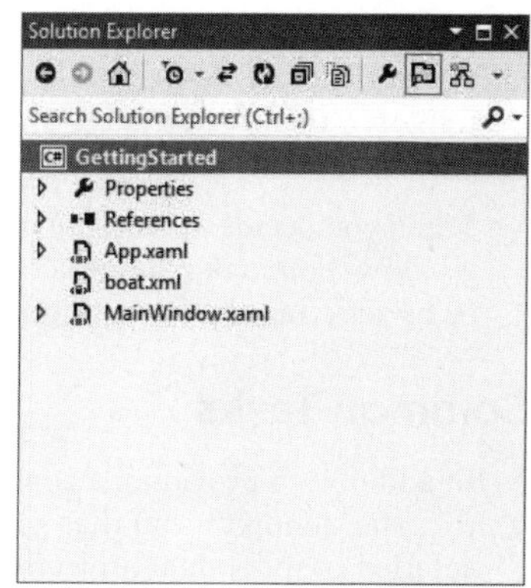

FIGURE 2-3

Along with navigating down the solution using the Scope to This option, the Solution Explorer also allows for moving backward and forward through the navigation. At the top left of the Solution Explorer's toolbar, there is a left arrow that you can use to navigate up the hierarchy. So if that arrow were clicked, the full solution would be displayed, as shown in Figure 2-2. And there is also a right-facing arrow that, when clicked, navigates forward into the scoped view.

New to Visual Studio 2012, the expanded view also shows the properties and methods for a given class. When you click the icon to the left of a code file, the properties and methods become visible. The context menus have also changed to reflect the selected item. When you right-click a class, the context menu includes Base Types, Derived Types, and Is Used By options. These options change the scope of the Solution Explorer to the base class, the derived classes, and the classes used by the selected class, respectively.

As you continue navigating into the properties and methods, the context menu includes Calls, Is Called By, and Is Used By. These options scope the Solution Explorer to the classes that call this class, classes that are called by this class, and classes that are used by this class, respectively.

Previewing Files

One of the more interesting features of Visual Studio 2012 is the file preview capability of Solution Explorer. One of the buttons at the top of the Solution Explorer is Preview Selected Items (shown in Figure 2-4). When it has been selected, as you navigate through the files in the Solution Explorer (to "navigate," the file must be selected either with the mouse or by using the cursor), the file appears on the Preview tab (Figure 2-4).

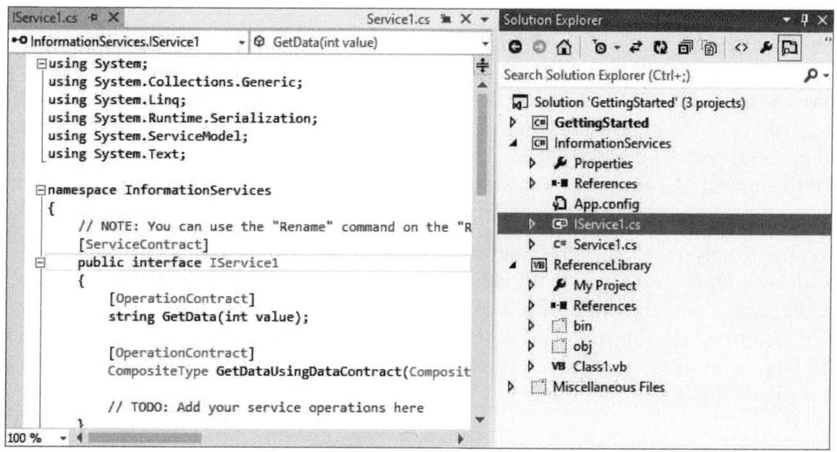

FIGURE 2-4

At this moment, the file has not been modified but is simply open to look at. You are free to navigate through the file as you would any other file. However, when you navigate to another file in the Solution Explorer, the Preview tab is replaced with the new file. In other words, it is no longer required to have a proliferation of tabs to view the contents of various files in your solution.

When you decide to stop previewing the file, it automatically moves to the tabs on the left side of your editor window. You make the choice to stop previewing either by editing the file directly (by typing, for example) or by selecting the Open option from the drop-down list on the right of the Preview tab.

Common Tasks

In addition to providing a convenient way to manage projects and items, the Solution Explorer has a dynamic context menu that gives you quick access to some of the most common tasks, such as building the solution or individual projects, accessing the build configuration manager, and opening files. Figure 2-5 shows how the context menu varies depending on which item is selected in the Solution Explorer.

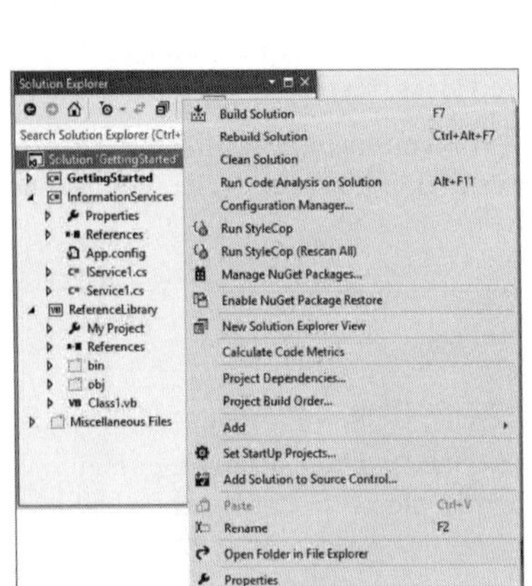

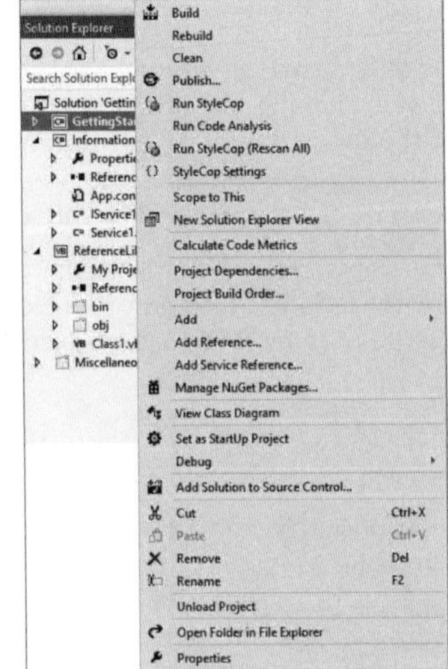

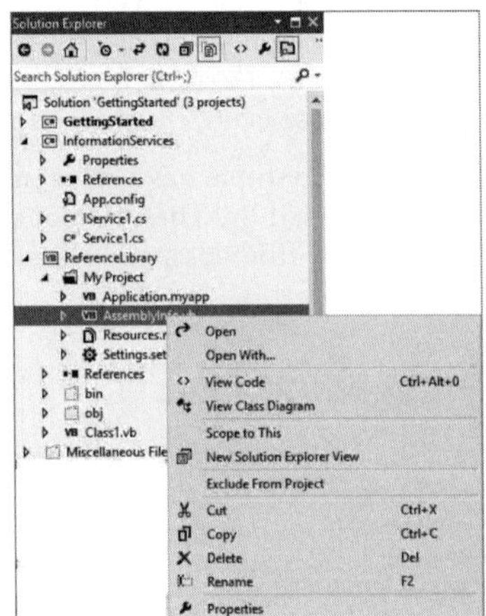

FIGURE 2-5

The first items in the left and center menus relate to building either the entire solution or the selected project. In most cases, selecting Build is the most efficient option, because it only builds projects where one or more of the contained files have changed. However, in some cases you may need to force a Rebuild, which builds all dependent projects regardless of their states. If you just want to remove all the additional files that are created during the build process, you can invoke Clean. This option can be useful if you want to package your solution to e-mail it to someone — you wouldn't want to include all the temporary or output files that are created by the build.

For most items in the Solution Explorer, the first section of the context menu is similar to the right menu in Figure 2-5: The default Open and Open With items allow you to determine how the item will be opened. This is of particular use when you work with XML resource files. Visual Studio 2012 opens this file type using the built-in resource editor, but this prevents you from making certain changes and doesn't support all data types you might want to include. (Chapter 39, "Resource Files," goes into how you can use your own data types in resource files.) By using the Open With menu item, you can use the XML Editor instead.

> **NOTE** *The context menu for the Solution, Project, and Folder nodes contains the Open Folder in Windows Explorer item. This enables you to open Windows Explorer quickly to the location of the selected item, saving you the hassle of having to navigate to where your solution is located, and then find the appropriate subfolder.*

Adding Projects and Items

The most common activities carried out in the Solution Explorer are the addition, removal, and renaming of projects and items. To add a new project to an existing solution, select Add ➪ New Project from the context menu off the Solution node. This invokes the dialog in Figure 2-6, which has undergone a few minor changes since earlier versions of Visual Studio. Project templates can now be sorted and searched. The pane on the right side displays information about the selected project, such as the type of project and its description. (Chapter 15, "Project and Item Templates," covers creating your own Project and Item templates, including setting these properties.)

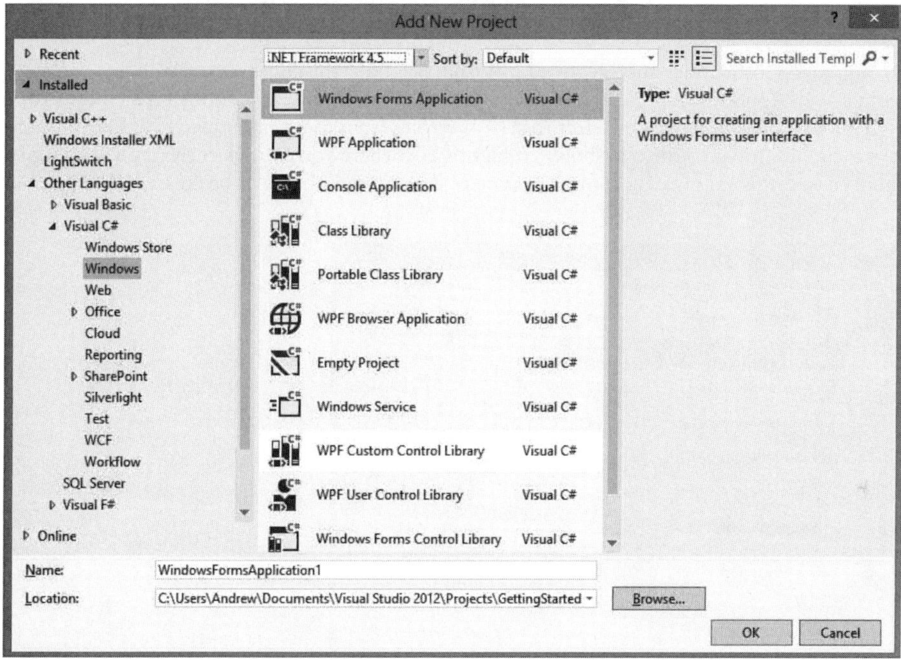

FIGURE 2-6

In the Installed templates hierarchy on the left side of the Add New Project dialog, the templates are primarily arranged by language, and then by technology. The templates include Office project types, enabling you to build both application- and document-level add-ins for most of the Office products. Though the Office add-ins still use Visual Studio Tools for Office (VSTO), this is built into Visual Studio 2012 instead of being an additional installation. Chapter 19, "Office Business Applications," shows how you can use these project types to build add-ins for the core Office applications. There are also tabs for Recent templates and Online templates. The Online templates can be sorted and searched in the same way as your Installed templates; although the sort criteria has been extended to include creation date, ratings, and downloaded frequency.

The other thing you will notice in this dialog is the ability to select different framework versions. If you have existing projects that you don't want to have to migrate forward to a more recent version of the .NET Framework, you can still immediately take advantage of the current features, such as improved IntelliSense. The alternative would have been to have both Visual Studio 2012 and a previous version installed to build projects for earlier framework versions. The framework selection is also included in the search criteria, limiting the list of available project templates to those that are compatible with the selected .NET Framework version.

> **NOTE** *When you open your existing solutions or projects in Visual Studio 2012, they will not necessarily go through the upgrade wizard (see Chapter 45, "Upgrading with Visual Studio 2012," for more information). If the projects are already in Visual Studio 2010, an upgrade might not be required. To be precise, the act of opening a project in Visual Studio 2012 might cause modifications to the project that allow it to be opened in both Visual Studio 2010 and Visual Studio 2012. This is both important and different enough to warrant additional comment. What this means for developers is that they might be able to use Visual Studio 2012 to modify projects (thus getting the benefits of using the latest version). At the same time, projects that have been opened in Visual Studio 2012 will still open in Visual Studio 2010. For projects that are from versions earlier than Visual Studio 2010, the upgrade wizard will be triggered. These matters are discussed further in Chapter 45, "Upgrading with Visual Studio 2012."*

One of the worst and most poorly understood features in Visual Studio is the concept of a Web Site project. This is distinct from a Web Application project, which can be added via the aforementioned Add New Project dialog. To add a Web Site project you need to select Add ➪ Web Site from the context menu off the Solution node. This displays a dialog similar to the one shown in Figure 2-7, where you can select the type of web project to be created. In most cases, this simply determines the type of default item that is to be created in the project.

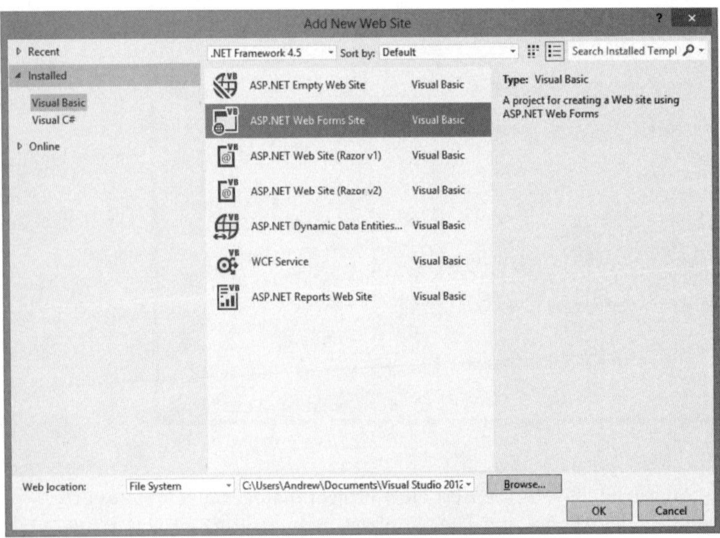

FIGURE 2-7

> **NOTE** *It is important to note that the types of web projects listed in Figure 2-7 are the same as the types listed under the Web node in the Add New Project dialog. However, understand that they will not generate the same results because significant differences exist between Web Site projects (created via the Add New Web Site dialog) and Web Application projects (created via the Add New Project dialog). The differences between these project types are covered in detail in Chapter 21, "ASP.NET Web Forms."*

When you have a project or two, you need to start adding items. You do this via the Add context menu item off the project node in the Solution Explorer. The first submenu, New Item, launches the Add New Item dialog, as shown in Figure 2-8.

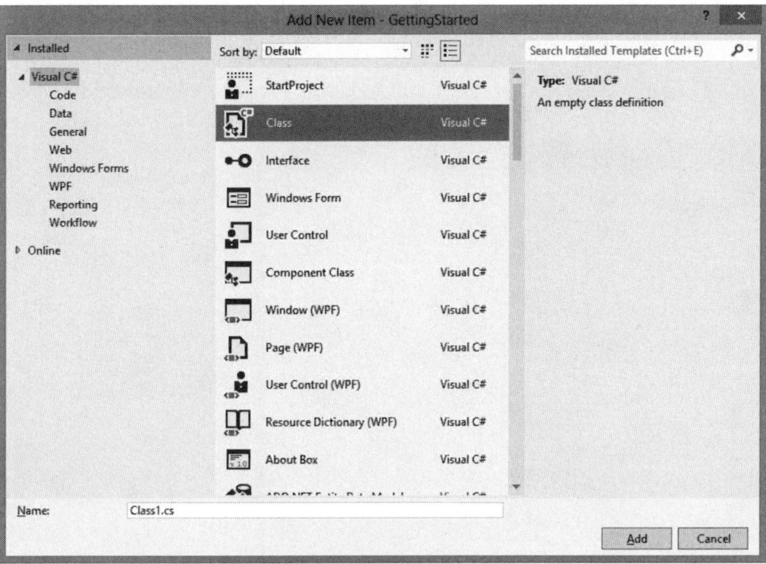

FIGURE 2-8

In addition to listing only those item templates that are relevant to the project you have selected, the Add New Item dialog enables you to search the installed templates, as well as go online to look for templates generated by third parties.

Returning to the Add context menu, you will notice a number of predefined shortcuts such as User Control and Class. The shortcuts that appear depend on the type of project to which the item is being added. These do little more than bypass the stage of locating the appropriate template within the Add New Item dialog. Regardless, the Add New Item dialog is still displayed because you need to assign a name to the item being created.

It is important to make the distinction that you are adding items rather than files to the project. Though a lot of the templates contain only a single file, some, like the Window or User Control, add multiple files to your project.

Adding References

Each new software development technology that is released promises better reuse, but few can actually deliver on this promise. One way that Visual Studio 2012 supports reusable components is via the references for a project. If you expand out any project, you can observe a number of .NET Framework libraries, such as System and System.Core, which need to be referenced by a project to be built. Essentially, a reference enables the compiler to resolve type, property, field, and method names back to the assembly where they are defined. If you want to reuse a class from a third-party library, or even your own .NET assembly, you need to add a reference to it via the Add Reference context menu item on the project node of the Solution Explorer.

When you launch the Reference Manager dialog, as shown in Figure 2-9, Visual Studio 2012 interrogates the local computer, the Global Assembly Cache, and your solution to present a list of known libraries that can be referenced. This includes both .NET and COM references that are separated into different lists, as well as projects and recently used references. In earlier versions of Visual Studio this dialog was notoriously slow to load. Visual Studio 2010 saw an improvement, but because the list of .NET assemblies was lazy loaded after the dialog was displayed, the resulting user experience was not completely satisfactory. Visual Studio 2012 appears to have finally gotten it right. The dialog displays almost instantly, showing the assemblies that are part of the .NET Framework first.

As in other project-based development environments going back as far as the first versions of VB, you can add references to projects contained in your solution, rather than adding the compiled binary components. The advantage to this model is that it's easier to debug into the referenced component and helps ensure you are running the latest version of all components, but for large solutions this may become unwieldy.

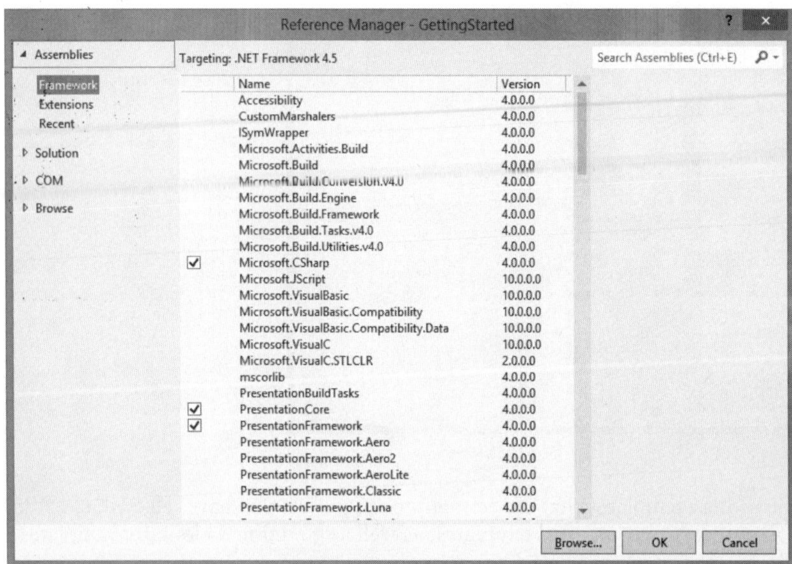

FIGURE 2-9

> **NOTE** *When you have a solution with a large number of projects (large can be relevant to your computer but typically anything more than 20), you may want to consider having multiple solutions that reference subsets of the projects. In previous versions, large solutions were notoriously slow to load and build. Microsoft put some effort into improving this and were quite successful. Loads and builds are actually done in parallel. Still, keeping the number of projects in your solution to a minimum does ensure a nice debugging experience throughout the entire application. But be warned. The segregation of projects into different solutions is not nearly as clear-cut as you might initially imagine. Not because it's difficult to do (it's actually easy), but you'll find there are a number of different approaches that might be the "best," depending on your goals. For example, you may want to create different solutions to support build configurations (see Chapter 46, "Build Customization") that build a subset of the projects.*

Adding Service References

The other type of reference that the Solution Explorer caters to is service references. In earlier versions of Visual Studio, these references were referred to as Web references, but with the advent of the Windows Communication Foundation (WCF) there is now a more generic Add Service Reference menu item. This invokes the Add Service Reference dialog, which you can see in Figure 2-10. In this example the drop-down feature of the Discover button has been used to look for Services in Solution.

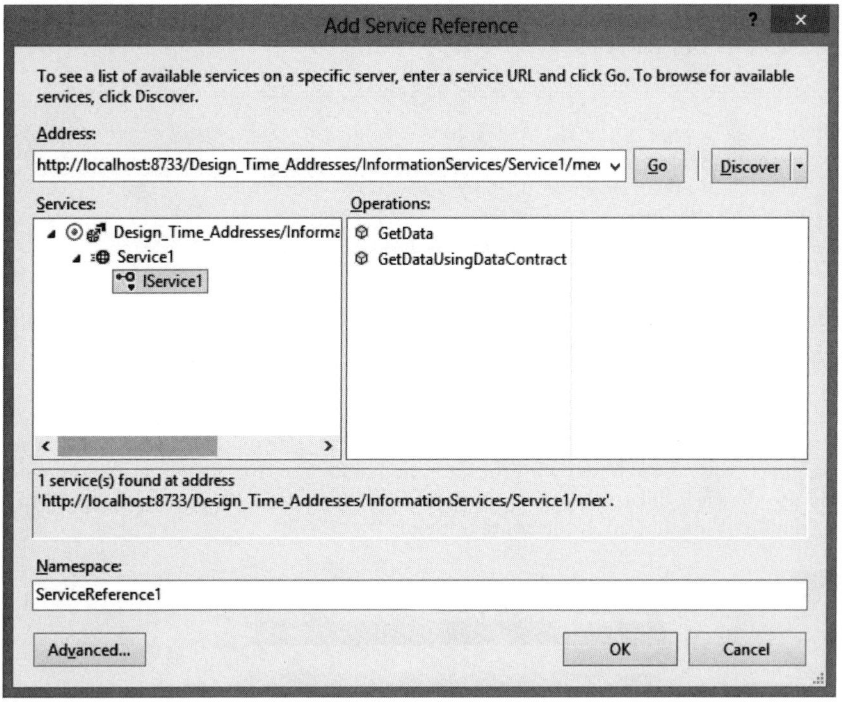

FIGURE 2-10

Unfortunately, this dialog is another case of Microsoft not understanding the usage pattern properly. Though the dialog itself is resizable, the status response message area is not, making it hard to read any errors generated. Luckily, if any errors are thrown while Visual Studio 2012 attempts to access the service information, a hyperlink is provided that opens the Add Service Reference Error dialog. This generally gives you enough information to resolve the problem.

In the lower left corner of Figure 2-10 is an Advanced button. The Service Reference Settings dialog that this launches enables you to customize which types are defined as part of the service reference. By default, all the types used by the service are re-created in the client application unless they are implemented in an assembly that is referenced by both the service and the application. The Data Type area of this dialog is used to change this behavior. There is also an Add Web Reference button in the lower left corner of the Service Reference Settings dialog, which enables you to add more traditional .NET Web service references. This might be important if you have some limitations or are trying to support intersystem operability. Adding services to your application is covered in more detail in Chapter 32, "Windows Communication Foundation (WCF)."

THE TOOLBOX

One of the major advantages over many other IDEs that Microsoft has offered developers is true drag-and-drop placement of elements during the design of both web and rich client applications. These elements are all available in the Toolbox (Ctrl+Alt+X), a tool window accessible via the View menu.

The Toolbox window contains all the available components for the currently active document being shown in the main workspace. These can be visual components, such as buttons and textboxes; invisible, service-oriented objects, such as timers and system event logs; or even designer elements, such as class and interface objects used in the Class Designer view.

> **NOTE** *An interesting feature of the Toolbox is that you can copy snippets of code into the Toolbox by simply selecting a region and dragging it onto the Toolbox. You can rename and reorder your code snippets, making it useful for presentations or storing chunks of code you use frequently.*

Visual Studio 2012 presents the available components in groups rather than as one big mess of controls. This default grouping enables you to more easily locate the controls you need — for example, data-related components are in their own Data group.

By default, groups are presented in List view (see the left side of Figure 2-11). Each component is represented by its own icon and the name of the component. This differs from the very old way of displaying the available objects when the Toolbox was simply a stacked list of icons that left you guessing as to what some of the more obscure components were, as shown with the Common WPF Controls group on the right side of Figure 2-11. You can change the view of each control group individually — right-click anywhere within the group area and deselect the List View option in the context menu.

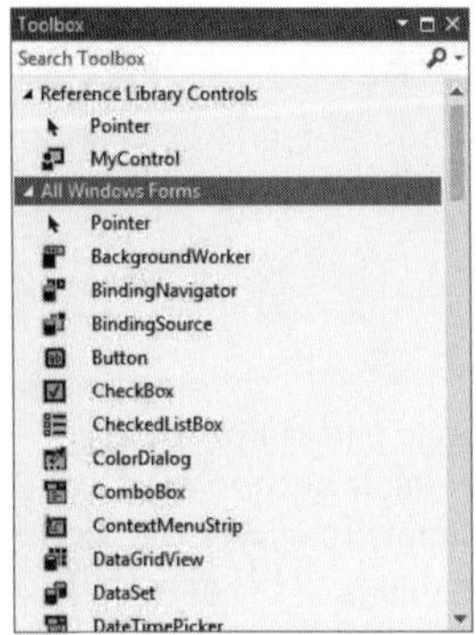

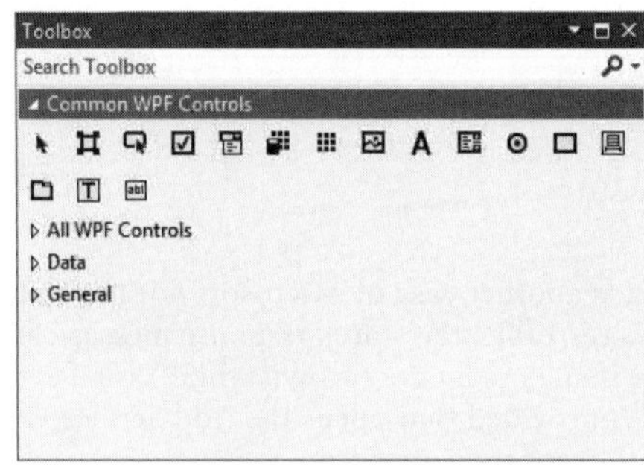

FIGURE 2-11

Regardless of how the components are presented, the way they are used in a program is usually the same: Click and drag the desired component onto the design surface of the active document, or double-click the component's entry for Visual Studio to automatically add an instance. Visual components, such as buttons and textboxes, appear in the design area where they can be repositioned, resized, and otherwise adjusted via the property grid. Nonvisual components, such as the Timer control, appear as icons, with associated labels, in a nonvisual area below the design area, as shown in Figure 2-12.

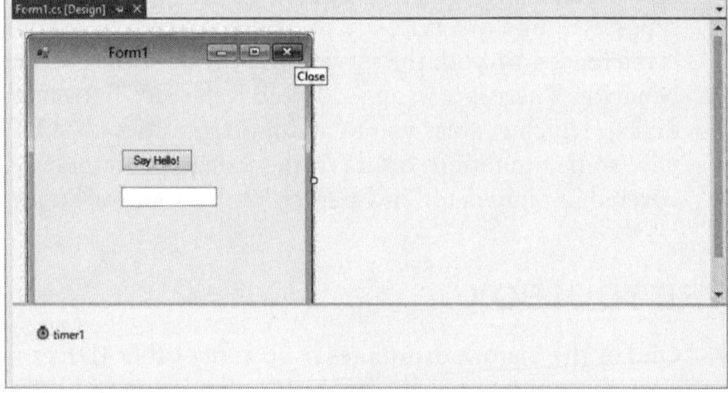

FIGURE 2-12

At the top-left side of Figure 2-11 is a group called Reference Library Controls with a single component, MyControl. Reference_Library is actually the name of a class library that is defined in the same solution, and it contains the MyControl control. When you start to build your own components or controls, instead of your having to manually create a new tab and go through the process of adding each item to the Toolbox, Visual Studio 2012 automatically interrogates all the projects in your solution. If any components or controls are identified (essentially any class that implements *System.ComponentModel.IComponent* or *System.Windows.FrameworkElement* for WPF and Silverlight), a new tab is created for that project and the appropriate items are added with a default icon and class name (in this case MyControl), as you can see on the left in Figure 2-11. For components, this is the same icon that appears in the nonvisual part of the design area when you use the component.

> **NOTE** *Visual Studio 2012 interrogates all projects in your solution, both at startup and after build activities. This can take a significant amount of time if you have a large number of projects. If this is the case, you should consider disabling this feature by setting the AutoToolboxPopulate property to false under the Windows Forms Designer node of the Options dialog (Tools ⇨ Options).*

To customize how your items appear in the Toolbox, you need to add a 16 × 16 pixel bitmap to the same project as your component or control. Next, select the newly inserted bitmap in the Solution Explorer and navigate to the Properties window. Make sure the Build property is set to Embedded Resource. All you now need to do is attribute your control with the `ToolboxBitmap` attribute:

VB

```
<ToolboxBitmap(GetType(MyControl), "MyControlIcon.bmp")>
Public Class MyControl
```

C#

```
[ToolboxBitmap(typeof(MyControl), "MyControlIcon.bmp")]
public class MyControl
```

This attribute uses the type reference for MyControl to locate the appropriate assembly from which to extract the `MyControlIcon.bmp` embedded resource. Other overloads of this attribute can use a file path as the only argument. In this case you don't even need to add the bitmap to your project.

Unfortunately, you can't customize the way the automatically generated items appear in the Toolbox. However, if you manually add an item to the Toolbox and select your components, you'll see your custom icon. Alternatively, if you have a component and you drag it onto a form, you'll see your icon appear in the nonvisual space on the designer.

It is also worth noting that customizing the Toolbox and designer experience for Windows Presentation Foundation (WPF) controls uses the notion of a Metadata store instead of attributes. This typically results in additional assemblies that can be used to tailor the design experience in both Visual Studio 2012 and Expression Blend.

Arranging Components

Having Toolbox items in alphabetical order is a good default because it enables you to locate items that are unfamiliar. However, if you're using only a handful of components and are frustrated by having to continuously scroll up and down, you can create your own groups of controls and move existing object types around.

Repositioning an individual component is easy. Locate it in the Toolbox, and click and drag it to the new location. When you're happy with where it is, release the mouse button and the component moves to the new spot in the list. You can move it to a different group in the same way — just keep dragging the component up or down the Toolbox until you have located the right group. These actions work in both List and Icon views.

If you want to copy the component from one group to another, rather than move it, hold down the Ctrl key as you drag, and the process duplicates the control so that it appears in both groups.

Sometimes it's nice to have your own group to host the controls and components you use the most. To create a new group in the Toolbox, right-click anywhere in the Toolbox area and select the Add Tab command. A new blank tab will be added to the bottom of the Toolbox with a prompt for you to name it. After you name the tab, you can then add components to it by following the steps described in this section.

When you first start Visual Studio 2012, the items within each group are arranged alphabetically. However, after moving items around, you may find that they're in a bewildering state and you may decide that you simply need to start again. All you have to do is right-click anywhere within the group and choose the Sort Items Alphabetically command.

By default, controls are added to the Toolbox according to their class names. This means you end up with some names that are hard to understand, particularly if you add COM controls to your Toolbox. Visual Studio 2012 enables you to modify a component's name to something more understandable.

To change the name of a component, right-click the component's entry in the Toolbox and select the Rename Item command. An edit field appears inline in place of the original caption, enabling you to name it however you like, even with special characters.

If you've become even more confused, with components in unusual groups, and you have lost sight of where everything is, you can choose Reset Toolbox from the same right-click context menu. This restores all the groups in the Toolbox to their original states, with components sorted alphabetically and in the groups in which they started.

> **NOTE** *Remember: Selecting Reset Toolbox permanently deletes any of your own custom-made groups of commands, so be sure you want to perform this function!*

New to Visual Studio 2012 is the search capability that is found in the Toolbox. At the top of the Toolbox, there is a Search area. As you type characters into this area, the components in the Toolbox are filtered to match. The search is implemented so that it finds the characters that have been typed anyplace they exist in the name of the control. Because the search is performed across all the groups, this is a convenient way to locate controls, provided that you know all or part of the name. Figure 2-13 shows what the Toolbox might look like after "Tex" has been entered into the Search area.

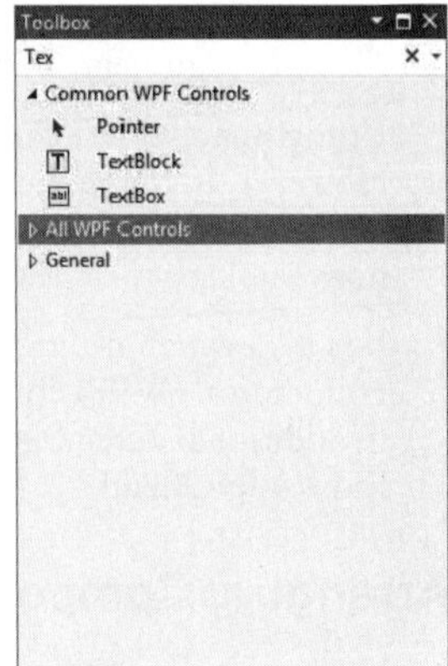

FIGURE 2-13

Adding Components

Sometimes you'll find that a particular component you need is not present in the lists displayed in the Toolbox. Most of the main .NET components are already present, but some are not. For example, the `WebClient` class component is not displayed in the Toolbox by default. Managed applications can also use COM components in their design. When added to the Toolbox, COM objects can be used in much the same way as regular .NET components, and if coded correctly you can program against them in precisely the same way using the Properties window and referring to their methods, properties, and events in code.

To add a component to your Toolbox layout, right-click anywhere within the group of components you want to add it to and select Choose Items. After a moment (this process can take a few seconds on a slower machine because the machine needs to interrogate the .NET cache to determine all the possible components you can choose from), you are presented with a list of .NET Framework components, as Figure 2-14 shows. One of the nice enhancements with Visual Studio 2012 is that there is now a progress bar indicating the assemblies that are being loaded. This is different from previous versions, where the only indication that this work was being done was the mouse cursor changing to its busy image.

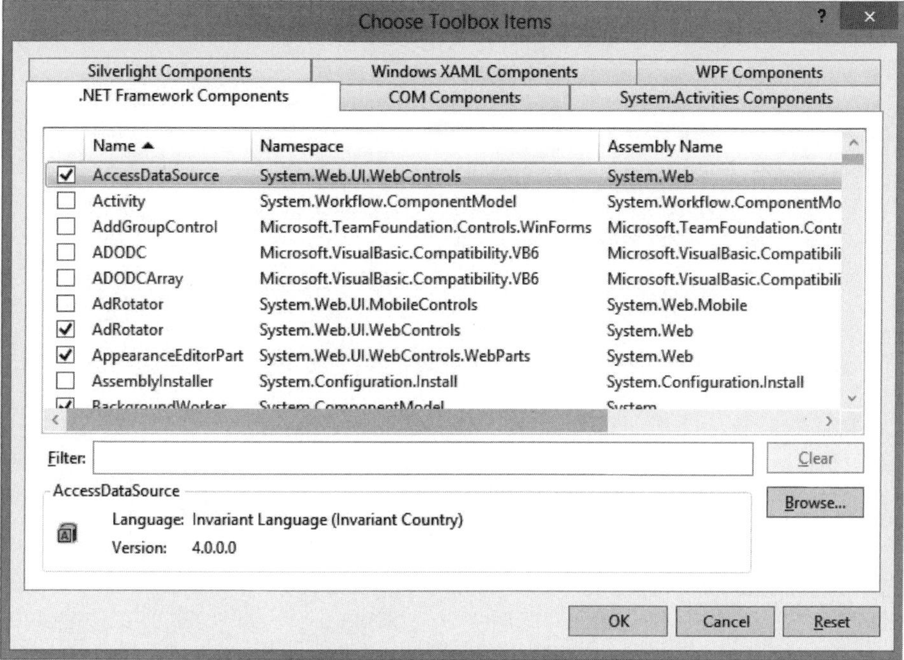

FIGURE 2-14

Scroll through the list to locate the item you want to add to the Toolbox and check the corresponding check box. You can add multiple items at the same time by selecting each of them before clicking the OK button to apply your changes. At this time you can also remove items from the Toolbox by deselecting them from the list. Note that this removes the items from any groups to which they belong, not just from the group you are currently editing.

If you find it hard to locate the item you need, you can use the Filter box, which filters the list based on name, namespace, and assembly name. On rare occasions the item may not be listed at all. This can happen with nonstandard components, such as ones that you build yourself or that are not registered in the Global Assembly Cache (GAC). You can still add them by using the Browse button to locate the physical file on the computer. After you select and deselect the items you need, click the OK button to save them to the Toolbox layout.

COM components, WPF components, Silverlight components, Workflow components, and Activities components can be added in the same manner. Simply switch over to the relevant tab in the dialog window to view the list of available, properly registered COM components to add. Again, you can use the Browse button to locate controls that may not appear in the list.

PROPERTIES

One of the most frequently used tool windows built into Visual Studio 2012 is the Properties window (F4), as shown in Figure 2-15. The Properties window is made up of a property grid and is contextually aware, displaying only relevant properties of the currently selected item, whether that item is a node in the

Solution Explorer or an element in the form design area. Each line represents a property with its name and corresponding value in two columns. The right side of Figure 2-15 shows the updated property grid for WPF applications, which includes a preview icon and search capabilities.

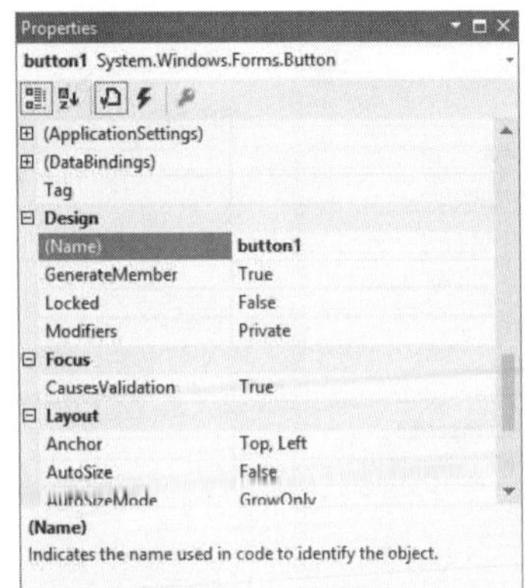

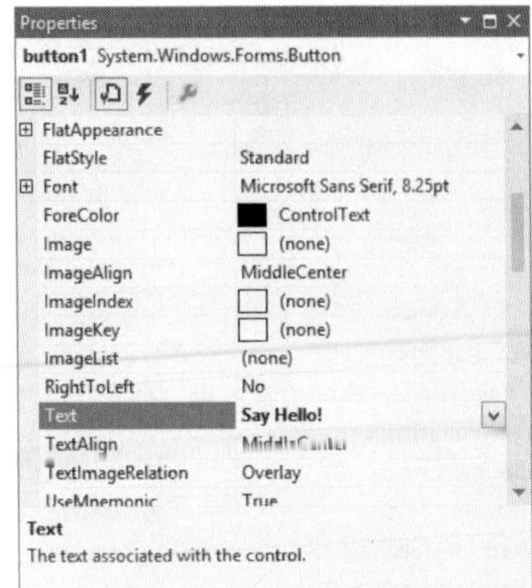

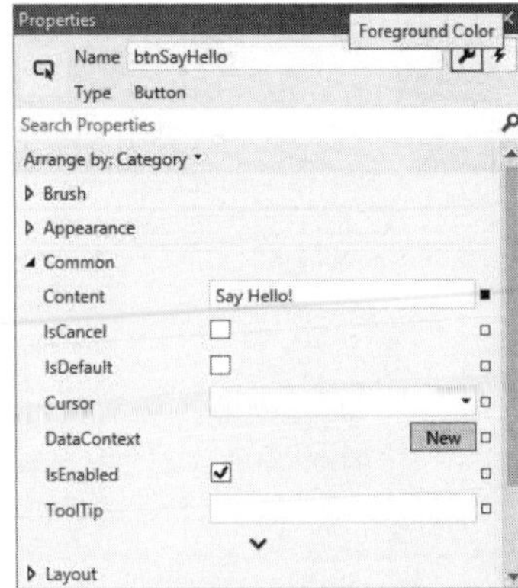

FIGURE 2-15

The Properties window is capable of grouping properties, or sorting them alphabetically — you can toggle this layout using the first two buttons at the top of the Properties window. It has built-in editors for a range of system types, such as colors, fonts, anchors, and docking, which are invoked when you click into the value column of the property to be changed. When a property is selected, as shown in the center of Figure 2-15, the property name is highlighted, and a description is presented in the lower region of the property grid.

In the Properties window, read-only properties are indicated in gray and you cannot modify their values. The value `Say Hello!!` for the `Text` property on the center of Figure 2-15 is boldfaced, which indicates that this is not the default value for this property. Similarly on the right side of Figure 2-15, the `Text` property has a filled-in black square to the right of the value, indicating the value has been specified. If you inspect the following code that is generated by the designer, you will notice that a line exists for each property that is boldfaced in the property grid — adding a line of code for every property on a control would significantly increase the time to render the form.

VB

```
Me.btnSayHello.Location = New System.Drawing.Point(12, 12)
Me.btnSayHello.Name = "btnSayHello"
Me.btnSayHello.Size = New System.Drawing.Size(100, 23)
Me.btnSayHello.TabIndex = 0
Me.btnSayHello.Text = "Say Hello!"
Me.btnSayHello.UseVisualStyleBackColor = True
```

C#

```
this.btnSayHello.Location = new System.Drawing.Point(12, 12);
this.btnSayHello.Name = "btnSayHello";
this.btnSayHello.Size = new System.Drawing.Size(100, 23);
this.btnSayHello.TabIndex = 0;
this.btnSayHello.Text = "Say Hello!";
this.btnSayHello.UseVisualStyleBackColor = true;
```

> **NOTE** *For Web and WPF applications, the properties set in the Properties window are persisted as markup in the aspx or xaml file, respectively. As with the Windows forms designer, only those values in the Properties window that have been set are persisted into markup.*

In addition to displaying properties for a selected item, the Properties window also provides a design experience for wiring up event handlers. The Properties window on the left side of Figure 2-16 illustrates the event view that is accessible via the lightning bolt button at the top of the Properties window. In this case, you can see that there is an event handler for the click event. To wire up another event, you can either select from a list of existing methods via a drop-down list in the value column, or you can double-click the value column. This creates a new event-handler method and wires it up to the event. If you use the first method you can notice that only methods that match the event signature are listed.

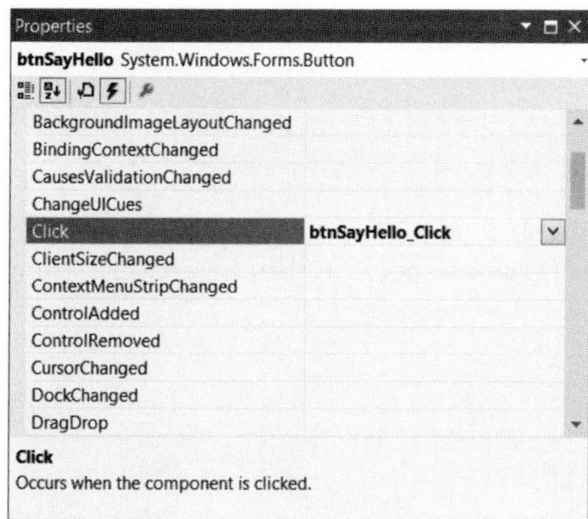

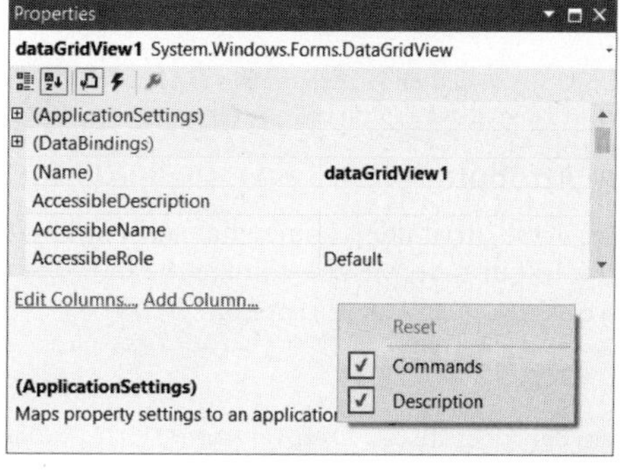

FIGURE 2-16

Certain components, such as the `DataGridView`, expose a number of commands, or shortcuts, which can be executed via the Properties window. On the right side of Figure 2-16 you can see two commands for the `DataGridView`: Edit Columns and Add Column. When you click either of these command links, you are presented with a dialog for performing that action. If the commands are not immediately visible, right-click the Properties window and select Commands from the context menu.

If the Properties window has only a small amount of screen real estate, it can be difficult to scroll through the list of properties. If you right-click in the property grid, you can uncheck the Command and Description options to hide these sections of the Properties window.

Extending the Properties Window

You have just seen how Visual Studio 2012 highlights properties that have changed by boldfacing the value. The question that you need to ask is, How does Visual Studio 2012 know what the default value is? The answer is that when the Properties window interrogates an object to determine what properties to display in the property grid, it looks for a number of design attributes. These attributes can be used to control which properties are displayed, the editor that is used to edit the value, and what the default value is. To show how you can use these attributes on your own components, start with adding a simple automatic property to your component:

VB

```
Public Property Description As String
```

C#

```
public string Description { get; set; }
```

The Browsable Attribute

By default, all public properties display in the property grid. However, you can explicitly control this behavior by adding the `Browsable` attribute. If you set it to `false` the property does not appear in the property grid:

VB

```
<System.ComponentModel.Browsable(False)>
Public Property Description As String
```

C#

```
[System.ComponentModel.Browsable(false)]
public string Description { get; set; }
```

DisplayName Attribute

The `DisplayName` attribute is somewhat self-explanatory; it enables you to modify the display name of the property. In our case, we can change the name of the property as it appears in the property grid from `Description` to `VS2012 Description`:

VB

```
<System.ComponentModel.DisplayName("VS2012 Description")>
Public Property Description As String
```

C#

```
[System.ComponentModel.DisplayName("VS2012 Description")]
public string Description { get; set; }
```

Description

In addition to defining the friendly or display name for the property, it is also worth providing a description, which appears in the bottom area of the Properties window when the property is selected. This ensures that users of your component understand what the property does:

VB

```
<System.ComponentModel.Description("My first custom property")>
Public Property Description As String
```

C#

```
[System.ComponentModel.Description("My first custom property")]
public string Description { get; set; }
```

Category

By default, any property you expose is placed in the Misc group when the Properties window is in grouped view. Using the `Category` attribute, you can place your property in any of the existing groups, such as Appearance or Data, or a new group if you specify a group name that does not yet exist:

VB

```
<System.ComponentModel.Category("Appearance")>
Public Property Description As String
```

C#

```
[System.ComponentModel.Category("Appearance")]
public string Description { get; set; }
```

DefaultValue

Earlier you saw how Visual Studio 2012 highlights properties that have changed from their initial or default values. The `DefaultValue` attribute is what Visual Studio 2012 looks for to determine the default value for the property:

VB

```
Private Const cDefaultDescription As String = "<enter description>"
<System.ComponentModel.DefaultValue(cDefaultDescription)>
Public Property Description As String = cDefaultDescription
```

C#

```
private const string cDefaultDescription = "<enter description>";
private string mDescription = cDefaultDescription;
[System.ComponentModel.DefaultValue(cDefaultDescription)]
public string Description
{
    get
    {
        return mDescription;
    }
    set
    {
        mDescription = value;
    }
}
```

In this case, if the value of the `Description` property is set to `"<enter description>"`, Visual Studio 2012 removes the line of code that sets this property. If you modify a property and want to return to the default value, you can right-click the property in the Properties window and select Reset from the context menu.

> **NOTE** *The `DefaultValue` attribute does not set the initial value of your property. It is recommended that if you specify the `DefaultValue` attribute you also set the initial value of your property to the same value, as done in the preceding code.*

AmbientValue

One of the features we all take for granted but that few truly understand is the concept of ambient properties. Typical examples are background and foreground colors and fonts. Unless you explicitly set these via the Properties window, they are inherited — not from their base classes, but from their parent control. A broader definition of an ambient property is a property that gets its value from another source.

Like the `DefaultValue` attribute, the `AmbientValue` attribute is used to indicate to Visual Studio 2012 when it should not add code to the designer file. Unfortunately, with ambient properties you can't hard-code a value for the designer to compare the current value to because it is contingent on the property's source value. Because of this, when you define the `AmbientValue` attribute, this tells the designer that it needs to look for a function called `ShouldSerializePropertyName`. For example, in our case, the designer would look for a method called `ShouldSerializeDescription`. This method is called to determine if the current value of the property should be persisted to the designer code file:

VB

```
Private mDescription As String = cDefaultDescription
<System.ComponentModel.AmbientValue(cDefaultDescription)>
Public Property Description As String
    Get
```

```
            If Me.mDescription = cDefaultDescription AndAlso
                                 Me.Parent IsNot Nothing Then
                Return Parent.Text
            End If
            Return mDescription
        End Get
        Set(ByVal value As String)
            mDescription = value
        End Set
    End Property

    Private Function ShouldSerializeDescription() As Boolean
        If Me.Parent IsNot Nothing Then
            Return Not Me.Description = Me.Parent.Text
        Else
            Return Not Me.Description = cDefaultDescription
        End If
    End function
```

C#

```
    private string mDescription = cDefaultDescription;
    [System.ComponentModel.AmbientValue(cDefaultDescription)]
    public string Description{
        get{
            if (this.mDescription == cDefaultDescription &&
                this.Parent != null){
                return Parent.Text;
            }
            return mDescription;
        }
        set{
            mDescription = value;
        }
    }

    private bool ShouldSerializeDescription(){
        if (this.Parent != null){
            return this.Description != this.Parent.Text;
        }
        else{
            return this.Description != cDefaultDescription;
        }
    }
```

When you create a control with this property, the initial value would be set to the value of the `DefaultDescription` constant, but in the designer you would see a value corresponding to the `Parent.Text` value. There would also be no line explicitly setting this property in the designer code file, as reflected in the Properties window by the value being non-boldfaced. If you change the value of this property to anything other than the `DefaultDescription` constant, you'll see that it becomes bold and a line is added to the designer code file. If you reset this property, the underlying value is set back to the value defined by `AmbientValue`, but all you'll see is that it has returned to displaying the `Parent.Text` value.

SUMMARY

In this chapter you have seen three of the most common tool windows in action. Knowing how to manipulate these windows can save you considerable time during development. However, the true power of Visual Studio 2012 is exposed when you start to incorporate the designer experience into your own components. This can be useful even if your components aren't going to be used outside your organization. Making effective use of the designer can improve not only the efficiency with which your controls are used, but also the performance of the application you are building.

Options and Customizations

WHAT'S IN THIS CHAPTER?

- Customizing the Visual Studio 2012 start page
- Tweaking options
- Controlling window layout

Now that you're familiar with the general layout of Visual Studio 2012, it's time to learn how you can customize the IDE to suit your working style. In this chapter you learn how to manipulate tool windows, optimize the code window for maximum viewing space, and change fonts and colors to reduce developer fatigue.

As Visual Studio has grown, so too has the number of settings that you can adjust to optimize your development experience. Unfortunately, unless you've periodically spent time sifting through the Options dialog (Tools ➪ Options), it's likely that you've overlooked one or two settings that might be important. Through the course of this chapter, you see a number of settings that might be worth further investigation.

A number of Visual Studio add-ins add their own nodes to the Options dialog because this provides a one-stop shop for configuring settings within Visual Studio. Note also that some developer setting profiles, as selected in Chapter 1, "A Quick Tour," show only a cut-down list of options. In this case, checking the Advanced check box shows the complete list of available options.

THE START PAGE

By default, when you open a new instance of Visual Studio 2012, you see the Start Page. You can adjust this behavior from the Environment ➪ Startup node of the Options dialog. Other alternatives are to display the Home Page (which you can set via the Environment ➪ Web Browser node), the last loaded solution, the open or new project dialogs, or no action at all.

The reason that most developers stick with the Start Page is that it provides a useful starting point from which to jump to any number of actions. In Figure 3-1, you can see that there are links down the left side for connecting to Team Foundation Server and for creating or opening projects. There is also a list of recent projects allowing you to quickly open projects that you have recently been working on. Hovering the mouse over the left side of a project displays a horizontal pin. Clicking the pin changes its orientation to vertical to indicate that the project has been pinned to the Recent Projects list. Alternatively, you can right-click a project and either open the containing folder (useful if you want to locate the project on disk rather than actually opening it) or remove the project from the list. In the lower-left corner there are two check boxes that control whether the Start Page is closed after opening a project and whether it's displayed at startup. If for whatever reason the Start Page is closed and you want to open it again, you can do so by selecting the View ➪ Start Page menu item.

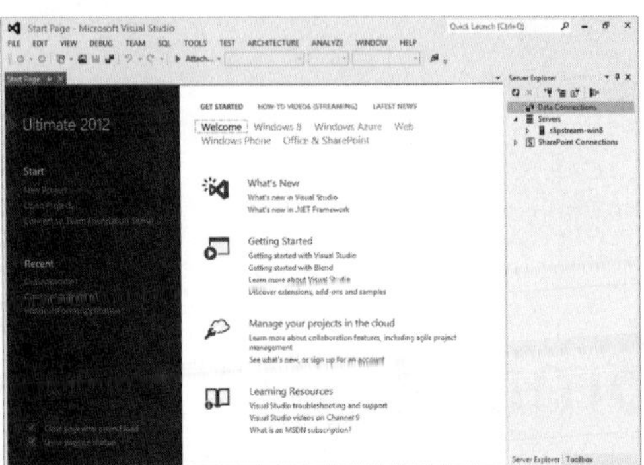

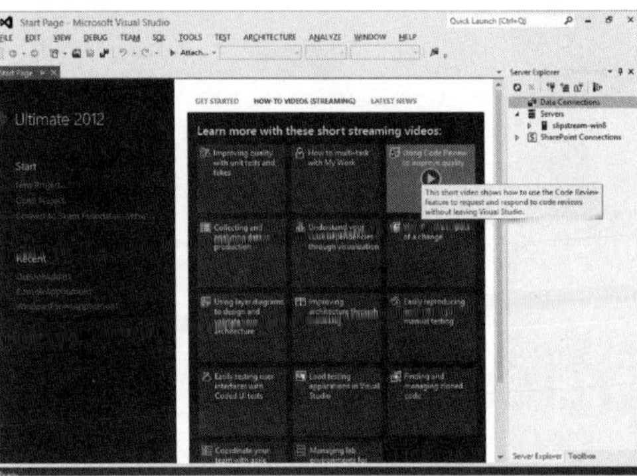

FIGURE 3-1

Near the top of the right side of the Start Page are a few clickable labels. The Get Started label (refer to Figure 3-1) contains various subsections on a variety of topics including Windows 8, Windows Azure, and the Web. Click any of these to find information on how to start working with these technologies and what's new in Visual Studio 2012. The How-To Videos provides a variety of helpful streaming videos. The Latest News label keeps you abreast of the latest happenings for Visual Studio 2012 and the .NET Framework. You can either use the default RSS feed or specify your own feed that you want to be displayed within the Start Page.

Customizing the Start Page

In Visual Studio 2012, the Start Page is a WPF control hosted within the IDE shell. You can tailor the Start Page to feature information or actions relevant to you. Rather than modifying the default Start Page, Visual Studio supports user-specific or Custom Start Pages. Unlike Visual Studio 2010, where there was a project template that gave you the basic components to create a custom start page, in Visual Studio 2012, this functionality is enabled by creating a Visual Studio Extension (VSIX) package. The details related to the creation and deployment of VSIX packages are covered in Chapter 53, "Managed Extensibility Framework (MEF)."

WINDOW LAYOUT

If you are unfamiliar with Visual Studio, the behavior of the numerous tool windows may strike you as erratic because they seem to appear in random locations and then come and go when you move between writing code (design time) and running code (run time). Actually, Visual Studio 2012 remembers the locations of tool windows in each of these modes. This way, you can optimize the way you write and debug code separately.

Also, if you are familiar with the toolbars in Visual Studio 2010, you'll see that the toolbars that are visible by default are much fewer in number (and in number of buttons). This was part of the user experience refactoring that was one of the design objectives of Visual Studio 2012. The simplification was based on a lot of user feedback (gathered both through questioning and metering) that identified the buttons which are most commonly used in the previous toolbars. The buttons that, for whatever reason, didn't make the cut are still available through customization. But the icons that remain are, for the most part, the ones most frequently used. Yes, it's difficult to adjust when someone changes a familiar interface. But over time, you'll find that Microsoft has done a good job at removing the buttons that you rarely used, leaving only the ones you click regularly.

As you open different items from the Solution Explorer, you can see that the number of toolbars across the top of the screen varies depending on the type of file being opened. Each toolbar (and, indeed, each button) has a built-in association to specific file extensions so that Visual Studio knows to display the toolbar (or enable/disable a button) when a file with one of those extensions is opened. If you close a toolbar when a file is open that has a matching file extension, Visual Studio remembers this when future files with the same extension are opened.

> **NOTE** *You can reset the association between toolbars and the file extensions via the Customize dialog (Tools ➪ Customize). On the Commands tab, select the appropriate toolbar, and click the Reset All button.*

Viewing Windows and Toolbars

After a tool window or toolbar has been closed, it can be difficult to locate it again. Luckily, most of the most frequently used tool windows are accessible via the View menu. Other tool windows, mainly related to debugging, are located under the Debug menu.

All the toolbars available in Visual Studio 2012 are listed under the View ➪ Toolbars menu item. Each toolbar currently visible is marked with a tick beside the appropriate menu item. You can also access the list of toolbars by right-clicking in any empty space in the toolbar area at the top of the Visual Studio window.

When a toolbar is visible, you can customize which buttons are displayed, either via View ➪ Toolbars ➪ Customize or Tools ➪ Customize. Alternatively, as shown in Figure 3-2, if you select the down arrow at the end of a toolbar, you see a list of all the buttons available on that toolbar, from which you can check the buttons you want to appear on the toolbar.

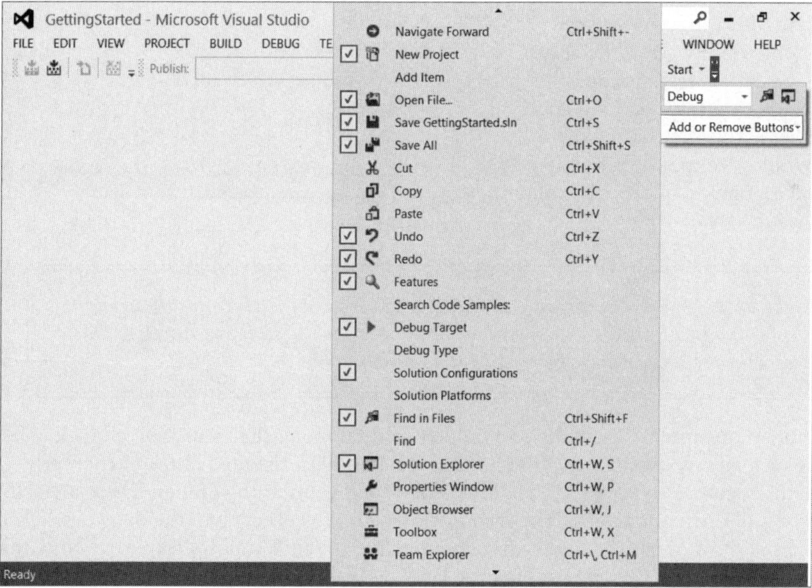

FIGURE 3-2

Navigating Open Items

After opening multiple items you notice that you run out of room across the top of the editor space and that you can no longer see the tabs for all the items you have open. Of course, you can go back to the Solution

Explorer window and select a specific item. If the item is already open it displays without reverting to its saved state. However, it is still inconvenient to have to find the item in the Solution Explorer.

Luckily, Visual Studio 2012 has a number of shortcuts to the list of open items. As with most document-based applications, Visual Studio has a Windows menu. When you open an item, its title is added to the bottom section of this menu. To display an open item, just select the item from the Windows menu, or click the generic Windows item, which displays a modal dialog from which you can select the item you want.

Another alternative is to use the drop-down menu at the end of the tab area of the editor space. Figure 3-3 shows the drop-down list of open items from which you can select the item you want to access.

The right side of Figure 3-3 is the same as the left side except for the drop-down icon. This menu also displays a down arrow, but this one has a line across the top. This line indicates that there are more tabs than can fit across the top of the editor space.

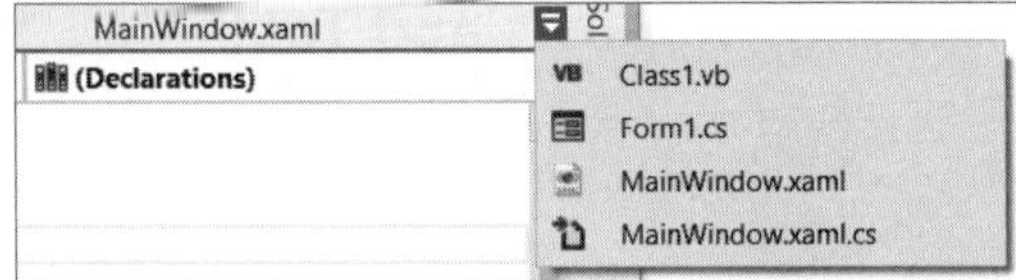

FIGURE 3-3

Another way to navigate through the open items is to press Ctrl+Tab, which displays a temporary window, as shown in Figure 3-4. It is a temporary window because when you release the Ctrl key it disappears. However, while the window is open, you can use the arrow keys or press Tab to move among the open windows.

The Ctrl+Tab window is divided into two sections, which include the active tool windows and the active files (this should actually be active items because it contains some items that don't correspond to a single file. As the number of either active files or active tool windows increases, the windows expand vertically until there are 15 items, at which point an additional column is formed.

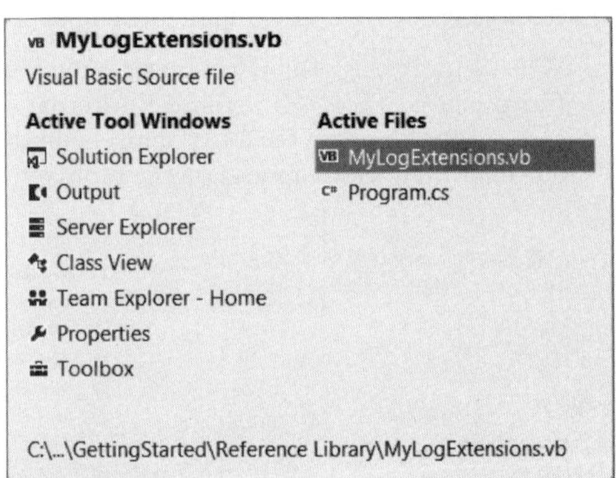

FIGURE 3-4

> **NOTE** *If you get to the point where you see multiple columns of active files, you might consider closing some or all of the unused files. The more files Visual Studio 2012 has open, the more memory it uses and the slower it performs.*

If you right-click the tab of an open item, you will see a hidden context menu that gives you a quick way to do common tasks such as save or close the file that's associated with the tab. Three particularly useful actions are Close All Documents, Close All but This, and Open Containing Folder. These are self-descriptive as the first closes all open documents, the second closes all tabs other than the one you clicked to get the context menu, and the third opens the folder that contains the file in Windows Explorer. Now that all windows are dockable, there are also actions to Float or Dock as Tabbed Document, which are enabled depending on what state the tab is in. There is also a new option in Visual Studio 2012, Copy Full Path, which copies the path to the physical file into the clipboard.

Docking

Each tool window has a default position, which it resumes when it is opened from the View menu. For example, View ⇨ Toolbox opens the Toolbox docked to the left edge of Visual Studio. When a tool window is opened and is docked against an edge, it has two states, pinned and unpinned. As you saw in Chapter 1, you can toggle between these states by clicking the vertical pin to unpin the tool window or the horizontal pin to pin the tool window.

As you unpin a tool window, it disappears back against the edge of the IDE, leaving visible a tag displaying the title of the tool window. To redisplay the tool window, the default behavior requires that you click the visible tag. If you would prefer the window to appear when the mouse hovers over the tag, go into the Options dialog and locate the Environment ➪ Tabs and Windows node. At the bottom, there is an option named Show Auto-Hidden Windows on Mouse Over. If you check this, then as you move your mouse over the tab, the hidden window becomes visible. Most developers accept the default location of tool windows, but occasionally you may want to adjust where the tool windows appear. Visual Studio 2012 has a sophisticated system for controlling the layout of tool windows. In Chapter 1 you saw how you could use the drop-down, next to the Pin and Close buttons at the top of the tool window, to make the tool window floating, dockable, or even part of the main editor space (using the Tabbed Document option).

When a tool window is dockable, you have a lot of control over where it is positioned. In Figure 3-5 you can see the top of the Properties window, which has been dragged away from its default position at the right of the IDE. To begin dragging, you need to click either the title area at the top of the tool window or the tab at the bottom of the tool window and drag the mouse in the direction you want the window to move. If you click in the title area, you see that all tool windows in that section of the IDE will also be moved. Clicking the tab results in only the corresponding tool window moving.

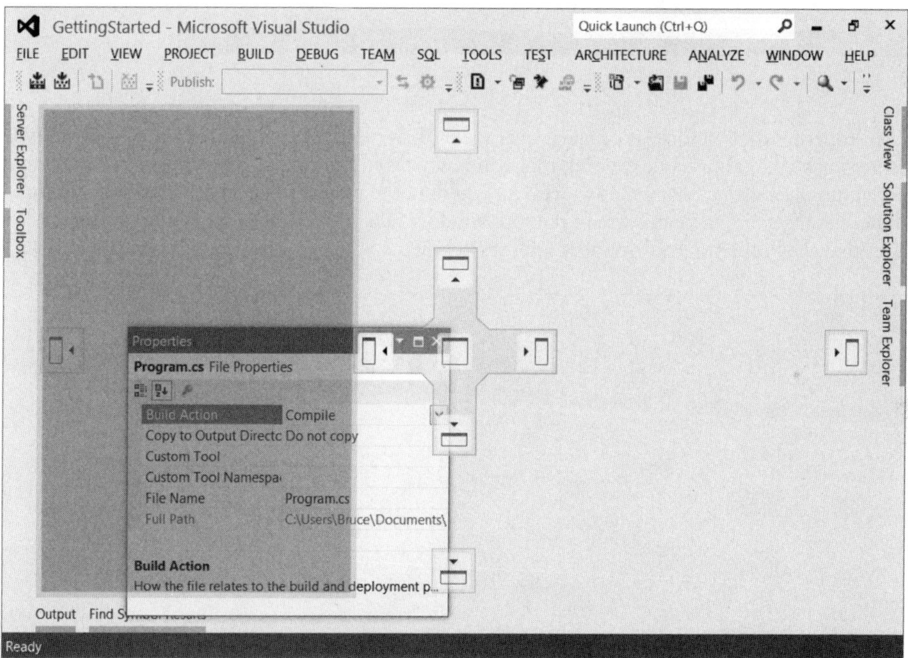

FIGURE 3-5

As you drag the tool window around Visual Studio 2012, you see that translucent icons appear at different locations around the IDE. These icons are a useful guide to help you position the tool window exactly where you want. In Figure 3-6 the SQL Server Object Explorer window has been pinned against the left side. Now when the Properties window is positioned over the left icon of the center image, the blue shading again appears on the inside of the existing tool window. This indicates that the Properties tool window will be pinned to the right of the SQL Server Object Explorer window and visible if this layout is chosen. If the far left icon were selected, the Properties tool window would again be pinned to the left of the IDE, but this time to the left of the SQL Server Object Explorer window.

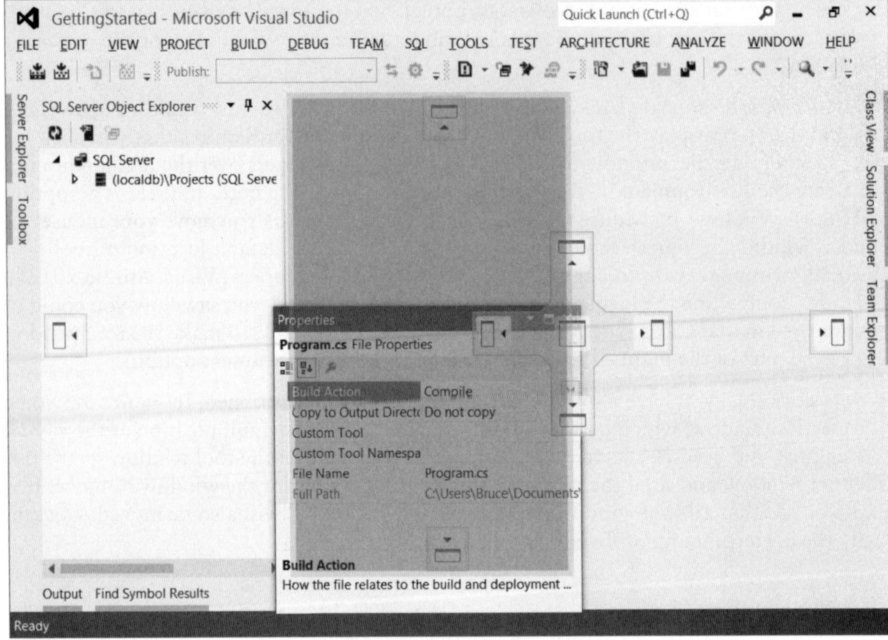

FIGURE 3-6

Alternatively, if the Properties tool window is dragged over the SQL Server Object Explorer window as shown in Figure 3-7, the center image moves over the existing tool window. This indicates that the Properties tool window will be positioned within the existing tool window area. As you drag the window over the different quadrants, you can see that the blue shading again indicates where the tool window will be positioned when the mouse is released. Figure 3-7 indicates that the Properties tool window appears below the SQL Server Object Explorer window.

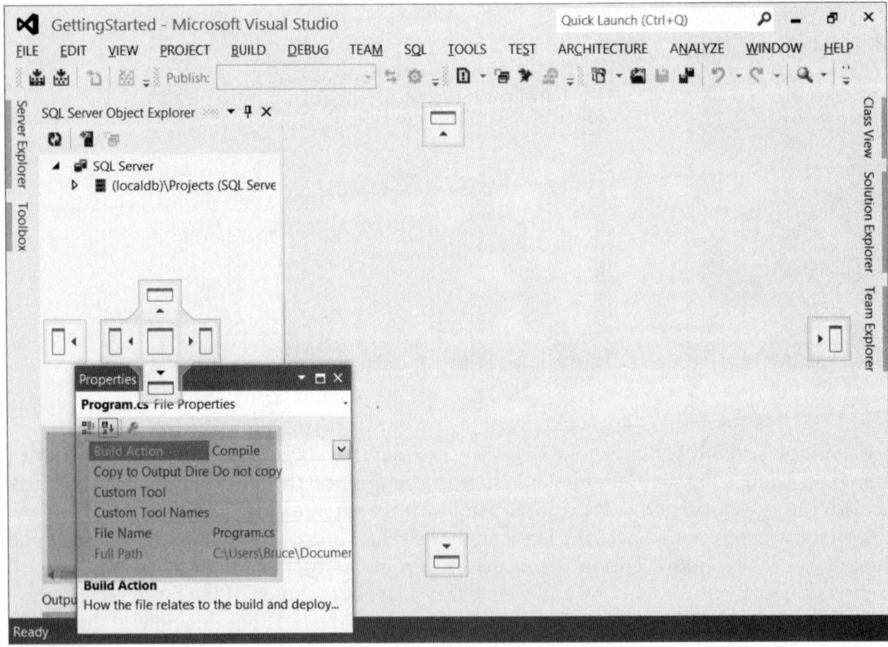

FIGURE 3-7

> **NOTE** *If you have a large screen or multiple screens, it is worth spending time laying out the tool windows you use frequently. With multiple screens, using floating tool windows means that you can position them away from the main editor space, maximizing your screen real estate. If you have a small screen, you may find that you continually have to adjust which tool windows are visible, so becoming familiar with the docking and layout options is essential.*

THE EDITOR SPACE

Like most IDEs, Visual Studio 2012 has been built up around the central code-editing window. Over time, it has evolved and is now much more than a simple text editor. Though most developers spend considerable time writing code in the editor space, an increasing number of designers are available for performing tasks such as building forms, adjusting project settings, and editing resources. Regardless of whether you write code or do form design, you are going to spend a lot of your time within Visual Studio 2012 in the editor space. Because of this, you must to know how to tweak the layout so that you can work more efficiently.

The basic look of Visual Studio 2012 is markedly different from previous versions. Whereas previous versions have been (relatively speaking) awash in colors and gradients, Visual Studio 2012 is much more stark. There are two main themes that are available: Dark and Light. For Light, the color choices are gray and black. For Dark, the color choices are black and white. Little, if any, gradients can be found. The only coloration appears in the icons used in the toolbar and the various tool windows.

The default theme is Light and is what the vast majority of images in this book were created in. Figure 3-8 shows the Dark theme.

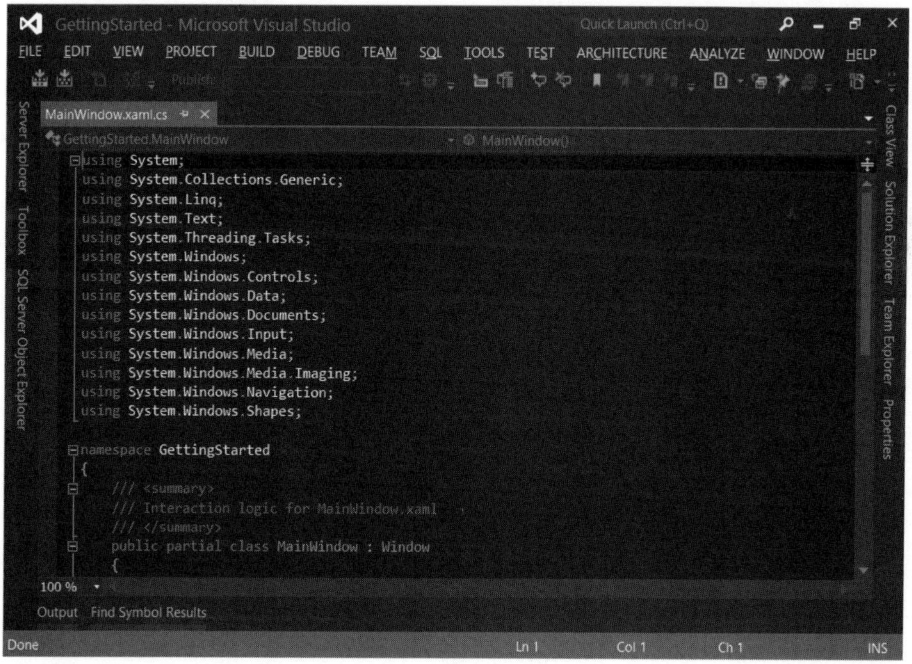

```
using System;
using System.Collections.Generic;
using System.Linq;
using System.Text;
using System.Threading.Tasks;
using System.Windows;
using System.Windows.Controls;
using System.Windows.Data;
using System.Windows.Documents;
using System.Windows.Input;
using System.Windows.Media;
using System.Windows.Media.Imaging;
using System.Windows.Navigation;
using System.Windows.Shapes;

namespace GettingStarted
{
    /// <summary>
    /// Interaction logic for MainWindow.xaml
    /// </summary>
    public partial class MainWindow : Window
    {
```

FIGURE 3-8

You can change the theme through the Options option on the Tools menu. You can select the color theme from the drop-down that appears in the Environment node.

Fonts and Colors

Some of the first things that presenters change in Visual Studio are the fonts and colors used in the editor space to make the code more readable. However, it shouldn't just be presenters who adjust these settings. Selecting fonts and colors that are easy for you to read and that aren't harsh on the eyes can make you more productive and enable you to code for longer without feeling fatigued. Figure 3-9 shows the Fonts and Colors node of the Options dialog, where you can make adjustments to the font, size, color, and styling of different display items. One thing to note about this node in the Options dialog is that it is slow to load, so try to avoid accidentally clicking it.

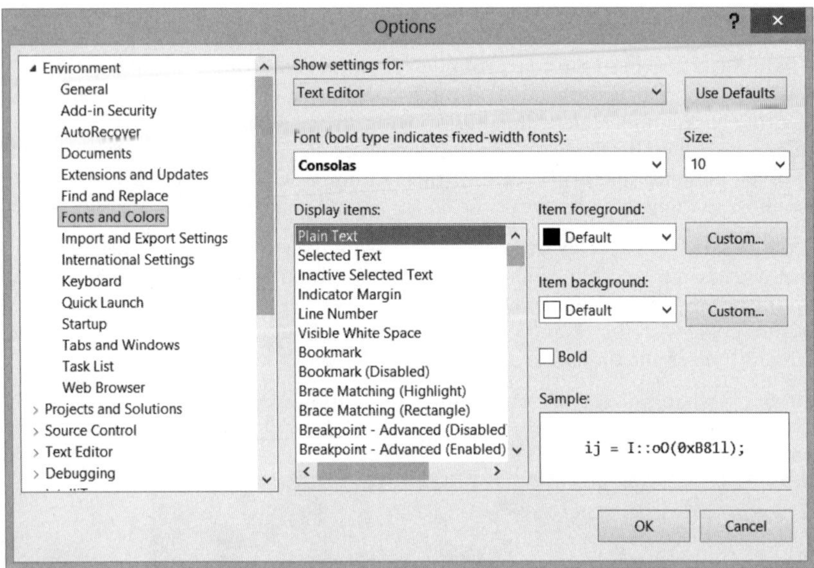

FIGURE 3-9

To adjust the appearance of a particular text item within Visual Studio 2012, you first need to select the area of the IDE that it applies to. In Figure 3-9, the Text Editor has been selected and has been used to determine which items should appear in the Display Items list. When you find the relevant item in this list, you can make adjustments to the font and colors.

> **NOTE** *Some items in the Display Items list, such as Plain Text, are reused by a number of areas within Visual Studio 2012, which can result in some unpredictable changes when you tweak fonts and colors.*

When choosing a font, remember that proportional fonts are usually not as effective for writing code as nonproportional fonts (also known as fixed-width fonts). Fixed-width fonts are distinguished in the list from the variable-width types, so they are easy to locate.

Visual Guides

When you edit a file, Visual Studio 2012 automatically colors the code based on the type of file. For example, VB code highlights keywords in blue, variable names and class references in black, and string literals in red. In Figure 3-10 you can see that there is a line running up the left side of the code. This is used to indicate where the code blocks are. You can click the minus sign to condense the `btnSayHello_Click` method or the entire `Form1` code block.

Various points about visual guides are shown in Figures 3-10 through 3-12. Those readers familiar with VB.NET realize that Figure 3-10 is missing the end of the line where the method is set to handle the `Click` event of the `btnSayHello` button. This is because the rest of the line is obscured by the edge of the code window. To see what is at the end of the line, the developer must either scroll the window to the right or use the keyboard to navigate the cursor to the end of the line. In Figure 3-11, word wrap has been enabled via the Options dialog. (See the Text Editor ⇨ All Languages ⇨ General node.)

Unfortunately, enabling word wrapping can make it hard to work out which lines have been wrapped. Luckily, Visual Studio 2012 has an option (immediately below the check box to enable word wrapping in the Options dialog) that can display visual glyphs at the end of each line that indicate a line has been wrapped to the next line (refer to Figure 3-12). There are also two other visual guides you can use. On the left, outside the code block markers, you can include line numbers. These can be enabled via the Line Numbers check box below both the Word Wrap and Visual Glyphs check boxes. The other guide is the use of dots that represent space in the code. Unlike the other visual guides, this one can be enabled via the Edit ⇨ Advanced ⇨ View White Space menu item when the code editor space has focus.

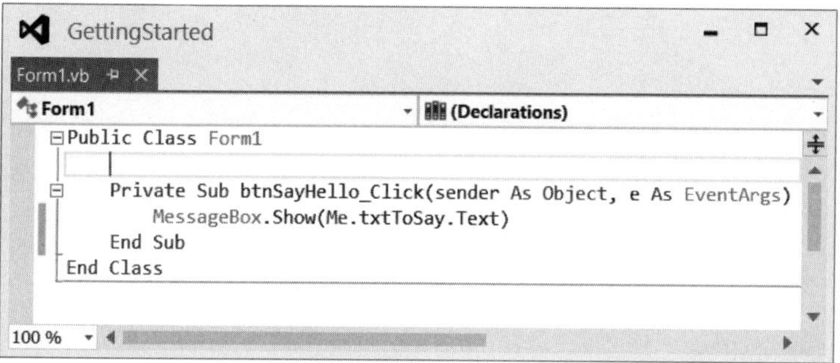

FIGURE 3-10

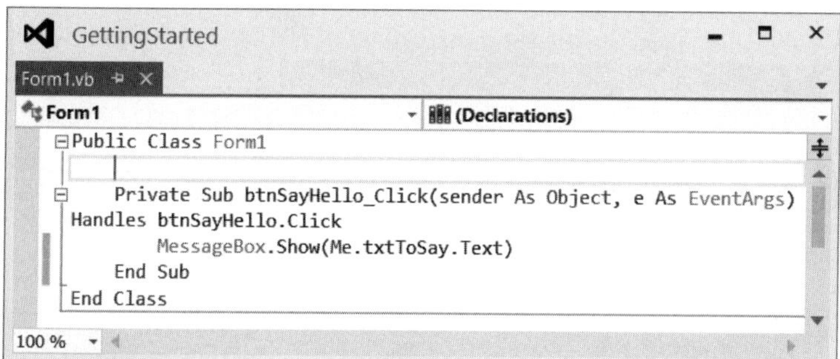

FIGURE 3-11

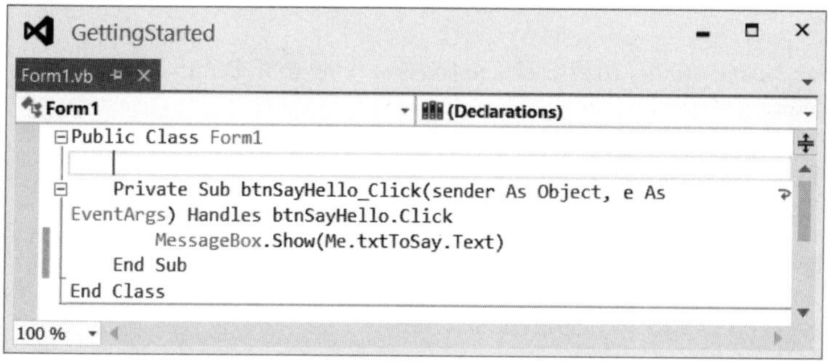

```
GettingStarted
Form1.vb
Form1                                   (Declarations)
Public Class Form1

    Private Sub btnSayHello_Click(sender As Object, e As
EventArgs) Handles btnSayHello.Click
        MessageBox.Show(Me.txtToSay.Text)
    End Sub
End Class
100 %
```

FIGURE 3-12

Full-Screen Mode

If you have a number of tool windows and multiple toolbars visible, you might have noticed that you quickly run out of space for actually writing code. For this reason, Visual Studio 2012 has a full-screen mode that you can access via the View ➪ Full Screen menu item. Alternatively, you can press Shift+Alt+Enter to toggle in and out of full-screen mode. Figure 3-13 shows the top of Visual Studio 2012 in full-screen mode. As you can see, no toolbars or tool windows are visible, and the window is completely maximized, even to the exclusion of the normal Minimize, Restore, and Close buttons.

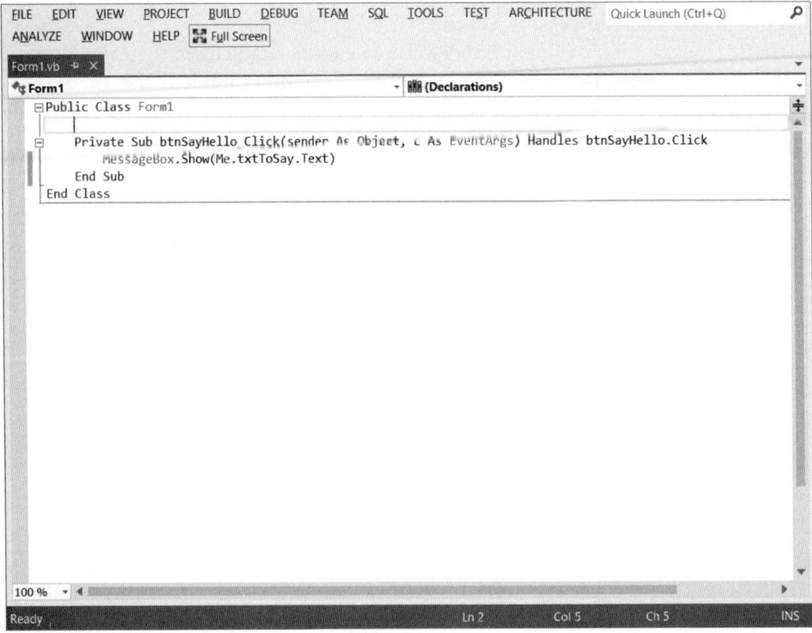

FIGURE 3-13

> **NOTE** *If you use multiple screens, full-screen mode can be particularly useful. Undock the tool windows and place them on the second monitor. When the editor window is in full-screen mode, you still have access to the tool windows, without having to toggle back and forth. If you undock a code window this will not be set to full screen.*

Tracking Changes

To enhance the experience of editing, Visual Studio 2012 uses line-level tracking to indicate which lines of code you have modified during an editing session. When you open a file to begin editing there will be no line coloring. However, when you begin to edit, you notice that a yellow (light gray for the Dark theme) mark appears next to the lines that have been modified. In Figure 3-14 you can see that the `MessageBox` line has been modified since this file was last saved.

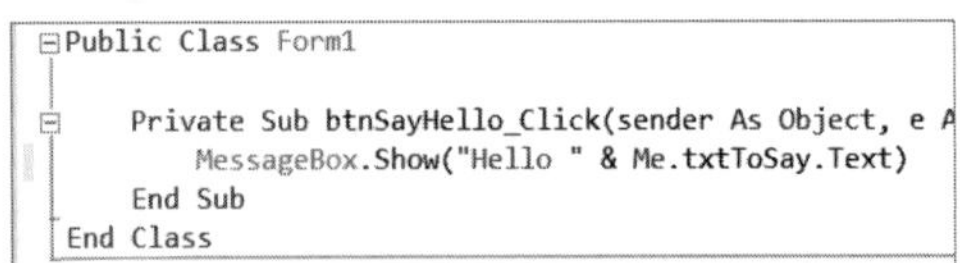

FIGURE 3-14

When the file is saved, the modified lines change to having a green (same color in the Dark theme) mark next to them. In Figure 3-15 the first `MessageBox` line has changed since the file was opened, but those changes have been saved to disk. However, the second `MessageBox` line has not yet been saved.

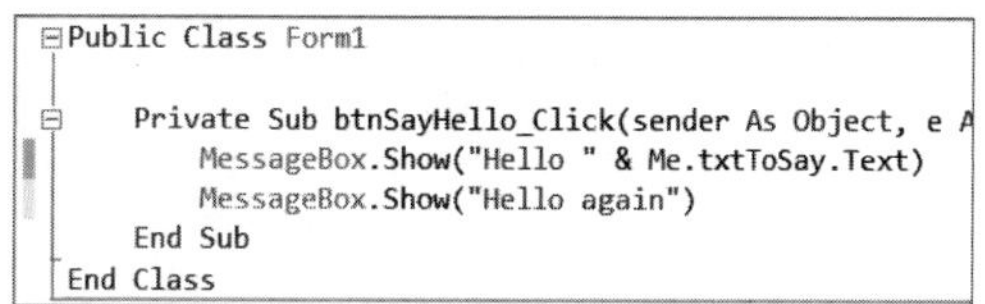

FIGURE 3-15

> **NOTE** *If you don't find tracking changes to be useful, you can disable this feature by unchecking the Text Editor ⇨ General ⇨ Track Change node in the Options dialog.*

OTHER OPTIONS

You can use many options that haven't yet been mentioned to tweak the way Visual Studio operates. Through the remainder of this chapter some of the more useful options that can help you be more productive are presented.

Keyboard Shortcuts

Visual Studio 2012 ships with many ways to perform the same action. Menus, toolbars, and various tool windows provide direct access to many commands, but despite the huge number available, many more are not accessible through the graphical interface. Instead, these commands are accessed (along with most of those in the menus and toolbars) via keyboard shortcuts.

These shortcuts range from the familiar Ctrl+Shift+S to save all changes, to the obscure Ctrl+Alt+E to display the Exceptions dialog window. As you might have guessed, you can set your own keyboard shortcuts and even change the existing ones. Even better, you can filter the shortcuts to operate only in certain contexts, meaning you can use the same shortcut differently depending on what you're doing.

Figure 3-16 shows the Keyboard node in the Environment section of the Options dialog with the default keyboard mapping scheme selected. If you want to change to use a different keyboard mapping scheme, simply select it from the drop-down, and press the Reset button.

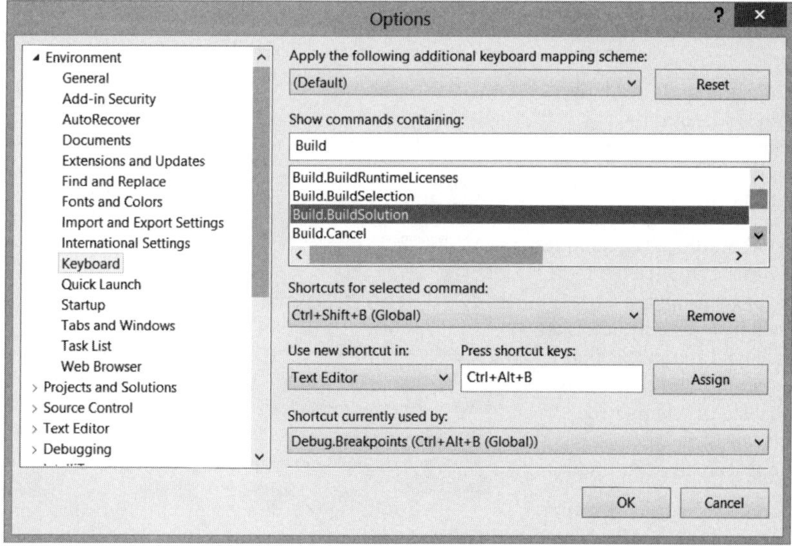

FIGURE 3-16

> **NOTE** *The keyboard mapping schemes are stored as VSK files at* `C:\Program Files\Microsoft Visual Studio 11.0\Common7\IDE`. *(or* `C:\Program Files (x86)\Microsoft Visual Studio 11.0\Common7\IDE` *if you are using the 64-bit version). This is the keyboard mapping file format used in versions of Visual Studio after Visual Studio 2005. To import keyboard mappings from Visual Studio 2005, use the import settings feature (see the end of this chapter); for earlier versions, copy the appropriate VSK file into the aforementioned folder, and you can select it from the mapping scheme drop-down the next time you open the Options dialog.*

The listbox in the middle of Figure 3-16 lists every command that is available in Visual Studio 2012. Unfortunately, this list is quite extensive and the Options dialog is not resizable, which makes navigating this list difficult. To make it easier to search for commands, you can filter the command list using the Show Commands Containing textbox. In Figure 3-16 the word *Build* has been used to filter the list down to all the commands starting with or containing that word. From this list the `Build.BuildSolution` command has been selected. Because there is already a keyboard shortcut assigned to this command, the Shortcuts for Selected Command drop-down and the Remove button have been enabled. It is possible to have multiple shortcuts for the same command, so the drop-down enables you to remove individual assigned shortcuts.

> **NOTE** *Having multiple shortcuts is useful if you want to keep a default shortcut — so that other developers feel at home using your setup — but also add your own personal one.*

The remainder of this dialog enables you to assign a new shortcut to the command you have selected. Simply move to the Press Shortcut Keys textbox, and as the label suggests, press the appropriate keys. In Figure 3-16 the keyboard chord Ctrl+Alt+B has been entered, but this shortcut is already being used by another command, as shown at the bottom of the dialog window. If you click the Assign button, this keyboard shortcut will be remapped to the `Build.BuildSolution` command.

To restrict a shortcut's use to only one contextual area of Visual Studio 2012, select the context from the Use New Shortcut In drop-down list. The Global option indicates that the shortcut should be applied across the entire environment, but we want this new shortcut to work only in the editor window, so the Text Editor item has been selected in Figure 3-16.

Quick Launch

The continuing proliferation of commands available in Visual Studio cannot be fully addressed by programming keyboard shortcuts. Aside from the sheer number of commands, it is also possible to run out of reasonable keyboard combinations.

To alleviate this problem, Visual Studio 2012 includes a new feature called Quick Launch. Opened from the top-left portion of the toolbar or by using the Ctrl+Q shortcut (and shown in Figure 3-17), visually, it looks like any other search textbox. The difference is that the scope of the search is every command that exists within Visual Studio. So regardless of whether the command is in the toolbar, on one of the menus, or not associated with either, the search box can find it.

The search box is also a progressive one. As you type characters, the list of possible matches displays. The

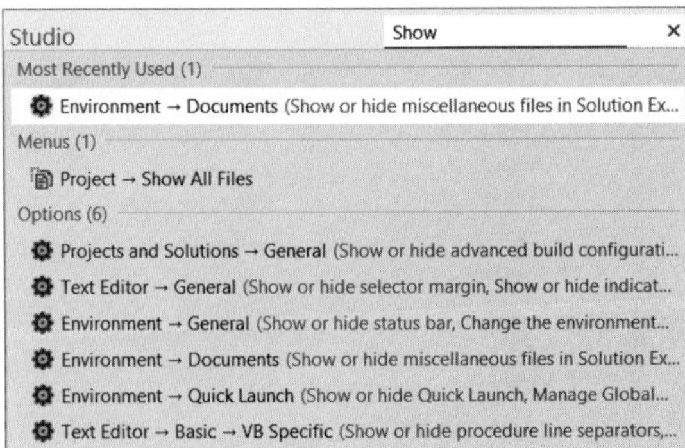

FIGURE 3-17

matches are placed in up to four different categories: Most Recently Used, Menus, Options, and Open Documents. Not all the matches are shown in each category. (The results would be too overwhelming, in some cases.) If you want to see more results from a particular category, you can use Ctrl+Q or Ctrl+Shift+Q to navigate back and forth through the categories, showing more from each category as appropriate.

You can also scope your search to the items in a specific category directory from the textbox. For example, entering the text **@mru font** would display the most recently used items that include the term "font." For the other categories, the scoping keyword are @menu, @otp, and @doc.

The default setting for Quick Launch is to not persist the search terms. After you move your cursor outside the Quick Launch area, the text area is cleared. If you want to modify this behavior so that the search terms are persisted, you can use the Quick Launch node in Tools ⇨ Options. Ensuring that the Show Search Results from Previous Search When Quick Launch Is Activated check box is checked allows your previous search terms to be preserved the next time you access Quick Launch.

Projects and Solutions

Several options relate to projects and solutions. The first of these is perhaps the most helpful — the default locations of your projects. By default, Visual Studio 2012 uses the standard Documents and Settings path common to many applications (see Figure 3-18), but this might not be where you want to keep your development work.

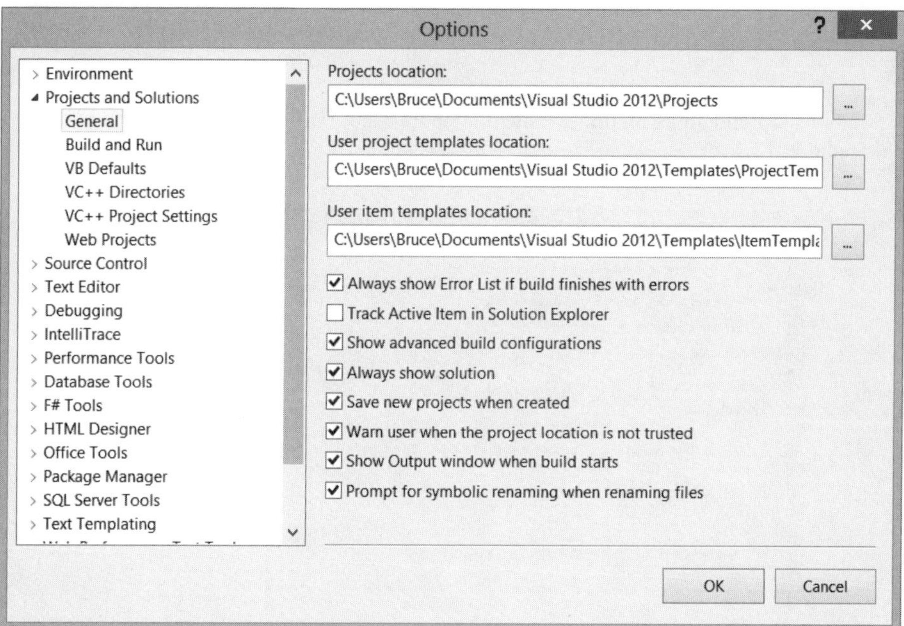

FIGURE 3-18

You can also change the location of template files at this point. If your organization uses a common network location for corporate project templates, you can change the default location in Visual Studio 2012 to point to this remote address rather than map the network drive.

You can adjust a number of other options to change how projects and solutions are managed in Visual Studio 2012. One of particular interest is Track Active Item in Solution Explorer. With this option enabled, the layout of the Solution Explorer changes as you switch among items to ensure the current item is in focus.

This includes expanding (but not collapsing again) projects and folders, which can be frustrating on a large solution because you are continually having to collapse projects so that you can navigate.

Another option that relates to solutions, but doesn't appear in Figure 3-18, is to list miscellaneous files in the Solution Explorer. Say you are working on a solution and you have to inspect an XML document that isn't contained in the solution. Visual Studio 2012 will happily open the file, but you will have to reopen it every time you open the solution. Alternatively, if you enable Environment ⇨ Documents ⇨ Show Miscellaneous Files in Solution Explorer via the Options dialog, the file will be temporarily added to the solution. The miscellaneous files folder to which this file is added is shown in Figure 3-19.

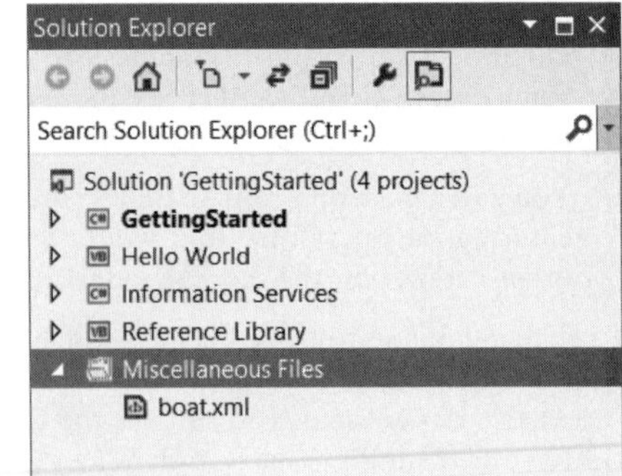

FIGURE 3-19

> **NOTE** *Visual Studio 2012 will automatically manage the list of miscellaneous files, keeping only the most recent ones, based on the number of files defined in the Options dialog. You can get Visual Studio to track up to 256 files in this list, and files will be evicted based on when they were last accessed.*

Build and Run

The Projects and Solutions ⇨ Build and Run node, shown in Figure 3-20, can be used to tailor the build behavior of Visual Studio 2012.

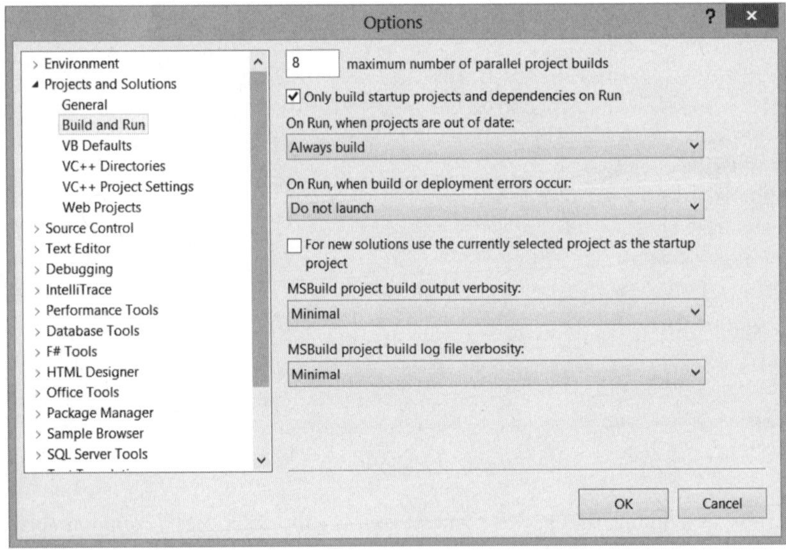

FIGURE 3-20

To reduce the amount of time it takes to build your solution, you may want to increase the maximum number of parallel builds that are performed. Visual Studio 2012 can build in parallel only those projects that are not dependent, but if you have a large number of independent projects, this might yield a noticeable benefit. Be aware that on a single-core or single-processor machine this may actually increase the time taken to build your solution.

Figure 3-20 shows that projects will Always Build when they are out of date, and that if there are build errors, the solution will not launch. Both these options can increase your productivity, but be warned that they eliminate dialogs letting you know what's going on.

> **NOTE** *The last option worth noting in Figure 3-20 is the MSBuild project build output verbosity. In most cases the Visual Studio 2012 build output is sufficient for debugging build errors. However, in some cases, particularly when building ASP.NET projects, you need to increase verbosity to diagnose a build error. Visual Studio 2012 has the capability to control the log file verbosity independently of the output.*

VB Options

VB programmers have four compiler options that can be configured at a project or a file level. You can also set the defaults on the Projects and Solutions ➪ VB Defaults node of the Options dialog. Before Visual Studio 2010, earlier versions of VB had an Option Explicit, which forced variables to be defined prior to their use in code. When it was introduced, many experts recommended that it be turned on permanently because it did away with many run-time problems in VB applications that were caused by improper use of variables.

Option Strict takes enforcing good programming practices one step further by forcing developers to explicitly convert variables to their correct types, rather than let the compiler try to guess the proper conversion method. Again, this results in fewer runtime issues and better performance.

> **NOTE** *We advise strongly that you use Option Strict to ensure that your code is not implicitly converting variables inadvertently. If you are not using Option Strict, with all the language features introduced in the last few versions of .NET Framework, you may not be making the most effective use of the language.*

IMPORTING AND EXPORTING SETTINGS

When you have the IDE in exactly the configuration you want, you may want to back up the settings for future use. You can do this by exporting the IDE settings to a file that can then be used to restore the settings or even transfer them to a series of Visual Studio 2012 installations so that they all share the same IDE setup.

> **NOTE** *The Environment ➪ Import and Export Settings node in the Options dialog enables you to specify a team settings file. This can be located on a network share, and Visual Studio 2012 can automatically apply new settings if the file changes.*

To export the current configuration, select Tools ➪ Import and Export Settings to start the Import and Export Settings Wizard. The first step in the wizard is to select the Export option and which settings are to be backed up during the export procedure.

As shown in Figure 3-21, a variety of grouped options can be exported. The screenshot shows the Options section expanded, revealing that the Debugging and Projects settings will be backed up along with the Text Editor and Windows Forms Designer configurations. As the small exclamation icon indicates, some settings are not included in the export by default because they contain information that may infringe on your privacy. You need to select such sections manually if you want them to be included in the backup. After you select the settings you want to export, you can progress through the rest of the wizard, which might take a few minutes depending on the number of settings being exported.

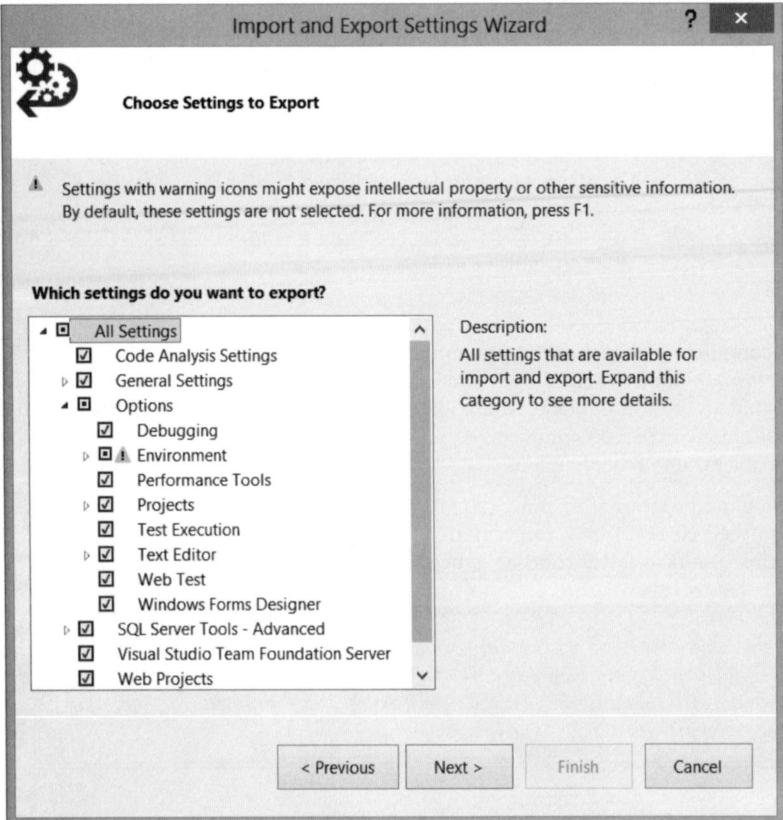

FIGURE 3-21

Importing a settings file is just as easy. The same wizard is used, but you select the Import option on the first screen. Rather than simply overwriting the current configuration, the wizard enables you to back up the current setup first.

You can then select from a list of preset configuration files — the same set of files from which you can choose when you first start Visual Studio 2012 — or browse to a settings file that you created previously. When the settings file has been chosen, you can then choose to import only certain sections of the configuration or import the whole lot.

The wizard excludes some sections by default, such as External Tools or Command Aliases so that you don't inadvertently overwrite customized settings. Make sure you select these sections if you want to do a full restore.

> **NOTE** *If you just want to restore the configuration of Visual Studio 2012 to one of the default presets, you can choose the Reset All Settings option in the opening screen of the wizard, rather than go through the import process.*

SUMMARY

This chapter covered only a core selection of the useful options available to you as you start to shape the Visual Studio interface to suit your own programming style; many other options are available. These numerous options enable you to adjust the way you edit your code, add controls to your forms, and even select the methods to use when debugging code.

The settings within the Visual Studio 2012 Options page also enable you to control how and where applications are created, and even to customize the keyboard shortcuts you use. Throughout the remainder of this book, you can see the Options dialog revisited according to specific functionality such as compiling, debugging, and writing macros.

The Visual Studio Workspace

WHAT'S IN THIS CHAPTER?

- Using the code editor
- Exploring the core Visual Studio tool windows
- Reorganizing your workspace

So far you have seen how to get started with Visual Studio 2012 and how to customize the IDE to suit the way that you work. In this chapter, you'll learn to take advantage of some of the built-in commands, shortcuts, and supporting tool windows that can help you to write code and design forms.

THE CODE EDITOR

As a developer you're likely to spend a considerable portion of your time writing code, which means that knowing how to tweak the layout of your code and navigating it effectively are particularly important. The WPF-based code editor provides numerous features, including navigating, formatting, using multiple monitors, creating tab groups, searching, and more.

The Code Editor Window Layout

When you open a code file for editing you are working in the code editor window, as shown in Figure 4-1. The core of the code editor window is the code pane in which the code displays.

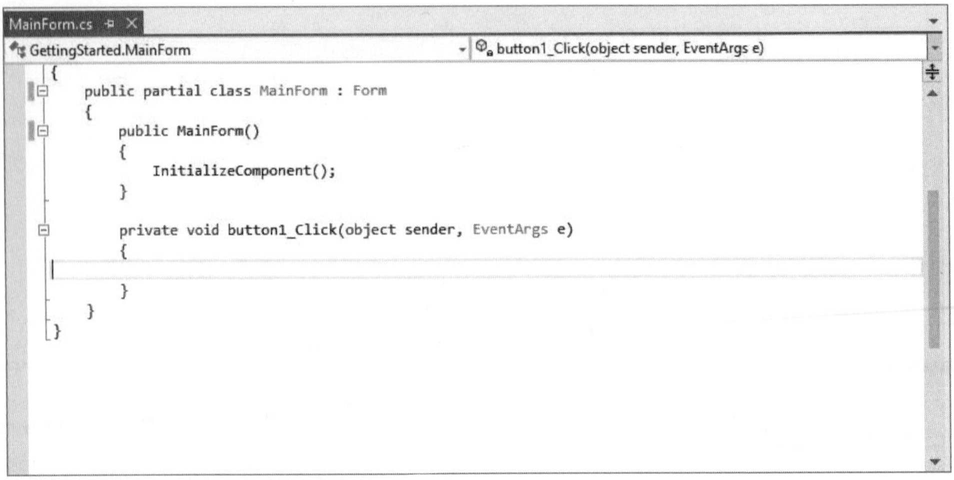

```
MainForm.cs
GettingStarted.MainForm          button1_Click(object sender, EventArgs e)
{
    public partial class MainForm : Form
    {
        public MainForm()
        {
            InitializeComponent();
        }

        private void button1_Click(object sender, EventArgs e)
        {

        }
    }
}
```

FIGURE 4-1

Above the code pane are two drop-down lists that can help you navigate the code file. The first drop-down lists the classes in the code file, and the second one lists the members of the selected class in the first drop-down. These are listed in alphabetical order, making it easier to find a method or member definition within the file.

As you modify the code in the code editor window, lines of code that you've modified since the file has been opened are marked in the left margin — yellow for unsaved changes and green for those that have been saved.

Regions

Effective class design usually results in classes that serve a single purpose and are not overly complex or lengthy. However, there will be times when you have to implement so many interfaces that your code file will become unwieldy. In this case, you have a number of options, such as partitioning the code into multiple files or using regions to condense the code, thereby making it easier to navigate.

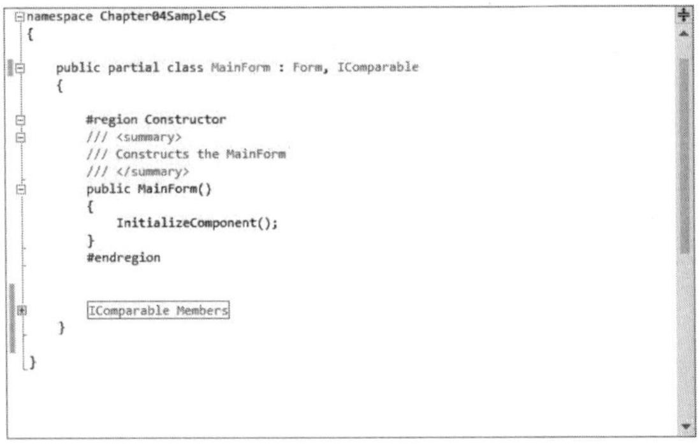

```
namespace Chapter04SampleCS
{
    public partial class MainForm : Form, IComparable
    {
        #region Constructor
        /// <summary>
        /// Constructs the MainForm
        /// </summary>
        public MainForm()
        {
            InitializeComponent();
        }
        #endregion

        IComparable Members
    }
}
```

FIGURE 4-2

The introduction of partial classes (where the definition of a class can be split over two or more files) means that at design time you can place code into different physical files representing a single logical class. The advantage of using separate files is that you can effectively group all methods that are related; for example, methods that implement an interface. The problem with this strategy is that navigating the code then requires continual switching between code files.

An alternative is to use named code regions to condense sections of code that are not currently in use. In Figure 4-2 you can see that two regions are defined, called `Constructor` and

`IComparable`. Clicking the minus sign next to `#region` condenses the region into a single line and clicking the plus sign expands it again.

> **NOTE** *You don't need to expand a region to see the code within it. Simply hover the mouse cursor over the region, and a tooltip displays the code within it.*

Outlining

In addition to regions that you have defined, you have the ability to auto-outline your code, making it easy to collapse methods, comments, and class definitions. Auto-outlining is enabled by default, but if it's not enabled you can enable it using the Edit ➪ Outlining ➪ Start Automatic Outlining menu item.

Figure 4-3 shows four condensable regions. One is a defined region called `Constructor`; however, there are also three other automatic regions, outlining the class, the XML comments, and the constructor method (which has been collapsed). Automatic outlines can be condensed and expanded in the same way as regions you define manually.

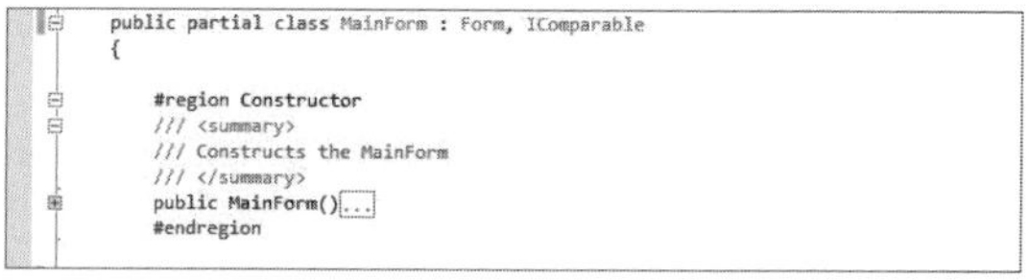

The Edit ➪ Outlining menu provides a number of commands to help in toggling outlining, such as collapsing the entire file to just method/property definitions (Edit ➪ Outlining ➪ Collapse to Definitions) and expanding it to display all collapsed code again (Edit ➪ Outlining ➪ Stop Outlining). The other way to expand and condense regions is via the keyboard shortcut Ctrl+M, Ctrl+M. This shortcut toggles between the two layouts.

```
public partial class MainForm : Form, IComparable
{
    #region Constructor
    /// <summary>
    /// Constructs the MainForm
    /// </summary>
    public MainForm()[...]
    #endregion
```

FIGURE 4-3

> **NOTE** *One trick for C# developers is that Ctrl+] enables you to easily navigate from the beginning of a region, outline, or code block to the end and back again.*

Code Formatting

By default, Visual Studio 2012 assists you in writing readable code by automatically indenting and aligning. However, it is also configurable so that you can control how your code is arranged. Common to all languages is the ability to control what happens when you create a new line. In Figure 4-4 you can see that there is a Tabs node under the Text Editor ➪ All Languages node of the Options dialog. Setting values here defines the default value for all languages, which you can then overwrite for an individual language using the Basic ➪ Tabs node (for VB.NET), C# ➪ Tabs, or other language nodes.

By default, the indenting behavior for both C# and VB.NET is smart indenting, which will, among other things, automatically add indentation as you open and close enclosures. Smart indenting is not available for all languages, in which case block indenting is used.

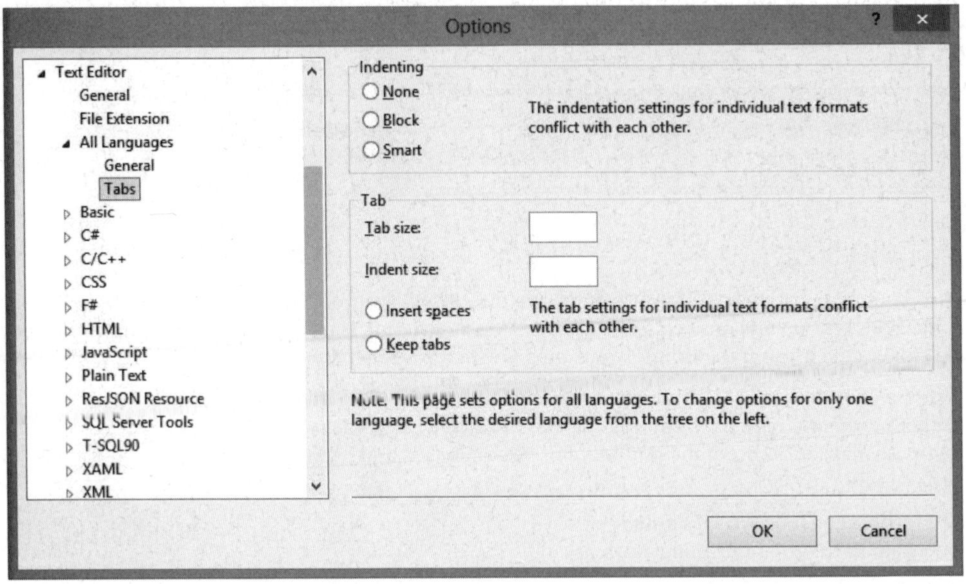

FIGURE 4-4

> **NOTE** *If you are working on a small screen, you might want to reduce the tab and indent sizes to optimize screen usage. Keeping the tab and indent sizes the same ensures that you can easily indent your code with a single tab keypress.*
>
> *What is interesting about this dialog is the degree of control C# users have over the layout of their code. Under the VB Specific node is a single check box entitled Pretty Listing (Reformatting) of Code, which if enabled keeps your code looking uniform without you worrying about aligning methods, closures, class definitions, or namespaces. C# users, on the other hand, can control nearly every aspect of how the code editor reformats code.*

Visual Studio's Smart Indenting does a good job of automatically indenting code as it is written or pasted into the code editor, but occasionally you can come across code that has not been properly formatted, making it difficult to read. To have Visual Studio reformat the entire document and set the brace locations and line indentations, select Edit ➪ Advanced ➪ Format Document or press Ctrl+K, Ctrl+D. To reformat just the selected code block, select Edit ➪ Advanced ➪ Format Selection or press Ctrl+K, Ctrl+F.

When writing code, to indent an entire block of code one level without changing each line individually, simply select the block and press Tab. Each line has a tab inserted at its start. To unindent a block one level, select it and press Shift+Tab.

> **NOTE** *You may have noticed the Tabify/Untabify Selected Lines commands under the Edit ➪ Advanced menu and wondered how these differ from the Format Selection command. These commands simply convert leading spaces in lines to tabs and vice versa, rather than recalculating the indenting as the Format Selection command does.*

Navigating Forward/Backward

As you move within and between items, Visual Studio 2012 tracks where you have been, in much the same way that a web browser tracks the sites you have visited. Using the Navigate Forward and Navigate Backward items from the View menu, you can easily go back and forth between the various locations in the project that you have changed. The keyboard shortcut to navigate backward is Ctrl+–. To navigate forward again it is Ctrl+Shift+–.

Additional Code Editor Features

The Visual Studio code editor is rich with far more features than we can cover in depth here. However, here are a few additional features that you may find useful.

Reference Highlighting

Another great feature is reference highlighting. All uses of the symbol (such as a method or property) under the cursor within its scope are highlighted (as shown in Figure 4-5). This makes it easy to spot where else this symbol is used within your code. You can easily navigate between the uses by Ctrl+Shift+Up/Down.

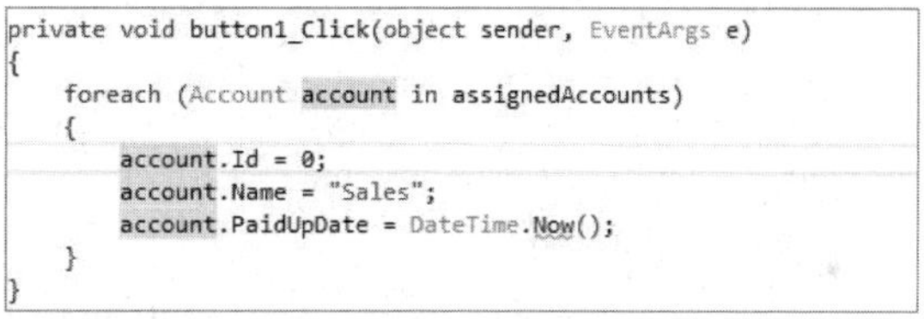

```
private void button1_Click(object sender, EventArgs e)
{
    foreach (Account account in assignedAccounts)
    {
        account.Id = 0;
        account.Name = "Sales";
        account.PaidUpDate = DateTime.Now();
    }
}
```

FIGURE 4-5

Code Zooming

You can use Ctrl+Mouse Wheel to zoom in and out of your code (effectively making the text larger or smaller). This feature can be especially useful when presenting to a group to enable the people at the back of the audience to see the code being demonstrated. The bottom left corner of the code editor also has a drop-down enabling you to select from some predefined zoom levels.

Word Wrap

You can turn on word wrap in the code editor from the options. Go to Tools ➪ Options, expand the Text Editor node, select the All Languages subnode, and select the Word wrap option. You can also choose to display a return arrow glyph where text has been wrapped by selecting the Show Visual Glyphs for Word Wrap option below the Word Wrap option.

You can turn this on for the current project by selecting Edit ➪ Advanced ➪ Word Wrap.

Line Numbers

To keep track of where you are in a code file, you may find it useful to turn on line numbers in the code editor (as shown in Figure 4-6). To turn line numbers on, go to Tools ➪ Options, expand the Text Editor node, select the All Languages sub-node, and select the Line Numbers option.

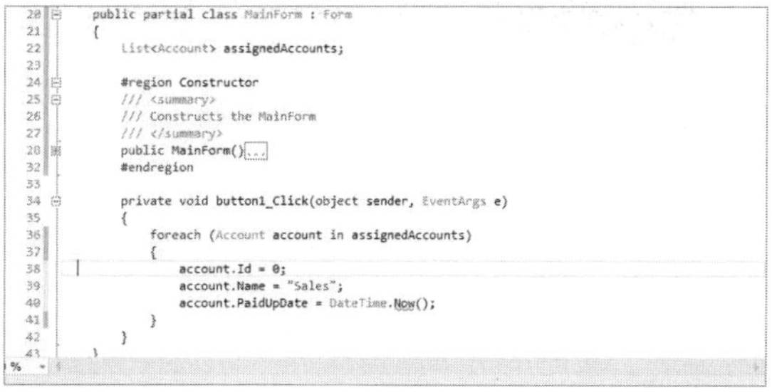

```
public partial class MainForm : Form
{
    List<Account> assignedAccounts;

    #region Constructor
    /// <summary>
    /// Constructs the MainForm
    /// </summary>
    public MainForm()...
    #endregion

    private void button1_Click(object sender, EventArgs e)
    {
        foreach (Account account in assignedAccounts)
        {
            account.Id = 0;
            account.Name = "Sales";
            account.PaidUpDate = DateTime.Now();
        }
    }
}
```

FIGURE 4-6

Split View

Sometimes you want to view two different parts of the same code file at the same time. Split view enables you to do this by splitting the active code editor window into two horizontal panes separated by a splitter bar. These can then be scrolled separately to display different parts of the same file simultaneously (as shown in Figure 4-7).

To split a code editor window, select Split from the Window menu. Alternatively, drag the handle directly above the vertical scroll bar down to position the splitter bar.

Drag the splitter bar up and down to adjust the size of each pane. To remove the splitter simply double-click the splitter bar, or select Remove Split from the Window menu.

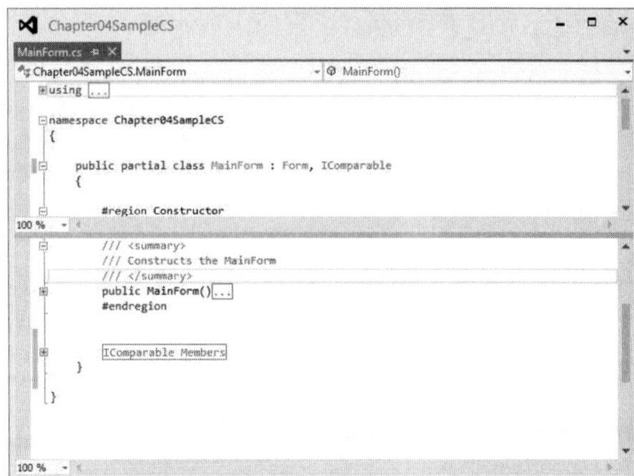

FIGURE 4-7

Tear Away (Floating) Code Windows

A great feature for those with multiple monitors is the ability to "tear off" or float code editor windows (and tool windows) and move them outside the main Visual Studio IDE window (as shown in Figure 4-8), including onto another monitor. This allows you to now make use of the extra screen real estate that having multiple monitors provides by enabling multiple code editor windows to be visible at the same time over separate monitors. It is also possible to place these floating windows onto a "raft" so that they can be moved together (as shown in Figure 4-9). To tear off a window, make sure it has the focus, and then select Float from the Window menu. Alternatively, right-click the title bar of the window, and select Float from the drop-down menu, or simply click and drag the tab for that window (effectively tearing it away from its docked position) and position it where you want it to be located.

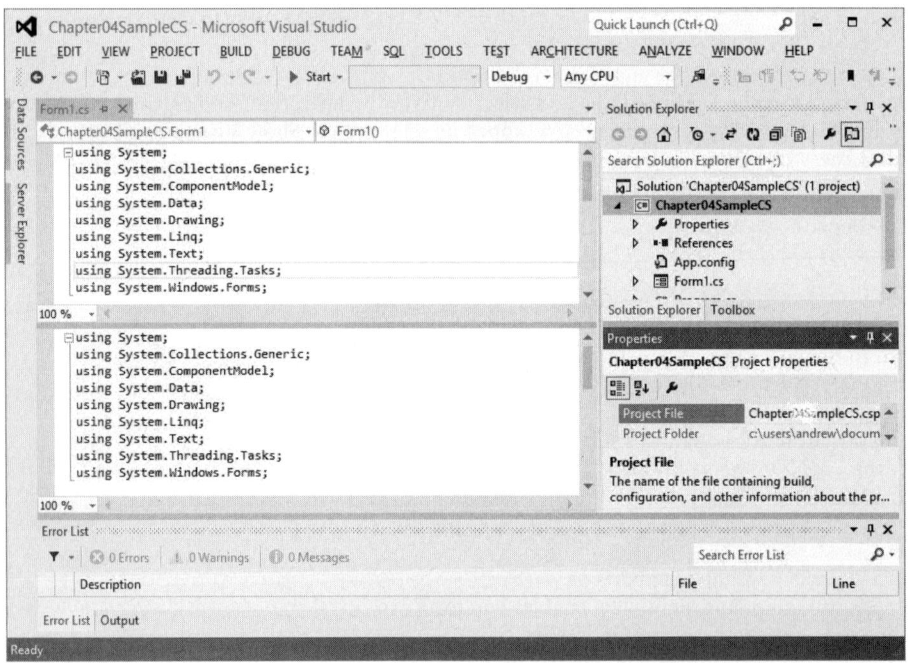

FIGURE 4-8

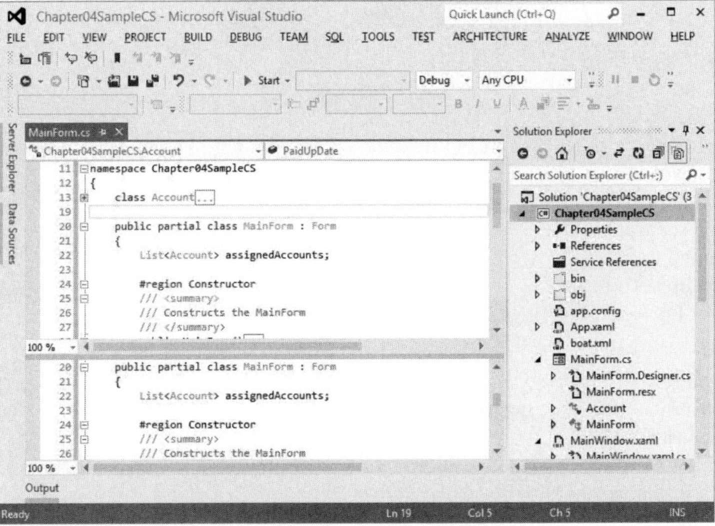

FIGURE 4-9

You may find halving the code editor window in split view (discussed in the previous section) to view different parts of a file at the same time too much of a limited view, so you might want to use the floating code windows feature instead to open another code editor window for the same file, and place it, say, on a different screen (if you have a multiple monitor setup). The trick to doing this (because double-clicking the file again in the Solution Explorer simply activates the existing code editor window instance for that file) is to select New Window from the Window menu. This opens the file currently being viewed in another window, which you can then tear away and position as you please.

Duplicating Solution Explorer

If you work in a multimonitor environment, a limitation in previous versions of Visual Studio was that only one copy of Solution Explorer was available. With Visual Studio 2012, this limitation has been lifted. Right click on one of the elements in the Solution Explorer and select New Solution Explorer View. When clicked, a new floating Solution Explorer window is created. This window can now be moved around, just like the windows previously described. Figure 4-10 illustrates the newly created Solution Explorer.

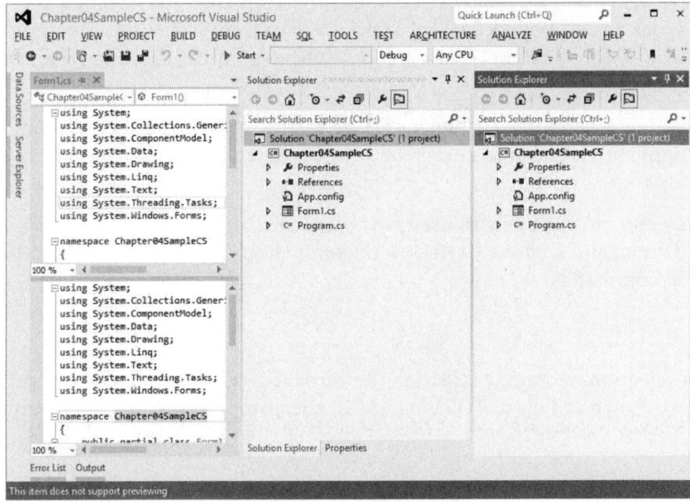

FIGURE 4-10

Creating Tab Groups

If you don't have the privilege of having more than one monitor, it is still possible to view more than one code editor window at the same time. You do this by creating tab groups and tiling these groups to display at the same time. As their name would indicate, a tab group is a group of code editor window tabs, with each tab group appearing in a separate tile. Multiple tab groups can be created, limited only by the amount of screen real estate they occupy. You can choose to tile the tab groups vertically or horizontally; you cannot use a mix of the two.

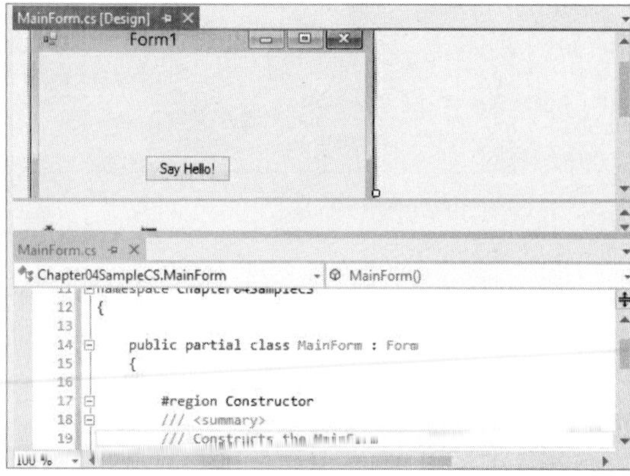

FIGURE 4-11

To start this process you need to have more than one tab open in the code editor window. Ensure a code editor tab has the focus then select Window ➪ New Horizontal Tab Group or Window ➪ New Vertical Tab Group from the menu displayed. This starts a new tab group and creates a tile for it (as shown in Figure 4-11).

Alternatively, you can simply drag a tab below or beside an existing one and dock it to achieve the same effect.

You can drag tabs between tab groups or move them between tab groups using Window ➪ Move to Next Tab Group and Window ➪ Move to Previous Tab Group. These options are also available from the drop-down menu when right-clicking a tab.

To restore the user interface to having a single tab group again, move the tabs from the new tab group(s) back into the original one again and the tiling will be removed.

Advanced Functionality

To be a truly productive developer, it can help to know various advanced features available in the code editor that are hidden away but can save you a lot of time. Here are some of the most useful commands that aren't immediately obvious within the code editor.

Commenting/Uncommenting a Code Block

Often you need to comment or uncomment a block of code, and you don't want to have to add/remove the comment characters to/from the start of each line, especially when there are many lines in the block. Of course, in C# you could wrap the block of code between a `/*` and `*/` to comment it out, but this type of comment isn't available in Visual Basic, and it can be problematic in C# when commenting out a block that already contains a comment using this style.

Visual Studio provides a means to comment/uncomment a block of code easily, by selecting the block and then selecting Edit ➪ Advanced ➪ Comment Selection to comment it out, or selecting Edit ➪ Advanced ➪ Uncomment Selection to uncomment it.

The easiest way to access these commands (you are likely to use these often) is via their shortcuts. Press Ctrl+K, Ctrl+C to comment a block of code, and Ctrl+K, Ctrl+U to uncomment it. The Text Editor toolbar is another simple means to access these commands.

Block Selection

Also known as box selection, column selection, rectangle selection, or vertical text selection, block selection is the ability to select text in a block (as shown in Figure 4-12) instead of the normal behavior of selecting lines of text (stream selection). To select a block of text, hold down the Alt key while selecting text with the mouse, or use Shift+Alt+Arrow with the keyboard. This feature can come in handy when, for example, you have code lined up and want to remove a vertical portion of that code (such as a prefix on variable declarations).

```
private readonly string string1 = string.Empty;
private readonly string string2 = string.Empty;
private readonly string string3 = string.Empty;
private readonly string string4 = string.Empty;
```

FIGURE 4-12

Multiline Editing

Multiline editing extends the abilities of block selection. With block selection, after selecting a vertical block of text you can only delete, cut, or copy the block. With multiline editing you can type after selecting a vertical block of text, which will replace the selected text with what's being typed on each line, as shown in Figure 4-13. This can be handy for changing a group of variables from private to protected, for example.

```
private con string string1 = string.Empty;
private con string string2 = string.Empty;
private con string string3 = string.Empty;
private con string string4 = string.Empty;
```

FIGURE 4-13

> **NOTE** *You can also insert text across multiple lines by creating a block with zero width and simply starting to type.*

The Clipboard Ring

Visual Studio keeps track of the last 20 snippets of text that have been copied or cut to the clipboard. To paste text that was previously copied to the clipboard but overwritten, instead of the normal Ctrl+V when pasting, use Ctrl+Shift+V. Pressing V while holding down Ctrl+Shift cycles through the entries.

Full-Screen View

You can maximize the view for editing the code by selecting View ➪ Full Screen, or using the Shift+Alt+Enter shortcut. This effectively maximizes the code editor window, hiding the other tool windows and the toolbars. To return to the normal view, press Shift+Alt+Enter again, or click the Full-Screen toggle button that has been added to the end of the menu bar.

Go to Definition

To quickly navigate to the definition of the class, method, or member under the cursor, right-click ➪ Go to Definition, or simply press F12.

Find All References

You can find where a method or property is called by right-clicking its definition and selecting Find All References from the drop-down menu, or placing the cursor in the method definition and pressing Shift+F12. This activates the Find Symbol Results tool window and displays the locations throughout your solution where that method or property is referenced. You can then double-click a reference in the results window to navigate to that result in the code editor window.

> **NOTE** *This feature has been somewhat made obsolete by the Call Hierarchy window, discussed later in this chapter. However, it can still be a quick way to view where a method is used without navigating through the Call Hierarchy window.*

THE COMMAND WINDOW

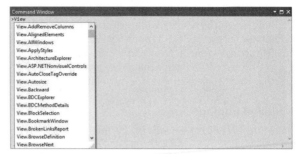

FIGURE 4-14

As you become more familiar with Visual Studio 2012, you will spend less time looking for functionality and more time using keyboard shortcuts to navigate and perform actions within the IDE. One of the tool windows that's often overlooked is the Command window, accessible via View ➪ Other Windows ➪ Command Window (Ctrl+Alt+A). From this window you can execute any existing Visual Studio command or macro, as well as any additional macros you may have recorded or written. Figure 4-14 illustrates the use of IntelliSense to show the list of commands that can be executed from the Command window. This list includes all macros defined within the current solution.

A full list of the Visual Studio commands is available via the Environment ➪ Keyboard node of the Options dialog (Tools ➪ Options). The commands all have a similar syntax based on the area of the IDE that they are derived from. For example, you can open the debugging output window (Debug ➪ Windows ➪ Output) by typing `Debug.Output` into the Command window.

The commands fall into three rough groups. Many commands are shortcuts to either tool windows (which are made visible if they aren't already open) or dialogs. For example, `File.NewFile` opens the new file dialog. Other commands query information about the current solution or the debugger. Using `Debug.ListThreads` lists the current threads, in contrast to `Debug.Threads`, which opens the Threads tool window. The third type includes those commands that perform an action without displaying a dialog. This would include most macros and a number of commands that accept arguments. (A full list of these, including the arguments they accept, is available within the MSDN documentation.) There is some overlap between these groups: For example, the `Edit.Find` command can be executed with or without arguments. If this command is executed without arguments, the Find and Replace dialog displays. Alternatively, the following command finds all instances of the string `MyVariable` in the current document (`/d`) and places a marker in the code window border against the relevant lines (`/m`):

```
>Edit.Find MyVariable /m /d
```

Although there is IntelliSense within the Command window, you may find typing a frequently used command somewhat painful. Visual Studio 2012 has the capability to assign an alias to a particular command. For example, the `alias` command can be used to assign an alias, `e?`, to the find command used previously:

```
>alias e? Edit.Find MyVariable /m /d
```

With this alias defined you can easily perform this command from anywhere within the IDE: Press Ctrl+Alt+A to give the Command Window focus, and then type **e?** to perform the find-and-mark command.

You will have imported a number of default aliases belonging to the environment settings when you began working with Visual Studio 2012. You can list these using the `alias` command with no arguments. Alternatively, if you want to find out what command a specific alias references, you can execute the command with the name of the alias. For example, querying the previously defined alias, `e?`, would look like the following:

```
>alias e?
alias e? Edit.Find SumVals /m /doc
```

Two additional switches can be used with the `alias` command. The `/delete` switch, along with an alias name, removes a previously defined alias. If you want to remove all aliases you may have defined and revert any changes to a predefined alias, you can use the `/reset` switch.

THE IMMEDIATE WINDOW

Quite often when you write code or debug your application, you want to evaluate a simple expression either to test a bit of functionality or to remind yourself of how something works. This is where the Immediate window comes in handy. This window enables you to run expressions as you type them. Figure 4-15 shows a number of statements — from basic assignment and print operations to more advanced object creation and manipulation.

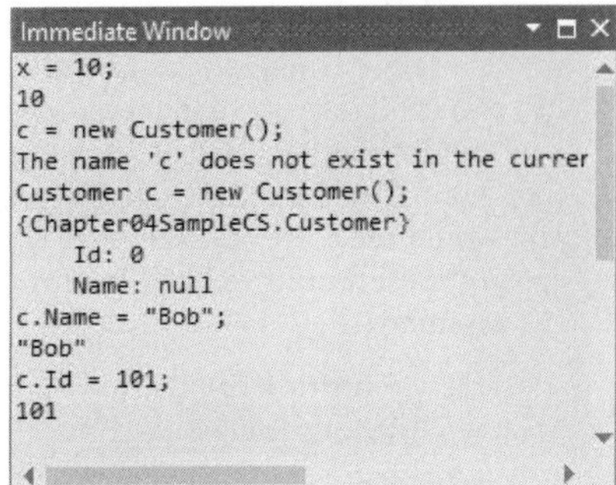

FIGURE 4-15

> **NOTE** *In Visual Basic you can't do explicit variable declaration in the Immediate window (for example, Dim x as Integer), but instead you do this implicitly via the assignment operator. The example shown in Figure 4-15 shows a new customer being created, assigned to a variable c, and then used in a series of operations. When using C#, new variables in the Immediate window must be declared explicitly before they can be assigned a value.*

The Immediate window supports a limited form of IntelliSense, and you can use the arrow keys to track back through the history of previous commands executed. Variable values can be displayed by means of the `Debug.Print` statement. Alternatively, you can use its `?` alias. Neither of these is necessary in C#; simply type the variable's name into the window, and press Enter to print its value.

When you execute a command in the Immediate window while in design mode, Visual Studio will build the solution before executing the command. If your solution doesn't compile, the expression cannot be evaluated until the compilation errors are resolved. If the command execute code has an active breakpoint, the command will break there. This can be useful if you work on a particular method that you want to test without running the entire application.

You can access the Immediate window via the Debug ➪ Windows ➪ Immediate menu or the Ctrl+Alt+I keyboard chord, but if you work between the Command and Immediate windows, you may want to use the predefined aliases `cmd` and `immed`, respectively.

> **NOTE** *To execute commands in the Immediate window, you need to add > as a prefix (for example, `>cmd` to go to the Command window); otherwise Visual Studio tries to evaluate the command.*
>
> *Also, you should be aware that the language used in the Immediate window is that of the active project. The examples shown in Figure 4-15 can work only if a Visual Basic project is currently active.*

THE CLASS VIEW

Although the Solution Explorer is probably the most useful tool window for navigating your solution, it can sometimes be difficult to locate particular classes and methods. The Class View tool window provides you with an alternative view of your solution that lists namespaces, classes, and methods so that you can easily navigate to them. Figure 4-16 shows a simple Windows application that contains a single form (MainForm), which is selected in the class hierarchy. Note that there are two Chapter04Sample nodes. The first is the name of the project (not the assembly as you might expect), and the second is the namespace that MainForm belongs to. If you were to expand the Project References node you would see a list of assemblies that this project references. Drilling further into each of these would yield a list of namespaces, followed by the classes contained in the assembly.

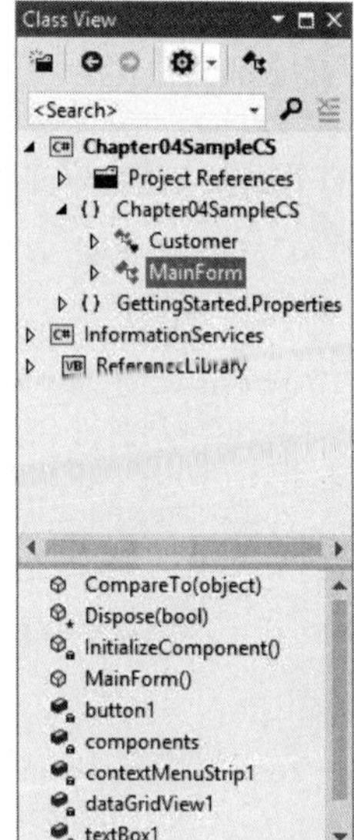

FIGURE 4-16

In the lower portion of Figure 4-16 you can see the list of members that are available for the class `MainForm`. Using the right-click shortcut menu, you can either filter this list based on accessibility, sort and group the list, or use it to navigate to the selected member. For example, clicking Go to Definition on `InitializeComponent()` would take you to the `MainForm.Designer.vb` file.

The Class View is useful for navigating to generated members, which are usually in a file hidden in the default Solution Explorer view (such as the designer file in the previous example). It can also be a useful way to navigate to classes that have been added to an existing
file — this would result in multiple classes in the same file, which is not a recommended practice. Because the file does not have a name that matches the class name, it becomes hard to navigate to that class using the Solution Explorer; hence the Class View is a good alternative.

THE ERROR LIST

The Error List window displays compile errors, warnings, and messages for your solution, as shown in Figure 4-17. You can open the Error List window by selecting View ➪ Error List, or by using the keyboard shortcut Ctrl+\, Ctrl+E. Errors appear in the list as you edit code and when you compile the project. Double-clicking an error in the list opens the file and takes you to the line of code that is in error.

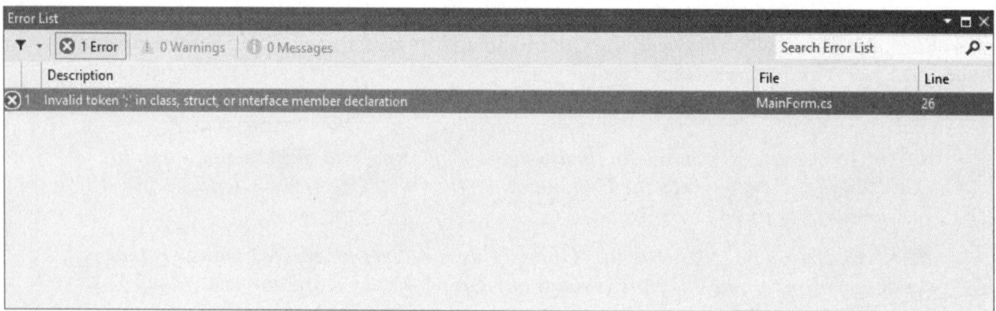

FIGURE 4-17

You can filter the entries in the list by toggling the buttons above the list to select the types of errors (Errors, Warnings, and Messages) you want to display.

THE OBJECT BROWSER

Another way to view the classes that make up your application is via the Object Browser. Unlike most other tool windows, which appear docked to a side of Visual Studio 2012 by default, the Object Browser appears in the editor space. To view the Object Browser window, select View ➪ Object Browser, or use the keyboard shortcut Ctrl+Alt+J (or F2, depending on your keyboard settings). As you can see in Figure 4-18, at the top of the Object Browser window is a drop-down box that defines the object browsing scope. This includes a set of predefined values, such as All Components, .NET Framework 4.5, and My Solution, as well as a Custom Component Set. Here, My Solution is selected and a search string of `sample` has been entered. The contents of the main window are then all the namespaces, classes, and members that match this search string.

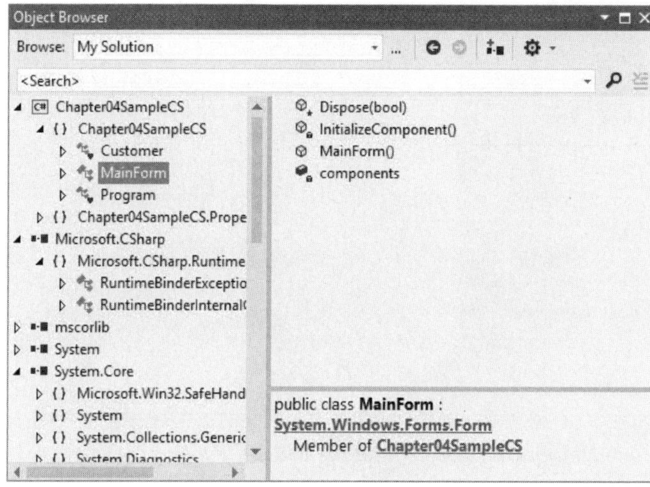

FIGURE 4-18

In the top right portion of Figure 4-18, you can see the list of members for the selected class (`MainForm`), and in the lower window the full class definition, which includes its base class and namespace information. One of the options in the Browse drop-down of Figure 4-18 is a Custom Component Set. To define what assemblies are included in this set, you can either click the ellipsis next to the drop-down or select Edit Custom Component Set from the drop-down itself. This presents you with an edit dialog similar to the one shown in Figure 4-19.

Selecting items in the top section and clicking Add inserts that assembly into the component set. Similarly, selecting an item in the lower section and clicking Remove deletes that assembly from the component set. When you finish customizing the component set, it is saved between Visual Studio sessions.

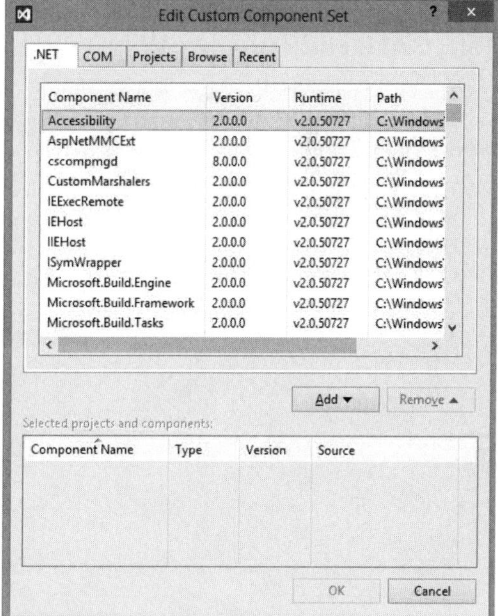

FIGURE 4-19

THE CODE DEFINITION WINDOW

When navigating around your code, you might come across a method call that you'd like to view the code for without leaving your current position in the code editor. This is where the Code Definition window can come in handy, to show the source of the method when the cursor has been placed within a reference to it (as shown in Figure 4-20). Access it via View ➪ Code Definition window (Ctrl+\, D). It's just like another code editor window with many of the same commands available (such as inserting a breakpoint, view call hierarchy, and so on) but is read-only. To edit the code for that method, right-click anywhere within the Code Definition window and select Edit Definition. The source code file for this method will be opened in a code editor window, and the method definition will be navigated to.

```
MainForm.cs   MainForm.cs [Design]
Chapter04SampleCS.MainForm      MainForm()

            InitializeComponent();
        }
    }

    class Customer
    {
        public string Name;
        public int Id;

Code Definition Wi...inForm.Designer.cs)

namespace Chapter04SampleCS
{
    partial class MainForm
    {
        /// <summary>
        /// Required designer variable.
        /// </summary>
        private System.ComponentModel.IContainer components = nul

        /// <summary>
```

FIGURE 4-20

> **NOTE** *You can also use the Code Definition window with the Class View and the Object Browser windows to view the code for the selected member of a class.*

THE CALL HIERARCHY WINDOW

The Call Hierarchy window displays all the calls to and from a method (or property or constructor, but each henceforth referred to as methods), enabling you to see where a method is being used and, in addition, what calls it makes to other methods. This enables you to easily follow the execution path and the flow of the code.

To view the call hierarchy for a method, select a method definition in the code editor window, and select View Call Hierarchy from the right-click context menu. This adds the method to the tree in the Call Hierarchy window with three subnodes — Calls To (MethodName), Calls From (MethodName), and Override, as shown in Figure 4-21.

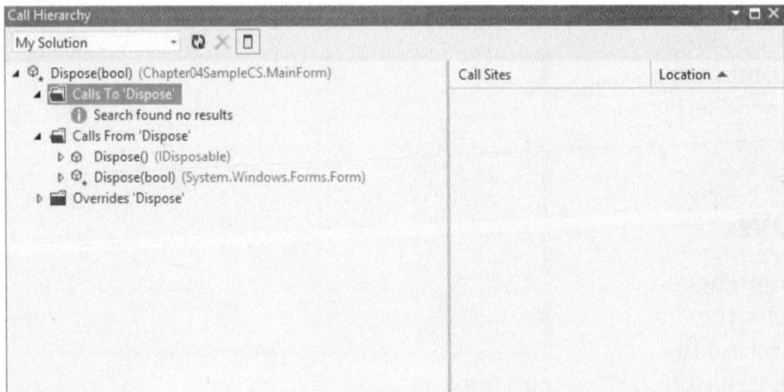

FIGURE 4-21

Expanding the Calls To (MethodName) lists all the methods that call the specified method. Expanding the Calls From (MethodName) lists all the other methods that are called by the specified method. For members that are virtual or abstract, an Overrides method name node appears. For interface members an Implements Method name node appears.

The Call Hierarchy window allows you to drill down through the results to build a hierarchy of the program execution flow — seeing which methods call the specified method, which methods call them, and so on.

Double-clicking a method navigates to that method definition in the code editor window.

> **NOTE** *You can view the call hierarchy for methods in the Class View window or the Object Browser window also by right-clicking the method and selecting View Call Hierarchy from the drop-down menu.*

Despite that the Call Hierarchy window can be left floating or be docked, it doesn't work in the same way as the Code Definition window. Moving around the code editor window to different methods cannot display the call hierarchy automatically for the method under the cursor — instead you need to explicitly request to view the call hierarchy for that method, at which point it is added to the Call Hierarchy window. The Call Hierarchy window can display the call hierarchy for more than just one method, and each time you view the call hierarchy for a method, it is added to the window rather than replacing the call hierarchy currently being viewed. When you no longer need to view the call hierarchy for a method, select it in the window and press Delete (or the red cross in the toolbar) to remove it.

> **NOTE** *This window can come in handy when working on an unfamiliar project or refactoring a project.*

THE DOCUMENT OUTLINE TOOL WINDOW

Editing HTML files, using either the visual designer or code view, is never as easy as it could be, particularly when you have a large number of nested elements. When Visual Studio .NET first arrived on the scene, a feature known as document outlining came to at least partially save the day. In fact, this feature was so successful for working with HTML files that it was repurposed for working with nonweb forms and controls. This section introduces you to the Document Outline window and demonstrates how effective it can be at manipulating HTML documents and forms and controls.

HTML Outlining

The primary purpose of the Document Outline window is to present a navigable view of HTML pages so that you could easily locate the different HTML elements and the containers they were in. Because it is difficult to get HTML layouts correct, especially with the many .NET components that could be included on an ASP.NET page, the Document Outline view provides a handy way to find the correct position for a specific component.

Figure 4-22 shows a typical HTML page. Without the Document Outline window, selecting an element in the designer can be rather tricky if it's small or not visible in the designer. The Document Outline pane (View ➪ Other Windows ➪ Document Outline), on the left of Figure 4-22, enables you to easily select elements in the hierarchy to determine where in the page they are located, and to enable you to set their properties.

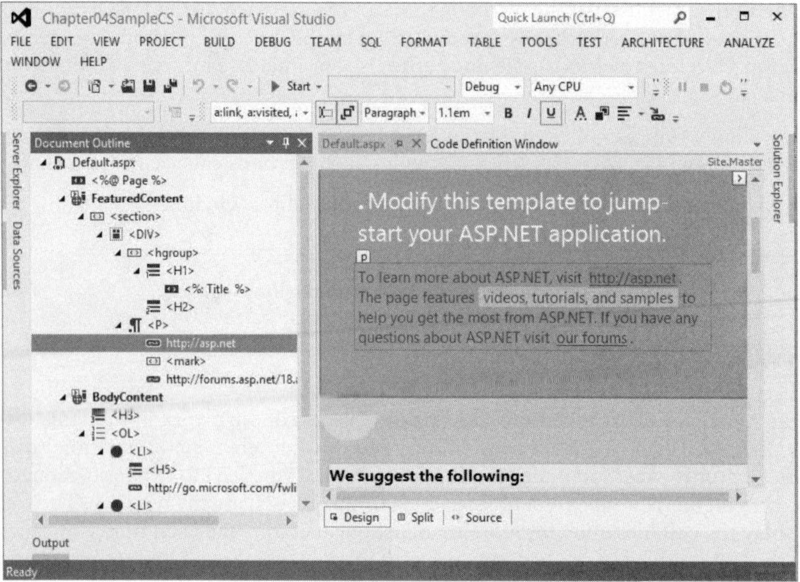

FIGURE 4-22

Visual Studio analyzes the content of the currently active file and populates it with a tree view containing every element in the page hierarchy. The Name or ID value of each element will be displayed in the tree (if they are assigned one), while unnamed elements are simply listed with their HTML tags.

As you select each entry in the Document Outline window, the Design view is updated to select the component and its children. In Figure 4-22, the hyperlink tag for the `http://asp.net` page is selected in the Document Outline window, highlighting the control in the Design view, and enabling you to see where it is located on the page. Correspondingly, selecting a control or element in the Design view selects the corresponding tag in the page hierarchy in the Document Outline window. (Although you need to set the focus back to the Document Outline window for it to update accordingly.)

Control Outlining

By their very nature, HTML pages are a hierarchical collection of visual and non-visual elements – controls within containers within forms within documents. In most situations, this fact is either transparent to the developer or irrelevant. However, there are a number of situations where knowing the details of the hierarchy are not just nice to have but make life significantly easier.

Consider, for instance, a typical complex form such as found in Figure 4-23. The many panels provide the UI structure and controls provide the visual elements. How easy is it to tell by looking whether this is implemented as an HTML table or a set of docked panels? What if you wanted to reside the panels or move a control from one container to another? Yes, it's doable, but is it easy? As you look at the menus, can you tell what options you put under the Tool menu?

It is for situations such as this that the Document Outline tool window was created. Each component on the page is represented in the Document Outline by its name and component type. It is possible to drag and drop elements from one container to another. And as each item is selected in the Document Outline window, the corresponding visual element is selected and displayed in the Design view.

This means that when the item is in a menu (as is the case in Figure 4-23) Visual Studio automatically opens the menu and selects the menu item ready for editing. As you can imagine, this is an incredibly useful way to navigate your form layouts, and it can often provide a shortcut for locating wayward items.

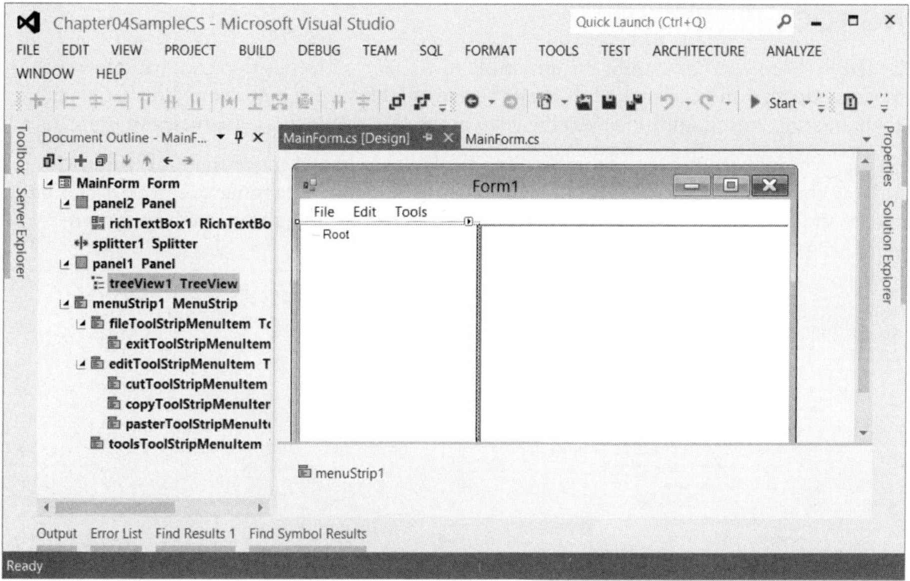

FIGURE 4-23

The Document Outline window has more functionality when used in Control Outline mode than just a simple navigation tool. Right-clicking an entry gives you a small context menu of actions that can be performed against the selected item. The most obvious is to access the Properties window.

One tedious chore is renaming components after you've added them to the form. You can select each one in turn and set its Name property in the Properties window, but by using the Document Outline window you can simply choose the Rename option in the context menu, and Visual Studio automatically renames the component in the design code, thus updating the Name property for you without your needing to scroll through the Properties list.

Complex form design can sometimes produce unexpected results. This often happens when a component is placed in an incorrect or inappropriate container control. In such a case you need to move the component to the correct container. Of course, you have to locate the issue before you even know that there is a problem.

The Document Outline window can help with both of these activities. First, using the hierarchical view, you can easily locate each component and check its parent container elements. The example shown in Figure 4-23 indicates that the treeView1 control is in panel1. In this way you can easily determine when a control is incorrectly placed on the form's design layout.

When you need to move a component, it can be quite tricky to get the layout right. In the Document Outline window it's easy. Simply drag and drop the control to the correct position in the hierarchy. For example, dragging the treeView1 control to panel2 results in its sharing the panel2 area with the richTextBox1 control.

You also have the option to cut, copy, and paste individual elements or whole sets of containers and their contents by using the right-click context menu. The copy-and-paste function is particularly useful because you can duplicate whole chunks of your form design in other locations on the form without having to use trial and error to select the correct elements in the Design view, or resort to duplicating them in the code-behind in the `Designer.vb` file.

> **NOTE** *When you cut an item, remember to paste it immediately into the destination location.*

REORGANIZING TOOL WINDOWS

The Visual Studio IDE has been designed to be customizable to enable you to position tool windows such that you can be the most productive and can make full use of your available screen real estate. You can dock tool windows, have them floating, or minimize them to the edge of the IDE displaying only their tab using auto hide.

When dragging a tool window around, a series of guides display to help you move the tool window to a docked position. Drag the tool window onto a guide to dock the window. Dragging over a part of a guide highlights the part of the IDE that the tool window would be docked to if you were to drop it there (as shown in Figure 4-24).

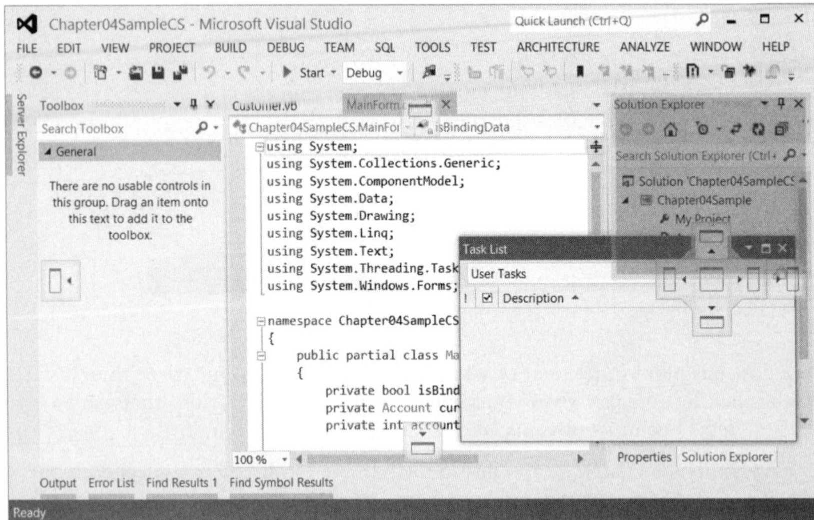

FIGURE 4-24

To float a docked tool window, simply click and drag it to a new position (making sure not to drop it on top of one of the guides that appears). Pressing the Ctrl key while moving the window prevents the guides from appearing and the window from snapping to them. When a tool window is docked and part of a tab group (that is, windows that occupy the same space and can be switched between by clicking their tabs), clicking and dragging the tab for the tool window moves just that window, whereas clicking and dragging the title bar for the tool window moves the entire tab group.

To access a tool window that is set to auto hide, put your mouse over its tab to make it slide out. To put a tool window into auto hide mode, click the pushpin button in the title bar for the window, and click it again while in the auto hide mode to return it to its docked position.

> **NOTE** *After dragging a tool window out of its docked position and moving it elsewhere (such as onto another monitor), simply double-click its title bar while holding the Ctrl key to return it to its previously docked position.*

SUMMARY

In this chapter you have seen a number of tool windows that can help you not only write code but also prototype and try it out. Making effective use of these windows can dramatically reduce the number of times you need to run your application to test the code you are writing. This, in turn, can improve your overall productivity and eliminate idle time spent waiting for your application to run.

Find and Replace and Help

WHAT'S IN THIS CHAPTER?

- Using Visual Studio's various Find and Replace tools
- Navigating Visual Studio's local help system

To be a productive developer, you need to navigate your way around a code base and find what you need quickly. Visual Studio 2012 provides not just one but a number of search functions, each suited to particular searching tasks. The first part of this chapter discusses each of these search functions and when and where to use them.

Visual Studio 2012 is an immensely complex development environment that encompasses multiple languages based on an extensive framework of libraries and components. You can find it almost impossible to know everything about the IDE, let alone each of the languages or even the full extent of the .NET Framework. As both the .NET Framework and Visual Studio evolve, it becomes increasingly difficult to stay abreast of all the changes; moreover, it is likely that you need to know only a subset of this knowledge. Of course, you periodically need to obtain more information on a specific topic. To help you in these situations, Visual Studio 2012 comes with comprehensive documentation in the form of the MSDN Library, Visual Studio 2012 Edition. The second part of this chapter walks you through the methods to research documentation associated with developing projects in Visual Studio 2012.

QUICK FIND/REPLACE

The simplest means to search in Visual Studio 2012 is via the Quick Find dialog.

The find-and-replace functionality in Visual Studio 2012 is split into two broad tiers with a shared dialog and similar features: Quick Find and the associated Quick Replace are for searches that you need to perform quickly on the document or project currently open in the IDE. These two tools have limited options to filter and extend the search, but as you'll see in a moment, even those options provide a powerful search engine that goes beyond what you can find in most applications.

> **NOTE** *This search tool is best suited for when you need to do a simple text-based search/replace (as opposed to searching for a symbol).*

Quick Find

Quick Find is the term that Visual Studio 2012 uses to refer to the most basic search functionality. By default, it enables you to search for a simple word or phrase within the current document, but even Quick Find has additional options that can extend the search beyond the active module, or even incorporate regular expressions in the search criteria.

> **NOTE** *While there is an option in Quick Find to allow you to utilize regular expressions, one feature that is missing is the ability to easily select from a list of commonly used patterns. The expectation (and it is based on metrics gathered by Microsoft) is that the vast majority of quick finds don't use regular expressions. Instead, the ability to select from a list of common patterns can be found in the Find In Files functionality described later in this chapter.*

To start a Find action, press the standard keyboard shortcut Ctrl+F or select Edit ➪ Find and Replace ➪ Quick Find. Visual Studio displays the basic Find window, with the default Quick Find action selected (see Figure 5-1).

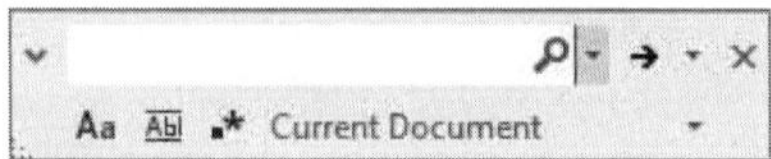

FIGURE 5-1

Compared to earlier versions, the dialog that appears in Visual Studio 2012 has changed significantly. However, the mechanism for performing the search is the same. Type the search criteria into the Find textbox, or select from previous searches by clicking the drop-down arrow and scrolling through the list of criteria that have been used. By default, the scope of the search is restricted to the current document or window you're editing, unless you have a number of lines selected, in which case the default scope is the selection.

The Quick Find dialog in Visual Studio 2012 implements functionality that was previously found in the Incremental Search in Visual Studio 2010. As you type each character into the search textbox, the editor moves to the next match for the text you entered. For example, typing **f** would find the first letter **f**, regardless of whether it is found within a word, such as in *offer*, or on its own. Typing an **o** would then move the cursor to the first instance of *fo* — such as *form*, and so on.

You can change the scope for the search; although it is less visible than before. Start by clicking the caret to the left of the search text. Use this to toggle between Find mode and Replace mode. At the bottom of the dialog, you'll see a Scope field. This drop-down list gives you additional options based on the context of the search itself, including Selection, Current Block, Current Document, Current Project, Entire Solution, and All Open Documents (shown in Figure 5-2).

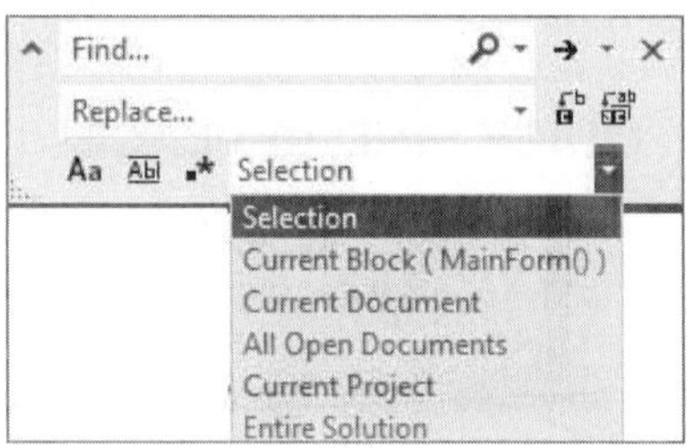

FIGURE 5-2

Find-and-replace actions always wrap around the selected scope looking for the search terms, stopping only when the find process has reached the starting point again. As Visual Studio finds each result, it highlights the match and scrolls the code window so that you can view it. If the match is already visible in the code window, Visual Studio does not scroll the code. Instead, it just highlights the new match. However, if it does need to scroll the window, it attempts to position the listing so that the match is in the middle of the code editor window.

> **NOTE** *After you perform the first Quick Find search, you no longer need the dialog to be visible. You can simply press F3 to repeat the same search.*

If you were comfortable using the Quick Find search box that was in the Standard toolbar, it is no longer part of the default configuration. You can still add it to the toolbar, but you need to do so manually.

Quick Replace

Performing a Quick Replace is similar to performing a Quick Find. You can switch between Quick Find and Quick Replace by clicking the caret to the left of the search textbox. If you want to go directly to Quick Replace, you can do so with the keyboard shortcut Ctrl+H or the menu command Edit ➪ Find and Replace ➪ Quick Replace. The Quick Replace options (see Figure 5-2) are the same as those for Quick Find, but with an additional field where you can specify what text should be used in the replacement.

> **NOTE** *A simple way to delete recurring values is to use the replace functionality with nothing specified in the Replacement Term text area. This enables you to find all occurrences of the search text and decide if it should be deleted.*

The Replacement Tem field works in the same way as Find — you can either type a new replacement string, or with the drop-down list provided choose any you previously entered.

Find Options

Sometimes you want to specify criteria and filter the search results in different ways. Click the triangle icon next to search text. A drop-down expands to show recently used search values (see Figure 5-3).

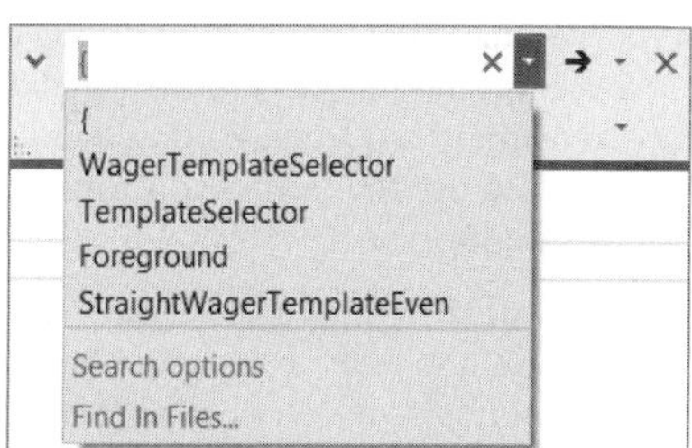

FIGURE 5-3

Also, below the search text, there are three buttons (shown in Figure 5-1). These are actually toggle buttons that enable you to refine the search to be case-sensitive (the left button) or to be an exact match (the middle button). You can also specify that you are performing a more advanced search that uses regular expressions (the right button). One of the differences between this Quick Find dialog in Visual Studio 2012 and the one found in Visual Studio 2010 is that there is no longer a list of commonly used regular expressions available. As you will see shortly, these are still found in the Find All Files dialog, but to use regular expressions in Quick Find, you need to write them from scratch."

Find and Replace Options

You can further configure the find-and-replace functionality with its own set of options in the Tools ➪ Options dialog. Found in the Environment group, the Find and Replace options enable you to enable/disable displaying informational and warning messages, as well as to indicate whether or not the Find What field should be automatically filled with the current selection in the editor window.

FIND/REPLACE IN FILES

The *Find in Files* and *Replace in Files* commands enable you to broaden the search beyond the current solution to whole folders and folder structures, and even to perform mass replacements on any matches for the given criteria and filters. Additional options are available to you when using these commands, and search results can be placed in one of two tool windows, so you can easily navigate them.

> **NOTE** *This search tool is best suited when you need to do a simple text-based search/replace across files that are not necessarily a part of your current solution.*

Find in Files

The powerful part of the search engine built into Visual Studio is in the Find in Files command. Rather than restrict yourself to files in the current solution, Find in Files gives you the ability to search entire folders (along with all their subfolders), looking for files that contain the search criteria.

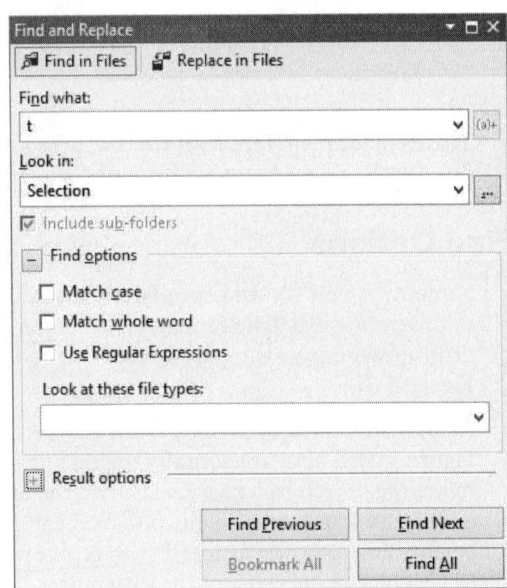

FIGURE 5-4

The Find in Files dialog, as shown in Figure 5-4, can be invoked via the menu command Edit ➪ Find. Alternatively, if you have the Quick Find dialog open, you can switch over to Find in Files mode by clicking the small drop-down arrow next to Quick Find and choosing Find in Files. You can also use the keyboard shortcut Ctrl+Shift+F to launch this dialog.

Most of the Quick Find options are still available to you, including regular expressions searching, but instead of choosing a scope from the project or solution, use the Look In field to specify where the search is to be performed. Either type the location you want to search or click the ellipsis to display the Choose Search Folders dialog, as shown in Figure 5-5.

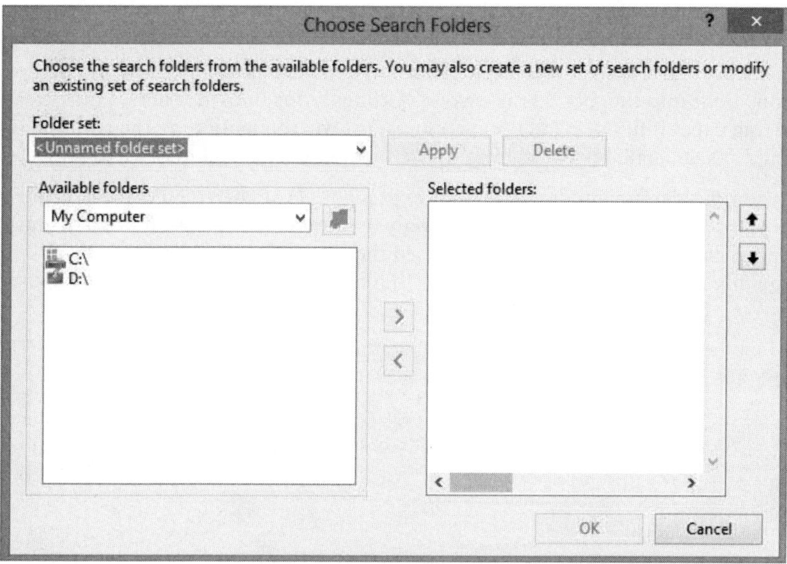

FIGURE 5-5

You can navigate through the entire filesystem, including networked drives, and add the folders you want to the search scope. This enables you to add disparate folder hierarchies to the one single search. Start by using the Available Folders list on the left to select the folders that you would like to search. Add them to the Selected Folders list by clicking the right arrow. Within this list you can adjust the search order using the up and down arrows. After you add folders to the search, you can simply click OK to return a semicolon-delimited list of folders. If you want to save this set of folders for future use, you can enter a name into the Folder Set drop-down and click Apply.

> **NOTE** *The process to save search folders is less than intuitive, but if you think of the Apply button as more of a Save button, then you can make sense of this dialog.*

Find Dialog Options

The options for the Find in Files dialog are similar to those for the Quick Find dialog. Because the search is performed on files that are not necessarily open within the IDE or are even code files, the Search Up option is therefore not present. There is an additional filter that can be used to select only specific file types to search in.

The Look at These File Types drop-down list contains several extension sets, each associated with a particular language, making it easy to search for code in Visual Basic, C#, J#, and other languages. You can type in your own extensions too, so if you work in a non-Microsoft language, or just want to use the Find in Files feature for non-development purposes, you can still limit the search results to those that correspond to the file types you want.

In addition to the Find options are configuration settings for how the results display. For searching, you can choose one of two results windows, which enables you to perform a subsequent search without losing your initial action. The results can be quite lengthy if you show the full output of the search, but if you're interested only in finding out which files contain the information you're looking for, check the Display Filenames Only option, and the results window will be populated with only one line per file.

Regular Expressions

Regular expressions take searching to a whole new level, with the capability to do complex text matching based on the full RegEx engine built into the .NET Framework. Although this book doesn't go into great detail on the advanced matching capabilities of regular expressions, it's worth mentioning the additional help provided by the Find and Replace dialog if you choose to use them in your search terms.

Figure 5-6 shows the Expression Builder for building a regular expression. From here you can easily build your regular expressions with a menu showing the most commonly used regular expression phrases and symbols, along with English descriptions of each. If you have used the Expression Builder in previous versions of Visual Studio, you might notice there are a lot more "built-in" patterns from which to choose.

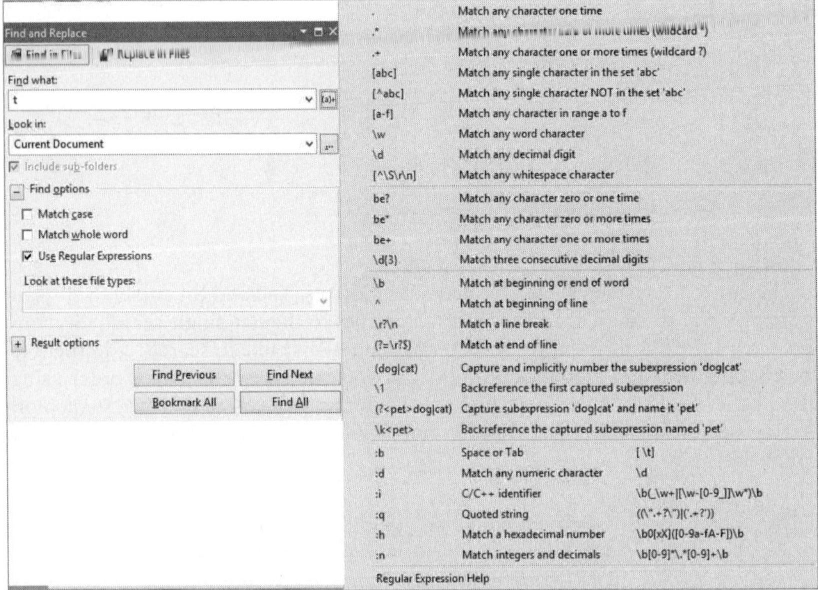

FIGURE 5-6

An example of where using regular expressions might come in handy is when reversing assignments. For example, if you have this code:

VB

```
Description = product.Description
Quantity = product.Quantity
SellPrice = product.SellPrice
```

C#

```
Description = product.Description;
Quantity = product.Quantity;
SellPrice = product.SellPrice;
```

and want to reverse the assignments like so:

VB

```
product.Description = Description
product.Quantity = Quantity
product.SellPrice = SellPrice
```

C#

```
product.Description = Description;
product.Quantity = Quantity;
product.SellPrice = SellPrice;
```

This would be a perfect use for performing a Quick Replace with regular expressions rather than modifying each line of code manually. Be sure you select Use Regular Expressions in the Find Options, and enter the following as the Find What text:

VB

```
{<.*} = {.*}
```

C#

```
{<.*} = {.*};
```

and the following as the Replace With text:

VB

```
\2 = \1
```

C#

```
\2 = \1;
```

As a brief explanation, you are searching for two groups (defined by the curly brackets) separated by an equals sign. The first group is searching for the first character of a word (<) and then any characters (.*). The second group is searching for any characters until an end-of-line character is found in the VB example or a semicolon is found in the C# example. Then when you do the replace, you are simply inserting the characters from the second group found in its place, an equals sign (surrounded by a space on each side), and then the characters from the first group found (followed by a semicolon in the C# example). If you aren't familiar with regular expressions, it may take some time to get your head around it, but it is a quick-and-easy way to perform an otherwise rather mundane manual process.

Results Window

When you perform a Find in Files action, results display in one of two Find Results windows. These appear as open tool windows docked to the bottom of the IDE workspace. For each line that contains the search criteria, the results window displays a full line of information, containing the filename and path, the line number that contained the match, and the actual line of text itself, so you can instantly see the context (see Figure 5-7).

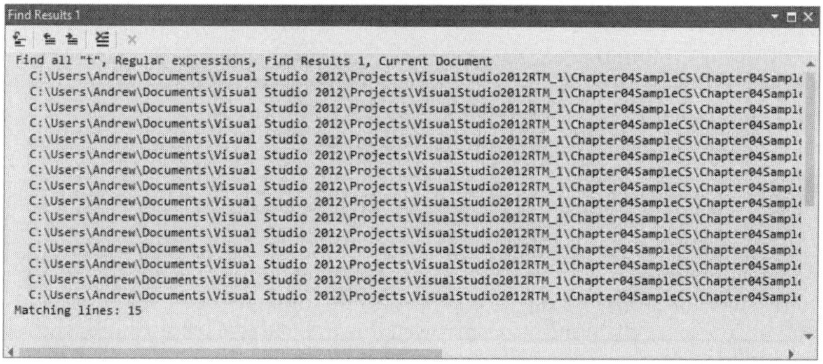

```
Find Results 1
Find all "t", Regular expressions, Find Results 1, Current Document
  C:\Users\Andrew\Documents\Visual Studio 2012\Projects\VisualStudio2012RTM_1\Chapter04SampleCS\Chapter04Sampl
  C:\Users\Andrew\Documents\Visual Studio 2012\Projects\VisualStudio2012RTM_1\Chapter04SampleCS\Chapter04Sampl
  C:\Users\Andrew\Documents\Visual Studio 2012\Projects\VisualStudio2012RTM_1\Chapter04SampleCS\Chapter04Sampl
  C:\Users\Andrew\Documents\Visual Studio 2012\Projects\VisualStudio2012RTM_1\Chapter04SampleCS\Chapter04Sampl
  C:\Users\Andrew\Documents\Visual Studio 2012\Projects\VisualStudio2012RTM_1\Chapter04SampleCS\Chapter04Sampl
  C:\Users\Andrew\Documents\Visual Studio 2012\Projects\VisualStudio2012RTM_1\Chapter04SampleCS\Chapter04Sampl
  C:\Users\Andrew\Documents\Visual Studio 2012\Projects\VisualStudio2012RTM_1\Chapter04SampleCS\Chapter04Sampl
  C:\Users\Andrew\Documents\Visual Studio 2012\Projects\VisualStudio2012RTM_1\Chapter04SampleCS\Chapter04Sampl
  C:\Users\Andrew\Documents\Visual Studio 2012\Projects\VisualStudio2012RTM_1\Chapter04SampleCS\Chapter04Sampl
  C:\Users\Andrew\Documents\Visual Studio 2012\Projects\VisualStudio2012RTM_1\Chapter04SampleCS\Chapter04Sampl
  C:\Users\Andrew\Documents\Visual Studio 2012\Projects\VisualStudio2012RTM_1\Chapter04SampleCS\Chapter04Sampl
  C:\Users\Andrew\Documents\Visual Studio 2012\Projects\VisualStudio2012RTM_1\Chapter04SampleCS\Chapter04Sampl
  C:\Users\Andrew\Documents\Visual Studio 2012\Projects\VisualStudio2012RTM_1\Chapter04SampleCS\Chapter04Sampl
  C:\Users\Andrew\Documents\Visual Studio 2012\Projects\VisualStudio2012RTM_1\Chapter04SampleCS\Chapter04Sampl
  C:\Users\Andrew\Documents\Visual Studio 2012\Projects\VisualStudio2012RTM_1\Chapter04SampleCS\Chapter04Sampl
Matching lines: 15
```

FIGURE 5-7

In the top left corner of each results window is a small toolbar, as shown in Figure 5-7 and magnified on the left side of Figure 5-8, for navigation within the results. These commands are also accessible through a context menu, as shown in Figure 5-8 (right).

Simply double-click a specific match to navigate to that line of code.

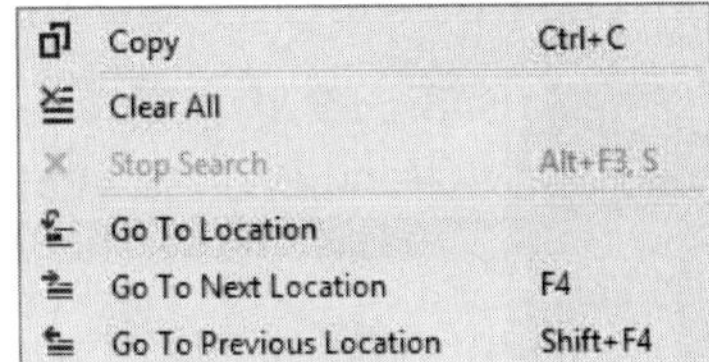

FIGURE 5-8

Replace in Files

Although it's useful to search a large number of files and find a number of matches to your search criteria, even better is the Replace in Files action. Accessed via the keyboard shortcut Ctrl+Shift+H or the drop-down arrow next to Quick Replace, Replace in Files performs in much the same way as Find in Files, with all the same options.

The main difference is that you can enable an additional Results option when you're replacing files. When you perform a mass replacement action like this, it can be handy to have a final confirmation before committing changes. To have this sanity check available to you, select the Keep Modified Files Open After Replace All check box (shown at the bottom of Figure 5-9).

Note that this feature works only when you use Replace All; if you just click Replace, Visual Studio opens the file containing the next match and leaves the file open in the IDE anyway.

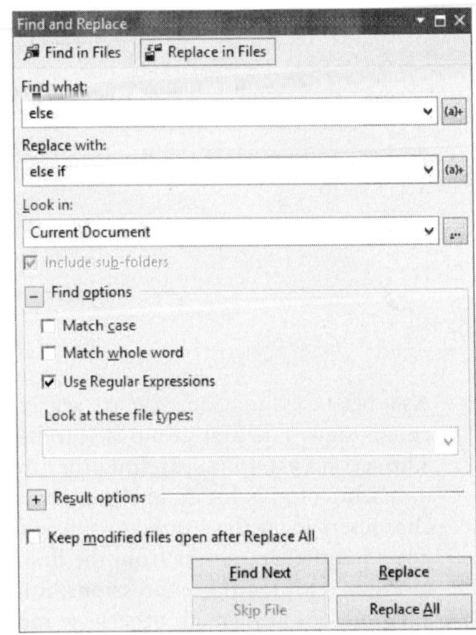

FIGURE 5-9

> **WARNING** *Important: If you leave the Keep Modified Files Open After Replace All option unchecked and perform a mass replacement on a large number of files, they will be changed permanently without your having any recourse to an undo action. Be very sure that you know what you're doing.*

Regardless of whether or not you have this option checked, after performing a Replace All action, Visual Studio reports back to you how many changes were made. If you don't want to see this dialog box, you have an option to hide the dialog with future searches.

NAVIGATE TO

Navigate To is a powerful search tool that provides an alternative to the standard find functions when searching for symbols. Unlike the other find functionality that we have covered, in Navigate To you are limited to only searching for symbols. Navigate To displays live results as you type the search text. The more of the search text you type, the more the results are narrowed down. Double-clicking one of the results closes the dialog and navigates to that result.

One of the most unique features of the Navigate To dialog, however, is in how it searches. Say you are looking for a method named BindAccountDetails. In this search tool, spaces are essentially AND operators, so typing **bi det** as the search text (that is, searching for *bi* and *det* in the same symbol name) returns the BindAccountDetails method as a result, as would typing in **det bi**.

The other unique search capability that it has is its camel case searching. To find the BindAccountDetails method you can simply search for *BD* (some of the capitals in its name) to return it as one of the results (as shown in Figure 5-10) — a powerful feature found only in this search tool.

If you enter the text to search for in lowercase, the matching will be noncase-specific. However, if you enter an uppercase character as a part of the search text, the search becomes case-specific.

The shortcut to open the Navigate To dialog is Ctrl+, (comma).

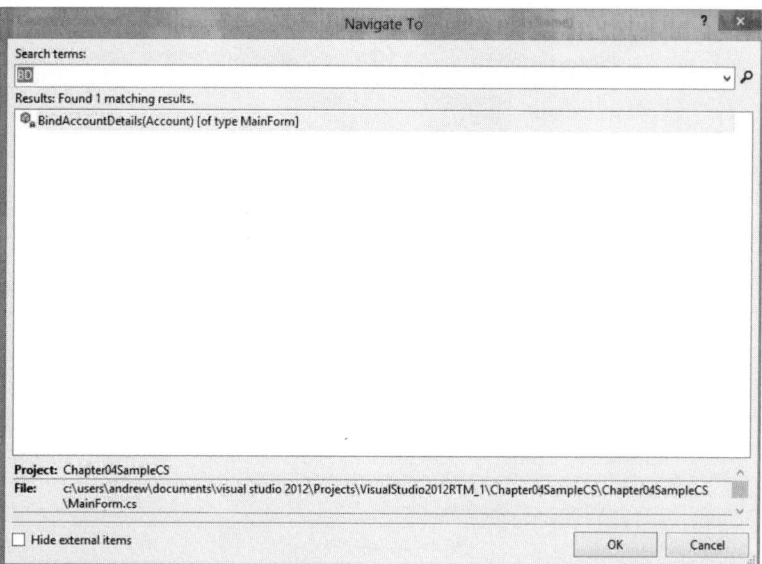

FIGURE 5-10

ACCESSING HELP

You are exposed to a wide range of technologies as a developer. Not only do they evolve at a rapid pace, but you are also constantly bombarded with additional new technologies that you must get up to speed on quickly. It's impossible to know everything about these technologies, and being a developer involves constantly learning. Often, knowing how to find information on using these technologies is as important a skill as actually implementing them. Luckily, you can choose from a multitude of information sources on these technologies. The inclusion of IntelliSense into IDEs over a decade ago was one of the most useful tools to help developers write code, but it's rarely a substitute for a full-blown help system that provides all the ins and outs of a technology. Visual Studio's help system provides this support for developers.

The easiest way to get help for Visual Studio 2012 is to use the same method you would use for almost every Windows application ever created: Press the F1 key, the universal shortcut key for help. Visual Studio 2012's help system uses Microsoft Help Viewer 2. Rather than using a special "shell" to host the help and enable you to navigate around and search it, the help system now runs in a browser window. To support some of the more complex features of the help system such as the search functionality (when using the offline help), there is now a help listener application that runs in your system tray and serves these requests. The address in the browser's address bar points to a local web server on your machine. The online and offline help modes look and behave similarly to one another, but this chapter specifically focuses on the offline help.

> **NOTE** *You may find that you receive a Service Unavailable message when using the help system. The likely cause of this error is that the help listener is no longer running in your system tray. Simply open the help system from within Visual Studio and the help listener automatically starts again.*

The help system in Visual Studio is contextual. This means that if the cursor is currently positioned on a .NET class usage in a project and you press F1, the help window opens immediately with a minitutorial about what the class is and how to use it, as shown in Figure 5-11.

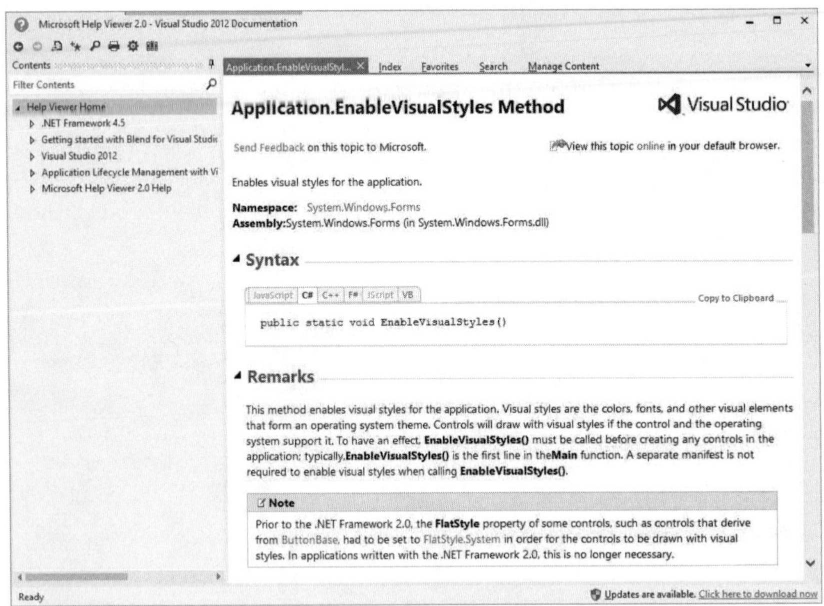

FIGURE 5-11

This is incredibly useful because more often than not if you simply press F1, the help system navigates directly to the help topic that deals with the problem you're currently researching.

However, in some situations you want to go directly to the table of contents within the help system. Visual Studio 2012 enables you to do this through the Visual Studio Documentation menu item in its main Help menu (see Figure 5-12).

In addition to the several help links, you also have shortcuts to MSDN forums and for reporting a bug.

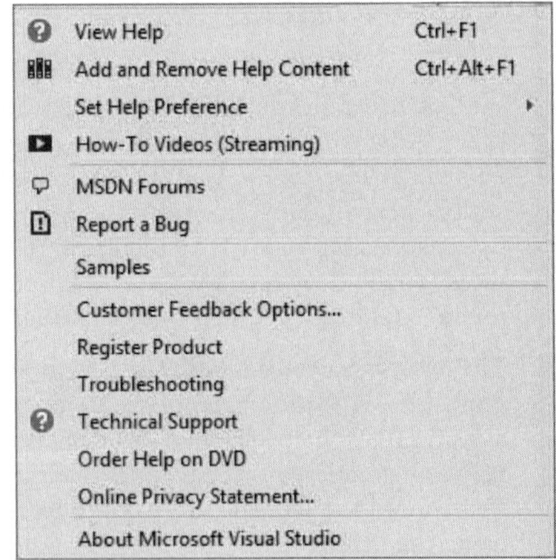

FIGURE 5-12

Navigating and Searching the Help System

Navigating through the help system should be familiar because it is essentially the same as navigating the MSDN documentation on the web. On the left side of the browser window, you can find links to pages in the same part of the help system as the page currently viewed, and you can also find links that might be related to the current page.

In the top left of the browser window, you can find a search textbox. Enter your search query here (in much the same way you would in a search engine such as Google or Bing). This search is a full text search of the pages in the help system, and your query does not necessarily need to appear in the title of the pages. This takes you to the results, which are again provided in a manner similar to the results from a search engine. A one-line extract from the page of each result displays to help you determine if it is the article you are after, and you can click through to view the corresponding page.

Configuring the Help System

When you first start using the help system, it's a good idea to configure it to your needs. To do so, select the Help ➪ Set Help Preferences menu. The menu provides two options: Use Online Help and Use Local Help.

The first option, Use Online Help, sets the help system to use the MSDN documentation on the web. Now pressing F1 or opening the help from the Help menu automatically navigates to the appropriate page in the documentation on MSDN online (for the current context in Visual Studio). Selecting the Use Local Help option navigates to the appropriate page in the documentation installed locally (assuming that the documentation has actually been installed on your machine).

The advantage of the online help over the offline help is that it is always up to date and won't consume space on your hard drive (assuming you don't install the help content). The disadvantage is that you must always have an active Internet connection, and at times (depending on your bandwidth) it may be slower than the offline version to access. Essentially it is a trade-off, and you must choose the most appropriate option for your work environment.

With the Use Local Help option selected, using F1 or opening help from the Help menu launches the Help Viewer. This viewer (refer to Figure 5-11) provides a user experience roughly the same as the Web documentation (navigation on the left, body of the content on the right).

The final option in the Help menu is Add and Remove Local Help Content, which enables you to remove product documentation sets from your local disk and free some disk space. The screen shows the documentation sets currently installed, and you can uninstall a documentation set by pressing the Remove hyperlink button next to its name.

SUMMARY

As you've seen in this chapter, Visual Studio 2012 comes with a number of search-and-replace tools, each suited to a particular type of search task to enable you to navigate and modify your code quickly and easily.

The help system is a powerful interface to the documentation that comes with Visual Studio 2012. The ability to switch easily between online and local documentation ensures that you can balance the speed of offline searches with the relevance of information found on the web. And the abstract paragraphs shown in all search results, regardless of their locations, help reduce the number of times you might click a false positive.

PART II
Getting Started

Solutions, Projects, and Items

WHAT'S IN THIS CHAPTER?

- Creating and configuring solutions and projects
- Controlling how an application is compiled, debugged, and deployed
- Configuring the many project-related properties
- Including resources and settings with an application
- Enforcing good coding practices with the Code Analysis Tools
- Modifying the configuration, packaging, and deployment options for web applications

Other than the simplest applications, such as Hello World, most applications require more than one source file. This raises a number of issues, such as how the files will be named, where they will be located, and whether they can be reused. Within Visual Studio 2012, the concept of a *solution*, containing a series of *projects*, made up of a series of *items*, is used to enable developers to track, manage, and work with their source files. The IDE has a number of built-in features that aim to simplify this process, while still allowing developers to get the most out of their applications. This chapter examines the structure of solutions and projects, looking at available project types and how they can be configured.

SOLUTION STRUCTURE

Whenever you work within Visual Studio, you have a solution open. When you edit an ad hoc file, this is a temporary solution that you can elect to discard when you complete your work. However, the solution enables you to manage the files that you're currently working with, so in most cases saving the solution means that you can return to what you were doing at a later date without having to locate and reopen the files on which you were working.

> **NOTE** *Solutions should be thought of as a container of related projects. The projects within a solution do not need to be of the same language or project type. For example, a single solution could contain an ASP.NET web application written in Visual Basic, an F# library, and a C# WPF application. The solution enables you to open all these projects together in the IDE and manage the build and deployment configuration for them as a whole.*

The most common way to structure applications written within Visual Studio is to have a single solution containing a number of projects. Each project can then be made up of a series of both code files and folders. The main window in which you work with solutions and projects is the Solution Explorer, as shown in Figure 6-1.

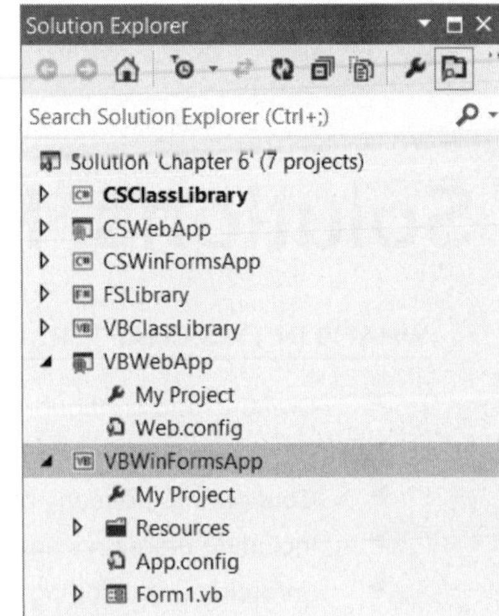

FIGURE 6-1

Within a project, you use folders to organize the source code that have no application meaning associated with them (with the exception of web applications, which can have specially named folders that have specific meaning in this context). Some developers use folder names that correspond to the namespace to which the classes belong. For example, if class `Person` is found within a folder called `DataClasses` in a project called FirstProject, the fully qualified name of the class could be `FirstProject.DataClasses.Person`.

Solution folders are a useful way to organize the projects in a large solution. Solution folders are visible only in the Solution Explorer — a physical folder is not created on the Filesystem. Actions such as Build or Unload can be performed easily on all projects in a solution folder. Solution folders can also be collapsed or hidden so that you can work more easily in the Solution Explorer. Projects that are hidden are still built when you build the solution. Because solution folders do not map to a physical folder, they can be added, renamed, or deleted at any time without causing invalid File references or source control issues.

> **NOTE** *Miscellaneous Files is a special solution folder that you can use to keep track of other files that have been opened in Visual Studio but are not part of any projects in the solution. The Miscellaneous Files solution folder is not visible by default. You can find the settings to enable it under Tools ➪ Options ➪ Environment ➪ Documents.*

There is a common misconception that projects necessarily correspond to .NET assemblies. Although this is generally true, it is possible for multiple projects to represent a single .NET assembly. However, this case is not supported by Visual Studio 2012, so this book assumes that a project corresponds to an assembly.

In Visual Studio 2012, although the format for the solution file has not changed, you cannot open a solution file that was created with Visual Studio 2012 with Visual Studio 2010. However, project files can be opened with both Visual Studio 2010 and Visual Studio 2012.

In addition to tracking which files are contained within an application, solution and project files can record other information, such as how a particular file should be compiled, project settings, resources, and much more. Visual Studio 2012 includes nonmodal dialog for editing project properties, whereas solution properties still open in a separate window. As you might expect, the project properties are those properties pertaining only to the project in question, such as assembly information and references, whereas solution properties determine the overall build configurations for the application.

SOLUTION FILE FORMAT

Visual Studio 2012 actually creates two files for a solution, with extensions `.suo` and `.sln` (solution file). The first of these is a rather uninteresting binary file and hence difficult to edit. It contains user-specific information — for example, which files were open when the solution was last closed and the location of breakpoints. This file is marked as hidden, so it won't appear in the solution folder using Windows Explorer unless you enable the option to show hidden files.

> **WARNING** *Occasionally the* `.suo` *file becomes corrupted and causes unexpected behavior when building and editing applications. If Visual Studio becomes unstable for a particular solution, you should exit and delete the* `.suo` *file. It will be re-created by Visual Studio the next time the solution is opened.*

The `.sln` solution file contains information about the solution, such as the list of projects, build configurations, and other settings that are not project-specific. Unlike many files used by Visual Studio 2012, the solution file is not an XML document. Instead, it stores information in blocks, as shown in the following example solution file:

```
Microsoft Visual Studio Solution File, Format Version 12.00
# Visual Studio 2012
Project("{F184B08F-C81C-45F6-A57F-5ABD9991F28F}") = "FirstProject",
    "FirstProject\FirstProject.vbproj", "{D4FAF2DD-A26C-444A-9FEE-2788B5F5FDD2}"
EndProject
Global
    GlobalSection(SolutionConfigurationPlatforms) = preSolution
         Debug|Any CPU = Debug|Any CPU
    EndGlobalSection
    GlobalSection(ProjectConfigurationPlatforms) = postSolution
     {D4FAF2DD-A26C-444A-9FEE-2788B5F5FDD2}.Debug|Any CPU.ActiveCfg = Debug|Any CPU
     {D4FAF2DD-A26C-444A-9FEE-2788B5F5FDD2}.Debug|Any CPU.Build.0 = Debug|Any CPU
    EndGlobalSection
    GlobalSection(SolutionProperties) = preSolution
        HideSolutionNode = FALSE
    EndGlobalSection
EndGlobal
```

In this example, the solution consists of a single project, FirstProject, and a `Global` section outlining settings that apply to the solution. For instance, the solution itself is visible in the Solution Explorer because the `HideSolutionNode` setting is `FALSE`. If you were to change this value to `TRUE`, the solution name would not display in Visual Studio.

> **NOTE** *As long as a solution consists of projects that do not target the .NET Framework version 4.5 or that do not contain projects that are not supported in Visual Studio 2010 (Windows Store apps being an obvious example), you can still open the solution with Visual Studio 2010.*

SOLUTION PROPERTIES

You can reach the solution Properties dialog by right-clicking the Solution node in the Solution Explorer and selecting Properties. This dialog contains two nodes to partition Common and Configuration properties, as shown in Figure 6-2.

The following sections describe the Common and Configuration properties nodes in more detail.

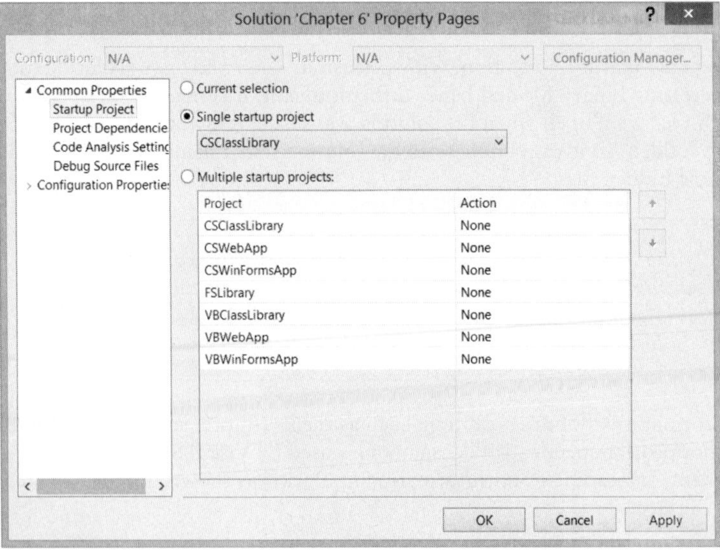

FIGURE 6-2

Common Properties

You have three options when defining the Startup Project for an application, and they're somewhat self-explanatory. Selecting Current Selection starts the project that has current focus in the Solution Explorer. Single Startup ensures that the same project starts up each time. This is the default selection because most applications have only a single startup project. You can use the drop-down list to indicate the single project that you need to start. The last option, Multiple Startup Projects, allows for multiple projects to be started in a particular order. This can be useful if you have a client/server application specified in a single solution and you want them both to be running. When running multiple projects, it is also relevant to control the order in which they start up. Use the up and down arrows next to the project list to control the order in which projects are started.

The Project Dependencies section is used to indicate other projects on which a specific project is dependent. For the most part, Visual Studio manages this for you as you add and remove Project references for a given project. However, sometimes you may want to create dependencies between projects to ensure that they are built in the correct order. Visual Studio uses its list of dependencies to determine the order in which projects should be built. This window prevents you from inadvertently adding circular references and from removing necessary project dependencies.

In the Debug Source Files section, you can provide a list of directories through which Visual Studio can search for source files when debugging. This is the default list that is searched before the Find Source dialog displays. You can also list source files that Visual Studio should not try to locate. If you click Cancel when prompted to locate a source file, the file will be added to this list.

The Code Analysis Settings section is available only in the Visual Studio Premium and Ultimate editions. This allows you to select the static code analysis rule set that will be run for each project. Code Analysis is discussed in more detail later in the chapter.

> **NOTE** *If you have never specified a code analysis run in Visual Studio, it's possible that the solution properties window won't have the Code Analysis Settings section even if you run one of the appropriate editions. To correct this, run Code Analysis directly from the menu. When the analysis finishes, this section becomes visible to you on the solution properties.*

Configuration Properties

Both projects and solutions have build configurations associated with them that determine which items are built and how. It can be somewhat confusing because there is actually no correlation between a project configuration, which determines how things are built, and a solution configuration, which determines which projects are built, other than they might have the same name. A new solution defines both Debug and Release (solution) configurations, which correspond to building all projects within the solution in Debug or Release (project) configurations.

For example, a new solution configuration called Test can be created, which consists of two projects: MyClassLibrary and MyClassLibraryTest. When you build your application in Test configuration, you want MyClassLibrary to be built in Release mode so that you're testing as close to what you would release as possible. However, to step through your test code, you want to build the test project in Debug mode.

When you build in Release mode, you don't want the Test solution to be built or deployed with your application. In this case, you can specify in the Test solution configuration that you want the MyClassLibrary project to be built in Release mode and that the MyClassLibraryTest project should not be built.

> **NOTE** *You can switch between configurations easily via the Configuration drop-down on the standard toolbar. However, it is not as easy to switch between platforms, because the Platform drop-down is not on any of the toolbars. To make this available, select View ➪ Toolbars ➪ Customize. From the Build category on the Commands, the Solution Platforms item can be dragged onto a toolbar.*

When you select the Configuration Properties node from the Solution Properties dialog, as shown in Figure 6-3, the Configuration and Platform drop-down boxes are enabled. The Configuration drop-down contains each of the available solution configurations (Debug and Release by default), Active and All. Similarly, the Platform drop-down contains each of the available platforms. Whenever these drop-downs appear and are enabled, you can specify the settings on that page on a per-configuration and per-platform basis. You can also use the Configuration Manager button to add additional solution configurations and platforms.

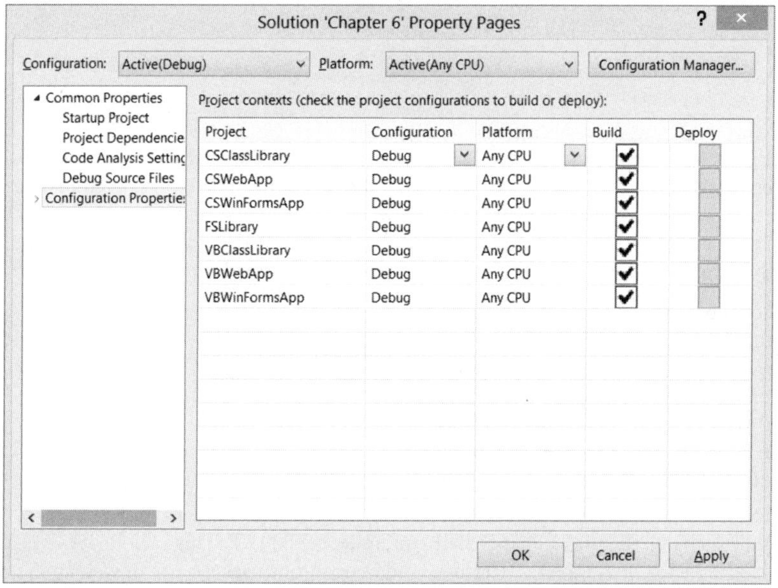

FIGURE 6-3

When adding additional solution configurations, there is an option (checked by default) to create corresponding project configurations for existing projects (projects will be set to build with this configuration by default for this new solution configuration), and an option to base the new configuration on an existing configuration. If the Create Project Configurations option is checked and the new configuration is based on an existing configuration, the new project configurations copies the project configurations specified for the existing configuration.

The options available for creating new platform configurations are limited by the types of CPU available: Itanium, x86, and x64. Again, the new platform configuration can be based on existing configurations, and the option to create project platform configurations is also available.

The other thing you can specify in the solution configuration file is the type of CPU for which you are building. This is particularly relevant if you want to deploy to 64-bit architecture machines.

You can reach all these solution settings directly from the right-click context menu from the Solution node in the Solution Explorer window. Whereas the Set Startup Projects menu item opens the solution configuration window, the Configuration Manager, Project Dependencies, and Project Build Order items open the Configuration Manager and Project Dependencies window. The Project Dependencies and Project Build Order menu items will be visible only if you have more than one project in your solution.

When the Project Build Order item is selected, this opens the Project Dependencies window and lists the build order, as shown in Figure 6-4. This tab reveals the order in which projects will be built, according to the dependencies. This can be useful if you maintain references to project binary assemblies rather than project references, and it can be used to double-check that projects are built in the correct order.

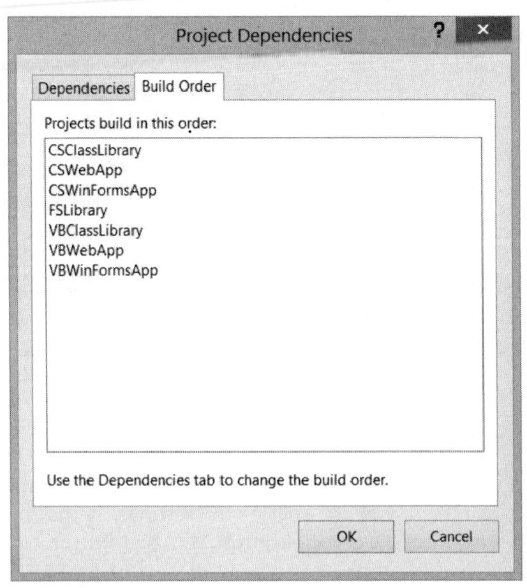

FIGURE 6-4

PROJECT TYPES

Within Visual Studio, the projects for Visual Basic and C# are broadly classified into different categories. With the exception of Web Site projects, which are discussed separately later in this chapter, each project contains a project file (`.vbproj` or `.csproj`) that conforms to the MSBuild schema. Selecting a project template creates a new project, of a specific project type, and populates it with initial classes and settings. Following are some of the more common categories of projects as they are grouped under Visual Studio:

- **Windows:** The Windows project category is the broadest category and includes most of the common project types that run on end-user operating systems. This includes the Windows Forms executable projects, Console application projects, and Windows Presentation Foundation (WPF) applications. These project types create an executable (`.exe`) assembly that is executed directly by an end user. The Windows category also includes several types of library assemblies that can easily be referenced by other projects. These include both class libraries and control libraries for Windows Forms and WPF applications. A class library reuses the familiar DLL extension. The Windows Service project type can also be found in this category.
- **Web:** The Web category includes the project types that run under ASP.NET. This includes ASP.NET web applications (including MVC), XML web services, and control libraries for use in web applications and rich AJAX-enabled web applications.

- **Extensibility:** This collection of templates is used to create add-ons to the Visual Studio IDE, including project and item templates, code editor extensions and a VSIX project that can be used to create deployment packages for the extensions.
- **Office:** As its name suggests, the Office category creates managed code add-ins for Microsoft Office products, such as Outlook, Word, or Excel. These project types use Visual Studio Tools for Office (VSTO) and are capable of creating add-ins for most products in the Office 2010 product suite.
- **Cloud:** By default, the cloud section contains only a link that can retrieve the Windows Azure SDK. After the SDK is installed, additional project templates related to the development of Azure applications appear.
- **Reporting:** This category includes a project type that is ideal for quickly generating complex reports against a data source.
- **SharePoint:** Another self-describing category, this contains projects that target Windows SharePoint Services, such as SharePoint Workflows or Team Sites.
- **Silverlight:** This contains project types for creating Silverlight Applications or Class Library projects.
- **Test:** The Test category includes a project type for projects that contain tests using the MSTest unit testing framework.
- **WCF:** This contains a number of project types for creating applications that provide Windows Communication Foundation (WCF) services.
- **Workflow:** This contains a number of project types for sequential and state machine workflow libraries and applications.
- **SQL Server:** The SQL Server category contains a project type for creating code that can be used with SQL Server. This includes stored procedures, user-defined types and functions, triggers, and custom aggregate functions.

The Add New Project dialog box, as shown in Figure 6-5, enables you to browse and create any of these project types. The target .NET Framework version is listed in a drop-down selector in the top center of this dialog box. If a project type is not supported by the selected .NET Framework version, such as a WPF application under .NET Framework 2.0, that project type will not display.

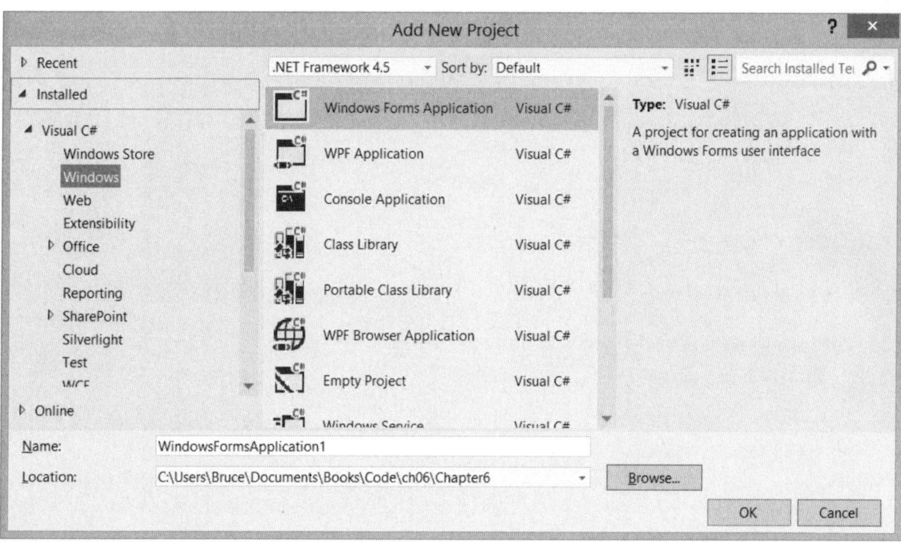

FIGURE 6-5

PROJECT FILES FORMAT

The project files (`.csproj`, `.vbproj`, or `.fsproj`) are text files in an XML document format that conforms to the MSBuild schema. The XML schema files for the latest version of MSBuild are installed with the .NET Framework, by default in `C:\WINDOWS\Microsoft.NET\Framework\v4.0.30319\MSBuild\Microsoft.Build.Core.xsd`.

> **NOTE** *To view the project file in XML format, right-click the project and select Unload. Then right-click the project again and select Edit <project name>. This displays the project file in the XML editor, complete with IntelliSense.*

The project file stores the build and configuration settings that have been specified for the project and details about all the files that are included in the project. In some cases, a user-specific project file is also created (`.csproj.user` or `.vbproj.user`), which stores user preferences such as startup and debugging options. The `.user` file is also an XML file that conforms to the MSBuild schema.

PROJECT PROPERTIES

You can reach the project properties by either right-clicking the Project node in Solution Explorer and then selecting Properties, or by double-clicking My Project (Properties in C#) just under the Project node. In contrast to solution properties, the project properties do not display in a modal dialog. Instead, they appear as an additional tab alongside your code files. This was done in part to make it easier to navigate between code files and project properties, but it also makes it possible to open project properties of multiple projects at the same time. Figure 6-6 illustrates the project settings for a Visual Basic Windows Forms project. This section walks you through the vertical tabs on the project editor for both Visual Basic and C# projects.

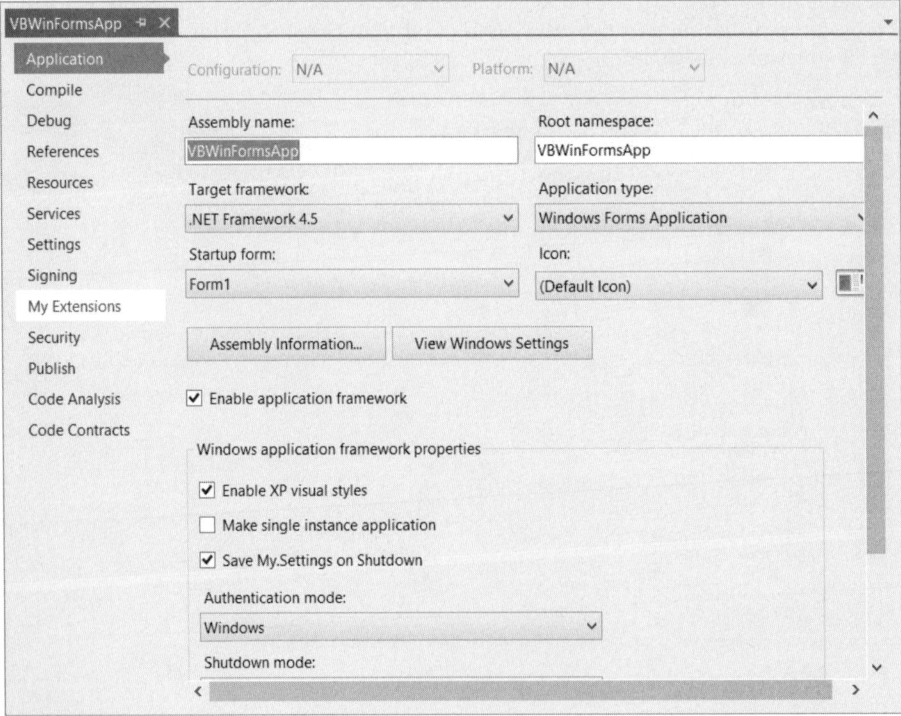

FIGURE 6-6

The project properties editor contains a series of vertical tabs that group the properties. As changes are made to properties in the tabs, a star is added to the corresponding vertical tab. This functionality is limited, however, because it does not indicate which fields within the tab have been modified.

Application

The Application tab, visible in Figure 6-6 for a Visual Basic Windows Forms project, enables the developer to set the information about the assembly that will be created when the project is compiled. These include attributes such as the output type (that is, Windows or Console Application, Class Library, Windows Service, or a Web Control Library), application icon, startup object, and the target .NET Framework version. This last attribute is newly added to Visual Studio 2012 for Visual Basic projects. The Application tab for C# applications, as shown in Figure 6-7, has a different format, and provides a slightly different (and reduced) set of options such as the ability to configure the application manifest directly.

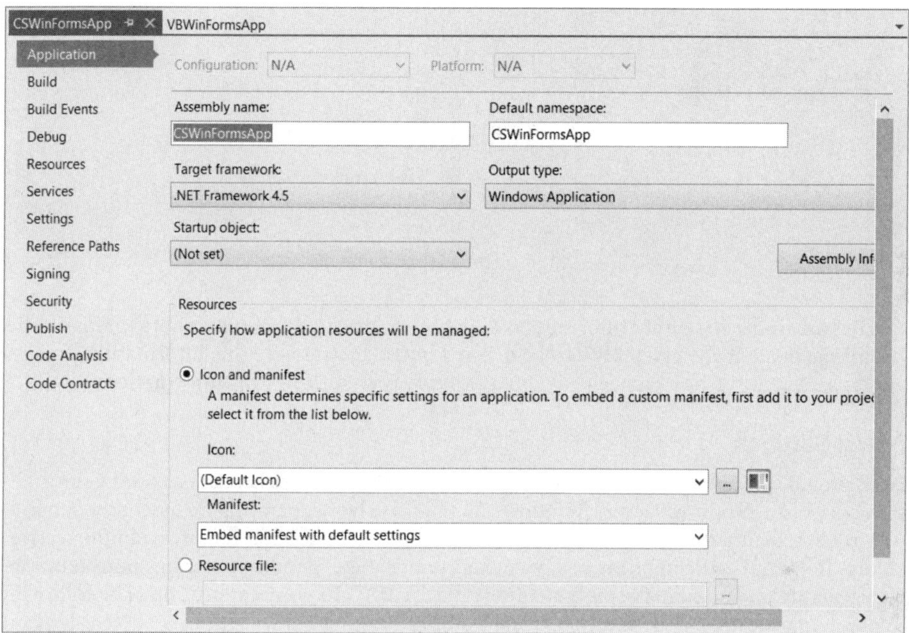

FIGURE 6-7

Assembly Information

Attributes that previously had to be configured by hand in the AssemblyInfo file contained in the project can also be set via the Assembly Information button. This information is important because it shows up when an application is installed and when the properties of a file are viewed in Windows Explorer. Figure 6-8 (left) shows the assembly information for a sample application and Figure 6-8 (right) shows the properties of the compiled executable.

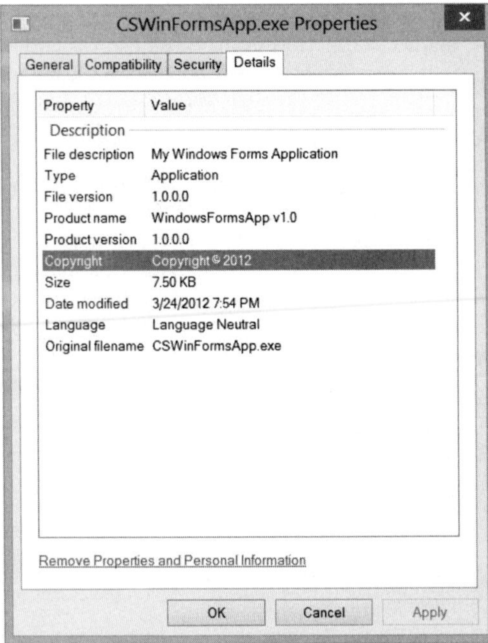

FIGURE 6-8

Each of the properties set in the Assembly Information dialog is represented by an attribute that is applied to the assembly. This means that the assembly can be queried in code to retrieve this information. In Visual Basic, the `My.Application.Info` namespace provides an easy way to retrieve this information.

User Account Control Settings

Visual Studio 2012 provides support for developing applications that work with User Account Control (UAC) under Windows Vista, Windows 7 and Windows 8. This involves generating an assembly manifest file, which is an XML file that notifies the operating system if an application requires administrative privileges on startup. In Visual Basic applications, you can use the View Windows Settings button on the Application tab to generate and add an assembly manifest file for UAC to your application. The following code shows the default manifest file generated by Visual Studio:

```
<?xml version="1.0" encoding="utf-8"?>
<asmv1:assembly manifestVersion="1.0" xmlns="urn:schemas-microsoft-com:asm.v1"
       xmlns:asmv1="urn:schemas-microsoft-com:asm.v1"
       xmlns:asmv2="urn:schemas-microsoft-com:asm.v2"
       xmlns:xsi="http://www.w3.org/2001/XMLSchema-instance">
  <assemblyIdentity version="1.0.0.0" name="MyApplication.app" />
  <trustInfo xmlns="urn:schemas-microsoft-com:asm.v2">
    <security>
      <requestedPrivileges xmlns="urn:schemas-microsoft-com:asm.v3">
        <!-- UAC Manifest Options
           If you want to change the Windows User Account Control level replace the
           requestedExecutionLevel node with one of the following.

        <requestedExecutionLevel  level="asInvoker" />
        <requestedExecutionLevel  level="requireAdministrator" />
        <requestedExecutionLevel  level="highestAvailable" />
```

```
            If you want to utilize File and Registry Virtualization for backward
            compatibility then delete the requestedExecutionLevel node.
          -->
          <requestedExecutionLevel level="asInvoker" />
        </requestedPrivileges>
        <applicationRequestMinimum>
          <defaultAssemblyRequest permissionSetReference="Custom" />
          <PermissionSet ID="Custom" SameSite="site" />
        </applicationRequestMinimum>
      </security>
    </trustInfo>
  </asmv1:assembly>
```

If the UAC-requested execution level is changed from the default `asInvoker` to `require Administrator`, Windows presents a UAC prompt when the application launches. If you have UAC enabled, Visual Studio 2012 also prompts to restart in administrator mode if an application requiring admin rights starts in Debug mode. Figure 6-9 shows the prompt that is shown in Windows allowing you to restart Visual Studio in administrator mode.

If you agree to the restart, Visual Studio not only restarts with administrative privileges, it also reopens your solution including all files you had opened. It even remembers the last cursor position.

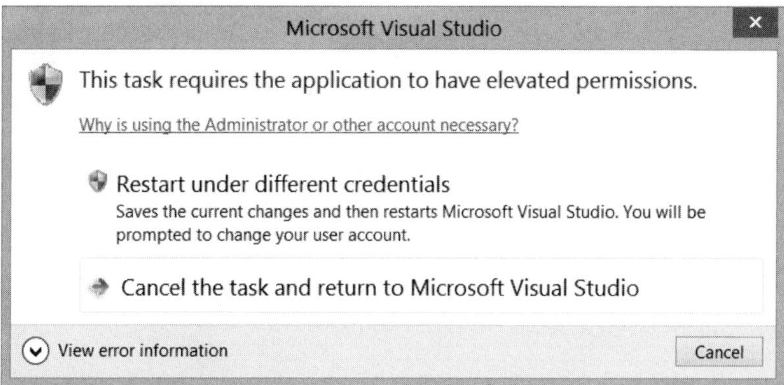

FIGURE 6-9

Application Framework (Visual Basic Only)

Additional application settings are available for Visual Basic Windows Forms projects because they can use the Application Framework that is exclusive to Visual Basic. This extends the standard event model to provide a series of application events and settings that control the behavior of the application. You can enable the Application Framework by checking the Enable Application Framework check box. The following three check boxes control the behavior of the Application Framework:

- **Enable XP Visual Styles:** XP visual styles are a feature that significantly improves the look and feel of applications, running on Windows XP or later, because it provides a much smoother interface through the use of rounded buttons and controls that dynamically change color as the mouse passes over them. Visual Basic applications enable XP styles by default and can be disabled from the Project Settings dialog, or controlled from within code through the `EnableVisualStyles` method on the Application class.
- **Make Single Instance Application:** Most applications support multiple instances running concurrently. However, an application opened more than two or three times may be run only once, with successive executions simply invoking the original application. Such an application could be a document editor, whereby successive executions simply open a different document. This functionality can be easily added by marking the application as a single instance.
- **Save My Settings on Shutdown:** Selecting the Save My Settings on Shutdown option ensures that any changes made to user-scoped settings will be preserved, saving the settings provided prior to the application shutting down.

This section also allows you to select an authentication mode for the application. By default this is set to Windows, which uses the currently logged-on user. Selecting Application-defined allows you to use a custom authentication module.

You can also identify a form to be used as a splash screen when the application first launches and specify the shutdown behavior of the application.

Compile (Visual Basic Only)

The Compile section of the project settings, as shown in Figure 6-10, enables the developer to control how and where the project is built. For example, the output path can be modified so that it points to an alternative location. This might be important if the output is to be used elsewhere in the build process.

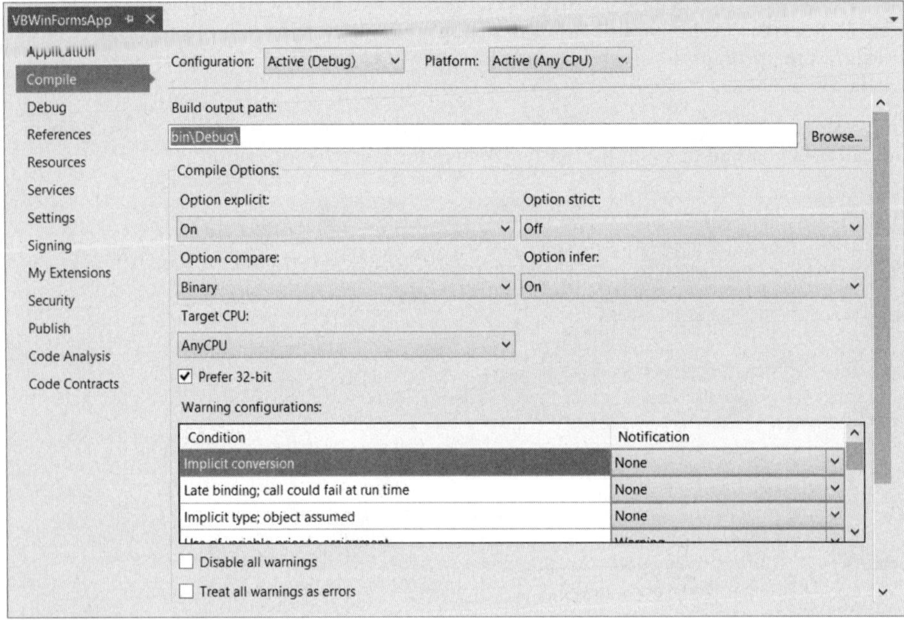

FIGURE 6-10

The Configuration drop-down selector at the top of the tab page allows different build settings for the Debug and Release build configuration.

If your dialog is missing the Configuration drop-down selector, you need to check the Show Advanced Build Configurations property in the Projects and Solutions node of the Options window, accessible from the Tools menu. Unfortunately, this property is not checked for some of the built-in setting profiles — for example, the Visual Basic Developer profile.

Some Visual Basic–specific properties can be configured in the Compile pane. Option Explicit determines whether variables that are used in code must be explicitly defined. Option Strict forces the type of variables to be defined, rather than it being late-bound. Option Compare determines whether strings are compared using binary or text comparison operators. Option Infer specifies whether to allow local type inference in variable declarations or whether the type must be explicitly stated.

> **NOTE** *All four of these compile options can be controlled at either the Project-or File-level. File-level compiler options override the Project-level options.*

The Compile pane also defines a number of different compiler options that can be adjusted to improve the reliability of your code. For example, unused variables may only warrant a warning, whereas a path that doesn't return a value is more serious and should generate a build error. It is possible either to disable all these warnings or treat all of them as errors.

Visual Basic developers also have the ability to generate XML documentation. Of course, because the documentation takes time to generate, it is recommended that you disable this option for debug builds. This can speed up the debugging cycle; however, when turned off warnings are not given for missing XML documentation.

The last element of the Compile pane is the Build Events button. Click this button to view commands that can be executed prior to and after the build. Because not all builds are successful, the execution of the post-build event can depend on a successful build. C# projects have a separate Build Events tab in the project properties pages for configuring pre- and post-build events.

Build (C# and F# Only)

The Build tab, as shown in Figure 6-11, is the C# equivalent of the Visual Basic Compile tab. This tab enables the developer to specify the project's build configuration settings. For example, the Optimize code setting can be enabled, which results in assemblies that are smaller, faster, and more efficient. However, these optimizations typically increase the build time, and as such are not recommended for the Debug build.

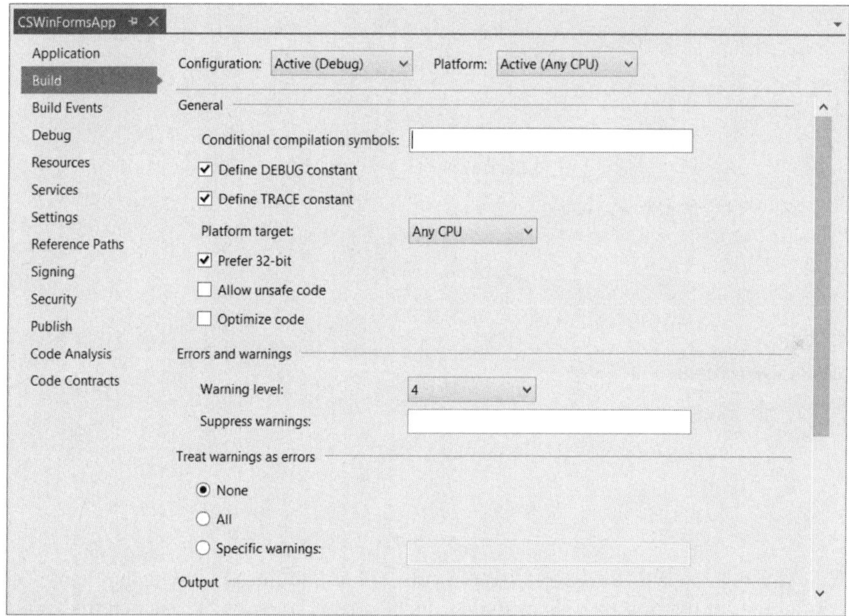

FIGURE 6-11

On the Build tab, the `DEBUG` and `TRACE` compilation constants can be enabled. Alternatively, you can easily define your own constants by specifying them in the Conditional compilation symbols textbox. The value of these constants can be queried from code at compile-time. For example, the `DEBUG` constant can be queried as follows:

C#

```
#if(DEBUG)
    MessageBox.Show("The debug constant is defined");
#endif
```

VB

```
#If DEBUG Then
    MessageBox.Show("The debug constant is defined")
#End If
```

The compilation constants are defined on the Advanced Compiler Settings dialog, which can be displayed by clicking the Advanced Compile Options button on the Compile tab.

The Configuration drop-down selector at the top of the tab page allows different build settings for the Debug and Release build configuration. You can find more information on the Build options in Chapter 46, "Build Customization."

Build Events (C# and F# Only)

The Build Events tab enables you to perform additional actions before or after the build process. In Figure 6-12, you can see a post-build event that executes the FXCop Static Code Analysis tool after every successful build.

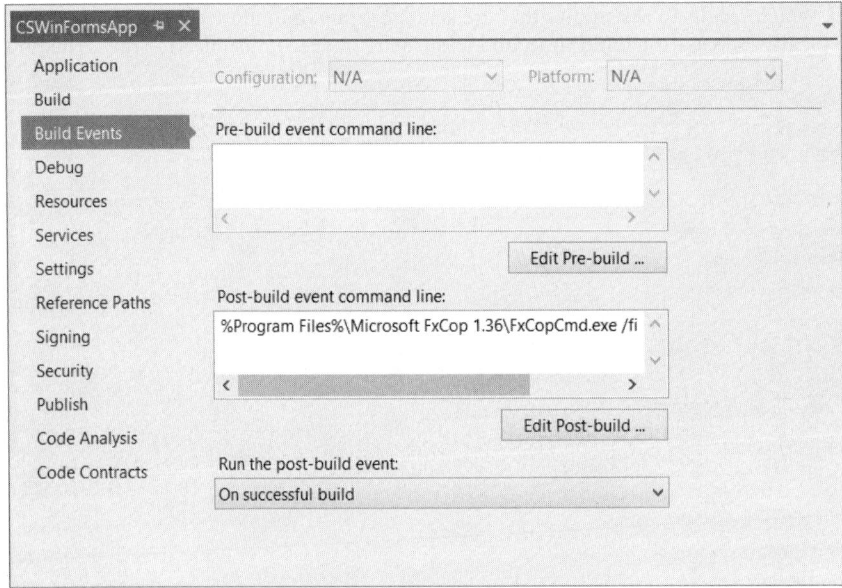

FIGURE 6-12

You can use environment variables such as `ProgramFiles` in your command lines by enclosing them with the percent character. A number of macros are also available, such as `ProjectPath`. These macros are listed when the Macros button on the Edit Pre-build and Edit Post-build dialog box is clicked and can be injected into the command wherever needed.

Debug

The Debug tab, shown in Figure 6-13, determines how the application will be executed when run from within Visual Studio 2012. This tab is not visible for web applications — instead the Web tab is used to configure similar options.

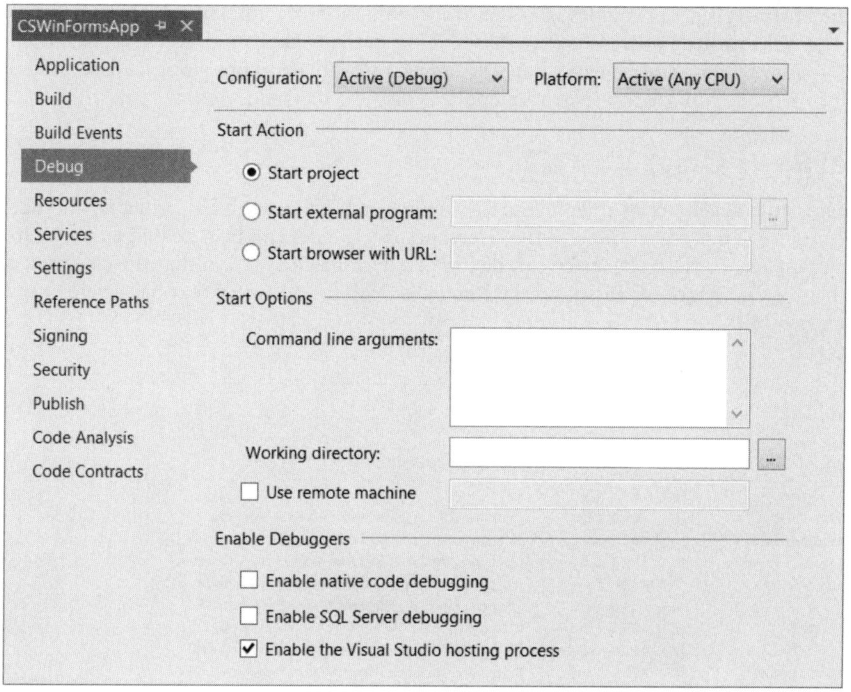

FIGURE 6-13

Start Action

When a project is set to start up, this set of radio buttons controls what actually happens when the application is run within Visual Studio. The default value is to start the project, which calls the Startup object specified on the Application tab. The other options are to either run an executable or launch a specific website.

Start Options

The options that can be specified when running an application are additional command-line arguments (generally used with an executable start action) and the initial working directory. You can also specify to start the application on a remote computer. Of course, this is possible only when debugging is enabled on the remote machine.

Enable Debuggers

Debugging can be extended to include unmanaged code and SQL Server. The Visual Studio hosting process can also be enabled here. This process has a number of benefits associated with the performance and functionality of the debugger. The benefits fall into three categories. First, the hosting process acts as a background host for the application you debug. To debug a managed application, various administrative tasks must be performed, such as creating an AppDomain and associating the debugger, which take time. With the hosting process enabled, these tasks are handled in the background, resulting in a much quicker load time during debugging.

Second, in Visual Studio 2012, it is quite easy to create, debug, and deploy applications that run under partial trust. The hosting process is an important tool in this process because it gives you the ability to run and debug an application in partial trust. Without this process, the application would run in full trust mode, preventing you from debugging the application in partial trust mode.

The last benefit that the hosting process provides is design-time evaluation of expressions. This is in effect an optical illusion, because the hosting process is actually running in the background. However, using the Immediate window as you write your code means that you can easily evaluate expressions, call methods, and even hit breakpoints without running up the entire application.

References (Visual Basic Only)

The References tab enables the developer to reference classes in other .NET assemblies, projects, and native DLLs. When the project or DLL has been added to the references list, a class can be accessed either by its full name, including namespace, or the namespace can be imported into a code file so that the class can be referenced by just the class name. Figure 6-14 shows the References tab for a project that has a reference to a number of framework assemblies.

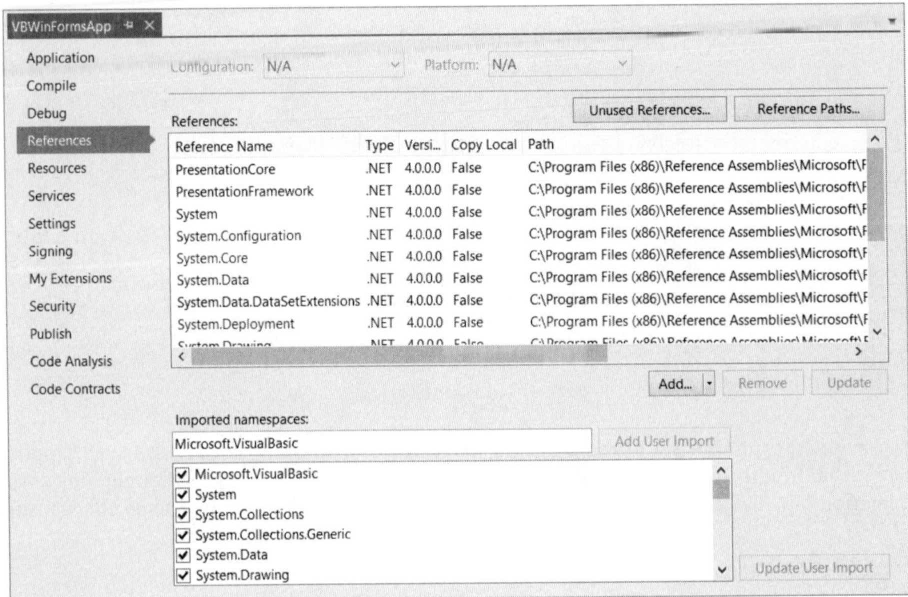

FIGURE 6-14

One of the features of this tab for Visual Basic developers is the Unused References button, which performs a search to determine which references can be removed. You can add a reference path, which includes all assemblies in that location.

> **NOTE** *Having unused references in your project is not generally a problem. Although some people don't like it because it makes the solution "messy," from a performance perspective, there is no impact. Assemblies that are not used are not copied to the output directory.*

When an assembly has been added to the reference list, any public class contained within that assembly can be referenced within the project. Where a class is embedded in a namespace (which might be a nested hierarchy), referencing a class requires the full class name. Both Visual Basic and C# provide a mechanism for importing namespaces so that classes can be referenced directly. The References section allows namespaces to be globally imported for all classes in the project, without being explicitly imported within the class file.

References to external assemblies can either be File references or Project references. File references are direct references to an individual assembly. You can create File references by using the Browse tab of the Reference Manager dialog box. Project references are references to a project within the solution. All assemblies that are output by that project are dynamically added as references. Create Project references by using the Solution tab of the Reference Manager dialog box.

> **WARNING** *You should generally not add a File reference to a project that exists in the same solution. If a project requires a reference to another project in that solution, a Project reference should be used.*

The advantage of a Project reference is that it creates a dependency between the projects in the build system. The dependent project will be built if it has changed since the last time the referencing project was built. A File reference doesn't create a build dependency, so it's possible to build the referencing project without building the dependent project. However, this can result in problems with the referencing project expecting a different version from what is included in the output.

Resources

You can add or remove Project resources via the Resources tab, as shown in Figure 6-15. In the example shown, four icons have been added to this application. Resources can be images, text, icons, files, or any other serializable class.

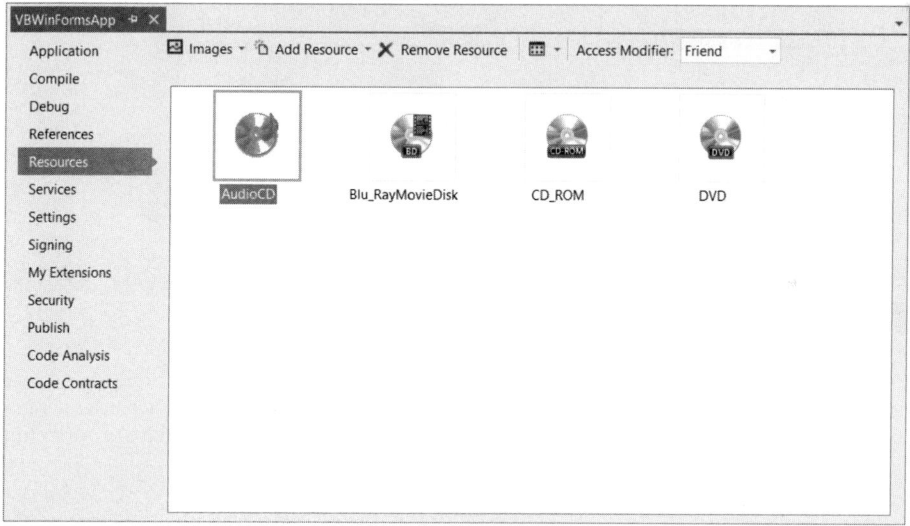

FIGURE 6-15

This interface makes working with resource files at design time easy. Chapter 39, "Resource Files," examines in more detail how you can use resource files to store application constants and internationalize your application.

Services

Client application services allow Windows-based applications to use the authentication, roles, and profile services that were introduced with Microsoft ASP.NET 2.0. The client services enable multiple web- and Windows-based applications to centralize user profiles and user-administration functionality.

Figure 6-16 shows the Services tab, which is used to configure client application services for Windows applications. When enabling the services, the URL of the ASP.NET service host must be specified for each service. This will be stored in the `app.config` file. The following client services are supported:

- **Authentication:** This enables the user's identity to be verified using either the native Windows authentication, or a custom forms-based authentication that is provided by the application.
- **Roles:** This obtains the roles an authenticated user has been assigned. This enables you to allow certain users access to different parts of the application. For example, additional administrative functions may be made available to admin users.
- **Web Settings:** This stores per-user application settings on the server, which allows them to be shared across multiple computers and applications.

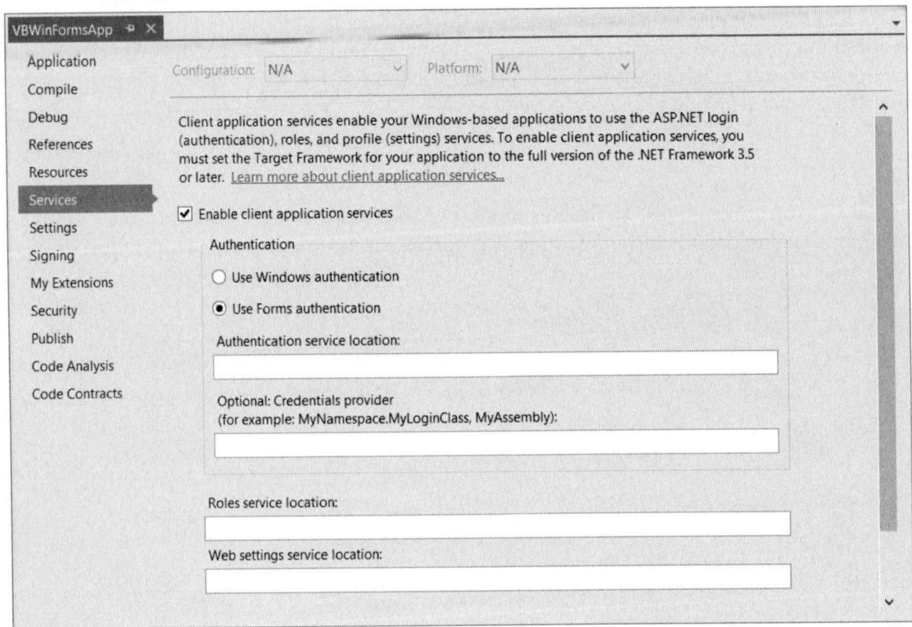

FIGURE 6-16

Client application services utilize a provider model for web services extensibility. The service providers include offline support that uses a local cache to ensure that it can still operate even when a network connection is not available.

Client application services are discussed further in Chapter 34, "Client Application Services."

Settings

Project settings can be of any type and simply reflect a name/value pair whose value can be retrieved at run time. Settings can be scoped to either the Application or the User, as shown in Figure 6-17. Settings are stored internally in the `Settings.settings` file and the `app.config` file. When the application is compiled, this file is renamed according to the executable generated — for example, `SampleApplication.exe.config`.

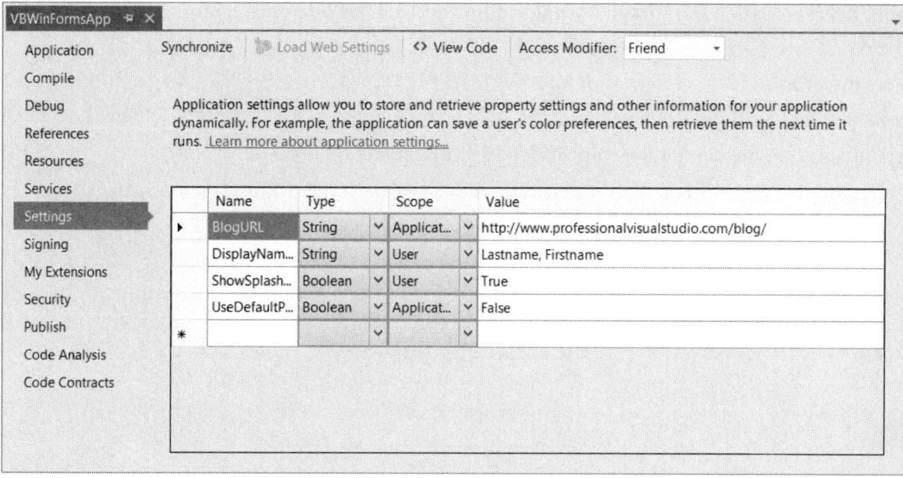

FIGURE 6-17

Application-scoped settings are read-only at run time and can be changed only by manually editing the config file. User settings can be dynamically changed at run time and may have a different value saved for each user who runs the application. The default values for User settings are stored in the `app.config` file, and the per-user settings are stored in a `user.config` file under the user's private data path.

Application and User settings are described in more detail in Chapter 37, "Configuration Files."

Reference Paths (C# and F# Only)

The Reference Paths tab, as shown in Figure 6-18, is used to specify additional directories that are searched for referenced assemblies.

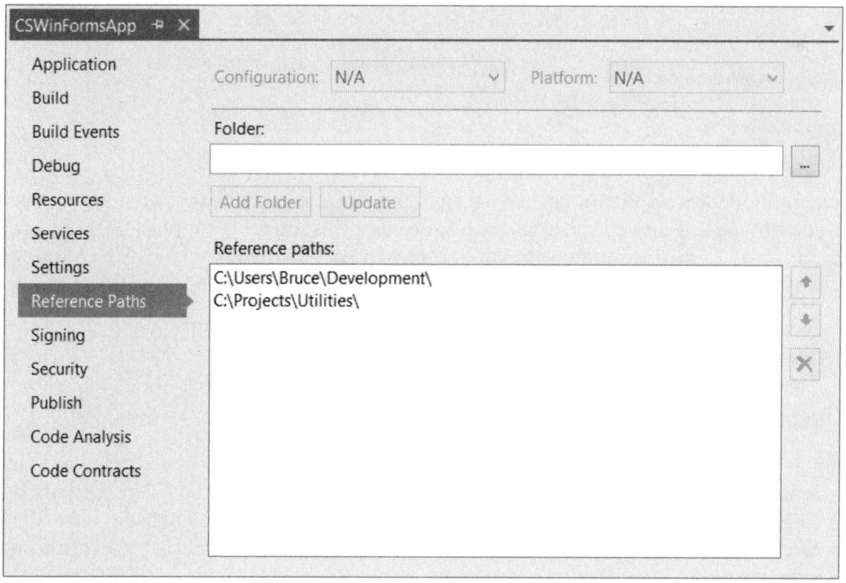

FIGURE 6-18

When an assembly reference has been added, Visual Studio resolves the reference by looking in the following directories in order:

1. The project directory.
2. Directories specified in this Reference Paths list.
3. Directories displaying files in the Reference Manager dialog box.
4. The obj directory for the project. This is generally only relevant to COM interop assemblies.

Signing

Figure 6-19 shows the Signing tab, which provides developers with the capability to determine how assemblies are signed in preparation for deployment. An assembly can be signed by selecting a key file. A new key file can be created by selecting <New...> from the file selector drop-down.

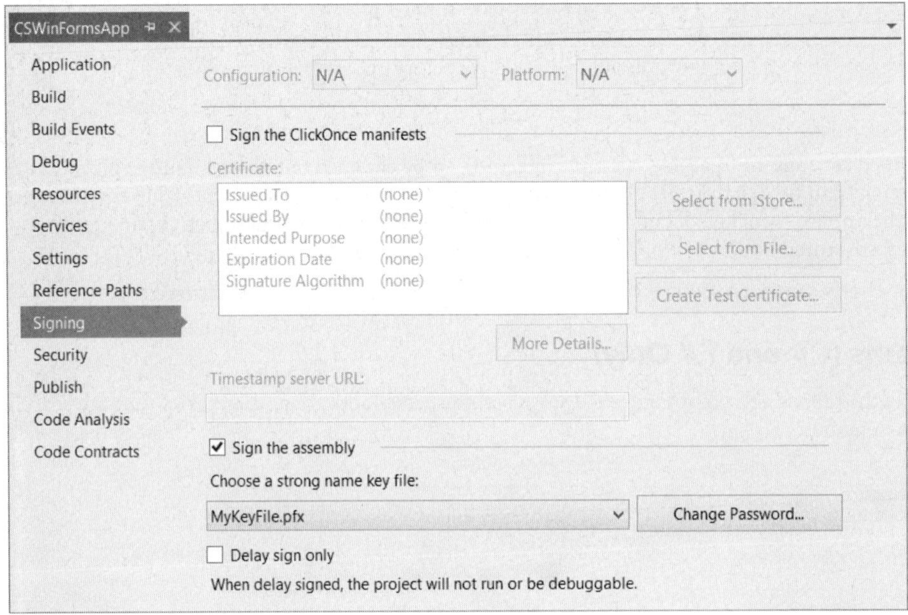

FIGURE 6-19

The ClickOnce deployment model for applications enables an application to be published to a website where a user can click once to download and install the application. Because this model is supposed to support deployment over the Internet, an organization must be able to sign the deployment package. The Signing tab provides an interface for specifying the certificate to use to sign the ClickOnce manifests.

Chapter 47, "Assembly Versioning and Signing," provides more detail on assembly signing and Chapter 49, "Packaging and Deployment," discusses ClickOnce deployments.

My Extensions (Visual Basic Only)

The My Extensions tab, as shown in Figure 6-20, enables you to add a reference to an assembly that extends the Visual Basic `My` namespace, using the extension methods feature. Extension methods were initially introduced to enable LINQ to be shipped without requiring major changes to the base class library. They allow developers to add new methods to an existing class, without having to use inheritance to create a subclass or recompile the original type.

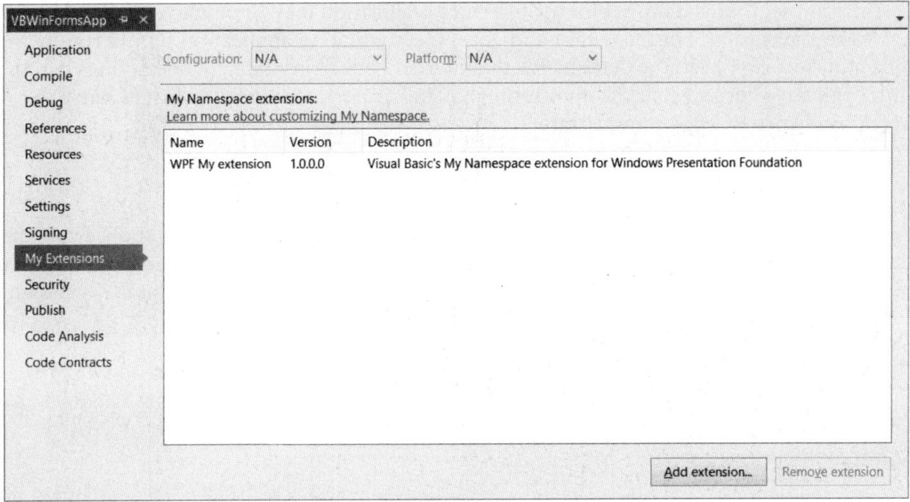

FIGURE 6-20

The `My` namespace was designed to provide simplified access to common library methods. For example, `My.Application.Log` provides methods to write an entry or exception to a log file using a single line of code. As such it is the ideal namespace to add custom classes and methods that provide useful utility functions, global state, or configuration information, or a service that can be used by multiple applications.

Security

Applications deployed using the ClickOnce deployment model may be required to run under limited or partial trust. For example, if a low-privilege user selects a ClickOnce application from a website across the Internet, the application needs to run with partial trust as defined by the Internet zone. This typically means that the application can't access the local Filesystem, has limited networking capability, and can't access other local devices such as printers, databases, and computer ports.

The Security tab, illustrated in Figure 6-21, allows you to define the trust level that is required by your application to operate correctly.

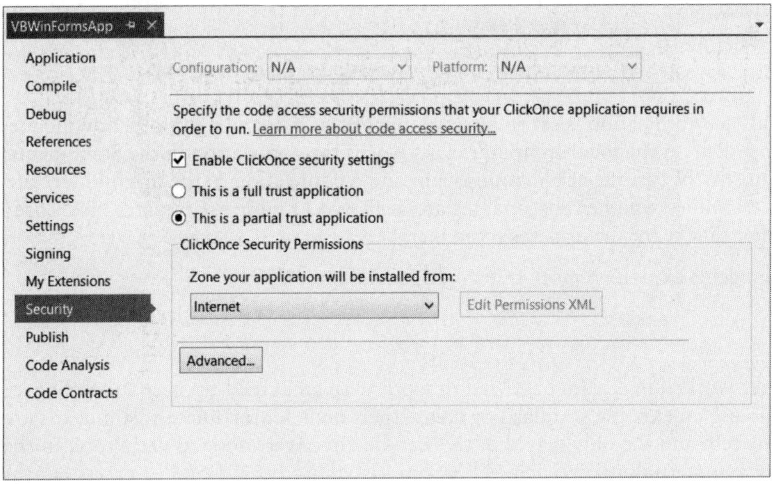

FIGURE 6-21

Modifying the permission set that is required for a ClickOnce application may limit who can download, install, and operate the application. For the widest audience, specify that an application should run in partial-trust mode with security set to the defaults for the Internet zone. Alternatively, specifying that an application requires full trust ensures that the application has full access to all local resources but necessarily limits the audience to local administrators.

Publish

The ClickOnce deployment model can be divided into two phases: initially publishing the application and subsequent updates, and the download and installation of both the original application and subsequent revisions. You can deploy an existing application using the ClickOnce model using the Publish tab, as shown in Figure 6-22.

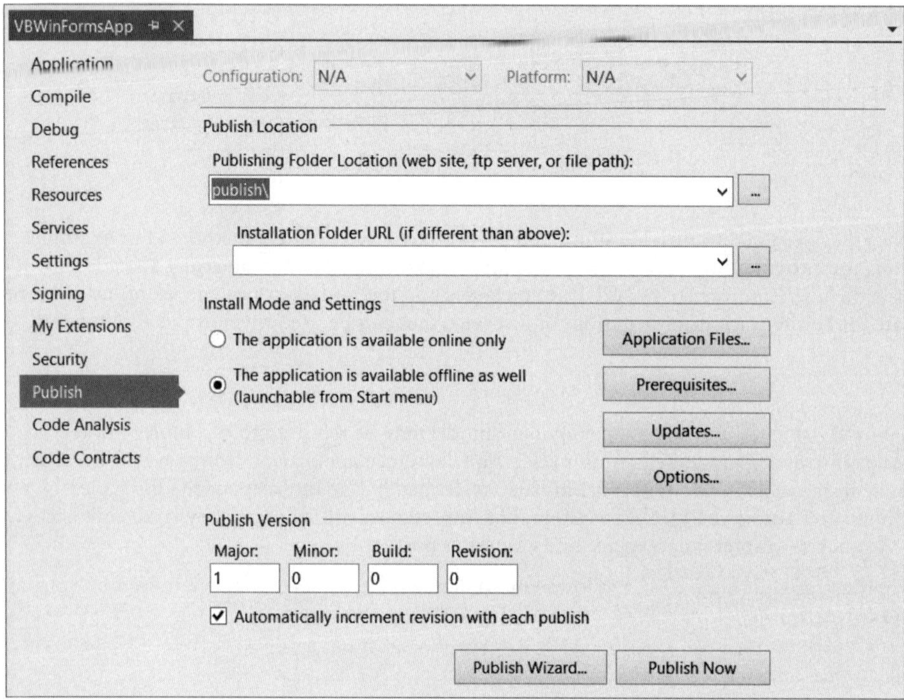

FIGURE 6-22

If the install mode for a ClickOnce application is set to be available offline when it is initially downloaded from the website, it will be installed on the local computer. This places the application in the Start menu and the Add/Remove Programs list. When the application is run and a connection to the original website is available, the application determines whether any updates are available. If there are updates, users are prompted to determine whether they want the updates to be installed.

The ClickOnce deployment model is explained more thoroughly in Chapter 49.

Code Analysis

Most developers who have ever worked in a team have had to work with an agreed-upon set of coding standards. Organizations typically use an existing standard or create their own. Unfortunately, standards are useful only if they can be enforced, and the only way that this can be effectively done to use a tool. In the past this had to be done using an external utility, such as FXCop. Visual Studio 2012 (all versions but the Express version) have the capability to carry out static code analysis from within the IDE.

The Code Analysis tab, as shown in Figure 6-23, can be used to enable code analysis as part of the build process. Because this can be quite a time-consuming process, it may be included only in release or test build configurations. Regardless of whether code analysis has been enabled for a project, it can be manually invoked from the Build menu.

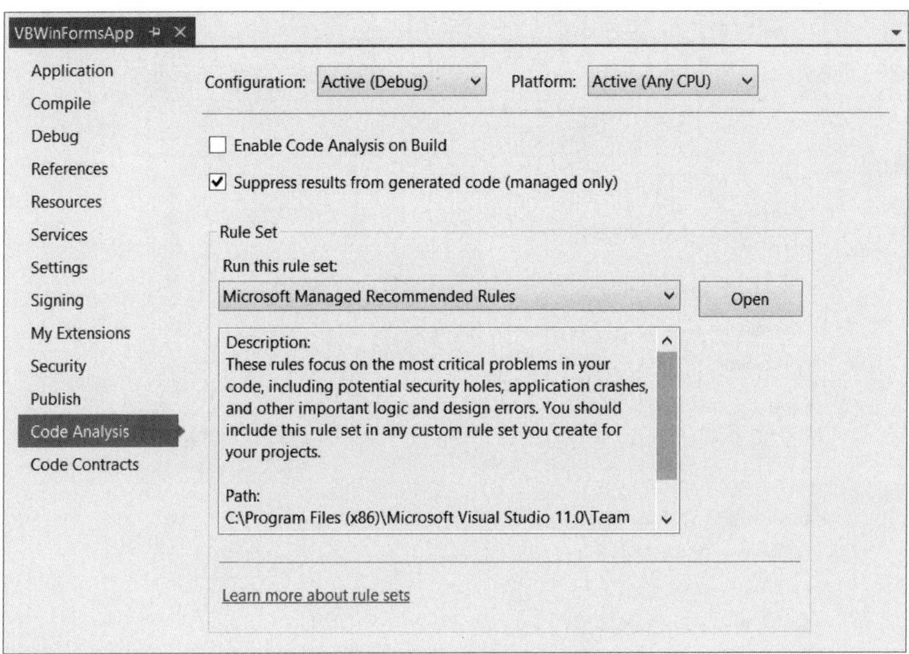

FIGURE 6-23

Not all rules defined in the Code Analysis pane are suitable for all organizations or applications. This pane gives the developer control over which rules are applied and whether they generate a warning or a build error. Deselecting the rule in the Rules column disables the rule. Double-clicking a cell in the Status column toggles what happens when a rule fails to be met between a warning and a build error.

FXCop and Code Contracts are covered in Chapter 13, "Code Consistency Tools," and the native Visual Studio Code Analysis tools are discussed further in Chapter 55, "Visual Studio Ultimate for Developers."

WEB APPLICATION PROJECT PROPERTIES

Due to the unique requirements of web applications, four additional project property tabs are available to ASP.NET Web Application projects. These tabs control how web applications run from Visual Studio as well as the packaging and deployment options.

Web

The Web tab, shown in Figure 6-24, controls how Web Application projects are launched when executed from within Visual Studio. Visual Studio ships with a built-in web server suitable for development purposes. The Web tab enables you to configure the port and virtual path that this runs under. You may also choose to enable NTLM authentication.

> **NOTE** *The Enable Edit and Continue option allows editing of code behind and stand-alone class files during a debug session. Editing of the HTML in an* `.aspx` *or* `.ascx` *page is allowed regardless of this setting; however, editing inline code in an* `.aspx` *page or an* `.ascx` *file is never allowed.*

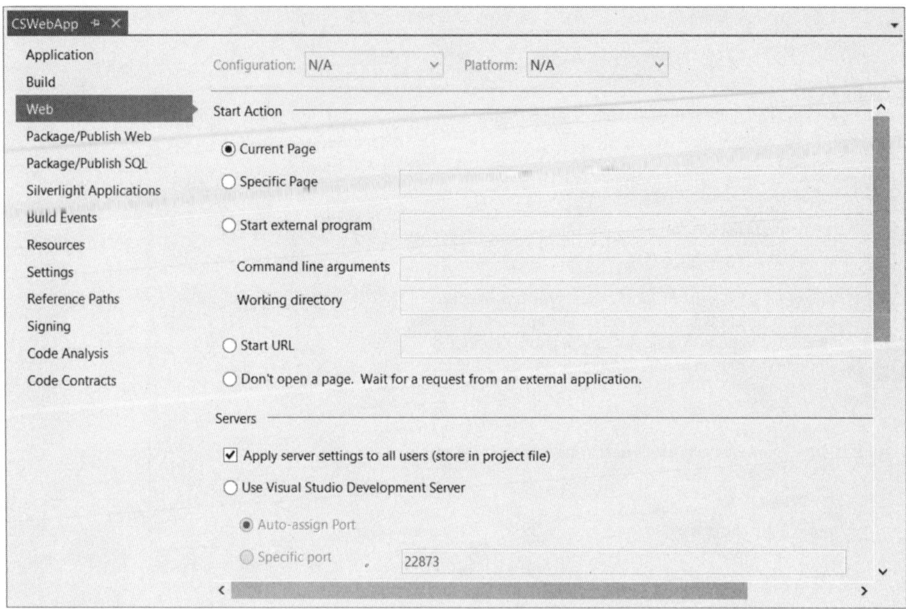

FIGURE 6-24

The debugging options for web applications are explored in Chapter 43, "Debugging Web Applications."

Silverlight Applications

The Silverlight Applications tab provides an easy way to provide a link to a Silverlight project and host it within an ASP.NET Web Application.

When you add a Silverlight application to a Web Application project, you can select an existing Silverlight project if one exists in the current solution or create a new Silverlight project, as shown in Figure 6-25. The dialog box allows you to select the location and language for the new project, as well as options for how the Silverlight application will be included in the current web application.

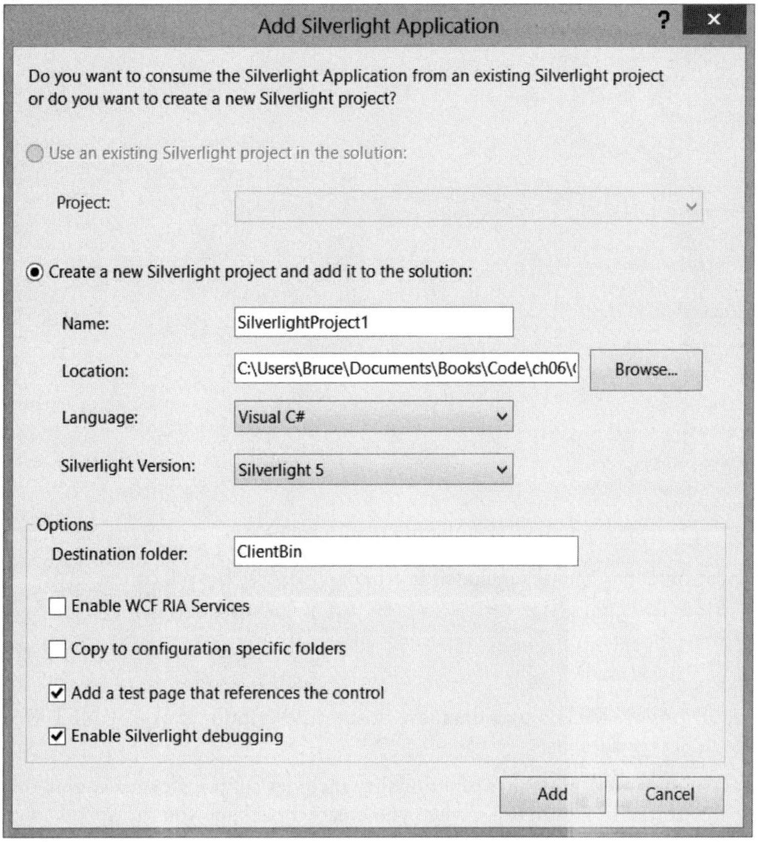

FIGURE 6-25

If you accept the defaults when you add a new Silverlight application, Visual Studio creates a reference to the new project and generates three files in the web application: a static HTML page, an ASP.NET web form, and a JavaScript file that contains logic for loading Silverlight applications and installing the run time if required.

Chapter 23, "Silverlight," explores the development of Silverlight applications and the options for hosting them within an existing web application.

Package/Publish Web

Application deployment has always been a difficult challenge, especially for complex web applications. A typical web application is composed of not only a large number of source files and assemblies, but also images, stylesheets, and JavaScript files. To complicate matters further, it may be dependent on a specific configuration of the IIS web server.

Visual Studio 2012 simplifies this process by enabling you to package a Web Application project with all the necessary files and settings contained in a single compressed (`.zip`) file. Figure 6-26 shows the packaging and deployment options that are available to an ASP.NET Web Application.

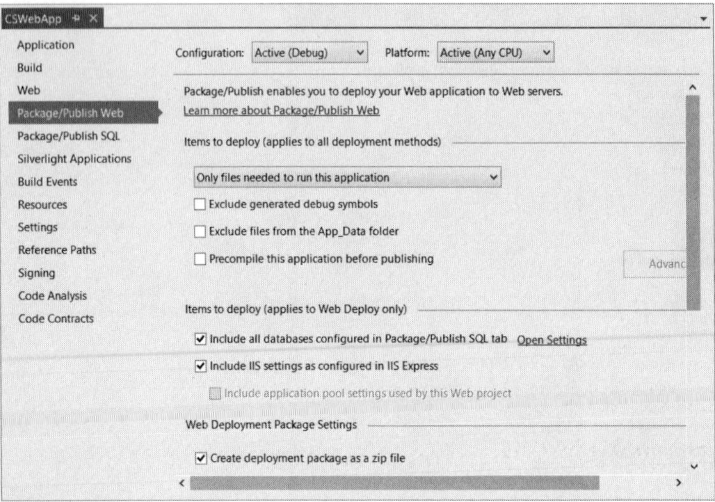

FIGURE 6-26

Further discussion on web application deployment is included in Chapter 50, "Web Application Deployment."

Package/Publish SQL

All but the simplest of web applications are backed by a database of some description. For ASP.NET Web applications this is typically a SQL Server database.

The Visual Studio 2012 web packaging and deployment functionality includes support for packaging one or more SQL Server databases. As illustrated in Figure 6-27, when you create a package you can specify a connection string for your source database. You can allow Visual Studio to create SQL scripts for the database schema only or schema and data. You can also provide custom SQL scripts to be executed either before or after the auto-generated script.

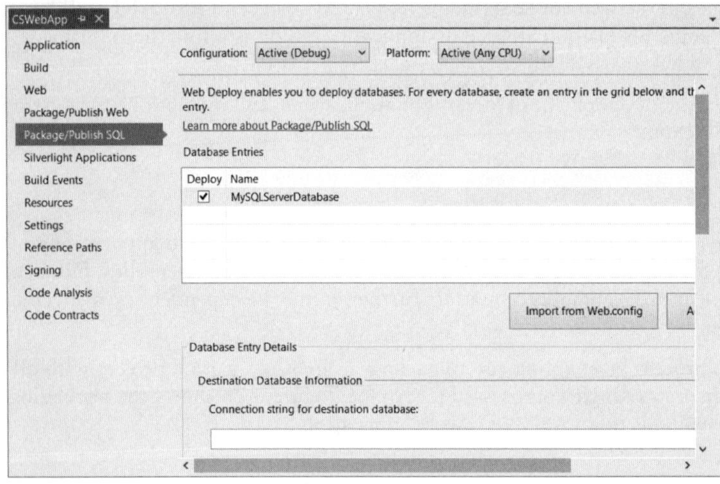

FIGURE 6-27

Chapter 50 explores the web application deployment options in more detail.

WEB SITE PROJECTS

The Web Site project functions quite differently from other project types. Web Site projects do not include a `.csproj` or `.vbproj` file, which means they have a number of limitations for build options, project resources, and managing references. Instead, Web Site projects use the folder structure to define the contents of the project. All files within the folder structure are implicitly part of the project.

Web Site projects provide the advantage of dynamic compilation, which allows pages to be edited without rebuilding the entire site. The file can be saved and simply reloaded in the browser. As such, they enable extremely short code and debug cycles. Microsoft first introduced Web Site projects with Visual Studio 2005; however, it was quickly inundated with customer feedback to reintroduce the Application Project model, which had been provided as an additional download. By the release of Service Pack 1, Web Application projects were back within Visual Studio as a native project type.

> **NOTE** *Since Visual Studio 2005, an ongoing debate has been raging about which is better — Web Site projects or Web Application projects. Unfortunately, there is no simple answer to this debate. Each has its own pros and cons, and the decision comes down to your requirements and your preferred development workflow.*

You can find further discussion on Web Site and Web Application projects in Chapter 21, "ASP.NET Web Forms."

SUMMARY

In this chapter you have seen how a solution and projects can be configured using the user interfaces provided within Visual Studio 2012. In particular, this chapter showed you how to do the following:

- Create and configure solutions and projects
- Control how an application is compiled, debugged, and deployed
- Configure the many project-related properties
- Include resources and settings with an application
- Enforce good coding practices with the Code Analysis Tools
- Modify the configuration, packaging, and deployment options for web applications

In subsequent chapters many of the topics, such as building and deploying projects and the use of resource files, are examined in more detail.

7

IntelliSense and Bookmarks

WHAT'S IN THIS CHAPTER?

- Improving efficiency with contextual help
- Detecting and fixing simple errors
- Reducing keystrokes
- Generating code
- Navigating source code with bookmarks

One of the design goals of Visual Studio has always been to improve the productivity of developers. IntelliSense is one of those functions that fit perfectly into this category. It has been around for more than a decade, and it has become so deeply embedded into the day-to-day world of coders that we pretty much take it for granted. And yet, from version to version, Microsoft is still able to find tweaks and improvements that make it even more useful. This chapter illustrates the many ways in which IntelliSense helps you write your code. Among the topics covered are detecting and repairing syntax errors, harnessing contextual information, and variable name completion. You'll also learn how to set and use bookmarks in your code for easier navigation.

INTELLISENSE EXPLAINED

IntelliSense is the general term for automated help and actions in a Microsoft application. The most commonly encountered aspects of IntelliSense are those wavy lines you see under words that are not spelled correctly in Microsoft Word, or the small visual indicators in a Microsoft Excel spreadsheet that inform you that the contents of the particular cell do not conform to what was expected.

Even these basic indicators enable you to quickly perform related actions. Right-clicking a word with red wavy underlining in Word displays a list of suggested alternatives. Other applications have similar features.

The good news is that Visual Studio has had similar functionality for a long time. In fact, the simplest IntelliSense features go back to tools such as Visual Basic 6. With each release of Visual Studio, Microsoft has refined the IntelliSense features, making them more context-sensitive and putting them in more places so that you should always have the information you need right at your fingertips.

In Visual Studio 2012, the IntelliSense name is applied to a number of different features, from visual feedback for bad code and smart tags for designing forms to shortcuts that insert whole slabs of code. These features work together to provide you with deeper insight, efficiency, and control of your code. Some of Visual Studio's features, such as suggestion mode and Generate From Usage, are designed to support the alternative style of application development known as test-driven development (TDD).

General IntelliSense

The simplest feature of IntelliSense gives you immediate feedback about bad code in your code listings. Figure 7-1 shows one such example, in which an unknown data type is used to instantiate an object. Because the data type is unknown where this code appears, Visual Studio draws a red (C# and C++) or blue (VB) wavy line underneath to indicate a problem.

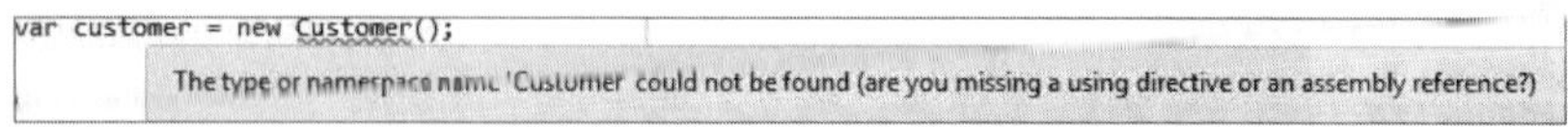

FIGURE 7-1

> **NOTE** *You can adjust the formatting of this color feedback in the Fonts and Colors group of Options.*

Hovering the mouse over the offending piece of code displays a tooltip to explain the problem. In this example the cursor was placed over the data type, with the resulting tooltip The Type Or Namespace Name 'Customer' Could Not Be Found.

Visual Studio can look for this kind of error by continually compiling the code you write in the background, and looking for anything that can produce a compilation error. If you were to add the `Customer` class to your project, Visual Studio would automatically process this and remove the IntelliSense marker.

Figure 7-2 displays the smart tag associated with the error. This applies only to errors for which Visual Studio 2012 can offer you corrective actions. Just below the problem code, a small blue (C#) or red (VB) rectangle displays. Placing the mouse cursor over this marker displays the smart tag action menu associated with the type of error — in this case the action menu provides options for generating your `Customer` class from what Visual Studio can determine from the way you have used it.

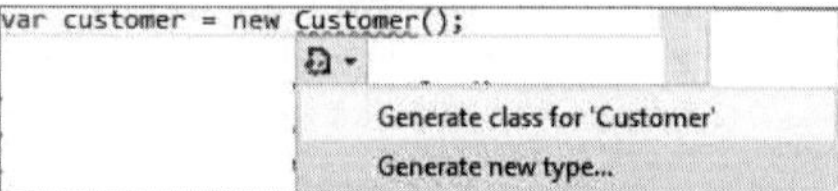

FIGURE 7-2

> **NOTE** *The standard shortcut key used by all Microsoft applications to activate an IntelliSense smart tag is Shift+Alt+F10, but Visual Studio 2012 provides the more wrist-friendly Ctrl+. (period) shortcut for the same action.*

The smart tag technology found in Visual Studio is not solely reserved for the code window. In fact, Visual Studio 2012 also includes smart tags on visual components when you edit a form or user control in Design view (see Figure 7-3).

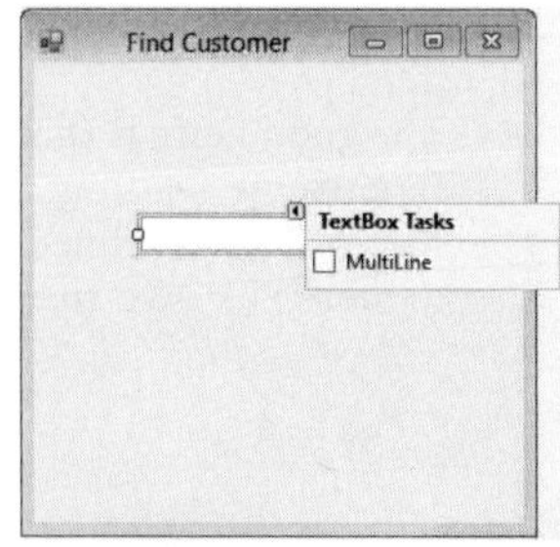

FIGURE 7-3

> **NOTE** *The keyboard shortcuts for opening smart tags also work for visual controls.*

When you select a control that has a smart tag, a small triangle appears at the top-right corner of the control. Click this button to open the smart tag Tasks list — Figure 7-3 shows the Tasks list for a standard TextBox control.

IntelliSense and C++

One of the major IntelliSense additions in Visual Studio 2012 is that C++/CLI is now fully supported. Now, to be fair, it's not like C++ hasn't had some IntelliSense support over the years. It has. However, there have always been limitations. Large projects would result in degraded performance for the IDE. Auto completion, Quick Information, and Parameter Help were there. But tools like Navigate To used a combination of browsing and IntelliSense to fulfill their function.

However, that has changed with Visual Studio 2012. For the first time, all of the topics in the following sections are of interest to C++ developers. Changes have been made to the underlying infrastructure to improve IntelliSense performance in a number of previous pain points. And features that were previously absent have found a home. So C++ developers rejoice and bask in the warm glow of IntelliSense.

Completing Words and Phrases

The power of IntelliSense in Visual Studio 2012 becomes apparent as soon as you start writing code. As you type, various drop-down lists are displayed to help you choose valid members, functions, and parameter types, thus reducing the potential for compilation errors before you even finish writing your code. When you become familiar with the IntelliSense behavior, you'll notice that it can greatly reduce the amount of code you actually have to write. This can be a significant savings to developers using more verbose languages such as Visual Basic.

In Context

In Visual Studio 2012, IntelliSense appears almost as soon as you begin to type within the code window. Figure 7-4 illustrates the IntelliSense displayed during the creation of a `For` loop in Visual Basic. On the left side of the image, IntelliSense appeared as soon as the f was entered, and the list of available words progressively shrank as each subsequent key was pressed. As you can see, the list is made up of all the alternatives, such as statements, classes, methods, or properties, that match the letters entered (in this case those containing the word `For`).

Notice the difference in the right image of Figure 7-4, where a space has been entered after the word `for`. Now the IntelliSense list has expanded to include all the alternatives that could be entered at this position in the code. In addition, there is a tooltip that indicates the syntax of the `For` statement. Lastly, there is a <new variable> item just above the IntelliSense list. This is to indicate that it's possible for you to specify a new variable at this location.

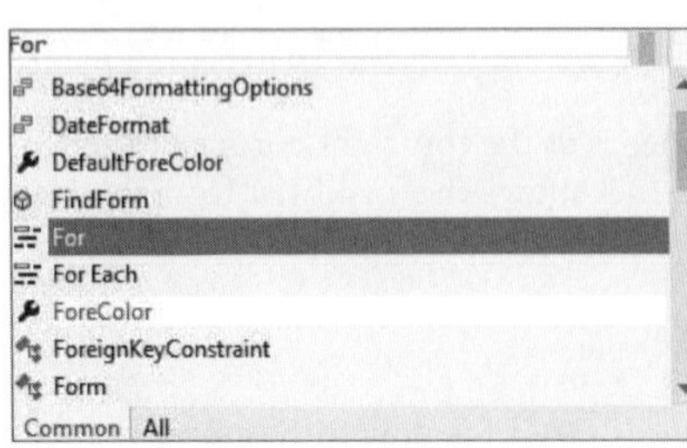

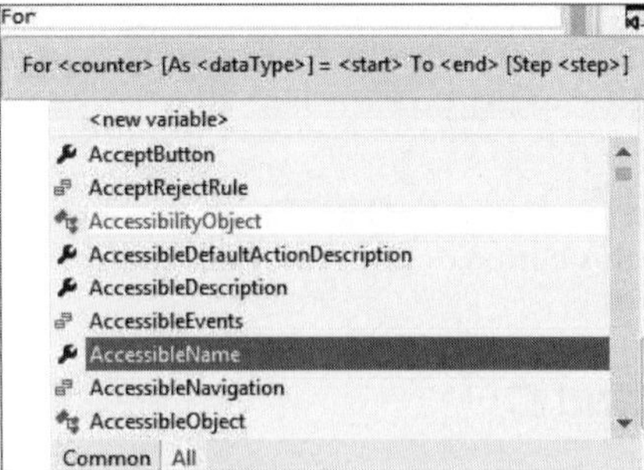

FIGURE 7-4

> **NOTE** *The <new variable> item appears only for Visual Basic users.*

Although it can be useful that the IntelliSense list is reduced based on the letters you enter, this feature is a double-edged sword. Quite often you will be looking for a variable or member but won't quite remember what it is called. In this scenario, you might enter the first couple of letters of a guess and then use the scrollbar to locate the right alternative. Clearly, this won't work if the letters you have entered have already eliminated the alternative. To bring up the full list of alternatives, simply press the Backspace key with the IntelliSense list visible. Alternatively, Ctrl+Space lists all of the alternatives if the IntelliSense list is not visible.

In older versions of Visual Studio, IntelliSense was only able to help you find members that began with the same characters that you typed into the editor. This changed with Visual Studio 2010. Now you can find words that appear in the middle of member names as well. IntelliSense does this by looking for word boundaries within the member names. Figure 7-5 shows an example in C# where typing **`Console.in`** will find `In`, `InputEncoding`, `IsInputRedirected`, `OpenStandardInput`, `SetIn`, and `TreatControlCAsInput` but does not find `LargestWindowHeight` despite the fact that it contains the substring "in."

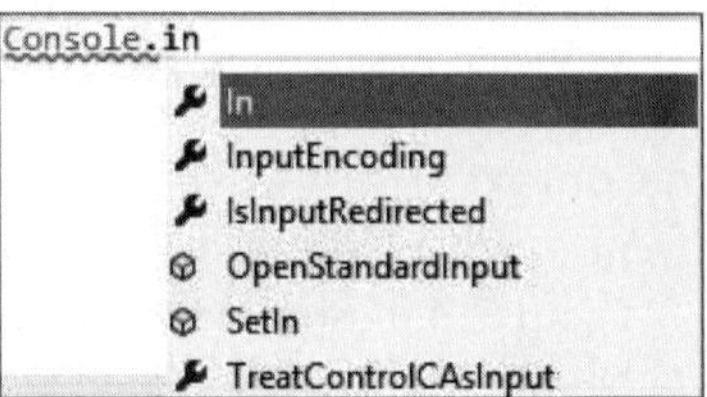

FIGURE 7-5

> **NOTE** *If you know exactly what you are looking for, you can save even more keystrokes by typing the first character of each word in uppercase. As an example, if you type* `System.Console.OSI` *then* `OpenStandardInput` *will be selected by IntelliSense.*

If you find that the IntelliSense information is obscuring other lines of code, or you simply want to hide the list, you can press Esc. Alternatively, if you simply want to view what is hidden behind the IntelliSense list without closing it completely, you can hold down the Ctrl key. This makes the IntelliSense list translucent, enabling you to read the code behind it, as shown in Figure 7-6.

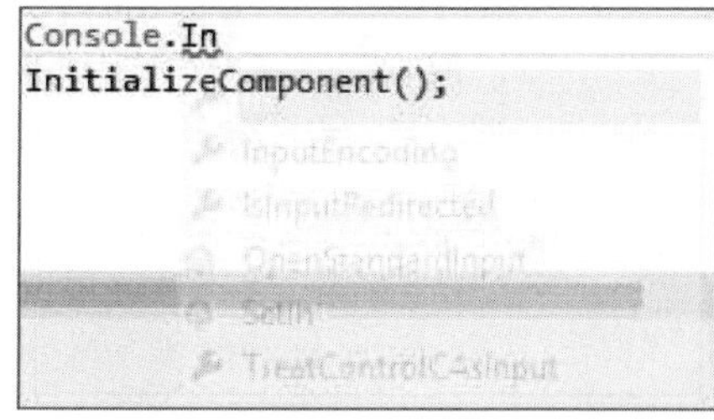

FIGURE 7-6

The IntelliSense list is not just for informational purposes. You can select an item from this list and have Visual Studio actually insert the full text into the editor window for you. You have a number of ways to select an item from the list. You can double-click the wanted item with the mouse; you can use the arrow keys to change which item is highlighted and then press the Enter or Tab keys to insert the text; and finally, when an item is highlighted in the list, it will automatically be selected if you enter a *commit character*. Commit characters are those that are not normally allowed within member names. Examples include parentheses, braces, mathematical symbols, and semicolons.

List Members

Because IntelliSense has been around for so long, most developers are familiar with the member list that appears when you type the name of an object and immediately follow it by a period. This indicates that you are going to refer to a member of the object, and Visual Studio automatically displays a list of members available to you for that object (see Figure 7-7). If this is the first time you've accessed the member list for a particular object, Visual Studio simply shows the member list in alphabetical order with the top of the list visible. However, if you've used it before, it highlights the last member you accessed to speed up the process for repetitive coding tasks.

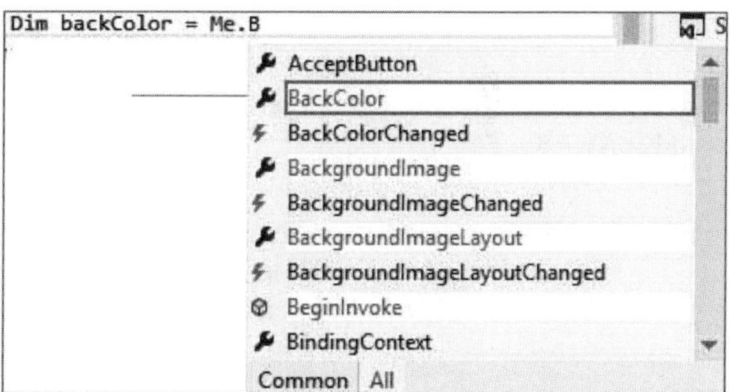

FIGURE 7-7

Figure 7-7 also shows another helpful aspect of the member list for Visual Basic programmers. The Common and All tabs (at the bottom of the member list) enable you to view either just the commonly used members or a comprehensive list.

> **NOTE** *Only Visual Basic gives you the option to filter the member list down to commonly accessed properties, methods, and events.*

Suggestion Mode

By default, when Visual Studio 2012 shows the IntelliSense member list, one member is selected, and as you type, the selection is moved to the item in the list that best matches the characters entered. If you press Enter, Space, or type one of the commit characters (such as an open parenthesis), the currently selected member is inserted into the editor window. This default behavior is known as *completion mode*.

In most cases completion mode provides the wanted behavior and can save you a great deal of typing, but it can be problematic for some activities. One such activity is test-driven development where references are frequently made to members that have not yet been defined. This causes IntelliSense to select members that you didn't intend it to and insert text that you do not want.

To avoid this issue you can use the IntelliSense *suggestion mode*. When IntelliSense is in suggestion mode, one member in the list will have focus but will not be selected by default. As you type, IntelliSense moves the focus indicator to the item that most closely matches the characters you typed, but it will not automatically select it. Instead, the characters that you type are added to the top of the IntelliSense list, and if you type one of the commit characters or press Space or Enter, the exact string that you typed is inserted into the editor window.

Figure 7-8 shows an example of the problem that suggestion mode is designed to address. On the left side you can write a test for a new method called `Load` on the `CustomerData` class. The `CustomerData` class does not have a method called `Load` yet, but it does have a method called `LoadAll`.

On the right side of Figure 7-8, you can type **`Load`** followed by the open parenthesis character. IntelliSense incorrectly assumes that you wanted the `LoadAll` method and inserts it into the editor.

To avoid this behavior you can turn on suggestion mode by pressing Ctrl+Alt+Space. Now when you type `Load,` it appears at the top of the IntelliSense list. When you type the open parenthesis character, you get `Load` as originally intended (see Figure 7-9).

> **NOTE** *You can still make a selection from the IntelliSense list by using the arrow keys. Also, you can select the item that has focus in the member list by pressing the Tab key.*

FIGURE 7-8

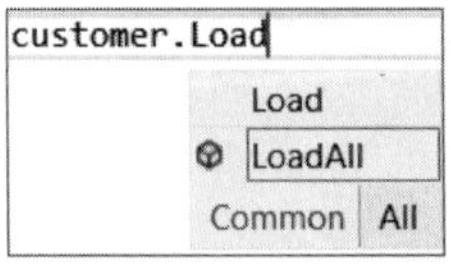

FIGURE 7-9

> **NOTE** *IntelliSense remains in suggestion mode until you press Ctrl+Alt+Space again to revert back to completion mode.*

Stub Completion

In addition to word and phrase completion, the IntelliSense engine has another feature known as *stub completion*. This feature can be seen in Visual Basic when you create a function by writing the declaration of the function and pressing Enter. Visual Studio automatically reformats the line, adding the appropriate `ByVal` keyword for parameters that don't explicitly define their contexts, and also adding an `End Function` line to enclose the function code. Another example can be seen when editing an XML document. When you type the open tag of a new element, Visual Studio automatically puts the closing tag in for you.

Visual Studio 2012 takes stub completion an extra step by enabling you to do the same for interface and method overloading. When you add certain code constructs, such as an interface in a C# class definition, Visual Studio gives you the opportunity to automatically generate the code necessary to implement the interface. To show you how this works, the following steps outline a task in which the IntelliSense engine generates an interface implementation in a simple class:

1. Start Visual Studio 2012 and create a C# Windows Forms Application project. When the IDE has finished generating the initial code, open `Form1.cs` in the code editor.
2. At the top of the file, add a `using` statement to provide a shortcut to the `System.Collections` namespace:

```
using System.Collections;
```

3. Add the following line of code to start a new class definition:

```
public class MyCollection: IEnumerable
```

As you type the `IEnumerable` interface, Visual Studio first adds a red wavy line at the end to indicate that the class definition is missing its curly braces, and then adds a smart tag indicator at the beginning of the interface name (see Figure 7-10).

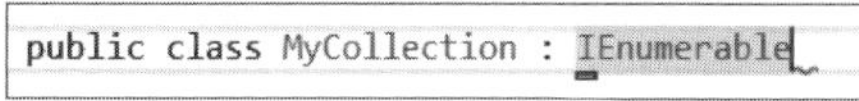

FIGURE 7-10

4. Hover your mouse pointer over the smart tag indicator. When the drop-down icon appears, click it to open the menu of possible actions, as shown in Figure 7-11.

```
public class MyCollection : IEnumerable
```

Implement interface 'IEnumerable'

Explicitly implement interface 'IEnumerable'

FIGURE 7-11

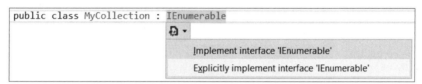

5. Click either of the options to Implement Interface 'IEnumerable' and Visual Studio 2012 automatically generates the rest of the code necessary to implement the minimum interface definition. Because it detects that the class definition itself isn't complete, it also adds the braces to correct that issue at the same time. Figure 7-12 shows what the final interface will look like.

```
public class MyCollection : IEnumerable
{
    public IEnumerator GetEnumerator()
    {
        throw new NotImplementedException();
    }
}
```

FIGURE 7-12

> **NOTE** *Though generated properties and classes can be used as they are, method stubs are generated to throw a* `NotImplementedException`.

Event handlers can also be automatically generated by Visual Studio 2012. The IDE does this much as it performs interface implementation. When you write the first portion of the statement (for instance, `myBase.OnClick +=`), Visual Studio gives you a suggested completion that you can select simply by pressing Tab.

Generate From Usage

Rather than generating code from a definition that already exists, sometimes it is more convenient to generate the definition of a code element from the way you have used it. This is especially true if you practice test-driven development where you write tests for classes that have not been defined yet. It would be convenient to generate the classes from the tests themselves, and this is the purpose of the Generate from Usage feature in C# and Visual Basic.

To understand how you might use this in practice, the following steps outline the creation of a simple `Customer` class by writing some client code that uses it, and then generating the class from that usage:

1. Start Visual Studio 2012 and create a C# Console Application project. When the IDE is ready, open the `Program.cs` file.
2. Update the `Main` method with the following code:

C#

```
Customer c = new Customer
{
  FirstName = "Joe",
  LastName = "Smith"
};

Console.WriteLine(c.FullName);
c.Save();
```

3. You should see a red wiggly line underneath both instances of the class name `Customer`. Right-click one of them, and select Generate ➪ Class. This should create a new class in your project called `Customer`. If you open `Customer.cs` you'll see an empty class declaration. Visual Studio can discover that `FirstName`, `LastName`, `FullName`, and `Save` are not members of this class.
4. For each property that does not exist, right-click it and select Generate ➪ Property. Now go and look at `Customer.cs` again, and note that Visual Studio has provided an implementation for you.
5. You can do the same for the `Save` method by right-clicking and selecting Generate ➪ Method Stub.

> **NOTE** *When you generate a method stub in this manner, you might notice that the method is always marked as being internal. The reason for this has to do with a "best practices" approach that Microsoft code-generator is taking. Specifically, it is giving the minimum access required for a method to be invoked from the call site. An internal method can be called from within the assembly but is not accessible from outside the assembly. This meets the security best practice of "least privilege."*

If the undefined code that you want to generate is a type, you have the option to Generate Class or Generate New Type. If you select Generate New Type, the Generate New Type dialog displays (see Figure 7-13). This dialog gives you more options to configure your new type, including class, enumeration, interface, or structure; if the new type should be public, private, or internal; and where the new type should go.

FIGURE 7-13

Parameter Information

In old versions of Microsoft development tools, such as Visual Basic 6, as you created the call to a function, IntelliSense would display the parameter information as you typed. Thankfully, this incredibly useful feature is still present in Visual Studio 2012.

The problem with the old way parameter information was displayed was that it would be shown only if you were actually modifying the function call. Therefore, you could see this helpful tooltip as you created the function call or when you changed it but not if you were just viewing the code. The result was that programmers sometimes inadvertently introduced bugs into their code because they intentionally modified function calls so that they could view the parameter information associated with the calls.

Visual Studio 2012 eliminates that risk by providing an easily accessible command to display the information without modifying the code. The keyboard shortcut Ctrl+K, Ctrl+I displays the information about the function call, as displayed in Figure 7-14. You can also access this information through the Edit ➪ IntelliSense ➪ Parameter Info menu command.

```
PrintGreeting("Mike");
  void MyCollection.PrintGreeting(string customerName, [string format = "Hello {0}!"])
```

FIGURE 7-14

> **NOTE** *In Figure 7-14 the* `vmethod` *takes two parameters. The second parameter is optional and displays in square brackets with an assignment showing its default value if you don't provide one. VB programmers will be familiar with this syntax, and it has been included in C# ever since version 4.0 was introduced.*

Quick Info

In a similar vein, sometimes you want to see the information about an object or interface without modifying the code. The Ctrl+K, Ctrl+I keyboard shortcut or hovering over the object name with the mouse displays a brief tooltip explaining what the object is and how it was declared (see Figure 7-15).

```
Dim backColor = frm.BackColor
  Private frm As VBWinFormsApp.Form1
```

FIGURE 7-15

You can also display this tooltip through the Edit ➪ IntelliSense ➪ Quick Info menu command.

JAVASCRIPT INTELLISENSE

If you build web applications, you can work in JavaScript to provide a richer client-side experience for your users. Unlike C# and Visual Basic, which are compiled languages, JavaScript is an interpreted language, which means that traditionally the syntax of a JavaScript program has not been verified until it is loaded into the browser. Although this can give you a lot of flexibility at run time, it requires discipline, skill, and a heavy emphasis on testing to avoid a large number of common mistakes.

In addition to this, while developing JavaScript components for use in a browser, you must keep track of a number of disparate elements. This can include the JavaScript language features, HTML DOM elements, and handwritten and third-party libraries. Luckily Visual Studio 2012 can provide a full IntelliSense experience for JavaScript, which can help you to keep track of all these elements and warn you of syntax errors.

As you type JavaScript into the code editor window, Visual Studio lists keywords, functions, parameters, variables, objects, and properties just as if you were using C# or Visual Basic. This works for built-in JavaScript functions and objects as well as those you define in your own custom scripts and those found in third-party libraries. Visual Studio can also detect and highlight syntax errors in your JavaScript code.

> **NOTE** *The keyboard shortcuts for each Visual Studio 2012 install depend on the settings selected (that is, Visual Basic Developer, Visual C# Developer, and so on). All the shortcut keys in this chapter are based on using the General Developer Profile setting.*

> **NOTE** *Since Internet Explorer 3.0, Microsoft has maintained its own dialect of JavaScript called JScript. Technically, the JavaScript tools in Visual Studio 2012 are designed to work with Jscript, so you sometimes see menu options and window titles containing this name. In practice, the differences between the two languages are so minor that the tools work equally well with either one.*

The JavaScript IntelliSense Context

To prevent you from accidentally referring to JavaScript elements that are not available, Visual Studio 2012 builds up an IntelliSense context based on the location of the JavaScript block that you edit. The context is made up of the following items:

- The current script block. This includes inline script blocks for `.aspx`, `.ascx`, `.master`, `.html`, and `.htm` files.
- Any script file imported into the current page via a `<script />` element or a ScriptManager control. In this case the imported script file must have the `.js` extension.
- Any script files that are referenced with a references directive (see the section "Referencing Another JavaScript File").
- Any references made to XML Web Services.
- The items in the Microsoft AJAX Library (if you work in an AJAX-enabled ASP.NET web application).

Referencing Another JavaScript File

Sometimes one JavaScript file builds upon the base functionality of another. When this happens they are usually referenced together by any page using them but have no direct reference explicitly defined. Because there is no explicit reference, Visual Studio 2012 cannot add the file with the base functionality to the JavaScript IntelliSense context, and you won't get full IntelliSense support. The exception to this is when you create Javascript-based Windows Store applications where all the references are traversed to provide full IntelliSense context.

> **NOTE** *Visual Studio keeps track of files in the context and updates JavaScript IntelliSense whenever one of them changes. Sometimes this update may be pending and the JavaScript IntelliSense data will be out of date. You can force Visual Studio to update the JavaScript IntelliSense data by selecting Edit ⇨ IntelliSense ⇨ Update JScript IntelliSense.*

To allow Visual Studio to discover the base file and add it to the context, you can provide a reference to it by using a references directive. A references directive is a special kind of comment that provides information about the location of another file. You can use references directives to make a reference to any of the following:

- **Other JavaScript files:** This includes `.js` files and JavaScript embedded in assemblies. It does not include absolute paths, so the file you reference must be a part of the current project.
- **Web Service (.asmx) files:** These also must be a part of the current project, and Web Service files in Web Application projects are not supported.
- **Pages containing JavaScript:** One page may be referred to in this way. If any page is referenced, no other references can be made.

Following are some examples of references directives. These must appear before any other code in your JavaScript file.

JAVASCRIPT

```
// JavaScript file in current folder
/// <reference path="Toolbox.js" />

// JavaScript file in parent folder
/// <reference path="../Toolbox.js" />

// JavaScript file in a path relative to the root folder of the site
/// <reference path="~/Scripts/Toolbox.js" />

// JavaScript file embedded in Assembly
/// <reference name="Ajax.js" path="System.Web.Extensions, ..." />

// Web Service file
/// <reference path="MyService.asmx" />

// Standard Page
/// <reference path="Default.aspx" />
```

> **NOTE** *A few restrictions exist on how far references directives will work. First, references directives that refer to a path outside of the current project are ignored. Second, references directives are not recursively evaluated, so only those in the file currently being edited are used to help build the context. References directives inside other files in the context are not used.*

INTELLISENSE OPTIONS

Visual Studio 2012 sets up a number of default options for your experience with IntelliSense, but you can change many of these in the Options dialog if they don't suit your own way of doing things. Some of these items are specific to individual languages.

General Options

The first options to look at are in the Environment section under the Keyboard group. Every command available in Visual Studio has a specific entry in the keyboard mapping list (see the Options dialog shown in Figure 7-16, accessible via Tools ➪ Options).

You can override the predefined keyboard shortcuts or add additional ones. The commands for the IntelliSense features are shown in Table 7-1.

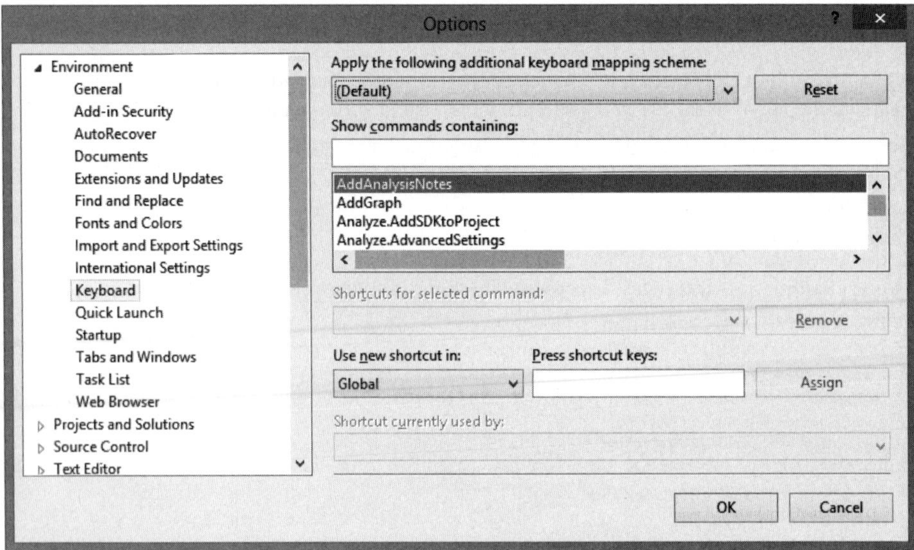

FIGURE 7-16

TABLE 7-1: IntelliSense Commands

COMMAND NAME	DEFAULT SHORTCUT	COMMAND DESCRIPTION
`Edit.QuickInfo`	Ctrl+K, Ctrl+I	Displays the Quick Info information about the selected item
`Edit.CompleteWord`	Ctrl+Space	Attempts to complete a word if there is a single match, or displays a list to choose from if multiple items match
`Edit.ToggleCompletionMode`	Ctrl+Alt+Space	Toggles IntelliSense between suggestion and completion modes
`Edit.ParameterInfo`	Ctrl+Shift+Space	Displays the information about the parameter list in a function call
`Edit.InsertSnippet`	Ctrl+K, Ctrl+X	Invokes the Code Snippet Picker from which you can select a code snippet to insert code automatically (see the next chapter)
`Edit.GenerateMethod`	Ctrl+K,Ctrl+M	Generates the full method stub from a template

COMMAND NAME	DEFAULT SHORTCUT	COMMAND DESCRIPTION
`Edit.ImplementAbstractClassStubs`	None	Generates the abstract class definitions from a stub
`Edit.ImplementInterfaceStubsExplicitly`	None	Generates the explicit implementation of an interface for a class definition
`Edit.ImplementInterfaceStubsImplicitly`	None	Generates the implicit implementation of an interface for a class definition

Use the techniques discussed in Chapter 3 to add additional keyboard shortcuts to any of these commands.

Statement Completion

You can control how IntelliSense works on a global language scale (see Figure 7-17) or per individual language. In the General tab of the language group in the Options dialog, you'll want to change the Statement Completion options to control how member lists should be displayed, if at all.

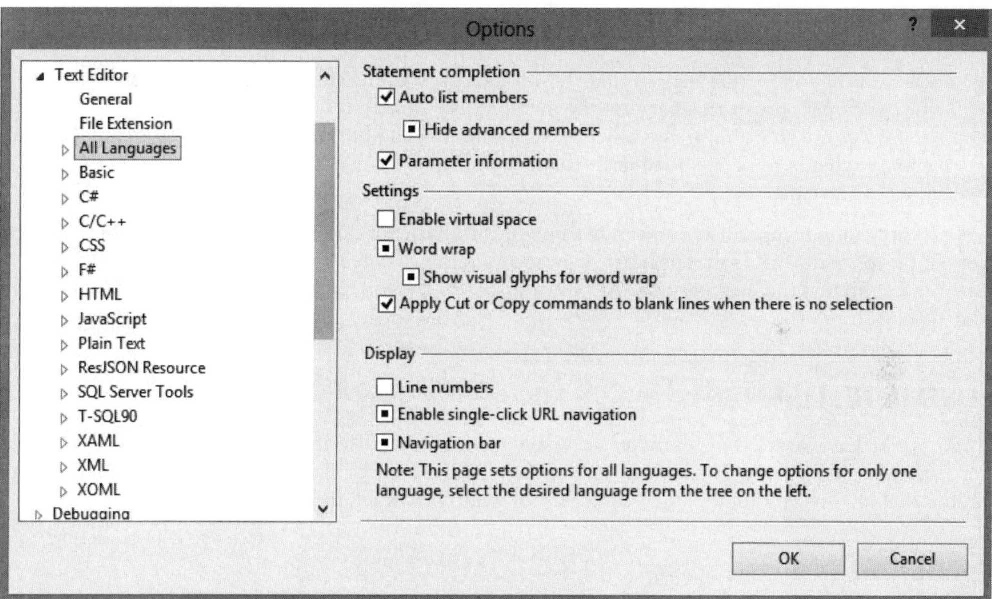

FIGURE 7-17

C#-Specific Options

Besides the general IDE and language options for IntelliSense, some languages, such as C#, provide an additional IntelliSense tab in their own sets of options. Displayed in Figure 7-18, the IntelliSense for C# can be further customized to fine-tune how the IntelliSense features should be invoked and used.

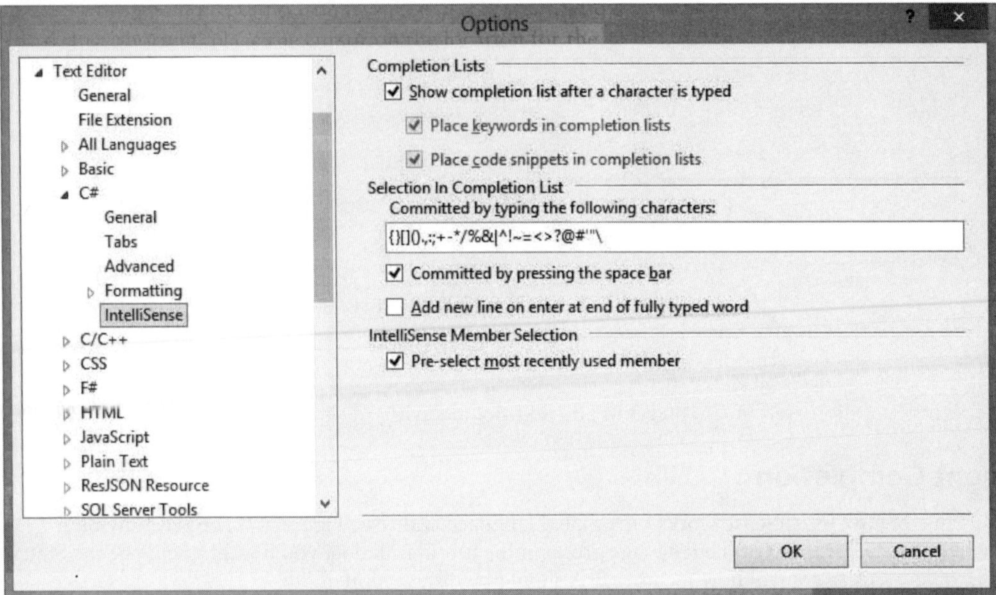

FIGURE 7-18

First, you can turn off completion lists so that they do not appear automatically, as discussed earlier in this chapter. Some developers prefer this because the member lists don't get in the way of their code listings. If the completion list is not to be automatically displayed, but instead only shown when you manually invoke it, you can choose what is to be included in the lists in addition to the normal entries, including keywords and code snippet shortcuts.

To select an entry in a member list, you can use any of the characters shown in the Selection In Completion List section, or optionally after the spacebar is pressed. Finally, as mentioned previously, Visual Studio automatically highlights the member in a list that was last used. You can turn this feature off for C# or just clear the history.

EXTENDED INTELLISENSE

In addition to the basic aspects of IntelliSense, Visual Studio 2012 also implements extended IDE functionality that falls into the IntelliSense feature set. These features are discussed in detail in Chapters 8 and 12, but this section provides a quick summary of what's included in IntelliSense.

Code Snippets

Code snippets are sections of code that can be automatically generated and pasted into your own code, including associated references and `using` statements, with variable phrases marked for easy replacement. To invoke the Code Snippets dialog, press Ctrl+K, Ctrl+X. Navigate the hierarchy of snippet folders (shown in Figure 7-19) until you find the one you need. If you know the shortcut for the snippet, you can simply type it and press Tab, and Visual Studio

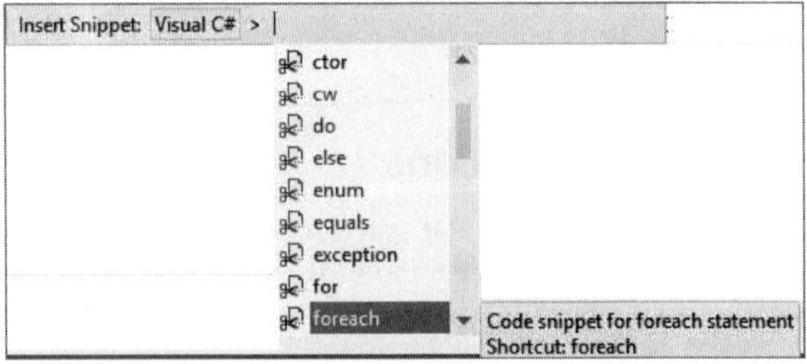

FIGURE 7-19

invokes the snippet without displaying the dialog. In Chapter 8, "Code Snippets and Refactoring," you'll see just how powerful code snippets are.

XML Comments

XML comments are described in Chapter 12, "Documentation with XML Comments," as a way to provide automated documentation for your projects and solutions. However, another advantage to use XML commenting in your program code is that Visual Studio can use it in its IntelliSense engine to display tooltips and parameter information beyond the simple variable-type information you see in normal user-defined classes.

Adding Your Own IntelliSense

You can also add your own IntelliSense schemas, normally useful for XML and HTML editing, by creating a correctly formatted XML file and installing it into the `Common7\Packages\schemas\xml` subfolder inside your Visual Studio installation directory. (The default location is `C:\Program Files\Microsoft Visual Studio 11.0`.) An example of this would be extending IntelliSense support for the XML editor to include your own schema definitions. The creation of such a schema file is beyond the scope of this book, but you can find schema files on the Internet by searching for IntelliSense Schema in Visual Studio.

BOOKMARKS AND THE BOOKMARK WINDOW

Bookmarks in Visual Studio 2012 enable you to mark places in your code modules so that you can easily return to them later. They are represented by indicators in the left margin of the code, as shown in Figure 7-20.

To toggle between bookmarked and not bookmarked on a line, use the shortcut Ctrl+K, Ctrl+K. Alternatively, you can use the Edit ➪ Bookmarks ➪ Toggle Bookmark menu command to do the same thing.

```
public void PrintGreeting(string name)
{
    Console.WriteLine("Hello " + name);
}

public void PrintClosingMessage()
{
    Console.WriteLine("Goodbye.");
}
```

FIGURE 7-20

> **NOTE** *Remember that* toggle *means just that. If you use this command on a line already bookmarked, it removes the bookmark.*

Figure 7-20 shows a section of the code editor window with two bookmarks set. The top bookmark is in its normal state, represented by a dark rectangle. The lower bookmark has been disabled and is represented by a hatched gray rectangle. Disabling a bookmark enables you to keep it for later use while excluding it from the normal bookmark-navigation functions.

To enable or disable a bookmark use the Edit ➪ Bookmarks ➪ Enable Bookmark toggle menu command. Use the same command to re-enable the bookmark. This seems counterintuitive because you actually want to disable an active bookmark, but for some reason the menu item isn't updated based on the cursor context.

Along with the ability to add and remove bookmarks, Visual Studio provides a Bookmarks tool window, shown in Figure 7-21. You can display this tool window by pressing Ctrl+K, Ctrl+W or via the View Bookmark Window menu item. By default, this window is docked to the bottom of the IDE and shares space with other tool windows, such as the Task List and Find Results windows.

> **NOTE** *You may want to set up a shortcut for disabling and enabling bookmarks if you plan to use them a lot in your code management. To do so, access the Keyboard Options page in the Environment group in Options and look for* `Edit.EnableBookmark`.

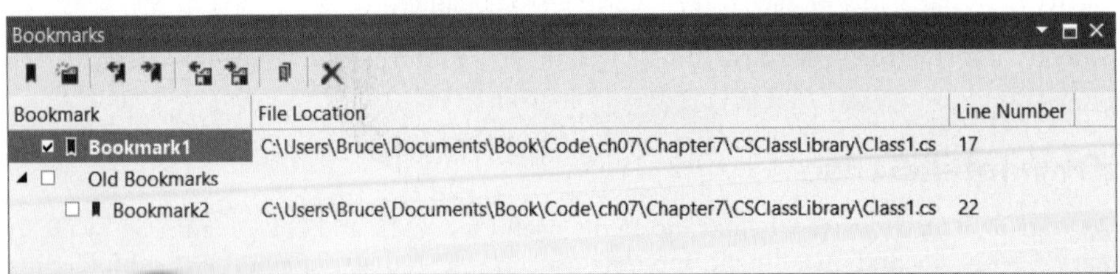

FIGURE 7-21

Figure 7-21 illustrates some useful features of bookmarks in Visual Studio 2012. The first feature is the ability it gives you to create folders that can logically group the bookmarks. In the example list, notice that a folder named Old Bookmarks contains a bookmark named Bookmark2.

To create a folder of bookmarks, click the New Folder icon in the toolbar along the top of the Bookmarks window. (It's the second button from the left.) This creates an empty folder (using a default name of Folder1, followed by Folder2, and so on) with the name of the folder in focus so that you can make it more relevant. You can move bookmarks into the folder by selecting their entries in the list and dragging them into the wanted folder. Note that you cannot create a hierarchy of folders, but it's unlikely that you'll want to. Bookmarks can be renamed in the same way as folders, and for permanent bookmarks, renaming can be more useful than accepting the default names of Bookmark1, Bookmark2, and so forth. Folders are not only a convenient way of grouping bookmarks; they also provide an easy way for you to enable or disable a number of bookmarks in one go, simply by using the check box beside the folder name.

To navigate directly to a bookmark, double-click its entry in the Bookmarks tool window. Alternatively, if you want to cycle through all the enabled bookmarks defined in the project, use the Previous Bookmark (Ctrl+K, Ctrl+P) and Next Bookmark (Ctrl+K, Ctrl+N) commands. You can restrict this navigation to only the bookmarks in a particular folder by first selecting a bookmark in the folder and then using the Previous Bookmark in Folder (Ctrl+Shift+K, Ctrl+Shift+P) and Next Bookmark in Folder (Ctrl+Shift+K, Ctrl+Shift+N) commands.

The last two icons in the Bookmarks window are Toggle All Bookmarks, which can be used to disable (or re-enable) all the bookmarks defined in a project, and Delete, which can be used to delete a folder or bookmark from the list.

> **NOTE** *Deleting a folder also removes all the bookmarks contained in the folder. Visual Studio provides a confirmation dialog to safeguard against accidental loss of bookmarks. Deleting a bookmark is the same as toggling it off.*

Bookmarks can also be controlled via the Bookmarks submenu, which is found in the Edit main menu. In Visual Studio 2012, bookmarks are also retained between sessions, making permanent bookmarks a much more viable option for managing your code organization.

Task lists are customized versions of bookmarks displayed in their own tool windows. The only connection that still exists between the two is that there is an Add Task List Shortcut command still in the Bookmarks menu. Be aware that this does not add the shortcut to the Bookmarks window but instead to the Shortcuts list in the Task List window.

SUMMARY

IntelliSense functionality extends beyond the main code window. Various other windows, such as the Command and Immediate tool windows, can harness the power of IntelliSense through statement and parameter completion. Any keywords, or even variables and objects, known in the current context during a debugging session can be accessed through the IntelliSense member lists.

IntelliSense in all its forms enhances the Visual Studio experience beyond most other tools available to you. Constantly monitoring your keystrokes to give you visual feedback or automatic code completion and generation, IntelliSense enables you to be extremely effective at writing code quickly and correctly the first time. In the next chapter you'll dive into the details behind code snippets, a powerful addition to IntelliSense.

In this chapter you've also seen how you can set and navigate between bookmarks in your code. Becoming familiar with using the associated keystrokes can help you improve your coding efficiency.

Code Snippets and Refactoring

WHAT'S IN THIS CHAPTER?

- Using code snippets
- Creating your own code snippets
- Refactoring code

One of the advantages of using an integrated development environment (IDE) over a plain text editor is that it's designed to help you be more productive and efficient by enabling you to write code faster. Two of Visual Studio 2012's most powerful features that help increase your productivity are its support for code snippets and the refactoring tools that it provides.

Code snippets are small chunks of code that can be inserted into an application's code base and then customized to meet the application's specific requirements. They do not generate full-blown applications or whole files, unlike project and item templates. Instead, code snippets are used to insert frequently used code structures or obscure program code blocks that are not easy to remember. In the first part of this chapter, you see how using code snippets can improve your coding efficiency enormously.

This chapter also focuses on Visual Studio 2012's refactoring tools — refactoring is the process of reworking code to improve it without changing its functionality. This might entail simplifying a method, extracting a commonly used code pattern, or even optimizing a section of code to make it more efficient.

Although refactoring tools are implemented for C# in Visual Studio, unfortunately they haven't been implemented for VB. To fill this hole in functionality in earlier versions of Visual Studio, Microsoft licensed the VB version of Refactor! from Developer Express. As of Visual Studio 2010, CodeRush Xpress (also from Developer Express) took over from Refactor! to implement refactoring for VB. Even though Microsoft has licensed CodeRush Xpress, it still needs to be downloaded and installed separately from Visual Studio (as an add-in). You can download it from the VB developer center at `http://msdn.microsoft.com/vbasic/`; follow the link to Downloads and locate the section titled Additional Downloads. In Additional Downloads, there is a link that goes to the CodeRush Xpress for C# and Visual Basic. On that page, you will find a link that allows you to download the current version of CodeRush Xpress.

CodeRush Xpress provides a range of additional refactoring support that complements the integrated support available for C# developers. However, this chapter's discussion is restricted to the built-in refactoring support provided within Visual Studio 2012 (for C# developers) and the corresponding action in CodeRush Xpress (for VB developers).

CODE SNIPPETS REVEALED

Visual Studio 2012 includes extensive code snippet support that allows a block of code along with predefined replacement variables to be inserted into a file, making it easy to customize the inserted code to suit the task at hand.

Storing Code Blocks in the Toolbox

Before looking at code snippets, this section looks at the simplest means Visual Studio provides to insert predefined blocks of text into a file. Much like it can hold controls to be inserted on a form, the Toolbox can also hold blocks of text (such as code) that can be inserted into a file. To add a block of code (or other text) to the Toolbox, simply select the text in the editor and drag it over onto the Toolbox. This creates an entry for it in the Toolbox with the first line of the code as its name. You can rename, arrange, and group these entries like any other element in the Toolbox. To insert the code block you simply drag it from the Toolbox to the wanted location in a file, as shown in Figure 8-1, or simply double-click the Toolbox entry to insert it at the current cursor position in the active file.

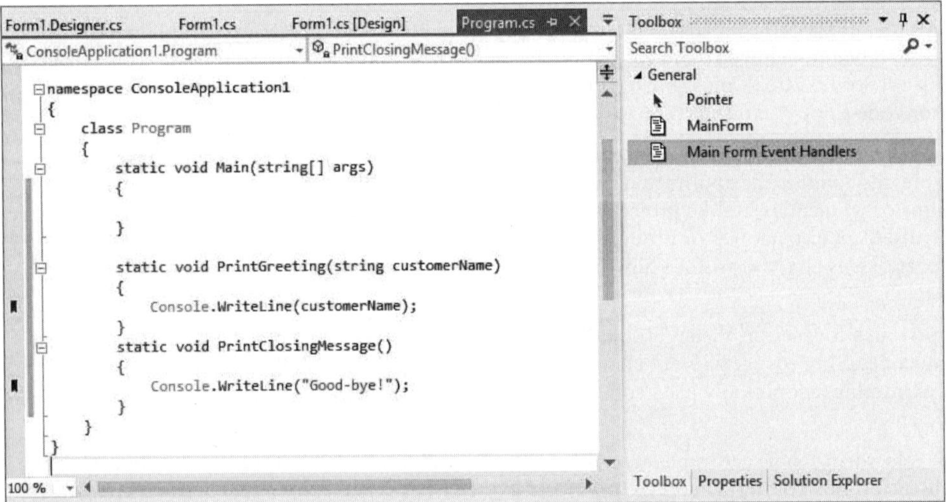

FIGURE 8-1

> **NOTE** *Many presenters use this simple feature to quickly insert large code blocks when writing code live in presentations.*

This is the simplest form of code snippet behavior in Visual Studio 2012, but with its simplicity comes limited functionality, such as the lack of ability to modify and share them. Nevertheless, this method of keeping small sections of code can prove useful in some scenarios to maintain a series of code blocks for short-term use.

Code Snippets

Now we come to a much more useful way to insert blocks of code into a file: *code snippets*. Code snippets are defined in individual XML files, each containing a block of code that programmers may want to insert into their code, and may also include replaceable parameters making it easy to then customize the inserted snippet for the current task. They are integrated with Visual Studio's IntelliSense, making them easy to find and insert into a code file.

> **NOTE** *VB code snippets also give you the ability to add assembly references and insert* `Imports` *statements.*

Visual Studio 2012 ships with many predefined code snippets for the two main languages, VB and C#, along with snippets for JavaScript, HTML, XML, CSS, C++, and SQL Server. These snippets are arranged hierarchically in a logical fashion so that you can easily locate the appropriate snippet. Rather than locate the snippet in the Toolbox, you can use menu commands or keyboard shortcuts to bring up the main list of groups.

In addition to the predefined code snippets, you can create your own code snippets and store them in this code snippet library. Because each snippet is stored in a special XML file, you can even share them with other developers.

Following are three scopes under which a snippet can be inserted:

- **Class Declaration:** The snippet actually generates an entire class.
- **Member Declaration:** This snippet scope includes code that defines members, such as methods, properties, and event handler routines. This means it should be inserted outside an existing member.
- **Member Body:** This scope is for snippets that are inserted into an already defined member, such as a method.

Using Snippets in C#

Insert Snippet is a special kind of IntelliSense that appears inline in the code editor. Initially, it displays the words Insert Snippet along with a drop-down list of code snippet groups from which to choose. After you select the group that contains the snippet you require (using up and down arrows, followed by the Tab key), it shows you a list of snippets, and you can simply double-click the one you need. (Alternatively, pressing Tab or Enter with the required snippet selected has the same effect.)

To insert a code snippet in C#, simply locate the position where you want to insert the generated code, and then the easiest way to bring up the Insert Snippet list is to use the keyboard shortcut combination of Ctrl+K, Ctrl+X. You have two additional methods to start the Insert Snippet process. The first is to right-click at the intended insertion point in the code window and select Insert Snippet from the context menu that is displayed. The other option is to use the Edit ➪ IntelliSense ➪ Insert Snippet menu command.

At this point, Visual Studio brings up the Insert Snippet list, as Figure 8-2 demonstrates. As you scroll through the list and hover the mouse pointer over each entry, a tooltip displays to indicate what the snippet does and a shortcut that you can use to insert it.

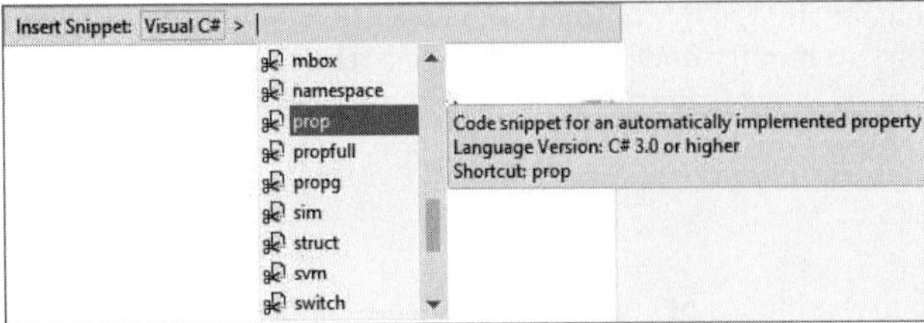

FIGURE 8-2

To use the shortcut for a code snippet, simply type it into the code editor (note that it appears in the IntelliSense list) and press the Tab key twice to insert the snippet at that position.

```
namespace ConsoleApplication1
{
    class Program
    {
        public int MyProperty { get; set; }
        static void Main(string[] args)
        {

        }

        static void PrintGreeting(string customerName)
        {
            Console.WriteLine(customerName);
        }
        static void PrintClosingMessage()
        {
            Console.WriteLine("Good-bye!");
        }
    }
}
```

FIGURE 8-3

Figure 8-3 displays the result of selecting the Automatically Implemented Property snippet. To help you modify the code to your own requirements, the sections you would normally need to change (the replacement variables) are highlighted, with the first one conveniently selected.

When you change the variable sections of the generated code snippet, Visual Studio 2012 helps you even further. Pressing the Tab key moves to the next highlighted value, ready for you to override the value with your own. Shift+Tab navigates backward, so you have an easy way to access the sections of code that need changing without needing to manually select the next piece to modify. Some code snippets use the same variable for multiple pieces of the code snippet logic. This means changing the value in one place results in it changing in all other instances.

To hide the highlighting of these snippet variables when you finish, you can simply continue coding, or press either Enter
or Esc.

Using Snippets in VB

Code snippets in VB have additional features over what is available in C#, namely the ability to automatically add references to assemblies in the project, and insert `Imports` statements into a file that the code needs to compile.

To use a code snippet, first locate where you want the generated code to be placed in the program listing, and position the cursor at that point. You don't have to worry about the associated references and `Imports` statements; they will be placed in the correct location. Then, as with C# snippets, you can use one of the following methods to display the Insert Snippet list:

- Use the keyboard chord Ctrl+K, Ctrl+X.
- Right-click and choose Insert Snippet from the context menu.
- Run the Edit ⇨ IntelliSense ⇨ Insert Snippet menu command.

VB also has an additional way to show the Insert Snippet List: Simply type **?** and press Tab.

Now navigate through the hierarchy and insert a snippet named Draw a Pie Chart. Figure 8-4 demonstrates how you might navigate through the hierarchy to find the snippet and insert it into your project.

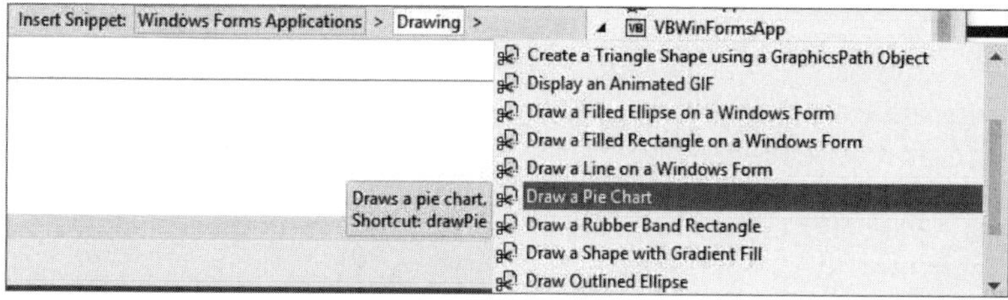

FIGURE 8-4

You might have noticed in Figure 8-4 that the tooltip text includes the words Shortcut: drawPie. This text indicates that the selected code snippet has a text shortcut that you can use to automatically invoke the code snippet behavior without navigating the code snippet hierarchy. As with C# all you need to do is type the shortcut into the code editor and press the Tab key once for it to be inserted. In VB the shortcut isn't case-sensitive, so you can generate this example by typing **drawpie** and pressing Tab. Note that shortcuts don't appear in IntelliSense in VB as they do in C#.

After inserting the code snippet, if it contains replacement variables, you can enter their values and then navigate between these by pressing Tab as described for C#. To hide the highlighting of these snippet variables when you are done, you can simply continue coding, or right-click and select Hide Snippet Highlighting. If you want to highlight all the replacement variables of the code snippets inserted since the file was opened, right-click and select Show Snippet Highlighting.

Surround With Snippet

The last refactoring action, available in C# (and VB with CodeRush Xpress), is the capability to surround an existing block of code with a code snippet. For example, to wrap an existing block with a conditional `try-catch` block, right-click and select Surround With, or select the block of code and press Ctrl+K, Ctrl+S. This displays the Surround With drop-down that contains a list of surrounding snippets that are available to wrap the selected line of code, as shown in Figure 8-5.

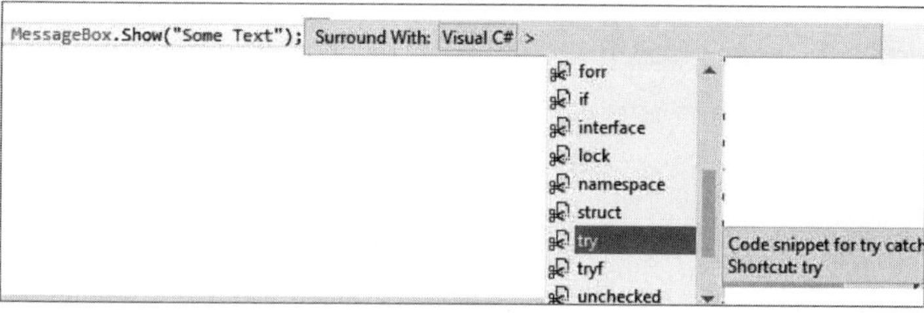

FIGURE 8-5

Selecting the `try` snippet results in the following code:

VB

```
Public Sub MethodXYZ(ByVal name As String)
    Try
```

```
            MessageBox.Show(name)
        Catch ex As Exception
            Throw
        End Try
    End Sub
```

C#

```
public void MethodXYZ(string name)
{
    try
    {
        MessageBox.Show(name);
    }
    catch (Exception)
    {
        throw;
    }
}
```

Code Snippets Manager

The Code Snippets Manager is the central library for the code snippets known to Visual Studio 2012. You can access it via the Tools ➪ Code Snippet Manager menu command or the keyboard shortcut chord Ctrl+K, Ctrl+B.

When it is initially displayed, the Code Snippets Manager shows the HTML snippets available, but you can change it to display the snippets for the language you are using via the Language drop-down list. Figure 8-6 shows how it looks when you're editing a C# project. The hierarchical folder structure follows the same set of folders on the PC by default, but as you add snippet files from different locations and insert them into the different groups, the new snippets slip into the appropriate folders.

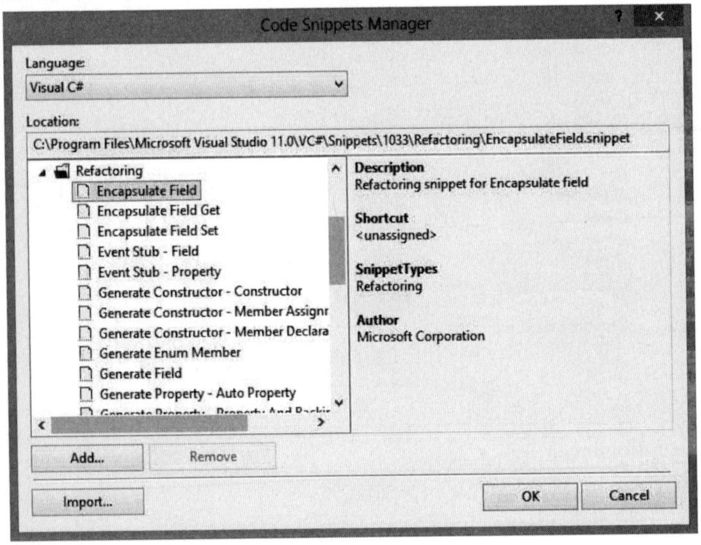

FIGURE 8-6

If you have an entire folder of snippets to add to the library, such as when you have a corporate setup and need to import the company-developed snippets, use the Add button. This brings up a dialog that you use to browse to the required folder. Folders added in this fashion appear at the root level of the tree — on the same level as the main groups of default snippets. However, you can add a folder that contains subfolders, which will be added as child nodes in the tree.

Removing a folder is just as easy — actually it's dangerously easy. Select the root node that you want to remove, and click the Remove button. Instantly, the node and all child nodes and snippets are removed from the Snippets Manager without a confirmation window. If you do this by accident, you should click the Cancel button and open the dialog again. If you've made changes you don't want to lose, you can add them back by following the steps explained in the previous walkthrough, but it can be frustrating trying to locate a default snippet folder that you inadvertently deleted from the list.

The location for the code snippets installed with Visual Studio 2012 is deep within the installation folder. By default, the code snippet library when running on 32-bit Windows is installed in `%programfiles%\Microsoft Visual Studio 11.0\VB\Snippets\1033` for VB snippets and `%programfiles%\Microsoft Visual Studio 11.0\VC#\Snippets\1033` for C#. For 64-bit Windows, replace `%programfiles%` with `%programfiles(x86)%`. You can import individual snippet files into the library using the Import button. The advantage of this method over the Add button is that you get the opportunity to specify the location of each snippet in the library structure.

Creating Snippets

Visual Studio 2012 does not ship with a code snippet creator or editor. However, Bill McCarthy's Snippet Editor allows you to create, modify, and manage your snippets (including support for VB, C#, HTML, JavaScript, and XML snippets). Starting as an internal Microsoft project, the Snippet Editor is now an open-source project hosted on CodePlex where Bill fixed the outstanding issues and proceeded to add functionality. With the help of other MVPs, it is now also available in a number of different languages. You can download the snippet editor from `http://snippeteditor.codeplex.com`.

Creating code snippets by manually editing the `.snippet` XML files can be a tedious and error-prone process, so the Snippet Editor makes it a much more pleasant experience. When you start the Snippet Editor, you can notice a drop-down list in the top left corner. If you select SnippetEditor.Product.Utility from the list, a tree containing all of the known snippets appears. By expanding a node you can see a set of folders similar to those in the code snippet library.

Reviewing Existing Snippets

An excellent feature of the Snippet Editor is the view it offers of the structure of any snippet file in the system. This means you can browse the default snippets installed with Visual Studio, which can provide insight into how to better build your own snippets.

Browse to the snippet you're interested in, and double-click its entry to display it in the Editor window. Figure 8-7 shows a simple snippet to Display a Windows Form. Four main panes contain all the associated information about the snippet. From top to bottom, these panes are described in Table 8-1.

TABLE 8-1: Information Panes for Snippets

PANE	FUNCTION
Properties	The main properties for the snippet, including title, shortcut, and description.
Code	Defines the code for the snippet, including all Literal and Object replacement regions.
References	If your snippet requires assembly references, this tab enables you to define them.
Imports	Similar to the References tab, this tab enables you to define any `Imports` statements required for your snippet to function correctly.

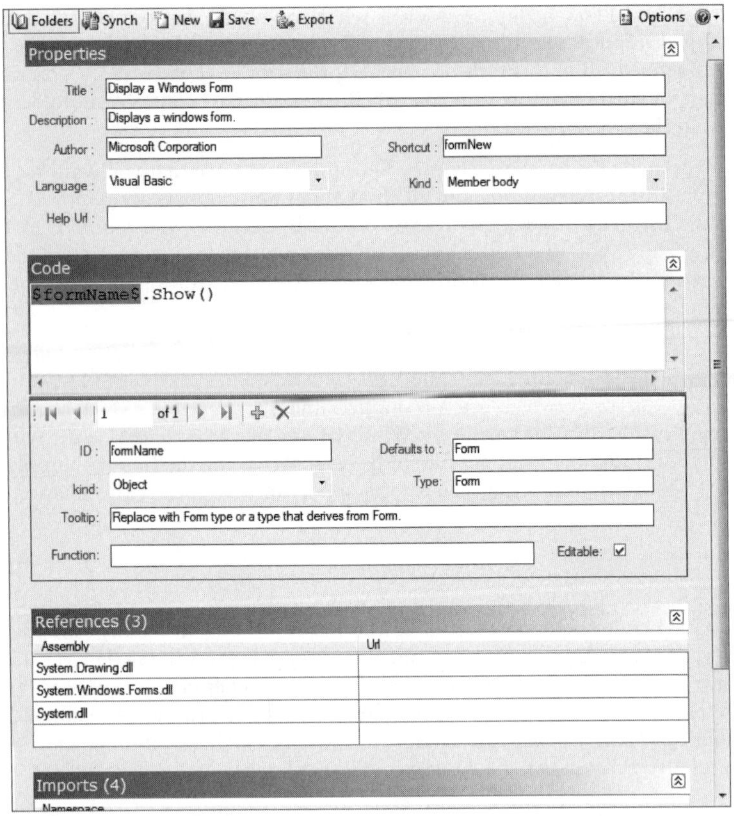

FIGURE 8-7

Browsing through these panes enables you to analyze an existing snippet for its properties and replacement variables. In Figure 8-7, there is a single replacement region with an ID of `formName` and a default value of `Form`.

To demonstrate how the Snippet Editor makes creating your own snippets straightforward, follow this next exercise to create a snippet that creates three subroutines, including a helper subroutine:

1. Start the Snippet Editor and create a new snippet. To do this, select a destination folder in the tree, right-click, and select Add New Snippet from the context menu displayed.
2. When prompted, name the snippet **Create A Button Sample** and click OK. Double-click the new entry to open it in the Editor pane.

> **NOTE** *Creating the snippet does not automatically open the new snippet in the Editor — don't overwrite the properties of another snippet by mistake!*

3. The first thing you need to do is edit the Title, Description, and Shortcut fields (see Figure 8-8):

   - Title: **Create A Button Sample**
   - Description: **This snippet adds code to create a button control and hook an event handler to it.**
   - Shortcut: **CreateAButton**

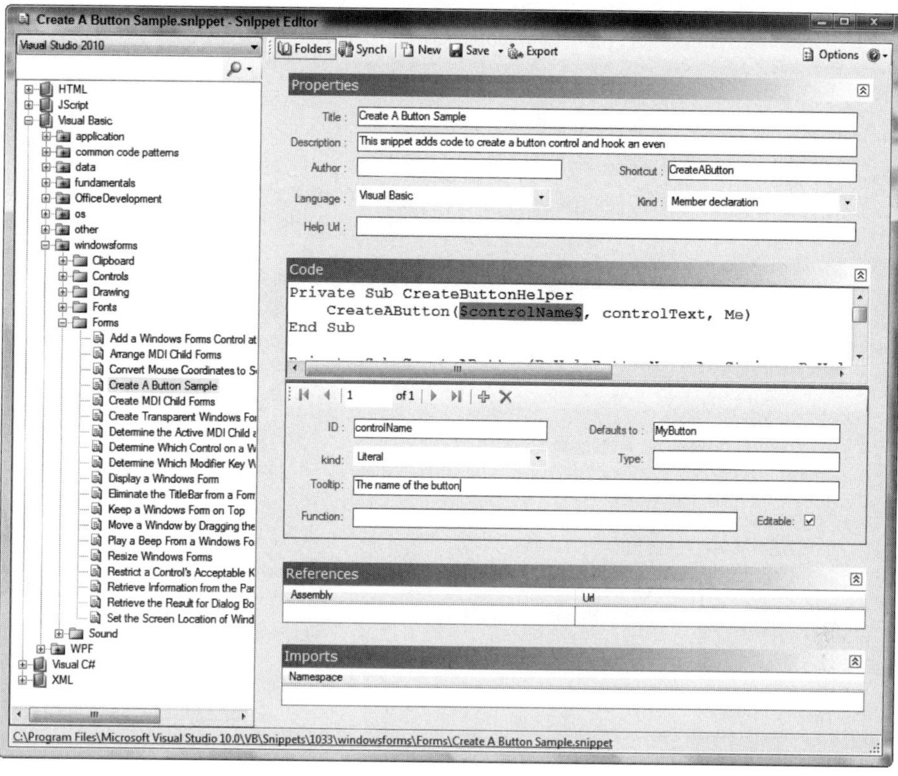

FIGURE 8-8

4. Because this snippet contains member definitions, set the Type to Member Declaration.
5. In the Editor window, insert the code necessary to create the three subroutines:

VB

```
Private Sub CreateButtonHelper
    CreateAButton(controlName, controlText, Me)
End Sub

Private Sub CreateAButton(ByVal ButtonName As String, _
                          ByVal ButtonText As String, _
                          ByVal Owner As Form)
    Dim MyButton As New Button

    MyButton.Name = ButtonName
    MyButton.Text = ButtonName
    Owner.Controls.Add(MyButton)

    MyButton.Top = 0
    MyButton.Left = 0
    MyButton.Text = ButtonText
    MyButton.Visible = True

    AddHandler MyButton.Click, AddressOf ButtonClickHandler
End Sub

Private Sub ButtonClickHandler(ByVal sender As System.Object, _
```

```
                                  ByVal e As System.EventArgs)
    MessageBox.Show("The " & sender.Name & " button was clicked")
End Sub
```

C#

```
private void CreateButtonHelper()
{
    CreateAButton(controlName, controlText, this);
}

private void CreateAButton(string ButtonName, string ButtonText,
                           Form Owner)
{
    Button MyButton = new Button();

    MyButton.Name = ButtonName;
    MyButton.Text = ButtonName;
    Owner.Controls.Add(MyButton);

    MyButton.Top = 0;
    MyButton.Left = 0;
    MyButton.Text = ButtonText;
    MyButton.Visible = true;

    MyButton.Click += MyButton_Click;
}

private void  MyButton_Click(object sender, EventArgs e)
{
    MessageBox.Show("The " + sender.Name + " button was clicked");
}
```

6. Your code differs from that shown in Figure 8-8 in that the word `controlName` does not appear highlighted. In Figure 8-8, this argument has been made a replacement region. You can do this by selecting the entire word, right-clicking, and selecting Add Replacement (or alternatively, clicking the Add button in the area below the code window).
7. Change the replacement properties like so:
   - ID: **controlName**
   - Defaults to: **"MyButton"**
   - Tooltip: The name of the button
8. Repeat this for `controlText`:
   - ID: **controlText**
   - Defaults to: **"Click Me!"**
   - Tooltip: The text property of the button

Your snippet is now done and ready to use. You can use Visual Studio 2012 to insert the snippet into a code window.

ACCESSING REFACTORING SUPPORT

There are a number of ways to invoke the refactoring tools in Visual Studio 2012, including from the right-click context menu, smart tags, and the Refactor menu in the main menu (for C# developers only).

Figure 8-9 shows the Refactor context menu available for C# developers. The full list of refactoring actions available to C# developers within Visual Studio 2012 includes Rename, Extract Method, Encapsulate Field, Extract Interface, Promote Local Variable to Parameter, Remove Parameters, and Reorder Parameters. You can also use Generate Method Stub and Organize Usings, which can be loosely classified as refactoring.

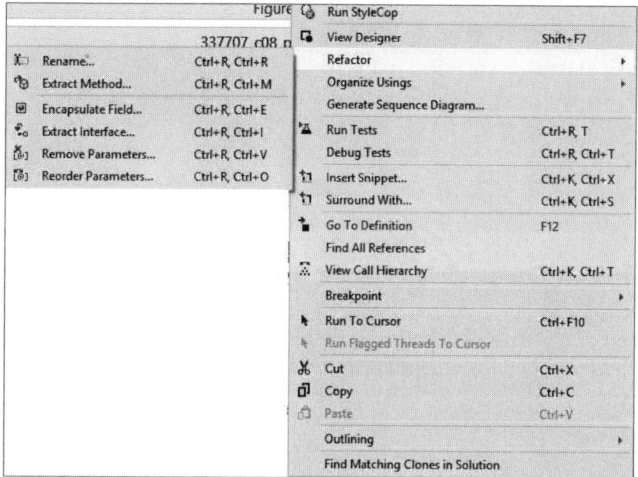

FIGURE 8-9

The built-in refactoring support provided by Visual Studio 2012 for VB developers is limited to the symbolic Rename and Generate Method Stub. Additional refactoring support for VB developers is provided by CodeRush Xpress, which can be accessed via the right-click context menu (which dynamically changes so that only valid refactoring actions display), or via the smart tags (as shown in Figure 8-10) that it displays when a refactoring is available for the current selection (which can be clicked or activated by pressing Ctrl+').

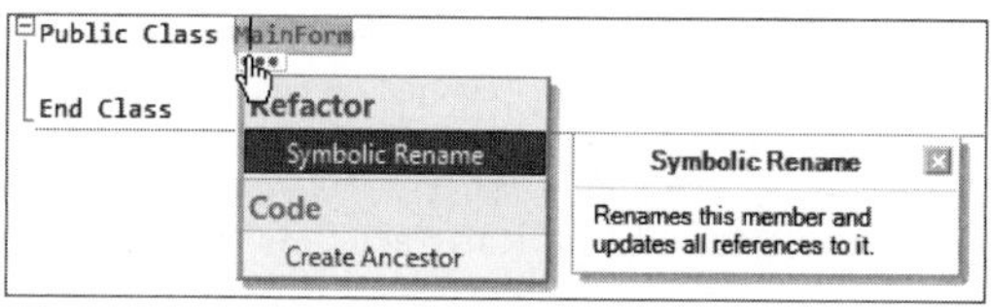

FIGURE 8-10

CodeRush Xpress adds support for all the refactoring tools that C# has, and it adds many more (to both languages). Examples of additional refactorings include Create Overload, Flatten Conditional, Inline Temp, Introduce Constant, Introduce Local, Move Declaration Near Reference, Move Initialization to Declaration, Remove Assignments to Parameters, Rename, Reorder Parameters, Replace Temp with Query, Reverse Conditional, Safe Rename, Simplify Expression, Split Initialization from Declaration, and Split Temporary Variable.

REFACTORING ACTIONS

The following sections describe each of the refactoring options and provide examples of how to use built-in support for both C# and CodeRush Xpress for VB.

Extract Method

One of the best ways to start refactoring a long method is to break it up into several smaller methods. The Extract Method refactoring action is invoked by selecting the region of code you want moved out of the original method and selecting Extract Method from the context menu. In C#, this prompts you to enter a new method name, as shown in Figure 8-11. If there are variables within the block of code to be extracted that were used earlier in the original method, they automatically appear as variables in the method signature. After the name has been confirmed, the new method is created immediately after the original method. A call to the new method replaces the extracted code block.

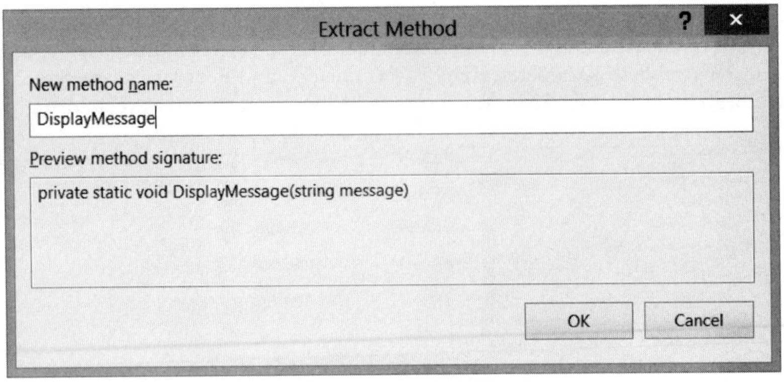

FIGURE 8-11

For example, in the following code snippet, if you want to extract the conditional logic into a separate method, you can select the code, shown in bold, and choose Extract Method from the right-click context menu:

C#

```
private void button1_Click(object sender, EventArgs e)
{
    string connectionString = Properties.Settings.Default.ConnectionString;
    if (connectionString == null)
    {
        connectionString = "DefaultConnectionString";
    }
    MessageBox.Show(connectionString);
    /* ... Much longer method ... */
}
```

This would automatically generate the following code in its place:

C#

```
private void button1_Click(object sender, EventArgs e)
{
    string connectionString = Properties.Settings.Default.ConnectionString;
    connectionString = ValidateConnectionString(output);
    MessageBox.Show(connectionString);
    /* ... Much longer method ... */
 }

private static string ValidateConnectionString(string connectionString)
{
    if (connectionString == null)
    {
        connectionString = "DefaultConnectionString";
    }
    return connectionString;
}
```

CodeRush Xpress handles this refactoring action slightly differently for VB developers. After you select the code you want to replace, CodeRush Xpress prompts you to select a place in your code where you want to insert the new method. This can help developers organize their methods in groups, either alphabetically or according to functionality.

Figure 8-12 illustrates the aid that appears that enables you to position where the method should be inserted using the cursor keys.

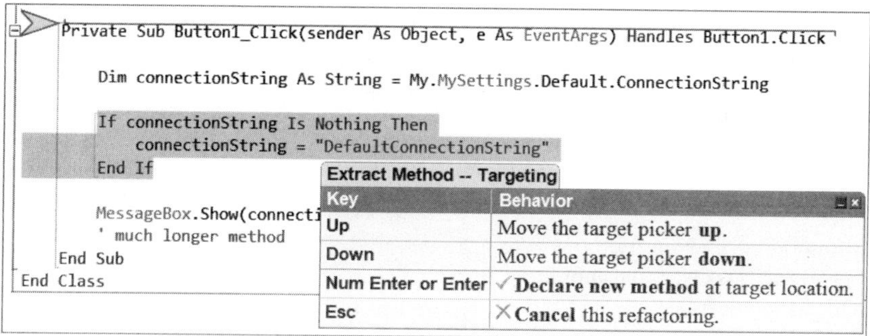

FIGURE 8-12

After selecting the insert location, CodeRush Xpress inserts the new method, giving it an arbitrary name. In doing so it highlights the method name, enabling you to rename the method either at the insert location or where the method is called (see Figure 8-13).

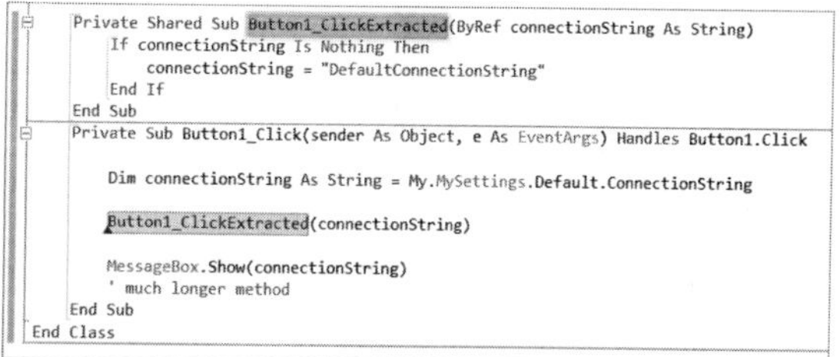

FIGURE 8-13

Using the Extract Method refactoring on the following code:

VB

```
Private Sub Button1_Click(ByVal sender As System.Object,
                          ByVal e As System.EventArgs) Handles Button1.Click
    Dim connectionString As String = My.MySettings.Default.ConnectionString
    If connectionString Is Nothing Then
        connectionString = "DefaultConnectionString"
    End If
    MessageBox.Show(connectionString)
    'Much longer method
End Sub
```

And renaming the method to give it an appropriate name results in the following code:

VB

```
Private Sub Button1_Click(ByVal sender As System.Object,
                          ByVal e As System.EventArgs) Handles Button1.Click
    Dim connectionString As String = My.MySettings.Default.ConnectionString
    ValidateConnectionString(connectionString)
    MessageBox.Show(connectionString)
    'Much longer method
End Sub

Private Shared Sub ValidateConnectionString(ByRef connectionString As String)
    If connectionString Is Nothing Then
        connectionString = "DefaultConnectionString"
    End If
End Sub
```

Encapsulate Field

Another common task when refactoring is to encapsulate an existing class variable with a property. This is what the Encapsulate Field refactoring action does. To invoke this action, select the variable you want to encapsulate, and then choose the appropriate refactoring action from the context menu. This gives you the opportunity to name the property and elect where to search for references to the variable, as shown in Figure 8-14.

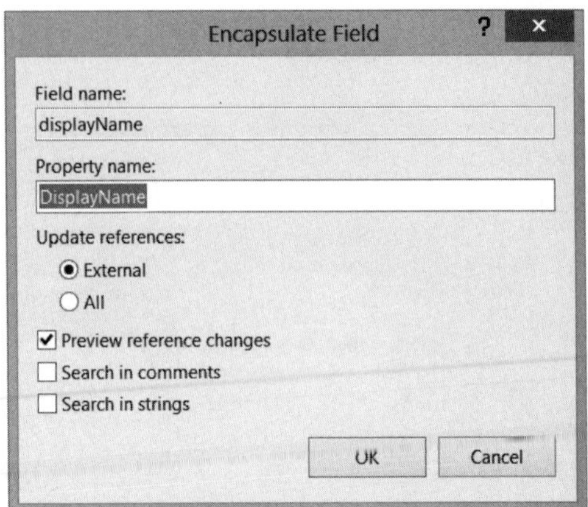

FIGURE 8-14

The next step after specifying the new property name is to determine which references to the class variable should be replaced with a reference to the new property. Figure 8-15 shows the preview window that is returned after the reference search has been completed. In the top pane is a tree indicating which files and methods have references to the variable. For each row where a replacement will be made, a check box will appear. Selecting a row in the top pane brings that line of code into focus in the lower pane. After each of the references has been validated, the encapsulation can proceed. The class variable is updated to be private, and the appropriate references are also updated.

The Encapsulate Field refactoring action using CodeRush Xpress works in a similar way, except that it automatically assigns the name of the property based on the name of the class variable. The interface for updating references is also different, as shown in Figure 8-16. Instead of a modal dialog, CodeRush Xpress presents a visual aid that can be used to navigate through the references. (Or you can navigate between references using the Tab key.) Where a replacement is required, click the checkmark or press Enter. Unlike the C# dialog box, in which the check boxes can be checked and unchecked as many times as needed, after you accept a replacement, there is no way to undo this action.

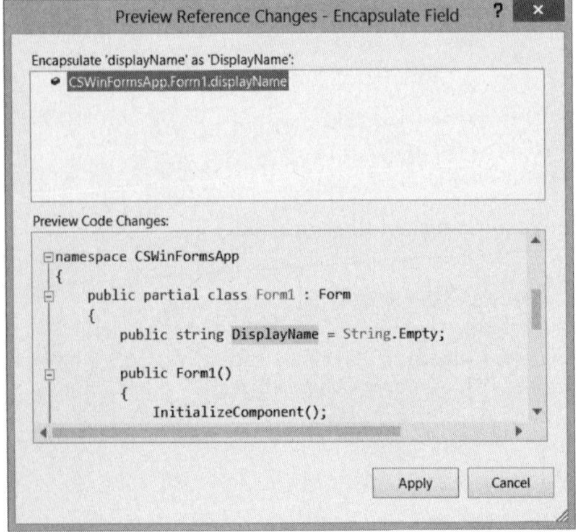

FIGURE 8-15

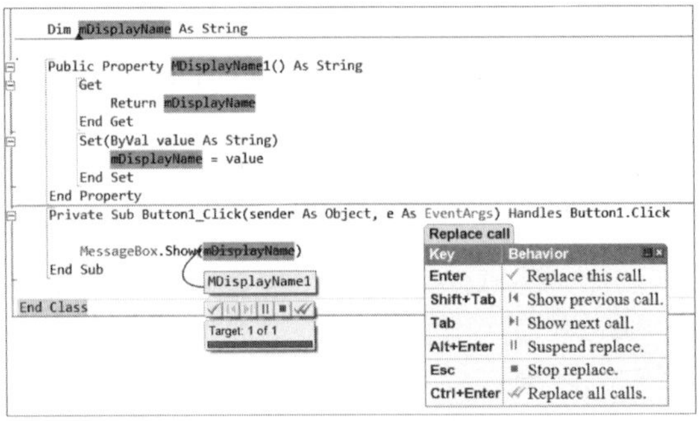

FIGURE 8-16

Extract Interface

As a project goes from prototype or early-stage development to a full implementation or growth phase, it's often necessary to extract the core methods for a class into an interface to enable other implementations or to define a boundary between disjointed systems. In the past you could do this by copying the entire method to a new file and removing the method contents, so you were just left with the interface stub. The Extract Interface refactoring action enables you to extract an interface based on any number of methods within a class. When this refactoring action is invoked on a class, the dialog in Figure 8-17 displays, which enables you to select which methods are included in the interface. When selected, those methods are added to the new interface. The new interface is also added to the original class.

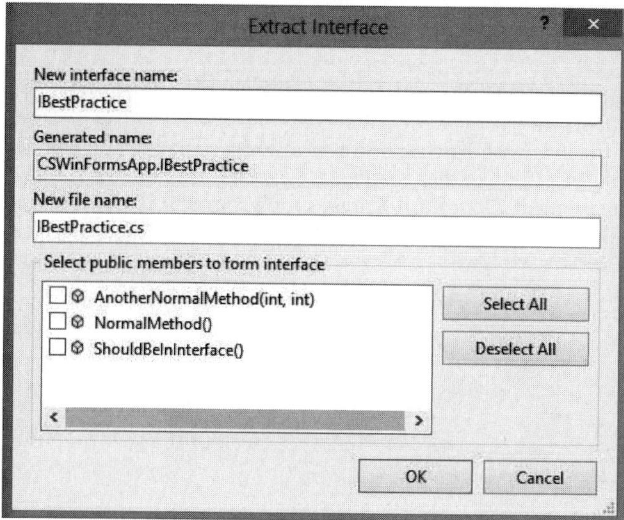

FIGURE 8-17

In the following example, the first method needs to be extracted into an interface:

C#

```
public class ConcreteClass
{
    public void ShouldBeInInterface()
    { /* ... */ }

    public void AnotherNormalMethod(int ParameterA, int ParameterB)
    { /* ... */ }

    public void NormalMethod()
    { /* ... */ }
}
```

Selecting Extract Interface from the right-click context menu and selecting only the `ShouldBeInInterface` method to be extracted from the Extract Interface dialog introduces a new interface (in a new file) and updates the original class as follows:

C#

```
interface IBestPractice
{
    void ShouldBeInInterface();
```

```
    }

    public class ConcreteClass: Chapter08Sample.IBestPractice
    {
        public void ShouldBeInInterface()
        { /* ... */ }

        public void NormalMethod(int ParameterA, int ParameterB)
        { /* ... */ }

        public void AnotherNormalMethod()
        { /* ... */ }
    }
```

Extracting an interface is also available within CodeRush Xpress; however it doesn't allow you to choose which methods you want to include in the interface. Unlike the C# interface extraction, which places the interface in a separate file (which is recommended), CodeRush Xpress simply extracts all public class methods into an interface in the same code file. For example, using CodeRush Xpress's Extract Interface refactoring action on the following class:

VB

```
Public Class ConcreteClass
    Public Sub ShouldBeInInterface()
        '...
    End Sub

    Public Sub NormalMethod(ByVal ParameterA As Integer,
                            ByVal ParameterB As Integer)
        '...
    End Sub

    Public Sub AnotherNormalMethod()
        '...
    End Sub
End Class
```

results in the following code:

VB

```
Public Interface IConcreteClass
    Sub ShouldBeInInterface()
    Sub NormalMethod(ByVal ParameterA As Integer, ByVal ParameterB As Integer)
    Sub AnotherNormalMethod()
End Interface
Public Class ConcreteClass
    Implements IConcreteClass
    Public Sub ShouldBeInInterface() Implements IConcreteClass.ShouldBeInInterface
        '...
    End Sub

    Public Sub NormalMethod(ByVal ParameterA As Integer,
                            ByVal ParameterB As Integer) _
                            Implements IConcreteClass.NormalMethod
        '...
    End Sub

    Public Sub AnotherNormalMethod() Implements IConcreteClass.AnotherNormalMethod
        '...
    End Sub
End Class
```

Reorder Parameters

Sometimes it's necessary to reorder parameters. This is often for cosmetic reasons, but it can also aid readability and is sometimes warranted when implementing interfaces. The Reorder Parameters dialog, as shown in Figure 8-18, enables you to move parameters up and down in the list according to the order in which you want them to appear.

After you establish the correct order, you're given the opportunity to preview the changes. By default, the parameters in every reference to this method are reordered according to the new order. The Preview dialog, similar to the one shown in Figure 8-15, enables you to control which references are updated.

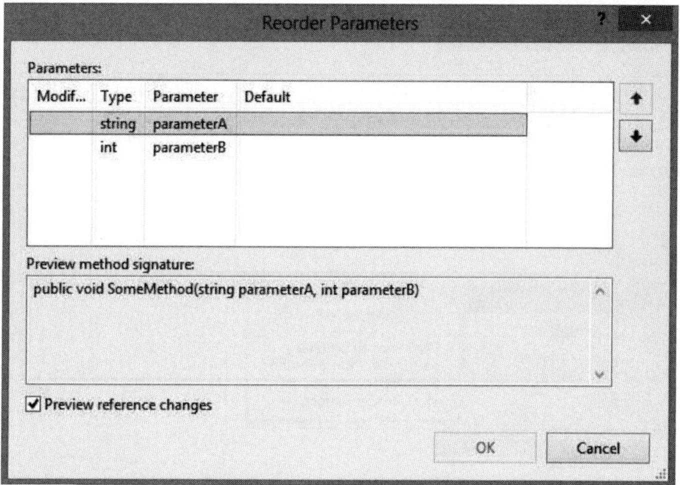

FIGURE 8-18

Remove Parameters

When removing a parameter from a method, using the refactoring function to do this considerably reduces the amount of searching that must be done for compile errors that can occur when a parameter is removed. The other time this action is particularly useful is when there are multiple overloads for a method, and removing a parameter may not generate compile errors; in such a case, run time errors may occur due to semantic, rather than syntactical, mistakes.

Figure 8-19 illustrates the Remove Parameters dialog that is used to remove parameters from the parameters list. If a parameter is accidentally removed, it can be easily restored until the correct parameter list is arranged. As the warning on this dialog indicates, removing parameters can often result in unexpected functional errors, so it is important to review the changes made. Again, you can use the preview window to validate the proposed changes.

CodeRush Xpress supports removing only unused parameters, as shown in Figure 8-20.

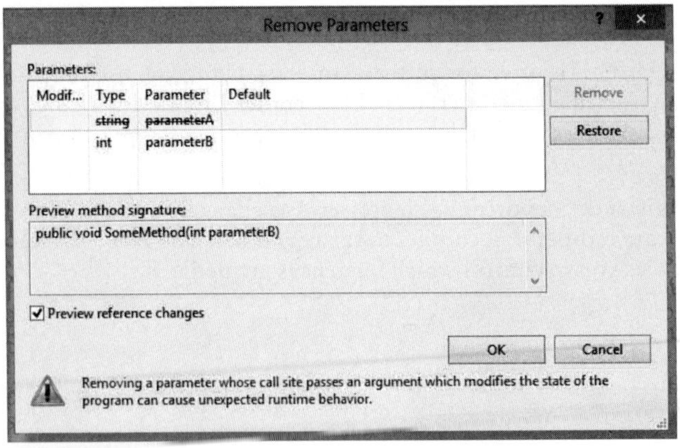

FIGURE 8-19

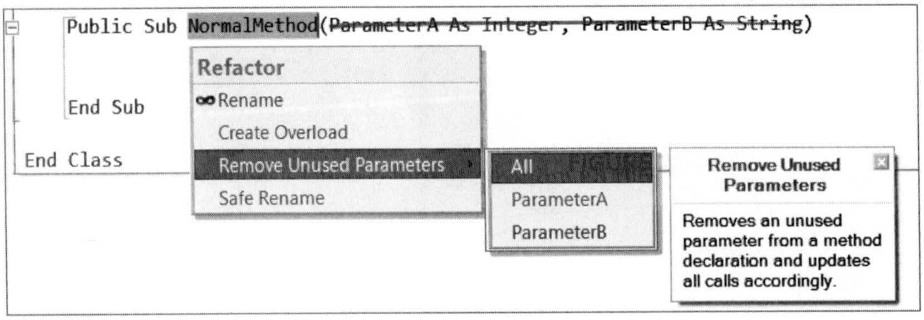

FIGURE 8-20

Rename

Visual Studio 2012 provides rename support in both C# and VB. The Rename dialog for C# is shown in Figure 8-21; it is similar in VB although it doesn't have the options to search in comments or strings.

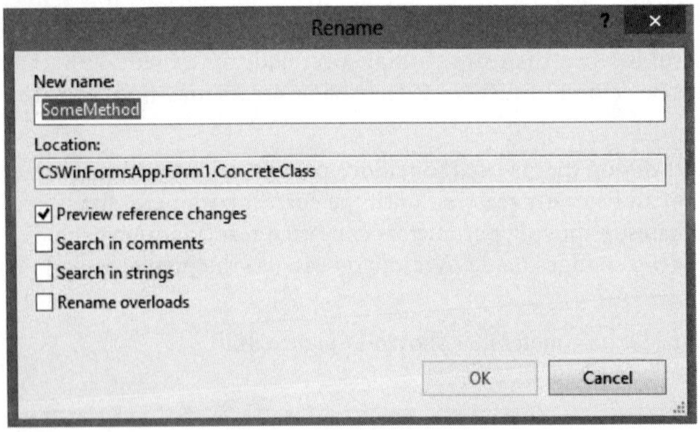

FIGURE 8-21

Unlike the C# rename support, which displays the preview window so that you can confirm your changes, the rename capability in VB simply renames all references to that variable.

Generate Method Stub

As you write code, you may realize that you need to call a method that you haven't written yet. For example, the following snippet illustrates a new method that you need to generate at some later stage:

VB

```
Private Sub MethodA()
    Dim InputA As String
    Dim InputB As Double
    Dim OutputC As Integer = NewMethodIJustThoughtOf(InputA, InputB)
End Sub
```

C#

```
public void MethodA()
{
    string InputA;
    double InputB;
    int OutputC = NewMethodIJustThoughtOf(InputA, InputB);
}
```

Of course, the preceding code generates a build error because this method has not been defined. Using the Generate Method Stub refactoring action (available as a smart tag in the code), you can generate a method stub. As you can see from the following sample, the method stub is complete with input parameters and output type:

VB

```
Private Function NewMethodIJustThoughtOf(ByVal InputA As String,
                                         ByVal InputB As Double) As Integer
    Throw New NotImplementedException
End Function
```

C#

```
private int NewMethodIJustThoughtOf(string InputA, double InputB)
{
    throw new Exception("The method or operation is not implemented.");
}
```

Organize Usings

It's good practice to maintain a sorted list of Using statements in each file (in C#), and reference only those namespaces that are actually required within that file. The Organize Usings menu (available from the context menu when right-clicking in the code editor, as shown in Figure 8-22) can help you in both these cases.

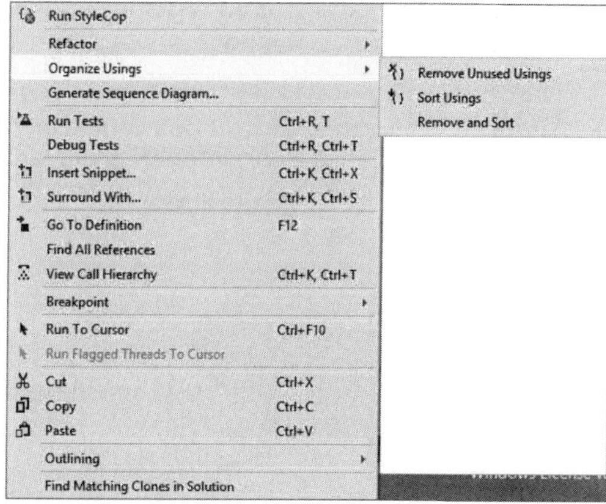

FIGURE 8-22

After a major refactoring of your code, you may find that you have a number of using directives at the top of your code file that are no longer used. Rather than going through a process of trial and error to determine what is and isn't used, you can use an operation in Visual Studio to do this for you by right-clicking in the code editor and choosing Organize Usings ➪ Remove Unused Usings (C# only). Using directives, using aliases, and external assembly aliases not used in the code file are removed.

> **NOTE** *VB developers don't have a way to sort and remove unused* `Imports` *statements. However, on the References tab on the Project Properties dialog, it's possible to mark namespaces to be imported into every code file. This can save significantly on the number of* `Imports` *statements. On this page you also have the ability to remove unused assembly references.*

It's good practice to organize the using directives in alphabetical order to make it easy to manage what namespaces are referenced. To save you doing this manually, you can right-click in the code editor and choose Organize Usings ➪ Sort Usings to have Visual Studio do this for you. The using directives from the `System` namespace appear first; then the using directives from other namespaces appear in alphabetical order. If you have aliases defined for namespaces, these are moved to the bottom of the list, and if you use external assembly aliases (using the `extern` keyword in C#), these are moved to the top of the list.

To sort using directives and remove those that are not used in one action, right-click in the code editor and choose Organize Usings ➪ Remove and Sort.

> **NOTE** *The default Visual Studio template code files have the* `using` *statements at the top of the file outside the namespace block. However, if you follow the StyleCop guidelines, these specify that using statements should be contained within the namespace block. The Organize Usings functions handle either situation based upon the current location of the* `using` *statements in the file and retaining that location.*

SUMMARY

Code snippets are a valuable inclusion in the Visual Studio 2012 feature set. You learned in this chapter how to use them, and how to create your own, including variable substitution (and `Imports` and reference associations for VB snippets). With this information you can create your own library of code snippets from functionality that you use frequently, saving you time in coding similar constructs later.

This chapter also provided examples of each of the refactoring actions available within Visual Studio 2012. Although VB developers do not get complete refactoring support out-of-the-box, CodeRush Xpress provides a wide range of refactoring actions that enable them to easily refactor their projects.

Server Explorer

WHAT'S IN THIS CHAPTER?

- Querying hardware resources and services on local and remote computers
- Using the Server Explorer to easily add code to your applications that works with computer resources

The Server Explorer is one of the few tool windows in Visual Studio that is not specific to a solution or project. It allows you to explore and query hardware resources and services on local or remote computers. You can perform various tasks and activities with these resources, including adding them to your applications.

The Server Explorer, as shown in Figure 9-1, has three types of resources to which it can connect out of the box. The first, under the Servers node, enables you to access hardware resources and services on a local or remote computer. This functionality is explored in detail in this chapter. The second type of resources is under the Data Connections node and allows you to work with all aspects of data connections, including the ability to create databases, add and modify tables, build relationships, and even execute queries. Chapter 27, "Visual Database Tools," covers the Data Connections functionality in detail. Finally, you can add a connection to a SharePoint server and browse SharePoint-specific resources such as Content Types, Lists, Libraries, and Workflows. SharePoint connections are covered in more detail in Chapter 25, "SharePoint." Figure 9-1 also shows some Azure connection types. The visible connection types depend on the SDKs that you have installed.

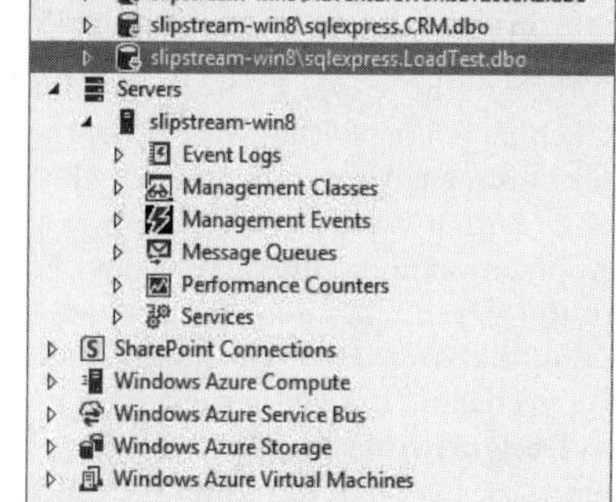

FIGURE 9-1

SERVER CONNECTIONS

The Servers node would be better named Computers because you can use it to attach to and interrogate any computer to which you have access, regardless of whether it is a server or a desktop workstation. Each computer is listed as a separate node under the Servers node. Below each computer node is a list of the hardware, services, and other components that belong to that computer. Each of these contains a number of activities or tasks that can be performed. Several software vendors have components that extend the functionality provided by the Server Explorer.

To access Server Explorer, on the View menu, select Server Explorer. By default, the local computer appears in the Servers list. To add another computer, right-click the Servers node, and select Add Server from the context menu.

Entering a computer name or IP address initiates an attempt to connect to the machine using your credentials. If you do not have sufficient privileges, you can elect to connect using a different username by clicking the appropriate link. The link appears to be disabled, but clicking it does bring up a dialog, as shown in Figure 9-2, in which you can provide an alternative username and password.

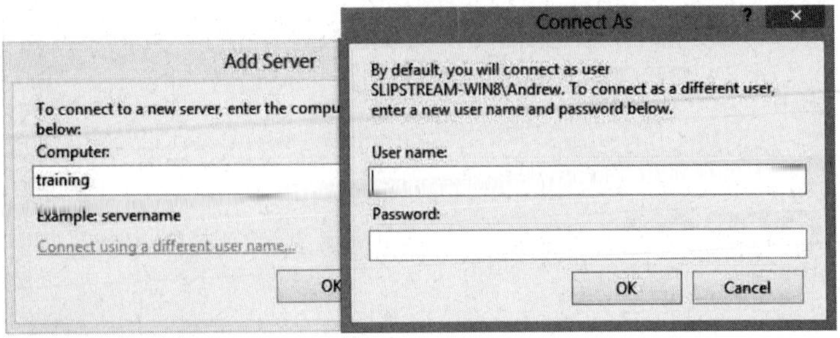

FIGURE 9-2

> **NOTE** *You need Administrator privileges on any server that you want to access through the Server Explorer.*

Event Logs

The Event Logs node gives you access to the machine event logs. You can launch the Event Viewer from the right-click context menu. Alternatively, as shown in Figure 9-3, you can drill into the list of event logs to view the events for a particular application. Clicking any of the events displays information about the event in the Properties window.

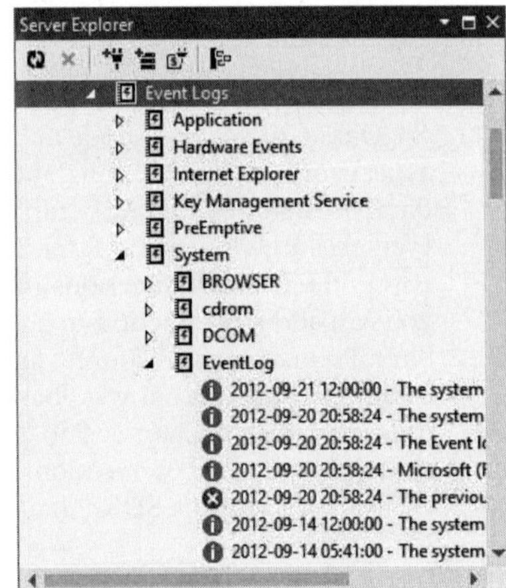

FIGURE 9-3

Although the Server Explorer is useful for interrogating a machine while writing your code, the true power comes with the component creation you get when you drag a resource node onto a Windows Form. For example, if you drag the Application node onto a Windows Form, you get an instance of the `System.Diagnostics.EventLog` class added to the nonvisual area of the designer. The same can be done by right-clicking the log in the Server Explorer and selecting Add to Designer from the context menu. You can then write an entry to this event log using the following code:

C#

```
this.eventLog1.Source = "My Server Explorer App";
this.eventLog1.WriteEntry("Something happened",
                          System.Diagnostics.EventLogEntryType.Information);
```

VB

```
Me.EventLog1.Source = "My Server Explorer App"
Me.EventLog1.WriteEntry("Something happened",
                        System.Diagnostics.EventLogEntryType.Information)
```

> **NOTE** *Because the preceding code creates a new Source in the Application Event Log, it requires administrative rights to execute. If you run Windows Vista, Windows 7, or Windows 8 with User Account Control enabled, you should create an application manifest. This is discussed in Chapter 6, "Solutions, Projects, and Items."*

After you run this code, you can view the results directly in the Server Explorer. Click the Refresh button on the Server Explorer toolbar to ensure that the new Event Source displays under the Application Event Log node.

For Visual Basic programmers, an alternative to adding an `EventLog` class to your code is to use the built-in logging provided by the `My` namespace. For example, you can modify the previous code snippet to write a log entry using the `My.Application.Log.WriteEntry` method:

VB

```
My.Application.Log.WriteEntry("Button Clicked", TraceEventType.Information)
```

You can also write exception information using the `My.Application.Log.WriteException` method, which accepts an exception and two optional parameters that provide additional information.

Using the `My` namespace to write logging information has a number of additional benefits. In the following configuration file, an `EventLogTraceListener` is specified to route log information to the event log. However, you can specify other trace listeners — for example, the `FileLogTraceListener`, which writes information to a log file by adding it to the `SharedListeners` and `Listeners` collections:

```
<?xml version="1.0" encoding="utf-8" ?>
<configuration>
    <system.diagnostics>
        <sources>
            <source name="DefaultSource" switchName="DefaultSwitch">
                <listeners>
                    <add name="EventLog"/>
                </listeners>
            </source>
        </sources>
        <switches>
            <add name="DefaultSwitch" value="Information"/>
        </switches>
        <sharedListeners>
            <add name="EventLog"
                 type="System.Diagnostics.EventLogTraceListener"
                 initializeData="ApplicationEventLog"/>
        </sharedListeners>
    </system.diagnostics>
</configuration>
```

This configuration also specifies a switch called `DefaultSwitch`. This switch is associated with the trace information source via the `switchName` attribute and defines the minimum event type that will be sent to the listed listeners. For example, if the value of this switch were `Critical`, events with the type Information would not be written to the event log. The possible values of this switch are shown in Table 9-1.

TABLE 9-1: Values for DefaultSwitch

DEFAULTSWITCH	EVENT TYPES WRITTEN TO LOG
Off	No Events
Critical	Critical Events
Error	Critical and Error Events
Warning	Critical, Error, and Warning Events
Information	Critical, Error, Warning, and Information Events
Verbose	Critical, Error, Warning, Information, and Verbose Events
ActivityTracing	Start, Stop, Suspend, Resume, and Transfer Events
All	All Events

Note that there are overloads for both `WriteEntry` and `WriteException` that do not require an event type to be specified. In this case the event types defaults to Information and Error, respectively.

Management Classes

Figure 9-4 shows the full list of management classes available via the Server Explorer. Each node exposes a set of functionalities specific to that device or application. For example, right-clicking the Printers node enables you to add a new printer connection, whereas right-clicking the named node under My Computer enables you to add the computer to a domain or workgroup. The one thing common to all these nodes is that they provide a strongly typed wrapper around the Windows Management Instrumentation (WMI) infrastructure. In most cases, it is simply a matter of dragging the node representing the information in which you're interested across to the form. From your code you can then access and manipulate that information.

To give you an idea of how these wrappers can be used, this section walks through how you can use the management classes to retrieve information about a computer. Under the My Computer node, you can see a node with the name of the local computer. Selecting this node and dragging it onto the form gives you a `ComputerSystem` component in the nonvisual area of the form. Also add a Label control, a TextBox control, a Button, and a PropertyGrid control from the All Windows Forms tab on the Toolbox and arrange them on the Form, as shown in Figure 9-5.

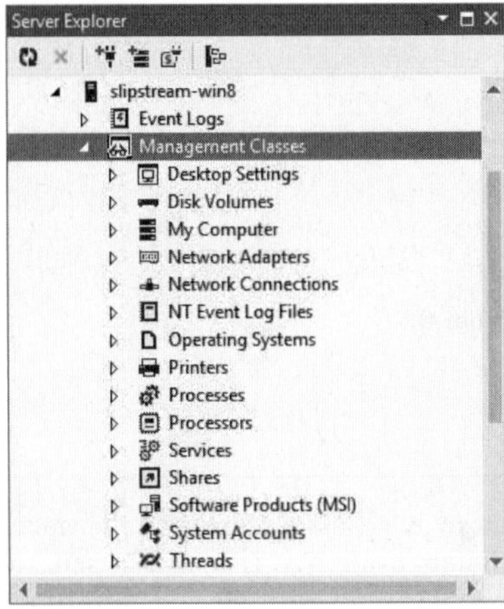

FIGURE 9-4

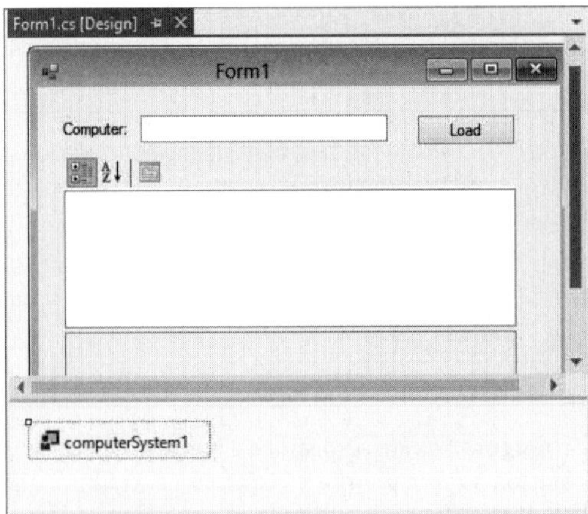

FIGURE 9-5

If you look in the Solution Explorer, you'll see that it has also added a custom component called `root.CIMV2.Win32_ComputerSystem` (or similar depending on the computer configuration). This custom component is generated by the Management Strongly Typed Class Generator (`Mgmtclassgen.exe`) and includes the `ComputerSystem` and other classes, which can enable you to expose WMI information.

If you click the `computerSystem1` object on the form, you can see the information about that computer in the Properties window. In this application, however, you're not that interested in that particular computer; that computer was selected as a template to create the `ComputerSystem` class. The `ComputerSystem1` object can be deleted, but before deleting it, take note of the `Path` property of the object. The `Path` is used, combined with the computer name entered in the form in Figure 9-5, to load the information about that computer. You can see this in the following code that is added to the button click event handler for the Load button:

C#

```
const string compPath = "\\\\{0}\\root\\CIMV2:Win32_ComputerSystem.Name=\"{0}\"";

if (!string.IsNullOrEmpty(this.textBox1.Text))
{
    string computerName = this.textBox1.Text;
    string pathString = string.Format(compPath, computerName);
    var path = new System.Management.ManagementPath(pathString);
    ROOT.CIMV2.ComputerSystem cs = new ROOT.CIMV2.ComputerSystem(path);

    this.propertyGrid1.SelectedObject = cs;
}
```

VB

```
Const compPath As String = "\\{0}\root\CIMV2:Win32_ComputerSystem.Name=""{0}"""

If Not Me.TextBox1.Text = "" Then
    Dim computerName As String = Me.TextBox1.Text
    Dim pathString As String = String.Format(compPath, computerName)
    Dim path As New System.Management.ManagementPath(pathString)
    Dim cs As New ROOT.CIMV2.ComputerSystem(path)

    Me.PropertyGrid1.SelectedObject = cs
End If
```

In this example, the `Path` property, which was obtained earlier from the `computerSystem1` object, has been used in a string constant with the string replacement token `{0}` where the computer name should go. When the button is clicked, the computer name entered into the textbox is combined with this path using `String.Format` to generate the full WMI path. The path is then used to instantiate a new `ComputerAccount` object, which is in turn passed to the PropertyGrid control. The result of this at run time is shown in Figure 9-6.

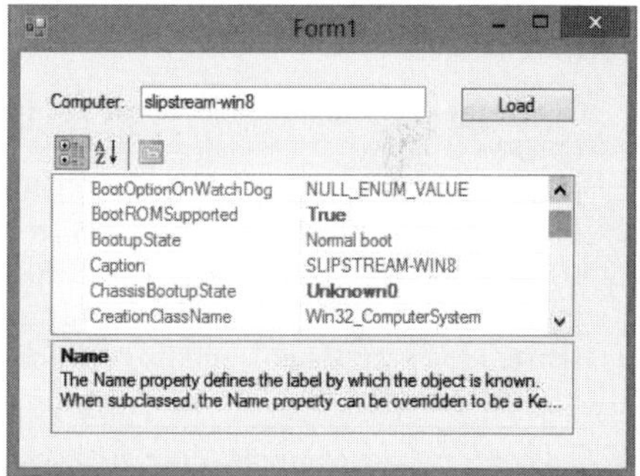

FIGURE 9-6

> **NOTE** *The generated code doesn't handle unsupported functionality gracefully. For example, if you run the application on a machine that does not support power management, the* `computerSystem1` *component raises an exception while it is being instantiated. This might require you to modify the generated code before your application can run successfully.*

Though most properties are read-only, for those fields that are editable, changes made in this PropertyGrid are immediately committed to the computer. This behavior can be altered by changing the `AutoCommit` property on the `ComputerSystem` class.

Management Events

In the previous section you learned how you can drag a management class from the Server Explorer onto the form and then work with the generated classes. The other way to work with the WMI interface is through the Management Events node. A management event enables you to monitor any WMI data type and have an event raised if an object of that type is created, modified, or deleted. By default, this node is empty, but you can create your own by right-clicking the Management Events node and selecting Add Event Query, which invokes the dialog shown in Figure 9-7.

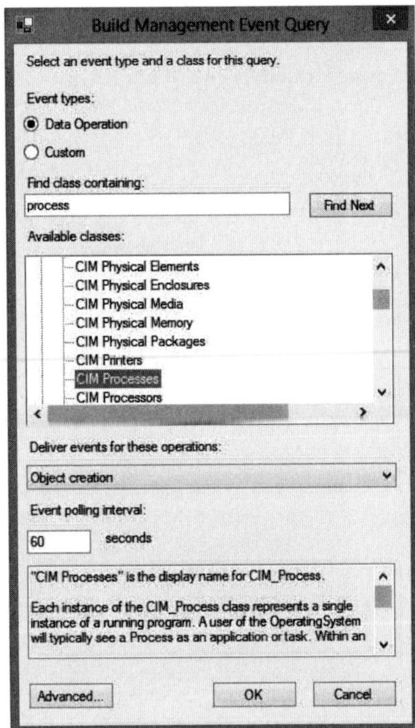

FIGURE 9-7

Use this dialog to locate the WMI data type in which you are interested. Because there are literally thousands of these, it is useful to use the Find box. In Figure 9-7, the search term "process" was entered, and the class CIM Processes was found under the root\CIMV2 node. Each instance of this class represents a single process running on the system. You are only interested in being notified when a new process is created, so ensure that Object Creation is selected from the drop-down menu.

After clicking OK, a CIM Processes Event Query node is added to the Management Events node. If you open a new instance of an application on your system, such as Notepad, you'll see events being progressively added to this node. In the Build Management Event Query dialog, as shown in Figure 9-7, the default polling interval was set to 60 seconds, so you may need to wait up to 60 seconds for the event to show up in the tree after you have made the change.

When the event does finally show up, it will initially appear in the Output window. Once it does, you can refresh the Event Query node (right-click and select Refresh from the context menu) to see the event in Server Explorer. The output is shown in Figure 9-8. If you select the event, you'll notice that the Properties window is populated with a large number of properties that don't make any sense. However, when you know which of the properties to query, it is quite easy to trap, filter, and respond to system events.

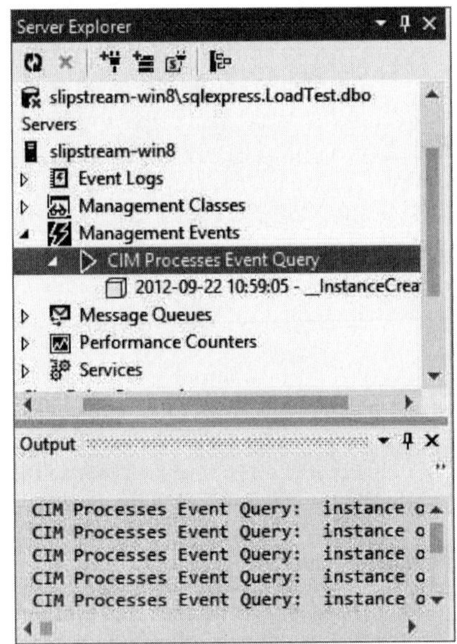

FIGURE 9-8

To continue the example, drag a CheckBox control and a ListBox control from the Toolbox onto a new Windows Form.

Next, drag the CIM Processes Event Query node from the Server Explorer onto a new form. This generates an instance of the `System.Management.ManagementEventWatcher` class, with properties configured, so it can listen for the creation of a new process. You can access the actual via the `QueryString` property of the nested `ManagementQuery` object. As with most watcher classes, the `ManagementEventWatcher` class triggers an event when the watch conditions are met — in this case, the `EventArrived` event. To handle this event, add the following code:

C#

```
private void managementEventWatcher1_EventArrived(System.Object sender,
                                        System.Management.EventArrivedEventArgs e)
{
    foreach (System.Management.PropertyData p in e.NewEvent.Properties)
    {
        if (p.Name == "TargetInstance")
        {
            var mbo = (System.Management.ManagementBaseObject)p.Value;
            string[] sCreatedProcess = {(string)mbo.Properties["Name"].Value,
                                        (string)mbo.Properties["ExecutablePath"].
                                        Value };
            this.BeginInvoke(new LogNewProcessDelegate(LogNewProcess),
                             sCreatedProcess);
        }
    }
}

delegate void LogNewProcessDelegate(string ProcessName, string ExePath);
private void LogNewProcess(string ProcessName, string ExePath)
{
    this.listBox1.Items.Add(string.Format("{0}—{1}", ProcessName, ExePath));
}

private void checkBox1_CheckedChanged(System.Object sender, System.EventArgs e)
{
    if (this.checkBox1.Checked)
    {
        this.managementEventWatcher1.Start();
    }
    else
    {
        this.managementEventWatcher1.Stop();
    }
}
```

VB

```
Private Sub ManagementEventWatcher1_EventArrived(ByVal sender As System.Object, _
                              ByVal e As System.Management.EventArrivedEventArgs)
    For Each p As System.Management.PropertyData In e.NewEvent.Properties
        If p.Name = "TargetInstance" Then
            Dim mbo As System.Management.ManagementBaseObject = _
                           CType(p.Value, System.Management.ManagementBaseObject)
            Dim sCreatedProcess As String() = {mbo.Properties("Name").Value, _
                                         mbo.Properties("ExecutablePath").Value}
            Me.BeginInvoke(New LogNewProcessDelegate(AddressOf LogNewProcess), _
                           sCreatedProcess)
        End If
    Next
End Sub

Delegate Sub LogNewProcessDelegate(ByVal ProcessName As String, _
                                   ByVal ExePath As String)
Private Sub LogNewProcess(ByVal ProcessName As String, ByVal ExePath As String)
    Me.ListBox1.Items.Add(String.Format("{0}—{1}", ProcessName, ExePath))
```

```
    End Sub

    Private Sub CheckBox1_CheckedChanged(ByVal sender As System.Object, _
                                            ByVal e As System.EventArgs) _
                                            Handles CheckBox1.CheckedChanged
        If Me.CheckBox1.Checked Then
            Me.ManagementEventWatcher1.Start()
        Else
            Me.ManagementEventWatcher1.Stop()
        End If
    End Sub
```

In the event handler, you'll need to iterate through the `Properties` collection on the `NewEvent` object. Where an object has changed, two instances are returned: `PreviousInstance`, which holds the state at the beginning of the polling interval, and `TargetInstance`, which holds the state at the end of the polling interval. It is possible for the object to change state multiple times within the same polling period. If this is the case, an event will be triggered only when the state at the end of the period differs from the state at the beginning of the period. For example, no event is raised if a process is started and then stopped within a single polling interval.

The event handler constructs a new `ManagementBaseObject` from a value passed into the event arguments to obtain the display name and executable path of the new process. Because UI controls can be updated only from the UI thread, you cannot directly update the ListBox. Instead you must call `BeginInvoke` to execute the `LogNewProcess` function on the UI thread. The last pieces that need to be put in place in order to see it function is to wire up the CheckChanged event for the CheckBox and the EventArrived even for the ManagementEventWatcher. Select the control in the designer, click the Events button on the Property Window, then use the drop-down for the event to select the Event Handler. Figure 9-9 shows the form in action.

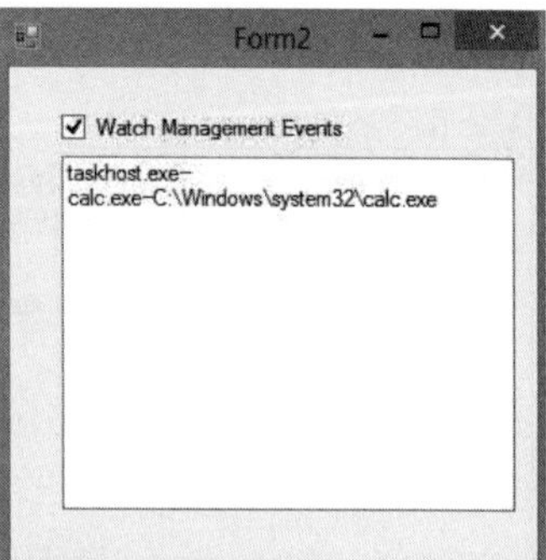

FIGURE 9-9

Message Queues

The Message Queues node, expanded in Figure 9-10, gives you access to the message queues available on your computer. You can use three types of queues: private, which does not appear when a foreign computer queries your computer; public, which appears; and system, which is used for unsent messages and other exception reporting.

> **NOTE** *To use the Message Queues node, you need to ensure that MSMQ is installed on your computer. You can do this via Programs and Features in the Control Panel. Select the Turn Windows Features On or Off task menu item, and then select the check box to enable the Microsoft Message Queue (MSMQ) Server feature.*

In Figure 9-10, a message queue called samplequeue has been added to the Private Queues node by selecting Create Queue from the right-click context menu. After you create a queue, you can create a properly configured instance of the `MessageQueue` class by dragging the queue onto a new Windows Form. To demonstrate the functionality of the `MessageQueue` object, add two TextBoxes and a button to the form, laid out as shown in Figure 9-11. The Send button is wired to use the `MessageQueue` object to send the message entered in the first textbox. In the `Load` event for the form, a background thread is created that continually polls the queue to retrieve messages, which can populate the second textbox:

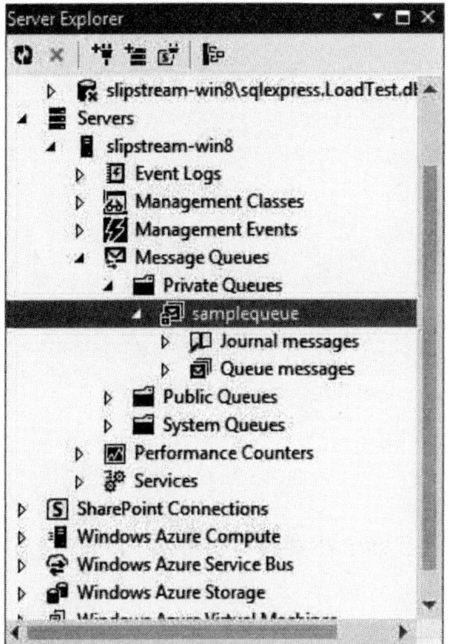

FIGURE 9-10

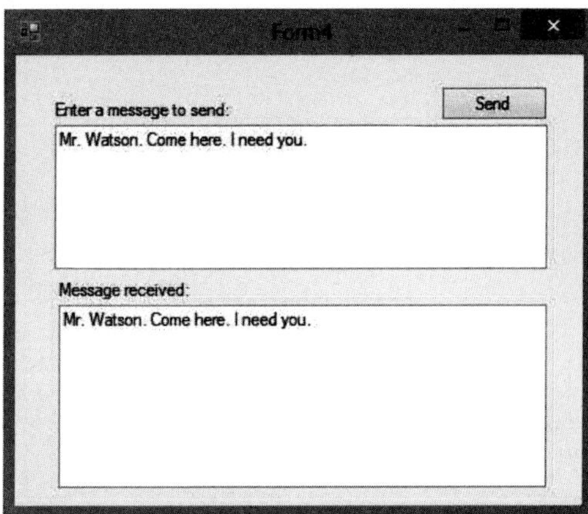

FIGURE 9-11

C#

```
public Form4()
{
    InitializeComponent();
    var monitorThread = new System.Threading.Thread(MonitorMessageQueue);
    monitorThread.IsBackground = true;
    monitorThread.Start();
    this.button1.Click +=new EventHandler(btn_Click);
}

private void btn_Click(object sender, EventArgs e)
{
    this.messageQueue1.Send(this.textBox1.Text);
}

private void MonitorMessageQueue()
{
    var m = default(System.Messaging.Message);
    while (true)
    {
        try
        {
            m = this.messageQueue1.Receive(new TimeSpan(0, 0, 0, 0, 50));
            this.ReceiveMessage((string)m.Body);
        }
        catch (System.Messaging.MessageQueueException ex)
        {
            if (!(ex.MessageQueueErrorCode ==
                  System.Messaging.MessageQueueErrorCode.IOTimeout))
            {
                throw ex;
            }
        }
        System.Threading.Thread.Sleep(10000);
    }
}

private delegate void MessageDel(string msg);
private void ReceiveMessage(string msg)
```

```
{
    if (this.InvokeRequired)
    {
        this.BeginInvoke(new MessageDel(ReceiveMessage), msg);
        return;
    }
    this.textBox2.Text = msg;
}
```

VB

```
Private Sub Form_Load(ByVal sender As Object, ByVal e As System.EventArgs) _
                      Handles Me.Load
    Dim monitorThread As New Threading.Thread(AddressOf MonitorMessageQueue)
    monitorThread.IsBackground = True
    monitorThread.Start()
End Sub

Private Sub btn_Click(ByVal sender As System.Object, ByVal e As System.EventArgs) _
                          Handles Button1.Click
    Me.MessageQueue1.Send(Me.TextBox1.Text)
End Sub

Private Sub MonitorMessageQueue()
    Dim m As Messaging.Message
    While True
        Try
            m = Me.MessageQueue1.Receive(New TimeSpan(0, 0, 0, 0, 50))
            Me.ReceiveMessage(m.Body)
        Catch ex As Messaging.MessageQueueException
            If Not ex.MessageQueueErrorCode = _
                    Messaging.MessageQueueErrorCode.IOTimeout Then
                Throw ex
            End If
        End Try
        Threading.Thread.Sleep(10000)
    End While
End Sub

Private Delegate Sub MessageDel(ByVal msg As String)
Private Sub ReceiveMessage(ByVal msg As String)
    If Me.InvokeRequired Then
        Me.BeginInvoke(New MessageDel(AddressOf ReceiveMessage), msg)
        Return
    End If
    Me.TextBox2.Text = msg
End Sub
```

Note in this code snippet that the background thread is never explicitly closed. Because the thread has the `IsBackground` property set to `True`, it is automatically terminated when the application exits. As with the previous example, because the message processing is done in a background thread, you need to switch threads when you update the user interface using the `BeginInvoke` method. Putting this all together, you get a form like the one shown in Figure 9-11.

As messages are sent to the message queue, they appear under the appropriate queue in Server Explorer. Clicking the message displays its contents in the Properties window.

Performance Counters

One of the most common things developers forget to consider when building an application is how it will be maintained and managed. For example, consider an application that was installed a year ago and has been operating without any issues. All of a sudden, requests start taking an unacceptable amount of time. It is clear that the application is not behaving correctly, but there is no way to determine the cause of the misbehavior. One strategy to identify where the performance issues are is to use performance counters. Windows has many built-in performance counters that you can use to monitor operating system activity, and a lot of third-party software also installs performance counters so administrators can identify any rogue behavior.

The Performance Counters node in the Server Explorer tree, expanded in Figure 9-12, has two primary functions. First, it enables you to view and retrieve information about the currently installed counters. You can also create new performance counters, as well as edit or delete existing counters. As you can see in Figure 9-12, under the Performance Counters node is a list of categories and under those is a list of counters.

> **NOTE** *You must run Visual Studio with Administrator rights to view the Performance Counters under the Server Explorer. As well, the ability to edit categories is limited to those categories that you created.*

To edit either the category or the counters, select Edit Category from the right-click context menu for the category. To add a new category and associated counters, right-click the Performance Counters node, and select Create New Category from the context menu. Both of these operations use the dialog shown in Figure 9-13. Here, a new performance counter category has been created that will be used to track a form's open and close events.

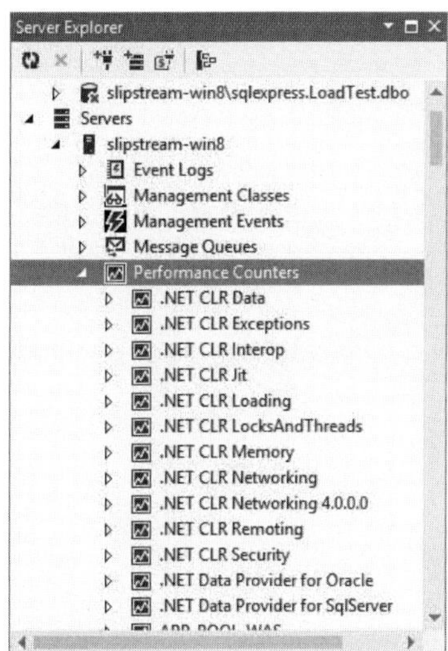

FIGURE 9-12

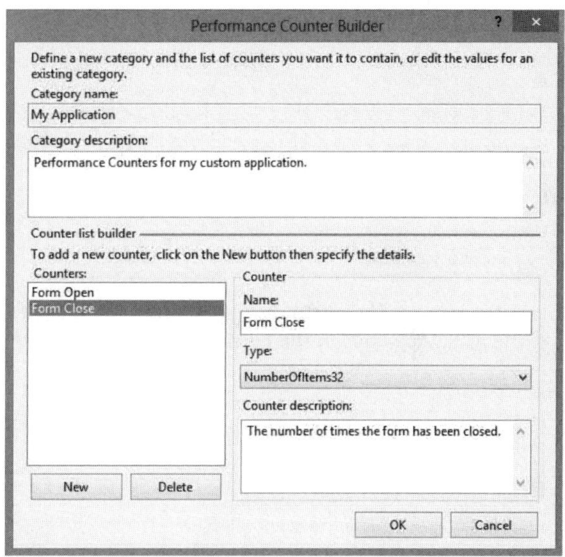

FIGURE 9-13

The second function of the Performance Counters section is to provide an easy way for you to access performance counters via your code. By dragging a performance counter category onto a form, you gain access to read and write to that performance counter. To continue with this chapter's example, drag the new My Application performance counters, Form Open and Form Close, onto a new Windows Form. Also add a couple of textboxes and a button so that you can display the performance counter values. Finally, rename the performance counters so they have friendly names. This should give you a form similar to the one shown in Figure 9-14.

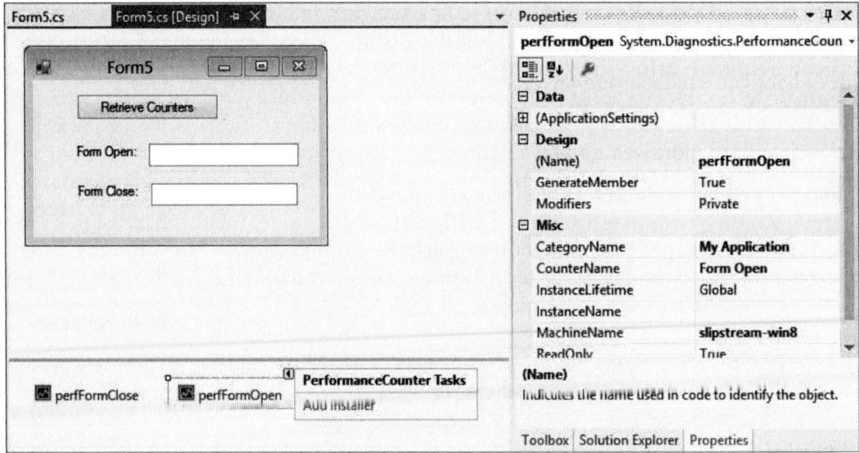

FIGURE 9-14

In the properties for the selected performance counter, you can see that the appropriate counter — in this case, Form Open — has been selected from the My Application category. You can also notice a `MachineName` property, which is the computer from which you are retrieving the counter information, and a `ReadOnly` property, which needs to be set to `False` if you want to update the counter. (By default, the `ReadOnly` property is set to `True`.) To complete this form, add the following code to the Retrieve Counters' button click event handler:

C#

```
this.textBox1.Text = this.perfFormOpen.RawValue.ToString();
this.textBox2.Text = this.perfFormClose.RawValue.ToString();
```

VB

```
Me.textBox1.Text = Me.perfFormOpen.RawValue
Me.textBox2.Text = Me.perfFormClose.RawValue
```

You also need to add code to the application to update the performance counters. For example, you might have the following code in the Form `Load` event handlers:

C#

```
this.perfFormOpen.Increment();
```

VB

```
Me.perfFormOpen.Increment()
```

When you dragged the performance counter onto the form, you may have noticed a *smart tag* (small arrow that appears near the top-right corner when a control is selected) on the performance counter component that had a single item, Add Installer. When the component is selected, you can notice the same action at the bottom of the Properties window. Clicking this action in either place adds an `Installer` class to your solution that can be used to install the performance counter as part of your installation process. Of course, for this installer to be called, the assembly it belongs to must be added as a custom action for the deployment project. For more information on custom actions, see Chapter 49, "Packaging and Deployment."

To create multiple performance counters, you can simply select each additional performance counter and click Add Installer. Visual Studio 2012 directs you back to the first installer that was created and has automatically added the second counter to the `Counters` collection of the `PerformanceCounterInstaller` component, as shown in Figure 9-15.

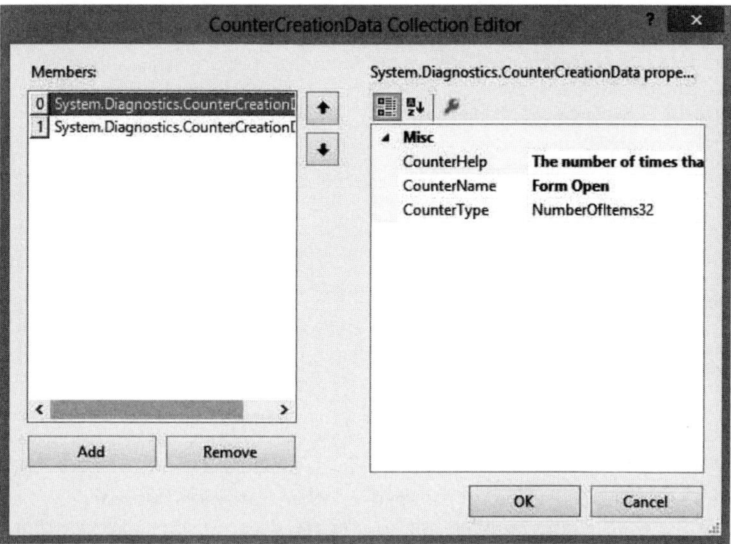

FIGURE 9-15

You can also add counters in other categories by adding additional `PerformanceCounterInstaller` components to the design surface. You are now ready to deploy your application with the knowledge that you can use a tool such as PerfMon to monitor how your application behaves.

Services

The Services node, expanded in Figure 9-16, shows the registered services for the computer. Each node indicates the state of that service in the bottom-right corner of the icon. Possible states are Stopped, Running, or Paused. Selecting a service displays additional information about the service, such as other service dependencies, in the Properties window.

FIGURE 9-16

As with other nodes in the Server Explorer, each service can be dragged onto the design surface of a form. This generates a `ServiceController` component in the nonvisual area of the form. By default, the `ServiceName` property is set to the service that you dragged across from the Server Explorer, but this can be changed to access information and control any service. Similarly, the `MachineName` property can be changed to connect to any computer to which you have access. The following code shows how you can stop a Service using `ServiceController` component:

C#

```
this.serviceController1.Refresh();
if (this.serviceController1.CanStop)
```

```
{
    if (this.serviceController1.Status ==
            System.ServiceProcess.ServiceControllerStatus.Running)
    {
        this.serviceController1.Stop();
        this.serviceController1.Refresh();
    }
}
```

VB

```
Me.ServiceController1.Refresh()
If Me.ServiceController1.CanStop Then
   If Me.ServiceController1.Status = _
         ServiceProcess.ServiceControllerStatus.Running Then
      Me.ServiceController1.Stop()
      Me.ServiceController1.Refresh()
   End If
End If
```

In addition to the three main states — Running, Paused, or Stopped — other transition states are ContinuePending, PausePending, StartPending, and StopPending. If you are about to start a service that may be dependent on another service that is in one of these transition states, you can call the `WaitForStatus` method to ensure that the service starts properly.

DATA CONNECTIONS

The Data Connections node enables you to connect to a database and perform a large range of administrative functions. You can connect to a wide variety of data sources including any edition of SQL Server, Microsoft Access, Oracle, or a generic ODBC data source. Figure 9-17 shows the Server Explorer connected to a SQL Server database file.

The Server Explorer provides access to the Visual Database, which allows you to perform a large range of administrative functions on the connected database. You can create databases; add and modify tables, views, and stored procedures; manage indexes, execute queries, and much more. Chapter 27 covers all aspects of the Data Connections functionality.

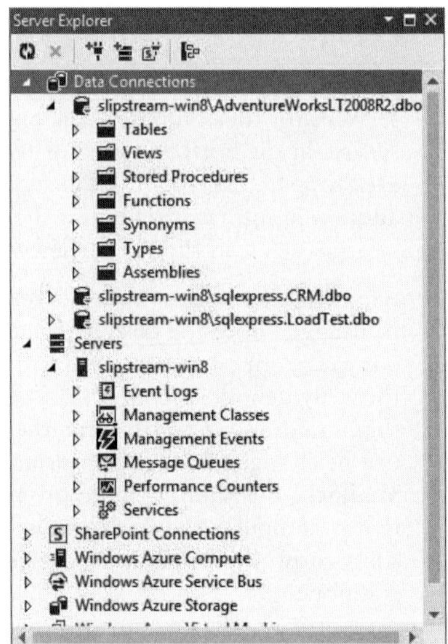

FIGURE 9-17

SHAREPOINT CONNECTIONS

One of the great features of Visual Studio 2012 is the ability to connect to a Microsoft Office SharePoint Server with the Server Explorer. This feature allows you to navigate and view many of the SharePoint resources and components.

The Server Explorer provides only read-only access to SharePoint resources— you cannot, for example, create or edit a list definition. Even so, it can be useful to have ready access to this information in

Visual Studio when developing a SharePoint application. As with many of the components under the Servers node, you can also drag and drop certain SharePoint resources directly onto the design surface of your SharePoint project.

Using the Server Explorer to browse SharePoint resources is covered in detail in Chapter 25.

SUMMARY

In this chapter you learned how you can use Server Explorer to manage and work with computer resources and services. Chapter 27 continues the discussion on the Server Explorer, covering the Data Connections node in more detail. Chapter 25 provides an in-depth look at managing SharePoint resources using the Server Explorer.

10

Modeling with the Class Designer

WHAT'S IN THIS CHAPTER?

- Using the Class Designer to create a graphical visualization of your class architecture
- Easily generating and refactoring your classes with the Class Designer
- Using the Modeling Power Toys for Visual Studio 2012 add-in to better work with large-class hierarchies

Traditionally, software modeling has been performed separately from coding, often during a design phase that is completed before coding begins. More often than not, the modeling diagrams constructed during design are not kept up to date as the development progresses, and they quickly lose their value as design changes are inevitably made.

In Visual Studio 2012, class diagrams are constructed dynamically from the source code. Any change made to the source code is immediately reflected in the class diagram, and any change to the diagram is also made to the code. This means that they are always up to date, which allows them to become a more integral and useful part of the development process.

This chapter looks at the Class Designer in detail and explains how you can use it to design, visualize, and refactor your class architecture.

CREATING A CLASS DIAGRAM

The design process for an application typically involves at least a sketch of the classes that are going to be created and how they interact. Visual Studio 2012 provides a design surface, called the Class Designer, onto which classes can be drawn to form a class diagram. Fields, properties, and methods can then be added to the classes, and relationships can be established between classes. Although this design is called a class diagram, it supports classes, structures, enumerations, interfaces, abstract classes, and delegates.

There is more than one way to add a Class Diagram to your project. One way to add a Class Diagram is through the Add New Item dialog, as shown in Figure 10-1. This creates a new blank Class Diagram within the project.

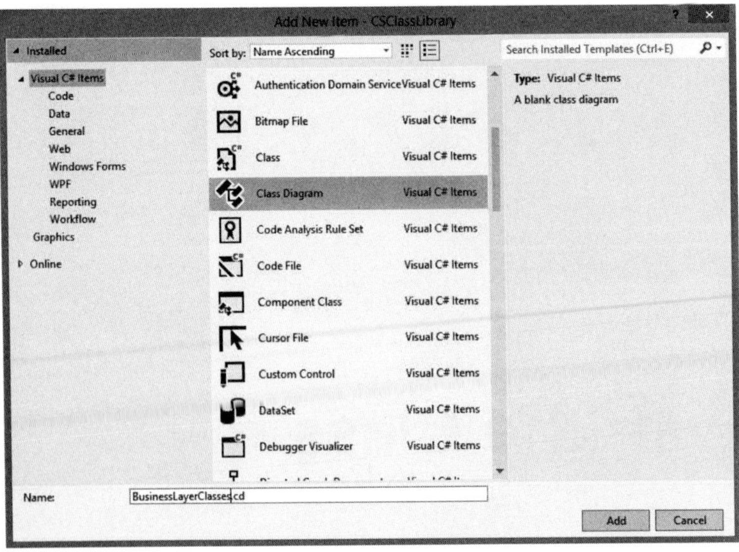

FIGURE 10-1

You can also add a new Class Diagram to your project by right-clicking a project or class in the Solution Explorer and selecting the View Class Diagram menu item. If the project is selected when you create a Class Diagram in this way, Visual Studio automatically adds all the types defined within the project to the initial class diagram. Although this may be desirable in some instances, for a project that contains a large number of classes, the process of creating and laying out the diagram can be time-consuming.

Unlike some tools that require all types within a project to be on the same diagram, the class diagram can include as many or as few of your types as you want. This makes it possible to add multiple class diagrams to a single solution.

> **NOTE** *The scope of the Class Designer is limited to a single project. You cannot add types to a class diagram that are defined in a different project, even if it is part of the same solution.*

The Class Designer can be divided into four components: the design surface, the Toolbox, the Class Details window, and the property grid. Changes made to the class diagram are saved in a `.cd` file, which works in parallel with the class code files to generate the visual layout shown in the Class Designer.

THE DESIGN SURFACE

The design surface of the Class Designer enables the developer to interact with types using a drag-and-drop-style interface. You can add existing types to the design surface by dragging them from either the class view or the Solution Explorer. If a file in the Solution Explorer contains more than one type, they are all added to the design surface.

Figure 10-2 shows a simple class diagram that contains two classes, `Customer` and `Order`, and an enumeration, `OrderStatus`. Each class contains fields, properties, methods, and events. There is an association between the classes. The link between `Customer` and `Order` is one-to-many (indicated by the two arrowheads). As an implementation, it will appear in the `Customer` class as a property called `Orders` that is a list of `Order` objects. The link between `Order` and `Customer` is one-to-one (the single arrowhead is the indicator) and would be implemented as a `Customer` property in the `Order` class. Finally, the `Order` class implements the IDataErrorInfo interface. All this information can be gleaned from this class diagram.

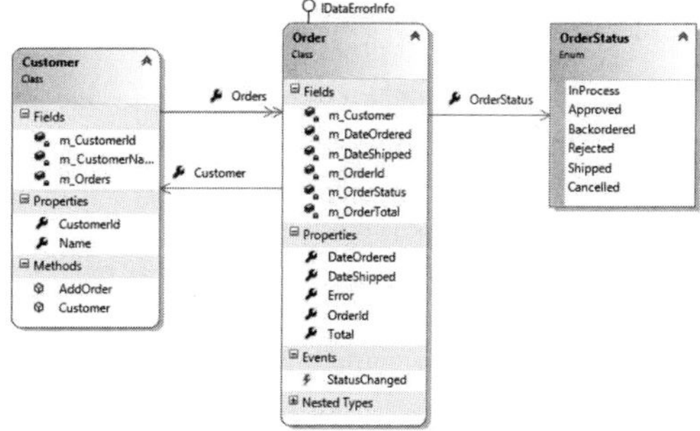

FIGURE 10-2

Each class appears as an entity on the class diagram, which can be dragged around the design surface and resized as required. A class is made up of fields, properties, methods, and events. In Figure 10-2, these components are grouped into compartments. You can select alternative layouts for the class diagram, such as listing the components in alphabetical order or grouping the components by accessibility.

The Class Designer is often used to view multiple classes to get an understanding of how they are associated. In this case, it is convenient to hide the components of a class to simplify the diagram. To hide all the components at once, use the toggle in the top-right corner of the class on the design surface. If only certain components need to be hidden, they can be individually hidden, or the entire compartment can be hidden, by right-clicking the appropriate element and selecting the Hide menu item. Alternatively, the Class Details form includes a Hide column where the individual components can be hidden or unhidden as required.

THE TOOLBOX

To facilitate items being added to the class diagram, there is a Class Designer tab in the Toolbox. To create most items, drag the item from the Toolbox onto the designer surface or simply double-click it. Figure 10-3 shows the Toolbox with the Class Designer tab visible. The items in the Toolbox can be classified as either entities or connectors. Note the Comment item, which can be added to the Class Designer but does not appear in any of the code; it is there simply to aid documentation of the class diagram.

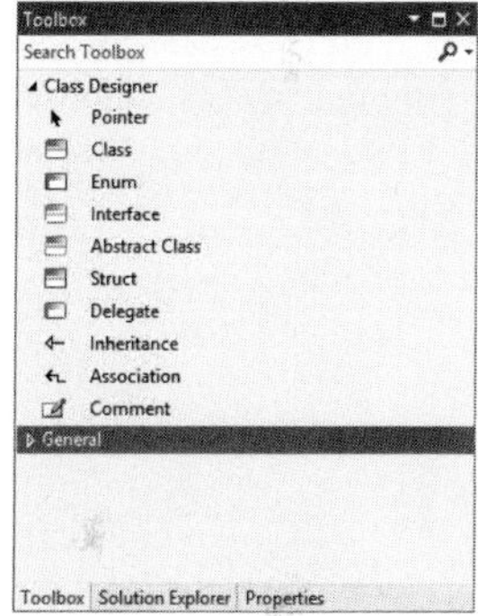

FIGURE 10-3

Entities

The entities that can be added to the class diagram all correspond to types in the .NET Framework. When you add a new entity to the design surface, you need to give it a name. In addition, you need to indicate whether it should be added to a new file or an existing file.

You can remove entities from the diagram by right-clicking and selecting the Remove from Diagram menu item. This does not remove the source code; it simply removes the entity from the diagram. In cases in which you want to delete the associated source code, select the Delete Code menu item.

You can view the code associated with an entity by either double-clicking the entity or selecting View Code from the right-click context menu.

The following list explains the entities in the Toolbox:

- **Class:** Fields, properties, methods, events, and constants can all be added to a class via the right-click context menu or the Class Details window. Although a class can support nested types, they cannot be added using the designer surface. Classes can also implement interfaces. In Figure 10-2, the `Order` class implements the IDataErrorInfo interface.
- **Enum:** An enumeration can contain only a list of members that can have a value assigned to them. Each member also has a summary and remarks property, but these appear only as an XML comment against the member.

- **Interface:** Interfaces define properties, methods, and events that a class must implement. Interfaces can also contain nested types, but recall that adding a nested type is not supported by the Designer.
- **Abstract Class:** Abstract classes behave the same as classes except that they appear on the design surface with an italic name and are marked as `Abstract` (C#) or `MustInherit` (VB).
- **Struct:** A structure is the only entity, other than a comment, that appears on the Designer in a rectangle. Similar to a class, a structure supports fields, properties, methods, events, and constants. It, too, can contain nested types. However, unlike a class, a structure cannot have a destructor.
- **Delegate:** Although a delegate appears as an entity on the class diagram, it can't contain nested types. The only components it can contain are parameters that define the delegate signature.

Connectors

Two types of relationships can be established between entities. These are illustrated on the class diagram using connectors and are explained in the following list:

- **Inheritance:** The Inheritance connector is used to show the relationship between classes that inherit from each other.
- **Association:** Where a class makes reference to another class, there is an association between the two classes. This is shown using the Association connector.

If a relationship is based around a collection — for example, a list of `Order` objects — this can be represented using a *collection association*. A collection association called `Orders` is shown in Figure 10-2 connecting the `Customer` and `Order` classes.

A *class association* can be represented as either a field or property of a class, or as an association link between the classes. You can use the right-click context menu on either the field or property or the association to toggle between the two representations.

> **NOTE** *To show a property as a collection association, you need to right-click the property in the class and select Show as Collection Association. This hides the property from the class and displays it as a connector to the associated class on the diagram.*

The creation of an inheritance or association relationship in the class diagram is done by selecting the desired relationship in the Toolbox. Then click on one of the two classes (for inheritance, you click on the derived class; for association, you click on the class that will contain the association property) and then hold down the left button and drag the mouse over the second class and release.

THE CLASS DETAILS

You can add a component to an entity by right-clicking and selecting the appropriate component to add. Unfortunately, this is a time-consuming process and doesn't afford you the ability to add method parameters or return values. The Class Designer in Visual Studio 2012 includes a Class Details window, which provides a user interface that enables components to be quickly entered. This window is illustrated in Figure 10-4 for the `Customer` class previously shown in Figure 10-2.

Class Details - Customer

Name	Type	Modifier	Summary	Hide
Methods				
AddOrder	void	public	Adds an order for this customer	
Customer		public	Constructor for Customer	
<add method>				
Properties				
CustomerId	Guid	public	Gets the unique Id for the custome	
Name	string	public	The display name for this custome	
Orders	List<Order>	public		
<add property>				
Fields				
m_CustomerId	Guid	private		
m_CustomerName	string	private		
m_Orders	List<Order>	private		
<add field>				
Events				
<add event>				

FIGURE 10-4

On the left side of the window are buttons that can aid in navigating classes that contain a large number of components. The top button can be used to add methods, properties, fields, or events to the class. The remaining buttons can be used to bring any of the component groups into focus. For example, the second button is used to navigate to the list of methods for the class. You can navigate between components in the list using the up and down arrow keys.

Because Figure 10-4 shows the details for a class, the main region of the window is divided into four alphabetical lists: Methods, Properties, Fields, and Events. Other entity types may have other components, such as Members and Parameters. Each row is divided into five columns that show the name, the return type, the modifier or accessibility of the component, a summary, and whether the item is hidden on the design surface. In each case, the Summary field appears as an XML comment against the appropriate component. Events differ from the other components in that the Type column must be a delegate. You can navigate between columns using the left and right arrow keys, Tab (next column), and Shift+Tab (previous column).

To enter parameters on a method, use the right arrow key to expand the method node so that a parameter list appears. Selecting the Add Parameter node adds a new parameter to the method. Once added, the new parameter can be navigated to by using the arrow keys.

> **NOTE** *You might notice that the list of properties that are included in the Class Details view in Figure 10-4 is a little different than the properties in the Class Diagram in Figure 10-2. The reason for this is that some properties shown in Class Details are represented as lines in the Class Diagram. Take the Orders property, for example. In the Class Diagram, this is shown as a line connecting Customer to Order. However, it is actually implemented as a collection property and that is what is visible through the Class Details view.*

THE PROPERTIES WINDOW

Although the Class Details window is useful it does not provide all the information required for entity components. For example, properties can be marked as read-only, which is not displayed in the Class Details window. The Properties window in Figure 10-5 shows the full list of attributes for the `Orders` property of the `Customer` class.

Figure 10-5 shows that the `Orders` property is read-only and that it is not static. It also shows that this property is defined in the `Customer.cs` file. With partial classes, a class may be separated over multiple files. When a partial class is selected, the File Name property shows all files defining that class as a comma-delimited list. Although some of these properties are read-only in this window, they can, of course, be adjusted within the appropriate code file.

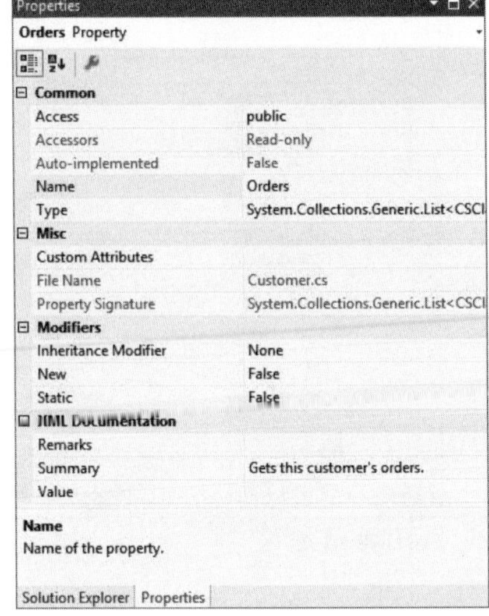

FIGURE 10-5

LAYOUT

Because the class diagram is all about visualizing classes, you have several toolbar controls at your disposal to create the layout of the entities on the Designer. Figure 10-6 shows the full toolbar that appears as part of the designer surface. The default toolbar contains fewer buttons.

The first three buttons control the size of the elements on the design surface by allowing you to zoom in and out of the entities. The next button is used to display the Class Details windows. The next three buttons modify the layout of entity components. From left to right, the buttons are Group by Kind, Group by Access, and Sort Alphabetically.

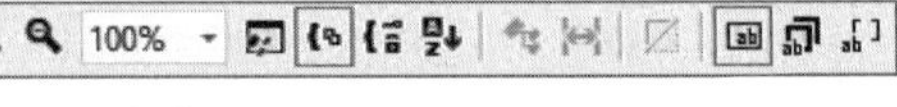

FIGURE 10-6

The next two buttons are used to automate the process of arranging the entities on the design surface. On the left is the Layout Diagram button, which automatically repositions the entities on the design surface. It also minimizes the entities, hiding all components. The right button, Adjust Shapes Width, adjusts the size of the entities so that all components are fully visible. If a single component is selected, the Adjust Shapes Width button adjusts the width of only that component. If no components are selected, the width of all components are adjusted.

Entity components, such as fields, properties, and methods, can be hidden using the Hide Member button.

The display style of entity components can be adjusted using the next three buttons. The left button, Display Name, sets the display style to show only the name of the component. This can be extended to show both the name and the component type using the Display Name and Type button. The right button, Display Full Signature, sets the display style to be the full component signature. This is often the most useful; although, it takes more space to display.

EXPORTING DIAGRAMS

Quite often, the process to design which classes will be part of the system architecture is a part of a much larger design or review process. Therefore, it is a common requirement to export the class diagram for inclusion in reports.

You can export a class diagram either by right-clicking the context menu from any space on the Class Designer or via the Class Diagram menu. Either way, selecting the Export Diagram as Image menu item opens a dialog prompting you to select an image format and filename for saving the diagram.

You can also copy and paste an image directly into Microsoft Word or a drawing program such as Visio. To do this, you must first select one or more classes on the diagram.

Lastly, you can also print Class Diagrams directly from Visual Studio through the normal File ➪ Print menu option.

CODE GENERATION AND REFACTORING

One of the core goals of Visual Studio 2012 and the .NET Framework is to reduce the amount of code that developers have to write. This goal is achieved in two ways: Either reduce the total amount of code that has to be written or reduce the amount that actually has to be written manually. The first approach is supported through a rich set of base classes included in the .NET Framework. The second approach, reduce the amount of code that is written manually, is supported by the code generation and refactoring tools included with the Class Designer.

Drag-and-Drop Code Generation

Almost every action performed on the class diagram results in a change in the underlying source code and essentially provides some level of code generation. We've already covered a number of these changes, such as adding a property or method to a class in the Class Details window. However, some more advanced code generation actions can be performed by manipulating the class diagram.

As explained earlier in the chapter, you can use the Inheritance connector to establish an inheritance relationship between a parent class and an inheriting class. When you do this, the code file of the derived class is updated to reflect this change. However, when the parent class is abstract, as in the case of the `Product` class in Figure 10-7, the Class Designer can perform some additional analysis and code generation. If the parent class is an abstract class and contains any abstract members, those members are automatically implemented in the inheriting classes. This is shown in Figure 10-7 (right) where the abstract properties `Description`, `Price`, and `SKU` have been added to the `Book` class. The method `GetInventory` was not implemented because it was not marked as abstract.

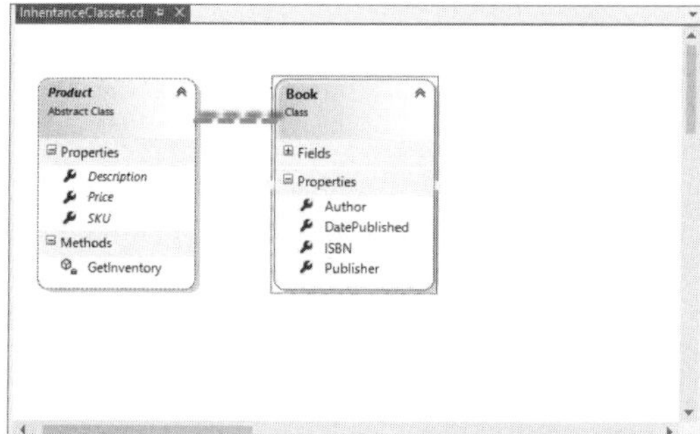

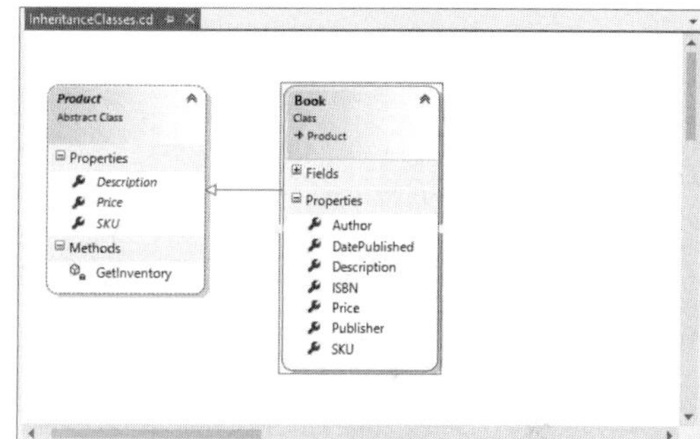

FIGURE 10-7

The Inheritance connector can be used in one more way that results in automatic code generation. In Figure 10-8 (left) an interface, ICrudActions, has been added to the diagram. When the Inheritance connector is dragged from a class to the interface, all the members of the interface are implemented on the class, as shown in Figure 10-8 (right).

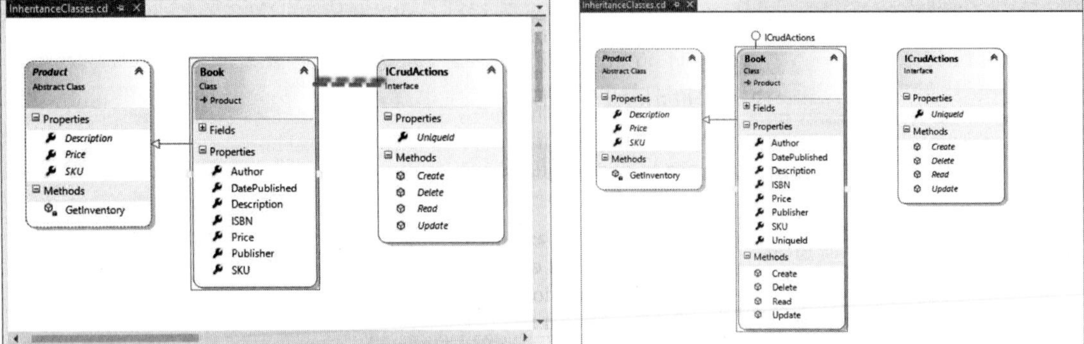

FIGURE 10-8

The following code is automatically generated when the ICrudActions interface is added to the `Book` class.

C#

```
#region ICrudActions Members
    public Guid UniqueId
    {
        get
        {
            throw new NotImplementedException();
        }
        set
        {
            throw new NotImplementedException();
        }
    }
    public void Create()
    {
        throw new NotImplementedException();
    }

    public void Update()
    {
        throw new NotImplementedException();
    }

    public void Read()
    {
        throw new NotImplementedException();
    }

    public void Delete()
    {
        throw new NotImplementedException();
    }
#endregion
```

VB

```
#Region ICrudActions Members
    Public Property UniqueId As Guid
        Get
            throw new NotImplementedException()
```

```
        End Get
        Set
            throw new NotImplementedException()
        End Set
    End Property

    Public Sub Create()
        throw new NotImplementedException()
    End Sub

    Public Sub Update()
        throw new NotImplementedException()
    End Sub

    Public Sub Read()
        throw new NotImplementedException()
    End Sub

    Public Sub Delete()
        throw new NotImplementedException()
    End Sub
#End Region
```

IntelliSense Code Generation

The rest of the code generation functions in the Class Designer are available under the somewhat unintuitively named IntelliSense submenu. Because these code generation functions apply only to classes, this menu is visible only when a class or abstract class has been selected on the diagram. The two code generation functions included on this menu are Implement Abstract Class and Override Members.

The Implement Abstract Class function ensures that all abstract members from the base class are implemented in the inheriting class. To access this function, right-click the inheriting class, choose IntelliSense, and then choose Implement Abstract Class.

Somewhat related is the Override Members function, which is used to select public properties or methods from a base class that you would like to override. To access this function, right-click the inheriting class, choose IntelliSense, and then choose Override Members. The dialog box shown in Figure 10-9 displays, populated with the base classes and any properties or methods that have not already been overridden.

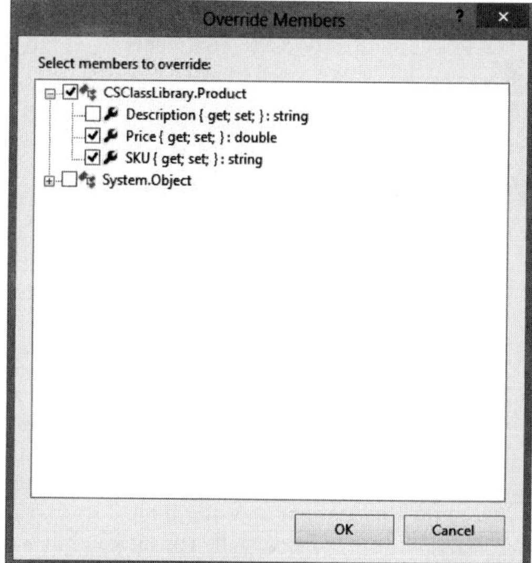

FIGURE 10-9

Refactoring with the Class Designer

In Chapter 8, "Code Snippets and Refactoring," you saw how Visual Studio 2012 provides support for refactoring code from the code editor window. The Class Designer also exposes a number of these refactoring functions when working with entities on a class diagram.

The refactoring functions in the Class Designer are available by right-clicking an entity, or any of its members, and choosing an action from the Refactor submenu. The following refactoring functions are available:

- **Rename Types and Type Members:** Allows you to rename a type or a member of a type on the class diagram or in the Properties window. Renaming a type or type member changes it in all code locations where the old name appeared. You can even ensure that the change is propagated to any comments or static strings.
- **Encapsulate Field:** Enables you to quickly create a new property from an existing field and then seamlessly update your code with references to the new property.
- **Reorder or Remove Parameters (C# only):** Enables you to change the order of method parameters in types or to remove a parameter from a method.
- **Extract Interface (C# only):** You can extract the members of a type into a new interface. This function allows you to select only a subset of the members that you want to extract into the new interface.

> **NOTE** *You can also use the standard Windows Cut, Copy, and Paste actions to copy and move members between types.*

MODELING POWER TOYS FOR VISUAL STUDIO

Although the Class Designer is a useful tool for designing and visualizing a class hierarchy, it can be cumbersome and unwieldy when trying to work with large diagrams. To ease this burden you can either break up the diagram into multiple class diagrams, or install the Modeling Power Toys for Visual Studio 2012.

Modeling Power Toys is a free add-in to Visual Studio that extends the functionality of the Class Designer in several ways. It includes enhancements that enable you to work more effectively with large diagrams including panning and zooming, improved scrolling, and diagram search. It also provides functions that address some of the limitations of the Class Designer such as the ability to create nested types and new derived classes and display XML comments.

The add-in, including source code, is available from `http://modeling.codeplex.com/`. The download includes an MSI file for easy installation.

Visualization Enhancements

The Modeling Power Toys for Visual Studio 2012 provides some useful enhancements for visualizing and working with large class diagrams. The diagram search feature is one of the more useful; it allows you to search the entities on a diagram for a specific search term. The search dialog, shown in Figure 10-10, is invoked via the standard Find menu item or Ctrl+F shortcut.

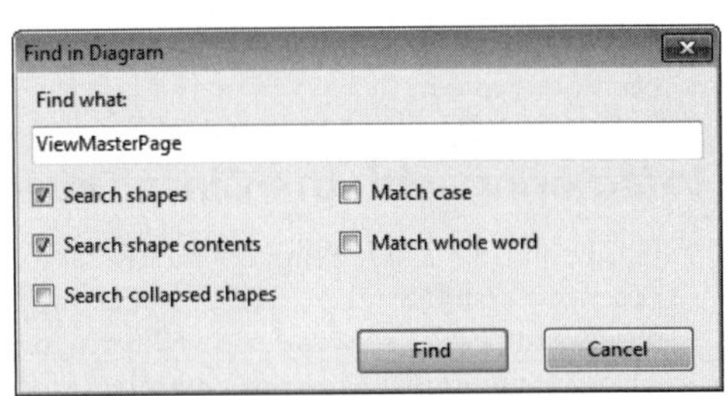

FIGURE 10-10

Another useful tool for large diagrams is the panning tool, which provides an easy way to see an overview of the entire diagram and navigate to different areas without changing the zoom level. You can invoke this tool by clicking an icon that appears in the bottom right of the window, which displays the panning window, as shown in Figure 10-11.

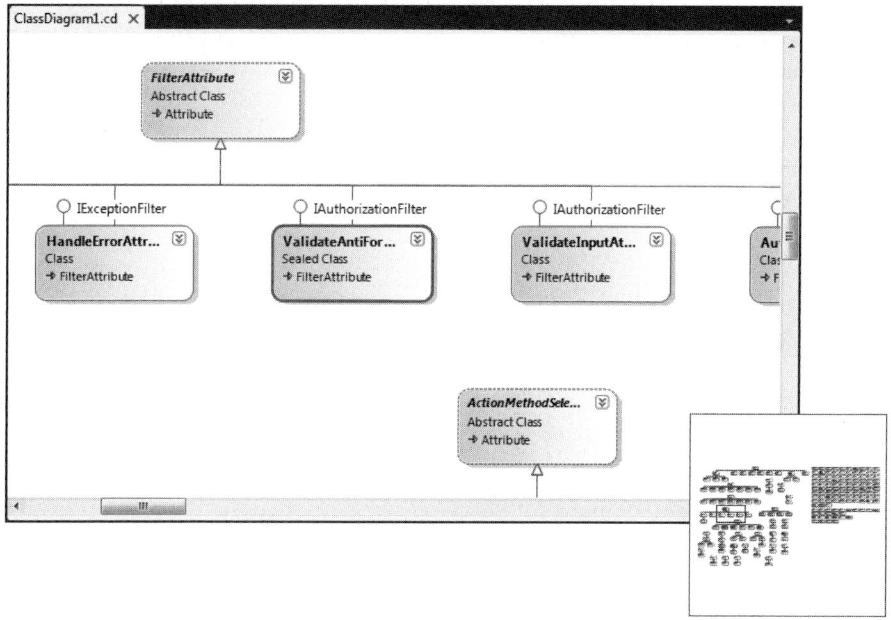

FIGURE 10-11

The Modeling Power Toys also allows quite fine control over what is displayed on the diagram via the filtering options. These are available via the Class Diagram menu, and include

- **Hide Inheritance Lines:** Hides all inheritance lines in the selection.
- **Show All Inheritance Lines:** Shows all hidden inheritance lines on the diagram.
- **Show All Public Associations:** Shows all possible public associations on the diagram.
- **Show All Associations:** Shows all possible associations on the diagram.
- **Show Associations As Members:** Shows all association lines as members.
- **Hide Private:** Hides all private members.
- **Hide Private and Internal:** Hides all private and/or internal members.
- **Show Only Public:** Hides all members except for public; all hidden public members are shown.
- **Show Only Public and Protected:** Hides all members except for public and protected; hidden public and/or protected members are shown.
- **Show All Members:** Shows all hidden members.

Functionality Enhancements

Modeling Power Toys includes a number of enhancements that address some of the functional limitations of the Class Designer. Though the Class Designer can display nested types, you cannot create them using the design surface.

This constraint is addressed by the Modeling Power Toys by enabling you to add nested types including classes, enumerations, structures, or delegates. You can also easily add several new member types, such as read-only properties and indexers.

There are also some improvements around working with interfaces. Often it is difficult to understand what members of a class have been used to implement an interface. The Modeling Power Toys simplifies this by adding a Select Members menu item to the interface lollipop label on a type. For example, in Figure 10-12, the Select Members command is invoked on the ICrudActions interface.

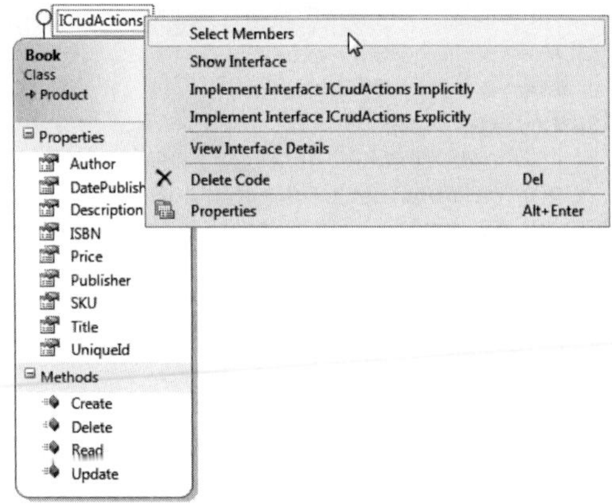

FIGURE 10-12

In addition to those mentioned here, many other minor enhancements and functionality improvements are provided by the Modeling Power Toys that add up to make it a useful extension.

SUMMARY

This chapter focused on the Class Designer, one of the best tools built into Visual Studio 2012 for generating and understanding code. The design surface and supporting toolbars and windows provide a rich user interface with which complex class hierarchies and associations can be modeled and designed.

PART III
Digging Deeper

11

Unit Testing

WHAT'S IN THIS CHAPTER?

- Generating a test harness from existing code
- Making assertions about the behavior of your code
- Executing custom code during test life-cycle events
- Creating data-driven tests
- Testing private members and code contracts
- Managing lists of tests

Application testing is one of the most important parts of writing software. Research into the costs of software maintenance have revealed that a software defect can cost up to 25 times more to fix if it makes it to a production environment than if it had been caught during development. At the same time, a lot of testing involves repetitive, dull, and error-prone work that must be undertaken every time you make a change to your code base. The easiest way to counter this is to produce repeatable automated tests that can be executed by a computer on demand. This chapter looks at a specific type of automated testing that focuses on individual components, or units, of a system. Having a suite of automated unit tests gives you the power to verify that your individual components all work as specified even after making radical changes to them.

Visual Studio 2012 has a built-in framework for authoring, executing, and reporting on test cases. Many of the testing tools that were once only included in the Team System Edition of Visual Studio are now available in the Professional Edition. This means a much wider audience can more easily obtain the benefits of automated, robust testing. This chapter focuses on creating, configuring, running, and managing a suite of unit tests as well as adding support to drive the tests from a set of data.

YOUR FIRST TEST CASE

Writing test cases is not a task easily automated because the test cases must mirror the functionality of the software developed. In fact, there are solid arguments against automating all but the simplest of unit tests. However, at several steps in the process, code stubs can be generated by a tool. To illustrate this, start with a straightforward snippet of code to learn to write test cases that fully exercise the code. Setting the scene is a `Subscription` class with a public property called `CurrentStatus`, which returns the status of the current subscription as an enumeration value:

VB

```
Public Class Subscription
    Public Enum Status
        Temporary
        Financial
        Unfinancial
        Suspended
    End Enum

    Public Property PaidUpTo As Nullable(Of Date)

    Public ReadOnly Property CurrentStatus As Status
        Get
            If Not Me.PaidUpTo.HasValue Then Return Status.Temporary
            If Me.PaidUpTo > Now Then
                Return Status.Financial
            Else
                If Me.PaidUpTo >= Now.AddMonths(-3) Then
                    Return Status.Unfinancial
                Else
                    Return Status.Suspended
                End If
            End If
        End Get
    End Property
End Class
```

C#

```
public class Subscription
{
    public enum Status
    {
        Temporary,
        Financial,
        Unfinancial,
        Suspended
    }

    public DateTime? PaidUpTo { get; set; }

    public Status CurrentStatus
    {
        get
        {
            if (this.PaidUpTo.HasValue == false)
                return Status.Temporary;
            if (this.PaidUpTo > DateTime.Today)
                return Status.Financial;
            else
            {
                if (this.PaidUpTo >= DateTime.Today.AddMonths(-3))
                    return Status.Unfinancial;
                else
                    return Status.Suspended;
            }
        }
    }
}
```

As you can see from the code snippet, four code paths need to be tested for the CurrentStatus property. To test this property you create a separate SubscriptionTest test class in a new test project, into which you add a test method that contains the code necessary to instantiate a Subscription object, set the PaidUpTo property, and check that the CurrentStatus property contains the correct result. Then you keep adding test methods until all the code paths through the CurrentStatus property have been executed and tested.

In Visual Studio 2010, there was a wizard that generated unit tests for a given tasks. For a number of reasons, this functionality has been removed for Visual Studio 2012. As a result, the creation of proper unit test code is now left in the hands of the developer.

Although Visual Studio no longer supports the automatic generation of unit tests, it does provide a run-time engine that can run the test cases, monitor its progress, and report on any outcome from the test. Therefore, all you need to do is write the code to test the property in question.

The lack of automated unit test generation means that the developer has to know what makes a particular method a unit test. To see the basic template of a test class, make sure that the test project is selected in Solution Explorer and then select Project ➪ Add Unit Test. This creates a test class and a single test method. The Unit Test template includes just a basic unit test class containing just a single method, shown in the code sample below. For this example, the test class has been named SubscriptionTest (as opposed to the default UnitTest1) to indicate the class being tested:

VB

```
Imports Microsoft.VisualStudio.TestTools.UnitTesting

<TestClass()>
Public Class SubscriptionTest


    <TestMethod()>
    Public Sub TestMethod1()
    End Sub
End Class
```

C#

```
using System;
using Microsoft.VisualStudio.TestTools.UnitTesting;

[TestClass]
public class SubscriptionTest
{

    [TestMethod]
    public void TestMethod1()
    {
    }
}
```

While there are a number of techniques that can be used to write your own unit tests, there are two main ideas that you should keep in mind. One is that, given a large number of unit tests in a project, it can quickly become difficult to manage them. To address this issue, it is suggested that a naming convention be used. As you might expect, there are many different conventions that can be used, but a popular one is MethodName_StateUnderTest_ExpectedBehavior. This simple naming convention ensures that test cases can easily be found and identified.

A second idea is to approach each test using an Arrange/Act/Assert paradigm. Start by setting up and initializing the values used in the test (the Arrange portion). Then execute the method being tested (Act). Finally, determine the outcome of the test (Assert). If you follow this approach, you end up with unit tests that look like the following:

VB

```
<TestMethod()>
Public Sub CurrentStatus_NothingPaidUpToDate_TemporaryStatus()
    ' Arrange
    Dim s as New Subscription()
    s.PaidUpTo = Nothing

    ' Act
    Dim actual as Subscription.Status = s.CurrentStatus

    ' Assert
    Assert.Inconclusive()
End Sub
```

C#

```
[TestMethod]
public void CurrentStatus_NullPaidUpToDate_TemporaryStatus()
{
    // Arrange
    Subscription s = new Subscription();
    s.PaidUpTo = null;

    // Act
    Subscription.Status actual = s.CurrentStatus;

    //Assert
    Assert.Inconclusive();
}
```

Before going any further, run this test case to see what happens by right-clicking in the code window and selecting Run Tests. The result is the Test Explorer, as shown in Figure 11-1.

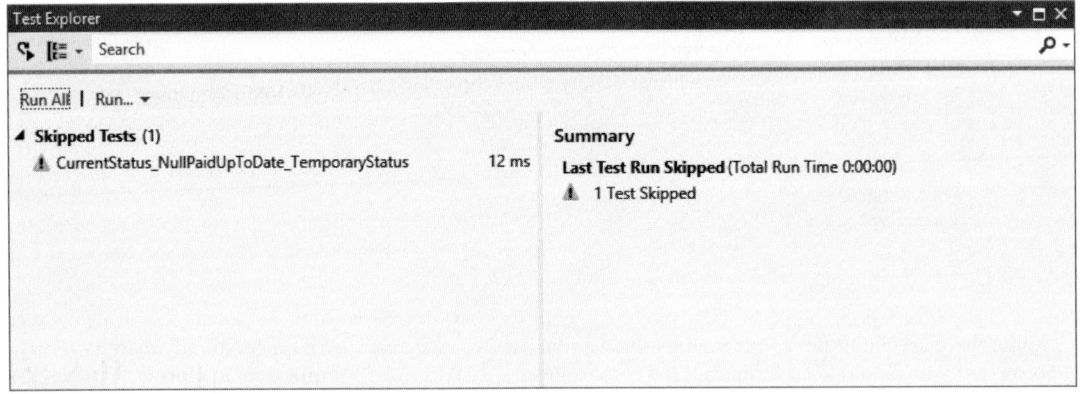

FIGURE 11-1

> **NOTE** *The context menu is just one way to select and run a test case. There is a Test menu that includes a Run submenu that allows for the execution of all or selected tests. Or you can open the Test Explorer window directly and run all or selected tests using the links (refer to Figure 11-1). In addition to each of these methods, you can also set breakpoints in your code and run test cases in the debugger by selecting one of the Debug Tests options from the main toolbar.*

You can see from Figure 11-1 that the test case has returned an inconclusive result. Essentially, this indicates either that a test is not complete or that the results should not be relied upon because changes may have been made that would make this test invalid.

You can get more information on the result of any particular test result by clicking it. Figure 11-2 shows the result of clicking the inconclusive result for the example. The results show basic information about the test, the result, and other useful environmental information such as the computer name, test execution duration, and start and end times.

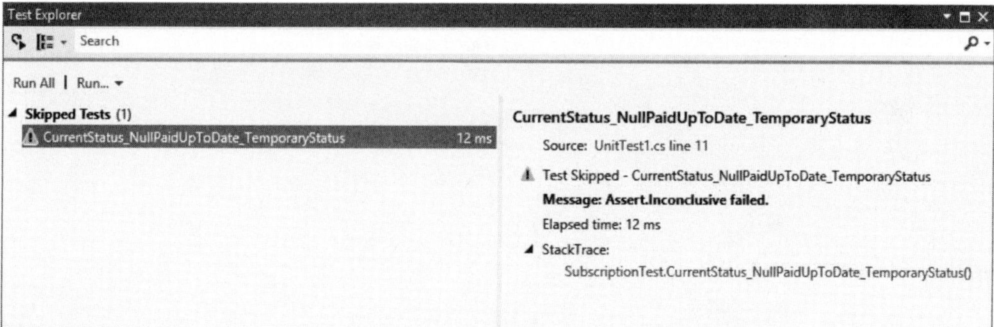

FIGURE 11-2

In creating this unit test, the `Assert.Inconclusive` statement was inserted by hand. To complete the unit test, it is necessary to actually perform the appropriate analysis of the results to ensure that the test passed. This is accomplished by replacing the `Assert.Inconclusive` statement with `Assert.AreEqual`, as shown in the following code:

VB

```
<TestMethod()>
    Public Sub CurrentStatusTest()
        Dim target As Subscription = New Subscription
        Dim actual As Subscription.Status
        actual = target.CurrentStatus
        Assert.AreEqual(Subscription.Status.Temporary, actual, _
                        "Subscription.CurrentStatus was not set correctly.")
    End Sub
```

C#

```
[TestMethod()]
public void CurrentStatusTest()
{
    Subscription target = new Subscription();
```

```
        Subscription.Status actual;
        actual = target.CurrentStatus;
        Assert.AreEqual(Subscription.Status.Temporary, actual,
                        "Subscription.CurrentStatus was not set correctly.");
    }
```

Although it is not apparent from the work you have done to this point, the completed tests are grouped into one of four categories: Failed Tests, Passed Tests, Skipped Tests, and Not Run Tests. It is possible to run all the tests, only the tests from a specific category, or just the tests that you select. The Run link at the top of the Test Explorer contains a drop-down where you can select the category of tests to run. To select individual tests to run, click the desired tests (using the standard Ctrl+click or Shift+Ctrl+click to add tests after the first one), and then right-click and choose Run Selected Tests. After you fix the code that caused the tests to fail, click the Run All button to rerun these test cases and produce a successful result, as shown in Figure 11-3.

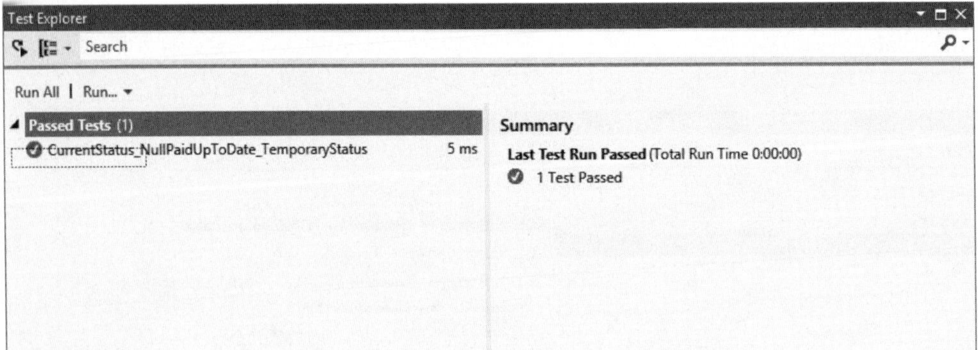

FIGURE 11-3

> **NOTE** *There is one thing to be aware of regarding unit tests. Put simply, the default behavior for a unit test method is to "pass." And the way that you change this behavior is by adding Assert statements to the method, the idea being that if one of the Assert statements file, the unit test is considered to have "failed." However, when you manually create a brand new unit test, there are no assertions present, which means that the unit test doesn't start out "failing." To address this, an* `Assert.Inconclusive` *is automatically placed into unit tests when they are created. When you remove the Assert.Inconclusive statement, you are indicating that the test case is complete.*

In this example, we have exercised only one code path, and you should add further test cases that fully exercise the other three. While you could add additional assertions to the one test method that you've created, this is not considered to be the best practice for writing unit tests. The general approach is to have each test method test one and only one thing. This means that (ideally) there is only one Assert in the method.

The reason for this is that more granular tests means that if the test fails, the cause is usually more readily apparent. Also, keep in mind that the method does not continue executing past the first failed Assert. Multiple assertions in a method just makes it a little more difficult to determine the cause of the failure. That having been said, it is common to have two or three assertions, and there is a parameter that can be passed into the Assert statement for the message that gets displayed if the test fails.

One of the differences between unit test creation in Visual Studio 2010 and 2012 is the `.testsettings` file. The `.testsettings` file is a Test Run Configuration file. This is an XML file that stores settings that control how a set of tests, called a test run, is executed. You can create and save multiple run configurations that represent different scenarios, and then make a specific run configuration active using the Test ➪ Select Active Test Run Configuration menu item. This defines which of the test run configurations should be used when tests are run.

In Visual Studio 2010, this file was created automatically and included in the solution where the text project resides. However, in Visual Studio 2012, the file is not created, as a way to improve the performance of testing. In fact, if you upgrade a Visual Studio 2010 test project to Visual Studio 2012, it is recommended that you remove the `.testsettings` file unless it is needed.

Identifying Tests Using Attributes

Before going any further with this scenario, take a step back to consider how testing is carried out within Visual Studio 2012. As mentioned earlier, all test cases must exist within test classes that reside in a test project. But what actually distinguishes a method, class, or project as containing test cases? Starting with the test project, if you look at the underlying XML project file, you can see that there is virtually no difference between a test project file and a normal class library project file. In fact, the only difference appears to be the project type: When this project is built, it simply outputs a standard .NET class library assembly. The key difference is that Visual Studio recognizes this as a test project and automatically analyzes it for any test cases to populate the various test windows.

Classes and methods used in the testing process are marked with an appropriate attribute. The attributes are used by the testing engine to enumerate all the test cases within a particular assembly.

TestClass

All test cases must reside within a test class that is appropriately marked with the `TestClass` attribute. Although it may appear that there is no reason for this attribute other than to align test cases with the class and member that they are testing, you later see some benefits associated with grouping test cases using a test class. For testing the `Subscription` class, a test class called `SubscriptionTest` was created and marked with the `TestClass` attribute. Because Visual Studio uses attributes to locate classes that contain test cases, the name of this class is irrelevant. However, adopting a naming convention, such as adding the Test suffix to the class being tested, makes it easier to manage a large number of test cases.

TestMethod

Individual test cases are marked with the `TestMethod` attribute, which is used by Visual Studio to enumerate the list of tests that can be executed. The `CurrentStatus_NullPaidUpToDate_TemporaryStatus` method in the `SubscriptionTest` class is marked with the `TestMethod` attribute. Again, the actual name of this method is irrelevant, because Visual Studio uses only the attributes. However, the method name is used in the various test windows when the test cases are listed, so it is useful for test methods to have meaningful names. This is especially true when reviewing test results.

Additional Test Attributes

As you have seen, the unit-testing subsystem within Visual Studio uses attributes to identify test cases. A number of additional properties can be set to provide further information about a test case. This information is then accessible either via the Properties window associated with a test case or within the other test windows. This section goes through the descriptive attributes that can be applied to a test method.

Description

Because test cases are listed by the test method name, a number of tests may have similar names, or names that are not descriptive enough to indicate what functionality they test. The `Description` attribute, which takes a `String` as its sole argument, can be applied to a test method to provide additional information about a test case.

Owner

The `Owner` attribute, which also takes a `String` argument, is useful for indicating who owns, wrote, or is currently working on a particular test case.

Priority

The `Priority` attribute, which takes an `Integer` argument, can be applied to a test case to indicate the relative importance of a test case. Though the testing framework does not use this attribute, it is useful for prioritizing test cases when you are determining the order in which failing, or incomplete, test cases are resolved.

TestCategories

The `TestCategory` attribute accepts a single `String` identifying one user-defined category for the test. Like the `Priority` attribute, the `TestCategory` attribute is essentially ignored by Visual Studio but is useful for sorting and grouping related items together. A test case may belong to many categories but must have a separate attribute for each one.

WorkItems

The `WorkItem` attribute can be used to link a test case to one or more work items in a work-item-tracking system such as Team Foundation Server. If you apply one or more `WorkItem` attributes to a test case, you can review the test case when making changes to existing functionality. You can read more about Team Foundation Server in Chapter 57, "Team Foundation Server."

Ignore

You can temporarily prevent a test method from running by applying the `Ignore` attribute to it. Test methods with the `Ignore` attribute will not be run and will not show up in the results list of a test run.

> **NOTE** *You can apply the* `Ignore` *attribute to a test class as well to switch off all the test methods within it.*

Timeout

A test case can fail for any number of reasons. A performance test, for example, might require a particular functionality to complete within a specified time frame. Instead of the tester writing complex multithreading tests that stop the test case when a particular timeout has been reached, you can apply the `Timeout` attribute to a test case with a timeout value in milliseconds, as shown in the following code. This ensures that the test case fails if that timeout is reached.

VB

```
<TestMethod()>
<Owner("Mike Minutillo")>
<Description("Tests the functionality of the Current Status Property")>
<Priority(3)>
```

```
<Timeout(10000)>
<TestCategory("Financial")>
Public Sub CurrentStatusTest()
    Dim target As Subscription = New Subscription
    Dim actual As Subscription.Status
    actual = target.CurrentStatus
    Assert.AreEqual(Subscription.Status.Temporary, actual, _
                    "Subscription.CurrentStatus was not set correctly.")
End Sub
```

C#

```
[TestMethod()]
[Owner("Mike Minutillo")]
[Description("Tests the functionality of the Current Status Method")]
[Priority(3)]
[Timeout(10000)]
[TestCategory("Financial")]
public void CurrentStatusTest()
{
    Subscription target = new Subscription();
    Subscription.Status actual;
    actual = target.CurrentStatus;
    Assert.AreEqual(Subscription.Status.Temporary, actual,
                    "Subscription.CurrentStatus was not set correctly.");
}
```

This snippet augments the original `CurrentStatusTest` method with some of these attributes to illustrate their usage. In addition to providing additional information about what the test case does and who wrote it, this code assigns the test case a priority of `3` and a category of `"Financial"`. Lastly, the code indicates that this test case should fail if it takes more than 10 seconds (10,000 milliseconds) to execute.

ASSERTING THE FACTS

So far, this chapter has examined the structure of the test environment and how test cases are nested within test classes in a test project. What remains is to look at the body of the test case and review how test cases either pass or fail. (When a test case is generated, you saw that an `Assert.Inconclusive` statement is added to the end of the test to indicate that it is incomplete.)

The idea behind unit testing is that you start with the system, component, or object in a known state, and then run a method, modify a property, or trigger an event. The testing phase comes at the end, when you need to validate that the system, component, or object is in the correct state. Alternatively, you may need to validate that the correct output was returned from a method or property. You do this by attempting to assert a particular condition. If this condition is not true, the testing system reports this result and ends the test case. A condition is asserted, not surprisingly, via the `Assert` class. There is also a `StringAssert` class and a `CollectionAssert` class, which provide additional assertions for dealing with `String` objects and collections of objects, respectively.

The Assert Class

The `Assert` class in the `UnitTesting` namespace, not to be confused with the `Debug.Assert` or `Trace.Assert` method in the `System.Diagnostics` namespace, is the primary class used to make assertions about a test case. The basic assertion has the following format:

VB

```
Assert.IsTrue(variableToTest, "Output message if this fails")
```

C#

```
Assert.IsTrue(variableToTest, "Output message if this fails");
```

As you can imagine, the first argument is the condition to be tested. If this is true, the test case continues operation. However, if it fails, the output message is emitted and the test case exits with a failed result.

This statement has multiple overloads whereby the output message can be omitted or `String` formatting parameters supplied. Because quite often you won't be testing a single positive condition, several additional methods simplify making assertions within a test case:

- `IsFalse`: Tests for a negative, or false, condition
- `AreEqual`: Tests whether two arguments have the same value
- `AreSame`: Tests whether two arguments refer to the same object
- `IsInstanceOfType`: Tests whether an argument is an instance of a particular type
- `IsNull`: Tests whether an argument is nothing

This list is not exhaustive — several more methods exist, including negative equivalents of those listed. Also, many of these methods have overloads that allow them to be invoked in several different ways.

The StringAssert Class

The `StringAssert` class does not provide any additional functionality that cannot be achieved with one or more assertions via the `Assert` class. However, it not only simplifies the test case code by making it clear that `String` assertions are being made; it also reduces the mundane tasks associated with testing for particular conditions. The additional assertions are as follows:

- `Contains`: Tests whether a `String` contains another `String`
- `DoesNotMatch`: Tests whether a `String` does not match a regular expression
- `EndsWith`: Tests whether a `String` ends with a particular `String`
- `Matches`: Tests whether a `String` matches a regular expression
- `StartsWith`: Tests whether a `String` starts with a particular `String`

The CollectionAssert Class

Similar to the `StringAssert` class, `CollectionAssert` is a helper class used to make assertions about a collection of items. Some of the assertions are as follows:

- `AllItemsAreNotNull`: Tests that none of the items in a collection is a null reference
- `AllItemsAreUnique`: Tests that no duplicate items exist in a collection
- `Contains`: Tests whether a collection contains a particular object
- `IsSubsetOf`: Tests whether a collection is a subset of another collection

The ExpectedException Attribute

Sometimes test cases have to execute paths of code that can cause exceptions to be raised. Though exception coding should be avoided, conditions exist where this might be appropriate. Instead of writing a test case that includes a `Try-Catch` block with an appropriate assertion to test that an exception was raised, you can mark the test case with an `ExpectedException` attribute. For example, change the `CurrentStatus` property to throw an exception if the `PaidUp` date is prior to the date the subscription opened, which in this case is a constant:

VB

```
Public Const SubscriptionOpenedOn As Date = #1/1/2000#
Public ReadOnly Property CurrentStatus As Status
    Get
        If Not Me.PaidUpTo.HasValue Then Return Status.Temporary
        If Me.PaidUpTo > Now Then
            Return Status.Financial
        Else
            If Me.PaidUpTo >= Now.AddMonths(-3) Then
                Return Status.Unfinancial
            ElseIf Me.PaidUpTo > SubscriptionOpenedOn Then
                Return Status.Suspended
            Else
                Throw New ArgumentOutOfRangeException( _
          "Paid up date is not valid as it is before the subscription opened.")
            End If
        End If
    End Get
End Property
```

C#

```
public static readonly DateTime SubscriptionOpenedOn = new DateTime(2000, 1, 1);
public Status CurrentStatus
{
    get
    {
        if (this.PaidUpTo.HasValue == false)
            return Status.Temporary;
        if (this.PaidUpTo > DateTime.Today)
            return Status.Financial;
        else
        {
            if (this.PaidUpTo >= DateTime.Today.AddMonths(-3))
                return Status.Unfinancial;
            else if (this.PaidUpTo >= SubscriptionOpenedOn)
                return Status.Suspended;
            else
                throw new ArgumentOutOfRangeException(
             "Paid up date is not valid as it is before the subscription opened");
        }
    }
}
```

Using the same procedure as before, you can create a separate test case for testing this code path, as shown in the following example:

VB

```
<TestMethod()>
<ExpectedException(GetType(ArgumentOutOfRangeException),
    "Argument exception not raised for invalid PaidUp date.")>
Public Sub CurrentStatusExceptionTest()
    Dim target As Subscription = New Subscription

    target.PaidUpTo = Subscription.SubscriptionOpenedOn.AddMonths(-1)

    Dim expected = Subscription.Status.Temporary

    Assert.AreEqual(expected, target.CurrentStatus, _
                    "This assertion should never actually be evaluated")
End Sub
```

C#

```
[TestMethod()]
[ExpectedException(typeof(ArgumentOutOfRangeException),
   "Argument Exception not raised for invalid PaidUp date.")]
public void CurrentStatusExceptionTest()
{
    Subscription target = new Subscription();
    target.PaidUpTo = Subscription.SubscriptionOpenedOn.AddMonths(-1);

    var expected = Subscription.Status.Temporary;

    Assert.AreEqual(expected, target.CurrentStatus,
        "This assertion should never actually be evaluated");
}
```

The `ExpectedException` attribute not only catches any exception raised by the test case it also ensures that the type of exception matches the type expected. If no exception is raised by the test, case, this attribute causes the test to fail.

INITIALIZING AND CLEANING UP

There are occasions where you have to write a lot of setup code, code that is executed whenever you run a test case. For example, where a unit test uses a database, that database should be returned to its initial state after each test to ensure that the test cases are completely repeatable. This is also true for unit tests that modify other resources such as the filesystem. Visual Studio provides support for writing methods that can be used to initialize and clean up around test cases. (Again, attributes are used to mark the appropriate methods that should be used to initialize and clean up the test cases.)

The attributes for initializing and cleaning up around test cases are broken down into three levels: those that apply to individual tests, those that apply to an entire test class, and those that apply to an entire test project.

TestInitialize and TestCleanup

As their names suggest, the `TestInitialize` and `TestCleanup` attributes indicate methods that should be run before and after each test case within a particular test class. These methods are useful for allocating and subsequently freeing any resources needed by all test cases in the test class.

ClassInitialize and ClassCleanup

Sometimes, instead of setting up and cleaning up after each test, it can be easier to ensure that the environment is in the correct state at the beginning and end of running an entire test class. Previously, we explained that test classes are a useful mechanism for grouping test cases; this is where you put that knowledge to use. Test cases can be grouped into test classes that contain one method marked with the `ClassInitialize` attribute and another marked with the `ClassCleanup` attribute. These methods must both be marked as `static`, and the one marked with `ClassInitialize` must take exactly one parameter that is of type `UnitTesting.TestContext`, which is explained later in this chapter.

AssemblyInitialize and AssemblyCleanup

The final level of initialization and cleanup attributes is at the assembly, or project, level. Methods intended to initialize the environment before running an entire test project, and cleaning up after, can be marked with the AssemblyInitialize and AssemblyCleanup attributes, respectively. Because these methods apply to any test case within the test project, only a single method can be marked with each of these attributes. Like the class-level equivalents, these methods must both be static, and the one marked with AssemblyInitialize must take a parameter of type UnitTesting.TestContext.

For both the assembly-level and class-level attributes, it is important to remember that even if only one test case is run, the methods marked with these attributes will also be run.

> **NOTE** *It is a good idea to put the methods marked with* AssemblyInitialize *and* AssemblyCleanup *together into their own test class to make them easy to find. If there is more than one method marked with either of these attributes, then running any tests in the project results in a run-time error.*

TESTING CONTEXT

When you write test cases, the testing engine can assist you in a number of ways, including by managing sets of data so that you can run a test case with a range of data, and by enabling you to output additional information for the test case to aid in debugging. This functionality is available through the TestContext object generated within a test class and passed into the AssemblyInitialize and ClassInitialize methods.

Data

The CurrentStatus_NullPaidUpToDate_TemporaryStatus method written in the first section of this chapter tested only a single path through the CurrentStatus property. To fully test this property, you could have written additional methods, each with their own setup and assertions. However, this process is fairly repetitive and would need to be updated if you ever changed the structure of the CurrentStatus property. An alternative is to provide a DataSource for the CurrentStatus_NullPaidUpToDate_TemporaryStatus method whereby each row of data tests a different path through the property. To add appropriate data to this method, use the following process:

1. Create a LocalDB database and database table to store the various test data. (The details on how to do this can be found in Chapter 27, "Visual Database Tools.") In this case, create a database called LoadTest with a table called Subscription_CurrentStatus. The table has an Identity bigint column called Id, a nullable datetime column called PaidUp, and an nvarchar(20) column called Status.
2. Add appropriate data values to the table to cover all paths through the code. Test values for the CurrentStatus property are shown in Figure 11-4.
3. Add a DataSource attribute to the test case. This attribute is used by the testing engine to load the appropriate data from the specified table. This data is then exposed to the test case through the TestContext object.

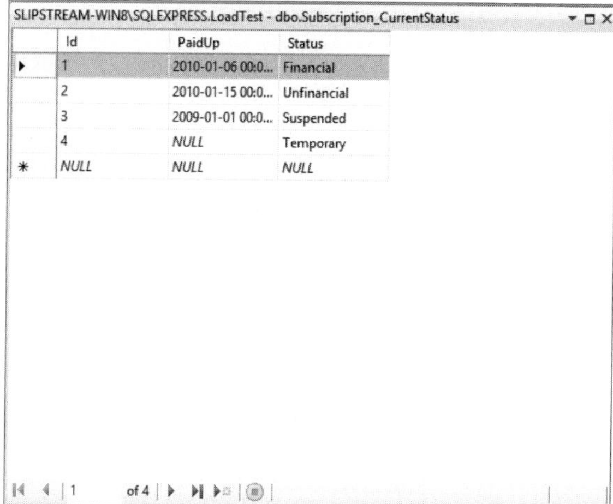

FIGURE 11-4

> **NOTE** *If you are using a LocalDB database or an Excel file, you'll also want to add a* `DeploymentItem` *attribute. This ensures that the data source will be copied if the test assembly is deployed to another location.*

4. Modify the test case to access data from the `TestContext` object, and use the data to drive the test case, which gives you the following `CurrentStatus_NullPaidUpToDate_TemporaryStatus` method:

VB

```
<DataSource("System.Data.SqlServerCe.4.0", _
    "data source=|DataDirectory|\LoadTest.sdf", _
    "Subscription_CurrentStatus", DataAccessMethod.Sequential)> _
<DeploymentItem("SubscriptionTest\LoadTest.sdf")> _
<TestMethod()>_
Public Sub CurrentStatus_NullPaidUpToDate_TemporaryStatus()
    Dim target As Subscription = New Subscription
    If Not IsDBNull(Me.TestContext.DataRow.Item("PaidUp")) Then
        target.PaidUpTo = CType(Me.TestContext.DataRow.Item("PaidUp"), Date)
    End If
    Dim val As Subscription.Status = _
        CType([Enum].Parse(GetType(Subscription.Status), _
         CStr(Me.TestContext.DataRow.Item("Status"))), Subscription.Status)

    Assert.AreEqual(val, target.CurrentStatus, _
        "Subscripiton.CurrentStatus was not set correctly.")
End Sub
```

C#

```
[DataSource("System.Data.SqlServerCe.4.0",
    "data source=|DataDirectory|\\LoadTests.sdf",
    "Subscription_CurrentStatus",
    DataAccessMethod.Sequential)]
[DeploymentItem("SubscriptionTest\\LoadTests.sdf")]
[TestMethod()]
public void CurrentStatus_NullPaidUpToDate_TemporaryStatus()
{
    var target = new Subscription();
    var date = this.TestContext.DataRow["PaidUp"] as DateTime?;
    if (date != null)
    {
      target.PaidUpTo = date;
    }

    var val = Enum.Parse(typeof(Subscription.Status),
      this.TestContext.DataRow["Status"] as string);

    Assert.AreEqual(val, target.CurrentStatus,
      "Subscription.CurrentStatus was not set correctly.");

}
```

> **NOTE** *The value of the first parameter in the* `DataSource` *attribute depends on the version of SQL Server CE that you have installed on your system. The code presumes that you're using version 4.0.*

When this test case is executed, the `CurrentStatus_NullPaidUpToDate_TemporaryStatus` method is executed four times (once for each row of data in the database table). Each time it is executed, a `DataRow` object is retrieved and exposed to the test method via the `TestContext.DataRow` property. If the logic within the `CurrentStatus` property changes, you can add a new row to the `Subscription_CurrentStatus` table to test any code paths that may have been created.

Before moving on, take one last look at the `DataSource` attribute that was applied to the `CurrentStatus_NullPaidUpToDate_TemporaryStatus` method. This attribute takes four arguments, the first three of which are used to determine which `DataTable` needs to be extracted. The remaining argument is a `DataAccessMethod` enumeration, which determines the order in which rows are returned from the `DataTable`. By default, this is `Sequential`, but it can be changed to `Random` so the order is different every time the test is run. This is particularly important when the data is representative of end user data but does not have to be processed in any particular order.

> **NOTE** *Data-driven tests are not just limited to database tables; they can be driven by Excel spreadsheets or even from Comma-Separated Values (CSV) files.*

Writing Test Output

Writing unit tests is all about automating the process of testing an application. Because of this, these test cases can be executed as part of a build process, perhaps even on a remote computer. This means that the normal output windows, such as the console, are not a suitable place for outputting test-related information. Clearly, you also don't want test-related information interspersed throughout the debugging or trace information being generated by the application. For this reason, there is a separate channel for writing test-related information so that it can be viewed alongside the test results.

The `TestContext` object exposes a `WriteLine` method that takes a `String` and a series of `String.Format` arguments that can be used to output information to the results for a particular test. For example, adding the following line to the `CurrentStatusDataTest` method generates additional information with the test results:

VB

```
TestContext.WriteLine("No exceptions thrown for test id {0}", _
    CInt(Me.TestContext.DataRow.Item(0)))
```

C#

```
TestContext.WriteLine("No exceptions thrown for test id {0}",
                this.TestContext.DataRow[0]);
```

> **NOTE** *Although you should use the* `TestContext.WriteLine` *method to capture details about your test executions, the Visual Studio test tools will collect anything written to the standard error and standard output streams and add that data to the test results.*

After the test run is completed, the Test Explorer window is displayed, listing all the test cases that were executed in the test run along with their results. Figure 11-5 shows this run with the completed (and passing) unit tests.

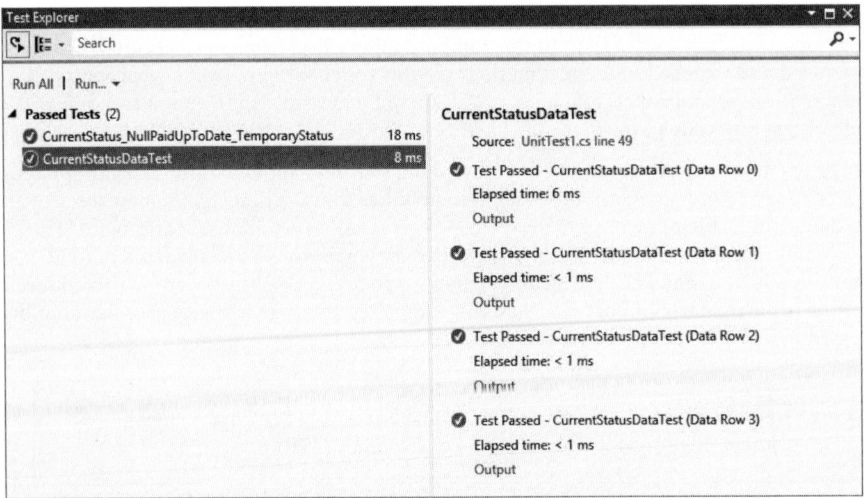

FIGURE 11-5

You might notice in Figure 11-5 that there is a link called Output. By clicking on this link you can go directly to the Test Output for the test. And in the Test Output, you can see in the Standard Output section in Figure 11-6 the output from the `WriteLine` method you added to the test method. Although you added only one line to the test method, the `WriteLine` method was executed for each row in the database table. And because each of the data-driven tests has its own test results, the line appears in each of them.

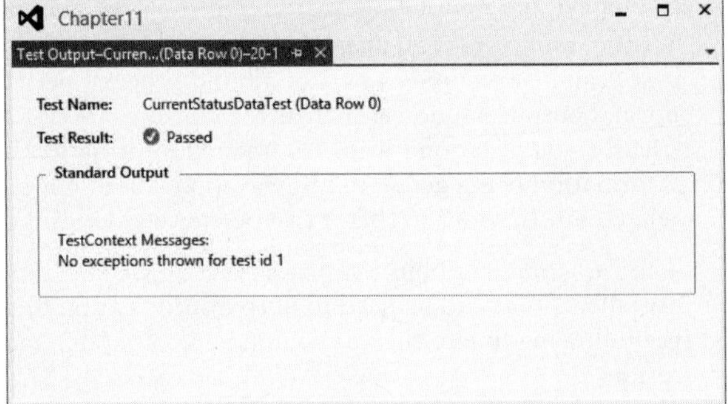

FIGURE 11-6

ADVANCED UNIT TESTING

Up until now, you have seen how to write and execute unit tests. This section examines how you can add custom properties to a test case, and how you can use the same framework to test private methods and properties.

Custom Properties

The testing framework provides a number of test attributes that you can apply to a method to record additional information about a test case. This information can be edited via the Properties window and updates the appropriate attributes on the test method. At times you might want to drive your test methods by specifying your own properties, which can also be set using the Properties window. To do this, add `TestProperty` attributes to the test method. For example, the following code adds two attributes to the test method to enable you to specify an arbitrary date and an expected status. This might be convenient for ad hoc testing using the Test View and Properties window:

VB

```
<TestMethod()>
<TestProperty("SpecialDate", "1/1/2008")>
<TestProperty("SpecialStatus", "Suspended")>
```

```
Public Sub SpecialCurrentStatusTest()
    Dim target As New Subscription
    target.PaidUpTo = CType(Me.TestContext.Properties.Item("SpecialDate"), _
        Date)
    Dim val As Subscription.Status = _
        [Enum].Parse(GetType(Subscription.Status), _
        CStr(Me.TestContext.Properties.Item("SpecialStatus")))
    Assert.AreEqual(val, target.CurrentStatus, _
        "Correct status not set for Paidup date {0}", target.PaidUpTo)
End Sub
```

C#

```
[TestMethod]
[TestProperty("SpecialDate", "1/1/2008")]
[TestProperty("SpecialStatus", "Suspended")]
public void SpecialCurrentStatusTest()
{
    var target = new Subscription();

    target.PaidUpTo = this.TestContext.Properties["SpecialDate"] as DateTime?;
    var val = Enum.Parse(typeof(Subscription.Status),
        this.TestContext.Properties["SpecialStatus"] as string);

    Assert.AreEqual(val, target.CurrentStatus,
        "Correct status not set for Paidup date {0}", target.PaidUpTo);

}
```

> **NOTE** *In earlier versions of Visual Studio, the* `TestContext.Properties` *dictionary was not automatically filled in and you had to do this by hand in your* `TestInitialize` *method. In Visual Studio 2010 this was all handled for you. However, with some of the unit test simplifications found in Visual Studio 2012, you are back to coding the values by hand.*

Testing Private Members

One of the selling points of unit testing is that it is particularly effective for testing the internals of your class to ensure that they function correctly. The assumption here is that if each of your components works in isolation, there is a better chance that they will work together correctly; and in fact, you can use unit testing to test classes working together. However, you might wonder how well the unit-testing framework handles testing private methods.

One of the features of the .NET Framework is the capability to reflect over any type that has been loaded into memory and to execute any member regardless of its accessibility. This functionality does come at a performance cost because the reflection calls obviously include an additional level of redirection, which can prove costly if done frequently. Nonetheless, for testing, reflection enables you to call into the inner workings of a class and not worry about the potential performance penalties for making those calls.

The other, more significant issue with using reflection to access nonpublic members of a class is that the code to do so is somewhat messy. Although Visual Studio 2010 generated a wrapper class to simplify the testing of private methods, this functionality is not present in Visual Studio 2012. However, you can still utilize reflection to accomplish the same goal. On the `Subscription` class, let's set up for the test by returning to the `CurrentStatus` property and change its access from `public` to `private`.

Back in the unit test, modify the body so that it looks like the following:

VB

```
<TestMethod(), _
 DeploymentItem("Subscriptions.dll")> _
Public Sub Private CurrentStatusTest()
    ' Arrange
    Dim s = new Subscription()
    s.PaidUpTo = null

    ' Act
    Dim t = s.GetType()
    Dim result As Object
    Result =  t.InvokeMember("CurrentStatus", BindingFlags.GetProperty |
       BindingFlags.Instance |BindingFlags.Public | BindingFlags.NonPublic, null, s, null)

    ' Assert
    Assert.IsInstanceOfType(result, GetType(Subscription.Status))
    Assert.AreEqual(Subscription.Status.Temporary, Cast(result, Subscription.Status))

End Sub
```

C#

```
[TestMethod()]
[DeploymentItem("Subscriptions.dll")]
public void Private CurrentStatusTest()
{
    // Arrange
    Subscription s = new Subscription();
    s.PaidUpTo = null;

    // Act
    Type t = s.GetType();
    object result =  t.InvokeMember("CurrentStatus", BindingFlags.GetProperty |
       BindingFlags.Instance |BindingFlags.Public | BindingFlags.NonPublic, null, s, null);

    // Assert
    Assert.IsInstanceOfType(result, typeof(Subscription.Status));
    Assert.AreEqual(Subscription.Status.Temporary, (Subscription.Status)result);
}
```

As you can see, the preceding example uses reflection, in the form of the `InvokeMember` method. Specifically, it retrieves the type (that would be the Subscription class) and then calls `InvokeMember` to retrieve (the `GetProperty` binding flag) the `CurrentStatus` property value. The result is then asserted to be of the type `Subscription.Status` and equal to `Temporary`.

TESTING CODE CONTRACTS

If you are using the Code Contracts feature described in Chapter 13, "Code Consistency Tools," then you might want to write tests that verify the behavior of your contracts. The simplest way to do this is to open the Code Contracts project properties page and uncheck the Assert on Contract Failure check box. When you do this the Code Contracts API raises exceptions instead of causing Assertion failures. You can check for these exceptions with an `ExpectedException` attribute if you know the type of exception to expect. By default, the Code Contracts tools generate the exceptions that will be thrown, and their type cannot be known at run time. Many of the contract methods have an overload that accepts an exception type as a generic parameter.

Here is a simple class that performs a mathematical operation on positive integers and a unit test to check the case where a negative number is passed in:

VB

```
Class Calculator
  Public Function Factorial(ByVal n As Integer) As Integer
    Contract.Requires(Of ArgumentOutOfRangeException)(n >= 0, "n")

    If n = 0 Then Return 1
    Return n * Factorial(n - 1)

  End Function
End Class


<TestMethod(), ExpectedException(GetType(ArgumentOutOfRangeException))>
Public Sub NegativeTest()

  Dim generator As New Calculator()
  Dim actual = generator.Factorial(-1)

  Assert.Fail("Contract not working")
End Sub
```

C#

```
class Calculator
{
  public int Factorial(int n)
  {
    Contract.Requires<ArgumentOutOfRangeException>(n >= 0, "n");

    if (n == 0) return 1;
    return n * Factorial(n - 1);
  }
}

[TestMethod, ExpectedException(typeof(ArgumentOutOfRangeException))]
public void NegativeTest()
{
  var generator = new Calculator();
  var actual = generator.Factorial(-1);

  Assert.Fail("Contract not working");
}
```

Although this method of testing Code Contracts works, it is not recommended because it may cover up errors in the code. A better option is to hook into the Code Contracts system and override its default behavior from within the test project. You do this by registering for the `ContractFailed` event on the static `Contract` class inside of an `AssemblyInitialize` method. Inside of the event handler, you tell the Code Contracts API that you have handled the contract failure and that you would like to throw an appropriate exception.

VB

```
<AssemblyInitialize()>
Public Shared Sub AssemblyInitialize(ByVal testContext As TestContext)

  AddHandler Contract.ContractFailed, Sub(sender As Object,
                      e As ContractFailedEventArgs)
```

```
                    e.SetHandled()
                    e.SetUnwind()
                  End Sub
End Sub

<TestMethod(), ExpectedException(GetType(Exception), AllowDerivedTypes:=True)>
Public Sub NegativeTest()

  Dim generator As New Calculator()
  Dim actual = generator.Factorial(-1)

  Assert.Fail("Contract not working")
End Sub
```

C#

```
[AssemblyInitialize]
public static void AssemblyInitialize(TestContext testContext)
{
  Contract.ContractFailed += (s, e) =>
  {
    e.SetHandled();
    e.SetUnwind();
  };
}

[TestMethod, ExpectedException(typeof(Exception), AllowDerivedTypes = true)]
public void NegativeTest()
{
  var generator = new Calculator();
  var actual = generator.Factorial(-1);
  Assert.Fail("Contract not working");
}
```

> **NOTE** *When Code Contracts are configured to cause Asserts, the intended exception is lost, so the code sample checks for any subclass of* `Exception`. *The actual exception that gets thrown is a* `System.Diagnostics.Contracts.ContractException`, *which is private to the .NET Framework, so you can't detect it directly.*

SUMMARY

This chapter described how you can use unit testing to ensure the correct functionality of your code. The unit-testing framework within Visual Studio is quite comprehensive, enabling you to both document and manage test cases.

You can fully exercise the testing framework using an appropriate data source to minimize the repetitive code you need to write. You can also extend the framework to test all the inner workings of your application.

Visual Studio Premium and Ultimate contain even more functionality for testing, including the capability to track and report on code coverage, and support for load and web application testing. Chapter 56, "Visual Studio Ultimate for Testers," provides more detail on these advanced testing capabilities.

12

Documentation with XML Comments

WHAT'S IN THIS CHAPTER?

- Adding inline documentation to your code using XML comments
- Using the GhostDoc Visual Studio Add-In to automatically generate XML comments
- Producing standalone documentation from XML comments with Sandcastle
- Using Task List comments to keep track of pending coding tasks and other things to do

Documentation is a critical, and often overlooked, feature of the development process. Without documentation, other programmers, code reviewers, and project managers have a more difficult time analyzing the purpose and implementation of code. You can even have problems with your own code when it becomes complex, and having good internal documentation can aid in the development process.

XML comments are a way to provide that internal documentation for your code without having to go through the process to manually create and maintain a separate document. Instead, as you write your code, you include meta data at the top of every definition to explain the intent of your code. When the information has been included in your code, it can be consumed by Visual Studio to provide Object Browser and IntelliSense information.

GhostDoc is a free third-party add-in for Visual Studio that can automatically insert an XML comment block for a class or member.

Sandcastle is a set of tools that act as a documentation compiler. You can use these tools to easily create standalone documentation in Microsoft compiled HTML help or Microsoft Help 2 format from the XML comments you have added to your code.

INLINE COMMENTING

All programming languages supported by Visual Studio provide a method for adding inline documentation. By default, all inline comments are highlighted in green.

C# supports both single-line comments and comment blocks. Single-line comments are denoted by `//` at the beginning of the comment. Block comments typically span multiple lines and are opened by `/*` and closed off by `*/`, as shown in the following code:

C#

```
// Calculate the factorial of an integer
public int Factorial(int number)
{
   /* This function calculates a factorial using an
    * iterative approach.
    */
    int intermediateResult = 1;
    for (int factor = 2; factor <= number; factor++)
    {
       intermediateResult = intermediateResult * factor;
    }
    return intermediateResult;   //The calculated factorial
}
```

VB just uses a single quote character to denote anything following it to be a comment, as shown in the following code:

VB

```
' Calculate the factorial of an integer
Public Function Factorial(ByVal number As Integer) As Integer
   ' This function calculates a factorial using an
   ' iterative approach.
   '
   Dim intermediateResult As Integer = 1
   For factor As Integer = 2 To number
      intermediateResult = intermediateResult * factor
   Next
   Return intermediateResult 'The calculated factorial
End Function
```

XML COMMENTS

XML comments are specialized comments that you include in your code. When the project goes through the build process, Visual Studio can optionally include a step to generate an XML file based on these comments to provide information about user-defined types such as classes and individual members of a class (user defined or not), including events, functions, and properties.

XML comments can contain any combination of XML and HTML tags. Visual Studio performs special processing on a particular set of predefined tags, as you'll see throughout the bulk of this chapter. Any other tags are included in the generated documentation file as is.

Adding XML Comments

XML comments are added immediately before the property, method, or class definition they are associated with. Visual Studio automatically adds an XML comment block when you type the shortcut code `///` in C# before a member or class declaration. In some cases the XML comments will already be present in code generated by the supplied project templates, as shown in Figure 12-1.

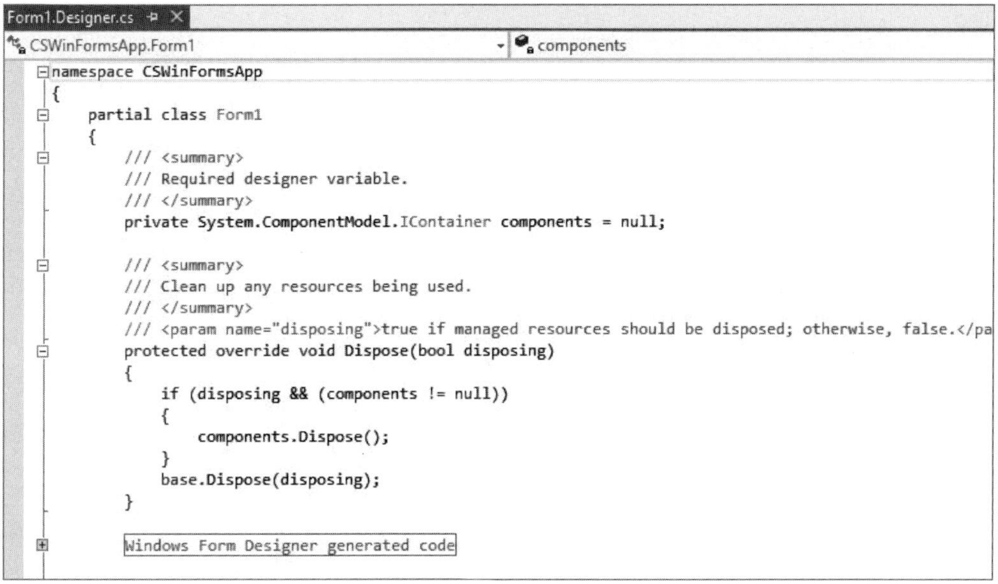

```
Form1.Designer.cs
CSWinFormsApp.Form1                                  components
namespace CSWinFormsApp
{
    partial class Form1
    {
        /// <summary>
        /// Required designer variable.
        /// </summary>
        private System.ComponentModel.IContainer components = null;

        /// <summary>
        /// Clean up any resources being used.
        /// </summary>
        /// <param name="disposing">true if managed resources should be disposed; otherwise, false.</pa
        protected override void Dispose(bool disposing)
        {
            if (disposing && (components != null))
            {
                components.Dispose();
            }
            base.Dispose(disposing);
        }

        Windows Form Designer generated code
```

FIGURE 12-1

> **NOTE** *The automatic insertion of the summary section can be enabled or disabled in the Visual Studio options. Select Tools ➪ Options, and then choose Text Editor ➪ C# ➪ Advanced from the navigation tree. Uncheck the Generate XML Documentation Comments for /// option to disable this feature.*

Adding an XML comment block to VB is achieved by using the “'” shortcut code. In this way it replicates the way C# documentation is generated.

In both languages, after the comments have been added, Visual Studio automatically adds a collapsible region to the left margin, so you can hide the documentation when you're busy writing code. Hovering over the collapsed area displays a tooltip message containing the first few lines of the comment block.

XML Comment Tags

Though you can use any kind of XML comment structure you like, including your own custom XML tags, Visual Studio's XML comment processor recognizes a number of predefined tags and automatically formats them appropriately. The Sandcastle document compiler, which is discussed later in this chapter, has support for a number of additional tags, and you can supplement these further with your own XML schema document.

> **NOTE** *If you need to use angle brackets in the text of a documentation comment, use the entity references* `<` *and* `>`*.*

Because documentation is so important, the next section details each of these predefined tags, their syntax, and how you would use them in your own documentation.

The <c> Tag

The <c> tag indicates that the enclosed text should be formatted as code, rather than normal text. It's used for code that is included in a normal text block. The structure of <c> is simple, with any text appearing between the opening and closing tags being marked for formatting in the code style.

```
<c>code-formatted text</c>
```

The following example shows how <c> might be used in the description of a property:

C#

```
/// <summary>
/// The <c>UserId</c> property is used in conjunction with other properties
/// to set up a user properly. Remember to set the <c>Password</c> field too.
/// </summary>
public string UserId { get; set; }
```

VB

```
''' <summary>
''' The <c>UserId</c> property is used in conjunction with other properties
''' to set up a user properly. Remember to set the <c>Password</c> field too.
''' </summary>
Public Property UserId() As String
```

The <code> Tag

If the amount of text in the documentation you need to format as code is more than just a phrase within a normal text block, you can use the <code> tag instead of <c>. This tag marks everything within it as code, but it's a block-level tag, rather than a character-level tag. The syntax of this tag is a simple opening and closing tag with the text to be formatted inside, as shown here:

```
<code>
Code-formatted text
Code-formatted text
</code>
```

The <code> tag can be embedded inside any other XML comment tag. The following code shows an example of how it could be used in the summary section of a property definition:

C#

```
/// <summary>
/// The <c>UserId</c> property is used in conjunction with other properties
/// to set up a user properly. Remember to set the <c>Password</c> field too.
/// For example:
/// <code>
/// myUser.UserId = "daveg"
/// myUser.Password = "xg4*Wv"
/// </code>
/// </summary>
public string UserId { get; set; }
```

VB

```
''' <summary>
''' The <c>UserId</c> property is used in conjunction with other properties
''' to set up a user properly. Remember to set the <c>Password</c> field too.
```

```
''' For example:
''' <code>
''' myUser.UserId = "daveg"
''' myUser.Password = "xg4*Wv"
''' </code>
''' </summary>
Public Property UserId() As String
```

The <example> Tag

A common requirement for internal documentation is to provide an example of how a particular procedure or member can be used. The `<example>` tags indicate that the enclosed block should be treated as a discrete section of the documentation, dealing with a sample for the associated member. Effectively, this doesn't do anything more than help organize the documentation, but used with an appropriately designed XML style sheet or processing instructions, the example can be formatted properly.

The other XML comment tags, such as `<c>` and `<code>`, can be included in the text inside the `<example>` tags to give you a comprehensively documented sample. The syntax of this block-level tag is simple:

```
<example>
Any sample text goes here.
</example>
```

Using the example from the previous discussion, the following code moves the `<code>` formatted text out of the `<summary>` section into an `<example>` section:

C#

```
/// <summary>
/// The <c>UserId</c> property is used in conjunction with other properties
/// to set up a user properly. Remember to set the <c>Password</c> field too.
/// </summary>
/// <example>
/// <code>
/// myUser.UserId = "daveg"
/// myUser.Password = "xg4*Wv"
/// </code>
/// </example>
public string UserId { get; set; }
```

VB

```
''' <summary>
''' The <c>UserId</c> property is used in conjunction with other properties
''' to set up a user properly. Remember to set the <c>Password</c> field too.
''' </summary>
''' <example>
''' <code>
''' myUser.UserId = "daveg"
''' myUser.Password = "xg4*Wv"
''' </code>
''' </example>
Public Property UserId() As String
```

The <exception> Tag

The `<exception>` tag is used to define any exceptions that could be thrown from within the member associated with the current block of XML documentation. Each exception that can be thrown should be defined with its own `<exception>` block, with an attribute of `cref` identifying the fully qualified type name of an exception that could be thrown. Note that the Visual Studio 2012 XML comment processor checks the syntax of the exception block to enforce the inclusion of this attribute. It also ensures that you don't have multiple `<exception>` blocks with the same attribute value. The full syntax is as follows:

```
<exception cref="exceptionName">
Exception description.
</exception>
```

Extending the examples from the previous tag discussions, the following code adds two exception definitions to the XML comments associated with the `UserId` property: `System.TimeoutException`, and `System.UnauthorizedAccessException`.

C#

```
/// <summary>
/// The <c>UserId</c> property is used in conjunction with other properties
/// to set up a user properly. Remember to set the <c>Password</c> field too.
/// </summary>
/// <exception cref="System.TimeoutException">
/// Thrown when the code cannot determine if the user is valid within a reasonable
/// amount of time.
/// </exception>
/// <exception cref="System.UnauthorizedAccessException">
/// Thrown when the user identifier is not valid within the current context.
/// </exception>
/// <example>
/// <code>
/// myUser.UserId = "daveg"
/// myUser.Password = "xg4*Wv"
/// </code>
/// </example>
public string UserId { get; set; }
```

VB

```
''' <summary>
''' The <c>UserId</c> property is used in conjunction with other properties
''' to set up a user properly. Remember to set the <c>Password</c> field too.
''' </summary>
''' <exception cref="System.TimeoutException">
''' Thrown when the code cannot determine if the user is valid within a reasonable
''' amount of time.
''' </exception>
''' <exception cref="System.UnauthorizedAccessException">
''' Thrown when the user identifier is not valid within the current context.
''' </exception>
''' <example>
''' <code>
''' myUser.UserId = "daveg"
''' myUser.Password = "xg4*Wv"
''' </code>
''' </example>
Public Property UserId() As String
```

The <include> Tag

You'll often have documentation that needs to be shared across multiple projects. In other situations, one person may be responsible for the documentation while others are doing the coding. Either way, the `<include>` tag will prove useful. The `<include>` tag enables you to refer to comments in a separate XML file, so they are brought inline with the rest of your documentation. Using this method, you can move the actual documentation out of the code, which can be handy when the comments are extensive.

The syntax of <include> requires that you specify which part of the external file is to be used in the current context. The path attribute is used to identify the path to the XML node and uses standard XPath terminology:

```
<include file="filename" path="XPathQuery" />
```

The external XML file containing the additional documentation must have a section that can be navigated to by using XPath notation. That notation is specified in the path attribute. As well, the XPath value must be able to uniquely identify the specific section of the XML document to be included.

You can include files in either VB or C# using the same tag. The following code takes the samples used in the <exception> tag discussion and moves the documentation to an external file:

C#

```
/// <include file="externalFile.xml" path="MyDoc/Properties[@name='UserId']/*" />
public string UserId { get; set; }
```

VB

```
''' <include file="externalFile.xml" path="MyDoc/Properties[@name='UserId']/*" />
Public Property UserId() As String
```

The external file's contents would be populated with the following XML document structure to synchronize it with what the <include> tag processing expects to find:

```
<MyDoc>
  <Properties name="UserId">
    <summary>
      The <c>sender</c> object is used to identify who invoked the procedure.
    </summary>
    <summary>
      The <c>UserId</c> property is used in conjunction with other properties
      to set up a user properly. Remember to set the <c>Password</c> field too.
    </summary>
    <exception cref="System.TimeoutException">
      Thrown when the code cannot determine if the user is valid within a
      reasonable amount of time.
    </exception>
    <exception cref="System.UnauthorizedAccessException">
      Thrown when the user identifier is not valid within the current context.
    </exception>
    <example>
      <code>
        myUser.UserId = "daveg"
        myUser.Password = "xg4*Wv"
      </code>
    </example>
  </Procedures>
</MyDoc>
```

The <list> Tag

Some documentation requires lists of various descriptions, and with the <list> tag you can generate numbered and unnumbered lists along with two-column tables. All three take two parameters for each entry in the list — a term and a description — represented by individual XML tags, but they instruct the processor to generate the documentation in different ways.

To create a list in the documentation, use the following syntax, where `type` can be one of the following values: `bullet`, `numbered`, or `table`:

```
<list type="type">
   <listheader>
      <term>termName</term>
      <description>description</description>
   </listheader>
   <item>
      <term>myTerm</term>
      <description>myDescription</description>
   </item>
</list>
```

The `<listheader>` block is optional and is usually used for table-formatted lists or definition lists. For definition lists, the `<term>` tag must be included, but for bullet lists, numbered lists, or tables, the `<term>` tag can be omitted.

The XML for each type of list can be formatted differently using an XML style sheet. An example of how to use the `<list>` tag appears in the following code. Note how the sample has omitted the `listheader` tag because it was unnecessary for the bullet list:

C#

```
/// <summary>
/// This function changes a user's password. The password change could fail for
/// several reasons:
/// <list type="bullet">
/// <item>
/// <term>Too Short</term>
/// <description>The new password was not long enough.</description>
/// </item>
/// <item>
/// <term>Not Complex</term>
/// <description>The new password did not meet the complexity requirements. It
/// must contain at least one of the following characters: lowercase, uppercase,
/// and number.
/// </description>
/// </item>
/// </list>
/// </summary>
public bool ChangePwd(string oldPwd, string newPwd)
{
    //...code...
    return true;
}
```

VB

```
''' <summary>
''' This function changes a users password. The password change could fail for
''' several reasons:
''' <list type="bullet">
''' <item>
''' <term>Too Short</term>
''' <description>The new password was not long enough.</description>
''' </item>
''' <item>
''' <term>Not Complex</term>
''' <description>The new password did not meet the complexity requirements. It
```

```
''' must contain at least one of the following characters: lowercase, uppercase,
''' and number.
''' </description>
''' </item>
''' </list>
''' </summary>
Public Function ChangePwd(ByVal oldPwd As String, ByVal newPwd As String) _
                          As Boolean
    '...code...
    Return True
End Function
```

The <para> Tag

Without using the various internal block-level XML comments such as <list> and <code>, the text you add to the main <summary>, <remarks>, and <returns> sections all just runs together. To break it up into readable chunks, you can use the <para> tag, which simply indicates that the text enclosed should be treated as a discrete paragraph. The syntax is simple:

```
<para>This text will appear in a separate paragraph.</para>
```

The <param> Tag

To explain the purpose of any parameters in a function declaration, you can use the <param> tag. This tag will be processed by the Visual Studio XML comment processor with each instance requiring a name attribute that has a value equal to the name of one of the properties. Enclosed between the opening and closing <param> tag is the description of the parameter:

```
<param name="parameterName">Definition of parameter.</param>
```

The XML processor will not allow you to create multiple <param> tags for the one parameter, or tags for parameters that don't exist, producing warnings that are added to the Error List in Visual Studio if you try. The following example shows how the <param> tag is used to describe two parameters of a function:

C#

```
/// <param name="oldPwd">Old password-must match the current password</param>
/// <param name="newPwd">New password-must meet the complexity requirements</param>
public bool ChangePwd(string oldPwd, string newPwd)
{
    //...code...
    return true;
}
```

VB

```
''' <param name="oldPwd">Old password-must match the current password</param>
''' <param name="newPwd">New password-must meet the complexity requirements</param>
Public Function ChangePwd(ByVal oldPwd As String, ByVal newPwd As String) _
                          As Boolean
    '...code...
    Return True
End Function
```

> **NOTE** *The* <param> *tag is especially useful for documenting preconditions for a method's parameters, such as if a null value is not allowed.*

The <paramref> Tag

If you refer to the parameters of the method definition elsewhere in the documentation other than the `<param>` tag, you can use the `<paramref>` tag to format the value, or even link to the parameter information depending on how you code the XML transformation. The compiler does not require that the name of the parameter exist, but you must specify the text to be used in the `name` attribute, as the following syntax shows:

```
<paramref name="parameterName" />
```

Normally, `<paramref>` tags are used when you refer to parameters in the larger sections of documentation such as the `<summary>` or `<remarks>` tags, as the following example demonstrates:

C#

```
/// <summary>
/// This function changes a user's password. This will throw an exception if
/// <paramref name="oldPwd" /> or <paramref name="newPwd" /> are nothing.
/// </summary>
/// <param name="oldPwd">Old password-must match the current password</param>
/// <param name="newPwd">New password-must meet the complexity requirements</param>
public bool ChangePwd(string oldPwd, string newPwd)
{
    //...code...
    return true;
}
```

VB

```
''' <summary>
''' This function changes a user's password. This will throw an exception if
''' <paramref name="oldPwd" /> or <paramref name="newPwd" /> are nothing.
''' </summary>
''' <param name="oldPwd">Old password-must match the current password</param>
''' <param name="newPwd">New password-must meet the complexity requirements</param>
Public Function ChangePwd(ByVal oldPwd As String, ByVal newPwd As String) _
                          As Boolean
    '...code...
    Return True
End Function
```

The <permission> Tag

To describe the code access security permission set required by a particular method, use the `<permission>` tag. This tag requires a `cref` attribute to refer to a specific permission type:

```
<permission cref="permissionName">
   description goes here
</permission>
```

If the function requires more than one permission, use multiple `<permission>` blocks, as shown in the following example:

C#

```
/// <permission cref="System.Security.Permissions.RegistryPermission">
/// Needs full access to the Windows Registry.
/// </permission>
/// <permission cref="System.Security.Permissions.FileIOPermission">
/// Needs full access to the .config file containing application information.
/// </permission>
public string UserId { get; set; }
```

VB

```
''' <permission cref="System.Security.Permissions.RegistryPermission">
''' Needs full access to the Windows Registry.
''' </permission>
''' <permission cref="System.Security.Permissions.FileIOPermission">
''' Needs full access to the .config file containing application information.
''' </permission>
Public Property UserId() As String
```

The <remarks> Tag

The `<remarks>` tag is used to add an additional comment block to the documentation associated with a particular method. Discussion on previous tags has shown the `<remarks>` tag in action, but the syntax is as follows:

```
<remarks>
   Any further remarks go here
</remarks>
```

Normally, you would create a summary section, briefly outline the method or type, and then include the detailed information inside the `<remarks>` tag, with the expected outcomes of accessing the member.

The <returns> Tag

When a method returns a value to the calling code, you can use the `<returns>` tag to describe what it could be. The syntax of `<returns>` is like most of the other block-level tags, consisting of an opening and closing tag with any information detailing the return value enclosed within:

```
<returns>
   Description of the return value.
</returns>
```

A simple implementation of `<returns>` might appear like the following code:

C#

```
/// <summary>
/// This function changes a user's password.
/// </summary>
/// <returns>
/// This function returns:
/// <c>True</c> which indicates that the password was changed successfully,
/// or <c>False</c> which indicates that the password change failed.
/// </returns>
public bool ChangePwd(string oldPwd, string newPwd)
{
    //...code...
    return true;
}
```

VB

```
''' <summary>
''' This function changes a user's password.
''' </summary>
''' <returns>
''' This function returns:
''' <c>True</c> which indicates that the password was changed successfully,
''' or <c>False</c> which indicates that the password change failed.
''' </returns>
```

```
Public Function ChangePwd(ByVal oldPwd As String, ByVal newPwd As String) _
                          As Boolean
    '...code...
    Return True
End Function
```

> **NOTE** *In addition to return value of a function, the* `<returns>` *tag is especially useful for documenting any post-conditions that should be expected.*

The <see> Tag

You can add references to other items in the project using the `<see>` tag. Like some of the other tags already discussed, the `<see>` tag requires a `cref` attribute with a value equal to an existing member, whether it is a property, method, or class definition. The `<see>` tag is used inline with other areas of the documentation such as `<summary>` or `<remarks>`. The syntax is as follows:

```
<see cref="memberName" />
```

When Visual Studio processes the `<see>` tag, it produces a fully qualified address that can then be used as the basis for a link in the documentation when transformed via style sheets. For example, referring to an application with a class containing a function named `ChangePwd` would result in the following `cref` value:

```
<see cref="applicationName.className.ChangePwd"/>
```

The following example uses the `<see>` tag to provide a link to another function called `CheckUser`:

C#

```
/// <remarks>
/// Use <see cref="CheckUser" /> to verify that the user exists before calling
/// ChangePwd.
/// </remarks>
public bool ChangePwd(string oldPwd, string newPwd)
{
    //...code...
    return true;
}
```

VB

```
''' <remarks>
''' Use <see cref="CheckUser" /> to verify that the user exists before calling
''' ChangePwd.
''' </remarks>
Public Function ChangePwd(ByVal oldPwd As String, ByVal newPwd As String) _
                          As Boolean
    '...code...
    Return True
End Function
```

> **NOTE** *In VB only, if the member specified in the* `cref` *value does not exist, Visual Studio uses IntelliSense to display a warning and adds it to the Error List.*

The <seealso> Tag

The <seealso> tag is used to generate a separate section containing information about related topics within the documentation. Rather than being inline like <see>, the <seealso> tags are defined outside the other XML comment blocks, with each instance of <seealso> requiring a cref attribute containing the name of the property, method, or class to which to link. The full syntax appears like so:

```
<seealso cref="memberName" />
```

Modifying the previous example, the following code shows how the <seealso> tag can be implemented in code:

C#

```
/// <remarks>
/// Use <see cref="CheckUser" /> to verify that the user exists before calling
/// ChangePwd.
/// </remarks>
/// <seealso cref="ResetPwd" />
public bool ChangePwd(string oldPwd, string newPwd)
{
    //...code...
    return true;
}
```

VB

```
''' <remarks>
''' Use <see cref="CheckUser" /> to verify that the user exists before calling
''' ChangePwd.
''' </remarks>
''' <seealso cref="ResetPwd" />
Public Function ChangePwd(ByVal oldPwd As String, ByVal newPwd As String) _
                          As Boolean
    '...code...
    Return True
End Function
```

The <summary> Tag

The <summary> tag is used to provide the brief description that appears at the top of a specific topic in the documentation. As such it is typically placed before all public and protected methods and classes. In addition, the <summary> area is used for Visual Studio's IntelliSense engine when using your own custom-built code. The syntax to implement <summary> is as follows:

```
<summary>
   A description of the function or property goes here.
</summary>
```

The <typeparam> Tag

The <typeparam> tag provides information about the type parameters when dealing with a generic type or member definition. The <typeparam> tag expects an attribute of name containing the type parameter being referred to:

```
<typeparam name="typeName">
   Description goes here.
</typeparam>
```

You can use <typeparam> in either C# or VB, as the following code shows:

C#

```
/// <typeparam name="T">
/// Base item type (must implement IComparable)
/// </typeparam>
public class myList<T> where T : IComparable
{
    //...code...
}
```

VB

```
''' <typeparam name="T">
''' Base item type (must implement IComparable)
''' </typeparam>
Public Class myList(Of T As IComparable)
    '...code...
End Class
```

The <typeparamref> Tag

If you refer to a generic type parameter elsewhere in the documentation other than the <typeparam> tag, you can use the <typeparamref> tag to format the value, or even link to the parameter information depending on how you code the XML transformation.

```
<typeparamref name="parameterName" />
```

Normally, <typeparamref> tags are used when you refer to parameters in the larger sections of documentation such as the <summary> or <remarks> tags, as the following code demonstrates:

C#

```
/// <summary>
/// Creates a new list of arbitrary type <typeparamref name="T"/>
/// </summary>
/// <typeparam name="T">
/// Base item type (must implement IComparable)
/// </typeparam>
public class myList<T> where T : IComparable
{
    //...code...
}
```

VB

```
''' <summary>
''' Creates a new list of arbitrary type <typeparamref name="T"/>
''' </summary>
''' <typeparam name="T">
''' Base item type (must implement IComparable)
''' </typeparam>
Public Class myList(Of T As IComparable)
    '...code...
End Class
```

The <value> Tag

Normally used to define a property's purpose, the <value> tag gives you another section in the XML where you can provide information about the associated member. The <value> tag is not used by IntelliSense.

```
<value>The text to display</value>
```

When used with a property, you would normally use the <summary> tag to describe what the property is for, whereas the <value> tag is used to describe what the property represents:

C#

```
/// <summary>
/// The <c>UserId</c> property is used in conjunction with other properties
/// to set up a user properly. Remember to set the <c>Password</c> field too.
/// </summary>
/// <value>
/// A string containing the UserId for the current user
/// </value>
public string UserId { get; set; }
```

VB

```
''' <summary>
''' The <c>UserId</c> property is used in conjunction with other properties
''' to set up a user properly. Remember to set the <c>Password</c> field too.
''' </summary>
''' <value>
''' A string containing the UserId for the current user
''' </value>
Public Property UserId() As String
```

USING XML COMMENTS

When you have the XML comments inline with your code, you'll most likely want to generate an XML file containing the documentation. In VB this setting is on by default, with an output path and filename specified with default values. However, C# has the option turned off as its default behavior, so if you want documentation you need to turn it on manually.

To ensure that your documentation is generated where you require, open the property pages for the project through the Solution Explorer's right-click context menu. Locate the project for which you want documentation, right-click its entry in the Solution Explorer, and select Properties.

The XML documentation options are located in the Build section (see Figure 12-2). Below the general build options is an Output section that contains a check box that enables XML documentation file generation. When this check box is checked, the text field next to it becomes available for you to specify the filename for the XML file that will be generated.

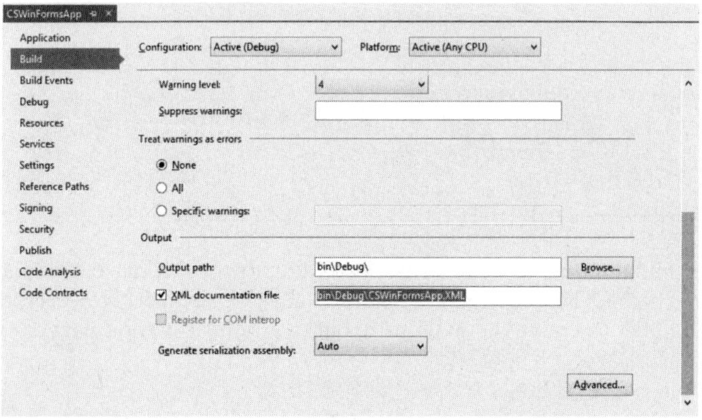

FIGURE 12-2

For VB applications, the option to generate an XML documentation file is on the Compile tab of the project properties.

After you save these options, the next time you perform a build, Visual Studio adds the `/doc` compiler option to the process so that the XML documentation is generated as specified.

> **NOTE** *Generating an XML documentation file can slow down the compile time. If this is impacting your development or debugging cycle, you can disable it for the Debug build while leaving it enabled for the Release build.*

The XML file generated contains a full XML document that you can apply XSL transformations against, or process through another application using the XML document object model. All references to exceptions, parameters, methods, and other "see also" links will be included as fully addressed information, including namespace, application, and class data. Later in this chapter you'll see how you can make use of this XML file to produce professional-looking documentation using Sandcastle.

IntelliSense Information

The other useful advantage of using XML comments is how Visual Studio consumes them in its own IntelliSense engine. As soon as you define the documentation tags that Visual Studio understands, it will generate the information into its IntelliSense, which means you can refer to the information elsewhere in your code.

You can access IntelliSense in two ways. If the member referred to is within the same project or is in another project within the same solution, you can access the information without having to build or generate the XML file. However, you can still take advantage of IntelliSense even when the project is external to your current application solution.

The trick is to ensure that when the XML file is generated by the build process, it must have the same name as the .NET assembly being built. For example, if the compiled output is `MyApplication.exe`, the associated XML file should be named `MyApplication.xml`. In addition, this generated XML file should be in the same folder as the compiled assembly so that Visual Studio can locate it.

GENERATING DOCUMENTATION WITH GHOSTDOC

Although most developers will agree that documentation is important, it still takes a lot of time and commitment to write. The golden rule of "if it's easy the developer will have more inclination to do it" means that any additional enhancements to the documentation side of development will encourage more developers to embrace it.

> **NOTE** *You can always take a more authoritarian approach to documentation and use a source code analysis tool such as StyleCop to enforce a minimum level of documentation. StyleCop ships with almost 50 built-in rules specifically for verifying the content and formatting of XML documentation. StyleCop is discussed in more detail in Chapter 13, "Code Consistency Tools."*

GhostDoc is an add-in for Visual Studio that attempts to do just that, providing the capability to set up a keyboard shortcut that automatically inserts the XML comment block for a class or member. However, the true power of GhostDoc is not in the capability to create the basic stub, but to automate a good part of the documentation.

> **NOTE** *As of this writing, in order to use GhostDoc with Visual Studio 2012, you need to be running GhostDoc v4.*

Through a series of lists that customize how different parts of member and variable names should be interpreted, GhostDoc generates simple phrases that get you started in creating your own documentation. For example, consider the list shown in Figure 12-3 (which is displayed by selecting the Tools ➪ GhostDoc ➪ Options menu item), where words are defined as trigger points for "Of the" phrases. Whenever a variable or member name has the string "color" as part of its name, GhostDoc attempts to create a phrase that can be used in the XML documentation.

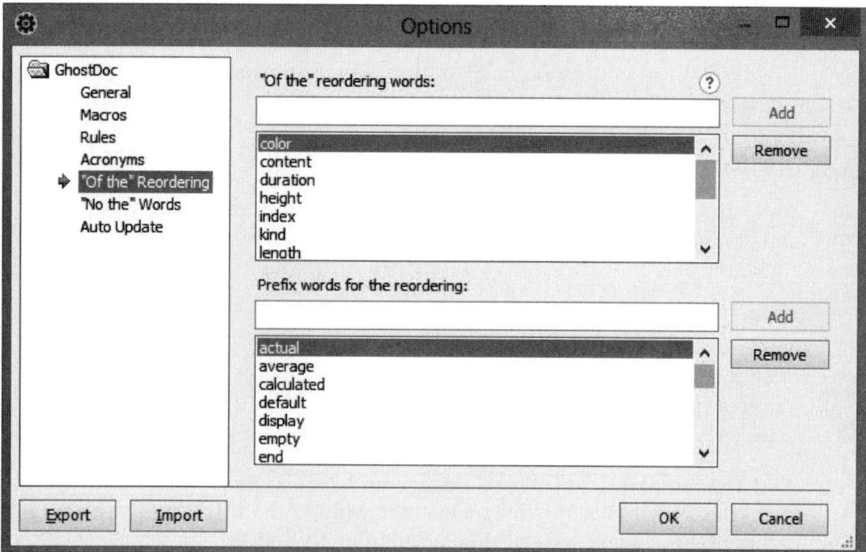

FIGURE 12-3

For instance, a property called `NewBackgroundColor` can generate a complete phrase of `New color of the background`. The functionality of GhostDoc also recognizes common parameter names and their purpose. Figure 12-4 shows this in action with a default `Click` event handler for a button control. The `sender` and `e` parameters were recognized as particular types in the context of an event handler, and the documentation that was generated by GhostDoc reflects this accordingly.

```
/// <summary>
/// Handles the Click event of the btnClose control.
/// </summary>
/// <param name="sender">The source of the event.</param>
/// <param name="e">The <see cref="EventArgs" /> instance containing the event data.</param>
private void btnClose_Click(object sender, EventArgs e)
{

}
```

FIGURE 12-4

GhostDoc is an excellent resource for those who find documentation difficult. You can find it at its official website, `http://submain.com/ghostdoc`.

COMPILING DOCUMENTATION WITH SANDCASTLE

Sandcastle is a set of tools published by Microsoft that act as documentation compilers. You can use these tools to easily create professional-looking external documentation in Microsoft compiled HTML help (`.chm`) or Microsoft Help 2 (`.hsx`) format.

The primary location for information on Sandcastle is the Sandcastle blog at `http://blogs.msdn.com/sandcastle/`. There is also a project on CodePlex, Microsoft's open source project hosting site at `http://sandcastle.codeplex.com/`. You can find documentation, a discussion forum, and a link to download the latest Sandcastle installer package on this site.

By default, Sandcastle installs to `c:\Program Files\Sandcastle` (if you're installing on a 64-bit system, the installation location is `c:\Program Files (x86)\Sandcastle` by default). When it is run, Sandcastle creates a large number of working files and the final output file under this directory. Unfortunately, all files and folders under Program Files require administrator permissions to write to, which can be problematic, particularly if you run on Windows Vista with UAC enabled. Therefore, it is recommended that you install it to a location where your user account has write permissions.

Out of the box, Sandcastle is used from the command line only. A number of third parties have put together GUI interfaces for Sandcastle, which are linked to on the Wiki.

To begin, open a Visual Studio 2012 Command Prompt from Start Menu ⇨ All Programs ⇨ Microsoft Visual Studio 2012 ⇨ Visual Studio Tools, and change the directory to `<Sandcastle Install Directory>\Examples\sandcastle\`.

> **NOTE** *The Visual Studio 2012 Command Prompt is equivalent to a normal command prompt except that it also sets various environment variables, such as directory search paths, which are often required by the Visual Studio 2012 command-line tools.*

In this directory, you can find an example class file, `test.cs`, and an MSBuild project file, `build.proj`. The example class file contains methods and properties commented with the standard XML comment tags that were explained earlier in this chapter, as well as some additional Sandcastle-specific XML comment tags. You can compile the class file and generate the XML documentation file by entering the following command:

```
csc /t:library test.cs /doc:example.xml
```

> **NOTE** *In Windows 7, the Sandcastle installation directory is in Program Files, which is (by default) restricted. Which means that when you execute this command, you're going to run into security problems. To address this, you can either give write access to the Examples subdirectory (and all sub directories) or you can run the Visual Studio 2012 Command Prompt as an administrator.*

When that has completed, you are now ready to generate the documentation help file. The simplest way to do this is to execute the example MSBuild project file that ships with Sandcastle. This project file has been hard-coded to generate the documentation using `test.dll` and `example.xml`. Run the MSBuild project by entering the following command:

```
msbuild build.proj
```

The MSBuild project will call several Sandcastle tools to build the documentation file, including MRefBuilder, BuildAssembler, and XslTransform.

> **NOTE** *Rather than manually running Sandcastle every time you build a release version, it would be better to ensure that it is always run by executing it as a post-build event. Chapter 6, "Solutions, Projects, and Items," describes how to create a build event.*

You may be surprised at how long the documentation takes to generate. This is partly because the MRefBuilder tool uses reflection to inspect the assembly and all dependent assemblies to obtain information about all the types, properties, and methods in the assembly and all dependent assemblies. In addition, any time it comes across a base .NET Framework type, it will attempt to resolve it to the MSDN online documentation to generate the correct hyperlinks in the documentation help file.

> **NOTE** *The first time you run the MSBuild project, it generates reflection data for all the .NET Framework classes, so you can expect it to take even longer to complete.*

By default, the `build.proj` MSBuild project generates the documentation with the vs2005 look and feel, as shown in Figure 12-5, in the directory `<Sandcastle Install Directory>\Examples\sandcastle\chm\`. You can choose a different output style by adding one of the following options to the command line:

```
/property:PresentationStyle=vs2005
/property:PresentationStyle=hana
/property:PresentationStyle=prototype
```

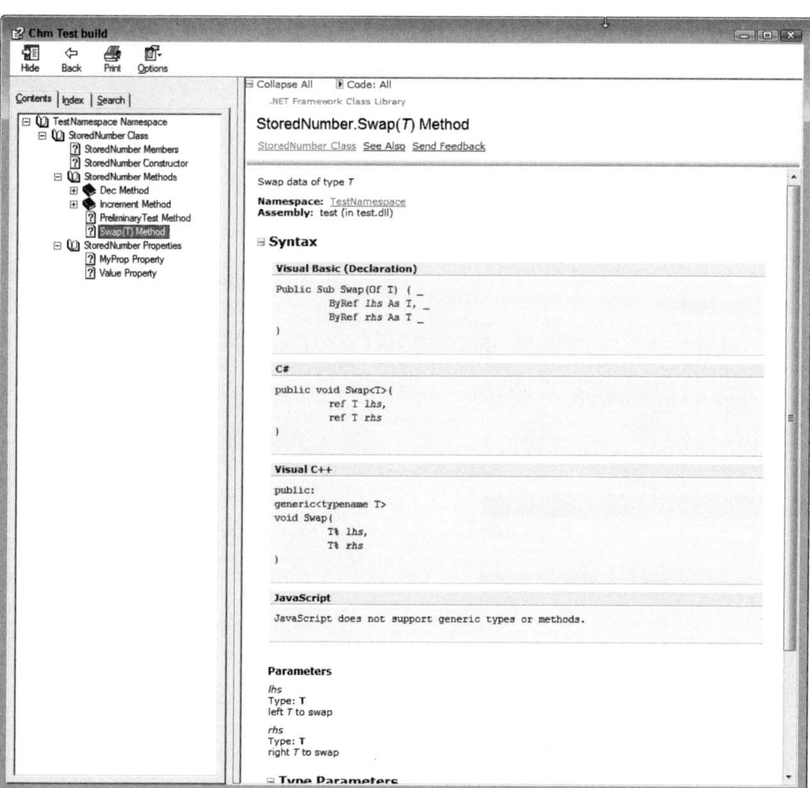

FIGURE 12-5

The following code shows the source code section from the example class file, `test.cs`, which relates to the page of the help documentation shown in Figure 12-5.

```
/// <summary>
/// Swap data of type <typeparamref name="T"/>
/// </summary>
/// <param name="lhs">left <typeparamref name="T"/> to swap</param>
/// <param name="rhs">right <typeparamref name="T"/> to swap</param>
/// <typeparam name="T">The element type to swap</typeparam>
public void Swap<T>(ref T lhs, ref T rhs)
{
    T temp;
    temp = lhs;
    lhs = rhs;
    rhs = temp;
}
```

The default target for the `build.proj` MSBuild project is "Chm," which builds a CHM-compiled HTML Help file for the `test.dll` assembly. You can also specify one of the following targets on the command line:

```
/target:Clean  - removes all generated files
/target:HxS    - builds HxS file for Visual Studio in addition to CHM
```

> **NOTE** *The Microsoft Help 2 (.HxS) is the format that the Visual Studio help system uses. You must install the Microsoft Help 2.x SDK to generate .HxS files. This is available and included as part of the Visual Studio 2012 SDK.*

TASK LIST COMMENTS

The Task List window is a feature of Visual Studio 2012 that allows you to keep track of any coding tasks or outstanding activities you have to do. Tasks can be manually entered as User Tasks, or automatically detected from the inline comments. You can open the Task List window by selecting View ⇨ Task List, or using the keyboard shortcut CTRL+\, CTRL+T. Figure 12-6 shows the Task List window with some User Tasks defined.

> **NOTE** *User Tasks are saved in the solution user options (.suo) file, which contains user-specific settings and preferences. It is not recommended that you check this file into source control and, as such, multiple developers working on the same solution cannot share User Tasks.*

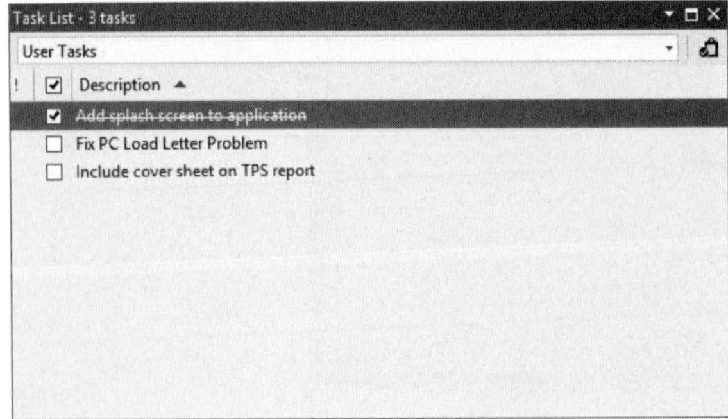

FIGURE 12-6

> **NOTE** *The Task List has a filter in the top-left corner that toggles the code between Comment Tasks and manually entered User Tasks.*

When you add a comment into your code that begins with a *comment token*, the comment will be added to the Task List as a Comment Task. The default comment tokens that are included with Visual Studio 2012 are `TODO`, `HACK`, `UNDONE`, and `UnresolvedMergeConflict`.

The following code shows a `TODO` comment. Figure 12-7 shows how this comment appears as a task in the Task List window. You can double-click the Task List entry to go directly to the comment line in your code.

C#

```
using System;
using System.Windows.Forms;

namespace CSWindowsFormsApp
{
    public partial class Form1 : Form
    {
        public Form1()
        {
            InitializeComponent();
            //TODO: The database should be initialized here
        }
    }
}
```

You can edit the list of comment tokens from an options page under Tools ➪ Options ➪ Environment ➪ Task List, as shown in Figure 12-8. Each token can be assigned a priority: Low, Normal, or High. The default token is `TODO`, and it cannot be renamed or deleted. You can, however, adjust its priority.

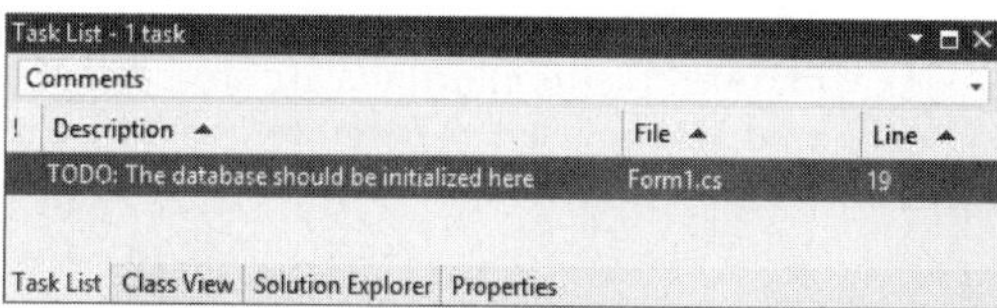

FIGURE 12-7

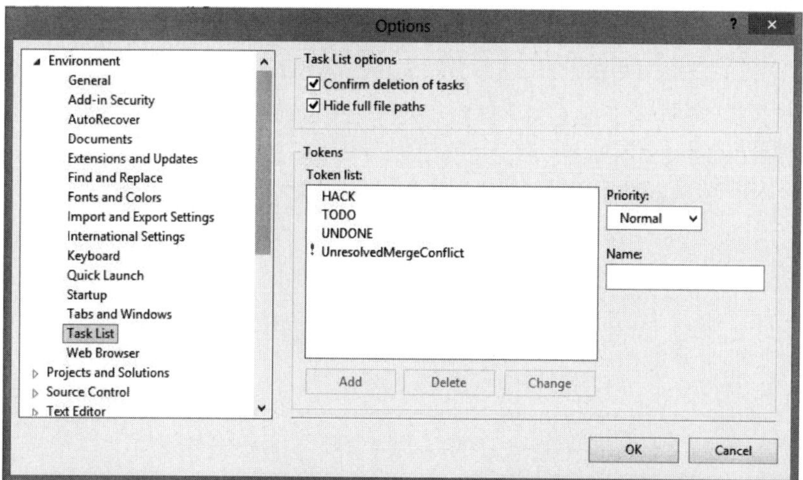

FIGURE 12-8

In addition to User Tasks and Comments, you can also add shortcuts to code within the Task List. To create a Task List Shortcut, place the cursor on the location for the shortcut within the code editor and select Edit ➪ Bookmarks ➪ Add Task List Shortcut. This places an arrow icon in the gutter of the code editor, as shown in Figure 12-9.

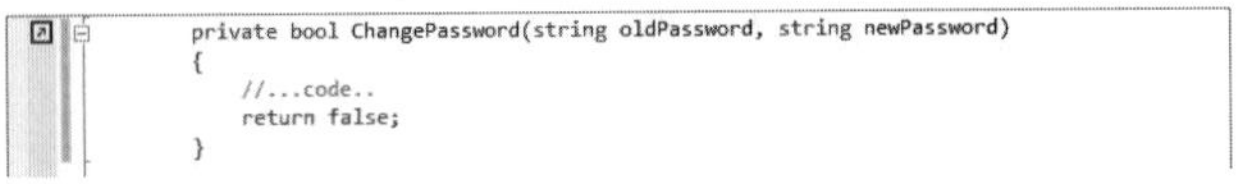

```
private bool ChangePassword(string oldPassword, string newPassword)
{
    //...code..
    return false;
}
```

FIGURE 12-9

If you now go to the Task List window, you can see a category called Shortcuts listed in the drop-down list, as shown in Figure 12-10. By default the description for the shortcut contains the line of code; however, you can edit this and enter whatever text you like. Double-clicking an entry takes you to the shortcut location in the code editor.

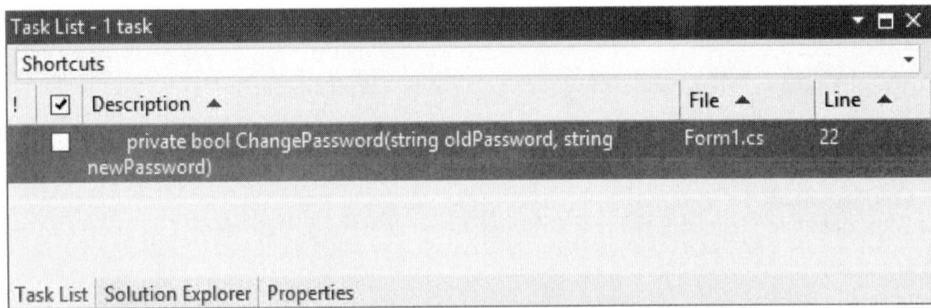

FIGURE 12-10

As with User Tasks, Shortcuts are stored in the `.suo` file and aren't typically checked into source control or shared among users. Therefore, they are a great way to annotate your code with private notes and reminders.

SUMMARY

XML comments are not only extremely powerful but also easy to implement in a development project. Using them enables you to enhance the existing IntelliSense features by including your own custom-built tooltips and Quick Info data. You can automate the process of creating XML comments with the GhostDoc Visual Studio add-in. Using Sandcastle, you can generate professional-looking standalone documentation for every member and class within your solutions. Finally, Task List comments are useful for keeping track of pending coding tasks and other outstanding activities.

13

Code Consistency Tools

WHAT'S IN THIS CHAPTER?

- Working with source control
- Creating, adding, and updating code in a source repository
- Defining and enforcing code standards
- Adding contracts to your code

If you are building a small application by yourself, it's easy to understand how all the pieces fit together and to make changes to accommodate new or changed requirements. Unfortunately, even on such a small project, the codebase can easily go from being well structured and organized to being a mess of variables, methods, and classes. This problem is amplified if the application is large and complex, and if it has multiple developers working on it concurrently.

In this chapter, you'll learn about how you and your team can use features of Visual Studio 2012 to write and maintain consistent code. The first part of this chapter is dedicated to the use of source control to assist you in tracking changes to your codebase over time. Use of source control facilitates sharing of code and changes among a team, but more importantly, gives you a history of changes made to an application over time.

In the remainder of the chapter, you'll learn about FxCop and StyleCop, which you can use to set up and enforce coding standards. Adhering to a set of standards and guidelines ensures the code you write will be easier to understand, leading to fewer issues and shorter development times. You'll also see how you can use Code Contracts to write higher quality code.

SOURCE CONTROL

Many different methodologies for building software applications exist, and though the theories about team structure, work allocation, design, and testing often differ, one point that the theories agree on is that there should be a repository for all source code for an application. Source control is the process of storing source code (referred to as checking code in) and accessing it again (referred to as checking code out) for editing. When we refer to source code, we mean any resources, configuration files, code files, or even documentation that is required to build and deploy an application.

Source code repositories also vary in structure and interface. Basic repositories provide a limited interface through which files can be checked in and out. The storage mechanism can be as simple as a file share, and no history may be available. Yet this repository still has the advantage that all developers working on a project can access the same file, with no risk of changes being overwritten or lost. More sophisticated repositories not only provide a rich interface for checking in and out, they also assist with file merging and conflict resolution. They can also be used from within Visual Studio to manage the source code. Other functionality that a source control repository can provide includes versioning of files, branching, and remote access.

Most organizations start using a source control repository to provide a mechanism for sharing source code between participants in a project. Instead of developers having to manually copy code to and from a shared folder on a network, the repository can be queried to get the latest version of the source code. When developers finish their work, any changes can simply be checked into the repository. This ensures that everyone on the team can access the latest code. Also, having the source code checked into a single repository makes it easy to perform regular backups.

Version tracking, including a full history of what changes were made and by whom, is one of the biggest benefits of using a source control repository. Although most developers would like to think that they write perfect code, the reality is that quite often a change might break something else. Reviewing the history of changes made to a project makes it possible to identify which change caused the breakage. Tracking changes to a project can also be used for reporting and reviewing purposes because each change is date stamped and its author indicated.

Selecting a Source Control Repository

Visual Studio 2012 does not ship with a source control repository, but it does include rich support for checking files in and out, as well as merging and reviewing changes. To make use of a repository from within Visual Studio 2012, it is necessary to specify which repository to use. Visual Studio 2012 supports deep integration with Team Foundation Server (TFS), Microsoft's premier source control and project tracking system. In addition, Visual Studio supports any source control client that uses the Source Code Control (SCC) API. Products that use the SCC API include Microsoft Visual SourceSafe and the free, open-source, source-control repositories Subversion and CVS.

> **NOTE** *You would be forgiven for thinking that Microsoft Visual SourceSafe is no longer available, considering that all the press mentions is TFS. However, Microsoft Visual SourceSafe 2005 is still available and compatible with Visual Studio 2012. There is, however, a licensing option for TFS, which is specifically designed for small development teams as a replacement for SourceSafe.*

To get Visual Studio 2012 to work with a particular source control provider, you must configure the appropriate information under the Options item on the Tools menu. The Options window, with the Source Control tab selected, is shown in Figure 13-1.

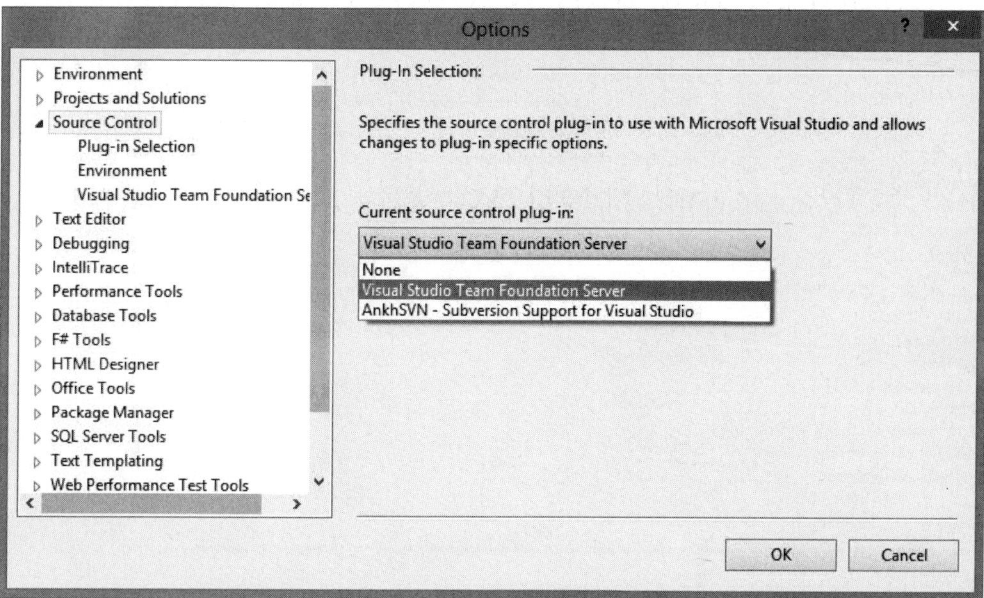

FIGURE 13-1

> **NOTE** *You might notice that the drop-down shown in Figure 13-1 includes AnkhSVN as one of the options. This choice is not available out of the box, but is available once you have installed the AnkhSVN plugin. You can find the AnkhSVN plug-in at* `http://ankhsvn.open.collab.net`. *Another well-regarded SVN plug-in, albeit one that does cost, is VisualSVN, which you can find at* `www.visualsvn.com`.

Initially, few settings for source control appear. However, after a provider has been selected, additional nodes are added to the tree to control how source control behaves. These options are specific to the source control provider that has been selected.

Chapter 57, "Team Foundation Server," covers the use of Team Foundation, which offers much richer integration and functionality as a source control repository. As a result, the remainder of this chapter focuses on the use of Subversion, a free source control repository, which can be integrated with Visual Studio 2012. Subversion has a number of plug-ins that allow it to be integrated with Visual Studio. We will be working with AnkhSVN, which itself is free.

Environment Settings

After a source control repository has been selected from the plug-in menu, it is necessary to configure the repository for that machine. Most source control repositories define a series of settings that must be configured so that Visual Studio 2012 can connect to and access information from the repository. These settings are usually unique to the repository.

In Figure 13-2 the Subversion Environment tab is shown, illustrating the options that control when files are checked in and out of the repository. There are also options available for setting up a proxy and maintaining your authentication cache.

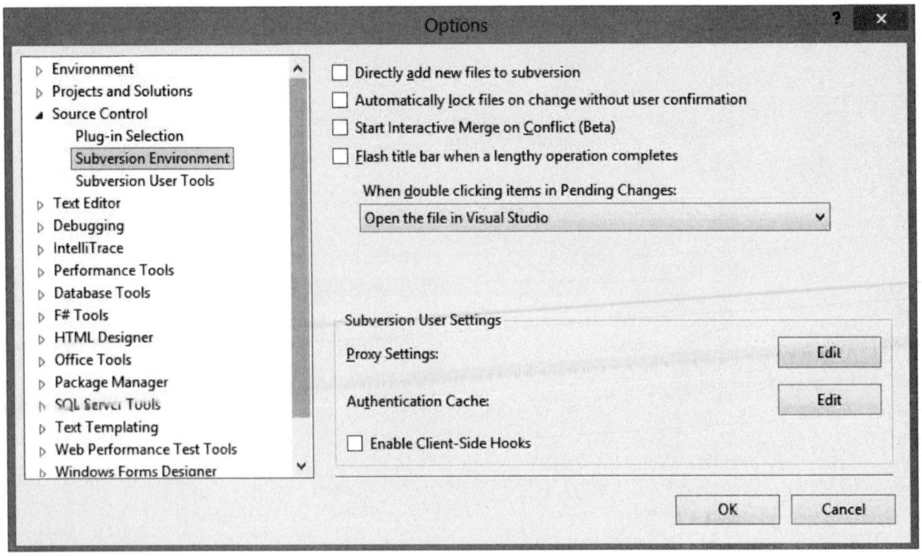

FIGURE 13-2

Many source control repositories need some additional settings to integrate with Visual Studio 2012. These would be found in additional panes that are part of the Settings form. For Ankh, the tools used to perform differencing, merging, and patching can be identified. However, these values are specific to the plug-in, so making generalized statements about the details is not feasible. Suffice it to say that the plug-in can provide the information necessary for you to properly configure it.

Accessing Source Control

This section walks through the process to add a solution to a Subversion repository; however, the same principles apply regardless of the repository chosen. This process can be applied to any new or existing solution that is not already under source control. We assume here that you have access to a Subversion repository and that it has been selected as the source control repository within Visual Studio 2012.

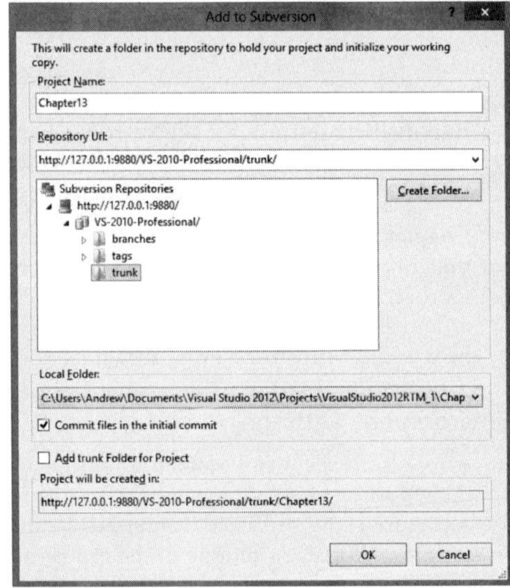

FIGURE 13-3

Adding the Solution

To begin the process to add a solution to source control, navigate to the File menu, and select Subversion ➪ Add Solution to Subversion, which opens the Add to Subversion dialog box as shown in Figure 13-3. Alternatively, if you create a new solution, select the Add to Subversion check box on the New Project dialog to immediately add your new solution to a source control repository.

For Subversion, this includes the project name and the path to the repository. You might notice in Figure 13-3 that a path to the Subversion repository has been provided and the location within that path where the code will be placed has been selected. In order to add a solution to Subversion, a Subversion repository already needs to exist. There are a number of hosting solutions for Subversion, one of which (`www.assembla.com`) is used in the figure. If you are using Subversion in a corporate environment, the URL to the repository is typically provided by the group that maintains the repository. Specific instructions on how to set up your own repository will depend on where the repository is hosted and is beyond the scope of the book. However, for outside hosting companies (like assembla.com), the details are available on their website.

When the solution has been added, these values can be updated through the File ➪ Subversion ➪ Change Source Control option, which opens the screen shown in Figure 13-4.

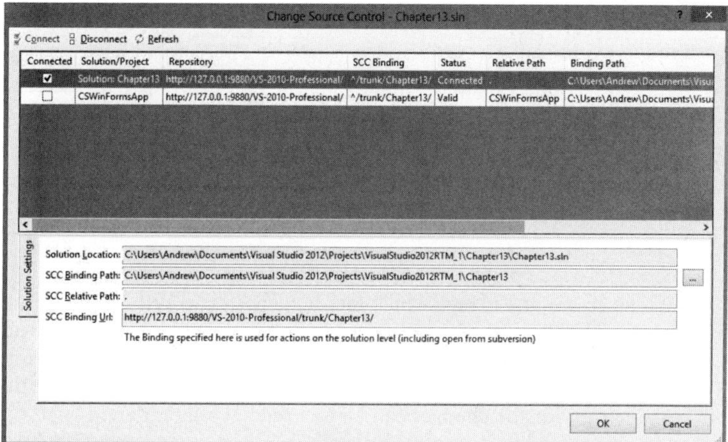

FIGURE 13-4

> **NOTE** *The Source Code Control (SCC) API assumes that the `.sln` solution file is located in the same folder or a direct parent folder as the project files. If you place the `.sln` solution file in a different folder hierarchy than the project files, then you should expect some "interesting" source control maintenance issues.*

Solution Explorer

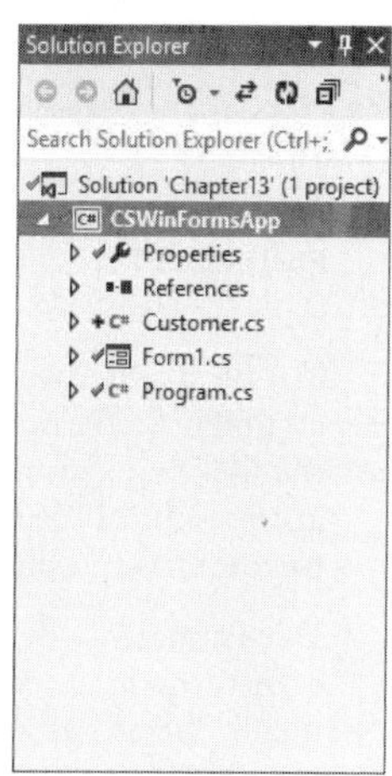

FIGURE 13-5

The first difference that you see after adding your solution to source control is that Visual Studio 2012 adjusts the icons within the Solution Explorer to indicate their source control status. Figure 13-5 illustrates three file states. When the solution is initially added to the source control repository, the files all appear with a little check mark icon next to the file type icon. This indicates that the file has been checked in and is not currently checked out by anyone. For example, the solution file and Properties have this icon.

When a solution is under source control, all changes are recorded, including the addition and removal of files. Figure 13-5 illustrates the addition of `Customer.cs` to the solution. The plus sign next to `Customer.cs` indicates that this is a new file. The red check mark next to the CSWinFormsApp project signifies that the file has been edited since it was last checked in.

Locking

Subversion has a locking concept similar to the checking in and out that is found in TFS. But there is a significant difference. If you edit a file, Subversion recognizes that the file has been changed. However, other developers can also change the file. To prevent others from editing the file, you need to lock them. If you are used to using Visual SourceSafe, you will find this behavior a little unusual; however, it is completely in line with how most source control management tools (including TFS and Subversion) currently work.

Locking is performed manually through the right-click shortcut menu associated with an item in the Solution Explorer. When a solution is under source control, the context menu includes a Subversion option, which expands to show the submenu shown in Figure 13-6.

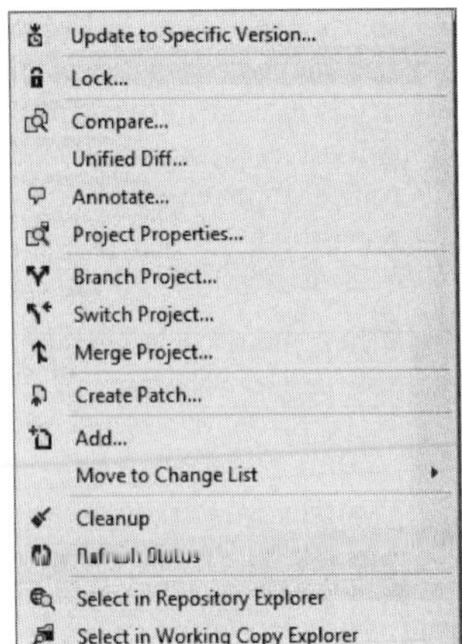

FIGURE 13-6

Along with the basic locking functionality, the context menu includes Branching, Differencing, reviewing annotations, and more. Detailed descriptions of what these functions are and how they operate are beyond the scope of this book, but details are readily available through AnkhSVN or Subversion documentation.

Pending Changes

In a large application, it can often be difficult to see at a glance which files have been checked out for editing or recently added or removed from a project. The Pending Changes window (which is available via the View menu), as shown in Figure 13-7, is useful for seeing which files are waiting to be checked into the repository. It also provides a space into which a comment can be added. This comment is attached to the files when they are checked into the repository so that the reason for the changes can be reviewed at a later date.

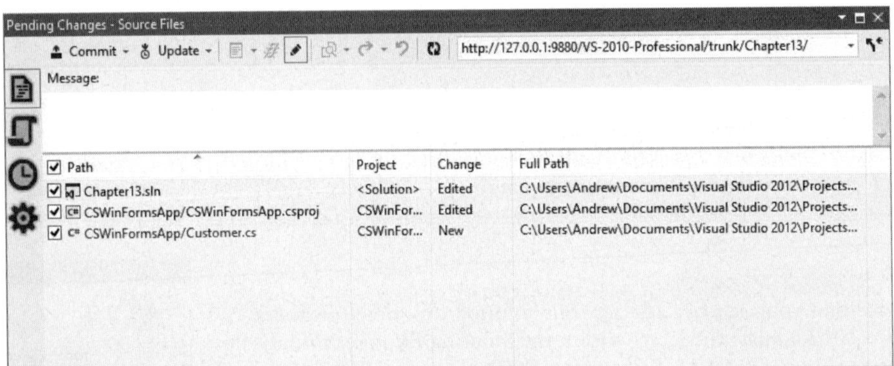

FIGURE 13-7

To check a file back in, you should ensure that there is a check against the file in the list, add an appropriate comment in the space provided, and then select the Commit button. If you want to maintain any locks on the files being committed, specify the Commit Keeping Locks option (found by selecting the drop-down at the right of the Commit button). This can be useful if you are in the middle of a set of changes and want to commit your current changes so that other developers can access them.

Occasionally, a developer may decide that changes made previously are no longer required and want to revert to what is contained in the repository. Through the Subversion option on the right-click context menu, there is an option to Update to Specific Version. Through the dialog that appears (Figure 13-8), it is possible to revert to a number of different versions, including the committed version.

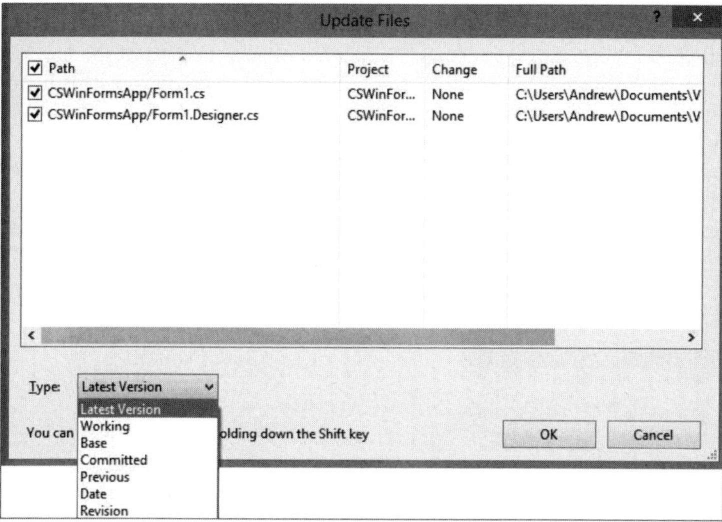

FIGURE 13-8

Merging Changes

Occasionally, changes might be made to the same file by multiple developers. In some cases, these changes can be automatically resolved if they are unrelated, such as the addition of a method to an existing class. However, when changes are made to the same portion of the file, there needs to be a process by which the changes can be mediated to determine the correct code.

For AnkhSVN, there are no built-in differencing or merging tools. However, it is possible to configure AnkhSVN to use the tools of your choice through the Tools ➪ Options menu (specifically, on the Subversion User Tools pane of the Source Control section, as shown in Figure 13-9).

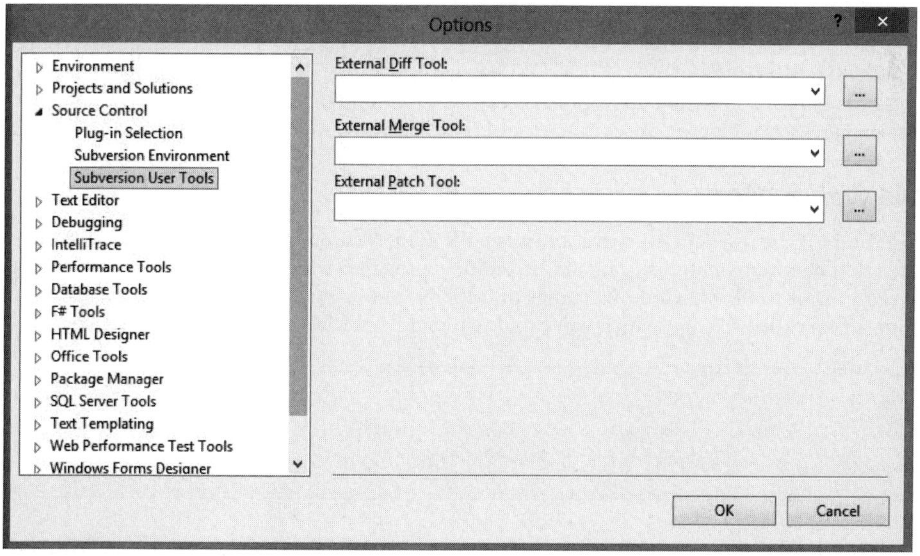

FIGURE 13-9

History

Anytime a file is updated in the Subversion repository, a history is recorded of each version of the file. Use the View History option on the right-click shortcut menu from the Solution Explorer to review this history. Figure 13-10 shows what a brief history of a file would look like. This dialog enables developers to view previous versions (you can see that the current file has two previous versions) and look at the comments related to each version (which appear in the Message column). The functionality offered on this screen is dependent on the source control plug-in that is being used. For AnkhSVN, these functions are the main ones available on this screen. However, if you utilize Team Foundation Server as your source control plug-in, then toolbar items and context menu options on this form allow you to get the particular version, mark a file as being checked out, compare different versions of the file, roll the file back to a previous version (which erases newer versions), and report on the version history.

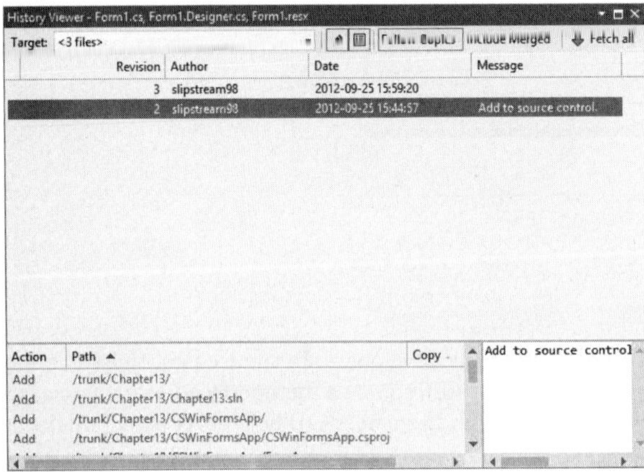

FIGURE 13-10

CODING STANDARDS

As software development projects and teams grow, there is a tendency for code to rapidly become a mixed bag of styles, standards, and approaches. This can lead to a maintenance nightmare, often resulting in new features being parked due to an abundance of bugs and issues that need to be addressed. Luckily, some great tools are both built into Visual Studio 2012 and available as add-ins that can enforce things like naming conventions and the ordering of methods, and ensure appropriate comments are written. In this section you'll learn about some tools that you can use to improve the consistency of the code you and your team write.

Code Analysis with FxCop

Over several iterations of the .NET Framework and Visual Studio, Microsoft has put together a set of coding standards that development teams can choose to adhere to. These are well documented under the topic of Code Analysis for Managed Code Warnings on MSDN (`http://msdn.microsoft.com`) and can be enforced using a tool called FxCop, which you can download from the Microsoft download site.

> **NOTE** *Visual Studio 2012 Premium edition and above include the Managed Code Analysis tool, which is essentially a version of FxCop that is integrated into the IDE. This is discussed in Chapter 55, "Visual Studio Ultimate for Developers."*

The latest version of FXCop (which is version 10.0, as of this writing) is available as part of the Microsoft Windows SDK for Windows 7 download. After you download the SDK, one of the options available is to install FxCop (the installer is at `%ProgramFiles%\Microsoft SDKs\Windows\v7.1\Bin\FXCop\FxCopSetup.exe`). Once installed, you'll run FxCop as a standalone tool from the Start menu. If you want to run FxCop as part of your build process, you can run it from the command line using the `FxCopCmd.exe` found in the install folder.

When FxCop launches through the Windows Start menu, it automatically creates and opens a new project. If you are using FxCop in conjunction with a real project (as opposed to a sample project that you've created to work through the ideas in this book), save the project into the folder alongside the solution file for your application.

An empty FxCop project is not of much use. To analyze the output from projects, you need to add targets to the project. From the Project menu in FxCop, select Add Targets, and choose the assemblies (dlls and exes) that make up the application you which the evaluate. When all of the assemblies have been chosen, click the Analyze button to run the code analysis over all of the targets; the result should look similar to Figure 13-11.

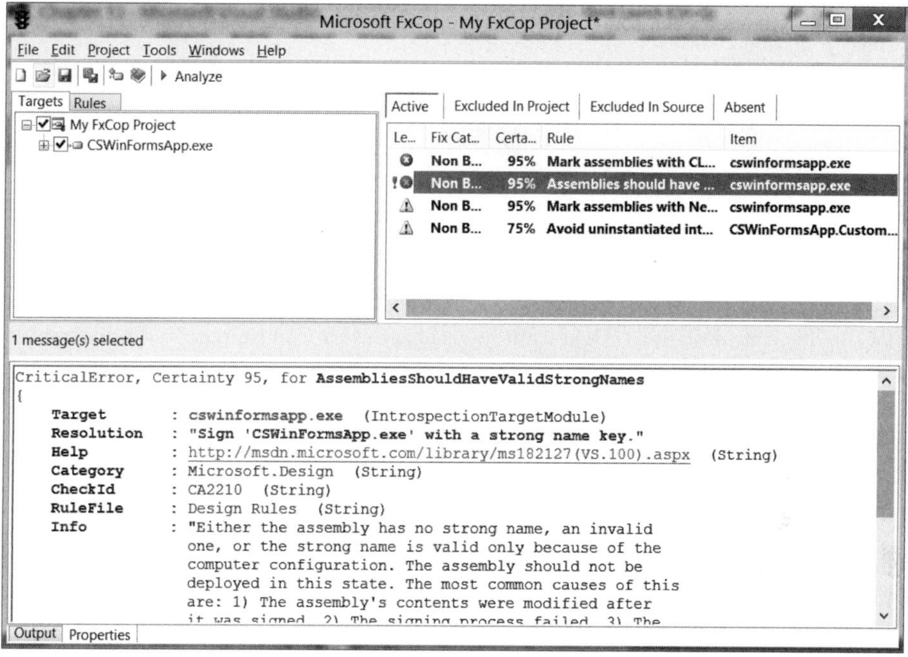

FIGURE 13-11

As you can see from Figure 13-11, there are three errors (including one marked as critical) and one warning. Although you can ignore the warnings, they quite often indicate an area of concern, either to do with the architecture or security of your code, so it is wise to try to minimize or eliminate where possible the number of warnings and errors. In this example, the first error is easy to resolve; you can just code sign the application and the error will go away. However, it may not be possible to mark your assembly with the `CLSCompliant` attribute, which is what the second error requires. So that this error doesn't appear each time in the active errors list, you can right-click the error and select Exclude. You'll be prompted to add a comment so that you can justify the exclusion of that error. After you click OK, the excluded error appears in the Excluded in Project tab, as shown in the background of Figure 13-12. Double-clicking this error opens the details for the error in which you can find your comment in the Notes section.

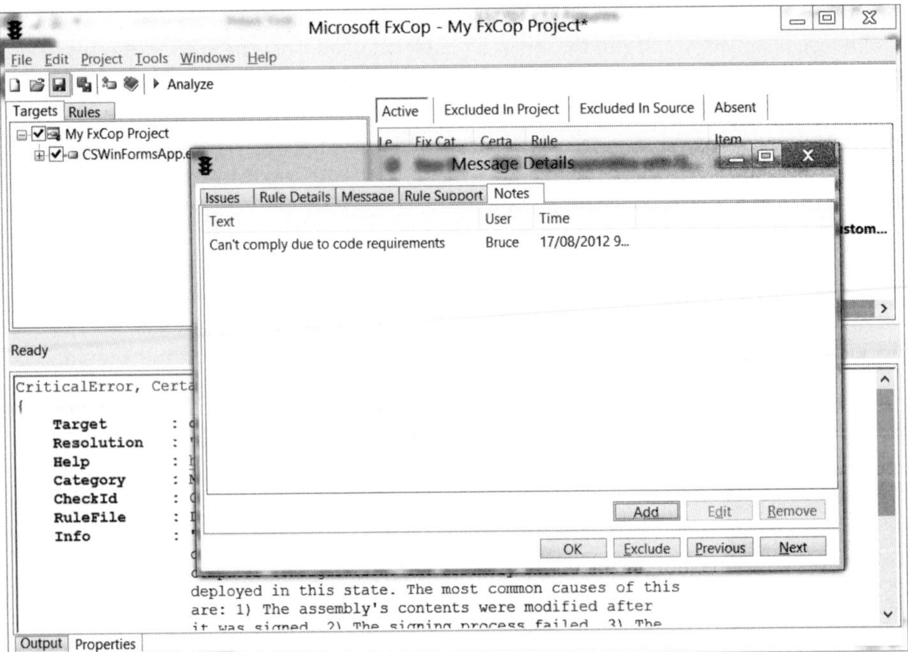

FIGURE 13-12

The third error in Figure 13-11 points out that the `MessageBoxOptions` parameter hasn't been specified. In this case, this is by design, so you'll want to exclude the error in source. To do this, add the `SuppressMessage` attribute to the method calling `MessageBox.Show` as in the following code. The parameters supplied are the Category, CheckId, and Name of the error as found in the Message Details window for the error.

C#

```
[System.Diagnostics.CodeAnalysis.SuppressMessage("Microsoft.Globalization",
                                        "CA1300:SpecifyMessageBoxOptions",
                    Justification="MessageBoxOptions omitted intentionally")]
private void SayHelloButton_Click(object sender, EventArgs e){
    MessageBox.Show("Hello World!");
}
```

VB

```
<System.Diagnostics.CodeAnalysis.SuppressMessage("Microsoft.Globalization",
                                              "CA1300:SpecifyMessageBoxOptions",
                    Justification:="MessageBoxOptions omitted intentionally")>
Private Sub SayHelloButton_Click(ByVal sender As System.Object, _
                     ByVal e As System.EventArgs) Handles SayHelloButton.Click
    MessageBox.Show("Hello World!")
End Sub
```

To get FxCop to notice the `SuppressMessage` attribute, you'll also need to set the `CODE_ANALYSIS` compilation flag. You do this by adding the `CODE_ANALYSIS` keyword to the Custom Constants textbox in the Advanced Compile Options dialog (from the Compile tab of the project properties page) for VB, or by adding the same keyword to the Conditional compilation symbols textbox (on the Build tab of the project properties page) for C#. After saving, rebuilding your application and rerunning the Analysis (note that you don't need to restart or even reload the project within FxCop) you can see that the error has been moved to the Excluded in Source tab. Again, double-clicking the error and going to the Notes tab reveals the contents of the `Justification` parameter specified as part of the `SuppressMessage` attribute. (You may need to import the `System.Diagnostic.CodeAnalysis` namespace to use this attribute.)

You have two other ways to control how FxCop is applied to your code. The first is to use the Targets window to enable/disable the running of rules on sections of code. The left image of Figure 13-13 shows the Targets window with the SourceSafeSample expanded to view the `IsAdminUser` property. In this example the check boxes have been unchecked to indicate that rules should not be run on this property.

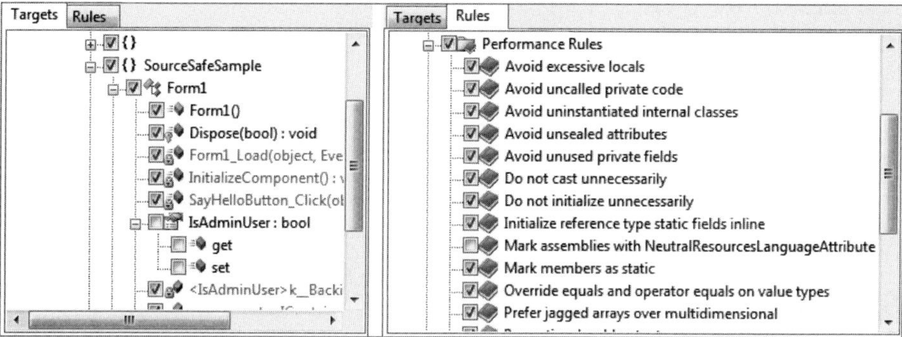

FIGURE 13-13

In the right image of Figure 13-13, you can see the Rules list that has been expanded to show the Mark assemblies with `NeutralResourcesLanguageAttribute` rule. This was the rule that was generating a warning in Figure 13-11 and has been unchecked to prevent this rule being used in the analysis.

> **NOTE** *Excluding an entire rule is generally not a good practice because it can hide errors at a later date. For example, if an assembly is added to the project, this rule will never be run on that assembly, even though it may be important for the rule to be applied to that assembly.*

FxCop comes with a large selection of rules that may or may not align with the way you and your team write code. If you want to enforce your own standards, you can extend the default set of rules by writing your own, using the FxCop SDK that comes with FxCop as a reference.

Style Using StyleCop

StyleCop, which is available at `http://stylecop.codeplex.com`, is great for maintaining a common coding style. StyleCop integrates into the Visual Studio 2012 IDE, allowing you to invoke the analysis from the Tools menu, as shown in Figure 13-14.

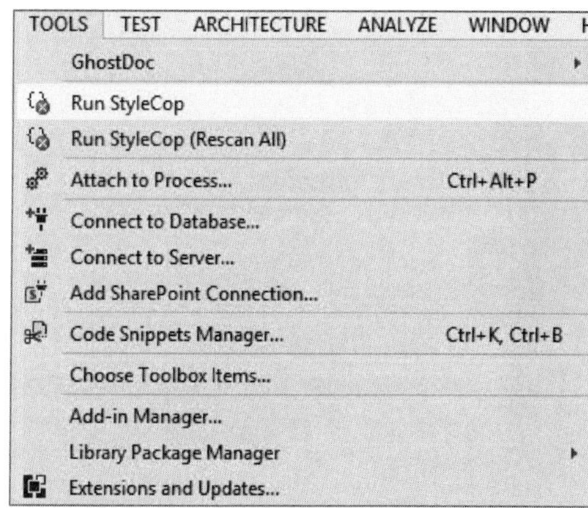

FIGURE 13-14

After running StyleCop, you can see that any issues are by default reported as warnings, as in Figure 13-15. If you want to enforce StyleCop you need to tell Visual Studio 2012 to treat warnings as errors.

Error List

0 Errors | 38 Warnings | 0 Messages | Search Error List

	Description	File	Line
1	SA1600: The class must have a documentation header.	Customer.cs	8
2	SA1633: The file has no header, the header Xml is invalid, or the header is not located at the top of the file.	Customer.cs	1
3	SA1400: The class must have an access modifier.	Customer.cs	8
4	SA1200: All using directives must be placed inside of the namespace.	Customer.cs	1
5	SA1200: All using directives must be placed inside of the namespace.	Customer.cs	2
6	SA1200: All using directives must be placed inside of the namespace.	Customer.cs	3
7	SA1200: All using directives must be placed inside of the namespace.	Customer.cs	4
8	SA1600: The class must have a documentation header.	Program.cs	8
9	SA1633: The file has no header, the header Xml is invalid, or the header is not located at the top of the file.	Program.cs	1
10	SA1400: The class must have an access modifier.	Program.cs	8

FIGURE 13-15

You can elect to ignore rules via the StyleCop settings, or suppress rules in specific instances by adding the `SuppressMessage` attribute. You will most likely have to right-click the warning and select Show Error Help to access the Category, CheckId, and Name of the warning you are going to suppress. The format for the `SuppressMessage` arguments are `("[Category]", "[CheckId]:[Name]")`, so for example, `("Maintainability Rules", "SA1400:AccessModifierMustBeDeclared")`.

Code Contracts

The last tool that we're going to cover is Microsoft Code Contracts, which, unlike in previous versions, has been built into the .NET Framework. More specifically, it's part of the System.Diagnostics.Contracts namespace.

Once the appropriate using/Imports statement has been added to your file, you can add contracts in the form of pre- and post-conditions to your code. In the following code snippet, you can see a precondition set for the `Divide` method that requires (using `Contract.Requires`) that the denominator is not zero. Similarly, there is a post-condition that ensures (using `Contract.Ensure`) the `Add` method increments the field `currentValue` by the correct amount.

C#

```
private double currentValue;
private double Divide(double denominator){
    Contract.Requires(denominator != 0);
    return currentValue / denominator;
}
private void Add(double valueToAdd){
    Contract.Ensures(currentValue == Contract.OldValue(currentValue) + valueToAdd);
    // Do nothing so that contract fails
}

private void InvokeDivision(){
    currentValue = 7.0;
    double c = Divide(0); // fails validation because b == 0
}
private void InvokeAddition(){
    currentValue = 13.0;
    Add(6);
}
```

VB

```
Private currentValue As Double
Private Function Divide(ByVal denominator As Double) As Double
```

```
        Contract.Requires(denominator <> 0)
        Return currentValue / denominator
    End Function
    Private Sub Add(ByVal valueToAdd As Double)
        Contract.Ensures(currentValue = Contract.OldValue(currentValue) + valueToAdd)
        ' Do nothing so that contract fails
    End Sub

    Private Sub InvokeDivision()
        currentValue = 7.0
        Dim c = Divide(0.0) 'fails validation because b == 0
    End Sub

    Private Sub InvokeAddition()
        currentValue = 13.0
        Add(6)
    End Sub
```

With these contracts in place, you'll need to enable contract verification via the Code Contracts tab of the project properties page, as shown in Figure 13-16. Now when you build and run your application, you can see an Assert dialog thrown when either `InvokeDivision` or `InvokeAddition` are called, reflecting the contract that has been violated.

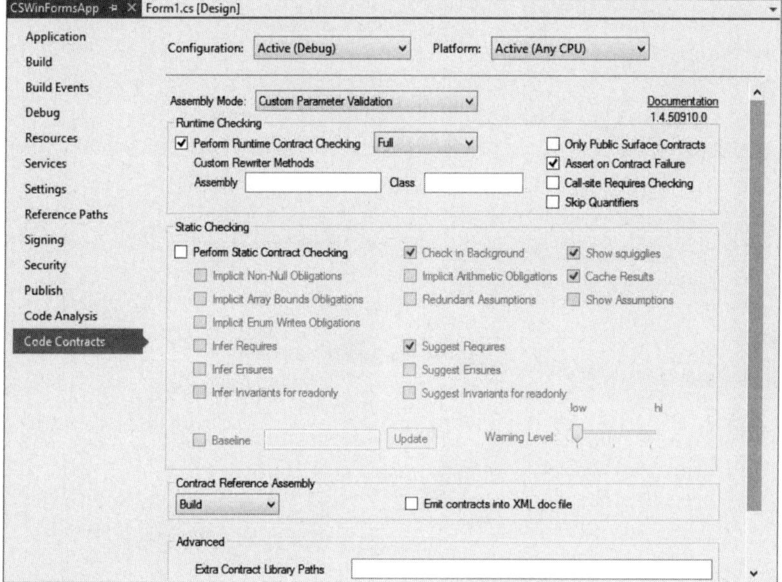

FIGURE 13-16

Here you can see that run-time checking has been enabled and that it has been set to raise an Assert on Contract Failure. If you disable this option a `ContractException` is raised instead, which you can handle via code.

> **NOTE** *In the middle of Figure 13-16, there is an area dedicated to configuring Static Checking options. These are available if you install Code Contracts for Visual Studio 2012 Premium and above. This enables further static checking to attempt to ensure contracts are not violated at design time, rather than waiting for them to fail at run time.*

SUMMARY

This chapter demonstrated the rich interface of Visual Studio 2012 when using a source control repository to manage files associated with an application. Checking files in and out can be done using the Solution Explorer window, and more advanced functionality is available via the Pending Changes window.

Although we have been covering Subversion and AnkhSVN as source code tools, they are not the only options available. Git (`http://git-scm.com/`) is a popular choice, and the newly introduced cloud-based version of TFS (`www.tfspreview.com`) is gaining some traction. And Chapter 57, "Team Foundation Server," discusses the advantages and additional functionality that is provided by Team Foundation Server, an enterprise-class source control repository system.

This chapter also introduced you to FxCop, StyleCop, and Code Contracts, which can be used to improve the quality, reliability, and consistency of your code. Their close integration into or with Visual Studio 2012 makes them invaluable tools for development teams of any size.

14

Code Generation with T4

WHAT'S IN THIS CHAPTER?

- Using T4 templates to generate text and code
- Troubleshooting T4 templates
- Creating Runtime T4 template to include templating in your projects

Frequently, when writing software applications, you'll have large areas of boilerplate code in which the same pattern is repeated over and over. Working on these areas of code can be time-consuming and tedious, which leads to inattention and easily avoidable errors. Writing this code is a task best suited to automation.

Code generation is a common software engineering practice where some mechanism, rather than a human engineer, is used to write program components automatically. The tool used to generate the code is known as a *code generator*. A number of commercial and free code generators are available in the market, from the general to those targeted toward a specific task.

Visual Studio 2012 includes a code generator that can generate files from simple template definitions. This code generator is the Text Template Transformation Toolkit, or more commonly, T4.

T4 was originally introduced as part of the Domain Specific Languages Toolkit, which was an add-in for Visual Studio 2005. T4 was included out of the box in Visual Studio 2008, but it was poorly documented, and there were few hints in the IDE that it existed. Visual Studio 2010 made T4 a first-class citizen so that Text Template is now one of the options in the File ➪ New dialog.

This chapter explores the creation, configuration, and execution of T4 templates. You'll also see how to troubleshoot templates when they go wrong. Finally, you'll create a Runtime Text Template that enables you to create reusable T4 templates that you can easily call from your own code.

CREATING A T4 TEMPLATE

In earlier versions of Visual Studio, creating a new T4 template was a hidden feature that involved creating a text file with the `.tt` extension. Ever since Visual Studio 2010, you can create a T4 template simply by selecting Text Template from the General page of the Add New Item dialog, as shown in Figure 14-1.

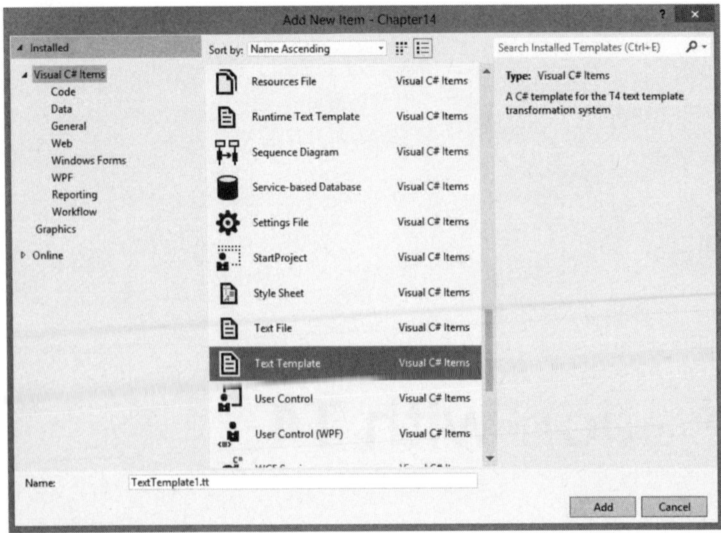

FIGURE 14-1

When a new T4 template is created or saved, Visual Studio displays the warning dialog, as shown in Figure 14-2. T4 templates execute normal .NET code and can theoretically be used to run *any* sort of .NET code. T4 templates are executed every time they are saved, so you will likely see this warning a lot. There is an option to suppress these warnings, but it is global to all templates in all solutions. If you do turn it off and decide you'd rather have the warnings, you can reactivate them by changing Show Security Message to True in Tools ➪ Options ➪ Text Templating.

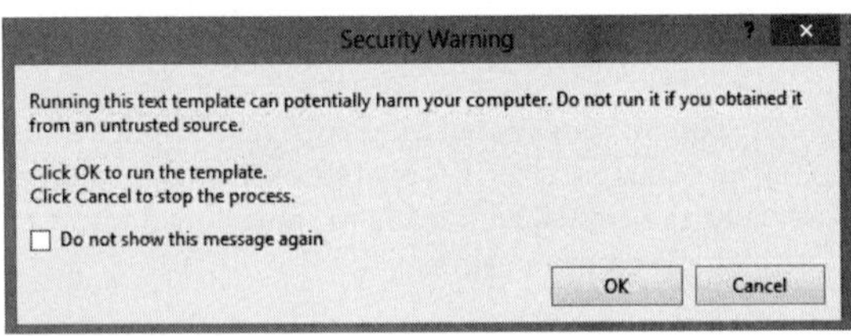

FIGURE 14-2

After you create the template, it appears in the Solution Explorer window as a file with the `.tt` extension. The template file can be expanded to reveal the file it generates. Each template generates a single file, which has the same name as the template file and a different extension. Figure 14-3 shows a template file and the file it generates in Solution Explorer.

HelloWorld.tt
HelloWorld.txt

FIGURE 14-3

> **NOTE** *If you use VB you need to enable Show All Files for the project to see the generated file.*

The generated file is initially empty because no output has been defined in the template file. The template file is not empty, however. When it is first generated, it contains the following two lines:

```
<#@ template debug="false" hostspecific="false" language="C#" #>
<#@ output extension=".txt" #>
```

Each of these two lines is a T4 *directive*, which controls some aspect of the way in which the template is executed. T4 directives are discussed in the "T4 Directives" section, but there are a few things of interest here. The `template` directive contains an attribute specifying which `language` the template will use. Each template file can include code statements that are executed to generate the final file, and this attribute tells Visual Studio which language those statements will be in.

> **NOTE** *The template language has no impact on the file generated. You can generate a C# file from a template that uses the VB language and vice versa. This defaults to the language of the current project but can be changed. Both C# and VB templates are supported in projects of either language.*

The second thing of note is the `extension` attribute on the `output` directive. The name of the generated file is always the same as that of the template file except that the `.tt` extension is replaced by the contents of this attribute. If Visual Studio recognizes the extension of the generated file, it treats it the same as if you had created it from the Add New Item dialog. In particular, if the extension denotes a code file, such as `.cs` or `.vb`, Visual Studio adds the generated file to the build process of your project.

> **NOTE** *When the output extension of a template is changed, the previously generated file is deleted the next time the template is run. As long as you are not editing the generated file, this shouldn't be an issue.*

At the bottom of the template file add a single line containing the words `Hello World` and save the template.

C#

```
<#@ template debug="false" hostspecific="false" language="C#" #>
<#@ output extension=".txt" #>
Hello World
```

VB

```
<#@ template debug="false" hostspecific="false" language="VB" #>
<#@ output extension=".txt" #>
Hello World
```

As mentioned previously, templates are run every time they are saved, so the generated file will be updated with the new contents of the template. Open up the generated file to see the text `Hello World`.

Although each individual template file can always be regenerated by opening it and saving it again, the template can be generated using either the Run Custom Tool option on the right-click menu from within Solution Explorer or the Run Custom Tool menu option from the Project menu. Clicking this button transforms all the templates in the solution.

As mentioned previously, if the `output` directive specifies an extension that matches the language of the current project, the resulting generated file is included in the project. You can get full IntelliSense from types and members declared within generated files. The next code snippet shows a T4 template along with the code that it generates. You can access the generated class by other parts of the program and a small console application demonstrating this follows.

C#

```
<#@ template debug="false" hostspecific="false" language="C#" #>
<#@ output extension=".cs" #>
namespace AdventureWorks {
```

```
    class GreetingManager {
      public static void SayHi() {
        System.Console.WriteLine("Aloha Cousin!");
      }
    }
  }
  namespace AdventureWorks {
    class GreetingManager {
      public static void SayHi() {
        System.Console.WriteLine("Aloha Cousin!");
      }
    }
  }
  namespace AdventureWorks {
    class Program {
      static void Main(string[] args) {
        GreetingManager.SayHi();
      }
    }
  }
```

VB

```
<#@ template debug="false" hostspecific="false" language="VB" #>
<#@ output extension=".vb" #>
Public Class GreetingManager
  Public Shared Sub SayHi
    System.Console.WriteLine( "Aloha Cousin!" )
  End Sub
End Class
Public Class GreetingManager
    Public Shared Sub SayHi()
        System.Console.WriteLine("Aloha Cousin!")
    End Sub
End Class
Module Module1
  Sub Main()
    GreetingManager.SayHi()
  End Sub
End Module
```

> **NOTE** *Although the rest of your application will get IntelliSense covering your generated code, the T4 template files have no IntelliSense or syntax highlighting in Visual Studio 2012. A few third-party editors and plug-ins are available that provide a richer design-time experience for T4.*

This example works, but it doesn't actually demonstrate the power and flexibility that T4 can offer. This is because the template is completely static. To create useful templates, more dynamic capabilities are required.

T4 BUILDING BLOCKS

Each T4 template consists of a number of *blocks* that affect the generated file. The line `Hello World` from the first example is a Text block. Text blocks are copied verbatim from the template file into the generated file. They can contain any kind of text and can contain other blocks.

In addition to Text blocks, three other types of blocks exist: Expression blocks, Statement blocks, and Class Feature blocks. Each of the other types of block is surrounded by a specific kind of markup to identify it. Text blocks are the only type of block that has no special markup.

Expression Blocks

An Expression block is used to pass some computed value to the generated file. Expression blocks normally appear inside of Text blocks and are denoted by `<#=` and `#>` tags. Here is an example of a template that outputs the date and time that the file was generated.

C#

```
<#@ template debug="false" hostspecific="false" language="C#" #>
<#@ output extension=".txt" #>
This file was generated: <#=System.DateTime.Now #>
```

VB

```
<#@ template debug="false" hostspecific="false" language="VB" #>
<#@ output extension=".txt" #>
This file was generated: <#=System.DateTime.Now #>
```

The expression inside the block may be any valid expression in the template language specified in the `template` directive. Every time it is run, the template evaluates the expression and then calls `ToString()` on the result. This value is then inserted into the generated file.

Statement Blocks

A Statement block is used to execute arbitrary statements when the template is run. Code inside a Statement block might log the execution of the template, create temporary variables, or delete a file from your computer, so you need to be careful. In fact, the code inside a Statement block can consist of any valid statement in the template language. Statement blocks are commonly used to implement flow control within a template, manage temporary variables, and interact with other systems. A Statement block is denoted by `<#` and `#>` tags that are similar to Expression block delimiters but without the equals sign. The following example produces a file with all 99 verses of a popular drinking song.

C#

```
<#@ template debug="false" hostspecific="false" language="C#" #>
<#@ output extension=".txt" #>
<# for( int i = 99; i > = 1; )
   { #>
<#=i #> Bottles of Non-alcoholic Carbonated Beverage on the wall
<#=i #> Bottles of Non-alcoholic Carbonated Beverage
Take one down
And pass it around
<# if( i-1 == 0 ) { #>
There's no Bottles of Non-alcoholic Carbonated Beverage on the wall
<# } else { #>
There's <#=i-1 #> Bottles of Non-alcoholic Carbonated Beverage on the wall
<# } #>
  <# } #>
```

VB

```
<#@ template debug="false" hostspecific="false" language="VB" #>
<#@ output extension=".txt" #>
<# For i As Integer = 99 To 1 Step -1 #>
  <#= i #> Bottles of Non-alcoholic Carbonated Beverage on the wall
  <#= i #> Bottles of Non-alcoholic Carbonated Beverage
  Take one down
  And pass it around
```

```
<# If i - 1 = 0 Then #>
  There's no Bottles of Non-Alcoholic Carbonated Beverage on the wall.
<# Else #>
  There's <#= i-1 #> Bottles of Non-alcoholic Carbonated Beverage on the wall.
<# End If #>
<# Next #>
```

> **NOTE** *In the preceding example the Statement block contains another Text block, which in turn contains a number of Expression blocks. Using these three block types alone enables you to create some powerful templates*

Although the Statement block in the example contains other blocks, it doesn't need to. From within a Statement block you can write directly to the generated file using the `Write()` and `WriteLine()` methods. Here is the example again using this method.

C#

```
<#@ template debug="false" hostspecific="false" language="C#" #>
<#@ output extension=".txt" #>
<#
for( int i = 99; i > 1; i-- )
{
  WriteLine( "{0} Bottles of Non-alcoholic Carbonated Beverage on the wall", i);
  WriteLine( "{0} Bottles of Non-alcoholic Carbonated Beverage", i );
  WriteLine( "Take one down" );
  WriteLine( "And pass it around" );
  if( i - 1 == 0 ) {
    WriteLine(
      "There's no Bottles of Non-alcoholic Carbonated Beverage on the wall." );
  } else {
    WriteLine(
      "There's {0} Bottles of Non-alcoholic Carbonated Beverage on the wall.",i-1);
  }
  WriteLine( "" );
} #>
```

VB

```
<#@ template debug="false" hostspecific="false" language="VB" #>
<#@ output extension=".txt" #>
<# For i As Integer = 99 To 1 Step -1
  Me.WriteLine("{0} Bottles of Non-alcoholic Carbonated Beverage on the wall", i)
  Me.WriteLine("{0} Bottles of Non-alcoholic Carbonated Beverage", i)
  Me.WriteLine("Take one down")
  Me.WriteLine("And pass it around")
  If i - 1 = 0 Then
    WriteLine("There's no Bottles of Non-Alcoholic Carbonated Beverage on the" & _
      " wall.")
  Else
    WriteLine("There's {0} Bottles of Non-alcoholic Carbonated Beverage on the" & _
      " wall.",i-1)
  End If
  Me.WriteLine( "" )
  Next #>
```

The final generated results for these two templates are the same. Depending on the template, you might find one technique or the other easier to understand. It is recommended that you use one technique exclusively in each template to avoid confusion.

Class Feature Blocks

The final type of T4 block is the Class Feature block. These blocks contain arbitrary code that can be called from Statement and Expression blocks to help in the production of the generated file. This often includes custom formatting code or repetitive tasks. Class Feature blocks are denoted using <#+ and #> tags that are similar to those that denote Expression blocks except that the equals sign in the opening tag becomes a plus character. The following template writes the numbers from –5 to 5 using a typical financial format where every number has two decimal places, is preceded by a dollar symbol, and negatives are written as positive amounts but are placed in brackets.

C#

```
<#@ template debug="false" hostspecific="false" language="C#" #>
<#@ output extension=".txt" #>
Financial Sample Data
<# for( int i = -5; i <= 5; i++ )
   {
     WriteFinancialNumber(i);
         WriteLine( "" );
   } #>
End of Sample Data
 <#+
   void WriteFinancialNumber(decimal amount)
   {
     if( amount < 0 )
       Write("(${0:#0.00})", System.Math.Abs(amount) );
     else
        Write("${0:#0.00}", amount);
   }
   #>
```

VB

```
<#@ template debug="true" hostspecific="false" language="VB" #>
<#@ output extension=".txt" #>
Financial Sample Data
<# For i as Integer = -5 To 5
   WriteFinancialNumber(i)
   WriteLine( "" )
 Next  #>
End of Sample Data
<#+
Sub WriteFinancialNumber(amount as Decimal)
  If amount < 0 Then
    Write("(${0:#0.00})", System.Math.Abs(amount) )
  Else
    Write("${0:#0.00}", amount)
  End If
End Sub
#>
```

Class Feature blocks can contain Text blocks and Expression blocks but they cannot contain Statement blocks. In addition to this, no Statement blocks are allowed to appear after the first Class Feature block is encountered.

Now that you know the different types of T4 blocks that can appear within a template file, it's time to see how Visual Studio 2012 can use them to generate the output file.

HOW T4 WORKS

The process to generate a file from a T4 template is composed of two basic steps. In the first step, the `.tt` file is used to generate a standard .NET class. This class inherits from the `abstract` (`MustInherit`) `Microsoft.VisualStudio.TextTemplating.TextTransformation` class and overrides a method called `TransformText()`.

In the second step, an instance of this class is created and configured, and the `TransformText` method is called. This method returns a string used as the contents of the generated file.

Normally, you won't see the generated class file but you can configure the T4 engine to make a copy available by turning debugging on for the template. This simply involves setting the `debug` attribute of the `template` directive to `true` and saving the template file.

After a T4 template is executed in Debug mode, a number of files are created in the temporary folder of the system. One of these files will have a random name and a `.cs` or a `.vb` extension (depending on the template language). This file contains the actual generator class.

> **NOTE** *You can find the temporary folder of the system by opening a Visual Studio command prompt and entering the command* `echo %TEMP%`.

This code contains a lot of preprocessor directives that support template debugging but make the code quite difficult to read. Here are the contents of the code file generated from the `FinancialSample.tt` template presented in the previous section reformatted and with these directives removed.

C#

```
namespace Microsoft.VisualStudio.TextTemplatingBE7601CBE8A6858147D586FD8FC4C6F9
{
  using System;
  public class GeneratedTextTransformation :
         Microsoft.VisualStudio.TextTemplating.TextTransformation
  {
    public override string TransformText()
    {
      try
      {
        this.Write("\r\nFinancial Sample Data\r\n");

        for( int i = -5; i <= 5; i++ )
        {
          WriteFinancialNumber(i);
          WriteLine( "" );
        }

        this.Write("End of Sample Data\r\n\r\n ");
      }
      catch (System.Exception e)
      {
        System.CodeDom.Compiler.CompilerError error = new
                     System.CodeDom.Compiler.CompilerError();
        error.ErrorText = e.ToString();
        error.FileName = "C:\\dev\\Chapter 14\\Chapter 14\\Finance.tt";
        this.Errors.Add(error);
      }
      return this.GenerationEnvironment.ToString();
    }
```

```
      void WriteFinancialNumber(decimal amount)
      {
        if( amount < 0 )
          Write("({0:#0.00})", System.Math.Abs(amount) );
        else
          Write("{0:#0.00}", amount);
      }
    }
  }
```

VB

```
Imports System
Namespace Microsoft.VisualStudio.TextTemplating2739DD4202E83EF5273E1D1376F8FC4E
  Public Class GeneratedTextTransformation
    Inherits Microsoft.VisualStudio.TextTemplating.TextTransformation
    Public Overrides Function TransformText() As String
      Try
        Me.Write(""&Global.Microsoft.VisualBasic.ChrW(13) _
          & Global.Microsoft.VisualBasic.ChrW(10) _
          & "Financial Sample Data" _
          & Global.Microsoft.VisualBasic.ChrW(13) _
          & Global.Microsoft.VisualBasic.ChrW(10)) _

        For i as Integer = -5 To 5
          WriteFinancialNumber(i)
          WriteLine( "" )
        Next

        Me.Write("End of Sample Data" _
          & Global.Microsoft.VisualBasic.ChrW(13) _
          & Global.Microsoft.VisualBasic.ChrW(10) _
          & Global.Microsoft.VisualBasic.ChrW(13) _
          & Global.Microsoft.VisualBasic.ChrW(10)&" ")
      Catch e As System.Exception
        Dim [error] As System.CodeDom.Compiler.CompilerError = _
           New System.CodeDom.Compiler.CompilerError()
        [error].ErrorText = e.ToString
        [error].FileName = "C:\\dev\\Chapter 14\\Chapter 14\\Finance.tt"
        Me.Errors.Add([error])
      End Try
      Return Me.GenerationEnvironment.ToString
    End Function

    Sub WriteFinancialNumber(amount as Decimal)
      If amount < 0 Then
        Write("(${0:#0.00})", System.Math.Abs(amount) )
      Else
        Write("${0:#0.00}", amount)
      End If
    End Sub

  End Class
End Namespace
```

Note a few things of interest in this code. First, the template is executed by running the `TransformText()` method. The contents of this method run within the context of a try-catch block where all errors are captured and stored. Visual Studio 2012 knows how to retrieve these errors and displays them in the normal errors tool window.

The next interesting thing is the use of `Write()`. You can see that each Text block has been translated into a single string, which is passed to the `Write()` method. Under the covers, this is added to the `GenerationEnvironment` property, which is then converted into a string and returned to the T4 engine.

The Statement blocks and the Class Feature blocks are copied verbatim into the generated class. The difference is in where they end up. Statement blocks appear inside the `TransformText()` method, but Class Feature blocks appear after it and exist at the same scope. This should give you some idea as to the kinds of things you could declare within a Class Feature block.

Finally, Expression blocks are evaluated and the result is passed into `Microsoft.VisualStudio.TextTemplating.ToStringHelper.ToStringWithCulture()`. This method returns a string, which is then passed back into `Write()` as if it were a Text block. Note that the `ToStringHelper` takes a specific culture into account when producing a string from an expression. This culture can be specified as an attribute of the `template` directive.

When the `TransformText()` method finishes execution, it passes a string back to the host environment, which in this case is Visual Studio 2012. It is up to the host to decide what to do with it. Visual Studio uses the `output` directive for this task. Directives are the subject of the next section.

> **NOTE** *Before moving on, the previous text implied that T4 does not need to run inside Visual Studio. There is a command-line tool called* `TextTransform.exe`, *which you can find in the* `%CommonProgramFiles%\microsoft shared\TextTemplating\11.0\` *folder (*`C:\Program Files(x86)\Common Files\microsoft shared\TextTemplating\11.0\` *on 64-bit machines). Although you can use this to generate files during a build process, T4 relies on the presence of certain libraries installed with Visual Studio to run. This means that if you have a separate build machine, you need to install Visual Studio on it. Within Visual Studio, files with the* `.tt` *extension are processed with a custom tool referred to as* `TextTemplatingFileGenerator`.

T4 DIRECTIVES

A T4 template can communicate with its execution environment by using directives. Each directive needs to be on its own line and is denoted with `<#@` and `#>` tags. This section discusses the five standard directives.

Template Directive

The `template` directive controls a number of diverse options about the template. It contains the following attributes:

- `language`: Defines the .NET language used throughout the template inside of Expression, Statement, and Class Feature blocks. Valid values are `C#` and `VB`.
- `inherits`: Determines the base class of the generated class used to produce the output file. This can be overridden to provide additional functionality from within template files. Any new base class must derive from `Microsoft.VisualStudio.TextTemplating.TextTransformation`, which is the default value for the attribute.

> **NOTE** *If you want to inherit from a different base class, you need to use an* `assembly` *directive (see the "Assembly Directive" section) to make it available to the T4 template.*

- `culture`: Selects a localization culture for the template to be executed within. Values should be expressed using the standard xx-XX notation (en-US, ja-JP, and so on). The default value is a blank string that specifies the Invariant Culture.

- `debug`: Turns on Debug mode. This causes the code file containing the generator class to be dumped into the temporary folder of the system. It can be set to `true` or `false`. It defaults to `false`.
- `hostspecific`: Indicates that the template file is designed to work within a specific host. If set to `true`, a `Host` property is exposed from within the template. When running in Visual Studio 2012, this property is of type `Microsoft.VisualStudio.TextTemplating.VSHost.TextTemplatingService`. It defaults to `false`. It is beyond the scope of this book, but you can write your own host for T4 and use it to execute template files.

Output Directive

The `output` directive is used to control the file generated by the template. It contains two properties.

- `extension`: The extension that will be added to the generator name to create the filename of the output file. The contents of this property basically replace `.tt` in the template filename. By default, this is `.cs` but it may contain any sequence of characters that the underlying file system allows.
- encoding: Controls the encoding of the generated file. This can be the result of any of the encodings returned by `System.Text.Encoding.GetEncodings()`; that is, UTF-8, ASCII, and Unicode. The value is Default, which makes the encoding equal to the current ANSI code page of the system the template is run on.

Assembly Directive

The `assembly` directive is used to give code within the template file access to classes and types defined in other assemblies. It is similar to adding a reference to a normal .NET project. It has a single attribute called `name`, which should contain one of the following items:

- **The filename of the assembly:** The assembly will be loaded from the same directory as the T4 template.
- **The absolute path of the assembly:** The assembly will be loaded from the exact path provided.
- **The relative path of the assembly:** The assembly will be loaded from the relative location with respect to the directory in which the T4 template is located.
- **The strong name of the assembly:** The assembly will be loaded from the Global Assembly Cache (CAG).

Import Directive

The `import` directive is used to provide easy access to items without specifying their full namespace-qualified type name. It works in the same way as the `Import` statement in VB or the `using` statement from C#. It has a single attribute called `namespace`. By default, the `System` namespace is already imported for you. The following example shows a small Statement block both with and without an `import` directive.

C#

```
<#
  var myList = new System.Collections.Generic.List<string>();
  var myDictionary = new System.Collections.Generic.Dictionary<string,
 System.Collections.Generic.List <string>>();
#>
```

VB

```
<#
Dim myList As New System.Collections.Generic.List(Of String)
Dim myDictionary As New System.Collections.Generic.Dictionary(Of System.String,
System.Collections.Generic.List(Of String))
#>
```

C#

```
<#@ import namespace="System.Collections.Generic" #>
<#
  var myList = new List<string>();
  var myDictionary = new Dictionary<string, List<string>>();
#>
```

VB

```
<#@ import namespace="System.Collections.Generic" #>
<#
Dim myList As New List(Of String)
Dim myDictionary As New Dictionary(Of String, List(Of String))
#>
```

> **NOTE** *The code that benefits from the* `import` *and* `assembly` *directives is the code that is executed when the T4 template is run, not the code contained within the final output file. If you want to access resources in other namespaces in the generated output file, you must include* `using` *or* `Import` *statements of your own into the generated file and add references to your project as normal.*

Include Directive

The `include` directive allows you to copy the contents of another file directly into your template file. It has a single attribute called `file`, which should contain a relative or absolute path to the file to be included. If the other file contains T4 directives or blocks, they are executed as well. The following example inserts the BSD License into a comment at the top of a generated file.

```
' Copyright (c) <#=DateTime.Now.Year#>, <#=CopyrightHolder#>
' All rights reserved.
' Redistribution and use in source and binary forms, with or without
...
```

C#

```
<#@ template debug="false" hostspecific="false" language="C#" #>
<#@ output extension=".generated.cs" #>
<# var CopyrightHolder = "AdventureWorks Inc."; #>
/*
<#@ include file="License.txt" #>
*/
namespace AdventureWorks {
  // ...
}
```

VB

```
<#@ template debug="false" hostspecific="false" language="VB" #>
<#@ output extension=".vb" #>
<# Dim CopyrightHolder = "AdventureWorks Inc." #>
<#@ include file="License.txt" #>
Namespace AdventureWorks
  ' ...
End Namespace
```

TROUBLESHOOTING

As template files get bigger and more complicated, the potential for errors grows significantly. This is not helped by the fact that errors might occur at several main stages, and each needs to be treated slightly differently. Remember that even though T4 runs these processes one at a time, any might occur when a template file is executed, which occurs every time the file is saved or the project is built.

When making any changes to T4 template files, it is highly recommended that you take small steps to regenerate often and immediately reverse out any change that breaks things.

Design-Time Errors

The first place where errors might occur is when Visual Studio attempts to read a T4 template and use it to create the temporary .NET class. In Figure 14-4 there is a missing hash symbol in the opening tag for the Expression block. The resulting template is invalid. The Error List window at the bottom of Figure 14-4 shows Visual Studio identifying this sort of issue quite easily. It can even correctly determine the line number where the error occurs.

The other type of error commonly encountered at design time relates to directive issues. In many cases when a problem arises with an attribute of a directive, a warning is raised and the default value is used. When there are no sensible defaults, such as with the `import`, `include`, and `assembly` directives, an error is raised instead.

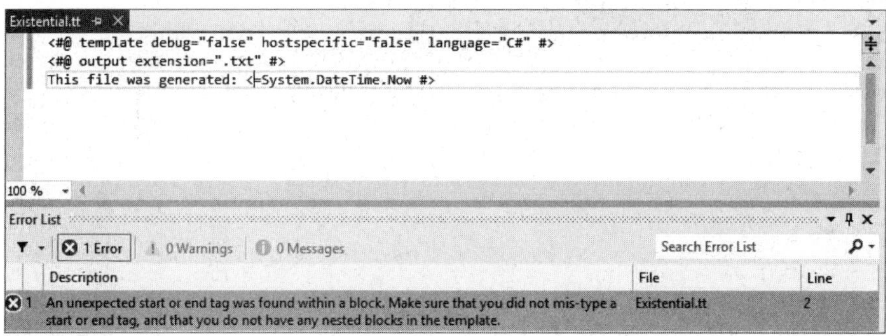

FIGURE 14-4

> **NOTE** *One interesting exception to the way that Visual Studio handles invalid directives is the* `extension` *attribute of the* `output` *directive. If the value supplied is invalid in any way, a warning is raised, but the generated file is not produced. If you have other code that depends on the contents of the generated file, the background compilation process can quickly find a cascade of errors, which can be overwhelming. Check to see if the file is generated before attempting to fix the template by temporarily removing all the contents of the template file except for the* `template` *and* `output` *directives.*

Compiling Transformation Errors

The next step in the T4 pipeline where an error might occur is when the temporary .NET code file containing the code generator class is compiled into an assembly. Errors that occur here typically result from malformed code inside Expression, Statement, or Class Feature blocks. Again, Visual Studio does a good job finding and exposing these errors, but the file and line number references point to the generated file. Each error found by the engine at this point is prefixed with the string Compiling Transformation, which make them easy to identify.

The first step to fixing these errors is to turn Debug mode on in the template directive. This forces the engine to dump copies of the files that it is using to try and compile the code into the temporary folder. When these files are dumped out, double-clicking the error line in the Error List window opens the temporary file, and you can see what is happening. Because this file will be a `.cs` or `.vb` file, Visual Studio can provide syntax highlighting and IntelliSense to help isolate the problem area. When the general issue has been discovered it is then much easier to find and update the relevant area of the template.

> **NOTE** *One of the other files generated by turning debugging on is a* `.cmdline` *file, which contains arguments passed to* `csc.exe` *or* `vbc.exe` *when T4 compiles the template. You can use this file to re-create the compilation process. There is also a file with the* `.out` *extension, which contains the command-line call to the compiler and its results.*

Executing Transformation Errors

The final step in the T4 pipeline that might generate errors is when the code generator is actually instantiated and executed to produce the contents of the generated file. This stage is essentially running arbitrary .NET code and is the most likely to encounter trouble with environmental conditions or faulty logic. Like Compiling Transformation errors, errors found during this stage have a prefix of Executing Transformation, which makes them easy to spot.

The best way to handle Executing Transformation errors is to code defensively. From within the T4 template, if you can detect an error condition such as a file missing or being unable to connect to a database, you can use the `Error()` method to notify the engine of the specific problem. These errors appear as Executing Transformation errors just like all the others; except they'll have a more contextual, and, hence, more useful message associated with them:

```
if( !File.Exists(fileName) ) {
  this.Error("Cannot find file");
}
```

In addition to `Error()` there is an equivalent `Warning()` method to raise warnings.

If the T4 template encounters an error that is catastrophic, such as not connecting to the database that it gets its data from, it can throw an exception to halt the execution process. The details about the exception are gathered and included in the Error List tool window.

Generated Code Errors

Although not technically a part of the T4 process, the generated file can just as easily contain compile-time or run-time errors. For compile-time errors, Visual Studio can simply detect these as normal. For run-time errors it is probably a good idea to unit test complex types anyway, even those that have been generated.

Now that you know what to do when things go wrong, it is time to look at a larger example.

GENERATING CODE ASSETS

When you develop enterprise applications, you frequently come across reference data that rarely changes and is represented in code as an enumeration type. The task to keep the data in the database and the values of the enumerated type in sync is time-consuming and repetitive, which makes it a perfect candidate to automate with a T4 template. The template presented in this section connects to the AdventureWorks example database and creates an enumeration based on the contents of the `Person.ContactType` table.

C#

```
<<#@ template debug="false" hostspecific="false" language="C#" #>
<#@ output extension=".generated.cs" #>
<#@ assembly name="System.Data" #>
<#@ import namespace="System.Data.SqlClient" #>
<#@ import namespace="System.Text.RegularExpressions" #>
<#
var connectionString = "Data Source=.\\SQLEXPRESS; Initial Catalog=AdventureWorks;"
   + "Integrated Security=true;";
var sqlString = "SELECT ContactTypeID, [Name] FROM [Person].[ContactType]";
#>
// This code is generated. Please do not edit it directly
// If you need to make changes please edit ContactType.tt instead
namespace AdventureWorks {
  public enum ContactType {
<#
using(var conn = new SqlConnection(connectionString))
using(var cmd = new SqlCommand(sqlString, conn))
{
  conn.Open();

  var contactTypes = cmd.ExecuteReader();

  while( contactTypes.Read() )
  {
  #>
    <#= ValidIdentifier( contactTypes[1].ToString() ) #> = <#=contactTypes[0]#>,
  <#}

  conn.Close();
}
#>
  }
}
<#+
  public string ValidIdentifier(string input)
  {
    return  Regex.Replace(input, @"[^a-zA-Z0-9]", String.Empty );
  }
#>
```

VB

```
<#@ template debug="false" hostspecific="false" language="VB" #>
<#@ output extension=".generated.vb" #>
<#@ assembly name="System.Data" #>
<#@ import namespace="System.Data.SqlClient" #>
<#@ import namespace="System.Text.RegularExpressions" #>
<#
Dim ConnectionString as String = "Data Source=.\SQLEXPRESS; " _
& "Initial Catalog=AdventureWorks; Integrated Security=true;"
Dim SqlString as String = "SELECT ContactTypeID,[Name] FROM [Person].[ContactType]"
#>
' This code is generated. Please do not edit it directly
' If you need to make changes please edit ContactType.tt instead
Namespace AdventureWorks
  Enum ContactType

<#
Using Conn As New SqlConnection(ConnectionString), _
      Cmd As New SqlCommand(SqlString, Conn)
```

```
        Conn.Open()

        Dim ContactTypes As SqlDataReader = Cmd.ExecuteReader()

        While ContactTypes.Read()
#>
        <#= ValidIdentifier( contactTypes(1).ToString() ) #> = <#=contactTypes(0)#>
<#
    End While
    Conn.Close()
End Using
#>
    End Enum
End Namespace
<#+
    Public Function ValidIdentifier(Input as String) As String
        Return Regex.Replace(Input, "[^a-zA-Z0-9]", String.Empty )
    End Function
#>
```

> **NOTE** *The above example utilizes the AdventureWorks database, which can be downloaded from* `http://msftdbprodsamples.codeplex.com`. *Instructions on how to install the database can be found at that site and the connection string that is used in the example might need to be modified for your own SQL environment.*

The first section consists of T4 directives. The first two specify the language for the template and the extension of the output file. The third attaches an assembly to the generator (to provide access to the `System.Data.SqlClient` namespace), and the final two import namespaces into the template that the template code requires.

The next section is a T4 Statement block. It contains some variables that the template will be using. Putting them at the top of the template file makes them easier to find later on in case they need to change.

After the variable declarations there is a T4 Text block containing some explanatory comments along with a namespace and an enumeration declaration. These are copied verbatim into the generated output file. It's usually a good idea to provide a comment inside the generated file explaining where they come from and how to edit them. This prevents nasty accidents when changes are erased after a file is regenerated.

A Statement block takes up the bulk of the rest of the template. This block creates and opens a connection to the `AdventureWorks` database using the variables defined in the first Statement block. It then queries the database to retrieve the wanted data with a data reader.

For each record retrieved from the database, a Text block is produced. This Text block consists of two Expression blocks separated by an equals sign. The second expression merely adds the ID of the Contact Type to the generated output file. The first one calls a helper method called `ValidIdentifier`, which is defined in a Class Feature block that creates a valid identifier for each contact type by removing all invalid characters from the Contact Type Name.

The generated output file is shown in the following listing. The end result looks fairly simple in comparison to the script used to generate it, but this is a little deceiving. The T4 template can remain the same as rows of data are added to and removed from the ContactType table. In fact, the items in the database can be completely reordered, and your code will still compile. With a little modification this script can even be used to generate enumerated types from a number of different tables at once.

C#

```
// This code is generated. Please do not edit it directly
// If you need to make changes please edit ContactType.tt instead
namespace AdventureWorks {
  public enum ContactType {
      AccountingManager = 1,
      AssistantSalesAgent = 2,
      AssistantSalesRepresentative = 3,
      CoordinatorForeignMarkets = 4,
      ExportAdministrator = 5,
      InternationalMarketingManager = 6,
      MarketingAssistant = 7,
      MarketingManager = 8,
      MarketingRepresentative = 9,
      OrderAdministrator = 10,
      Owner = 11,
      OwnerMarketingAssistant = 12,
      ProductManager = 13,
      PurchasingAgent = 14,
      PurchasingManager = 15,
      RegionalAccountRepresentative = 16,
      SalesAgent = 17,
      SalesAssociate = 18,
      SalesManager = 19,
      SalesRepresentative = 20,
    }
}
```

VB

```
' This code is generated. Please do not edit it directly
' If you need to make changes please edit ContactType.tt instead
Namespace AdventureWorks
  Enum ContactType

    AccountingManager = 1
    AssistantSalesAgent = 2
    AssistantSalesRepresentative = 3
    CoordinatorForeignMarkets = 4
    ExportAdministrator = 5
    InternationalMarketingManager = 6
    MarketingAssistant = 7
    MarketingManager = 8
    MarketingRepresentative = 9
    OrderAdministrator = 10
    Owner = 11
    OwnerMarketingAssistant = 12
    ProductManager = 13
    PurchasingAgent = 14
    PurchasingManager = 15
    RegionalAccountRepresentative = 16
    SalesAgent = 17
    SalesAssociate = 18
    SalesManager = 19
    SalesRepresentative = 20
  End Enum
End Namespace
```

RUNTIME TEXT TEMPLATES

Text Template Transformation is a powerful technique and shouldn't be restricted to a design-time activity. Visual Studio 2012 makes it easy to take advantage of the T4 engine to create your text template generators to use in your projects. These generators are called Runtime Text Templates.

To create a new Runtime Text Template, open the Add New Item dialog, select the General page, and select Runtime Text Template from the list of items. The newly created file has the same `.tt` extension as normal T4 template files and contains a number of T4 directives:

C#

```
<#@ template language="C#" #>
<#@ assembly name="System.Core" #>
<#@ import namespace="System.Linq" #>
<#@ import namespace="System.Text" #>
<#@ import namespace="System.Collections.Generic" #>
```

VB

```
<#@ template language="VB" #>
<#@ assembly name="System.Core" #>
<#@ import namespace="System.Linq" #>
<#@ import namespace="System.Text" #>
<#@ import namespace="System.Collections.Generic" #>
```

Note that there is no `output` directive. The generated file will have the same filename as the template file but the `.tt` will be replaced with `.vb` or `.cs` depending on your project language. When this file is saved, it generates an output file like the following.

C#

```
// ------------------------------------------------------------------------------
// <auto-generated>
//     This code was generated by a tool.
//     Runtime Version: 10.0.0.0
//
//     Changes to this file may cause incorrect behavior and will be lost if
//     the code is regenerated.
// </auto-generated>
// ------------------------------------------------------------------------------
namespace Chapter_14
{
  using System;
  using System.Linq;
  using System.Text;
  using System.Collections.Generic;

  public partial class NewTemplate
  {
    // region Fields
    // region Properties
    // region Transform-time helpers
    public virtual string TransformText()
    {
      return this.GenerationEnvironment.ToString();
    }
  }
}
```

VB

```
Imports System
Imports System.Linq
Imports System.Text
Imports System.Collections.Generic
'------------------------------------------------------------------------------
'<auto-generated>
'     This code was generated by a tool.
'     Runtime Version: 11.0.0.0
'
'     Changes to this file may cause incorrect behavior and will be lost if
'     the code is regenerated.
'</auto-generated>
'------------------------------------------------------------------------------
Namespace My.Templates
  Partial Public Class NewTemplate
    ' Region "Fields"
    ' Region "Properties"
    ' Region "Transform-time helpers"
    Public Overridable Function TransformText() As String
      Return Me.GenerationEnvironment.ToString
    End Function
  End Class
End Namespace
```

This is similar to the interim code file produced by T4 for a normal template. This generated class is now just a class inside the project, which means you can instantiate it, fill in its properties, and call `TransformText()` on it.

> **NOTE** *Just as with a normal Text Template, Visual Studio uses a Custom Tool to generate the output file of a Runtime Text Template. Instead of using the* `TextTemplatingFileGenerator` *custom tool, Runtime Text Templates are transformed using the* `TextTemplatingFilePreprocessor` *custom tool, which adds the code generator class to your project instead of the results of executing the code generator.*

Using Runtime Text Templates

To demonstrate how to use a Runtime Text Template within your own code, this section presents a simple scenario. The project needs to send a standard welcome letter to new club members when they join the AdventureWorks Cycle club. The following Runtime Text Template contains the basic letter to be produced.

C#

```
<#@ template language="C#" #>
Dear <#=Member.Salutation#> <#=Member.Surname#>,
  Welcome to our Bike Club!

Regards,
The AdventureWorks Team
<#= Member.DateJoined.ToShortDateString() #>
<#+ public ClubMember Member { get; set; } #>
```

VB

```
<#@ template language="VB" #>
Dear <#=Member.Salutation#> <#=Member.Surname#>,
  Welcome to our Bike Club!
```

```
Regards,
The AdventureWorks Team
<#= Member.DateJoined.ToShortDateString() #>
<#+ Public Member as ClubMember #>
```

This file generates a class called `WelcomeLetter` and relies on the following simple data class, which is passed into the template via its `Member` property.

C#

```
public class ClubMember
{
  public string Salutation { get; set; }
  public string Surname { get; set; }
  public DateTime DateJoined { get; set; }
}
```

VB

```
Public Class ClubMember
    Public Surname As String
    Public Salutation As String
    Public DateJoined As Date
End Class
```

Finally, to create the letter, you instantiate a `WelcomeLetter` object, set the `Member` property to a `ClubMember` object, and call `TransformText()`.

C#

```
// ...
var member = new ClubMember
{
  Surname = "Fry",
  Salutation = "Mr",
  DateJoined = DateTime.Today
};
var letterGenerator = new WelcomeLetter();
letterGenerator.Member = member;
var letter = letterGenerator.TransformText();
// ...
```

VB

```
' ...
Dim NewMember As New ClubMember
With NewMember
   .Surname = "Fry"
   .Salutation = "Mr"
   .DateJoined = Date.Today
End With
Dim LetterGenerator As New WelcomeLetter
LetterGenerator.Member = NewMember
Dim Letter = LetterGenerator.TransformText()
' ...
```

This can look awkward but `WelcomeLetter` is a partial class, so you can change the API to be whatever you want. Often you make the constructor of the generator private and create a few static methods to handle the creation and use of generator instances.

C#

```
public partial class WelcomeLetter
{
  private WelcomeLetter() { }
  public static string Create(ClubMember member)
  {
    return new WelcomeLetter { Member = member }.TransformText();
  }
}
```

VB

```
Namespace My.Templates
  Partial Public Class WelcomeLetter
    Private Sub New()
    End Sub
    Public Shared Function Create(ByVal Member As ClubMember) As String
      Dim LetterGenerator As New WelcomeLetter()
      LetterGenerator.Member = Member
      Return LetterGenerator.TransformText()
    End Function
  End Class
End Namespace
```

> **NOTE** *The generator contains a* `StringBuilder`*, which it uses internally to build up the input when* `TransformText` *is executed. This* `StringBuilder` *is not cleared out when you run the* `TransformText` *method, which means that each time you run it the results are appended to the results of the previous execution. This is why the* `Create` *method presented creates a new* `WelcomeLetter` *object each time instead of keeping one in a* `static` *(*`Shared`*) variable and reusing it.*

Differences Between Runtime Text Templates and Standard T4 Templates

Aside from which aspect of the generation process is included in your project, a few other key differences exist between a Runtime Text Template and a standard T4 template. First, Runtime Text Templates are completely standalone classes. They do not inherit from a base class by default and therefore do not rely on Visual Studio to execute. The `TransformText()` method of the generator class does not run within a `try/catch` block, so you need to watch for and handle errors when executing the generator.

Not all T4 directives make sense in a Runtime Text Template, and for those that do, some attributes no longer make much sense. Here is a quick summary.

The `template` directive is still used but not all the attributes make sense. The `culture` and `language` attributes are fully supported. The `language` attribute must match that of the containing language or the generator class cannot be compiled. The `debug` attribute is ignored because you can control the debug status of the generator class by setting the project configuration as you would with any other class.

The `inherits` attribute is supported and has a significant impact on the generated class. If you do not specify a base class, the generated file will be completely standalone and will contain implementations of all the helper functions such as `Write` and `Error`. If you do specify a base class, it is up to the base class to specify these implementations, and the generated class will rely on those implementations to perform the generation work.

The `hostspecific` attribute is supported and generates a `Host` property on the generator class. This property is of the `Microsoft.VisualStudio.TextTemplating.ITextTemplatingEngineHost` type, which resides in the `Microsoft.VisualStudio.TextTemplating.10.0` assembly. You must add a reference to this assembly to your project and to provide a member of the appropriate type before calling the `TransformText` method.

The `import` directive works as normal. The referenced namespaces are included in the generator code file with `using` statements in C# and `Import` statements in VB. The `include` directive is also fully supported.

The `output` and `assembly` directives are ignored. To add an assembly to the template, you simply add a reference to the project as normal. The output filename is selected based on the template filename and the selected language.

Finally, you can set the namespace of the generator class in the Properties window of the template file, as shown in Figure 14-5. The namespace is normally based on the project defaults and the location of the template file within the folder structure of the project.

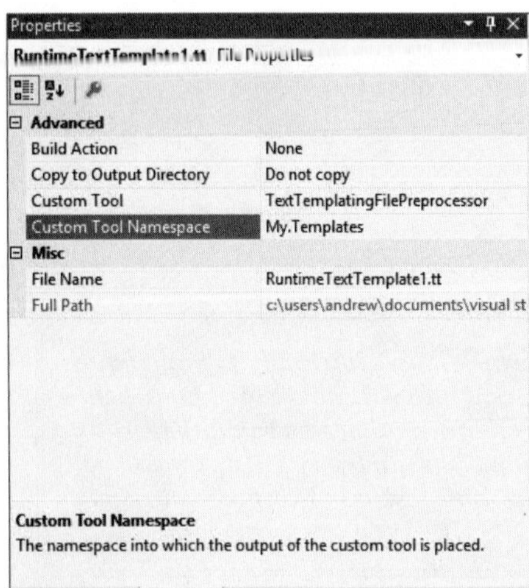

FIGURE 14-5

TIPS AND TRICKS

The following are a few things that might help you to take full advantage of T4:

- Write the code you intend to generate first for one specific case as a normal C# or VB code file. When you are satisfied that everything works as intended, copy the entire code file into a `.tt` file. Now start slowly making the code less specific and more generic by introducing Statement blocks and Expression blocks, factoring out Class Feature blocks as you go.
- Save frequently as you make changes. As soon as a change breaks the generated code or the generator, simply reverse it and try again.
- Never make changes directly to a generated file. The next time the template is saved, those changes will be lost.
- Make generated classes partial. This makes the generated classes extensible, allowing you to keep some parts of the class intact and regenerate the other parts. This is one of the reasons that the partial class functionality exists.
- Use an extension that includes the word *generated* such as `.generated.cs` and `.generated.vb`. This is a convention used by Visual Studio and will discourage other users from making changes to template files.
- Similarly, include a comment toward the top of the generated file stating that the file is generated along with instructions for how to change the contents and regenerate the file.

- Make T4 template execution a part of your build process. This ensures that the content of the generated files doesn't get stale with respect to the meta data used to generate it.
- If you don't have a lot of things dependent upon the generated code produced by a normal T4 Text Template, switch the custom tool over to make the template a Runtime Template while you develop it. This brings the code generator into your project and allows you to write unit tests against it.
- Don't use T4 to generate `.tt` files. If you try to use a code generator to generate template files, the level of complexity when things go wrong increases substantially. At this point it might be wise to consider a different strategy for your project.
- Finally, an absolutely invaluable resource for anyone getting started with T4 is `www.olegsych.com`. Oleg Sych is a Visual C# MVP who maintains a blog with a large collection of articles about T4.

SUMMARY

Code generation can be a fantastic productivity gain for your projects, and Visual Studio 2012 includes some powerful tools for managing the process out-of-the-box. In this chapter you have seen how to create and use T4 templates to speed up common and generic coding tasks. Learning when and how to apply T4 to your projects increases your productivity and makes your solutions flexible.

15

Project and Item Templates

WHAT'S IN THIS CHAPTER?

- Creating your own item templates
- Creating your own project templates
- Adding a wizard to your project templates

Most development teams build a set of standards that specify how they build applications. This means that every time you start a new project or add an item to an existing project, you have to go through a process to ensure that it conforms to the standard. Visual Studio 2012 enables you to create templates that can be reused without having to modify the standard item templates that ship with Visual Studio 2012. This chapter describes how you can create simple templates and then extend them with a wizard that can change how the project is generated using the `IWizard` interface.

CREATING TEMPLATES

Two types of templates exist: those that create new project items and those that create entire projects. Both types of templates essentially have the same structure, as you'll see later, except that they are placed in different template folders. The project templates appear in the New Project dialog, whereas the item templates appear in the Add New Item dialog.

Item Template

Although you can build a project item template manually, it is much quicker to create one from an existing project item and make changes as required. This section begins by looking at an item template — in this case an About form that contains some basic information, such as the application's version number and who wrote it.

To begin, create a new Windows Forms application (using your language of choice) called StarterProject. Instead of creating an About form from scratch, you can customize the About Box template that ships with Visual Studio. Right-click the StarterProject project, select Add ➪ New Item, and add a new About Box (name it AboutForm). Customize the default About form by deleting the logo and first column of the TableLayoutPanel control (by selecting the table layout panel, going to the Properties window, selecting the Columns property, clicking its ellipsis button (. . .), and deleting column 1). Figure 15-1 shows the customized About form.

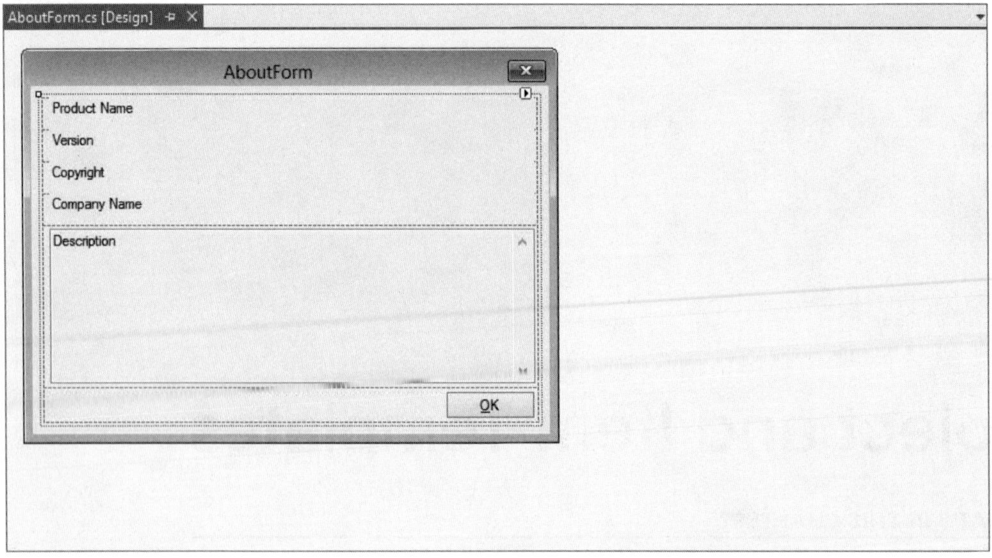

FIGURE 15-1

To make a template out of the About form, select the Export Template item from the File menu. This starts the Export Template Wizard, as shown in Figure 15-2. If you have unsaved changes in your solution, you will be prompted to save before continuing. The first step is to determine what type of template you want to create. In this case, select the Item Template radio button and make sure that the project in which the About form resides is selected in the drop-down list.

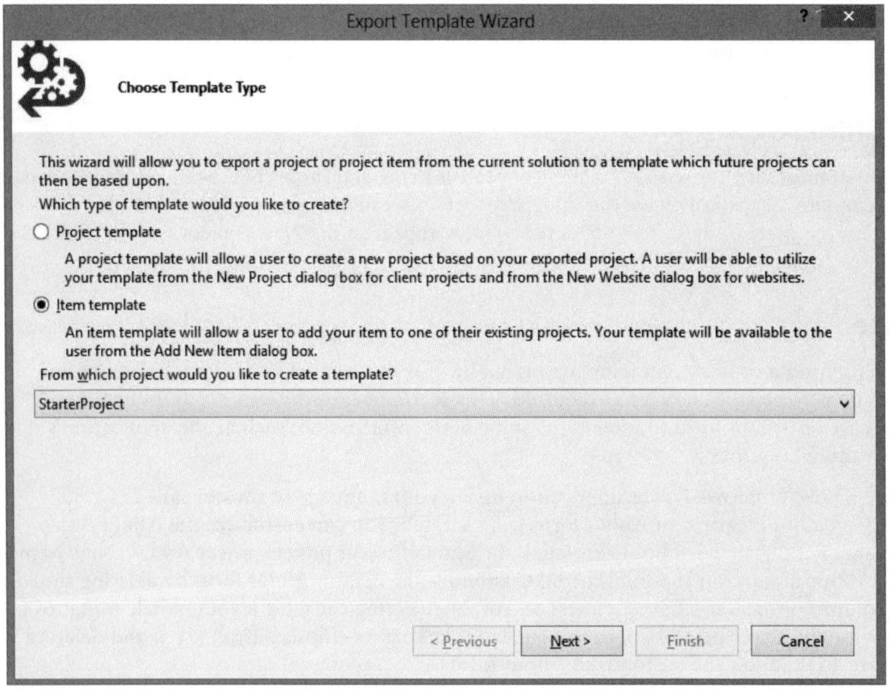

FIGURE 15-2

Click Next. You will be prompted to select the item on which you want to base the template. In this case, select the About form. The use of check boxes is slightly misleading because with item templates you can select only a single item on which to base the template (selecting a second item deselects the item already selected). After you make your selection and click Next, the dialog, as shown in Figure 15-3, enables you to include any assembly references that you may require. This list is based on the list of references in the project in which that item resides. Because this is a form, include a reference to the `System.Windows.Forms` library, which will be added to a project when adding a new item of this type (if it has not already been added). Otherwise, it is possible that the project won't compile if it did not have a reference to this assembly. (Class Library projects don't generally reference this assembly by default.)

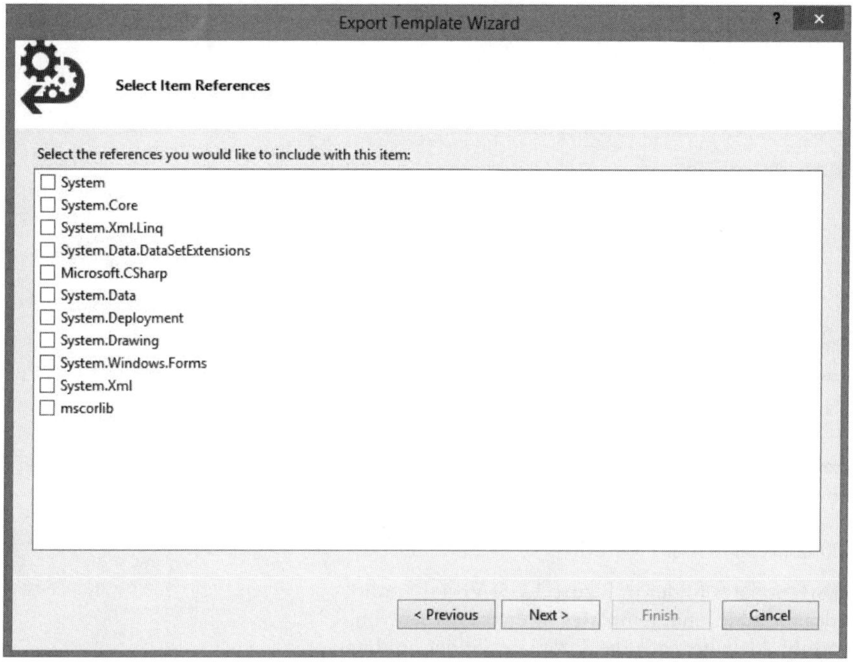

FIGURE 15-3

> **NOTE** *After selecting an assembly, a warning may display under the list stating that the selected assembly isn't preinstalled with Visual Studio and may prevent users from using your template if the assembly isn't available on their machine. Be aware of this issue, and only select assemblies that your item needs.*

The final step in the Export Template Wizard is to specify some properties of the template to be generated, such as the name, description, and icon that will appear in the Add New Item dialog.

Figure 15-4 shows the final dialog in the wizard. As you can see, there are two check boxes, one for displaying the output folder upon completion and one for automatically importing the new template into Visual Studio 2012.

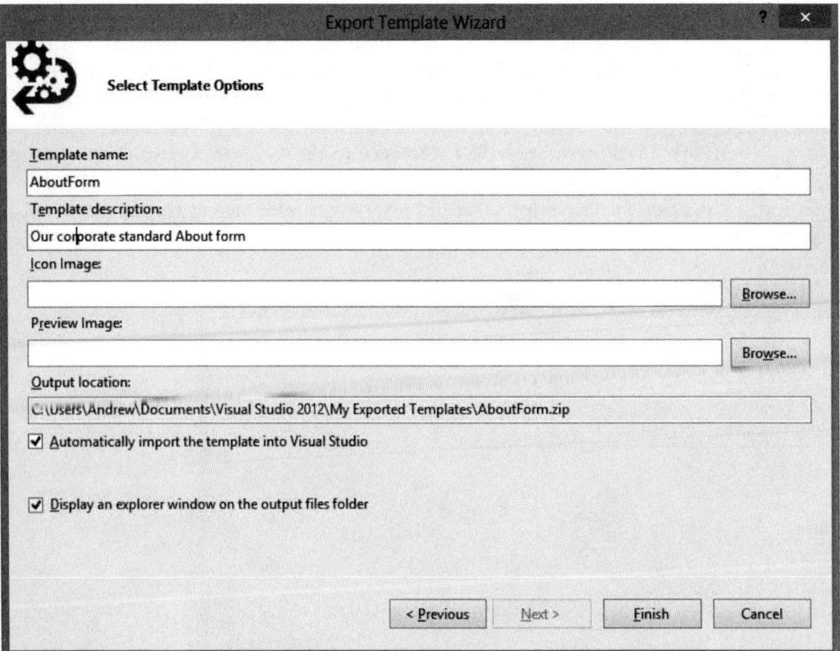

FIGURE 15-4

By default, exported templates are created in the My Exported Templates folder under the current user's `Documents\Visual Studio 2012` folder. Inside this root folder are a number of folders that contain user settings about Visual Studio 2012 (as shown in Figure 15-5).

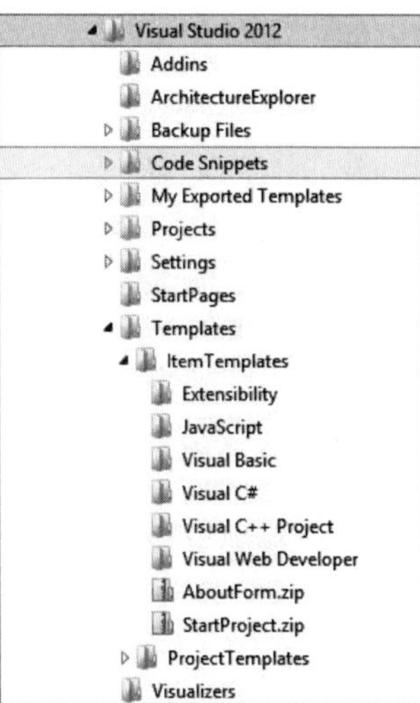

FIGURE 15-5

You can also notice the Templates folder in Figure 15-5. Visual Studio 2012 looks in this folder for additional templates to display when you create new items. Two subfolders beneath the Templates folder hold item templates and project templates, respectively. These are divided further by language. If you check the Automatically Import the Template into Visual Studio option on the final page of the Export Template Wizard, the new template will not only be placed in the output folder but will also be copied to the relevant location (depending on language and template type) within the Templates folder. Visual Studio 2012 automatically displays this item template the next time you display the Add New Item dialog, as shown in Figure 15-6.

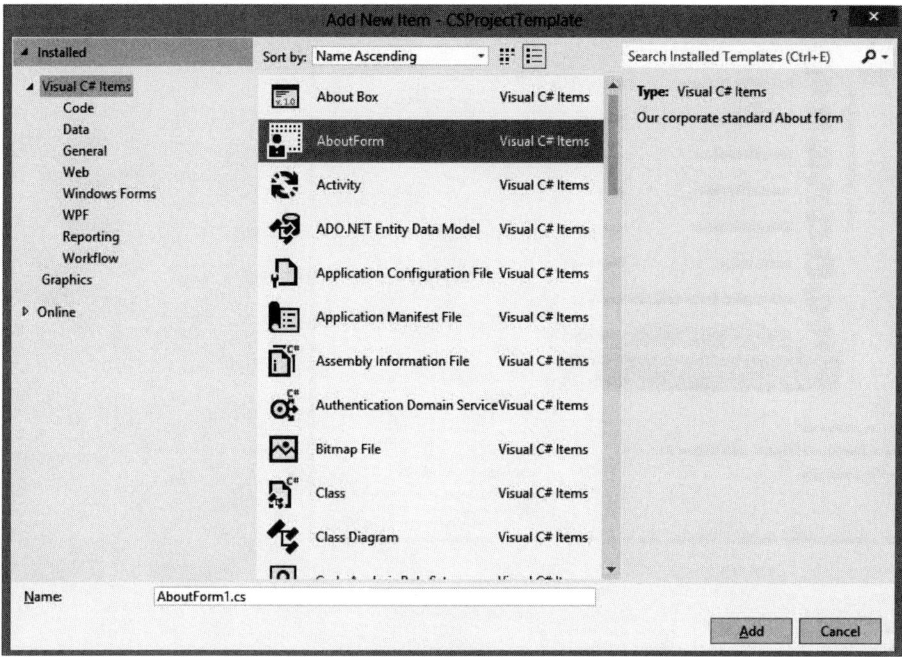

FIGURE 15-6

> **NOTE** *If you want an item or project template to appear under an existing category (or one of your own) in the Add New Item/New Project dialog (such as the Windows Forms category), simply create a folder with that name and put the template into it (under the relevant location as described for that template). The next time you open the Add New Item/New Project dialog, the template appears in the category with the corresponding folder name (or as a new category if a category matching the folder name doesn't exist).*

Project Template

You build a project template the same way you build an item template, but with one difference. Whereas the item template is based on an existing item, the project template needs to be based on an entire project. For example, you might have a simple project called ProjectTemplateExample (as shown in Figure 15-7) that has a main form, an About form, and a splash screen.

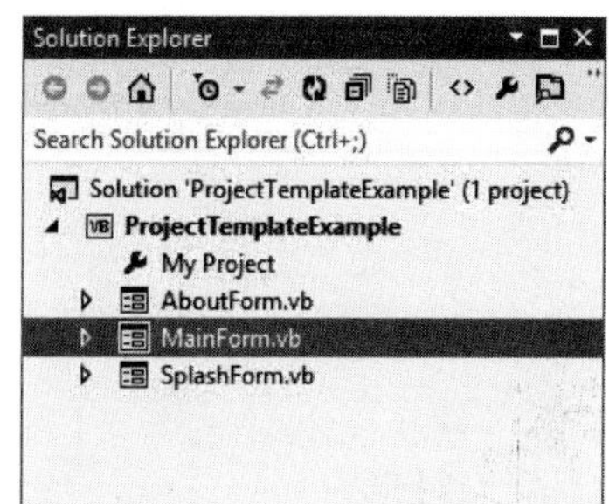

FIGURE 15-7

To generate a template from this project, follow the same steps you took to generate an item template, except that you need to select Project Template when asked what type of template to generate, and there is no step to select the items to be included. (All items within the project will be included in the template.) After you complete the Export Template Wizard, the new project template appears in the Add New Project dialog, as shown in Figure 15-8.

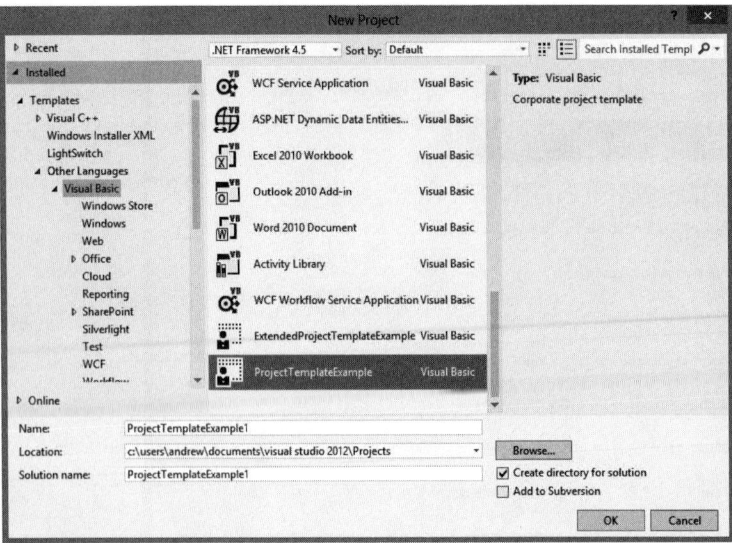

FIGURE 15-8

Template Structure

Before examining how to build more complex templates, you need to understand what the Export Template Wizard produces. If you look in the My Exported Templates folder, you can see that all the templates are exported as a single compressed zip file. The zip file can contain any number of files or folders, depending on whether they are templates for single files or full projects. However, the one common element of all template zip files is that they contain a `.vstemplate` file. This file is an XML document that holds the template configuration. The following listing is the `.vstemplate` file that was exported as a part of your project template earlier:

```
<VSTemplate Version="3.0.0" xmlns="http://schemas.microsoft.com/developer/vstemplate/2005"
Type="Project">
  <TemplateData>
    <Name>ProjectTemplateExample</Name>
    <Description>Project Template Example</Description>
    <ProjectType>VisualBasic</ProjectType>
    <ProjectSubType>
    </ProjectSubType>
    <SortOrder>1000</SortOrder>
    <CreateNewFolder>true</CreateNewFolder>
    <DefaultName>ProjectTemplateExample</DefaultName>
    <ProvideDefaultName>true</ProvideDefaultName>
    <LocationField>Enabled</LocationField>
    <EnableLocationBrowseButton>true</EnableLocationBrowseButton>
    <Icon>__TemplateIcon.ico</Icon>
  </TemplateData>
  <TemplateContent>
    <Project TargetFileName="ProjectTemplateExample.vbproj" File="ProjectTemplateExample.
vbproj"
ReplaceParameters="true">
      <ProjectItem ReplaceParameters="true" TargetFileName="AboutForm.vb">
AboutForm.vb</ProjectItem>
      <ProjectItem ReplaceParameters="true" TargetFileName="AboutForm.Designer.vb">
AboutForm.Designer.vb</ProjectItem>
      <ProjectItem ReplaceParameters="true" TargetFileName="AboutForm.resx">
AboutForm.resx</ProjectItem>
```

```
        <ProjectItem ReplaceParameters="true" TargetFileName="App.config">
App.config</ProjectItem>
        <ProjectItem ReplaceParameters="true" TargetFileName="MainForm.vb">
MainForm.vb</ProjectItem>
        <ProjectItem ReplaceParameters="true" TargetFileName="MainForm.Designer.vb">
MainForm.Designer.vb</ProjectItem>
        <Folder Name="My Project" TargetFolderName="My Project">
          <ProjectItem ReplaceParameters="true" TargetFileName="Application.myapp">
Application.myapp</ProjectItem>
          <ProjectItem ReplaceParameters="true" TargetFileName="Application.Designer.vb">
Application.Designer.vb</ProjectItem>
          <ProjectItem ReplaceParameters="true" TargetFileName="AssemblyInfo.vb">
AssemblyInfo.vb</ProjectItem>
          <ProjectItem ReplaceParameters="true" TargetFileName="Resources.resx">
Resources.resx</ProjectItem>
          <ProjectItem ReplaceParameters="true" TargetFileName="Resources.Designer.vb">
Resources.Designer.vb</ProjectItem>
          <ProjectItem ReplaceParameters="true" TargetFileName="Settings.settings">
Settings.settings</ProjectItem>
          <ProjectItem ReplaceParameters="true" TargetFileName="Settings.Designer.vb">
Settings.Designer.vb</ProjectItem>
        </Folder>
        <ProjectItem ReplaceParameters="true" TargetFileName="SplashForm.vb">
SplashForm.vb</ProjectItem>
        <ProjectItem ReplaceParameters="true" TargetFileName="SplashForm.Designer.vb">
SplashForm.Designer.vb</ProjectItem>
        <ProjectItem ReplaceParameters="true" TargetFileName="SplashForm.resx">
SplashForm.resx</ProjectItem>
      </Project>
    </TemplateContent>
</VSTemplate>
```

At the top of the file, the `VSTemplate` node contains a `Type` attribute that specifies if this is an item template (`Item`), a project template (`Project`), or a multiple project template (`ProjectGroup`). The remainder of the file is divided into `TemplateData` and `TemplateContent`. The `TemplateData` block includes information about the template, such as its name, description, and the icon that will be used to represent it in the New Project dialog, whereas the `TemplateContent` block defines the file structure of the template.

In the preceding example, the content starts with a `Project` node, which indicates the project file to use. The files contained in this template are listed by means of the `ProjectItem` nodes. Each node contains a `TargetFileName` attribute that can be used to specify the name of the file as it will appear in the project created from this template. For an item template, the `Project` node is missing and `ProjectItems` are contained within the `TemplateContent` node.

> **NOTE** *You can create templates for a solution that contains multiple projects. These templates contain a separate .*`vstemplate` *file for each project in the solution. They also have a global .*`vstemplate` *file, which describes the overall template and contains references to each projects' individual .*`vstemplate` *files. Creating this file is a manual process, however, because Visual Studio does not currently have a function to export a solution template.*

For more information on the structure of the .`vstemplate` file, see the full schema at `%programfiles%\Microsoft Visual Studio 11.0\Xml\Schemas\1033\vstemplate.xsd`.

Template Parameters

Both item and project templates support parameter substitution, which enables replacement of key parameters when a project or item is created from the template. In some cases these are automatically inserted. For example, when the About form was exported as an item template, the class name was removed and replaced with a template parameter, as shown here:

```
Public Class $safeitemname$
```

Table 15-1 lists 14 reserved template parameters that can be used in any project.

TABLE 15-1: Template Parameters

PARAMETER	DESCRIPTION
`Clrversion`	Current version of the common language run time.
`GUID[1-10]`	A GUID used to replace the project GUID in a project file. You can specify up to ten unique GUIDs (for example, GUID1, GUID2, and so on).
`Itemname`	The name provided by the user in the Add New Item dialog.
`machinename`	The current computer name (for example, computer01).
`projectname`	The name provided by the user in the New Project dialog.
`Registeredorganization`	The Registry key value that stores the registered organization name.
`rootnamespace`	The root namespace of the current project. This parameter is used to replace the namespace in an item being added to a project.
`safeitemname`	The name provided by the user in the Add New Item dialog, with all unsafe characters and spaces removed.
`safeprojectname`	The name provided by the user in the New Project dialog, with all unsafe characters and spaces removed.
`Time`	The current time on the local computer.
`Userdomain`	The current user domain.
`Username`	The current username.
`webnamespace`	The name of the current website. This is used in any web form template to guarantee unique class names.
`Year`	The current year in the format `YYYY`.

In addition to the reserved parameters, you can also create your own custom template parameters. You define these by adding a `<CustomParameters>` section to the `.vstemplate` file, as shown here:

```
<TemplateContent>
    ...
    <CustomParameters>
        <CustomParameter Name="$timezoneName $" Value="(GMT+8:00) Perth"/>
        <CustomParameter Name="$timezoneOffset $" Value="+8"/>
    </CustomParameters>
</TemplateContent>
```

You can refer to this custom parameter in code as follows:

```
string tzName = "$timezoneName$";
string tzOffset = "$timezoneOffset$";
```

When a new item or project containing a custom parameter is created from a template, Visual Studio automatically performs the template substitution on both custom and reserved parameters.

Template Locations

By default, custom item and project templates are stored in the user's personal `Documents\Visual Studio 2012\Templates` folder, but you can redirect this to another location (such as a shared directory on a network so you use the same custom templates as your colleagues) via the Options dialog. Go to Tools ➪ Options, and select the Projects and Solutions node. You can then select a different location for the custom templates here.

EXTENDING TEMPLATES

Building templates based on existing items and projects limits what you can do. It assumes that every project or scenario requires exactly the same items. Instead of creating multiple templates for each different scenario (for example, one that has a main form with a black background and another that has a main form with a white background), with a bit of user interaction, you can accommodate multiple scenarios from a single template. Therefore, this section takes the project template created earlier and tweaks it so users can specify the background color for the main form. In addition, you can build an installer for both the template and the wizard that you create for the user interaction.

To add user interaction to a template, you need to implement the `IWizard` interface in a class library that is then signed and placed in the Global Assembly Cache (GAC) on the machine on which the template will be executed. For this reason, to deploy a template that uses a wizard, you also need rights to deploy the wizard assembly to the GAC.

Template Project Setup

Before plunging in and implementing the `IWizard` interface, follow these steps to set up your solution so that you have all the bits and pieces in the same location, which makes it easy to make changes, perform a build, and then run the installer:

1. Create a new project with the Project Template Example project template that you created earlier in the chapter, and name it **ExtendedProjectTemplateExample**. Make sure that this solution builds and runs successfully before proceeding. Any issues with this solution will be harder to detect later because the error messages that appear when a template is used are somewhat cryptic.
2. Into this solution add a Class Library project, called **WizardClassLibrary**, in which you will place the `IWizard` implementation.
3. Add to the WizardClassLibrary a new empty class file called **`MyWizard`**, and a blank Windows Form called **ColorPickerForm**. These will be customized later.
4. To access the `IWizard` interface, add to the Class Library project `EnvDTE.dll` and `Microsoft.VisualStudio.TemplateWizardInterface.dll` as references. `EnvDTE.dll` can be found at `%programfiles%\Common Files\Microsoft Shared\MSEnv` while `Microsoft.VisualStudio.TemplateWizardInterface.dll` is located at `%programfiles%\Microsoft Visual Studio 11.0\Common7\IDE\PublicAssemblies\`.
5. You also need to add a Setup project to the solution. One of the things that has been removed in Visual Studio 2012 is the Setup and Deployment project template. Instead, it is expected that you use either the InstallShield Limited Edition (LE) tool or an open-source toolkit such as WiX. WiX is covered in Chapter 49, "Packaging and Deployment," so here we'll focus on InstallShield LE. To do this, select File ➪ Add ➪ New Project, expand the Other Project Types category and select Setup and Deployment. A template appears on the right that says Enable InstallShield Setup and Deployment. Select this option and click OK. A web page appears that walks you through the process of installing InstallShield Limited Edition. Once it has been installed, open Visual Studio 2012 and your project. Then go through the same steps as you did before (that is File ➪ Add ➪ New Project, select Project TypesSetup and Deployment, and choose the Install Shield project template) and give the project a name

like ExtendedProjectTemplateSetup. Click OK a second time and follow the wizard to include both the Primary Output and Content Files from WizardClassLibrary.

This should result in a solution that looks similar to what is shown in Figure 15-9.

Next perform the following steps to complete the configuration of the Installer project:

1. When you add primary outputs and content files from projects in the solution to the installer, they are added to the Application folder. However, you want the primary output of the class library to be placed in the GAC, and its content files to go into the user's Visual Studio Templates folder. These are predefined folders for InstallShield, but they need to be identified within the setup project. From the Solution Explorer, double-click the Project Assistant in the ExtendedProjectTemplateSetup project.
2. In the Application Files step, right-click the Destination Computer, and select Show Predefined Folders ➪ [Global Assembly Cache]. This causes the folder to appear under the Destination Computer. Do the same steps, adding the [TemplateFolder] to the layout. The setup project should now look like Figure 15-10.

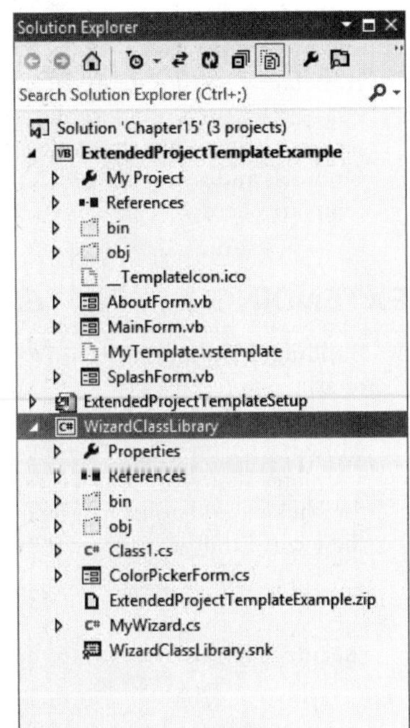

FIGURE 15-9

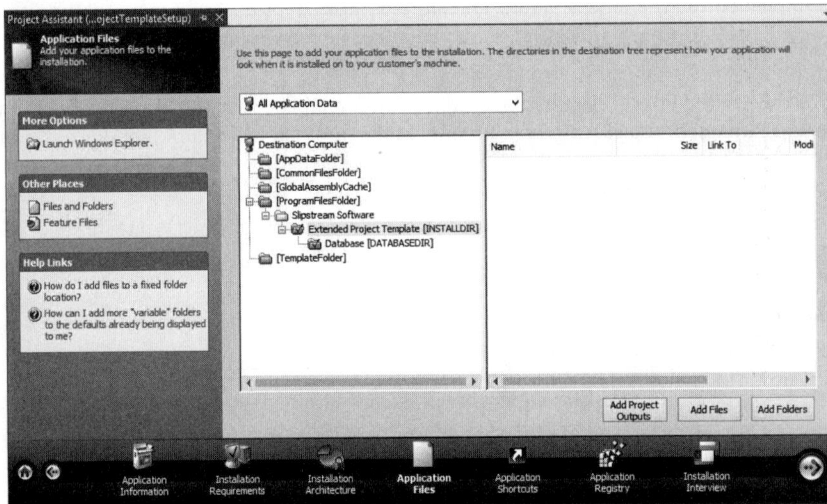

FIGURE 15-10

3. Click the folder that appears under the [ProgramFilesFolder]. The project output and content items appear in the list to the right. Drag the Project Output item to the [GlobalAssemblyCache]. Then drag the Content files to the [TemplateFolder].

IWizard

Now that you've completed the installer, you can start work on the wizard class library. You have a form (ColorPickerForm) and a class (`MyWizard`) (refer to Figure 15-9). The former is a simple form that you can use to specify the color of the background of the main form. To this form you need to add a Color Dialog control, called ColorDialog1, a Panel called ColorPanel, a Button called PickColorButton (with the text Pick Color), and a Button called AcceptColorButton (with the text Accept Color).

Rather than use the default icon that Visual Studio uses on the form, you can select a more appropriate icon from the Visual Studio 2012 Image Library. The Visual Studio 2012 Image Library is a collection of standard icons, images, and animations that are used in Windows, Office, and other Microsoft software. You can use any of these images royalty-free to ensure that your applications are visually consistent with Microsoft software.

The Image Library is installed with Visual Studio as a compressed file called `VS2012ImageLibrary.zip`. By default, you can find this under `%programfiles%\Microsoft Visual Studio 11.0\Common7\VS2012ImageLibrary\1033\`. Extract the contents of this zip file to a more convenient location, such as a directory under your profile.

To replace the icon on the form, first go to the Properties window, and then select the Form in the drop-down list at the top. On the `Icon` property, click the ellipsis button (...) to load the file selection dialog. Select the icon file you want to use, and click OK. (For this example use `VS2012ImageLibrary\Objects\ico_format\WinVista\Settings.ico`.)

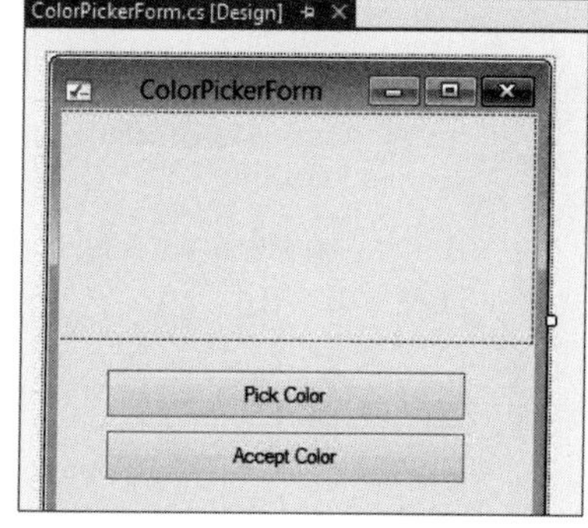

FIGURE 15-11

When completed, the ColorPickerForm should look similar to the one shown in Figure 15-11.

The following code listing can be added to this form. The main logic of this form is in the event handler for the Pick Color button, which opens the ColorDialog that is used to select a color:

VB

```
Public Class ColorPickerForm
    Public ReadOnly Property SelectedColor() As Drawing.Color
        Get
            Return ColorPanel.BackColor
        End Get
    End Property

    Private Sub PickColorButton_Click(ByVal sender As System.Object, _
                        ByVal e As System.EventArgs) Handles
                        PickColorButton.Click
        ColorDialog1.Color = ColorPanel.BackColor
        If ColorDialog1.ShowDialog() = Windows.Forms.DialogResult.OK Then
            ColorPanel.BackColor = ColorDialog1.Color
        End If
    End Sub

    Private Sub AcceptColorButton_Click(ByVal sender As System.Object, _
                        ByVal e As System.EventArgs) Handles
                        AcceptColorButton.Click
        Me.DialogResult = Windows.Forms.DialogResult.OK
        Me.Close()
    End Sub
End Class
```

C#

```
using System;
using System.Drawing;
using System.Windows.Forms;
```

```
namespace WizardClassLibrary
{
    public partial class ColorPickerForm : Form
    {
        public ColorPickerForm()
        {
            InitializeComponent();

            PickColorButton.Click += PickColorButton_Click;
            AcceptColorButton.Click += AcceptColorButton_Click;
        }

        public Color SelectedColor
        {
            get { return ColorPanel.BackColor; }
        }

        private void PickColorButton_Click(object sender, EventArgs e)
        {
            ColorDialog1.Color = ColorPanel.BackColor;

            if (ColorDialog1.ShowDialog() == DialogResult.OK)
            {
                ColorPanel.BackColor = ColorDialog1.Color;
            }
        }

        private void AcceptColorButton_Click(object sender, EventArgs e)
        {
            this.DialogResult = DialogResult.OK;
            this.Close();
        }
    }
}
```

The `MyWizard` class implements the `IWizard` interface, which provides a number of opportunities for user interaction throughout the template process. Add some code to the `RunStarted` method, which is called just after the project-creation process starts. This provides the perfect opportunity to select and apply a new background color for the main form:

VB

```
Imports Microsoft.VisualStudio.TemplateWizard
Imports System.Collections.Generic
Imports System.Windows.Forms

Public Class MyWizard
    Implements IWizard

    Public Sub BeforeOpeningFile(ByVal projectItem As EnvDTE.ProjectItem) _
                                             Implements IWizard.BeforeOpeningFile
    End Sub

    Public Sub ProjectFinishedGenerating(ByVal project As EnvDTE.Project) _
                                    Implements IWizard.ProjectFinishedGenerating
    End Sub

    Public Sub ProjectItemFinishedGenerating _
                              (ByVal projectItem As EnvDTE.ProjectItem) _
                              Implements IWizard.ProjectItemFinishedGenerating
```

```
    End Sub

    Public Sub RunFinished() Implements IWizard.RunFinished

    End Sub

    Public Sub RunStarted(ByVal automationObject As Object, _
                          ByVal replacementsDictionary As  _
    Dictionary(Of String, String), _
                          ByVal runKind As WizardRunKind, _
                          ByVal customParams() As Object) _
    Implements IWizard.RunStarted
        Dim selector As New ColorPickerForm
        If selector.ShowDialog = DialogResult.OK Then
            Dim c As Drawing.Color = selector.SelectedColor
            Dim colorString As String = "System.Drawing.Color.FromArgb(" & _
    c.R.ToString & "," & _
    c.G.ToString & "," & _
    c.B.ToString & ")"
            replacementsDictionary.Add _
                                ("Me.BackColor = System.Drawing.Color.Silver", _
                                 "Me.BackColor = " & colorString)
        End If
    End Sub

    Public Function ShouldAddProjectItem(ByVal filePath As String) As Boolean _
                                          Implements IWizard.ShouldAddProjectItem
        Return True
    End Function
End Class
```

C#

```
using System;
using System.Drawing;
using System.Windows.Forms;
using System.Collections.Generic;
using Microsoft.VisualStudio.TemplateWizard;

namespace WizardClassLibrary
{
    public class MyWizard : IWizard
    {
        public void BeforeOpeningFile(EnvDTE.ProjectItem projectItem)
        {
        }

        public void ProjectFinishedGenerating(EnvDTE.Project project)
        {
        }

        public void ProjectItemFinishedGenerating(EnvDTE.ProjectItem projectItem)
        {
        }

        public void RunFinished()
        {
        }

        public void RunStarted(object automationObject, Dictionary<string, string>
            replacementsDictionary, WizardRunKind runKind, object[] customParams)
        {
```

```
                ColorPickerForm selector = new ColorPickerForm();

                if (selector.ShowDialog() == DialogResult.OK)
                {
                    Color c = selector.SelectedColor;
                    string colorString = "Color.FromArgb(" +
                        c.R.ToString() + "," +
                        c.G.ToString() + "," +
                        c.B.ToString() + ")";
                    replacementsDictionary.Add
                                 ("this.BackColor = System.Drawing.Color.Silver",
                                  "this.BackColor = " + colorString);
                }
            }

            public bool ShouldAddProjectItem(string filePath)
            {
                return true;
            }
        }
    }
```

In the `RunStarted` method, you prompt the user to select a new color and then use that response to add a new entry into the replacements dictionary. In this case, you replace `"Me.BackColor = System.Drawing.Color.Silver"` (VB) or `"this.BackColor = System.Drawing.Color.Silver"` (C#) with a concatenated string made up of the RGB values of the color specified by the user. The replacements dictionary is used when the files are created for the new project because they will be searched for the replacement keys. Upon any instances of these keys being found, they will be replaced by the appropriate replacement values. In this case, look for the line specifying that the `BackColor` is `Silver`, and replace it with the new color supplied by the user.

The class library containing the implementation of the `IWizard` interface must be a strongly named assembly capable of being placed into the GAC. To ensure this, use the Signing tab of the Project Properties dialog to generate a new signing key, as shown in Figure 15-12.

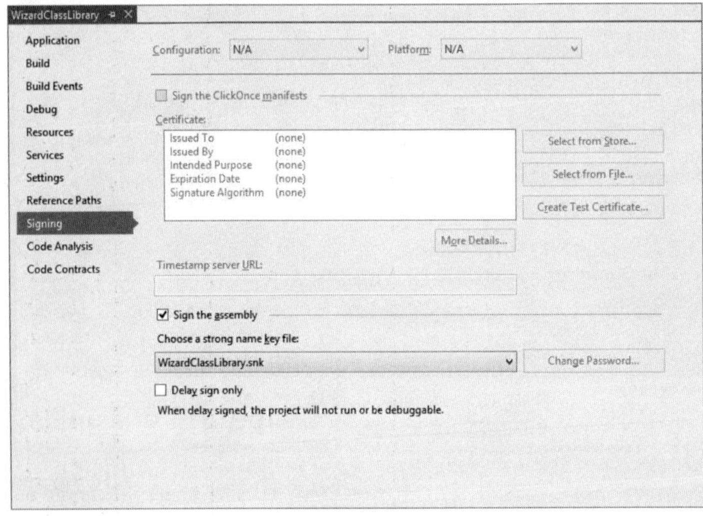

FIGURE 15-12

After you check the Sign the Assembly check box, there will be no default value for the key file. To create a new key, select <New . . .> from the drop-down list. Alternatively, you can use an existing key file using the <Browse . . .> item in the drop-down list.

Generating the Extended Project Template

You're basing the template for this example on the ExtendedProjectTemplateExample project, and you need to make minor changes for the wizard you just built to work correctly. In the previous section you added an entry in the replacements dictionary, which searches for instances in which the `BackColor` is set to `Silver`. If you want the `MainForm` to have the `BackColor` specified while using the wizard, you need to ensure that the replacement value is found. To do this, simply set the `BackColor` property of the `MainForm` to `Silver`. This adds the line `"Me.BackColor = System.Drawing.Color.Silver"` to the `MainForm.Designer.vb` file (VB) or `"this.BackColor = System.Drawing.Color.Silver"` to the `MainForm.Designer.cs` file so that it is found during the replacement phase.

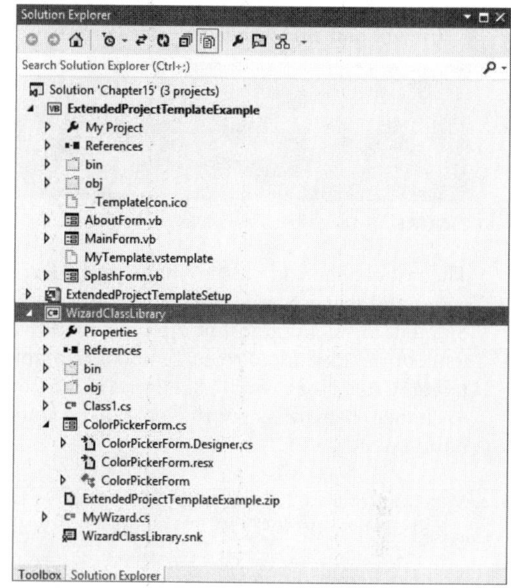

FIGURE 15-13

Now you need to associate the wizard with the project template so that it is called when creating a new project from this template. Unfortunately, this is a manual process, but you can automate it after you make these manual changes upon subsequent rebuilds of the project. Start by exporting the ExtendedProjectTemplateExample as a new project template as per the previous instructions. Find the `.zip` file for this template in Windows Explorer and unzip it. Take the `.vstemplate` file and the icon file and put it into the folder containing the ExtendedProjectTemplateExample project. The other files from the unzipped template can be disregarded — these are just the same files from the project folder that you will use in your template's output instead, so you now have all the files you need in the project folder. Make sure that you do *not* include these files in the ExtendedProjectTemplateExample; they should appear as excluded files, as shown in Figure 15-13.

Notice the `.zip` file in the WizardClassLibrary project — this is the template file that Visual Studio exported (which you want compiled into the setup project). For the moment, take the project template `.zip` file that Visual Studio created, and copy it into the WizardClassLibrary project folder. Show all files for the project (as per Figure 15-13), right-click the file, and select Include in Project. In the Properties window, set its Build Action property to Content. This is for the installer you set up earlier — it includes the Content files from the class library in the setup file, and these will be placed in the Visual Studio Templates folder as part of the installation process.

To have the wizard triggered when you create a project from this template, add some additional lines to the `MyTemplate.vstemplate` file:

```
<VSTemplate Version="2.0.0"
 xmlns="http://schemas.microsoft.com/developer/vstemplate/2005" Type="Project">
  <TemplateData>
  ...
  </TemplateData>
  <TemplateContent>
  ...
  </TemplateContent>
  <WizardExtension>
    <Assembly>WizardClassLibrary, Version=1.0.0.0, Culture=neutral,
       PublicKeyToken=022e960e5582ca43, Custom=null</Assembly>
    <FullClassName>WizardClassLibrary.MyWizard</FullClassName>
  </WizardExtension>
</VSTemplate>
```

The `<WizardExtension>` node added in the sample indicates the class name of the wizard and the strong-named assembly in which it resides. You have already signed the wizard assembly, so all you need to do is determine the `PublicKeyToken`. The easiest way to do this is to open the Visual Studio 2012 Command Prompt and navigate to the directory that contains the WizardLibrary.dll. Then execute the `sn -T <assemblyName>` command. Figure 15-14 shows the output for this command. The `PublicKeyToken` value in the `.vstemplate` file needs to be replaced with the value you found using Reflector.

```
C:\Users\Andrew\Documents\Visual Studio 2012\Projects\Chapter15\WizardClassLibra
ry\bin\Debug>sn -T WizardClassLibrary.dll

Microsoft (R) .NET Framework Strong Name Utility  Version 4.0.30319.17929
Copyright (c) Microsoft Corporation.  All rights reserved.

Public key token is 9764e75da5f8bae4

C:\Users\Andrew\Documents\Visual Studio 2012\Projects\Chapter15\WizardClassLibra
ry\bin\Debug>
```

FIGURE 15-14

The last change you need to make to the ExtendedProjectTemplateExample is to add a post-build event command that zips this project into a project template. (This example uses 7-zip, available at `www.7-zip.org`, but any command-line zip utility will work.) Make a call to the 7-zip executable, which zips the contents of the ExtendedProjectTemplateExample folder (recursively, but excluding the bin and obj folders) into `ExtendedProjectTemplateExample.zip`, and place it into the WizardClassLibrary folder. You may need to change the path as per the location of your zip utility. Put the following command (on one line) as a post-build event:

```
"C:\Program Files\7-Zip\7z.exe" a -tzip ..\..\..\WizardClassLibrary\
ExtendedProjectTemplateExample.zip ..\..\*.* -r -x!bin -x!obj
```

You have now completed the individual projects required to create the project template (ExtendedProjectTemplateExample), added a wizard to modify the project as it is created (WizardClassLibrary), and built an installer to deploy your template to other machines. One last step is to correct the solution dependency list to ensure that the ExtendedProjectTemplateExample is rebuilt (and hence the template zip file re-created) prior to the installer being built. Because there is no direct dependency between the Installer project and the ExtendedProjectTemplateExample, you need to open the solution properties and indicate that there is a dependency, as illustrated in Figure 15-15.

Your solution is now complete and can be used to install the ExtendedProjectTemplateExample and associated `IWizard` implementation. When the solution is installed, you can create a new project from the ExtendedProjectTemplateExample you have just created.

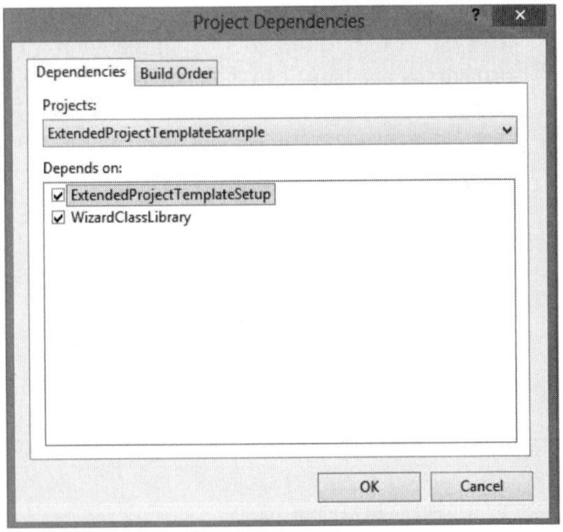

FIGURE 15-15

STARTER KITS

A Starter Kit is essentially the same as a template but differs somewhat in terms of intent. Whereas project templates create the basic shell of an application, Starter Kits create an entire sample application with documentation on how to customize it. Starter Kits appear in the New Project window in the same way project templates do. Starter Kits can give you a big head start on a project (if you can find one focused toward your project type), and you can create your own to share with others in the same way that you created the project template previously.

ONLINE TEMPLATES

Visual Studio 2012 integrates nicely with the online Visual Studio Gallery (`http://www.visualstudio-gallery.com`) enabling you to search for templates created by other developers that they uploaded to the gallery for other developers to download and use. You can browse the gallery and install selected templates from within Visual Studio in two ways: via the Open Project window and from the Extension Manager.

When you open the New Project window in Visual Studio, you are looking at the templates installed on your machine; however, you can browse and search the templates available online by selecting Online from the sidebar. Visual Studio then enables you to browse the templates online. When you select a template it will be downloaded and installed on your machine, and a new project will be created using it.

Visual Studio 2012 includes the Extensions and Updates window (as shown in Figure 15-16), which you can get to from Tools ➪ Extensions and Updates. The Extensions and Updates window integrates the online Visual Studio Gallery (`http://www.visualstudiogallery.com`) into Visual Studio. It also allows you to browse the Visual Studio Gallery and download and install templates, as well as controls and tools.

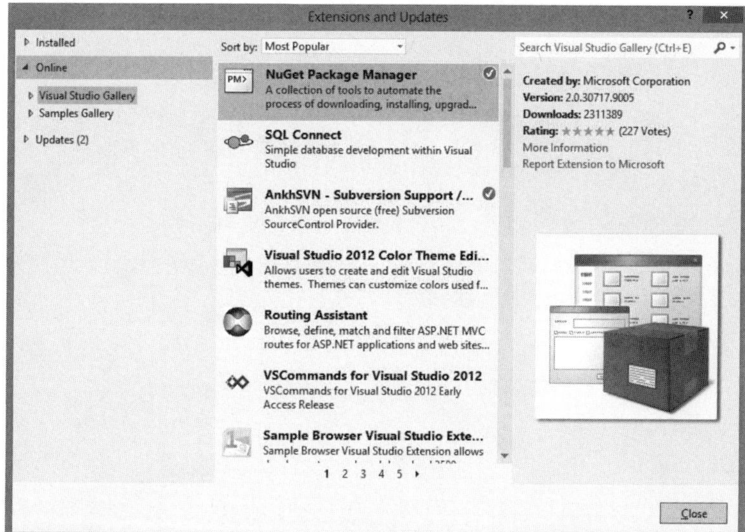

FIGURE 15-16

SUMMARY

This chapter provided an overview of how to create both item and project templates with Visual Studio 2012. Existing projects or items can be exported into templates that you can deploy to your colleagues. Alternatively, you can build a template manually and add a user interface using the `IWizard` interface. From what you learned in this chapter, you can now build a template solution to create a project template, build and integrate a wizard interface, and finally build an installer for your template.

16

Language-Specific Features

WHAT'S IN THIS CHAPTER?

- Choosing the right language for the job
- Working with the new C# and VB language features
- Understanding and getting started with Visual F#

The .NET language ecosystem is alive and well. With literally hundreds of languages targeting the .NET Framework (you can find a fairly complete list at `www.dotnetpowered.com/languages.aspx`), .NET developers have a huge language arsenal at their disposal. Because the .NET Framework was designed with language interoperability in mind, these languages are also able to talk to each other, allowing for a creative cross-pollination of languages across a cross-section of programming problems. You can literally choose the right language tool for the job.

This chapter explores some of the latest language paradigms within the ecosystem, each with particular features and flavors that make solving those tough programming problems just a little bit easier. After a tour of some of the programming language paradigms, you'll learn about some of the new language features introduced in Visual Studio 2012.

HITTING A NAIL WITH THE RIGHT HAMMER

You need to be a flexible and diverse programmer. The programming landscape requires elegance, efficiency, and longevity. Gone are the days of picking one language and platform and executing like crazy to meet the requirements of your problem domain. Different nails sometimes require different hammers.

Given that hundreds of languages are available on the .NET platform, what makes them different from each other? Truth be told, most are small evolutions of each other and are not particularly useful in an enterprise environment. However, it is easy to class these languages into a range of programming paradigms.

Programming languages can be classified in various ways, but by taking a broad-strokes approach, you can put languages into four broad categories: imperative, declarative, dynamic, and functional. This section takes a quick look at these categories and what languages fit within them.

Imperative

Your classic all-rounder — imperative languages describe how, rather than what. Imperative languages were designed from the get-go to raise the level of abstraction of machine code. It's said that when Grace Hopper invented the first-ever compiler, the A–0 system, her machine code programming colleagues complained that she would put them out of a job.

It includes languages where language statements primarily manipulate program state. Object-oriented languages are classic state manipulators through their focus on creating and changing objects. The C and C++ languages fit nicely in the imperative bucket, as do favorites VB and C#.

They're great at describing real-world scenarios through the world of the type system and objects. They are strict — meaning the compiler does a lot of safety checking for you. Safety checking (or type soundness) means you can't easily change a Cow type to a Sheep type — so, for example, if you declare that you need a Cow type in the signature of your method, the compiler (and the run time) make sure that you don't hand that method a Sheep instead. They usually have fantastic reuse mechanisms, too — code written with polymorphism in mind can easily be abstracted away so that other code paths, from within the same module through to entirely different projects, can leverage the code that was written. They also benefit from being the most popular. They're clearly a good choice if you need a team of people working on a problem.

Declarative

Declarative languages describe what, rather than how (in contrast to imperative, which describes the how through program statements that manipulate state). Your classic well-known declarative language is HTML. It describes the layout of a page: what font, text, and decoration are required, and where images should be shown. Parts of another classic, SQL, are declarative — it describes what it wants from a relational database. A recent example of a declarative language is eXtensible Application Markup Language (XAML), which leads a long list of XML-based declarative languages.

Declarative languages are great for describing and transforming data, and as such, we've invoked them from our imperative languages to retrieve and manipulate data for years.

Dynamic

The dynamic category includes all languages that exhibit "dynamic" features such as late-bound binding and invocation, Read Eval Print Loops (REPL), duck typing (non-strict typing, that is, if an object looks like a duck and walks like a duck it must be a duck), and more.

Dynamic languages typically delay as much compilation behavior as they possibly can to run time. Whereas your typical C# method invocation `Console.WriteLine()` would be statically checked and linked to at compile time, a dynamic language would delay all this to run time. Instead, it looks up the `WriteLine()` method on the `Console` type while the program is actually running, and, if it finds it, invokes it at run time. If it does not find the method or the type, the language may expose features for the programmer to hook up a failure method so that the programmer can catch these failures and programmatically try something else.

Other features include extending objects, classes, and interfaces at run time (meaning modifying the type system on the fly); dynamic scoping (for example, a variable defined in the global scope can be accessed by private or nested methods); and more.

Compilation methods like this have interesting side effects. If your types don't need to be fully defined up front (because the type system is so flexible), you can write code that consumes strict interfaces (such as COM, or other .NET assemblies, for example) and make that code highly resilient to failure and versioning of that interface. In the C# world, if an interface you're consuming from an external assembly changes, you typically need a recompile (and a fix-up of your internal code) to get it up and running again. From a dynamic language, you could hook the "method missing" mechanism of the language, and when a particular interface has changed, simply do some "reflective" lookup on that interface and decide if you can invoke anything else. This means you can write fantastic glue code that glues together interfaces that may not be versioned dependently.

Dynamic languages are great at rapid prototyping. Not having to define your types up front (something you would do straightaway in C#) allows you to concentrate on code to solve problems, rather than on the type constraints of the implementation. The REPL enables you to write prototypes line by line and immediately see the changes reflected in the program instead of wasting time doing a compile-run-debug cycle.

If you're interested in looking at dynamic languages on the .NET platform, you're in luck. Microsoft has released IronPython (`www.codeplex.com/IronPython`), which is a Python implementation for the .NET Framework. The Python language is a classic example of a dynamic language and is wildly popular in the scientific computing, systems administration, and general programming space. If Python doesn't tickle your fancy, you can also download and try out IronRuby (`www.ironruby.net/`), which is an implementation of the Ruby language for the .NET Framework. Ruby is a dynamic language that's popular in the web space, and though it's still relatively young, it has a huge popular following.

Functional

The functional category focuses on languages that treat computation like mathematical functions. They try hard to avoid state manipulation, instead concentrating on the results of functions as the building blocks for solving problems. If you've done any calculus before, the theory behind functional programming might look familiar.

Because functional programming typically doesn't manipulate state, the surface area of side effects generated in a program is much smaller. This means it is fantastic for implementing parallel and concurrent algorithms. The holy grail of highly concurrent systems is the avoidance of overlapping "unintended" state manipulation. Deadlocks, race conditions, and broken invariants are classic manifestations of not synchronizing your state manipulation code. Concurrent programming and synchronization through threads, shared memory, and locks is incredibly hard, so why not avoid it altogether? Because functional programming encourages the programmer to write stateless algorithms, the compiler can then reason about automatic parallelism of the code. This means you can exploit the power of multicore processors without the heavy lifting of managing threads, locks, and shared memory.

Functional programs are terse. There's usually less code required to arrive at a solution than with its imperative cousin. Less code typically means fewer bugs and less surface area to test.

What's It All Mean?

These categories are broad by design: Languages may include features common to one or more of these categories. The categories should be used as a way to relate the language features that exist in them to the particular problems that they are good at solving.

Languages such as C# and VB.NET are leveraging features from their dynamic and functional counterparts. Language Integrated Query (LINQ) is a great example of a borrowed paradigm. Consider the following C# 3.0 LINQ query:

```
var query =   from c in customers
              where c.CompanyName == "Microsoft"
              select new { c.ID, c.CompanyName };
```

This has a few borrowed features. The `var` keyword says "infer the type of the query specified," which looks a lot like something out of a dynamic language. The actual query itself, `from c in ...`, looks and acts like the declarative language SQL, and the `select new { c.ID ...` creates a new anonymous type, again something that looks fairly dynamic. The code-generated results of these statements are particularly interesting: they're actually not compiled into classic IL (intermediate language); they're instead compiled into what's called an expression tree and then interpreted at run time — something that's taken right out of the dynamic language playbook.

The truth is, these categories don't particularly matter too much for deciding which tool to use to solve the right problem. Cross-pollination of feature sets from each category into languages is in fashion at the moment, which is good for a programmer, whose favorite language typically picks up the best features from each category. Currently the trend is for imperative/dynamic languages to be used by application developers, whereas functional languages have excelled in solving domain-specific problems.

If you're a .NET programmer, you have even more to smile about. Language interoperation through the Common Language Specification (CLS) works seamlessly, meaning you can use your favorite imperative language for the majority of the problems you're trying to solve and then call into a functional language for your data manipulation, or maybe some hard-core math you need to solve a problem.

A TALE OF TWO LANGUAGES

Since the creation of the .NET Framework, there has been an ongoing debate as to which language developers should use to write their applications. In a lot of cases, teams choose between C# and VB based upon prior knowledge of either C/C++, Java, or VB6. However, this decision was made harder by a previous divergence of the languages. In the past, the language teams within Microsoft made additions to their languages independently, resulting in a number of features appearing in one language and not the other. For example, VB has integrated language support for working with XML literals, whereas C# has anonymous methods and iterators. Although these features benefited the users of those languages, it made it difficult for organizations to choose which language to use. In fact, in some cases organizations ended up using a mix of languages attempting to use the best language for the job at hand. Unfortunately, this either means that the development team needs to read and write both languages, or the team gets fragmented with some working on the C# and some on the VB code.

With Visual Studio 2010 and the .NET Framework 4.0, a decision was made within Microsoft to co-evolve the two primary .NET languages, C# and VB. This co-evolution would seek to minimize the differences in capabilities between the two languages (often referred to as *feature parity*). However, this isn't an attempt to merge the two languages; actually, it's quite the opposite. Microsoft has clearly indicated that each language may implement a feature in a different way to ensure it is in line with the way developers already write and interact with the language.

In the coming sections, you'll learn about the language features that have been added in Visual Studio 2012. You'll start by looking at the features common to both languages before going through changes to the individual languages, most of which are discussed in the context of feature parity, and how the introduced feature matches a feature already in the other language.

The Async Keyword

As has already been mentioned, writing code that supports multiple threads is difficult to accomplish. At least, it's difficult to do so without introducing bugs that can be challenging to identify and remove. For the last few versions of C#, Microsoft has been working toward the goal of making writing multithreaded applications easier. You've seen this with the introduction of classes such as `BackgroundWorker` and widespread use of the Event-based Asynchronous Pattern. Each of these was focused on the idea of removing the need for a developer to create threads as part of their code. In .NET 4.0, the Task Parallel Library (TPL) made some multithreading concepts (such as separating loop iterations or LINQ queries into parallel threads) more readily available to the average developer. .NET 4.5 goes a step further with the introduction of the `async` keyword.

The main goal of the Async feature is to call methods in an asynchronous manner without needing to write continuations and without requiring you to split code across different methods. It isn't that this work isn't done. It's just that you don't have to write it because the developer takes care of that for you.

There are actually two keywords added as part of the Async feature. The async modifier on a method signature indicates that a particular method will return either a Task object or a Task generic object. The difference between the two being that the Task returns void (or Nothing) and the Task generic (in the form of Task<TResult>) returns an object of type TResult. This object represents the ongoing state of the method. As such, it contains information about the status of the task. The idea is that the caller can then use this information to operate on and with the running task.

The second keyword is await. This keyword is actually an operator and it operates on a Task. When this is done, the execution of the current method is suspended until the asynchronous method represented by the task is complete. While waiting, control is returned to the caller of the method that is suspended.

To see what this looks like in action, consider the following method named GetContentsAtUrl. It takes a URL as a parameter and returns a byte array of the contents found at the location:

C#

```
private byte[] GetContentsAtUrl(string url)
{
    var contents = new MemoryStream();

    var webReq = (HttpWebRequest)WebRequest.Create(url);

    using (var webResp = webReq.GetResponse())
    {
        using (Stream responseStream = webResp.GetResponseStream())
        {
            responseStream.CopyTo(contents);
        }
    }

    return contents.ToArray();
}
```

This is a synchronous method. Therefore, you need to wait for the response to come back (initiated by the call to the GetResponse method) before the method can complete. And while you're waiting, the caller's thread is suspended.

To change this, now modify this method to be an asynchronous method with this code:

C#

```
private async Task<byte[]> GetContentsAtUrlAsync(string url)
{
    var contents = new MemoryStream();

    var webReq = (HttpWebRequest)WebRequest.Create(url);

    using (WebResponse response = await webReq.GetResponseAsync())
    {
        using (Stream responseStream = response.GetResponseStream())
        {
            await responseStream.CopyToAsync(contents);
        }
    }
    return contents.ToArray();
}
```

The first change (besides the async keyword) is the return value for the method. Instead of a byte array, it returns a generic Task object declared with the byte array. This allows it to be used as part of the await operator. You might also notice that the name of the method has changed. This is a convention (appending the word `Async` to the method name) that is intended to help developers recognize that a method can be called asynchronously.

Four lines into the routine, you'll notice another difference. Instead of calling `GetResponse`, the call is made to `GetResponseAsync`. This method wraps the `GetResponse` functionality in a Task. Because `GetResponseAsync` returns a task, it can be used with the `await` keyword. When this statement is executed, the `GetContentsAtUrlAsync` method is suspended, a separate thread is spun up to run the `GetResponse` function, and control is returned to the calling application.

When the `GetResponseAsync` method is complete, the `GetContentsAtUrlAsync` method will be unsuspended (the correct term is actually "continued"), with execution continuing at the statement immediately following the `GetContentsAtUrlAsync` method.

Just so that you're clear, `async` methods do not block on the current thread. This may seem a little odd, but what happens in the compilation process is that the remainder of the method (that is, after the `await` call) is built out as a continuation. After the method call (`GetResponseAsync`, in this case) is complete, this continuation is executed on the original thread (when the thread is idle). This eliminates even the need to marshal callbacks onto the UI thread, as would have been done in asynchronous programming in previous versions.

Caller Information

There are times when it might be useful to find out information about who is calling a particular method. In .NET 4.5, this is available through the use of Caller Info attributes. To see this in action, consider the following method:

C#

```
public void TraceMessage(string message)
{
    Trace.WriteLine("Message: " + message);
}
```

In this case, a message is passed in and written to any trace listeners. But what if you want to know the name of the method making the call? In .NET 4.5, you would add some parameters to the method and decorate them with Caller Info attributes, as shown here:

C#

```
public void TraceMessage(string message,
        [CallerMemberName] string memberName = "",
        [CallerFilePath] string sourceFilePath = "",
        [CallerLineNumber] int sourceLineNumber = 0)
{
    Trace.WriteLine("Message: " + message);
    Trace.WriteLine("Member Name: " + memberName);
    Trace.WriteLine("Source File Path: " + sourceFilePath);
    Trace.WriteLine("Source Line Number: " + sourceLineNumber);
}
```

A number of parameters have now been added to the methods. These are actually optional parameters, in that if the values are not provided, then they are given default values. But by specifying the `CallerMemberName`, `CallerFilePath`, and `CallerLineNumber` attributes, the default values are actually the name of the method, the path to the source code, and the line number within the source code. These values are now available for use as you see fit.

VISUAL BASIC

In the spirit of feature parity, two of the new features offered in this version of Visual Basic are the same as the two found in C#. Both Caller Info attributes and the Async feature are included. The difference between the C# code and the VB code is just syntactical. There is an `Async` keyword that modifies a method declaration and an `Await` operator the works on a Task object. And there are `CallerMemberName`, `CallerFilePath`, and `CallerLineNumber` attributes that can be used to provide values to optional method parameters. So instead of rehashing, let's concentrate on the features that are new for just Visual Basic.

Iterators

Although iterators have been around in C# since Visual Studio 2005, they have not been available in Visual Basic until more recently. They are a fairly infrequently used concept that, when you need it, is incredibly useful. In a nutshell, the `iterator` keyword allows a developer to create a custom iteration across a collection.

Start with a simple method that returns an `IEnumerable` value and how it would be used in a `For Each` statement:

VB

```
Sub Main()
    For Each number As Integer In GetNumbers()
        Console.Write(number & ",")
    Next
End Sub

Private Iterator Function GetNumbers() As System.Collections.IEnumerable
    Yield 9
    Yield 12
    Yield 14
    Yield 16
End Function
```

In the code snippet, you'll see a method named `GetNumbers` that returns an `IEnumerable` value. The body of the method is just a set of four `Yield` statements. In the `Main` subroutine, there is a `For Each` statement that loops across each of the elements returned by `GetNumbers`.

The purpose of the `Yield` is to indicate that the specified value is the next value in the enumeration. When the `GetNumbers` enumerator is next evaluated for the next value, the method continues executing immediately after the previous `Yield` until another one is found. So in the case of the preceding code snippet, the output would be `9, 12, 14,` and `16`.

The Global Keyword

You can create a nested hierarchy of namespaces that can prevent you from having access to some of the built-in .NET data types. For example, consider the following code snippet:

VB

```
Namespace MyNameSpace
    Namespace System
        Class Sample
            Function getValue() As System.Double
                Dim d As System.Double
                Return d
            End Function
        End Class
    End Namespace
End Namespace
```

The preceding code will not compile because the attempt is made to resolve the `System` namespace (as seen in `System.Double`) with the `System` namespace found in `MyNameSpace`. And because there is no class called `Double`, the compiler throws up its virtual hands and gives you an error message.

The `Global` keyword enables you to avoid this problem. When `Global` is used with a namespace, it tells the compiler to start resolving the data type back at the root level namespace. The following code snippet corrects the problem:

VB

```
Namespace MyNameSpace
    Namespace System
        Class Sample
            Function getValue() As Global.System.Double
                Dim d As Global.System.Double
                Return d
            End Function
        End Class
    End Namespace
End Namespace
```

You can see that the `Global` keyword has been added to the two places where a `System.Double` is defined, allowing the compiler to successfully resolve the data type.

Visual Basic PowerPacks

One of the challenges often put forward by VB6 developers is that doing tasks in .NET requires many more steps or is more complex than it was in VB6. To encourage VB6 developers to move to the .NET Framework, VB introduced the `My` namespace, which provides a set of shortcut methods to get frequently performed tasks done. The VB team has also released the Visual Basic PowerPacks for previous versions of Visual Studio that add a number of useful controls and other classes to aid VB developers.

Ever since Visual Studio 2010, the Visual Basic Power Pack has shipped with the product. As you can see in Figure 16-1, an additional tab in the Toolbox contains a number of drawing controls such as Line, Oval, and Rectangle. These can be used to generate simple graphics, such as the one on the right side of Figure 16-1.

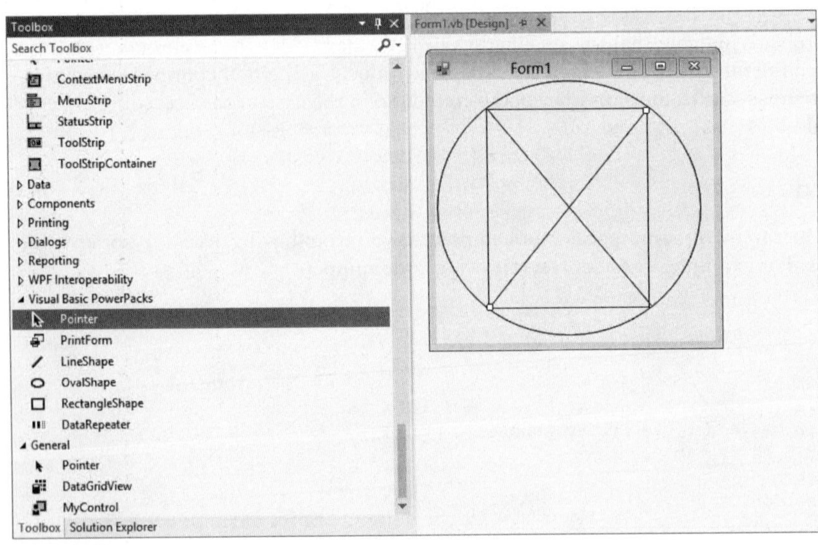

FIGURE 16-1

Although the Visual Basic PowerPacks are available by default to VB developers, there is no reason why C# developers can't access the same controls. To use these controls in a C# project, simply add a reference to the PowerPacks assembly and then add the controls to your Toolbox. From there you can use them on any Windows Forms application.

F#

F# (pronounced F Sharp) is a language incubated out of Microsoft Research in Cambridge, England, by the guy that brought generics to the .NET Framework, Don Syme. F# ships with Visual Studio 2012 and is a multiparadigm functional language. This means it's primarily a functional language but supports other flavors of programming, such as imperative and object-oriented programming styles.

Your First F# Program

Fire up Visual Studio 2012 and create a new F# project. As Figure 16-2 shows, the F# Application template is located in the Visual F# node in the New Project dialog. Give it a name and click OK.

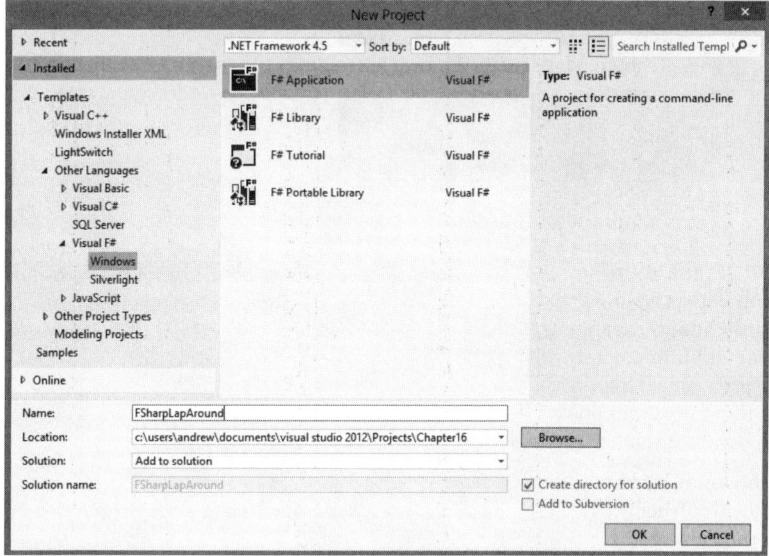

FIGURE 16-2

The F# Application template simply creates an F# project with a single source file, `Program.fs`, which is empty except for a reference to the F# Developer Center, `http://fsharp.net`. If you want to learn more about F#, a great place to start is the F# Tutorial template. This creates a normal F# project except for the main source file, `Tutorial.fs`, which contains approximately 280 lines of documentation on how to start with F#. Walking down this file and checking out what language features are available is an interesting exercise in itself. For now, return to the `Program.fs` and quickly get the canonical "Hello World" example up and running to see the various options available for compilation and interactivity. Add the following code:

```
#light

printfn "Hello, F# World!"
let x = System.Console.ReadLine();
```

The first statement, `#light`, is a compile flag to indicate that the code is written using the optional lightweight syntax. With this syntax, whitespace indentation becomes significant, reducing the need for certain tokens such as `in` and `;;`. The second statement simply prints out `"Hello, F# World!"` to the console.

> **NOTE** *If you have worked with earlier versions of F#, you may find that your code now throws compiler errors. F# was born out of a research project and now has been converted into a commercial offering. As such, there has been a refactoring of the language, and some operations have been moved out of FSharp.Core into supporting assemblies. For example, the* `print_endline` *command has been moved into the* `FSharp.PowerPack.dll` *assembly. The F# Powerpack is available for download via the F# Developer Center at* `http://fsharp.net`.

You can run an F# program in two ways. The first is to simply run the application as you would normally. (Press F5 to start debugging.) This compiles and runs your program, as shown in Figure 16-3.

FIGURE 16-3

The other way to run an F# program is to use the F# Interactive window from within Visual Studio. This allows you to highlight and execute code from within Visual Studio and immediately see the result in your running program. It also allows you to modify your running program on the fly!

The F# Interactive window (shown in Figure 16-4) is available from the View ➪ Other Windows ➪ F# Interactive menu item, or by pressing the Ctrl+Alt+F key combination.

In the Interactive window, you can start interacting with the F# compiler through the REPL prompt. This means that for every line of F# you type, it compiles and executes that line immediately. REPLs are great if you want to test ideas quickly and modify programs on the fly. They allow for quick algorithm experimentation and rapid prototyping.

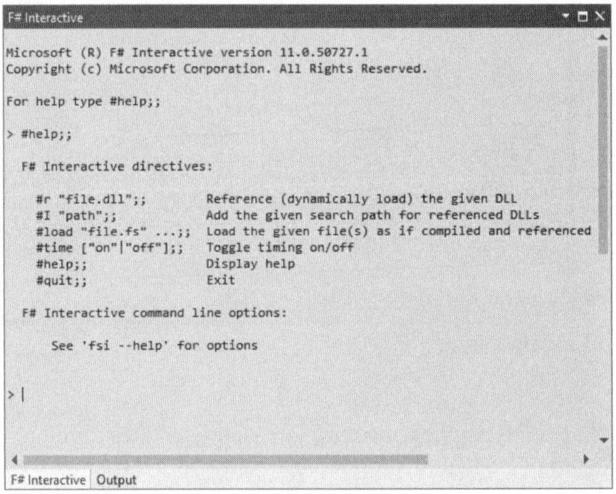

FIGURE 16-4

However, from the REPL prompt in the F# Interactive window, you essentially miss out on the value that Visual Studio delivers through IntelliSense, code snippets, and so on. The best experience is that of both worlds: Use the Visual Studio text editor to create your programs, and pipe that output through to the Interactive Prompt. You can do this by pressing Alt+Enter on any highlighted piece of F# source code.

Alternatively, you can use the right-click context menu to send a selection to the Interactive window, as shown in Figure 16-5.

Pressing Alt+Enter, or selecting Execute in Interactive, pipes the highlighted source code straight to the Interactive window prompt and executes it immediately, as shown in Figure 16-6.

Figure 16-6 also shows the right-click context menu for the F# Interactive window where you can either Cancel Interactive Evaluation (for long-running operations) or Reset Interactive Session (where any prior state will be discarded).

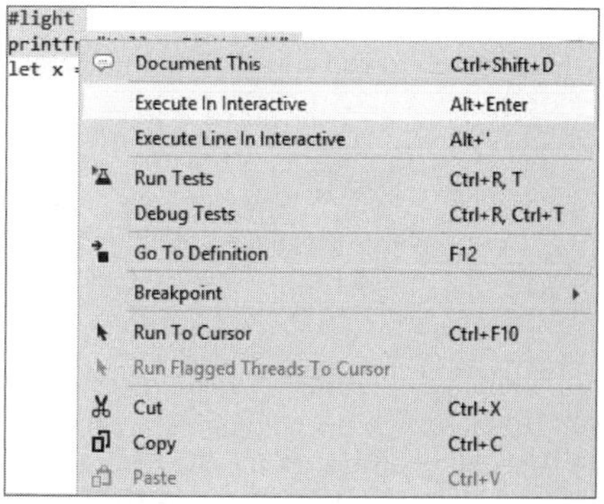

FIGURE 16-5

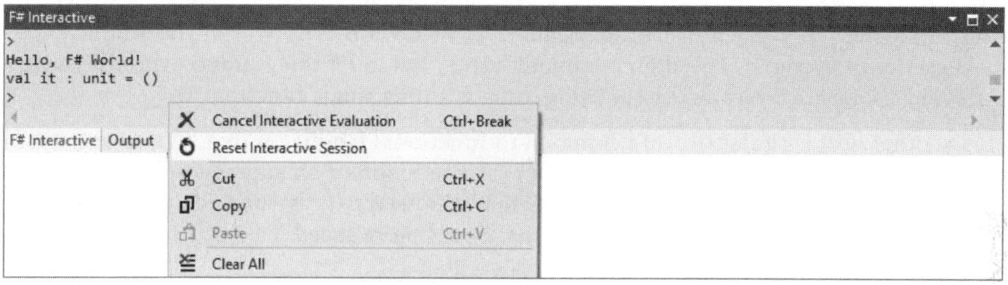

FIGURE 16-6

Exploring F# Language Features

A primer on the F# language is beyond the scope of this book, but it's worth exploring some of the cooler language features that it supports. If anything, it should whet your appetite for F# and act as a catalyst to learn more about this great language.

A common data type in the F# world is the list. It's a simple collection type with expressive operators. You can define empty lists, multidimensional lists, and your classic flat list. The F# list is immutable, meaning you can't modify it after it's created; you can take only a copy. F# exposes a feature called List Comprehensions to make creating, manipulating, and comprehending lists easier and more expressive. Consider the following:

```
#light

let countInFives = [ for x in 1 .. 20 do if x % 5 = 0  then yield x ]

printf "%A" countInFives
System.Console.ReadLine()
```

The expression in braces does a classic `for` loop over a list that contains elements 1 through 20 (the ". ." expression is shorthand for creating a new list with elements 1 through 20 in it). The `do` is a comprehension that the `for` loop executes for each element in the list. In this case, the action to execute is to `yield` x where the if condition "when x module 5 equals 0" is true. The braces are shorthand for "create a new list with all returned elements in it." And there you have it — an expressive way to define a new list on the fly in one line.

F#'s Pattern Matching feature is a flexible and powerful way to create control flow. In the C# world, you have the switch (or simply a bunch of nested "if else's"), but you're usually constrained to the type of what you're switching over. F#'s pattern matching is similar, but more flexible, allowing the test to be over whatever types or values you specify. For example, take a look at defining a Fibonacci function in F# using pattern matching:

```
let rec fibonacci x =
    match x with
    | 0 | 1 -> x
    | _ -> fibonacci (x - 1) + fibonacci (x - 2)

printfn "fibonacci 15 = %i" (fibonacci 15)
```

The pipe operator (|) specifies that you want to match the input to the function against an expression on the right side of the pipe. The first says return the input of the function `x` when `x` matches either `0` or `1`. The second line says return the recursive result of a call to Fibonacci with an input of `x - 1`, adding that to another recursive call where the input is `x - 2`. The last line writes the result of the Fibonacci function to the console.

Pattern matching in functions has an interesting side effect — it makes dispatch and control flow over different receiving parameter types much easier and cleaner. In the C#/VB.NET world, you would traditionally write a series of overloads based on parameter types, but in F# this is unnecessary because the pattern matching syntax allows you to achieve the same thing within a single function.

Lazy evaluation is another neat language feature common to functional languages that F# also exposes. It simply means that the compiler can schedule the evaluation of a function or an expression only when it's needed, rather than precomputing it up front. This means that you need to only run code you absolutely have to — fewer cycles spent executing and less working set means more speed.

Typically, when you have an expression assigned to a variable, that expression gets immediately executed to store the result in the variable. Leveraging the theory that functional programming has no side effects, there is no need to immediately express this result (because in-order execution is not necessary), and as a result, you should execute only when the variable result is actually required. Take a look at a simple case:

```
let lazyDiv = lazy ( 10 / 2 )
printfn "%A" lazyDiv
```

First, the `lazy` keyword is used to express a function or expression that will be executed only when forced. The second line prints whatever is in `lazyDiv` to the console. If you execute this example, what you actually get as the console output is "(unevaluated)." This is because under the hood the input to `printfn` is similar to a delegate. You actually need to force, or invoke, the expression before you'll get a return result, as in the following example:

```
let lazyDiv2 = lazy ( 10 / 2 )
let result = lazyDiv2.Force()
print_any result
```

The `lazyDiv2.Force()` function forces the execution of the `lazyDiv2` expression.

This concept is powerful when optimizing for application performance. Reducing the amount of working set, or memory, that an application needs is extremely important in improving both startup performance and run-time performance. Lazy evaluation is also a required concept when dealing with massive amounts of data. If you need to iterate through terabytes of data stored on disk, you can easily write a Lazy evaluation wrapper over that data so that you slurp up the data only when you actually need it. The Applied Games Group in Microsoft Research has a great write-up of using F#'s Lazy evaluation feature with exactly that scenario: `http://blogs.technet.com/apg/archive/2006/11/04/dealing-with-terabytes-with-f.aspx`.

Type Providers

The concept of a type provider, as it applies to F#, is relatively straightforward. Modern development involves bringing data in from a disparate number of sources. And to work with this data, it needs to be marshaled into classes and objects that can be manipulated by your application. The creation of all these classes by hand is not only tedious, but also increases the possibility of bugs. Frequently, a code generator would be used to address this issue. But if you use F# in an interactive mode, traditional code generators are not the best. Every time a service reference is adjusted, the code would need to be regenerated and that can be annoying.

To address this, F# has introduced a number of build-time type providers aimed at addressing common data access situations. These include access to SQL relational database, Open Data (OData) services, and WSDL-defined services. Or you have the ability to create and use your own custom type providers.

As an example of how type providers would be used to access a SQL Server database, consider the following code:

F#

```
#r "System.Data.dll"
#r "FSharp.Data.TypeProviders.dll"
#r "System.Data.Linq.dll"

type dbSchema = SqlDataConnection<"Data Source=.\SQLEXPRESS;Initial
Catalog=AdventureWorksLT2008R2;Integrated Security=SSPI;">
let db = dbSchema.GetDataContext()

let qry =
        query {
            for row in db.Customers do
            select row
        }
qry |> Seq.iter (fun row -> printfn "%s, %s" row.Name row.City)
;;
```

> **NOTE** *In order to run the above code, you need to add a number of references to your project. This is true even if you are running in F# Interactive mode. Specifically, the System.Data and System.Data.Linq assemblies need to be added. For the SQLDataConnection class and related F# data functionality, you need to add the FSharp.Data.TypeProviders assembly.*

After adding references to the necessary namespaces, the type provider is accessed through the use of the `type` declaration. This allows the `dbSchema` variable to be created as the type, which contains all the generated types representing the database tables in the AdventureWorksLT2008 R2 database. And after `GetDataContext` is invoked, the `db` variable has as its properties all the table names, allowing for rows to be iterated across and the name and city of the customers to be printed for each one.

Query Expressions

Earlier versions of F# were lacking in support for LINQ. As many C# and VB developers have discovered, LINQ is a powerful syntax for querying many different data sources and shaping the resulting data as required by the application. With F# 3.0, LINQ queries can be built and executed, extending the expressibility of the language. Consider the code snippet shown here:

F#

```
open System
open System.Data
open System.Data.Linq
open Microsoft.FSharp.Data.TypeProviders
open Microsoft.FSharp.Linq

type dbSchema = SqlDataConnection<"Data Source=.\SQLEXPRESS;Initial
Catalog=AdventureWorksLT2008R2;Integrated Security=SSPI;">
let db = dbSchema.GetDataContext()

let qry =
        query {
            for row in db.Customers do
            where (row.City == "London")
            select row
        }
qry |> Seq.iter (fun row -> printfn "%s, %s" row.Name row.City)
```

This code snippet performs almost exactly the same function as the one found in the previous section. The difference is that only customers in the city of London are displayed. But the LINQ syntax is visible in the query statement, including the ability to filter out rows based on specified criteria. And although the keywords are a little different, most of the same functionality as LINQ found in C# and VB is available as well.

Auto-Implemented Properties

Properties in F# can be defined in one of two ways. The difference is whether or not you want the property to have an explicit backing store. The "traditional" way to create a property is to define a private variable that holds the value of the property. Then this value can be exposed through the `get` and `set` methods of the property. If, on the other hand, you don't need or want to create that private variable, F# can generate one for you. This is the concept behind auto-implemented properties. The following code snippet shows both the traditional and auto-implemented approaches:

F#

```
type Person() =
   member val FirstName
      with get () = privateFirstName
      and set (value) = privateFirstNam <- value
   member val LastName = "" with get, set
```

The last line is actually the auto-implemented property. Unlike the `FirstName` property, which has explicit `get` and `set` methods (and uses the `privateFirstName` variable as the backing store), `LastName` is defined as defaulting to an empty string and uses whatever variable the compiler generates.

SUMMARY

In this chapter you learned about the different styles of programming languages and about their relative strengths and weaknesses. Visual Studio 2012 brings together the two primary .NET languages, C# and VB, with the goal of reaching feature parity. The co-evolution of these languages can help reduce the cost of development teams and projects, allowing developers to more easily switch between languages. You also learned about Visual F#. As the scale of problems that you seek to solve increases, so does the complexity introduced by the need to write highly parallel applications. You can use Visual F# to tackle these problems through the execution of parallel operations without adding to the complexity of an application.

PART IV
Rich Client Applications

17

Windows Forms Applications

WHAT'S IN THIS CHAPTER?

- Creating a new Windows Forms application
- Designing the layout of forms and controls using the Visual Studio designers and control properties
- Using container controls and control properties to ensure that your controls automatically resize when the application resizes

Since its earliest days, Visual Studio has excelled at providing a rich visual environment for rapidly developing Windows applications. From simple drag-and-drop procedures to place graphical controls onto the form, to setting properties that control advanced layout and behavior of controls, the designer built into Visual Studio 2012 provides you with immense power without having to manually create the UI from code.

This chapter walks you through the rich designer support and comprehensive set of controls available for you to maximize your efficiency when creating Windows Forms applications.

GETTING STARTED

The first thing you need to start is to create a new Windows Forms project. Select the File ⇨ New ⇨ Project menu to create the project in a new solution. If you have an existing solution to which you want to add a new Windows Forms project, select File ⇨ Add ⇨ New Project.

Windows Forms applications can be created with either VB or C#. In both cases, the Windows Forms Application project template is the default selection when you open the New Project dialog box and select the Windows category, as shown in Figure 17-1.

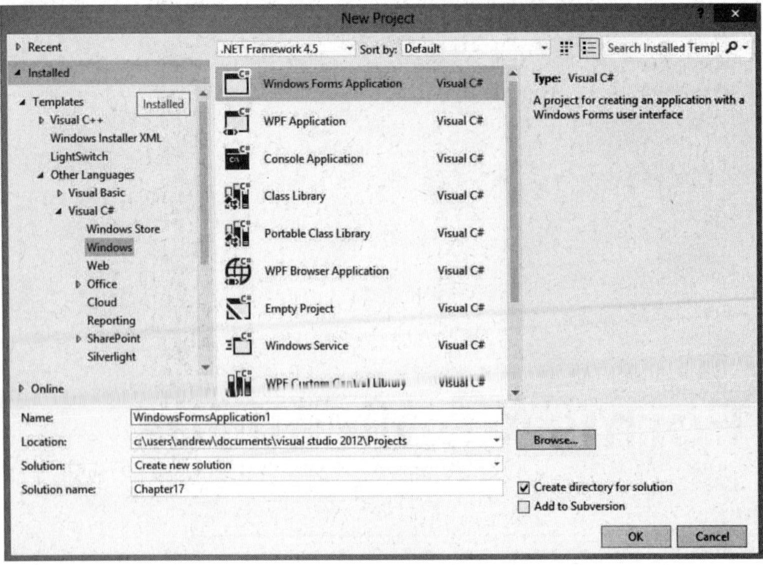

FIGURE 17-1

The New Project dialog allows you to select the .NET Framework version you are targeting. Unlike WPF applications, Windows Forms projects have been available since version 1.0 of the .NET Framework and will stay in the list of available projects regardless of which version of the .NET Framework you select. After entering an appropriate name for the project, click OK to create the new Windows Forms Application project.

THE WINDOWS FORM

When you create a Windows application project, Visual Studio 2012 automatically creates a single blank form ready for your user interface design (see Figure 17-2). You can modify the visual design of a Windows Form in two common ways: by using the mouse to change the size or position of the form or a control or by changing the value of the control's properties in the Properties window.

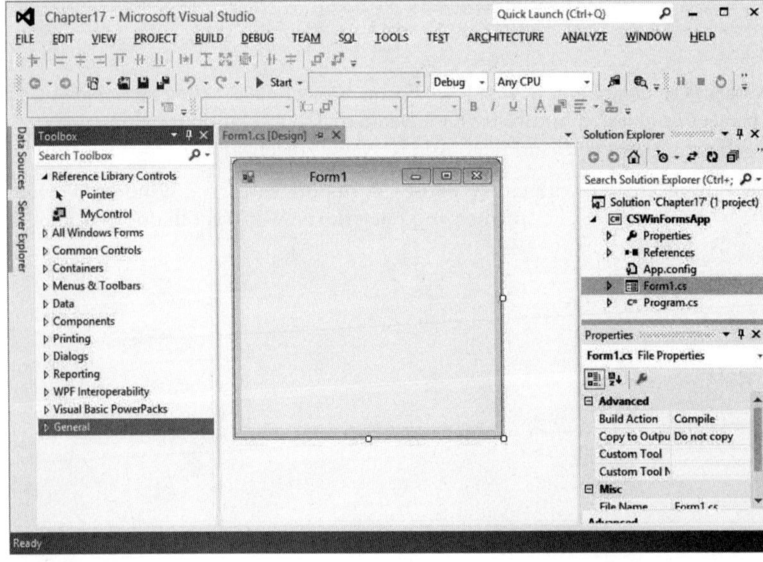

FIGURE 17-2

Almost every visual control, including the Windows Form, can be resized using the mouse. Resize grippers appear when the form or control has focus in the Design view. For a Windows Form, these are visible only on the bottom, the right side, and the bottom-right corner. Use the mouse to grab the gripper, and drag it to the size you want. As you resize, the dimensions of the form are displayed on the bottom right of the status bar.

There is a corresponding property for the dimensions and position of Windows Forms and controls. As you may recall from Chapter 2, "The Solution Explorer, Toolbox, and Properties," the Properties window, as shown on the right side of Figure 17-2, shows the current value of many of the attributes of the form. This includes the `Size` property, a compound property made up of the `Height` and `Width`. Click the expand icon to display the individual properties for any compound properties. You can set the dimensions of the form in pixels by entering either an individual value in both the `Height` and `Width` properties or a compound `Size` value in the format width, height.

The Properties window, as shown in Figure 17-3, displays some of the available properties for customizing the form's appearance and behavior.

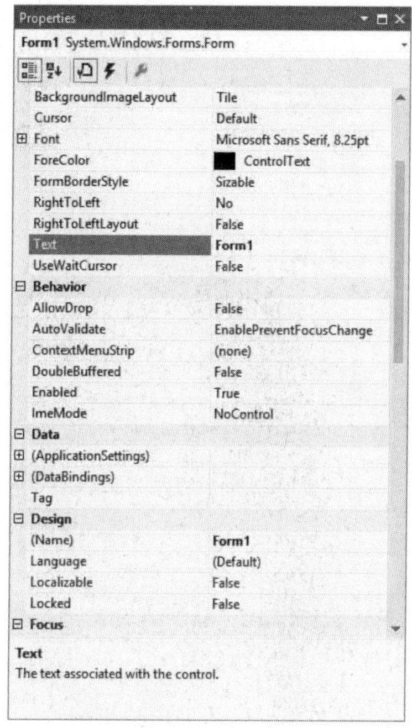

FIGURE 17-3

Properties display in one of two views: either grouped together in categories or in alphabetical order. The view is controlled by the first two icons in the toolbar of the Properties window. The following two icons toggle the attribute list between displaying Properties and Events.

Three categories cover most of the properties that affect the overall look and feel of a form: Appearance, Layout, and Window Style. Many of the properties in these categories are also available on Windows controls.

Appearance Properties

The Appearance category covers the colors, fonts, and form border style. Many Windows Forms applications leave most of these properties as their defaults. The `Text` property is one that you typically change because it controls what display in the form's caption bar.

If the form's purpose differs from the normal behavior, you may need a fixed-size window or a special border, as is commonly seen in tool windows. The `FormBorderStyle` property controls how this aspect of your form's appearance is handled.

Layout Properties

In addition to the `Size` properties discussed earlier, the Layout category contains the `MaximumSize` and `MinimumSize` properties, which control how small or large a window can be resized to. The `StartPosition` and `Location` properties can be used to control where the form displays on the screen. You can use the `WindowState` property to initially display the form minimized, maximized, or normally according to its default size.

Window Style Properties

The Window Style category includes properties that determine what is shown in the Windows Form's caption bar, including the maximize and minimize boxes, help button, and form icon. The `ShowInTaskbar` property determines whether the form is listed in the Windows taskbar. Other notable properties in this category include the `TopMost` property, which ensures that the form always appears on top of other windows, even when it does not have focus, and the `Opacity` property, which makes a form semi-transparent.

FORM DESIGN PREFERENCES

You can modify some Visual Studio IDE settings that simplify your user interface design phase. In the Options dialog (as shown in Figure 17-4), two pages of preferences deal with the Windows Forms Designer.

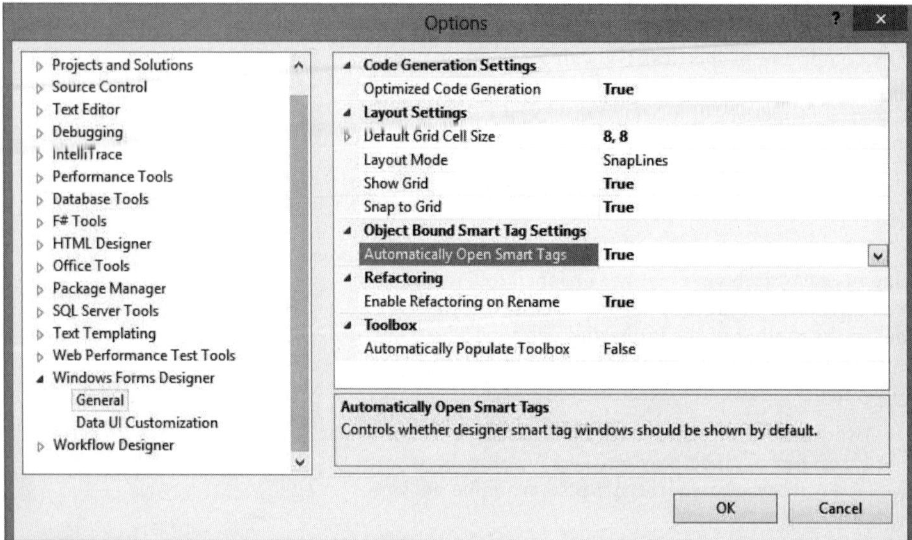

FIGURE 17-4

The main settings that affect your design are the layout settings. By default, Visual Studio 2012 uses a layout mode called SnapLines. Rather than position visible components on the form via an invisible grid, SnapLines helps you position them based on the context of surrounding controls and the form's own borders. You see how to use this mode in a moment, but if you prefer the older style of form design that originated in Visual Basic 6 and was used in the first two versions of Visual Studio .NET, you can change the `LayoutMode` property to `SnapToGrid`.

> **NOTE** *The SnapToGrid layout mode is still used even if the LayoutMode is set to SnapLines. SnapLines becomes active only when you are positioning a control relative to another control. At other times, SnapToGrid will be active and allow you to position the control on the grid vertex.*

You can use the `GridSize` property when positioning and sizing controls on the form. As you move controls around the form, they snap to specific points based on the values you enter here. Most of the time, you can find a grid of 8 × 8 (the default) too large for fine-tuning, so changing this to something such as 4 × 4 might be more appropriate.

> **NOTE** *Both SnapToGrid and SnapLines are aids for designing user interfaces using the mouse. After the control has been roughly positioned, you can use the keyboard to fine-tune control positions by "nudging" the control with the arrow keys.*

`ShowGrid` displays a network of dots on your form's design surface when you're in SnapToGrid mode, so you can more easily see where the controls will be positioned when you move them. You need to close the designer and reopen it to see any changes to this setting. Finally, setting the `SnapToGrid` property to False deactivates the layout aids while in SnapToGrid mode and results in pure free-form form design.

While you're looking at this page of options, you may want to change the Automatically Open Smart Tags value to False. The default setting of True pops open the smart tag task list associated with any control you add to the form, which can be distracting during your initial form design phase. Smart tags are discussed later in this chapter in the section titled "Smart Tag Tasks."

The other page of preferences that you can customize for the Windows Forms Designer is the Data UI Customization section (see Figure 17-5). This is used to automatically bind various controls to data types when connecting to a database.

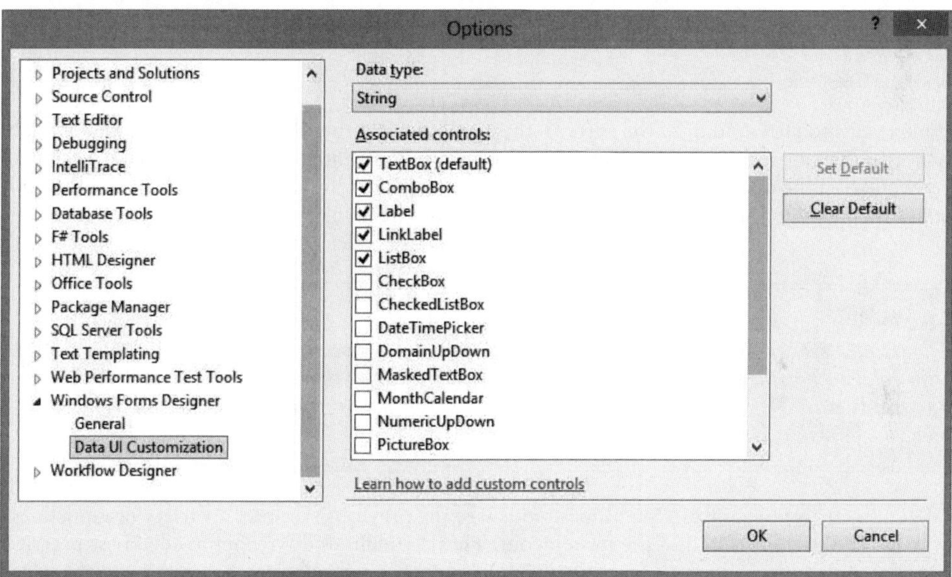

FIGURE 17-5

As you can see in the screenshot, the `String` data type is associated with five commonly used controls, with the TextBox control set as the default. Whenever a database field that is defined as a `String` data type is added to your form, Visual Studio automatically generates a TextBox control to contain the value.

The other controls marked as associated with the data type (ComboBox, Label, LinkLabel, and ListBox) can be optionally used when editing the data source and style.

> **NOTE** *It's worth reviewing the default controls associated with each data type at this time to make sure you're happy with the types chosen. For instance, all* `DateTime` *data type variables will automatically be represented with a DateTime Picker control, but you may want it to be bound to a MonthCalendar.*

Working with data-bound controls is discussed further in Chapter 28, "Datasets and Data Binding."

ADDING AND POSITIONING CONTROLS

You can add two types of controls to a Windows Form: graphical components that actually reside on the form, and components that do not have a specific visual interface displaying on the form.

You can add graphical controls to your form in one of two ways. The first method is to locate the control you want to add in the Toolbox and double-click its entry. Visual Studio 2012 places it in a default location on the form — the first control will be placed adjacent to the top and left borders of the form, with subsequent controls placed down and to the right.

> **NOTE** *If the Toolbox is closed, it won't be automatically displayed next time the Windows Forms designer is opened. You can display it again by selecting View ⇨ Toolbox from the menu.*

The second method is to click and drag the entry in the Toolbox onto the form. As you drag over available space on the form, the mouse cursor changes to show you where the control will be positioned. This enables you to directly position the control where you want it, rather than first adding it to the form and then moving it to the desired location. Either way, when the control is on the form, you can move it as many times as you like, so it doesn't matter how you get the control onto the form's design surface.

> **NOTE** *There is actually a third method to add controls to a form: Copy and paste a control or set of controls from another form. If you paste multiple controls at once, the relative positioning and layout of the controls to each other will be preserved. Any property settings will also be preserved; although the control names may be changed because they must be unique.*

When you design your form layouts in SnapLines mode (see the previous section), a variety of guidelines display as you move controls around in the form layout. These guidelines are recommended best practice for positioning and sizing markers, so you can easily position controls in context to each other and the edge of the form.

Figure 17-6 shows a Button control being moved toward the top-left corner of the form. As it gets near the recommended position, the control snaps to the exact recommended distance from the top and left borders, and small blue guidelines display.

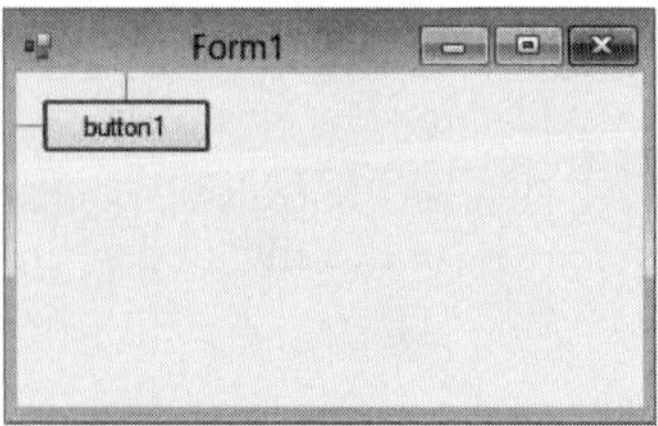

FIGURE 17-6

These guidelines work for both positioning and sizing a control, enabling you to snap to any of the four borders of the form — but they're just the tip of the SnapLines iceberg. When additional components are present on the form, many more guidelines begin to appear as you move a control around.

In Figure 17-7, you can see a second Button control being moved. The guideline on the left is the same as previously discussed, indicating the ideal distance from the left border of the form. However, now three additional guidelines display. Two blue vertical lines appear on either side of the control, confirming that the control is aligned with both the left and right sides of the other Button control already on the form. (This is expected because the buttons are the same width.) The other vertical line indicates the ideal gap between two buttons.

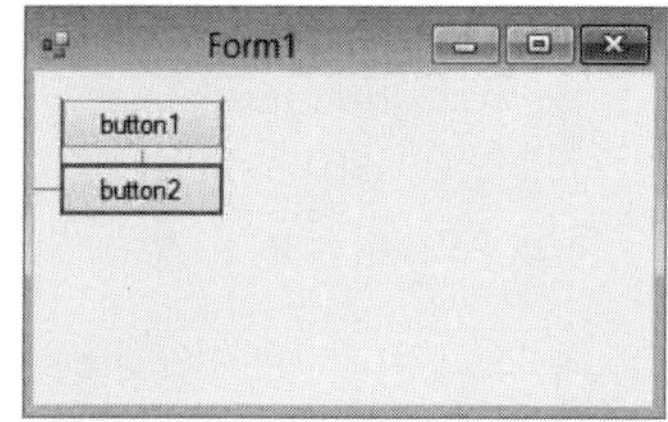

FIGURE 17-7

Vertically Aligning Text Controls

One problem with alignment of controls is that the vertical alignment of the text displayed within a TextBox is different compared to a Label. The problem is that the text within each control is at a different vertical distance from the top border of the control. If you simply align these different controls according to their borders, the text contained within these controls would not be aligned.

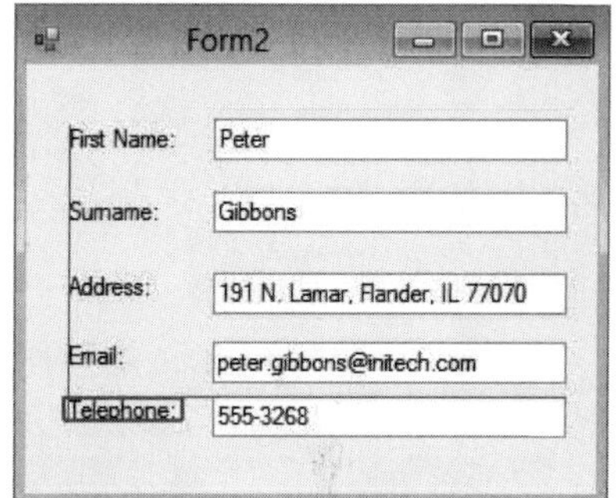

FIGURE 17-8

As shown in Figure 17-8, an additional guideline is available when lining up controls that have text aspects to them. In this example, the Telephone label is lined up with the TextBox containing the actual Telephone value. A line, colored magenta by default, appears and snaps the control in place. You can still align the label to the top or bottom borders of the TextBox by shifting it slightly and snapping it to their guidelines, but this guideline takes the often painful guesswork out of lining up text.

The other guidelines show how the label is horizontally aligned with the Label controls above it, and it is positioned the recommended distance from the TextBox.

Automatic Positioning of Multiple Controls

Visual Studio 2012 gives you additional tools to automatically format the appearance of your controls after they are positioned approximately where you want them. The Format menu, as shown in Figure 17-9, is normally only accessible when you're in the Design view of a form. From here you can have the IDE automatically align, resize, and position groups of controls, as well as set the order of the controls in the event that they overlap each other. These commands are also available via the design toolbar and keyboard shortcuts.

The form displayed in Figure 17-9 contains several TextBox controls that originally had differing widths. This looks messy and should be cleaned up by setting them all to the same width as the widest control. The Format menu provides you with the capability to automatically resize the controls to the same width, using the Make Same Size ➪ Width command.

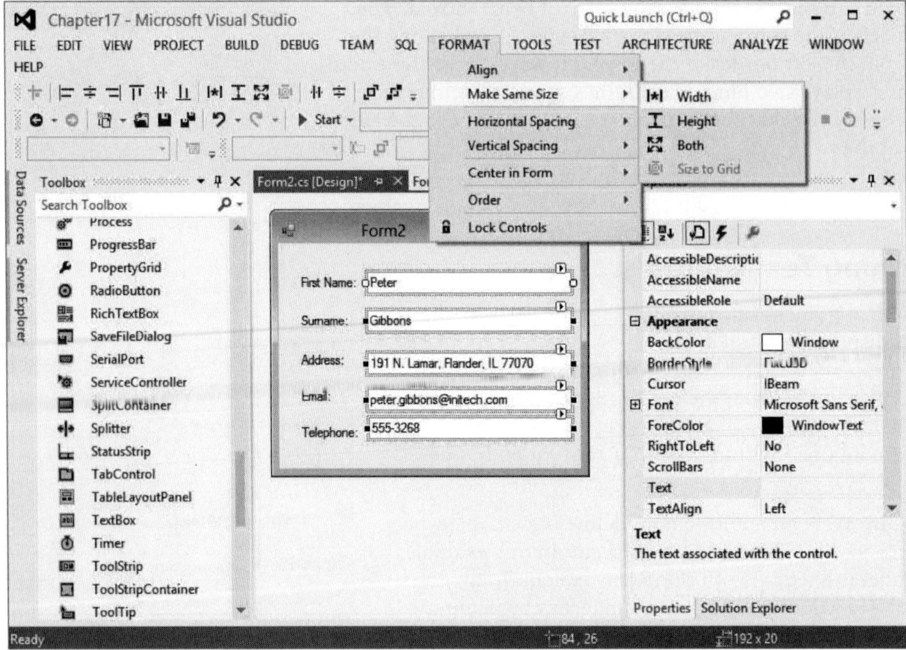

FIGURE 17-9

> **NOTE** *The commands in the Make Same Size menu use the first control selected as the template for the dimensions. You can first select the control to use as the template and then add other controls to the selection by holding down the Ctrl key and clicking them. Alternatively, when all controls are the same size, you can simply ensure they are still selected and resize the group at the same time with the mouse.*

You can perform automatic alignment of multiple controls in the same way. First, select the item whose border should be used as a base, and then select all the other elements that should be aligned with it. Next, select Format ➪ Align, and choose which alignment should be performed. In this example, the Label controls have all been positioned with their right edges aligned. This could have been done using the guidelines, but often it's easier to use this mass alignment option.

Two other handy functions are the horizontal and vertical spacing commands. These automatically adjust the spacing between a set of controls according to the particular option you have selected.

Tab Order and Layering Controls

Many users find it faster to use the keyboard rather than the mouse when working with an application, particularly those that require a large amount of data entry. Therefore it is essential that the cursor moves from one field to the next in the expected manner when the user presses the Tab key.

By default, the tab order is the same as the order in which controls were added to the form. Beginning at zero, each control is given a value in the `TabIndex` property. The lower the `TabIndex`, the earlier the control is in the tab order.

> **NOTE** *If you set the* `TabStop` *property to False, the control will be skipped over when the Tab key is pressed, and there will be no way for a user to set its focus without using the mouse. Some controls can never be given the focus, such as a Label. These controls still have a* `TabIndex` *property; however, they are skipped when the Tab key is pressed.*

Visual Studio provides a handy feature to view and adjust the tab order of every control on a form. If you select View ➪ Tab Order from the menu, the `TabIndex` values display in the designer for each control, as shown in Figure 17-10. In this example the `TabIndex` values assigned to the controls are not in order, which would cause the focus to jump all over the form as the Tab key is pressed.

You can click each control to establish a new tab order. When you finish, press the Esc key to hide the tab order from the designer.

If more than one control on a form has the same `TabIndex`, the *z-order* is used to determine which control is next in the tab order. The z-order is the layering of controls on a form along the form's z-axis (depth) and is generally only relevant if controls must be layered on top of each other. The z-order of a control can be modified using the Bring to Front and Send to Back commands under the Format ➪ Order menu.

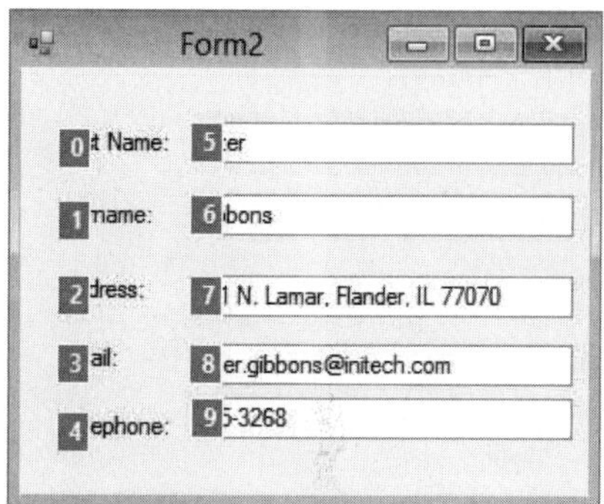

FIGURE 17-10

Locking Control Design

When you're happy with your form design, you will want to start applying changes to the various controls and their properties. However, in the process of selecting controls on the form, you may inadvertently move a control from its desired position, particularly if you're not using either of the snap layout methods or if you have many controls that are being aligned with each other.

Fortunately, Visual Studio 2012 provides a solution in the form of the Lock Controls command, available in the Format menu. When controls are locked, you can select them to change their properties, but you cannot use the mouse to move or resize them, or the form itself. The location of the controls can still be changed via the Properties grid.

Figure 17-11 shows how small padlock icons display on controls that are selected while the Lock Controls feature is active.

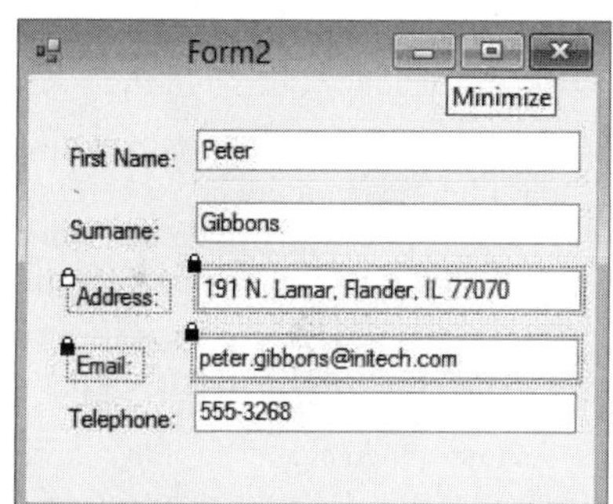

FIGURE 17-11

> **NOTE** *You can also lock controls on an individual basis by setting the* `Locked` *property of the control to True in the Properties window.*

Setting Control Properties

You set the properties on controls using the Properties window, just as you would for a form's settings. In addition to simple text value properties, Visual Studio 2012 has a number of property editor types, which aid you in setting the values efficiently by restricting them to a particular subset appropriate to the type of property.

Many advanced properties have a set of subordinate properties that can be individually accessed by expanding the entry in the Properties window. Figure 17-12 (left) displays the Properties window for a Label, with the `Font` property expanded to show the individual properties available.

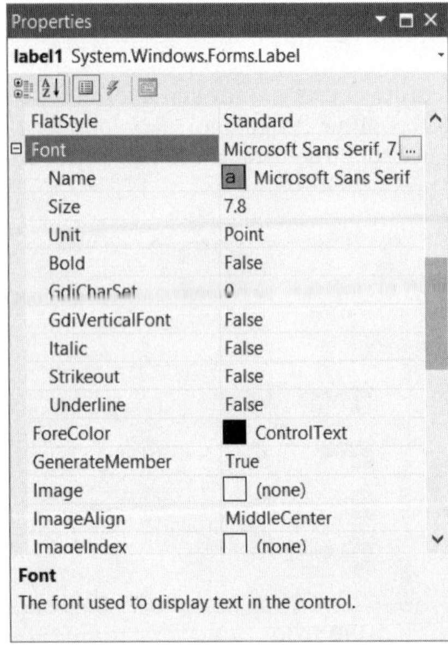

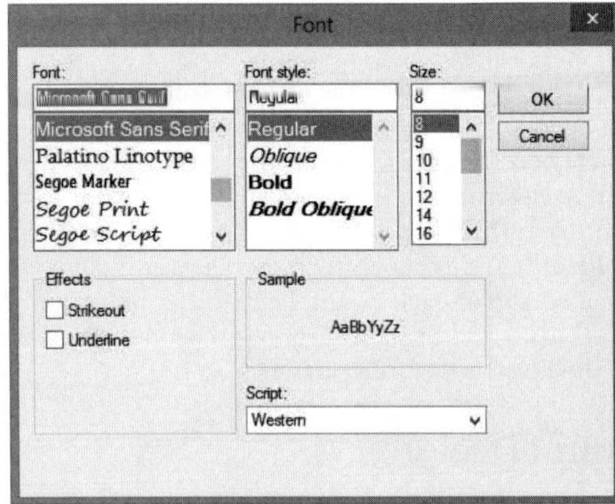

FIGURE 17-12

Many properties also provide extended editors, as is the case for Font properties. In Figure 17-12 (right), the extended editor button in the `Font` property has been selected, causing the Font dialog to appear.

Some of these extended editors invoke full-blown wizards, such as the Data Connection property on some data-bound components, whereas others have custom-built inline property editors. An example of this is the `Dock` property, for which you can choose a visual representation of how you want the property docked to the containing component or form.

Service-Based Components

As mentioned earlier in this chapter, two kinds of components can be added to a Windows Form — those with visual aspects to them and those without. Service-based components such as timers and dialogs, or extender controls such as tooltip and error provider components, can all be used to enhance your application.

Rather than place these components on the form, when you double-click one in the Toolbox, or drag and drop it onto the design surface, Visual Studio 2012 creates a tray area below the Design view of the form and puts the new instance of the component type there, as shown in Figure 17-13.

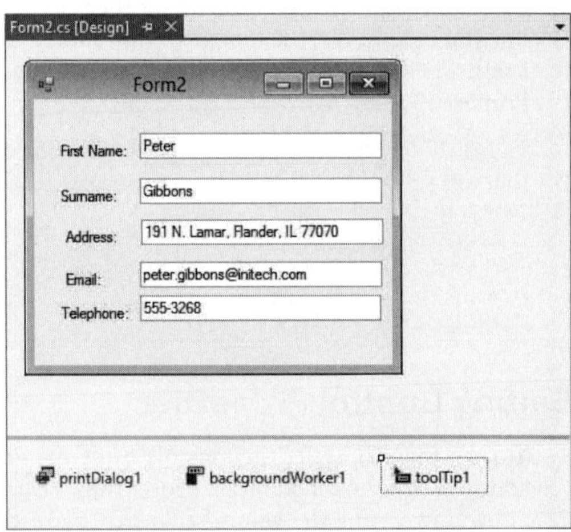

FIGURE 17-13

To edit the properties of one of these controls, locate its entry in the tray area and open the Properties window.

> **NOTE** *In the same way that you can create your own custom visual controls by inheriting from* `System.Windows.Forms.Control`*, you can create nonvisual service components by inheriting from* `System.ComponentModel.Component`*. In fact,* `System.ComponentModel.Component` *is the base class for* `System.Windows.Forms.Control`*.*

Smart Tag Tasks

Smart tag technology was introduced in Microsoft Office. It provides inline shortcuts to a small selection of actions you can perform on a particular element. In Microsoft Word, this might be a word or phrase, and in Microsoft Excel it could be a spreadsheet cell. Visual Studio 2012 supports the concept of design-time smart tags for a number of the controls available to you as a developer.

Whenever a selected control has a smart tag available, a small right-pointing arrow displays on the top-right corner of the control. Clicking this smart tag indicator opens up a Tasks menu associated with that particular control.

Figure 17-14 shows the tasks for a newly added DataGridView control. The various actions that can be taken usually mirror properties available to you in the Properties window (such as the `Multiline` option for a TextBox control), but sometimes they provide quick access to more advanced settings for the component.

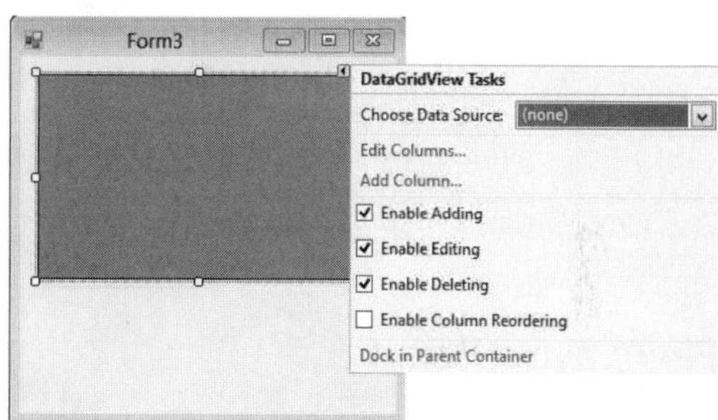

FIGURE 17-14

The Edit Columns and Add Column commands shown in Figure 17-14 are not listed in the DataGridView's Properties list, and the Data Source and Enable settings directly correlate to individual properties. (For example, Enable Adding is equivalent to the `AllowUserToAddRows` property.)

CONTAINER CONTROLS

Several controls, known as *container controls*, are designed specifically to help you with your form's layout and appearance. Rather than have their own appearance, they hold other controls within their bounds. When a container houses a set of controls, you no longer need to move the child controls individually, but instead just move the container. Using a combination of `Dock` and `Anchor` values, you can have whole sections of your form's layout automatically redesign themselves at run time in response to the resizing of the form and the container controls that hold them.

Panel and SplitContainer

The Panel control is used to group components that are associated with each other. When placed on a form, it can be sized and positioned anywhere within the form's design surface. Because it's a container control, clicking within its boundaries selects anything inside it. To move it, Visual Studio 2012 places a move icon at the top-left corner of the control. Clicking and dragging this icon enables you to reposition the Panel.

The SplitContainer control (as shown in Figure 17-15) automatically creates two Panel controls when added to a form (or another container control). It divides the space into two sections, each of which you can control individually. At run time, users can resize the two spaces by dragging the splitter bar that divides them. SplitContainers can be either vertical (refer to Figure 17-15) or horizontal, and they can be contained with other SplitContainer controls to form a complex layout that can then be easily customized by the end user without you needing to write any code.

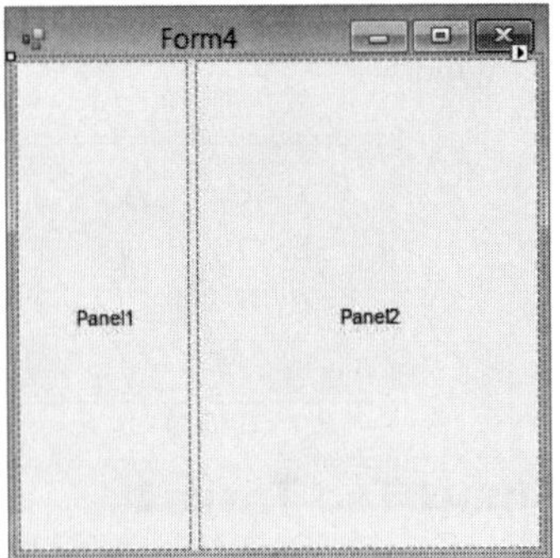

FIGURE 17-15

> **NOTE** *Sometimes it's hard to select the actual container control when it contains other components, such as in the case of the SplitContainer housing the two Panel controls. To gain direct access to the SplitContainer control, you can either locate it in the drop-down list in the Properties window, or right-click one of the Panel controls and choose the Select command that corresponds to the SplitContainer. This context menu contains a Select command for every container control in the hierarchy of containers, right up to the form.*

FlowLayoutPanel

The FlowLayoutPanel control enables you to create form designs with a behavior similar to web browsers. Rather than explicitly position each control within this particular container control, Visual Studio simply sets each component you add to the next available space. By default, the controls flow left to right, and then top to bottom, but you can use the `FlowDirection` property to reverse this order in any configuration depending on the requirements of your application.

Figure 17-16 displays the same form with six button controls housed within a FlowLayoutPanel container. The FlowLayoutPanel's `Dock` property was set to fill the entire form's design surface, so as the form is resized, the container is also automatically sized. As the form gets wider and there is available space, the controls begin to realign to flow left to right before descending down the form.

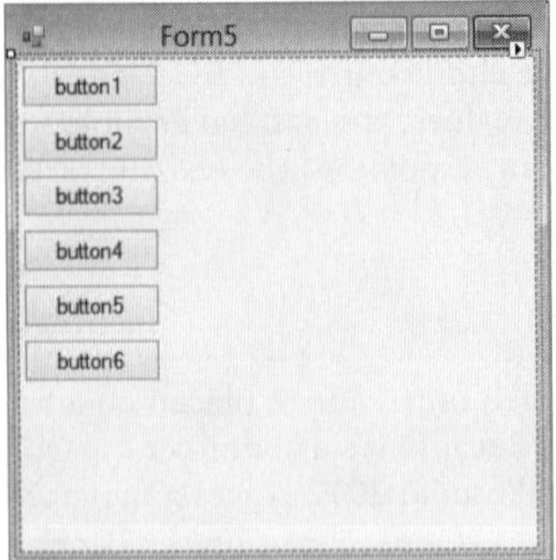

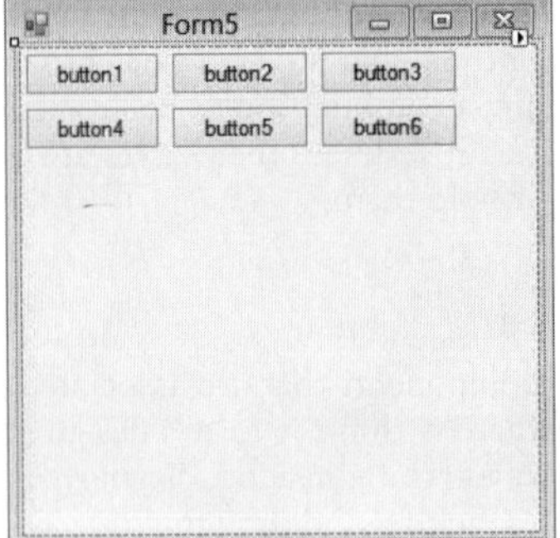

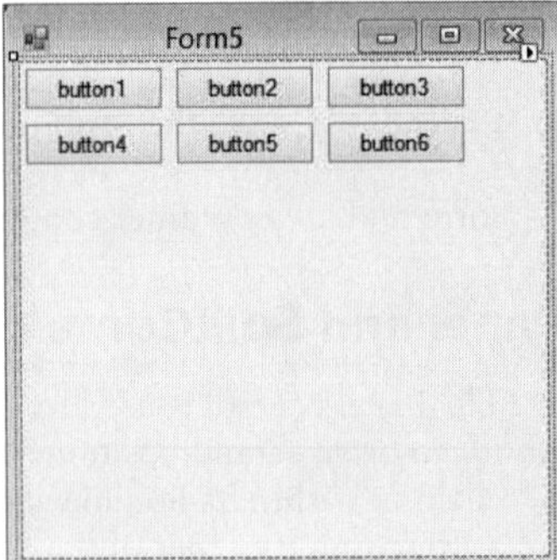

FIGURE 17-16

TableLayoutPanel

An alternative to the previously discussed container controls is the TableLayoutPanel container. This control works much like a table in Microsoft Word or in a typical web browser, with each cell acting as an individual container for a single control.

> **NOTE** *You cannot add multiple controls within a single cell directly. You can, however, place another container control, such as a Panel, within the cell, and then place the required components within that child container.*

Placing a control directly into a cell automatically positions the control to the top-left corner of the table cell. You can use the `Dock` property to override this behavior and position it as required. This property is discussed further in the section "Docking and Anchoring Controls."

The TableLayoutPanel container enables you to easily create a structured, formal layout in your form with advanced features, such as the capability to automatically grow by adding more rows as additional child controls are added.

Figure 17-17 shows a form with a TableLayoutPanel added to the design surface. The smart tag tasks were then opened and the Edit Rows and Columns command executed. As a result, the Column and Row Styles dialog displays, so you can adjust the individual formatting options for each column and row. The dialog displays several tips for designing table layouts in your forms, including spanning multiple rows and columns and how to align controls within a cell. You can change the way the cells are sized here as well as add or remove additional columns and rows.

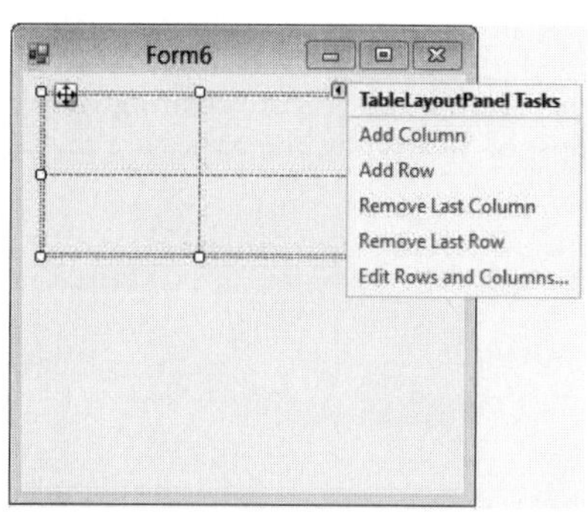

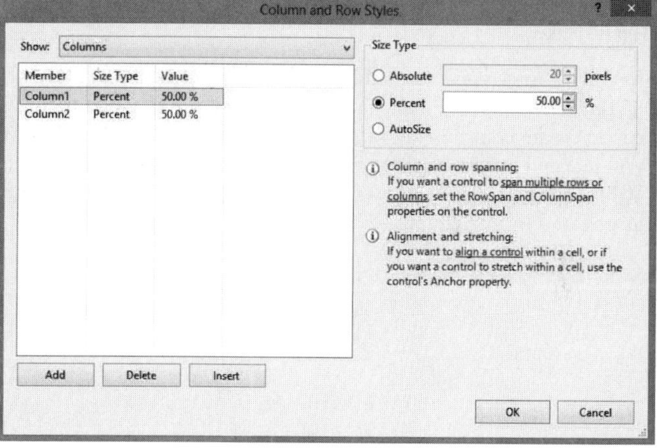

FIGURE 17-17

DOCKING AND ANCHORING CONTROLS

It's not enough to design layouts that are nicely aligned according to the design-time dimensions. At run time, a user will likely resize the form, and ideally the controls on your form will resize automatically to fill the modified space. The control properties that have the most impact on this are `Dock` and `Anchor`. Figure 17-18 shows how the controls on a Windows Form properly resize after you set the correct `Dock` and `Anchor` property values.

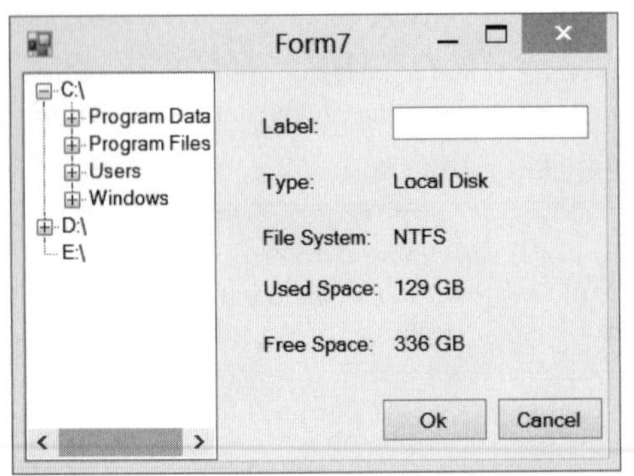

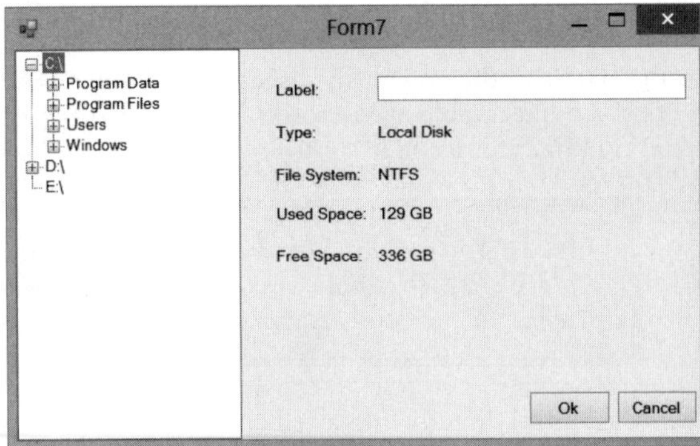

FIGURE 17-18

The `Dock` property controls which borders of the control are bound to the container. For example, in Figure 17-18 (left), the TreeView control `Dock` property has been set to `Fill` to fill the left panel of a SplitContainer, effectively docking it to all four borders. Therefore, no matter how large or small the left side of the SplitContainer is made, the TreeView control always resizes itself to fill the available space.

The `Anchor` property defines the edges of the container to which the control is bound. In Figure 17-18 (left), the two button controls have been anchored to the bottom-right of the form. When the form is resized, as shown in 17-18 (right), the button controls maintain the same distance between to the bottom-right of the form. Similarly, the TextBox control has been anchored to the left and right, which means that it can auto-grow or auto-shrink as the form is resized.

SUMMARY

In this chapter you received a good understanding of how Visual Studio can help you to quickly design the layout of Windows Forms applications. The various controls and their properties enable you to quickly and easily create complex layouts that can respond to user interaction in a large variety of ways. The techniques you learned in this chapter are user interface technology independent. So whether you are creating websites, WPF applications, Windows Store applications, Windows Phone apps, or Silverlight, the basics are the same as covered in this chapter.

18

Windows Presentation Foundation (WPF)

WHAT'S IN THIS CHAPTER?

- Learning the basics of XAML
- Creating a WPF application
- Styling your WPF application
- Hosting WPF content in a Windows Forms project
- Hosting Windows Forms content in a WPF project
- Using the WPF Visualizer

When starting a new Windows client application in Visual Studio, you have two major technologies to choose from — a standard Windows Forms–based application, or a Windows Presentation Foundation (WPF)–based application. Both are essentially a different API for managing the presentation layer for your application. WPF is extremely powerful and flexible, and was designed to overcome many of the shortcomings and limitations of Windows Forms. In many ways you could consider WPF a successor to Windows Forms. However, WPF's power and flexibility comes with a price in the form of a rather steep learning curve because it does things quite differently than Windows Forms.

This chapter guides you through the process to create a basic WPF application in Visual Studio 2012. It's beyond the scope of this book to cover the WPF framework in any great detail — it would take an entire book to do so. Instead, what you see is an overview of Visual Studio 2012's capabilities to help you rapidly build user interfaces using XAML.

WHAT IS WPF?

Windows Presentation Foundation is a presentation framework for Windows. But what makes WPF unique, and why should you consider using it over Windows Forms? Whereas Windows Forms uses the raster-based GDI/GDI+ as its rendering engine, WPF instead contains its own vector-based rendering engine, so it essentially isn't creating windows and controls in the standard Windows manner and look. WPF takes a radical departure from the way things are done in Windows Forms. In Windows Forms you generally define the user interface using the visual designer, and in doing so it automatically creates the code (in the language your project targets) in a `.designer` file to define that user interface — so essentially your user interface is defined and driven in C# or VB code. However, user interfaces in WPF are actually defined in an XML-based markup language called Extensible Application Markup Language (generally referred to as XAML, pronounced "zammel") specifically designed for this purpose by Microsoft. XAML is the underlying technology to WPF that gives it its power and flexibility, enabling the design of much richer user experiences and more unique user interfaces than was possible in Windows Forms. Regardless of which language your project targets, the XAML defining the user interface will be the same. Consequently, along with the capabilities of the user interface controls there are a number of supporting concepts on the code side of things, such as the introduction of dependency properties (properties that can accept an expression that must be resolved as their value — which is required in many binding scenarios to support XAML's advanced binding capabilities). However, you can find that the code-behind in a WPF application is much the same as a standard Windows Forms application — the XAML side of things is where you need to do most of your learning.

When developing WPF applications, you need to think differently than the way you think when developing Windows Forms applications. A core part of your thought processes should be to take full advantage of XAML's advanced binding capabilities, with the code-behind no longer acting as the controller for the user interface but serving it instead. Instead of the code "pushing" data into the user interface and telling it what to do, the user interface should ask the code what it should do, and request (that is, "pull") data from it. It's a subtle difference, but it greatly changes the way in which the presentation layer of your application will be defined. Think of it as having a user interface that is in charge. The code can (and should) act as a decision manager, but no longer provides the muscle.

There are also specific design patterns for how the code and the user interface elements interact, such as the popular Model-View-ViewModel (MVVM) pattern, which enables much better unit testing of the code serving the user interface and maintains a clean separation between the designer and developer elements of the project. This results in changing the way you write the code-behind, and ultimately changes the way you design your application. This clear separation supports the designer/developer workflow, enabling a designer to work in Expression Blend on the same part of the project as the developer (working in Visual Studio) without clashing.

By taking advantage of the flexibility of XAML, WPF enables you to design unique user interfaces and user experiences. At the heart of this is WPF's styling and templating functionality that separates the look of controls from their behavior. This enables you to alter the appearance of controls easily by simply defining an alternative "style" on that particular use without having to modify the control.

Ultimately, you could say that WPF uses a much better way of defining user interfaces than Windows Forms does, through its use of XAML to define user interfaces, along with a number of additional supporting concepts thrown in. The bad news is that the flexibility and power of XAML comes with a corresponding steep learning curve that takes some time to climb, even for the experienced developer. If you are a productive developer in Windows Forms, WPF will no doubt create considerable frustration for you while you get your head around its concepts, and it actually requires a change in your developer mindset to truly get a grasp on it and how things hold together. Many simple tasks will initially seem a whole lot harder than they should be, and would have been were you to implement the same functionality or feature in Windows Forms. However, if you can make it through this period, you will start to see the benefits and appreciate the possibilities that WPF and XAML provide. Because Silverlight shares a lot conceptually with WPF (both being XAML-based, with Silverlight not quite a subset of WPF, but close), by learning and understanding WPF you are also learning and understanding how to develop Silverlight applications.

> **NOTE** *If you've looked at earlier versions of WPF (those that shipped in the .NET Framework 3.0 and 3.5 versions) you may have noticed that text rendered in WPF often took on a rather blurry appearance instead of being crisp and sharp, generating numerous complaints from the developer community. Fortunately in the .NET Framework 4.0, the text rendering was vastly improved, and if this has held you back from developing WPF applications previously, it is probably time to take another look. Microsoft demonstrated its faith in WPF by rewriting Visual Studio's code editor in WPF for the 2010 version in order to take advantage of its power and flexibility. And although the initial results were a little under-performing, improvements in both Visual Studio and the XAML rendering engine have come a long way toward eliminating that particular issue.*

GETTING STARTED WITH WPF

When you open the New Project dialog you see WPF Application, WPF Browser Application, WPF Custom Control Library, and WPF User Control Library and a number of other built-in project templates that ship with Visual Studio 2012, as shown in Figure 18-1.

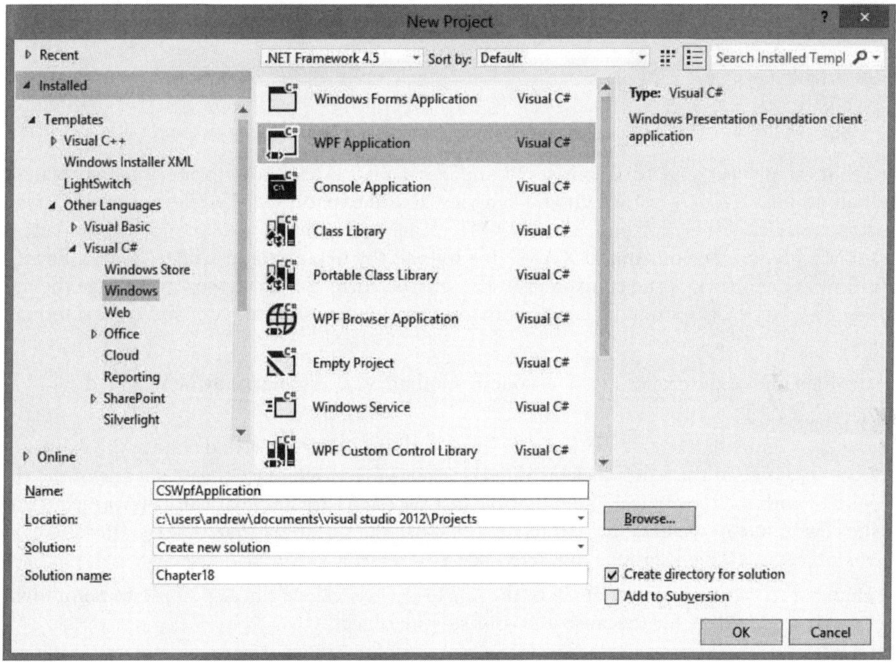

FIGURE 18-1

You can notice that these projects are for the most part a direct parallel to the Windows Forms equivalent. The exception is the WPF Browser Application, which generates an XBAP file that uses the browser as the container for your rich client application (in much the same way as Silverlight does, except an XBAP application targets the full .NET Framework, which must be installed on the client machine).

For this example you create a project using the WPF Application template, but most of the features of Visual Studio 2012 discussed herein apply equally to the other project types. The project structure generated should look similar to Figure 18-2.

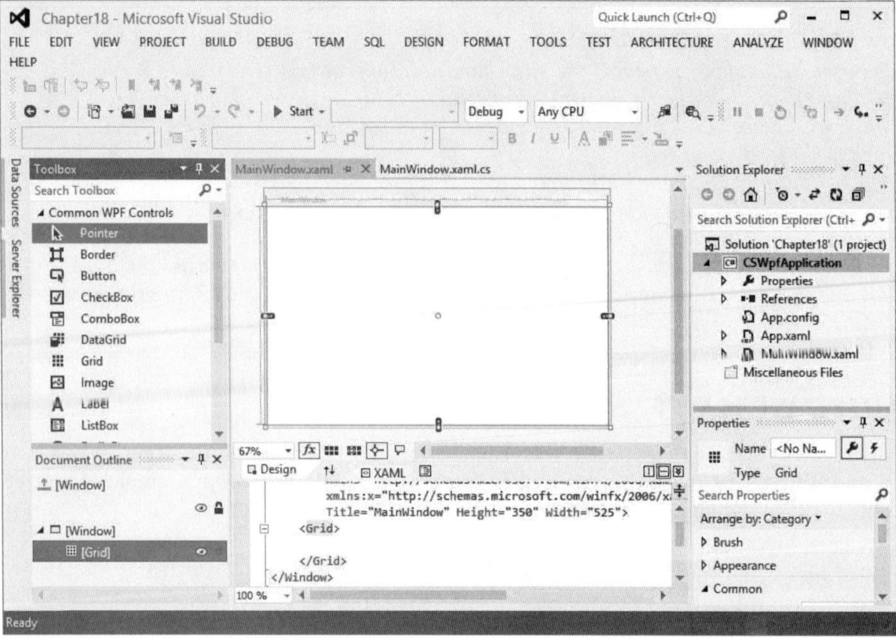

FIGURE 18-2

Here, you can see that the project structure consists of `App.xaml` and `MainWindow.xaml`, each with a corresponding code-behind file (`.cs` or `.vb`), which you can view if you expand out the relevant project items. At this stage the `App.xaml` contains an Application XAML element, which has a `StartupUri` attribute used to define which XAML file will be your initial XAML file to load (by default `MainWindow.xaml`). For those familiar with Windows Forms, this is the equivalent of the startup form. So if you were to change the name of `MainWindow.xaml` and its corresponding class to something more meaningful, you would need to make the following changes:

- Change the filename of the `.xaml` file. The code-behind file will automatically be renamed accordingly.
- Change the class name in the code-behind file, along with its constructor, and change the value of the `x:Class` attribute of the `Window` element in the `.xaml` file to reference the new name of the class (fully qualified with its namespace). Note that the last two steps are automatically performed if you change the class name in the code-behind file first and use the smart tag that appears after doing so to rename the object in all the locations that reference it.
- Finally, change the `StartupUri` attribute of the `Application` element in `App.xaml` to point toward the new name of the `.xaml` file (because it is your startup object).

As you can see, a few more changes need to be made when renaming a file in a WPF project than you would have to do in a standard Windows Forms project; however, it's reasonably straightforward when you know what you are doing. (And using the smart tag reduces the number of steps required.)

Working around the Visual Studio layout of Figure 18-2, you can see that the familiar Toolbox tool window attached to the left side of the screen has been populated with WPF controls that are similar to what you would be used to when building a Windows Forms application. Below this window, still on the left side, is the Document Outline tool window. As with both Windows Forms and Web Applications, this gives you a hierarchical view of the elements on the current window. Selecting any of these nodes in this window highlights the appropriate control in the main editor window, making it easier to navigate more complex documents. An interesting feature of the Document Outline when working with WPF is that as you hover over an item you get a mini-preview of the control. This helps you identify that you are selecting the correct control.

> **NOTE** *If the Document Outline tool window is not visible, it may be collapsed against one of the edges of Visual Studio. Alternatively, you may need to force it to display by selecting it from the View ➪ Other Windows menu.*

On the right side of Figure 18-2 is the Properties tool window. You may note that it has a similar layout and behavior to the Windows Forms designer Properties tool window. However, this window in the WPF designer has additional features for editing WPF windows and controls. Finally, in the middle of the screen is the main editor/preview space, which is currently split to show both the visual layout of the window (above) and the XAML code that defines it (below).

XAML Fundamentals

If you have some familiarity working with XML (or to some extent HTML), you should find the syntax of XAML relatively straightforward because it is XML-based. XAML can have only a single root-level node, and elements are nested within each other to define the layout and content of the user interface. Every XAML element maps to a .NET class, and the attribute names map to properties/events on that class. Note that element and attribute names are case-sensitive.

Take a look at the default XAML file created for the `MainWindow` class:

```
<Window x:Class="CSWpfApplication.MainWindow"
    xmlns="http://schemas.microsoft.com/winfx/2006/xaml/presentation"
    xmlns:x="http://schemas.microsoft.com/winfx/2006/xaml"
    Title="MainWindow" Height="300" Width="300">
    <Grid>

    </Grid>
</Window>
```

Here you have `Window` as your root node and a `Grid` element within it. To make sense of it, think of it in terms of "your window contains a grid." The root node maps to its corresponding code-behind class via the `x:Class` attribute, and also contains some namespace prefix declarations (discussed shortly) and some attributes used to set the value of properties (`Title`, `Height`, and `Width`) of the `Window` class. The value of all attributes (regardless of type) should be enclosed within quotes.

Two namespace prefixes are defined on the root node, both declared using `xmlns` (the XML attribute used for declaring namespaces). You could consider XAML namespace prefix declarations to be somewhat like the `using`/`Imports` statements at the top of a class in C#/VB, but not quite. These declarations assign a unique prefix to the namespaces used within the XAML file, with the prefix used to qualify that namespace when referring to a class within it (that is, specify the location of the class). Prefixes reduce the verbosity of XAML by letting you use that prefix rather than including the whole namespace when referring to a class within it in your XAML file. The prefix is defined immediately following the colon after `xmlns`. The first definition actually doesn't specify a prefix because it defines your default namespace (the WPF namespace). However, the second namespace defines *x* as its prefix (the XAML namespace). Both definitions map to URIs rather than specific namespaces — these are consolidated namespaces (that is, they cover multiple namespaces) and hence reference the unique URI used to define that consolidation. However, you don't need to worry about this concept — leave these definitions as they are, and simply add your own definitions following them. When adding your own namespace definitions, they almost always begin with `clr-namespace` and reference a CLR namespace and the assembly that contains it, for example:

```
xmlns:wpf="clr-namespace:Microsoft.Windows.Controls;assembly=WPFToolkit"
```

Prefixes can be anything of your choosing, but it is best to make them short yet meaningful. Namespaces are generally defined on the root node in the XAML file. This is not necessary because a namespace prefix can be defined at any level in a XAML file, but it is generally a standard practice to keep them together on the root node for maintainability purposes.

If you want to refer to a control in the code-behind or by binding it to another control in the XAML file (such as `ElementName` binding) you need to give your control a name. Many controls implement the `Name` property for this purpose, but you may also find that controls are assigned a name using the `x:Name` attribute. This is defined in the XAML namespace (hence the `x:` prefix) and can be applied to any control. If the `Name` property is implemented (which it will be in most cases because it is defined on the base classes that most controls inherit from), it simply maps to this property anyway, and they serve the same purpose, for example:

```
<Button x:Name="OKButton" Content="OK" />
```

is the same as

```
<Button Name="OKButton" Content="OK" />
```

Either way is technically valid. (Although in Silverlight most controls don't support the `Name` attribute, and you must use the `x:Name` attribute instead.) After one of these properties is set, a field is generated (in the automatically generated code that you won't see) that you can use to refer to that control.

The WPF Controls

WPF contains a rich set of controls to use in your user interfaces, roughly comparable to the standard controls for Windows Forms. If you looked at previous versions of WPF, you may have noticed a number of controls (such as the `Calendar`, `DatePicker`, `DataGrid`, and so on), which are included in the standard controls for Windows Forms but were not included in the standard controls for WPF. Instead, you had to turn to the free WPF Toolkit hosted on CodePlex to obtain these controls. This toolkit was developed by Microsoft over time to help fill this hole in the original WPF release by providing some of the missing controls. As WPF has matured over a number of versions, you can find many of the controls that were previously part of the WPF Toolkit are now included within WPF's standard controls, providing a reasonably complete set of controls out-of-the-box. Of course, you can still use third-party controls where the standard set doesn't suffice, but you have a reasonable base to work from.

Although the controls set for WPF are somewhat comparable to that of Windows Forms, their properties are quite different to their counterparts. For example, there is no longer a `Text` property on many controls; although you can find a `Content` property instead. The `Content` property is used to assign content to the control (hence its name). You can for the most part treat this as you would the `Text` property for a Windows Forms control and simply assign some text to this property to be rendered. However, the `Content` property can accept any WPF element, allowing almost limitless ability to customize the layout of a control without necessarily having to create your own custom control — a powerful feature for designing complex user interfaces. You may note that many controls don't have properties to accomplish what was straightforward in Windows Forms, and you may find this somewhat confusing. For example, there is no `Image` property on the WPF Button control to assign an image to a button as there is in Windows Forms. This may initially make you think WPF is limited in its capabilities, but you would be mistaken because this is where the `Content` property comes into its own. Because the `Content` property can have any WPF control assigned to it to define the content of its control, you can assign a `StackPanel` (discussed in the next section) containing both an `Image` control and a `TextBlock` control to achieve the same effect. Though this may initially appear to be more work than it would be to achieve the same outcome in Windows Forms, it does enable you to easily lay out the content of the button in whatever form you choose (rather than how the control chooses to implement the layout), and demonstrates the incredible flexibility of WPF and XAML. The XAML for the button in Figure 18-3 is as follows:

```
<Button HorizontalAlignment="Left" VerticalAlignment="Top" Width="100" Height="30">
    <Button.Content>
        <StackPanel Orientation="Horizontal">
            <Image Source="Resources/FloppyDisk.ico" Width="16" Height="16" />
            <TextBlock Margin="5,0,0,0" Text="Save" VerticalAlignment="Center" />
        </StackPanel>
    </Button.Content>
</Button>
```

FIGURE 18-3

Other notable property name changes from Windows Forms include the `IsEnabled` property (which was simply `Enabled` in Windows Forms) and the `Visibility` property (which was `Visible` in Windows Forms). Like `IsEnabled`, you can notice that most Boolean properties are prefixed with `Is` (for example, `IsTabStop`, `IsHitTestVisible`, and so on), conforming to a standard naming scheme. The `Visibility` property, however, is no longer a boolean value — instead it is an enumeration that can have the value `Visible`, `Hidden`, or `Collapsed`.

> **NOTE** *Keep an eye on the WPF Toolkit at* `http://wpf.codeplex.com` *because new controls for WPF will continue to be developed and hosted there that you may find useful.*

The WPF Layout Controls

Windows Forms development used absolute placement for controls on its surface (that is, each control had its *x* and *y* coordinates explicitly set); although over time the `TableLayoutPanel` and `FlowLayoutPanel` controls were added, in which you could place controls to provide a more advanced means of laying out the controls on your form. However, the concepts around positioning controls in WPF are slightly different than how controls are positioned in Windows Forms. Along with controls that provide a specific function (for example, buttons, TextBoxes, and so on), WPF also has a number of controls used specifically for defining the layout of your user interface.

Layout controls are invisible controls that handle the positioning of controls upon their surface. In WPF there isn't a default surface for positioning controls as such — the surface you are work with is determined by the layout controls further up the hierarchy, with a layout control generally used as the element directly below the root node of each XAML file to define the default layout method for that XAML file. The most important layout controls in WPF are the `Grid`, the `Canvas`, and the `StackPanel`, so this section takes a look at each of those. For example, in the default XAML file created for the `MainWindow` class provided earlier, the `Grid` element was the element directly below the `Window` root node, and thus would act as the default layout surface for that window. Of course, you could change this to any layout control to suit your requirements, and use additional layout controls within it if necessary to create additional surfaces that change the way their containing controls are positioned.

The next section looks at how to layout your forms using the designer surface, but look at the XAML to use these controls first.

In WPF, if you want to place controls in your form using absolute coordinates (similar to the default in Windows Forms) you would use the `Canvas` control as a "surface" to place the controls on. Defining a `Canvas` control in XAML is straightforward:

```
<Canvas>

</Canvas>
```

To place a control (for example, a `TextBox` control) within this surface using given *x* and *y* coordinates (relative to the location of the top-left corner of the canvas) you need to introduce the concept of *attached properties* within XAML. The `TextBox` control doesn't actually have properties to define its location because its positioning within the layout control it is contained within is totally dependent on the type of control. So correspondingly, the properties that the `TextBox` control requires to specify its position within the layout control must come from the layout control itself. (Because it will be handling the positioning of the controls within it.) This is where attached properties come in. In a nutshell, attached properties are properties assigned a value on a control, but the property is actually defined on and belongs to another control higher up in the hierarchy. When using the property, the name of the property is qualified by the name of the control that the property is actually defined on, followed by a period, and then the name of the property on that control you are using (for example, `Canvas.Left`). By setting that value on another control that is hosted within it (such as your TextBox), the `Canvas` control is actually storing that value and will manage that TextBox's position using that value. For example, this is the XAML required to place the TextBox at coordinates 15, 10 using the `Left` and `Top` properties defined on the `Canvas` control.

```
<Canvas>
    <TextBox Text="Hello" Canvas.Left="15" Canvas.Top="10" />
</Canvas>
```

Although absolute placement is the default for controls in Windows Forms, best practice in WPF is to actually use the `Grid` control for laying out controls. The `Canvas` control should be used only sparsely and where necessary, because the `Grid` control is actually far more powerful for defining form layouts and is a better choice in most scenarios. One of the big benefits of the `Grid` control is that its contents can automatically resize when its own size is changed. So you can easily design a form that automatically sizes to fill all the area available to it — that is, the size and location of the controls within it are determined dynamically.

> **NOTE** *One of the controls available in the WPF Toolkit is a layout control called a* `ViewBox`*. When a* `Canvas` *element is placed inside a* `ViewBox`*, the positioning of the elements on the* `Canvas` *will be dynamically changed based on the size of the* `ViewBox` *container. This is a big deal for people who want absolute positioning but still want the benefit of dynamic positioning.*

The `Grid` control allows you to divide its area into regions (cells) into which you can place controls. These cells are created by defining a set of rows and columns on the grid, and are defined as values on the `RowDefinitions` and `ColumnDefinitions` properties on the grid. The intersections between rows and columns become the cells that you can place controls within.

To support defining rows and columns, you need to know how to define complex values in XAML. Up until now you have been assigning simple values to controls, which map to either .NET primitive data types, the name of an enumeration value, or have a type converter to convert the string value to its corresponding object. These simple properties had their values applied as attributes within the control definition element. However, complex values cannot be assigned this way because they map to objects (which require the value of multiple properties on the object to be assigned), and must be defined using *property element syntax* instead. Because the `RowDefinitions` and `ColumnDefinitions` properties of the `Grid` control are collections, they take complex values that need to be defined with property element syntax. For example, here is a grid that has two rows and three columns defined using property element syntax:

```
<Grid>
    <Grid.RowDefinitions>
        <RowDefinition />
        <RowDefinition />
```

```
    </Grid.RowDefinitions>
    <Grid.ColumnDefinitions>
        <ColumnDefinition Width="100" />
        <ColumnDefinition Width="150" />
        <ColumnDefinition />
    </Grid.ColumnDefinitions>
</Grid>
```

To set the RowDefinitions property using property element syntax, you need to create a child element of the Grid to define it. Qualifying it by adding Grid before the property name indicates that the property belongs to a control higher in the hierarchy (as with attached properties), and making the property an element in XAML indicates you are assigning a complex value to the specified property on the Grid control.

The RowDefinitions property accepts a collection of RowDefinitions, so you are instantiating a number of RowDefinition objects that are then populating that collection. Correspondingly, the ColumnDefinitions property is assigned a collection of ColumnDefinition objects. To demonstrate that ColumnDefinition (like RowDefinition) is actually an object, the Width property of the ColumnDefinition object has been set on the first two column definitions.

To place a control within a given cell, you again make use of attached properties, this time telling the container grid which column and row it should be placed in:

```
<CheckBox Grid.Column="0" Grid.Row="1" Content="A check box" IsChecked="True" />
```

The StackPanel is another important container control for laying out controls. It stacks the controls contained within it either horizontally or vertically (depending on the value of its Orientation property). For example, if you had two buttons defined within the same grid cell (without a StackPanel) the grid would position the second button directly over the first. However, if you put the buttons within a StackPanel control, it would control the position of the two buttons within the cell and lay them out next to one another.

```
<StackPanel Orientation="Horizontal">
    <Button Content="OK" Height="23" Width="75" />
    <Button Content="Cancel" Height="23" Width="75" Margin="10,0,0,0" />
</StackPanel>
```

THE WPF DESIGNER AND XAML EDITOR

With each new version of Visual Studio, the WPF designer and XAML editor have had a number of improvements. These include stability improvements (the Visual Studio 2008 WPF designer was notoriously unstable) and performance upgrades. And, most notably, the designer now supports drag-and-drop binding.

The WPF designer is similar in layout to Windows Form's designer, but supports a number of unique features. To take a closer look at some of these, Figure 18-4 isolates this window, so you can see in more detail the various components.

First, you can notice that the window is split into a visual designer at the top and a code window at the bottom. If you prefer the other way around, you can simply click the up/down arrows between the Design and XAML tabs. In Figure 18-4 the second icon on the right side is highlighted to indicate that the screen is split horizontally. Selecting the icon to its left instead splits the screen vertically.

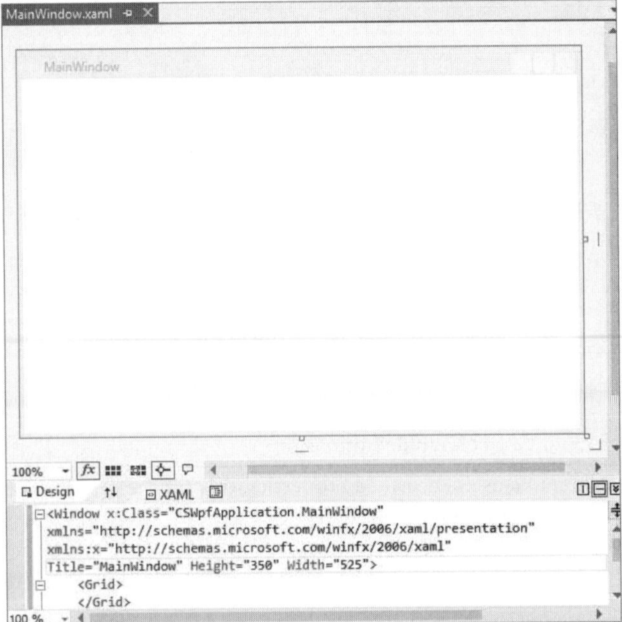

FIGURE 18-4

> **NOTE** *You will probably find that working in split mode is the best option when working with the WPF designer because you are likely to find yourself directly modifying the XAML regularly but want the ease of use of the designer for general tasks.*

If you prefer not to work in split-screen mode, you can double-click either the Design or XAML tab. This makes the relevant tab fill the entire editor window, as shown in Figure 18-5, and you can click the tabs to switch between each view. To return to split-screen mode, you just need to click the Expand Pane icon, which is the rightmost icon on the splitter bar.

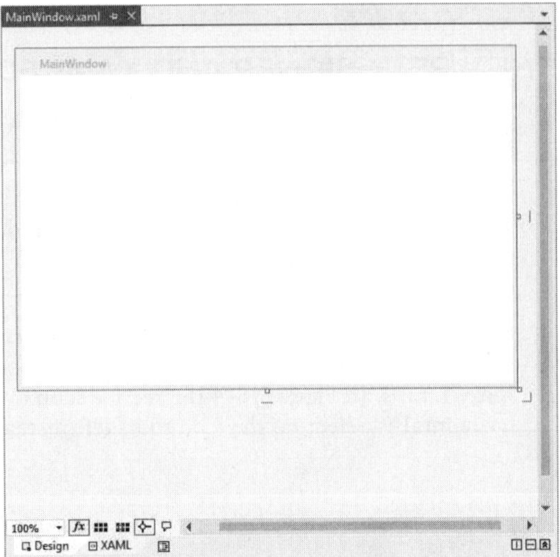

FIGURE 18-5

Unlike Visual Studio 2010, the only way to zoom in or out of the design surface is through a combo box at the bottom left of the designer. Along with having a number of fixed percentages, there is also the ability to fill all and fit the selection. The first zooms the designer out far enough so that all the controls are visible. The second zooms the designer in so that all the selected item is visible. This can be extremely handy when making small fiddly adjustments to the layout.

Working with the XAML Editor

Working with the XAML editor is somewhat similar to working with the HTML editor in Visual Studio. Numerous IntelliSense improvements have been made in this editor since Visual Studio 2008, making writing XAML directly quick and easy.

One neat feature with the XAML editor is the ability to easily navigate to an event handler after it has been assigned to a control. Simply right-click the event handler assignment in XAML, and select the Navigate To Event Handler item from the pop-up menu, as shown in Figure 18-6.

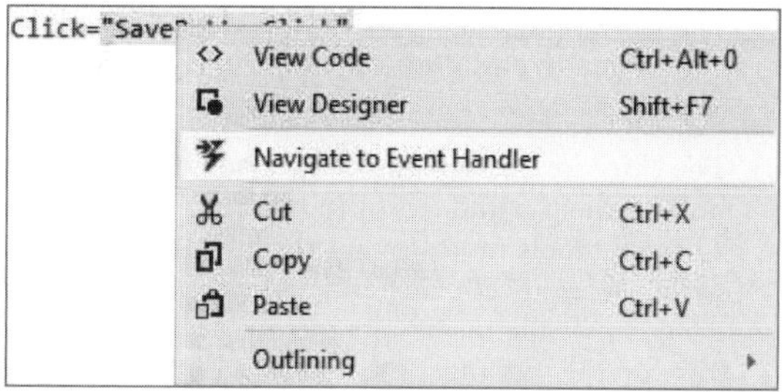

FIGURE 18-6

Working with the WPF Designer

Although it is important to familiarize yourself with writing XAML in the XAML editor, Visual Studio 2012 also has a good designer for WPF, comparable to the Windows Forms designer, and in some respects even better. This section takes a look at some of the features of the WPF designer.

Figure 18-7 shows some of the snap regions, guides, and glyphs added when you select, move, and resize a control.

Note the glyph that appears on the right of the window toward its bottom-right corner in the first image in Figure 18-7. Clicking it allows you to easily switch between the window having a fixed width/height and having it automatically size to fit its contents. When you click the glyph, the glyph changes (indicating what sizing mode it is in), and the `SizeToContent` property on the window sets accordingly. Clicking the glyph again changes the window back to having a fixed width/height. This option appears only on the root node.

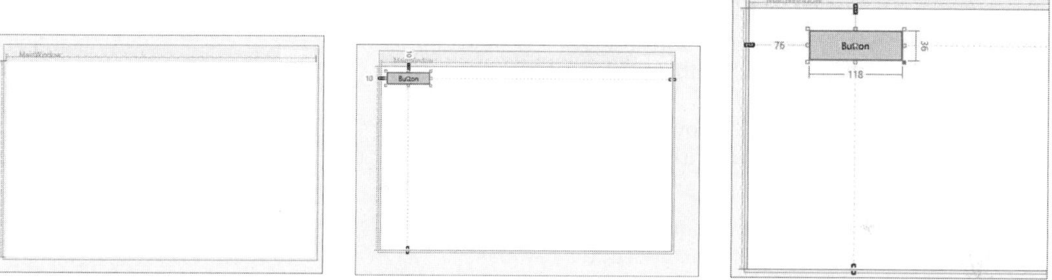

FIGURE 18-7

> **NOTE** *If you wonder why the size of the window doesn't change in the designer when you click the glyph for it to size to content, the* `Height` *and* `Width` *properties of the window are replaced with "designer" height/width properties that retain these values for use by the WPF designer so that the* `SizeToContent` *property doesn't interfere while designing the form. These properties are then switched back to the standard* `Height` *and* `Width` *properties if you return to fixed-size mode.*

The second image in Figure 18-7 demonstrates the snap regions that appear when you move a control around the form (or resize it). These snap regions are similar to snap lines in the Windows Forms designer, and help you align controls to a standard margin within their container control, or easily align a control to other controls. Hold down ALT while you move a control if you don't want these snap regions to appear and your control to snap to them.

The third image in Figure 18-7 demonstrates the rulers that appear when you resize a control. This feature allows you to easily see the new dimensions of a control as you resize it to help you adjust it to a particular size.

The third image in Figure 18-7 also contains some anchor points (that is, the symbols that look like a chain link on the top and left of the button, and the "broken" chain link on the bottom and right of the button). These symbols indicate that the button has a margin applied to it, dictating the placement of the button within its grid cell. Currently, these symbols indicate that the button has a top and left margin applied, effectively "anchoring" its top and left sides to the top and left of the grid containing it. However, it is easy to swap the top anchor so that the button is anchored by its bottom edge, and swap the left anchor so that the button is anchored by its right edge instead. Simply click the top anchor symbol to have the button anchored by its bottom edge, and click the left anchor symbol to have the button anchored by its right edge. The anchor symbol `swap` positions, and you can simply click them again to return them back to their original anchor points. You can also anchor both sides (that is, left/right or top/bottom) of a control such that it stretches as the grid cell it is hosted within is resized. For example, if the left side of the TextBox is anchored to the grid cell, you can also anchor its right side by clicking the small circle to the right of the TextBox. To remove the anchor from just one side, click the anchor symbol on that side to remove it.

As previously mentioned, the most important control for laying out your form is the `Grid` control. Take a look at the some of the special support that the WPF designer has for working with this control. By default your `MainWindow.xaml` file was created with a single grid element without any rows or columns defined. Before you commence adding elements, you might want to define some rows and columns, which can be used to control the layout of the controls within the form. To do this, start by selecting the grid by clicking in the blank area in the middle of the window, selecting the relevant node from the Document Outline tool window, or placing the cursor within the corresponding grid element in the XAML file itself (when in split view).

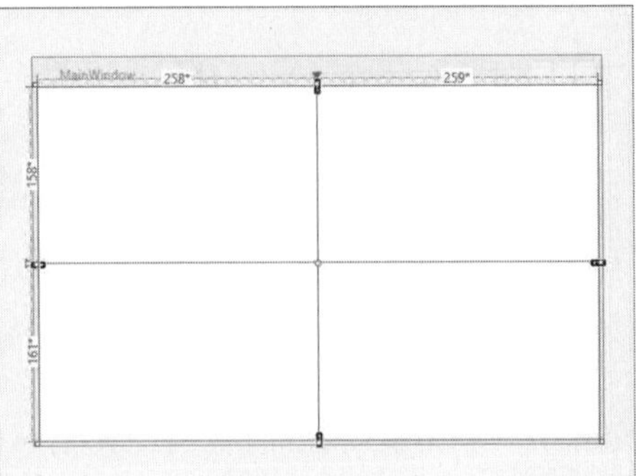

FIGURE 18-8

When the grid element is selected, a border appears around the top and left edges of the grid, highlighting both the actual area occupied by the grid and the relative sizing of each of the rows and columns, as shown in Figure 18-8. This figure currently shows a grid with two rows and two columns.

You can add additional rows or columns by simply clicking at a location within the border. When added, the row or column markers can be selected and dragged to get the correct sizing. You will notice when you are initially placing the markers that there is no information about the size of the new row/column displayed, which is unfortunate; however, these will appear after the marker has been created.

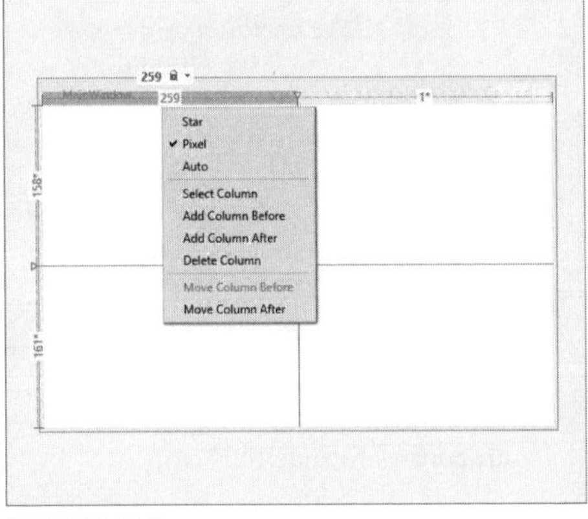

FIGURE 18-9

When you move the cursor over the size display for a row or column, a small indicator appears above or to the left of the label. In Figure 18-9, it's a lock symbol with a drop-down arrow. By selecting the drop-down, you can specify whether the row/column should be fixed (Pixel), a weighted proportion (Star), or determined by its contents (Auto). Alternatively, there is a drop-down menu that lets you specify this information, as well as performing some common grid operations.

> **NOTE** *Weighted proportion is a similar concept to specifying a percentage of the space available (compared to other columns). After fixed and auto-sized columns/rows have been allocated space, columns/rows with weighted proportions will divide up the remaining available space. This division will be equal, unless you prefix the asterisk with a numeric multiplier. For example, say you have a grid with a width of 1000 (pixels) and two columns. If both have * as their specified width, they each will have a width of 500 pixels. However, if one has a width of *, and the other has a width of 3*, then the 1000 pixels will divide into 250 pixel "chunks," with one chunk allocated to the first column (thus having a width of 250 pixels), and three chunks allocated to the second column (thus having a width of 750 pixels).*

To delete a row or column, click the row or column, and drag it outside of the grid area. It will be removed, and the controls in the surrounding cells will be updated accordingly.

> **NOTE** *When you create a control by dragging and dropping it on a grid cell, remember to "dock" it to the left and top edges of the grid cell (by dragging it until it snaps into that position). Otherwise a margin will be defined on the control to position it within the grid cell, which is probably not the behavior you want.*

The Properties Tool Window

When you've placed a control on your form, you don't have to return to the XAML editor to set its property values and assign event handlers. Like Windows Forms, WPF has a Properties window; although there are quite a few differences in WPF's implementation, as shown in Figure 18-10.

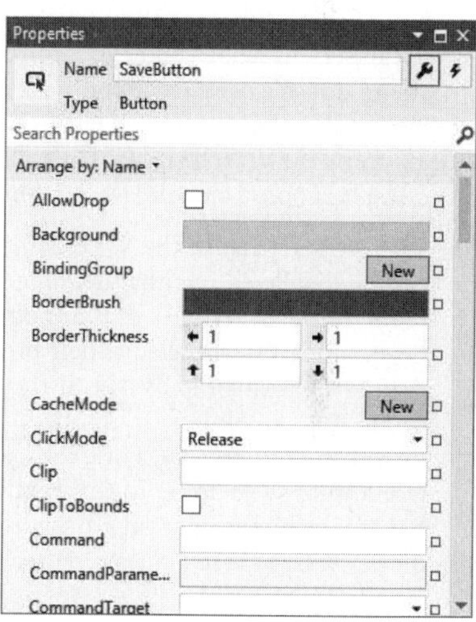

FIGURE 18-10

> **NOTE** *If you are upgrading from Visual Studio 2008, you'll notice that the Properties window has had a huge makeover in terms of functionality. In many ways, the new window more closely resembles the Properties window found in Expression Blend. In some cases, you'll find the changes make it easier to set certain values. For others, you'll miss the "old" Properties way of setting values.*

The Properties tool window for Windows Forms development allows you to select a control to set the properties via a drop-down control selector above the properties/events list. However, this drop-down is missing in WPF's Properties window. Instead, you must select the control on the designer, via the Document Outline tool window, or by placing the cursor within the definition of a control in XAML view.

> **NOTE** *The Properties window can be used while working in both the XAML editor and the designer. However, if you want to use it from the XAML editor, the designer must have been loaded (you may need to switch to designer view and back if you have opened the file straight into the XAML editor), and if you have invalid XAML you may find you need to fix the errors first.*

The `Name` property for the control is not within the property list but has a dedicated TextBox above the property list. If the control doesn't already have a name, it assigns the value to its `Name` property (rather than `x:Name`). However, if the `x:Name` attribute is defined on the control element and you update its name from the Properties window, it continues to use and update that attribute.

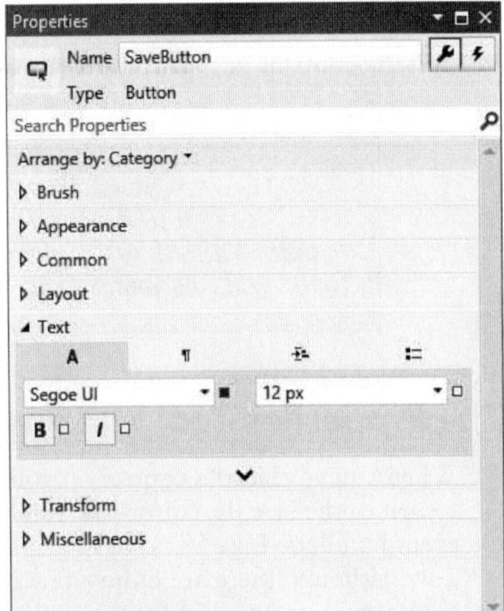

FIGURE 18-11

Controls can have many properties or events, and navigating through the properties/events lists in Windows Forms to find the one you are after can be a chore. To make finding a specific property easier for developers, the WPF Properties window has a search function that dynamically filters the properties list based on what you type into the TextBox. Your search string doesn't need to be the start of the property/event name, but retains the property/event in the list if any part of its name contains the search string. Unfortunately, this search function doesn't support camel-case searching.

The property list in the WPF designer (like for Windows Forms) can be displayed in either a Category or Alphabetical order. None of the properties that are objects (such as Margin) can be expanded to show/edit their properties (which they do for Windows Forms). However, if the list displays in the Category, order you can observe a unique feature of WPF's property window: category editors. For example, if you select a Button control and browse down to the Text category, you find that it has a special editor for the properties in the Text category to make setting these values a better experience, as shown in Figure 18-11.

Various attached properties available to a control also appear in the property list, as shown in Figure 18-12.

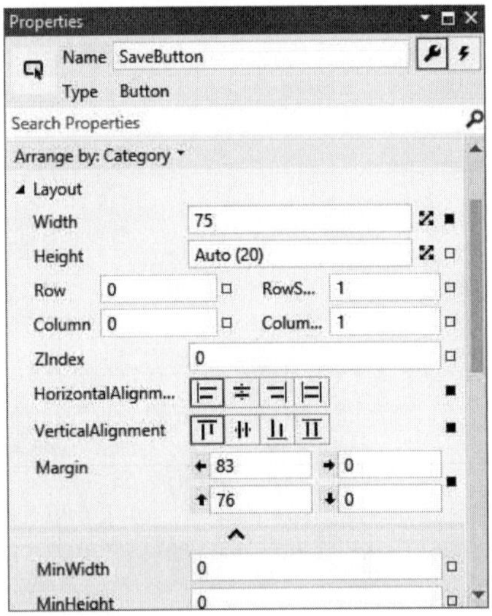

FIGURE 18-12

You may have noticed that each property name has a small square to its right. This is a feature called *property markers*. A property marker indicates what the source for that property's value is. Placing your mouse cursor over a square shows a tooltip describing what it means. The icon changes based on where the value is to be sourced from. Figure 18-13 demonstrates these various icons, which are described here:

- A light gray square indicates that the property has no value assigned to it and will use its default value.
- A black square indicates that the property has a local value assigned to it (that is, has been given a specific value).
- A yellow square indicates that the property has a data binding expression assigned to it. (Data binding is discussed later in the section "Data Binding Features.")
- A green square indicates that the property has a resource assigned to it.
- A purple square indicates that the property is inheriting its value from another control further up the hierarchy.

Clicking a property marker icon displays a pop-up menu providing some advanced options for assigning the value of that property, as shown in Figure 18-14.

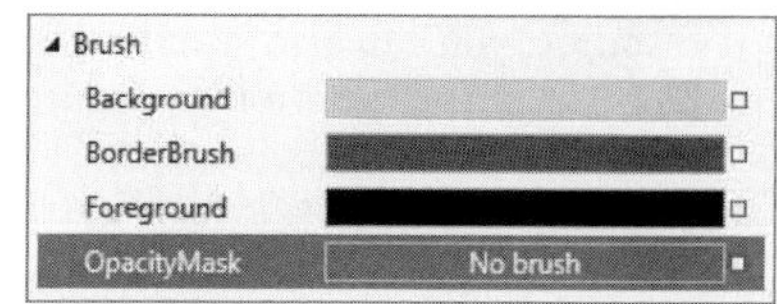

FIGURE 18-13

The Create Data Binding option provides a pop-up editor to select various binding options to create a data binding expression for that value. WPF supports numerous binding options, and these and this window are described further in the next section.

The Custom Expression allows you to directly edit the binding expression that you would like to use for the property.

The Reset option is available if there is a specific value provided for a property through data binding, resource assignment or local values. When Reset is clicked, all of the binding for this property is removed and the value reverts to its default.

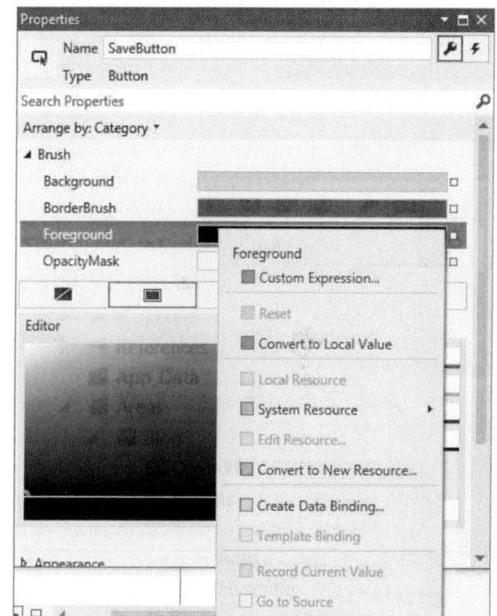

FIGURE 18-14

The Convert to Local Value takes the current value of the property and assigns it in the control's attribute directly. It is not set up as a reusable resource, nor is the value changeable through any data. It is just a static value defined through an attribute.

The first two Resource options, Local Resource and System Resource, enable you to select a resource that you've created (or is defined by WPF) and assign it as the value of the selected property. Selecting one of the options causes the available choices to appear in a fly-away menu.

Resources are essentially reusable objects and values, similar in concept to constants in code. The resources are all the resources available to this property (that is, within scope and of the same type), grouped by their resource dictionary. Along with the menus, you can see the resources grouped at the bottom of the category. Figure 18-15 shows a resource of the same type as this property (RedBrushKey) that is defined within the current XAML file (under the Local grouping) along with the system-defined resources that meet the same criteria. (That is, they have the same type.) Because this is a property of type SolidColorBrush, the window displays all the color brush resources predefined in WPF for you to choose from.

Returning to the other options in the menu shown in Figure 18-14, the Edit Resource option is used to edit a resource that has previously been assigned to the property's value. The dialog that gets displayed depends on the type of property. For instance, a brush property, such as the one in the example, will display a color picker dialog. Any values that are edited through this editor will affect any other property that is bound to the edited resource.

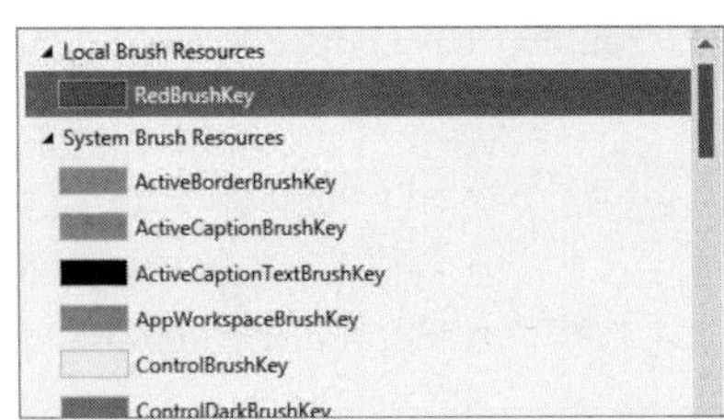

FIGURE 18-15

The Convert to New Resource option takes the value of the current property and turns it into a resource, with options to place the resource at one of a number of different levels. When selected, a dialog similar to the one shown in Figure 18-16 appears.

When a new resource is created, a XAML element is added to some part of the XAML file (or another XAML file). Along with specifying the name of the resource, you can also specify the level where it will be placed. At the bottom of Figure 18-16, you see a radio buttons for Application, This Document, and Resource Dictionary. If Application is selected, the resource will be added to the `App.xaml` file. If you specify This Document, the resource will be created in the current XAML file. And if you select Resource Dictionary, the resource will be added to a separate XAML file created specifically to hold resources. Within this document, you can also select a more detailed level, starting from the top-level Window element down to the element whose property you are currently modifying. Regardless of where you put the resource, it can be reused in other places by referencing the unique key you give it.

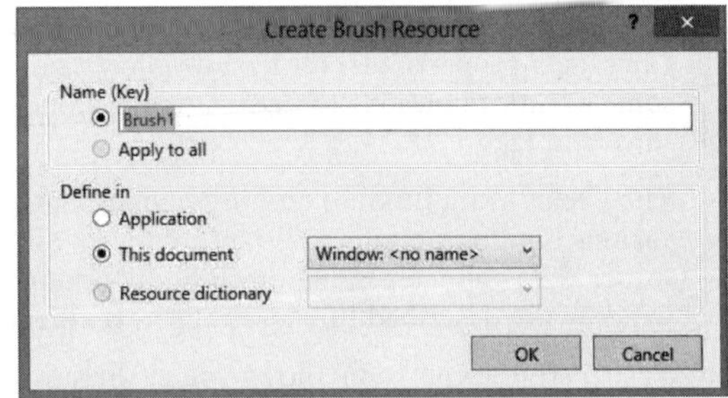

FIGURE 18-16

When the resource has been created, the value of the property is automatically updated to use this resource. For example, using this option on the `Background` property of a control that has a value of `#FF8888B7` defines the following resource in `Window.Resources` with the name `BlueVioletBrushKey`:

```
<SolidColorBrush x:Key="BlueVioletBrushKey">#FF8888B7</SolidColorBrush>
```

The control will reference this resource as such:

```
Background="{StaticResource BlueVioletBrushKey}"
```

You can then apply this resource to other controls using the same means in XAML, or you can apply it by selecting the control and the property to apply it to, and using the Apply Resource option on the property marker menu described previously.

In the designer you can find that (as with Windows Forms) double-clicking a control automatically creates an event handler for that control's default event in the code-behind. You can also create event handlers for any of the control's events using the Properties window as you would in Windows Forms. Clicking the lightning icon in the Properties window takes you to the Events view, as shown in Figure 18-17. This shows a list of events that the control can raise, and you can double-click the event to automatically create the appropriate event handler in the code-behind.

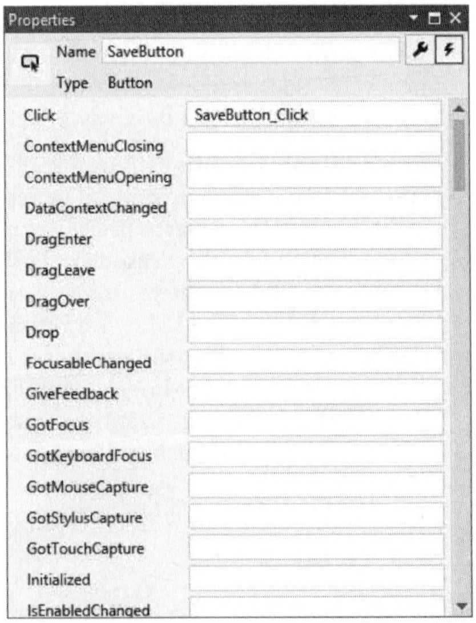

FIGURE 18-17

> **NOTE** *For VB.NET developers, double-clicking the Button control or creating the event via the Properties window wires up the event using the Handles syntax. Therefore, the event handler is not assigned to the event as an attribute. If you use this method to handle the event, you won't see the event handler defined in the XAML for the control, and thus you can't use the Navigate to Event Handler menu (from Figure 18-6) when in the XAML editor to navigate to it.*

Data Binding Features

Data binding is an important concept in WPF, and is one of its core strengths. Data binding syntax can be a bit confusing initially, but Visual Studio 2012 makes creating data bound forms easy in the designer. Visual Studio 2012 helps with data binding in two ways: with the Create Data Binding option on a property in the Properties tool window, and the drag-and-drop data binding support from the Data Sources window. This section looks at these two options in turn.

In WPF you can bind to objects (which also include datasets, ADO.NET Entity Framework entities, and so on), resources, and even properties on other controls. So there are rich binding capabilities in WPF, and you can bind a property to almost anything you want. Hand-coding these complex binding expressions in XAML can be quite daunting, but the Data Binding editor enables you to build these expressions via a point-and-click interface.

To bind a property on a control, first select the control in the designer, and find the property you want to bind in the Properties window. Click the property marker icon, and select the Create Data Binding option. Figure 18-18 shows the window that appears.

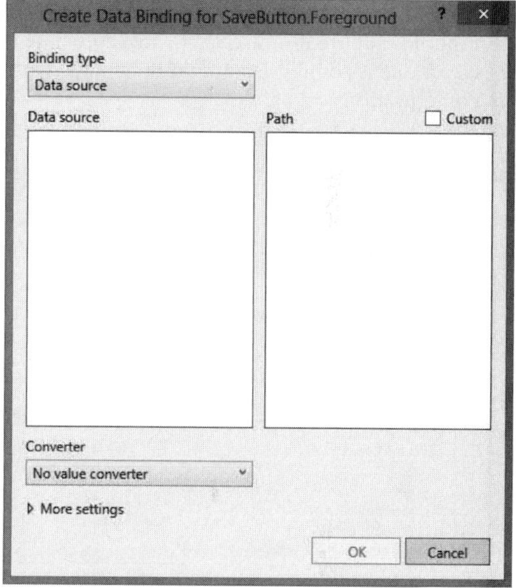

FIGURE 18-18

This window contains a number of options that help you create a binding: Binding Type, Data Source, Converter, and More Settings.

Generally the first step is to define the Binding Type. This is a drop-down list that allows you to specify the type of binding that you want to create. The choices are as follows:

- **Data Context:** Uses the current data context for the element
- **Data Source:** Allows you use an existing data source in your project
- **Element Name:** Uses a property on an element elsewhere in your XAML
- **Relative Source – Find Ancestor:** Navigates up the hierarchy of XAML elements looking for a specific element
- **Relative Source – Previous data:** In a list or items controls, references the data context used by the previous element in the list
- **Relative Source – Self:** Uses a property on the current element
- **Relative Source – Templated Parent:** Uses a property defined on the template for the element
- **Static Resource:** Uses a statically defined resource in the XAML file

Depending on the option selected in the Binding Type, the area immediately below the combo box changes. For example, if you select Data Context, you will be presented with a list of the properties visible on the data context for the element. If you select Element Name, you see a list of the elements that are in your current XAML page (as shown in Figure 18-19). The details about what these and the other binding types do are specific to XAML and therefore not within the scope of the book. But ultimately, the purpose of the binding type and the other controls is to allow you to specify not only the type of binding to use but also the path to the data.

The Converter section is where any value converter can be specified. The *value converter* is a class (one that implements the IValueConverter interface) that converts data as it moves back and forth from the data source and the bound property.

Finally, there is the More Settings option. These settings allow you to configure properties related to the binding that are not directly related to where the property value is coming from. Figure 18-20 illustrates these configuration settings.

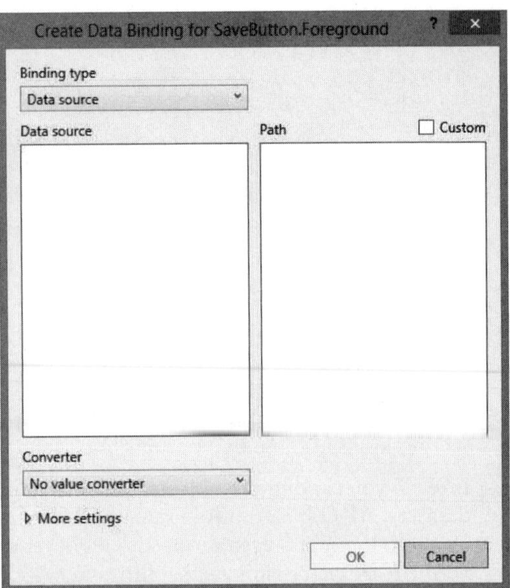

FIGURE 18-19

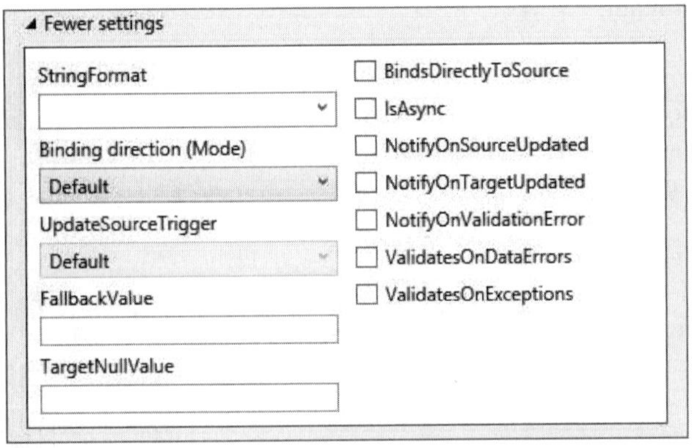

Fewer settings
StringFormat
Binding direction (Mode)
Default
UpdateSourceTrigger
Default
FallbackValue
TargetNullValue
BindsDirectlyToSource
IsAsync
NotifyOnSourceUpdated
NotifyOnTargetUpdated
NotifyOnValidationError
ValidatesOnDataErrors
ValidatesOnExceptions

FIGURE 18-20

As you can see, this binding expression builder makes creating the binding expression much easier, without requiring you to learn the data binding syntax. This is a good way to learn the data binding syntax because you can then see the expression produced in the XAML.

Now you will look at the drag-and-drop data binding features of Visual Studio 2012. The first step is to create something to bind to. This can be an object, a dataset, or an ADO.NET Entity Framework entity, among many other binding targets. For this example, you create an object to bind to. Create a new class in your project called `ContactViewModel`, and create a number of properties on it such as `FirstName`, `LastName`, `Company`, `Phone`, `Fax`, `Mobile`, and `Email` (all strings).

> **NOTE** *The name of your object is called* `ContactViewModel` *because it is acting as your* `ViewModel` *object, which pertains to the Model-View-ViewModel (MVVM) design pattern mentioned earlier. This design pattern will not be fully fleshed out in this example, however, to reduce its complexity and save potential confusion.*

Now compile your project. (This is important or otherwise the class won't appear in the next step.) Return to the designer of your form, and select Add New Data Source from the Data menu. Select Object as your data source type, click Next, and select the `ContactViewModel` class from the tree. (You need to expand the nodes to find it within the namespace hierarchy.) Click the Finish button, and the Data Sources tool window appears with the `ContactViewModel` object listed and its properties below, as shown in Figure 18-21.

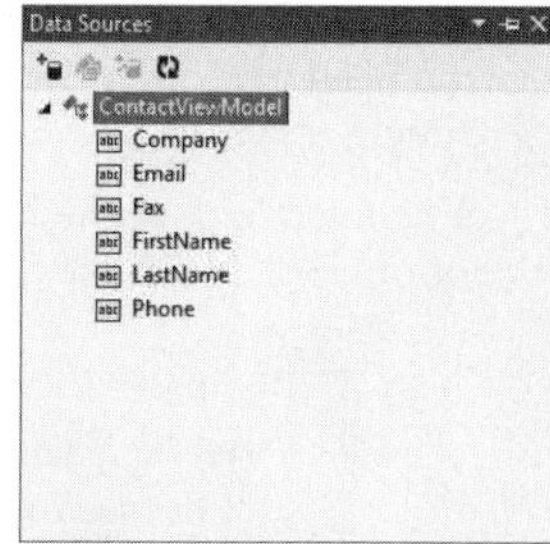

FIGURE 18-21

Now you are set to drag and drop either the whole object or individual properties onto the form, which creates one or more controls to display its data. By default a `DataGrid` control is created to display the data, but if you select the ContactViewModel item, it shows a button that, when clicked, displays a drop-down menu (as shown in Figure 18-22) allowing you to select between DataGrid, List, and Details.

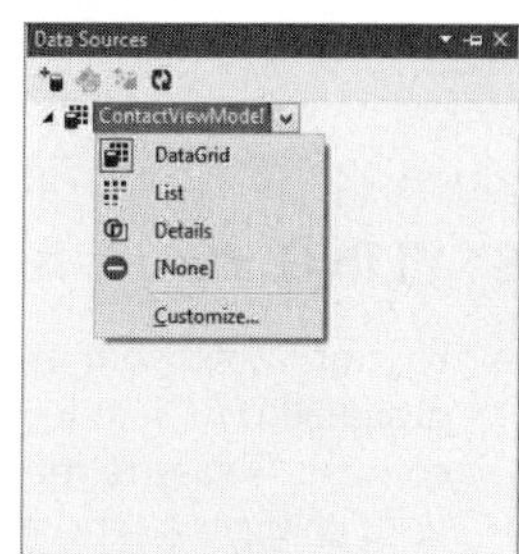

FIGURE 18-22

- The DataGrid option creates a `DataGrid` control, which has a column for each property of the object.
- The List option creates a `List` control with a data template containing fields for each of the properties.
- The Details option creates a `Grid` control with two columns: one for labels and one for fields. A row will be created for each property on the object, with a Label control displaying the field name (with spaces intelligently inserted before capital letters) in the first column, and a field (whose type depends on the data type of the property) in the second column.

A resource is created in the Resources property of the Window, which points to the `ContactViewModel` object that can then be used as the data context or items source of the controls binding to the object. This can be deleted at a later stage if you want to set the data source from the code-behind. The controls also have the required data binding expressions assigned. The type of controls created on the form to display the data depend on your selection on the `ContactViewModel` item.

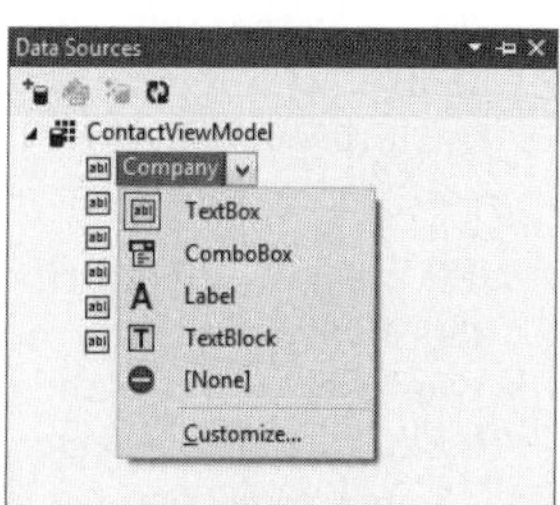

FIGURE 18-23

The type of control created for each property has a default based upon the data type of the property, but like the `ContactViewModel` item, you can select the property to show a button that, when clicked, displays a drop-down menu allowing you to select a different control type (as shown in Figure 18-23). If the type of control isn't in the list (such as if you want to use a third-party control), you can use the Customize option to add it to the list for the corresponding data type. If you don't want a field created for that property, select None from the menu.

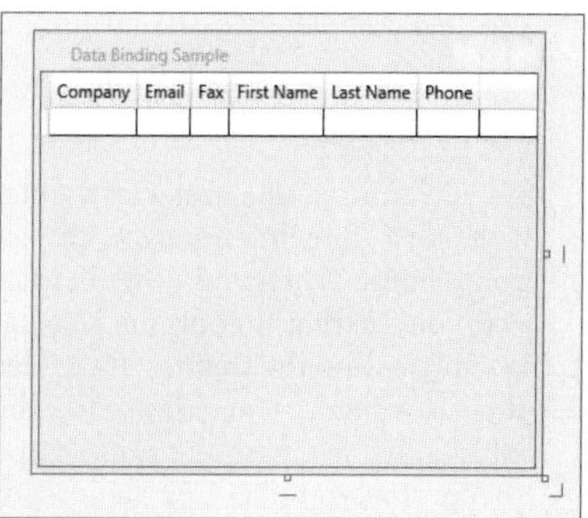

FIGURE 18-24

For this example, you create a details form, so select Details on the `ContactViewModel` item in the Data Sources window. You can change the control generated for each property if you want, but for now leave each as a TextBox and have each property generated in the details form. Now select the `ContactViewModel` item from the Data Sources window, and drop it onto your form. A grid will be created along with a field for each property, as shown in Figure 18-24.

Unfortunately, there is no way in the Data Sources window to define the order of the fields in the form, so you need to reorder the controls in the grid manually (either via the designer or by modifying the XAML directly).

When you look at the XAML generated, you see that this drag-and-drop data binding feature can save you a lot of work and make the process of generating forms a lot faster and easier.

> **NOTE** *If you write user/custom controls that expose properties that may be assigned a data binding expression, you need to make these* dependency properties. *Dependency properties are a special WPF/Silverlight concept whose values can accept an expression that needs to be resolved (such as data binding expression). Dependency properties need to be defined differently than standard properties. The discussion of these is beyond the scope of this chapter, but essentially only properties that have been defined as dependency properties can be assigned a data binding expression.*

STYLING YOUR APPLICATION

Up until now, your application has looked plain — it couldn't be considered much plainer if you had designed it in Windows Forms. The great thing about WPF, however, is that the visual appearance of the controls is easy to modify, allowing you to completely change the way they look. You can store commonly used changes to specific controls as *styles* (a collection of property values for a control stored as a resource that can be defined once and applied to multiple controls), or you can completely redefine the XAML for a control by creating a new *control template* for it. These resources can be defined in the `Resources` property of any control in your layout along with a key, which can then be used by any controls further down the hierarchy that refer to it by that key. For example, if you want to define a resource available for use by any control within your MainWindow XAML file, you can define it in `Window.Resources`. Or if you want to use it throughout the entire application, you can define it in the `Application.Resources` property on the `Application` element in `App.xaml`.

Taking it one step further, you can define multiple control templates/styles in a resource dictionary and use this as a *theme*. This theme could be applied across your application to automatically style the controls in your user interface and provide a unique and consistent look for your application. This is what this section looks at. Rather than creating your own themes, you can actually use the themes available from the WPF Themes project on CodePlex: `http://wpfthemes.codeplex.com`.

These themes were initially designed (most by Microsoft) for use in Silverlight applications but have been converted (where it was necessary) so they can be used in WPF applications. Use one of these themes to create a completely different look for your application.

Start by creating a new application and adding some different controls on the form, as shown in Figure 18-25.

As you can see this looks fairly bland, so try applying a theme and seeing how you can easily change its look completely. When you download the WPF Themes project, you see that it contains a solution with two projects: one providing the themes and a demonstration project that uses them. You can use the themes slightly differently, however. Run the sample application and find a theme that you like. For the purposes of demonstration, choose the Shiny Blue theme. In the `WPF.Themes` project under the `ShinyBlue` folder, find a `Theme.xaml` file. Copy this into the root of your own project (making sure to include it in your project in Visual Studio).

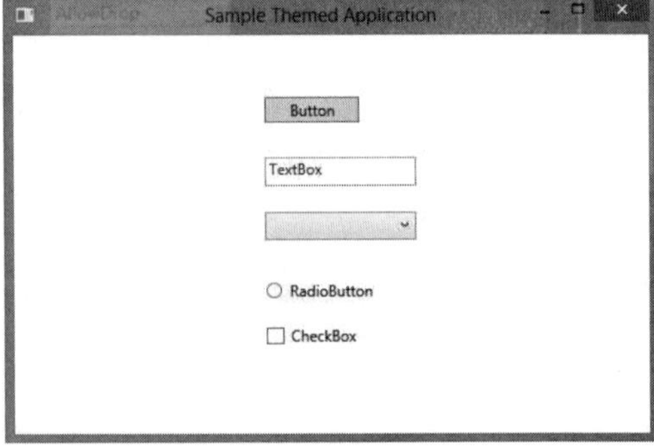

FIGURE 18-25

Open up `App.xaml` and add the following XAML code to `Application.Resources`. You might already see it there, having been added when you included the `Theme.xaml` file in your project.

```
<ResourceDictionary>
    <ResourceDictionary.MergedDictionaries>
        <ResourceDictionary Source="Theme.xaml" />
    </ResourceDictionary.MergedDictionaries>
</ResourceDictionary>
```

This XAML code simply merges the resources from the theme file into your application resources, which applies the resources application-wide and overrides the default styling of the controls in your project with the corresponding ones defined in the theme file.

One last change to make is to set the background style for your windows to use the style from the theme file (because this isn't automatically assigned). In your `Window` element add the following attribute:

```
Background="{StaticResource WindowBackgroundBrush}"
```

Now run your project, and you can find the controls in your form look completely different, as shown in Figure 18-26.

To change the theme to a different one, you can simply replace the `Theme.xaml` file with another one from the `WPF.Themes` project and recompile your project.

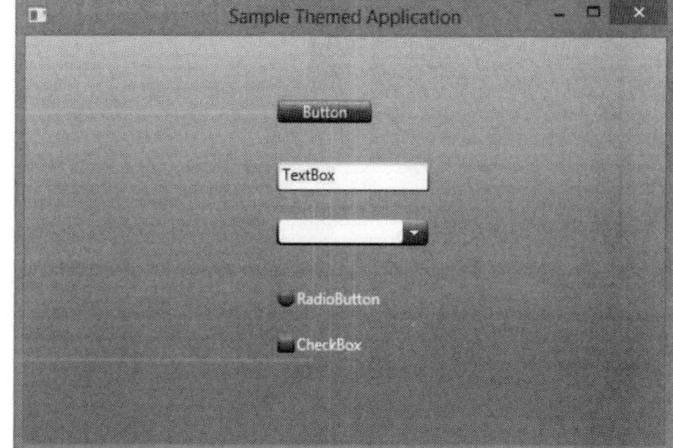

FIGURE 18-26

> **NOTE** *If you plan to extensively modify the styles and control templates for your application, you may find it much easier to do so in Expression Blend — a tool specifically designed for graphics designers who work with XAML. Expression Blend is much better suited to designing graphics and animations in XAML, and provides a much better designer for doing so than Visual Studio (which is focused more toward developers). Expression Blend can open up Visual Studio solutions and can also view/edit code and compile projects; although, it is best suited to design-related tasks. This integration of Visual Studio and Expression Blend helps to support the designer/developer workflow. Both of these tools can have the same solution/project open at the same time (even on the same machine), enabling you to quickly switch between them when necessary. If a file is open in one when you save a change to a file in the other, a notification dialog appears asking if you want to reload the file. To easily open a solution in Expression Blend from Visual Studio, right-click a XAML file, and select the Open in Expression Blend option.*

WINDOWS FORMS INTEROPERABILITY

Up until now you have seen how you can build a WPF application; however the likelihood is that you already have a significant code base in Windows Forms and are unlikely to immediately migrate it all to WPF. You may have a significant investment in that code base and not want to rewrite it all for technology's sake. To ease this migration path, Microsoft has enabled WPF and Windows Forms to work together within the same application. Bidirectional interoperability is supported by both WPF and Windows Forms applications, with WPF controls hosted in a Windows Forms application, and Windows Forms controls hosted in a WPF application. This section looks at how to implement each of these scenarios.

Hosting a WPF Control in Windows Forms

To begin with, create a new project in your solution to create the WPF control in. This control (for the purpose of demonstration) is a simple username and password entry control. From the Add New Project dialog (see Figure 18-27), select the WPF User Control Library project template. This already includes the XAML and code-behind files necessary for a WPF user control. If you examine the XAML of the control, you can see that it is essentially the same as the original XAML for the window you started with at the beginning of the chapter except that the root XAML element is `UserControl` instead of `Window`.

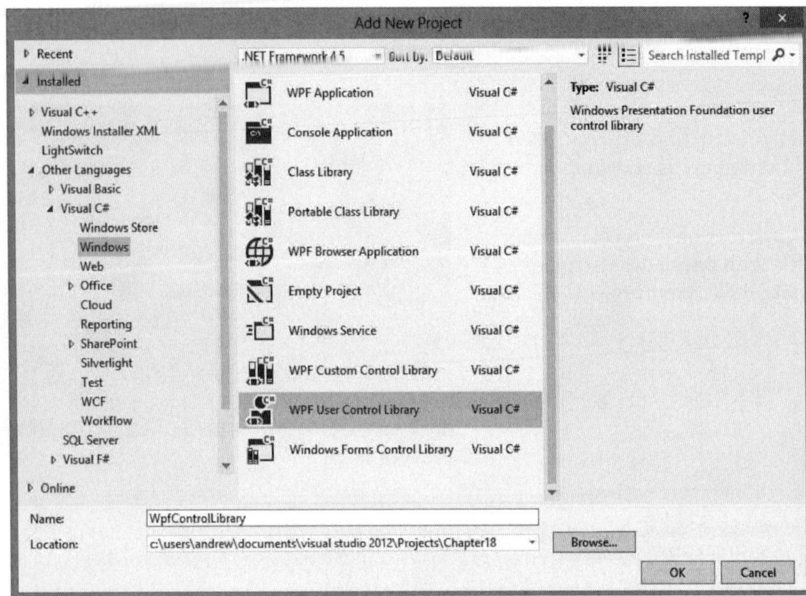

FIGURE 18-27

Rename the control to `UserLoginControl`, and add a grid, two text blocks, and two TextBoxes to it, as demonstrated in Figure 18-28.

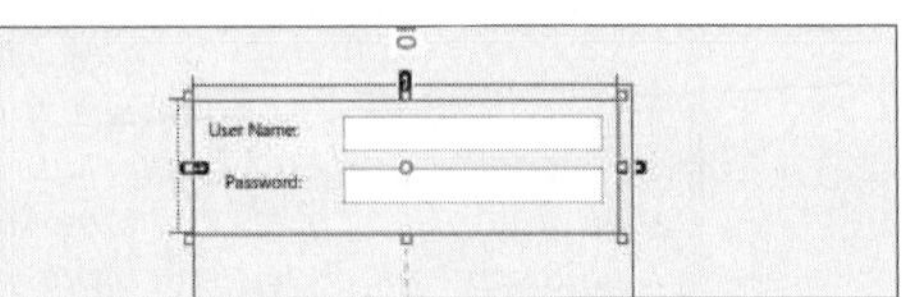

FIGURE 18-28

In the code-behind add some simple properties to expose the contents of the TextBoxes publicly (getters and setters):

VB

```
Public Property UserName As String
    Get
        Return txtUserName.Text
    End Get
    Set(ByVal value As String)
        txtUserName.Text = value
    End Set
End Property

Public Property Password As String
    Get
        Return txtPassword.Text
    End Get
    Set(ByVal value As String)
```

```
        txtPassword.Text = value
    End Set
End Property
```

C#

```
public string Username
{
    get { return txtUserName.Text; }
    set { txtUserName.Text = value; }
}

public string Password
{
    get { return txtPassword.Text; }
    set { txtPassword.Text = value; }
}
```

Now that you have your WPF control, build the project and create a new Windows Forms project to host it in. Create the project and add a reference to your WPF project that contains the control (using the Add Reference menu item when right-clicking the References in the project).

Open the form that will host the WPF control in the designer. Because the WPF control library you built is in the same solution, your `UserLoginControl` control appears in the Toolbox and can simply be dragged and dropped onto the form to be used. This automatically adds an `ElementHost` control (which can host WPF controls) and references the control as its content.

However, if you need to do this manually, the process is as follows. In the Toolbox there is a WPF Interoperability tab, under which there is a single item called the ElementHost. Drag and drop this onto the form, as shown in Figure 18-29, and you see that there is a smart tag that prompts you to select the WPF control that you want to host. If the control doesn't appear in the drop-down, you may need to build your solution.

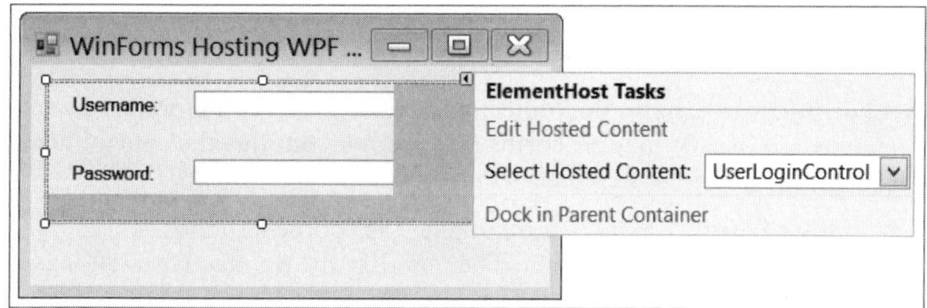

FIGURE 18-29

The control loads into the ElementHost control and is automatically given a name to refer to it in code (which you can change via the `HostedContentName` property).

Hosting a Windows Forms Control in WPF

Now take a look at the opposite scenario — hosting a Windows Forms control in a WPF application. Create a new project using the Class Library project template called `WinFormsControlLibrary`. Delete the `Class1` class, and add a new User Control item to the project and call it `UserLoginControl`.

Open this item in the designer, and add two text blocks and two TextBoxes to it, as demonstrated in Figure 18-30.

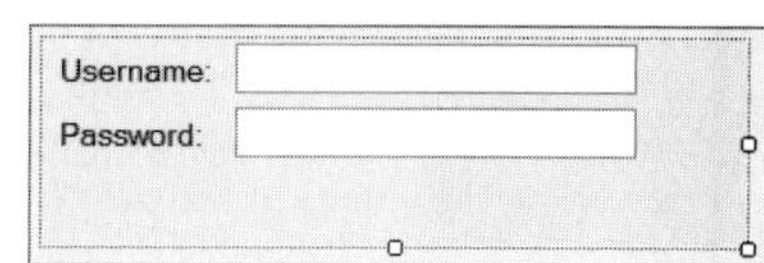

FIGURE 18-30

In the code-behind add some simple properties to expose the contents of the TextBoxes publicly (getters and setters):

VB

```
Public Property UserName As String
    Get
        Return txtUserName.Text
    End Get
    Set(ByVal value As String)
        txtUserName.Text = value
    End Set
End Property

Public Property Password As String
    Get
        Return txtPassword.Text
    End Get
    Set(ByVal value As String)
        txtPassword.Text = value
    End Set
End Property
```

C#

```
public string Username
{
    get { return txtUserName.Text; }
    set { txtUserName.Text = value; }
}

public string Password
{
    get { return txtPassword.Text; }
    set { txtPassword.Text = value; }
}
```

Now that you have your Windows Forms control, build the project and create a new WPF project to host it in. Create the project and add a reference to your Windows Forms project that contains the control (using the Add Reference menu item when right-clicking the References in the project).

Open the form that will host the Windows Forms control in the designer. Select the `WindowsFormsHost` control from the Toolbox, and drag and drop it onto your form. Then modify the `WindowsFormsHost` element to host your control by setting the `Child` property to refer to the Windows Forms control, which when run renders the control, as shown in Figure 18-31.

DEBUGGING WITH THE WPF VISUALIZER

Identifying problems in your XAML/visual tree at run time can be difficult, but fortunately a feature called the WPF Visualizer is available in Visual Studio 2012 to help you debug your WPF application's visual tree. For example, an element may not be visible when it should be, may not appear where it should, or may not be styled correctly. The WPF Visualizer can help you track these sorts of problems by enabling you to view the visual tree, view the values of the properties for a selected element, and view where properties get their styling from.

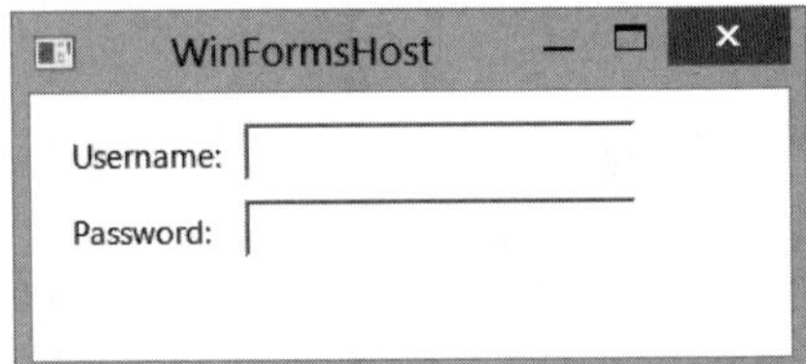

FIGURE 18-31

To open the WPF Visualizer, you must first be in break mode. Using the Autos, Locals, or Watch tool window, find a variable that contains a reference to an element in the XAML document to debug. You can then click the little magnifying glass icon next to a WPF user interface element listed in the tool window to open the visualizer (as shown in Figure 18-32). Alternatively, you can place your mouse cursor over a variable that references a WPF user interface element (to display the DataTip popup) and click the magnifying glass icon there.

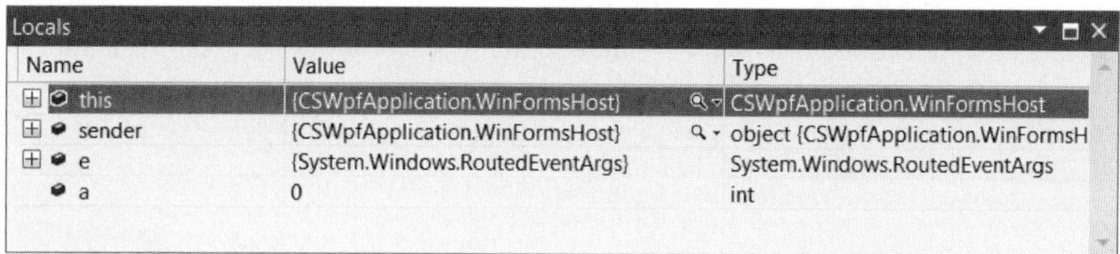

FIGURE 18-32

The WPF Visualizer is shown in Figure 18-33. On the left side of the window you can see the visual tree for the current XAML document and the rendering of the selected element in this tree below it. On the right side is a list of all the properties of the selected element in the tree, their current values, and other information associated with each property.

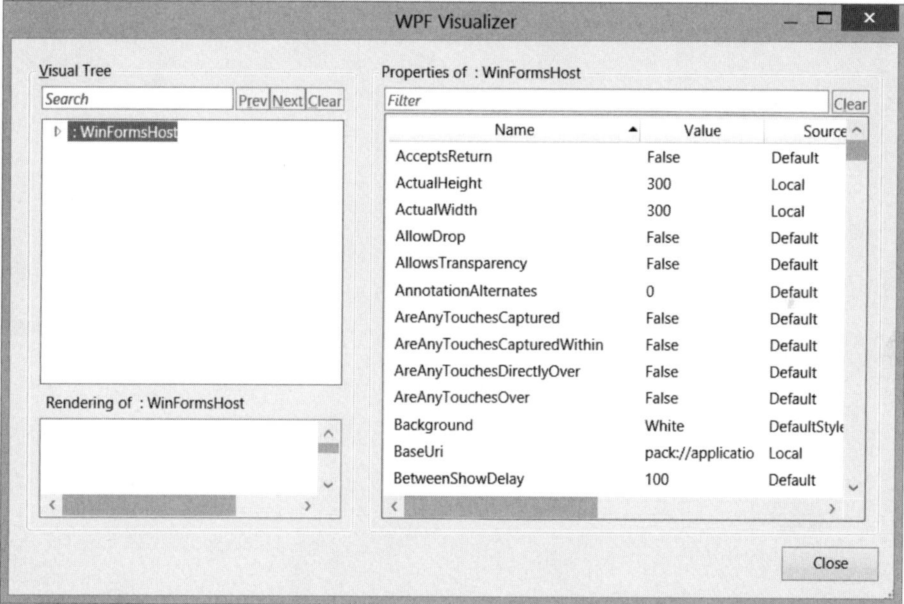

FIGURE 18-33

Because a visual tree can contain thousands of items, finding the one you are after by traversing the tree can be difficult. If you know the name or type of the element you are looking for, you can enter this into the search TextBox above the tree and navigate through the matching entries using the Next and Prev buttons. You can also filter the property list by entering a part of the property name, value, style, or type that you are searching for.

Unfortunately, there's no means to edit a property value or modify the property tree, but inspecting the elements in the visual tree and their property values (and the source of the values) should help you track problems in your XAML much more easily than in previous versions of Visual Studio.

SUMMARY

In this chapter you have seen how you can work with Visual Studio 2012 to build applications with WPF. You've learned some of the most important concepts of XAML, how to use the unique features of the WPF designer, looked at styling an application, and used the interoperability capabilities between WPF and Windows Forms.

19

Office Business Applications

WHAT'S IN THIS CHAPTER?

- Exploring the different ways to extend Microsoft Office
- Creating a Microsoft Word document customization
- Creating a Microsoft Outlook add-in
- Launching and debugging an Office application
- Packaging and deploying an Office application

Microsoft Office applications have always been extensible via add-ins and various automation techniques. Even Visual Basic for Applications (VBA), which was widely known for various limitations in accessing system files, had the capability to write applications that used an instance of an Office application to achieve certain tasks, such as Word's spell-checking feature.

When Visual Studio .NET was released in 2002, Microsoft soon followed with the first release of Visual Studio Tools for Office (known by the abbreviation VSTO, pronounced "visto"). This initial version of VSTO didn't actually produce anything new except for an easier way to create application projects that would use Microsoft Word or Microsoft Excel. However, subsequent versions of VSTO quickly evolved and became more powerful, enabling you to build more functional applications that ran on the Office platform.

The latest version of VSTO was shipped as part of Visual Studio 2010. It provides many useful features, including support for Office 2010, support for the Ribbon user interface, and packaging and deployment functionality.

This chapter begins with a look at the types of applications you can build with VSTO. It then guides you through the process to create a document-level customization to a Word document, including a custom Actions Pane. Following this, the chapter provides a walkthrough, showing how to create an Outlook add-in complete with an Outlook Form region. Finally, the chapter provides some important information regarding the debugging and deployment of Office applications.

CHOOSING AN OFFICE PROJECT TYPE

As you might expect, the versions of applications you can create using VSTO under Visual Studio have been updated since the previous version. You have the ability to create applications that target the Microsoft Office 2010 applications. However, creating Microsoft Office 2007 applications is not supported.

In Visual Studio 2012, add-in applications can be created for almost every product in the Office suite, including Excel, InfoPath, Outlook, PowerPoint, Project, Visio, and Word. For Excel and Word, these solutions can either be attached to a single document, created as a template, or be loaded every time that application launches.

You can create a new Office application by selecting File ➪ New ➪ Project. Select your preferred language (Visual Basic or Visual C#), and then select the Office project category, as shown in Figure 19-1.

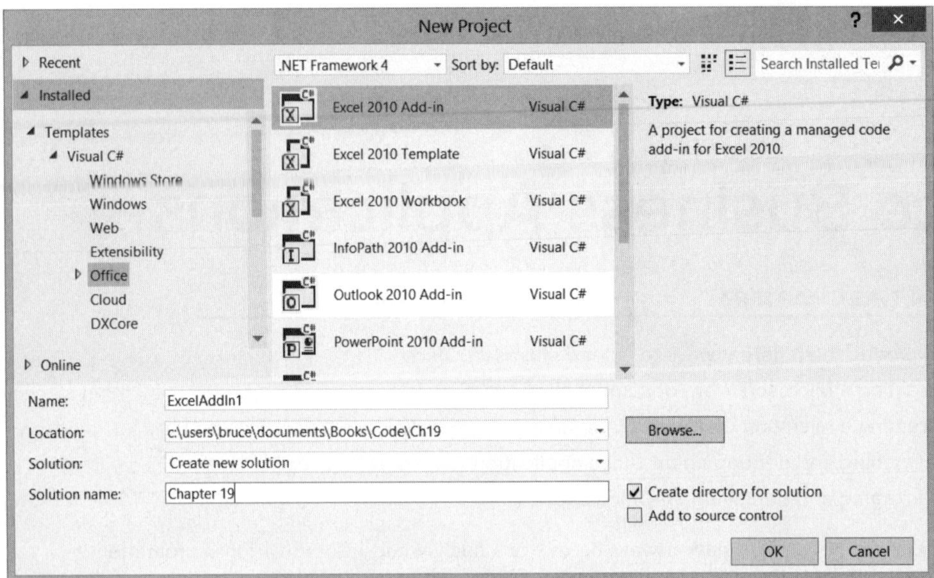

FIGURE 19-1

Two types of project templates are available for Office applications: document-level customizations and application-level add-ins.

Document-Level Customizations

A document-level customization is a solution based on a single document. To load the customization, an end user must open a specific document. Events in the document, such as loading the document or clicking buttons and menu items, can invoke event handler methods in the attached assembly. Document-level customizations can also be included with an Office template, which ensures that the customization is included when you create a new document from that template.

Visual Studio 2012 allows you to create document-level customizations for the following types of documents:

- Microsoft Excel Workbook
- Microsoft Excel Template
- Microsoft Word Document
- Microsoft Word Template

Using a document-level customization, you can modify the user interface of Word or Excel to provide a unique solution for your end users. For example, you can add new controls to the Office Ribbon or display a customized Actions Pane window.

Microsoft Word and Microsoft Excel also include a technology called *smart tags*, which enable developers to track the user's input and recognize when text in a specific format has been entered. Your solution can use this technology by providing feedback or even actions that the user could take in response to certain recognized terms, such as a phone number or address.

Visual Studio also includes a set of custom controls specific to Microsoft Word. Called *content controls*, they are optimized for both data entry and print. You'll see content controls in action later in this chapter.

Application-Level Add-ins

Unlike a document-level customization, an application-level add-in is always loaded regardless of the document currently open. In fact, application-level add-ins run even if the application runs with no documents open.

Earlier versions of VSTO had significant limitations for application-level add-ins. For example, you could create add-ins only for Microsoft Outlook, and even then you could not customize much of the user interface.

Fortunately, in Visual Studio 2012, such restrictions do not exist, and you can create application-level add-ins for almost every product in the Microsoft Office 2010 suite, including Excel, InfoPath, Outlook, PowerPoint, Project, Visio, and Word. You can create the same UI enhancements as you can with a document-level customization, such as adding new controls to the Office Ribbon.

You can also create a custom Task Pane as part of your add-in. Task Panes are similar to the Action Panes available in document-level customization projects. However, custom Task Panes are associated with the application, not a specific document, and as such can be created only within an application-level add-in.

An Actions Pane, on the other hand, is a specific type of Task Pane that is customizable and is attached to a specific Word document or Excel workbook. You cannot create an Actions Pane in an application-level add-in.

Also included in Visual Studio 2012 is the ability to create custom Outlook form regions in Outlook add-in projects. Form regions are the screens displayed when an Outlook item is opened, such as a Contact or Appointment. You can either extend the existing form regions or create a completely custom Outlook form. Later in this chapter, in the section named "Creating an Application Add-in," you'll walk through the creation of an Outlook 2010 add-in that includes a custom Outlook form region.

CREATING A DOCUMENT-LEVEL CUSTOMIZATION

This section walks through the creation of a Word document customization. This demonstrates how to create a document-level customization complete with Word Content Controls and a custom Actions Pane.

Your First VSTO Project

When you create a document-level customization with Visual Studio 2012, you can either create the document from scratch or jump-start the design by using an existing document or template. A great source of templates, particularly for business-related forms, is the free templates available from Microsoft Office Online at `http://office.microsoft.com/templates/`.

> **NOTE** *All the templates available for download from the Office Online website are provided in the older Word 97–2003 format (`.dot`). Unfortunately, some features, such as the Word Content Controls, are only available for documents saved with the Open XML format (`.dotx`). Therefore, you need to ensure that the template is saved in the latest format if you want to use all the available features.*

This example uses the Employee warning notice that is available under the Forms category but is more easily located by typing **Employee Warning Notice** in the search box. When you download a template from the Office Online website using Internet Explorer, you are prompted to save it to the default templates location. When saved, Microsoft Word then opens with a new document based on the template. Save this new document to a convenient folder on your computer as a Word Template in the Open XML format (`.dotx`), as shown in Figure 19-2.

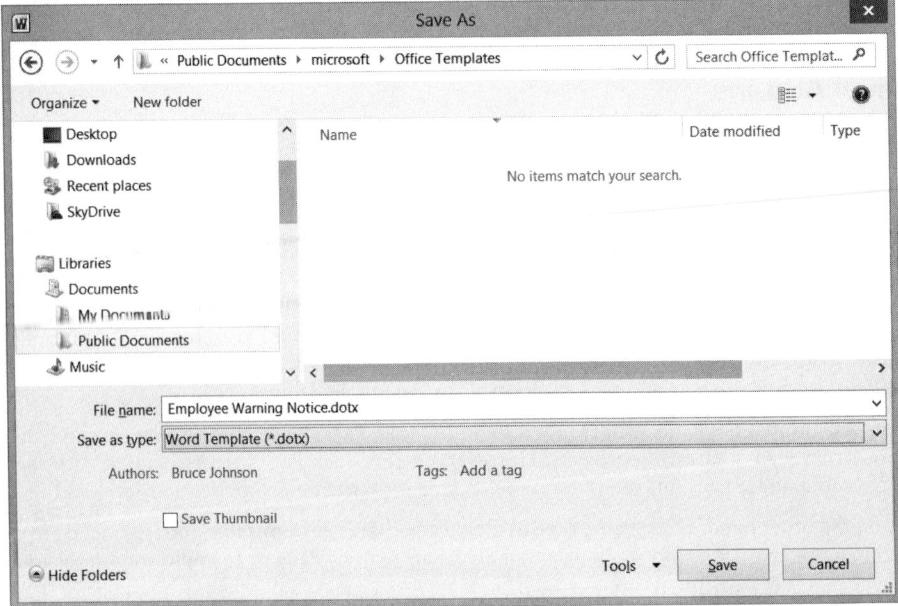

FIGURE 19-2

Next, launch Visual Studio 2012 and select File ➪ New ➪ Project. Filter the project types by selecting your preferred language (C# or Visual Basic) followed by Office, and then choose a new Word 2010 Template. You are presented with a screen that prompts you to create a new document or copy an existing one. Select the option to copy an existing document, and then navigate to and select the document template you saved earlier. When you click OK, the project is created and the document opens in the Designer, as shown in Figure 19-3.

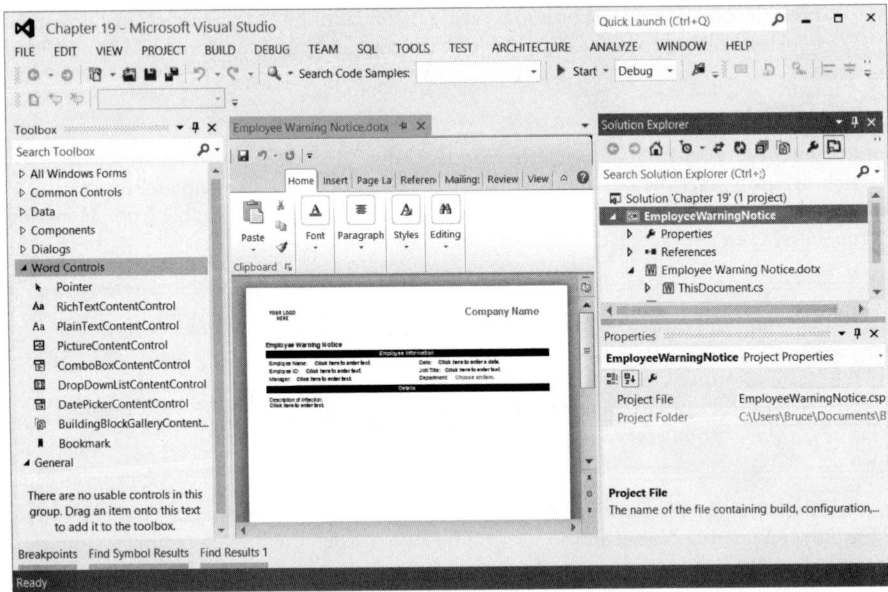

FIGURE 19-3

> **NOTE** *VSTO requires access to Visual Basic for Applications (VBA) even though the projects do not use VBA. Therefore, the first time you create an Office application you are prompted to enable access to VBA. You must grant this access even if you work exclusively in C#.*

A few things are worth pointing out in Figure 19-3. First, notice that along the top of the Designer is the Office Ribbon. This is the same Ribbon displayed in Word, and you can use it to modify the layout and design of the Word document. Second, in the Solution Explorer to the right, the file currently open is called `ThisDocument.cs` (or `ThisDocument.vb` if you use Visual Basic). You can right-click this file and select either View Designer to display the design surface for the document (refer to Figure 19-3) or View Code to open the source code behind this document in the code editor. Finally, in the Toolbox to the left, there is a tab group called Word Controls, which contains a set of controls that allow you to build rich user interfaces for data input and display.

To customize this form, first drag four PlainTextContentControl controls onto the design surface for the Employee Name, Employee ID, Job Title, and Manager. Rename these controls to `txtEmpName`, `txtEmpID`, `txtJobTitle`, and `txtManager`, respectively.

Next, drag a DatePickerContentControl for the Date field, and rename it to be `dtDate`. Then drag a DropDownListContentControl next to the Department field, and rename it `ddDept`.

Following this, drag a RichTextContentControl into the Details section of the document, and place it under the Description of Infraction label.

Finally, to clean up the document a little, remove the sections titled Type of Warning and Type of Offense, and all the text below the RichTextContentControl you added. After you have done this, your form should look similar to what is shown in Figure 19-4.

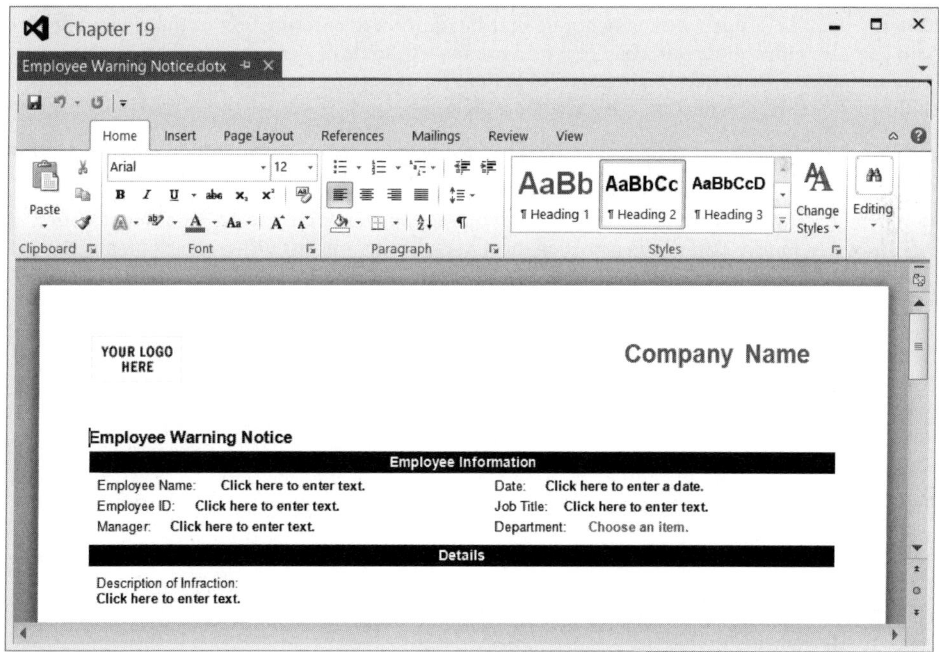

FIGURE 19-4

Before you run this project, you need to populate the Department drop-down list. Although you can do this declaratively via the Properties field, for this exercise you'll perform it programmatically. Right-click the `ThisDocument` file in the Solution Explorer, and select View Code to display the managed code that is behind this document. Two methods will be predefined: a function that is run during startup when the document is opened, and a function that is run during shutdown when the document is closed.

Add the following code for the `ThisDocument_Startup` method to populate the Department drop-down list:

C#

```
ddDept.PlaceholderText = "Select your department";
ddDept.DropDownListEntries.Add("Finance", "Finance", 0);
ddDept.DropDownListEntries.Add("HR", "HR", 1);
ddDept.DropDownListEntries.Add("IT", "IT", 2);
ddDept.DropDownListEntries.Add("Marketing", "Marketing", 3);
ddDept.DropDownListEntries.Add("Operations", "Operations", 4);
```

VB

```
ddDept.PlaceholderText = "Select your department"
ddDept.DropDownListEntries.Add("Finance", "Finance", 0)
ddDept.DropDownListEntries.Add("HR", "HR", 1)
ddDept.DropDownListEntries.Add("IT", "IT", 2)
ddDept.DropDownListEntries.Add("Marketing", "Marketing", 3)
ddDept.DropDownListEntries.Add("Operations", "Operations", 4)
```

You can run the project in Debug mode by pressing F5. This compiles the project and opens the document in Microsoft Word. You can test out entering data in the various fields to obtain a feel for how they behave.

Protecting the Document Design

While you have the document open, you may notice that in addition to entering text in the control fields that you added, you can also edit the surrounding text and even delete some of the controls. This is obviously not ideal in this scenario. Fortunately, Office and VSTO provide a way to prevent the document from undesirable editing. For this, you need to show the Developer tab.

For Word 2010, click the File tab, and then click the Options button. In the Word Options dialog window, select Customize Ribbon, and then check the box next to Developer under the Main Tabs list.

When you stop debugging and return to Visual Studio, you see the Developer tab on the toolbar above the Ribbon, as shown in Figure 19-5. This provides some useful functions for Office development-related tasks.

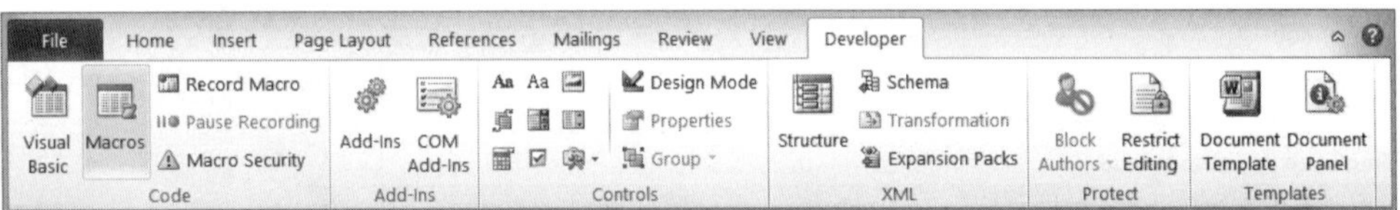

FIGURE 19-5

To prevent the document from being edited, you must perform a couple steps. First, ensure that the Designer is open and then press Ctrl+A to select everything in the document (text and controls). On the Developer tab click Group ⇨ Group. This allows you to treat everything on the document as a single entity and easily apply properties to all elements in one step.

With this new group selected, open the Properties window and set the `LockContentControl` property to `True`. Now when you run the project, you'll find that the standard text on the document cannot be edited or deleted, and you can only input data into the content controls that you have added.

Adding an Actions Pane

The final customization you'll add to this document is an Actions Pane window. An Actions Pane is typically docked to one side of a window in Word and can be used to display related information or provide access to additional information. For example, on an employee leave request form, you could add an Actions Pane that retrieves and displays the current employees' available leave balance.

> **NOTE** *An Actions Pane, or custom Task Pane in the case of application-level add-ins, is nothing more than a standard user control. In the case of an Actions Pane, Visual Studio has included an item template; under the covers, however, this does little more than add a standard user control to the project with the Office namespace imported. For application-level add-ins there is no custom Task Panes item template, so you can simply add a standard user control to the project.*

To add an Actions Pane to this document customization, right-click the project in the Solution Explorer, and select Add ➪ New Item. Select Actions Pane Control, provide it with a meaningful name, and click Add. The Actions Pane opens in a new designer window. You are simply going to add a button that retrieves the username of the current user and adds it to the document. Drag a button control onto the form and rename it `btnGetName`. Then double-click the control to register an event handler, and change the code for the button click event to the following:

C#

```
private void btnGetName_Click(object sender, EventArgs e)
{
    var myIdent = System.Security.Principal.WindowsIdentity.GetCurrent();
    Globals.ThisDocument.txtEmpName.Text = myIdent.Name;
}
```

VB

```
Private Sub btnGetName_Click(ByVal sender As System.Object, _
                             ByVal e As System.EventArgs) _
                             Handles btnGetName.Click
   Dim myIdent = System.Security.Principal.WindowsIdentity.GetCurrent()
   Globals.ThisDocument.txtEmpName.Text = myIdent.Name
End Sub
```

The Actions Pane components are not added automatically to the document because you may want to show different Actions Panes, depending on the context users find themselves in when editing the document. However, if you have a single Actions Pane component and simply want to add it immediately when the document is opened, add the component to the `ActionsPane.Controls` collection of the document at startup, as demonstrated in the following code:

C#

```
private void ThisDocument_Startup(object sender, System.EventArgs e)
{
    this.ActionsPane.Controls.Add(new NameOfActionsPaneControl());
}
```

VB

```
Private Sub ThisDocument_Startup() Handles Me.Startup
    Me.ActionsPane.Controls.Add(new NameOfActionsPaneControl())
End Sub
```

For application-level add-ins, add the user control to the `CustomTaskPanes` collection.

The next time you run the project, it will display the document in Word with the Actions Pane window shown during startup, as shown in Figure 19-6.

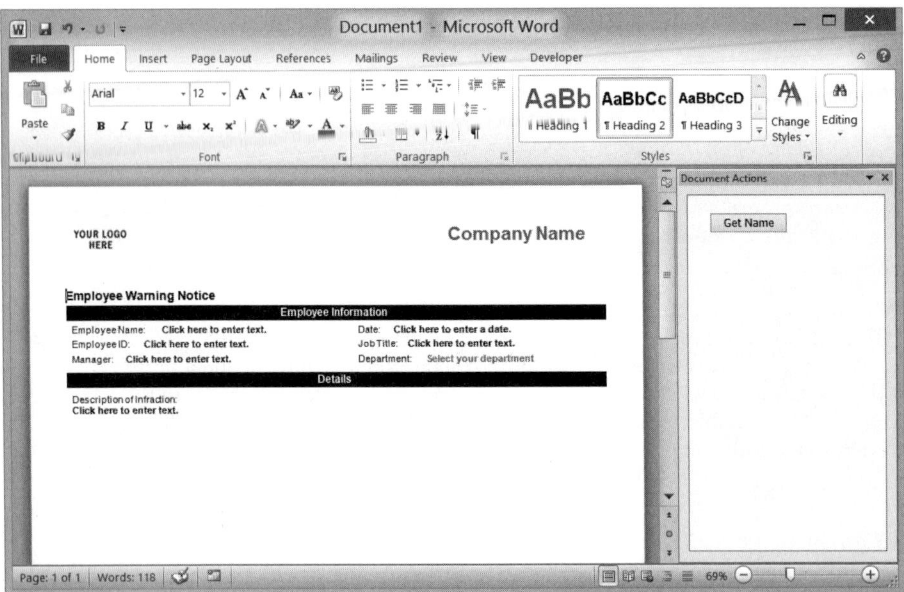

FIGURE 19-6

CREATING AN APPLICATION ADD-IN

This section walks through the creation of an add-in to Microsoft Outlook 2010. This demonstrates how to create an application-level add-in that includes a custom Outlook form region for a Contact item.

> **WARNING** *Never develop Outlook add-ins using your production e-mail account! There's too much risk that you will accidentally do something that you will regret later, such as deleting all the e-mail in your Inbox. With Outlook, you can create a separate mail profile: one for your normal mailbox and one for your test mailbox.*

Some Outlook Concepts

Before creating an Outlook add-in, it is worth understanding some basic concepts that are specific to Outlook development. Though there is a reasonable degree of overlap, Outlook has always had a slightly different programming model from the rest of the products in the Office suite.

The Outlook object model is a heavily collection-based API. The `Application` class is the highest-level class and represents the Outlook application. This can be directly accessed from code as a property of the add-in: `this.Application` in C# or `Me.Application` in Visual Basic. With the `Application` class, you can access classes that represent the *Explorer* and *Inspector* windows.

An Explorer window in Outlook is the main window displayed when Outlook is first opened and displays the contents of a folder, such as the Inbox or Calendar. Figure 19-7 (left) shows the Calendar in the Explorer window. The `Explorer` class represents this window and includes properties, methods, and events that you can use to access the window and respond to actions.

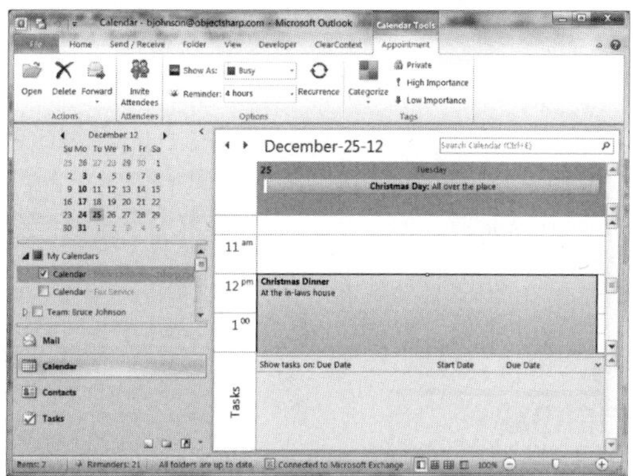

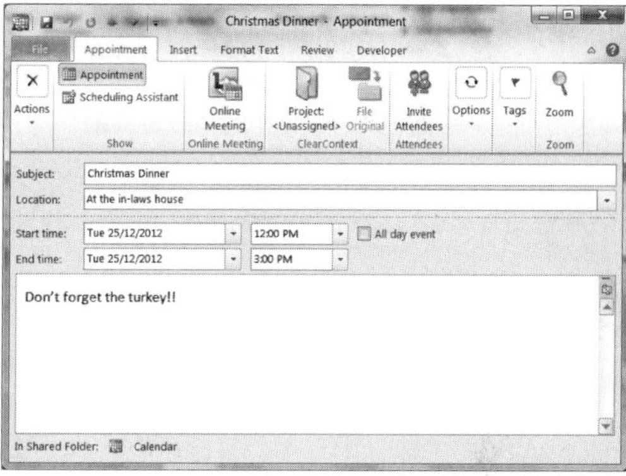

FIGURE 19-7

An Inspector window displays an individual item such as an e-mail message, contact, or appointment. Figure 19-7 (right) shows an Inspector window displaying an appointment item. The `Inspector` class includes properties and methods to access the window, and events that can be handled when certain actions occur within the window. Outlook form regions are hosted within Inspector windows.

The `Application` class also contains a `Session` object, which represents everything to do with the current Outlook session. This object provides you with access to the available address lists, mail stores, folders, items, and other Outlook objects. A mail folder, such as the Inbox or Calendar, is represented by a `MAPIFolder` class and contains a collection of items. Within Outlook, every item has a message class property that determines how it is presented within the application. For example, an e-mail message has a message class of `IPM.Note`, and an appointment has a message class of `IPM.Appointment`.

Creating an Outlook Form Region

Now that you understand the basics of the Outlook object model, you can create your first Outlook add-in. In Visual Studio 2012, select File ➪ New ➪ Project. Filter the project types by selecting Visual C# followed by Office, and then choose a new Outlook 2010 Add-in project.

Unlike a document-level customization, an application-level add-in is inherently code-based. In the case of a Word or Excel add-in, there may not even be a document open when the application is first launched. An Outlook add-in follows a similar philosophy; when you first create an Outlook add-in project, it consists of a single nonvisual class called `ThisAddIn.cs` (or `ThisAddIn.vb`). You can add code here that performs some actions during startup or shutdown.

To customize the actual user interface of Outlook, you can add an Outlook form region. This is a user control hosted in an Outlook Inspector window when an item of a certain message class is displayed.

To add a new Outlook form region, right-click the project in the Solution Explorer, and select Add ➪ New Item. From the list of available items, select Outlook Form Region, provide it with a meaningful name, and click Add. Visual Studio then opens the New Outlook Form Region Wizard that can obtain some basic properties needed to create the new item.

The first step of the wizard asks you to either design a new form or import an Outlook Form Storage (`.ofs`) file, which is a form designed in Outlook. Select Design a New Form Region, and click Next.

The second step in the wizard enables you to select what type of form region to create. The wizard provides a handy visual representation of each type of form region, as shown in Figure 19-8. Select the Separate option and click Next.

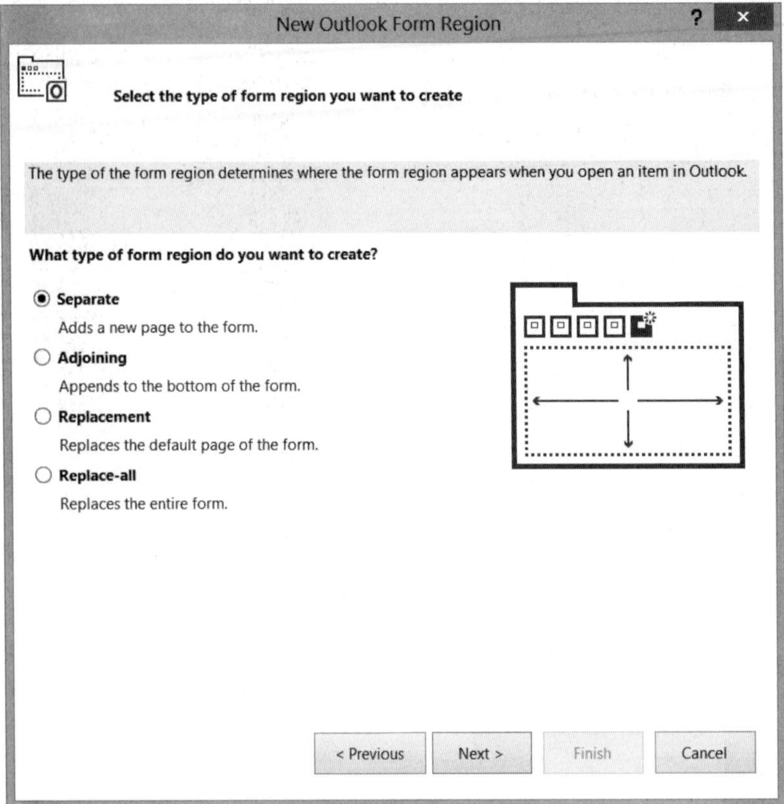

FIGURE 19-8

The next step in the wizard allows you to enter a friendly name for the form region, and, depending on the type of form region you've chosen, a title and description. This step also allows you to choose the display mode for the form region. *Compose mode* displays when an item is first created, such as when you create a new e-mail message. *Read mode* displays when you subsequently open an e-mail message that has already been sent or received. Ensure that both of these check boxes are ticked, enter Custom Details as the name, and click Next.

The final step in the wizard enables you to choose what message classes display the form region. You can select from any of the standard message classes, such as mail message or appointment, or specify a custom message class. Select the Contact message class, as shown in Figure 19-9, and click Finish to close the wizard.

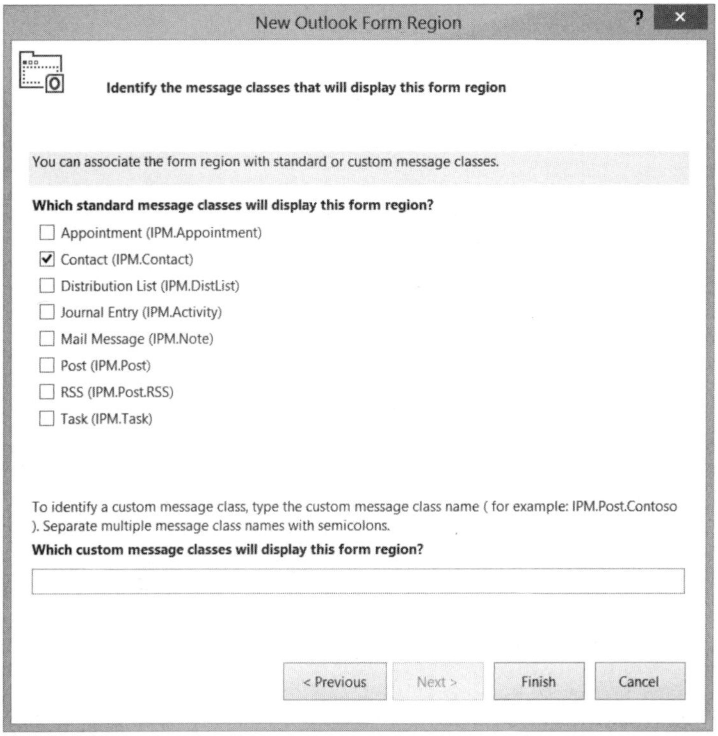

New Outlook Form Region

Identify the message classes that will display this form region

You can associate the form region with standard or custom message classes.

Which standard message classes will display this form region?

- [ ] Appointment (IPM.Appointment)
- [x] Contact (IPM.Contact)
- [ ] Distribution List (IPM.DistList)
- [ ] Journal Entry (IPM.Activity)
- [ ] Mail Message (IPM.Note)
- [ ] Post (IPM.Post)
- [ ] RSS (IPM.Post.RSS)
- [ ] Task (IPM.Task)

To identify a custom message class, type the custom message class name (for example: IPM.Post.Contoso). Separate multiple message class names with semicolons.

Which custom message classes will display this form region?

< Previous | Next > | Finish | Cancel

FIGURE 19-9

After the wizard exits, the new form region is created and opened in the Designer. As mentioned earlier, an Outlook form region, like an Actions Pane and a Task Pane, is simply a user control. However, unlike an Actions Pane, it contains an embedded manifest that defines how the form region appears in Outlook. To access the manifest, ensure that the form is selected in the Designer, and open the Properties window. This shows a property called `Manifest`, under which you can set various properties to how it appears. This property can also be accessed through code at run time.

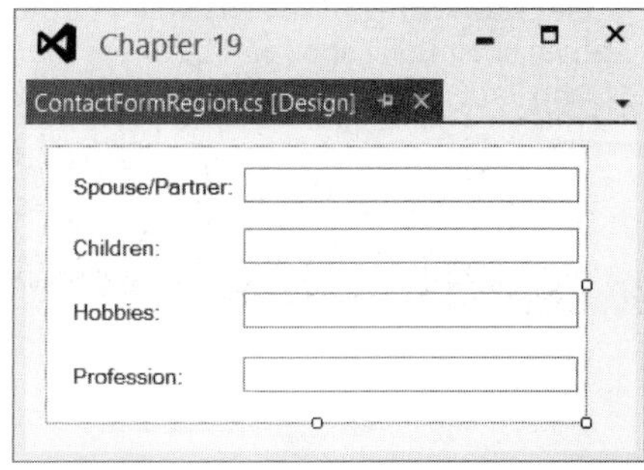

FIGURE 19-10

In this scenario you'll use the Outlook form region to display some additional useful information about a Contact. The layout of an Outlook form region is created in the same way as any other user control. Drag four Label controls and four TextBox controls onto the design surface and align them, as shown in Figure 19-10. Rename the textbox controls `txtPartner`, `txtChildren`, `txtHobbies`, and `txtProfession`, and change the text on the labels to match these fields.

The `ContactItem` class contains a surprisingly large number of properties that are not obviously displayed in a standard Contact form in Outlook. In fact, with more than 100 contact-specific fields, there is a high chance that any custom property you want to display for a contact is already defined. In this case, the fields displayed on this form (Spouse/Partner, Children, Hobbies, and Profession) are available as existing properties. You can also store a custom property on the item by adding an item to the `UserProperties` collection.

The code behind the form region already has stubs for the `FormRegionShowing` and `FormRegionClosed` event handlers. Add code to those methods to access the current Contact item, and retrieve and save these custom properties. They should look similar to the following (taking into consideration the name that you gave the form):

C#

```
private void CustomFormRegion_FormRegionShowing(object sender, System.EventArgs e)
{
    var myContact = (Outlook.ContactItem)this.OutlookItem;
    this.txtPartner.Text = myContact.Spouse;
    this.txtChildren.Text = myContact.Children;
    this.txtHobbies.Text = myContact.Hobby;
    this.txtProfession.Text = myContact.Profession;
}
private void CustomFormRegion_FormRegionClosed(object sender, System.EventArgs e)
{
    var myContact = (Outlook.ContactItem)this.OutlookItem;
    myContact.Spouse = this.txtPartner.Text;
    myContact.Children = this.txtChildren.Text;
    myContact.Hobby = this.txtHobbies.Text;
    myContact.Profession = this.txtProfession.Text;
}
```

VB

```
Private Sub CustomFormRegion_FormRegionShowing(ByVal sender As Object, _
                                               ByVal e As System.EventArgs) _
                                               Handles MyBase.FormRegionShowing
    Dim myContact = CType(Me.OutlookItem, Outlook.ContactItem)
    myContact.Spouse = Me.txtPartner.Text
    myContact.Children = Me.txtChildren.Text
    myContact.Hobby = Me.txtHobbies.Text
    myContact.Profession = Me.txtProfession.Text
End Sub
Private Sub CustomFormRegion_FormRegionClosed(ByVal sender As Object, _
                                              ByVal e As System.EventArgs) _
                                              Handles MyBase.FormRegionClosed
    Dim myContact = CType(Me.OutlookItem, Outlook.ContactItem)
    myContact.Spouse = Me.txtPartner.Text
    myContact.Children = Me.txtChildren.Text
    myContact.Hobby = Me.txtHobbies.Text
    myContact.Profession = Me.txtProfession.Text
End Sub
```

Press F5 to build and run the add-in in Debug mode. If the solution compiled correctly, Outlook opens with your add-in registered. Open the Contacts folder and create a new Contact item. To view your custom Outlook form region, click the Custom Details button in the Show tab group of the Office Ribbon. Figure 19-11 shows how the Outlook form region should appear in the Contact Inspector window.

FIGURE 19-11

DEBUGGING OFFICE APPLICATIONS

You can debug Office applications by using much the same process as you would with any other Windows application. All the standard Visual Studio debugger features, such as the ability to insert breakpoints and watch variables, are available when debugging Office applications.

The VSTO run time, which is responsible for loading add-ins into their host applications, can display any errors that occur during startup in a message box or write them to a log file. By default, these options are disabled, and they can be enabled through environment variables.

To display any errors in a message box, create an environment variable called `VSTO_SUPPRESSDISPLAYALERTS` and assign it a value of 0. Setting this environment variable to 1, or deleting it altogether, can prevent the errors from displaying.

To write the errors to a log file, create an environment variable called `VSTO_LOGALERTS` and assign it a value of 1. The VSTO run time creates a log file called `<manifestname>.manifest.log` in the same folder as the application manifest. Setting the environment variable to 0, or deleting it altogether, stops errors from being logged.

Unregistering an Add-in

When an application-level add-in is compiled in Visual Studio 2012, it automatically registers the add-in to the host application. Visual Studio does not automatically unregister the add-in from your application unless you run Build ⇨ Clean Solution. Therefore, you may find your add-in will continue to be loaded every time you launch the application. Rather than reopen the solution in Visual Studio, you can unregister the add-in directly from Office.

To unregister the application, you need to open the Add-Ins window. Under Outlook 2010, select File ⇨ Options ⇨ Add-Ins to bring up the window shown in Figure 19-12. For all the other Microsoft Office applications, open the File or Office menu, and click the Options button on the bottom of the menu screen.

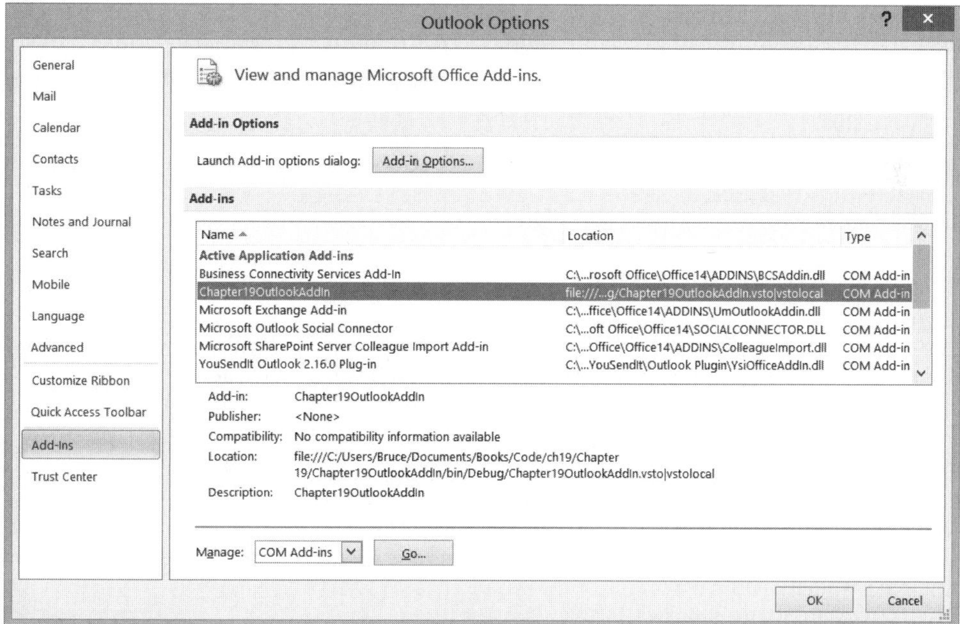

FIGURE 19-12

If it is registered and loaded, your application will be listed under the Active Application Add-ins list. Select COM Add-Ins from the drop-down list at the bottom of the window, and click the Go button. This brings up the COM Add-Ins window, as shown in Figure 19-13, which enables you to remove your add-in from the application.

You can also disable your add-in by clearing the checkbox next to the add-in name in this window.

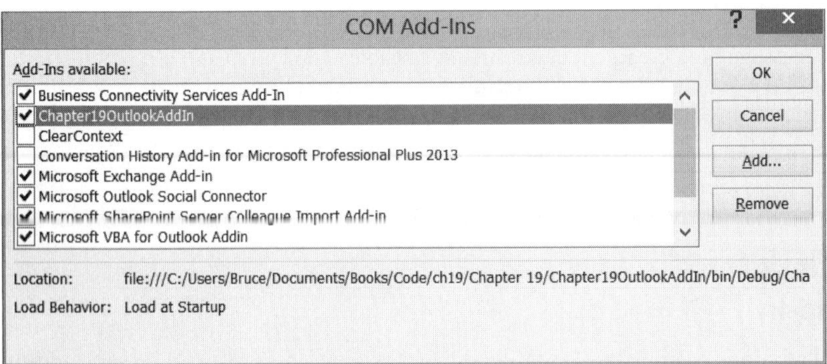

FIGURE 19-13

Disabled Add-ins

When developing Office applications, you will inevitably do something that will generate an unhandled exception and cause your add-in to crash. If your add-in happens to crash when it is being loaded, the Office application will disable it. This is called *soft disabling.*

A soft-disabled add-in will not be loaded and will appear in the Trust Center under the Inactive Application Add-ins list. Visual Studio 2012 automatically re-enables a soft-disabled add-in when it is recompiled. You can also use the COM Add-Ins window (refer to Figure 19-13) to re-enable the add-in by ticking the check box next to the add-in name.

An add-in will be flagged to be *hard disabled* when it causes the host application to crash, or when you stop the debugger, while the constructor or the Startup event handler is executing. The next time the Office application is launched, you will be presented with a dialog box similar to the one shown in Figure 19-14. If you select Yes the add-in will be hard disabled.

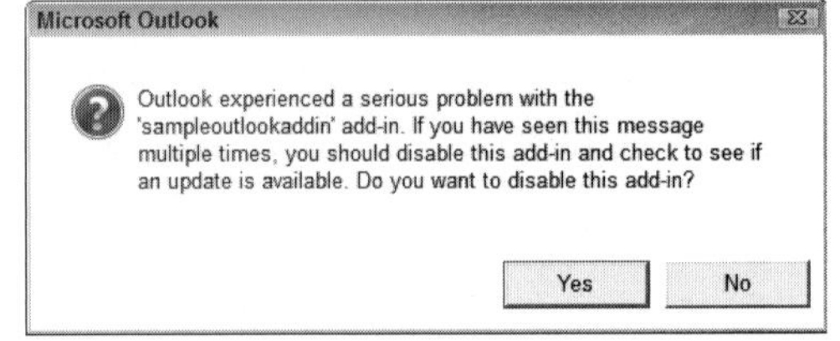

FIGURE 19-14

When an add-in is hard disabled it cannot be re-enabled from Visual Studio. If you attempt to debug a hard-disabled add-in, you will be presented with a warning message that the add-in has been added to the Disabled Items list and will not be loaded.

To remove the application from the Disabled Items list, start the Office application, and open the Add-Ins window (File ➪ Options ➪ Add-ins from Outlook 2010). Select Disabled Items from the drop-down list at the bottom of the window, and click the Go button. This displays the Disabled Items window, as shown in Figure 19-15. Select your add-in and click Enable to remove it from this list. You must restart the application for this to take effect.

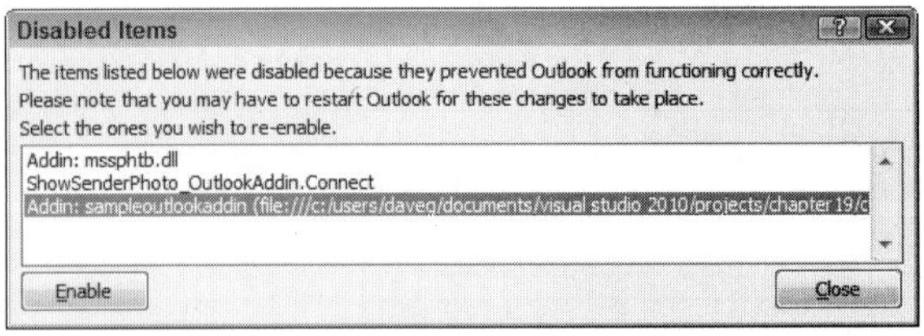

FIGURE 19-15

DEPLOYING OFFICE APPLICATIONS

The two main ways to deploy Office applications are either using a traditional MSI setup project or using the support for ClickOnce deployment that is built into Visual Studio 2012.

In earlier versions of VSTO, configuring code access security was a manual process. Although VSTO hides much of the implementation details from you, in the background it still needs to invoke COM+ code to communicate with Office. Because the Common Language Runtime (CLR) cannot enforce code access security for nonmanaged code, the CLR requires any applications that invoke COM+ components to have full trust to execute.

Fortunately, the ClickOnce support for Office applications that is built into Visual Studio 2012 automatically deploys with full trust. As with other ClickOnce applications, each time it is invoked, it automatically checks for updates.

When an Office application is deployed, it must be packaged with the required prerequisites. For Office applications, the following prerequisites are required:

- Windows Installer 3.1
- .NET Framework 4.5, .NET Framework 4, .NET Framework 4 Client Profile, or .NET Framework 3.5
- Visual Studio 2012 Tools for Office run time

If you use version 3.5 of the .NET Framework, you also need to package the Microsoft Office primary interop assemblies (PIAs). A PIA is an assembly that contains type definitions of types implemented with COM. The PIAs for Office 2010 are shipped with Visual Studio Tools for Office and are automatically included as references when the project is created. In Figure 19-16 (left), you can see a reference to `Microsoft.Office.Interop.Outlook`, which is the PIA for Outlook 2010.

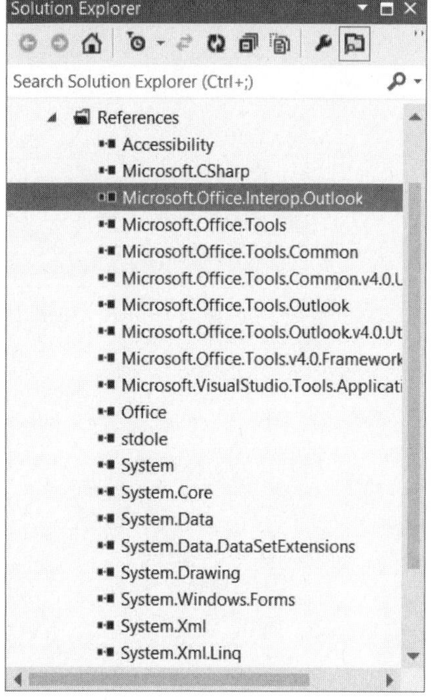

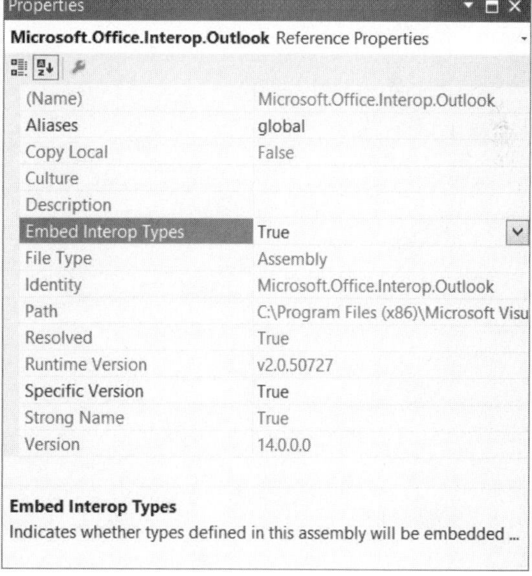

FIGURE 19-16

You do not need to deploy the PIAs with your application if you use .NET Framework 4 or higher because of a feature called Type Equivalence. When *Type Equivalence* is enabled, Visual Studio embeds the referenced PIA as a new namespace within the target assembly. CLR then ensures that these types are considered equivalent when the application is executed.

Type Equivalence is enabled for individual references by setting the Embed Interop Types property to True, as shown in Figure 19-16 (right). Rather than include the entire interop assembly, Visual Studio embeds only those portions of the interop assemblies that an application actually uses. This results in smaller and simpler deployment packages.

More information on ClickOnce and MSI setup projects is available in Chapter 49, "Packaging and Deployment."

SUMMARY

This chapter introduced you to the major features in Visual Studio Tools for Office. It is easy to build feature-rich applications using Microsoft Office applications because the development tools are fully integrated into Visual Studio 2012. You can create .NET solutions that customize the appearance of the Office user interface with your own components at both the application level and the document level. This enables you to have unprecedented control over how end users interact with all the products in the Microsoft Office suite.

20

Windows Store Applications

WHAT'S IN THIS CHAPTER?

- The major characteristics and considerations of a Windows Store application
- The Windows Store project templates
- How to use the Windows Store Simulator to test your application
- The basic structure of a data-bound Windows Store application

If you have been paying attention to the Windows development world in the last few years, you would be hard pressed to avoid the topic of Windows Store applications. After making its debut in Windows Phone 7 (when it was still code-named Metro), the Windows Store has become the focal point of the design sensibilities in Microsoft. When Windows 8 was introduced to the world, lo and behold the Windows Store took center stage.

But what exactly is the Windows Store? And, more important, what tools and techniques are available in Visual Studio 2012 to enable you to create Windows Store applications? In this chapter you'll learn the basic components of Windows Store applications, as well as how to create them and debug them using Visual Studio 2012.

WHAT IS A WINDOWS STORE APPLICATION?

When you look at Windows Phone 7 or Windows 8, the first visual impression is given by the Windows Store. And this impression is consistency and elegance. The navigation paradigms are intuitive. The applications (see Figure 20-1) fill the entire screen, providing an immersive experience for the user. The chrome that has surrounding applications since Windows 3.0 is gone, leaving nothing in the way of the user. All that is left is the app.

FIGURE 20-1

But there is more to the Windows Store than just the look and feel. Windows Store applications have the capability to work together, integrating tightly with search functionality. Contracts supported by Windows Store applications allow for the sending of content between otherwise independent applications, staying up to date (while connected to the Internet), and having that data reflected immediately on the screen.

From a technology perspective, developers can create Windows Store applications using languages with which they are already familiar. This includes Visual Basic and C#, as well as JavaScript and C++. But before getting into the technical side, look at the traits that make up the Windows Store:

- Surfacing the content
- Snapping
- Scaling
- Semantic zoom
- Contracts
- Tiles
- Embracing the cloud

Content Before Chrome

The purpose of your application is to surface content. It doesn't matter if that information is an RSS feed, pictures coming from your camera, or data retrieved from your corporate database, what the user cares about is the content. So when you design a Windows Store application, focus needs to be placed on surfacing the content.

One way to accomplish this is to use layout to improve readability. This typically involves leaving breathing space between the visual elements. Use typography to create the sense of hierarchy instead of the typical tree view commonly found in non-Windows Store applications. In general, this is done by arranging the visual elements into a graduated series. It takes advantage of how the human mind organizes things. When you look at a screen, you generally notice the big and bold things first. As a result, the most important visual elements in your design should also be the biggest and boldest. You also mentally group elements together if they are visually segregated from other elements. So if you want to create a two-level hierarchy, you can create a number of large areas spaced to be obviously independent. Then within the large area, you can place smaller areas. And if you want, you can add more levels by embedding additional elements in the already existing areas.

Snap and Scale

The Windows Store is designed to be used in a number of different configurations. The desktop or laptop configuration that you're used to is fine. But it is instructive to consider how your application can appear in other form factors. For example, the Windows Store is going to be available on a number of tablet devices, including the Surface. While running on a tablet, your application is going to be moved from landscape to portrait and back again. Although not every application needs to be this flexible (games, for example, are typically oriented in one direction), many can benefit from flowing between the different orientations.

Along with orientation, you also need to consider screen resolution. One of the benefits of Windows 8 is that the low end of screen resolution is now 1024 x 768, so you have no more concerns about needing to support 800 x 640. However, there is still a decent range of resolutions that you need to consider: Two displays with the same resolution may not have the same pixel density (that is, pixels/cm^2).

Even more important is how the user interface works at lower resolutions. Windows 8 is designed for touch. On low-resolution screens, you need to ensure that your touchable controls are still easily touchable — that is to say, not too small and not too close to other controls.

One further consideration is the Snap mode. In this mode, the Windows Store application is placed (snapped) to the left side of the display. While in this mode, the application still runs. (And the user can receive input, see messages, and so on.) However, in the rest of the screen, a separate application can run, which is conceptually not complicated, but your application must take advantage of this mode to participate well with the Windows 8 ecosystem.

Semantic Zoom

One of the common gestures in a touch interface is called the pinch. You use your thumb and forefinger to make a pinching motion on the screen to shrink the interface viewed. The opposite gesture (pushing your thumb and forefinger out) causes the interface to grow in size. If you have operated most smartphones, you're probably quite comfortable with the gesture and the expected outcome.

When your interface shows a large amount of data, even if it is pictorial, you can use this gesture to implement a semantic zoom. Conceptually, this is like a drill down into a report. Start at a high level of the information displayed. Then as you pinch, the more detailed view of the information displays. To be fair, it is not necessary that there be a more/less detailed relationship between the two views — only that there is a semantic relationship. Although more or less details certainly fits into this category, so too would a list of locations in a city and a map showing them as pushpins.

Contracts

As you swipe in from the right of a Windows 8 display, a collection of Charms appears. By using these Charms, you can access commonly available functionality (settings and search are two that fit this category) through a standard mechanism. However, to take advantage of this, your application needs to implement the right contract.

When you start to create Windows Store applications, you'll probably notice that there is a greater dependence on interfaces that would be found in a typical Windows Forms application. The many interfaces provide a great deal of flexibility for creating and testing applications. And they also enable Charms to do their job. If you want to have a search within your application, implement the interface that the Search Charm expects. If you need to display settings for your applications, implement the interface that the Settings Charm expects. By doing so you not only create an application that integrates seamlessly with Windows 8, but also one that is intuitive for your users to use.

Tiles

Although it might seem trite, even in the world of applications, first impressions are important. And when you create a Windows Store application, the first impression that a user gets comes from your tile. Your tile is the doorway through which users access your app. Spend the time to make sure that it is nicely designed. As much as you can in the space allowed, make your tile attractive and loveable.

But beyond simple appearance, the tiles in Windows 8 and Windows Phone are alive. When pinned to the main menu, your tile can provide information to the user before they go through the front door. For some applications, this is critical. Would you want to need to open a weather application to see what the current temperature is? So think about the information that your application provides to your users, and decide if some of the more useful data can be put into a more immediately accessible location: your tile.

Embrace the Cloud

It is understandable if you are tired of hearing about the cloud. It has been at the forefront of many marketing pushes and sales pitches for a couple of years. And, at the time, it's fairly safe to say that the hype got ahead of the reality. But that was then and this is now. Now, the cloud is right at the edge of becoming significant in how users interact with both their application and their data.

Specifically, look at some of the demonstrations of new technology. One of the key selling points is the ubiquitous nature of the data. Start watching a video on Xbox, pause it, and then launch the video on your desktop. It remembers the place you were at when you paused and continues the video from that point. Create a document on your Surface tablet while on the commute home. Save the document, and then when you get home, launch your laptop, and your document is there, ready to be used. It even remembers where in the document you were at.

All this functionality is made possible by using the cloud as your backing storage. Windows Store applications interact well with Windows Azure. Make sure you take advantage of this as you consider the different storage modes and locations that your application might find useful.

CREATING A WINDOWS STORE APPLICATION

It is a good idea to create your Windows Store application using a language with which you are already familiar. Fortunately, you can write Windows Store apps in most .NET languages including Visual Basic and C#. Also, Visual Studio provides the ability to create Windows Store applications using HTML and JavaScript.

That last combination is aimed at making it easy for web developers to create Windows Store apps. The form of JavaScript used to create Windows Store apps is known as WinJS. This form is syntactically the same as regular JavaScript, but it uses the WinRT libraries to perform its tasks. This requirement has the unfortunate side effect of making Windows Store applications incompatible with browsers.

To create your Windows Store application, start by creating a new Project. Use the File ➪ New ➪ Project menu option to launch the New Project dialog. In the Installed Templates selection, under the language of your choice, you'll see a section named Windows Store (see Figure 20-2).

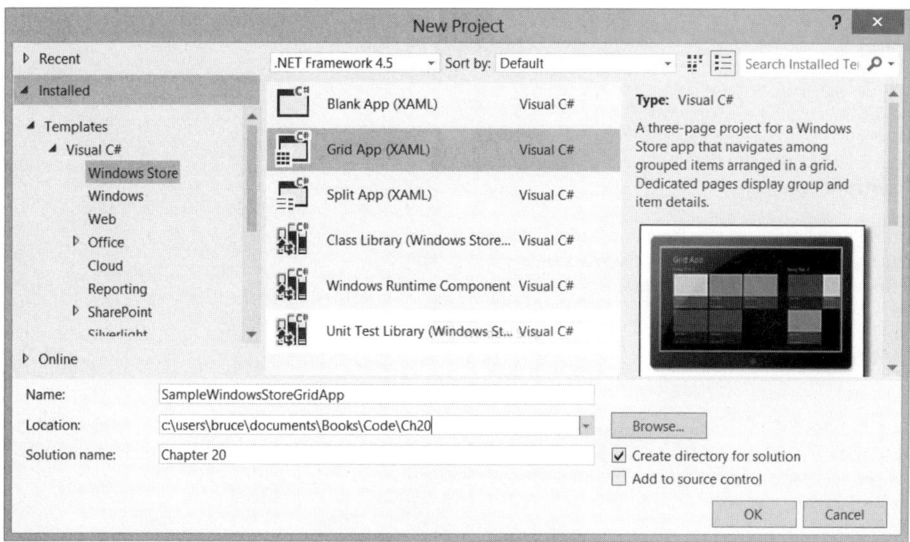

FIGURE 20-2

There are six different Windows Store project templates available to you. The Class Library and Windows Runtime Component create assemblies used by Windows Store applications. The Unit Test Library template creates a project that can unit test Windows Store libraries. The remaining three templates, Blank, Grid, and Split, are the ones that have more bearing on how your Windows Store application functions.

The Grid template navigates through multiple layers of content. As you move from one layer to the other, the details of a particular layer are contained within each page. The Split template navigates between groups of items. It is a two-page template where the first page contains the groups, while the second contains the items contained within the group. The Blank template contains a single page with no predefined navigation.

As you might expect, your choice of application template depends greatly on the type and relationship that exists within the content that you want to display. It is difficult to make generalizations (such as saying that a Line of Business application always uses a Grid template) because of this fact. Only you can identify the content and context, and the same set of data can be effectively displayed using either a Grid or a Split template. So it's best to try the templates before you commit to one or the other for a significant application.

> **NOTE** *To develop Windows Store applications, there are two requirements that must be met. First, you need to make sure that .NET Framework 4.5 is the targeted framework. Second, you need to run Windows 8. It is not possible (as of this writing) to create Windows Store applications unless you run Visual Studio in Windows 8.*

A Grid template is used for the sample Windows Store application. So select the Grid App on the New Project dialog, and click OK. This begins the process of creating a Windows Store project, starting with retrieving a Developer License.

One of the differences with Windows Store applications created within Visual Studio is that you need to have a Developer License to actually do so. This license is easily obtained, but it does require that you have a Microsoft Account to do so. If you have not already received your Windows 8 developer license, you will be prompted to do so during project creation. Also, the developer license is only good for a month, so if you have not renewed the license within that period, you will also be prompted. The renewal prompt is shown in Figure 20-3.

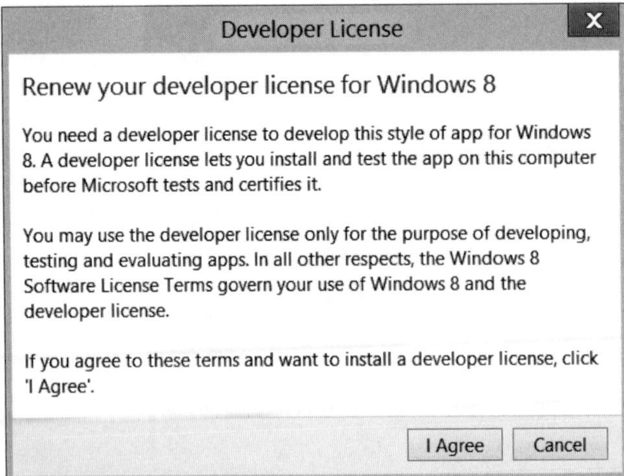

FIGURE 20-3

After your license has been validated, the project can be created normally. As with most other project templates, a number of files are created, as shown in Figure 20-4.

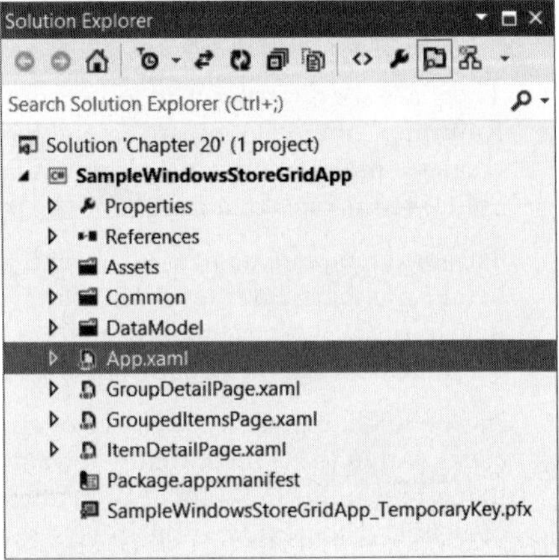

FIGURE 20-4

The starting point for the application is the GroupedItemsPage. You can see this if you examine the code behind for the App.xaml file. This page displays the top-level groups that are part of the application's data model. And you might notice that in Figure 20-4 there is a DataModel folder. If you examine the contents, you'll see that the project template has a sample data source used as the starting point for the application. The advantage of this sample data is that the application can be run immediately upon creation. The files included in the project template are:

- **App.xaml:** Contains the resources (or links to other resource dictionary files) used by the application. Here you can find fonts, brushes, control styles, control templates, and the application name.
- **CollectionSummaryPage.xaml:** Displays the details/summary of a collection.
- **GroupDetailPage.xaml:** Displays the details of a particular group.
- **GroupedItemsPage.xaml:** Displays the collection that is at the top level of the data model object.
- **ItemDetailPage.xaml:** Displays the details of a particular item.
- **Package.appxmanifest:** Defines the attributes of the application that will display in the marketplace.
- ***appname*_TemporaryKey.pfx:** The key pair used to provide hashing or encryption for your application.

Along with the files, the Grid project template contains a number of folders, which contain some additional elements for your application. The DataModel folder contains the classes that implement the group/item hierarchy. The Assets folder contains images that are part of the application. The Common folder is where you can find code not related to the pages. In the template, this includes code to support data binding, a couple of value converters, and the styles used by the application.

But before running the application, a couple of options are available. You are probably (by now) familiar with the Run button that appears on the Visual Studio toolbar. The Windows Store applications are no different; however, the options available to you do vary slightly.

The Windows 8 Simulator

To the right of the Run button, there is a caption that reads Local Machine (see Figure 20-5). With this setting, if you run the Windows Store application, it is deployed onto the local machine. From a debugging perspective, this is just fine. All the Visual Studio debugging functionality is available for you to use in this mode. However, depending on the machine on which you work, using the local machine might not be sufficient. If you develop on a desktop or laptop, it might be difficult to rotate your screen 90 degrees to convert from landscape to portrait mode. It also might be challenging to perform a pinch-zoom maneuver using a mouse. To accommodate this situation, Visual Studio includes a Windows 8 Simulator.

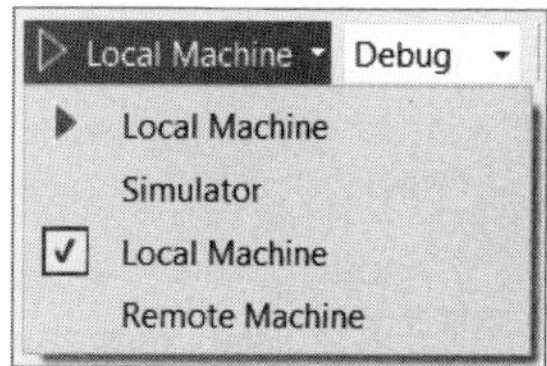

FIGURE 20-5

When you start the simulator, it appears to load your operating system. And, just to be clear, the term "appears" is appropriate in the last sentence. It does not actually load up a clean or new version of Windows 8. Instead, the simulator establishes a remote desktop connection to your Windows 8 machine. As a result, you have access to your current operating system, complete with all the background services, defaults, and customizations that you have made. When the desktop is ready to be used, your Windows Store application is deployed onto the virtual machine, resulting in a screen similar to the one in Figure 20-6.

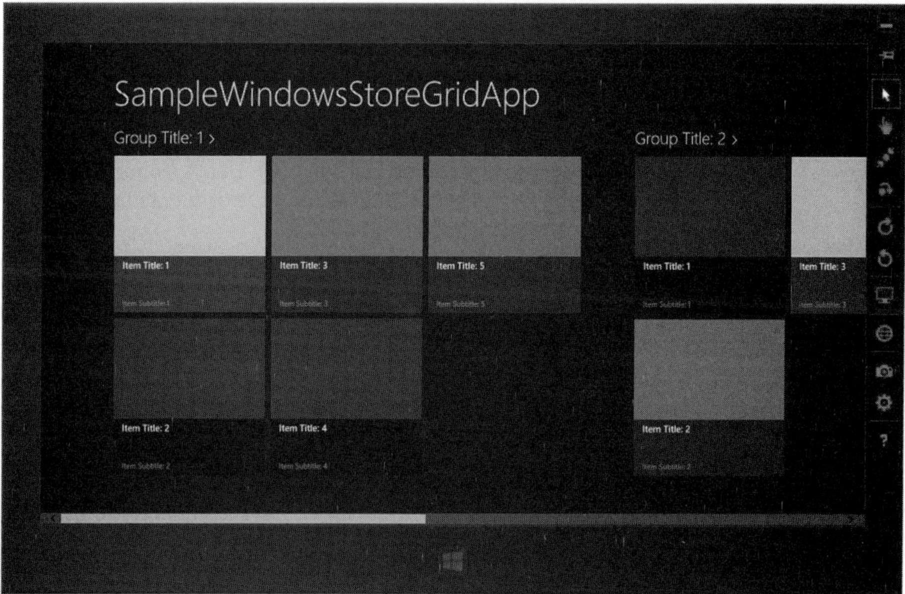

FIGURE 20-6

On the right side of the simulator, there are a number of icons. These icons enable you to act on the simulator as if it were a mobile device. Now consider some of the functionality provided through these icons, starting at the top.

The top icon on the right (the pushpin) is used to keep the simulator on top of the other windows on your computer. When pinned, the simulator will not be covered up by other applications you might have running. When unpinned, the simulator behaves as any other window. The remaining icons shown on the right side of the Simulator (as shown in Figure 20-6) are described in the following sections.

Interaction Mode

The simulator provides for two different interaction modes. This is set through the second and third icons on the right. The top icon (the arrow) sets the interaction modes to mouse gestures. The second icon (the finger) sets the interaction mode to touch gestures.

The purpose of the interaction mode is to enable you to emulate touch gestures with the use of a mouse. With mouse mode, your interactions with the simulator are what you would consider "typical." You click the mouse, and the click is picked up by the Windows Store application, which is the same for double-clicks and drags. However, when the interaction mode is set to touch, the mouse is used to generate touch interactions. For example, the mouse can be used to perform a swiping action.

Two-Finger Gestures

One of the more common touch gestures is the pinch and zoom. This is used, as an example, when performing a semantic zoom from within your application. And as you might expect, this would be a difficult gesture to emulate using just a mouse.

However, if you click the touch emulation icon (the fourth icon on the right side of Figure 20-6, which looks like two diagonal arrows pointing to a dot between them), you can use the combination of mouse button and mouse wheel to perform the zoom. Start by clicking the left mouse button at the desired location. Then rotate the mouse button backward to zoom in and forward to zoom out.

Another touch gesture requiring two fingers is the rotate. Two fingers are placed on the surface and then moved in a circular motion. In the simulator, the fifth icon (it resembles an arrow circling around a dot) is used to activate rotate mode. Using the mouse, the technique is similar to the pinch and zoom. Move the cursor over the desired location (the center point) and then use the mouse wheel the rotate left or right.

Device Characteristics

Another touch interaction that is difficult to emulate using a laptop is the orientation. If you try to spin your laptop around, it seems that the screen's orientation just won't change. But the simulator offers two icons to rotate the simulator. The icons are visually similar. (One is an arrow that circles in a clockwise direction, and the other is an arrow that circles in a counter-clockwise direction, as shown in the middle of the right side of Figure 20-6.) They rotate the simulator clockwise and counter-clockwise by 90 degrees. Along with rotating the image of the application, it also rotates the simulator.

> **NOTE** *The simulator does not respect the AutoRotationPreferences property of a project. This property can be used to lock the application so that it displays only in a particular orientation (like landscape for certain games). However, if your project has that restriction, it cannot prevent the simulator from rotating and resizing the image. If you want to test out this functionality, you need to use an actual device.*

Along with orientation, the simulator enables you to change the resolution of the virtual device. The icon looks like a square (actually like a flat-screen desktop monitor), and when clicked you are presented with a list of valid screen sizes and resolution. If you do change the resolution, it is only a simulated change. The coordinates of the points of interaction (like a touch) are converted to the coordinates that would be found if the device were the selected resolution.

Location

The last piece of simulated functionality provided by the simulator is geolocation. To be fair, it's not necessary that the location be simulated. The location can be taken from the device on which the application runs using a number of different techniques. However, unless you plan to take a trip around the world as part of your test plan, using the simulated location is a useful addition.

The starting point for a simulated location is to click the Set Location icon (the globe on the right side of Figure 20-6). Location emulation requires a number of different requirements. If you are missing any requirements, you will be prompted with a dialog box listing the issues that need to be corrected. After they have been addressed, you can see the Set Location dialog, as shown in Figure 20-7.

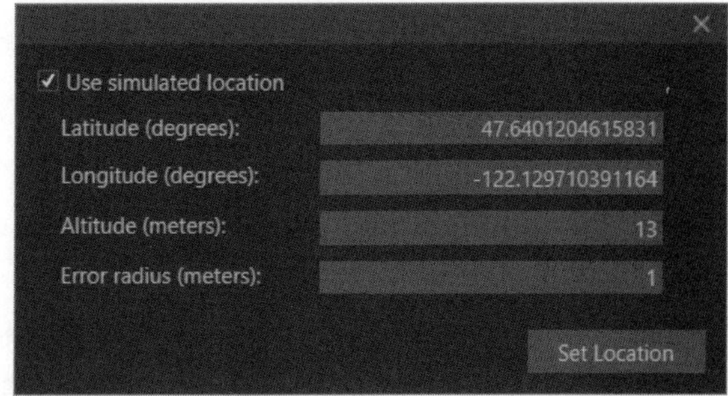

FIGURE 20-7

There are four attributes related to the dialog that can be set as part of this dialog. At the top of the dialog, you can notice a Use Simulated Location check box. If this value is unchecked, then the location information will be taken from your device (assuming that you can capture location information on your device). If the value is checked, the latitude and longitude values can be set by providing the wanted value in degrees. There is also an attribute that enables the third dimension (altitude) to be specified. Finally, the fourth attribute, error radius, is specified in meters and is used to simulate changes that occur with naturally occurring location information.

Screenshots

There are two icons related to the capturing of screenshots from within the simulator. This functionality is useful because capturing images is part of the submission process to the Windows Marketplace.

The Gear icon is used to change the settings for the screenshot. This includes whether the screenshot will be captured to both a clipboard and a file or just to the clipboard. As well, the location of the saved files can be specified.

After the settings have been set, you can capture a screenshot as required by clicking the icon (looks like a small camera on the right side of Figure 20-6). This takes the current image from within the simulator and stores it in the clipboard and file. The resolution of the image is dependent on the resolution set for the simulator, so be aware that your image might not be as crisp and clear as you'd like, depending on the resolution that has been set.

Your Windows Store Application

Now that you have looked at the simulator, use it to run the application. On the toolbar, make sure that Simulator is selected; then use the Run button. After a few moments (during which the operating system is loading), your application appears. The starting screen should resemble what you see in Figure 20-8.

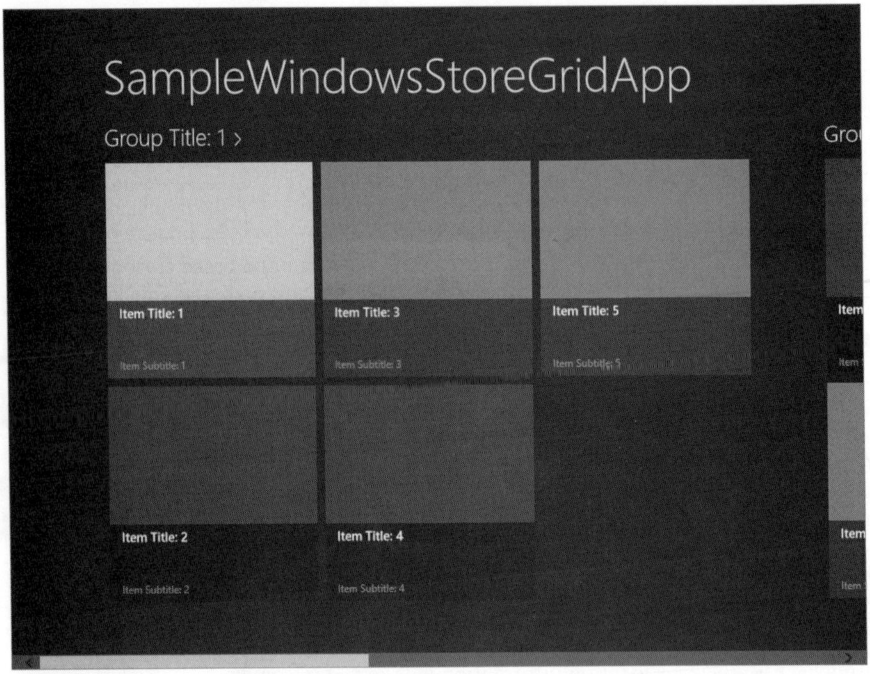

FIGURE 20-8

As you pan to the right and left, you can see the groups that have been defined in the sample data model. When you touch (or click, if you use a mouse) one of the collection names, you drill into the details of the collection (Figure 20-9). If you touch on an individual item, you are taken directly to the item detail page (Figure 20-10).

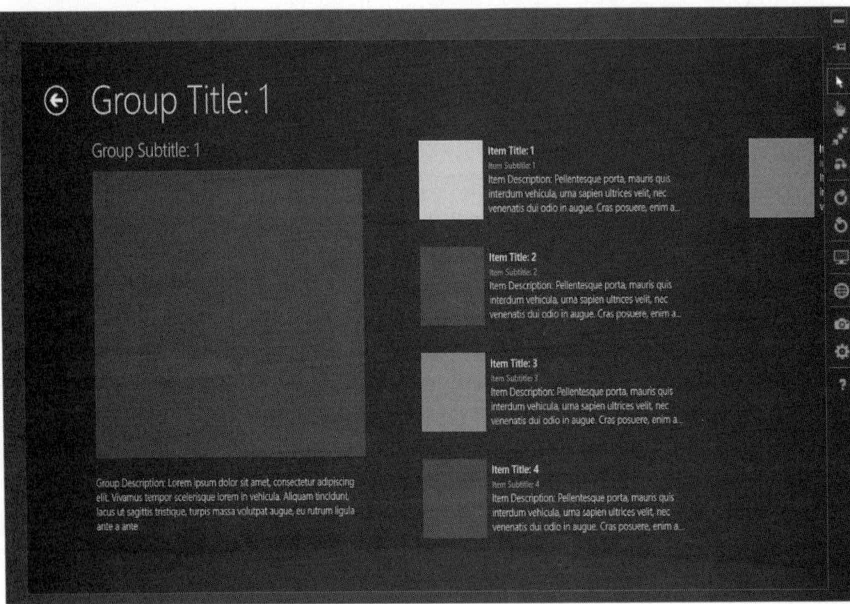

FIGURE 20-9

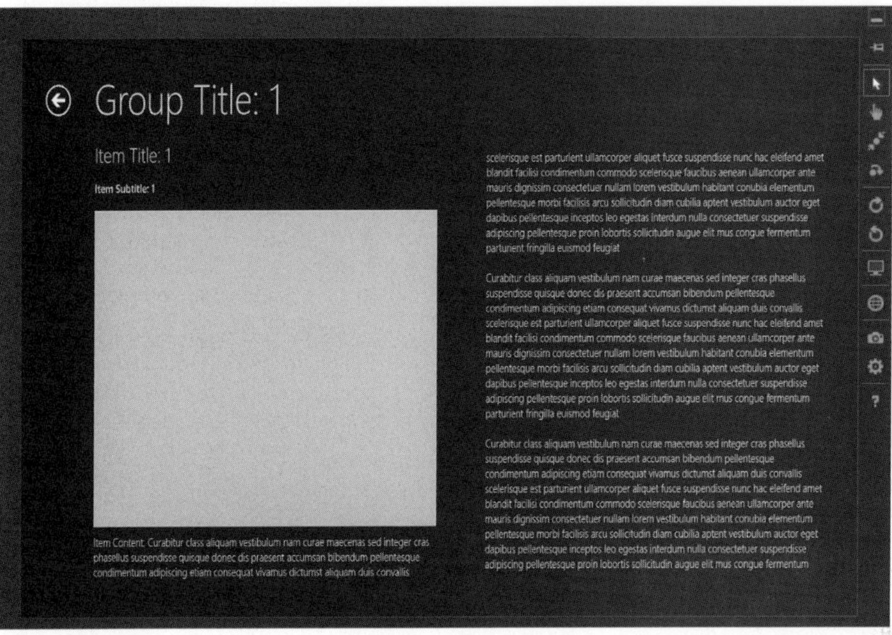

FIGURE 20-10

When you look at the collection detail page (after you touch the collection name), you can drill down to the same item detail page shown in Figure 20-10 simply by touching the wanted detail.

Finally, take a look at the application in Split mode. Touch the top of the screen and drag down to grab the application. Then drag your finger to the left, and the application snaps to the side of the screen (Figure 20-11).

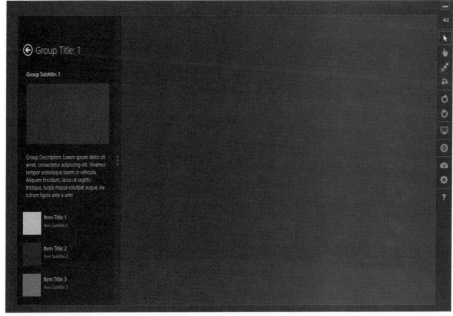

FIGURE 20-11

SUMMARY

In this chapter you learned how to create a Windows Store application using Visual Studio 2012. To start, you covered the fundamental elements of style that make up a Windows Store application. Then you looked at the components that make up the Windows Store project template. Finally, you examined the simulator, considering how you can use it to test some aspects of Windows 8 that are typically confined to a tablet or phone form factor.

PART V
Web Applications

21

ASP.NET Web Forms

WHAT'S IN THIS CHAPTER?

- The differences between Web Site and Web Application projects
- Using the HTML and CSS design tools to control the layout of your web pages
- Easily generating highly functional web applications with the server-side web controls
- Adding rich client-side interactions to your web pages with JavaScript and ASP.NET AJAX

When Microsoft released the first version of ASP.NET, one of the most talked-about features was the capability to create a full-blown web application in the same way as you would create a Windows application. The abstractions provided by ASP.NET coupled with the rich tooling support in Visual Studio allowed programmers to quickly develop feature-rich applications that ran over the web in a wholly integrated way.

ASP.NET version 2.0, which was released in 2005, was a major upgrade that included new features such as a provider model for everything from menu navigation to user authentication, more than 50 new server controls, a web portal framework, and built-in website administration, to name but a few. These enhancements made it even easier to build complex web applications in less time.

The last few versions of ASP.NET and Visual Studio have focused on improving the client-side development experience. These include enhancements to the HTML Designer and CSS editing tools; better IntelliSense and debugging support for JavaScript, HTML, and JavaScript snippets; and new project templates.

In this chapter you'll learn how to create ASP.NET Web Applications in Visual Studio 2012, as well as look at many of the features and components that Microsoft has included to make your web development life a little (and in some cases a lot) easier.

WEB APPLICATION VERSUS WEB SITE PROJECTS

With the release of Visual Studio 2005, a radically new type of project was introduced — the Web Site project. Much of the rationale behind the move to a new project type was based on the premise that websites, and web developers for that matter, are fundamentally different from other types of applications (and developers), and would therefore benefit from a different model. Although Microsoft did a good job extolling the virtues of this new project type, many developers found it difficult to work with, and clearly expressed their displeasure to Microsoft.

Fortunately, Microsoft listened to this feedback, and a short while later released a free add-on download to Visual Studio that provided support for a new Web Application project type. It was also included with Service Pack 1 of Visual Studio 2005.

The major differences between the two project types are fairly significant. The most fundamental change is that a Web Site project does not contain a Visual Studio project file (`.csproj` or `.vbproj`), whereas a Web Application project does. As a result, there is no central file that contains a list of all the files in a Web Site project. Instead, the Visual Studio solution file contains a reference to the root folder of the Web Site project, and the content and layout are directly inferred from its files and subfolders. If you copy a new file into a subfolder of a Web Site project using Windows Explorer, then that file, by definition, belongs to the project. In a Web Application project, you must explicitly add all files to the project from within Visual Studio.

The other major difference is in the way the projects are compiled. Web Application projects are compiled in much the same way as any other project under Visual Studio. The code is compiled into a single assembly that is stored in the `\bin` directory of the web application. As with all other Visual Studio projects, you can control the build through the property pages, name the output assembly, and add pre- and post-build action rules.

On the contrary, in a Web Site project all the classes that aren't code-behind-a-page or user control are compiled into one common assembly. Pages and user controls are then compiled dynamically as needed into a set of separate assemblies.

The big advantage of more granular assemblies is that the entire website does not need to be rebuilt every time a page is changed. Instead, only those assemblies that have changes (or have a down-level dependency) are recompiled, which can save a significant amount of time, depending on your preferred method of development.

Microsoft has pledged that it will continue to support both the Web Site and Web Application project types in all future versions of Visual Studio.

So which project type should you use? The official position from Microsoft is "it depends," which is certainly a pragmatic, although not particularly useful, position to take. All scenarios are different, and you should always carefully weigh each alternative in the context of your requirements and environment. However, the anecdotal evidence that has emerged from the .NET developer community over the past few years, and the experience of the authors, is that in most cases the Web Application project type is the best choice.

> **NOTE** *Unless you are developing a large web project with hundreds of pages, it is actually not too difficult to migrate from a Web Site project to a Web Application project and vice versa. So don't get too hung up on this decision. Pick one project type and migrate it later if you run into difficulties.*

CREATING WEB PROJECTS

In addition to the standard ASP.NET Web Application and Web Site projects, Visual Studio 2012 provides support and templates for several specialized web application scenarios. These include web services, WCF services, server control libraries, and reporting applications. However, before discussing these you should understand how to create the standard project types.

Creating a Web Site Project

As mentioned previously, creating a Web Site project in Visual Studio 2012 is slightly different from creating a regular Windows-type project. With normal Windows applications and services, you pick the type of project, name the solution, and click OK. Each language has its own set of project templates, and you have no real options when you create the project. Web Site project development is different because you can create the development project in different locations, from the local Filesystem to a variety of FTP and HTTP locations that are defined in your system setup, including the local Internet Information Services (IIS) server or remote FTP folders.

Because of this major difference in creating these projects, Microsoft has separated out the Web Site project templates into their own command and dialog. Selecting New Web Site from the File ➪ New submenu displays the New Web Site dialog, where you can choose the type of project template you want to use (see Figure 21-1).

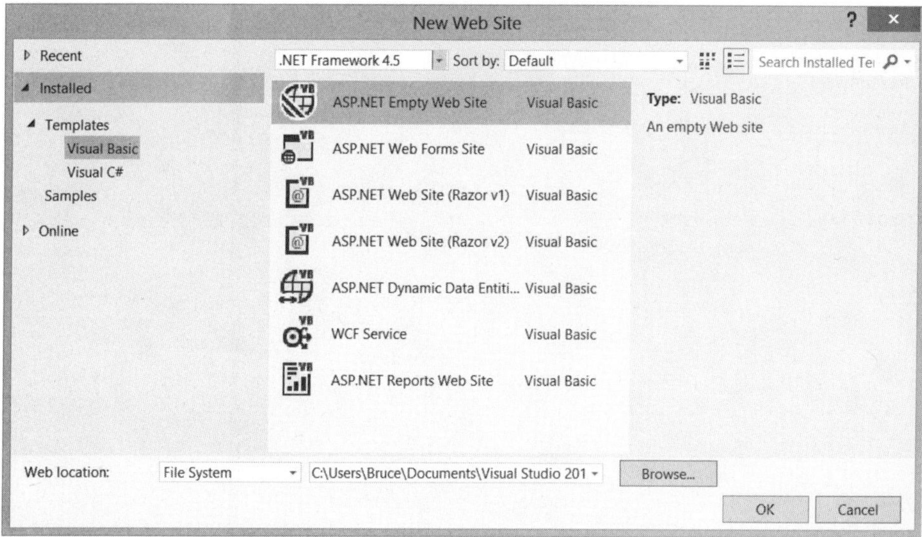

FIGURE 21-1

Most likely, you'll select the ASP.NET Web Forms Site project template. This creates a website populated with a starter web application that ensures you that your initial application is structured in a logical manner. The template creates a project that demonstrates how to use a master page, menus, the account management controls, CSS, and the jQuery JavaScript library.

In addition to the ASP.NET Web Forms Site project template, there is an ASP.NET Empty Web Site project template that creates nothing more than an empty folder and a reference in a solution file. The remaining templates, which are for the most part variations on the Web Site template, are discussed later in this chapter. Regardless of which type of web project you're creating, the lower section of the dialog enables you to choose where to create the project.

By default, Visual Studio expects you to develop the website or service locally, using the normal Filesystem. The default location is under the `My Documents/Visual Studio 2012/WebSites` folder for the current user, but you can change this by overtyping the value, selecting an alternative location from the drop-down list, or clicking the Browse button.

The Web Location drop-down list also contains HTTP and FTP as options. Selecting HTTP or FTP changes the value in the filename textbox to a blank `http://` or `ftp://` prefix ready for you to type in the destination URL. You can either type in a valid location or click the Browse button to change the intended location of the project.

The Choose Location dialog (shown in Figure 21-2) is shown when you click the Browse button and enables you to specify where the project should be stored. Note that this isn't necessarily where the project will be deployed because you can specify a different destination for that when you're ready to ship, so don't expect that you are specifying the ultimate destination here.

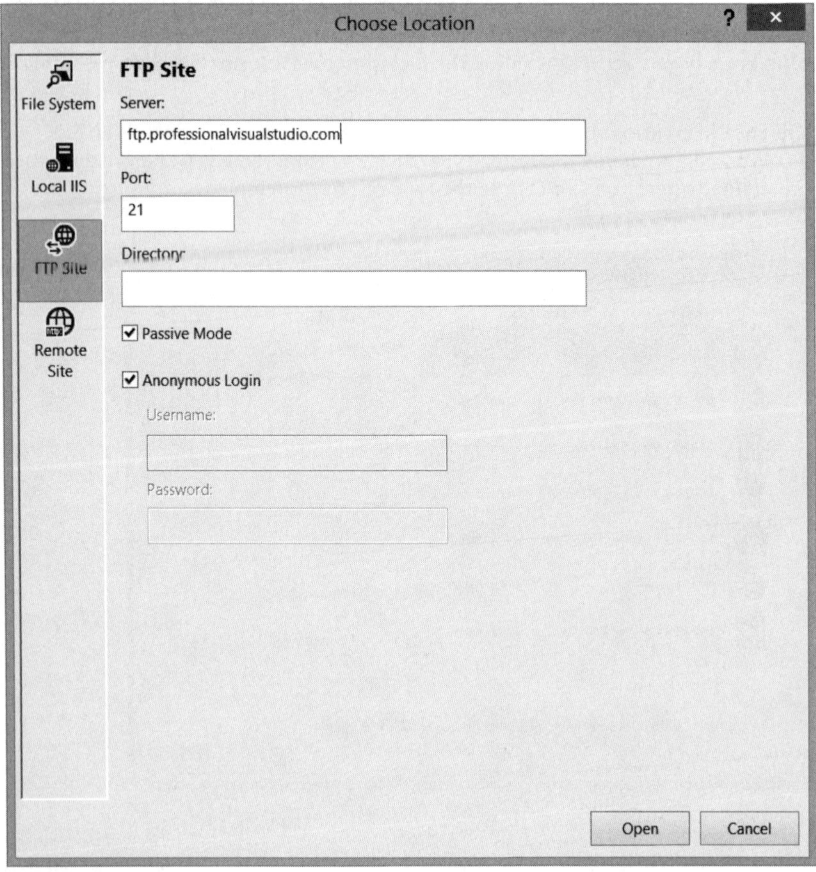

FIGURE 21-2

The File System option enables you to browse through the folder structure known to the system, including the My Network Places folders, and gives you the option to create subfolders where you need them. This is the easiest way to specify where you want the web project files, and the way that makes the files easiest to locate later.

> **NOTE** *Although you can specify where to create the project files, by default the solution file is created in a new folder under the* `My Documents/Visual Studio 2012/Projects` *folder for the current user. You can move the solution file to a folder of your choice without affecting the projects.*

If you use a local IIS server to debug your Web Site project, you can select the File System option and browse to your wwwroot folder to create the website. However, a much better option is to use the local IIS location type and drill down to your preferred location under the Default Web Site folders. This interface enables you to browse virtual directory entries that point to websites that are not physically located within the wwwroot folder structure but are actually aliases to elsewhere in the Filesystem or network. You can create your application in a new Web Application folder or create a new virtual directory entry in which you browse to the physical file location and specify an alias to appear in the website list.

The FTP site location type (refer to Figure 21-2) gives you the option to log in to a remote FTP site anonymously or with a specified user. When you click Open, Visual Studio saves the FTP settings for when you create the project, so be aware that it won't test whether or not the settings are correct until it attempts to create the project files and them to the specified destination.

> **NOTE** *You can save your project files to any FTP server to which you have access, even if that FTP site doesn't have .NET installed. However, you cannot run the files without .NET, so you can only use such a site as a file store.*

The last location type is a remote site, which enables you to connect to a remote server that has FrontPage extensions installed on it. If you have such a site, you can simply specify where you want the new project to be saved, and Visual Studio 2012 confirms that it can create the folder through the FrontPage extensions.

After you choose the intended location for your project, clicking OK tells Visual Studio 2012 to create the project files and store them in the desired location. After the web application has finished initializing, Visual Studio opens the `Default.aspx` page and populates the Toolbox with the components available to you for web development.

The Web Site project has only a small subset of the project configuration options available under the property pages of other project types, as shown in Figure 21-3. To access these options, right-click the project and select Property Pages.

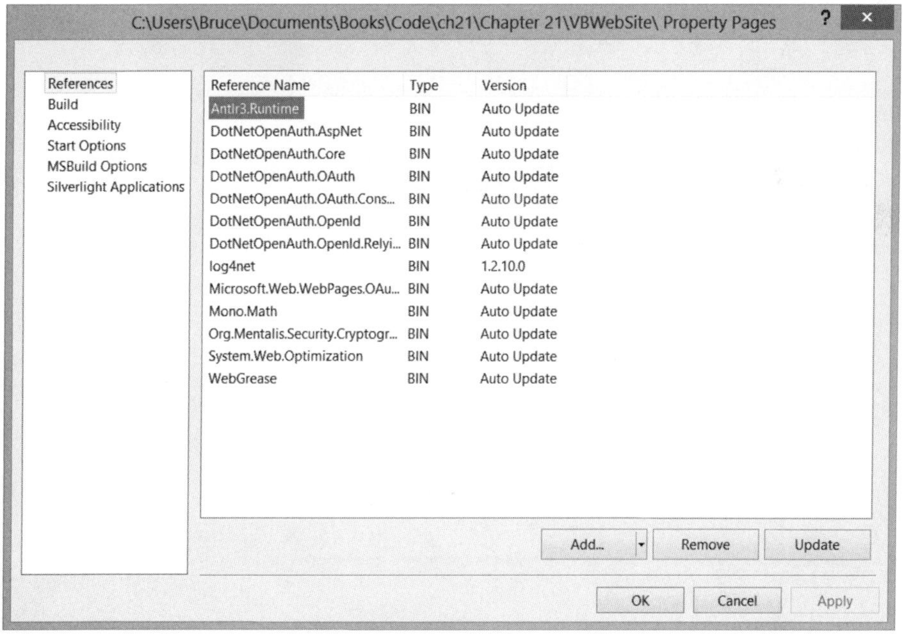

C:\Users\Bruce\Documents\Books\Code\ch21\Chapter 21\VBWebSite\ Property Pages

References
Build
Accessibility
Start Options
MSBuild Options
Silverlight Applications

Reference Name	Type	Version
Antlr3.Runtime	BIN	Auto Update
DotNetOpenAuth.AspNet	BIN	Auto Update
DotNetOpenAuth.Core	BIN	Auto Update
DotNetOpenAuth.OAuth	BIN	Auto Update
DotNetOpenAuth.OAuth.Cons...	BIN	Auto Update
DotNetOpenAuth.OpenId	BIN	Auto Update
DotNetOpenAuth.OpenId.Relyi...	BIN	Auto Update
log4net	BIN	1.2.10.0
Microsoft.Web.WebPages.OAu...	BIN	Auto Update
Mono.Math	BIN	Auto Update
Org.Mentalis.Security.Cryptogr...	BIN	Auto Update
System.Web.Optimization	BIN	Auto Update
WebGrease	BIN	Auto Update

Add... Remove Update

OK Cancel Apply

FIGURE 21-3

The References property page (refer to Figure 21-3) enables you to define references to external assemblies or web services. If you add a binary reference to an assembly that is not in the Global Assembly Cache (GAC), the assembly is copied to the `\bin` folder of your web project along with a `.refresh` file, which is a small text file that contains the path to the original location of the assembly. Every time the website is built, Visual Studio compares the current version of the assembly in the `\bin` folder with the version in the original location and, if necessary, updates it. If you have a large number of external references, this can slow the compile time considerably. Therefore, it is recommended that you delete the associated `.refresh` file for any assembly references that are unlikely to change frequently.

The Build, Accessibility, and Start Options property pages provide some control over how the website is built and launched during debugging. The accessibility validation options are discussed later in this chapter, and the rest of the settings on those property pages are reasonably self-explanatory.

The MSBuild Options property page provides a couple of interesting advanced options for web applications. If you uncheck the Allow This Precompiled Site to be Updatable option, all the content of the `.aspx` *and* `.ascx` pages is compiled into the assembly along with the code behind. This can be useful if you want to protect the user interface of a website from being modified. Finally, the Use Fixed Naming and Single Page Assemblies option specifies that each page be compiled into a separate assembly rather than the default, which is an assembly per folder.

The Silverlight Applications property page allows you to add or reference a Silverlight project that can be embedded into the website. This is discussed in more detail in Chapter 23, "Silverlight."

Creating a Web Application Project

Creating a Web Application project with Visual Studio 2012 is much the same as creating any other project type. Select File ➪ New ➪ Project, and you are presented with the New Project dialog box, as shown in Figure 21-4. By filtering the project types by language, and then by the Web category, you are given a selection of templates that is partially similar to those available for Web Site projects.

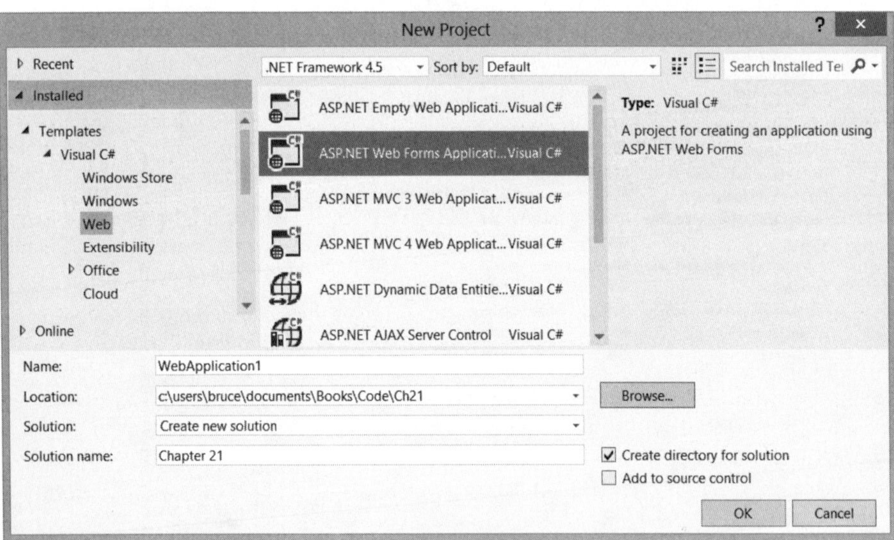

FIGURE 21-4

The notable difference in available project templates is that the reporting template is not available as a Web Application project. However, the Web Application project type includes templates for creating several different types of server controls.

After you click OK your new Web Application project will be created with a few more items than the Web Site projects. It includes an `AssemblyInfo` file, a References folder, and a My Project item under the Visual Basic or Properties node under C#.

You can view the project properties pages for a Web Application project by double-clicking the Properties or My Project item. The property pages include an additional Web page, as shown in Figure 21-5.

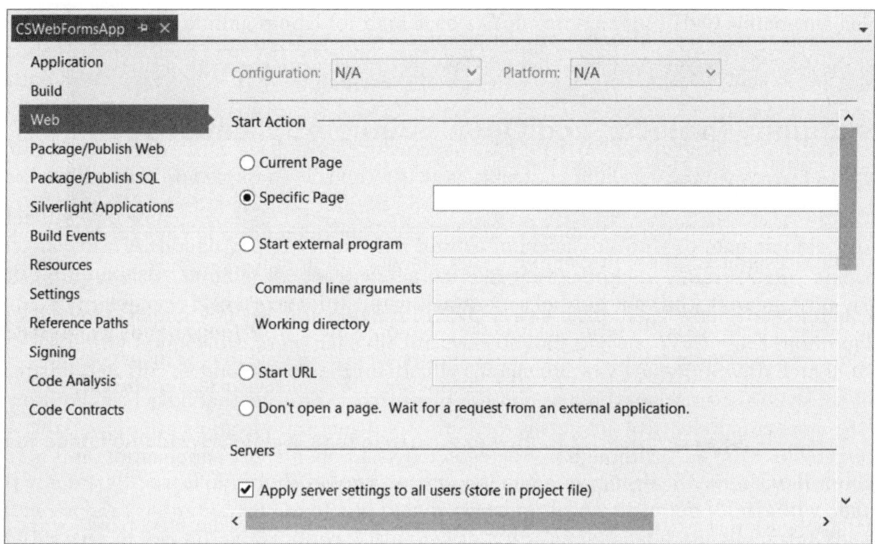

FIGURE 21-5

The options on the Web page are all related to debugging an ASP.NET web application and are covered in Chapter 43, "Debugging Web Applications," and Chapter 44, "Advanced Debugging Techniques."

Other Web Projects

In addition to the standard ASP.NET Web Site and Web Application project templates are templates that provide solutions for more specific scenarios:

- **ASP.NET 3 or 4 Web Application:** This creates a web application using the Model-View-Controller (MVC) architecture. This is only available as a Web Application project and is discussed in Chapter 22, "ASP.NET MVC."
- **ASP.NET Web Service:** This creates a default web service called `Sevice.asmx`, which contains a sample web method. This is only available as a Web Application project when the target is .NET Framework 3.5 or earlier.
- **ASP.NET Reports Web Site:** This creates an ASP.NET website with a report (`.rdlc`) and a ReportViewer control bound to the report. This is only available as a Web Site project and is explained in Chapter 31, "The ADO.NET Entity Framework."
- **ASP.NET Crystal Reports Web Site:** This creates an ASP.NET website with a sample Crystal Report. This is only available as a Web Site project.
- **ASP.NET Server Control:** Server controls include standard elements such as buttons and textboxes, and also special-purpose controls such as a calendar, menus, and tree view control. This template is only available as a Web Application project.
- **ASP.NET AJAX Server Control:** This contains the ASP.NET web server controls that enable you to add AJAX functionality to an ASP.NET web page. This is only available as a Web Application project.

- **ASP.NET AJAX Server Control Extender:** ASP.NET AJAX extender controls improve the client-side behavior and capabilities of standard ASP.NET web server controls. This is only available as a Web Application project.
- **Dynamic Data Web Site and Web Application:** Dynamic Data provides a quick way to build data-bound web applications that use either LINQ to SQL or Entity Framework. These are available for both Web Site and Web Application projects and are covered in Chapter 24, "Dynamic Data."

From time to time, Microsoft releases additional project templates as a separate download. For example, in Visual Studio 2008 the ASP.NET MVC and Silverlight 2.0 project types were released in this manner.

Starter Kits, Community Projects, and Open-Source Applications

One of the best ways to learn any new development technology is to review a sample application. The Microsoft ASP.NET website contains a list of starter kits and community projects at `http://www.asp.net/community/projects`. These web applications are excellent reference implementations for demonstrating best practices and good use of ASP.NET components and design.

Unfortunately, many of the starter kits have not been maintained and still run on older versions of the .NET Framework. However, they are still useful because they demonstrate a wide range of advanced ASP.NET technologies and techniques, including multiple CSS themes, master-detail pages, and user management.

The Microsoft ASP.NET site also contains a list of popular open-source projects that have been built on ASP.NET. One of the more comprehensive projects is the DinnerNow.net sample application, available at `http://dinnernow.codeplex.com/`. Although it is categorized as an open-source application, it is actually a reference implementation of many of the latest technologies from Microsoft.

The DinnerNow.net application is a fictitious marketplace where customers can order food from local restaurants for delivery to their homes or offices. In addition to the latest ASP.NET components, it demonstrates the use of IIS7, ASP.NET AJAX Extensions, LINQ, Windows Communication Foundation, Windows Workflow Foundation, Windows Presentation Foundation, Windows PowerShell, and the .NET Compact Framework.

Another great place to find a large number of excellent open-source examples is CodePlex, Microsoft's open-source project-hosting website. Located at `http://www.codeplex.com/`, CodePlex is a veritable wellspring of the good, the bad, and the ugly in Microsoft open-source applications.

DESIGNING WEB FORMS

One of the strongest features in Visual Studio 2012 for web developers is the visual design of web applications. The HTML Designer allows you to change the positioning, padding, and margins in Design view, using visual layout tools. It also provides a split view that enables you to simultaneously work on the design and markup of a web form. Finally, Visual Studio 2012 supports rich CSS editing tools for designing the layout and styling of web content.

The HTML Designer

The HTML Designer in Visual Studio is one of the main reasons it's so easy to develop ASP.NET applications. Because it understands how to render HTML elements as well as server-side ASP.NET controls, you can simply drag and drop components from the Toolbox onto the HTML Designer surface to quickly build up a web user interface. You can also quickly toggle between viewing the HTML markup and the visual design of a web page or user control.

The modifications made to the View menu of the IDE are a great example of what Visual Studio does to contextually provide you with useful features depending on what you're doing. When you edit a web page in Design view, additional menu commands become available for adjusting how the design surface appears (see Figure 21-6).

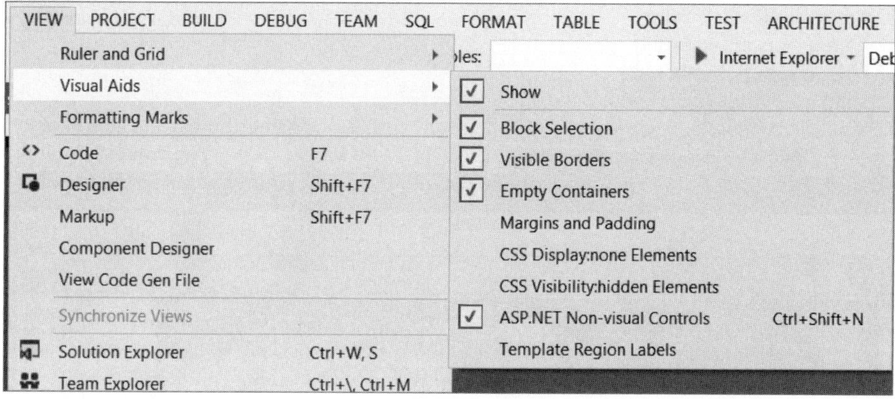

FIGURE 21-6

The three submenus at the top of the View menu — Ruler and Grid, Visual Aids, and Formatting Marks — provide you with a lot of useful tools to assist with the overall layout of controls and HTML elements on a web page.

For example, when the Show option is toggled on the Visual Aids submenu, it draws gray borders around all container controls and HTML tags such as `<table>` and `<div>` so that you can easily see where each component resides on the form. It also provides color-coded shading to indicate the margins and padding around HTML elements and server controls. Likewise, on the Formatting Marks submenu, you can toggle options to display HTML tag names, line breaks, spaces, and much more.

The HTML Designer also supports a split view, as shown in Figure 21-7, which shows your HTML markup and visual design at the same time. You activate this view by opening a page in design mode and clicking the Split button on the bottom left of the HTML Designer window.

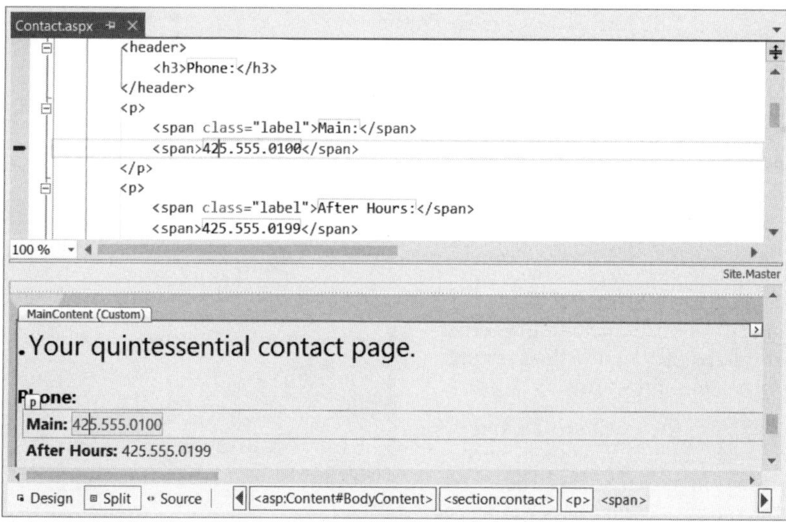

FIGURE 21-7

When you select a control or HTML element on the design surface, the HTML Designer highlights it in the HTML markup. Likewise, if you move the cursor to a new location in the markup, it highlights the corresponding element or control on the design surface.

If you make a change to anything on the design surface, that change is immediately reflected in the HTML markup. However, changes to the markup are not always shown in the HTML Designer immediately. Instead, you are presented with an information bar at the top of the Design view stating that it is out of sync with the Source view (see Figure 21-8). You can either click the information bar or press Ctrl+Shift+Y to synchronize the views. Saving your changes to the file also synchronizes it.

Design view is out of sync with Source view. Click here to synchronize views.

FIGURE 21-8

> **NOTE** *If you have a wide-screen monitor, you can orient the split view vertically to take advantage of your screen resolution. Select Tools ➪ Options, and then click the HTML Designer node in the TreeView. You can use a number of settings here to configure how the HTML Designer behaves, including an option called Split Views Vertically.*

Another feature worth pointing out in the HTML Designer is the tag navigator breadcrumb that appears at the bottom of the design window. This feature, which is also in the Silverlight and WPF Designers, displays the hierarchy of the current element or control and all its ancestors. The breadcrumb displays the type of the control or element and the ID or CSS class if it has been defined. If the tag path is too long to fit in the width of the HTML Designer window, the list is truncated, and a couple arrow buttons display, so you can scroll through the tag path.

The tag navigator breadcrumb displays the path only from the current element to its top-level parent. It does not list any elements outside that path. If you want to see the hierarchy of all the elements in the current document, you should use the Document Outline window, as shown in Figure 21-9. Select View ➪ Other Windows ➪ Document Outline to display the window. When you select an element or control in the Document Outline, it is highlighted in the Design and Source views of the HTML Designer. However, selecting an element in the HTML Designer does not highlight it in the Document Outline window.

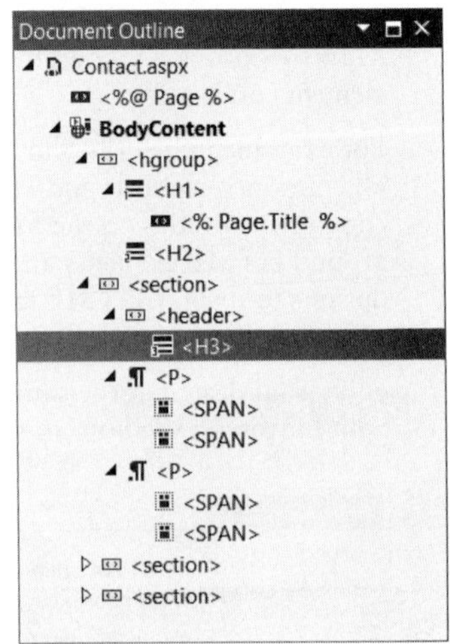

FIGURE 21-9

Positioning Controls and HTML Elements

One of the trickier parts of building web pages is the positioning of HTML elements. Several attributes can be set that control how an element is positioned, including whether or not it uses a relative or absolute position, the float setting, the z-index, and the padding and margin widths.

Fortunately, you don't need to learn the exact syntax and names of all these attributes and manually type them into the markup. As with most things in Visual Studio, the IDE is there to assist with the specifics. Begin by selecting the control or element that you want to position in Design view. Then choose Format ➪ Position from the menu to bring up the Position window, as shown in Figure 21-10.

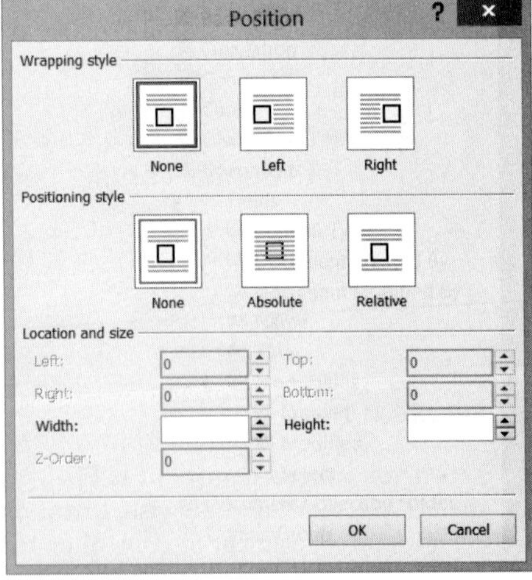

FIGURE 21-10

After you click OK, the wrapping and positioning style you have chosen and any values you have entered for location and size are saved to a style attribute on the HTML element.

If an element has relative or absolute positioning, you can reposition it in the Design view. Beware, though, of how you drag elements around the HTML Designer because you may be doing something you didn't intend! Whenever you select an element or control in Design view, a white tag appears at the top-left corner of the element. This displays the type of element, as well as the ID and class name if they are defined.

If you want to reposition an element with relative or absolute positioning, drag it to the new position using the white control tag. If you drag the element using the control itself, it does not modify the HTML positioning but instead moves it to a new line of code in the source.

Figure 21-11 shows a button that has relative positioning and has been repositioned 45 px down and 225 px to the right of its original position. The actual control is shown in its new position, and blue horizontal and vertical guidelines are displayed, which indicate that the control is relatively positioned. The guidelines are shown only while the element is selected.

Lorem ipsum dolor sit amet, consectetur adipisicing elit, sed do eiusmod tempor incididunt ut labore et dolore magna aliqua. Ut enim ad minim veniam, quis nostrud exercitation ullamco laboris nisi ut aliquip ex ea commodo consequat.

asp:Button#Button1

Button

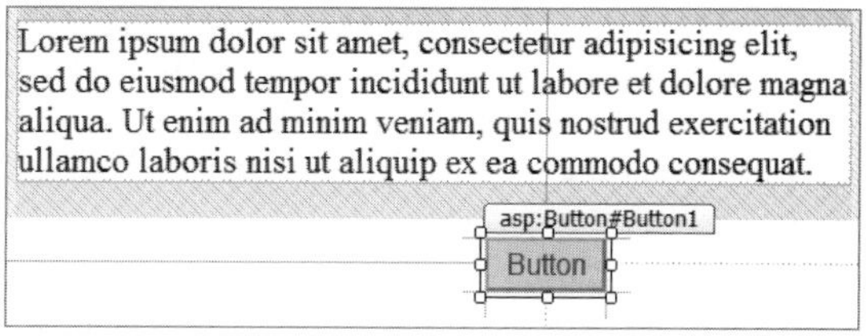

FIGURE 21-11

> **NOTE** *If a control uses absolute positioning, two additional guidelines display that extend from the bottom and right of the control to the edge of the container.*

The final layout technique discussed here is setting the padding and margins of an HTML element. Many web developers are initially confused about the difference between these display attributes — which is not helped by the fact that different browsers render elements with these attributes differently. Though not all HTML elements display a border, you can *generally* think of padding as the space inside the border and margins as the space outside.

If you look closely within the HTML Designer, you may notice some gray lines extending a short way horizontally and vertically from all four corners of a control (see Figure 21-12). These are only visible when the element is selected in the Design view. These are called *margin handles* and allow you to set the width of the margins. Hover the mouse over the handle until it changes to a resize cursor, and then drag it to increase or decrease the margin width (see Figure 21-12).

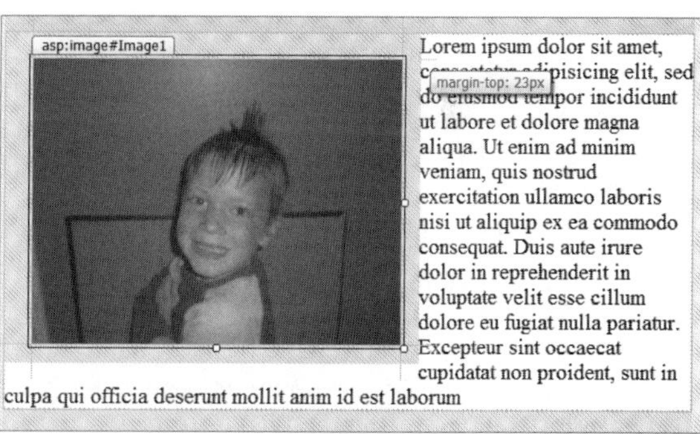

FIGURE 21-12

Finally, within the HTML Designer you can set the padding around an element. If you select an element and then hold down the Shift key, the margin handles become padding handles. Keeping the Shift key pressed, you can drag the handles to increase or decrease the padding width. When you release the Shift key, they revert to margin handles again. Figure 21-12 shows how an HTML image element looks in the HTML Designer when the margin and padding widths have been set on all four sides.

At first, this means of setting the margins and padding can feel counterintuitive because it does not behave consistently. To increase the top and left margins, you must drag the handlers into the element, and to increase the top and left padding, you must drag the handlers away. However, just to confuse things, dragging the bottom and right handlers away from the element increases both margin and padding widths.

When you have your HTML layout and positioning the way you want them, you can follow good practices by using the CSS tools to move the layout off the page and into an external style sheet. These tools are discussed in the section after the upcoming section.

Formatting Controls and HTML Elements

In addition to the Position dialog window discussed in the previous section, Visual Studio 2012 provides a toolbar and a range of additional dialog windows that enable you to edit the formatting of controls and HTML elements on a web page.

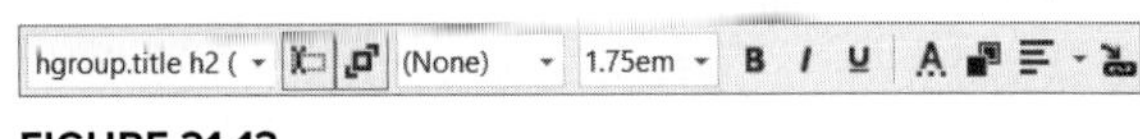

FIGURE 21-13

The Formatting toolbar, as shown in Figure 21-13, provides easy access to most of the formatting options. The leftmost drop-down list lets you control how the formatting options are applied and includes options for inline styling or CSS rules. The next drop-down list includes all the common HTML elements that can be applied to text, including the <h1> through <h6> headers, <ul>, <ol>, and <blockquote>.

Most of the other formatting dialog windows are listed as entries on the Format menu. These include windows for setting the foreground and background colors, font, alignment, bullets, and numbering. These dialog windows are similar to those available in any word processor or WYSIWYG interface, and their uses are immediately obvious.

The Insert Table dialog window, as shown in Figure 21-14, provides a way for you to easily define the layout and design of a new HTML table. Open it by positioning the cursor on the design surface where you want the new table to be placed and selecting Table ➪ Insert Table.

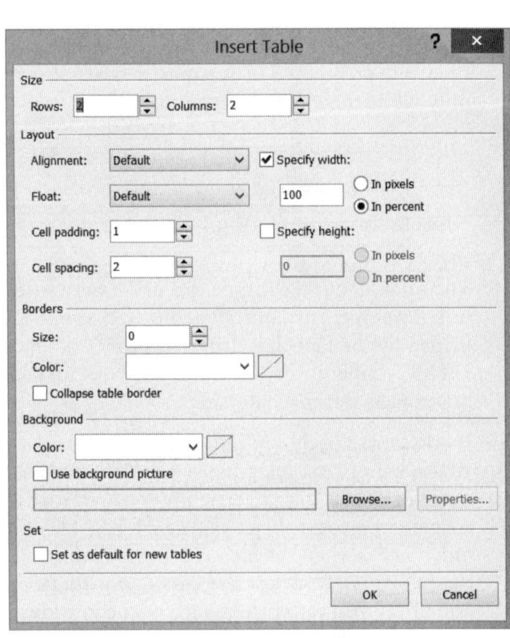

FIGURE 21-14

One final and quite useful feature on the Insert Table dialog window is under the color selector. In addition to the list of Standard Colors, there is also the Document Colors list, as shown in Figure 21-15. This lists all the colors that have been applied in some way or another to the current page, for example as foreground, background, or border colors. This saves you from having to remember custom RGB values for the color scheme that you have chosen to apply to a page.

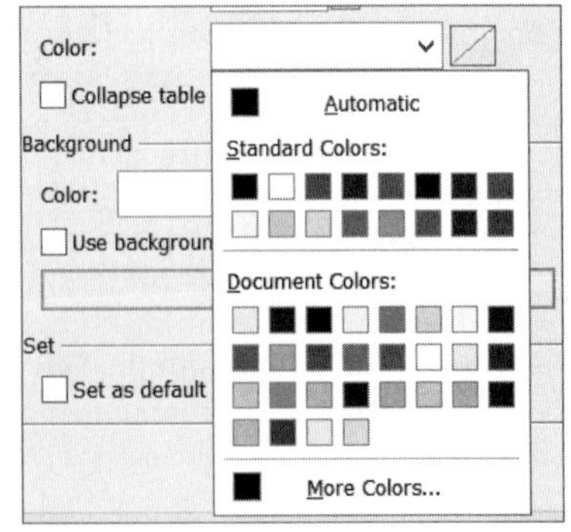

FIGURE 21-15

CSS Tools

Once upon a time, the HTML within a typical web page consisted of a mishmash of both content and presentation markup. Web pages made liberal use of HTML tags that defined *how* the content should be rendered, such as `<font>`, `<center>`, and `<big>`. These days, designs of this nature are frowned upon — best practice dictates that HTML documents should specify only the content of the web page, wrapped in semantic tags such as `<h1>`, `<ul>`, and `<div>`. Elements requiring special presentation rules should be assigned a `class` attribute, and all style information should be stored in external CSS.

Visual Studio 2012 has several features that provide a rich CSS editing experience in an integrated fashion. As you saw in the previous section, you can do much of the work of designing the layout and styling the content in Design view. This is supplemented by the Manage Styles window, the Apply Styles window, and the CSS Properties window, which are all accessible from the View menu when the HTML Designer is open.

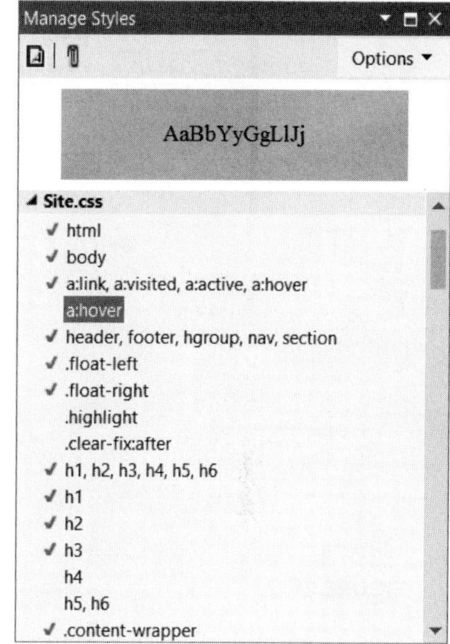

FIGURE 21-16

The Manage Styles window lists all the CSS styles that are internal, inline, or in an external CSS file linked through to the current page. The objective of this tool window is to provide you with an overall view of the CSS rules for a particular page, and to enable you to edit and manage those CSS classes.

All the styles are listed in a TreeView with the style sheet forming the top-level nodes, as shown in Figure 21-16. The styles are listed in the order in which they appear in the style sheet file, and you can drag and drop to rearrange the styles, or even move styles from one style sheet to another.

When you hover over a style, the tooltip shows the CSS properties in that style. The Options menu drop-down enables you to filter the list of styles to show only those that are applicable to elements on the current page or, if you have an element selected in the HTML Designer, only those that are relevant to the selected element.

> **NOTE** *The selected style preview, which is at the top of the Manage Styles window, is generally not what will actually be displayed in the web browser. This is because the preview does not take into account any CSS inheritance rules that might cause the properties of the style to be overridden.*

One of the big changes for the Manage Styles window (as compared to Visual Studio 2010) is the use of icons. Rather than a complex set of icons, the Visual Studio 2012 version of Manage Styles shows a check mark if the style is used in the current page. If a style is not used, then no icon appears.

When you right-click a style in the Manage Styles window, you are given the option to create a new style from scratch, create a new style based on the selected style, or modify the selected style. Any of these three options launch the Modify Style dialog box, as shown in Figure 21-17. This dialog provides an intuitive way to define or modify a CSS style. Style properties are grouped into familiar categories, such as Font, Border, and Position, and a useful preview displays toward the bottom of the window.

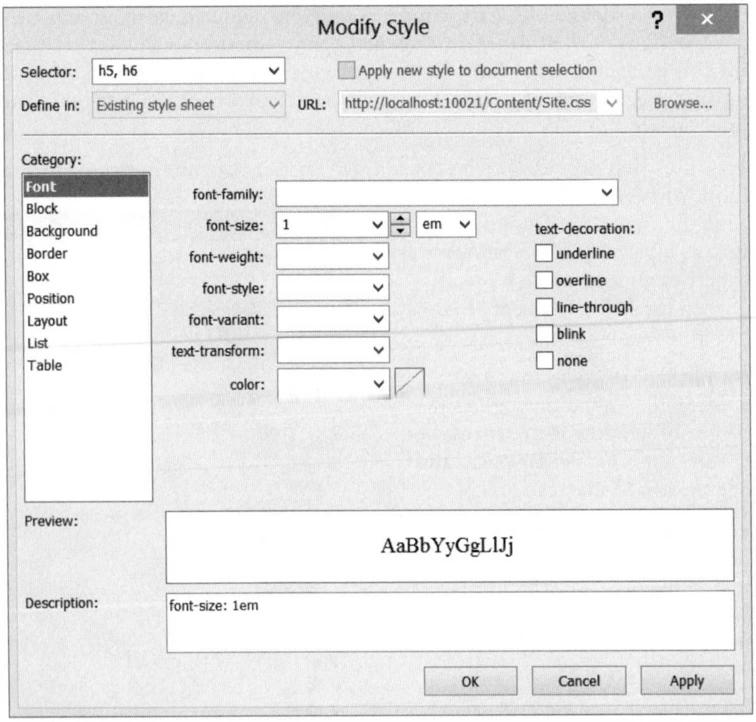

Modify Style

Selector: h5, h6 Apply new style to document selection

Define in: Existing style sheet URL: http://localhost:10021/Content/Site.css Browse...

Category:
Font
Block
Background
Border
Box
Position
Layout
List
Table

font-family:
font-size: 1 em
font-weight:
font-style:
font-variant:
text-transform:
color:

text-decoration:
underline
overline
line-through
blink
none

Preview: AaBbYyGgLlJj

Description: font-size: 1em

OK Cancel Apply

FIGURE 21-17

The second of the CSS windows is the Apply Styles window. Though this has a fair degree of overlap with the Manage Styles window, its purpose is to enable you to easily apply styles to elements on the web page. Select View ➪ Apply Styles to open the window, which is shown in Figure 21-18. As in the Manage Styles window, all the available styles are listed in the window, and you can filter the list to show only the styles that are applicable to the current page or the currently selected element. The window uses the same check mark icon to indicate whether or not the style is being used. You can also hover over a style to display all the properties in the CSS rule.

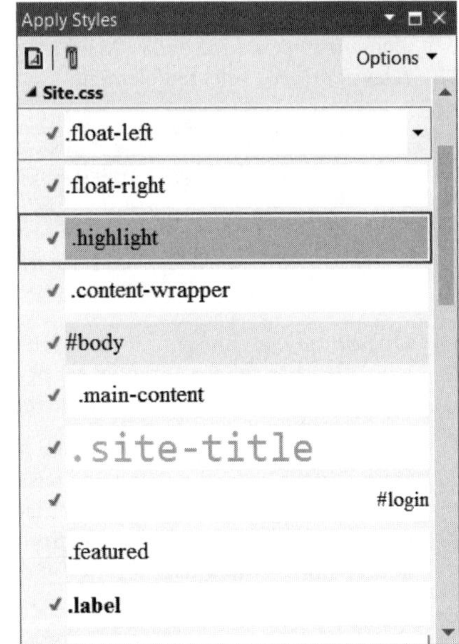

FIGURE 21-18

However, the Apply Styles window displays a much more visually accurate representation of the style than the Manage Styles window. It includes the font color and weight, background colors or images, borders, and even text alignment.

When you select an HTML element in the Designer, a blue border in the Apply Styles window surrounds the styles applied to that element. Refer to Figure 21-18, where the `.highlight` (and `.float-left`) style is active for the selected element. When you hover the mouse over any of the styles, a drop-down button appears over it, providing access to a context menu. This menu has options for applying that style to the selected element or, if the style has already been applied, for removing it. Simply clicking the style also applies it to the current HTML element.

The third of the CSS windows in Visual Studio 2012 is the CSS Properties window, as shown in Figure 21-19. This displays a property grid with all the styles used by the HTML element that is currently selected in the

HTML Designer. In addition, the window gives you a comprehensive list of all the available CSS properties. This enables you to add properties to an existing style, modify properties that you have already set, and create new inline styles.

Rather than display the details of an individual style, as was the case with the Apply Styles and Manage Styles windows, the CSS Properties window instead shows a cumulative view of all the styles applicable to the current element, taking into account the order of precedence for the styles. At the top of the CSS Properties window is the Applied Rules section, which lists the CSS styles in the order in which they are applied. Styles that are lower on this list override the styles above them.

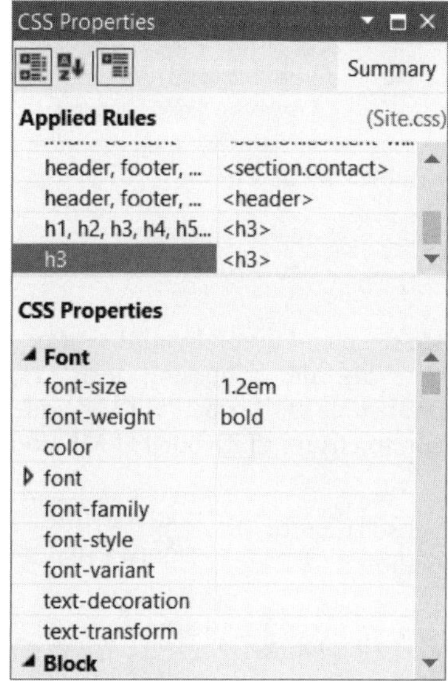

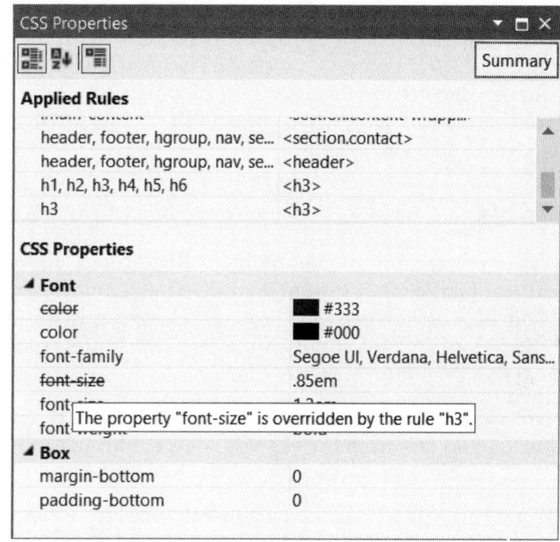

FIGURE 21-19

Selecting a style in the Applied Rules section shows all the CSS properties for that style in the lower property grid. In Figure 21-19 (left) the `h3` CSS rule has been selected, which has a definition for the `font-size` and `font-weight` CSS properties. You can edit these properties or define new ones directly in this property grid.

The CSS Properties window also has a Summary button, which displays all the CSS properties applicable to the current element. This is shown in Figure 21-19 (right). CSS properties that have been overridden are shown with a strikethrough, and hovering the mouse over the property displays a tooltip with the reason for the override.

Visual Studio 2012 also includes a Target Rule selector on the Formatting toolbar, as shown in Figure 21-20, which enables you to control where style changes you made using the formatting toolbars and dialog windows are saved. These include the Formatting toolbar and the dialog windows under the Format menu, such as Font, Paragraph, Bullets and Numbering, Borders and Shading, and Position.

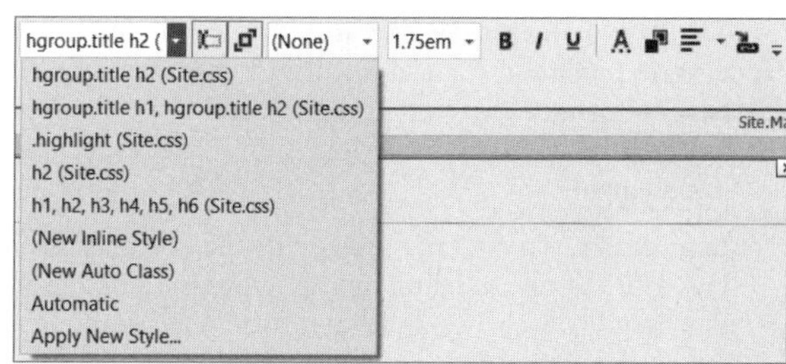

FIGURE 21-20

The Target Rule selector has two modes: Automatic and Manual. In Automatic mode Visual Studio automatically chooses where the new style is applied. In Manual mode you have full control over where the resulting CSS properties are created. Visual Studio

2012 defaults to Manual mode, and any changes to this mode are remembered for the current user.

The Target Rule selector is populated with a list of styles that have already been applied to the currently selected element. Inline styles display with an entry that reads `<inline style>`. Styles defined inline in the current page have `(Current Page)` appended, and styles defined in an external style sheet have the filename appended.

Finally, in Visual Studio 2012 there is IntelliSense support for CSS in both the CSS editor and HTML editor. The CSS editor, which is opened by default when you double-click a CSS file, provides IntelliSense prompts for all the CSS attributes and valid values, as shown in Figure 21-21. After the CSS styles are defined, the HTML editor subsequently detects and displays a list of valid CSS class names available on the web page when you add the `class` attribute to a HTML element.

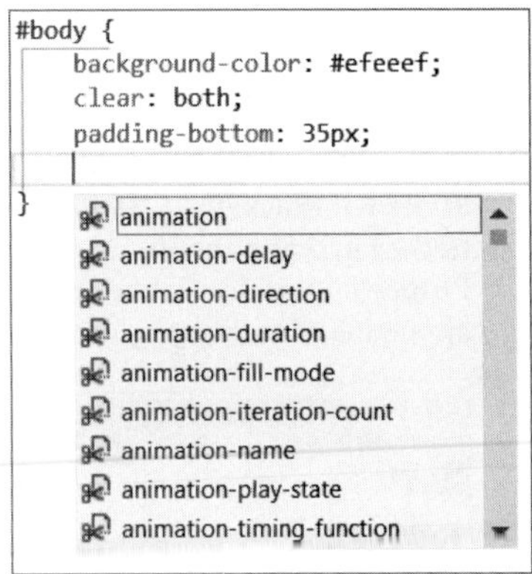

FIGURE 21-21

Validation Tools

Web browsers are remarkably good at hiding badly formed HTML code from end users. Invalid syntax that would cause a fatal error if it were in an XML document, such as out-of-order or missing closing tags, often renders fine in your favorite web browser. However, if you view that same malformed HTML code in a different browser, it may look totally different. This is one good reason to ensure that your HTML code is standards-compliant.

The first step to validating your standards compliance is to set the target schema for validation. You can do this from the HTML Source Editing toolbar, as shown in Figure 21-22.

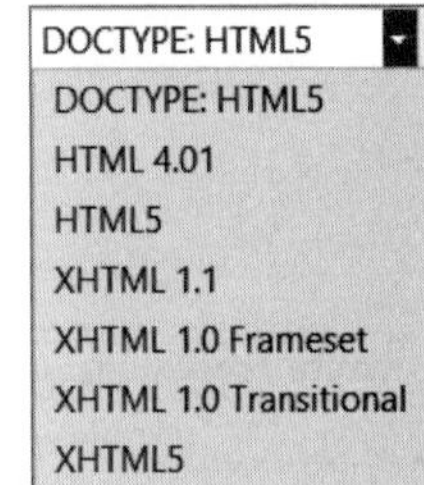

FIGURE 21-22

Your HTML markup will be validated against the selected schema. Validation works like a background spell-checker, examining the markup as it is entered and adding wavy green lines under the elements or attributes that are not valid based on the current schema. As shown in Figure 21-23, when you hover over an element marked as invalid, a tooltip appears showing the reason for the validation failure. A warning entry is also created in the Error List window.

Schema validation will go a long way toward helping your web pages render the same across different browsers. However, it does not ensure that your site is accessible to everyone. There may be a fairly large group of people with some sort of physical impairment who find it extremely difficult to access your site due to the way the HTML markup has been coded.

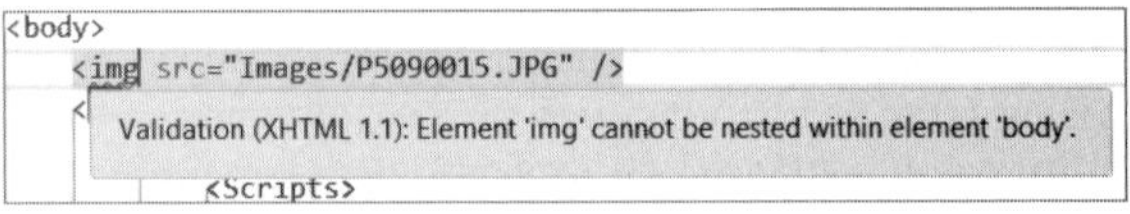

FIGURE 21-23

The World Health Organization has estimated that approximately 314 million people worldwide are visually impaired (World Health Organization, 2009). In the United States, more than 21 million people have reported experiencing significant vision loss (National Center for Health Statistics, 2006). That's a large body of people by anyone's estimate, especially given that it doesn't include those with other physical impairments.

In addition to reducing the size of your potential user base, if you do not take accessibilities into account, you may run the risk of being on the wrong side of a lawsuit. A number of countries have introduced legislation that requires websites and other forms of communication to be accessible to people with disabilities.

Fortunately, Visual Studio 2012 includes an accessibility-validation tool that checks HTML markups for compliance with accessibility guidelines. The Web Content Accessibility Checker, launched from Tools ➪ Check Accessibility, enables you to check an individual page for compliance against several accessibility guidelines, including Web Content Accessibility Guidelines (WCAG) version 1.0 and the Americans with Disabilities Act Section 508 Guidelines, commonly referred to as Section 508.

Select the guidelines to check for compliance and click Validate to begin. After the web page has been checked, any issues display as errors or warnings in the Error List window, as shown in Figure 21-24.

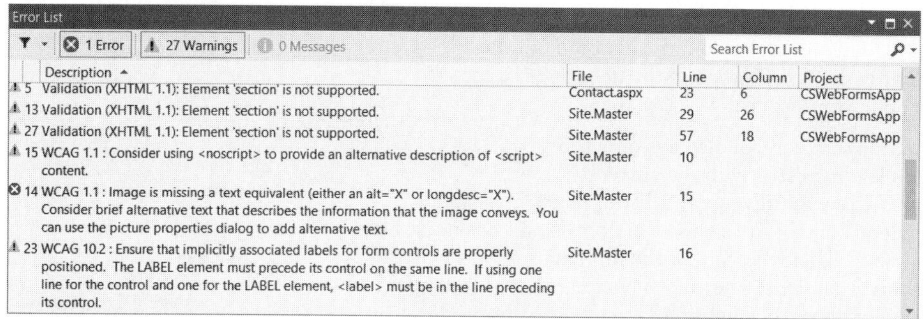

FIGURE 21-24

> **NOTE** *Previous versions of the ASP.NET web controls rendered markup that generally did not conform to HTML or accessibility standards. Fortunately, for the most part, this has been fixed as of ASP.NET version 4.0.*

WEB CONTROLS

When ASP.NET version 1.0 was first released, a whole new way to build web applications was enabled for Microsoft developers. Instead of using HTML elements mingled with a server-side scripting language, as was the case with languages such as classic ASP, JSP, and Perl, ASP.NET introduced the concept of feature-rich controls for web pages that acted in ways similar to their Windows counterparts.

Web controls such as button and textbox components have familiar properties such as `Text`, `Left`, and `Width`, along with just as recognizable methods and events such as `Click` and `TextChanged`. In addition to these, ASP.NET 1.0 provided a limited set of web-specific components, some dealing with data-based information, such as the DataGrid control, and others providing common web tasks, such as an ErrorProvider to give feedback to users about problems with information they entered into a web form.

Subsequent versions of ASP.NET introduced more than 50 web server controls including navigation components, user authentication, web parts, and improved data controls. Third-party vendors have also released numerous server controls and components that provide even more advanced functionality.

Unfortunately, there isn't room in this book to explore all the server controls available to web applications in much detail. In fact, many of the components, such as TextBox, Button, and Checkbox, are simply the web equivalents of the basic user interface controls that you may well be familiar with already. However, it can be useful to provide an overview of some of the more specialized and functional server controls that reside in the ASP.NET web developers' toolkit.

Navigation Components

ASP.NET includes a simple way to add sitewide navigation to your web applications with the sitemap provider and associated controls. To implement sitemap functionality into your projects, you must manually create the site data by default in a file called `Web.sitemap`, and keep it up to date as you add or remove web pages from the site. Sitemap files can be used as a data source for a number of web controls, including SiteMapPath, which automatically keeps track of where you are in the site hierarchy, as well as the Menu and TreeView controls, which can present a custom subset of the sitemap information.

After you have your site hierarchy defined in a `Web.sitemap` file, the easiest way to use it is to drag and drop a SiteMapPath control onto your web page design surface (see Figure 21-25). This control automatically binds to the default sitemap provider, as specified in the `Web.config` file, to generate the nodes for display.

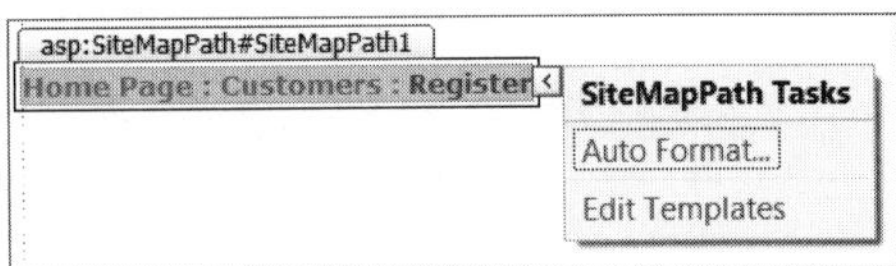

FIGURE 21-25

Though the SiteMapPath control displays only the breadcrumb trail leading directly to the currently viewed page, at times you will want to display a list of pages in your site. The ASP.NET Menu control can be used to do this and has modes for both horizontal and vertical viewing of the information. Likewise, the TreeView control can be bound to a sitemap and used to render a hierarchical menu of pages in a website. Figure 21-26 shows a web page with a SiteMapPath, Menu, and TreeView that have each been formatted with one of the built-in styles.

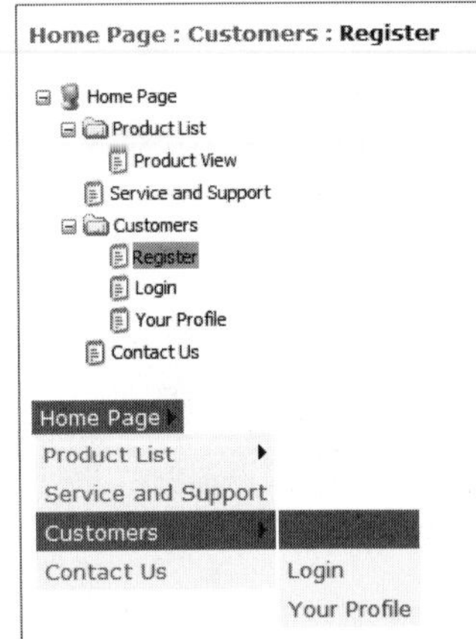

FIGURE 21-26

User Authentication

Perhaps the most significant additions to the web components in ASP.NET version 2.0 were the new user authentication and login components. Using these components, you can quickly and easily create the user-based parts of your web application without having to worry about how to format them or what controls are necessary.

Every web application has a default data source added to its ASP.NET configuration when it is first created. The data source is a SQL Server Express database with a default name pointing to a local Filesystem location. This data source is used as the default location for your user authentication processing, storing information about users and their current settings.

The benefit of having this automated data store generated for each website is that Visual Studio can have an array of user-bound web components that can automatically save user information without your needing to write any code.

Before you can sign in as a user on a particular site, you first need to create a user account. Initially, you can do that in the administration and configuration of ASP.NET, which is discussed later in this chapter in the "ASP.NET Web Site Administration" section, but you may also want to allow visitors to the site to create their own user accounts. The CreateUserWizard component does just that. It consists of two wizard pages with information about creating an account and indicates when account creation is successful.

After users have created their accounts, they need to log in to the site, and the Login control fills this need. Adding the Login component to your page creates a small form containing User Name and Password fields, along with the option to remember the login credentials, and a Log In button (see Figure 21-27).

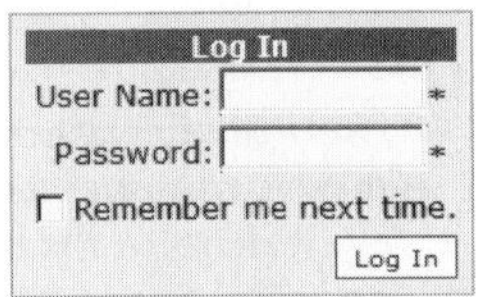

FIGURE 21-27

The trick to getting this to work straightaway is to edit your `Web.config` file and change the authentication to Forms. The default authentication type is Windows, and without the change the website authenticates you as a Windows user because that's how you are currently logged in. Obviously, some web applications require Windows authentication, but for a simple website that you plan to deploy on the Internet, this is the only change you need to make for the Login control to work properly.

You can also use several controls that will detect whether or not the user has logged on, and display different information to an authenticated user as opposed to an anonymous user. The LoginStatus control is a simple bi-state component that displays one set of content when the site detects that a user is currently logged in, and a different set of content when there is no logged-in user. The LoginName component is also simple; it just returns the name of the logged-in user.

There are also controls that allow end users to manage their own passwords. The ChangePassword component works with the other automatic user-based components to enable users to change their passwords. However, sometimes users forget their passwords, which is where the PasswordRecovery control comes into play. This component, shown in Figure 21-28, has three views: UserName, Question, and Success. The idea is that users first enter their username so the application can determine and display the security question, and then wait for an answer. If the answer is correct, the component moves to the Success page and sends an e-mail to the registered e-mail address.

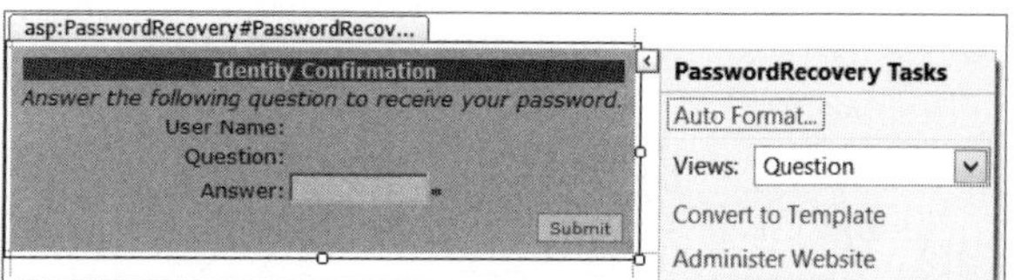

FIGURE 21-28

The last component in the Login group on the Toolbox is the LoginView object. LoginView enables you to create whole sections on your web page that are visible only under certain conditions related to who is (or isn't) logged in. By default, you have two views: the AnonymousTemplate, which is used when no user is logged in, and the LoggedInTemplate, used when any user is logged in. Both templates have an editable area that is initially completely empty.

However, because you can define specialized roles and assign users to these roles, you can also create templates for each role you have defined in your site (see Figure 21-29). The Edit RoleGroups command on the smart-tag Tasks list associated with LoginView displays the typical collection editor and enables you to build role groups that can contain one or multiple roles. When the site detects that the user logs in with a certain role, the display area of the LoginView component is populated with that particular template's content.

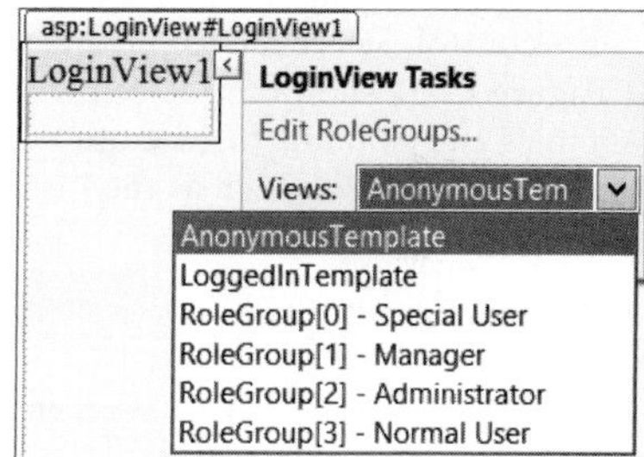

FIGURE 21-29

> **NOTE** *See the "ASP.NET Web Site Administration" section later in this chapter for information on how to create and manage roles.*

What's amazing about all these controls is that with only a couple of manual property changes and a few extra entries in the `Web.config` file, you can build a complete user-authentication system into your web application. In fact, as you'll see in the "ASP.NET Web Site Administration" section later in this chapter, you can edit all these settings without needing to edit the `Web.config` file directly. Now that's efficient coding!

Data Components

Data components were introduced to Microsoft web developers with the first version of Visual Studio .NET and have evolved to be even more powerful with each subsequent release of Visual Studio. Each data control has a smart-tag Tasks list associated with it that enables you to edit the individual templates for each part of the displayable area. For example, the DataList has several templates, each of which can be individually customized (see Figure 21-30).

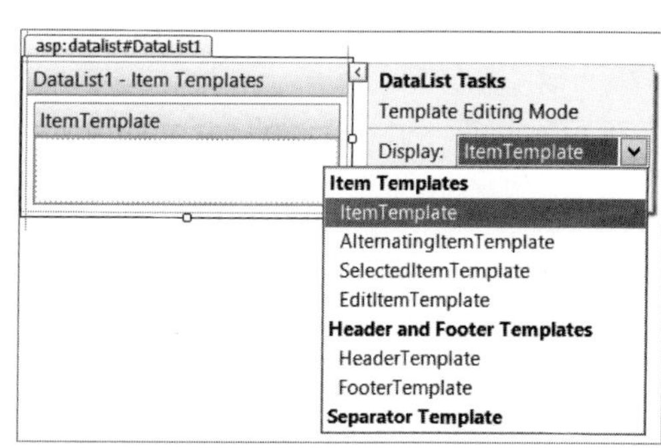

FIGURE 21-30

Data Source Controls

The data source control architecture in ASP.NET provides a simple way for UI controls to bind to data. The data source controls that were released with ASP.NET 2.0 include SqlDataSource and AccessDataSource for binding to SQL Server or Access databases, ObjectDataSource for binding to a generic class, XmlDataSource for binding to XML files, and SiteMapDataSource for the site navigation tree for the web application.

ASP.NET 3.5 shipped with a LinqDataSource control that enables you to directly bind UI controls to data sources using Language Integrated Query (LINQ). The EntityDataSource control, released with ASP.NET 3.5 SP1, supports data binding using the ADO.NET Entity Framework. These controls provide you with a designer-driven approach that automatically generates most of the code necessary for interacting with the data.

All data source controls operate in a similar way. For the purposes of this discussion, the remainder of this section uses the LinqDataSource as an example.

Before you can use LinqDataSource, you must already have a `DataContext` class created. The data context wraps a database connection to provide object lifecycle services. Chapter 29, "Language Integrated Queries (LINQ)," explains how to create a new `DataContext` class in your application.

You can then create a LinqDataSource control instance by dragging it from the Toolbox onto the design surface. To configure the control, launch the Configure Data Source Wizard under the smart tag for the control. Select the data context class, and then choose the data selection details you want to use. Figure 21-31 shows the screen within the Configure Data Source Wizard that enables you to choose the tables and columns to generate a LINQ to SQL query. It is then a simple matter to bind this data source to a UI server control, such as the ListView control, to provide read-only access to your data.

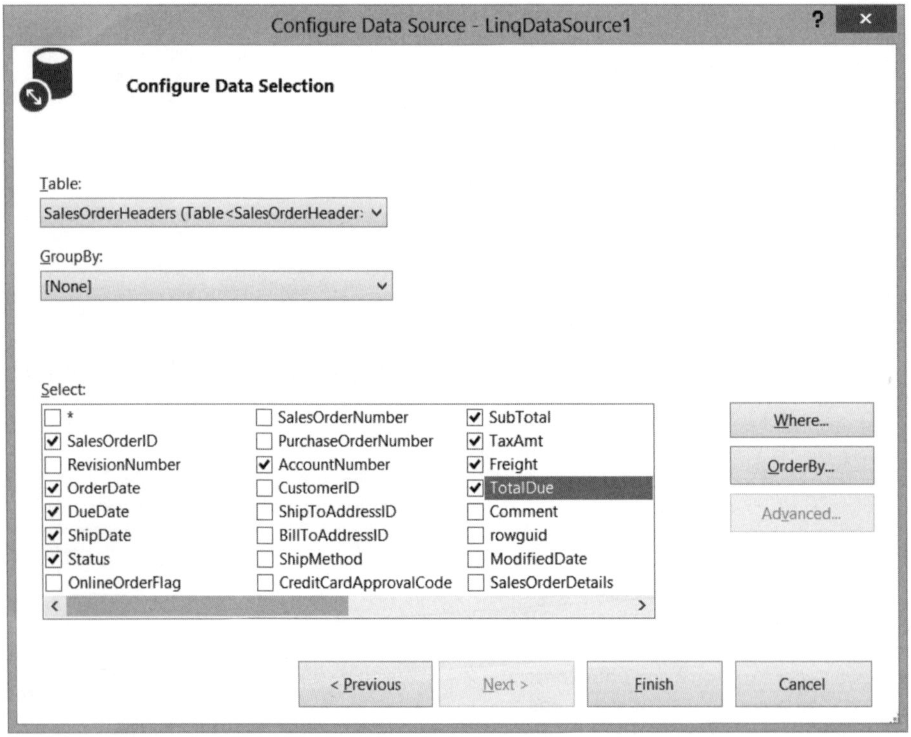

FIGURE 21-31

You can easily take advantage of more advanced data access functionality supported by LINQ, such as allowing inserts, updates, and deletes, by setting the `EnableInsert`, `EnableUpdate`, and `EnableDelete` properties on LinqDataSource to `true`. You can do this either programmatically in code or through the property grid.

You can find more information on LINQ in Chapter 29.

Data View Controls

After you specify a data source, it is a simple matter to use one of the data view controls to display this data. ASP.NET ships with built-in web controls that render data in different ways, including Chart, DataList, DetailsView, FormView, GridView, ListView, and Repeater. The Chart control is used to render data graphically using visualizations such as a bar chart or line chart and is discussed in Chapter 31, "Reporting,"

A common complaint about the ASP.NET server controls is that developers have little control over the HTML markup they generate. This is especially true of many of the data view controls such as GridView, which always uses an HTML table to format the data it outputs, even though in some situations an ordered list would be more suitable.

The ListView control provides a good solution to the shortcomings of other data controls in this area. Instead of surrounding the rendered markup with superfluous `<table>` or `<span>` elements, it enables you to specify the exact HTML output that is rendered. The HTML markup is defined in the templates that ListView supports:

- AlternatingItemTemplate
- EditItemTemplate
- EmptyDataTemplate
- EmptyItemTemplate
- GroupSeparatorTemplate
- GroupTemplate
- InsertItemTemplate
- ItemSeparatorTemplate
- ItemTemplate
- LayoutTemplate
- SelectedItemTemplate

The two most useful templates are LayoutTemplate and ItemTemplate. LayoutTemplate specifies the HTML markup that surrounds the output, and ItemTemplate specifies the HTML used to format each record that is bound to the ListView.

When you add a ListView control to the design surface, you can bind it to a data source and then open the Configure ListView dialog box, as shown in Figure 21-32, via smart-tag actions. This provides a code-generation tool that automatically produces HTML code based on a small number of predefined layouts and styles.

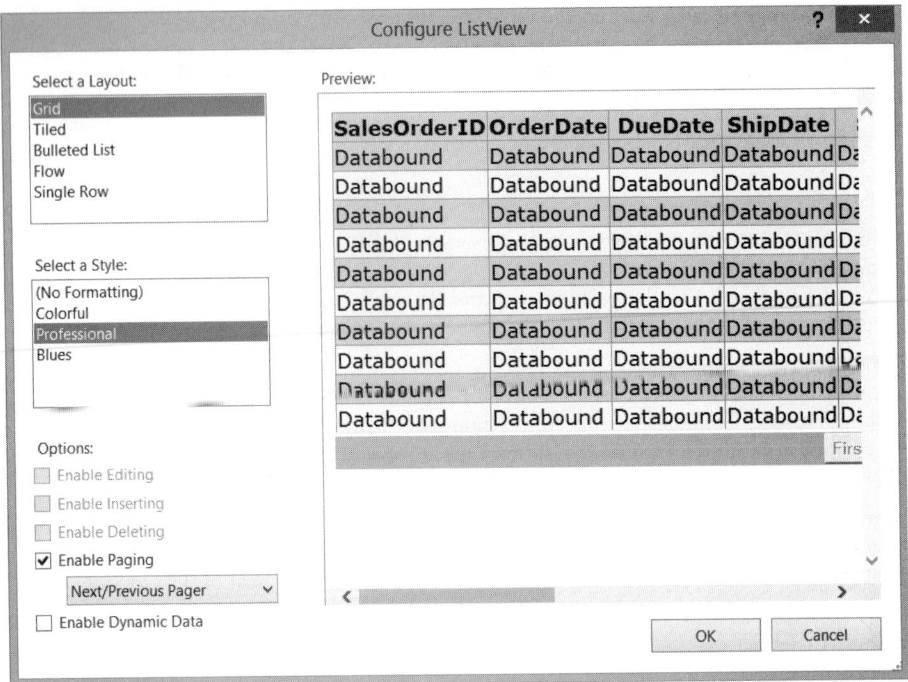

FIGURE 21-32

> **NOTE** *Because you have total control over the HTML markup, the Configure ListView dialog box does not even attempt to parse any existing markup. Instead, if you reopen the window, it simply shows the default layout settings.*

Data Helper Controls

The DataPager control is used to split the data that is displayed by a UI control into multiple pages, which is necessary when you work with large data sets. It natively supports paging via either a NumericPagerField object, which lets users select a page number, or a NextPreviousPagerField object, which lets users navigate to the next or previous page. As with the ListView control, you can also write your own custom HTML markup for paging by using the TemplatePagerField object.

Finally, the QueryExtender control, introduced in ASP.NET version 4.0, provides a way to filter data from an EntityDataSource or LinqDataSource in a declarative manner. It is particularly useful for searching scenarios.

Web Parts

Another excellent feature in ASP.NET is the ability to create Web Parts controls and pages. These allow certain pages on your site to be divided into chunks that either you or your users can move around, and show and hide, to create a unique viewing experience. Web Parts for ASP.NET are loosely based on custom web controls but owe their inclusion in ASP.NET to the huge popularity of Web Parts in SharePoint Portals.

With a Web Parts page, you first create a WebPartManager component that sits on the page to look after any areas of the page design that are defined as parts. You then use WebPartZone containers to set where you want customizable content on the page, and then finally place the actual content into the WebPartZone container.

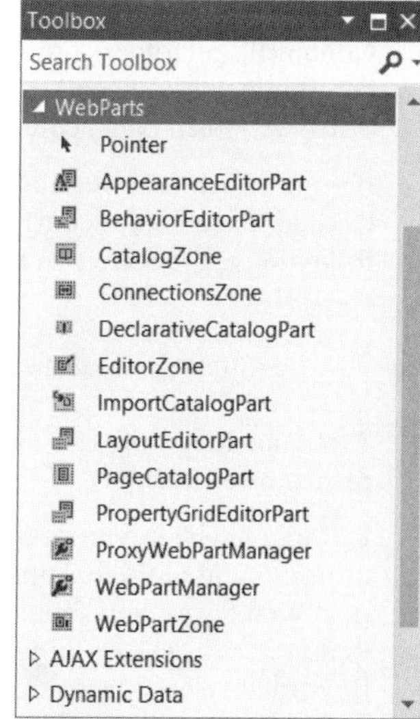

FIGURE 21-33

Though these two components are the core of Web Parts, you need look at only the WebParts group in the Toolbox to discover a whole array of additional components (see Figure 21-33). You use these additional components to enable your users to customize their experience of your website.

Unfortunately, there is not enough space in this book to cover the ASP.NET web controls in any further detail. If you want to learn more, check out the massive *Professional ASP.NET 4 in C# and VB* by Bill Evjen, Scott Hanselman, and Devin Rader.

MASTER PAGES

A useful feature of web development in Visual Studio is the ability to create *master pages* that define sections that can be customized. This enables you to define a single page design that contains the common elements that should be shared across your entire site, specify areas that can house individualized content, and inherit it for each of the pages on the site.

To add a master page to your Web Application project, use the Add New Item command from the website menu or from the context menu in the Solution Explorer. This displays the Add New Item dialog, as shown in Figure 21-34, which contains a large number of item templates that can be added to a web application. You'll notice that besides Web Forms (`.aspx`) pages and Web User Controls, you can also add plain HTML files, style sheets, and other web-related file types. To add a master page, select the Master Page template, choose a name for the file, and click Add.

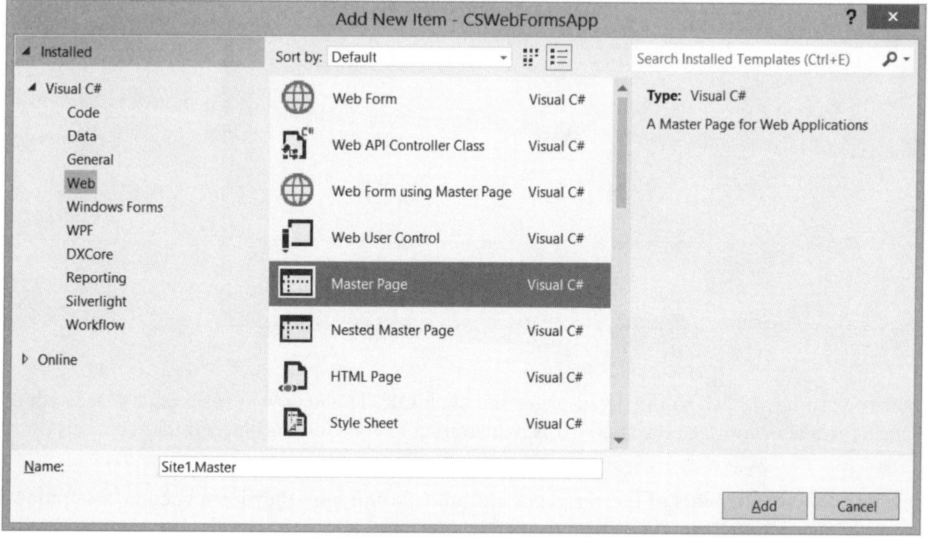

FIGURE 21-34

When a master page is added to your website, it starts out as a minimal web page template with two empty ContentPlaceHolder components — one in the body of the web page and one in the head. This is where the detail information can be placed for each individual page. You can create the master page as you would any other web form page, complete with ASP.NET and HTML elements, CSSs, and theming.

If your design requires additional areas for detail information, you can either drag a new ContentPlaceHolder control from the Toolbox onto the page, or switch to Source view and add the following tags where you need the additional area:

```
<asp:ContentPlaceHolder id="aUniqueid" runat="server">
</asp:ContentPlaceHolder>
```

After the design of your master page has been finalized, you can use it for the detail pages for new web forms in your project.

Unfortunately, the process to add a form that uses a master page is slightly different depending on whether or not you use a Web Application or Web Site project. For a Web Application project, rather than adding a new Web Form, you should add a new Web Form using Master Page. This displays the Select a Master Page dialog box, as shown in Figure 21-35. In a Web Site project, the Add New Item window contains a check box titled Select Master Page. If you check this, the Select a Master Page dialog displays.

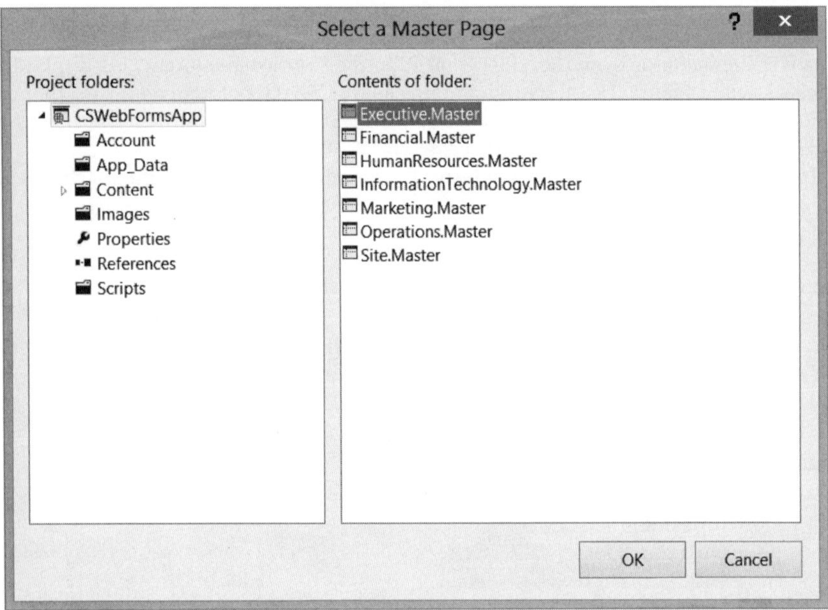

FIGURE 21-35

Select the master page to be applied to the detail page, and click OK. The new web form page that is added to the project includes one or more Content controls, which map to the ContentPlaceHolder controls on the master page.

It doesn't take long to see the benefits of master pages and understand why they have become a popular feature. However, it is even more useful to create nested master pages.

Working with nested master pages is not much different from working with normal master pages. To add one, select Nested Master Page from the Add New Item window. You are prompted to select the parent master page via the Select a Master Page window (refer to Figure 21-35). When you subsequently add a new content web page, any nested master pages are also shown in the Select a Master Page window.

RICH CLIENT-SIDE DEVELOPMENT

In the past couple of years the software industry has seen a fundamental shift toward emphasizing the importance of the end user experience in application development. Nowhere has that been more apparent than in the development of web applications. Fueled by technologies such as AJAX and an increased appreciation of JavaScript, you are expected to provide web applications that approach the richness of their desktop equivalents.

Microsoft has certainly recognized this and includes a range of tools and functionality in Visual Studio 2012 that support the creation of rich client-side interactions. There is integrated debugging and IntelliSense support for JavaScript. ASP.NET AJAX is shipped with Visual Studio 2012, and there is support in the IDE for AJAX Control Extenders. These tools make it much easier for you to design, build, and debug client-side code that provides a much richer user experience.

Developing with JavaScript

Writing JavaScript client code has long had a reputation for being difficult, even though the language is quite simple. Because JavaScript is a dynamic, loosely typed programming language — different from the strong typing enforced by Visual Basic and C# — JavaScript's reputation is even worse in some .NET developer circles.

Thus, one of the most useful features of Visual Studio for web developers is IntelliSense support for JavaScript. The IntelliSense begins immediately as you start typing, with prompts for native JavaScript functions and keywords such as `var`, `alert`, and `eval`.

Furthermore, the JavaScript IntelliSense in Visual Studio 2012 automatically evaluates and infers variable types to provide more accurate IntelliSense prompts. For example, in Figure 21-36 you can see that IntelliSense has determined that `optSelected` is an HTML object because a call to the `document .getElementByID` function returns that type.

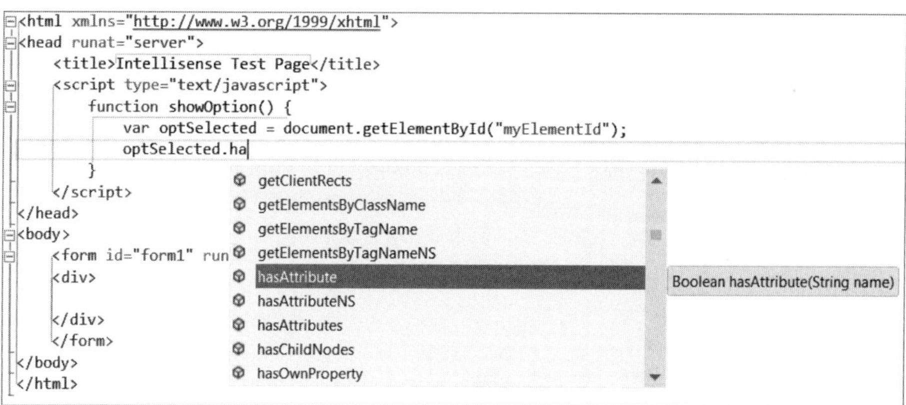

FIGURE 21-36

In addition to displaying IntelliSense within web forms, Visual Studio also supports IntelliSense in external JavaScript files. It also provides IntelliSense help for referenced script files and libraries, such as the Microsoft AJAX library.

Microsoft has extended the XML commenting system in Visual Studio to recognize comments on JavaScript functions. IntelliSense detects these XML code comments and displays the summary, parameters, and return type information for the function.

Although Visual Studio constantly monitors changes to files in the project and updates the IntelliSense as they happen, a couple limitations could prevent the JavaScript IntelliSense from displaying information in certain circumstances, including:

- A syntax or other error in an external referenced script file.
- Invoking a browser-specific function or object. Most web browsers provide a set of objects that is proprietary to that browser. You can still use these objects, and many popular JavaScript frameworks do; however, you won't get IntelliSense support for them.
- Referencing files outside the current project.

One feature of ASP.NET that is a boon to JavaScript developers is the `ClientIDMode` property that is available for web server controls. In earlier versions, the value that was generated for the `id` attribute on generated HTML controls made it difficult to reference these controls in JavaScript. The `ClientIDMode` property fixes this by defining two modes (`Static` and `Predictable`) for generating these ids in a simpler and more predictable way.

The updated JavaScript IntelliSense support, combined with the improved client-side debugging and better control over client IDs, significantly reduces the difficulty to develop JavaScript code with Visual Studio 2012.

Working with ASP.NET AJAX

The ASP.NET AJAX framework provides web developers with a familiar server-control programming approach for building rich client-side AJAX interactions.

ASP.NET AJAX includes both server-side and client-side components. A set of server controls, including the popular UpdatePanel and UpdateProgess controls, can be added to web forms to enable asynchronous partial-page updates without your needing to make changes to any existing code on the page. The client-side Microsoft AJAX Library is a JavaScript framework that can be used in any web application, such as PHP on Apache, and not just ASP.NET or IIS.

The following walkthrough demonstrates how to enhance an existing web page by adding the ASP.NET AJAX UpdatePanel control to perform a partial-page update. In this scenario you have a simple web form with a DropDownList server control, which has an AutoPostBack to the server enabled. The web form handles the `DropDownList.SelectedIndexChanged` event and saves the value that was selected in the DropDownList to a TextBox server control on the page. The code listing for this page follows:

AJAXSAMPLEFORM.ASPX

```
<%@ Page Language="vb" AutoEventWireup="false"
   CodeBehind="AjaxSampleForm.aspx.vb"
   Inherits="ASPNetWebApp.AjaxSampleForm" %>
<!DOCTYPE html PUBLIC "-//W3C//DTD XHTML 1.0 Transitional//EN"
   "http://www.w3.org/TR/xhtml1/DTD/xhtml1-transitional.dtd">
<html xmlns="http://www.w3.org/1999/xhtml" >
<head runat="server">
    <title>ASP.NET AJAX Sample</title>
</head>
<body>
    <form id="form1" runat="server">
        <div>
        Select an option:
        <asp:DropDownList ID="DropDownList1" runat="server" AutoPostBack="True">
            <asp:ListItem Text="Option 1" Value="Option 1" />
            <asp:ListItem Text="Option 2" Value="Option 2" />
            <asp:ListItem Text="Option 3" Value="Option 3" />
        </asp:DropDownList>
        <br />
```

```
        Option selected:
        <asp:TextBox ID="TextBox1" runat="server"></asp:TextBox>
    </div>
    </form>
</body>
</html>
```

AJAXSAMPLEFORM.ASPX.VB

```
Public Partial Class AjaxSampleForm
    Inherits System.Web.UI.Page
    Protected Sub DropDownList1_SelectedIndexChanged(ByVal sender As Object, _
                                                     ByVal e As EventArgs) _
                                        Handles
DropDownList1.SelectedIndexChanged
        System.Threading.Thread.Sleep(2000)
        Me.TextBox1.Text = Me.DropDownList1.SelectedValue
    End Sub
End Class
```

Notice that in the `DropDownList1_SelectedIndexChanged` method you added a statement to sleep for 2 seconds. This exaggerates the server processing time, thereby making it easier to see the effect of the changes you will make. When you run this page and change an option in the drop-down list, the whole page will be refreshed in the browser.

The first AJAX control that you need to add to your web page is a ScriptManager. This is a nonvisual control that's central to ASP.NET AJAX and is responsible for tasks such as sending script libraries and files to the client and generating any required client proxy classes. You can have only one ScriptManager control per ASP.NET web page, which can pose a problem when you use master pages and user controls. In that case, you should add the ScriptManager to the topmost parent page and a ScriptManagerProxy control to all child pages.

After you add the ScriptManager control, you can add any other ASP.NET AJAX controls. In this case, add an UpdatePanel control to the web page, as shown in the following listing. Notice that `TextBox1` is now contained within the UpdatePanel control.

```
<%@ Page Language="vb" AutoEventWireup="false"
   CodeBehind="AjaxSampleForm.aspx.vb"
   Inherits="ASPNetWebApp.AjaxSampleForm" %>
<!DOCTYPE html PUBLIC "-//W3C//DTD XHTML 1.0 Transitional//EN"
   "http://www.w3.org/TR/xhtml1/DTD/xhtml1-transitional.dtd">
<html xmlns="http://www.w3.org/1999/xhtml" >
<head runat="server">
    <title>ASP.NET AJAX Sample</title>
</head>
<body>
    <form id="form1" runat="server">
    <asp:ScriptManager ID="ScriptManager1" runat="server"></asp:ScriptManager>
    <div>
        Select an option:
        <asp:DropDownList ID="DropDownList1" runat="server" AutoPostBack="True">
            <asp:ListItem Text="Option 1" Value="Option 1" />
            <asp:ListItem Text="Option 2" Value="Option 2" />
            <asp:ListItem Text="Option 3" Value="Option 3" />
        </asp:DropDownList>
        <br />
        Option selected:
        <asp:UpdatePanel ID="UpdatePanel1" runat="server">
            <ContentTemplate>
                <asp:TextBox ID="TextBox1" runat="server"></asp:TextBox>
```

```
                </ContentTemplate>
                <Triggers>
                    <asp:AsyncPostBackTrigger ControlID="DropDownList1"
                                              EventName="SelectedIndexChanged" />
                </Triggers>
            </asp:UpdatePanel>
        </div>
        </form>
    </body>
    </html>
```

The web page now uses AJAX to provide a partial-page update. When you now run this page and change an option in the drop-down list, the whole page is no longer refreshed. Instead, just the text within the textbox is updated. In fact, if you run this page you can notice that AJAX is too good at just updating part of the page. There is no feedback, and if you didn't know any better, you would think that nothing is happening. This is where the UpdateProgress control becomes useful. You can place an UpdateProgress control on the page, and when an AJAX request is invoked, the HTML within the ProgressTemplate section of the control is rendered. The following listing shows an example of an UpdateProgress control for your web form:

```
<asp:UpdateProgress ID="UpdateProgress1" runat="server">
    <ProgressTemplate>
        Loading.
    </ProgressTemplate>
</asp:UpdateProgress>
```

The final server control in ASP.NET AJAX that hasn't been mentioned is the Timer control, which enables you to perform asynchronous or synchronous client-side postbacks at a defined interval. This can be useful for scenarios such as checking with the server to see if a value has changed.

After you have added some basic AJAX functionality to your web application, you can further improve the client user experience by adding one or more elements from the AJAX Control Toolkit, which is discussed in the following section.

Using AJAX Control Extenders

AJAX Control Extenders provide a way to add AJAX functionality to a standard ASP.NET server control. The best-known set of control extenders is the AJAX Control Toolkit, a free open-source library of client behaviors that includes dozens of control extenders. These either provide enhancements to existing ASP.NET web controls or provide completely new rich-client UI elements. Figure 21-37 shows a Calendar Extender that has been attached to a TextBox control.

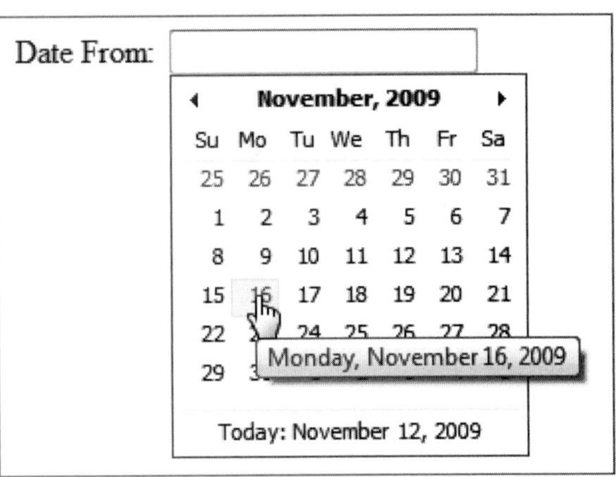

FIGURE 21-37

The ASP.NET AJAX Control Toolkit is available for download via a link from `http://ajaxcontroltoolkit.codeplex.com`. The binary version of the download includes an assembly called `AjaxControlToolkit.dll`. Copy this to a directory where you won't accidentally delete it.

To add the controls to the Visual Studio Control Toolbox, you should first create a new tab to house them. Right-click anywhere in the Toolbox window, choose Add Tab, and then rename the new tab something meaningful, such as AJAX Control Toolkit. Next, right-click in the new tab, and select Choose Items. Click the Browse button, and locate the `AjaxControlToolkit.dll` to add the AJAX controls to the list of available .NET Framework Components. Click OK and the tab will be populated with all the controls in the AJAX Control Toolkit.

Visual Studio 2012 provides designer support for any AJAX Control Extenders, including the AJAX Control Toolkit. After you have added the controls to the Toolbox, Visual Studio adds an entry to the smart-tag Tasks list of any web controls with extenders, as shown in Figure 21-38.

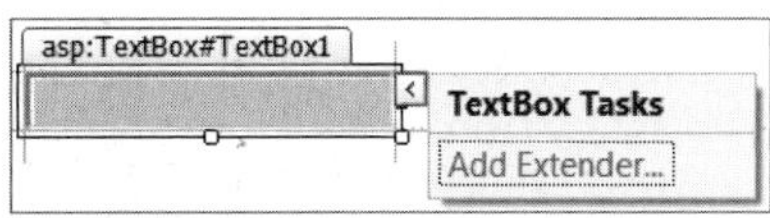

FIGURE 21-38

When you select the Add Extender task, it launches the Extender Wizard, as shown in Figure 21-39. Choose an extender from the list, and click OK to add it to your web form. In most cases, the Extender Wizard also automatically adds a reference to the AJAX Control Toolkit library. However, if it does not, you can manually add a binary reference to the `AjaxControlToolkit.dll` assembly.

> **NOTE** *Because the Extender Controls are built on top of ASP.NET AJAX, you need to ensure that a ScriptManager control is on your web form.*

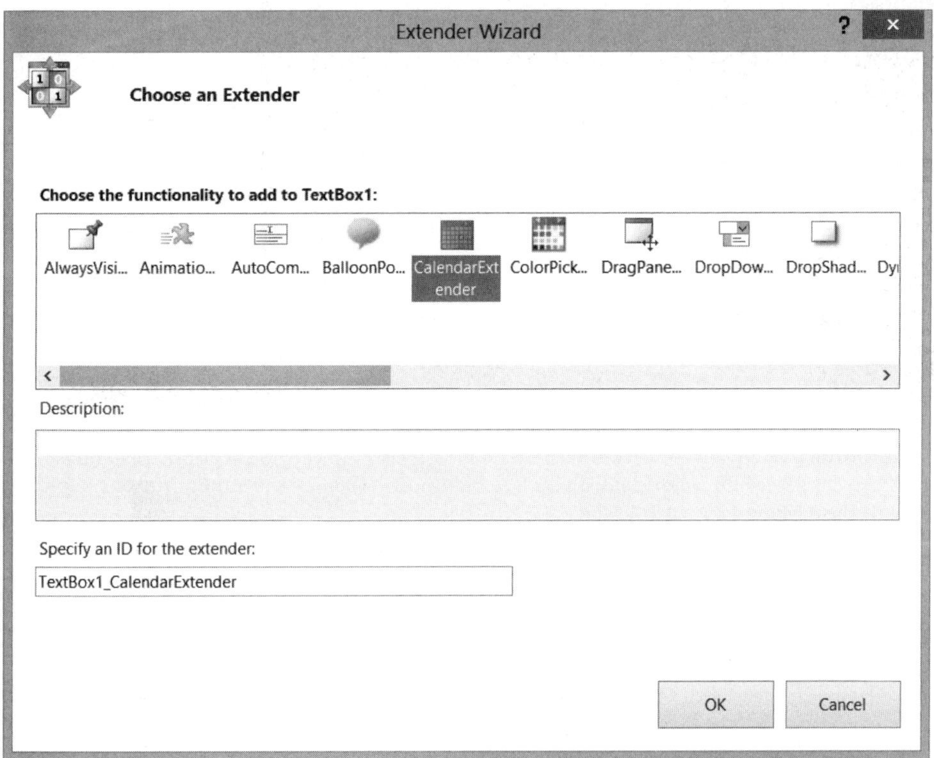

FIGURE 21-39

As shown in Figure 21-40, Visual Studio 2012 includes all the properties for the control extender in the property grid, under the control to which the extender is attached.

Because the AJAX Control Toolkit is open source, you can customize or further enhance any of the control extenders it includes. Visual Studio 2012 also ships with C# and Visual Basic project templates to create your own AJAX Control Extenders and ASP.NET AJAX Controls. This makes it easy to build rich web applications with UI functionality that can be easily reused across your web pages and projects.

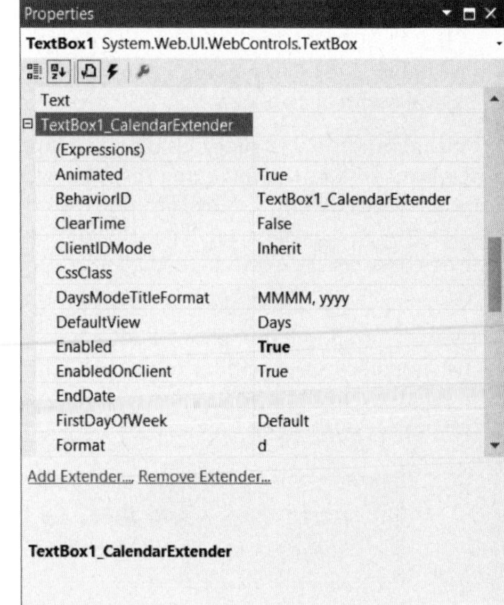

FIGURE 21-40

ASP.NET WEB SITE ADMINISTRATION

Although running your web application with default behavior works in most situations, sometimes you need to manage the application settings beyond simply setting the properties of components and page items. The Web Site Administration Tool provides you with a web-based configuration application that enables you to define various security-related settings, such as users and roles, as well as application-wide settings that can come in handy, such as a default error page, and global SMTP e-mail settings that are used by various components, such as the PasswordRecovery control.

To start the Administration Tool, use the Project ➪ ASP.NET Configuration menu command for Web Application projects, or Website ➪ ASP.NET Configuration for Web Site projects. When the tool is launched, Visual Studio 2012 instantiates a temporary web server on a unique port and opens a web browser to the Administration Tool home page for the application you're currently administering.

> **WARNING** *In some cases, you might receive a timeout message while launching the Web Site Administration Tool page. There can be a number of causes for the message, but in most cases, performing an iisreset to restart IIS will resolve the problem.*

You can determine whether or not the web server is active by looking in the notification area of your taskbar and finding the development server icon connected to the port that Visual Studio 2012 allocated when it was started up. You can stop an active web server by right-clicking its icon in the notification area and selecting Show Details. When the server information displays (see Figure 21-41), click the Stop button to stop the specific instance of the development web server.

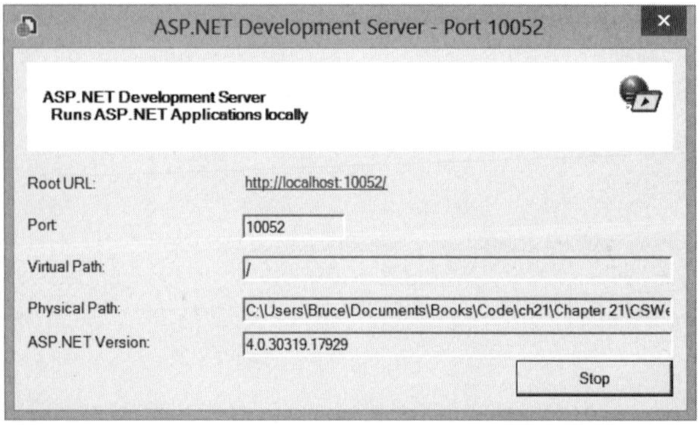

FIGURE 21-41

> **NOTE** *Stopping an active web server won't affect any other development servers currently running.*

When the Administration Tool displays in your web browser, it shows the application name, accompanied by the name of the current Windows-based authenticated user. The tool has three main sections: security for the creation and maintenance of users, roles, and authentication; application configuration to control application-specific key-value pairs, SMTP settings, and debug configurations; and provider configuration to control the way the user administration data is stored for the site.

Security

The security section of the tool provides you with a summary of the users and roles defined in the site and the authentication mode. You can change individual settings from this summary page by clicking their associated links, or use the Security Setup Wizard to step through each section of the security settings in turn.

The authentication mode is controlled by the access method page (shown in the wizard in Figure 21-42). If you choose From the Internet, the tool sets the authentication mode to Forms, whereas the From a Local Area Network option results in an authentication mode of Windows.

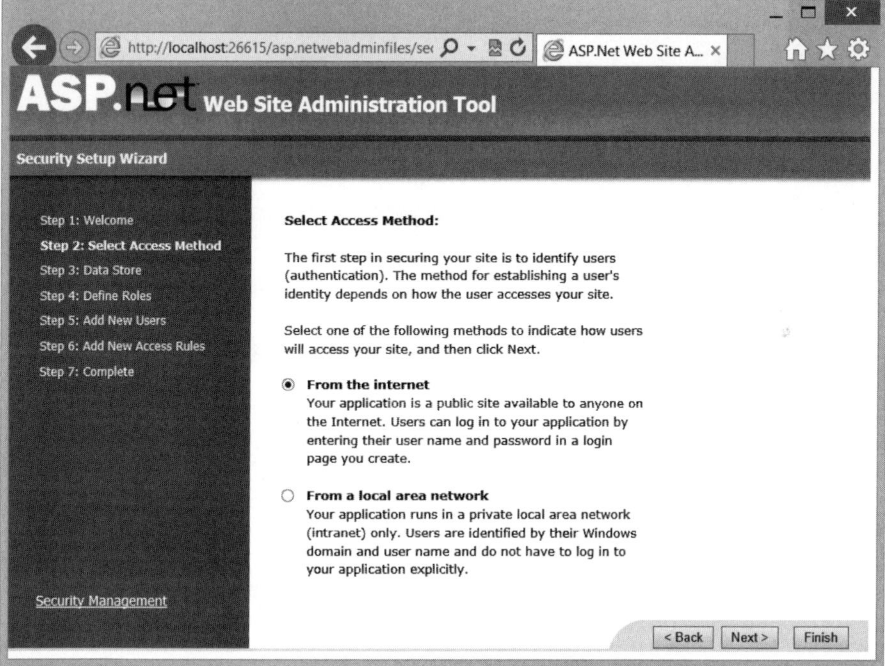

FIGURE 21-42

The most useful part of this tool is the ability it gives you to add and edit roles. In the wizard you first need to enable role management by checking the Enable Roles for This Web Site option. After roles are active you can define them either through the wizard or from the summary page. Each role is defined by a single string value, and it's up to you to control how that role will be used in your web application (with the exception of access rules, which are discussed in a moment).

The next step in the wizard is to create user accounts. The information on this page is a replication of the CreateUserAccount component and enables you to create an initial user who can serve as administrator for your website.

The access rules page (as shown in Figure 21-43) enables you to restrict access to certain parts of your site to a specific role or user, or to grant access only when any user is logged in. By default there is a single rule (which is actually implicitly defined and inherited from the server) that defines full access to the entire site for all users.

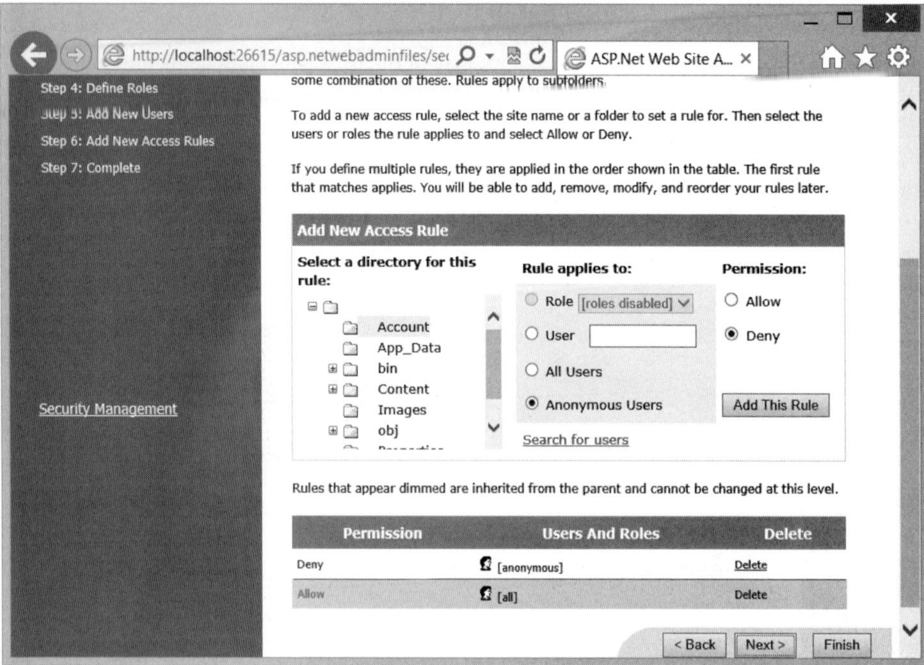

FIGURE 21-43

Website processing looks at the rules in the order in which they are defined, stopping at the first rule that applies to the particular context. For example, if you define first a rule that allows access to the Admin folder for anyone belonging to the Administrator's role, and then define a subsequent rule that denies access to the same folder for all users, it effectively blocks access to the Admin folder for all users who do not belong to the Administrator's role.

After you have users, roles, and rules defined in your site, you can then start applying the access by clicking the Manage Users link from the summary security page. This presents you with a list of all users defined in the system. Click the Edit User or Edit Roles link to specify the roles to which each user belongs.

This information can be used to customize the content in your web pages with the LoginView component discussed earlier in this chapter.

Application Settings

The application section of the Web Site Administration Tool enables you to define and edit application-specific settings in the form of key-value pairs, as well as to configure SMTP e-mail settings, including the default SMTP mail server and sender's e-mail address.

You can also specify what level of debugging you want to perform on the application and customize the tracing information being kept as you run the application.

ASP.NET Configuration in IIS

If you have already deployed an ASP.NET application to a production server, you can edit the configuration settings directly within Internet Information Services (IIS), located in the Administrative Tools section of the Control Panel. When ASP.NET is installed on a machine, you can find that each website (including virtual directories) has a set of configuration tools in IIS under the property pages, as shown in Figure 21-44.

FIGURE 21-44

The tools included in IIS enable you to manage all the settings you saw earlier, including the creation and management of users, roles, application settings, and SMTP settings. You are also given access to more powerful administration tools that enable you to configure advanced settings such as the .NET compilation behavior, .NET trust level, and session state configuration. These tools enable you to maintain a web application running on any IIS server without needing to resort to editing the `Web.config` configuration file.

SUMMARY

In this chapter you learned how to create ASP.NET applications using the Web Site and Web Application projects. The power of the HTML Designer and the CSS tools in Visual Studio 2012 provide you with great power over the layout and visual design of web pages. The vast number of web controls included in ASP.NET enables you to quickly put together highly functional web pages. Through the judicious use of JavaScript, ASP.NET AJAX, and control extenders in the AJAX Control Toolkit, you can provide a rich user experience in your web applications.

Of course, there's much more to web development than covered here. Chapters 22 and 23 continue the discussion on building rich web applications by exploring the latest web technologies from Microsoft: ASP.NET MVC and Silverlight. Chapter 43 provides detailed information about the tools and techniques available for effective debugging of web applications. Finally, Chapter 50, "Web Application Deployment," walks you through the deployment options for web applications. If you want more information after this, you should check out *Professional ASP.NET 4 in C# and VB* by Bill Evjen, Scott Hanselman, and Devin Rader. Weighing in at more than 1,600 pages, this is the best and most comprehensive resource available to web developers who are building applications on the latest version of ASP.NET.

22

ASP.NET MVC

WHAT'S IN THIS CHAPTER?

- Understanding the Model-View-Controller design pattern
- Developing ASP.NET MVC applications
- Designing URL routes
- Validating user input
- Integrating with jQuery

When Microsoft introduced the first version of the .NET Framework in 2002, it added a new abstraction for the development of web applications called ASP.NET Web Forms. Where traditional Active Server Pages (ASP) had up until this point operated like simple templates containing a mix of HTML markup and server-side code, Web Forms was designed to bring the web application development experience closer to the desktop application programming model. This model involves dragging components from a toolbox onto a design surface, and then configuring those components by setting property values and writing code to handle specific events.

Although Web Forms has been and continues to be successful, it is not without criticism. Without strong discipline it is easy for business logic and data-access concerns to creep into the user interface, making it hard to test without sitting in front of a browser. It heavily abstracts away the stateless request/response nature of the web, which can make it frustrating to debug. It relies heavily on controls rendering their own HTML markup, which can make it difficult to control the final output of each page.

In 2004, the release of a simple open source framework for building web applications called Ruby on Rails heralded a renewed interest in an architectural pattern called Model-View-Controller (MVC). The MVC pattern divides the parts of a user interface into three classifications with well-defined roles. This makes applications easier to test, evolve, and maintain.

Microsoft first announced the ASP.NET MVC framework at an ALT.NET conference in late 2007. This framework enables you to build applications based on the MVC architecture while taking advantage of the .NET Framework's extensive set of libraries and language options. ASP.NET MVC has been developed in an open manner with many of its features shaped by community feedback, and in April 2009 the entire source code for the framework was released as open source under the Ms-PL license.

> **NOTE** *Microsoft has been careful to state that ASP.NET MVC is not a replacement for Web Forms. It is simply an alternative way to build web applications that some people will find preferable. Microsoft has made it clear that it will continue to support both ASP.NET Web Forms and ASP.NET MVC.*

MODEL VIEW CONTROLLER

If you have never heard of it before, you might be surprised to learn that this "new" Model-View-Controller architectural pattern was first described in 1979 by Trygve Reenskaug, a researcher working on an implementation of SmallTalk.

In the MVC architecture, applications are separated into the following components.

- **Model:** The model consists of classes that implement domain-specific logic for the application. Although the MVC architecture does not concern itself with the specifics of the data access layer, it is understood that the model should encapsulate any data access code. Generally, the model calls separate data access classes responsible for retrieving and storing information in a database.
- **View:** The views are classes that take the model and render it into a format where the user can interact with it.
- **Controller:** The controller is responsible for bringing everything together. A controller processes and responds to events, such as a user clicking a button. The controller maps these events onto the model and invokes the appropriate view.

These descriptions aren't actually helpful until you understand how they interact together. The request life cycle of an ASP.NET MVC application normally consists of the following:

1. The user performs an action that triggers an event, such as entering a URL or clicking a button. This generates a request to the controller.
2. The controller receives the request and invokes the relevant action on the model. Often this can cause a change in the model's state, although not always.
3. The controller retrieves any necessary data from the model and invokes the appropriate view, passing it the data from the model.
4. The view renders the data and sends it back to the user.

The most important thing to note here is that both the view and controller depend on the model. However, the model has no dependencies, which is one of the key benefits of the architecture. This separation is what provides better testability and makes it easier to manage complexity.

> **NOTE** *Different MVC framework implementations have minor variations in the preceding life cycle. For example, in some cases the view queries the model for the current state, instead of receiving it from the controller.*

Now that you understand the Model-View-Controller architectural pattern, you can begin to apply this newfound knowledge to build your first ASP.NET MVC application.

GETTING STARTED WITH ASP.NET MVC

This section details the creation of a new ASP.NET MVC application and describes some of the standard components. To create a new MVC application, go to File ➪ New Project, and select ASP.NET MVC 4 Web Application from the Web section. After you give a name to the project and select OK, Visual Studio asks for a number of setup parameters, such as the project template, the view engine, and whether or not a unit test project for the application should be created (shown in Figure 22-1).

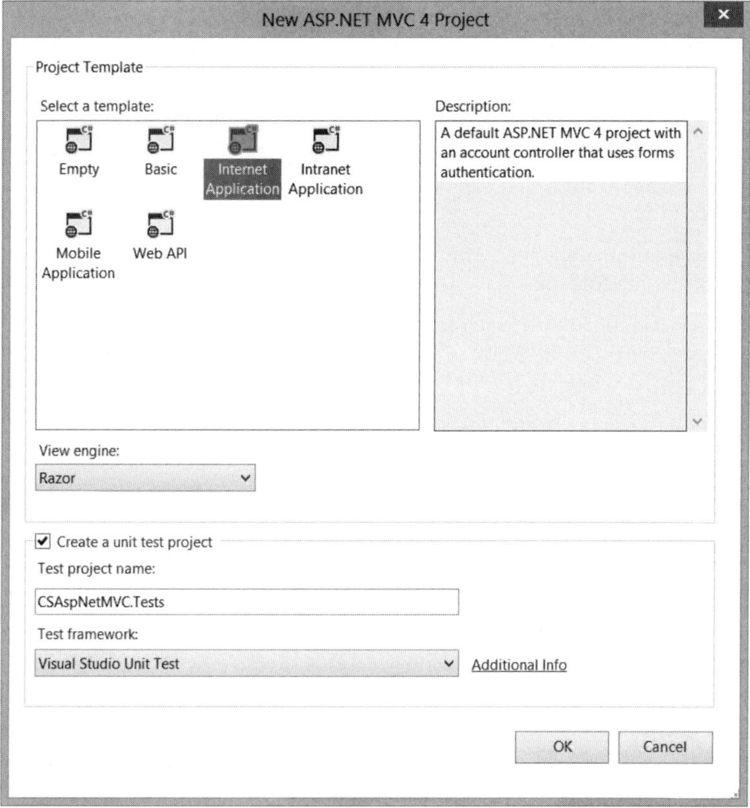

FIGURE 22-1

Your first option in defining the MVC project is to select a project template, such as Empty, Basic, Internet Application, Intranet Application, Mobile Application, and Web API. The choice you make impacts some of the files that are downloaded. For example, the Mobile Application template includes the jQuery Mobile libraries. So consider this choice to be just a further refinement of the project template options available from the New Project dialog.

The choice for the View Engine is a little more interesting. First, from the perspective of MVC, the view engine is responsible for rendering the view into HTML, XML, or into whatever format is required. In general, the difference between the various view engines relates to how easy or hard it is to express the desired output.

For example, Visual Studio 2012 ships with two view engines: ASPX and Razor. For the initial release of ASP.NET MVC, only the ASPX engine was shipped. This engine basically replicates the Web Form model (which was familiar to ASP.NET developers) using the MVC pattern. However, more recently Microsoft released the Razor engine, which bears much less resemblance to Web Forms and is therefore (at least in the context of MVC) easier to use. Beyond these two view engines, the ASP.NET MVC community has also contributed a number of other view engines, including two popular ones named Spark and NHaml.

Finally, you have the option to create a unit test project for the application. Although this is not required, it is highly recommended because improved testability is one of the key advantages of using the MVC framework. You can always add a test project later if you want.

> **NOTE** *Visual Studio 2012 can create test projects for MVC applications using a number of unit testing frameworks. The default choice (refer to Figure 22-1) is to use the built-in unit testing tools in Visual Studio. If you prefer to use a different unit testing technology, see the vendor for instructions on how to add to this list.*

When an ASP.NET MVC application is first created, it generates a number of files and folders. The MVC application generated from the project template is a complete application that can be run immediately.

Figure 22-2 shows the folder structure automatically generated by Visual Studio and includes the following folders:

- **Content:** A location to store static content files such as themes and CSS files.
- **Controllers:** Contains the Controller files. Two sample controllers called `HomeController` and `AccountController` are created by the project template.
- **Images:** A location to store static image files.
- **Models:** Contains model files. This is also a good place to store any data access classes that are encapsulated by the model. The MVC project template does not create an example model.
- **Scripts:** Contains JavaScript files. By default, this folder contains script files for JQuery and Microsoft AJAX along with some helper scripts to integrate with MVC.
- **Views:** Contains the view files. The MVC project template creates a number of folders and files in the Views folder. The Home subfolder contains two example view files invoked by the `HomeController`. The Shared subfolder contains a master page used by these views.

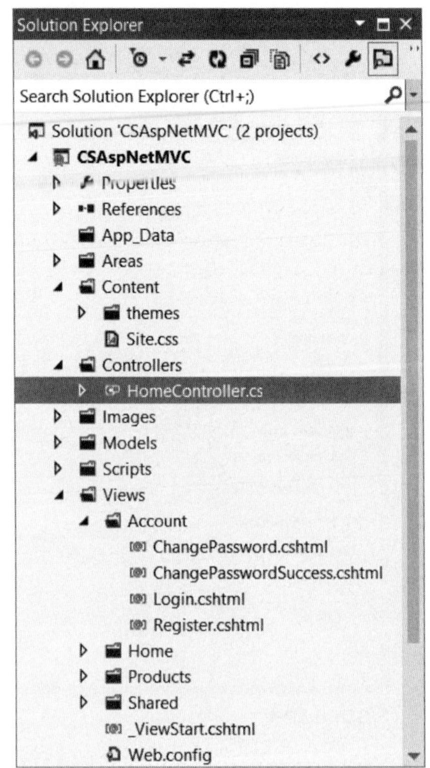

FIGURE 22-2

Visual Studio also creates a `Global.asax` file, which is used to configure the routing rules (more on that later).

Finally, if you elected to create a test project, this is created with a Controllers folder that contains a unit test stub for the `HomeController`.

Although it doesn't do much yet, you can run the MVC application by pressing F5. Exactly what it does depends on the template that you select.

CHOOSING A MODEL

In the previous section it was noted that the MVC project template does not create a sample model for you. Actually, the application can run without a model altogether. While in practice your applications are likely to have a full model, MVC provides no guidance as to which technology you should use. This gives you a great deal of flexibility.

The model part of your application is an abstraction of the business capabilities that the application provides. If you build an application to process orders or organize a leave schedule, your model should express these concepts. This is not always easy. It is frequently tempting to allow some of these details to creep in the View-controller part of your application.

The examples in this chapter use a simple LINQ-to-SQL model based on a subset of the AdventureWorksDB sample database as shown in Figure 22-3. You can download this sample database from `http://msftdbprodsamples.codeplex.com/`. Chapter 29, "Language Integrated Queries (LINQ)," explains how to create a new LINQ-to-SQL model.

The next section explains how you can build your own controller, followed by some interesting views that render a dynamic user interface.

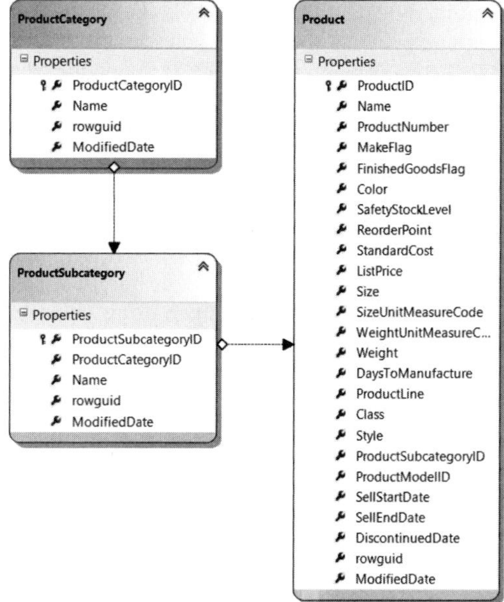

FIGURE 22-3

CONTROLLERS AND ACTION METHODS

A controller is a class that responds to some user action. Usually, this response involves updating the model in some way, and then organizing for a view to present content back to the user. Each controller can listen for and respond to a number of user actions. Each of these is represented in the code by a normal method referred to as an action method.

Begin by right-clicking the Controllers folder in the Solution Explorer and selecting Add ➪ Controller to display the Add Controller dialog, as shown in Figure 22-4. This dialog allows you to select a name for your new controller. By convention, the MVC framework requires that all controller classes have names that end in "Controller," so this part is already filled in for you. There is also a drop-down list allowing you to specify some scaffolding options for the controller. The available choices are covered in the next section.

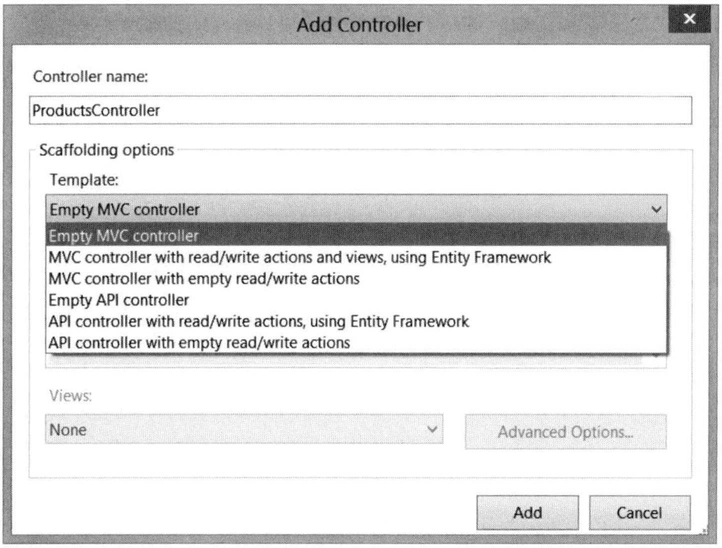

FIGURE 22-4

MVC Scaffolding

Scaffolding is a mechanism that is used in a couple of different technologies throughout .NET. It will be covered in Chapter 24, "Dynamic Data", where it is used to dynamically generate web pages based on the underlying database. For ASP.NET MVC, scaffolding is used to create a collection of pages that relate to the type of controller that you're adding. If you think of the scaffolding as a template, you're close. Typically a template is used to generate a single file from a given set of parameters. In this particular case, adding a controller using scaffolding results in a number of different files being added. The specific files and the functionality that are found therein depend on the type of scaffolding that is selected.

In Figure 22-4, you'll notice that the choices fall into two basic categories. Three of them relate to an MVC controller. The other three relate to a controller based on the ASP.NET Web API. You also notice that, within each of the groups, there are three different options: an empty controller, a controller that uses the Entity Framework to perform CRUD (Create/Read/Update/Delete) operations, and a controller that has the methods to perform CRUD, but no implementation. So the selection of the template should be based on whether or not you plan on using MVC or the Web API and secondarily on how much of the CRUD functions you would like to be automatically generated.

> **NOTE** *The ASP.NET Web API is a framework that allows a broad range of clients, from browsers to mobile devices, that consume HTTP services. On the server side, the Web API assists in the construction of easily consumable HTTP services. In terms of how it differs from MVC, in general, the answer can be given in terms of how it utilizes HTTP. MVC using a REST-based notation to identify the server-side resources that are retrieved. REST notations utilizes HTTP verbs (GET, PUT, DELETE, and POST) to perform their operations. The Web API takes advantage of all of the capabilities of HTTP (including headers, the body, and full URI addressing) to create a rich and interoperable way to access resources.*

Give the new controller a name of `ProductsController`, select an Empty MVC Controller as the template, and click Add.

> **NOTE** *You can quickly add a controller to your project by using the Ctrl+M, Ctrl+C shortcut as well.*

New controller classes inherit from the `System.Web.Mvc.Controller` base class, which performs all the hefty lifting in terms of determining the relevant method to call for an action and mapping of URL and POST parameter values. This means that you can concentrate on the implementation details of your actions, which typically involve invoking a method on a model class, and then selecting a view to render.

A newly created controller class will be populated with a default action method called `Index`. You can add a new action simply by adding a public method to the class. If a method is public, it will be visible as an action on the controller. You can stop a public method from being exposed as an action by adding the `System.Web.Mvc.NonAction` attribute to the method. The following listing contains the controller class with the default action that simply renders the `Index` view, and a public method that is not visible as an action:

C#

```
public class ProductsController : Controller
{
  //
  // GET: /Products/

  public ActionResult Index()
  {
    return View();
  }

  [NonAction]
  public void NotAnAction()
```

```
    {
      // This method is not exposed as an action.
    }
  }
```

VB

```
Public Class ProductsController
    Inherits System.Web.Mvc.Controller

    '
    ' GET: /Products/

    Function Index() As ActionResult
        Return View()
    End Function

    <NonAction()>
    Sub NotAnAction()
        ' This method is not exposed as an action.
    End Sub

End Class
```

> **NOTE** *The comment that appears above the* `Index` *method is a convention that indicates how the action is triggered. Each action method is placed at a URL that is a combination of the controller name and the action method name formatted like /controller/action. The comment has no control over this convention but is used to indicate where you can expect to find this action method. In this case it is saying that the index action is triggered by executing an HTTP GET request against the URL /Products/. This is just the name of the controller because an action named* `Index` *is assumed if one is not explicitly stated by the URL. This convention is revisited in the section on routing.*

The result of the `Index` method is an object that derives from the `System.Web.Mvc.ActionResult` abstract class. This object is responsible for determining what happens after the action method returns. A number of standard classes inherit from `ActionResult` that allow you to perform a number of standard tasks, including redirection to another URL, generating some simple content in a number of different formats, or in this case, rendering a view.

> **NOTE** *The* `View` *method on the* `Controller` *base class is a simple method that creates and configures a* `System.Web.Mvc.ViewResult` *object. This object is responsible for selecting a view and passing it any information that it needs to render its contents.*

It is important to note that `Index` is just a normal .NET method and `ProductsController` is just a normal .NET class. There is nothing special about either of them. This means that you can easily instantiate a `ProductsController` in a test harness, call its `Index` method, and then make assertions about the `ActionResult` object it returns.

Before moving on, update the `Index` method to retrieve a list of Products, and pass them onto the view, as shown in the following code listing:

C#

```
public ActionResult Index()
```

```
{
    List<Product> products;

    using (var db = new ProductsDataContext())
    {
        products = db.Products.ToList();
    }

    return View(products);
}
```

VB

```
Function Index() As ActionResult
  Dim products As New List(Of Product)

  Using db As New ProductsDataContext
    products = db.Products.ToList()
  End Using

  Return View(products)
End Function
```

Now that you have created a model and a controller, all that is needed is to create the view to display the UI.

RENDERING A UI WITH VIEWS

In the previous section you created an action method that gathers the complete list of products and passes that list to a view. Each view belongs to a single controller and is stored in a subfolder in the Views folder, which is named after the controller that owns it. In addition, there is a Shared folder, which contains a number of shared views that are accessible from a number of controllers. When the view engine looks for a view, it checks the controller-specific area first and then checks in the shared area.

> **NOTE** *You can specify the full path to a view as the view name if you need to refer to a view that is not in the normal view engine search areas.*

The look that a particular view has depends greatly on the view engine that is used. An ASPX view looks similar to a standard ASP.NET Web Forms `Page` or `Control` having either an `.aspx` or `.ascx` extension. A Razor view has some superficial resemblance to an ASPX page, but syntactically there are significant differences. However, in general, views contain some mix of HTML markup and code blocks. They can even have master pages and render some standard controls. However, a number of important differences exist that need to be highlighted.

First, a view doesn't have a code behind page. As such, there is nowhere to add event handlers for any controls that the view renders, including those that normally happen behind the scenes. Instead, it is expected that a controller will respond to user events and that the view will expose ways for the user to trigger action methods. Second, instead of inheriting from `System.Web.Page`, a view inherits from `System.Web.Mvc.ViewPage`. This base class exposes a number of useful properties and methods that can be used to help render the HTML output. One of these properties contains a dictionary of objects that were passed into the view from the controller. Finally, in the markup you can notice that there is no form control with a `runat="server"` attribute. No server form means that there is no View State emitted with the page. The majority of the ASP.NET server controls must be placed inside a server form. Some controls such as a Literal or Repeater control work fine outside a form; however, if you try to use a Button or DropDownList control, your page throws an exception at run time.

You can create a View in a number of ways, but the easiest is to right-click the title of the action method and select Add View, which brings up the Add View dialog, as shown in Figure 22-5.

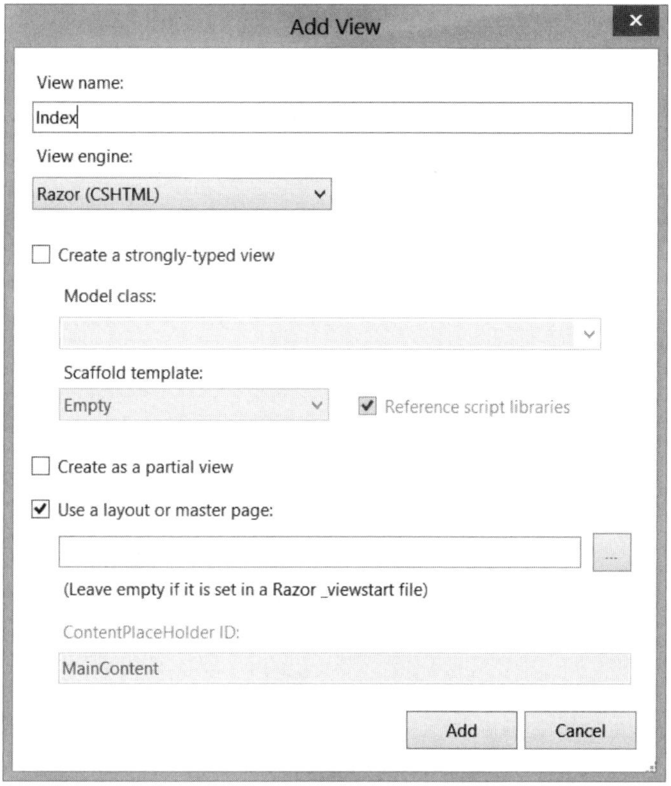

FIGURE 22-5

> **NOTE** *You can use the shortcut Ctrl+M, Ctrl+V when the cursor is inside an action method to open the Add View dialog as well.*

This dialog contains a number of options. By default, the name is set to match the name of the action method. If you change this, you need to change the constructor of the `View` to include the view name as a parameter. Check the box to create a strongly typed view and then choose `Models.Product` from the Model Class drop-down. If you don't see the Product class straight away, you might need to build the application before adding the view.

> **NOTE** *If you do not opt to create a strongly typed view, it will contain a dictionary of objects that need to be converted back into their real types before you can use them. It is recommended to always use strongly typed views. If you require your views to be weakly typed and you use C#, you should create a strongly typed view of the dynamic type and pass it* `ExpandoObject` *instances.*

When you create a strongly typed view, you also enable the Scaffold Template drop down. This drop down contains a number of view templates that are used to determine the type of view that is created. For example, a Create template would create a view that allows for a new product to be added. Change the Scaffold Template drop-down to List. This tells Visual Studio to generate a list page for Product objects.

When you click Add, the view should be generated and opened in the main editor window. It will look like this:

C#

```
<%@ Page Title="" Language="C#" MasterPageFile="~/Views/Shared/Site.Master"
Inherits="System.Web.Mvc.ViewPage<IEnumerable<CSProductsMVC.Models.Product>>" %>
<asp:Content ID="Content1" ContentPlaceHolderID="TitleContent" runat="server">
    Index
</asp:Content>
<asp:Content ID="Content2" ContentPlaceHolderID="MainContent" runat="server">
    <h2>Index</h2>
    <table>
        <tr>
            <th></th>
            <th>ProductID</th>
            <th>Name</th>
            <th>ProductNumber</th>
            <th>MakeFlag</th>
            <th>FinishedGoodsFlag</th>
            <th>Color</th>
            <th>SafetyStockLevel</th>
            <th>ReorderPoint</th>
            <th>StandardCost</th>
            <th>ListPrice</th>
            <th>Size</th>
            <th>SizeUnitMeasureCode</th>
            <th>WeightUnitMeasureCode</th>
            <th>Weight</th>
            <th>DaysToManufacture</th>
            <th>ProductLine</th>
            <th>Class</th>
            <th>Style</th>
            <th>ProductSubcategoryID</th>
            <th>ProductModelID</th>
            <th>SellStartDate</th>
            <th>SellEndDate</th>
            <th>DiscontinuedDate</th>
            <th>rowguid</th>
            <th>ModifiedDate</th>
        </tr>

    <% foreach (var item in Model) { %>

        <tr>
            <td>
                <%= Html.ActionLink("Edit", "Edit", new { id=item.ProductID }) %> |
                <%= Html.ActionLink("Details", "Details", new
                { id=item.ProductID })%>
            </td>
            <td><%= Html.Encode(item.ProductID) %></td>
            <td><%= Html.Encode(item.Name) %></td>
            <td><%= Html.Encode(item.ProductNumber) %></td>
            <td><%= Html.Encode(item.MakeFlag) %></td>
            <td><%= Html.Encode(item.FinishedGoodsFlag) %></td>
            <td><%= Html.Encode(item.Color) %></td>
            <td><%= Html.Encode(item.SafetyStockLevel) %></td>
            <td><%= Html.Encode(item.ReorderPoint) %></td>
            <td><%= Html.Encode(String.Format("{0:F}", item.StandardCost)) %></td>
            <td><%= Html.Encode(String.Format("{0:F}", item.ListPrice)) %></td>
            <td><%= Html.Encode(item.Size) %></td>
            <td><%= Html.Encode(item.SizeUnitMeasureCode) %></td>
            <td><%= Html.Encode(item.WeightUnitMeasureCode) %></td>
```

```
            <td><%= Html.Encode(String.Format("{0:F}", item.Weight)) %></td>
            <td><%= Html.Encode(item.DaysToManufacture) %></td>
            <td><%= Html.Encode(item.ProductLine) %></td>
            <td><%= Html.Encode(item.Class) %></td>
            <td><%= Html.Encode(item.Style) %></td>
            <td><%= Html.Encode(item.ProductSubcategoryID) %></td>
            <td><%= Html.Encode(item.ProductModelID) %></td>
            <td><%= Html.Encode(String.Format("{0:g}", item.SellStartDate)) %></td>
            <td><%= Html.Encode(String.Format("{0:g}", item.SellEndDate)) %></td>
            <td><%= Html.Encode(String.Format("{0:g}",
            item.DiscontinuedDate)) %></td>
            <td><%= Html.Encode(item.rowguid) %></td>
            <td><%= Html.Encode(String.Format("{0:g}", item.ModifiedDate)) %></td>
        </tr>

    <% } %>
    </table>
    <p>
        <%= Html.ActionLink("Create New", "Create") %>
    </p>
</asp:Content>
```

VB

```
<%@ Page Title="" Language="VB" MasterPageFile="~/Views/Shared/Site.Master"
Inherits="System.Web.Mvc.ViewPage(Of IEnumerable (Of ProductsMVC.Product))" %>
<asp:Content ID="Content1" ContentPlaceHolderID="TitleContent" runat="server">
    Index
</asp:Content>
<asp:Content ID="Content2" ContentPlaceHolderID="MainContent" runat="server">
    <h2>Index</h2>
    <p>
        <%=Html.ActionLink("Create New", "Create")%>
    </p>

    <table>
        <tr>
            <th></th>
            <th>ProductID</th>
            <th>Name</th>
            <th>ProductNumber</th>
            <th>MakeFlag</th>
            <th>FinishedGoodsFlag</th>
            <th>Color</th>
            <th>SafetyStockLevel</th>
            <th>ReorderPoint</th>
            <th>StandardCost</th>
            <th>ListPrice</th>
            <th>Size</th>
            <th>SizeUnitMeasureCode</th>
            <th>WeightUnitMeasureCode</th>
            <th>Weight</th>
            <th>DaysToManufacture</th>
            <th>ProductLine</th>
            <th>Class</th>
            <th>Style</th>
            <th>ProductSubcategoryID</th>
            <th>ProductModelID</th>
            <th>SellStartDate</th>
            <th>SellEndDate</th>
            <th>DiscontinuedDate</th>
            <th>rowguid</th>
            <th>ModifiedDate</th>
        </tr>
```

```
<% For Each item In Model%>

    <tr>
        <td>
            <%=Html.ActionLink("Edit", "Edit", New With
            {.id = item.ProductID})%> |
            <%=Html.ActionLink("Details", "Details", New With
            {.id = item.ProductID})%>
        </td>
        <td><%= Html.Encode(item.ProductID) %></td>
        <td><%= Html.Encode(item.Name) %></td>
        <td><%= Html.Encode(item.ProductNumber) %></td>
        <td><%= Html.Encode(item.MakeFlag) %></td>
        <td><%= Html.Encode(item.FinishedGoodsFlag) %></td>
        <td><%= Html.Encode(item.Color) %></td>
        <td><%= Html.Encode(item.SafetyStockLevel) %></td>
        <td><%= Html.Encode(item.ReorderPoint) %></td>
        <td><%= Html.Encode(String.Format("{0:F}", item.StandardCost)) %></td>
        <td><%= Html.Encode(String.Format("{0:F}", item.ListPrice)) %></td>
        <td><%= Html.Encode(item.Size) %></td>
        <td><%= Html.Encode(item.SizeUnitMeasureCode) %></td>
        <td><%= Html.Encode(item.WeightUnitMeasureCode) %></td>
        <td><%= Html.Encode(String.Format("{0:F}", item.Weight)) %></td>
        <td><%= Html.Encode(item.DaysToManufacture) %></td>
        <td><%= Html.Encode(item.ProductLine) %></td>
        <td><%= Html.Encode(item.Class) %></td>
        <td><%= Html.Encode(item.Style) %></td>
        <td><%= Html.Encode(item.ProductSubcategoryID) %></td>
        <td><%= Html.Encode(item.ProductModelID) %></td>
        <td><%= Html.Encode(String.Format("{0:g}", item.SellStartDate)) %></td>
        <td><%= Html.Encode(String.Format("{0:g}", item.SellEndDate)) %></td>
        <td><%= Html.Encode(String.Format("{0:g}",
        item.DiscontinuedDate)) %></td>
        <td><%= Html.Encode(item.rowguid) %></td>
        <td><%= Html.Encode(String.Format("{0:g}", item.ModifiedDate)) %></td>
    </tr>

<% Next%>
</table>
</asp:Content>
```

This view presents the list of Products in a simple table. The bulk of the work is done in a loop, which iterates over the list of products and renders an HTML table row for each one.

C#

```
<% foreach (var item in Model) { %>

        <tr>
            <!-- ... -->
            <td><%= Html.Encode(item.ProductID) %></td>
            <td><%= Html.Encode(item.Name) %></td>
            <!-- ... -->
        </tr>

    <% } %>
```

VB

```
<% For Each item In Model%>

        <tr>
            <!-- ... -->
            <td><%= Html.Encode(item.ProductID) %></td>
```

```
        <td><%= Html.Encode(item.Name) %></td>
        <!-- ... -->
    </tr>

<% Next%>
```

> **NOTE** *Visual Studio can infer the type of model because you created a strongly typed view. In the page directive you can see that this view doesn't inherit from* `System.Web.Mvc.Page`*. Instead, it inherits from the generic version, which states that the model will be an* `IEnumerable` *collection of* `Product` *objects. This in turn exposes a* `Model` *property with that type. You can still pass the wrong type of item to the view from the controller. In the case of a strongly typed view, this results in a run-time exception.*

Each of the properties of the products is HTML encoded before it is rendered using the `Encode` method on the `Html` helper property. This prevents common issues with malicious code injected into the application masquerading as valid user data. ASP.NET MVC can take advantage of the `<%: ... %>` markup, which uses a colon in the place of the equals sign in ASP.NET 4 to more easily perform this encoding. Here is the same snippet again taking advantage of this technique:

C#

```
<% foreach (var item in Model) { %>

    <tr>
        <!-- ... -->
        <td><%: item.ProductID %></td>
        <td><%: item.Name %></td>
        <!-- ... -->
    </tr>

<% } %>
```

VB

```
<% For Each item In Model%>

    <tr>
        <!-- ... -->
        <td><%: item.ProductID %></td>
        <td><%: item.Name %></td>
        <!-- ... -->
    </tr>

<% Next%>
```

In addition to the `Encode` method, one other `Html` helper method is used by this view: the `ActionLink` helper. This method emits a standard HTML anchor tag designed to trigger the specified action. Two forms are in use here. The simplest of these is the one designed to create a new Product record:

C#

```
<p>
  <%= Html.ActionLink("Create New", "Create") %>
</p>
```

VB

```
<p>
  <%=Html.ActionLink("Create New", "Create")%>
</p>
```

The first parameter is the text that will be rendered inside the anchor tag. This is the text that will be presented to the user. The second parameter is the name of the action to trigger. Because no controller has been specified, the current controller is assumed.

The more complex use of `ActionLink` is used to render the edit and delete links for each product.

C#

```
<td>
  <%= Html.ActionLink("Edit", "Edit", new { id=item.ProductID }) %> |
  <%= Html.ActionLink("Details", "Details", new { id=item.ProductID })%>
</td>
```

VB

```
<td>
  <%=Html.ActionLink("Edit", "Edit", New With {.id = item.ProductID})%> |
  <%=Html.ActionLink("Details", "Details", New With {.id = item.ProductID})%>
</td>
```

The first two parameters are the same as before and represent the link text and the action name, respectively. The third parameter is an anonymous object that contains data to be passed to the action method when it is called.

When you run the application and enter `/products/` in your address bar, you will be presented with the page displayed in Figure 22-6. Trying to click any of the links causes a run-time exception because the target action does not yet exist.

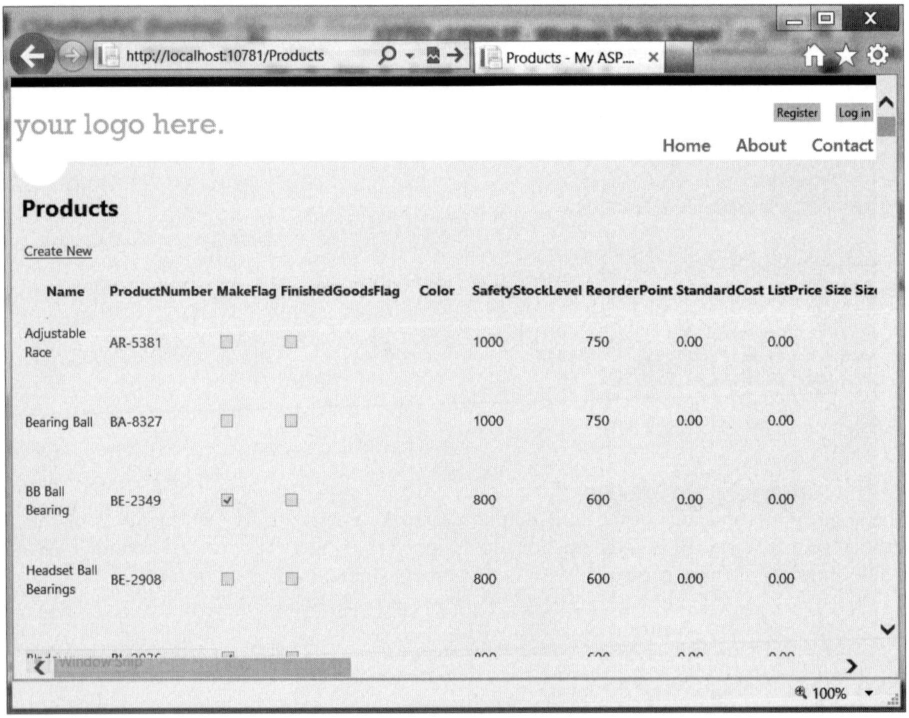

FIGURE 22-6

> **NOTE** *After you have a view and a controller, you can use the shortcut Ctrl+M, Ctrl+G to toggle between the two.*

ADVANCED MVC

This section provides an overview for some of the more advanced features of ASP.NET MVC.

Routing

As you were navigating around the MVC site in your web browser, you might have noticed that the URLs are quite different from a normal ASP.NET website. They do not contain file extensions and do not match up with the underlying folder structure. These URLs are mapped to action methods and controllers with a set of classes that belong to the routing engine, which is located in the `System.Web.Routing` assembly.

> **NOTE** *The routing engine was originally developed as a part of the ASP.NET MVC project but was released as a standalone library before MVC shipped. Although it is not described in this book, it is possible to use the routing engine with ASP.NET Web Forms projects.*

In the previous example you created a simple list view for products. This list view was based on the standard List template, which renders the following snippet for each Product in the database being displayed:

C#

```
<td>
  <%= Html.ActionLink("Edit", "Edit", new { id=item.ProductID }) %> |
  <%= Html.ActionLink("Details", "Details", new { id=item.ProductID })%>
</td>
```

VB

```
<td>
  <%=Html.ActionLink("Edit", "Edit", New With {.id = item.ProductID})%> |
  <%=Html.ActionLink("Details", "Details", New With {.id = item.ProductID})%>
</td>
```

If you examine the generated HTML markup of the final page, you should see that this becomes the following:

HTML

```
<td>
  <a href="/Products/Edit/2">Edit</a> |
  <a href="/Products/Details/2">Details</a>
</td>
```

These URLs are made up of three parts:

- Products is the name of the controller. There is a corresponding `ProductsController` in the project.
- Edit and Details are the names of action methods on the controller. The `ProductsController` will have methods called `Edit` and `Details`.
- 2 is a parameter that is called id.

Each of these components is defined in a *route*, which is set up in the `Global.asax.cs` file (or the `Global.asax.vb` file for VB) in a method called `RegisterRoutes`. When the application first starts, it calls this method and passes in the `System.Web.Routing.RouteTable.Routes` static collection. This collection contains all the routes for the entire application.

C#

```
public static void RegisterRoutes(RouteCollection routes)
{
```

```
        routes.IgnoreRoute("{resource}.axd/{*pathInfo}");

        routes.MapHttpRoute(
            name: "DefaultApi",
            routeTemplate: "api/{controller}/{id}",
            defaults: new { id = RouteParameter.Optional }
        );

        routes.MapRoute(
            name: "Default",
            routeTemplate: "{controller}/{action}/{id}",
            defaults: new { controller = "Home", action = "Index", id =
                  UrlParameter.Optional }
        );

    }
```

VB

```
    Shared Sub RegisterRoutes(ByVal routes As RouteCollection)
        routes.IgnoreRoute("{resource}.axd/{*pathInfo}")

        routes.MapHttpRoute( _
            "DefaultApi", _
            "api/{controller}/{id}", _
            New { .id = RouteParameter.Optional } _
        )

        routes.MapRoute( _
            "Default", _
            "{controller}/{action}/{id}", _
            New With {.controller = "Home", .action = "Index", .id = _
                UrlParameter.Optional } _
        )

    End Sub
```

The first method call tells the routing engine that it should ignore all requests for `.axd` files. When an incoming URL matches this route, the engine will completely ignore it and allow other parts of the application to handle it. This method can be handy if you want to integrate Web Forms and MVC into a single application. All you need to do is ask the routing engine to ignore `.aspx` and `.asmx` files.

The second method call defines a new `Route` and adds it to the collection. This overload of `MapRoute` method takes three parameters. The first parameter is a name, which can be used as a handle to this route later on. The second parameter is a URL template. This parameter can have normal text along with special tokens inside of braces. These tokens will be used as placeholders that are filled in when the route matches a URL. Some tokens are reserved and will be used by the MVC routing engine to select a controller and execute the correct action. The final parameter is a dictionary of default values. You can see that this "Default" route matches any URL in the form `/controller/action/id` where the default controller is Home, the default action is Index, and the id parameter defaults to an empty string.

When a new HTTP request comes in, each route in the `RouteCollection` tries to match the URL against its URL template in the order that they are added. The first route that can do so fills in any default values that haven't been supplied. When these values have all been collected, a `Controller` is created and an action method is called.

Routes are also used to generate URLs inside of views. When a helper needs a URL, it consults each route (in order again) to see if it can build a URL for the specified controller, action, and parameter values. The first route to match generates the correct URL. If a route encounters a parameter value that it doesn't know about, it becomes a query string parameter in the generated URL.

The following snippet declares a new route for an online store that allows for two parameters: a category and a subcategory. Assuming that this MVC application has been deployed to the root of a web server, requests for the URL `http://servername/Shop/Accessories/Helmets` will go to the List action on the Products controller with the parameters Category set to Accessories and Subcategory set to Helmets:

C#

```
public static void RegisterRoutes(RouteCollection routes)
{
  routes.IgnoreRoute("{resource}.axd/{*pathInfo}");

  routes.MapRoute(
    "ProductsDisplay",
    "Shop/{category}/{subcategory}",
    new {
      controller = "Products",
      action = "List",
      category = "",
      subcategory = ""
    }
  );

  routes.MapRoute(
    "Default",
    "{controller}/{action}/{id}",
    new { controller = "Home", action = "Index", id = "" }
  );
}
```

VB

```
Shared Sub RegisterRoutes(ByVal routes As RouteCollection)
  routes.IgnoreRoute("{resource}.axd/{*pathInfo}")

  routes.MapRoute( _
    "ProductsDisplay", _
    "Shop/{category}/{subcategory}", _
    New With { _
    .controller = "Products", .action = "List", _
    .category = "", .subcategory = "" _
    })

  routes.MapRoute( _
    "Default", _
    "{controller}/{action}/{id}", _
    New With {.controller = "Home", .action = "Index", .id = ""} _
  )

End Sub
```

> **NOTE** *When a* `Route` *in a* `RouteCollection` *matches the URL, no other* `Route` *gets the opportunity. Because of this, the order in which* `Routes` *are added to the* `RouteCollection` *can be quite important. If the previous snippet had placed the new route after the Default one, it would never get to match an incoming request because a request for* `/Shop/Accessories/Helmets` *would be looking for an Accessories action method on a* `ShopController` *with an id of Helmets. Because there isn't a* `ShopController`*, the whole request will fail. If your application is not going to the expected controller action method for a URL, you might want to add a more specific* `Route` *to the* `RouteCollection` *before the more general ones or remove the more general ones altogether while you figure out the problem.*

Finally, you can also add constraints to the Route to prevent it from matching a URL unless some other condition is met. This can be a good idea if your parameters are going to be converted into complex data types, such as date times later, and require a specific format. The most basic kind of restraint is a string, which is interpreted as a regular expression that a parameter must match for the route to take effect. The following route definition uses this technique to ensure that the `zipCode` parameter is exactly five digits:

C#

```
routes.MapRoute(
  "StoreFinder",
  "Stores/Find/{zipCode}",
  new { controller = "StoreFinder", action = "list" },
  new { zipCode = @"^\d{5}$" }
);
```

VB

```
routes.MapRoute( _
 "StoreFinder", _
 "Stores/Find/{zipCode}", _
 New With {.controller = "StoreFinder", .action = "list"}, _
 New With {.zipCode = "^\d{5}$"} _
)
```

The other type of constraint is a class that implements `IRouteConstraint`. This interface defines a single method `Match` that returns a boolean value indicating whether or not the incoming request satisfies the constraint. There is one out-of-the-box implementation of `IRouteConstraint` called `HttpMethodConstraint`. This constraint can be used to ensure that the correct HTTP method, such as GET, POST, HEAD, or DELETE, is used. The following route accepts only HTTP POST requests:

C#

```
routes.MapRoute(
  "PostOnlyRoute",
  "Post/{action}",
  new { controller = "Post" },
  new { post = new HttpMethodConstraint("POST") }
);
```

VB

```
routes.MapRoute(
  "PostOnlyRoute", _
  "Post/{action}", _
  New With {.controller = "Post"}, _
  New With {.post = New HttpMethodConstraint("POST")} _
)
```

The URL routing classes are powerful and flexible and allow you to easily create "pretty" URLs. This can aid users navigating around your site and even improve your site's ranking with search engines.

Action Method Parameters

All the action methods in previous examples do not accept any input from outside of the application to perform their tasks; they rely entirely on the state of the model. In real-world applications this is an unlikely scenario. The ASP.NET MVC framework makes it easy to parameterize action methods from a variety of sources.

As mentioned in the previous section, the Default route exposes an id parameter, which defaults to an empty string. To access the value of the id parameter from within the action method, you can just add it to the signature of the method as the following snippet shows:

C#

```
public ActionResult Details(int id)
{
  using (var db = new ProductsDataContext())
  {
    var product = db.Products.SingleOrDefault(x => x.ProductID == id);

    if (product == null)
      return View("NotFound");

    return View(product);
  }
}
```

VB

```
Public Function Details(ByVal id As Integer) As ActionResult
  Using db As New ProductsDataContext
    Dim product = db.Products.FirstOrDefault(Function(p As Product)
    p.ProductID = id)

    Return View(product)
  End Using
End Function
```

When the MVC framework executes the Details action method, it searches through the parameters that have been extracted from the URL by the matching route. These parameters are matched up with the parameters on the action method by name, and then passed in when the method is called. As the details method shows, the framework can convert the type of the parameter on the fly. Action methods can also retrieve parameters from the query string portion of the URL and from HTTP POST data using the same technique.

> **NOTE** *If the conversion cannot be made for any reason, an exception is thrown.*

In addition, an action method can accept a parameter of the `FormValues` type that aggregates all the HTTP POST data into a single parameter. If the data in the `FormValues` collection represents the properties of an object, you can simply add a parameter of that type, and a new instance will be created when the action method is called. The Create action, shown in the following snippet, uses this to construct a new instance of the `Product` class, and then saves it:

C#

```
public ActionResult Create()
{
  return View();
}

[HttpPost]
public ActionResult Create([Bind(Exclude="ProductId")]Product product)
{
  if (!ModelState.IsValid)
    return View();

  using (var db = new ProductsDataContext())
  {
    db.Products.InsertOnSubmit(product);
    db.SubmitChanges();
  }
  return RedirectToAction("List");
}
```

VB

```
<HttpPost()>
Function Create(<Bind(Exclude:="id")> ByVal product As Product)

  If (Not ModelState.IsValid) Then
    Return View()
  End If

  Using db As New ProductsDataContext
    db.Products.InsertOnSubmit(product)
    db.SubmitChanges()
  End Using
  Return RedirectToAction("List")
End Function
```

> **NOTE** *There are two Create action methods here. The first one simply renders the Create view. The second one is marked up with an* `HttpPostAttribute`, *which means that it can be selected only if the HTTP request uses the POST verb. This is a common practice in designing ASP.NET MVC websites. In addition to* `HttpPostAttribute` *there are also corresponding attributes for the* `GET`, `PUT`, *and* `DELETE` *verbs.*

Model Binders

The process to create the new Product instance is the responsibility of a *model binder.* The model binder matches properties in the HTTP POST data with properties on the type that it is attempting to create. This works in this example because the template that was used to generate the Create view renders the HTML INPUT fields with the correct name as this snippet of the rendered HTML shows:

HTML

```
<p>
  <label for="ProductID">ProductID:</label>
  <input id="ProductID" name="ProductID" type="text" value="" />
</p>
<p>
  <label for="Name">Name:</label>
  <input id="Name" name="Name" type="text" value="" />
</p>
```

A number of ways exist to control the behavior of a model binder including the `BindAttribute`, which is used in the `Create` method shown previously. This attribute is used to include or exclude certain properties and to specify a prefix for the HTTP POST values. This can be useful if multiple objects in the POST collection need to be bound.

Model binders can also be used from within the action method to update existing instances of your model classes using the `UpdateModel` and `TryUpdateModel` methods. The chief difference is that `TryUpdateModel` returns a boolean value indicating whether or not it built a successful model, and `UpdateModel` just throws an exception if it can't. The Edit action method shows this technique:

C#

```
[HttpPost]
public ActionResult Edit(int id, FormCollection formValues)
{
  using (var db = new ProductsDataContext())
```

```
    {
      var product = db.Products.SingleOrDefault(x => x.ProductID == id);

      if (TryUpdateModel(product))
      {
        db.SubmitChanges();
        return RedirectToAction("Index");
      }
      return View(product);
    }
  }
```

VB

```
<HttpPost()>
Function Edit(ByVal id As Integer, ByVal formValues As FormCollection)
  Using db As New ProductsDataContext
    Dim product = db.Products.FirstOrDefault(Function(p As Product)
    p.ProductID = id)

    If TryUpdateModel(product) Then
      db.SubmitChanges()
      Return RedirectToAction("Index")
    End If
    Return View(product)
  End Using
End Function
```

Areas

An *area* is a self-contained part of an MVC application that manages its own models, controllers, and views. You can even define routes specific to an area. To create a new area, select Add ➪ Area from the project context menu in the Solution Explorer. The Add Area dialog, as in Figure 22-7, prompts you to provide a name for your area.

After you click Add, many new files are added to your project to support the area. Figure 22-8 shows a project with two areas added to it named Blog and Shop, respectively.

In addition to having its own controllers and views, each area has a class called `AreaNameAreaRegistration` that inherits from the abstract base class `AreaRegistration`. This class contains an abstract property for the name of your area and an abstract method for integrating your area with the rest of the application. The default implementation registers the standard routes.

Add Area

Area name:

Shop

Add Cancel

FIGURE 22-7

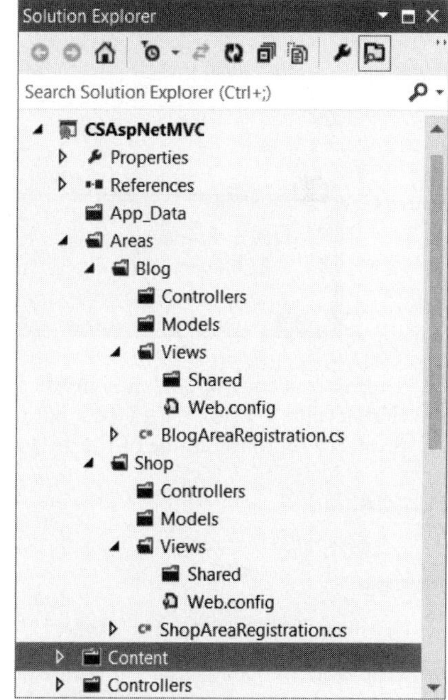

FIGURE 22-8

C#

```
public class BlogAreaRegistration : AreaRegistration
{
  public override string AreaName
  {
    get
    {
      return "Blog";
    }
  }

  public override void RegisterArea(AreaRegistrationContext context)
  {
    context.MapRoute(
      "Blog_default",
      "Blog/{controller}/{action}/{id}",
      new { action = "Index", id = "" }
    );
  }
}
```

VB

```
Public Class BlogAreaRegistration
  Inherits AreaRegistration

  Public Overrides ReadOnly Property AreaName() As String
    Get
      Return "Blog"
    End Get
  End Property

  Public Overrides Sub RegisterArea(ByVal context As AreaRegistrationContext)
    context.MapRoute( _
      "Blog_default", _
      "Blog/{controller}/{action}/{id}", _
      New With {.action = "Index", .id = ""} _
    )
  End Sub
End Class
```

> **NOTE** *The* `RegisterArea` *method of the* `BlogAreaRegistration` *class defines a route in which every URL is prefixed with* `/Blog/` *by convention. This can be useful while debugging routes but is not necessary as long as area routes do not clash with any other routes.*

To link to a controller that is inside another area, you need to use an overload of `Html.ActionLink` that accepts a `routeValues` parameter. The object you provide for this parameter must include an `area` property set to the name of the area that contains the controller you link to.

C#

```
<%= Html.ActionLink("Blog", "Index", new { area = "Blog" }) %>
```

VB

```
<%= Html.ActionLink("Blog", "Index", New With {.area = "Blog"})%>
```

One issue frequently encountered when adding area support to a project is that the controller factory becomes confused when multiple controllers have the same name. To avoid this issue you can limit the namespaces that a route uses to search for a controller to satisfy any request. The following code snippet limits the namespaces for the global routes to `MvcApplication.Controllers`, which do not match any of the area controllers.

C#

```
routes.MapRoute(
  "Default",
  "{controller}/{action}/{id}",
  new { controller = "Home", action = "Index", id = "" },
  null,
  new[] { "MvcApplication.Controllers" }
);
```

VB

```
routes.MapRoute( _
  "Default", _
  "{controller}/{action}/{id}", _
  New With {.controller = "Home", .action = "Index", .id = ""}, _
  Nothing, _
  New String() {"MvcApplication.Controllers"} _
)
```

> **NOTE** *The* `AreaRegistrationContext` *automatically includes the area namespace when you use it to specify routes, so you should need to supply only namespaces to the global routes.*

Validation

In addition to just creating or updating it, a model binder can decide whether or not the model instance that it operates on is valid. The results of this decision are found in the `ModelState` property. Model binders can pick up some simple validation errors by default, usually for incorrect types. Figure 22-9 shows the result of attempting to save a Product when the form is empty. Most of these validation errors are based on the fact that these properties are non-nullable value types and require a value.

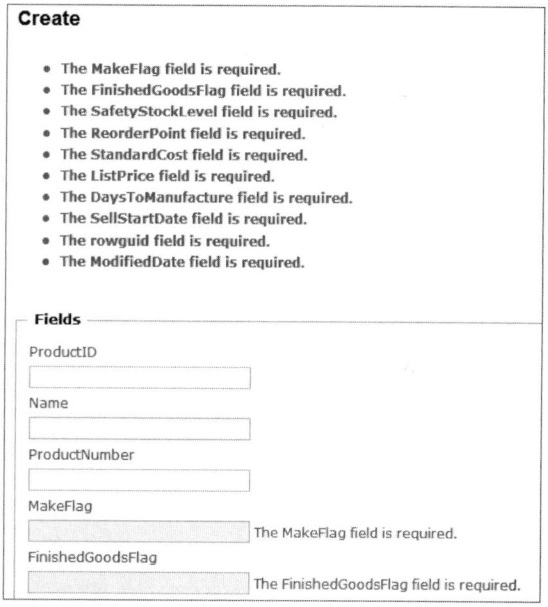

The user interface for this error report is provided by the `Html.ValidationSummary` call, which is made on the view. This helper method examines the `ModelState`, and if it finds any errors, it renders them as a list along with a header message.

Create
The MakeFlag field is required.
The FinishedGoodsFlag field is required.
The SafetyStockLevel field is required.
The ReorderPoint field is required.
The StandardCost field is required.
The ListPrice field is required.
The DaysToManufacture field is required.
The SellStartDate field is required.
The rowguid field is required.
The ModifiedDate field is required.
Fields
ProductID
Name
ProductNumber
MakeFlag
The MakeFlag field is required.
FinishedGoodsFlag
The FinishedGoodsFlag field is required.

FIGURE 22-9

You can add additional validation hints to the properties of the model class by marking them up using the attributes in the `System.ComponentModel.DataAnnotations` assembly. Because the `Product` class is created by LINQ to SQL you should not update it directly. The LINQ to SQL generated classes are defined as partial, so you can extend them, but there is no easy way to attach meta data to the generated properties this way. Instead, you need to create a *meta data proxy* class with the properties you want to mark up, provide them with the correct data annotation attributes, and then mark up the partial class with a `MetadataTypeAttribute` identifying the proxy class. The following code snippet shows this technique used to provide some validation meta data to the `Product` class:

C#

```
[MetadataType(typeof(ProductValidationMetadata))]
public partial class Product
{
```

```
    }

    public class ProductValidationMetadata
    {
        [Required, StringLength(256)]
        public string Name { get; set; }

        [Range(0, 100)]
        public int DaysToManufacture { get; set; }
    }
```

VB

```
Imports System.ComponentModel.DataAnnotations

<MetadataType(GetType(ProductMetaData))>
Partial Public Class Product

End Class

Public Class ProductMetaData
    <Required(), StringLength(256)>
    Property Name As String

    <Range(0, 100)>
    Property DaysToManufacture As Integer
End Class
```

Now, attempting to create a new Product with no name and a negative Days to Manufacture produces the errors shown in Figure 22-10.

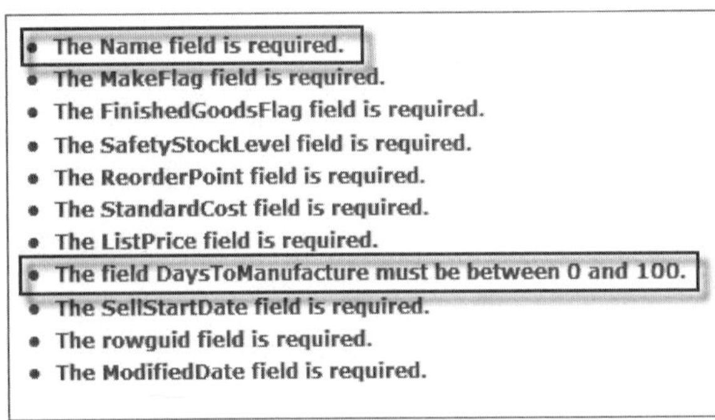

• The Name field is required.
• The MakeFlag field is required.
• The FinishedGoodsFlag field is required.
• The SafetyStockLevel field is required.
• The ReorderPoint field is required.
• The StandardCost field is required.
• The ListPrice field is required.
• The field DaysToManufacture must be between 0 and 100.
• The SellStartDate field is required.
• The rowguid field is required.
• The ModifiedDate field is required.

FIGURE 22-10

> **NOTE** *You might notice that along with the error report at the top of the page, for each field that has a validation error, the textbox is colored red and has an error message after it. The first effect is caused by the* `Html.TextBox` *helper, which accepts the value of the property that it is attached to. If it encounters an error in the model state for its attached property, it adds an* `input-validation-error` *CSS class to the rendered* `INPUT` *control. The default style sheet defines the red background. The second effect is caused by the* `Html.ValidationMessage` *helper. This helper is also associated with a property and renders the contents of its second parameter if it detects that its attached property has an error associated with it.*

Partial Views

At times you have large areas of user interface markup that you would like to reuse. In the ASP.NET MVC framework a reusable section of view is called a partial view. Partial views act similar to views except that they have an `.ascx` extension and inherit from `System.Web.Mvc.ViewUserControl`. To create a partial view, check the Create a Partial View check box on the same Add View dialog that you use to create other views.

To render a partial view, you can use the `Html.RenderPartial` method. The most common overload of this method accepts a view name and a model object. Just as with a normal view, a partial view can be either controller-specific or shared. After the partial view has been rendered, its HTML markup is inserted into the main view. This code snippet renders a "Form" partial for the current model:

C#

```
<% Html.RenderPartial("Form", Model); %>
```

VB

```
<% Html.RenderPartial("Form", Model) %>
```

> **NOTE** *You can call a partial view directly from an action using the normal View method. If you do this, only the HTML rendered by the partial view will be included in the HTTP response. This can be useful if you return data to jQuery.*

Dynamic Data Templates

Dynamic Data is a feature of ASP.NET Web Forms that enables you to render UI based on meta data associated with the model. Although ASP.NET MVC does not integrate directly with Dynamic Data, a number of features in ASP.NET MVC 4 are similar in spirit. Templates in ASP.NET MVC 4 can render parts of your model in different ways, whether they are small and simple such as a single string property or large and complex like the whole product class. The templates are exposed by Html helper methods. There are templates for display and templates for editing purposes.

Display Templates

The Details view created by the Add View dialog contains code to render each property. Here is the markup for just two of these properties:

C#

```
<p>
  ProductID:
  <%= Html.Encode(Model.ProductID) %>
</p>
<p>
  Name:
  <%= Html.Encode(Model.Name) %>
</p>
```

VB

```
<p>
  ProductID:
  <%= Html.Encode(Model.ProductID) %>
</p>
<p>
  Name:
  <%= Html.Encode(Model.Name) %>
</p>
```

With the templates feature, you can change this to the following:

C#

```
<p>
  <%= Html.LabelFor(x => x.ProductID) %>
  <%= Html.DisplayFor(x => x.ProductID) %>
</p>
<p>
  <%= Html.LabelFor(x => x.Name) %>
  <%= Html.DisplayFor(x => x.Name) %>
</p>
```

VB

```
<p>
  <%: Html.LabelFor(Function(x As ProductsMVC.Product) x.ProductID)%>
  <%: Html.DisplayFor(Function(x As ProductsMVC.Product) x.ProductID) %>
</p>
<p>
  <%: Html.LabelFor(Function(x As ProductsMVC.Product) x.Name)%>
  <%: Html.DisplayFor(Function(x As ProductsMVC.Product) x.Name) %>
</p>
```

This has a number of immediate advantages. First, the label is no longer hard-coded into the view. Because the label is now strongly typed, it updates if you refactor your model class. In addition to this you can apply a `System.ComponentModel.DisplayName` attribute to your model (or to a model meta data proxy) to change the text that displays to the user. This helps to ensure consistency across the entire application. The following code snippet shows the Product meta data proxy with a couple of `DisplayNameAttributes`, and Figure 22-11 shows the rendered result:

C#

```
public class ProductValidationMetadata
{
    [DisplayName("ID")]
    public int ProductID { get; set; }

    [Required, StringLength(256)]
    [DisplayName("Product Name")]
    public string Name { get; set; }

    [Range(0, 100)]
    public int DaysToManufacture { get; set; }
}
```

VB

```
Public Class ProductMetaData
    <DisplayName("ID")>
    Property ProductID As Integer

    <Required(), StringLength(256)> _
    <DisplayName("Product Name")>
    Property Name As String

    <Range(0, 100)>
    Property DaysToManufacture As Integer
End Class
```

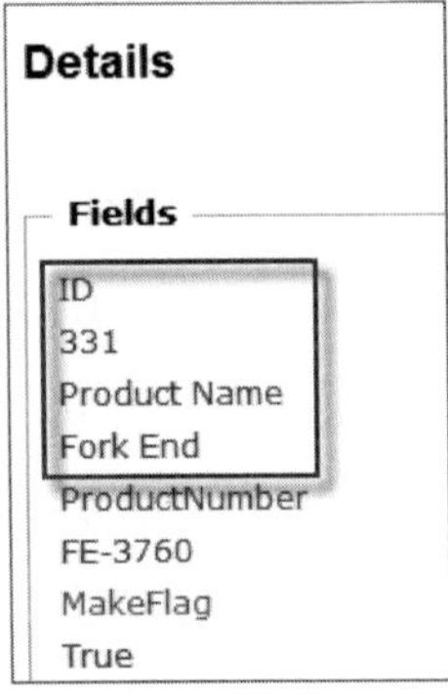

FIGURE 22-11

The `DisplayFor` helper also provides a lot of hidden flexibility. It selects a template based on the type of the property that it displays. You can override each of these type-specific views by creating a partial view named after the type in the `Shared\DisplayTemplates` folder. Figure 22-12 shows a String template, and Figure 22-13 shows the output result:

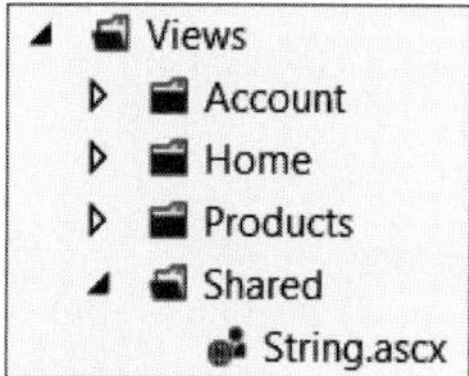

FIGURE 22-12

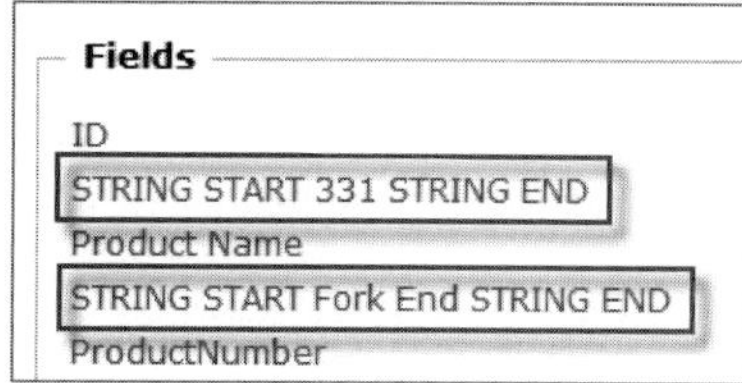

FIGURE 22-13

C#

```
<%@ Control Language="C#" Inherits="System.Web.Mvc.ViewUserControl" %>

STRING START
<%= Html.Encode(ViewData.TemplateInfo.FormattedModelValue) %>
STRING END
```

VB

```
<%@ Control Language="VB" Inherits="System.Web.Mvc.ViewUserControl" %>

STRING START
<%= Html.Encode(ViewData.TemplateInfo.FormattedModelValue) %>
STRING END
```

> **NOTE** *You can also create controller-specific templates by putting them inside a* `DisplayTemplates` *subfolder of the controller-specific Views folder.*

Although the display template is selected based on the type of the property by default, you can override this by either supplying the name of the template to the `DisplayFor` helper or applying a `System.ComponentModel.DataAnnotations.UIHintAttribute` to the property. This attribute takes a string that identifies the type of template to use. When the framework needs to render the display for the property, it tries to find the display template described by the UI Hint. If one is not found, it looks for a type-specific template. If a template still hasn't been found, the default behavior is executed.

If you simply apply `LabelFor` and `DisplayFor` for every property on your model, you can use the `Html.DisplayForModel` helper method. This method renders a label and a display template for each property on the model class. You can prevent a property from displaying by this helper by annotating it with a `System.ComponentModel.DataAnnotations.ScaffoldColumnAttribute` passing it the value `false`.

> **NOTE** *If you want to change the way the* `DisplayForModel` *renders, you can create a type-specific template for it. If you want to change the way it renders generally, create an* `Object` *display template.*

A number of built-in display templates are available that you can use out of the box. Be aware that if you want to customize the behavior of one of these, you need to re-create it from scratch:

- **String:** No real surprises, just renders the string contents itself. This template does HTML encode the property value, though.
- **Html:** The same as string but without the HTML encoding. This is the rawest form of display that you can have. Be careful using this template because it is a vector for malicious code injection such as Cross Site Scripting Attacks (XSS).
- **EmailAddress:** Renders an e-mail address as a mailto: link.
- **Url:** Renders a URL as an HTML anchor.
- **HiddenInput:** Does not render the property at all unless the `ViewData.ModelMetaData.HideSurroundingHtml` property is `false`.
- **Decimal:** Renders the property to two decimal places.
- **Boolean:** Renders a read-only check box for non-nullable values and a read-only drop-down list with True, False, and Not Set options for nullable properties.
- **Object:** Renders complex objects and null values.

Edit Templates

It probably comes as no surprise that there are corresponding `EditorFor` and `EditorForModel` Html helpers that handle the way properties and objects are rendered for edit purposes. Editor templates can be overridden by supplying partial views in the EditTemplates folder. Edit Templates can use the same UI hint system that Display Templates use. Just as with Display Templates, you can use a number of built-in editor templates out of the box:

- **String:** Renders a standard textbox, initially populated with the value if provided and named after the property. This ensures that it will be used correctly by the model binder to rebuild the object on the other side.
- **Password:** The same as string but renders an HTML `PASSWORD` input instead of a textbox.
- **MultilineText:** Creates a multiline textbox. There is no way to specify the number of rows and columns for this textbox here. It is assumed that you will use CSS to do that.
- **HiddenInput:** Similar to the display template, renders an HTML `HIDDEN` input.
- **Decimal:** Similar to the display template but renders a textbox to edit the value.
- **Boolean:** If the property type is non-nullable, this renders a check box control. If this template is applied to a nullable property, it renders a drop-down list containing the same three items as the display template.
- **Object:** Renders complex editors.

jQuery

jQuery is an open-source JavaScript framework included by default with the ASP.NET MVC framework. The basic element of jQuery is the function $(). This function can be passed a JavaScript DOM element or a string describing elements via a CSS selector. The $() function returns a jQuery object that exposes a number of functions that affect the elements contained. Most of these functions also return the same jQuery object, so these function calls can be chained together. As an example, the following snippet selects all the H2 tags and adds the word "section" to the end of each one:

JAVASCRIPT

```
$("h2").append("section");
```

To make use of jQuery, you need to create a reference to the jQuery library found in the /Scripts folder by adding the following to the head section of your page:

HTML

```
<script type="text/javascript" src="/Scripts/jquery-1.3.2.js"></script>
```

You can use jQuery to make an HTTP request by using the `$.get` and `$.post` methods. These methods accept a URL and can optionally have a callback function to provide the results to. The following view renders the time inside two div tags called `server` and `client`, respectively. There is also a button called update, which when clicked makes a GET request to the `/time` URL. When it receives the results, it updates the value displayed in the client div but not the server one. In addition to this it uses the `slideUp` and `slideDown` functions to animate the client time in the UI.

C#

```
<%@ Page Language="C#" Inherits="System.Web.Mvc.ViewPage<System.String>" %>
<!DOCTYPE html PUBLIC "-//W3C//DTD XHTML 1.0 Transitional//EN"
"http://www.w3.org/TR/xhtml1/DTD/xhtml1-transitional.dtd">
<html xmlns="http://www.w3.org/1999/xhtml">
<head runat="server">
  <title>Index</title>
  <script type="text/javascript" src="/Scripts/jquery-1.3.2.js"></script>
  <script type="text/javascript">
    $(document).ready(function () {
      $('#updater').click(UpdateNow);
    });
    function UpdateNow() {
      $.get('/time', function (data) {
        $('#clientTime').slideUp('fast', function () {
          $('#clientTime').empty().append(data).slideDown();
        });
      });
    }
  </script>
</head>
<body>
    <div>
        <h2>
            Server</h2>
        <div id="serverTime">
            <%:Model %></div>
        <h2>
            Client</h2>
        <div id="clientTime">
            <%:Model %></div>
        <input type="button" value="Update" id="updater"  />
    </div>
</body>
</html>
```

Here is the action method that controls the previous view. It uses the `IsAjaxRequest` extension method to determine if the request has come from jQuery. If it has, it returns just the time as a string; otherwise it returns the full view.

C#

```
public ActionResult Index()
{
  var now = DateTime.Now.ToLongTimeString();
  if (Request.IsAjaxRequest())
    return Content(now);
  return View(now as object);
}
```

VB

```
Function Index() As ActionResult
  Dim timeNow = Now.ToString()
  If Request.IsAjaxRequest() Then
    Return Content(timeNow)
  End If
  Return View(CType(timeNow, Object))
End Function
```

jQuery is a rich client-side programming tool with an extremely active community and a large number of plug-ins. For more information about jQuery, including a comprehensive set of tutorials and demos, see `http://jquery.com`.

SUMMARY

The ASP.NET MVC framework makes it easy to build highly testable, loosely coupled web applications that embrace the nature of HTTP. The 2.0 release has a lot of productivity gains, including Templates and Visual Studio integration. For more information about ASP.NET MVC, see `http://asp.net/mvc`.

23

Silverlight

WHAT'S IN THIS CHAPTER?

- Creating your first Silverlight application
- Using the Navigation Framework
- Theming your Silverlight application
- Running a Silverlight application outside of the browser

Silverlight has been getting a lot of traction from within Microsoft and the developer community due to its huge potential as a development platform. New major versions are released regularly, demonstrating that it is progressing fast. At the time of writing, Silverlight had reached version 5, which is already showing a lot of maturity for a reasonably young technology, and although there has been nothing officially announced, it is likely that this is the last version of Silverlight (at least for a while).

In earlier versions of Visual Studio, it was quite a chore to configure the IDE for Silverlight development, requiring Service Pack 1 along with the Silverlight Tools to be installed just to start. Since Visual Studio 2010, Silverlight development is configured out-of-the-box, making it easy to start. Also, Visual Studio 2008 had no designer for Silverlight user interfaces (initially there was a preview view but this was later abandoned), requiring developers to write the XAML and run their application to view the results, or use Expression Blend if they had access to it (which did have a designer). This was improved in Visual Studio 2010, which included a capable designer that makes it much easier for developers to create user interfaces in Silverlight. It is still not perfect, and there are a number of scenarios in which Expression Blend is the better choice, but it has definitely improved.

Because Silverlight shares a large number of similarities with Windows Presentation Foundation (WPF), you can find that many of the Visual Studio features for WPF detailed in Chapter 18, "Windows Presentation Foundation (WPF)," also apply to Silverlight, and thus aren't repeated here. Of course, Silverlight has no Windows Forms interoperability (due to it running in a sandboxed environment and not using the full .NET Framework), but the other Visual Studio features detailed for WPF development can also be used when developing Silverlight applications. This chapter takes you through the features of Visual Studio specific to Silverlight but don't apply to WPF.

WHAT IS SILVERLIGHT?

When starting Silverlight development you notice its similarity to WPF. Both technologies revolve around their use of XAML for defining the presentation layer and are similar to develop with. However, they do differ greatly in how they are each intended to be used. Silverlight could essentially be considered a trimmed-down version of WPF, designed to be deployed via the Web and run in a web browser — what is generally called a Rich Internet Application (RIA). WPF, on the other hand, is for developing rich client (desktop) applications. It could be pointed out that WPF applications can be compiled to a XAML Browser Application (XBAP) and deployed and run in the same manner as Silverlight applications, but these require the .NET Framework to be installed on the client machine and can run only on Windows — neither of which is true for Silverlight applications. Many of the advances in Silverlight in the last couple of versions are aimed at narrowing the gap between it and WPF. Out-Of-Browser installations, the ability to access local functionality through COM, and elevated permissions have, in many scenarios, made Silverlight the equal of WPF for desktop application.

One of the great benefits of Silverlight is that it doesn't require the .NET Framework to be installed on the client machine (which can be quite a sizable download if it isn't installed). Instead, the Silverlight run time is just a small download (approximately 5 MB), and installs itself as a browser plug-in. If the user navigates to a web page that has Silverlight content but the client machine doesn't have the Silverlight run time installed, the user is prompted to download and install it. The install happens automatically after the user agrees to it, and the Silverlight application opens when the install completes. With such a small download size for the run time, the Silverlight plug-in can be installed and running the Silverlight application in under 2 minutes. This makes it easy to deploy your application. Though not as prevalent as Adobe Flash, Silverlight is rapidly expanding its install base, and eventually it's expected that its install base will come close to that of Flash.

One of the advantages Silverlight applications (and RIA applications in general) have over ASP.NET applications is that they allow you to write rich applications that run solely on the client and communicate with the server only when necessary (generally to send or request data). Essentially, you can write web applications in much the same way as you write desktop applications. This includes the ability to write C# or VB.NET code that runs on the client — enabling you to reuse your existing codebase and not have to learn new languages (such as JavaScript).

Another great benefit of Silverlight is that Silverlight applications can run in all the major web browsers and most excitingly can also run on the Mac as well as Windows, enabling you to build cross-browser and cross-platform applications easily. Support for Linux is provided by Moonlight (developed by the Mono team at Novell); although its development is running somewhat behind the versions delivered by Microsoft. This means that Silverlight can be the ideal way to write web-deployed, cross-platform applications. Silverlight applications render exactly the same across different web browsers, removing the pain of regular web development where each browser can render your application differently.

> **NOTE** *Some of the advanced features, such as using COM objects, are not available on platforms other than Windows. So you must ensure that your application respects these limitations if your goal is cross-platform compatibility.*

The downsides of Silverlight are that it includes only a subset of the .NET Framework to minimize the size of the run-time download, and that the applications are run in a sandboxed environment — preventing access to the client machine (a good thing for security but reduces the uses of the technology). There are trade-offs to be made when choosing between WPF and Silverlight, and if you choose Silverlight, you should be prepared to make these sacrifices to obtain the benefits.

Ultimately, you could say that Silverlight applications are a cross between rich client and web applications, bringing the best of both worlds together.

GETTING STARTED WITH SILVERLIGHT

Visual Studio 2012 comes configured with the main components you need for Silverlight development. Silverlight is supported out-of-the-box with Visual Studio 2012, but if a new version of Silverlight has been released that you want to target, you need to download the SDK for that version. The best place to check if a new SDK has been released and download any required (or related) components is `http://www.silverlight.net/getstarted`.

Create a new project and select the Silverlight category (see Figure 23-1). You can find a number of project templates for Silverlight to start your project.

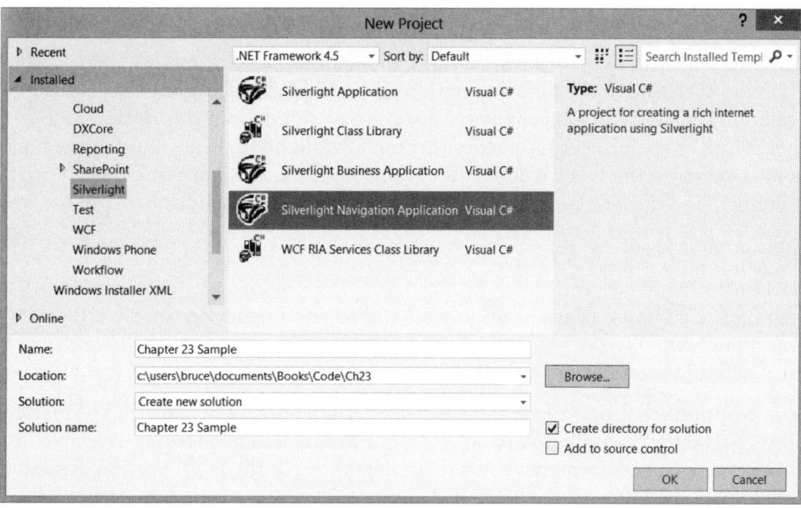

FIGURE 23-1

The Silverlight Application project template is essentially a blank slate, providing a basic project to start with (best if you create a simple gadget). The Silverlight Navigation Application project template, however, provides you with a much better structure if you plan to build an application with more than one screen or view, providing a user interface framework for your application and some sample views. The Silverlight Class Library project template generates exactly the same output as a standard Class Library project template but targets the Silverlight run time instead of the full .NET Framework.

Use the Silverlight Navigation Application template for your sample project because it gives you a good base to work from. When you create the project, you are presented with the template wizard screen that is shown in Figure 23-2 to configure the project.

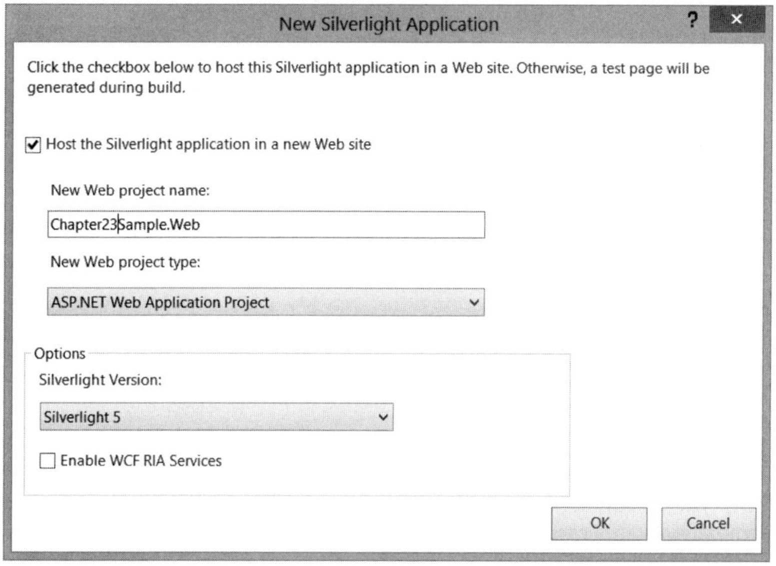

FIGURE 23-2

Most of the options in this window are dedicated to configuring the web project that will be generated in the same solution as the Silverlight project. Designed primarily to be accessed via a web browser, Silverlight applications need to be hosted by a web page. Therefore, you also need a separate web project with a page that can act as the host for the Silverlight application in the browser.

So that the wizard generates a web project to host the Silverlight application, select the Host the Silverlight Application in a New or Existing Web Site in the Solution option. If you add a Silverlight project to a solution with an existing web project that will host the application, you can uncheck this option and manually configure the project link in the project properties (for the Silverlight application). A default name for the web project will already be set in the New Web Project Name textbox, but you can change this if you want. The final option for configuring the web project is to select its type. The options are

- ASP.NET Web Application Project
- ASP.NET Web Site Project

Which of these web project types you choose to use is up to you, and has no impact on the Silverlight project. The sample application uses the Web Application Project, but how you intend to develop the website that will host the application will ultimately determine the appropriate web project type.

In the Options group are some options that pertain to the Silverlight application. The Silverlight Version drop-down list allows you to choose the Silverlight version you want to target. The versions available in this list depend on the individual Silverlight SDKs you have installed, defaulting to the latest version available. Because RIA Services are discussed in Chapter 36, "WCF RIA Services," disregard the Enable WCF RIA Services option for now, and leave it unchecked for the sample application.

> **NOTE** *You can change the properties in the Options group later via the project properties pages for the Silverlight project.*

Now take a tour through the structure of the solution that has been generated (as shown in Figure 23-3). As was previously noted you have two projects: the Silverlight project and a separate web project to host the compiled Silverlight application. The web project is the startup project in the solution because it's actually this that is opening in the browser and then loading the Silverlight application.

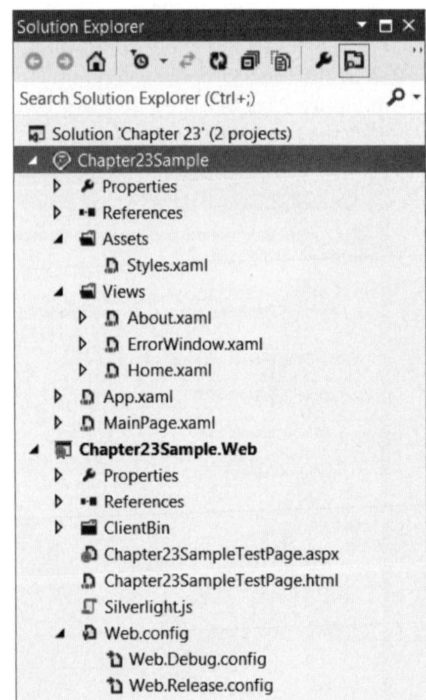

FIGURE 23-3

The web project is linked to the Silverlight project such that after the Silverlight application compiles, its output (that is, the `.xap` file) is automatically copied into the web project (into the ClientBin folder), where it can be accessed by the web browser. If you haven't already done so, compile the solution, and you can see the `.xap` file appear under the ClientBin folder.

The web project includes two different pages that can be used to host the Silverlight application: a standard HTML page and an ASPX page. Both do exactly the same thing, so it's up to you which one you use, and you can delete the other.

Looking at the Silverlight project now, you can see an `App.xaml` file and a `MainPage.xaml` file — similar to the initial structure of a WPF project. The `MainPage.xaml` file fills the browser window, shows a header at the top with buttons to navigate around the application, and hosts different "views" inside the Frame control that it contains. So you can think of `MainPage.xaml` as the shell for the content in your application.

The project template includes two default content views: a Home view and an About view. Modifying and adding new views is covered in the next section. This folder also contains `ErrorWindow.xaml`, which inherits from ChildWindow (essentially a modal dialog control in Silverlight) and pops up when an unhandled exception occurs. (The unhandled exception event is handled in the code-behind for `App.xaml` and displays this control.)

The Assets folder contains `Styles.xaml`, which is composed of the theme styles used by the application. This is discussed in the "Theming" section in this chapter.

Now take a look at what options are available in the project properties pages of the Silverlight project. The property page unique to Silverlight applications is the Silverlight page, as shown in Figure 23-4.

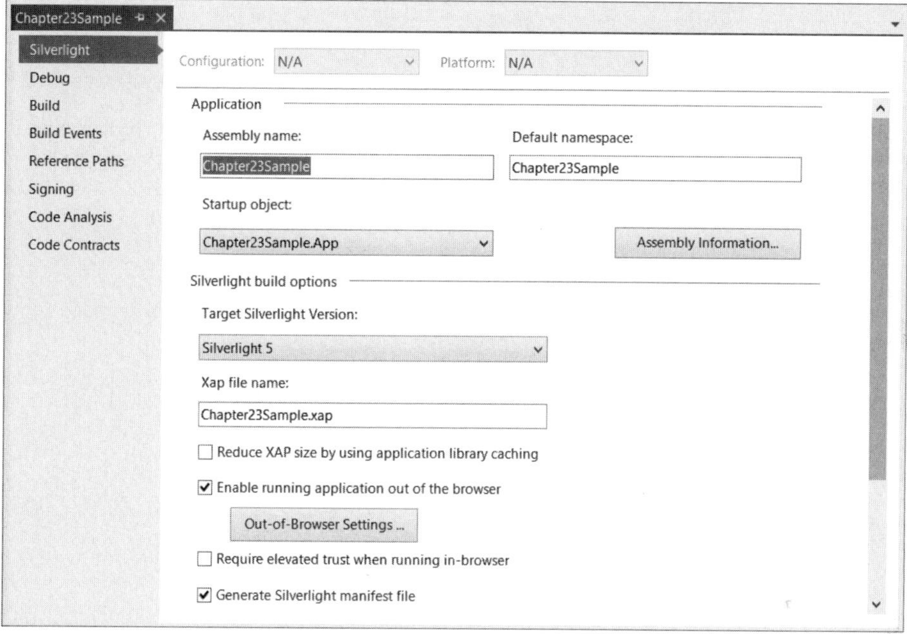

FIGURE 23-4

A number of options are of particular interest here. The Xap file name option allows you to set the name of the `.xap` file that your Silverlight project and all its references (library and control assemblies, and so on) will be compiled into. A `.xap` file is simply a zip file with a different extension, and opening it in a zip file manager enables you to view its contents. If your project is simple (that is, was created using the Silverlight Application project template and doesn't reference any control libraries), it will probably contain only your project's assembly and a manifest file. However, if you reference other assemblies in your project (such as if you use the DataGrid control that exists in the System.Windows.Controls.Data.dll assembly) you will find that your `.xap` file blows out in size quickly because these are also included in the `.xap` file. This would mean that each time you make a minor change to your project and deploy it that the users will be redownloading the assemblies (such as the assembly containing the DataGrid) that haven't changed simply because they are included again in the `.xap` file. Fortunately, there is a way to improve this scenario, and that's to use application library caching. This is easy to turn on, simply requiring the Reduce XAP Size by Using Application Library Caching option to be checked. The next time the project is compiled, the referenced assemblies will be separated out into different files and downloaded separately from the application's `.xap` file.

One caveat is that for assemblies to be cached they must have an extension map XML file, which is included in the `.xap` file and points to the zip file containing the assembly. Most controls from Microsoft already have one of these, so you should not have to worry about this issue. Now when you compile your project again, take a look at the ClientBin folder under the web project. You can find one or more `.zip` files — one for each external assembly referenced by your Silverlight project, which isn't included in the core Silverlight run time. Your `.xap` file will also be much smaller because it will no longer contain these assemblies. The first time the user runs your application all the required pieces will be downloaded. Then when you update your project and compile it only the `.xap` file will need to be downloaded again. The benefits of this include less bandwidth being used for both the server and the client (updates will be much smaller to download), and updates will be much quicker, meaning less time for the users to wait before they can continue to use your application.

> **NOTE** *Unfortunately, application library caching cannot be used in applications that are configured to run in Out-Of-Browser mode (detailed later in this chapter), because Out-Of-Browser mode requires all the assemblies to be in the* `.xap` *file. If you attempt to set both options, a message box appears stating as such.*

Now return to see how the Silverlight project and the web project are linked together. This project link is managed by the web project and can be configured from its project properties page. Open the properties for this project, and select the Silverlight Applications tab to see the Silverlight projects currently linked to the web project (Figure 23-5).

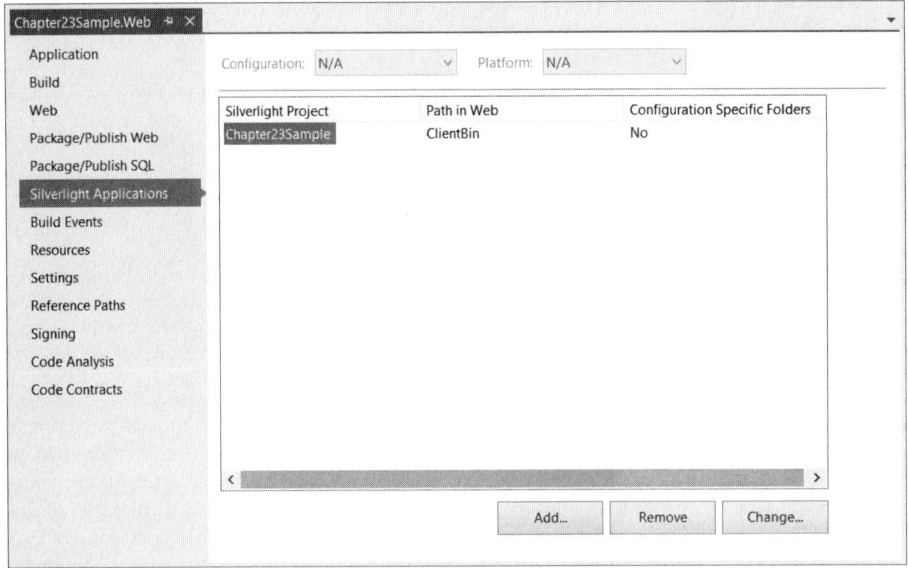

FIGURE 23-5

You will most likely need to use only this property page if the web project needs to host multiple Silverlight applications, or you have added a Silverlight project to a solution already containing a web project and you need to link the two. Project links can only be added or removed (not modified), so you will generally find you will use this property page only when a Silverlight project has been added or removed from the solution.

This property page displays a list of the Silverlight projects in this solution to which the current web project has a link. You have three options here: you can add another link to a Silverlight project, you can remove a project link, or you can change a project link. (Although this change option is not what you might initially expect, as discussed shortly.)

Click the Add button to link another Silverlight project to the web project. Figure 23-6 shows the window used to configure the new link.

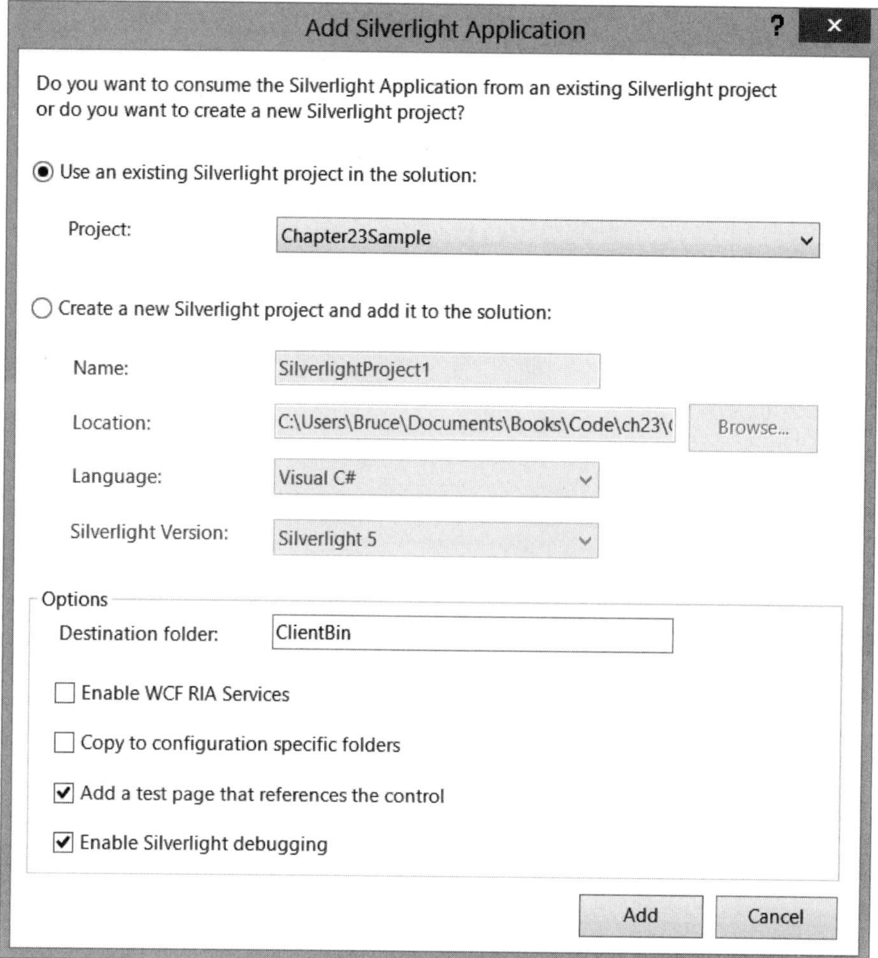

FIGURE 23-6

You have two choices when adding a link to a Silverlight project. The first is to link to a Silverlight project already in the solution, where you can simply select a project from the drop-down list to link to. You also have the choice to create a new Silverlight project and have it automatically link to the current web project. Unfortunately, you don't have the ability to select the project template to use, so it will only generate a new project based upon the Silverlight Application project template, somewhat limiting its use.

The Destination Folder option enables you to specify the folder underneath the web project that this Silverlight project will be copied to when it has been compiled. The test pages that are generated (if selected to be created) to host the Silverlight application will point to this location.

If the Copy to configuration specific folders option is set, the Silverlight application will not be copied directly under the specified destination folder, but an additional folder will be created underneath it with the name of the current configuration (Debug, Release, and so on) and the Silverlight application will be copied under it instead. Note that when this setting is turned on, the test pages still point to the destination folder, not the subfolder with the name of the current configuration which is now where the Silverlight application is located. If you want to use this option you need to manually update the test pages to point to the path as per the current configuration, and update this each time you switch between configurations. By default, this option is not set, and it is probably best not to use it unless necessary.

Selecting the Add a test page that references the control option adds both an HTML page and an ASPX page to the web project, already configured to host the output of the Silverlight project being linked. (You can delete the one you don't want to use.)

The Enable Silverlight debugging option turns on the ability to debug your Silverlight application (that is, stop on breakpoints, step through code, and so on). The downside to enabling this option is that it disables JavaScript debugging for the web project because enabling debugging for both at the same time is not possible.

Returning to the list of linked Silverlight projects (refer to Figure 23-5), the Remove button removes a link as you'd expect, but the Change button probably won't do what you'd initially assume it would. This button is used simply to toggle between using and not using configuration-specific folders (described earlier).

Now that you have learned the structure of the project, you can try running it. You can see that the Silverlight Navigation Application project template gives you a good starting point for your application and can form the basis of your application framework (as shown in Figure 23-7).

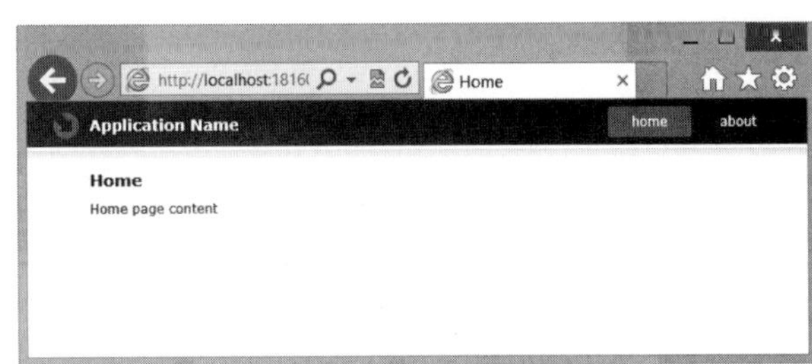

FIGURE 23-7

NAVIGATION FRAMEWORK

Because you have used the Silverlight Navigation Application project template for your project, you should take a quick look at Silverlight's Navigation Framework. The Navigation Framework was introduced in Silverlight 3 and makes it easy to create an application with multiple views and navigate between them. `MainPage.xaml` contains a Frame control (a part of the Navigation Framework), which is used to host the individual views when they are required to be shown.

Views must inherit from the Page control to be hosted in the frame. If you take a look at `Home.xaml`, you can notice that the root element is `navigation:Page` instead of `UserControl`. To create a new view, right-click the Views folder and select Add ➪ New Item. Select the Silverlight Page item template, give it a name (such as `Test.xaml`), and click OK. Add content to the view as required.

Each view needs a URI to point to it, and this URI will be used when you want to navigate to that view. You may want to set up a mapping from a chosen URI to the path (within the project) of its corresponding view file. These mappings are defined on the `UriMapper` property of the Frame control (in `MainPage.xaml`). These mappings allow wildcards, and a wildcard mapping has already been created that allows you to simply use the name of the XAML file (without the `.xaml` on the end). It looks for a XAML file with that name with a `.xaml` extension in the Views folder. This means you don't need to set up a mapping if you want to navigate to your `Test.xaml` file using `/Test` as the URI.

Now you need to add a button that allows you to navigate to the new view. In `MainPage.xaml` you can find some HyperlinkButton controls (named Link1 and Link2). Copy one of these, and paste it as a new line below it. (You may want to create another divider element by copying the existing one, too.) Change the `NavigateUri` to one that maps to your view (in this case it will be `/Test`), give the control a new name, and set the text to display on the button (in the `Content` property).

Now run the project. The new button appears in the header area of the application, and clicking it navigates to the new view.

> **NOTE** *The bookmark on the URL (the part after the # in the URL in the address bar of the browser) changes as you navigate between pages. You can also use the browser's Back and Next buttons to navigate backward and forward through the history of which views were previously navigated to. It also enables deep linking, such that views have a unique URL that can automatically be opened to. The Navigation Framework provides all this functionality.*

THEMING

Like WPF, Silverlight has extensive styling and theming capabilities; although their styling models are implemented slightly differently from one another. Silverlight introduced the Visual State Manager (VSM), a feature that WPF did not originally have (until WPF 4), which enables a control contract to be explicitly defined for the boundary between the control's behavior (that is, the code) and its look (that is, the XAML). This permits a strict separation to be maintained between the two. This contract defines a model for control templates called the Parts and States model, which consists of parts, states, transitions, and state groups. Further discussion of this is beyond the scope of this chapter; however, the VSM in Silverlight manages this model. This is considered a much better way to manage styles than WPF's original method to use triggers, and thus the VSM has been incorporated into WPF 4. However, until Silverlight 4, Silverlight did not support implicit styling (unlike WPF, which did), where it could be specified that all controls of a given type should use a particular style (making applying a theme to your project somewhat difficult). To make theming easier, Microsoft created the ImplicitStyleManager control, which shipped in the Silverlight Toolkit control library. Silverlight 4 finally introduced implicit styling, making the ImplicitStyleManager control somewhat redundant. The only reason to continue using the ImplicitStyleManager is if you need to write code that runs across multiple versions of Silverlight, including Silverlight 3.

> **NOTE** *You can download the free Silverlight Toolkit from CodePlex at* `http://silverlight.codeplex.com`*. It also contains numerous useful controls that aren't included in the Silverlight SDK (such as charts, tab control, TreeView, and so on).*

So despite their differences, WPF and Silverlight both have controls in their respective toolkit projects that enable similar styling and theming behavior between the two.

Now take a look at applying a different theme to your project to completely change the way the controls look. Conceptually, a theme is just a collection of styles. And Silverlight has the same themes available as demonstrated in Chapter 18 (in fact, the themes were originally developed for Silverlight and ported to WPF) and can be found in the Silverlight Toolkit. You can call these *control themes* to separate them from the *application themes* discussed shortly.

You have a couple of ways to use these control themes. One is to take one of the XAML theming files from the Silverlight Toolkit, copy it into your project's root folder, and include it in your project (setting its Build Action to Content at the same time). For this example you use the `System.Windows.Controls.Theming.ExpressionDark.xaml` theme file. Since Silverlight 5 supports implicit styles (that is, styles that can be associated with a control type and then used for every that control is found within the application), all that is required is to add a reference to the XAML theme file. This can be done in the `App.xaml` file, as shown below.

```
<Application
  x:Class="Chapter23Sample.App"
  xmlns="http://schemas.microsoft.com/winfx/2006/xaml/presentation"
  xmlns:x="http://schemas.microsoft.com/winfx/2006/xaml">

  <Application.Resources>
    <ResourceDictionary>
```

```
      <ResourceDictionary.MergedDictionaries>
        <ResourceDictionary
            Source="System.Windows.Controls.Theming.ExpressionDark.xaml"/>
      </ResourceDictionary.MergedDictionaries>
    </ResourceDictionary>
  </Application.Resources>

</Application>
```

If you want to change the theme for your application, add the XAML file for the theme to your project and change the Source attribute in `App.xaml`.

This is not a particularly flexible approach. To be fair, it's flexible if you want to set your theme at design time. But if you have the need to change the theme at run time, then you can do so programmatically.

Start by adding all of the themes that you want to use to your project. Select the default theme and add it to the `App.xaml` as has already been demonstrated. From a user experience perspective, the next step is to create the user interface that allows the user to change the theme. It could be a ComboBox. It could be a link. The interface is not particularly important. What is important is that the following methods be called from the event handler for the interface that you choose to use.

VB

```
Private Sub RemoveCurrentSource(source As String)

   Dim res As ResourceDictionary = _
      Application.Current.Resources.MergedDictionaries.Where
        (Function(d)d.Source.OriginalString = source).FirstOrDefault()
   If res <> Nothing Then
       Application.Current.Resources.MergedDictionaries.Remove(res)
   End If
End Sub

Private Sub AddNewSource(source As String)

   Dim res As ResourceDictionary =
      Application.Current.Resources.MergedDictionaries.Where
         (Function(d) d.Source.OriginalString = source).FirstOrDefault()
   If res Is Nothing Then
       Dim stylePath = New Uri(source, UriKind.Relative)
       Dim newResource = New ResourceDictionary()
       newResource.Source = stylePath
       Application.Current.Resources.MergedDictionaries.Add(newResource)
   End If

End Sub
```

C#

```
private void RemoveCurrentSource(string source)
{
   ResourceDictionary res =
      Application.Current.Resources.MergedDictionaries.Where
        (d => d.Source.OriginalString == source).FirstOrDefault();
   if (res != null)
   {
       Application.Current.Resources.MergedDictionaries.Remove(res);
   }
}

private void AddNewSource(string source)
{
```

```
        ResourceDictionary res =
           Application.Current.Resources.MergedDictionaries.Where
              (d => d.Source.OriginalString == source).FirstOrDefault();
        if (res == null)
        {
            Uri stylePath = new Uri(source, UriKind.Relative);
            ResourceDictionary newResource = new ResourceDictionary();
            newResource.Source = stylePath;
            Application.Current.Resources.MergedDictionaries.Add(newResource);
        }
    }
```

The idea is to call the RemoveCurrentSource method to remove whatever style XAML file is currently being used. Then call AddNewSource with the name of the XAML file that contains the theme that you want to use.

If you create your project using the Silverlight Navigation Application template or the Silverlight Business Application template, you can also take advantage of some alternative application themes that have been created to give your application a whole new look. You can find the application theme styles in the `Styles.xaml` file under the Assets folder in your Silverlight project. The `App.xaml` file merges the styles from this file into its own if your project is based on the Silverlight Navigation Application project template. `MainPage.xaml` uses the styles that have been defined in `Styles.xaml` to specify its layout and look. Therefore, all you need to do is replace this file with one with the same styles defined but with different values to completely change the way the application looks. A number of alternative application theme files for projects based upon the Silverlight Navigation Application project template have been created by Microsoft and the community and can be downloaded from `http://gallery.expression.microsoft.com` (look in the Themes category). For example, simply replacing the `Styles.xaml` file for the project (refer to Figure 23-7) with the theme file from the gallery called "Frosted Cinnamon Toast" completely changes the way it looks, as shown in Figure 23-8.

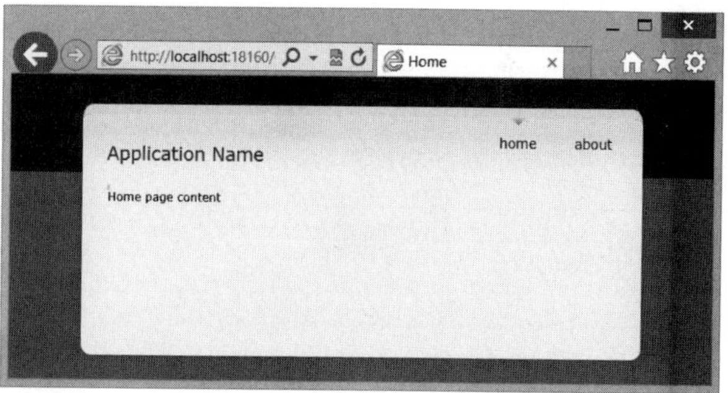

FIGURE 23-8

ENABLING RUNNING OUT OF BROWSER

Though Silverlight was initially designed as a browser-based plug-in, Silverlight 3 introduced the ability to run a Silverlight application outside the browser as if it were a standard application, and it was no longer necessary to run your Silverlight application within a browser. In fact, you don't even need to be online to run a Silverlight application after it has been installed to run in Out-Of-Browser mode. Out-Of-Browser applications are delivered initially via the browser and can then be installed on the machine (if enabled by the developer). This install process can be initiated from the right-click menu or from code — the only criteria being that the install process must be user initiated, so random applications can't install themselves on users' machines without their approval.

> **NOTE** *If you aren't seeing an option to install your application when you right-click on it, make sure that your Web project, not your Silverlight project, is set as the startup project in your solution.*

By default, your Silverlight application will not be configured for Out-Of-Browser mode, and you must explicitly enable this in your application for the feature to be available. The easiest way to enable this is in the project properties for the Silverlight application (refer to Figure 23-4). When you put a check in the Enable Running Application Out of the Browser option, the Out-of-Browser Settings button becomes enabled, and clicking this button pops up the window shown in Figure 23-9.

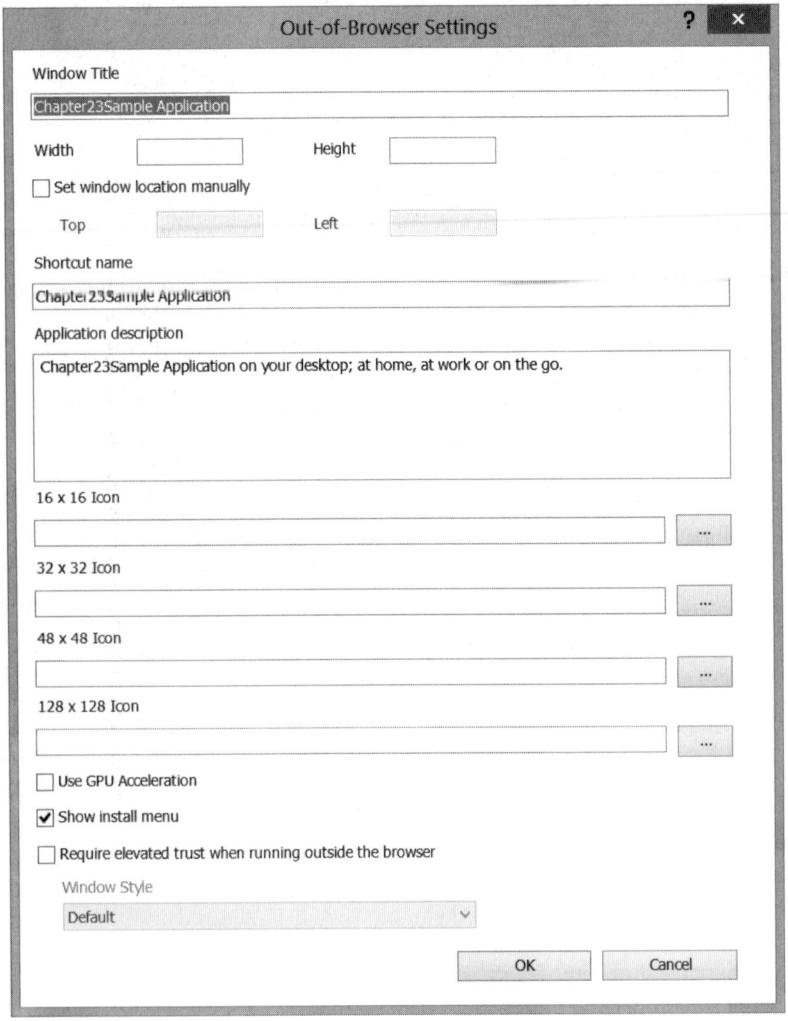

FIGURE 23-9

This window enables you to configure various options for when the application is running in Out-Of-Browser mode. Most of the options are fairly self-explanatory. You can set the window title and its starting dimensions. (The window is resizable.) You can also configure the start menu/desktop shortcuts, set the text for the shortcut (the shortcut name), set the text that will appear when the mouse hovers over the icon (the application description), and set the various-sized icons to use for the shortcut. These icons must be PNG files that have already been added as files in your Silverlight project. Select the appropriate image for each icon size. If you leave any of these icons blank, it simply uses the default Out-Of-Browser icon for that icon size instead. The two check boxes at the bottom enable you to set whether Out-Of-Browser mode should use GPU acceleration (for Silverlight applications running inside the browser this setting is set on the Silverlight plug-in), and the Show install menu check box specifies whether the user should have the option to install the application via the right-click menu. (Otherwise, the install process must be initiated from code.)

> **NOTE** *Your Silverlight application is still sandboxed when running outside the browser and will have no more access to the user's computer than it did while running inside the browser, unless the user has been granted a request for running with elevated trust. If it is not running with elevated trust, even though it may appear to be running as if it were a standard application, it's still restricted by the same security model as when it's running inside the browser. However, with elevated trust, Silverlight has the capability for Out-Of-Browser applications to utilize COM automation, access local files, and perform PInvokes against DLLs stored locally.*

After you configure the Out-Of-Browser settings, you can run the project and try it out. When your application is running, right-click anywhere on your application, and select the Install *XXXX* onto your computer option, as shown in Figure 23-10, to initiate the install process (where *XXXX* is the name of the application).

Silverlight
Install Chapter23Sample Application onto this computer...

FIGURE 23-10

The window shown in Figure 23-11 appears with options for the user to select which types of shortcuts to the application should be set up.

This installs the application locally (under the user's profile), configures the selected desktop/start menu shortcuts, and automatically starts the application in Out-Of-Browser mode.

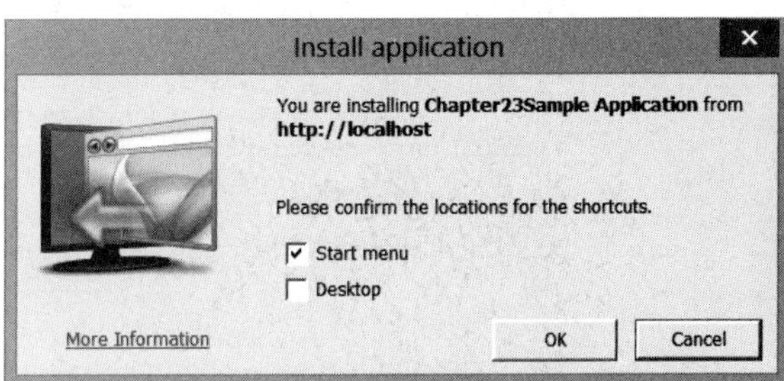

FIGURE 23-11

> **NOTE** *To uninstall the application, simply right-click it, and select the Remove This Application option.*

Of course, you need to update your application at some point in time and have the existing instances that were installed updated accordingly. Luckily, this is easy to do but does require some code. This code could be used anywhere in your application, but you'll put it in the code-behind for the `App.xaml` file, and start the update available check as soon as the application has started as follows:

VB

```
Private Sub Application_Startup(ByVal o As Object, ByVal e As StartupEventArgs) _
                                                                    Handles Me.Startup
    Me.RootVisual = New MainPage()

    If Application.Current.IsRunningOutOfBrowser Then
        Application.Current.CheckAndDownloadUpdateAsync()
    End If
End Sub

Private Sub App_CheckAndDownloadUpdateCompleted(ByVal sender As Object, _
                        ByVal e As _
                        System.Windows.CheckAndDownloadUpdateCompletedEventArgs) _
                        Handles Me.CheckAndDownloadUpdateCompleted
    If e.UpdateAvailable Then
        MessageBox.Show("A new version of this application is available and " &
                        "has been downloaded.  Please close the application and " &
                        "restart it to use the new version.",
                        "Application Update Found", MessageBoxButton.OK)
```

```
    End If
End Sub
```

C#

```
private void Application_Startup(object sender, StartupEventArgs e)
{
    this.RootVisual = new Page();

    if (Application.Current.IsRunningOutOfBrowser)
    {
        Application.Current.CheckAndDownloadUpdateCompleted +=
                Current_CheckAndDownloadUpdateCompleted;
        Application.Current.CheckAndDownloadUpdateAsync();
    }
}

private void Current_CheckAndDownloadUpdateCompleted(object sender,
                      CheckAndDownloadUpdateCompletedEventArgs e)
{
    if (e.UpdateAvailable)
    {
        MessageBox.Show("A new version of this application is available and " +
            "has been downloaded.  Please close the application and restart " +
            "it to use the new version.", "Application Update Found",
            MessageBoxButton.OK);
    }
}
```

As you can see, if the application is running in Out-Of-Browser mode, you check to see if there are any updates. This asynchronously goes back to the URL that the application was installed from and checks if there is a new version (during which the application continues to load and run). If so it automatically downloads it. Whether an update was found, it raises the `CheckAndDownloadUpdateCompleted` event when the check (and potential download of a new version) is complete. Then you just need to see if an update had been found and notify the user if so. The update is automatically installed the next time the application is run, so to start using the new version, the user needs to close the application and reopen it again.

To test the update process, start by including the update check code in your application. Run the application and install it using the method described earlier. Close both it and the instance that was running in the browser, and return to Visual Studio. Make a change to the application (one that allows you to spot the difference if it is updated correctly) and recompile it. Now run the previously installed version (from the Start menu or desktop icon). The application starts, and shortly afterward the message box appears stating that the new version has been downloaded and to restart the application. When you reopen the application again, you should see that you are indeed now running the new version.

SUMMARY

In this chapter you have seen how you can work with Visual Studio 2012 to build applications with Silverlight and run them both within and outside the browser. To learn about one of the many means to communicate between the client and the server and transferring data, see Chapter 36.

24

Dynamic Data

WHAT'S IN THIS CHAPTER?

- Creating a data-driven web application without writing any code using Dynamic Data's scaffolding functionality
- Customizing the data model and presentation layer of a Dynamic Data application
- Adding Dynamic Data features to an existing web application

Most developers spend an inordinately large amount of time writing code that deals with data. This is so fundamental to what developers do on a daily basis that an acronym has appeared to describe this type of code — *CRUD*, which stands for *Create, Read, Update, Delete*, which are the four basic functions that can be performed on data.

For example, consider a simple application to maintain a Tasks or To Do list. At the very least the application must provide the following functionality:

- **Create:** Create a new task and save it in the database.
- **Read:** Retrieve a list of tasks from the database and display them to the user. Retrieve and display all the properties of an individual task.
- **Update:** Modify the properties of an existing task and save the changes to the database.
- **Delete:** Delete a task from the database that is no longer required.

ASP.NET Dynamic Data is a framework that takes away the need to write much of this low-level CRUD code. Dynamic Data can discover the data model and automatically generate a fully functioning, data-driven web site at run time. This allows developers to focus instead on writing rock-solid business logic, enhancing the user experience, or performing some other high-value programming task.

LESS IS MORE: SCAFFOLDING AND CONVENTION OVER CONFIGURATION

Scaffolding is the name for the mechanism that ASP.NET Dynamic Data uses to dynamically generate web pages based on the underlying database. The generated pages include all the functionality you would expect in any decent data-driven application including paging and sorting. In addition to the benefits of freeing developers from writing low-level data access code, scaffolding provides built-in data validation based on the database schema and full support for foreign keys and relationships between tables.

Scaffolding was popularized by the Ruby on Rails web development framework. Along with scaffolding, ASP.NET Dynamic Data includes several other principles and practices that are clearly inspired by Ruby on Rails. One such principle is *Convention over Configuration*, which means that certain things are implicitly assumed through a standard convention. For example, at run time, Dynamic Data can detect the file `List.aspx` under the folder called Products and use it to render a custom web page for the Product database table. Because the folder name is the same (pluralized) name as the database table, there is no need to explicitly tell Dynamic Data that this file exists, or that it is associated with the Product table.

Less code means fewer places for mistakes.

This chapter demonstrates how to use Dynamic Data scaffolding to create a data-driven web application with little or no code. You also learn how flexible Dynamic Data is by customizing the data model and web pages.

Although Dynamic Data is somewhat synonymous with scaffolding and building a data-driven web application from scratch, at the end of this chapter you see that you can get a number of benefits by adding Dynamic Data functionality to your existing web application.

CREATING A DYNAMIC DATA WEB APPLICATION

Before you can create and run a Dynamic Data web application, you need a database. The examples in this chapter use the SQL Server 2008 AdventureWorksLT2008R2 database, which you can download from the CodePlex web site at `http://msftdbprodsamples.codeplex.com/`.

After you download your database, open Visual Studio and select File ➪ New ➪ Project. In the Web project category of both Visual Basic and C#, you see a project template for Dynamic Data, the Dynamic Data Entities Web Application, which supports the ADO.NET Entity Framework as the underlying data access mechanism.

NOTE *If you prefer to work with Web Site projects instead of Web Application projects, you can still use Dynamic Data. Under the New Web Site dialog you find the equivalent template for creating a new Entities Dynamic Data Web Site project.*

THE ADO.NET ENTITY FRAMEWORK

The ADO.NET Entity Framework is one of the two main data access options (the other is LINQ to SQL) currently promoted by Microsoft. Both have their pros and cons, and both work perfectly well for many of the more common scenarios.

However, where LINQ to SQL works only with Microsoft SQL Server database, the ADO .NET Entity Framework allows for a data model different from the underlying database schema. You can map multiple database tables to a single .NET class, or a single database table to multiple .NET classes. The Entity Framework also supports a number of different databases including Oracle, MySQL, and DB2.

You can find out more about the ADO.NET Entity Framework in Chapter 30, "The ADO .NET Framework."

Select the ASP.NET Dynamic Data Entities Web Application project, and click OK. When the new project is created, it generates a large number of files and folders, as shown in Figure 24-1. Most of these files are templates that can be modified to customize the user interface. These are located under the DynamicData root folder and are discussed later in this chapter.

The project template also creates a standard web form, `Default.aspx`, as the start page for the web application. As with the standard ASP.NET Web Application project, the application encourages best practices by making use of the master page feature and an external CSS file, and includes the JQuery JavaScript library. See Chapter 21, "ASP.NET Web Forms," for further information on these features.

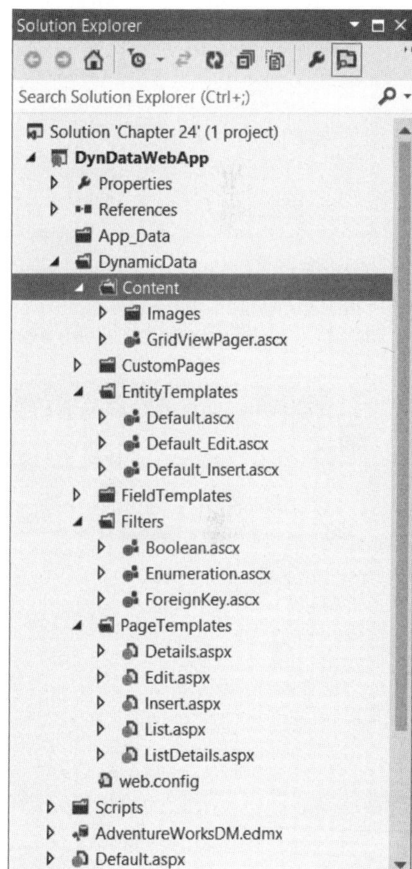

FIGURE 24-1

Adding a Data Model

After you create your new project, the next step is to create the data model. Right-click the project in the Solution Explorer, and select Add ➪ New Item. Select the ADO.NET Entity Data Model item from the Data category and name it `AdventureWorksDM.edmx`.

After you create your new project, the next step is to create the data model. Right-click the project in the Solution Explorer, and select Add ➪ New Item. Select the ADO.NET Entity Data Model item from the Data category and name it `AdventureWorksDM.edmx`. After you click Add, the Entity Data Model Wizard launches. Select the Generate from Database option, and click Next. On the subsequent page, the connection to the database is specified. In this case, use an existing connection to the AdventureWorksLT2008R2 database or create a new one if necessary. Figure 24-2 shows the form as it should be filled out for this exercise.

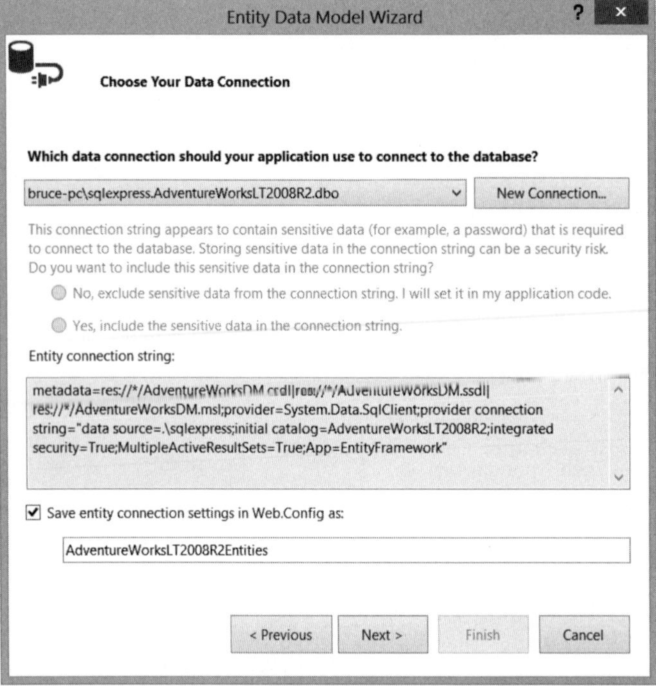

FIGURE 24-2

The definition of the wanted connection leads to the next step, which is identifying the entities in that database to be modeled. For this exercise, select all the tables in SalesLT, as shown in Figure 24-3.

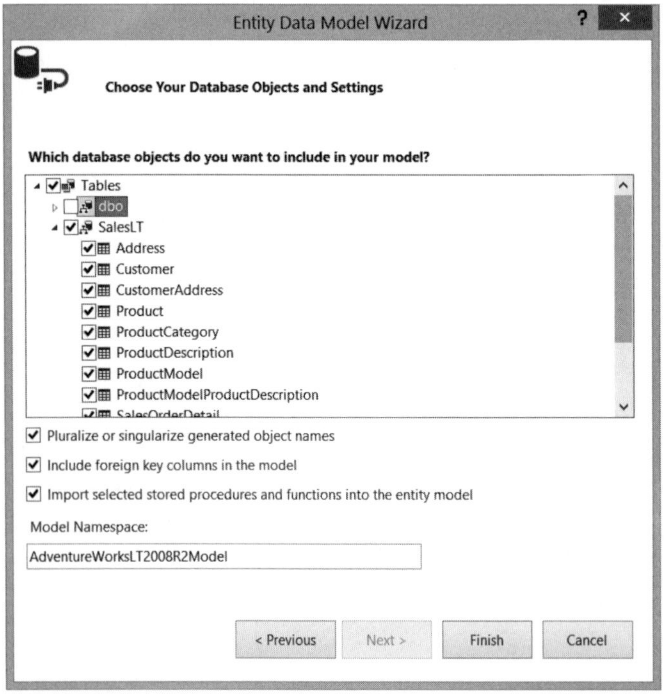

FIGURE 24-3

After you complete this step, the Entity Model is generated and added to your solution. You need to register your data model with Dynamic Data and enable scaffolding. Open the `Global.asax.cs` (or `Global.asax.vb` if you use Visual Basic) and locate the following line of code. Uncomment this line and change the `YourDataContextType` to `AdventureWorksLT2008R2Entities`. Finally, change the `ScaffoldAllTables` property to `true`.

C#

```
DefaultModel.RegisterContext(typeof(AdventureWorksLT2008R2Entities),
                             new ContextConfiguration()
                             { ScaffoldAllTables = true });
```

VB

```
DefaultModel.RegisterContext(GetType(AdventureWorksLT2008R2Entities), _
                             New ContextConfiguration() _
                             With {.ScaffoldAllTables = True})
```

That is all you need to do to get a data-driven web application with full CRUD support up and running.

Exploring a Dynamic Data Application

When you run the application, it opens with the home page, `Default.aspx`, which displays a list of hyperlinks for all the tables you added to the data model (see Figure 24-4). Note that the names listed on this page are pluralized versions of the table name.

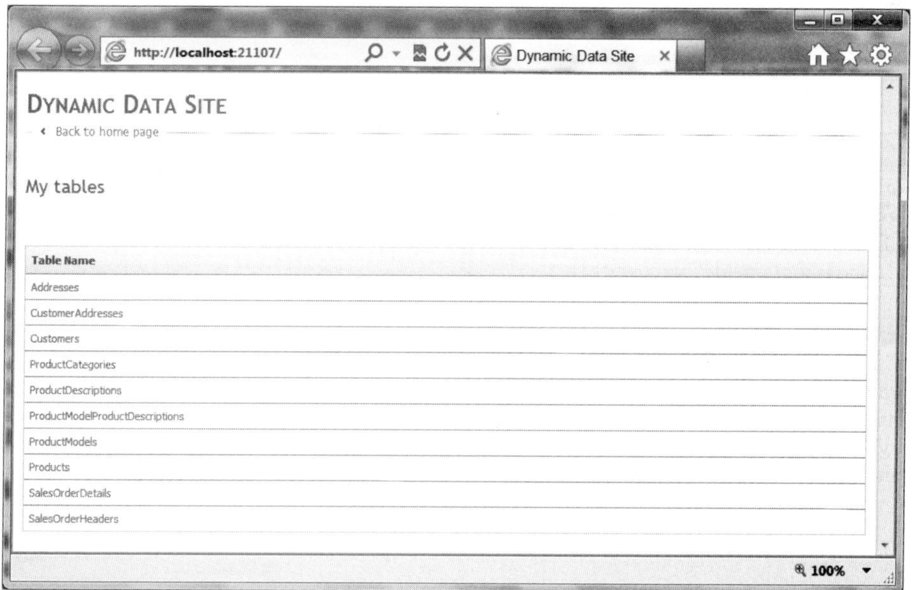

FIGURE 24-4

When you click one of these links, the `List.aspx` page displays, as shown in Figure 24-5, for the selected table. This page, along with the `Details.aspx` page for an individual record, represents the "Read" function of your CRUD application and includes support for paging and filtering of the records by the foreign key. This page also displays links to view details, edit, or delete a record. Any foreign keys display as links to a details page for that foreign key record.

> **NOTE** *Some database fields are missing from the web page, such as ProductID and ThumbNailPhoto. By default, Dynamic Data does not scaffold Identity columns, binary columns, or computed columns. This can be overridden, as you find out later in this chapter.*

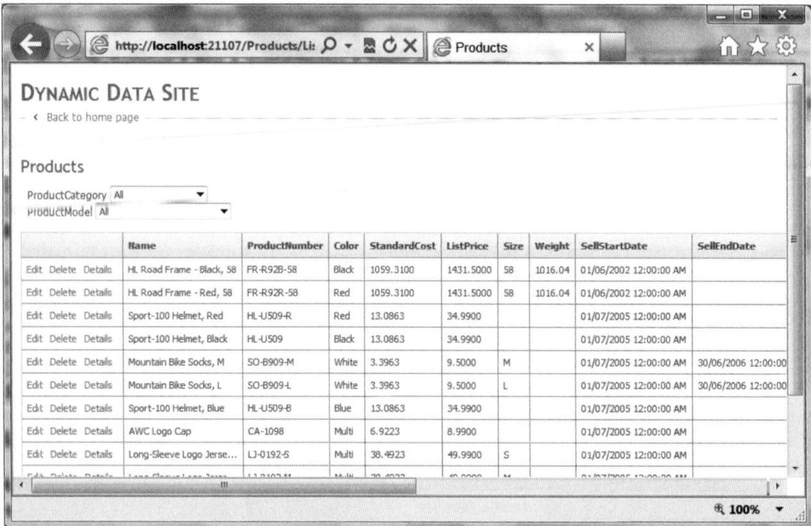

FIGURE 24-5

The "Update" CRUD function is accessed by clicking the Edit link against a record. This displays the `Edit.aspx` page, as shown in Figure 24-6. The textboxes are different widths — this is determined based on the length of the database field. This page also includes a number of ASP.NET validation controls based on database field information. For example, the ProductNumber field has a `RequiredFieldValidator` because the underlying database field is not nullable. Likewise, the Weight field uses a `CompareValidator` to ensure that the value entered is a decimal.

Foreign keys are also handled by drop-down selectors. For example, in Figure 24-6 the ProductCategory and ProductModel fields are foreign keys. Tables that use the selected table as a foreign key display as hyperlinks, as shown in the SalesOrderDetails field in Figure 24-6.

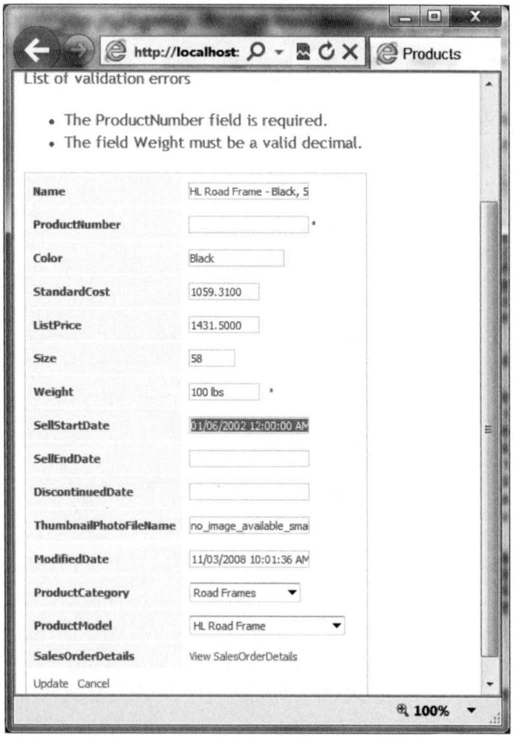

FIGURE 24-6

CUSTOMIZING THE DATA MODEL

Although scaffolding an entire database makes for an impressive demo, it is unlikely that you would actually want to expose every table and field in your database to end users. Fortunately, Dynamic Data has been designed to handle this scenario, and many others, by customizing the data model.

Scaffolding Individual Tables

Before you begin customizing the data model, disable automatic scaffolding of all tables. Open the `Global.asax.cs` file and change the `ScaffoldAllTables` property to `false`.

The next step is to selectively enable scaffolding for individual tables. Begin by adding a new class file to the project called `Product.cs`. This class must be a partial class because Product is already defined in the Entity data model. To enable scaffolding for the Product table, decorate the class with the `ScaffoldTable` attribute. When completed, the class should look similar to the following code:

C#

```
using System.ComponentModel.DataAnnotations;

namespace DynDataWebApp
{
    [ScaffoldTable(true)]
    public partial class Product
    {
    }
}
```

VB

```
Imports System.ComponentModel.DataAnnotations

<ScaffoldTable(True)> _
Partial Public Class Product
End Class
```

If you run the application now, only the Product table will be listed and editable.

> **NOTE** *You can achieve the same result by leaving the* `ScaffoldAllTables` *property to* `true` *and selectively hiding tables by decorating their corresponding classes with the* `ScaffoldTable` *attribute set to* `false`.

Customizing Individual Data Fields

In many cases you want certain fields in a table to be either read-only or hidden. This is useful if the table contains sensitive data such as credit card information.

For example, when you edit a record in the Product table, it displays a link to the SalesOrderDetails table. This link is disabled because the SalesOrderDetails table has not been enabled for scaffolding. Therefore, displaying this field provides the user with no useful information. Also the ModifiedDate field, although useful for end users to know, is not something that you would typically want them to edit directly. Therefore, it would be better to display this field as read-only and allow the database to modify it with an `Update` trigger.

These requirements are supported by Dynamic Data by adding a *meta data class* to your data model class. In the `Product.cs` file add a new class to the bottom of the file called `ProductMetadata`. This class can be associated by applying the `MetadataType` attribute to the `Product` class.

In the `ProductMetadata` class, create public fields with the same name as each data field that you want to customize. Because Dynamic Data can read the type of this field from the data model class rather than the meta data class, you can use `object` as the type for these fields.

Add the `ScaffoldColumn` attribute to the `SalesOrderDetails` field, and set it to `false` to hide the field. To make the `ModifiedDate` field read-only, decorate it with an `Editable` attribute set to `false`.

The following code shows these changes:

C#

```
namespace DynDataWebApp
{
    [ScaffoldTable(true)]
    [MetadataType(typeof(ProductMetadata))]
    public partial class Product
    {
    }
    public class ProductMetadata
    {
        [ScaffoldColumn(false)]
        public object SalesOrderDetails;

        [Editable(false)]
        public object ModifiedDate;
    }
}
```

VB

```
<ScaffoldTable(True)> _
<MetadataType(GetType(ProductMetadata))> _
Partial Public Class Product
End Class
Public Class ProductMetadata
    <ScaffoldColumn(False)> _
    Public SalesOrderDetails As Object

    <Editable(False)> _
    Public ModifiedDate As Object
End Class
```

Figure 24-7 shows the results of these changes in action. On the left is the original edit screen for the Product table. On the right is the new edit screen after the data model has been customized.

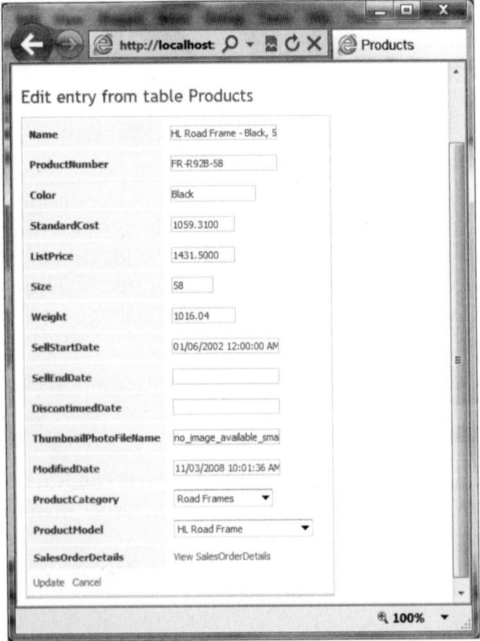

FIGURE 24-7

Adding Custom Validation Rules

As mentioned earlier, Dynamic Data includes some built-in support for validation rules inferred from the underlying database schema. For example, if a field in a database table is marked as not nullable, a `RequiredFieldValidator` will be added to the Update page.

However, in some cases there are business rules about the format of data that isn't supported by the built-in validation rules. For example, in the Product table, the values saved in the ProductNumber field all follow a specific format that begins with two uppercase letters followed by a hyphen. This format can be enforced by decorating the ProductNumber field with a `RegularExpression` attribute, as shown in the following code:

C#

```
[ScaffoldTable(true)]
[MetadataType(typeof(ProductMetadata))]
public partial class Product
{
}

public class ProductMetadata
{
   [RegularExpression("^[A-Z]{2}-[A-Z0-9]{4}(-[A-Z0-9]{1,2})?$",
    ErrorMessage="Product Number must be a valid format")]
   public object ProductNumber;
}
```

VB

```
<ScaffoldTable(True)> _
<MetadataType(GetType(ProductMetadata))> _
Partial Public Class Product
End Class

Public Class ProductMetadata
    <RegularExpression("^[A-Z]{2}-[A-Z0-9]{4}(-[A-Z0-9]{1,2})?$", _
     ErrorMessage:="Product Number must be a valid format")> _
    Public ProductNumber As Object
End Class
```

There is also a `Range` attribute, which is useful for specifying the minimum and maximum allowed values for a numeric field. Finally, you can apply the `Required` or `StringLength` attributes if you want to enforce these constraints on a field in the data model without specifying them in the underlying database.

Although useful, the attribute-based validations don't support all scenarios. For example, a user could attempt to enter a date for the Product SellEndDate that is earlier than the SellStartDate value. Due to a database constraint on this field, this would result in a run-time exception rather than a validation error, which is presented to the user.

For each property that is in the data model, Entity Framework defines two methods that are called during an edit: the `On`*`FieldName`*`Changing` method, which is called just before the field is changed, and the `On`*`FieldName`*`Changed` method, which is called just after. Naturally, the *`FieldName`* in the method would match the name of the property. So for a property named FirstName, the methods would be `OnFirstNameChanging` and `OnFirstNameChanged`. To handle complex validation rules, you can complete the appropriate partial method declaration in the data model, adding the validation your application requires.

The following code shows a validation rule that ensures a value entered for the Product SellEndDate field is not earlier than the SellStartDate:

C#

```
[ScaffoldTable(true)]
[MetadataType(typeof(ProductMetadata))]
public partial class Product
```

```
{
    partial void OnSellEndDateChanging(DateTime? value)
    {
        if (value.HasValue && value.Value < this._SellStartDate)
        {
            throw new ValidationException(
                     "Sell End Date must be later than Sell Start Date");
        }
    }
}
```

VB

```
<ScaffoldTable(True)> _
<MetadataType(GetType(ProductMetadata))> _
Partial Public Class Product
    Private Sub OnSellEndDateChanging(ByVal value As Nullable(Of DateTime))
        If value.HasValue AndAlso value.Value < Me._SellStartDate Then
            Throw New ValidationException( _
                     "Sell End Date must be later than Sell Start Date")
        End If
    End Sub
End Class
```

Figure 24-8 shows how this custom validation rule is enforced by Dynamic Data.

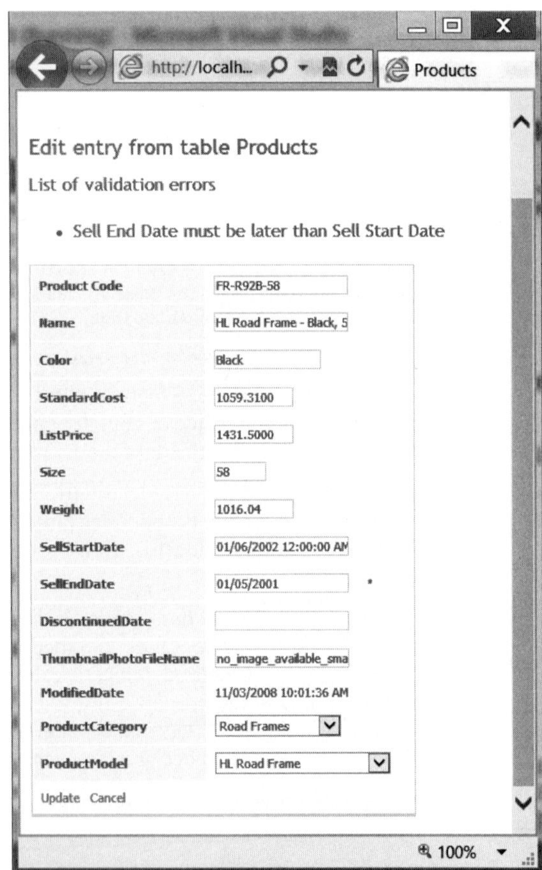

FIGURE 24-8

Customizing the Display Format

The default way that some of the data types are formatted is less than ideal. For example, the Product StandardCost and ListPrice fields, which use the SQL `money` data type, are displayed as numbers to four decimal places. Also, the Product SellStartDate and SellEndDate fields, which have a SQL `datetime` data type, are formatted showing both the date and time, even though the time portion is not actually useful information.

The display format of these fields can be customized in two ways: globally for a specific data type by customizing the field template; or on an individual field basis by customizing the data model. Field template customization is discussed in the section "Field Templates" later in this chapter.

First, to specify how the fields will be formatted in the user interface, decorate the corresponding property in the data model with the `DisplayFormat` attribute. This attribute has a `DataFormatString` property that accepts a .NET format string. The attribute also includes a number of additional parameters to control rendering including the `HtmlEncode` parameter, which indicates whether the field should be HTML encoded, and the `NullDisplayText` attribute, which sets the text to be displayed when the field's value is null. The following code shows how the `DisplayFormat` attribute can be applied:

C#

```
[DisplayFormat(DataFormatString="{0:C}")]
public object ListPrice;

[DisplayFormat(DataFormatString="{0:MMM d, yyyy}",
               NullDisplayText="Not Specified")]
public object SellEndDate;
```

VB

```
<Display(Name:="List Price")> _
<DisplayFormat(DataFormatString:="{0:C}")> _
Public ListPrice As Object

<Display(Name:="Sell End Date")> _
<DisplayFormat(DataFormatString:="{0:MMM d, yyyy}",
               NullDisplayText:="Not Specified")> _
Public SellEndDate As Object
```

> **NOTE** *By default, the display format will be applied only to the Read view. To apply this formatting to the Edit view, set the* `ApplyFormatInEditMode` *property to* `true` *on the* `DisplayFormat` *attribute.*

Second, it's unlikely that you want to use the database field names in the user interface. It would be much better to provide descriptive names for all of your fields. You can use the `Display` attribute to control how the field labels render. This attribute accepts a number of parameters, including `Name`, to specify the actual label and `Order` to control the order in which fields should be listed. In the following code, the ProductNumber field has been given a display name of "Product Code" and an order value of 1 to ensure it is always displayed as the first field:

C#

```
[Display(Name="Product Code", Order=1)]
public object ProductNumber;
```

VB

```
<Display(Name:="Product Code", Order:=1)> _
Public ProductNumber As Object
```

Figure 24-9 shows how these formatting changes are rendered by Dynamic Data.

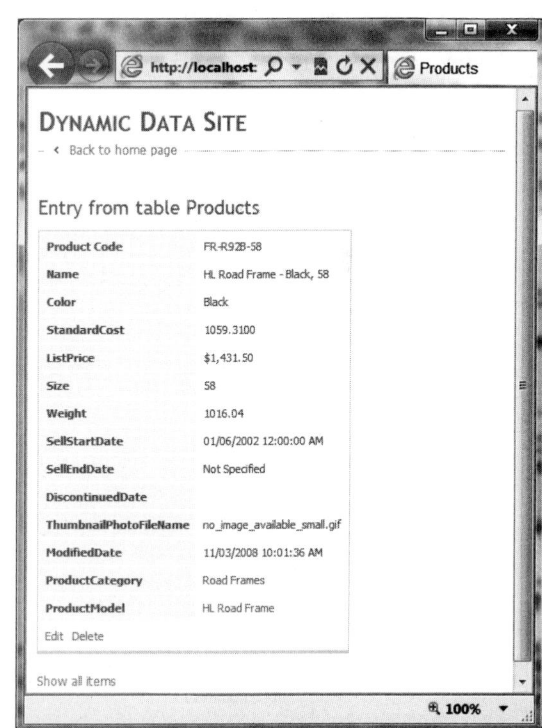

FIGURE 24-9

CUSTOMIZING THE PRESENTATION

Chances are the way that Dynamic Data renders a website by default will not be exactly what you require. The previous section demonstrated how many aspects of the data model could be customized to control how the database tables and fields are rendered. However, limitations exist as to what can be achieved simply by customizing the data model. Fortunately, Dynamic Data uses a rich template system that is fully customizable and allows you complete control over the UI.

The Dynamic Data template files are stored under a number of subfolders in the `DynamicData` folder, which is in the root of the web application. Following the Convention over Configuration principle, these template files do not need to be manually registered with Dynamic Data. Instead, each different type of template should be stored in a specific folder and the framework can use the location, as well as the template filename, to determine when to load it at run time.

Page Templates

Page templates are used to provide the default rendering of a database table. The master page templates are stored in the `DynamicData\PageTemplates` folder. Dynamic Data ships with the following five page templates for viewing and editing data:

- **Details.aspx:** Renders a read-only view of an existing entry from a table.
- **Edit.aspx:** Displays an editable view of an existing entry from a table.
- **Insert.aspx:** Displays a view that allows users to add a new entry to a table.
- **List.aspx:** Renders an entire table using a grid view with support for paging and sorting.
- **ListDetails.aspx:** Used when Dynamic Data is configured with the combined-page mode, where the Detail, Edit, Insert, and List tasks are performed by the same page. This mode can be enabled by following the comment instructions in the `Global.asax` file.

You can edit any of these default page templates if there are changes that you would like to affect all tables by default. You can also override the default page templates by creating a set of custom templates for a table. Custom pages templates are stored under the `DynamicData\CustomPages` folder.

In the AdventureWorksLT2008R2 database, the SalesOrderHeader table is a good candidate for a custom page template. Before creating the template, you need to enable scaffolding for this table. Enabling scaffolding was demonstrated earlier in the "Adding a Data Model" and "Scaffolding Individual Tables" sections. Create a new data model partial class for the SalesOrderHeader table, and enable scaffolding, as shown in the following code:

C#

```
using System.ComponentModel.DataAnnotations;

namespace DynDataWebApp
{
    [ScaffoldTable(true)]
    public partial class SalesOrderHeader
    {
    }
}
```

VB

```
Imports System.ComponentModel.DataAnnotations

<ScaffoldTable(True)> _
Partial Public Class SalesOrderHeader
End Class
```

Next, create a subfolder called SalesOrderHeaders under the `DynamicData\CustomPages` folder. This folder contains the custom templates for the SalesOrderHeader table. Copy the existing `List.aspx` template from the `DynamicData\PageTemplates` folder to the `DynamicData\CustomPages\SalesOrderHeaders` folder.

> **NOTE** *The folder name for custom page templates should generally be named with the plural form of the table name. The exceptions to this are if the data model uses the ADO.NET Entity Framework version 3.5 or if the default option Pluralize or Singularize Generated Object Names has been changed. In this case the folder name should have the same name as the table.*

Because the template was copied, and therefore a duplicate class was created, your application will no longer compile. The easiest way to fix this is to change the namespace to any unique value in both the markup and code-behind files of the new template, as shown in the following code:

C#

```
<%@ Page Language="C#" MasterPageFile="~/Site.master" CodeBehind="List.aspx.cs"
    Inherits="DynDataWebApp._SalesOrderHeaders.List" %>
namespace DynDataWebApp._SalesOrderHeaders
{
    public partial class List : System.Web.UI.Page
    {
        // Code snipped
    }
}
```

VB

```
<%@ Page Language="VB" MasterPageFile="~/Site.master" CodeBehind="List.aspx.vb"
    Inherits="DynDataWebApp._SalesOrderHeader.List" %>
Namespace _SalesOrderHeader
    Class List
        Inherits Page
        ' Code Snipped
    End Class
End Namespace
```

You can now customize the template in whatever manner you want. For example, you may want to reduce the number of columns that appear in the List view, while still ensuring that all data fields appear in the Insert and Edit views. This degree of customization is only possible by creating a table-specific page template.

Make this change by locating the GridView control in `List.aspx`. Disable the automatic rendering of all data fields by adding the property `AutoGenerateColumns="False"`. Then, manually specify the fields that you want to display by adding a set of DynamicField controls, as shown in the following code:

```
<asp:GridView ID="GridView1" runat="server" DataSourceID="GridDataSource"
              EnablePersistedSelection="True" AllowPaging="True"
              AllowSorting="True" CssClass="DDGridView"
              AutoGenerateColumns="False" RowStyle-CssClass="td"
              HeaderStyle-CssClass="th" CellPadding="6">
   <Columns>
      <asp:TemplateField>
         <ItemTemplate>
            <asp:DynamicHyperLink runat="server" Text="Details" />
         </ItemTemplate>
      </asp:TemplateField>
      <asp:DynamicField DataField="AccountNumber" HeaderText="Account No" />
```

```
            <asp:DynamicField DataField="PurchaseOrderNumber" HeaderText="PO Number" />
            <asp:DynamicField DataField="OrderDate" DataFormatString="{0:d-MMM-yyyy}"
                              HeaderText="Order Date" />
            <asp:DynamicField DataField="ShipDate" DataFormatString="{0:d-MMM-yyyy}"
                              HeaderText="Ship Date" />
            <asp:DynamicField DataField="SubTotal" DataFormatString="{0:c}"
                              HeaderText="Sub Total" />
            <asp:DynamicField DataField="TaxAmt" DataFormatString="{0:c}"
                              HeaderText="Tax Amount" />
            <asp:DynamicField DataField="Freight" DataFormatString="{0:c}"
                              HeaderText="Freight" />
        </Columns>

        <HeaderStyle CssClass="th" />

        <PagerStyle CssClass="DDFooter"/>
        <PagerTemplate>
            <asp:GridViewPager runat="server" />
        </PagerTemplate>
        <EmptyDataTemplate>
            There are currently no items in this table.
        </EmptyDataTemplate>
        <RowStyle CssClass="td" />
    </asp:GridView>
```

Figure 24-10 shows the customized List view of the SalesOrderHeader table with this reduced set of columns.

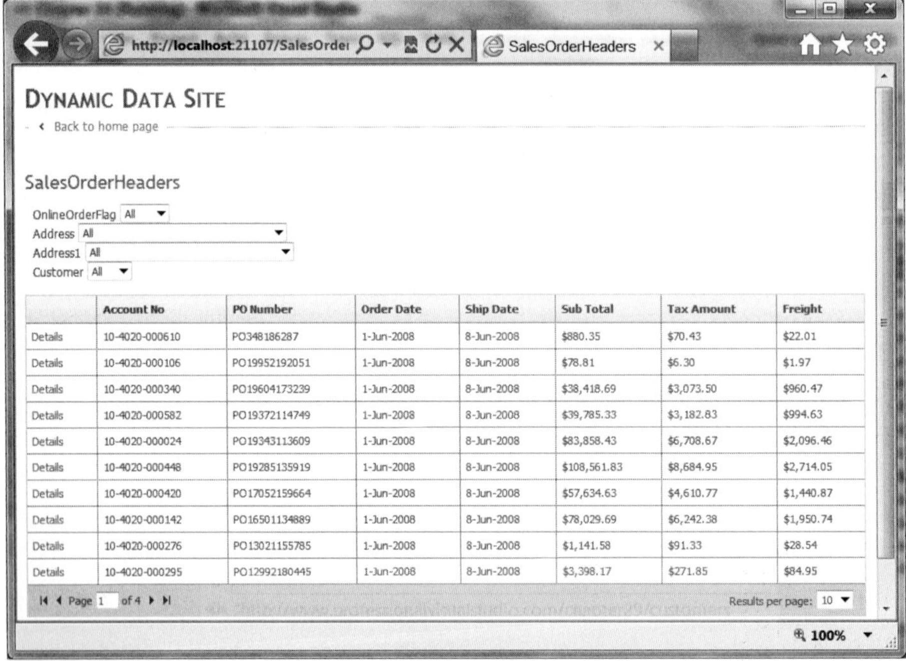

FIGURE 24-10

Field Templates

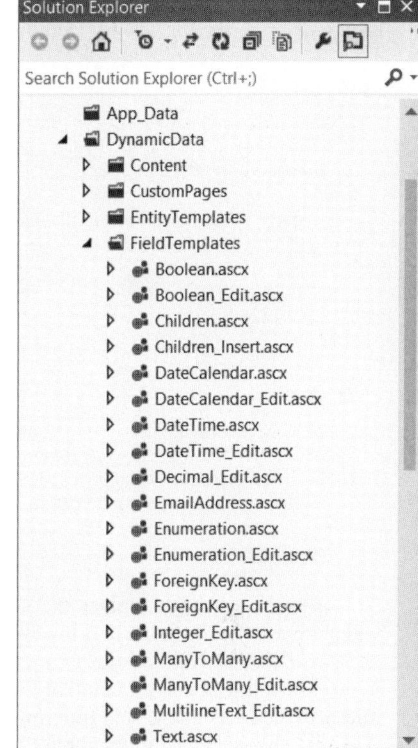

FIGURE 24-11

Field templates are used to render the user interface for individual data fields. There are both view and edit field templates. The field templates are named according to the name of the data type, with the suffix `_Edit` for the edit view. For example, the view template for a Text field is called `Text.ascx` and renders the field using an ASP.NET Literal control. The corresponding edit template is called `Text_Edit.ascx` and renders the field using an ASP.NET TextBox control. The edit template also contains several validation controls, which are enabled as required and handle any validation exceptions thrown by the data model.

Dynamic Data ships with a large number of field templates, as shown in Figure 24-11. As with page templates, you can customize the default field templates or create new ones. All field templates, including any new templates that you create, are stored in the `DynamicData\FieldTemplates` folder.

Several date fields in the SalesOrderHeader table of the AdventureWorksLT2008R2 database are rendered with both the date and time, even though the time portion is not relevant.

The DateTime field template in Dynamic Data displays a simple TextBox control for its Edit view. If the data field requires only the date to be entered, and not the time, it would be nice to display a Calendar control instead of a TextBox.

Begin by creating a copy of the `DateTime.ascx` template and renaming it to `DateCalendar.ascx`. Then open both the markup file and the code-behind file for `DateCalendar.ascx` and rename the class from `DateTimeField` to `DateCalendarField`, as shown in the following code:

C#

```
<%@ Control Language="C#" CodeBehind="DateCalendar.ascx.cs"
            Inherits="DynDataWebApp.DateCalendarField" %>
namespace DynDataWebApp
{
    public partial class DateCalendarField : FieldTemplateUserControl
    {
        // Code snipped
    }
}
```

VB

```
<%@ Control Language="VB" CodeBehind="DateCalendar.ascx.vb"
            Inherits="DynDataWebApp.DateCalendarField" %>
Class DateCalendarField
    Inherits FieldTemplateUserControl
    ' Code Snipped
End Class
```

Next, create a copy of the `DateTime_Edit.ascx` template and rename it to `DateCalendar_Edit.ascx`. As before, open both the markup file and the code-behind file for `DateCalendar_Edit.ascx` and rename the class from DateTime_EditField to DateCalendar_EditField. The following code shows how it should look when renamed:

C#

```
<%@ Control Language="C#" CodeBehind="DateCalendar_Edit.ascx.cs"
           Inherits="DynDataWebApp.DateCalendar_EditField" %>
namespace DynDataWebApp
{
    public partial class DateCalendar_EditField : FieldTemplateUserControl

    {
        // Code snipped
    }
}
```

VB

```
<%@ Control Language="VB" CodeBehind="DateCalendar_Edit.ascx.vb"
           Inherits="DynDataWebApp.DateCalendar_EditField" %>
Class DateCalendar_EditField
    Inherits FieldTemplateUserControl
    ' Code Snipped
End Class
```

At this point you could replace the TextBox control in the DateCalendar_Edit.ascx file with a standard Calendar web server control. However, this would require a number of changes in the code-behind file to get it working with this type of control. A far easier solution is to use the Calendar control from the AJAX Control Toolkit. This is a Control Extender, which means it attaches to an existing TextBox on a web page and provides new client-side functionality. You can find more information about Control Extenders and the AJAX Control Toolkit in Chapter 21.

You can download the AJAX Control Toolkit from http://ajaxcontroltoolkit.codeplex.com/. Follow the instructions in Chapter 21 to add the controls in the AJAX Control Toolkit to the Visual Studio Toolbox. When this has been done, add a CalendarExtender control onto the DateCalendar_Edit.ascx template. Then set the TargetControlID property and Format property, as shown in the following code:

```
<cc1:CalendarExtender ID="CalendarExtender1" TargetControlID="TextBox1"
      Format="d-MMM-yyyy" runat="server">
</cc1:CalendarExtender>
```

The final step is to associate some fields in the data model with the new field templates. In this example, the OrderDate, ShipDate, and DueDate fields from the SalesOrderHeader table should be associated. Modify the SalesOrderHeader partial class and create a meta data class, as described earlier. The UIHint attribute is used to associate the specified fields with the custom field template, as shown in the following code:

C#

```
namespace DynDataWebApp
{
    [ScaffoldTable(true)]
    [MetadataType(typeof(SalesOrderHeaderMetadata))]
    public partial class SalesOrderHeader
    {
    }
    public class SalesOrderHeaderMetadata
    {
        [DisplayFormat(DataFormatString = "{0:dd-MMM-yyyy}",
                       ApplyFormatInEditMode = true)]
        [UIHint("DateCalendar")]
        public object OrderDate;
```

```
            [DisplayFormat(DataFormatString = "{0:dd-MMM-yyyy}",
                           ApplyFormatInEditMode = true)]
            [UIHint("DateCalendar")]
            public object DueDate;

            [DisplayFormat(DataFormatString = "{0:dd-MMM-yyyy}",
                           ApplyFormatInEditMode = true)]
            [UIHint("DateCalendar")]
            public object ShipDate;
        }
    }
```

VB

```
<ScaffoldTable(True)> _
<MetadataType(GetType(SalesOrderHeaderMetadata))> _
Partial Public Class SalesOrderHeader
End Class
Public Class SalesOrderHeaderMetadata
    <DisplayFormat(DataFormatString:="{0:dd-MMM-yyyy}",
                   ApplyFormatInEditMode:=True)> _
    <UIHint("DateCalendar")> _
    Public OrderDate As Object

    <DisplayFormat(DataFormatString:="{0:dd-MMM-yyyy}",
                   ApplyFormatInEditMode:=True)> _
    <UIHint("DateCalendar")> _
    Public DueDate As Object

    <DisplayFormat(DataFormatString:="{0:dd-MMM-yyyy}",
                   ApplyFormatInEditMode:=True)> _
    <UIHint("DateCalendar")> _
    Public ShipDate As Object
End Class
```

Figure 24-12 shows the custom field template in the Edit view of an entry in the SalesOrderHeader table.

Entity Templates

Entity templates render the user interface for an individual entry from a table. The default entity templates are stored in the `DynamicData\EntityTemplates` folder and include templates to create, edit, and display a record. These templates work with the default page templates and render the UI using a two-column HTML table: label in the left column, data field in the right.

Customizing the existing entity templates affects all tables. You can also create a new custom entity template for a specific table. This allows you to provide a different layout when editing an entry from a database table compared to when the entry is simply viewed.

To create a new entity template, right-click the `DynamicData\EntityTemplate` folder and select Add ➪ New Item. Choose a new Web User Control and name it `SalesOrderHeaders.ascx`.

The default templates use an EntityTemplate control, which is more or less equivalent to a Repeater web

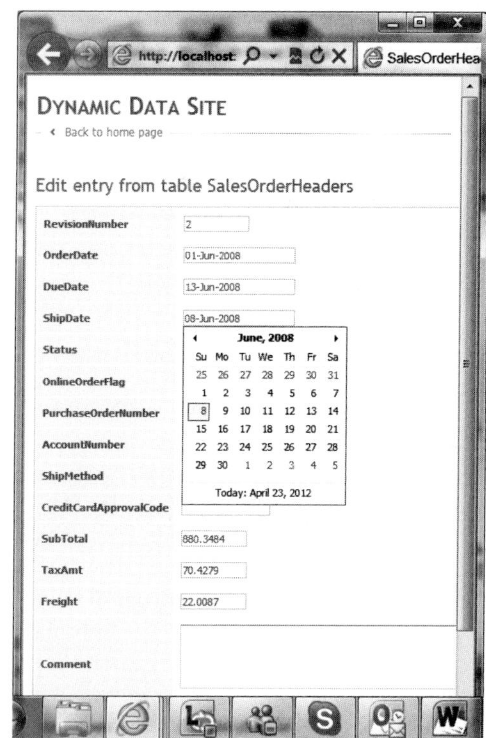

FIGURE 24-12

server control. This control dynamically generates all the fields for this table from the data model. In this case, instead of using an EntityTemplate control, you can manually specify the fields to be displayed. The following code lists a custom markup for the entity template that displays a subset of the data:

```
<tr>
   <td class="DDLightHeader">
      <asp:Label ID="Label1" runat="server" Text="Customer" />
   </td>
   <td>
      Acct No:
      <asp:DynamicControl ID="DynamicControl1" runat="server"
           DataField="AccountNumber" />
      <br/>
      PO No:
      <asp:DynamicControl ID="DynamicControl2" runat="server"
           DataField="PurchaseOrderNumber" />
   </td>
</tr>
<tr>
   <td class="DDLightHeader">
      <asp:Label ID="Label2" runat="server" Text="Dates" />
   </td>
   <td>
      Ordered:
      <asp:DynamicControl ID="DynamicControl3" runat="server"
           DataField="OrderDate" />
      <br/>
      Due:
      <asp:DynamicControl ID="DynamicControl4" runat="server"
           DataField="DueDate" />
      <br/>
      Shipped:
      <asp:DynamicControl ID="DynamicControl5" runat="server"
           DataField="ShipDate" />
   </td>
</tr>
<tr>
   <td class="DDLightHeader">
      <asp:Label ID="Label3" runat="server" Text="Amount" />
   </td>
   <td>
      Sub Total:
      <asp:DynamicControl ID="DynamicControl6" runat="server"
           DataField="SubTotal" DataFormatString="{0:c}" />
      <br/>
      Tax:
      <asp:DynamicControl ID="DynamicControl7" runat="server"
           DataField="TaxAmt" DataFormatString="{0:c}" />
      <br/>
      Freight:
      <asp:DynamicControl ID="DynamicControl8" runat="server"
           DataField="Freight" DataFormatString="{0:c}" />
   </td>
</tr>
```

Finally, change the web user control to inherit from `System.Web.DynamicData.EntityTemplateUserControl` instead of `System.Web.UI.UserControl`:

C#

```
public partial class SalesOrderHeaders :
        System.Web.DynamicData.EntityTemplateUserControl
```

VB

```
Public Class SalesOrderHeaders
    Inherits System.Web.DynamicData.EntityTemplateUserControl
```

You can now build and run the project to test the new entity template. Figure 24-13 shows the default entity template (left) and the new customized template (right) for the SalesOrderHeader table. The Edit and Insert views are unchanged because the read-only Details template was the only template that was customized.

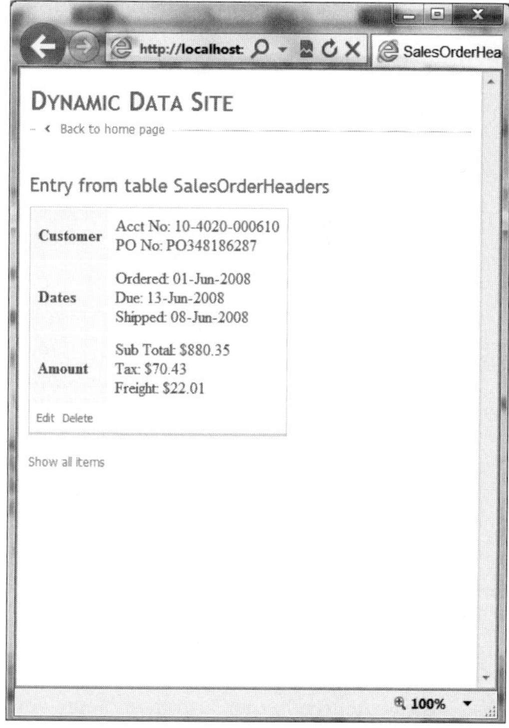

FIGURE 24-13

Filter Templates

Filter templates are used to display a control that filters the rows that display for a table. Dynamic Data ships with three filter templates, stored in the `DynamicData\Filters` folder. These filters have self-explanatory names: The `Boolean` filter is used for boolean data types, the `Enumeration` filter is used when the data type is mapped to an enum, and the `ForeignKey` filter is used for foreign key relationships.

Figure 24-14 shows the four filter templates that render by default for the SalesOrderHeader table. The first filter, OnlineOrderFlag, is a boolean filter and contains only three options: All, True, and False. The remaining three filters are generated from foreign keys, and each has a large number of entries.

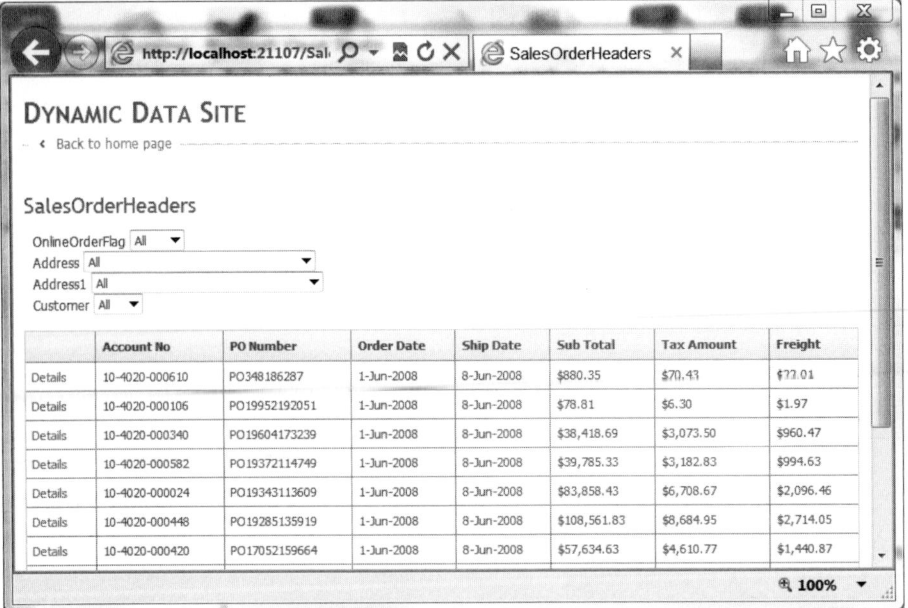

FIGURE 24-14

> **NOTE** *You may have noticed that the values displayed in the Customer drop-down list are simply the customer's title (Mr., Mrs., and so on), which are next to useless. To select the field that is displayed for foreign keys, Dynamic Data finds the first field on the table with a string type. This can be overridden to any other field on the table by decorating the data model class with a* `DisplayColumn` *attribute. However, in the case of the Customer table what you really want is to display a string containing a number of fields (FirstName, LastName). To do this, simply override the* `ToString` *method of the Customer data model class.*

Unfortunately, drop-down lists are only useful if they contain less than a couple hundred entries. Anything more than this and the rendering of the web page slows down and the list is difficult to navigate. As the number of customers in the database grows to thousands, or more, the use of a drop-down list for the Address, Address1, and Customer foreign keys renders this page unusable.

If you want to keep these filters, you could do something advanced such as customize the default ForeignKey filter with a search control that performed a server callback and displayed a list of valid entries that matched the search, all within an AJAX request of course! However, such an exercise is well beyond the scope of this book, so instead you can learn how to control which fields render as filters.

> **NOTE** *The remainder of this section assumes you have created a custom page template for the SalesOrderDetails table, as described earlier in this chapter.*

Open the custom `List.aspx` template for the SalesOrderHeader table from `DynamicData\CustomPages\SalesOrderHeaders`. Locate the QueryableFilterRepeater control on this page. This control is used to dynamically generate the list of filters. Delete this control, and in its place add a DynamicFilter control, as shown in the following code. The `DataField` property must be set to the correct data field for the filter, and the `FilterUIHint` property should be set to the correct filter template.

Online Order:

```
<asp:DynamicFilter ID="OnlineOrderFilter" runat="server"
           DataField="OnlineOrderFlag" FilterUIHint="Boolean"
           OnFilterChanged="DynamicFilter_FilterChanged">
</asp:DynamicFilter>
```

Next, locate the QueryExtender control toward the bottom of the page. This control is used to "wire up" the DynamicFilter control to the data source so that the correct query is used when the filter changes. Modify the `ControlID` property to match the name of the DynamicFilter control you just added, as shown in the following code:

```
<asp:QueryExtender TargetControlID="GridDataSource" ID="GridQueryExtender"
                   runat="server">
   <asp:DynamicFilterExpression ControlID="OnlineOrderFilter" />
</asp:QueryExtender>
```

Finally, you need to remove some code that was required only by the QueryableFilterRepeater control. Open the code-behind file (`List.aspx.cs` or `List.aspx.vb`) and remove the `Label_PreRender` method. When you save the changes and run the project, you can see only a single filter displayed for the SalesOrderHeader table, as shown in Figure 24-15.

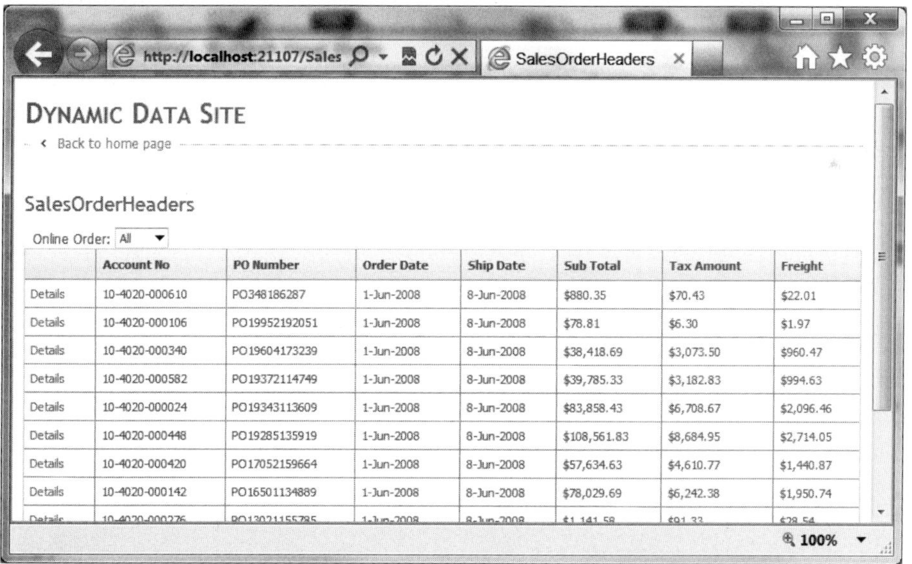

FIGURE 24-15

ENABLING DYNAMIC DATA FOR EXISTING PROJECTS

Dynamic Data is undoubtedly a powerful way to create a new data-driven web application from scratch. However, with the version of Dynamic Data that ships with Visual Studio 2012, you can use some of the features of Dynamic Data in an existing Web Application or Web Site project.

The `EnableDynamicData` extension method has been introduced to enable this functionality. This method can be called on any class that implements the `System.Web.UI.INamingContainer` interface. This includes the Repeater, DataGrid, DataList, CheckBoxList, ChangePassword, LoginView, Menu, SiteMapNodeItem, and RadioButtonList controls.

Adding this functionality to an existing web control does not require the application to use LINQ to SQL or the Entity Framework. In fact, the application could use any data access option including plain old ADO.NET. This is because the Dynamic Data functionality enabled in this way does not include any of the scaffolding functionality. Instead, it enables both field templates and the validation and display attributes that were described earlier.

For example, to enable Dynamic Data on a GridView control, call the `EnableDynamicData` extension method, as shown in the following code:

C#

```
GridView1.EnableDynamicData(typeof(Product));
```

VB

```
GridView1.EnableDynamicData(GetType(Product))
```

You can now create a `Product` class with public properties that match the data displayed in GridView1. Each of these properties can be decorated with attributes from the `System.ComponentModel.DataAnnotations` namespace, such as `Required`, `StringLength`, `RegularExpression`, or `DisplayFormat`. ASP.NET interprets these attributes at run time and automatically applies the relevant validations and formatting.

This allows any application to leverage Dynamic Data without making any significant changes to the application.

SUMMARY

In this chapter you learned how to use ASP.NET Dynamic Data to create a data-driven web application with little or no code. More important, you also learned how flexible Dynamic Data is by customizing the data model and web pages.

By freeing developers from needing to write reams of low-level data access code, Dynamic Data enables faster development time so that developers can build features that add more value to end users.

25

SharePoint

WHAT'S IN THIS CHAPTER?

- Setting up a development environment for SharePoint
- Developing custom SharePoint components such as Web Parts, lists, and workflows
- Debugging and testing SharePoint projects
- Packaging and deploying SharePoint components

Over the past couple of years the level of interest — and number of deployments — in Microsoft SharePoint has reached the point where SharePoint is now one of Microsoft's fastest growing product lines. Sure, it seems that SharePoint has been around for a while. And it has been, in various forms. However, a lot of effort has gone into improving the development story for SharePoint. Although it is not "perfect," writing SharePoint components using Visual Studio has gone from painful and cumbersome (needing to run Visual Studio on Windows Server, needing to run as an administrator) to not bad (you still have to run it as an administrator, but debugging is easy, and you can develop most components in 64-bit Windows 7). This chapter discusses some of the great features that you can expect.

SharePoint is a collection of related products and technologies that broadly service the areas of document and content management, web-based collaboration, and search. SharePoint is also a flexible application hosting platform, which enables you to develop and deploy everything from individual Web Parts to full-blown web applications.

Although you can use it to host websites for anonymous external visitors, SharePoint is more ideally suited for websites that involve registered users, particularly those that service the needs of employees within an organization. SharePoint provides much of the low-level integration code often required in these environments including built-in authentication and authorization, integration with Microsoft Office, access to external data, provisioning of sites, and collaborative workflow.

This chapter runs through the SharePoint development tools in Visual Studio 2012 and demonstrates how to build, debug, and deploy SharePoint solutions.

> **NOTE** *In addition to using Visual Studio 2012, you can create SharePoint solutions using the free SharePoint Designer 2010. SharePoint Designer provides a different implementation approach by presenting the elements of a SharePoint solution in a high-level logical way that hides the underlying implementation details. It also includes some excellent WYSIWYG tools to browse and edit components in existing SharePoint sites. As such, SharePoint Designer is often considered the tool of choice for nondevelopers (IT Professionals and end users). However, it is still useful to developers as certain development and configuration tasks, such as building page layouts and master pages, are much easier to perform using SharePoint Designer. Typically, you can find more experienced SharePoint developers using both tools to provision their solutions.*

PREPARING THE DEVELOPMENT ENVIRONMENT

One of the common complaints about early versions of SharePoint had been the requirement to use Windows Server for the local development environment. This was because SharePoint 2007 and earlier could run only on a server operating system, and you needed to have SharePoint running locally to perform any debugging and integration testing.

Fortunately, this was addressed in SharePoint 2010. In addition to Windows Server 2008, you can install SharePoint on either Windows 7 or Windows Vista (Service Pack 1 or later). Unfortunately, you need some reasonably powerful hardware for your local development machine. SharePoint 2010 requires a 64-bit operating system and a recommended 4 GB of RAM for SharePoint Foundation and 6 GB to 8 GB of RAM for SharePoint Server.

SHAREPOINT SERVER VERSUS SHAREPOINT FOUNDATION

SharePoint 2010 comes in two editions: SharePoint Server and SharePoint Foundation. SharePoint Foundation was called Windows SharePoint Services (WSS) in SharePoint 2007 and earlier versions and is the free version targeted at smaller organizations or deployments. It includes support for Web Parts and web-based applications, document management, and web collaboration functionality such as blogs, wikis, calendars, and discussions.

SharePoint Server, on the other hand, is aimed at large enterprises and advanced deployment scenarios. It has a cost for the server product as well as requiring a client access license (CAL) for each user. SharePoint Server includes all the features of SharePoint Foundation as well as providing multiple SharePoint sites, enhanced navigation, indexed search, access to back-end data, personalization, and Single Sign On.

It is recommended that unless you are building a solution that requires the advanced features of SharePoint Server, you should take advantage of the lower system requirements and install SharePoint Foundation on your development machine. Because SharePoint Server is built on top of SharePoint Foundation, anything that can run under SharePoint Foundation can also run under SharePoint Server.

Installing the Prerequisites

The installation of SharePoint is quite straightforward if you target Windows Server. The setup ships with a Prerequisite Installer tool (`PrerequisiteInstaller.exe`), which checks and installs the required prerequisites. However, this tool does not run on Windows 7 or Windows Vista. If you install SharePoint 2010 onto one of these client operating systems, you must install and configure a large number of prerequisites manually.

Regardless of which operating system you use, you must first install the WCF Hotfix for Microsoft Windows. You can download it from the following links:

- For Windows Vista or Windows Server 2008: `http://go.microsoft.com/fwlink/?linkID=160770`
- For Windows 7 or Windows Server 2008 R2: `http://go.microsoft.com/fwlink/?LinkID=166231`

> **NOTE** *The following instructions assume that your copy of SharePoint is in the form of a self-extracting executable called* `SharePoint.exe` *for SharePoint Foundation or* `OfficeServer.exe` *for SharePoint Server. If instead you install from a CD/DVD of SharePoint, you can skip the following step because the contents and folder structure on the disc are the same as the extracted files.*

Begin by creating a folder for the installation files, for example `c:\SharePoint`, and copy the setup executable to this folder. Next, extract the installation files by running the following from a command prompt (for SharePoint Foundation):

```
c:\SharePoint\SharePoint.exe /extract:c:\SharePoint
```

For SharePoint Server, replace `SharePoint.exe` with `OfficeServer.exe`.

If you install SharePoint on Windows Server, you can now run the Prerequisite Installer tool (`PrerequisiteInstaller.exe`) and then proceed to the next section ("Installing SharePoint 2010"). Otherwise, if you target Windows Vista or Windows 7, you must manually install the prerequisites as described in the remainder of this section.

The following prerequisites are required for Windows Vista only:

- **NET Framework 3.5 SP1:** If you have installed Visual Studio 2010, this will already be installed.
- **Windows PowerShell 2.0**
- **Windows Installer 4.5 Redistributable**

The following prerequisites are required for Windows 7 and Windows Vista:

- **Microsoft FilterPack 2.0:** This ships with the SharePoint installation files. Run the installer package at `c:\SharePoint\PrerequisiteInstallerFiles\FilterPack\FilterPack.msi`.
- **Microsoft Sync Framework:** If you installed Visual Studio 2010 or Visual Studio 2012, this is already installed.
- **SQL Server 2008 Native Client:** If you installed Visual Studio 2010 or Visual Studio 2012, this is already installed.
- **Windows Identity Foundation Runtime:** Formerly known as codename "Geneva" Framework.
- **ADO.NET Data Services:** Select the run time only.
- **Chart Controls:** This is not required for SharePoint Foundation.
- **Microsoft ADOMD.NET:** This is not required for SharePoint Foundation.

The final step is to enable all the required Windows Features. Figure 25-1 lists the features that must be enabled using the Programs and Features Control Panel item.

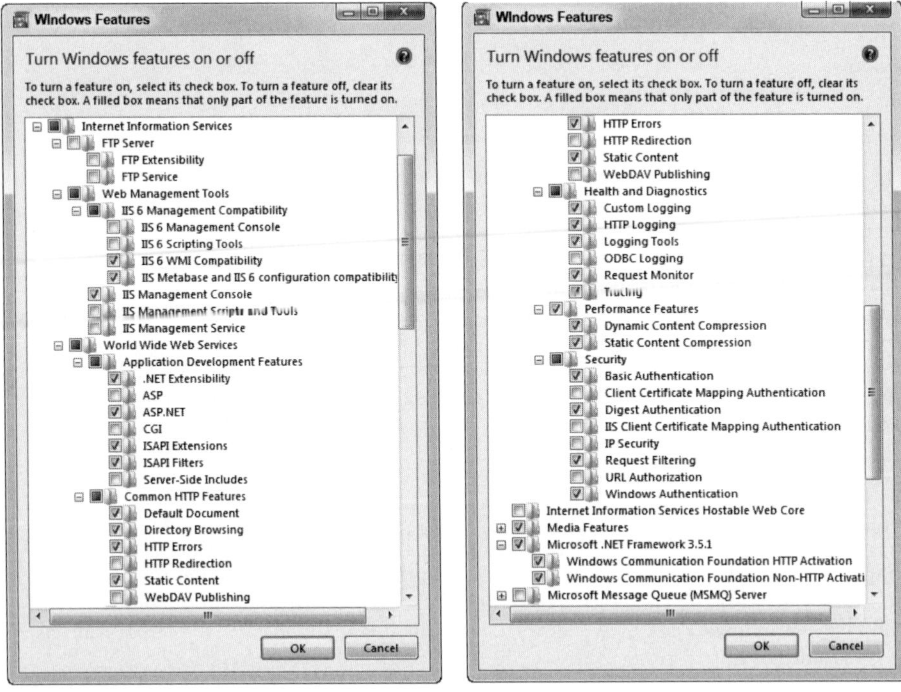

FIGURE 25-1

> **NOTE** *SharePoint is constantly evolving, so it's possible that some of the instructions may have changed. If any important changes are required, you can find corrections and updated instructions at* `www.wrox.com`*. Just search for this book by the ISBN number 978-1-118-33770-7, and look for Chapter 25 under errata.*

Installing SharePoint 2010

Now that the prerequisites have been installed, you can install either SharePoint Foundation or SharePoint Server. If you install on Windows Server, you can simply launch the installer, `setup.exe`. However, if you install to Windows 7 or Windows Vista, you see the error shown in Figure 25-2 if you try to run the installer.

To remove this limitation, you need to edit the configuration file, `config.xml`, which is located in the `c:\SharePoint\files\Setup` folder. Add the following line to the `<configuration>` tag:

```
<Setting Id="AllowWindowsClientInstall" Value="True" />
```

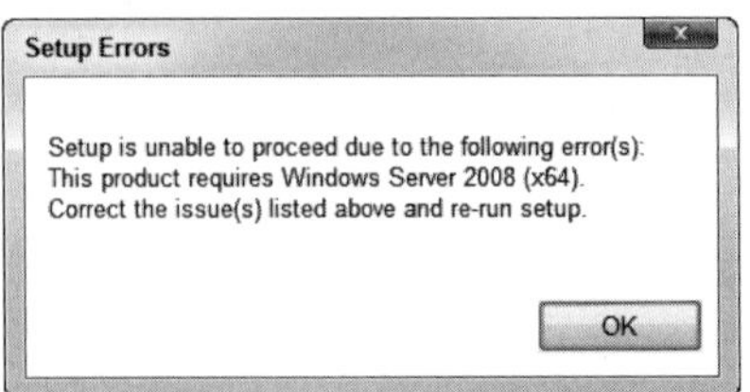

FIGURE 25-2

After you save the configuration file, run `setup.exe`. Follow the instructions on the installer, and select the Standalone installation. (Install single server standalone using default settings.) After the installer completes, you are prompted to run the SharePoint

Products Configuration Wizard. When the wizard completes, the default SharePoint site opens in a new browser window, as shown in Figure 25-3.

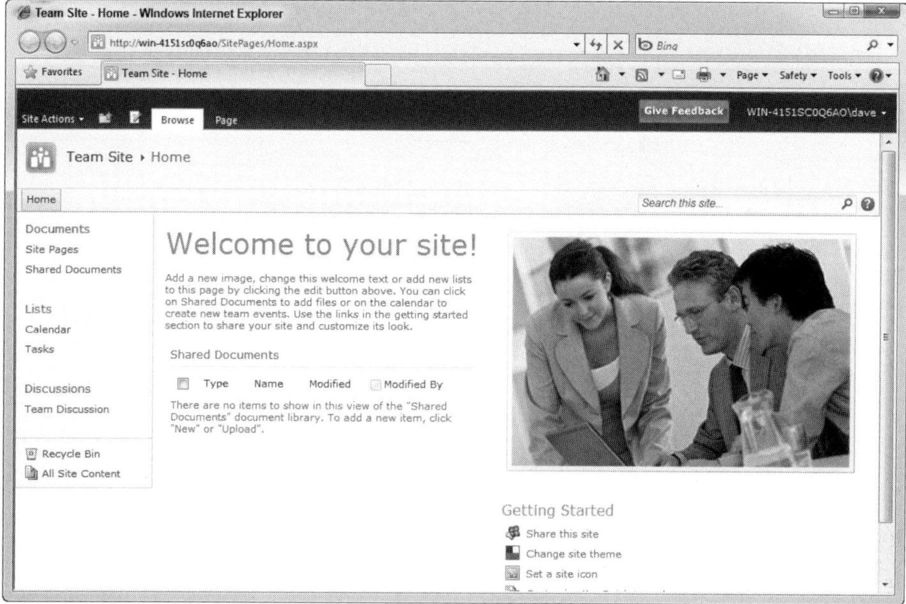

FIGURE 25-3

EXPLORING SHAREPOINT 2010

The first time you peak under the covers at SharePoint, it can be somewhat overwhelming. One reason for this is because so much of the terminology used by SharePoint is unfamiliar to web developers, even those who know ASP.NET inside out. Before you begin developing a SharePoint solution, it's helpful to understand the meaning of SharePoint components such as content types, Features, event receivers, lists, workflows, and Web Parts.

The Server Explorer in Visual Studio 2012 provides the ability to explore a SharePoint site and browse through its components. To connect to a SharePoint site, or develop and debug a SharePoint solution, you must run Visual Studio with administrator rights. Right-click the Visual Studio 2012 shortcut, and select Run as Administrator.

> **NOTE** *To always launch Visual Studio 2012 with administrator rights, right-click the shortcut, and select Properties; then select the Compatibility tab, and check the Run This Program as an Administrator check box.*

Open the Server Explorer by selecting View ➪ Server Explorer. You can connect to SharePoint only if you have installed SharePoint locally. By default, a connection to the local SharePoint installation is automatically listed under the SharePoint Connections node. You can add a connection to a remote server by right-clicking the SharePoint Connections node and selecting Add Connection.

When you select a SharePoint component in the Server Explorer, the properties of that component will be listed in the Properties window. The Server Explorer provides read-only access to SharePoint. Figure 25-4 shows the Server Explorer and the properties for a SharePoint site.

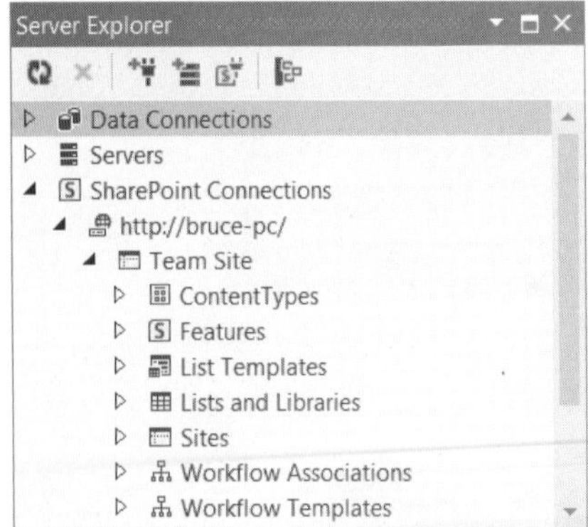

FIGURE 25-4

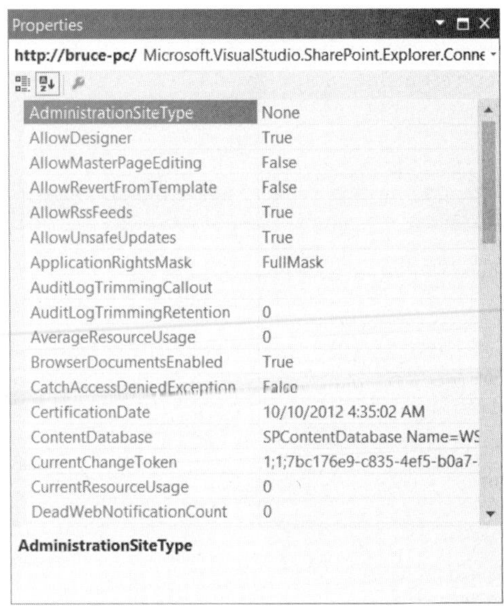

Now that you know how to connect to and browse a SharePoint site, it's worth spending some time understanding some of the main concepts used in SharePoint.

Content types provide a way to define distinct types of SharePoint content, such as a document or an announcement. A content type has a set of fields associated with it that define the meta data of the content. For example, the Document content type shown in Figure 25-5 has fields such as the title and the date the document was last modified. A content type has properties that define settings such as the template to use for displaying, editing, or creating a new instance of that content type.

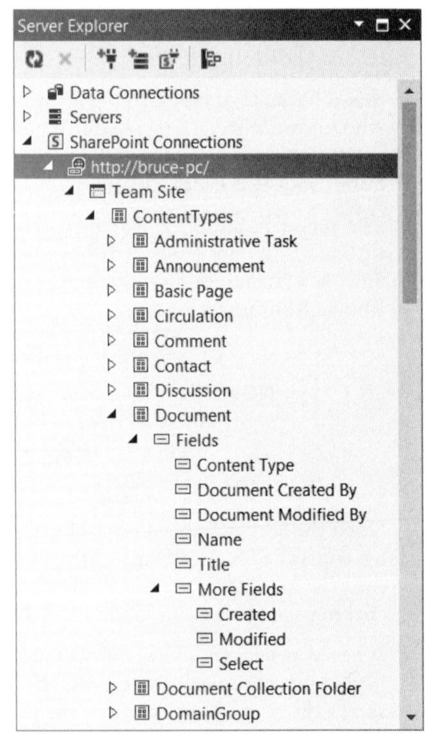

FIGURE 25-5

Features are a collection of resources that describe a logical set of functionality. For example, SharePoint ships with Features such as discussion lists, document libraries, and survey lists. Features contain templates, pages, list definitions, event receivers, and workflows. A Feature can also include resources such as images, JavaScript files, or CSS files.

Features also contain *event receivers*, which are event handlers invoked when a Feature is activated, deactivated, installed, uninstalled, or upgraded. Event receivers can also be created for other SharePoint items such as lists or SharePoint sites.

Lists are fundamental to SharePoint that are used almost everywhere. Features such as surveys, issues, and *document libraries* are all built upon lists. A *list definition* specifies the fields, forms, views (`.aspx` pages), and content types associated with the list. A concrete implementation of a list definition is called a *list instance*.

Workflows under SharePoint 2010 automate business processes. SharePoint workflows are actually built upon the same workflow engine (Windows Workflow Foundation) that ships with .NET v3.5. Workflows can be associated with a particular SharePoint site, list, or content type.

Finally, *Web Parts* are web server controls hosted on a Web Part page in SharePoint. Users can personalize a Web Part page and choose to display one or more Web Parts on that page. Web Parts can display anything as simple as a static label that provides some content for a web page, through to a complete data entry form for submitting line of business data.

CREATING A SHAREPOINT PROJECT

Now that you have some background on the main concepts behind SharePoint development, you can create your first SharePoint solution. In Visual Studio 2012 select File ➪ New ➪ Project. Filter the project types by selecting Visual C# or Visual Basic followed by SharePoint, and then 2010. The available SharePoint project types display, as shown in Figure 25-6.

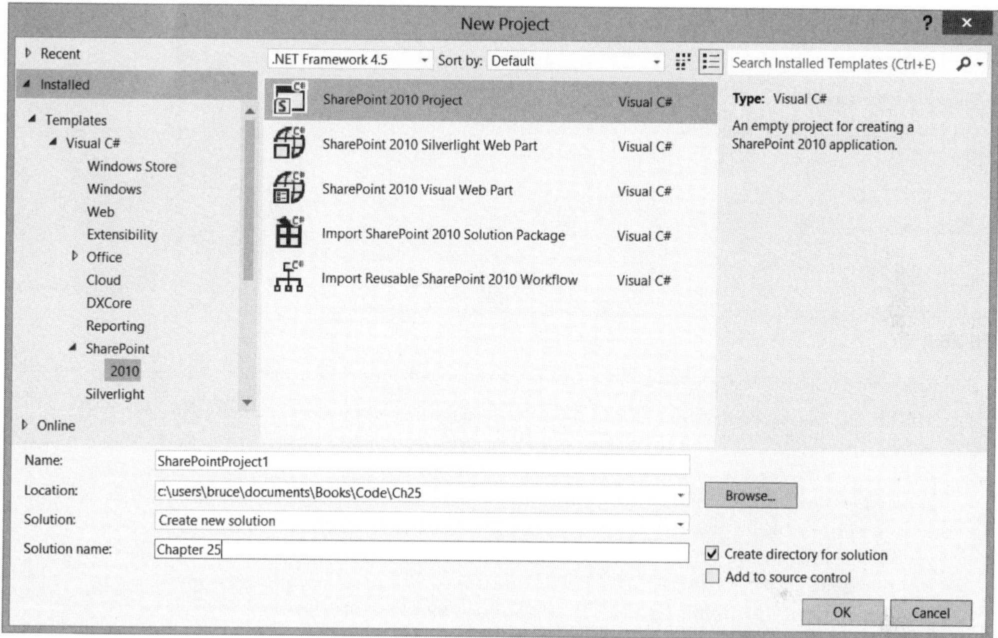

FIGURE 25-6

A number of SharePoint project templates ship with Visual Studio 2012. Most of the SharePoint components that can be created with these project templates can also be created as individual items in an existing SharePoint solution. For this reason, select a new Empty SharePoint Project.

When you click OK, Visual Studio launches the SharePoint Customization Wizard, as shown in Figure 25-7. You will be prompted to specify the site and a security level for debugging. Because it is not possible to debug SharePoint sites running on remote computers, you can select only a local SharePoint site. You must also select the trust level that the SharePoint solution will be deployed with during debugging. Select Deploy as a Farm Solution, and click Finish.

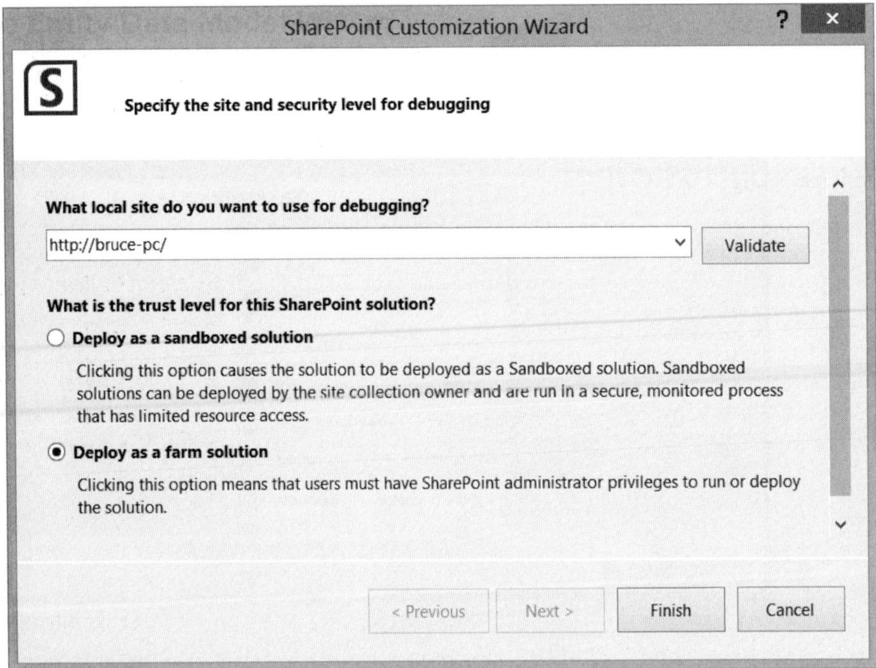

FIGURE 25-7

> **NOTE** *Sandboxed solutions run in a partially trusted environment with access to a limited subset of functionality. The sandbox environment monitors a range of performance-related measures including CPU execution time, memory consumption, and database query time. In addition, sandbox solutions cannot be activated unless they pass a validation process. This provides SharePoint administrators with the confidence that a rogue component won't impact the rest of the SharePoint environment. Also, choosing either a Sandboxed or a Farm solution is not a one-time decision. You can always change your mind by modify the Sandboxed Solution property on the solution.*

When the SharePoint project is created, you can notice two unique nodes listed in the Solution Explorer. These nodes are found in every SharePoint project and cannot be deleted, moved, or renamed.

The *Features* node can contain one or more SharePoint features. As mentioned in the previous section, a Feature is a collection of resources that describe a logical set of functionality. Any time you add a new item, such as a Visual Web Part or a content type, it is added to a Feature under the Features node. Depending on the *scope* of the item, it is either added to an existing Feature or a new Feature is created. Features are discussed in the "Working with Features" section.

The *Package* node contains a single file that serves as the deployment mechanism for a SharePoint project. A package has a `.wsp` extension and is logically equivalent to an installer file. The package contains a set of Features, site definitions, and additional assemblies deployed to a SharePoint site. Packages are discussed in the "Packaging and Deployment" section.

To add a SharePoint component to this solution, right-click the project in the Solution Explorer, and select Add ➪ New Item. As you can see in Figure 25-8, Visual Studio ships with templates for a large number of SharePoint components. Select a new Application Page item, enter `MyPage.aspx` as the name, and click Add.

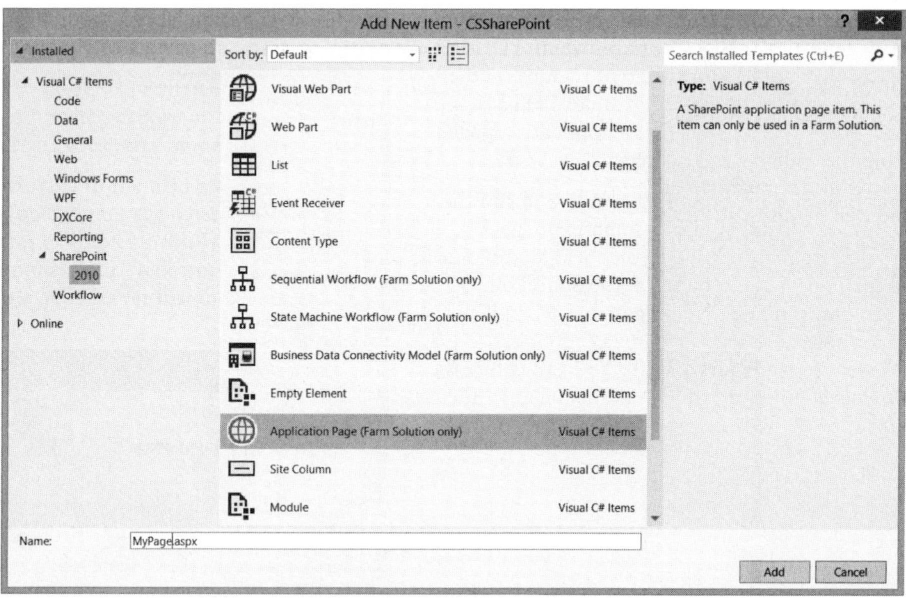

FIGURE 25-8

An *application page* is one of the two types of ASP.NET web pages found in SharePoint sites. Most of the pages that end users interact with in SharePoint are actually *content pages*. Visual Studio does not include a template for content pages. Instead, content pages are created and edited by tools such as the SharePoint Designer or using the SharePoint Foundation object model. Content pages can be added to a SharePoint page library and can also host dynamic Web Parts.

> **NOTE** *The SharePoint Foundation 2010 object model consists of more than 70 namespaces and provides an API that enables you to perform most administrative and user tasks programmatically. The bulk of the classes are contained in the* `Microsoft.SharePoint.dll` *and* `Microsoft.SharePoint.Client.dll` *assemblies. These classes can be used only to work with a local SharePoint Foundation or SharePoint Server environment.*

Although application pages cannot do many of the things that content pages can, they do have much better support for custom application code. For this reason, application pages are often used for nonuser administration functions.

When the application page is added to the project, it is not added to the root of the project. Instead, it is placed into a subfolder with the same name as your project, under a new folder called Layouts. The Layouts folder cannot be changed, but you can rename the subfolder at any time.

The Layouts folder is an example of a *SharePoint Mapped Folder*, which is essentially a shortcut to a standard SharePoint folder that can save you from needing to specify the full path to the folder in your SharePoint solution. You can add additional Mapped Folders to your project by right-clicking the project and selecting Add ➪ SharePoint Mapped Folder. The dialog box with all the available SharePoint folders displays, as shown in Figure 25-9.

By default, application pages are rendered using a SharePoint master page at run time and as such contain several ASP.NET Content controls as placeholders for different regions on the master page. You can add static content, standard HTML controls, and ASP.NET web controls on an application page in addition to editing the code behind the page.

As with any other project type, press F5 to build and run the project in Debug mode. Visual Studio automatically packages and deploys the application page to the local SharePoint installation and then opens the browser at the SharePoint site home page. You must manually navigate to the application page at `http://ServerName/_layouts/ProjectName/MyPage.aspx` to view it (see Figure 25-10). You can debug the application page in the same way you would debug any other ASP.NET web form.

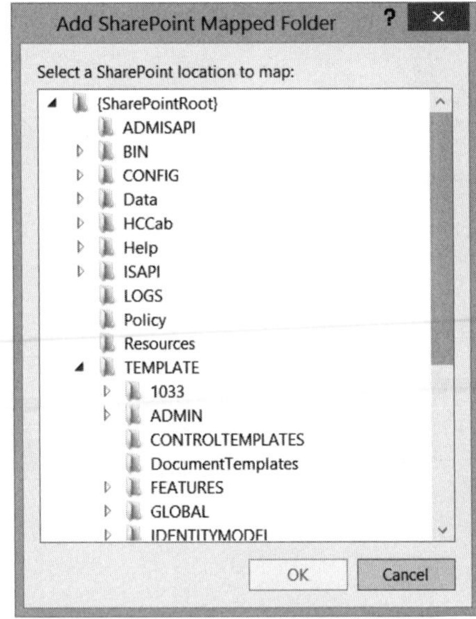

FIGURE 25-9

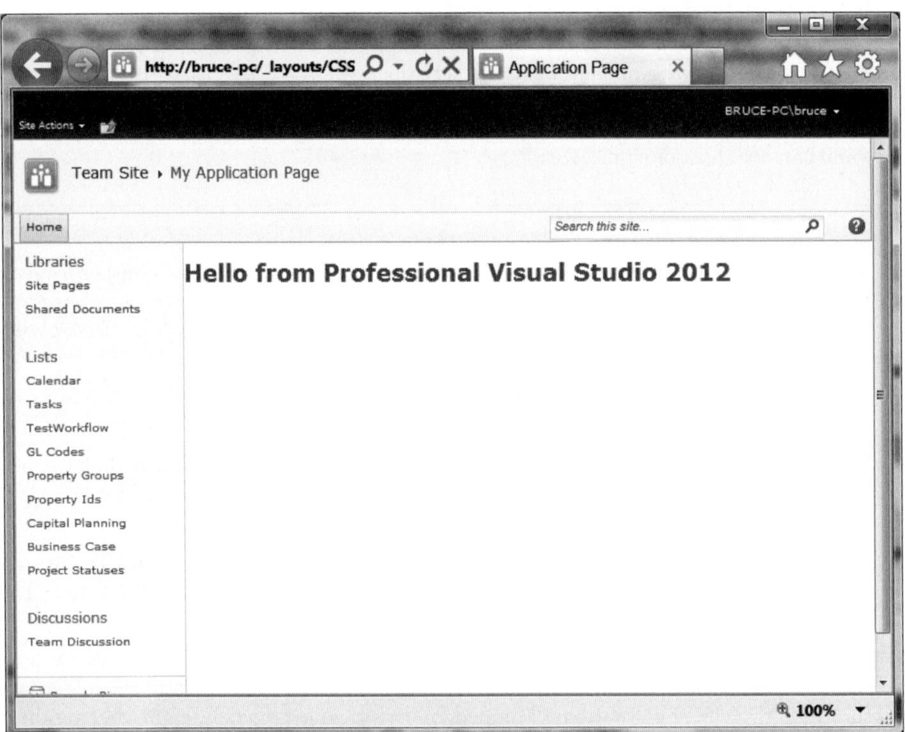

FIGURE 25-10

BUILDING CUSTOM SHAREPOINT COMPONENTS

This section walks you through the development activities associated with some of the more common SharePoint components.

Developing Web Parts

You can create three types of Web Parts in Visual Studio 2012: Visual Web Parts, SharePoint-based Web Parts, and Silverlight Web Parts.

Visual Web Parts, which were introduced in SharePoint 2010 as ASP.NET Web Parts, inherit from `System.Web.UI.WebControls.WebParts.WebPart` and can be used outside of SharePoint in any ASP.NET web application that implements the ASP.NET Web Parts functionality. And Visual Studio 2012 includes a designer for Visual Web Parts, making it easier to compose your user interface.

If you used Visual Web Parts in Visual Studio 2010, you are in for a pleasant surprise. The implementation for Visual Web Parts includes an `.ascx` file (the typical file for an ASP.NET user control). Because this physical file needed to be deployed onto the SharePoint server for the control the work, it was not possible to use Visual Web Parts in a sandboxed solution. However, with Visual Studio 2012, the Visual Web Part adapts to this restriction. Instead of creating a physical file, the compilation process converts the `.ascx` file into code, along the Web part to be deployed without a physical file. This allows it to be included in sandboxed solutions.

SharePoint-based Web Parts are a legacy control and inherit from the `Microsoft.SharePoint.WebPartPages.WebPart` class. SharePoint-based Web Parts can be used only in SharePoint sites. There is no designer support for SharePoint-based Web Parts in Visual Studio 2012. Instead, you must build up the design in code by overriding the `CreateChildControls()` or `Render()` methods.

Visual Web Parts are recommended for new Web Part development. To create a new Visual Web Part, right-click the project in the Solution Explorer, and select Add ⇨ New Item. Select the Visual Web Part template, enter `MyWebPart` as the name, and click Add.

Several files are added to the project when a new Web Part is created. `MyWebPart.cs` (or `MyWebPart.vb` if you use VB) is the entry point for the Web Part and the class that is instantiated when the Web Part is loaded at run time. `Elements.xml` and `MyWebPart.webpart` are XML-based manifest files that provide meta data to SharePoint about the Web Part. Finally, `MyWebPart.ascx` is the .NET user control that provides the UI for the Web Part. This is where you should customize the layout and add web control and code behind as required.

After you design your Web Part and add the necessary logic, build and run the project. Visual Studio automatically packages and deploys the Web Part to the local SharePoint site. You can add the Web Part to an existing page in SharePoint by selecting Site Actions ⇨ Edit Page. Click the tab labeled Insert on the Ribbon, and then click Web Part to view the list of available Web Parts. Your Web Part displays under the Custom category by default, as shown in Figure 25-11.

> **NOTE** *You can change the category that your Web Part appears under by editing the* `Elements.xml` *file.*

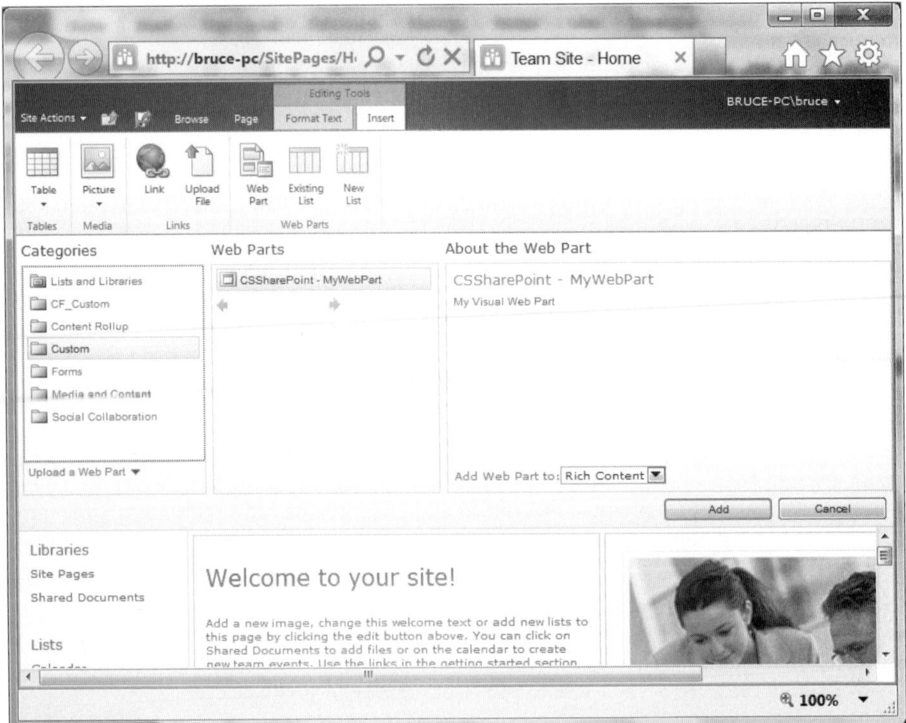

FIGURE 25-11

Creating Content Types and Lists

Content types and lists are two of the fundamental building blocks of SharePoint and can implement many of the features provided out-of-the-box.

Create a new custom content type by right-clicking the project in the Solution Explorer and selecting Add ➪ New Item. Select the Content Type template, enter **MyContentType** as the name, and click Add. In the SharePoint Customization Wizard, choose Task as the base content type to inherit from and click Finish. Visual Studio creates the custom content type, which is simply an XML-based definition of the content type in the `Elements.xml` file.

One of the additions to Visual Studio 2012 is a List and Content Type designer, as shown in Figure 25-12. This is actually the same designer with the goal to provide a user an easy way to create the XML that needs to go into the `Elements.xml` file.

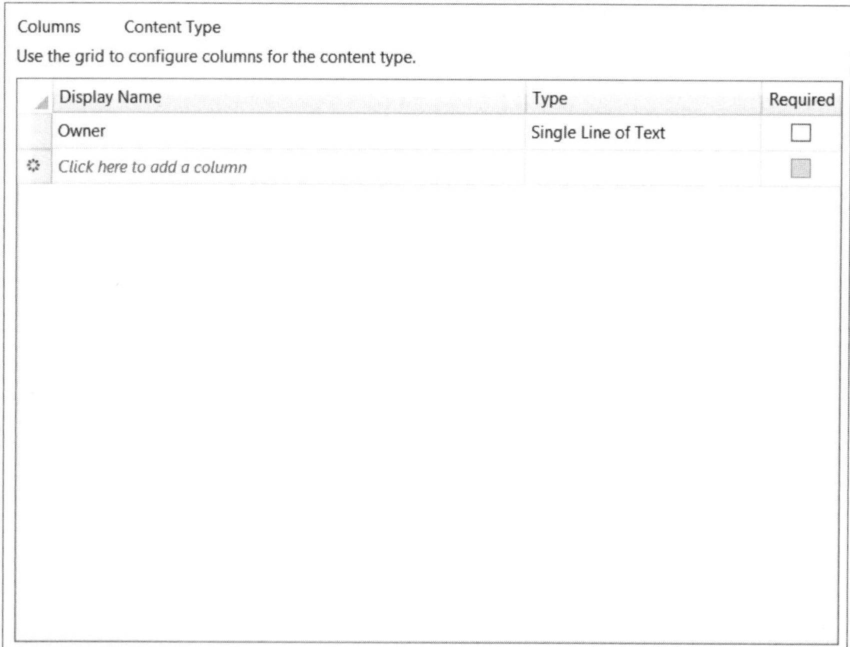

FIGURE 25-12

Each column in the content type has three values to be set: the display name; the type; and whether the column is required. The Display Name is actually a drop-down list, as the columns in the content type must be previously defined site columns. The Type comes from the site column definition, so it can't be changed. And the Required value is a check box.

If you want to create a custom field that can be used by the new content type, you can add a site solution. This is done from the Add New Item dialog, selecting a new Site Column template. Then enter **Owner** as the name, and click Add. This adds an `Elements.xml` file for the site column to the solution. Because the default type is text, you should modify the XML so that it looks like the following within the `<Elements>` node:

```
<Field ID="{3BA8B2E2-4BEA-4305-ACD2-9511C5E45738}"
       Type="User"
       Name="Owner"
       DisplayName="Task Owner"
       Required="FALSE"
       Group="Custom Site Columns">
</Field>
```

> **NOTE** *Each custom field that you create must have a unique ID. You can generate a new GUID within Visual Studio by selecting Tools ⇨ Create GUID.*

Now go back to the designer for `MyContentType`. When you add a column, you can now see that the Owner is listed as one of the possible columns.

Next, create a new SharePoint list definition for this content type. From the Add New Item dialog, select the List template, specify **MyCustomTasksList** as the name, and click Add. Visual Studio displays the

SharePoint Customization Wizard, as shown in Figure 25-13. Enter a display name, and then ensure that list is customized based on a blank list. You need to do this so that you can use the content type. But if you want the list to be based on another existing list, you can select the wanted list from the drop-downs.

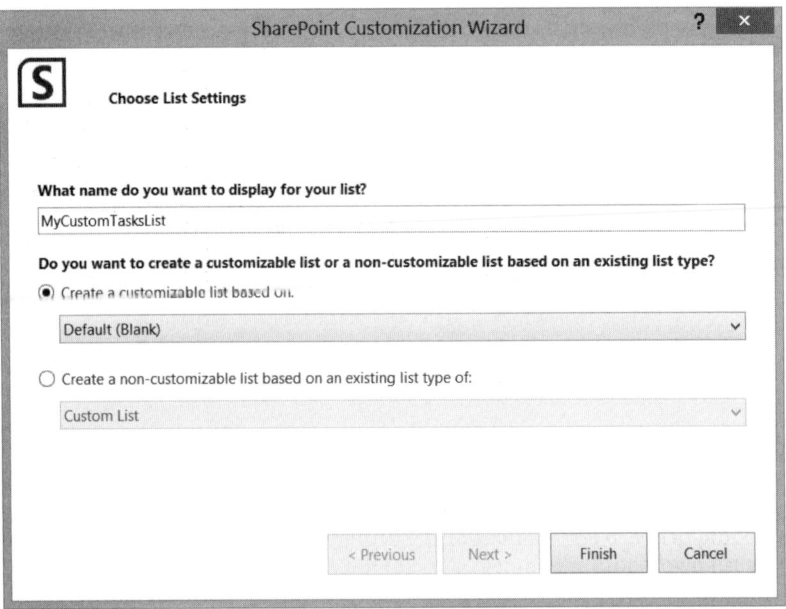

FIGURE 25-13

To add the content type, click the Content Types button at the bottom of the List designer. This launches the dialog shown in Figure 25-14. Select the content from the drop-down, and it is added to your list instance. Notice two other tabs on the List designer. The Views tab contains the .ASPX forms used to view, edit, and create items for the list. The List tab contains information about the list, such as the title, the URL, and the description. Save the file, and press F5 to build and run the project.

When the SharePoint site opens, you see a new list in the left column of the Home page. Click the list and then click the Items tab in the Ribbon. Click the New Item button to display the New Item dialog, as shown in Figure 25-15. Note the new custom field is shown at the bottom of the dialog.

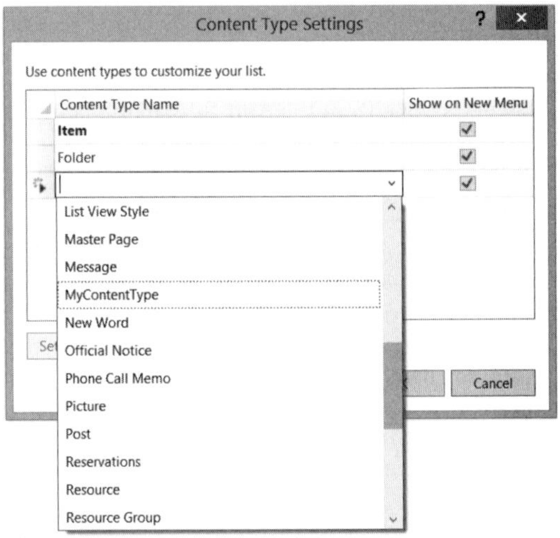

FIGURE 25-14

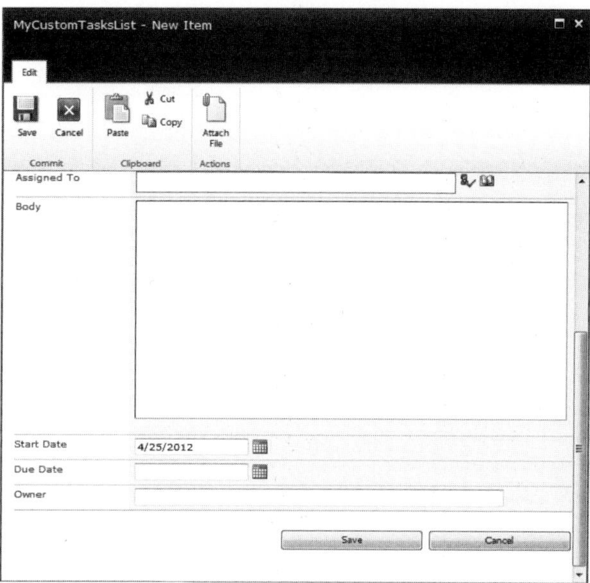

FIGURE 25-15

> **NOTE** *You can customize many aspects of the list, including which fields should display in the default view by modifying the list definition* `Schema.xml` *file.*

Adding Event Receivers

Event receivers can be added to many different SharePoint types, including lists, items in a list, workflows, Features, and SharePoint site administrative tasks. This walkthrough adds a new event receiver to the custom list created in the previous section.

Begin by selecting a new Event Receiver from the Add New Item dialog. When you click Add, the SharePoint Customization Wizard displays, as shown in Figure 25-16. Select List Item Events as the type of event receiver and the custom task list as the event source. Tick the check box next to the An Item Was Added event and click Finish.

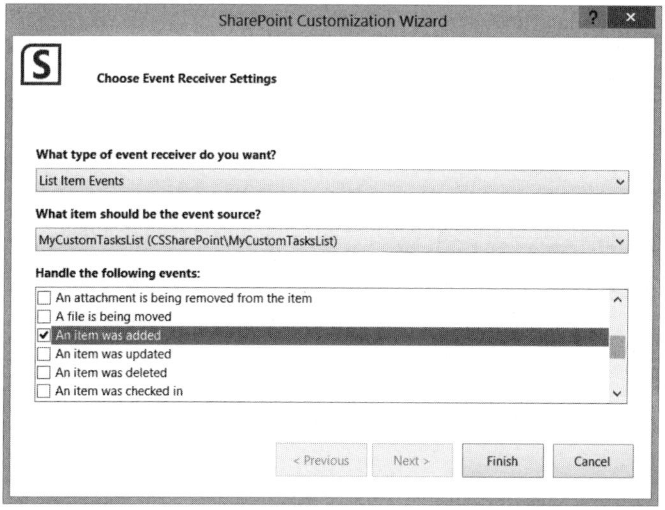

FIGURE 25-16

Visual Studio creates the new event receiver as a class that inherits from the `Microsoft.SharePoint.SPItemEventReceiver` base class. The `ItemAdded` method is overridden. Modify this by adding the following code that sets the Due Date of a new task to five days from the Start Date:

C#

```
public override void ItemAdded(SPItemEventProperties properties)
{
    var startDate = DateTime.Parse(properties.ListItem["Start Date"].ToString());
    properties.ListItem["Due Date"] = startDate.AddDays(5);
    properties.ListItem.Update();
    base.ItemAdded(properties);
}
```

VB

```
Public Overrides Sub ItemAdded(ByVal properties As SPItemEventProperties)
    Dim startDate = DateTime.Parse(properties.ListItem("Start Date").ToString())
    properties.ListItem("Due Date") = startDate.AddDays(5)
    properties.ListItem.Update()
    MyBase.ItemAdded(properties)
End Sub
```

You may be prompted with a deployment conflict, as shown in Figure 25-17, when you try to build and run the project. Check the option so that you are not prompted more than once, and click Resolve Automatically.

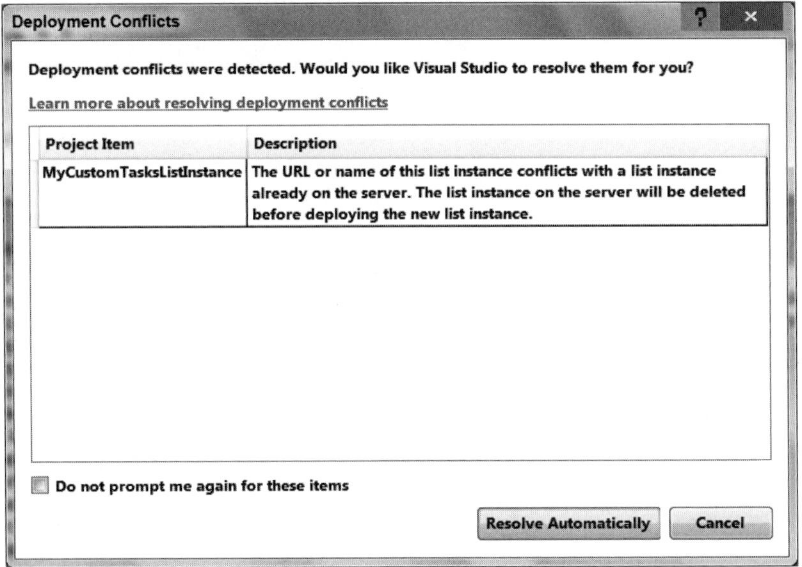

FIGURE 25-17

Now when you add a new task to the custom tasks list, the Due Date is automatically set when the item is saved.

Creating SharePoint Workflows

Visual Studio 2012 includes support for two types of SharePoint workflows: a sequential workflow and a state machine workflow.

A sequential workflow represents the workflow as a set of steps executed in order. For example, a document is submitted that generates an e-mail to an approver. The approver opens the document in SharePoint and either approves or rejects it. If approved, the document is published. If rejected, an e-mail is sent back to the submitter with the details of why it was rejected.

A state machine workflow represents the workflow as a set of states, transitions, and actions. You define the start state for the workflow, and it transitions to a new state based on an event. For example, you may have states such as Document Created and Document Published and events that control the transition to these states such as Document Submitted and Document Approved.

To create a new SharePoint workflow, right-click the project in the Solution Explorer and select Add ➪ New Item. Select the Sequential Workflow template, enter `MyWorkflow` as the name, and click Add.

Visual Studio launches the SharePoint Customization Wizard. On the first screen enter a meaningful name for the workflow, and ensure the type of workflow template to create is set to List Workflow, as shown in Figure 25-18.

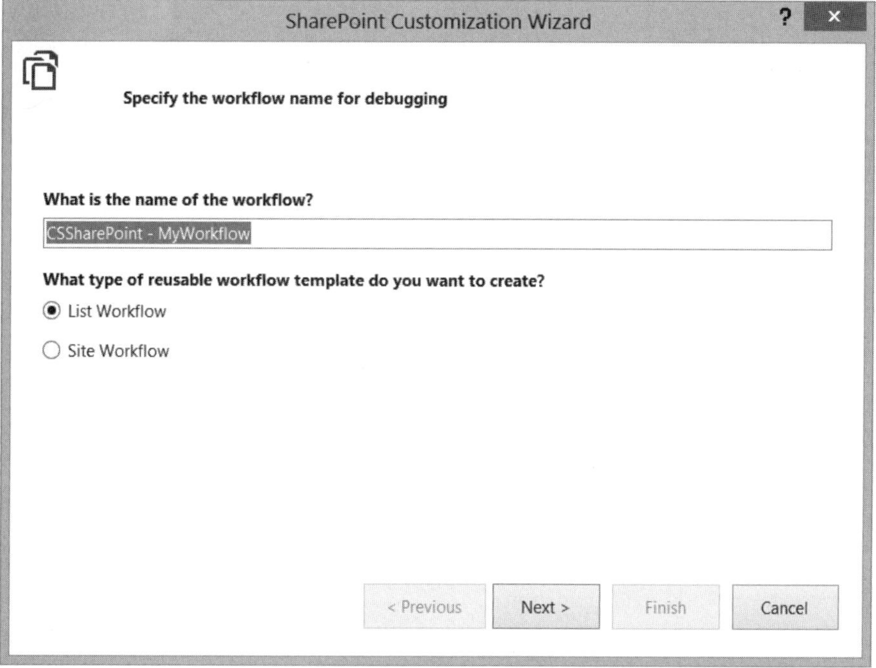

FIGURE 25-18

On the next screen, specify the automatic workflow association that should be created when a debug session starts. The default options, as shown in Figure 25-19, can associate the workflow with the Shared Documents document library. Leave the defaults and click Next.

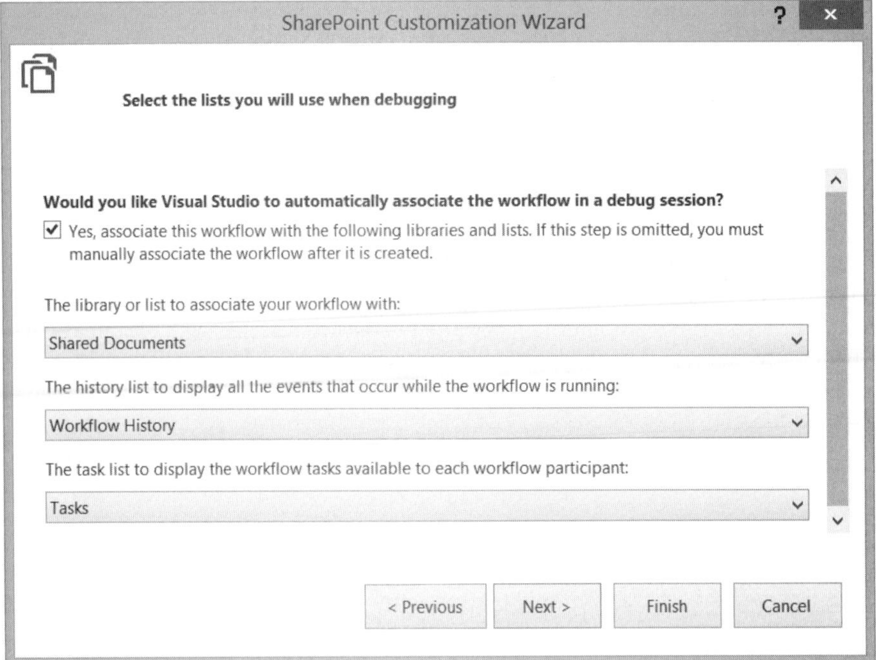

FIGURE 25-19

The final step in the SharePoint Customization Wizard is to specify how the workflow starts. Leave the defaults (manually started as well as when an item is created) and click Finish. Visual Studio creates the workflow and opens it in the Workflow Designer, as shown in Figure 25-20.

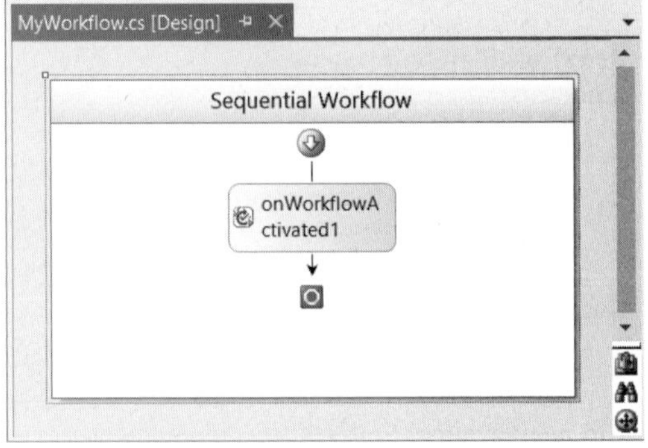

FIGURE 25-20

Because workflows in SharePoint are built on the Windows Workflow engine, this chapter doesn't explore how you can customize the workflow. Instead, refer to Chapter 33, "Windows Workflow Foundation (WF)," for a detailed look at Windows Workflow. One thing to note though is that SharePoint 2010 workflows run only on version 3.5 of Windows Workflow.

You can test your workflow by running it against the local SharePoint installation. When you run the solution, Visual Studio automatically packages and deploys the workflow with the associations that were specified earlier. When you add a new document to the Shared Documents library, the workflow is invoked. You can debug the workflow by setting breakpoints in the code behind and stepping through the execution in the same way you would any other Visual Studio project.

WORKING WITH FEATURES

Features are primarily targeted at SharePoint Administrators and provide them with a way to manage related items. Every time you create an item in a SharePoint project, it is added to a Feature.

Features are stored under the Features node in your SharePoint project. Visual Studio includes a Feature Designer (as shown in Figure 25-21), which displays when you double-click a Feature.

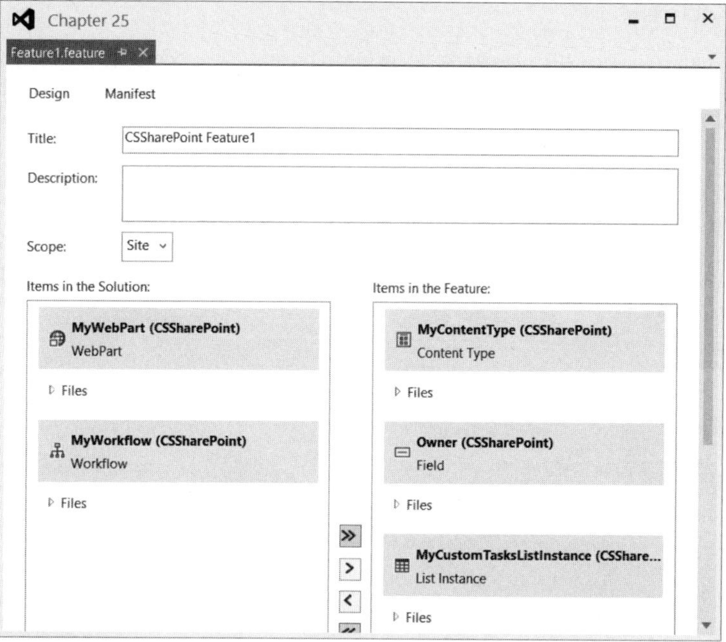

FIGURE 25-21

The Feature Designer enables you to set a title and description for the Feature that displays in SharePoint. You can also set the scope of the Feature to an entire server farm, all websites in a site collection, a specific website, or all websites in a web application.

You can choose to include or exclude certain items in a Feature with the Feature Designer. For example, in Figure 25-21, all SharePoint items in the project except for `MyWorkflow` and `MyWebPart` are included in the Feature. If you have more than one Feature in a project, you can also set dependencies that ensure one Feature cannot be activated unless another Feature has been.

In SharePoint, Administrators can activate or deactivate Features using the Manage Site Features or Site Collection Administration Features administration screens under Site Actions ➪ Site Settings (see Figure 25-22).

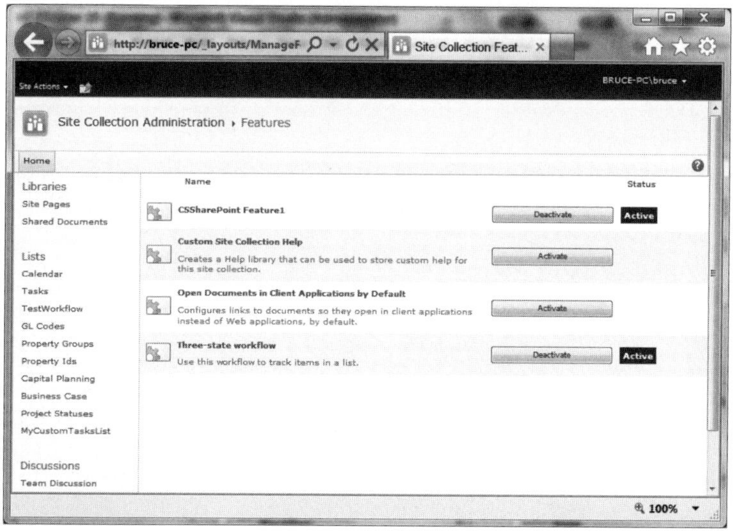

FIGURE 25-22

PACKAGING AND DEPLOYMENT

SharePoint provides a custom packaging format called Windows SharePoint Package (WSP). WSP files can contain Features, site definitions, templates and application pages, and additional required assemblies. WSP files are created in the `bin/debug` or `bin/release` folder when you build a SharePoint solution with Visual Studio. The WSP file can then be installed on a remote SharePoint server by an administrator.

When you create a SharePoint project, a package definition file is also created in the project under the Packages node. The package definition file describes what should go into the WSP file. Visual Studio includes a Package Designer and Packaging Explorer tool window to assist with building packages. If you double-click the package file, it opens the file with these design tools. Figure 25-23 shows a package file that includes an application page and a single Feature.

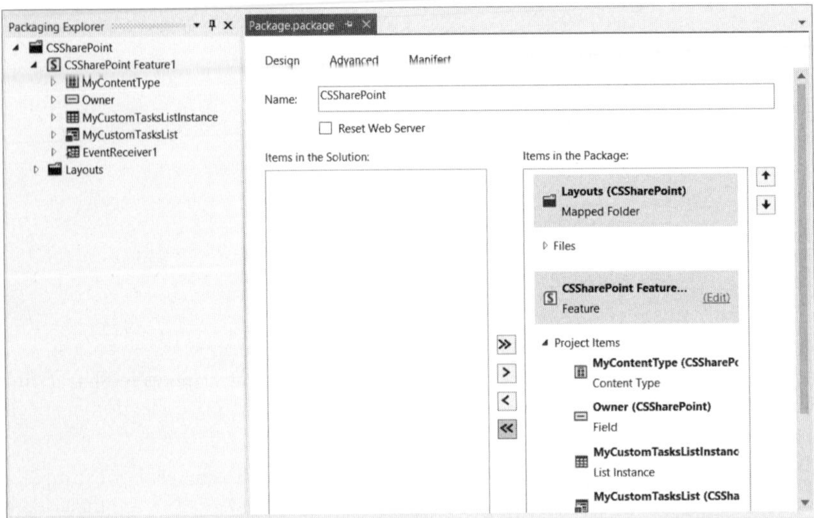

FIGURE 25-23

When you press F5 in a SharePoint project, Visual Studio saves you a lot of time by automatically deploying all the items in your project to the local SharePoint installation. The deployment steps are specified under a SharePoint-specific project property page, as shown in Figure 25-24. To display this property page, right-click the project in the Solution Explorer, and select Properties.

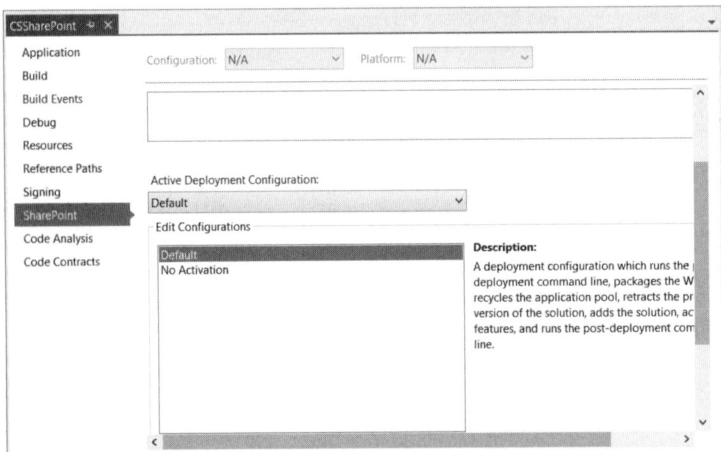

FIGURE 25-24

You can specify a command-line program or script to run before and after Visual Studio deploys the solution to the local SharePoint installation. The actual deployment steps are specified as a deployment configuration. Double-click the configuration in the Edit Configurations list to display the list of deployment steps. Figure 25-25 shows the default deployment configuration.

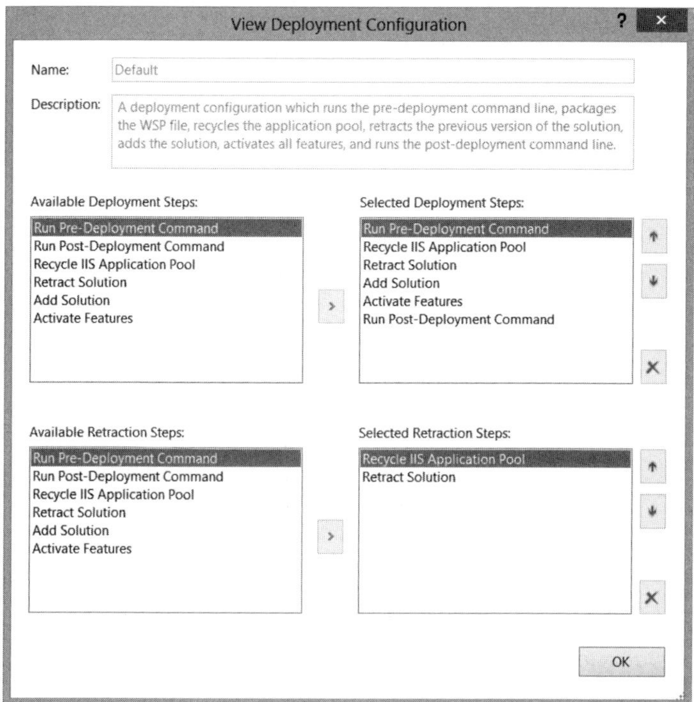

FIGURE 25-25

Finally, you can right-click a project in the Solution Explorer and select Retract to remove the SharePoint components from the local SharePoint installation.

The creation of the .wsp file is done through the Solution Explorer as well. A new feature for Visual Studio 2012 is the capability to publish to remote SharePoint servers. If you right-click the Solution and select Publish, the dialog in Figure 25-26 appears.

To create the .wsp file, select the Publish to File System option and specify the directory into which the .wsp should be placed. However, if you want to publish remotely (and your solution is a sandboxed solution), you can specify the remote URL in the first option.

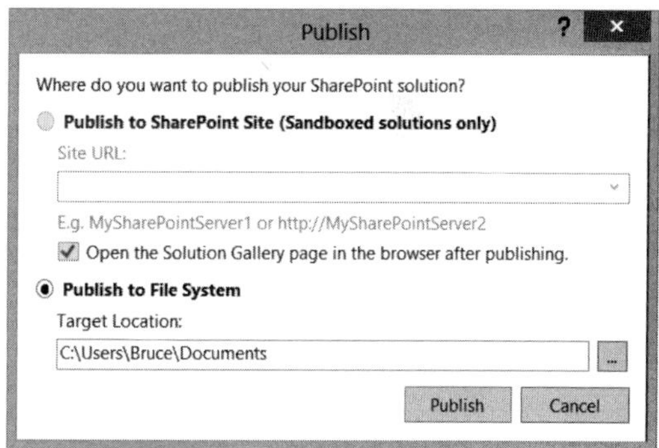

FIGURE 25-26

SUMMARY

In this chapter you learned how to build solutions for Microsoft SharePoint 2010. The development tools in Visual Studio 2012 enable you to easily develop Web Parts, workflows, custom lists, and complete web applications that run under SharePoint's rich hosting environment.

This chapter just scratched the surface of what is possible with SharePoint 2010 development. If you are interested in diving deeper into this topic, visit the SharePoint Developer Center at `http://msdn.microsoft.com/sharepoint`, the SharePoint Dev Wiki at `http://www.sharepointdevwiki.com`, or pick up a copy of *Professional SharePoint 2010 Development* by Tom Rizzo, Reza Alirezaei, Jeff Fried, and Paul Swider.

26

Windows Azure

WHAT'S IN THIS CHAPTER?

- Understanding Windows Azure
- Building, testing, and deploying applications using Windows Azure
- Storing data in Windows Azure tables, blobs, and queues
- Using SQL Azure from your application
- Understanding the AppFabric

Over the past couple of years, the adoption of cloud computing has taken off with Google, Amazon.com, and a host of other providers entering the market. Originally, Microsoft's approach to cloud computing was the same as its approach to desktop, mobile, and server computing, offering a development platform on top of which both ISVs and Microsoft could build great software. But the new release of Azure added a number of features to the platform, features that moved it from being "just" a development platform to an environment that enables it to become an important part of any company's cloud computing strategy.

A formal definition of cloud computing is challenging to give. More precisely, it's challenging to reach an agreement on a definition. It seems as if there are as many different definitions as there are vendors. For the purpose of this book, consider "the cloud" to be any service or server accessible through the Internet that can provide functionality to devices running both on-premises (within a typical corporate infrastructure) and in the cloud. This covers almost any scenario from a single, standalone web server to a completely virtualized infrastructure.

This chapter covers the Windows Azure Platform, SQL Azure, and the AppFabric. The Windows Azure Platform hosts your web application, enabling you to dynamically vary the number of concurrent instances running. It also provides storage services in the form of tables, blobs, and queues. SQL Azure provides a true database service hosted in the cloud. Finally, you can use the AppFabric to authenticate users, control access to your application and services, and simplify the process of exposing services from within your organization. This chapter also discusses some of the newly added features to Windows Azure that might impact some of the choices that you make for development and deployment.

THE WINDOWS AZURE PLATFORM

As with most Microsoft technologies, starting with the Windows Azure platform is as easy as creating a new application, building it, and then running it. You notice that there is a node in the New Project dialog titled Cloud, which has a single project template, called Windows Azure Cloud Service, as shown in Figure 26-1.

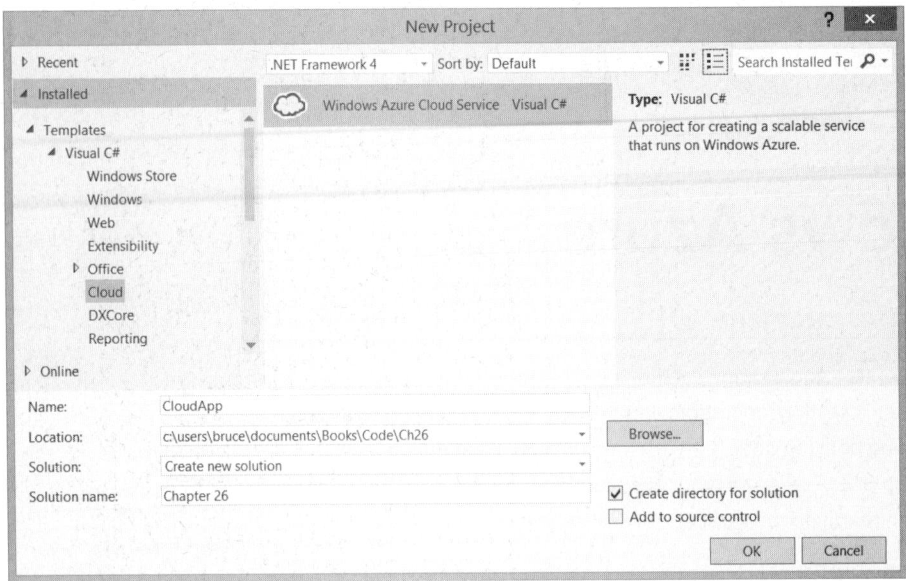

FIGURE 26-1

> **NOTE** *You might notice that the .NET Framework version is set to .NET 4.0. To see the Cloud Service project template, you need to set the framework to that version. The reason is that, as of this writing, .NET 4.5 is not supported on the web or worker role for Windows Azure.*

After selecting the Cloud Service project template, you are prompted to add one or more roles to your application. An Azure project can be broken into different roles based on the type of work they are going to do and whether they accept user input. Simply put, Web Roles can accept user input via an inbound connection (for example, HTTP on port 80), whereas Worker Roles cannot. A typical scenario would consist of a Web Role used to accept data. This may be a website or a web service of some description. The Web Role would hand off the data, for example, via a queue, to a Worker Role, which would then carry out any processing to be done. This separation means that the two tiers can be scaled out independently, improving the elasticity of the application.

In Figure 26-2, both an ASP.NET Web Role and a Worker Role have been added to the cloud services solution by selecting the role and clicking the right arrow button. Selecting a role and clicking the edit symbol allows you to rename the role before clicking OK to complete the creation of your application.

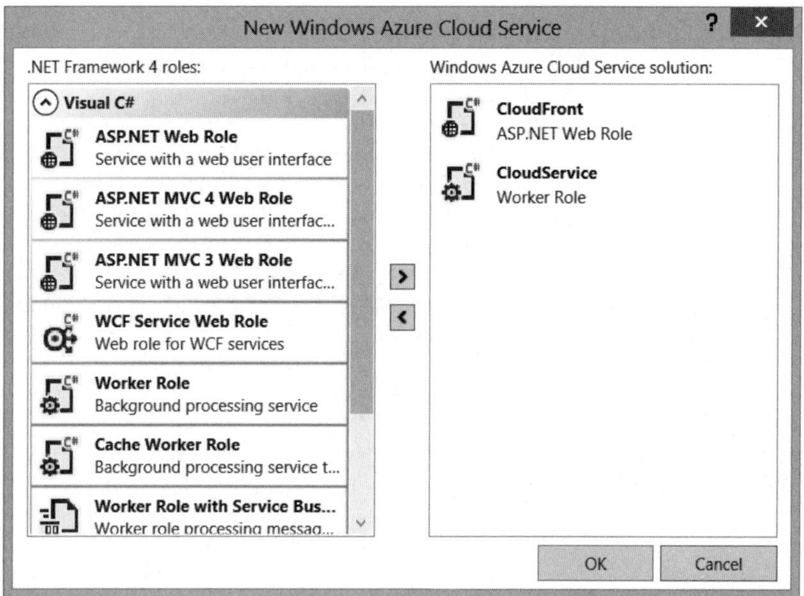

FIGURE 26-2

FIGURE 26-3

As you can see in Figure 26-3, the application created consists of a project for each role selected (CloudFront and CloudService, respectively) and an additional project, FirstCloudApplication, that defines the list of roles and other information about your Azure application.

The CloudFront project is essentially just an ASP.NET web application project. If you right-click this project and select Set as Startup Project, you can run this project as with any normal ASP.NET project. On the other hand, the CloudService project is simply a class library with a single class, WorkerRole, which contains the entry point for the worker.

To run your Azure application, make sure the FirstCloudApplication project is set as the Startup Project, and then press F5 to start debugging. If this is your first time running an Azure application, you can notice a dialog appears that initializes the Development Storage. This process takes 1–2 minutes to complete; when done you can see that two icons have been added to the Windows taskbar. The first icon enables you to control the Compute and Storage Emulator services. These services mirror the table, blob, and queue storage (the Storage Emulator), and the computational functionality (the Compute Emulator) available in the Azure platform. The second icon is the IIS Express instance that provides a hosting environment in which you can run, debug, and test your application.

After the Development Storage has been initialized you should notice that the default page of the CloudFront project launches within the browser. Although you see only a single browser instance; multiple instances of the web role are all running in the Compute Emulator.

The Compute Emulator

In the FirstCloudApplication project are three files that define attributes about your Azure application. The first, `ServiceDefinition.csdef`, defines the structure and attributes of the roles that make up your application. For example, if one of your roles needs to write to the file system, you can stipulate a `LocalStorage` property, giving the role restricted access to a small amount of disk space in which to read and write temporary files. This file also defines any settings that the roles require at run time. Defining settings is a great way to make your roles more adaptable at run time without needing to rebuild and publish them.

The second and third files relate to the run-time configuration of the roles. The names of the files have the same basic structure (`ServiceConfiguration.`*`location`*`.cscfg` file) and define the run time configuration of the roles. The *location* component of the filename determines when a particular configuration file should be used. Use the *local* instance when you debug your application. Use the *cloud* instance when you publish your application to Windows Azure. If you consider these to be similar to the debug and release versions of the `web.config` file, you are correct.

Included in these configuration files is the number of instances of each role that should be running, as well as any settings that you have defined in the `ServiceDefinition` file. If you modify values in the local configuration file, such as, changing the count attribute of the `Instances` element to 4 for both roles, and rerun your application, it runs with the new configuration values in the local Compute Emulator.

If you right-click the Emulator icon on the Windows taskbar and select Show Compute Emulator UI, you can see a hierarchical representation of the running applications within the emulator, as shown in Figure 26-4. As you drill-down into the deployments, you can see the FirstCloudApplication and then the two roles, CloudFront and CloudService.

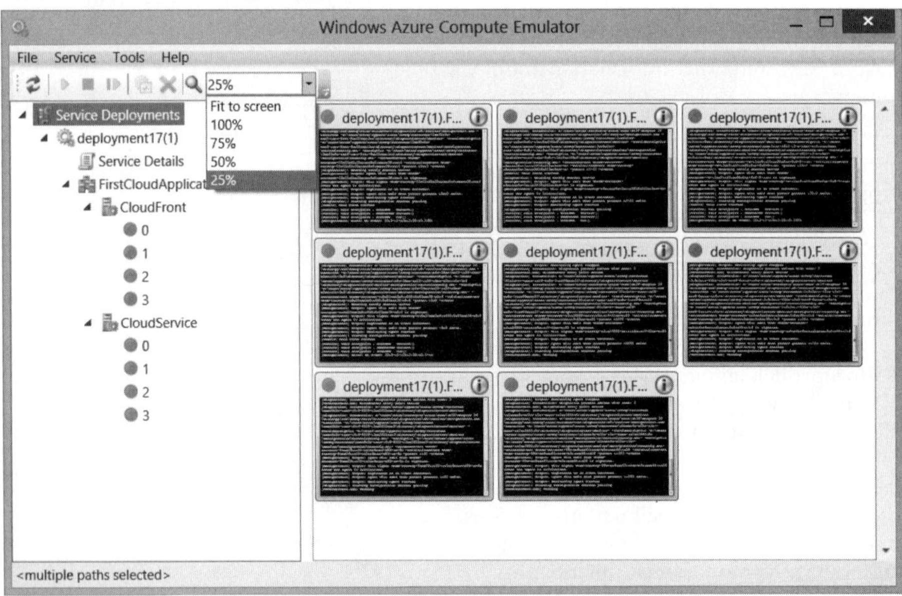

FIGURE 26-4

Within each of the roles, you can see the number of running (green dot) instances, which in Figure 26-4 is 4. In the right pane you can see the log output for each of the running instances. Clicking the title bar on any of the instances toggles that instance to display in the full pane. The icon in the top-right corner of each instance indicates the logging level. You can adjust this by right-clicking the title and selecting the wanted value from the Logging Level menu item.

Table, Blob, and Queue Storage

So far you have a web role with no content and a worker role that doesn't do anything. You can add content to the web role by simply adding controls to the `Default.aspx` page in the same way that you would for a normal web application. Start by removing the HTML markup from the Content element that has the ContentPlaceHolderId attribute with a value of `FeaturedContent`. Then add a textbox called JobDetailsText and a button called SubmitJob. Double-click the button to bring up the code behind file.

You can pass data between web and worker roles by writing to table (structured data), blob (single binary objects), or queue (messages) storage. You work with this storage within the Azure platform via its REST interface. However, as .NET developers, this is not a pleasant or efficient coding experience. Luckily, the Azure team has put together a wrapper for this functionality that makes it easy for your application to use Windows Azure storage. If you look at the references for both the Web and Worker Role projects, you can see a reference for `Microsoft.WindowsAzure.StorageClient.dll`, which contains the wrapper classes and methods that you can use from your application.

In the code behind file for the `Default.aspx` page, replace the Click event handler created when you double-clicked with the following code. This code obtains a queue reference and then adds a simple message to the queue. Note that you may need to add using statements to your code file where necessary.

C#

```
protected void SubmitJob_Click(object sender, EventArgs e){
    // read account configuration settings
    CloudStorageAccount.SetConfigurationSettingPublisher((configName, configSetter) =>
       {
           configSetter(CloudConfigurationManager.GetSetting(configName));
       });
    var storageAccount = CloudStorageAccount.
           FromConfigurationSetting("DataConnectionString");

    // create queue to communicate with worker role
    var queueStorage = storageAccount.CreateCloudQueueClient();
    var queue = queueStorage.GetQueueReference("sample");
    queue.CreateIfNotExist();
    queue.AddMessage(new CloudQueueMessage(this.JobDetailsText.Text));
}
```

VB

```
Protected Sub SubmitJob_Click(ByVal sender As Object,
                              ByVal e As EventArgs) Handles SubmitJob.Click
    ' read account configuration settings
    CloudStorageAccount.SetConfigurationSettingPublisher(
               Function(configName, configSetter)
                     configSetter(CloudConfigurationManager.GetSetting(configName)))
    Dim storageAccount = CloudStorageAccount.
                      FromConfigurationSetting("DataConnectionString")

    ' create queue to communicate with worker role
    Dim queueStorage = storageAccount.CreateCloudQueueClient()
    Dim queue = queueStorage.GetQueueReference("sample")
    queue.CreateIfNotExist()
    queue.AddMessage(New CloudQueueMessage(Me.JobDetailsText.Text))
End Sub
```

This code takes the value supplied in the JobDetailsText textbox and adds it to the queue, wrapped in a message.

Now, to process this message after it has been added to the queue, you need to update the worker role to pop messages off the queue and carry out the appropriate actions. The following code retrieves the next message on the queue, and simply writes the response out to the log, before deleting the message off the queue. If you don't delete the message from the queue, it is pushed back onto the queue after a configurable timeout to ensure all messages are handled at least once, even if a worker role dies mid-processing. This code replaces all the code in the WorkerRole file in the CloudService application.

C#

```
public override void Run(){
    DiagnosticMonitor.Start("DiagnosticsConnectionString");

    Microsoft.WindowsAzure.CloudStorageAccount.
            SetConfigurationSettingPublisher((configName, configSetter) =>{
        configSetter(Microsoft.WindowsAzure.ServiceRuntime.RoleEnvironment.
            GetConfigurationSettingValue(configName));
            });

    Trace.TraceInformation("Worker entry point called");

    // read account configuration settings
    var storageAccount = CloudStorageAccount.
                    FromConfigurationSetting("DataConnectionString");


    // create queue to communicate with web role
    var queueStorage = storageAccount.CreateCloudQueueClient();
    var queue = queueStorage.GetQueueReference("sample");
    queue.CreateIfNotExist();

    Trace.TraceInformation("CloudService entry point called");
    while (true){
        try{
            // Pop the next message off the queue
            CloudQueueMessage msg = queue.GetMessage();
            if (msg != null){
                // Parse the message contents as a job detail
                string jd = msg.AsString;
                Trace.TraceInformation("Processed {0}", jd);
                // Delete the message from the queue
                queue.DeleteMessage(msg);
            }
            else{
                Thread.Sleep(10000);
            }
            Trace.TraceInformation("Working");
        }
        catch (Exception ex){
            Trace.TraceError(ex.Message);
        }
    }
}
```

VB

```
Public Overrides Sub Run()
    DiagnosticMonitor.Start("Diagnostics.ConnectionString")
```

```
        CloudStorageAccount.SetConfigurationSettingPublisher(
                  Function(configName, configSetter)
                        configSetter(RoleEnvironment.
                            GetConfigurationSettingValue(configName)))
        Trace.TraceInformation("Worker entry point called")

        ' read account configuration settings
        Dim storageAccount = CloudStorageAccount.
                        FromConfigurationSetting("DataConnectionString")
        ' create queue to communicate with web role
        Dim queueStorage = storageAccount.CreateCloudQueueClient()
        queue = queueStorage.GetQueueReference("sample")
        queue.CreateIfNotExist()

        Trace.TraceInformation("CloudService entry point called.")
        Do While (True)
            Try
                ' Pop the next message off the queue
                Dim msg As CloudQueueMessage = queue.GetMessage()
                If (msg IsNot Nothing) Then
                    ' Parse the message contents as a job detail
                    Dim jd As String = msg.AsString
                    Trace.TraceInformation("Processed {0}", jd)
                    ' Delete the message from the queue
                    queue.DeleteMessage(msg)
                Else
                    Thread.Sleep(10000)
                End If
                Trace.TraceInformation("Working")
            Catch ex As StorageClientException
                Trace.TraceError(ex.Message)
            End Try
        Loop
    End Function
```

This code overrides the Run method. This method loads configuration values and sets up local variables for working with Windows Azure storage. It then starts an infinite while loop that processes messages off the queue.

Before you can run your modified roles, you need to specify the location of the queue storage that you will use. Though this will eventually be an Azure storage account, during development you need to specify the details of the local Storage Emulator. You do this in the `ServiceConfiguration` file:

```
<?xml version="1.0"?>
<ServiceConfiguration serviceName="FirstCloudApplication"
    xmlsn="http://schemas.microsoft.com/ServiceHosting/2008/10/ServiceConfiguration"
   osFamily="1" osVersion="*" schemaVersion="2012-05.1.7">
   <Role name="CloudFront">
      <Instances count="2" />
      <ConfigurationSettings>
         <Setting name="Microsoft.WindowsAzure.Plugins.Diagnostics.ConnectionString"
             value="UseDevelopmentStorage=true" />
         <Setting name="DiagnosticsConnectionString" value="UseDevelopmentStorage=true" />
<!-- <Setting name="DeploymentConnectionString" value="DefaultEndpointsProtocol=
https;AccountName=[YOUR_ACCOUNT_NAME];AccountKey=[YOUR_ACCOUNT_KEY]" /> -->
      </ConfigurationSettings>
   </Role>
   <Role name="CloudService">
      <Instances count="2" />
      <ConfigurationSettings>
```

```
            <Setting name="Microsoft.WindowsAzure.Plugins.Diagnostics.ConnectionString"
               value="UseDevelopmentStorage=true" />
            <Setting name="DiagnosticsConnectionString" value="UseDevelopmentStorage=true" />
        </ConfigurationSettings>
    </Role>
</ServiceConfiguration>
```

For both the CloudService and CloudFront roles, settings for `DataConnectionString` and `Diagnostics.ConnectionString` have been defined. In this case, the value has been set to use the development storage account. When you deploy to Windows Azure, you need to replace this with a connection string that includes the account name and key, in the format illustrated by the `DeploymentConnectionString`. And you actually need to put those connection strings (with the account name and key) into the cloud version of the configuration file.

Before these values are accessible to your roles, you also need to update the `ServiceDefinition` file to indicate which settings are defined for each role. Only the `DataConnectionString` appears in the configuration file shown here because the `Microsoft.WindowsAzure.Plugins.Diagnostics.ConnectionString` is actually a built-in value that has no need to be included explicitly in the configuration file.

```
<?xml version="1.0" encoding="utf-8"?>
<ServiceDefinition name="FirstCloudApplication"
   xmlsn="http://schemas.microsoft.com/ServiceHosting/2008/10/ServiceDefinition">
   <WebRole name="CloudFront" enableNativeCodeExecution="false">
      <InputEndpoints>
         <!-- Must use port 80 for http and port 443 for https when running in the cloud -->
         <InputEndpoint name="HttpIn" protocol="http" port="80" />
      </InputEndpoints>
      <ConfigurationSettings>
         <Setting name="DataConnectionString" />
      </ConfigurationSettings>
   </WebRole>
   <WorkerRole name="CloudService" enableNativeCodeExecution="false">
      <ConfigurationSettings>
         <Setting name="DataConnectionString" />
      </ConfigurationSettings>
   </WorkerRole>
</ServiceDefinition>
```

With these changes, try running your Azure application and noting that when you press the Submit button you see a Processed message appear in one of the running instances of the worker role in the Compute Emulator UI.

Application Deployment

After you build your Azure application using the Emulators, you must deploy it to the Windows Azure Platform. Before doing so you need to provision your Windows Azure account with both a hosting and a storage service. Start by going to `https://manage.windowsazure.com` and signing in using your Live ID to your Windows Azure account. After logging in, click the Go to the Windows Azure Developer Portal link. This opens the Windows Azure portal, which looks similar to Figure 26-5.

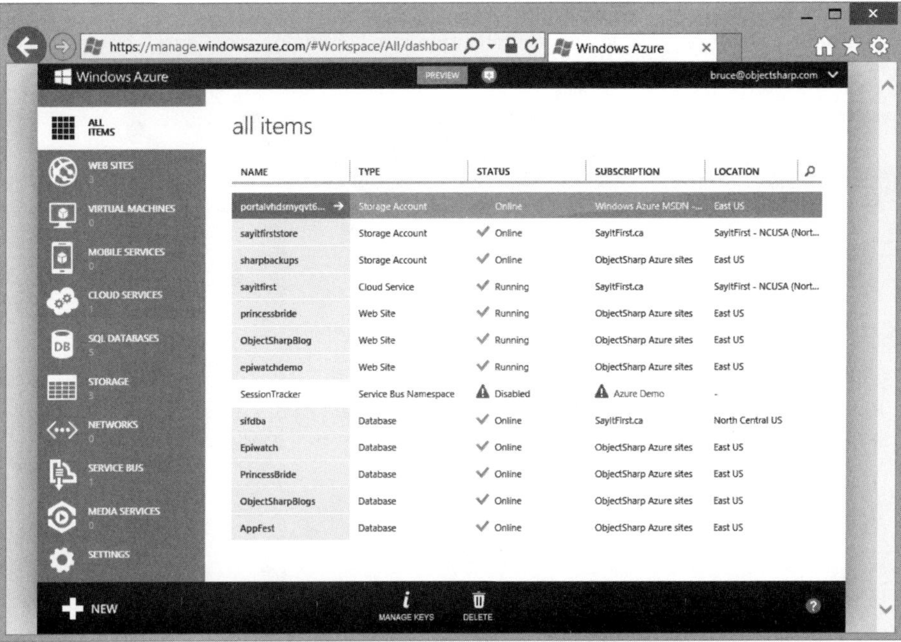

FIGURE 26-5

Click the New button, and then select the type of service you want to add. The FirstCloudApplication requires both web and storage roles, so select Cloud Service, followed by Custom Create. You see the dialog shown in Figure 26-6. Specify the header for the URL, along with the data center in which your application will run and the subscription used to pay for any charges you accrue.

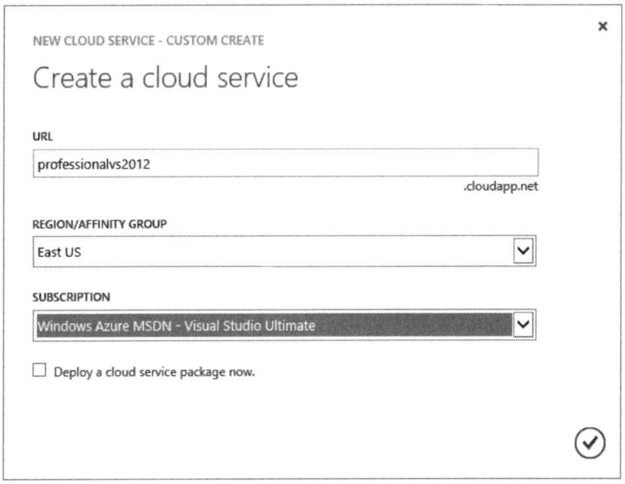

NEW CLOUD SERVICE - CUSTOM CREATE

Create a cloud service

URL

professionalvs2012

.cloudapp.net

REGION/AFFINITY GROUP

East US

SUBSCRIPTION

Windows Azure MSDN - Visual Studio Ultimate

☐ Deploy a cloud service package now.

FIGURE 26-6

After the account has been created, the dashboard for the account appears (see Figure 26-7). Through this dashboard, you have access to not only deploy your application into staging or production, but also to configure your environments.

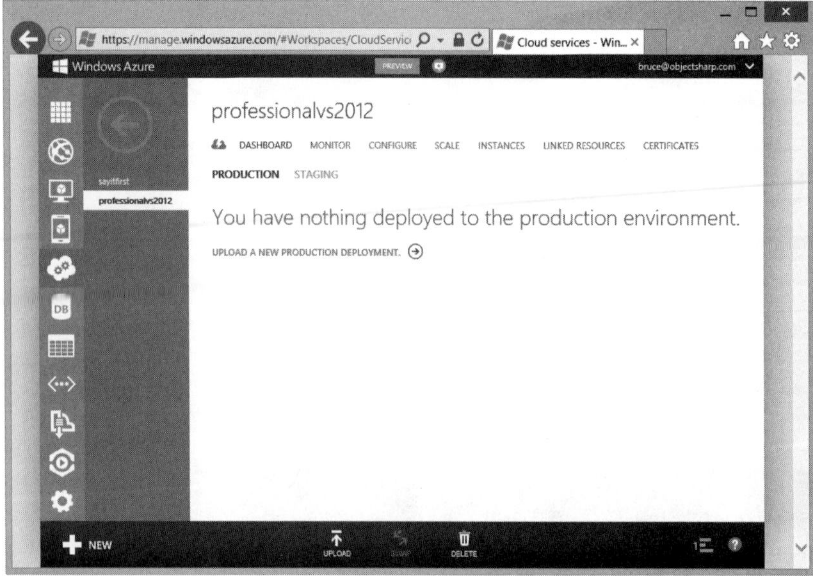

FIGURE 26-7

In Figure 26-7 you can see that you have two environments into which you can deploy: Production and Staging. As with all good deployment strategies, Azure supports deploying into Staging and then when you are comfortable, migrating that into Production.

Return to Visual Studio 2012, right-click the FirstCloudApplication project, and select Publish. This process starts by building your application and generates a deployment package and a configuration file. It also publishes those elements directly to Azure. The initial dialog in this process is shown in Figure 26-8.

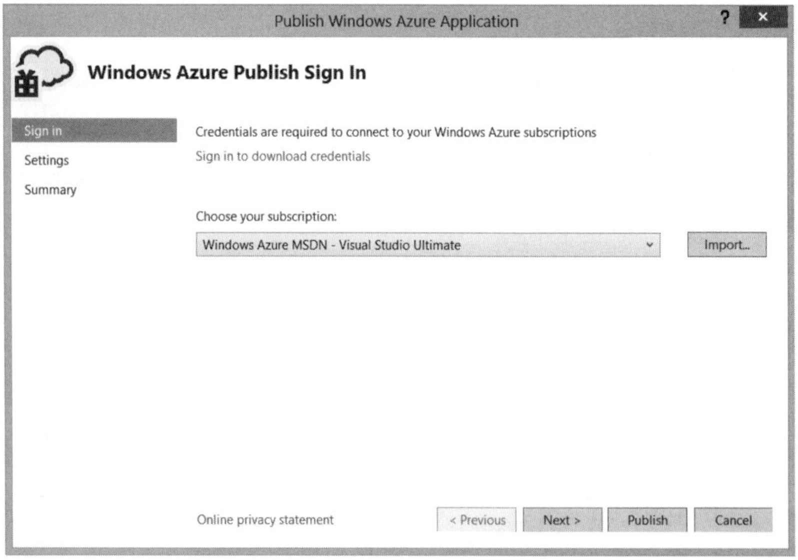

Publish Windows Azure Application

Windows Azure Publish Sign In

Sign in
Settings
Summary

Credentials are required to connect to your Windows Azure subscriptions
Sign in to download credentials

Choose your subscription:
Windows Azure MSDN - Visual Studio Ultimate
Import...

Online privacy statement
< Previous
Next >
Publish
Cancel

FIGURE 26-8

If this is the first time you publish an application, you need to set the publishing settings. In Figure 26-8, you can see a link titled Sign in to Download Credentials. When you click this link, you are prompted to log in to the Windows Live ID associated with your Azure account. Then the publication settings will be downloaded to your computer in the form of a publishsettings file. Then you can import this file into your profile using the Import button, also shown in Figure 26-8. After the file has been imported, you can select the account that you want to use and move to the next step.

The next step in publishing your application involves specifying the settings. The dialog shown in Figure 26-9 provides the mechanism to do this.

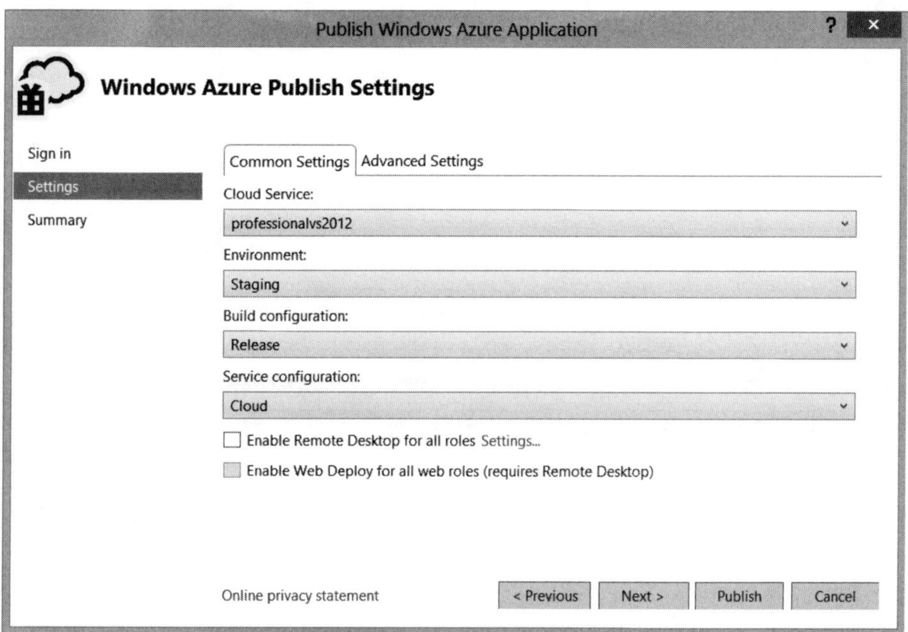

FIGURE 26-9

Through this dialog, the Cloud Service into which this project will be placed is specified, along with the environment (either Staging or Production), the build configuration (dependent on the configurations you have set up in your project), and the service configuration (either Cloud or Local). You can also enable Remote Desktop for the roles that you are deploying, and you can enable web deployment. Remote Desktop capabilities enable you to connect to the desktop of one of your roles so that you can troubleshoot issues or configure the role in ways that are not available through the configuration files.

After you specify the settings to match your requirements, click Next to display a summary screen. Click the Publish button to begin the deployment. The status of the deployment is visible in a separate window that, by default, is at the bottom of Visual Studio. As well, the Windows Azure dashboard displays the status. After a period of time (which might span 10–15 minutes and require a refresh of the Azure dashboard), you see that your application is deployed, as shown in Figure 26-10.

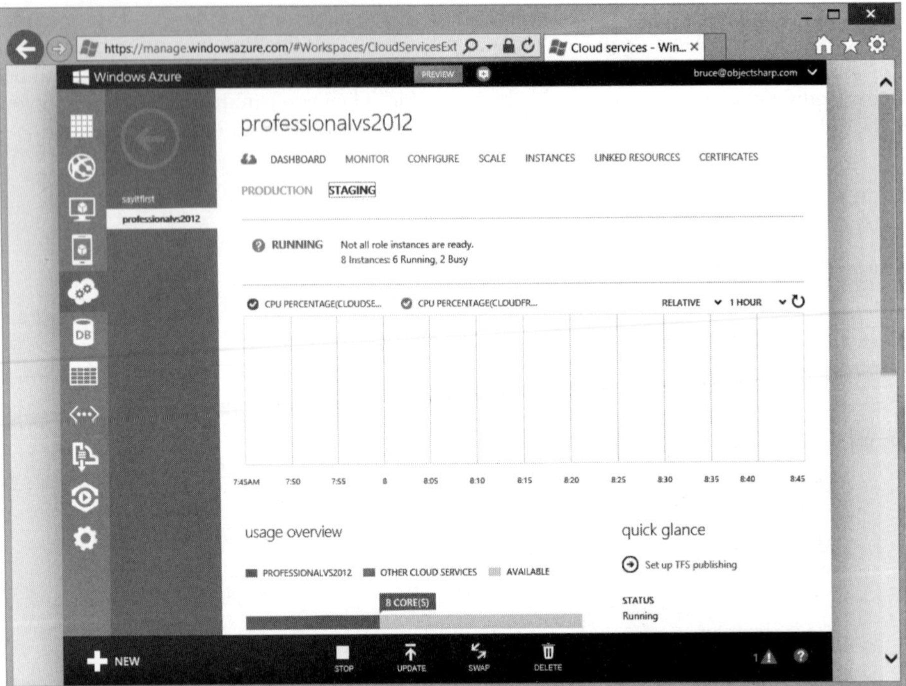

FIGURE 26-10

The last stage in this process is to promote what runs in the Staging environment into Production. The word "promote" is important because this transition is handled by an intelligent router. Because the cut over from one to the other will (depending on how quickly the router effects the change) be close to instantaneous, there should never be any time at which someone hitting the site receives a 404 or missing page. To promote Staging into Production, select the Swap button at the bottom of the dashboard (see Figure 26-10). To be precise, this button also moves the current production environment into staging. The benefit from this is that if after promoting your current version (staging) into production you find that there is a serious problem, you can perform a second swap and get the previous (and known-to-be-working) version back into production.

SQL AZURE

In addition to Azure table, blob, and queue storage, the Windows Azure Platform offers true relational data hosting in the form of SQL Azure. You can think of each SQL Azure database as being a hosted instance of a SQL Server 2008 or 2012 database running in high-availability mode. This means that at any point in time there are three synchronized instances of your database. If one of these instances fails, a new instance is immediately brought online, and the data is synchronized to ensure the availability of your data.

To create a SQL Azure database, sign into the Windows Azure portal and click the New icon. You see SQL Database as one of the options. Selecting that option and the Quick Create or Custom Create option gives you the options to specify the name and location of the database (Figure 26-11 illustrates the Quick Create option). After creating a database you can retrieve the connection string that you need to connect to the database by selecting the database and clicking the Show Connection Strings button, as shown in Figure 26-12.

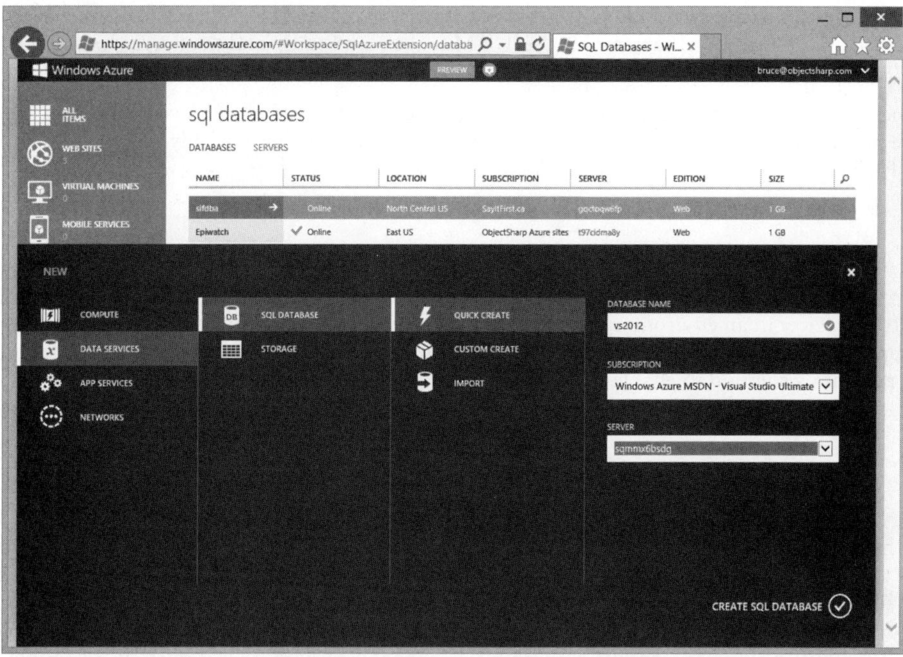

FIGURE 26-11

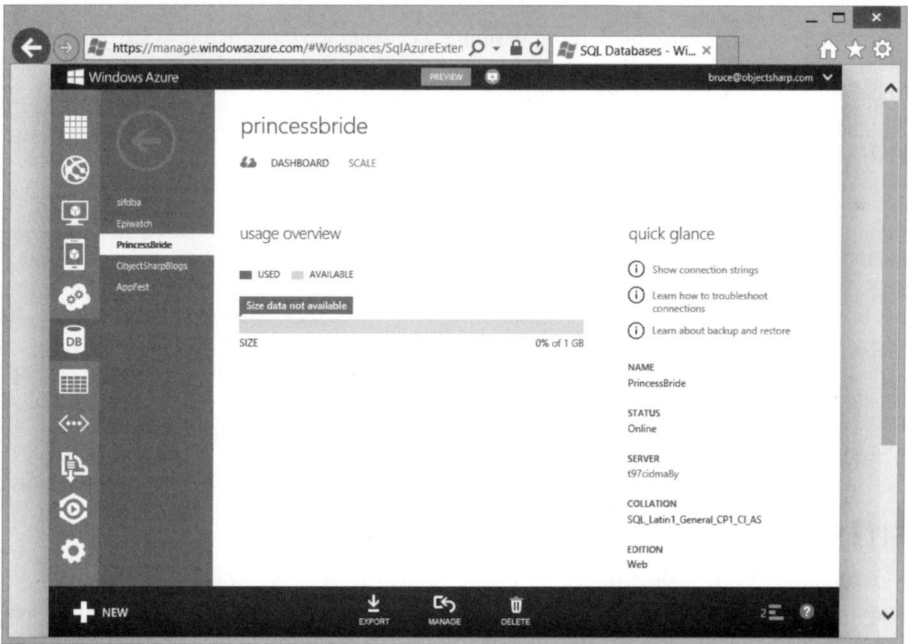

FIGURE 26-12

You have a number of ways to interact with a SQL Azure database. Because SQL Azure is based on SQL Server 2008 or 2012, graphical tools, such as SQL Server Management Studio and the Server Explorer in Visual Studio 2012, are the obvious choices.

From your application you can connect to SQL Azure using the connection string retrieved from the Windows Azure portal page. The list of connection strings includes versions for not only ADO.NET, but also JDBC and PHP.

APPFABRIC

The third component of the Windows Azure Platform is the AppFabric. This consists of the Service Bus and the Access Control Service. In an environment in which organizations are increasingly looking to host some or all of their applications in the cloud, significant challenges are posed around connectivity and security. The AppFabric provides a solution to enable enterprises to connect applications and unify application security.

Service Bus

Though most organizations have connectivity to the Internet, connectivity between offices or with individuals on the road is often the cause of frustration. Increasingly, companies operate behind one or more firewall devices that not only restrict the flow of traffic but also do network address translation. This means that computers sitting behind these devices cannot be easily addressable from outside the company network. In addition, as the number of public IPv4 addresses dwindles, more connections are dynamically allocated an IP address. This makes hosting an application within the company network that is publicly accessible almost impossible.

The Service Bus enables a service to be registered at a specific publicly addressable URL via the service registry. Requests made to this URL are directed to the service via an existing outbound connection made by the service. Working with the Service Bus can be as simple as changing your existing WCF bindings across to the new relay bindings. As part of running your service, it registers with the service registry and initiates the outbound connection required for all further communications.

Access Control Service

Where an organization wants to integrate multiple cloud-based applications and/or an on-premise application, there needs to be some way to control who (authentication) has access to particular resources (authorization). This is the function of the Access Control Service (ACS). Though still in its infancy, the ACS can verify a user's identity through the validation of input claims, performing claims translation, and the supply of output claims for specific applications. For example, you could sign into an application providing your e-mail address and a password. These input claims would be used to authenticate you, as well as determine that you belong in the fancy-hat group in application xyz that you want to access. The output claims may consist of your e-mail address and the fancy-hat group. Because there is a previously established trust relationship between application xyz and ACS (validated through signing of the output claims), application xyz can trust the output claims.

AZURE WEBSITES

A new addition to Windows Azure is the capability to use shared or reserved websites. The idea behind websites is a cross between web roles and web hosting. If you use the Azure website, you create your web application as you normally would. Then, when you finish, you can simply deploy the application to the website through a typical upload process (such as FTP or by using the Web Deploy functionality available in Visual Studio). At this point, your application runs on an instance of IIS and is ready to accept requests.

As you can see, this varies less from the traditional web application structure that web and worker roles do. If you can create a web application, you can create an application for your Azure website with no additional knowledge required. And if you were paying close attention to the first paragraph, you might have noticed that it didn't specify that the web application was an ASP.NET application. That's because, for Azure websites, ASP.NET is not a requirement. As of this writing, you can also create your application using PHP, Python, or `node.js`. If none of these appeals to you, check the Windows Azure website to see if your technology of choice is supported.

Along with support for different web technologies, Azure websites also provides for deploying using a tool that has become ubiquitous in the development world: Git. If you have created a Git repository for your source code, you can perform a Git Push to Azure Web Sites as a means to deploy your application. Also, if you use (the currently named) `http://www.tfspreview.com` site as your source code repository, you can also publish directly into Azure websites.

AZURE VIRTUAL MACHINES

The Windows Azure websites and Cloud Services that have already been covered fall into the Platform as a Service (PaaS) model of development. If you are just starting to build your application, these are very useful alternatives that are available to you. And although you can convert existing applications into this model, the level of effort involved can vary from almost zero to significant re-architecting. Not only that, there are many examples of applications that cannot be migrated into a PaaS environment.

To address this latter category, Windows Azure provides support for an Infrastructure as a Service (IaaS) model. One of the main components of this model is Windows Azure Virtual Machines. This is, as you might expect, a virtual machine that can support a wide variety of applications. This includes not only Windows-based applications, but also applications hosted in Linux. Access to the virtual machine is through a remote connection, and you are the administrator, configuring or installing as you want.

Along with providing a bare machine and operating system, the Windows Azure Portal also provides a gallery of Visual Machine types. For example, there are a number of different Linux distributions and SQL Server boxes, and it is anticipated that, over time, additional server offerings such as SharePoint will appear on the portal. And Microsoft has enabled other companies such as RightScale and Suse to provide Virtual Machine configuration and management services simplifying the deployment of different Virtual Machine instances.

Connectivity

To support the IaaS model, Windows Azure enables a number of different forms of connectivity. When thinking about the types of connectivity that are being defined, it's useful to think about what needs to be connected within a computing infrastructure (which, ultimately, is what Azure is implementing). Connectivity can take the form of publicly and privately available endpoints. As well, the endpoints can expose different types of functionality, including load balancing and port forwarding (and the more typical serving of Web pages).

Endpoints

Windows Azure endpoints are conceptually the same as the endpoints that have been available in WCF. They are IP addresses and ports exposed to other services or even to the public Internet. In the Windows Azure world, a Load Balancer can be associated with each endpoint so that the service behind the endpoint becomes scalable.

Cloud Services defines two types of public input endpoints: a simple input endpoint and an instance input endpoint. As well, there is an internal endpoint available only to Windows Azure services. The difference between the simple input and the instance input endpoints relates to how the load balancer handles traffic. For simple input endpoints, a round-robin algorithm is used to ensure an evenly shared flow of requests.

An instance input endpoint has traffic directed to a specific instance (such as a single Worker role). Typically, instance input endpoints are used to allow intraservice traffic within a cloud service.

For Virtual Machines, there are also two types of public endpoints (and they serve a different purpose than the Cloud Service endpoints). Load-balanced endpoints use a round-robin load balancing algorithm to direct traffic. Port forwarded endpoints use a mapping algorithm to redirect traffic from one port or endpoint to another.

Virtual Network

The inclusion of Virtual Machines into the Windows Azure world introduced the need to include those machines into a corporate network. With Virtual Network technology, it is possible to seamlessly extend a corporate network to include a Virtual Machine without increasing the security surface.

Windows Azure supports two types of VPN connectivity. The Virtual Network solution is a hardware-based, site-to-site VPN capability. This enables you to create a hybrid infrastructure that supports both on-premise services and Windows Azure-hosted services. To set up a Virtual Network within your environment, hardware within the corporate network might need to be modified.

The second option is named Windows Azure Connect. Unlike Virtual Network, this is a software-based VPN enabling developers to create connections between on-premise machines and Azure-based services. The software agent required to establish this connection is available only for Windows, which might limit the environments in which it can be used.

Along with the connectivity options, Windows Azure includes a number of other services designed to include the types of workloads that can be supported.

- **Windows Azure Traffic Manager:** Provides load-balancing capability for public HTTP endpoints exposed by Azure services. There is support for three different types of traffic distribution: geographical (traffic is directed to the server with the minimum latency from the current location); active-passive failover (traffic is sent to a backup service when the active service fails); and round-robin load balancing.
- **Windows Azure Service Bus:** Provides a mechanism that enables Azure services to communicate with one another. There are two different styles of services bus communication that are supported. With Relayed Messaging, the service and client both connect to a service bus endpoint. The Service Bus links these connections together, enabling two-way communication between the components. In Brokered Messaging, communication is enabled through a publish/subscribe model with durable message store. This is probably better recognized as a message queue model.

SUMMARY

In this chapter you learned about the Windows Azure Platform and how it represents Microsoft's entry into the cloud computing space. Using Visual Studio 2012, you can adapt an existing, or create a new, application or service for hosting in the cloud. The local Compute and Storage Emulators provide a great local testing solution, which means when you publish your application to Windows Azure, you can be confident that it will work without major issues.

Even if you don't want to migrate your entire application into the cloud, you can use SQL Azure and the AppFabric offerings to host your data, address connectivity challenges, or unify your application security.

PART VI
Data

27

Visual Database Tools

WHAT'S IN THIS CHAPTER?

- Understanding the data-oriented tool windows within Visual Studio 2012
- Creating and designing databases
- Navigating your data sources
- Entering and previewing data using Visual Studio 2012

Database connectivity is essential in almost every application you create, regardless of whether it's a Windows-based program or a website or service. When Visual Studio .NET was first introduced, it provided developers with a great set of options to navigate to the database files on their file systems and local servers, with a Server Explorer, data controls, and data-bound components. The underlying .NET Framework included ADO.NET, a retooled database engine more suited to the way applications are built today.

Visual Studio 2010 took those features and smoothed out the kinks, adding tools and functionality to the IDE to give you more direct access to the data in your application. Visual Studio 2012 continues this streamlining, adding tools to assist with designing tables and managing your SQL Server objects. This chapter looks at how you can create, manage, and consume data using the various tool windows provided in Visual Studio 2012, which can be collectively referred to as the Visual Database Tools.

DATABASE WINDOWS IN VISUAL STUDIO 2012

A number of windows specifically deal with databases and their components. From the Data Sources window that shows project-related data files and the Data Connections node in the Server Explorer, to the Database Diagram Editor and the visual designer for database schemas, you can find most of what you need directly within the IDE. It's unlikely that you need to venture outside of Visual Studio to work with your data.

Figure 27-1 shows the Visual Studio 2012 IDE with a current database-editing session. Notice how the windows, toolbars, and menus all update to match the particular context of editing a database table. In the main area is the list of columns belonging to the table. Below the column list is the SQL statement that can be used to create the table. The normal Properties tool window contains the properties for the current table. The next few pages take a look at each of these windows and describe their purposes so that you can use them effectively.

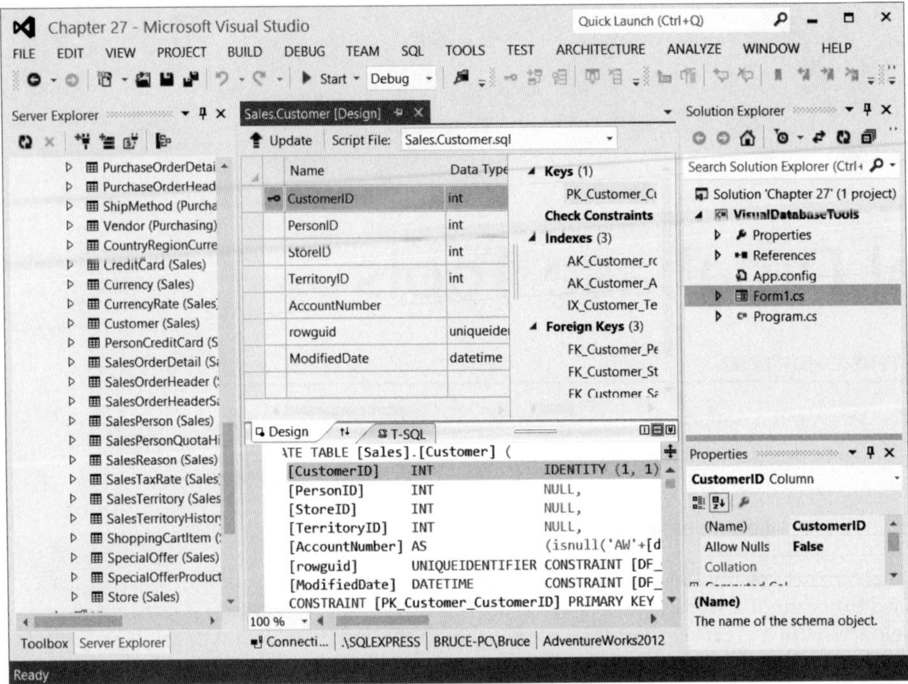

FIGURE 27-1

Server Explorer

You can use the Server Explorer to navigate the components that make up your system (or indeed the components of any server to which you can connect). One useful component of this tool window is the Data Connections node. Through this node, Visual Studio 2012 provides a significant subset of the functionality available through other products, such as SQL Server Management Studio, for creating and modifying databases.

Figure 27-1 shows the Server Explorer window with an active database connection (`AdventureWorksLT2008R2.dbo`). The database icon displays whether you are actively connected to the database and contains a number of child nodes dealing with the typical components of a modern database, such as Tables, Views, and Stored Procedures. Expanding these nodes lists the specific database components along with their details. For example, the Tables node contains a node for the `Customer` table, which in turn has nodes for each of the columns, such as `CustomerID`, `FirstName`, and `LastName`. Clicking these nodes enables you to quickly view the properties within the Properties tool window. This is the default database view; you can switch to either Object Type or Schema view by selecting Change View, followed by the view to change to, from the right-click context menu off the database node. Each of these views simply groups the information about the database into a different hierarchy.

To add a new database connection to the Server Explorer window, click the Connect to Database button at the top of the Server Explorer or right-click the Data Connections root node, and select the Add Connection command from the context menu.

If this is the first time you have added a connection, Visual Studio asks you what type of data source you are connecting to. Visual Studio 2012 comes packaged with a number of Data Source connectors, including Access, SQL Server, and Oracle, as well as a generic ODBC driver. It also includes a data source connector for Microsoft SQL Server Database File and Microsoft SQL Server Compact databases.

The Database File option borrows from the easy deployment model of its lesser cousins, Microsoft Access and MSDE. With SQL Server Database File, you can create a flat file for an individual database. This means you don't need to attach it to a SQL Server instance, and it's highly portable; you simply deliver the `.mdf` file containing the database along with your application. Alternatively, using a SQL Server Compact Edition (SQL CE) database can significantly reduce the system requirements for your application. Instead of requiring an instance of SQL Server to be installed, the SQL CE run time can be deployed alongside your application.

After you choose the data source type to use, the Add Connection dialog appears. Figure 27-2 shows this dialog for a SQL Server Database File connection with the settings appropriate to that data source type.

FIGURE 27-2

> **NOTE** *To be precise, you are taken directly to the Add Connection dialog only if you have previously defined a data connection in Visual Studio and chosen the Always Use This Selection check box in the Change Data Source dialog. This is the dialog that appears when you click the Change button (as described next) or if you have not previously checked Always Use This Selection.*

The Change button takes you to the Data Sources page, enabling you to add different types of database connections to your Visual Studio session. Note how easy it is to create a SQL Server Database File. Just type or browse to the location where you want the file and specify the database name for a new database. If you want to connect to an existing database, use the Browse button to locate it on the file system.

Generally, the only other task you need to perform is to specify whether your SQL Server configuration uses Windows or SQL Server Authentication. The default installation of Visual Studio 2012 includes an installation of SQL Server 2012 Express, which uses Windows Authentication as its base authentication model.

> **NOTE** *The Test Connection button displays an error message if you try to connect to a new database. This is because it doesn't exist until you click OK, so there's nothing to connect to!*

When you click OK, Visual Studio attempts to connect to the database. If successful, it adds it to the Data Connections node, including the children nodes for the main data types in the database, as discussed earlier. Alternatively, if the database doesn't exist, Visual Studio prompts you by asking if it should go ahead and create it. You can also create a new database by selecting the Create New SQL Server Database item from the right-click menu off the Data Connections node in the Server Explorer.

Table Editing

The easiest way to edit a table in the database is to double-click its entry in the Server Explorer. An editing window (Figure 27-3) then displays in the main workspace, consisting of three components. The top section is where you specify each field name, data type, and important information such as length of text fields, the default value for new rows, and whether the field is nullable.

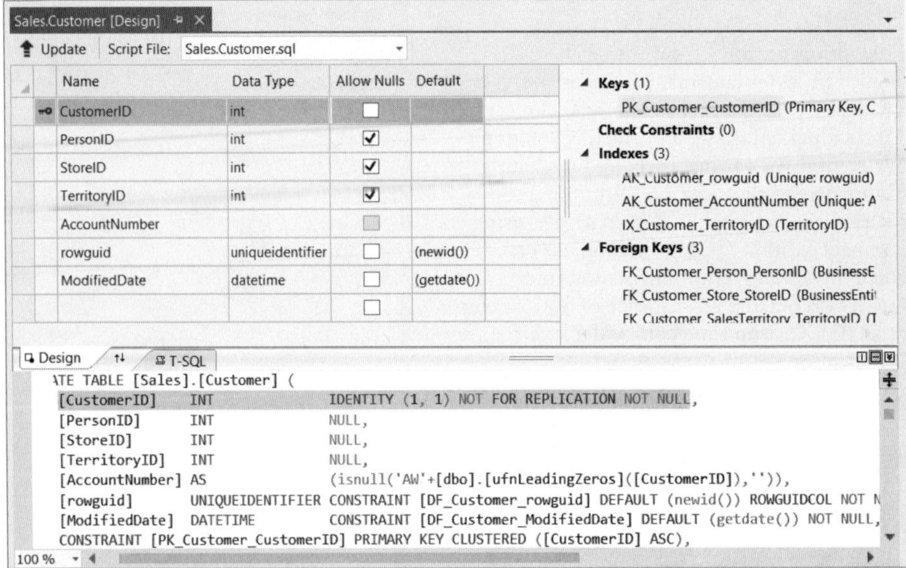

FIGURE 27-3

The lower half of the table editing workspace contains the SQL statement that, when executed, will create the table. On the right side of the workspace are additional table attributes. These include the keys, the indices, any constraints or foreign keys that are defined, and any triggers.

Right-clicking on one of the elements on the right gives you access to a set of commands that you can perform against the table (shown in Figure 27-3). Depending on which heading you right-click, the context menu allows you to add keys, indices, constraints, foreign keys and triggers.

For any of the columns in the table, the Properties window contains additional information beyond what is shown in the workspace. The column properties area enables you to specify all the available properties for the particular Data Source type. For example, Figure 27-4 shows the Properties window for a field, CustomerID, which has been defined with an identity clause automatically incremented by 1 for each new record added to the table.

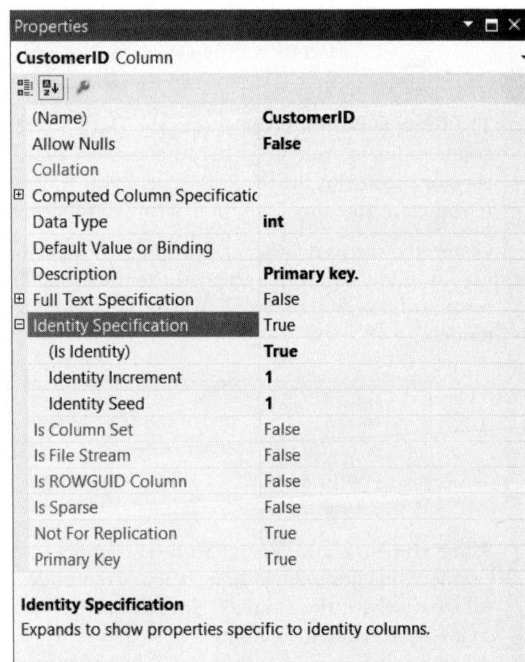

FIGURE 27-4

Relationship Editing

Most databases likely to be used by your .NET solutions are relational in nature, which means you connect tables together by defining relationships. To create a relationship, open one of the tables that will be part of the relationship, and right-click the Foreign Keys header at the right of the workspace. This creates a new entry in the list, along with a new fragment in the SQL statement (found at the bottom of the workspace). Unfortunately, this information is just a placeholder. In order to specify the details of the foreign key relationship, you need to modify the SQL fragment that was added, similarly to what is shown in Figure 27-5.

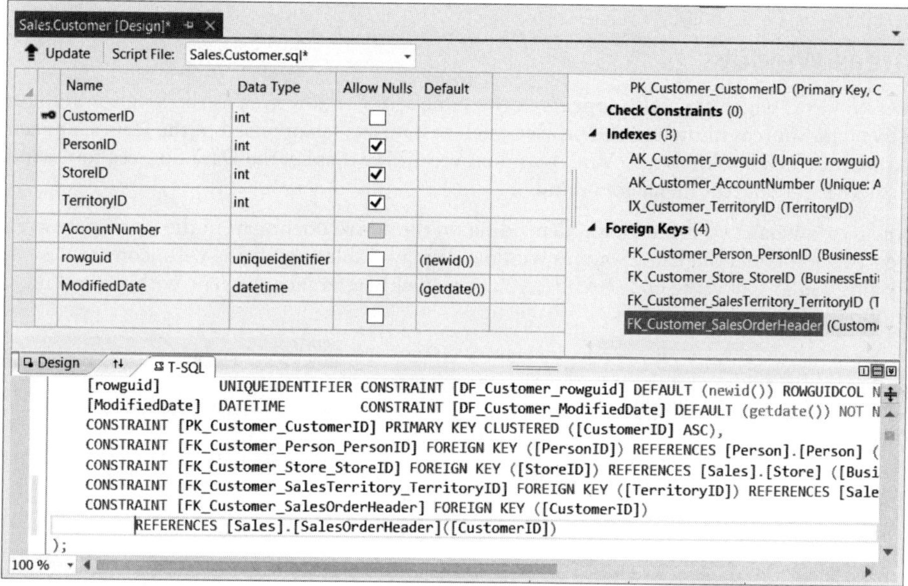

FIGURE 27-5

Views, Stored Procedures and Functions

To create and modify views, stored procedures and functions, Visual Studio 2012 uses a text editor, as shown in Figure 27-6. Because there is no IntelliSense to help you create your procedure and function definitions, Visual Studio doesn't allow you to save your code if it detects an error.

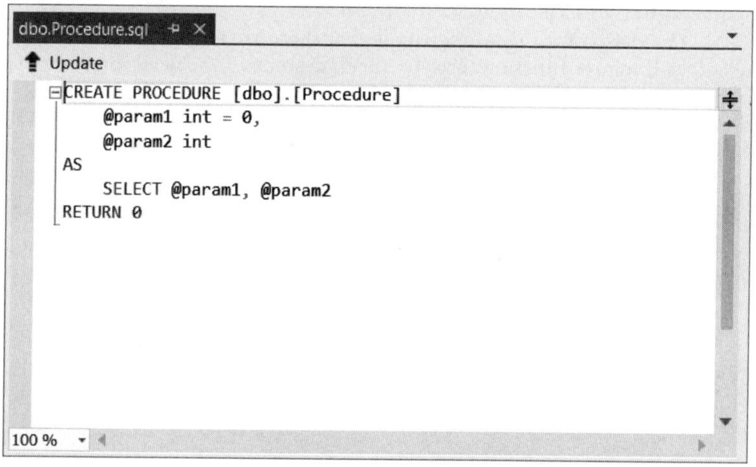

dbo.Procedure.sql

Update

```
CREATE PROCEDURE [dbo].[Procedure]
    @param1 int = 0,
    @param2 int
AS
    SELECT @param1, @param2
RETURN 0
```

100 %

FIGURE 27-6

To help you write and debug your stored procedures and functions, there are snippets available to be placed in your SQL statements. The right-click context menu includes an Insert Snippet option that has snippets for creating a stored procedure, a view, user defined type and a wide variety of other SQL artifacts. The context menu also includes options to execute the entire stored procedure or function. A word of warning about executing the SQL for existing artifacts. When you double click to look at the definition, the SQL that is procedure is the creation version. That is to say that double clicking on a view will display the CREATE VIEW SQL statement. If you execute that statement, you will attempt to create a view that already exists, resulting in a number of error statements. If you're attempting to modify the artifact, you need to change the statement to the alter version.

The Data Sources Window

The Data Sources window, which typically appears in the same tool window area as the Solution Explorer, contains any active data sources known to the project, such as datasets (as opposed to the Data Connections in the Server Explorer, which are known to Visual Studio overall). To display the Data Sources tool window, use the Data ➪ Show Data Sources menu command.

The Data Sources window has two main views, depending on the active document in the workspace area of the IDE. When you edit code, the Data Sources window displays tables and fields with icons representing their types. This aids you as you write code because you can quickly reference the type without looking at the table definition.

When you edit a form in Design view, however, the Data Sources view changes to display the tables and fields with icons representing their current default control types (initially set in the Data UI Customization page of Options). Figure 27-7 shows that the text fields use `TextBox` controls, whereas the `ModifiedDate` field uses a `DateTimePicker` control. The icons for the tables indicate that all tables will be inserted as `DataGridView` components by default as shown in the drop-down list.

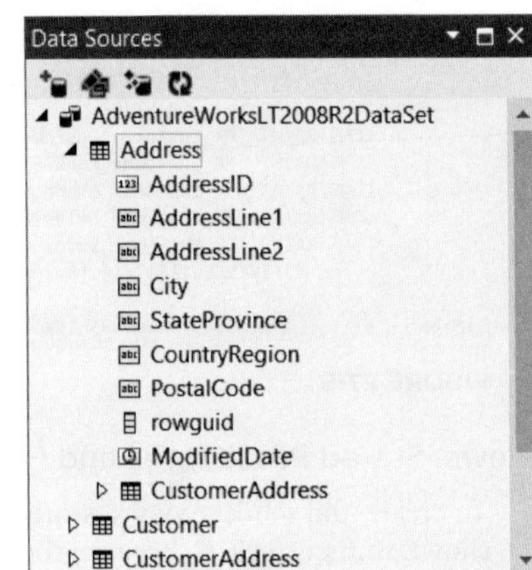

FIGURE 27-7

In the next chapter you learn how to add and modify data sources, as well as use the Data Sources window to bind your data to controls on a form. Data classes or fields can simply be dragged from the Data Sources window onto a form to wire up the user interface.

SQL Server Object Explorer

If you are a regular developer of database applications in Visual Studio, odds are that you're familiar with the SQL Server Management Studio (SSMS). The reason for the familiarity is that there are tasks that need to be performed that don't fit into the Server Explorer functionality. To alleviate some of the need to utilize SQL Server Management Studio, Visual Studio 2012 includes the SQL Server Object Explorer. Through this information, some of the functionality not found in the Server Explorer can be found in an interface that is somewhat reminiscent of SSMS. To launch the SQL Server Object Explorer, use the View ➪ SQL Server Object Explorer option.

To start working against an existing SQL Server instance, you need to add it to the Explorer. Right-click the SQL Server node, or click the Add SQL Server button (second from the left). The dialog that appears is the standard one that appears when connecting to SSMS. You need to provide the server name and instance, along with the authentication method that you want to use. Clicking the Connect button establishes the connection.

When the connection has been made, three nodes underneath the server appear. These are the Databases, Security items, and Server Objects that are part of that instance (see Figure 27-8).

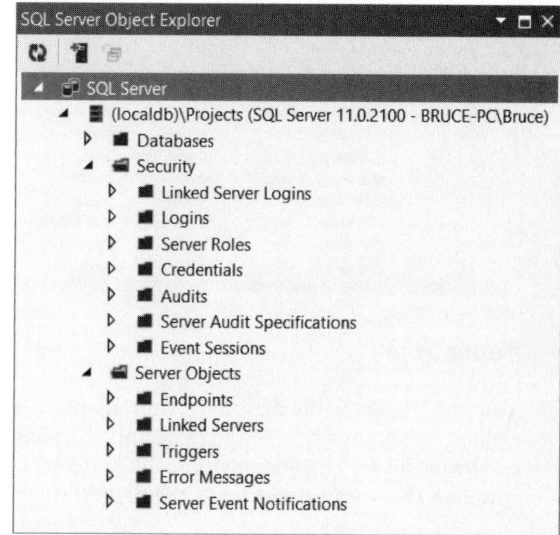

FIGURE 27-8

Under the Security and Server Objects nodes, a number of subfolders are available. These subfolders contain various server-level artifacts. These include logins, server roles, linked servers, triggers, and so on that are defined on the server. For each of the subfolders, you can add or modify the entities that are presented. For example, if you right-click the EndPoints node, the context menu provides the option to add either a TCP- or HTTP-based endpoint. When the Add option is selected, T-SQL code is generated and placed into a freshly opened designer tab. The T-SQL code, when executed, creates the artifact. Of course, you must modify the T-SQL so that when it is executed the results will be as wanted.

The Databases node also contains subfolders. The difference is that here each subfolder represents a database on the SQL Server instance. As you expand a database node, additional folders containing Tables, Views, Synonyms, Programmability items, Server Brokers Storage elements, and Security appear. For most of these items, the process to create or edit is commonplace. Right-clicking the subfolder and selecting the Add New option generates the SQL statement needed to create the selected item. (Naturally, you need to change a couple of values.) Or you could right-click on an existing item and select the View Properties or other similarly named menu options. This displays the T-SQL code that would alter the selected item. You can then change the appropriate values and execute the statement by clicking the Update button (see Figure 27-9).

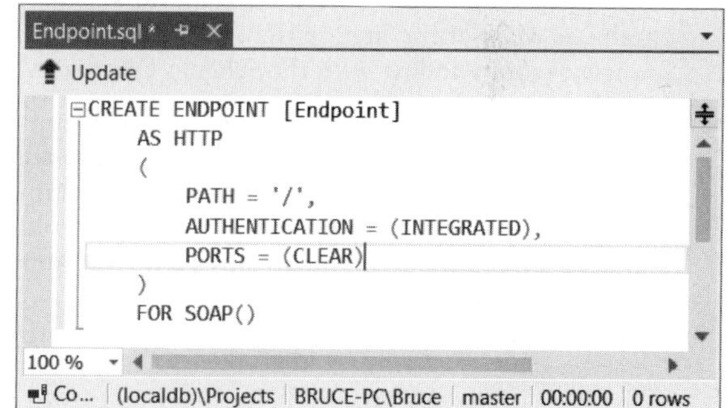

FIGURE 27-9

EDITING DATA

Visual Studio 2012 also has the capability to view and edit the data contained in your database tables. To edit the information, right-click on the table you want to view in the Server Explorer and select the Show Table Data option from the context menu. You see a tabular representation of the data in the table, as shown in Figure 27-10, enabling you to edit it to contain whatever default or test data you need to include. As you edit information, the table editor displays indicators next to fields that have changed.

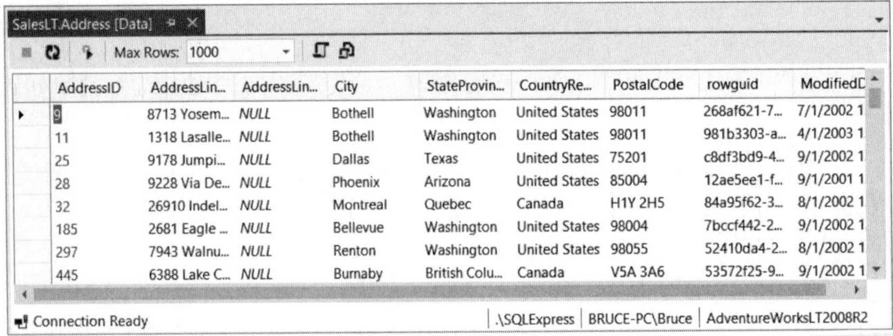

FIGURE 27-10

You can also show the diagram, criteria, and SQL panes associated with the table data you're editing by right-clicking anywhere in the table and choosing the appropriate command from the Pane submenu. This can be useful for customizing the SQL statement used to retrieve the data, for example, to filter the table for specific values or just to retrieve the first 50 rows.

SUMMARY

With the variety of tools and windows available in Visual Studio 2012, you can easily create and maintain databases without leaving the IDE. You can manipulate data and define database schemas visually using the Properties tool window with the Schema Designer view.

When you have your data where you want it, Visual Studio keeps helping you by providing a set of drag-and-drop components that can be bound to a data source. These can be as simple as a check box or textbox or as feature-rich as a DataGridView component with complete table views. In the next chapter you learn how being able to drag whole tables or individual fields from the Data Sources window onto a form and have Visual Studio automatically create the appropriate controls for you is a major advantage for rapid application development.

28

DataSets and DataBinding

WHAT'S IN THIS CHAPTER?

- Creating DataSets
- Connecting visual controls to a DataSet with DataBinding
- How BindingSource and BindingNavigator controls work together
- Chaining BindingSources and using the DataGridView
- Using Service and Object data sources

A large proportion of applications use some form of data storage. This might be in the form of serialized objects or XML data, but for long-term storage that supports concurrent access by a large number of users, most applications use a database. The .NET Framework includes strong support for working with databases and other data sources. This chapter examines how to use DataSets to build applications that work with data from a database.

In the second part of this chapter, you see how to use DataBinding to connect visual controls to the data they display. You see how they interact and how you can use the designers to control how data displays.

The examples in this chapter are based on the sample AdventureWorksLT2008R2 database available as a download from `http://msftdbprodsamples.codeplex.com`.

DATASETS OVERVIEW

The .NET Framework DataSet is a complex object approximately equivalent to an in-memory representation of a database. It contains DataTables that correlate to database tables. These in turn contain a series of DataColumns that define the composition of each DataRow. The DataRow correlates to a row in a database table. You can also establish relationships between DataTables within the DataSet in the same way that a database has relationships between tables.

One of the ongoing challenges for the object-oriented programming paradigm is that it does not align smoothly with the relational database model. The DataSet object goes a long way toward bridging this gap because it can be used to represent and work with relational data in an object-oriented fashion. However, the biggest issue with a raw DataSet is that it is weakly typed. Although the type of each column can be queried prior to accessing data elements, this adds overhead and can make code unreadable. Strongly typed DataSets combine the advantages of a DataSet with strong typing (in other words, creating strongly typed properties for all database fields) to ensure that data is accessed correctly at design time. This is done with the custom tool MSDataSetGenerator, which converts an XML schema into a strongly typed DataSet, essentially replacing a lot of run-time-type checking with code generated at design time. In the following code snippet, you can see the difference between using a raw DataSet in the first half of the snippet, and a strongly typed DataSet in the second half:

VB

```
'Raw DataSet
Dim nontypedAwds As DataSet = RetrieveData()
Dim nontypedcustomers As DataTable = nontypedAwds.Tables("Customer")
Dim nontypedfirstcustomer As DataRow = nontypedcustomers.Rows(0)
MessageBox.Show(nontypedfirstcustomer.Item("FirstName"))

'Strongly typed DataSet
Dim awds As AdventureWorksLT2008R2DataSet = RetrieveData()
Dim customers As AdventureWorksLT2008R2DataSet.CustomerDataTable = awds.Customer
Dim firstcustomer As AdventureWorksLT2008R2DataSet.CustomerRow = customers.Rows(0)
MessageBox.Show(firstcustomer.FirstName)
```

C#

```
// Raw DataSet
DataSet nontypedAwds = RetrieveData();
DataTable nontypedcustomers = nontypedAwds.Tables["Customer"];
DataRow nontypedfirstcustomer = nontypedcustomers.Rows[0];
MessageBox.Show(nontypedfirstcustomer["FirstName"].ToString());

// Strongly typed DataSet
AdventureWorksLT2008R2DataSet awds = RetrieveData();
AdventureWorksLT2008R2DataSet.CustomerDataTable customers = awds.Customer;
AdventureWorksLT2008R2DataSet.CustomerRow firstcustomer =
          customers.Rows[0] as AdventureWorksLT2008R2DataSet.CustomerRow;
MessageBox.Show(firstcustomer.FirstName);
```

Using the raw DataSet, both the table lookup and the column name lookup are done using string literals. As you are likely aware, string literals can be a source of much frustration and should be used only within generated code — and preferably not at all.

Adding a Data Source

You can manually create a strongly typed DataSet by creating an XSD using the XML schema editor. To create the DataSet, you set the custom tool value for the XSD file to be the MSDataSetGenerator. This creates the designer code file needed for strongly typed access to the DataSet.

Manually creating an XSD is difficult and not recommended unless you need to; luckily in most cases, the source of your data is a database, in which case Visual Studio 2012 provides a wizard that you can use to generate the necessary schema based on the structure of your database. Through the rest of this chapter, you see how you can create data sources and how they can be bound to the user interface. To start, create a new project called CustomerObjects, using the Windows Forms Application project template.

> **NOTE** *Although this functionality is not available for ASP.NET projects, a workaround is to perform all data access via a class library.*

To create a strongly typed DataSet from an existing database, follow these steps:

1. Right-click on the project in Solution Explorer and select Add -> New Item.
2. Navigate to the Data section on the left. You will see a number of choices, including ADO.NET Entity Data Model and DataSet. With ADO.NET, there are two different data models that you can choose to represent the mapping between database data and .NET entities: a DataSet or an Entity Data Model. The Entity Framework (which is used in the Entity Data Model) is covered in Chapter 30, "The ADO.NET Entity Framework." Double-click the DataSet icon to continue.
3. The link to the database which will be used for this DataSet is determined through the Server Explorer. If you don't already have a connection to the database that you want to use, you'll need to add it. At the top of the Server Explorer, there is a Connect to Database button that opens the Add Connection dialog. The attributes displayed in this dialog are dependent on the type of database you connect to. By default, the SQL Server provider is selected, which requires the Server name, authentication mechanism (Windows or SQL Server), and Database name to proceed. There is a Test Connection that you can use to ensure you have specified valid properties.
4. After specifying the connection, the next stage is to specify the data to be extracted. At this stage you can drag the tables and views from the Server Explorer onto the design surface for the DataSet. After you have moved at least one database object onto the DataSet designer, the connection string to the database is saved as an application setting in the application configuration file.

> **NOTE** *You can use a little-known utility within Windows to create connection strings, even if Visual Studio is not installed. Known as the Data Link Properties dialog, you can use it to edit Universal Data Link files, files that end in* `.udl`. *When you need to create or test a connection string, you can simply create a new text document, rename it to* `something.udl`, *and then double-click it from within Windows Explorer. This opens the Data Link Properties dialog, which enables you to create and test connection strings for a variety of providers. After you select the appropriate connection, this information is written to the UDL file as a connection string, which can be retrieved by opening the same file in Notepad. This can be particularly useful if you need to test security permissions and resolve other data connectivity issues.*

The DataSet Designer

When you drag a table or view onto the DataSet, Visual Studio uses the database schema to guess the appropriate .NET data type to use for the DataTable columns. In cases where the wizard gets information wrong, it can be useful to edit the DataSet directly. In the Solution Explorer, double-click on the DataSet. This opens the DataSet editor in the main window, as shown in the example in Figure 28-1.

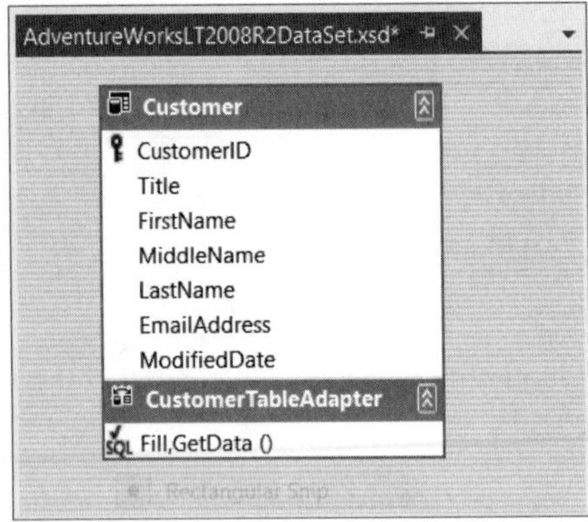

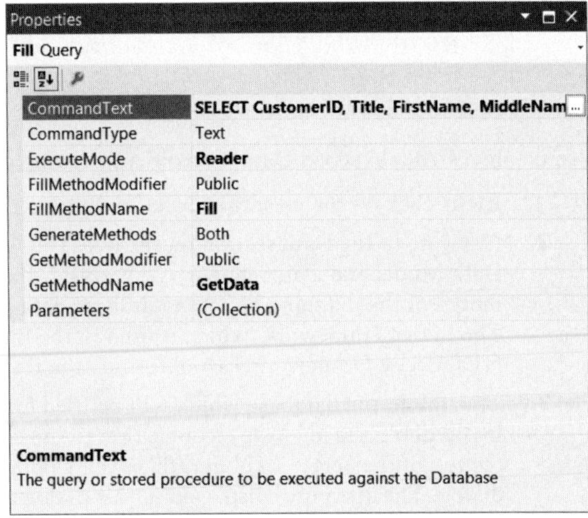

FIGURE 28-1

Here you start to see some of the power of using strongly typed DataSets. Not only has a strongly typed table (Customer) been added to the DataSet, you also have a CustomerTableAdapter. This TableAdapter is used for selecting from and updating the database for the DataTable to which it is attached. If you have multiple tables included in the DataSet, you can have a TableAdapter for each. Although a single TableAdapter can easily handle returning information from multiple tables in the database, it becomes difficult to update, insert, and delete records.

The CustomerTableAdapter has been created with `Fill` and `GetData` methods (refer to the right side of Figure 28-1), which are called to extract data from the database. The following code shows how you can use the `Fill` method to populate an existing strongly typed DataTable, perhaps within a DataSet. Alternatively, the `GetData` method creates a new instance of a strongly typed DataTable:

VB

```
Dim ta As New AdventureWorksLT2008R2DataSetTableAdapters.CustomerTableAdapter

'Option 1 - Create a new CustomerDataTable and use the Fill method
Dim customers1 As New AdventureWorksLT2008R2DataSet.CustomerDataTable
ta.Fill(customers1)

'Option 2 - Use the GetData method which will create a CustomerDataTable for you
Dim customers2 As AdventureWorksLT2008R2DataSet.CustomerDataTable = ta.GetData
```

The `Fill` and `GetData` methods appear as a pair because they make use of the same query (refer to Figure 28-1). The Properties window can be used to configure this query. A query can return data in one of three ways: using a text command (as the example illustrates), a stored procedure, or TableDirect (where the contents of the table name specified in the `CommandText` are retrieved). This is specified in the CommandType field. Although the `CommandText` can be edited directly in the Properties window, it is difficult to see the whole query and easy to make mistakes. Clicking the ellipsis button (refer to the top right of Figure 28-1) opens the Query Builder window, as shown in Figure 28-2.

> **NOTE** *Another option to open the Query Builder window is to right-click a table in the diagram, select Configure from the context menu and click on the Query Builder button to open the Query Builder window.*

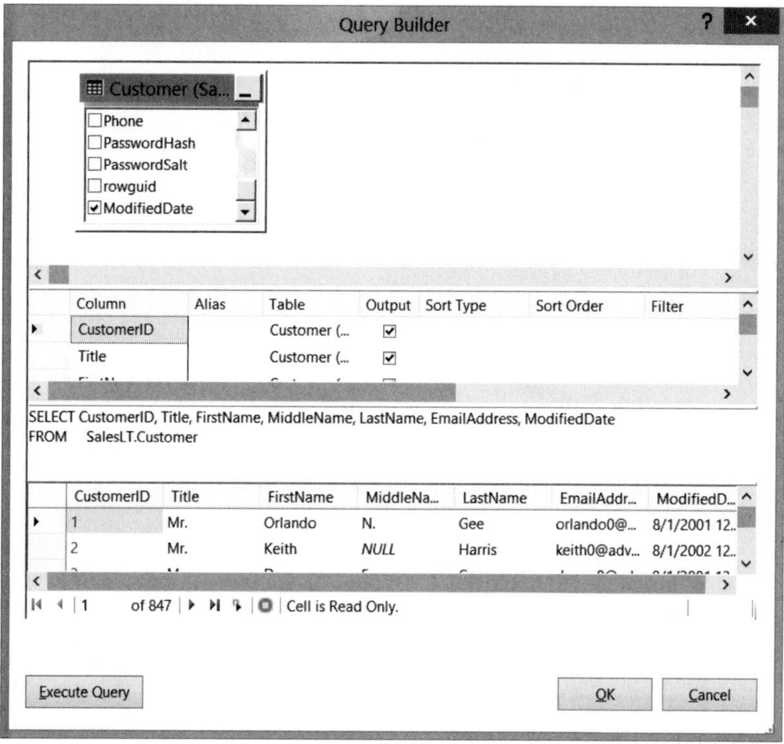

FIGURE 28-2

The Query Builder dialog is divided into four panes. In the top pane is a diagram of the tables involved in the query, and the selected columns. The second pane shows a list of columns related to the query. These columns are either output columns, such as FirstName and LastName, or a condition, such as the Title field, or both. The third pane is, of course, the SQL command that is to be executed. The final pane includes sample data that can be retrieved by clicking the Execute Query button. If there are parameters to the SQL statement (in this case, `@Title`), a dialog displays, prompting for values to use when executing the statement.

To change the query, you can make changes in any of the first three panes. As you move between panes, changes in one field are reflected in the others. You can hide any of the panes by unchecking that pane from the Panes item of the right-click context menu. Conditions can be added using the Filter column. These can include parameters (such as `@Title`), which must start with the `@` symbol.

Returning to the DataSet designer, and the Properties window associated with the `Fill` method, click the ellipsis to examine the list of parameters. This shows the Parameters Collection Editor, as shown in Figure 28-3. Occasionally, the Query Builder doesn't get the data type correct for a parameter, and you may need to modify it using this dialog.

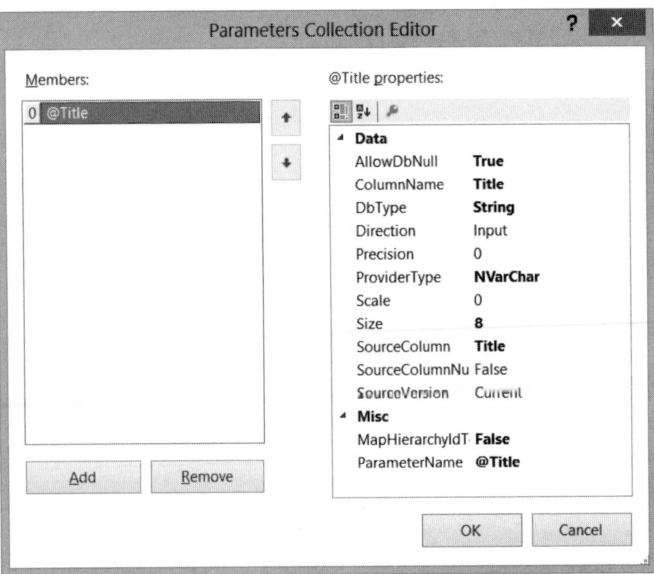

FIGURE 28-3

Also from the Properties window for the query, you can specify whether the `Fill` and `GetData` methods are created, using the `GenerateMethods` property, which has values `Fill`, `Get`, or `Both`. You can also specify the names and accessibility of the generated methods.

BINDING DATA

The most common type of application is one that retrieves data from a database, displays the data, allows changes to be made, and then persists those changes back to the database. The middle steps that connect the in-memory data with the visual elements are referred to as DataBinding, which often becomes the bane a of developer's existence because it has been difficult to get right. Most developers at some stage or another have resorted to writing their own wrappers to ensure that data is correctly bound to the controls on the screen. The recent versions of Visual Studio (including, of course Visual Studio 2012) dramatically reduce the pain of getting two-way DataBinding to work. The examples used in the following sections again work with the AdventureWorksLT2008R2 sample database. For simplicity, you work with a single Windows application, but the concepts discussed here can be extended over multiple tiers.

In this example, you build an application to assist you in managing the customers for AdventureWorks. To begin, you need to ensure that the `AdventureWorksLT2008R2DataSet` contains the Customer and Address tables. (You can reuse the `AdventureWorksLT2008R2DataSet` from earlier by clicking the Configure DataSet with Wizard icon in the Data Sources window and editing which tables are included in the DataSet.) With the form designer (any empty form in your project will do) and Data Sources window open, set the mode for the Customer table to Details using the drop-down list. Before creating the editing controls, tweak the list of columns for the Customer table. You're not that interested in the CustomerID, NameStyle, PasswordHash, PasswordSalt, or rowguid fields, so set them to None (again using the drop-down list for those nodes in the Data Sources window). ModifiedDate should be automatically set when changes are made, so this field should appear as a label, preventing the ModifiedDate from being edited.

Now you're ready to drag the Customer node onto the form design surface. This automatically adds controls for each of the columns you have specified. It also adds a `BindingSource`, a `BindingNavigator`, an `AdventureWorksLT2008R2DataSet`, a `CustomerTableAdapter`, a `TableAdapter Manager`, and a `ToolStrip` to the form, as shown in Figure 28-4.

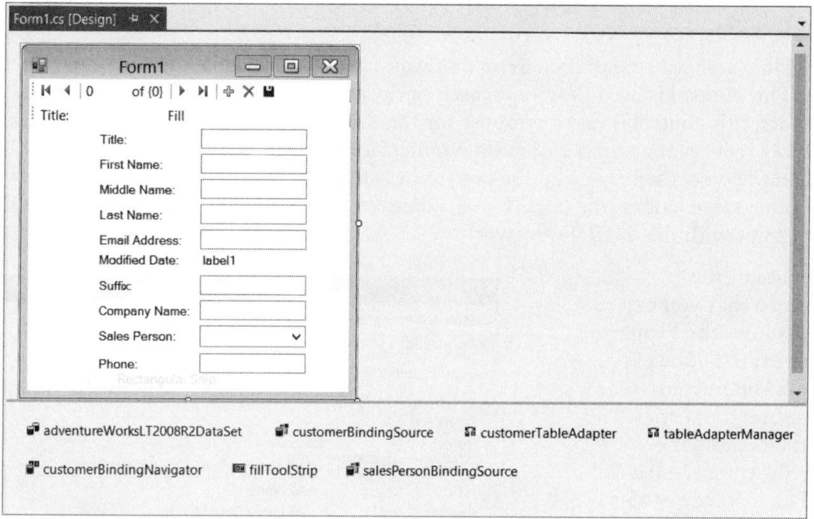

FIGURE 28-4

At this point you can build and run this application and navigate through the records using the navigation control, and you can also take the components apart to understand how they interact. Start with the `AdventureWorksLT2008R2DataSet` and the `CustomerTableAdapter` because they carry out the background grunt work to retrieve information and to persist changes to the database. The `AdventureWorksLT2008R2DataSet` added to this form is actually an instance of the `AdventureWorksLT2008R2DataSet` class created by the Data Source Configuration Wizard. This instance will be used to store information for all the tables on this form. To populate the DataSet, call the `Fill` method. If you open the code file for the form, you can see that the `Fill` command has been called from the `Click` event handler of the Fill button that resides on the toolstrip.

VB

```
Private Sub FillToolStripButton_Click(ByVal sender As Object,
                                      ByVal e As EventArgs) _
                                              Handles FillToolStripButton.Click
    Try
        Me.CustomerTableAdapter.Fill(Me.AdventureWorksLT2008R2DataSet.Customer,
                                     TitleToolStripTextBox.Text)
    Catch ex As System.Exception
        System.Windows.Forms.MessageBox.Show(ex.Message)
    End Try
End Sub
```

C#

```
private void fillToolStripButton_Click(object sender, EventArgs e){
    try{
        this.customerTableAdapter.Fill(
            this.adventureWorksLT2008R2DataSet.Customer, titleToolStripTextBox.Text);
    }
    catch (System.Exception ex){
        System.Windows.Forms.MessageBox.Show(ex.Message);
    }
}
```

As you extend this form, you add a `TableAdapter` for each table within the `AdventureWorksLT2008R2DataSet` that you want to work with.

BindingSource

The next item of interest is the `CustomerBindingSource` that was automatically added to the nonvisual part of the form designer. This control is used to wire up each of the controls on the design surface with the relevant data item. In fact, this control is just a wrapper for the `CurrencyManager`. However, using a `BindingSource` considerably reduces the number of event handlers and custom code that you have to write. Unlike the `AdventureWorksLT2008R2DataSet` and the `CustomerTableAdapter` (which are instances of the strongly typed classes with the same names) the `CustomerBindingSource` is just an instance of the regular `BindingSource` class that ships with the .NET Framework.

Take a look at the properties of the `CustomerBindingSource` so that you can see what it does. Figure 28-5 shows the Properties window for the `CustomerBindingSource`. The two items of particular interest are the `DataSource` and `DataMember` properties. The drop-down list for the `DataSource` property is expanded to illustrate the list of available data sources. The instance of the `AdventureWorksLT2008R2DataSet` added to the form is listed under CustomerForm List Instances. Selecting the `AdventureWorksLT2008R2DataSet` type under the Project Data Sources node creates another instance on the form instead of reusing the existing `DataSet`. In the DataMember field, you need to specify the table to use for DataBinding. Later, you see how the DataMember field can specify a foreign key relationship so that you can show linked data.

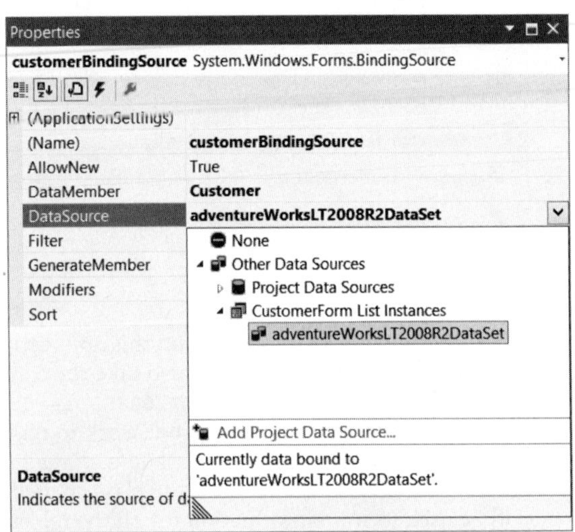

FIGURE 28-5

So far you have specified that the `CustomerBindingSource` binds data in the Customer table of the `AdventureWorksLT2008R2DataSet`. What remains is to bind the individual controls on the form to the `BindingSource` and the appropriate column in the Customer table. To do this you need to specify a DataBinding for each control. Figure 28-6 shows the Properties grid for the FirstNameTextBox, with the DataBindings node expanded to show the binding for the `Text` property.

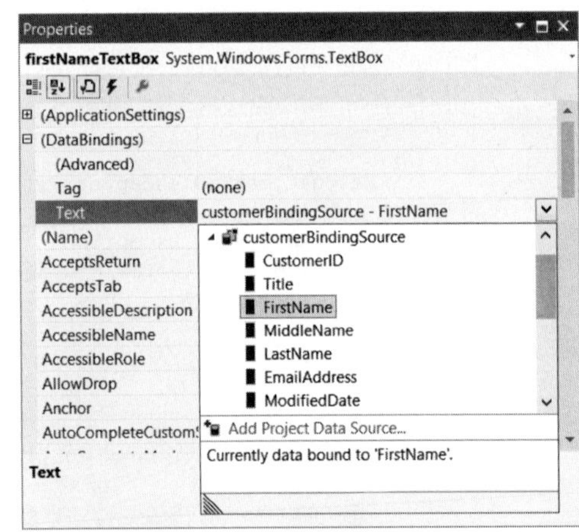

FIGURE 28-6

From the drop-down list you can see that the `Text` property is bound to the FirstName field of the `CustomerBindingSource`. Because the `CustomerBindingSource` is bound to the Customer table, this is actually the FirstName column in that table. If you look at the designer file for the form, you can see that this binding is set up using a new `Binding`, as shown in the following snippet:

```
Me.FirstNameTextBox.DataBindings.Add(
                    New System.Windows.Forms.Binding("Text",
                                                     Me.CustomerBindingSource,
                                                     "FirstName", True))
```

A `Binding` is used to ensure that two-way binding is set up between the Text field of the FirstNameTextBox and the FirstName field of the `CustomerBindingSource`. The controls for the other controls all have similar bindings between their `Text` properties and the appropriate fields on the `CustomerBindingSource`.

When you run the current application, you can notice that the Modified Date value displays as in the default string representation of a date, for example, 13/10/2004. Given the nature of the application, it might be more useful to have it in a format similar to October-13-04. To do this you need to specify additional properties as part of the DataBinding. Select the ModifiedDateLabel1 and in the Properties tool window, expand the DataBindings node and select the Advanced item. This opens up the Formatting and Advanced Binding dialog, as shown in Figure 28-7.

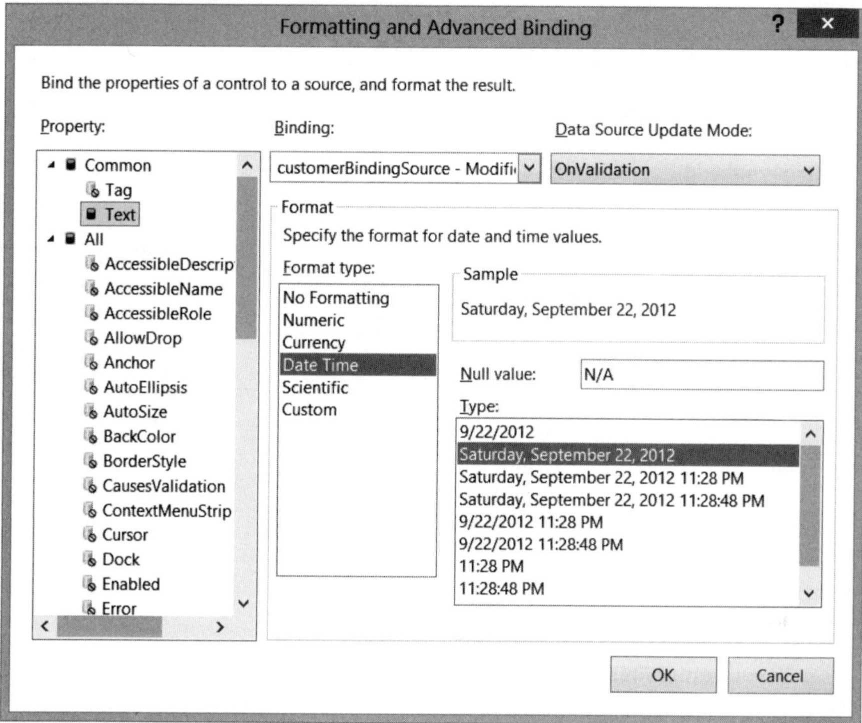

FIGURE 28-7

In Figure 28-7, you can see one of the predefined formatting types, Date Time. This then presents another list of formatting options in which Saturday, September 22, 2012 has been selected, which is an example of how the value will be formatted. This dialog also provides a Null value, "N/A," which displays if there is no Modified Date value for a particular row. In the following code you can see that three additional parameters have been added to create the DataBinding for the Modified Date value:

VB

```
Me.ModifiedDateLabel1.DataBindings.Add(
            New System.Windows.Forms.Binding("Text",
                        Me.CustomerBindingSource,
                        "ModifiedDate", True,
                        System.Windows.Forms.DataSourceUpdateMode.OnValidation,
                        "N/A", "D"))
```

The `OnValidation` value simply indicates that the data source updates when the visual control is validated. This is actually the default and is only specified here so that the next two parameters can be specified. The `"N/A"` is the value you specified for when there was no Modified Date value, and the `"D"` is actually a shortcut formatting string for the date formatting you selected.

BindingNavigator

Although the `CustomerBindingNavigator` component, which is an instance of the `BindingNavigator` class, appears in the nonvisual area of the design surface, it does have a visual representation in the form of the navigation toolstrip that is initially docked to the top of the form. As with regular toolstrips, this control can be docked to any edge of the form. In fact, in many ways the `BindingNavigator` behaves the same way as a toolstrip in that buttons and other controls can be added to the Items list. When the `BindingNavigator` is initially added to the form, a series of buttons are added for standard data functionality, such as moving to the first or last item, moving to the next or previous item, and adding, removing, and saving items.

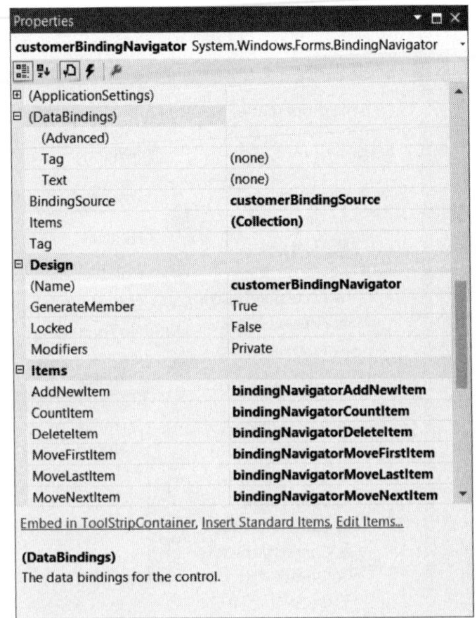

FIGURE 28-8

What is neat about the `BindingNavigator` is that it not only creates these standard controls, but also wires them up for you. Figure 28-8 shows the Properties window for the `BindingNavigator`, with the Data and Items sections expanded. In the Data section you can see that the associated `BindingSource` is the `CustomerBindingSource`, which will be used to perform all the actions implied by the various button clicks. The Items section plays an important role because each property defines an action, such as `AddNewItem`. The value of the property defines the `ToolStripItem` to which it will be assigned — in this case, the `BindingNavigatorAddNewItem` button.

Behind the scenes, when this application is run and this button is assigned to the `AddNewItem` property, the `OnAddNew` method is wired up to the `Click` event of the button. This is shown in the following snippet, extracted using Reflector from the `BindingNavigator` class. The `AddNewItem` property calls the `WireUpButton` method, passing in a delegate to the `OnAddNew` method:

VB

```
Public Property AddNewItem As ToolStripItem
    Get
        If ((Not Me.addNewItem Is Nothing) AndAlso Me.addNewItem.IsDisposed) Then
            Me.addNewItem = Nothing
        End If
        Return Me.addNewItem
    End Get
    Set(ByVal value As ToolStripItem)
        Me.WireUpButton(Me.addNewItem, value, _
                                         New EventHandler(AddressOf Me.OnAddNew))
    End Set
End Property

Private Sub OnAddNew(ByVal sender As Object, ByVal e As EventArgs)
      If (Me.Validate AndAlso (Not Me.bindingSource Is Nothing)) Then
```

```
            Me.bindingSource.AddNew
            Me.RefreshItemsInternal
        End If
    End Sub

    Private Sub WireUpButton(ByRef oldButton As ToolStripItem, _
                             ByVal newButton As ToolStripItem, _
                             ByVal clickHandler As EventHandler)
        If (Not oldButton Is newButton) Then
            If (Not oldButton Is Nothing) Then
                RemoveHandler oldButton.Click, clickHandler
            End If
            If (Not newButton Is Nothing) Then
                AddHandler newButton.Click, clickHandler
            End If
            oldButton = newButton
            Me.RefreshItemsInternal
        End If
    End Sub
```

The `OnAddNew` method performs a couple of important actions. First, it forces validation of the active field, which is examined in the "Validation" section later in this chapter. Second, and the most important aspect of the `OnAddNew` method, it calls the `AddNew` method on the `BindingSource`. The other properties on the `BindingNavigator` also map to corresponding methods on the `BindingSource`, and you need to remember that the `BindingSource`, rather than the `BindingNavigator`, does the work with the data source.

Data Source Selections

Now that you have seen how the `BindingSource` works, it's time to improve the user interface. At the moment, the Sales Person is displayed as a textbox, but this should actually be limited to just the sales staff at AdventureWorks. As such, instead of a textbox, it would be better to have the list of staff displayed as a drop-down box from which the user can select.

Start by removing the SalesPersonTextBox from the form. Next, add a ComboBox control from the toolbox. With the new ComboBox selected, note that a smart tag is attached to the control. Expanding this tag and checking the Use Data Bound Items check box opens the DataBinding Mode options, as shown in Figure 28-9.

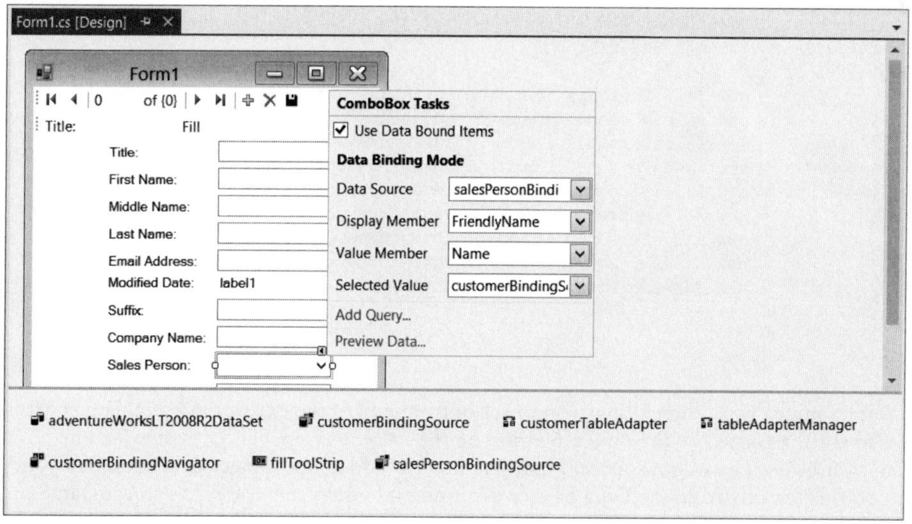

FIGURE 28-9

You need to define four things to get the DataBinding to work properly. The first is the data source for the list of staff the user should select from. Unfortunately, the list of staff is not contained in a database table. (This may be the case if the list of staff comes from a separate system such as Active Directory.) For this example, the list of staff is defined by a fixed array of `SalesPerson` objects.

VB

```
Public Class SalesPerson
    Public ReadOnly Property FriendlyName
        Get
            Return Name.Replace("adventure-works\", String.Empty)
        End Get
    End Property

    Public Property Name As String

    Public Shared Function Staff() As SalesPerson()
        Return {
            New SalesPerson() With {.Name = "adventure-works\pamela0"},
            New SalesPerson() With {.Name = "adventure-works\david8"},
            New SalesPerson() With {.Name = "adventure-works\jillian0"},
            New SalesPerson() With {.Name = "adventure-works\garrett1"},
            New SalesPerson() With {.Name = "adventure-works\jae0"},
            New SalesPerson() With {.Name = "adventure-works\linda3"},
            New SalesPerson() With {.Name = "adventure-works\josé1"},
            New SalesPerson() With {.Name = "adventure-works\michael9"},
            New SalesPerson() With {.Name = "adventure-works\shu0"}
        }
    End Function
End Class
```

C#

```
public class SalesPerson{
    public string FriendlyName{
        get{
            return Name.Replace(@"adventure-works\", String.Empty);
        }
    }

    public string Name { get; set; }
    public static SalesPerson[] Staff(){
        return new SalesPerson[]{
                        new SalesPerson() {Name= @"adventure-works\pamela0"},
                        new SalesPerson() {Name= @"adventure-works\david8"},
                        new SalesPerson() {Name= @"adventure-works\jillian0"},
                        new SalesPerson() {Name= @"adventure-works\garrett1"},
                        new SalesPerson() {Name= @"adventure-works\jae0"},
                        new SalesPerson() {Name= @"adventure-works\linda3"},
                        new SalesPerson() {Name= @"adventure-works\josé1"},
                        new SalesPerson() {Name= @"adventure-works\michael9"},
                        new SalesPerson() {Name= @"adventure-works\shu0"}
                    };
    }
}
```

Expanding the Data Source drop-down allows you to select from any of the existing project data sources. Although the list of staff, returned by the `Staff` method on the `SalesPerson` class, is contained in the project, it can't yet be used as a data source. First, you need to add a new Object data source to your project. You can do this directly from the Data Source drop-down by selecting the Add Project DataSource link. This displays the Data Source Configuration Wizard as you saw earlier in this chapter. However, this time you select Object as the type of data source. You then must select which objects you want to include in the data source, as shown in Figure 28-10.

FIGURE 28-10

When you select SalesPerson and click Finish, the data source is created and automatically assigned to the Data Source property of the Sales Person drop-down.

The Display Member and Value Member properties correspond to which properties on the SalesPerson object you want to be displayed and used to determine the selected item. In this case, the SalesPerson defines a read-only property, FriendlyName (which simply removes the adventure-works prefix), which should be displayed in the drop-down. However, the Value property needs to be set to the Name property so that it matches the value specified in the SalesPerson field in the Customer table. Lastly, the Selected Value property needs to be set to the SalesPerson property on the CustomerBindingSource. This is the property that is get/set to determine the Sales Person specified for the displayed Customer.

Although you have wired up the Sales Person drop-down list, if you run what you currently have, there would be no items in this list because you haven't populated the SalesPersonBindingSource. The BindingSource object has a DataSource property, which you need to set to populate the BindingSource. You can do this in the `Load` event of the form:

VB

```
Private Sub CustomerForm_Load(ByVal sender As Object,
                              ByVal e As EventArgs) Handles MyBase.Load
        Me.SalesPersonBindingSource.DataSource = SalesPerson.Staff
End SubPrivate
```

C#

```
private void CustomerForm_Load(object sender, EventArgs e){
    this.salesPersonBindingSource.DataSource = SalesPerson.Staff();
}
```

Now when you run the application, instead of having a textbox with a numeric value, you have a convenient drop-down list from which to select the SalesPerson.

Saving Changes

Now that you have a usable interface, you need to add support for making changes and adding new records. If you double-click the Save icon on the `CustomerBindingNavigator` toolstrip, the code window opens with a code stub that would normally save changes to the Customer table. As you can see in the following snippet, there are essentially three steps: the form is validated, each of the `BindingSources` has been instructed to end the current edit, and then the `UpdateAll` method is called on the `TableAdapterManager`:

VB

```
Private Sub CustomerBindingNavigatorSaveItem_Click(ByVal sender As Object,
                                         ByVal e As System.EventArgs) _
                              Handles CustomerBindingNavigatorSaveItem.Click
    Me.Validate()
    Me.CustomerBindingSource.EndEdit()
    Me.TableAdapterManager.UpdateAll(Me.AdventureWorksLT2008R2DataSet)
End Sub
```

C#

```
private void customerBindingNavigatorSaveItem_Click(object sender, EventArgs e){
    this.Validate();
    this.customerBindingSource.EndEdit();
    this.tableAdapterManager.UpdateAll(this.adventureWorksLT2008R2DataSet);
}
```

This code runs without modification, but it won't update the ModifiedDate field to indicate the Customer information has changed. You need to correct the `Update` method used by the `CustomerTableAdapter` to automatically update the ModifiedDate field. Using the DataSet designer, select the `CustomerTableAdapter`, open the Properties window, expand the UpdateCommand node, and click the ellipsis button next to the CommandText field. This opens the Query Builder dialog that you used earlier. Uncheck the boxes in the Set column for the rowguid row (because this should never be updated). In the New Value column, change `@ModifiedDate` to `getdate()` to automatically set the modified date to the date on which the query was executed. This should give you a query similar to the one shown in Figure 28-11.

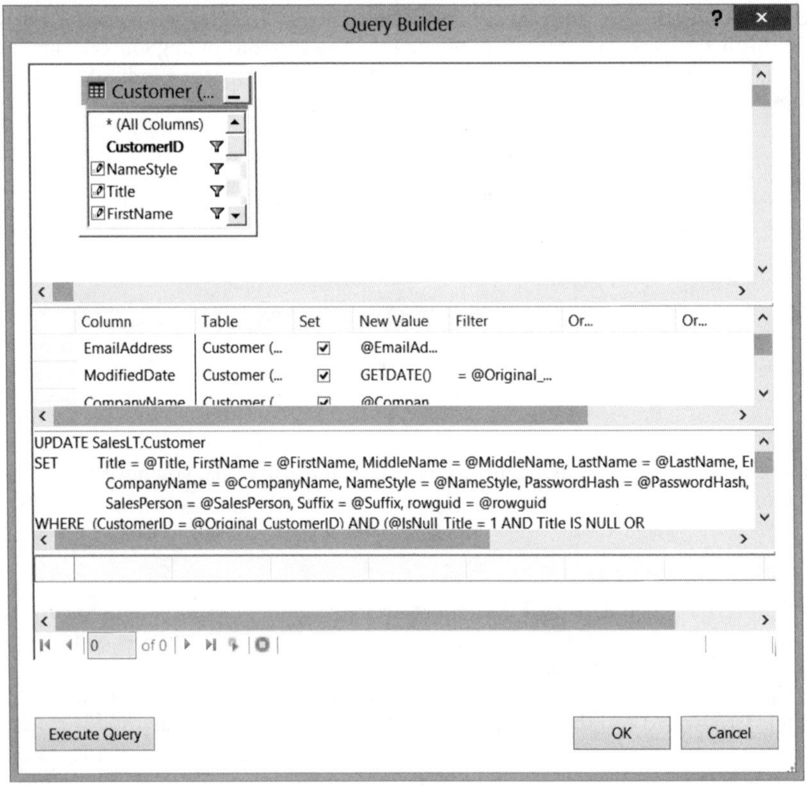

FIGURE 28-11

With this change, when you save a record the ModifiedDate is automatically set to the current date.

Inserting New Items

You now have a sample application that enables you to browse and make changes to an existing set of individual customers. The one missing piece is the capability to create a new customer. By default, the Add button on the `BindingNavigator` is automatically wired up to the `AddNew` method on the `BindingSource`, as shown earlier. In this case, you actually need to set some default values on the record created in the Customer table. To do this, you need to write your own logic behind the Add button.

The first step is to remove the automatic wiring by setting the `AddNewItem` property of the `CustomerBindingNavigator` to `(None)`; otherwise, you end up with two records created every time you click the Add button. Next, double-click the Add button to create an event handler for it. You can then modify the default event handler as follows to set initial values for the new customer, as well as create records in the other two tables:

VB

```
Private Sub BindingNavigatorAddNewItem_Click(ByVal sender As System.Object,
                                              ByVal e As System.EventArgs) _
                                            Handles BindingNavigatorAddNewItem.Click
    Dim drv As DataRowView

    'Create record in the Customer table
    drv = TryCast(Me.CustomerBindingSource.AddNew, DataRowView)
    Dim customer = TryCast(drv.Row, AdventureWorksLT2008R2DataSet.CustomerRow)
    customer.rowguid = Guid.NewGuid
    customer.PasswordHash = String.Empty
    customer.PasswordSalt = String.Empty
    customer.ModifiedDate = Now
    customer.FirstName = "<first name>"
    customer.LastName = "<last name>"
    customer.NameStyle = False
    Me.CustomerBindingSource.EndEdit()
End Sub
```

C#

```
private void bindingNavigatorAddNewItem_Click(object sender, EventArgs e){
    DataRowView drv;

    //Create record in the Customer table
    drv = this.customerBindingSource.AddNew() as DataRowView;
    var customer = drv.Row as AdventureWorksLT2008R2DataSet.CustomerRow;
    customer.rowguid = Guid.NewGuid();
    customer.PasswordHash = String.Empty;
    customer.PasswordSalt = String.Empty;
    customer.ModifiedDate = DateTime.Now;
    customer.FirstName = "<first name>";
    customer.LastName = "<last name>";
    customer.NameStyle = false;
    this.customerBindingSource.EndEdit();
}
```

From this example, it seems that you are unnecessarily setting some of the properties — for example, `PasswordSalt` and `PasswordHash` being equal to an empty string. This is necessary to ensure that the new row meets the constraints established by the database. Because these fields cannot be set by the user, you need to ensure that they are initially set to a value that can be accepted by the database. Clearly, for a secure application, the `PasswordSalt` and `PasswordHash` would be set to appropriate values.

Running the application with this method instead of the automatically wired event handler enables you to create a new Customer record using the Add button. If you enter values for each of the fields, you can save the changes.

Validation

In the previous section, you added functionality to create a new customer record. If you don't enter appropriate data upon creating a new record — for example, if you don't enter a first name — this record will be rejected when you click the Save button. The schema for the `AdventureWorksLT2008R2DataSet` contains a number of constraints, such as `FirstName` can't be null, which are checked when you perform certain actions, such as saving or moving between records. If these checks fail, an exception is raised. You have two options. One, you can trap these exceptions, which is poor programming practice because exceptions should not be used for execution control. Alternatively, you can preempt this by validating the data prior to the schema being checked. Earlier in the chapter, when you learned how the `BindingNavigator` automatically wires the `AddNew` method on the `BindingSource`, you saw that the `OnAddNew` method contains a call to a `Validate` method. This method in turn calls the `Validate` method on the active control, which returns a Boolean value that determines whether the action will proceed. This pattern is used by all the automatically wired events and should be used in the event handlers you write for the navigation buttons.

The `Validate` method on the active control triggers two events — `Validating` and `Validated` — that occur before and after the validation process, respectively. Because you want to control the validation process, add an event handler for the `Validating` event. For example, you could add an event handler for the `Validating` event of the FirstNameTextBox control:

VB

```
Private Sub FirstNameTextBox_Validating(ByVal sender As System.Object, _
                               ByVal e As System.ComponentModel.CancelEventArgs) _
                                                Handles FirstNameTextBox.Validating
        Dim firstNameTxt As TextBox = TryCast(sender, TextBox)
        If firstNameTxt Is Nothing Then Return
        e.Cancel = (firstNameTxt.Text = String.Empty)
End Sub
```

C#

```
private void firstNameTextBox_Validating(object sender, CancelEventArgs e){
    var firstNameTxt = sender as TextBox;
    if (firstNameTxt == null) return;
    e.Cancel = (firstNameTxt.Text == String.Empty);
}
```

Though this prevents users from leaving the textbox until a value has been added, it doesn't give them any idea why the application prevents them from proceeding. Luckily, the .NET Framework includes an ErrorProvider control that can be dragged onto the form from the Toolbox. This control behaves in a manner similar to the tooltip control. For each control on the form, you can specify an Error string, which, when set, causes an icon to appear alongside the relevant control, with a suitable tooltip displaying the Error string. This is illustrated in Figure 28-12, where the Error string is set for the FirstNameTextBox.

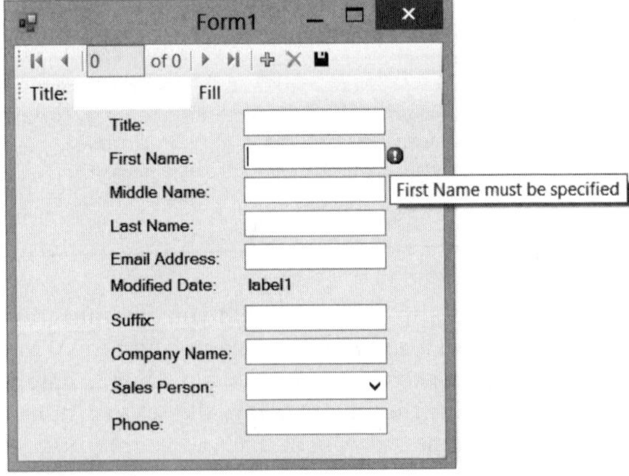

FIGURE 28-12

Clearly, you want to set only the Error string property for the FirstNameTextBox when there is no text. Following from the earlier example in which you added the event handler for the Validating event, you can modify this code to include setting the Error string:

VB

```
Private Sub FirstNameTextBox_Validating(ByVal sender As System.Object, _
                              ByVal e As System.ComponentModel.CancelEventArgs) _
                                          Handles FirstNameTextBox.Validating
    Dim firstNameTxt As TextBox = TryCast(sender, TextBox)
    If firstNameTxt Is Nothing Then Return
    e.Cancel = (firstNameTxt.Text = String.Empty)

    If String.IsNullOrWhiteSpace(firstNameTxt.Text) Then
        Me.ErrorProvider1.SetError(firstNameTxt, "First Name must be specified")
    Else
        Me.ErrorProvider1.SetError(firstNameTxt, Nothing)
    End If
End Sub
```

C#

```
private void firstNameTextBox_Validating(object sender, CancelEventArgs e){
    var firstNameTxt = sender as TextBox;
    if (firstNameTxt == null) return;
    e.Cancel = (firstNameTxt.Text == String.Empty);

    if (String.IsNullOrEmpty(firstNameTxt.Text)){
        this.errorProvider1.SetError(firstNameTxt, "First Name must be specified");
    }
    else{
        this.errorProvider1.SetError(firstNameTxt, null);
    }
}
```

You can imagine that having to write event handlers that validate and set the error information for each of the controls can be quite a lengthy process. Rather than having individual validation event handlers for each control, you may want to rationalize them into a single event handler that delegates the validation to a controller class. This helps ensure your business logic isn't intermingled within your user interface code.

Customized DataSets

At the moment, you have a form that displays some basic information about a customer. However, it is missing some of her address information, namely her Main Office and/or Shipping addresses. If you look at the structure of the AdventureWorksLT2008R2 database, you can notice that there is a many-to-many relationship between the Customer and Address tables, through the CustomerAddress linking table. The CustomerAddress has a column AddressType that indicates the type of address. Although this structure supports the concept that multiple Customers may have the same address, the user interface you have built so far is only interested in the address information for a particular customer. If you simply add all three of these tables to your DataSet, you cannot easily use DataBinding to wire up the user interface. As such it is worth customizing the generated DataSet to merge the CustomerAddress and Address tables into a single entity.

Open up the DataSet designer by double-clicking the `AdventureWorksLT2008R2DataSet.xsd` in the Solution Explorer. Select the AddressTableAdapter, which you should already have from earlier, expand out the SelectCommand property in the Properties tool window, and then click the ellipses next to the CommandText property. This again opens the Query Builder. Currently, you should have only the Address table in the diagram pane. Right-click in that pane, select Add Table, and then select the

CustomerAddress table. Check all fields in the CustomerAddress table except AddressID, and then go to the Criteria pane and change the Alias for the rowguid and ModifiedDate columns coming from the CustomerAddress table. The result should look similar to Figure 28-13.

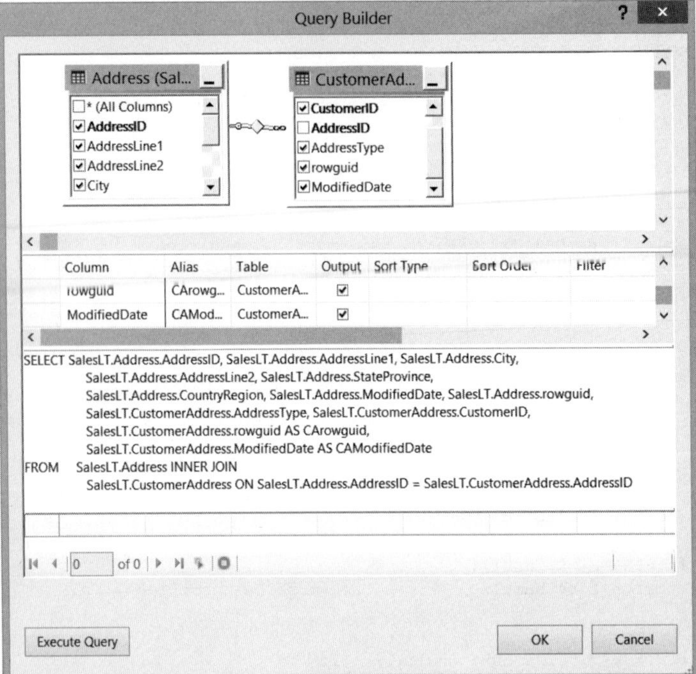

FIGURE 28-13

When you click the OK button, you are prompted to regenerate the `Update` and `Insert` statements. The code generator can't handle multiple table updates so it fails regardless of which option you select. This means that you need to manually define the update, insert, and delete statements. You can do this by defining stored procedures within the AdventureWorksLT2008R2 database and then by updating the CommandType and CommandText for the relevant commands in the AddressTableAdapter, as shown in Figure 28-14.

Now that your DataSet contains both Customer and Address DataTables, the only thing missing is the relationship connecting them. As you have customized the Address DataTable, the designer hasn't automatically created the relationship. To create a relation, right-click anywhere on the DataSet design surface, and select Add ➪ Relation. This opens the Relation dialog, as shown in Figure 28-15.

FIGURE 28-14

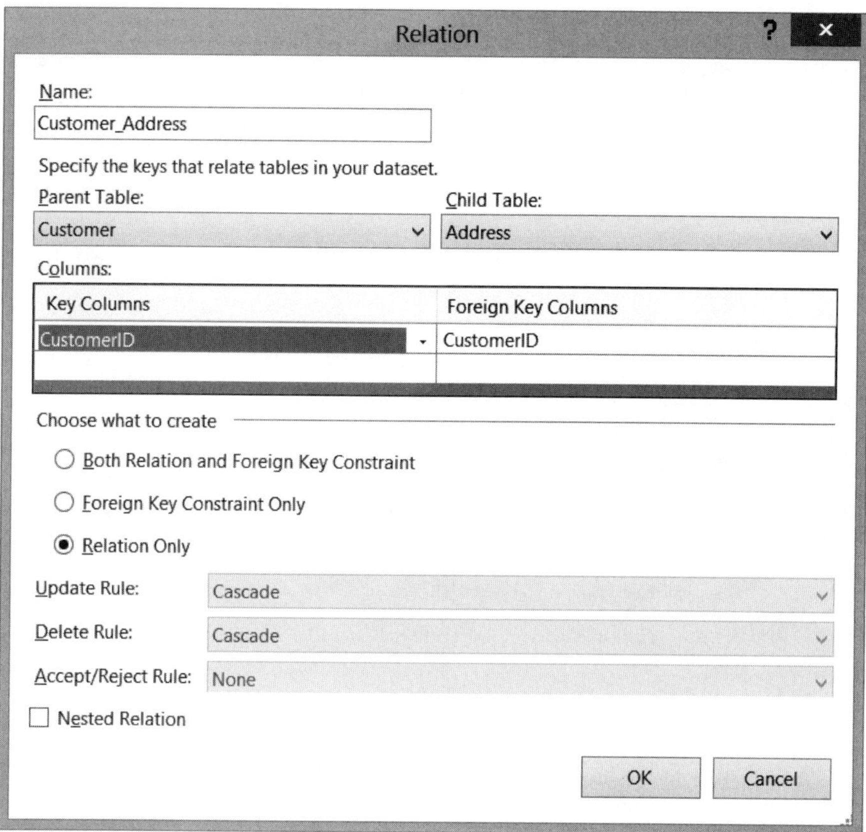

FIGURE 28-15

In accordance with the way the Address DataTable has been created by combining the CustomerAddress and Address tables, make the Customer DataTable the parent and the Address the child. When you accept this dialog, you can see a relationship line connecting the two DataTables on the DataSet design surface.

BindingSource Chains and the DataGridView

After completing the setup of the DataSet with the Customer and Address DataTables you are ready to data bind the Address table to your user interface. So far you've been working with simple input controls such as textboxes, drop-down lists, and labels, and you've seen how the BindingNavigator enables you to scroll through a list of items. Sometimes it is more convenient to display a list of items in a grid. This is where the DataGridView is useful because it enables you to combine the power of the BindingSource with a grid layout.

In this example, you extend the Customer Management interface by adding address information using a DataGridView. Returning to the Data Sources window, select the Address node from under the Customer node. From the drop-down list, select DataGridView and drag the node into an empty area on the form. This adds the appropriate BindingSource and TableAdapter to the form, as well as a DataGridView showing each of the columns in the Address table, as shown in Figure 28-16.

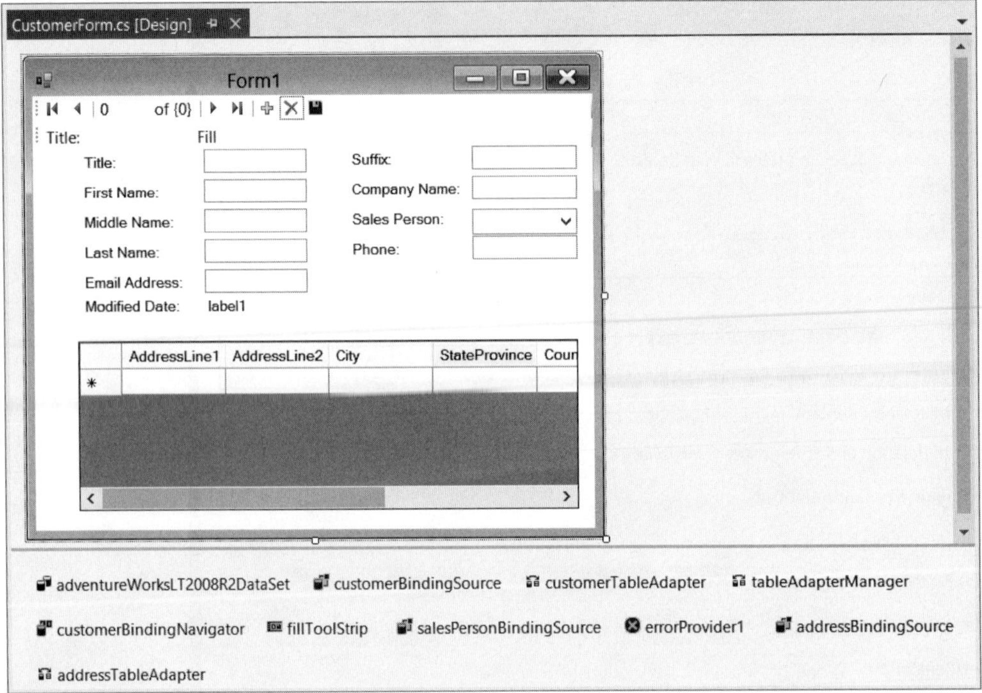

FIGURE 28-16

If you recall from earlier, the CustomerBindingSource has the AdventureWorksLT2008R2DataSet as its DataSource, with the Customer table set as the DataMember. This means that controls that are data bound using the CustomerBindingSource are binding to a field in the Customer table. If you look at the AddressBindingSource, you can see that its DataSource is actually the CustomerBindingSource, with its DataMember set to Customer_Address, which is the relationship you created between the two DataTables. As you would expect, any control being data bound using the AddressBindingSource is binding to a field in the Address table. However, the difference is that unlike the CustomerBindingSource, which returns all Customers, the AddressBindingSource is only populated with the Addresses associated with the currently selected Customer.

Unlike working with the Details layout, when you drag the DataGridView onto the form, it ignores any settings you might have specified for the individual columns. Instead, every column is added to the grid as a simple text field. To modify the list of columns that are displayed, you can either use the smart tag for the newly added DataGridView or select Edit Columns from the right-click context menu. This opens the Edit Columns dialog (shown in Figure 28-17), in which columns can be added, removed, and reordered.

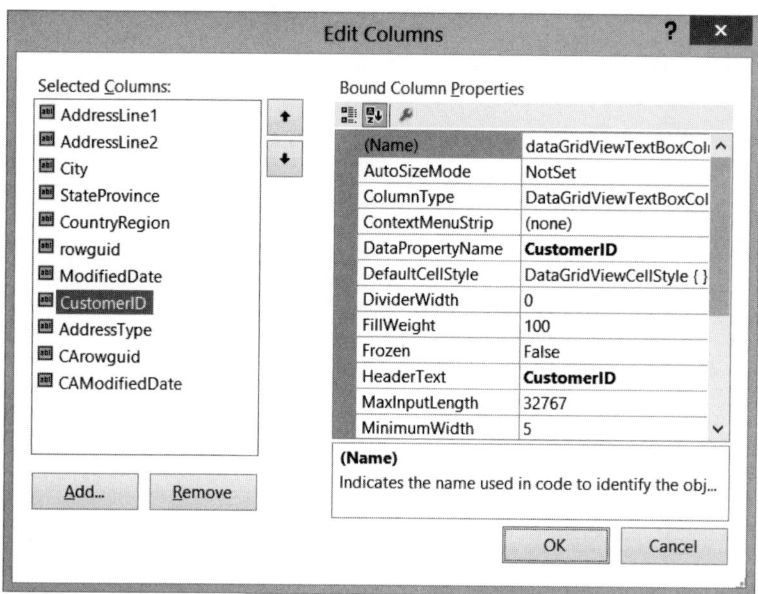

FIGURE 28-17

After specifying the appropriate columns, the finished application can be run, and the list of orders are visible for each customer in the database.

WORKING WITH DATA SOURCES

In this chapter you have been working with a strongly typed DataSet that contains a number of rows from the Customer table, based on a `Title` parameter. So far the example has had only one tier, which is the Windows Forms application. In this section you see how you can use Visual Studio 2012 to build a multitier application.

Start by creating two new projects, CustomerBrowser (Windows Forms Application) and CustomerService (WCF Service Application). In the CustomerBrowser project, add a reference to the CustomerObjects project that you had been working on in this chapter. Yes, they are both Windows Forms applications, but that doesn't mean that the classes contained therein cannot be included in another project.

In the CustomerService project, add a reference to the CustomerObjects project. Also change the name of the `Service1.svc` and `IService1` class files to `CustomerService.svc` and `ICustomerService`, respectively. This seemingly minor change (especially because Visual Studio has had a rename feature for a while) requires one more step to be complete. Open up the `CustomerService.svc` file as markup. (Right-click the file in the Solution Explorer and select View Markup.) Then change the Service attribute to `CustomerService.CustomerService`.

To get the service functioning as wanted, there are two steps. First, the interface implemented by the service needs to be updated to support retrieving and saving customers. In the `ICustomerService` file, replace the default `GetData` and `GetDataUsingDataContract` methods with `RetrieveCustomers` and `SaveCustomers`:

VB

```
Imports CustomerObjects

<ServiceContract()>
Public Interface ICustomerService
```

```
        <OperationContract()>
        Function RetrieveCustomers(ByVal Title As String) As _
            AdventureWorksLT2008R2DataSet.CustomerDataTable

        <OperationContract()>
        Sub SaveCustomers(ByVal changes As Data.DataSet)

    End Interface
```

C#

```
using CustomerObjects;

namespace CustomerService {
   [ServiceContract]
   public interface ICustomerService
   {
      [OperationContract]
      AdventureWorksLT2008R2DataSet.CustomerDataTable RetrieveCustomers(string Title);

      [OperationContract]
      void SaveCustomers(Data.DataSet changes);
   }
}
```

The second step involves creating an implementation for the methods described in the interface. Right-click the `CustomerService.svc` file and select View Code. Then change the code in the class so that it resembles the following:

VB

```
Imports CustomerObjects

Imports CustomerObjects

Public Class CustomerService
    Implements ICustomerService

    Public Function RetrieveCustomers(ByVal Title As String) _
        As AdventureWorksLT2008R2DataSet.CustomerDataTable Implements _
           ICustomerService.RetrieveCustomers
        Dim ta As New AdventureWorksLT2008R2DataSetTableAdapters.CustomerTableAdapter
        Return ta.GetData(Title)
    End Function

    Public Sub SaveCustomers(ByVal changes As Data.DataSet) Implements _
        ICustomerService.SaveCustomers
        Dim changesTable As Data.DataTable = changes.Tables("Customer")
        Dim ta As New AdventureWorksLT2008R2DataSetTableAdapters.CustomerTableAdapter
        ta.Update(changesTable.Select)
    End Sub

End Class
```

C#

```
using CustomerObjects;

namespace CustomerService {
   public class CustomerService : ICustomerService

   public AdventureWorksLT2008R2DataSet.CustomerDataTable RetrieveCustomers(string Title)
```

```
        {
            var ta = new AdventureWorksLT2008R2DataSetTableAdapters.CustomerTableAdapter();
            return ta.GetData(Title);
        }

        public void SaveCustomers(Data.DataSet changes)
        {
            var changesTable = changes.Tables("Customer");
            var ta = new AdventureWorksLT2008R2DataSetTableAdapters.CustomerTableAdapter();
            ta.Update(changesTable.Select);
        }
    }
```

The first method, as the name suggests, retrieves the list of customers based on the `Title` that is passed in. In this method, you create a new instance of the strongly typed TableAdapter and return the DataTable retrieved by the `GetData` method. The second method saves changes to a DataTable, again using the strongly typed TableAdapter. The DataSet passed in as a parameter to this method is not strongly typed. Unfortunately, the generated strongly typed DataSet doesn't provide a strongly typed `GetChanges` method, which is used later to generate a DataSet containing only data that has changed. This new DataSet is passed into the `SaveCustomers` method so that only changed data needs to be sent to the web service.

The Web Service Data Source

These changes to the WCF service complete the server side of the process, but your application still doesn't have access to this data. To access the data from your application, you need to add a data source to the application. Again, use the Add New Data Source Wizard, but this time select Service from the Data Source Type screen. Because the service is in the same project, click the Discover button. This launches the WCF service (behind the scenes) and displays CustomerService in the list of services. Change the namespace to CustomerService (see Figure 28-18) and click OK to add the reference.

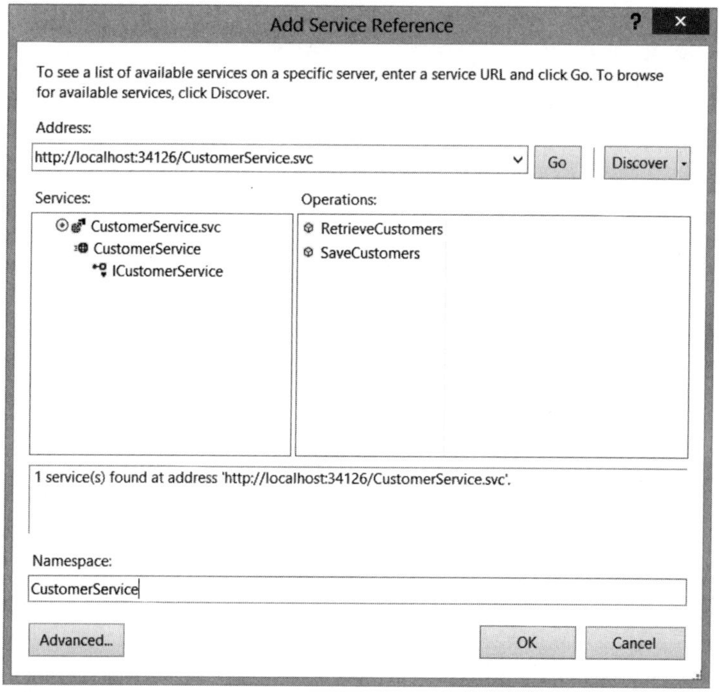

FIGURE 28-18

> **NOTE** *For you to add a service reference, the service application needs to be running. This means that the service project will be built and any compilation errors will stop this process from working.*

There is one additional step that is required due to the amount of data retrieved by the service. WCF has a default limit of 64 KB for the size of the returned message. However, given the number of customers, 64 KB is not sufficient to populate our list. To increase this default, open the `app.config` file in the CustomerBrowser project and locate the `binding` element. Add an appropriately large value for the `maxReceivedMessageSize` attribute, as shown below, to correct this potential problem.

```
<binding name="BasicHttpBinding_ICustomerService"
    maxReceivedMessageSize="2000000000"/>
```

Click the OK button to add an AdventureWorksLT2008R2DataSet to the Data Sources window under the CustomerService node. Examine the generated code and you can see that the data source is similar to the data source you had in the class library.

Browsing Data

To actually view the data being returned via the web service, you need to add some controls to your form. Open the form so that the designer appears in the main window. In the Data Sources window, click the Customer node, and select Details from the drop-down. This indicates that when you drag the Customer node onto the form, Visual Studio 2012 creates controls to display the details of the Customer table (for example, the row contents), instead of the default DataGridView. Next, select the attributes you want to display by clicking them and selecting the control type to use. When you drag the Customer node onto the form, you should have a layout similar to Figure 28-19.

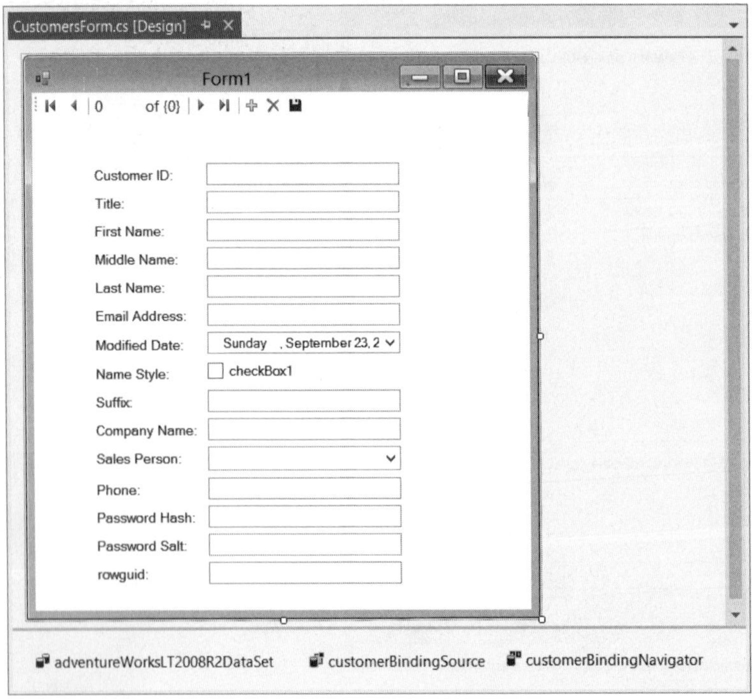

FIGURE 28-19

In addition to adding controls for the information to be displayed and edited, a Navigator control has also been added to the top of the form, and an `AdventureWorksLT2008R2DataSet` and a `CustomerBindingSource` have been added to the nonvisual area of the form.

The final stage is to wire up the `Load` event of the form to retrieve data from the web service and to add the Save button on the navigator to save changes. Right-click the save icon, and select Enabled to enable the Save button on the navigator control; then double-click the save icon to generate the stub event handler. Add the following code to load data and save changes via the web service you created earlier:

VB

```
Public Class CustomerForm
    Private Sub CustomerForm_Load(ByVal sender As System.Object,
                                  ByVal e As System.EventArgs) Handles Me.Load
        Me.CustomerBindingSource.DataSource = _
                 My.WebServices.CustomerService.RetrieveCustomers("%mr%")
    End Sub

    Private Sub CustomerBindingNavigatorSaveItem_Click _
                               (ByVal sender As System.Object,
                                ByVal e As System.EventArgs)
                                 Handles CustomerBindingNavigatorSaveItem.Click
        Me.CustomerBindingSource.EndEdit()
        Dim ds = CType(Me.CustomerBindingSource.DataSource,  _
                  CustomerService.AdventureWorksLT2008R2DataSet.CustomerDataTable)
        Dim changesTable As DataTable = ds.GetChanges()
        Dim changes As New DataSet
        changes.Tables.Add(changesTable)
        My.WebServices.CustomerService.SaveCustomers(changes)
    End Sub
End Class
```

C#

```
private void CustomersForm_Load(object sender, EventArgs e){
    var service = new CustomerService.CustomerService();
    this.CustomerBindingSource.DataSource = service.RetrieveCustomers("%mr%"); ;
}

private void CustomerBindingNavigatorSaveItem_Click(object sender, EventArgs e){
    this.CustomerBindingSource.EndEdit();
    var ds = this.CustomerBindingSource.DataSource
                  as CustomerService.AdventureWorksLT2008R2DataSet.CustomerDataTable;
    var changesTable = ds.GetChanges();
    var changes = new DataSet();
    changes.Tables.Add(changesTable);
    var service = new CustomerService.CustomerService();
    service.SaveCustomers(changes);
}
```

To retrieve the list of customers from the web service, all you need to do is call the appropriate web method — in this case, `RetrieveCustomers`. Pass in a parameter of `%mr%`, which indicates that only customers with a Title containing the letters "mr" should be returned. The `Save` method is slightly more complex because you have to end the current edit (to make sure all changes are saved), retrieve the DataTable, and then extract the changes as a new DataTable. Although it would be simpler to pass a DataTable to the SaveCustomers web service, only DataSets can be specified as parameters or return values to a web service. As such, you can create a new DataSet and add the changed DataTable to the list of tables. The new DataSet is then passed into the `SaveCustomers` method. As mentioned previously, the `GetChanges` method returns a raw DataTable, which is unfortunate because it limits the strongly typed data scenario.

This completes the chapter's coverage of the strongly typed DataSet scenario and provides you with a two-tiered solution to access and edit data from a database via a web service interface.

SUMMARY

This chapter provided an introduction to working with strongly typed DataSets. Support within Visual Studio 2012 for creating and working with strongly typed DataSets simplifies the rapid building of applications. This is clearly the first step in the process to bridge the gap between the object-oriented programming world and the relational world in which the data is stored.

Hopefully, this chapter has given you an appreciation for how the `BindingSource`, `BindingNavigator`, and other data controls work together to give you the ability to rapidly build data applications. Because the controls support working with either DataSets or your own custom objects, they can significantly reduce the amount of time it takes you to write an application.

29

Language Integrated Queries (LINQ)

WHAT'S IN THIS CHAPTER?

- Querying objects with LINQ
- Writing and querying XML with XLINQ
- Querying and updating data with LINQ to SQL

Language Integrated Queries (LINQ) was designed to provide a common programming model for querying data. In this chapter you see how you can take some verbose, imperative code and reduce it to a few declarative lines. This enables you to make your code more descriptive rather than prescriptive; that is, describing what you want to occur, rather than detailing how it should be done.

Although LINQ provides an easy way to filter, sort, and project from an in-memory object graph, it is more common for the data source to be either a database or a file type, such as XML. In this chapter you are introduced to LINQ to XML, which makes working with XML data dramatically simpler than with traditional methods such as using the document object model, XSLT, or XPath. You also learn how to use LINQ to SQL to work with traditional databases, such as SQL Server, enabling you to write LINQ statements that can query the database, pull back the appropriate data, and populate .NET objects that you can work with. In Chapter 30, "The ADO.NET Entity Framework," you are introduced to the ADO.NET Entity Framework for which there is also a LINQ provider. This means that you can combine the power of declarative queries with the fidelity of the Entity Framework to manage your data object life cycle.

LINQ PROVIDERS

One of the key tenets of LINQ is the capability to abstract away the query syntax from the underlying data store. LINQ sits behind the various .NET languages such as C# and VB and combines various language features, such as extension methods, type inferences, anonymous types, and Lambda expressions, to provide a uniform syntax for querying data.

A number of LINQ-enabled data sources come with Visual Studio 2012 and the .NET Framework 4.5: Objects, DataSets, SQL, Entities, and XML; each with its own LINQ provider that can query the corresponding data source. LINQ is not limited to just these data sources, and providers are available for querying all sorts of other data sources. For example, there is a LINQ provider for querying SharePoint. In fact, the documentation that ships with Visual Studio 2012 includes a walkthrough on creating your own LINQ provider.

In this chapter you see some of the standard LINQ operations as they apply to standard .NET objects. You then see how these same queries can be applied to both XML and SQL data sources. The syntax for querying the data remains constant with only the underlying data source changing.

OLD-SCHOOL QUERIES

Instead of walking through exactly what LINQ is, this section starts with an example that demonstrates some of the savings that these queries offer. The scenario is one in which a researcher investigates whether there is a correlation between the length of a customer's name and the customer's average order size by analyzing a collection of customer objects. The relationship between a customer and the orders is a simple one-to-many relationship, as shown in Figure 29-1.

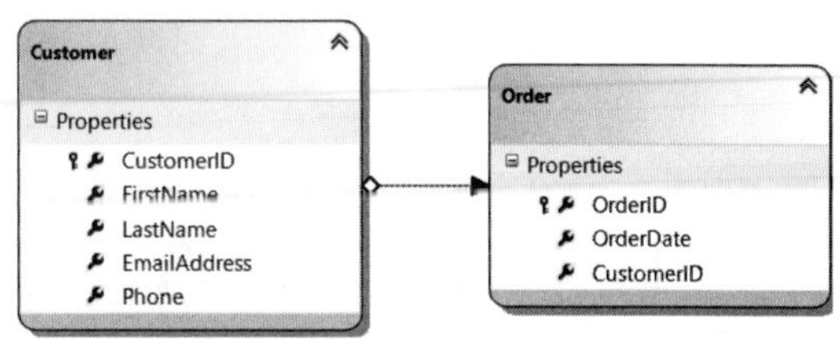

FIGURE 29-1

In the particular query you examine, the researchers look for the average Milk order for customers with a first name greater than or equal to five characters, ordered by the first name:

C#

```
private void OldStyleQuery(){
    Customer[] customers = BuildCustomers();
    List<SearchResult> results = new List<SearchResult>();
    SearchForProduct matcher = new SearchForProduct() { Product = "Milk" };
    foreach (Customer c in customers){
        if (c.FirstName.Length >= 5){
            Order[] orders = Array.FindAll(c.Orders, matcher.ProductMatch);
            if (orders.Length > 0){
                SearchResult cr = new SearchResult();
                cr.Customer = c.FirstName + " " + c.LastName;
                foreach (Order o in orders){
                    cr.Quantity += o.Quantity;
                    cr.Count++;
                }
                results.Add(cr);
            }
        }
    }
    results.Sort(CompareSearchResults);
    ObjectDumper.Write(results, Writer);
}
```

VB

```
Private Sub OldStyleQuery()
    Dim customers As Customer() = BuildCustomers()

    Dim results As New List(Of SearchResult)
    Dim matcher As New SearchForProduct() With {.Product = "Milk"}

    For Each c As Customer In customers
        If c.FirstName.Length >= 5 Then
```

```
            Dim orders As Order() = Array.FindAll(c.Orders, _
                                        AddressOf matcher.ProductMatch)
            If orders.Length > 0 Then
                Dim cr As New SearchResult
                cr.Customer = c.FirstName & " " & c.LastName
                For Each o As Order In orders
                    cr.Quantity += o.Quantity
                    cr.Count += 1
                Next
                results.Add(cr)
             End If
         End If
    Next
    results.Sort(AddressOf CompareSearchResults)

    ObjectDumper.Write(results, Writer)
End Sub
```

Before jumping in and seeing how LINQ can improve this snippet, examine how this snippet works. The opening line calls out to a method that simply generates `Customer` objects. This is used throughout the snippets in this chapter. The main loop in this method iterates through the array of customers searching for those customers with a first name longer than five characters. Upon finding such a customer, you use the `Array.FindAll` method to retrieve all orders where the predicate is true. Prior to the introduction of anonymous methods, you couldn't supply the predicate function inline with the method. As a result, the usual way to do this was to create a simple class that could hold the query variable (in this case, the product, Milk) that you were searching for, and that had a method that accepted the type of object you were searching through, in this case an `Order`. With the use of Lambda expressions, you can rewrite this line:

C#

```
var orders = Array.FindAll(c.Orders, order=>order.Product =="Milk");
```

VB

```
Dim orders = Array.FindAll(c.Orders,
                           Function(o As Order) o.Product = "Milk")
```

Here you have also taken advantage of type inferencing to determine the type of the variable orders, which is of course still an array of orders.

Returning to the snippet, after you locate the orders, you still need to iterate through them and sum up the quantity ordered and store this, along with the name of the customer and the number of orders. This is your search result; as you can see you use a `SearchResult` object to store this information. For convenience, the `SearchResult` object also has a read-only `Average` property, which simply divides the total quantity ordered by the number of orders. Because you want to sort the customer list, you use the `Sort` method on the `List` class, passing in the address of a comparison method. Again, using Lambda expressions, this can be rewritten as an inline statement:

C#

```
results.Sort((r1, r2) => string.Compare(r1.Customer, r2.Customer));
```

VB

```
results.Sort( Function(r1 as SearchResult, r2 as SearchResult) _
                                  String.Compare(r1.Customer, r2.Customer))
```

The last part of this snippet is to print out the search results. This is using one of the samples that ships with Visual Studio 2012 called `ObjectDumper`. This is a simple class that iterates through a collection of objects printing out the values of the public properties. In this case the output would look like Figure 29-2.

As you can see from this relatively simple query, the code to do this in the past was quite prescriptive and required additional classes to carry out the query logic and return the results. With the power of LINQ, you can build a single expression that clearly describes what the search results should be.

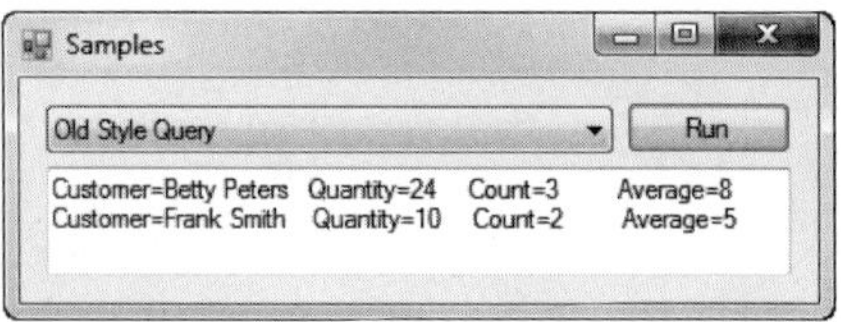

FIGURE 29-2

QUERY PIECES

This section introduces you to a number of the query operations that make up the basis of LINQ. If you have written SQL statements, these will feel familiar, although the ordering and syntax might take a little time to get used to. You can use a number of query operations, and numerous reference websites provide more information on how to use them. For the moment, focus on those operations necessary to improve the search query introduced at the beginning of this chapter.

From

Unlike SQL, where the first statement is `Select`, in LINQ the first statement is typically `From`. One of the key considerations in the creation of LINQ was providing IntelliSense support within Visual Studio. As you can see from the tooltip in Figure 29-3, the `From` statement consists of two parts, `<element>` and `<collection>`. The latter is the source collection from which you extract data, and the former is essentially an iteration variable that can be used to refer to the items being queried. This pair can then be repeated for each source collection.

```
Private Sub LinqQueryFromOnly()
    Dim customers = BuildCustomers()

    Dim results = From c In customers, o In c.Orders
                  From <element> In <collection>[, <element2> in <collection2>][, ...]
    ObjectDumper.Write(results, 1, Writer)
End Sub
```

FIGURE 29-3

In this case you can see you query the customer's collection, with an iteration variable `c`, and the orders collection `c.Orders` using the iteration variable `o`. There is an implicit join between the two source collections because of the relationship between a customer and that customer's orders. As you can imagine, this query results in the cross-product of items in each source collection. This leads to the pairing of a customer with each order that this customer has.

You don't have a `Select` statement because you are simply going to return all elements, but what does each result record look like? If you were to look at the tooltip for results, you would see that it is a generic IEnumerable of an anonymous type. The anonymous type feature is heavily used in LINQ so that you don't have to create classes for every result. If you recall from the initial code, you had to have a `SearchResult` class to capture each of the results. Anonymous types mean that you no longer need to create a class to store the results. During compilation, types containing the relevant properties are dynamically created, thereby giving you a strongly typed result set along with IntelliSense support. Though the tooltip for results may report only that it is an IEnumerable of an anonymous type, when you start to use the results collection, you see that the type has two properties, `c` and `o`, of type Customer and Order, respectively. Figure 29-4 displays the output of this code, showing the customer-order pairs.

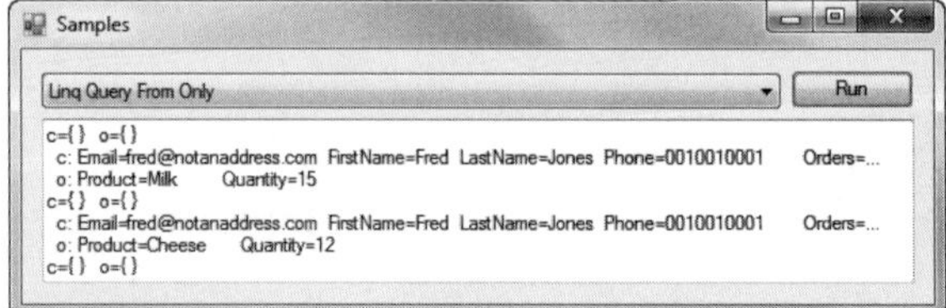

FIGURE 29-4

> **NOTE** *C# actually requires a* `Select` *clause to be present in all LINQ, even if you return all objects in the* `From` *clause.*

Select

In the previous code snippet, the result set was a collection of customer-order pairs, when what you want to return is the customer name and the order information. You can do this by using a `Select` statement in a way similar to the way you would when writing a SQL statement:

C#

```
private void LinqQueryWithSelect(){
    var customers = BuildCustomers();
    var results = from c in customers
                  from o in c.Orders
                  select new{c.FirstName,
                             c.LastName,o.Product,o.Quantity};
    ObjectDumper.Write(results, Writer);
}
```

VB

```
Private Sub LinqQueryWithSelect()
    Dim customers = BuildCustomers()

    Dim results = From c In customers, o In c.Orders
                  Select c.FirstName, c.LastName, o.Product, o.Quantity

    ObjectDumper.Write(results, Writer)
End Sub
```

Now when you execute this code, the result set is a collection of objects that have `FirstName`, `LastName`, `Product`, and `Quantity` properties. This is illustrated in the output shown in Figure 29-5.

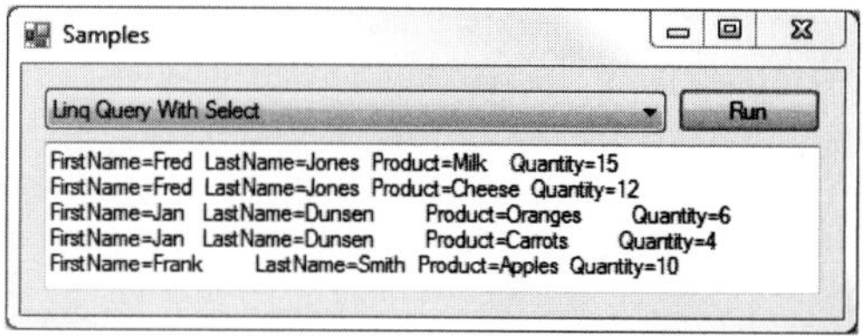

FIGURE 29-5

Where

So far all you have seen is how you can effectively flatten the customer-order hierarchy into a result set containing the appropriate properties. What you haven't done is filter these results so that they return only customers with a first name greater than or equal to five characters and who are ordering Milk. The following snippet introduces a `Where` statement, which restricts the source collections on both these axes:

C#

```
private void LinqQueryWithWhere(){
    var customers = BuildCustomers();

    var results = from c in customers
                  from o in c.Orders
                  where c.FirstName.Length >= 5 &&
                        o.Product == "Milk"
                  select new { c.FirstName, c.LastName, o.Product, o.Quantity };

    ObjectDumper.Write(results, Writer);
}
```

VB

```
Private Sub LinqQueryWithWhere()
    Dim customers = BuildCustomers()

    Dim results = From c In customers, o In c.Orders
                  Where c.FirstName.Length >= 5 And
                        o.Product = "Milk"
                  Select c.FirstName, c.LastName, o.Product, o.Quantity

    ObjectDumper.Write(results, Writer)
End Sub
```

The output of this query is similar to the previous one in that it is a result set of an anonymous type with the four properties `FirstName`, `LastName`, `Product`, and `Quantity`.

Group By

You are getting close to your initial query, except that your current query returns a list of all the Milk orders for all the customers. For a customer who might have placed two orders for Milk, this results in two records in the result set. What you actually want to do is to group these orders by customer and take an average of the quantities ordered. Not surprisingly, this is done with a `Group By` statement, as shown in the following snippet:

C#

```
private void LinqQueryWithGroupingAndWhere(){
    var customers = BuildCustomers();

    var results = from c in customers
                  from o in c.Orders
                  where c.FirstName.Length >= 5 &&
                        o.Product == "Milk"
                  group o by c into avg
                  select new { avg.Key.FirstName, avg.Key.LastName,
                               avg = avg.Average(o => o.Quantity) };
    ObjectDumper.Write(results, Writer);
}
```

VB

```
Private Sub LinqQueryWithGroupingAndWhere()
    Dim customers = BuildCustomers()

    Dim results = From c In customers, o In c.Orders _
                  Where c.FirstName.Length >= 5 And _
                        o.Product = "Milk" _
                  Group By c Into avg = Average(o.Quantity) _
                  Select c.FirstName, c.LastName, avg

    ObjectDumper.Write(results)
End Sub
```

What is a little confusing about the `Group By` statement is the syntax that it uses. Essentially, what it is saying is "group by dimension X" and place the results "Into" an alias that can be used elsewhere. In this case the alias is `avg`, which contains the average you are interested in. Because you group by the iteration variable `c`, you can still use this in the `Select` statement, along with the `Group By` alias. The C# example is slightly different in that although the grouping is still done on `c`, you then must access it via the `Key` property of the alias. Now when you run this, you get the output shown in Figure 29-6, which is much closer to your initial query.

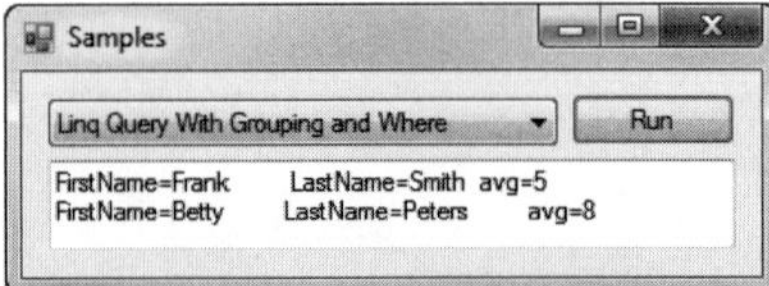

FIGURE 29-6

Custom Projections

You still need to tidy up the output so that you return a well-formatted customer name and an appropriately named average property, instead of the query results, `FirstName`, `LastName`, and `avg`. You can do this by customizing the properties contained in the anonymous type created as part of the `Select` statement projection. Figure 29-7 shows how you can create anonymous types with named properties.

```
Dim results = From c In customers, o In c.Orders
              Where c.FirstName.Length >= 5 And
                    o.Product = "Milk"
              Group By c Into avg = Average(o.Quantity)
              Select New With {.Name = c.FirstName & " " & c.LastName, .AverageMilkOrder = avg}

For Each cust In results
    cust.
Next     AverageMilkOrder   Public Property AverageMilkOrder As Double
         Name
         Common | All
```

FIGURE 29-7

This figure also illustrates that the type of the `AverageMilkOrder` property is indeed a Double, which is what you would expect based on the use of the `Average` function. It is this strongly typed behavior that can assist you in the creation and use of rich LINQ statements.

Order By

The last thing you have to do with the LINQ statement is to order the results. You can do this by ordering the customers based on their `FirstName` property, as shown in the following snippet:

C#

```
private void LinqQueryWithGroupingAndWhere(){
    var customers = BuildCustomers();

    var results = from c in customers
                  from o in c.Orders
                  orderby c.FirstName
                  where c.FirstName.Length >= 5 &&
                        o.Product == "Milk"
                  group o by c into avg
                  select new { Name = avg.Key.FirstName + " " + avg.Key.LastName,
                               AverageMilkOrder = avg.Average(o => o.Quantity) };
    ObjectDumper.Write(results, Writer);
}
```

VB

```
Private Sub FinalLinqQuery()
    Dim customers = BuildCustomers()

    Dim results = From c In customers, o In c.Orders
                  Order By c.FirstName
                  Where c.FirstName.Length >= 5 And
                        o.Product = "Milk
                  Group By c Into avg = Average(o.Quantity)
                  Select New With {.Name = c.FirstName & " " & c.LastName,
                                   .AverageMilkOrder = avg}

    ObjectDumper.Write(results)
End Sub
```

One thing to be aware of is how you can easily reverse the order of the query results. Here you can do this either by supplying the keyword `Descending` (`Ascending` is the default) at the end of the `Order By` statement, or by applying the `Reverse` transformation on the entire result set:

```
Order By c.FirstName Descending
```

or

```
ObjectDumper.Write(results.Reverse)
```

As you can see from the final query you have built up, it is much more descriptive than the initial query. You can easily see that you are selecting the customer name and an average of the order quantities. It is clear that you are filtering based on the length of the customer name and on orders for Milk, and that the results are sorted by the customer's first name. You also haven't needed to create any additional classes to help perform this query.

DEBUGGING AND EXECUTION

One of the things you should be aware of with LINQ is that the queries are not executed until they are used. Each time you use a LINQ query you find that the query is re-executed. This can potentially lead to some issues in debugging and some unexpected performance issues if you execute the query multiple times. In the code you have seen so far, you have declared the LINQ statement and then passed the results object to the `ObjectDumper`, which in turn iterates through the query results. If you were to repeat this call to the `ObjectDumper`, it would again iterate through the results.

Unfortunately, this delayed execution can mean that LINQ statements are hard to debug. If you select the statement and insert a breakpoint, all that happens is that the application stops where you have declared the LINQ statement. If you step to the next line, the results object simply states that it is an In-Memory Query. In C# the debugging story is slightly better because you can actually set breakpoints within the LINQ statement. As you can see from Figure 29-8, the breakpoint on the conditional statement has been hit. From the call stack you can see that the current execution point is no longer actually in the `FinalQuery` method; it is within the `ObjectDumper.Write` method.

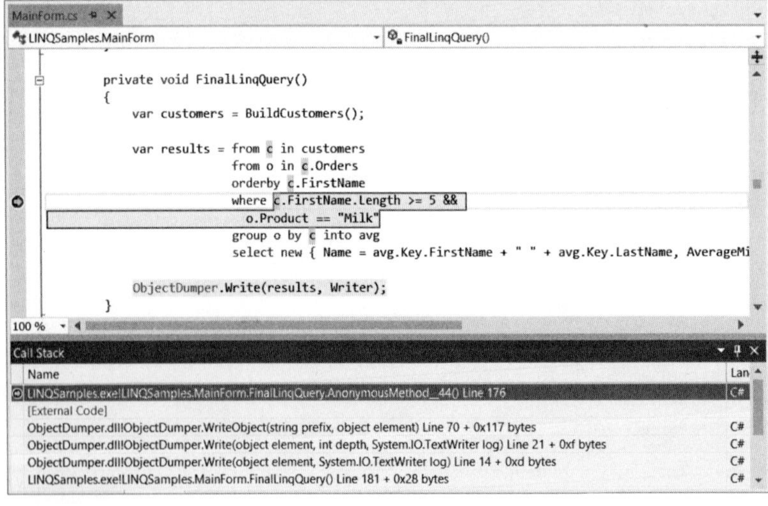

FIGURE 29-8

If you need to force the execution of a LINQ, you can call `ToArray` or `ToList` on the results object. This forces the query to execute, returning an Array or List of the appropriate type. You can then use this array in other queries, reducing the need for the LINQ to be executed multiple times.

> **NOTE** *When setting a breakpoint within a LINQ in C#, you need to place the cursor at the point you want the breakpoint to be set and press F9 (or use the right-click context menu to set a breakpoint), rather than clicking in the margin. Clicking in the margin sets a breakpoint on the whole LINQ statement, which is generally not what you want.*

LINQ TO XML

If you have ever worked with XML in .NET, you might recall that the object model isn't as easy to work with as you would imagine. For example, to create even a single XML element, you need to have an `XmlDocument`:

```
Dim x as New XmlDocument
x.AppendChild(x.CreateElement("Customer"))
```

As you see when you start to use LINQ to query and build XML, this object model doesn't allow for the inline creation of elements. To this end, an XML object model was created that resides in the `System.Xml.Linq` assembly, as shown in Figure 29-9.

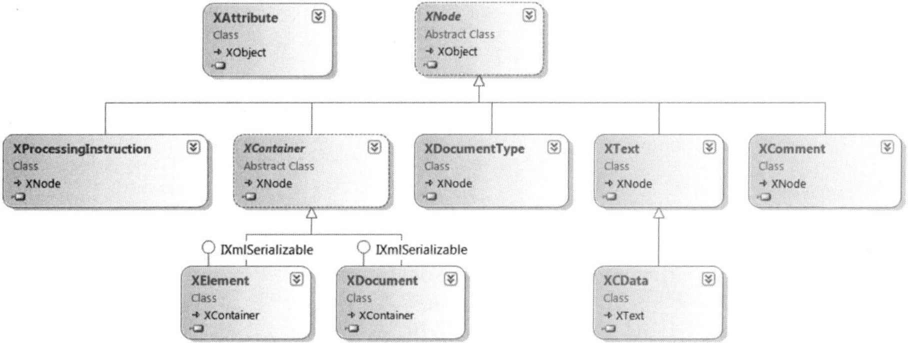

FIGURE 29-9

There are classes that correspond to the relevant parts of an XML document: `XComment`, `XAttribute`, and `XElement` (refer to Figure 29-9). The biggest improvement is that most of the classes can be instantiated by means of a constructor that accepts `Name` and `Content` parameters. In the following C# code, you can see that an element called `Customers` has been created that contains a single `Customer` element. This element, in turn, accepts an attribute, Name, and a series of `Order` elements.

C#

```
XElement x = new XElement("Customers",
                          new XElement("Customer",
                                       new XAttribute("Name","Bob Jones"),
                                       new XElement("Order",
                                             new XAttribute("Product", "Milk"),
                                             new XAttribute("Quantity", 2)),
                                       new XElement("Order",
```

```
                                new XAttribute("Product", "Bread"),
                                new XAttribute("Quantity", 10)),
                        new XElement("Order",
                                new XAttribute("Product", "Apples"),
                                new XAttribute("Quantity", 5))
                            )
            );
```

Though this code snippet is quite verbose and it's hard to distinguish the actual XML data from the surrounding .NET code, it is significantly better than with the old XML object model, which required elements to be individually created and then added to the parent node.

> **NOTE** *While you can write the same code in VB using the* `XElement` *and* `XAttribute` *constructors, the support for XML literals (as discussed in the next section) makes this capability redundant.*

VB XML Literals

One of the biggest innovations in the VB language is the support for XML literals. As with strings and integers, an XML literal is treated as a first-class citizen when you write code. The following snippet illustrates the same XML generated by the previous C# snippet as it would appear using an XML literal in VB:

VB

```
Dim cust = <Customers>
               <Customer Name="Bob Jones">
                   <Order Product="Milk" Quantity="2"/>
                   <Order Product="Bread" Quantity="10"/>
                   <Order Product="Apples" Quantity="5"/>
               </Customer>
           </Customers>
```

Not only do you have the ability to assign an XML literal in code, you also get designer support for creating and working with your XML. For example, when you enter the > on a new element, it automatically creates the closing XML tag for you. Figure 29-10 illustrates how the `Customers` XML literal can be condensed in the same way as other code blocks in Visual Studio 2012.

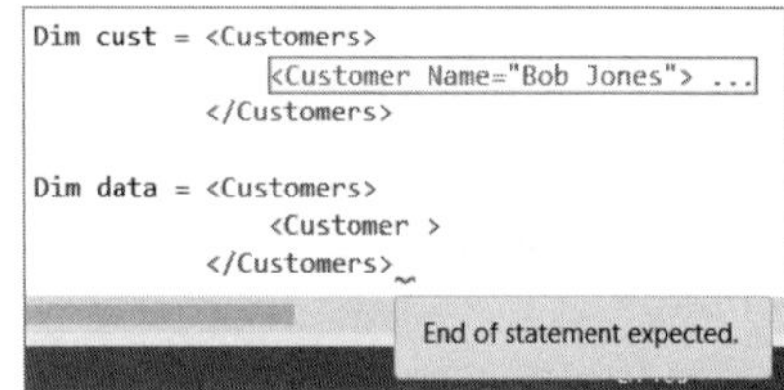

FIGURE 29-10

There is an error in the XML literal assigned to the data variable (refer to Figure 29-10). In this case there is no closing tag for the `Customer` element. Designer support is invaluable for validating your XML literals, preventing run-time errors when the XML is parsed into `XElement` objects.

Creating XML with LINQ

Although creating XML using the LINQ-inspired object model is significantly quicker than previously possible, the real power of the object model comes when you combine it with LINQ in the form of LINQ to XML (XLINQ). By combining the rich querying capabilities with the ability to create complex XML in a single statement, you can generate entire XML documents in a single statement. Now continue with the same example of customers and orders. In this case you have an array of customers, each of whom has any number of orders. What you want to do is create XML that lists the customers and their associated orders. Start by creating the customer list, and then introduce the orders.

To begin with, create an XML literal that defines the structure you want to create:

C#

```
XElement customerXml = new XElement("Customers",
                           new XElement("Customer",
                               new XAttribute("Name", "Bob Jones")));
```

VB

```
Dim customerXml = <Customers>
                      <Customer Name="Bob Jones">
                      </Customer>
                  </Customers>
```

Although you can simplify this code by condensing the `Customer` element into `<Customer Name="Bob Jones" />`, you add the orders as child elements, so you use a separate closing XML element.

Expression Holes

If you have multiple customers, the `Customer` element repeats for each one, with Bob Jones replaced by different customer names. Before you deal with replacing the name, you first need to get the `Customer` element to repeat. You do this by creating an expression hole, using a syntax familiar to anyone who has worked with ASP:

C#

```
XElement customerXml = new XElement("Customers",
                           from c in customers
                           select new XElement("Customer",
                                      new XAttribute("Name",
                                                     "Bob Jones")));
```

VB

```
Dim customerXml = <Customers>
                      <%= From c In customers _
                          Select <Customer Name="Bob Jones">
                                 </Customer> %>
                  </Customers>
```

Here you can see that in the VB code, `<%= %>` defines the expression hole, into which a LINQ statement has been added. This is not required in the C# syntax because the LINQ statement just becomes an argument to the `XElement` constructor. The `Select` statement creates a projection to an XML element for each `customer` in the Customers array based on the static value `"Bob Jones"`. To change this to return each of the customer names, you again must use an expression hole. Figure 29-11 shows how Visual Studio 2012 provides rich IntelliSense support in these expression holes.

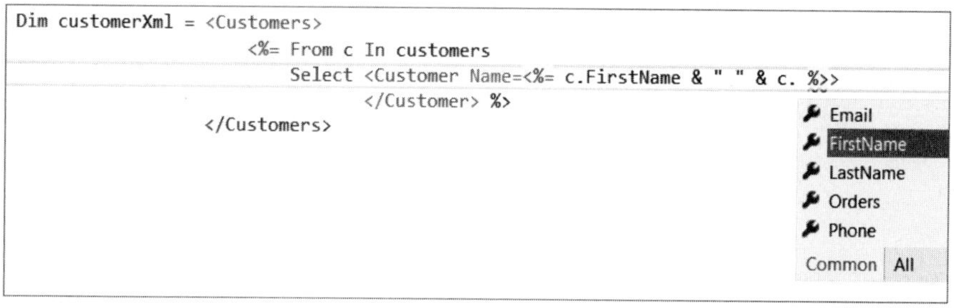

```
Dim customerXml = <Customers>
                      <%= From c In customers
                          Select <Customer Name=<%= c.FirstName & " " & c. %>>
                                 </Customer> %>
                  </Customers>
```

Email
FirstName
LastName
Orders
Phone
Common | All

FIGURE 29-11

The following snippet uses the loop variable `Name` so that you can order the customers based on their full names. This loop variable is then used to set the `Name` attribute of the customer node.

C#

```
XElement customerXml = new XElement("Customers",
                           from c in customers
                           let name = c.FirstName + " " + c.LastName
                           orderby name
                           select new XElement("Customer",
                                  new XAttribute("Name", name),
                                      from o in c.Orders
                                      select new XElement("Order",
                                             new XAttribute("Product", o.Product),
                                             new XAttribute("Quantity",
                                                           o.Quantity))));
```

VB

```
Dim customerXml = <Customers>
                      <%= From c In customers _
                          Let Name = c.FirstName & " " & c.LastName _
                          Order By Name _
                          Select <Customer Name=<%= Name %>>
                                     <%= From o In c.Orders _
                                         Select
                                          <Order
                                                Product=<%= o.Product %>
                                                Quantity=<%= o.Quantity %>
                                                     /> %>
                                         </Customer> %>
                          </Customers>
```

The other thing to notice in this snippet is that you have included the creation of the `Order` elements for each customer. Although it would appear that the second, nested LINQ statement is independent of the first, there is an implicit joining through the customer loop variable `c`. Hence, the second LINQ statement iterates through the orders for a particular customer, creating an `Order` element with attributes `Product` and `Quantity`.

As you can see, the C# equivalent is slightly less easy to read but is by no means more complex. There is no need for expression holes because C# doesn't support XML literals; instead, the LINQ statement just appears nested within the XML construction. For a complex XML document, this would quickly become difficult to work with, which is one reason VB includes XML literals as a first-class language feature.

QUERYING XML

In addition to enabling you to easily create XML, LINQ can also be used to query XML. The following `Customers` XML is used in this section to discuss the XLINQ querying capabilities:

```
<Customers>
    <Customer Name="Bob Jones">
        <Order Product="Milk" Quantity="2"/>
        <Order Product="Bread" Quantity="10"/>
        <Order Product="Apples" Quantity="5"/>
    </Customer>
</Customers>
```

The following two code snippets show the same query using VB and C#, respectively. In both cases the `customerXml` variable (an `XElement`) is queried for all `Customer` elements, from which the `Name` attribute is extracted. The Name attribute is then split over the space between names, and the result is used to create a new Customer object.

C#

```
var results = from cust in customerXml.Elements("Customer")
              let  nameBits = cust.Attribute("Name").Value.Split(' ')
              select new Customer() {FirstName = nameBits[0],
                                     LastName=nameBits[1] };
```

VB

```
Dim results = From cust In customerXml.<Customer>
              Let nameBits = cust.@Name.Split(" "c)
              Select New Customer() With {.FirstName = nameBits(0),
                                          .LastName = nameBits(1)}
```

As you can see, the VB XML language support extends to enabling you to query elements using .<elementName> and attributes using .@attributeName. Figure 29-12 shows the IntelliSense for the customerXml variable, which shows three XML query options.

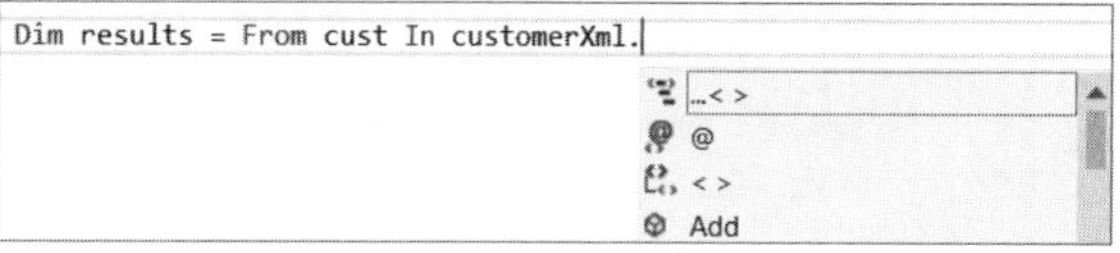

FIGURE 29-12

You have seen the second and third of these options in action in the previous query to extract attribute and element information, respectively. The third option enables you to retrieve all subelements that match the supplied element. For example, the following code retrieves all orders in the XML document, irrespective of which customer element they belong to:

```
Dim allOrders = From cust In customerXml.<Order>
                Select New Order With {.Product = cust.@Product,
                                       .Quantity = CInt(cust.@Quantity)}
```

SCHEMA SUPPORT

Although VB enables you to query XML using elements and attributes, it doesn't actually provide any validation that you have entered the correct element and attribute names. To reduce the chance of entering the wrong names, you can import an XML schema, which extends the default IntelliSense support to include the element and attribute names. You import an XML schema as you would any other .NET namespace. First, you need to add a reference to the XML schema to your project, and then you need to add an Imports statement to the top of your code file.

> **NOTE** *Unlike other import statements, an XML schema import can't be added in the Project Properties Designer, which means you need to add it to the top of any code file in which you want IntelliSense support.*

If you are working with an existing XML file but don't have a schema handy, manually creating an XML schema just so you can have better IntelliSense support seems like overkill. Luckily, the VB team has included the XML to Schema Inference Wizard in Visual Studio 2012. When installed, this wizard enables you to create a new XML schema based on an XML snippet or XML source file, or from a URL that contains the XML source. In this example, you start with an XML snippet that looks like the following:

```
<c:Customers xmlns:c="http://www.professionalvisualstudio.com/chapter29/customers">
    <c:Customer Name="Bob Jones">
```

```
            <c:Order Product="Milk" Quantity="2" />
            <c:Order Product="Cereal" Quantity="10" />
        </c:Customer>
        <c:Customer Name="Alastair Kelly">
            <c:Order Product="Milk" Quantity="9" />
            <c:Order Product="Bread" Quantity="7" />
        </c:Customer>
    </c:Customers>
```

Unlike the previous XML snippets, this one includes a namespace, which is necessary because the XML schema import is based on importing a namespace (rather than importing a specific XSD file). To generate an XML schema based on this snippet, start by right-clicking your project in the Solution Explorer and selecting Add New Item. With the XML to Schema Inference Wizard installed, there should be an additional XML to Schema item template, as shown in Figure 29-13.

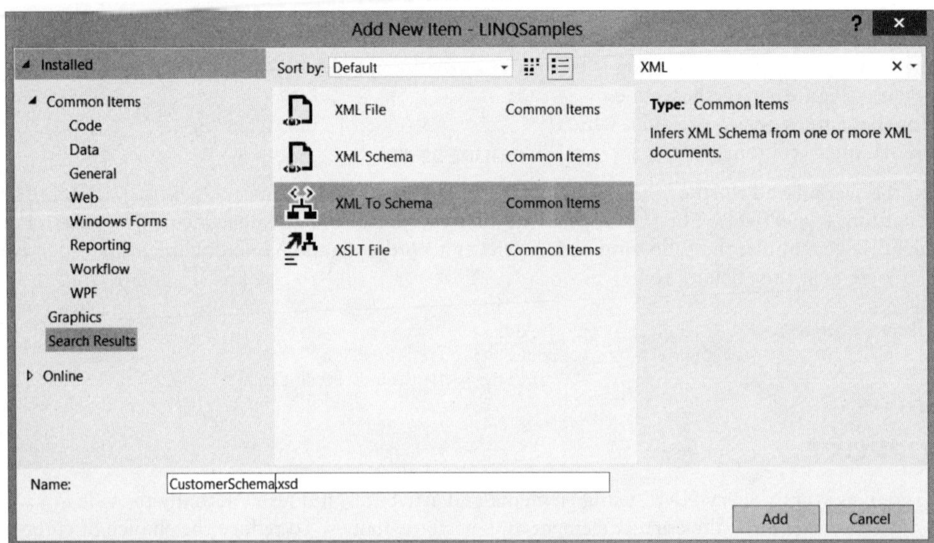

FIGURE 29-13

Selecting this item and clicking Add prompts you to select the location of the XML from which the schema should be generated. Select the Type or Paste XML button and paste the customers XML snippet from earlier into the text area provided. After you click OK, this generates the `CustomersSchema.xsd` file containing a schema based on the XML resources you have specified. The next step is to import this schema into your code file by adding an `Imports` statement to the XML namespace, as shown in Figure 29-14.

```
Imports <xmlns:c=
                    ""
                    "http://www.professionalvisualstudio.com/chapter29/customers"
```

FIGURE 29-14

Figure 29-14 also contains an alias, `c`, for the XML namespace, which will be used throughout the code for referencing elements and attributes from this namespace. In your XLINQs you now see that when you press < or @, the IntelliSense list contains the relevant elements and attributes from the imported XML schema. In Figure 29-15, you can see these new additions when you begin to query the `customerXml` variable. If you were in a nested XLINQ statement (for example, querying orders for a particular customer), you would see only a subset of the schema elements (that is, just the `c:Order` element).

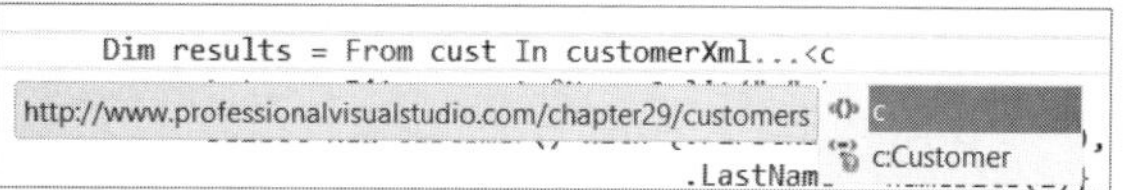

FIGURE 29-15

> **NOTE** *Importing an XML schema doesn't validate the elements or attributes you use. All it does is improve the level of IntelliSense available to you when you build your XLINQ.*

LINQ TO SQL

You may be thinking that you are about to be introduced to yet another technology for doing data access. Actually, what you will see is that everything covered in this chapter extends the existing ADO.NET data access model. LINQ to SQL is much more than just the ability to write LINQ statements to query information from a database. It provides an object to a relational mapping layer, capable of tracking changes to existing objects and allowing you to add or remove objects as if they were rows in a database.

Let's get started and look at some of the features of LINQ to SQL and the associated designers on the way. For this section you use the AdventureWorksLT2008R2 sample database (downloadable from `http://msftdbprodsamples.codeplex.com`. You end up performing a similar query to what you've seen earlier, which was researching customers with a first name greater than or equal to five characters and the average order size for a particular product. Earlier, the product was Milk, but because you are dealing with a bike company you will use the "HL Touring Seat/Saddle" product instead.

Creating the Object Model

For the purpose of this chapter you use a normal Visual Basic Windows Forms application from the New Project dialog. You also need to create a Data Connection to the AdventureWorksLT2008R2 database (covered in Chapter 28, "Datasets and DataBinding,"). The next step is to add a new LINQ to SQL Classes item, named `AdventureLite.dbml`, from the Add New Item dialog. This creates three files that will be added to your project. These are `AdventureLite.dbml`, which is the mapping file; `AdventureLite.dbml.layout`, which like the class designer used to lay out the mapping information to make it easier to work with; and finally, `AdventureLite.designer.vb`, which contains the classes into which data loads as part of LINQ to SQL.

> **NOTE** *These items may appear as a single item,* `AdventureLite.dbml` *if you don't have the Show All Files option enabled. Select the project and click the appropriate button at the top of the Solution Explorer tool window.*

Unfortunately, unlike some of the other visual designers in Visual Studio 2012 that have a helpful wizard, the LINQ to SQL designer initially appears as a blank design surface, as you can see in the center of Figure 29-16.

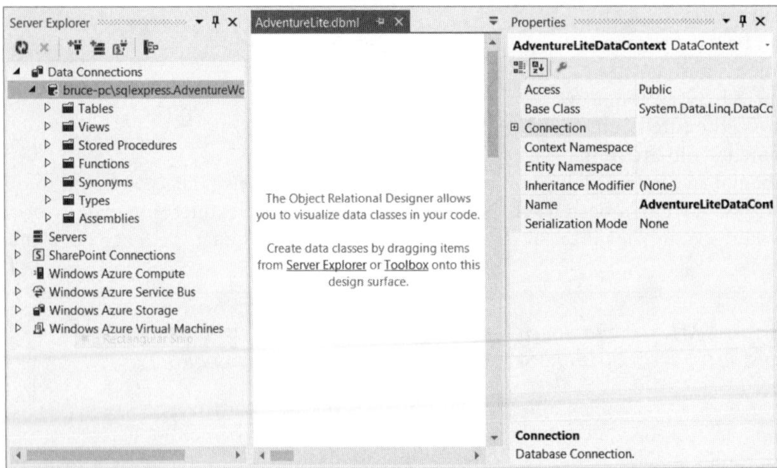

FIGURE 29-16

You can see the properties associated with the main design area (refer to the right side of Figure 29-16), which actually represents a DataContext. If you were to compare LINQ with ADO.NET, a LINQ statement equates approximately to a command, whereas a DataContext roughly equates to the connection. It equates only "roughly" because the DataContext actually wraps a database connection to provide object life-cycle services. For example, when you execute a LINQ to SQL statement, it is the DataContext that executes the request to the database, creating the objects based on the return data and then tracking those objects as they are changed or deleted.

If you have worked with the class designer, you will be at home with the LINQ to SQL designer. You can start to build your data mappings by dragging items from the Server Explorer or the Toolbox (refer to the instructions in the center of Figure 29-16). In this case you want to expand the Tables node, select the Customer, SalesOrderHeader, SalesOrderDetail, and Product tables and drag them onto the design surface. You can see from Figure 29-17 that a number of the classes and properties have been renamed to make the object model easier to read when you are writing LINQ statements. This is a good example of the benefits of separating the object model (for example, Order or OrderItem) from the underlying data (in this case, the SalesOrderHeader and SalesOrderDetail tables). Because you don't need all the properties that are automatically created, it is recommended that you select them in the designer and delete them. The end result should look like Figure 29-17.

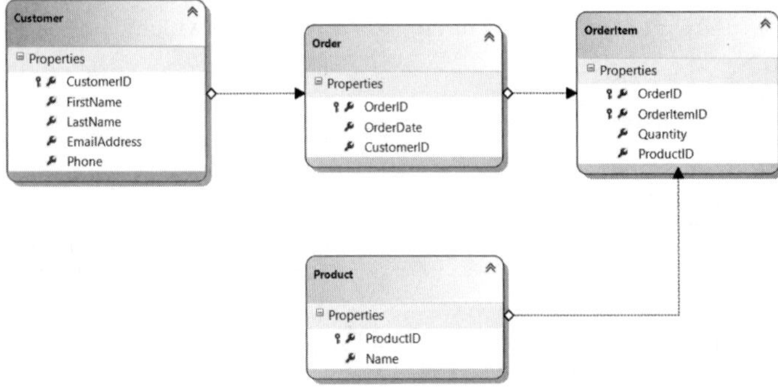

FIGURE 29-17

It is also worth noting that you can modify the details of the association between objects. Figure 29-18 shows the Properties tool window for the association between `Product` and `OrderItem`. Here you set the generation of the `Child Property` to `False` because you won't need to track back from a `Product` to all the `OrderItems`. You also rename the `Parent Property` to `Product` to make the association more intuitive. (However, the name in the drop-down at the top of the Properties window uses the original SQL Server table names.)

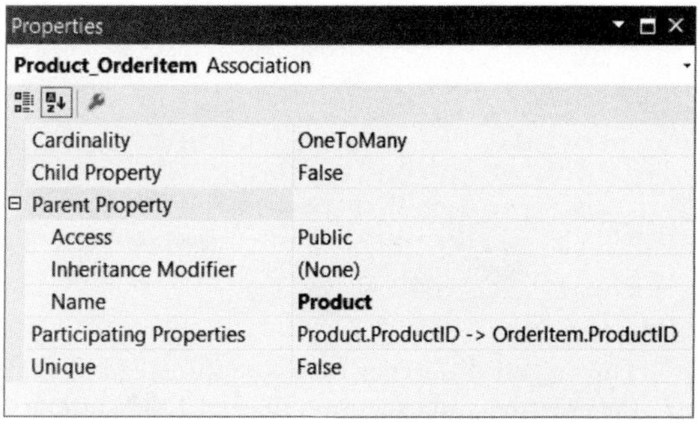

Properties	
Product_OrderItem Association	
Cardinality	OneToMany
Child Property	False
⊟ Parent Property	
Access	Public
Inheritance Modifier	(None)
Name	**Product**
Participating Properties	Product.ProductID -> OrderItem.ProductID
Unique	False

FIGURE 29-18

As you can see, you can control whether properties are created that can be used to navigate between instances of the classes. Though this might seem quite trivial, if you think about what happens if you attempt to navigate from an `Order` to its associated `OrderItems`, you can quickly see that there will be issues if the full object hierarchy hasn't been loaded into memory. For example, in this case if the `OrderItems` aren't already loaded into memory, LINQ to SQL intercepts the navigation, goes to the database, and retrieves the appropriate data to populate the `OrderItems`.

The other property of interest in Figure 29-18 is the `Participating Properties`. Editing this property launches an Association Editor window where you can customize the relationship between two LINQ to SQL classes. You can also reach this dialog by right-clicking the association on the design surface and selecting Edit Association. If you drag items from Server Explorer onto the design surface, you are unlikely to need the Association Editor. However, it is particularly useful if you manually create a LINQ to SQL mapping because you can control how the object associations align to the underlying data relationships.

Querying with LINQ to SQL

In the previous sections you have seen enough LINQ statements to understand how to put together a statement that filters, sorts, aggregates, and projects the relevant data. With this in mind, examine the following LINQ to SQL snippet:

C#

```
public void SampleLinqToSql(){
    using (var aw = new AdventureLiteDataContext()){

        var custs = from c in aw.Customers
                    from o in c.Orders
                    from oi in o.OrderItems
                    where c.FirstName.Length>=5 &&
                          oi.Product.Name == "HL Touring Seat/Saddle"
                    group oi by c into avg
                    let name = avg.Key.FirstName + " " + avg.Key.LastName
                    orderby name
                    select new { Name = name,
                                 AverageOrder = avg.Average(oi => oi.Quantity) };
        foreach (var c in custs){
            MessageBox.Show(c.Name + " = " + c.AverageOrder);
        }
    }
}
```

VB

```
Using aw As New AdventureLiteDataContext
    Dim custs = From c In aw.Customers, o In c.Orders, oi In o.OrderItems
                Where c.FirstName.Length >= 5 And
```

```
                    oi.Product.Name = "HL Touring Seat/Saddle"
                Group By c Into avg = Average(oi.Quantity)
                Let Name = c.FirstName & " " & c.LastName
                Order By Name
                Select New With {Name, .AverageOrder = avg}

    For Each c In custs
        MessageBox.Show(c.Name & " = " & c.AverageOrder)
    Next
End Using
```

The biggest difference here is that instead of the `Customer` and `Order` objects existing in memory before the creation and execution of the LINQ statement, all the data objects are loaded at the point of execution of the LINQ statement. The `AdventureLiteDataContext` is the conduit for opening the connection to the database, forming and executing the relevant SQL statement against the database and loading the return data into appropriate objects.

The LINQ statement must navigate through the Customers, Orders, OrderItems, and Product tables to execute the LINQ statement. Clearly, if this were to be done as a series of SQL statements, it would be horrendously slow. Luckily, the translation of the LINQ statement to SQL commands is done as a single unit.

> **NOTE** *There are some exceptions to this; for example, if you call* `ToList` *in the middle of your LINQ statement, this may result in the separation into multiple SQL statements. Though LINQ to SQL does abstract you from having to explicitly write SQL commands, you still need to be aware of the way your query will be translated and how it might affect your application performance.*

Inserts, Updates, and Deletes

You can see from the earlier code snippet that the DataContext acts as the conduit through which LINQ to SQL queries are processed. To get a better appreciation of what the DataContext does behind the scenes, look at inserting a new product category into the AdventureWorksLT2008R2 database. Before you can do this, you need to add the ProductCategory table to your LINQ to SQL design surface. In this case you don't need to modify any of the properties, so just drag the ProductCategory table onto the design surface. Then to add a new category to your database, all you need is the following code:

C#

```
using(var aw = new AdventureLiteDataContext()){
    var cat = new ProductCategory();
    cat.Name = "Extreme Bike";
    aw.ProductCategories.InsertOnSubmit(cat);
    aw.SubmitChanges();
}
```

VB

```
Using aw As New AdventureLiteDataContext
    Dim cat As New ProductCategory
    cat.Name = "Extreme Bike"
    aw.ProductCategories.InsertOnSubmit(cat)
    aw.SubmitChanges()
End Using
```

This code inserts the new category into the collection of product categories held in memory by the DataContext. When you then call `SubmitChanges` on the DataContext, it is aware that you have added a new product category, so it inserts the appropriate records. A similar process is used when making changes to existing items. In the following example, you retrieve the product category you just inserted using the Contains syntax. Because there is likely to be only one match, you can use the FirstOrDefault extension method to give you just a single product category to work with:

C#

```
using (var aw = new AdventureLiteDataContext()){
    var cat = (from pc in aw.ProductCategories
               where pc.Name.Contains("Extreme")
               select pc).FirstOrDefault();
    cat.Name = "Extreme Offroad Bike";
    aw.SubmitChanges();
}
```

VB

```
Using aw As New AdventureLiteDataContext
    Dim cat = (From pc In aw.ProductCategories
               Where pc.Name.Contains("Extreme")).FirstOrDefault
    cat.Name = "Extreme Offroad Bike"
    aw.SubmitChanges()
End Using
```

After the change to the category name has been made, you just need to call SubmitChanges on the DataContext for it to issue the update on the database. Without going into too much detail, the DataContext essentially tracks changes to each property on a LINQ to SQL object so that it knows which objects need updating when SubmitChanges is called. If you want to delete an object, you simply need to obtain an instance of the LINQ to SQL object, in the same way as for doing an update, and then call DeleteOnSubmit on the appropriate collection. For example, to delete a product category you would call aw.ProductCategories.DeleteOnSubmit(categoryToDelete), followed by aw.SubmitChanges.

Stored Procedures

One of the questions frequently asked about LINQ to SQL is whether you can use your own stored procedures in place of the run-time-generated SQL. The good news is that for inserts, updates, and deletes you can easily specify the stored procedure that should be used. You can also use existing stored procedures to create instances of LINQ to SQL objects. Start by adding a simple stored procedure to the AdventureWorksLT2008R2 database. To do this, right-click the Stored Procedures node under the database connection in the Server Explorer tool window, and select Add New Stored Procedure. This opens a code window with a new stored procedure template. In the following code you have selected to return the five fields that are relevant to your Customer object:

```
CREATE PROCEDURE dbo.GetCustomers
AS
BEGIN
    SET NOCOUNT ON
    SELECT c.CustomerID, c.FirstName, c.LastName, c.EmailAddress, c.Phone
    FROM SalesLT.Customer AS c
END;
```

After you save this stored procedure and you refresh the Server Explorer, it appears under the Stored Procedures node. If you now open up the AdventureLite LINQ to SQL designer, you can drag this stored procedure across into the right pane of the design surface. In Figure 29-19 you can see that the return type of the GetCustomers method is set to Auto-generated Type. This means that you can query only information in the returned object. Ideally, you would want to be able to make changes to these objects and be able to use the DataContext to persist those changes back to the database.

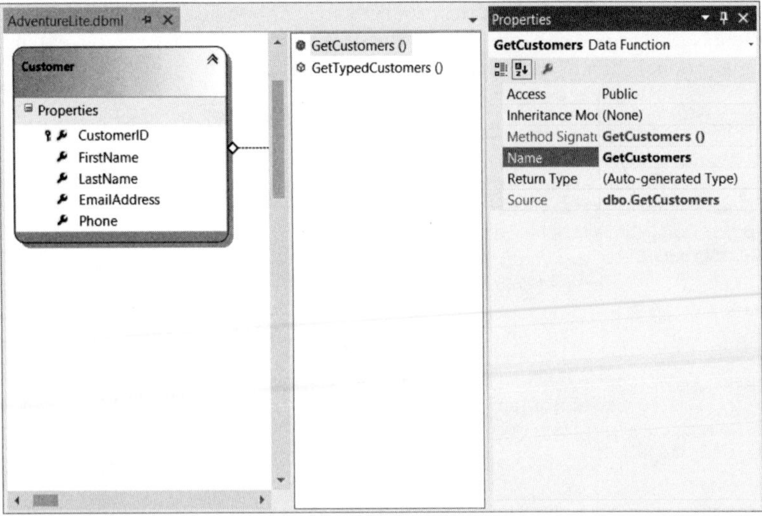

FIGURE 29-19

The second method, `GetTypedCustomers`, actually has the Return Type set as the `Customer` class. To create this method you can either drag the `GetCustomers` stored procedure to the right pane and then set the Return Type to `Customer`, or you can drag the stored procedure onto the `Customer` class in the left pane of the design surface. The latter still creates the method in the right pane, but it automatically specifies the return type as the `Customer` type.

> **NOTE** *You don't need to align properties with the stored procedure columns because this mapping is automatically handled by the DataContext. This is a double-edged sword: Clearly it works when the column names map to the source columns of the LINQ to SQL class, but it may cause a run-time exception if there are missing columns or columns that don't match.*

After you define these stored procedures as methods on the design surface, calling them is as easy as calling the appropriate method on the DataContext:

C#

```
using (var aw = new AdventureLiteDataContext()){
    var customers = aw.GetCustomers();
    foreach (var c in customers){
        MessageBox.Show(c.FirstName);
    }
}
```

VB

```
Using aw As New AdventureLiteDataContext
    Dim customers = aw.GetCustomers

    For Each c In customers
        MsgBox(c.FirstName)
    Next
End Using
```

Here you have seen how you can use a stored procedure to create instances of the LINQ to SQL classes. If you instead want to update, insert, or delete objects using stored procedures, follow a similar process except you need to define the appropriate behavior on the LINQ to SQL class. To begin with, create an insert stored procedure for a new product category:

```
CREATE PROCEDURE dbo.InsertProductCategory
    (
    @categoryName nvarchar(50),
    @categoryId int OUTPUT
    )
AS
BEGIN
    INSERT INTO SalesLT.ProductCategory (Name) VALUES (@categoryName)
    SELECT @categoryId=@@identity
END;
```

Following the same process as before, you need to drag this newly created stored procedure from the Server Explorer across into the right pane of the LINQ to SQL design surface. Then in the Properties tool window for the `ProductCategory` class, modify the `Insert` property. This opens the dialog shown in Figure 29-20. Here you can select whether you want to use the run-time-generated code or customize the method that is used. In Figure 29-20 the `InsertProductCategory` method has been selected. Initially, the Class Properties will be unspecified because Visual Studio 2012 wasn't able to guess which properties mapped to the method arguments. It's easy enough to align these to the `id` and `name` properties. Now when the DataContext goes to insert a ProductCategory, it can use the stored procedure instead of the run-time-generated SQL statement.

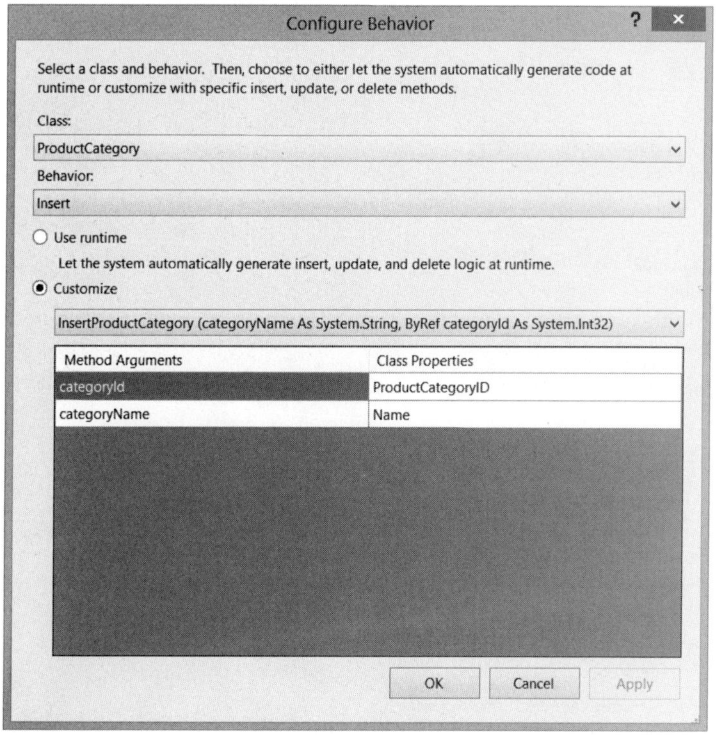

FIGURE 29-20

Binding LINQ to SQL Objects

The important thing to remember when using DataBinding with LINQ to SQL objects is that they are normal .NET objects. As well, you can add more classes to the diagram in the same way as before. That is, you can drag additional tables onto your designer. For instance, if you drag the Customer table onto the surface, it will add the appropriate class and set up the appropriate relationships (based on the database schema).

One of the things you will have noticed is that the columns on your OrderItems are not ideal. By default, you get Quantity, Order, and Product columns. Clearly, the last two columns are not going to display anything of interest, but you don't have an easy way to display the Name of the product in the order with the current LINQ to SQL objects. Luckily, there is an easy way to effectively hide the navigation from OrderItem to Product so that the name of the product appears as a property of OrderItem.

You do this by adding your own property to the `OrderItem` class. Each LINQ to SQL class is generated as a partial class, which means that extending the class is as easy as right-clicking the class in the LINQ to SQL designer and selecting View Code. This generates a custom code file, in this case `AdventureLite.vb` (or `AdventureLite.cs`), and includes the partial class definition. You can then proceed to add your own code. The following snippet added the `Product` property that can simplify access to the name of the product being ordered:

C#

```
partial class OrderItem{
    public string ProductName{
        get{
            return this.Product.Name;
        }
    }
}
```

VB

```
Partial Class OrderItem
    Public ReadOnly Property ProductName() As String
        Get
            Return Me.Product.Name
        End Get
    End Property
End Class
```

You can bind the Product column to this property by manually setting the `DataPropertyName` field in the Edit Columns dialog for the data grid.

The last thing to do is to actually load the data when the user clicks the button. To do this you can use the following code:

C#

```
private void btnLoadData_Click(object sender, EventArgs e){
    using (var aw = new AdventureLiteDataContext()){
        var cust = aw.Customers;
        this.customerBindingSource.DataSource = cust;
    }
}
```

VB

```
Private Sub btnLoad_Click(ByVal sender As System.Object, _
                          ByVal e As System.EventArgs) Handles btnLoad.Click
    Using aw As New AdventureLiteDataContext
        Dim custs = From c In aw.Customers
```

```
        Me.CustomerBindingSource.DataSource = custs
    End Using
End Sub
```

Your application can now run, and when the user clicks the button, the customer information will be populated in the top data grid. However, no matter which customer you select, no information appears in the Order information area. The reason for this is that LINQ to SQL uses lazy loading to retrieve information as it is required. Using the data visualizer you were introduced to earlier, if you inspect the query in this code, you see that it contains only the customer information:

```
SELECT [t0].[CustomerID], [t0].[FirstName], [t0].[LastName], [t0].[EmailAddress],
[t0].[Phone]
FROM [SalesLT].[Customer] AS [t0]
```

You have two ways to resolve this issue. The first is to force LINQ to SQL to bring back all the Order, OrderItem, and Product data as part of the initial query. To do this, modify the button click code to the following:

C#

```
private void btnLoadData_Click(object sender, EventArgs e){
    using (var aw = new AdventureLiteDataContext()){
        var loadOptions =new System.Data.Linq.DataLoadOptions();
        loadOptions.LoadWith<Customer>(c=>c.Orders);
        loadOptions.LoadWith<Order>(o=>o.OrderItems);
        loadOptions.LoadWith<OrderItem>(o=>o.Product);
        aw.LoadOptions = loadOptions;

        var cust = aw.Customers;
        this.customerBindingSource.DataSource = cust;
    }
}
```

VB

```
Private Sub btnLoad_Click(ByVal sender As System.Object,
                          ByVal e As System.EventArgs) Handles btnLoad.Click
    Using aw As New AdventureLiteDataContext
        Dim loadOptions As New System.Data.Linq.DataLoadOptions
        loadOptions.LoadWith(Of Customer)(Function(c As Customer) c.Orders)
        loadOptions.LoadWith(Of Order)(Function(o As Order) o.OrderItems)
        loadOptions.LoadWith(Of OrderItem)(Function(oi As OrderItem) _
                          oi.Product)
        aw.LoadOptions = loadOptions

        Dim custs = From c In aw.Customers
        Me.CustomerBindingSource.DataSource = aw.Customers
    End Using
End Sub
```

Essentially what this code tells the DataContext is that when it retrieves `Customer` objects it should forcibly navigate to the `Orders` property. Similarly, the `Order` objects navigate to the `OrderItems` property, and so on. One thing to be aware of is that this solution could perform badly if there are a large number of customers. As the number of customers and orders increases, this performs progressively worse, so this is not a great solution, but it does illustrate how you can use the `LoadOptions` property of the DataContext.

The other alternative is to not dispose of the DataContext. You need to remember what happens behind the scenes with DataBinding. When you select a customer in the data grid, this causes the OrderBindingSource to refresh. It tries to navigate to the `Orders` property on the customer. If you have disposed of the

DataContext, there is no way that the `Orders` property can be populated. So the better solution to this problem is to change the code to the following:

C#

```
private AdventureLiteDataContext aw = new AdventureLiteDataContext();
private void btnLoadData_Click(object sender, EventArgs e){
    var cust = aw.Customers;
    this.customerBindingSource.DataSource = cust;
}
```

VB

```
Private aw As New AdventureLiteDataContext()
Private Sub btnLoad_Click(ByVal sender As System.Object, _
                          ByVal e As System.EventArgs) Handles btnLoad.Click
    Dim custs = From c In aw.Customers
    Me.CustomerBindingSource.DataSource = custs
End Sub
```

Because the DataContext still exists, when the binding source navigates to the various properties, LINQ to SQL kicks in, populating these properties with data. This is much more scalable than attempting to populate the whole customer hierarchy when the user clicks the button.

LINQPAD

Although the intent behind LINQ was to make code more readable, in a lot of cases it has made writing and debugging queries much harder. Because LINQ expressions are executed only when the results are iterated, this can lead to confusion and unexpected results. One of the most useful tools to have by your side when writing LINQ expressions is Joseph Albahari's LINQPad (`http://www.linqpad.net`). Figure 29-21 illustrates how you can use the editor in the top-right pane to write expressions.

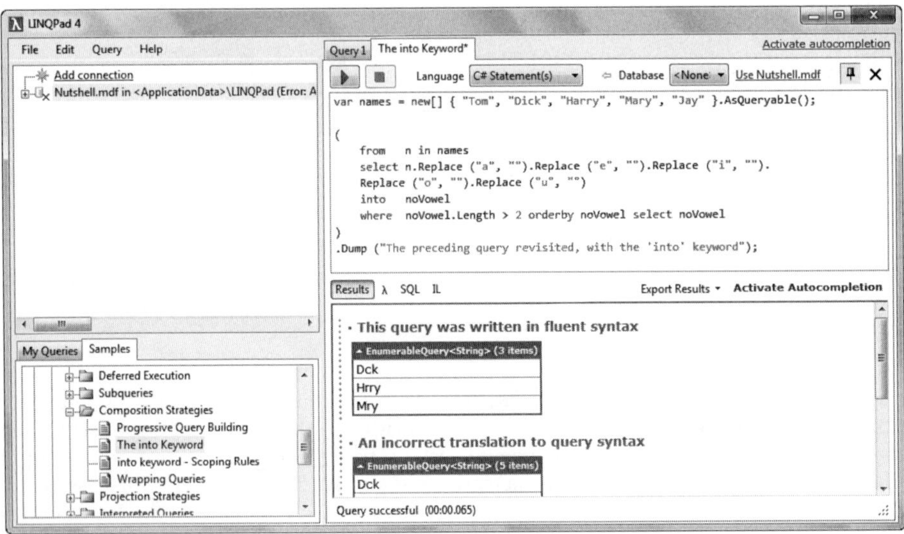

FIGURE 29-21

In the lower-right pane you can see the output from executing the expression. You can tweak your LINQ expression to get the correct output without having to build and run your entire application.

SUMMARY

In this chapter you were introduced to Language Integrated Queries (LINQ), a significant step toward a common programming model for data access. You can see that LINQ statements help to make your code more readable because you don't need to code all the details of how the data should be iterated, the conditional statements for selecting objects, or the code for building the results set.

You were also introduced to the LINQ-inspired XML object model, the XML redundant integration within VB, how LINQ can be used to query XML documents, and how Visual Studio 2012 IntelliSense enables a rich experience for working with XML in VB.

Finally, you were introduced to LINQ to SQL and how you can use it as a basic object-relational mapping framework. Although you are somewhat limited in being able only to map an object to a single table, it can still dramatically simplify working with a database.

In the next chapter you see how powerful LINQ is as a technology when you combine it with the ADO .NET Entity Framework to manage the life cycle of your objects. With much more sophisticated mapping capabilities, this technology can dramatically change the way you work with data in the future.

30

The ADO.NET Entity Framework

WHAT'S IN THIS CHAPTER?

- Understanding the Entity Framework
- Creating an Entity Framework model
- Querying Entity Framework models

One of the core requirements in business applications (and many other types of applications) is the ability to store and retrieve data in a database. However, that's easier said than done because the relational schema of a database does not blend well with the object hierarchies that you prefer to work with in code. To create and populate these object hierarchies required a lot of code to be written to transfer data from a data reader into a developer-friendly object model, which was then usually difficult to maintain. It was such a source of constant frustration that many developers turned to writing code generators or various other tools that automatically created the code to access a database based on its structure. However, code generators usually created a 1:1 mapping between the database structure and the object model, which was hardly ideal either, leading to a problem called "object relational impedance mismatch," where how data was stored in the database did not necessarily have a direct relationship with how developers wanted to model the data as objects. This led to the concept of Object Relational Mapping, where an ideal object model could be designed for working with data in code, which could then be mapped to the schema of a database. When the mapping is complete, the Object Relational Mapper (ORM) framework should take over the burden of translating between the object model and the database, leaving developers to focus on actually solving the business problem (rather than focusing on the technological issues of working with data).

To many developers, ORMs are the Holy Grail for working with data in a database as objects, and there's no shortage of debate over the strengths and pitfalls of the various ORM tools available, and how an ideal ORM should be designed. You won't delve into these arguments in this chapter, but simply look at how to use the ADO.NET Entity Framework — Microsoft's ORM tool and framework.

Looking through history, the .NET Framework added a number of means to access data in a database since its inception, all under the banner of ADO.NET. First, you had low-level access through SqlConnection (and connections for other types of databases) using means like data readers. Then you had a higher-level means of accessing data using Typed DataSets. LINQ to SQL appeared in the .NET Framework 3.5, providing the first built-in way to work with data as objects.

However, for a long time Microsoft did not include an ORM tool in the .NET Framework (despite a number of earlier attempts to do so with the failed ObjectSpaces). There were already a number of ORMs available for use with the .NET Framework, with nHibernate and LLBLGen Pro being among the most popular. Microsoft did eventually manage to release its own, which it called the ADO.NET Entity Framework, and shipped it with the .NET Framework 3.5 SP1.

The Entity Framework's eventual release (despite being long awaited) was not smooth sailing either — with controversy generated before it was even released by a vote of no confidence petition signed by many developers, including a number of Microsoft MVPs. Indeed, it was the technology that provided the catalyst leading to the rise of the ALT.NET movement. However, since then there have been many improvements in the Entity Framework implementation to reduce these perceived shortcomings.

This chapter takes you through the process of creating an Entity Framework model of a database, and how to use it to query and update the database. The Entity Framework is a huge topic, with entire books devoted to its use. Therefore, it would be impossible to go through all its features, so this chapter focuses on discussing some of its core features and how to start and create a basic entity model.

The Entity Framework model you create in this chapter will be used in a number of subsequent chapters where database access is required in the samples.

WHAT IS THE ENTITY FRAMEWORK?

Essentially, the Entity Framework is an Object Relational Mapper. Object Relational Mapping enables you to create a conceptual object model, map it to the database, and the ORM framework can take care of translating your queries over the object model to queries in the database, returning the data as the objects that you've defined in your model.

Comparison with LINQ to SQL

A common question from developers is regarding the Entity Framework's relationship with LINQ to SQL, and which technology they should use when creating data-centric applications. Now take a look at the advantages each has over the other.

LINQ to SQL advantages over the Entity Framework:

- It's easy to get started and query.

Entity Framework advantages over LINQ to SQL:

- Enables you to build a conceptual model of the database rather than purely working with a 1:1 domain model of the database as objects (such as having one object mapped to multiple database tables, inheritance support, and defining complex properties).
- Generates a database from your entity model.
- Support for databases other than just SQL Server.
- Support for many-to-many relationships.
- It works with Table-valued Functions.
- Lazy loading and eager loading support.
- Synchronization to get database updates will not lose your customizations to your model.
- Continues to evolve, whereas future LINQ to SQL development will be minimal.

Entity Framework Concepts

Here are some of the important concepts involved in the Entity Framework and some of the terms used throughout this chapter:

- **Entity Model:** The entity model you create using the Entity Framework consists of three parts:
  - **Conceptual model:** Represents the object model, including the entities, their properties, and the associations between them
  - **Store model:** Represents the database structure, including the tables/views/stored procedures, columns, foreign keys, and so on
  - **Mapping:** Provides the glue between the store model and the conceptual model (that is, between the database and the object model), by mapping one to the other

  Each of these parts is maintained by the Entity Framework as XML using a domain-specific language (DSL).
- **Entity:** Entities are essentially just objects (with properties) to which a database model is mapped.
- **Entity Set:** An entity set is a collection of a given entity. You can think of it as an entity being a row in a database, and an entity set being the table.
- **Association:** Associations define relationships between entities in your entity model and are conceptually the same as relationships in a database. Associations are used to traverse the data in your entity model between entities.
- **Mapping:** Mapping is the core concept of ORM. It's essentially the translation layer from a relational schema in a database to objects in code.

GETTING STARTED

To demonstrate some of the various features in the Entity Framework, the example in this section uses the AdventureWorksLT2008R2 sample database developed by Microsoft as one of the sample databases for SQL Server. AdventureWorksLT2008R2 is a simpler version of the full AdventureWorks database, making it somewhat easier to demonstrate the concepts of the Entity Framework without the additional complexity that using the full database would create.

The AdventureWorksLT2008R2 database is available for download from the CodePlex website as a database script here:

```
http://msftdbprodsamaples.codeplex.com
```

Adventure Works Cycles is a fictional bicycle sales chain, and the AdventureWorksLT2008R2 database is used to store and access its product sales data.

Follow the instructions from the CodePlex website detailing how to install the database from the downloaded script in a SQL Server instance (SQL Server Express Edition is sufficient) that is on or can be accessed by your development machine.

Now you will move on to create a project that contains an Entity Framework model of this database. Start by opening the New Project dialog and creating a new project. The sample project you create in this chapter uses the WPF project template. You can display data in a WPF DataGrid control defined in the `MainWindow.xaml` file named `dgEntityFrameworkData`.

Now that you have a project that can host and query an Entity Framework model, it's time to create that model.

CREATING AN ENTITY MODEL

You have two ways of going about creating an entity model. The usual means to do so is to create the model based on the structure of an existing database; however, with the Entity Framework it is also possible to start with a blank model and have the Entity Framework generate a database structure from it.

The sample project uses the first method to create an entity model based on the AdventureWorksLT2008R2 database's structure.

The Entity Data Model Wizard

Open the Add New Item dialog for your project, navigate to the Data category, and select ADO.NET Entity Data Model as the item template (as shown in Figure 30-1). Call it `AdventureWorksLTModel.edmx`.

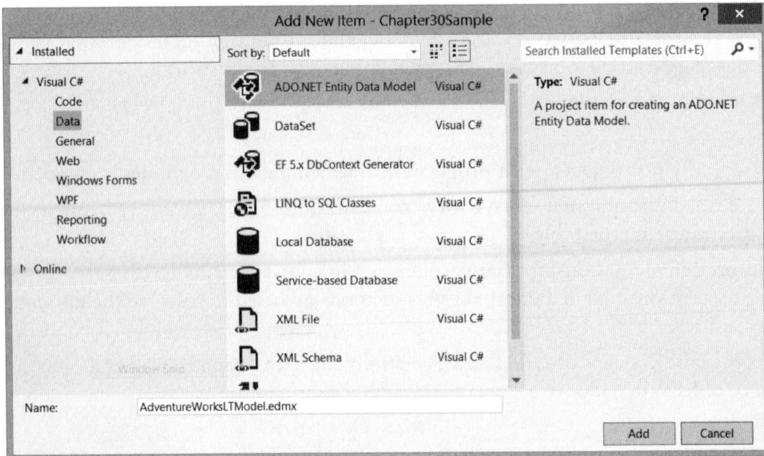

FIGURE 30-1

This starts the Entity Data Model Wizard that can help you start building an Entity Framework model.

This shows the dialog shown in Figure 30-2 that enables you to select whether you want to automatically create a model from a database (Generate from Database), or start with an empty model (Empty Model).

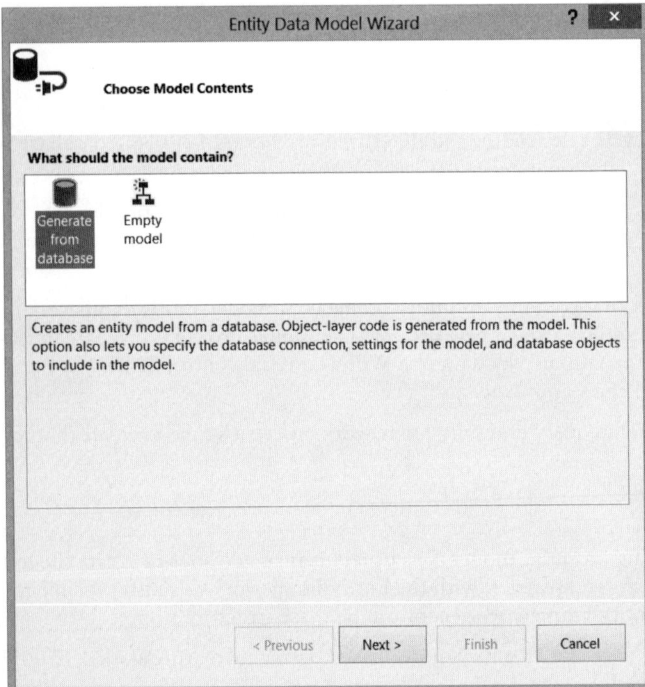

FIGURE 30-2

The Empty Model option is useful when you want to create your model from scratch, and either mapping it manually to a given database or letting the Entity Framework create a database based on your model.

However, as previously stated you create an entity model from the AdventureWorksLT2008R2 database, so for the purpose of this example use the Generate from Database option, and get the wizard to help you create the entity model from the database.

Moving to the next step, you now need to create a connection to the database (as shown in Figure 30-3). You can find the most recent database connection you've created in the drop-down list, but if it's not there (for example, if this is the first time you've created a connection to this database) you need to create a new connection. To do so, click the New Connection button, and go through the standard procedure to select the SQL Server instance, authentication credentials, and finally, the database.

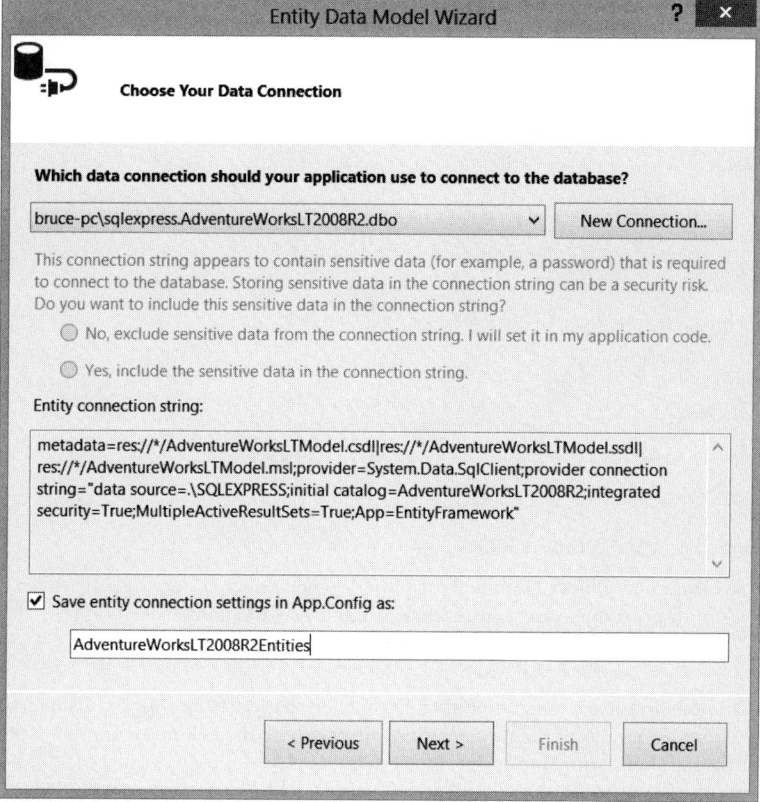

FIGURE 30-3

If you use a username and password as your authentication details, you can choose not to include those in the connection string (containing the details required to connect to the database) when it is saved because this string is saved in plain text that would enable anyone who sees it to have access to the database. In this case you would have to provide these credentials to the model before querying it for it to create a connection to the database. If you don't select the check box to save the connection settings in the `App.config` file, you also need to pass the model the details on how to connect to the database before you can query it.

In the next step, the wizard uses the connection created in the previous step to connect to the database and retrieve its structure (that is, its tables, views, and stored procedures), which displays in a tree for you to select the elements to be included in your model (see Figure 30-4).

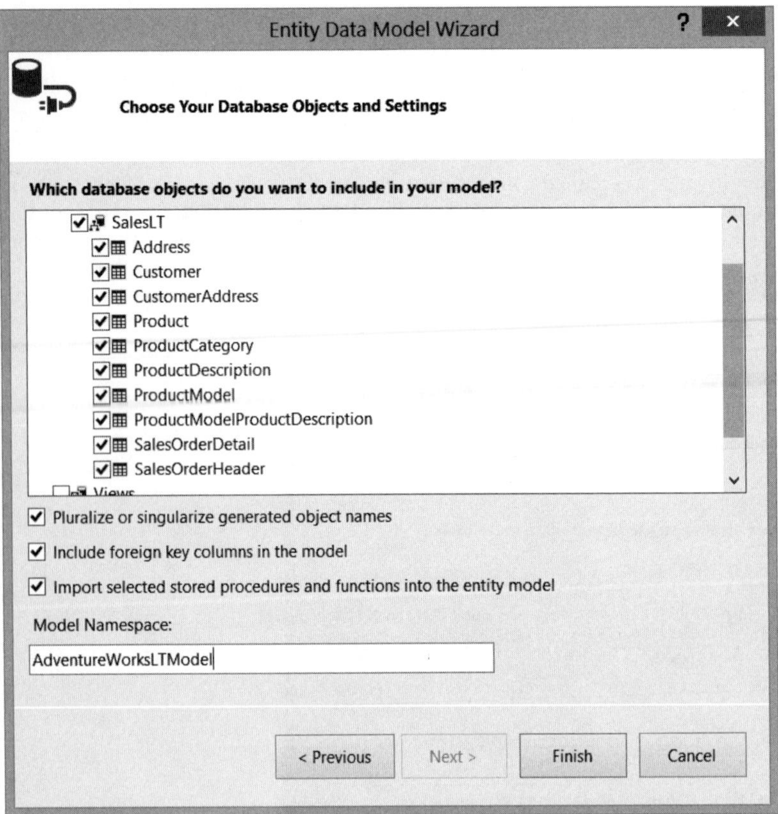

FIGURE 30-4

Other options that can be specified on this screen include:

- **Pluralize or Singularize Generated Object Names:** This option (when selected) intelligently takes the name of the table/view/stored procedure and pluralizes or singularizes the name based on how that name is used in the model. (Collections uses the plural form, entities use the singular form, and so on.)
- **Include Foreign Key Columns in the Model:** The Entity Framework supports two mechanisms for indicating foreign key columns. One is to create a relationship and hide the column from the entity, instead representing it through a relationship property. The other is to explicitly define the foreign key in the entity. If you wish to use the explicit definition, select this option to include it in your entities.
- **Import Selected Stored Procedures and Functions into the Entity Model:** While the entity data store supports the inclusion of stored procedures and functions, they need to be imported as functions in order to be accessible through the model. If you select this option, the stored procedures and functions that you choose in this dialog will automatically be imported into the model.
- **Model Namespace:** This enables you to specify the namespace in which all the classes related to the model will be created. By default, the model exists in its own namespace (which defaults to the name of the model entered in the Add New Item dialog) rather than the default namespace of the project to avoid conflict with existing classes with the same names in the project.

Select all the tables in the database to be included in the model. Clicking the Finish button in this screen creates an Entity Framework model that maps to the database. From here you can view the model in the Entity Framework, adjust it as per your requirements, and tidy it up as per your tastes (or standards) to make it ideal for querying in your code.

The Entity Framework Designer

After the Entity Framework model has been generated, it opens in the Entity Framework designer, as shown in Figure 30-5.

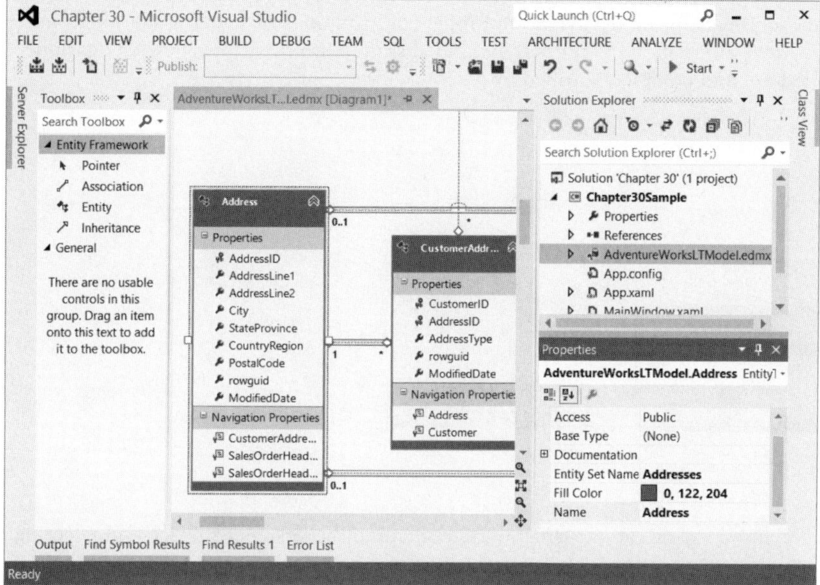

FIGURE 30-5

The designer has automatically laid out the entities that were created by the wizard, showing the associations it has created between them.

You can move entities around on the designer surface, and the designer automatically moves the association lines and tries to keep them neatly laid out. Entities automatically snap to a grid, which you can view by right-clicking the designer surface and selecting Grid ➪ Show Grid from the context menu. You can disable the snapping by right-clicking the designer surface and unchecking Grid ➪ Snap to Grid from the context menu to have finer control over the diagram layout, but entities line up better (and hence make the diagram neater) by leaving the snapping on.

As you move entities around (or add additional entities to) the diagram, you may find it gets a little messy, with association lines going in all directions to avoid getting "tangled." To get the designer to automatically lay out the entities neatly again according to its own algorithms, you can right-click the designer surface and select Diagram ➪ Layout Diagram from the context menu.

Entity Framework models can quickly become large and difficult to navigate in the Entity Framework designer. Luckily, the designer has a few tools to make navigating it a little easier. The designer enables you to zoom in and out using the zoom buttons in its bottom-right corner (below the vertical scrollbar — see Figure 30-6). The button sandwiched between these zoom in/out buttons zooms to 100% when clicked.

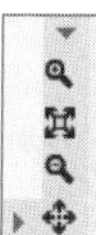

FIGURE 30-6

To zoom to a predefined percentage, right-click the designer surface, and select one of the options in the Zoom menu. In this menu you can also find a Zoom to Fit option (to fit the entire entity model within the visible portion of the designer), and a Custom option that pops up a dialog enabling you to type a specific zoom level.

In addition, selecting an entity in the Properties tool window (from the drop-down object selector) automatically selects that entity in the designer and brings it into view; right-clicking the entity in the Model Browser tool window (described shortly) and selecting the Show in Designer menu item does the same. These make it easy to navigate to a particular entity in the designer, so you can make any modifications as required.

You can minimize the space taken by entities by clicking the icon in the top-right corner of the entity. Alternatively, you can roll up the Properties/Navigation Properties groupings by clicking the +/– icons to their left. Figure 30-7 shows an entity in its normal expanded state, with the Properties/Navigation Properties groupings rolled up, and completely rolled up.

FIGURE 30-7

You can expand all the collapsed entities at one time by right-clicking the designer surface and selecting Diagram ➪ Expand All from the context menu. Alternatively, you can collapse all the entities in the diagram by right-clicking the designer surface and selecting Diagram ➪ Collapse All from the context menu.

A visual representation of an entity model (as provided by the Entity Framework designer) can serve a useful purpose in the design documentation for your application. The designer provides a means to save the model layout to an image file to help in this respect. Right-click anywhere on the designer surface, and select Diagram ➪ Export as Image from the context menu. This pops up the Save As dialog for you to select where to save the image. It defaults to saving as a bitmap (`.bmp`); — if you open the Save As Type drop-down list, you can see that it can also save to JPEG, GIF, PNG, and TIFF. PNG is probably the best choice for quality and file size.

It can often be useful (especially when saving a diagram for documentation) to display the property types against each property for an entity in the designer. You can turn this on by right-clicking the designer surface and selecting Scalar Property Format ➪ Display Name and Type from the context menu. You can return to displaying just the property name by selecting the Scalar Property Format ➪ Display Name item from the right-click context menu.

As with most designers in Visual Studio, the Toolbox and Properties tool windows are integral parts of working with the designer. The Toolbox (as shown in Figure 30-8) contains three controls: Entity, Association, and Inheritance. How to use these controls with the designer is covered shortly. The Properties tool window displays the properties of the selected items in the designer (an entity, association, or inheritance), enabling you to modify their values as required.

In addition to the Toolbox and Properties tool windows, the Entity Framework designer also incorporates two other tool windows specific to it — the Model Browser tool window and the Mapping Details tool window — for working with the data.

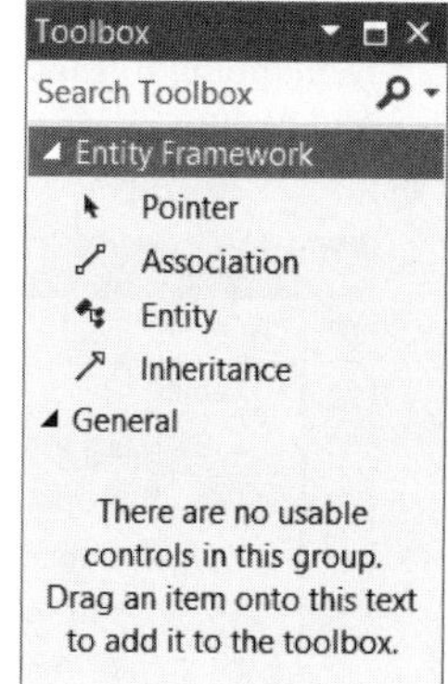

FIGURE 30-8

The Model Browser tool window (as shown in Figure 30-9) enables you to browse the hierarchy of both the conceptual entity model of the database and its storage model. Clicking an element in the Store model hierarchy shows its properties in the Properties tool window; however, these can't be modified (because this is an entity modeling tool, not a database modeling tool). The only changes you can make to the Store model is to delete tables, views, and stored procedures (which won't modify the underlying database). Clicking elements in the Conceptual model hierarchy also shows their properties in the Properties tool window (which can be modified), and its mappings display in the Mapping Details tool window. Right-clicking an entity in the hierarchy and selecting the Show in Designer menu item from the context menu brings the selected entity/association into view in the designer.

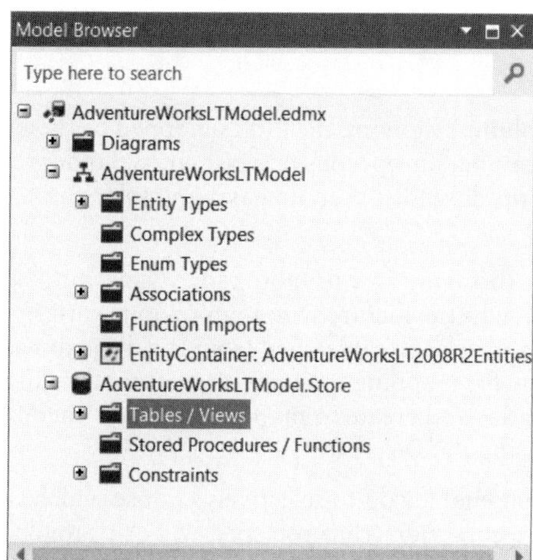

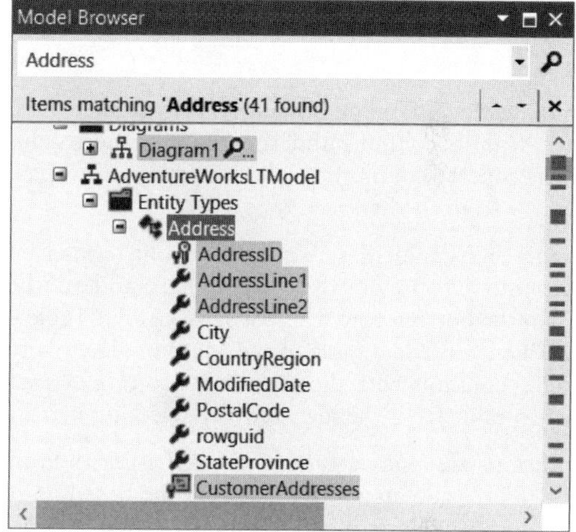

FIGURE 30-9

The second picture in Figure 30-9 demonstrates the searching functionality available in the Model Browser tool window. As previously discussed, because your entity model can get quite large, it can be difficult to find exactly what you are after. Therefore, a good search function is important. Type your search term in the search textbox at the top of the window, and press Enter. In this example the search term was Address, which highlighted all the names in the hierarchy (including entities, associations, properties, and so on) that contained the search term. The vertical scrollbar has the places in the hierarchy (which has been expanded) highlighted where the search terms have been found, making it easy to see where the results were found throughout the hierarchy. The number of results is shown just below the search textbox, next to which are an up arrow and a down arrow to enable you to navigate through the results. When you finish searching, you can click the cross icon next to these to return the window to normal.

The Mapping Details tool window (as shown in Figure 30-10) enables you to modify the mapping between the conceptual model and the storage model for an entity. Selecting an entity in the designer, the Model Browser tool window, or the Properties tool window shows the mappings in this tool window between the properties of the entity to columns in the database. You have two ways to map the properties of an entity to the database: either via tables and views, or via functions (that is, stored procedures). On the left side of the tool window are two icons, enabling you to swap the view between mapping to tables and views, to mapping to functions. However, focus here just on the features of mapping entity properties to tables and views.

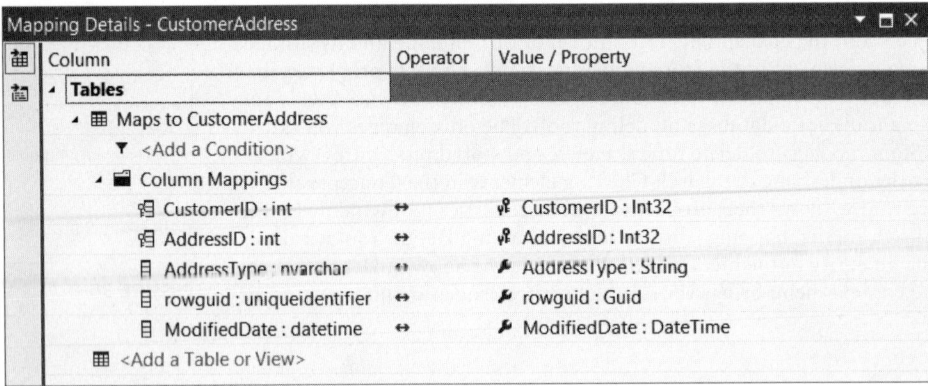

FIGURE 30-10

The table/view mapping has a hierarchy (under the Column column) showing the tables mapped to the entity, with its columns underneath it. To these columns you can map properties on your entity (under the Value/Property column) by clicking in the cell, opening the drop-down list that appears, and selecting a property from the list.

A single entity may map to more than one database table/view (bringing two or more tables/views into a single entity, as previously discussed). To add another table/view to the hierarchy to map to your entity, click in the bottom row where it says <Add a Table or View> and select a table/view from the drop-down list. When you add a table to the Mapping Details tool window for mapping to an entity, it automatically matches columns with the same name to properties on the entities and creates a mapping between them. Delete a table from the hierarchy by selecting its row and pressing the Delete key.

Conditions are a powerful feature of the Entity Framework that enable you to selectively choose which table you want to map an entity to at run time based on one or more conditions that you specify. For example, say you have a single entity in your model called Product that maps to a table called Products in the database. However, you have additional extended properties on your entity that map to one of two tables based on the value of the `ProductType` property on the entity — if the product is of a particular type, it maps the columns to one table, if it's another type, it maps the columns to the other table. You can do this by adding a condition to the table mapping. In the Mapping Details window, click in the row directly below a table to selectively map where it says <Add a Condition>. Open the drop-down list that appears, which contains all the properties on the entity. Select the property to base your condition on (in the given example it would be the `ProductType` property), select an operator, and enter a value to compare the property to. Note that there are only two operators: equals (=) and Is. You can add additional conditions as necessary to determine if the table should be used as the source of the data for the given properties.

> **NOTE** *A number of advanced features are available in the Entity Framework but not available in the Entity Framework designer (such as working with the store schema, annotations, referencing other models, and so on). However, these actions can be performed by modifying the schema files (which are XML files) directly.*

Creating/Modifying Entities

The Entity Data Model Wizard gave you a good starting point by building an entity model for you. In some cases this may be good enough, and you can start writing the code to query it, but you can now take the opportunity to go through the created model and modify its design as per your requirements.

Because the Entity Framework provides you with a conceptual model to design and work with, you are no longer limited to having a 1:1 relationship between the database schema and an object model in code, so the changes you make in the entity model won't affect the database in any way. So you may want to delete properties from entities, change their names, and so on, and it will have no effect on the database. In addition, because any changes you make are in the conceptual model, updating the model from the database will not affect the conceptual model (only the storage model), so your changes won't be lost.

Changing Property Names

Often you might work with databases that have tables and columns containing prefixes or suffixes, over/under use of capitalization, or even names that no longer match their actual function. This is where the use of an ORM like the Entity Framework can demonstrate its power because you can change all these in the conceptual layer of the entity model to make the model nice to work with in code (with more meaningful and standardized names for the entities and associations) without needing to modify the underlying database schema. Luckily, the tables and columns in the AdventureWorksLT2008R2 database have reasonably friendly names, but if you wanted to change the names, it would simply be a case of double-clicking the property in the designer (or selecting it and pressing F2), which changes the name display to a textbox enabling you to make the change. Alternatively, you can select the property in the designer, the Model Browser tool window, or the Properties tool window, and update the Name property in the Properties tool window.

Adding Properties to an Entity

Now look at the process of adding properties to an entity. Three types of properties exist:

- **Scalar properties:** Properties with a primitive type, such as string, integer, Boolean, and so on.
- **Complex properties:** A grouping of scalar properties in a manner similar to a structure in code. Grouping properties together in this manner can make your entity model a lot more readable and manageable.
- **Navigation properties:** Used to navigate across associations. For example, the SalesOrderHeader entity contains a navigation property called SalesOrderDetails that enables you to navigate to a collection of the SalesOrderDetail entities related to the current SalesOrderHeader entity. Creating an association between two entities automatically creates the required navigation properties.

The easiest way to try this is to delete a property from an existing entity and add it back again manually. Delete a property from an entity. (Select it in the designer and press the Delete key.) Now to add it back again, right-click the entity, and select Add ⇨ Scalar Property from the context menu. Alternatively, a much easier and less frustrating way when you are creating a lot of properties is to simply select a property or the Properties header and press the Insert key on your keyboard. A new property will be added to the entity, with the name displayed in a textbox for you to change as required.

The next step is to set the type of the property; you need to move over to the Properties tool window to set. The default type is string, but you can change this to the required type by setting its Type property.

Properties that you want to designate as entity keys (that is, properties used to uniquely identify the entity) need their Entity Key property set to True. The property in the designer will have a picture of a little key added to its icon, making it easy to identify which properties are used to uniquely identify the entity.

You can set numerous other properties on a property, including assigning a default value, a maximum length (for strings), and whether or not it's nullable. You can also assign the scope of the getter and setter for the property (public, private, and so on), useful for, say, a property that will be mapped to a column with a calculated value in the database where you don't want the consuming application to attempt to set the value (by making the setter private).

The final task is to map the property to the store model. You do this as described earlier using the Mapping Details tool window.

Creating Complex Types

Create a complex type on the Customer entity grouping the various customer name-related properties together in a complex type and thus making the Customer entity neater. Though you can create a complex type from scratch, the easiest way to create a complex type is to refactor an entity by selecting the scalar properties on the entity to be included in the complex type and having the designer create the complex type from those properties. Follow these instructions to move the name-related properties on the Customer entity to a complex type:

1. Select the name-related properties on the Customer entity (FirstName, LastName, MiddleName, NameStyle, Suffix, Title) by selecting the first property, and while holding down the Ctrl key selecting the other properties (so they are all selected at the same time).
2. Right-click one of the selected properties, and select the Refactor ➪ Move To New Complex Type menu item.
3. In the Model Browser will be the new complex type that it created, with its name displayed in a textbox for you to name to something more meaningful. For this example, simply call it CustomerName.
4. The Entity Framework designer will have created a complex type, added the selected properties to it, removed the selected properties from the entity, and added the complex type that it just created as a new property on the entity in their place. However, this property will just have ComplexProperty as its name, so you need to rename it to something more meaningful. Select the property in the designer, press F2, and enter Name in the textbox.

You will now find that by grouping the properties together in this way, the entity will be easier to work with in both the designer and in code.

Creating an Entity

So far you've been modifying existing entities as they were created by the Entity Data Model Wizard. However, now take a look at the process to create an entity from scratch and then mapping it to a table/view/stored procedure in your storage model. Most of these aspects have already been covered, but walk through the required steps to get an entity configured from scratch.

You have two ways to manually create entities. The first is to right-click the designer surface and select Add New ➪ Entity from the context menu. That pops up the dialog shown in Figure 30-11, which helps you set up the initial configuration of the entity. When you enter a name for the entity in the Entity Name field, you'll notice that the Entity Set field automatically updates to the plural form of the entity name. (Although you can change this entity set name to something else if required.) The Base Type drop-down list enables you to select an existing entity in your entity model that this entity inherits from (discussed shortly). There is also a section enabling you to specify the name and type of a property to automatically create on the entity and set as an entity key.

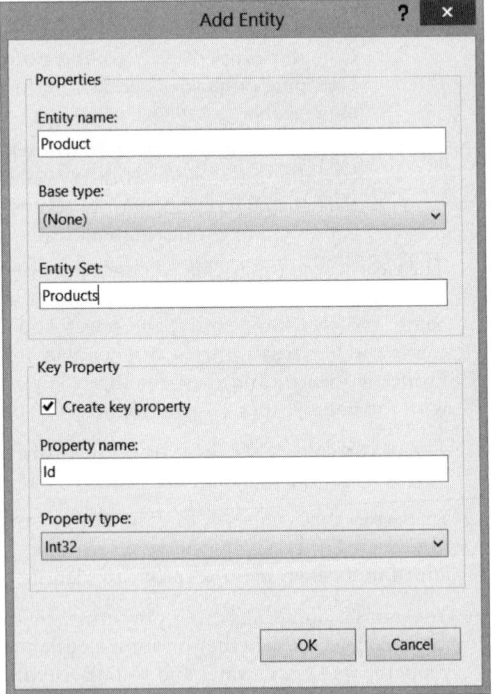

FIGURE 30-11

The other way to create an entity is to drag and drop the Entity component from the Toolbox onto the designer surface. However, it doesn't bring up the dialog from the previous method, instead opting to immediately create an entity with a default name, entity set name, and entity key property. You then have to use the designer to modify its configuration to suit your needs.

The steps needed to finish configuring the entity are as follows:

1. If required, create an inheritance relationship by specifying that the entity should inherit from a base entity.
2. Create the required properties on the entity, setting at least one as an entity key.
3. Using the Mapping Details tool window, map these properties to the storage schema.
4. Create any associations with other entities in the model.
5. Validate your model to ensure that the entity is mapped correctly.

> **NOTE** *All entities must have an entity key that can be used to uniquely identify the entity. Entity keys are conceptually the same as a primary key in a database.*

As discussed earlier, you aren't limited to mapping to a single database table/view per entity. This is one of the benefits of building a conceptual model of the database — you may have related data spread across a number of database tables, but through having a conceptual entity model layer in the Entity Framework, you can bring those different sources together into a single entity to make working with the data a lot easier in code.

> **NOTE** *Make sure you don't focus too much on the structure of the database when you create your entity model — the advantage of designing a conceptual model is that it enables you to design the model based on how you plan to use it in code. Therefore, focus on designing your entity model, and then you can look at how it maps to the database.*

Creating/Modifying Entity Associations

You have two ways of creating an association between two entities. The first is to right-click the header of one of the entities and select Add New ⇨ Association from the context menu. This displays the dialog shown in Figure 30-12.

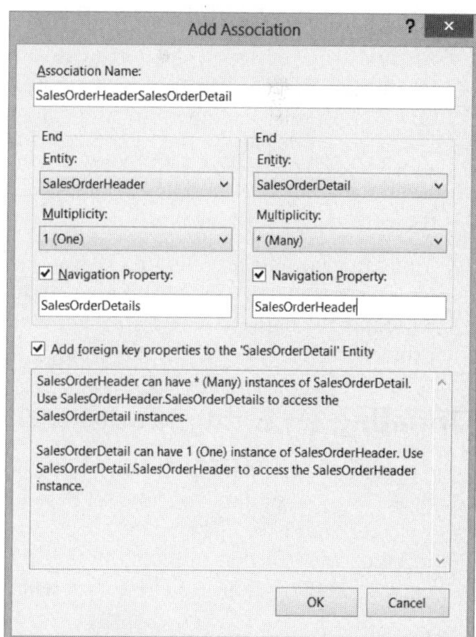

FIGURE 30-12

This dialog includes:

- **Association Name:** Give the association a name. This becomes the name of the foreign key constraint in the database if you update the database from the model.
- **Endpoints:** These specify the entities at each end of the association, the type of relationship (one-to-one, one-to-many, and so on), and the name of the navigation properties that it creates on both entities to navigate from one entity to the other over the association.
- **Add Foreign Key Properties to the Entity:** This enables you to create a property on the "foreign" entity that acts as a foreign key and map to the entity key property over the association. If you've already added the property that will form the foreign key on the associated entity, you should uncheck this check box.

The other way to create an association is to click the Association component in the Toolbox, click one entity to form an end on the association, and then click another entity to form the other end of the association. (If it is a one-to-many relationship, select the "one" entity first.) Using this method gives the association a default name, creates the navigation properties on both entities, and assumes a one-to-many relationship. It will not create a foreign key property on the "foreign" entity. You can then modify this association as required using the Properties tool window.

> **NOTE** *You cannot use the association component in a drag-and-drop fashion from the Toolbox.*

Despite having created the association, you aren't done yet unless you used the first method and also selected the option to create a foreign key property for the association. Now you need to map the property that acts as the foreign key on one entity to the entity key property on the other. The entity whose primary key is one endpoint in the association is known, but you have to tell the Entity Framework explicitly which property to use as the foreign key property. You can do this by selecting the association in the designer and using the Mapping Details tool window to map the properties.

When this is done, you may want to define a referential constraint for the association, which you can assign by clicking the association in the designer and finding the Referential Constraint property in the Properties tool window.

Entity Inheritance

In the same way that classes can inherit from other classes (a fundamental object-oriented concept), so can entities inherit from other entities. You have a number of ways to specify that one entity should inherit from another, but the most straightforward method is to select an entity in the designer, find its Base Type property in the Properties tool window, and select the entity from the drop-down list that this entity should inherit from.

Validating an Entity Model

At times your entity model may be invalid (such as when a property on an entity has not been mapped to the storage model, or its type cannot be converted from/to the mapped column's data type in the database); however, despite having an invalid entity model your project can still compile.

You can run a check to see if your model is valid by right-clicking the designer surface and selecting the Validate menu item from the context menu. This checks for any errors in your model and displays them in the Error List tool window.

You can also set the Validate On Build property for the conceptual model to True (click an empty space on the designer surface, and then you can find the property in the Properties tool window), which automatically validates the model each time you compile the project. However, again, an invalid model will not stop the project from successfully compiling.

Updating an Entity Model with Database Changes

The structure of databases tends to be updated frequently throughout the development of projects, so you need a way to update your model based on the changes in the database. To do so, right-click the designer surface, and select the Update Model from Database menu item. This opens the Update Wizard (as shown in Figure 30-13) that obtains the schema from the database, compares it to the current storage model, and extracts the differences. These differences display in the tabs in the wizard. The Add tab contains database objects that aren't in your storage model, the Refresh tab contains database objects that are different in the database from their corresponding storage model objects, and the Delete tab contains database objects that are in the storage model but no longer in the database.

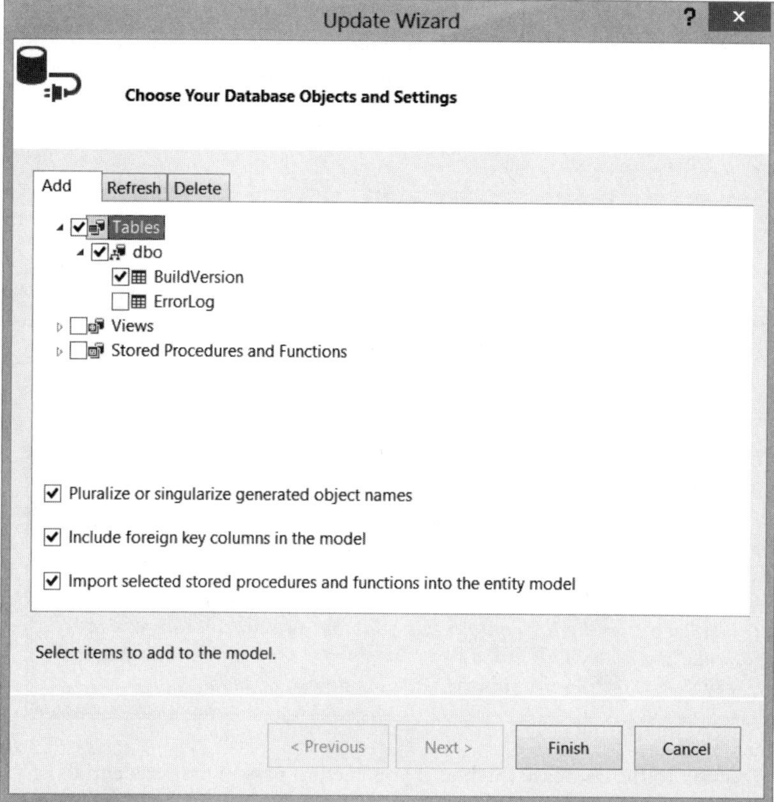

FIGURE 30-13

Select the items from these three tabs that you want to add, refresh, or delete, and click the Finish button to have your entity model updated accordingly.

QUERYING THE ENTITY MODEL

Now that you've created your entity model, you no doubt want to put it to the test by querying it, working with and modifying the data returned, and saving changes back to the database. The Entity Framework provides a number of ways to query your entity model, including LINQ to Entities, Entity SQL, and query builder methods. However, this chapter focuses specifically on querying the model with LINQ to Entities.

LINQ to Entities Overview

LINQ was covered in the previous chapter, specifically focusing on the use of LINQ to Objects, LINQ to SQL, and LINQ to XML; however, the Entity Framework has extended LINQ with its own implementation called LINQ to Entities. LINQ to Entities enables you to write strongly typed LINQ queries against your entity model and have it return the data as objects (entities). LINQ to Entities handles the mapping of your

LINQ query against the conceptual entity model to a SQL query against the underlying database schema. This is an extraordinarily powerful feature of the Entity Framework, abstracting away the need to write SQL to work with data in a database.

Getting an Object Context

To connect to your entity model, you need to create an instance of the object context in your entity model. So that the object context is disposed of when you finish, use a using block to maintain the lifetime of the variable:

VB

```
Using context As New AdventureWorksLTEntities()
    'Queries go here
End Using
```

C#

```
using (AdventureWorksLTEntities context = new AdventureWorksLTEntities())
{
    // Queries go here
}
```

> **NOTE** *Any queries placed within the scope of the* `using` *block for the object context aren't necessarily executed while the object context is in scope. As detailed in the "Debugging and Execution" section of Chapter 29, "Language Integrated Queries (LINQ)," the execution of LINQ queries is deferred until the results are iterated. (That is, the query is not run against the database until the code needs to use its results.) This means that if the variable containing the context has gone out of scope before you are actually using the results, the query will fail. Therefore, ensure that you have requested the results of the query before letting the context variable go out of scope.*

If you need to specify the connection to the database (such as if you need to pass in user credentials or use a custom connection string rather than what's in the `App.config` file) you can do so by passing the connection string to the constructor of the object context (in this case `AdventureWorksLT2008R2Entities`).

> **NOTE** *The connection string passed into the constructor is not quite the same as a connection string passed into the typical database connection object. In the case of the Entity Framework, the connection string includes a description of where to find the meta data for the entities.*

CRUD Operations

It would be hard to argue against the most important database queries being the CRUD (Create/Read/Update/Delete) operations. Read operations return data from the database, whereas the Create/Update/Delete operations make changes to the database. Create some LINQ to Entities queries to demonstrate retrieving some data from the database (as entities), modify these entities, and then save the changes back to the database.

> **NOTE** *While you get up to speed on writing LINQ to Entities queries, you may find LINQPad to be a useful tool, providing a "scratchpad" where you can write queries against an entity model and have them executed immediately so that you can test your query. You can get LINQPad from* `http://www.linqpad.net`.

Data Retrieval

Just like SQL, LINQ to Entity queries consist of `selects`, `where` clauses, `order by` clauses, and `group by` clauses. Take a look at some examples of these. The results of the queries can be assigned to the `ItemsSource` property of the DataGrid control created earlier in the `MainWindow.xaml` file, enabling you to visualize the results:

VB

```
dgEntityFrameworkData.ItemsSource = qry
```

C#

```
dgEntityFrameworkData.ItemsSource = qry;
```

There are actually a number of ways to query the entity model within LINQ to Entities, but you can just focus on one method here. Assume that the query is between the using block demonstrated previously, with the variable containing the instance of the object context simply called `context`.

To return the entire collection of customers in the database, you can write a select query like so:

VB

```
Dim qry = From c In context.Customers
          Select c
```

C#

```
var qry = from c in context.Customers
          select c;
```

You can filter the results with a `where` clause, which can even include functions/properties such as `StartsWith`, `Length`, and so on. This example returns all the customers whose last name starts with A:

VB

```
Dim qry = From c In context.Customers
          Where c.Name.LastName.StartsWith("A")
          Select c
```

C#

```
var qry = from c in context.Customers
          where c.Name.LastName.StartsWith("A")
          select c;
```

You can order the results with an `order by` clause — in this example you order the results by the customer's last name:

VB

```
Dim qry = From c In context.Customers
          Order By c.Name.LastName Ascending
          Select c
```

C#

```
var qry = from c in context.Customers
          orderby c.Name.LastName ascending
          select c;
```

You can group and aggregate the results with a group by clause — in this example you group the results by the salesperson, returning the number of sales per salesperson. Note that instead of returning a Customer entity you request that LINQ to Entities returns an implicitly typed variable containing the salesperson and his sales count:

VB

```
Dim qry = From c In context.Customers
          Group c By salesperson = c.SalesPerson Into grouping = Group
          Select New With
          {
                .SalesPerson = salesperson,
                .SalesCount = grouping.Count()
          }
```

C#

```
var qry = from c in context.Customers
          group c by c.SalesPerson into grouping
          select new
          {
              SalesPerson = grouping.Key,
              SalesCount = grouping.Count()
          };
```

> **NOTE** *It can be useful to monitor the SQL queries generated and executed by the Entity Framework to ensure that the interaction between the entity model and the database is what you'd expect. For example, you may find that because an association is being lazy loaded, traversing the entity hierarchy across this association in a loop actually makes repeated and excessive trips to the database. Therefore, if you have SQL Server Standard or higher, you can use the SQL Profiler to monitor the queries being made to the database and adjust your LINQ queries if necessary. If you use SQL Server Express, you can download a free open source SQL Server profiler called SQL Express Profiler from* `http://code.google.com/p/sqlexpressprofiler/downloads/list`.

Saving Data

The Entity Framework employs change tracking — where you make changes to data in the model, it tracks the data that has changed, and when you request that the changes are saved back to the database, it commits the changes to the database as a batch. This commit is via the `SaveChanges()` method on the object context:

VB

```
context.SaveChanges()
```

C#

```
context.SaveChanges();
```

A number of ways to update data exists (for different scenarios), but for purposes of simplicity, this example takes simple straightforward approaches.

Update Operations

Assume you want to modify the name of a customer (with an ID of 1), which you've retrieved like so:

VB

```
Dim qry = From c In context.Customers
          Where c.CustomerID = 1
          Select c

Dim customer As Customer = qry.FirstOrDefault()
```

C#

```
var qry = from c in context.Customers
          where c.CustomerID == 1
          select c;

Customer customer = qry.FirstOrDefault();
```

All you need to do is modify the name properties on the customer entity you've retrieved. The Entity Framework automatically tracks that this customer has changed, and then calls the `SaveChanges()` method on the object context:

VB

```
customer.Name.FirstName = "Chris"
customer.Name.LastName = "Anderson"

context.SaveChanges()
```

C#

```
customer.Name.FirstName = "Chris";
customer.Name.LastName = "Anderson";

context.SaveChanges();
```

Create Operations

To add a new entity to an entity set, simply create an instance of the entity, assign values to its properties, add the new entity to the related collection on the data context, and then save the changes:

VB

```
Customer customer = new Customer()
customer.Name.FirstName = "Chris"
customer.Name.LastName = "Anderson"
customer.Name.Title = "Mr."
customer.PasswordHash = "*****"
customer.PasswordSalt = "*****"
customer.ModifiedDate = DateTime.Now
context.Customers.AddObject(customer)

context.SaveChanges()
```

C#

```
Customer customer = new Customer();
customer.Name.FirstName = "Chris";
customer.Name.LastName = "Anderson";
customer.Name.Title = "Mr.";
customer.PasswordHash = "*****";
customer.PasswordSalt = "*****";
```

```
customer.ModifiedDate = DateTime.Now;
context.Customers.AddObject(customer);

context.SaveChanges();
```

After the changes are saved back to the database your entity can now have the primary key that was automatically generated for the row by the database assigned to its `CustomerID` property.

Delete Operations

To delete an entity, simply use the `DeleteObject()` method on its containing entity set:

VB

```
context.Customers.DeleteObject(customer)
```

C#

```
context.Customers.DeleteObject(customer);
```

Navigating Entity Associations

Of course, working with data rarely involves the use of a single table/entity, which is where the navigation properties used by associations are useful indeed. A customer can have one or more addresses, which is modeled in your entity model by the Customer entity having an association with the CustomerAddress entity (a one-to-many relationship), which then has an association with the Address entity (a many-to-one relationship). The navigation properties for these associations make it easy to obtain the addresses for a customer.

Start by using the query from earlier to return a customer entity:

VB

```
Dim qry = From c In context.Customers
          Where c.CustomerID = 1
          Select c

Dim customer As Customer = qry.FirstOrDefault()
```

C#

```
var qry = from c in context.Customers
          where c.CustomerID == 1
          select c;

Customer customer = qry.FirstOrDefault();
```

You can enumerate and work with the addresses for the entity via the navigation properties like so:

VB

```
For Each customerAddress As CustomerAddress In customer.CustomerAddresses
    Dim address As Address = customerAddress.Address
    'Do something with the address entity
Next customerAddress
```

C#

```
foreach (CustomerAddress customerAddress in customer.CustomerAddresses)
{
    Address address = customerAddress.Address;
    // Do something with the address entity
}
```

Note how you navigate through the CustomerAddress entity to get to the Address entity for the customer. Because of these associations there's no need for joins in the Entity Framework.

However, there is an issue here with what you're doing. At the beginning of the loop, a database query will made to retrieve the customer addresses for the current customer. Then, for each address in the loop, an additional database query will be made to retrieve the information associated with the Address entity! This is known as *lazy loading* — where the entity model requests data only from the database when it actually needs it. This can have some advantages in certain situations; however, in this scenario it results in a lot of calls to the database, increasing the load on the database server, reducing the performance of your application, and reducing your application's scalability. If you then did this for a number of customer entities in a loop, that would add even more strain to the system. So it's definitely not an ideal scenario as is.

Instead, you can request from the entity model when querying for the customer entity that it eagerly loads its associated CustomerAddress entities and their Address entities. This requests all the data in one database query, thus removing all the aforementioned issues, because when navigating through these associations the entity model now has the entities in memory and does not have to go back to the database to retrieve them. The way to request that the model does this is to use the `Include` method, specifying the path (as a string) of the navigation properties (dot notation) to the associated entities whose data you also want to retrieve from the database at the same time as the actual entities being queried:

VB

```
Dim qry = From c In context.Customers
                        .Include("CustomerAddresses")
                        .Include("CustomerAddresses.Address")
          Where c.CustomerID = 1
          Select c

Dim customer As Customer = qry.FirstOrDefault()
```

C#

```
var qry = from c in context.Customers
                        .Include("CustomerAddresses")
                        .Include("CustomerAddresses.Address")
          where c.CustomerID == 1
          select c;

Customer customer = qry.FirstOrDefault();
```

ADVANCED FUNCTIONALITY

There's too much functionality available in the Entity Framework to discuss in detail, but here's an overview of some of the more notable advanced features available that you can investigate further if you want.

Updating a Database from an Entity Model

As mentioned earlier, it's possible with the Entity Framework to create an entity model from scratch, and then have the Entity Framework create a database according to your model. Alternatively, you can start with an existing database, but then get the Entity Framework to update the structure of your database based on the new entities/properties/associations that you've added to your entity model. To update the structure of the database based on additions to your model, you can use the Generate Database Wizard by right-clicking the designer surface and selecting the Generate Database from Model menu item.

Adding Business Logic to Entities

Though you are fundamentally building a data model with the Entity Framework rather than business objects, you can add business logic to your entities. The entities generated by the Entity Framework are partial classes, enabling to you extend them and add your own code. This code may respond to various events on the entity, or it may add methods to your entity that the client application can use to perform specific tasks or actions.

For example, you might want to have the Product entity in your AdventureWorksLT2008 entity model automatically assign the value of the `SellEndDate` property when the `SellStartDate` property is set (only if the `SellEndDate` property does not have a value). Alternatively, you may have some validation logic or business logic that you want to execute when the entity is being saved.

Each property on the entity has two partial methods that you can extend: a `Changing` method (before the property is changed) and a `Changed` method (after the property is changed). You can extend these partial methods in your partial class to respond accordingly to the value of a property being changed.

Plain Old CLR Objects (POCO)

One of the big complaints with the first version of the Entity Framework was that your entities had to inherit from `EntityObject` (or implement a set of given interfaces), meaning that they had a dependency on the Entity Framework — which made them unfriendly for use in projects where test-driven development (TDD) and domain-driven design (DDD) practices were employed. In addition, many developers wanted their classes to be persistence ignorant — that is, contain no logic or awareness of how they were persisted.

By default, the entities generated from the Entity Model Data Wizard in the Entity Framework v4 still inherit from `EntityObject`, but you now have the ability to use your own classes that do not need to inherit from `EntityObject` or implement any Entity Framework interfaces, and whose design is completely under your control. These types of classes are often termed Plain Old CLR Objects, or POCO for short.

SUMMARY

In this chapter you learned that the Entity Framework is an Object Relational Mapper (ORM) that enables you to create a conceptual model of your database to interact with databases in a more productive and maintainable manner. You then learned how to create an entity model and how to write queries against it in code.

31

Reporting

WHAT'S IN THIS CHAPTER?

- Designing reports
- Generating reports
- Deploying reports

One of the key components of almost every business application is reporting. Businesses put data into the system to get useful information out of it, and this information is generally in the form of reports. Numerous reporting tools and engines are available, and it can often be hard to choose which one is best for your application or system. (They tend to work in different ways and have different pros and cons.)

Visual Studio 2012 contains a built-in report designer that saves to files using the RDL file specification — and reports built using this designer can be generated using the local report engine, or rendered on a remote report server running SQL Server Reporting Services.

GETTING STARTED WITH REPORTING

When you start designing reports, you either want to add a report to an existing project or start a completely new project (such as for a reporting application). If it is the latter, the easiest way to start is to create a new project using the Reports Application project template. This creates a Windows Forms project already set up with the necessary assembly references, a form with the Report Viewer control on it, and an empty report. Now look at the former scenario and how to manually get started (which actually isn't much extra work).

Reports can be viewed in either a Windows Forms application or an ASP.NET application using the Report Viewer control. There are two Report Viewer controls: one for use in web projects and one for use in Windows Forms projects. Both are almost identical in appearance and how you use them to render reports.

> **NOTE** *To render reports in a WPF application, you can use the Windows Forms interoperability feature detailed in Chapter 18, "Windows Presentation Foundation (WPF)," and use the Windows Forms control. (Because there is no Report Viewer control in WPF.) Displaying reports in Silverlight applications is a bit harder because Silverlight has no Report Viewer control either (nor support for printing). In this case it is probably best to render reports to PDF, stream them through to the client using a HTTP handler, and display them in a different browser window.*

Now you need to add some assembly references to your project that are required for using the Report Viewer control and the report engine. If you work with an ASP.NET project, you need to add a reference to `Microsoft.ReportViewer.WebForms.dll`, or if you work with a Windows Forms project you need to add a reference to `Microsoft.ReportViewer.WinForms.dll`. Alternatively, the Report Viewer control should be in your Toolbox for both project types, and dropping it onto your report automatically adds the required assembly reference to your project.

Now add a report definition file to your project. Add a new item to your project, and select the Reporting subsection, as shown in Figure 31-1.

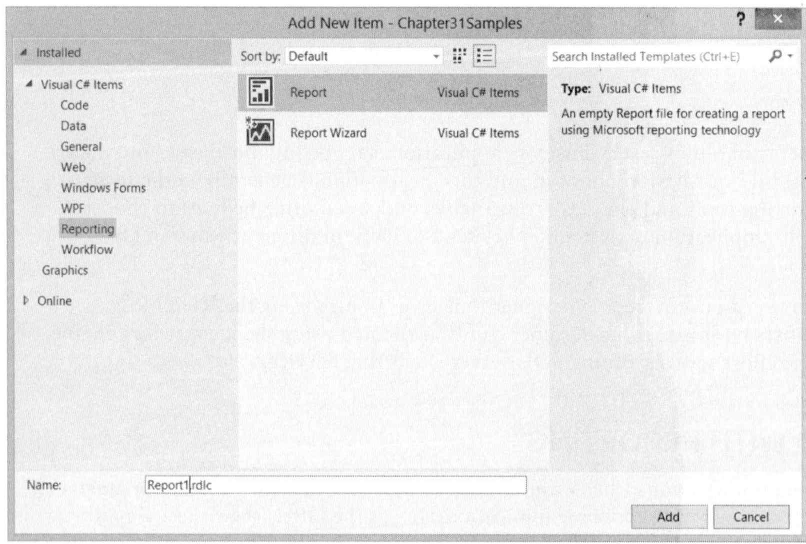

FIGURE 31-1

Selecting the Report item creates an empty report definition file — essentially a blank slate that you can start working with. Selecting the Report Wizard item creates a report definition file and automatically starts the Report Wizard (detailed in the "Report Wizard" section later in this chapter), which can design a report layout for you based upon your choices. You generally want to start your report by using the Report Wizard, and then modify its output to suit your requirements.

Before you get into designing the report, we must clarify the different parts of a reporting system, the terms you use when you reference each, and how they hang together. (Because this can be somewhat confusing initially.) There are six main parts:

- Report designer
- Report definition file

- Data sources
- Reporting engine
- Report
- Report Viewer

You use the *report designer* to design the *report definition file* (at design time), creating its structure and specifying the various rules of how the report will be laid out. At run time, you pass the *report definition file* and one or more *data sources* to the *reporting engine*. The *reporting engine* uses the two to generate the *report*, which it then renders in the *Report Viewer* (or a specified alternative output format such as PDF).

> **NOTE** *This can be confusing because the Report Viewer is the local report engine. So you pass the report definition file and the data sources to the Report Viewer, and it then both renders and displays it. From a conceptual perspective, however, it's probably best to think of these as separate components, which makes more sense.*

DESIGNING REPORTS

Take a look now at how to design a report. You will look at the manual process of designing a report, and then later take a look at how the Report Wizard automates the design process. For now, you work with an empty report that was created by adding a new item to the project and using the Report item template. When you create this item, it immediately opens in the report designer, as shown in Figure 31-2.

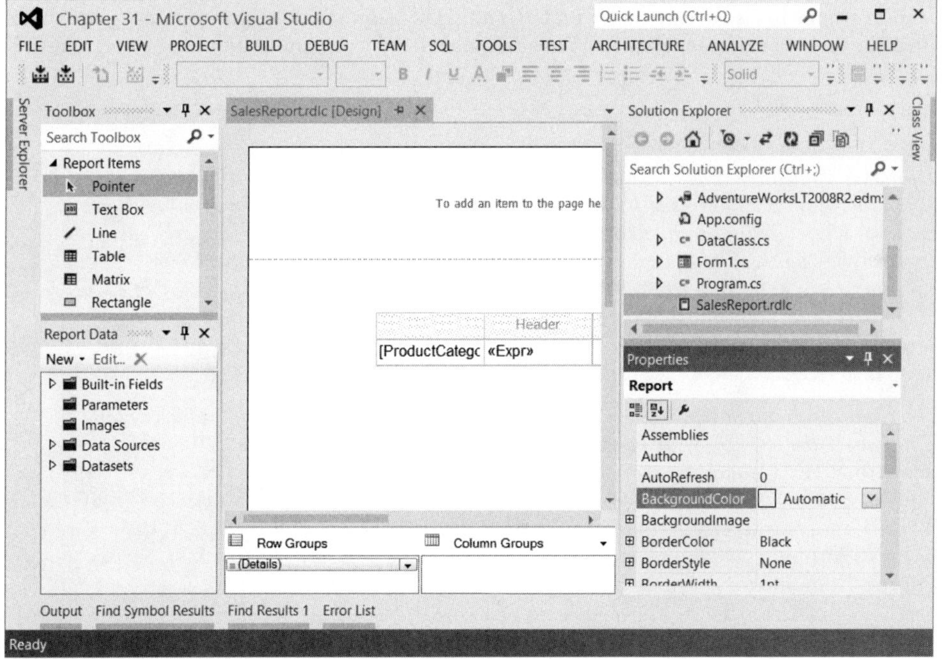

FIGURE 31-2

In the document area you have the design surface upon which you lay out the report. On the bottom left is the Report Data tool window, which contains the data fields that you can drag onto your report. If you accidentally close this window, you can open it again by using the View ➪ Report Data menu. Above it, the Toolbox window contains the controls that you can add to the report surface. When you work with the design surface of a report, a Report menu is also added to the menu bar.

> **NOTE** *Due to the nature of the local report engine, which can't query data sources itself (which is discussed shortly), there unfortunately is no way to preview the report in the designer. This means that in order to view the output of your report you must have previously set up a form with a Report Viewer control, and have written the code that populates the data structures and initiates the rendering process. This can make the report design process a little painful, and it is possibly worthwhile to create a temporary project that makes it easy to test your report. You can find the code required to do so later in this chapter.*

Defining Data Sources

Before you can design a report, you need to start with a data source because it dictates a large portion of the report's design. At design time the data sources won't contain any data, but the report needs the data sources for its structure.

An important concept to understand when starting with the *local* report engine is that you must pass it the data when generating the report — it doesn't query the data sources. The upside of this is that the data can come from a wide variety of sources; all you need to do is query the data, and you can then manipulate it and pass it to the report engine in a structure that it understands. The main structures you can use to populate your report (that the report engine understands) include DataSets, objects, and Entity Framework entities.

> **NOTE** *The* server *report engine (SQL Server Reporting Services) can query SQL Server databases (and some other various data sources via OLEDB and ODBC), and the query to obtain the data used by the report is stored in the report definition file. You can spot report definition files for use by SQL Server Reporting Services fairly easily because they have an* `.rdl` *extension, whereas the files for use by the local report engine have an* `.rdlc` *extension (the* `c` *stands for client-side processing). It's reasonably easy to convert reports from using the local report engine to using SQL Server Reporting Services because the underlying file formats are based upon the same Report Definition Language (RDL).*
>
> *The reason you might use SQL Server Reporting Services over the local report engine is to reduce the load on your server (such as the web server), and offload that to a separate server. Generating reports can be quite resource- and CPU-intensive, so you can make your system a lot more scalable by delegating this task to another server. SQL Server Reporting Services requires a full SQL Server license, but if you use SQL Server Express Edition, you can use a limited version of it if you install the free SQL Server Express Edition with Advanced Services.*

You can use an Entity Framework model for the data source for your report. However, a limitation of the local report engine is that you can't join data from separate data sources (in this case entities) in the report, which is often required in reporting (unless you have imported views from your database into your Entity Framework model that align with the requirements for your report). Therefore, you need to either create a Typed DataSet or create a class to populate with the joined data, which you can then pass to the report engine.

As an example, you simply use the AdventureWorksLT Entity Framework model that you created in Chapter 30, "The ADO.NET Entity Framework," as the source of the data for this report. The first step is to add an entity from this model as a data source for the report. To do so, click the New menu in the Report Data tool window, and select the Dataset menu item. This displays the Dataset Properties window, as shown in Figure 31-3.

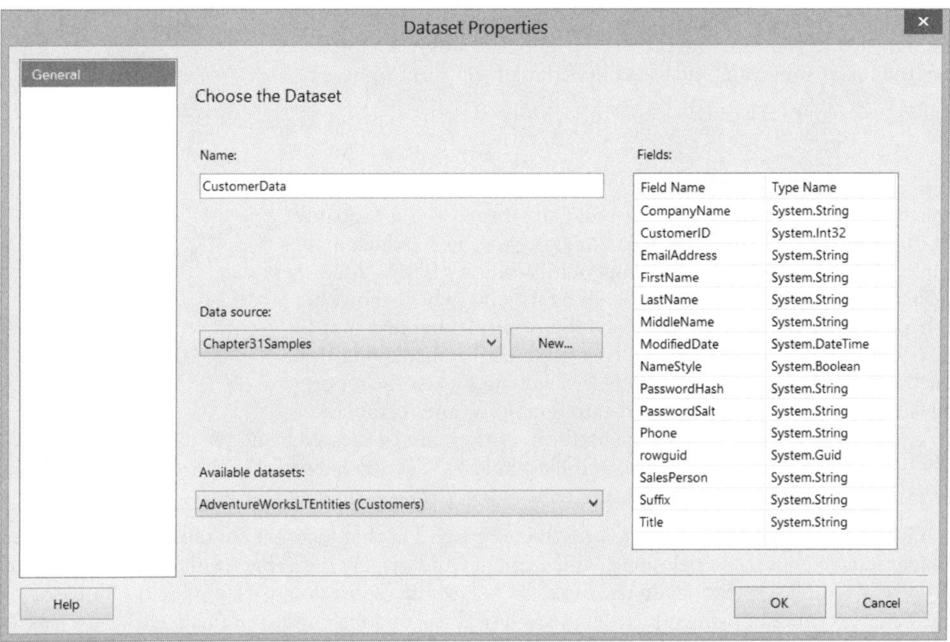

FIGURE 31-3

You should give the data source a meaningful name because you reference the data source name in code when you pass the local report engine the data to populate it with. Enter this name in the Name textbox.

Now you need to select the location of the data source from the Data Source drop-down list. The data source is usually in your project, so you can select it from the list. Click the New button to add a source of data to your project (such as to create a new entity model if it doesn't already exist). This opens the Data Source Configuration Wizard discussed in Chapter 28, "Datasets and Data Binding." You can assume the Entity Framework model of the AdventureWorksLT database that you created in Chapter 30 already exists in your project, so you can skip this step and simply select the type of entity objects that you want to pass to the report (for this example you want the Customer entities) from the Available Datasets drop-down box. Finding which item to select when dealing with Entity Framework entities can be rather confusing initially, but the parent entity is the first part of the item name, and the name of the actual entity you want to use in the report is in the brackets following it. So to select the Customer entity in the AdventureWorksLTEntities model, select the AdventureWorksLTEntities (Customer) item. When you select the item, the list of the fields it contains displays in the Fields list. This data source now displays in the Report Data tool window and lists the fields under it that you can use in your report.

If this data source changes (such as if a new field has been added to it), right-click it and select the Refresh item from the context menu to update it to its new structure.

Reporting Controls

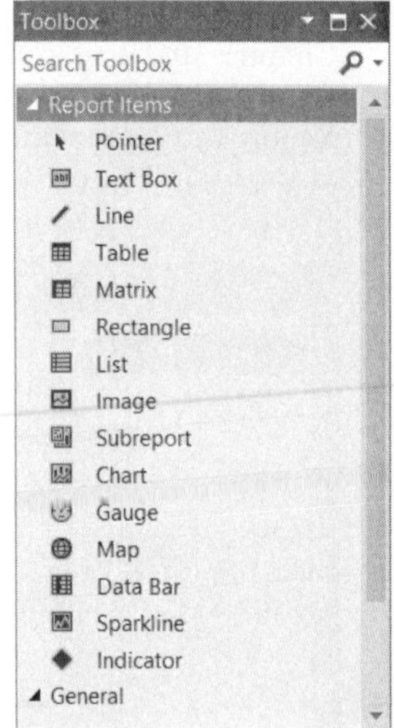

FIGURE 31-4

If you look at the Toolbox tool window, you can see that it contains the various types of controls that you can use in your report, as shown in Figure 31-4.

To use a control, simply drag and drop it on your report at the required position, and then you can set its properties using the Properties tool window. Alternatively, you can select the control in the Toolbox and draw the control on the report design surface. Another method is to right-click anywhere on your report, select the Insert submenu, and select the control you want to insert.

Now take a closer look at each of these controls.

Text Box

The name of the Text Box control is a little confusing because you probably immediately think of a control that the user can enter text into (which makes little sense in a report) like the Text Box control in Windows Forms and other platforms. This mental image is also backed up by its icon (which shows a textbox with a caret in it), but this control is only for displaying text, not for accepting text entry. The Text Box control isn't used just for displaying static text but can also contain expressions (which are evaluated when the report is generated, such as data field values, aggregate functions, and formulas). Expressions can be entered directly into the textbox, or they can be created using the expression builder (discussed in the "Expressions, Aggregates, and Placeholders" section later in this chapter) by right-clicking the textbox and selecting the Expression menu item.

When you drag a data field onto the report, a textbox is created at that location containing a placeholder. The placeholder has an expression behind it, which can get and display the value for that field. A placeholder is essentially a way to hide expressions in textboxes to reduce the report design's complexity. Think of it like a parameterless function, which has a name (referred to as a label) and contains code (known as an expression). In the report designer the textbox displays the label instead of the (potentially long and complex) expression.

> **NOTE** *Sometimes when you drag a data field onto your report, it displays <<Expr>>. This means it created a complex expression to refer to that field (such as getting the field's value in the first row in the dataset), which is hidden behind the <<Expr>> placeholder. If you don't want this behavior (such as showing a value in a report header or footer), it probably should be placed in a table, matrix, or a list to display the value of that field for each row in the dataset. However, if this is the behavior you want, first click the <<Expr>> placeholder, then right-click, select the Placeholder Properties menu item, and enter a meaningful name in the Label textbox.*

You can also drag a data field into an existing textbox. This creates a placeholder with an expression behind it to display the value of that field in the dropped location in the textbox. You may do this if, for example, you want to display the value of that field inline with some static text, or even combine the values of multiple fields in the one textbox.

> **NOTE** *You can quickly create an expression to display a data field value by typing the name of the field surrounded by square brackets (for example, [EmailAddress]). This text automatically turns into a placeholder with an expression behind it to display the corresponding field's value.*

To create a placeholder manually, put the textbox in edit mode (where it displays a cursor for you to type); then right-click and select the Create Placeholder menu item. Creating placeholders and expressions is discussed in the "Expressions, Aggregates, and Placeholders" section later in this chapter.

The format of the text in the Text Box (as a whole) can be set in a number of ways. You can find the formatting properties for the textbox in the Properties tool window, and there is also a Font tab in the Text Box Properties window for the Text Box. (Right-click the textbox, and select the Text Box Properties menu item.) Another way is to use the formatting options found on the Report Formatting toolbar. This is the easiest way but has another side benefit. If you select the textbox in the designer and choose formatting options from this toolbar, it applies these formatting options to all its text. However, the text within a textbox doesn't need to be all the same format, and selecting text *within* the textbox and choosing formatting options using this toolbar applies that formatting to just the selected text. Of course, you can use standard formatting shortcut keys, too, such as Ctrl+B for bold text, and so on.

When you display the value of a number or date data field, you quite often need to format it for display in the report. If your textbox contains just an expression, select the textbox, right-click, select the Text Box Properties menu item, and select the Number tab (as shown in Figure 31-5). Alternatively, if the textbox contains text or other field values, you can format just the value of the placeholder by selecting the placeholder in the textbox, right-clicking, selecting the Placeholder Properties menu item, and selecting the Number tab. Then select how you want the field to be formatted from the options available. If a standard format isn't available, you can select Custom from the Category list and enter a format string, or you can even write an expression to format the value by clicking the *fx* button.

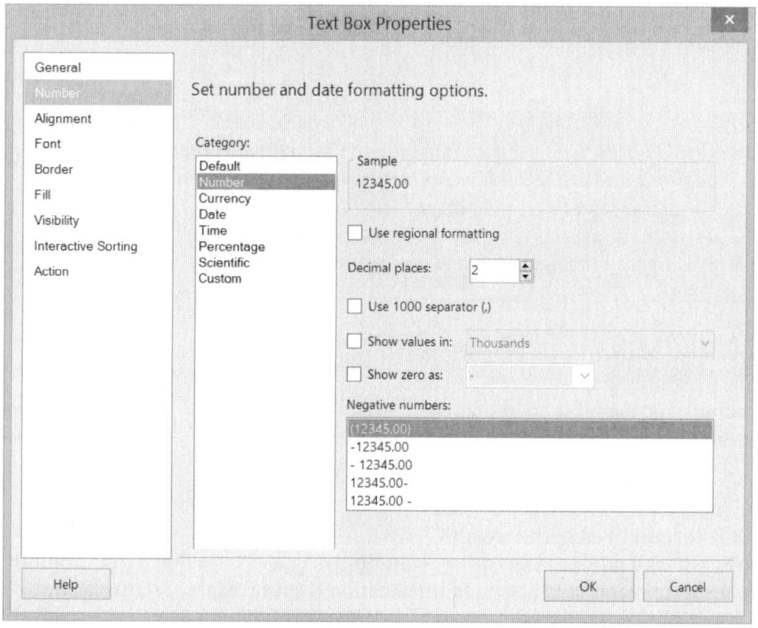

FIGURE 31-5

Line/Rectangle

The Line and Rectangle controls are shapes that you can use to draw on your report. The Line control is often used as a separator between various parts of a report. The Rectangle control is generally used to encapsulate an area in a report. The Rectangle control is a container control, meaning other controls can be placed on it, and when it is moved they will be moved along with it.

Table

The Table control displays the data in a tabular form, with fixed columns and a varying number of rows (depending on the data used to populate the report). In addition to the data, tables can also display column headers, row group headers, and totals rows.

By default, each of the cells in a table is a Text Box control. (Therefore, each cell has the same features described for the Text Box control.) However, a cell can contain any control from the Toolbox (such as an Image control, Chart, Gauge, and so on) by simply dragging the control from the Toolbox into the cell.

When you first drop a Table control onto your report, you'll see that it contains a header row and a data row, as shown in Figure 31-6.

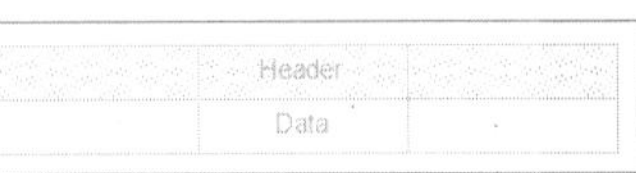

FIGURE 31-6

To display data in the table, drag a field from the appropriate data source in the Report Data tool window and drop it on a column in the table. It creates a placeholder with an expression behind it to display the value of that field in the data row, and it also automatically fills in the header row for that column to give it a title. This header name is the name of the field, but assuming the field name follows Pascal case naming rules, spaces have been intelligently inserted into the name before capital letters (so the CompanyName field automatically has Company Name inserted as its header). If this header name isn't suitable, you can change it by typing a new one in its place.

Another means of setting which field should display in a column is to mouse over a cell in the data row and click the icon that appears in its top-right corner, as shown in Figure 31-7. This displays a menu from which you can select the field to display in that column.

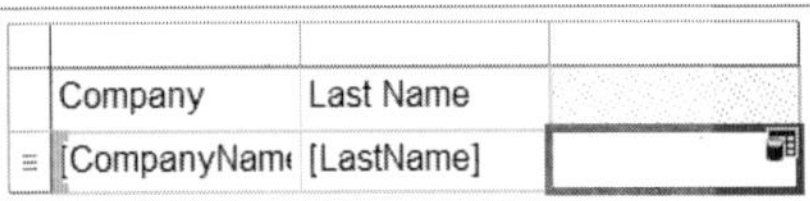

FIGURE 31-7

> **NOTE** *If you have multiple datasets in your report and you haven't specified the dataset that is the source of data for the table, clicking the icon in the top-right corner first requires you to drill down selecting the dataset first (before the field). The dataset selected will then be set as the source of the data for the table, and the next time you click the icon it will only display the fields from that dataset accordingly.*

The table has three columns when you drop it onto a report, but you can add additional columns by simply dragging another field from the Report Data tool window over the table such that the insertion point drawn on the table is at its right edge (as shown in Figure 31-8).

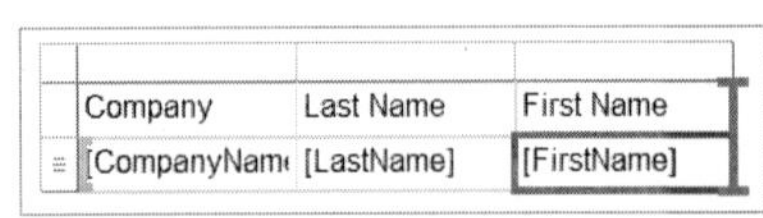

FIGURE 31-8

You can insert a column in the table by the same means, but position the insertion point at the location where the column should be inserted. Alternatively, you can add or insert a new column by right-clicking on a gray column handle, selecting the Insert Column submenu, and selecting the location (Left or Right) relative to the column selected.

To delete an unwanted column, right-click the gray column handle, and select Delete Columns from the menu.

> **NOTE** *Tables can contain only data from a single dataset; therefore, you can't join data from multiple data sources in the one table (such as including data from an Orders data source and a Customers data source to show each order and the name of the customer that placed the order in the table). Therefore you need to do this join in the data that you have passed to populate the report with.*

You can find which dataset is the source of the data for a table by selecting it and finding the DataSetName property in the Properties tool window. You can change which data source it uses by selecting an alternative one from the drop-down list.

Often you'll find that you need to display aggregate values at the bottom of the table, such as in a totals row. There are two ways to implement this. If you have a numeric field that you want to sum all the values in that column, right-click the cell (not the placeholder, but the entire cell) and select the Add Total menu item at the bottom of the menu. (This menu item is enabled only for numeric fields.) A new row will be added below the data row to display the totals, and a SUM aggregate expression for that field will be inserted, as shown in Figure 31-9.

Sales Order ID	Product ID	Unit Price	Line Total
[SalesOrderID]	[ProductID]	[UnitPrice]	[LineTotal]
			[Sum(LineTotal

FIGURE 31-9

Because the Add Total menu item is enabled only for numeric fields, you may need to create the totals row manually (such as if you want a count of items, for example). Right-click the data row's handle, and select Insert Row ➪ Outside Group - Below. Then you can write the aggregate expression in the newly inserted row as required.

If you want to change the type of aggregate function used by the total, you need to modify the expression. Instead of manually making the change, a quicker way to do this is to select the placeholder (and not the cell), right-click, select the Summarize By submenu, and select the alternative aggregate function from the submenu.

A table can filter and sort data from the data source before displaying it. Both of these can be configured in the Tablix Properties window. (Right-click the gray handle area for the table, and select the Tablix Properties menu item.) The Filter tab enables you to specify filters (each consisting of an expression, an operator, and a value). The Sorting tab enables you to specify one or more fields to sort the data by and the sort order for each.

You may also want to group rows in a table, showing a group header between each grouping. For example, you may want to group orders by customer, and show the customer's name in the group header row (which therefore doesn't need to be displayed as a column). You can have multiple levels of grouping, enabling complex nested hierarchies to be created. Again, there are multiple ways to set the grouping for a table. One is to select the table and drag a field from the Report Data tool window onto the Row Groups pane at the bottom of the report designer *above* the (Details) entry already there. Another way (that gives you additional options for the grouping) is to right-click the data row's gray handle and select Add Group ➪ Parent Group from the menu. This displays the Tablix Group window, as shown in Figure 31-10.

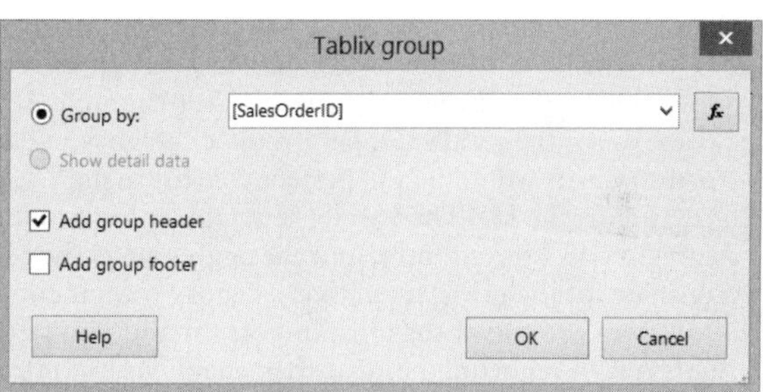

FIGURE 31-10

Here you can select the field or an expression to group by and there are also options to add group header or footer rows. For example, these additional options may be useful if you want to display the value of the group field in a header above the data for a group and totals in the footer below it.

By default (even if you select to create a group header row or if there is a column displaying the group field's value) a new column will be inserted to the left of the data configured to show the value of the group field. You can safely delete this column without affecting the grouping if this is not the behavior you are after.

> **NOTE** *When you add a group that has a group header row, here are some things that may improve your report layout. First, delete the column it added, and then set the first cell in the group header row to display the value of the field it is grouping by. Then select all the cells in the group header row, right-click, and select the Merge Cells menu item to turn them into a single cell (enabling the grouping field's value to stretch across the columns). You may also want to add a border or background color to the group header row so that it stands out.*

By default there is no formatting applied to the table apart from a solid light gray border around the cells (or technically the control in each cell). Often you want to have a border around the table, between columns, or even between individual cells. Or perhaps you want a line between the table header and the data, and the table footer and the data. In all of these cases the easiest way to set the borders is to select the cells to apply a border to and use the Report Borders toolbar (as shown in Figure 31-11) to set them.

FIGURE 31-11

Often you'll also want to set a background color for the header row (and a foreground color to match). The easiest way to do this is to select the cells and use the Background Color/Foreground Color buttons from the Report Formatting toolbar to select the color to use (shown in Figure 31-12).

FIGURE 31-12

Matrix

The Matrix control is used for cross-tab reports (similar to Pivot Tables in Excel). Essentially, a Matrix control groups data in two dimensions (both rows and columns), and you'll use it when you have two variables and an aggregate field for each combination of the two. So, for example, if you want to see the total sales per product category in each country, this would be the perfect control to use (see Figure 31-13). The variables would be the product category and the country, and the aggregate is the total revenue (of the products in that category to that country). Matrices are one of the most important and powerful controls in reporting because they enable useful information to be extracted from raw data.

	United Kingdom	United States
Bike Racks	$1584.00	$720.00
Bottles and Cages	$86.35	$71.86
Bottom Brackets	$777.52	$542.65
Brakes	$383.40	$447.30
Caps	$91.70	$185.67
Chains	$48.58	$48.58
Cleaners	$137.40	$114.48

FIGURE 31-13

What stands out about using the Matrix control (over the Table control) is that you don't know what columns there will be at design time. Both the number of rows and columns for the matrix (and their headers) will be dictated by the data.

> **NOTE** *The matrix is closely related to the Table control, and both (along with the List control, which is discussed shortly) are the same core control under the covers (called a Tablix). However, they are templated as separate controls to distinguish their different uses. If you were to delete the column group (and its related rows and columns), you effectively turn the Matrix control into a table.*

When you drop a Matrix control on your report, you'll see that it contains both a column header and a row header that intersect on a data cell (as shown in Figure 31-14), and that both the Row Groups and Column Groups panes at the bottom of the designer have grouping entries (whereas the Table control had only a row grouping entry).

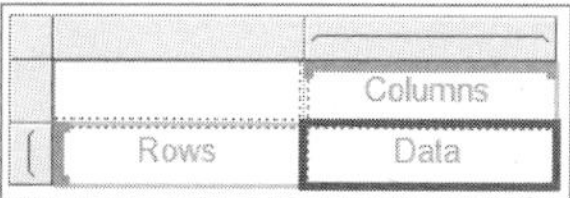

FIGURE 31-14

For this example, you will be using the example of displaying the total sales per product category in each country described earlier. Your data source (a collection of custom objects specifically created and populated as the source of data for this report) contains four fields: ProductCategory, Country, Revenue, and OrderQuantity. What you need to do is drag the ProductCategory field from the Report Data tool window onto the row header (marked Rows), and the Country field onto the column header (marked Columns). Then drag the Revenue field (or the OrderQuantity field — either one) onto the data cell (marked Data), and you're done! Assuming the field you aggregate is numeric, it will have automatically applied a SUM aggregate to the Revenue field.

> **NOTE** *The designer will have automatically inserted a header label into the top-left cell, but generally you want to delete it.*

The matrix in the report designer now looks like Figure 31-15, and after adding some formatting you get an output similar to that shown previously in Figure 31-13 when you generate the report.

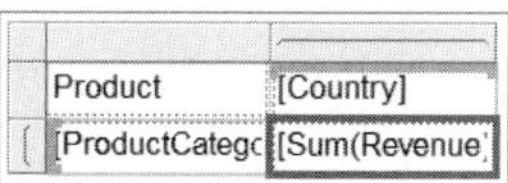

FIGURE 31-15

As with the Table control, you can display totals, but the Matrix control enables you to have column totals as well as row totals. When you right-click the data cell, the Add Total menu item is actually a submenu (unlike the Table control), from which you can select a Row total or a Column total.

The Matrix control doesn't limit you to having just one aggregate per "intersection." For example, you may want to show both the total revenue and quantity for each country/product category. Simply drag another field to aggregate (such as the OrderQuantity field) next to the Revenue field in the matrix, and it too appears for each country (as shown in Figure 31-16).

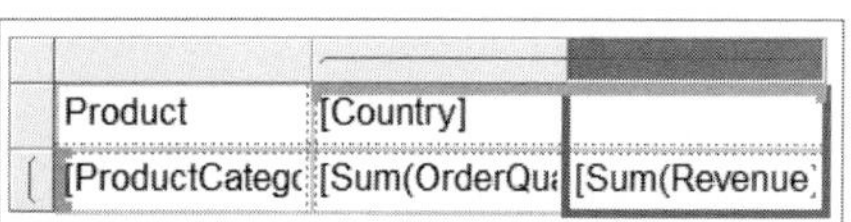

FIGURE 31-16

You can also extend the matrix to show additional "dimensions" by having multiple row or column groups. Again, simply drag the additional fields to group by into the appropriate position in the row/column grouping header area.

List

Lists are a more freeform means of displaying data than the Table and Matrix controls and provide a lot of flexibility in the display of the data. If you were to drop a field directly onto a report, you would find that it displays only the field's value in the dataset's first row, but the List control enables you to define a template (as shown in Figure 31-17) and enumerates through the data source, populating and displaying that template for each row (or group).

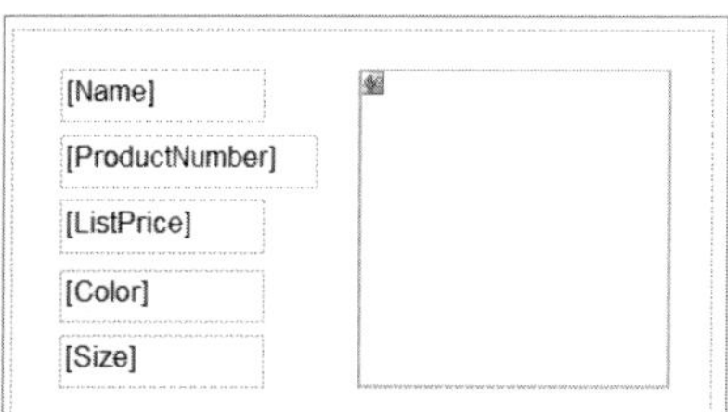

FIGURE 31-17

Being yet another form of the same base control used by the Table and Matrix controls, the List control shares many of the same features that they have.

Image

The Image control is used to display an image in your report. The source of this image can be from within your project (as an embedded image resource in your project), an external image (specified by a filesystem path or URL), or from a database field (a blob). When you drop this control on a report, a window is displayed enabling you to set these options (and others such as its size, border, and so on), as shown in Figure 31-18.

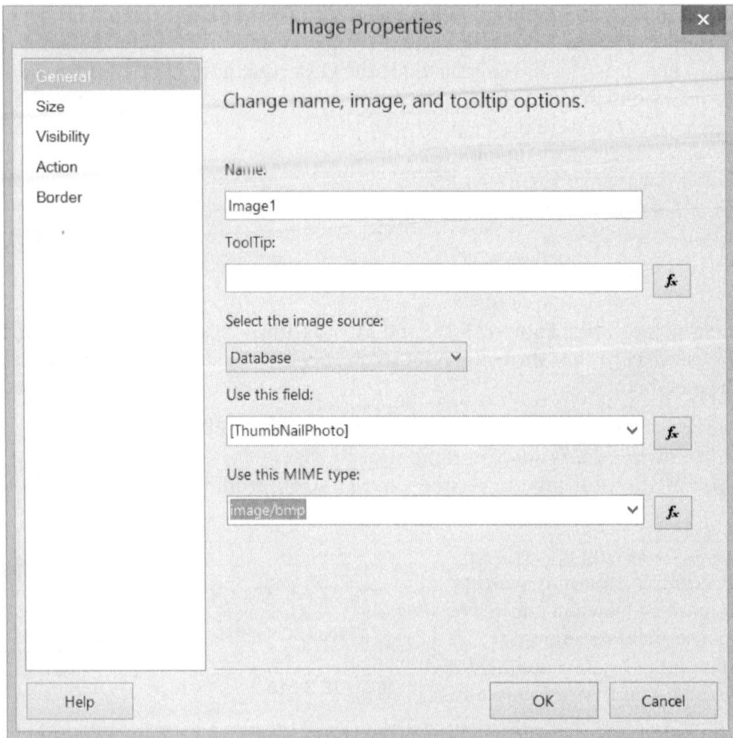

FIGURE 31-18

The options that appear depend on the source you selected for the image from the Select the Image Source drop-down box.

If you want to show external images (for example, from a file path) there are two things you must note. You must add a protocol prefix to the location you specify (for example, file://, http://, and so on), and you must also set the `EnableExternalImages` property on the `LocalReport` object to true because this is not enabled by default.

```
reportViewer.LocalReport.EnableExternalImages = true;
```

Subreport

The Subreport control is used as a placeholder where the contents of another report can be inserted into this report (enabling complex reports to be created). This is discussed in detail in the "Subreports" section later in this chapter.

Chart

Charts provide a more visual representation of data, enabling patterns and anomalies in the data to be easily identified.

When you drop a Chart control onto a report, it immediately opens the Select Chart Type window (as shown in Figure 31-19), allowing you to select from a wide range of available chart types.

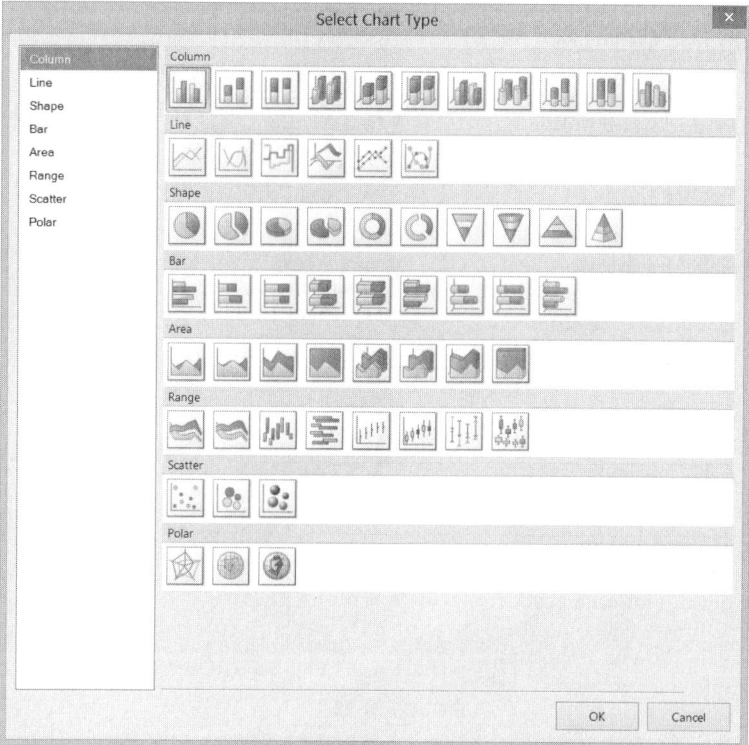

FIGURE 31-19

You can always change the type of chart at a later point by right-clicking it and selecting the Change Chart Type menu item.

Double-clicking a chart (like other controls) puts it into edit mode (as shown in Figure 31-20), which consists of a number of subcontrols. Depending on the type of chart you choose, it will have different controls arranged on its surface. All chart types, however, have a title and legend in addition to the chart itself. You can rearrange these components (or delete them) as you see fit.

Charts consist of categories, series, and data — each essentially representing an axis. Categories are used to group data, data specifies the source of the values to display, and series add additional "dimensions" that will be determined when the report is generated (the same concept upon which the Matrix control works). For simple charts you configure the categories and data axes; more complex charts also use the series axis.

When the chart is in edit mode, it displays drop zones (one for each axis) to the right of the chart, onto which you can drop the fields that each should use. For more advanced charts you can drop multiple fields in each drop zone for multiple groupings/value displays.

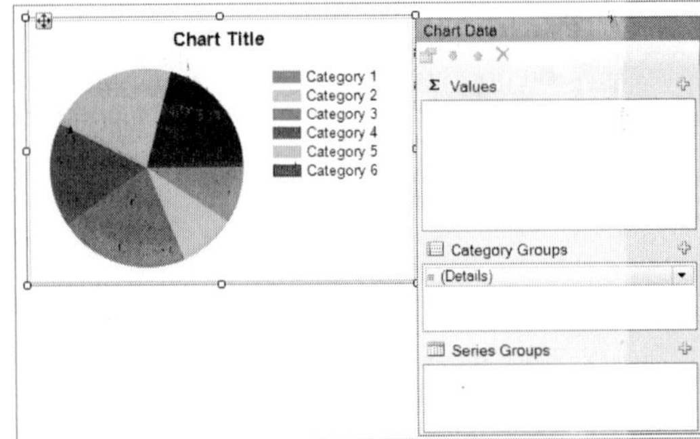

FIGURE 31-20

Using the same source of data that you used when generating the matrix report, you start by generating a simple bar chart (the total sales per product category). Drop the Chart control onto the report, set it to be a 3-D Clustered Bar chart, and double-click it to put it into edit mode. Drop the ProductCategory field onto the Category zone and the Revenue field onto the Data zone. Change the chart and axes titles as you see fit. Another thing you want to do (to show a label for every product category) is to right-click the vertical axis, select Axis Labels from the menu, and change the Interval from Auto to 1. Now when you generate the report, you get an output similar to Figure 31-21.

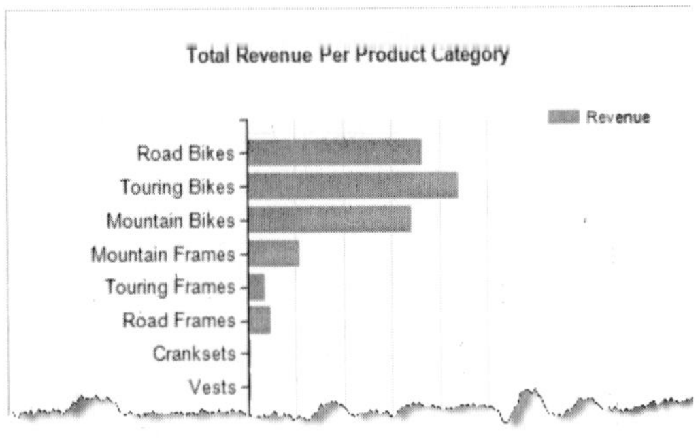

FIGURE 31-21

Note that currently the legend is of no real value because in a bar chart it is designed to show the series group values (which you aren't using in this chart).

Now generate a chart that works much like the Matrix control by setting the series grouping to add an additional dimension to your previous chart (so that it now displays the total quantity of sales for each product category per country). Drag the Country field onto the Series zone and run the report again. You have the total sales for each product category split out per country, as shown in Figure 31-22.

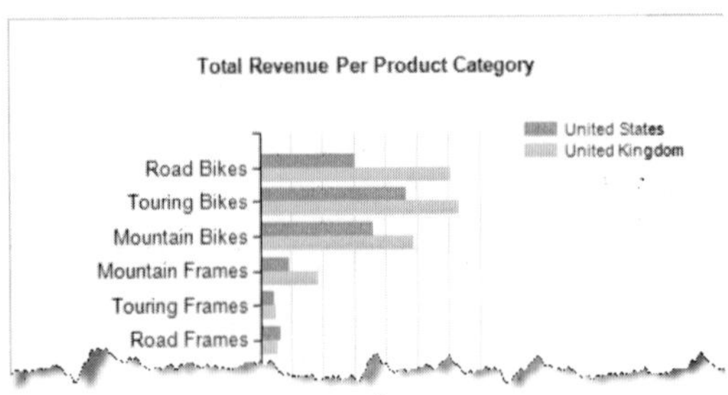

FIGURE 31-22

Note how the legend now shows which bar color represents each country because you are now making use of the series axis.

Gauge

The Gauge control is yet another means to visually represent the data. Gauges are generally designed to display a single value. (Although some gauges can each display a fixed number of separate values.) This can be quite useful in displaying Key Performance Indicators (KPIs), for example.

When you drop a Gauge control onto a report, it immediately opens the Select Gauge Type window, as shown in Figure 31-23, allowing you to select from a number of different linear and radial gauge types.

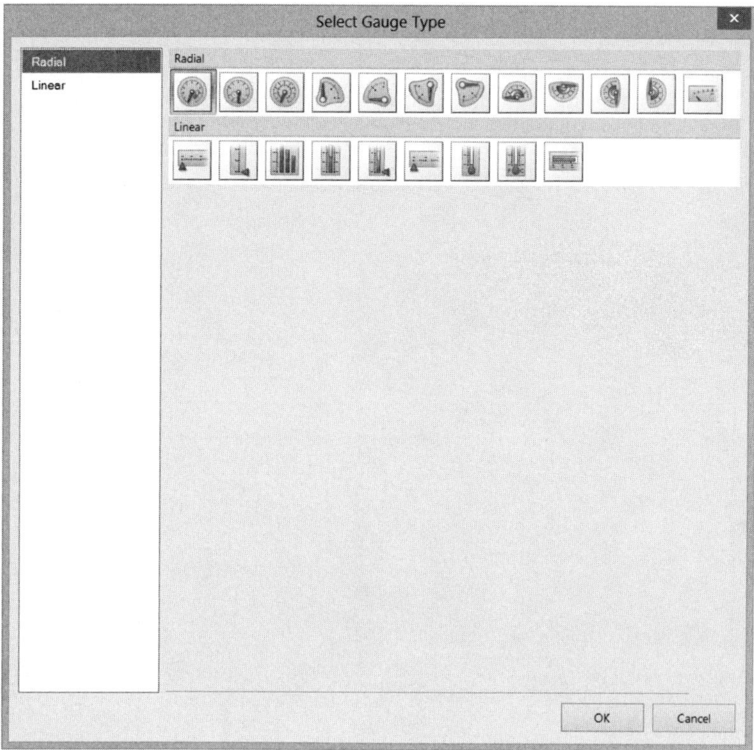

FIGURE 31-23

> **NOTE** *Unlike the Chart control, you cannot change the type of gauge after it has been created.*

For this example, use the Radial with Mini Gauge gauge. When you put the gauge into edit mode (by double-clicking it) it displays a drop zone to the right (as shown in Figure 31-24), which has one or more field placeholders (depending on how many values the gauge can display). Your selected gauge can display two values (one in the main gauge and one in the mini gauge), so it will have two field placeholders. When you drop a field from the Report Data window onto a field placeholder, it automatically applies an aggregate because it displays only a single value in its related gauge. Numeric fields automatically have a SUM aggregate applied, and other fields have a COUNT aggregate applied.

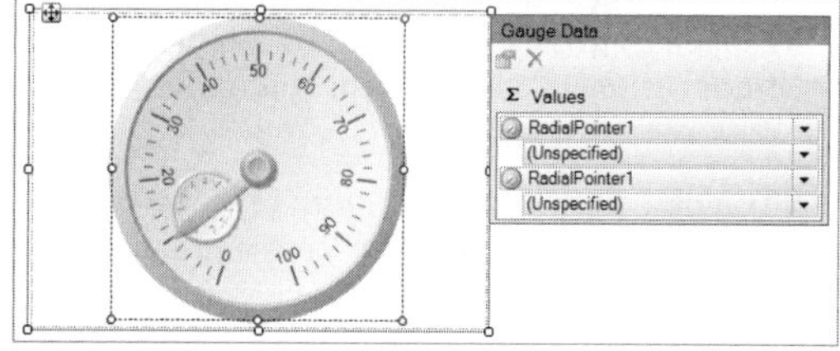

FIGURE 31-24

Gauges have a fixed scale, and you must specify the minimum and maximum values that it displays. The nature of the Gauge control means that it won't automatically determine these values. To change these values you need to select the scale (as shown in Figure 31-24); then right-click and select Scale Properties from the menu. This displays the window shown in Figure 31-25.

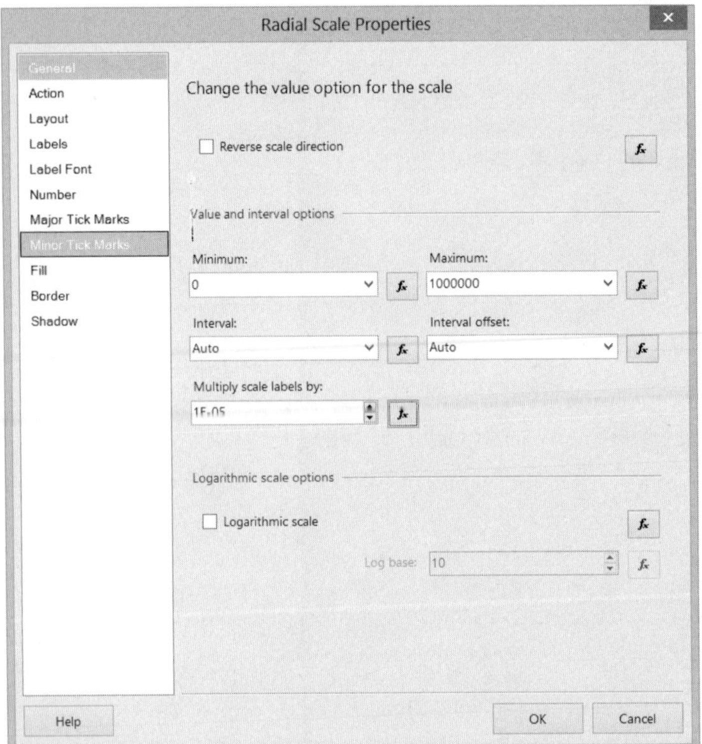

FIGURE 31-25

Your example will have expected values of up to 1 million, so you will set that as your maximum value. Leave the interval options to be automatically determined (this alters which scale labels display); although you can change these if the output is not as you want. When dealing with small or large values (as you are with this example), it may be useful to set the value of the Multiply Scale Labels By option. Instead of showing large numbers on the intervals, you can set the value labels to be multiplied by 0.00001, meaning that it displays 1 instead of 100000, 2 instead of 200000, and so on (making for a much less cluttered gauge). In this case it would be important to add a label to the gauge (right-click it and select Add Label from the menu) showing the multiplier that should be used with the label values to get the real value being represented.

You can also add one or more ranges to your gauge. For example, you might want to indicate that a range of values is acceptable by shading an area under the scale green, and shade another area red indicating the value should be of concern. Right-click your gauge and select Add Range from the menu. This automatically inserts a range into your gauge — to configure it, right-click and select Range Properties from the menu. From this window you can enter at what values the range should start and end, and you most likely (depending on your needs) want to change the start and end width of the range (generally so they are the same value). From the Fill tab you can change the color of the range to match its meaning (generally green = good, red = bad).

The final output of your gauge is shown in Figure 31-26.

FIGURE 31-26

Map

The purpose of the Map control is to allow geospatial information to be represented in a manner that is useful to view. In order to make use of a map to display data, you need to have some specific information available to you:

- **Spatial data –** More specifically, a set of coordinates that specify location information. The source for this data can be SQL Server, a spatial database, or an Environmental Systems Research Institute, Inc. (ESRI) Shapefile.
- **Analytical data –** The data that you want to display that is somehow correlated to location information. The "somehow" is part of the magic of using the Map control. It is possible, for example, to summarize information by state and represent the aggregated information on a map. But to accomplish this, there needs to be a connection between the analytical data and the spatial information, a connection that is typically in the form of some value (such as country, state, region) that can be converted into coordinates.

When you drag the Map control from the Toolbox onto the report surface, the Map Layer wizard is initiated. The steps involved in the wizard align with the need for both spatial and analytical data. You specify the spatial data source (which is most easily visualized as the map image), the visualization parameters of the spatial data (the scale, the data labels, the color theme), which can be an existing map gallery, the analytical data source, and the relationship between the spatial and analytical data.

Data Bar

The Data Bar control is a simplified version of the Chart control. The simplification is that it allows only horizontal or vertical bars. By restricting the options, the configuration of the controls is a lot simpler. As you can see in Figure 31-27, providing the aggregation value and the category group is sufficient to display the data in columnar form.

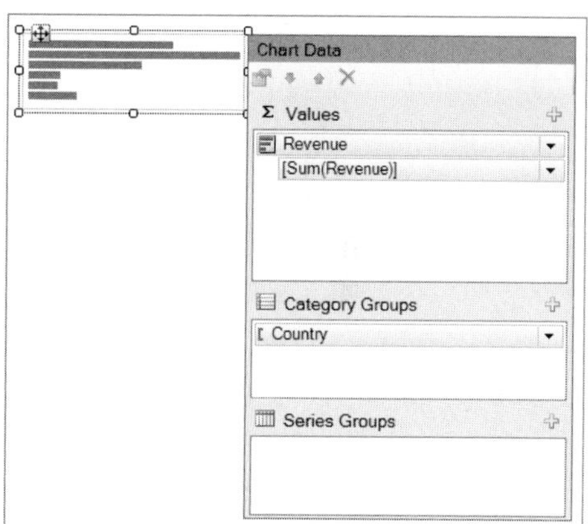

FIGURE 31-27

Sparkline

The Sparkline control performs a similar function to the Data Bar. That is to say that it's a simplified version of the Chart control that only allows visualization related to sparklines. A sparkline is a very small chart, typically a line chart, that is drawn without labels on either axis. Its purpose is to show the variation in data, typically over time. The major distinguishing characteristic between a sparkline and a full chart is that a full chart endeavors to display as much information as can be reasonably accommodated, whereas a sparkline is intended to give the impression of a trend with limited detail. Figure 31-28 illustrates what a sparkline might look like, along with how it can be configured with both aggregated and grouping values.

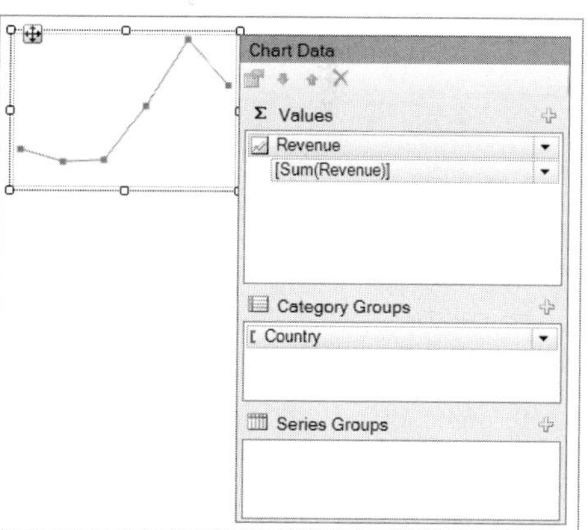

FIGURE 31-28

Indicator

The Indicator control is a simplified version of the Gauge control. Like the Gauge control, the Indicator control is frequently used to illustrate the status of a KPI, categorizing a value into three or four states (for example, red/yellow/green). The configuration of the Indicator control consists of two fundamental steps. The first is to select how you want the state to be visualized. The second is to identify the range of values that fall into each state. Figure 31-29 shows the dialog that is used to specify the range. This dialog can be accessed by right-clicking on the control, selecting Indicator properties from the context menu, and selecting the Value and States tab.

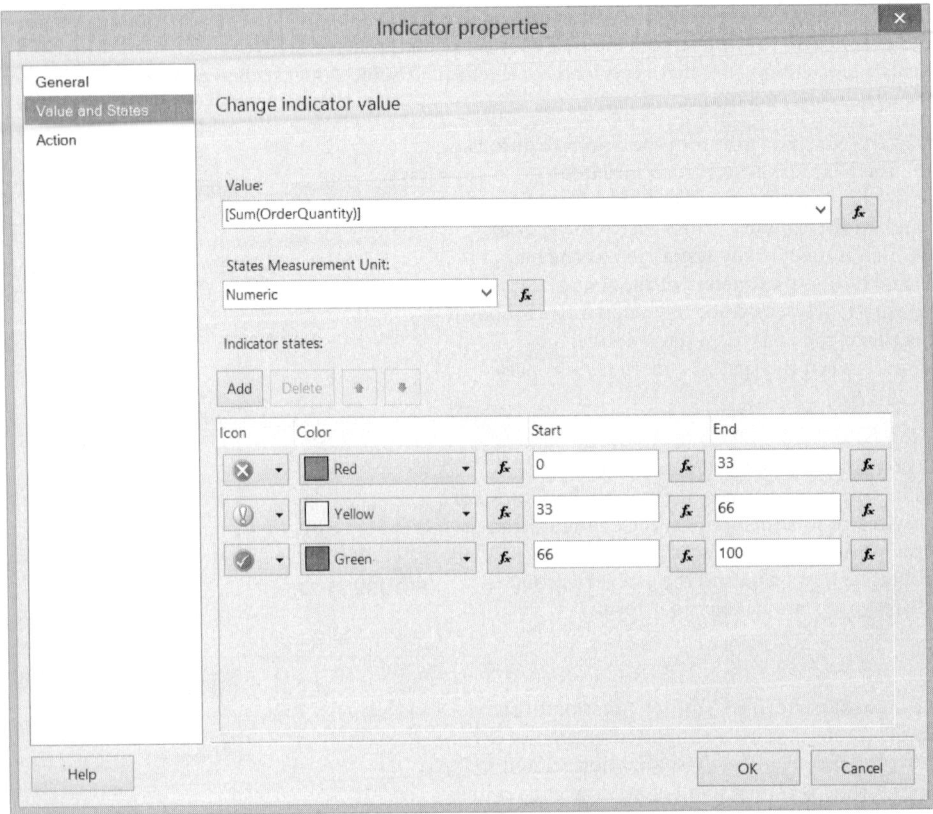

FIGURE 31-29

Expressions, Placeholders, and Aggregates

Expressions provide the flexibility and power in your report and are used everywhere from getting a value from a dataset, aggregating data, transforming data, and performing calculations through to decision-making processes using conditional statements (IIF, and so on). Anything dynamically inserted into the report when it is generated is handled by an expression. You might think of expressions as formulas that returns a value. Almost everything in a report can be controlled by an expression, including most control properties. So far you've already seen the expressions generated when you drag a field onto the report, and how the expression is "hidden" behind a placeholder, which can be used to hide its complexity. All expressions start with an equals (=) sign and return a single value.

Expressions can be categorized into simple expressions and complex expressions. Simple expressions refer only to a single field, which may have an aggregate function applied. Simple expressions display a simplified version of the underlying expression as the label of the placeholder when displayed in the report designer. An example of a simple expression is:

```
=Fields!Revenue.Value
```

This displays in the report designer simply as [Revenue].

Complex expressions, however, either reference multiple fields or include operators, and they appear in the report designer with <<Expr>> as their default placeholder label. (Although this can be changed in the placeholder properties to something more meaningful.) Complex expressions essentially use VB for their syntax; although, they still must consist of only a single line of code that returns a value. They can, however, make calls to more complicated multiline functions if necessary, as will be discussed in the next section. An example of a complex expression is:

```
=Fields!ProductCategory.Value + " sold to " + Fields!Country.Value
```

Now take a look at the process of creating an expression. As previously noted, when you drop a field onto a report, it creates an expression that returns the value of that field from the dataset. To see this in action, drop a table on a report and then drop a field from the Report Data window into one of its cells. As discussed earlier, what is displayed in the cell is a placeholder label. When you right-click the placeholder, you can select Expression from the menu to view and edit its underlying expression. This displays the Expression Builder window, as shown in Figure 31-30.

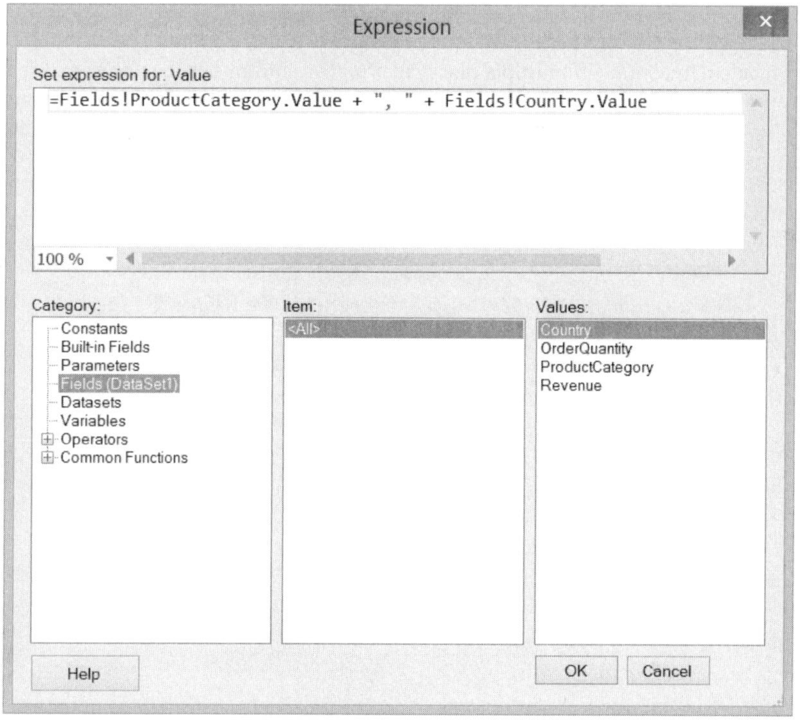

FIGURE 31-30

As its name might suggest, the Expression Builder helps you build expressions. At the top is the code area where you can type in the expression, and below it is the category tree, category items list, and a values list (which is only shown when values are available). The code area supports IntelliSense, tooltips (displaying function parameters), and syntax checking (squiggly red underlines to show errors); unfortunately it doesn't support syntax highlighting. The lower "builder areas" help you build an expression, which is especially helpful when you don't know the syntax or what functionality is available. The Category tree allows you to drill down to select a category (such as a dataset, an operator type, a function type, and so on). The Item list displays what is available in that category, and the Values list (if values are available) displays the values for that item. For functions and operators it displays some helpful information on the selected item (what it does and examples of how it is used) in place of the Values list.

When you create a report, many properties have an *fx* button next to them (in the dialog windows) or an Expression entry (in their drop-down list in the Properties tool window). This means that those properties can have expressions assigned to determine the value that should be applied to them, and clicking this button or selecting this item from the drop-down list opens the Expression Builder window in which you can create an expression to control the value of that property. This is extremely useful in conditional formatting scenarios, such as toggling the visibility or color of a control based upon the data displayed.

> **NOTE** *In conditional formatting scenarios you can find the IIF function (Inline If) useful to choose between two values based upon the result of a given expression (with the result applied as the value of the property). Other "program flow" functions that are useful are the Choose and Switch functions.*

Sometimes you want to use a calculated value in multiple places in a report, and rather than have the report recalculate the value multiple times, you'd like to calculate it once and reuse the value (speeding up the generation of the report in the process). This is where variables can be useful. Being named variables you may think that you can change their values (such as using them in a running totals scenario), but unfortunately that isn't the case. Their value can be set only once, and then this value is used from that point on without it needing to be recalculated.

> **NOTE** *Running totals are actually implemented in a report using the RunningValue function (built into the reporting engine) in an expression.*

There are two types of variables: report variables and group variables, with their name matching their scope. The value of report values is set in the Report ➪ Report Properties window, in the Variables tab, as shown in Figure 31-31.

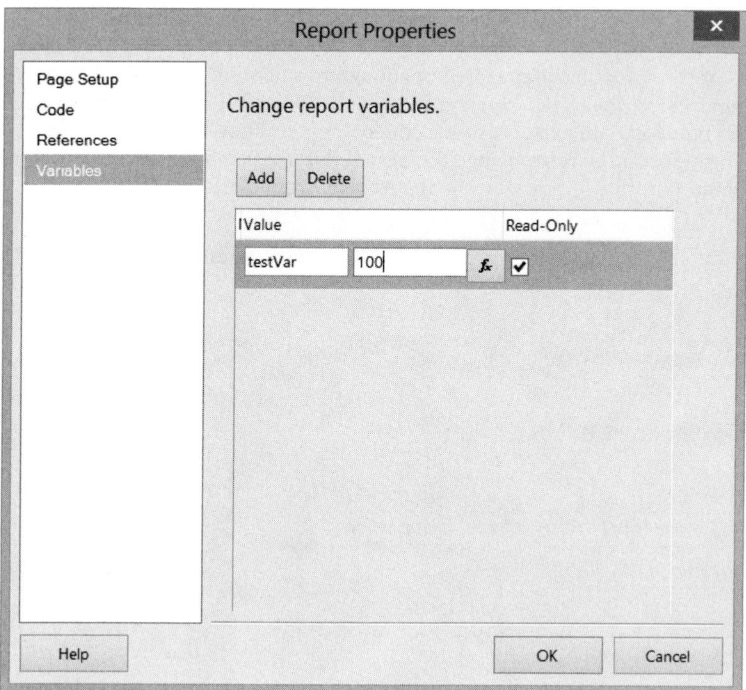

FIGURE 31-31

The variables defined here are available anywhere in the report. Click the Add button to create a new entry, where you can give the variable a name and a value. If it's a constant value, you can specify its value there, or you can click the *fx* button to create an expression that calculates the value. This calculation will be performed only once, and the value will be reused on subsequent references of the variable.

> **NOTE** *You can find the variables available to an expression in the Expression Builder under the Variables category.*

If you create a variable called `testVar`, you can use it in an expression like so:

```
=Variables!testVar.Value
```

You can also use report variables to define constant values. This enables you to centrally define values that are used in multiple places without having to "hard code" them in each individual place.

The other type of variable is the group variable. This works in much the same way as the report variables, except the scope of the calculated value is just the current grouping in a Table/Matrix/List control (and any child groupings). Its value is calculated each time the grouping changes, so if you have a calculation to make for each grouping (whose value is reused throughout that grouping), this is how you would implement it. To create a group variable, open the Group Properties window, go to the Variables tab, and then create and use the variable in the same way as demonstrated for the report variable. You can test the behavior of how the calculated value is reused and subsequently recalculated when the group changes by creating the following expression and seeing when its output changes:

```
=Round(Rnd() * 100)
```

Custom Code

Sometimes the built-in functions of the reporting engine are not enough to suit your purposes. When you need a complex multiline function to perform a calculation or make a decision, this must be written outside the expression builder (because expressions can exist only on a single line). You have two ways to achieve this: by embedding the code in the report or by referencing an external .NET assembly that contains your custom functions. You can set up both of these options at the report level from the Report ➪ Report Properties menu.

When you select the Code tab, you see what is shown in Figure 31-32. (A custom function is already entered for the demonstration.)

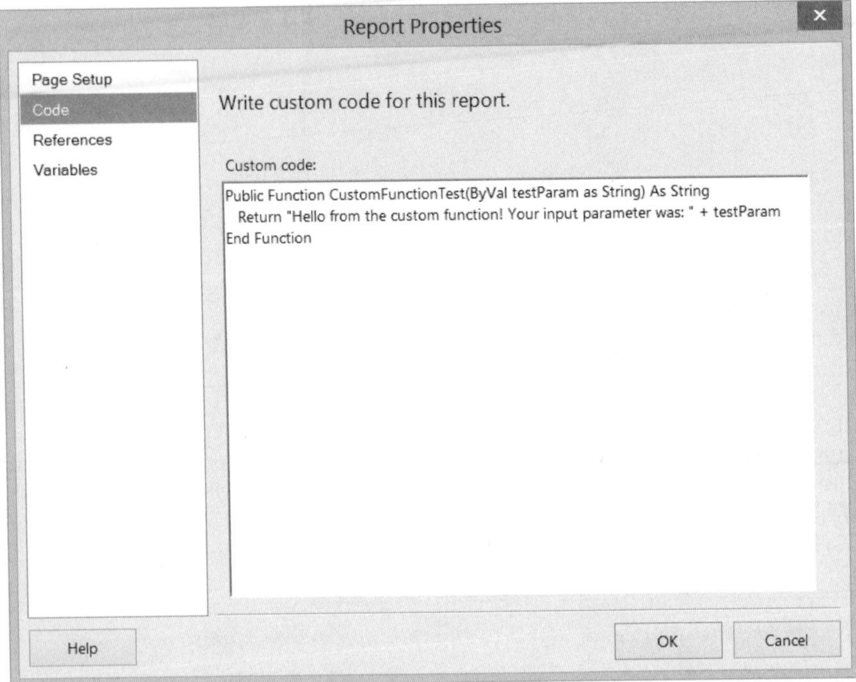

FIGURE 31-32

As you can see, this is a sparse code editor. There is no syntax highlighting, error checking, or IntelliSense, so it isn't friendly to use. If there is an error in your code, it will be caught when the project is compiled and the compilation will fail (pointing out the cause of the error in the Error List tool window). After you write your functions in here (using VB as the language) you can add a textbox to your report, open the expression builder, and call them like so:

```
=Code.CustomFunctionTest("Test Input")
```

> **NOTE** *The IntelliSense in the expression builder doesn't show the available function names when you type* `Code.` *in the editor, nor does it show what parameters the function takes. In addition, the only assemblies automatically referenced for use are the System.Convert, System.Math, and Microsoft.VisualBasic — if you need to use assemblies other than these, you need to add references to them in the References tab, which is discussed shortly.*

Calling the function shown in Figure 31-32 with this expression displays the following in the textbox:

```
Hello from the custom function!  Your input parameter was: Test Input
```

If you want to reuse the custom functions among multiple reports, you are better off writing the code in a .NET assembly and referencing it from each report that requires its functions. You can create a Class Library project, write the code (in either VB or C#), and then reference it in your report. Unfortunately, you will face a few difficulties in ensuring that the report can find the assembly and configuring its code access security settings so that the report has the permissions to execute its functions — so it's not a completely straightforward process. However, you are about to walk through the process required to get it working here.

Create a new project using the Class Library template called CustomReportingFunctions. Create a class called `MyFunctions`, and add the following function to it:

VB

```
Public Shared Function CustomFunctionTest(ByVal testParam As String) As String
    Return "Your input parameter was: " + testParam
End Function
```

C#

```
public static string CustomFunctionTest(string testParam)
{
    return "Your input parameter was: " + testParam;
}
```

You also need to add the following attribute to the assembly to enable it to be called by the reporting engine. This is added to `AssemblyInfo.vb` for VB developers (under the `My Project` folder, requiring the Show All Files option to be on in order to be seen), and to `AssemblyInfo.cs` for C# developers (under the `Properties` folder).

VB

```
<Assembly: System.Security.AllowPartiallyTrustedCallers>
```

C#

```
[assembly: System.Security.AllowPartiallyTrustedCallers]
```

For the report to find the assembly, it must be installed in the Global Assembly Cache (GAC). This means you need to give the assembly a strong name, by going to the Properties of the custom functions assembly, opening the Signing tab, checking in the Sign the Assembly check box, and choosing/creating a strong name key file. Now you can compile the project and then install the assembly in GAC by opening the Visual Studio Command Prompt, entering

```
gacutil -i <assembly_path>
```

and replacing `<assembly_path>` with the actual path to the compiled assembly.

> **NOTE** *Each time you update this assembly, remember to install it into the GAC again.*

Now you can reference the assembly in the report. Open the Report Properties window and go to the References tab (as shown in Figure 31-33). Click the Add button; then click the ellipsis button on the blank entry that appears. Find the assembly (you may need to browse by file to find it) and click OK.

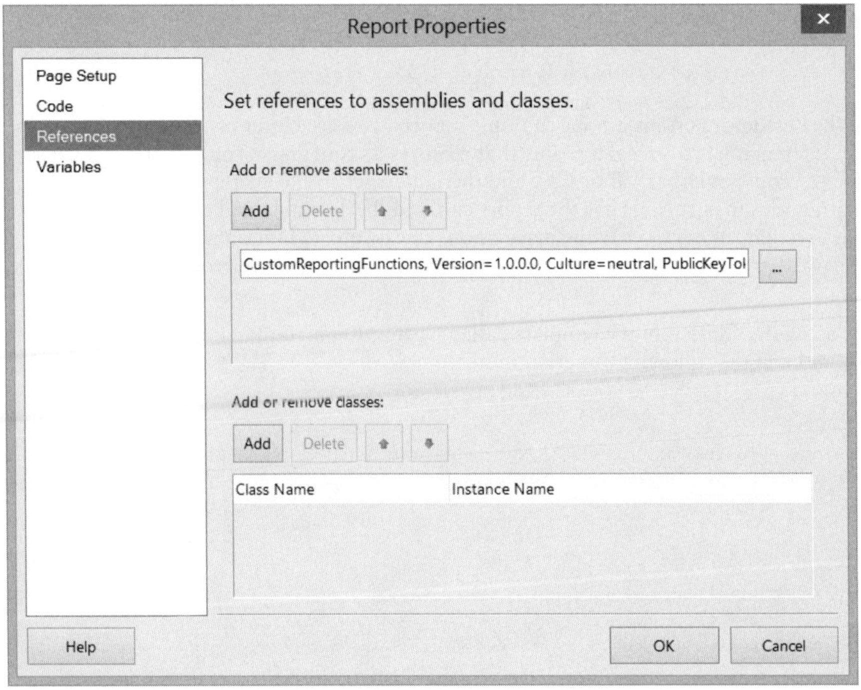

FIGURE 31-33

Note the Add or Remove Classes area below the Add or Remove Assemblies area. This is used to automatically create instances of classes in the referenced assemblies. You made your function shared (or static as it is referred to in C#) so you don't need an instance of the `MyFunctions` class. However, if the function was not shared/static and you need a class instance, you need to configure these instances here. (Because a class cannot be instantiated in an expression.) To do this, specify the class name (including its namespace) and give it an instance name (that is, the name of the variable that you will use in your expressions to refer to the instance of the class). The reporting engine handles instantiating the class and assigns the reference to a variable with the given name, so you can use it in your expressions.

Now you are ready to reference your function in an expression, although slightly differently from how you used the function when it was embedded in the report. You need to refer to the function by its full namespace, class, and function name, for example:

```
=CustomReportingFunctions.MyFunctions.CustomFunctionTest("Test Input")
```

You are almost done, but not quite. The final piece of the puzzle is to specify that the assembly should be run with full trust in the domain of the report engine. This is done when initiating the report rendering process (which is covered in the "Rendering Reports" section later in this chapter) and requires the strong name of the assembly:

VB

```
Dim customAssemblyName As String = "CustomReportingFunctions, Version=1.0.0.0, " &
                                   "Culture=neutral, PublicKeyToken=b9c8e588f9750854"

Dim customAssembly As Assembly = Assembly.Load(customAssemblyName)
Dim assemblyStrongName As StrongName = CreateStrongName(customAssembly)
reportEngine.AddFullTrustModuleInSandboxAppDomain(assemblyStrongName)
```

C#

```
string customAssemblyName = "CustomReportingFunctions, Version=1.0.0.0, " +
                            "Culture=neutral, PublicKeyToken=b9c8e588f9750854";

Assembly customAssembly = Assembly.Load(customAssemblyName);
StrongName assemblyStrongName = CreateStrongName(customAssembly);
reportEngine.AddFullTrustModuleInSandboxAppDomain(assemblyStrongName);
```

There are two things you can note from this code. The first is that you are loading the custom assembly from the GAC using its name (to obtain its strong name so you can notify the reporting engine that it's trusted), including its version, culture, and public key token. This string can be obtained by copying it from where you added the assembly reference to the report in its Report Properties dialog box.

The second is the use of the `GetStrongName` function to return the `StrongName` object, the code for which is here:

VB

```
Private Shared Function CreateStrongName(ByVal assembly As Assembly) As StrongName
    Dim assemblyName As AssemblyName = assembly.GetName()

    If assemblyName Is Nothing Then
        Throw New InvalidOperationException("Could not get assembly name")
    End If

    ' Get the public key blob
    Dim publicKey As Byte() = assemblyName.GetPublicKey()

    If publicKey Is Nothing OrElse publicKey.Length = 0 Then
        Throw New InvalidOperationException("Assembly is not strongly named")
    End If

    Dim keyBlob As New StrongNamePublicKeyBlob(publicKey)

    ' Finally create the StrongName
    Return New StrongName(keyBlob, assemblyName.Name, assemblyName.Version)
End Function
```

C#

```
private static StrongName CreateStrongName(Assembly assembly)
{
    AssemblyName assemblyName = assembly.GetName();

    if (assemblyName == null)
        throw new InvalidOperationException("Could not get assembly name");

    // Get the public key blob
    byte[] publicKey = assemblyName.GetPublicKey();

    if (publicKey == null || publicKey.Length == 0)
        throw new InvalidOperationException("Assembly is not strongly named");

    StrongNamePublicKeyBlob keyBlob = new StrongNamePublicKeyBlob(publicKey);

    // Finally create the StrongName
    return new StrongName(keyBlob, assemblyName.Name, assemblyName.Version);
}
```

Now when you run the report you have the same output as when you embedded the code in the report, but in a more reusable and maintainable form.

Report Layout

Generally reports are produced to be printed; therefore, you must consider how the printed report looks in your report design. The first thing to ensure is that the dimensions of your report match the paper size that it will be printed on. Open the Report Properties window via the Report ➪ Report Properties menu. The selected tab is the Page Setup tab from which you can select the paper size, the margins, and the orientation of the page (portrait or landscape).

Many reports tend to extend beyond one page, and it can be useful to show something at the top and bottom of each page to show which company and report it belongs to, and where that page belongs within the report (in case the pages are dropped, for example). So far you have been dealing just with the body of the report, but you can add a page header and footer to the report to use for these purposes. Page headers tend to be used for displaying the company logo, name, and information about the company (like a letterhead). Page footers tend to be used to display page numbers, the report title, and perhaps some totals for the information displayed on that page.

Add a page header to your report via the Report ➪ Add Page Header menu command. This adds a page header area in the report designer above the report body (see Figure 31-34), which you can resize to your needs, and upon which you can place various controls such as textboxes and images. You can even place other controls such as a Table or Gauge, although it's rare to do so. If you drag a field from the Report Data tool window directly onto the page header, it creates a complex expression (as it does on the report body), so add a table first if you want to display some totals, for example.

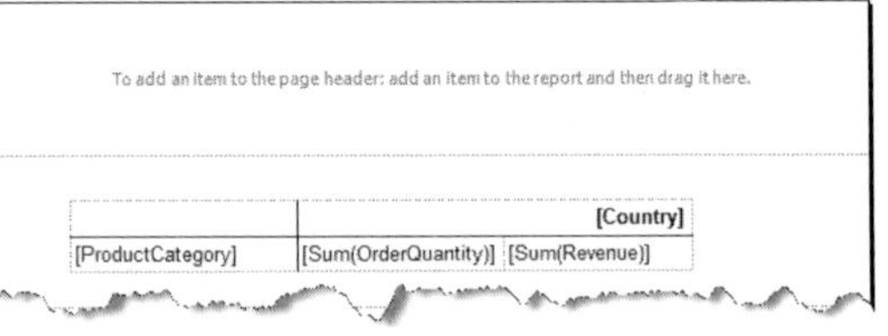

FIGURE 31-34

Adding a page footer is much the same process. Select the Report ➪ Add Page Footer menu to add a page footer area in the report designer below the body of the report (see Figure 31-35).

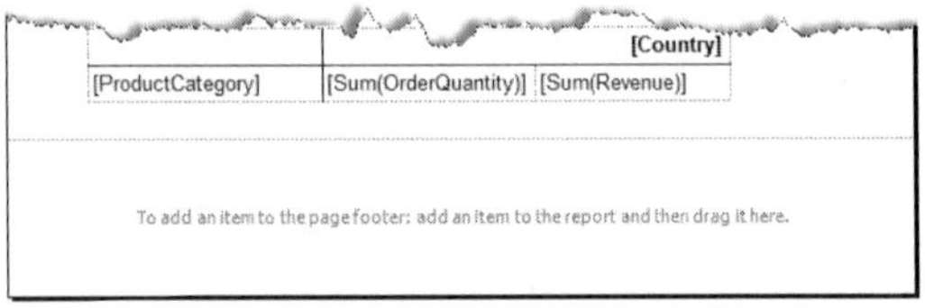

FIGURE 31-35

You can use the built-in report fields to display information such as the page number, the number of pages, the report name, the time the report was generated, and so on, which can be used anywhere in your report. You can find them in the Report Data tool window, under the Built-in Fields category.

> **NOTE** *The value for the Report Name field is retrieved from the filename of the report with the extension removed.*

Generally you want to show the page numbers in the form as Page 1 of 6. However, the page number and page count fields are separate, so it's best to drop a textbox in the footer and drop both fields in that:

```
Page [&PageNumber] of [&TotalPages]
```

The values in the square brackets automatically turn into placeholders with the correct expressions behind them (the `&` specifies that these are global variable references) that get the values from the built-in fields. You can alternatively drag these fields from the Report Data tool window into the textbox and add the static text in between.

> **NOTE** *Be careful that you don't remove the page header or footer after you create it (by selecting Remove Page Header or Remove Page Footer from the Report menu) because this deletes the content of the header/footer, and adding it back again won't restore its content. There is no warning displayed when you do this, so if you do so by accident, use the Undo function to restore it to its previous state.*

One question you may now have is how to create report headers and footers (that only appear on the first/last page of the report, rather than each page). An example of a report header would be to display the title of the report and other report information at the top of the report (on the first page only), and an example of a report footer would be to display some totals at the end of the report (on the last page only).

The report designer doesn't support report headers/footers as special areas of the report in the same way it does for page headers/footers because you can simply include them in the body of the report. By putting the report header content at the top of the body of your report, it displays only once; then it displays the content (which may expand to cover multiple pages). Finally, at the bottom of your report, you can put the report footer content. The only issue to deal with is that you won't want the page header on the first page of your report (because you will only want the report header), and you won't want the page footer on the last page (because you will only want the report footer). To do this, right-click your report header and select Header Properties from the menu. From the General tab (which will be the one selected), uncheck the Print on First Page check box. The process is much the same for the page footer: Right-click your report footer, select Footer Properties from the menu, and then uncheck the Print on Last Page check box.

The final thing you must consider with your report layout is where the page breaks occur. For example, you may want a table to appear all on the same page where possible rather than half on one page and half on another. Or perhaps you have its data grouped, and you want each group to start on a new page. You can do this by setting page break options on the controls that support them (Table, Matrix, List, Rectangle, Gauge, and Chart). Each of these controls has the PageBreak property. (Select the control in the report designer and find the property in the Properties tool window.) This gives you the option to start a new page before it displays the control, after it displays the control, or both before and after it displays the control. You can set KeepTogether to true so that if the output of the control stretches across two pages, it attempts to display it all on the one page by starting it on the next page instead. When you group data in a table, matrix, or list, you can also set the page break options for the group. When you view the properties of a group (right-click the group in the Row Groups pane at the bottom of the designer, and select Group Properties from the menu) you can note a Page Breaks tab. Here you can select whether or not there should be a page break between each group, and you can also select whether or not there should be an additional page break before and after each group.

Subreports

Subreports is a feature that enables you to insert the contents of one report into another. You can insert the contents (excluding headers and footers) of any report into another by adding a Subreport control to your main report and setting its ReportPath property to the path of the other report to display in that area. By merging a number of reports into a single output report, you can create complex report structures. Other uses of subreports include creating master-detail reports, drill-down reports, and splitting reports into predefined "components" that can be used by multiple reports — enabling each component to be defined once and used multiple times. This also has the advantage that changes can be made in a single place and automatically picked up by the other reports (such as a standard report header with company information, used by all the reports).

First, look at a scenario in which the contents of the subreport are not linked to the "master" report. Create a new report, and simply put a textbox on it with some text. Now add a Subreport control to your main report, and set the ReportName property to the filename of the other report (but without the extension).

> **NOTE** *Unfortunately, the report to be used as the subreport must be located in the same folder as the main report.*

When you run the project and view the report, you see that the contents of the subreport are merged into the main report.

Getting a little more complicated now, hook up a data source to the subreport and show some data in it (in a standalone fashion from the main report). The issue now is, because the data sources aren't shared between the main report and the subreport, how do you pass the data to that report? You do this by handling the `SubreportProcessing` event on the `LocalReport` object in the code that configures the Report Viewer control (discussed in the "Report Viewer Control" section later in this chapter). You need to add an event handler for this event like so:

VB

```
AddHandler reportViewer.LocalReport.SubreportProcessing, AddressOf ProcessSubreport
```

C#

```
reportViewer.LocalReport.SubreportProcessing += ProcessSubreport;
```

Add a function for this event handler that adds the data to the `SubreportProcessingEventArgs` object passed in as a parameter (including the name of the dataset), like so:

VB

```
Private Sub ProcessSubreport(ByVal sender As System.Object,
                             ByVal e As SubreportProcessingEventArgs)
    e.DataSources.Add(New ReportDataSource("DataSetName", data))
End Sub
```

C#

```
private void ProcessSubreport(object sender, SubreportProcessingEventArgs e)
{
    e.DataSources.Add(new ReportDataSource("DataSetName", data));
}
```

When you run the project now, the subreport is populated with data.

Now take a look at the slightly more complex scenario in which what displays in the subreport is dependent on data in the main report. Say, for example, the main report displays the details of each customer, but you also want to show the orders each customer made in the last month underneath their details using a subreport. So that the subreport knows which customer to retrieve the order details for, you need to make use of Report Parameters.

> **NOTE** *There are a lot of overheads in implementing this scenario in this way. There will be multiple calls to the database — one for each customer to return their order details, which puts strain on the database server. A better, more efficient way for this scenario would be to return a joined customer details + orders dataset from the database, and use the Table control to group by customer and display their order details. However, this scenario is just used as an example of how to pass information from the main report to subreports.*

Create a report (which will be the main report) to display the details of each customer (in a list), and another report (the subreport) that displays the orders that a customer has made. Under the customer details fields (but still in the list), add a Subreport control that points to the subreport you created, and hook up the code behind as previously described. When handling the `SubreportProcessing` event to return the order details data to the subreport, you need to know which customer to return the data for. (The subreport will be rendered for each customer; therefore, this event handler will be called to return the order details for each customer.) This is where you need to create a Report Parameter for the subreport that the main report will use to pass the current customer's ID to it.

To add a new parameter to the subreport, go to the Report Data tool window, right-click the Parameters folder, and select Add Parameter from the menu. Create the parameter with CustomerID as its name, and set its data type to Integer.

Back on the main report, select the Subreport control in the designer, right-click and select Subreport Properties from the menu; then go to the Parameters tab. Click the Add button, specify CustomerID as the parameter name, and enter [CustomerID] as its value. Now each time it renders the subreport, it passes it the current value of the customer ID field.

The final thing to do is retrieve the value of that parameter in your `ProcessSubreport` event handler, and filter the results returned accordingly, like so:

VB

```
Private Sub ProcessSubreport(ByVal sender As System.Object,
                              ByVal e As SubreportProcessingEventArgs)
    Dim customerID As Integer =
        Convert.ToInt32(e.Parameters("CustomerID").Values(0))
    Dim fromDate As DateTime = DateTime.Today.AddMonths(-1)

    Dim qry = From co In context.SalesOrderHeaders
              Where co.CustomerID = customerID AndAlso co.OrderDate > fromDate
              Select co

    e.DataSources.Add(New ReportDataSource("OrderData", qry))
End Sub
```

C#

```
public void ProcessSubreport(object sender, SubreportProcessingEventArgs e)
{
    int customerID = Convert.ToInt32(e.Parameters["CustomerID"].Values[0]);
    DateTime fromDate = DateTime.Today.AddMonths(-1);

    var qry = from co in context.SalesOrderHeaders
              where co.CustomerID == customerID && co.OrderDate > fromDate
              select co;

    e.DataSources.Add(new ReportDataSource("OrderData", qry));
}
```

The Report Wizard

The easiest place to start when designing a report is to make use of the Report Wizard. The Report Wizard leads you through all the main steps to generate a report, and based upon your input generates the report for you that you can then customize to your needs.

The Report Wizard takes you through the following steps:

- **Choosing/creating a data source:** Enables you to select an existing data source or create a new one as the source of data for the report. This step is exactly the same as was detailed earlier in the "Defining Data Sources" section.
- **Arranging fields:** Drag fields into the Values list to create a simple table, add fields in the Row Groups list to group the rows of the table by those fields, and add fields to the Column Groups list to group the columns by those fields (which turns it into a matrix).
- **Choose the layout:** Gives you the option to add subtotals and grand totals rows/columns.
- **Choose a style:** Allows you to choose different colors and styles used in the output. If you want to create your own color scheme, you can do so by modifying the `StyleTemplates.xml` file in the `C:\Program Files\Microsoft Visual Studio 11.0\Common7\IDE\PrivateAssemblies\1033` folder on your machine. (This path may differ on your machine based upon where Visual Studio has been installed.)

To start the Report Wizard you need to create a new report file. (You cannot use the Report Wizard on an existing file or after it has already been run.) Add a new item to your project, and from the Reporting subsection, add a new Report Wizard item.

The Report Wizard takes you through its series of steps to generate a basic report. When you complete the steps, it generates the report and opens it in the report designer for you to modify as required.

> **NOTE** *This is a great place to start when learning how to design reports, and when you become more familiar and comfortable with the process and designing more complicated reports, you will use it less and less.*

RENDERING REPORTS

Now that you have designed your report, it's time to actually generate it by populating it with data. This is where the Report Viewer control is used because it contains the local engine to generate the report from the report definition files and the data sources.

The Report Viewer Controls

There are two versions of the Report Viewer control: one for use in web applications and one for use in Windows applications. However, the way you use them to generate and display reports is virtually identical.

The Windows version of the control is shown in Figure 31-36.

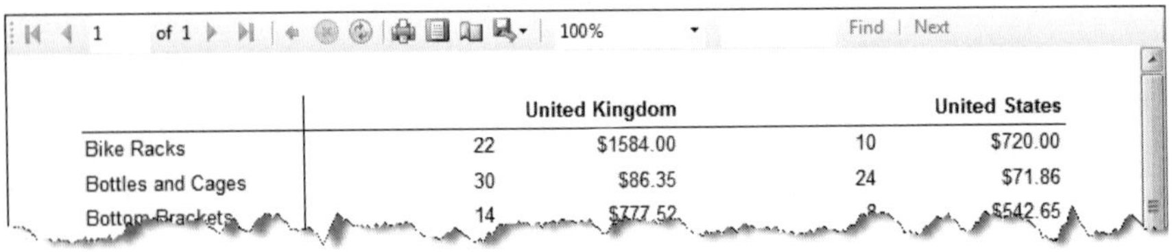

FIGURE 31-36

The Report Viewer contains a toolbar with various functions (such as Refresh, Export, Print, and so on) and a view of the report (page by page). Individual functions on this toolbar can be turned off via properties on the Report Viewer control, and each raises an event when clicked. (Although the corresponding behavior is performed by the Report Viewer control automatically unless canceled in the event handler.)

To use the Report Viewer control in your Windows Forms project, simply drop it on your form from the Toolbox.

The web version also looks quite similar (shown in Figure 31-37) but displays the report output in a browser.

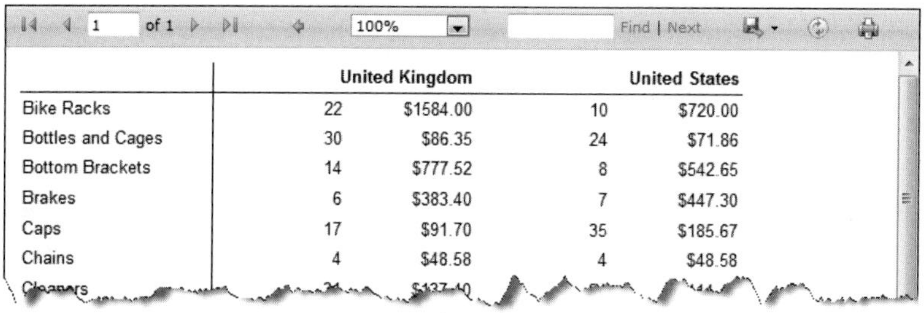

	United Kingdom		United States	
Bike Racks	22	$1584.00	10	$720.00
Bottles and Cages	30	$86.35	24	$71.86
Bottom Brackets	14	$777.52	8	$542.65
Brakes	6	$383.40	7	$447.30
Caps	17	$91.70	35	$185.67
Chains	4	$48.58	4	$48.58

FIGURE 31-37

To use the web version of the Report Viewer control, you can drop it on a page from the Toolbox (in the Reporting tab). This adds a namespace prefix (rsweb) for the `Microsoft.ReportViewer.WebForms` assembly/namespace and the following tag to use the Report Viewer control:

```
<rsweb:ReportViewer ID="reportViewer" runat="server" />
```

The web version of the Report Viewer control also requires a Script Manager to be on the page. If you don't have one on the page, drag this from the Toolbox (under the AJAX Extensions tab) and onto the page.

When you display a report in the web version of the Report Viewer control, you can find that it displays a Print button on the toolbar only in Internet Explorer (IE) and not in other browsers such as Firefox. This is because to print the report from the browser, the Report Viewer needs an ActiveX control to do the printing and ActiveX controls only work in IE. Because printing can't be done from other browsers, the Print button won't be displayed. When you click the Print button in IE the first time, it asks you for permission to install the ActiveX control.

Generating the Report

The process of generating a report is essentially to tell the report engine which report definition file to use, and pass it the data (objects, entities, data tables, and so on) to populate the report with.

By default the report definition file is embedded into the assembly; although it often is best to have it as a separate file so that it can be easily updated when necessary without having to recompile the assembly. However, embedding it into the assembly means that there are fewer files to distribute, and it may in some circumstances be preferable that the report definition file cannot (easily) be tampered with. Set the Build Action on the report definition file to Embedded Resource in order for it to be embedded in the assembly (which is the default value), or otherwise set it to be Content.

The following code is required to generate a report from a file-based report definition file and populate it with some data. (The `data` variable contains a collection of entities from the Entity Framework model, which is used to populate the CustomerData data source in the report.)

VB

```
Dim reportEngine As LocalReport = reportViewer.LocalReport
reportEngine.ReportPath = "CustomerReport.rdlc"
reportEngine.DataSources.Add(New ReportDataSource("CustomerData", data))
reportViewer.RefreshReport() 'Only for Windows Report Viewer
```

C#

```
LocalReport reportEngine = reportViewer.LocalReport;
reportEngine.ReportPath = "CustomerReport.rdlc";
reportEngine.DataSources.Add(new ReportDataSource("CustomerData", data));
reportViewer.RefreshReport(); // Only for Windows Report Viewer
```

Here you get the existing `LocalReport` object from the Report Viewer control, assign values to its properties, and then use the `RefreshReport` function on the Report Viewer control to start the report engine generating the report.

If you have chosen to embed the report in your assembly, then instead of setting the `ReportPath` property on the `LocalReport` object, you need to set the `ReportEmbeddedResource` property. This must be the qualified resource path (which is case-sensitive), including the namespace and the extension of the report, like so:

VB

```
reportEngine.ReportEmbeddedResource = "Chapter31Sample.CustomerReport.rdlc"
```

C#

```
reportEngine.ReportEmbeddedResource = "Chapter31Sample.CustomerReport.rdlc";
```

If you have one or more subreports in your report, you also have to handle the `SubreportProcessing` event of the `LocalReport` object, as was demonstrated when discussing the Subreport control. If you use custom assemblies, you need to include the code to specify that the custom assembly is trusted. In addition, you may need to set the properties on the `LocalReport` object to enable the report to use external images, hyperlinks, and so on. However, the code provided here is the core code required to generate a report and display it in the Report Viewer control.

Rendering Reports to Different Formats

It's not necessary to display a report in the Report Viewer control. In some instances you may want to generate the report and e-mail it as a PDF without any user interaction or return a PDF'd report as a result of a web service call. The Report Viewer control enables you to export the report to various formats (Excel, PDF, Word, and so on) as an option on its toolbar, and this can also be done via code. This is possible by creating a `LocalReport` object, setting the required properties, and then using the `Render` function on the `LocalReport` object to render it to a specified format (which is output to a stream or byte array).

The `Render` function has a number of overloads, but the simplest one to use is to just pass it the output format (in this case PDF) and it will return a byte array containing the report, for example:

VB

```
Dim reportOutput As Byte() = reportEngine.Render("PDF")
```

C#

```
byte[] reportOutput = reportEngine.Render("PDF");
```

The report engine can generate the report in a number of formats. Valid values include:

- **PDF:** Output to an Adobe Acrobat file
- **Word:** Output to a Microsoft Word document
- **Excel:** Output to an Microsoft Excel spreadsheet
- **Image:** Output to a TIFF image file

To output to a stream (such an HTTP Response stream or a file stream) you can turn the bytes into a stream:

VB

```
Dim stream As MemoryStream = New MemoryStream(reportOutput)
stream.Seek(0, SeekOrigin.Begin)
```

C#

```
MemoryStream stream = new MemoryStream(reportOutput);
stream.Seek(0, SeekOrigin.Begin);
```

Alternatively, for larger reports (where this may be too memory-intensive) you can write directly to a stream from the `Render` function using one of its overloads, passing in a callback function that creates and returns the stream to write to as the value for the `createStream` parameter:

VB

```
Private Function CreateReportFileStream(ByVal fileName As String,
                                         ByVal extension As String,
                                         ByVal encoding As Encoding,
                                         ByVal mimeType As String,
                                         ByVal willSeek As Boolean) As Stream
    Return New FileStream(fileName & "." & extension, FileMode.Create)
End Function
```

C#

```
private Stream CreateReportFileStream(string fileName, string extension,
                               Encoding encoding, string mimeType, bool willSeek)
{
    return new FileStream(fileName + "." + extension, FileMode.Create);
}
```

Then you can call the render function like so:

VB

```
Dim warnings As Warning() = Nothing
reportEngine.Render("PDF", Nothing, AddressOf CreateReportFileStream, warnings)
```

C#

```
Warning[] warnings;
reportEngine.Render("PDF", null, CreateReportFileStream, out warnings);
```

DEPLOYING REPORTS

Now that you've designed your report, you can deploy it to users as a part of your application. However, the Report Viewer control is not a part of the .NET Framework and needs to be installed separately. A search for "Report Viewer redistributable" on the web should help you find the installer for the Report Viewer assemblies.

An alternative is to simply distribute the Report Viewer assemblies that you have referenced with your application. Note, however, that this won't include the .cab installer for the ActiveX control that, when using the web report viewer control in web applications, enables reports to be printed (in IE only). If this is a feature you require in your application, it's best to use the Report Viewer redistributable installer instead.

SUMMARY

In this chapter you saw how to use Visual Studio's report designer to design a report, populate it with data, and display the output to the user. Unfortunately, reporting is an incredibly complex topic, and it is impossible to cover it completely and go through every option available in one chapter. Hopefully this has been a good introduction to the topic, however, and will guide you in the right direction for designing your own reports.

PART VII
Application Services

32

Windows Communication Foundation (WCF)

WHAT'S IN THIS CHAPTER?

- Understanding WCF services
- Creating a WCF service
- Configuring WCF service endpoints
- Hosting a WCF service
- Consuming a WCF service

Most systems require a means to communicate between their various components — most commonly between the server and the client. Many different technologies enable this sort of communication, but Windows Communication Foundation (WCF) brings a unified architecture to implementing them. This chapter takes you through the architecture of WCF services and how to create, host, and consume WCF services in your system.

WHAT IS WCF?

Within the .NET Framework there are a variety of ways that you can communicate among applications, including (but not limited to) remoting, web services, and a myriad of networking protocols. This has often frustrated application developers who not only had to pick the appropriate technology to use, but also had to write plumbing code that would allow their applications to use different technologies depending on where or how they would be deployed. For example, when users connect directly to the intranet, it is probably better for them to use a remoting or direct TCP/IP connection for their speed benefits. However, these aren't the ideal solution for communication when the application is outside the corporate firewall, in which case a secured web service would be preferable.

WCF is designed to solve this sort of problem by providing a means to build messaging applications that are technology-agnostic, which can then be configured (in text-based configuration files) to what technologies each service supports and how they are used. Therefore, you need to write only the one service, which can support all the various communication technologies supported by WCF. WCF is essentially a unified communication layer for .NET applications.

GETTING STARTED

A WCF service can be added to an existing project (such as a web application), or it can be created as a standalone project. For this example you create a standalone service so that you can easily see how a single service can be configured and hosted in many communication scenarios.

When you open the New Project dialog and click the WCF category (under either the VB or C# languages), you'll notice a number of different WCF project types, as shown in Figure 32-1.

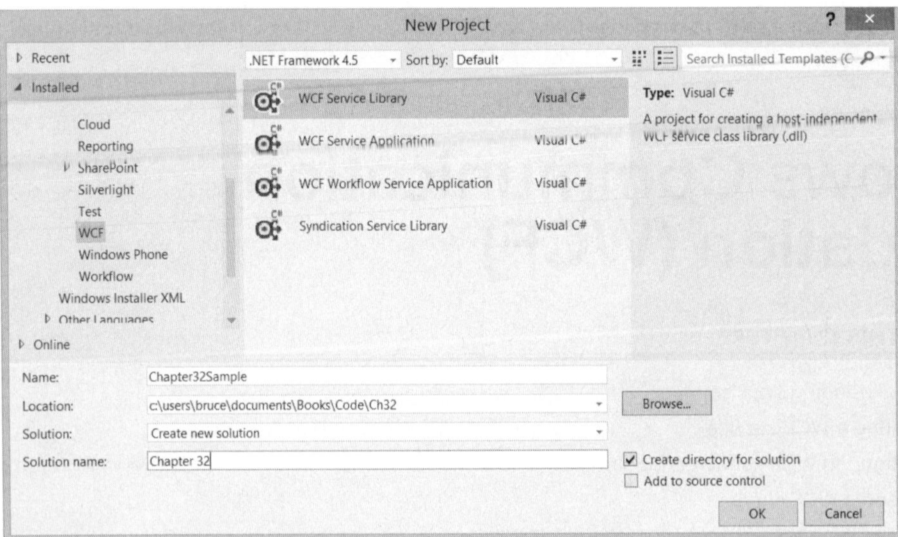

FIGURE 32-1

The WCF Workflow Service Application project template provides an easy way to expose a Windows Workflow (WF) publicly, which is discussed in Chapter 33, "Windows Workflow Foundation (WF)." The Syndication Service Library project template is used to expose data as an RSS feed. The WCF Service Application project template creates a project configured to be deployable into IIS. However, the project template you use in the example is the WCF Service Library project template.

> **NOTE** *In Visual Studio 2010, the WCF Service Application project template could be found in the Web category in the New Project dialog. For Visual Studio 2012, this template has been moved into the more appropriate WCF category.*

By default, a new WCF Service Library includes `IService1.vb` and `Service1.vb` (or `.cs` if you use C#), which define the contract and the implementation of a basic service, respectively. When you open these files, you'll see that they already expose some operations and data as an example of how to expose your own operations and data. This can all be cleared out until you simply have an interface with nothing defined (but with the `ServiceContract` attribute left in place), and a class that simply implements that interface. Or you can delete both files and start anew.

When you want to add additional services to your project, the WCF Service item template in the Add New Item dialog can add both an interface and a class to your project to use for the contract and implementation of the service.

DEFINING CONTRACTS

This example project exposes some data from the Entity Framework model that you created in Chapter 30, "The ADO.NET Framework," for the AdventureWorksLT2008R2 database and some operations that can be performed on that data. The way that you do so is by creating *contracts* that define the operations and the structure of the data that will be publicly exposed. Three core types of contracts exist: service contracts, data contracts, and message contracts.

- A *service contract* is a group of operations, essentially detailing the capabilities of the service.
- A *data contract* details the structure of the data passed between the service and the client.
- A *message contract* details the structure of the messages passed between the service and the client. This is useful when the service must conform to a given message format. This is an advanced topic and not required for basic services, so it isn't covered in this chapter.

These contracts are defined by decorating the classes/interfaces in the service with special attributes.

In this chapter you'll walk through an example of creating a WCF service exposing customer data from the AdventureWorksLT2008R2 database to client applications. To do this you'll expose operations for working with the customer data, which expose the actual customer data in the database.

For the purpose of this example start fresh — delete `IService1` (`.vb` or `.cs`) and `Service1` (`.vb` or `.cs`). Add a new item to the project using the WCF Service item template, called CustomerService. This adds two new files to your project — `CustomerService (.vb` or `.cs)` and `ICustomerService (.vb` or `.cs)`.

> **NOTE** *There are two primary approaches that you can take when designing services. You can take either an implementation-first approach (in which you write the code first and then apply attributes to it to create the contract), or you can take a contract-first approach (in which you design the schema/WSDL first and generate the code from it). An in-depth discussion of these approaches is beyond the scope of this chapter; however, WCF can support both approaches. The example in this chapter follows the contract-first approach.*

Creating the Service Contract

Focus on defining the service contract first. The operations you want to expose externally are:

- `AddCustomer`
- `GetCustomer`
- `UpdateCustomer`
- `DeleteCustomer`
- `GetCustomerList`

You may recognize the first four operations as standard CRUD (Create, Read, Update, and Delete) operations when you work with data. The final operation returns a list of all the customers in the database.

Now that you know what operations are required, you can define your service contract.

> **NOTE** *In the sample implementation in the WCF project template, all the service attributes were defined in the interface. However, creating an interface to decorate with the contract attributes is not essential — you don't need to create an interface, and you can decorate the class with the attributes instead. However, standard practice (and best practice) dictates that the contract should be defined as (and in) an interface, so you follow this best practice in the example.*

You define your operations in the ICustomerService interface. However, these operations expose data using a data class that you haven't defined as yet. In the meantime, create a stub data class, and you can flesh it out shortly. Add a new class to the project called `CustomerData` and leave it as it is to act as your stub. Each of the operations needs to be decorated with the `OperationContract` attribute:

VB

```
<ServiceContract([Namespace]:="http://www.professionalvisualstudio.com")>
Public Interface ICustomerService
    <OperationContract()>
    Function AddCustomer(ByVal customer As CustomerData) As Integer

    <OperationContract()>
    Function GetCustomer(ByVal customerID As Integer) As CustomerData

    <OperationContract()>
    Sub UpdateCustomer(ByVal customer As CustomerData)

    <OperationContract()>
    Sub DeleteCustomer(ByVal customerID As Integer)

    <OperationContract()>
    Function GetCustomerList() As List(Of CustomerData)
End Interface
```

C#

```
[ServiceContract(Namespace="http://www.professionalvisualstudio.com")]
public interface ICustomerService
{
    [OperationContract]
    int AddCustomer(CustomerData customer);

    [OperationContract]
    CustomerData GetCustomer(int customerID);

    [OperationContract]
    void UpdateCustomer(CustomerData customer);

    [OperationContract]
    void DeleteCustomer(int customerID);

    [OperationContract]
    List<CustomerData> GetCustomerList();
}
```

Both the `ServiceContract` and `OperationContract` attributes have a number of properties that you can apply values to, enabling you to alter their default behavior. For example, both have a name property (enabling you to specify the name of the service/operation as seen externally). Of particular note is the `ServiceContract`'s `Namespace` property, which you should always explicitly specify (as has been done in the preceding code). If a namespace has not been explicitly set, the schema and WSDL generated for the service uses `http://tempuri.org` as its namespace. However, to reduce the chance of collisions with other services, it's best to use something unique such as your company's URL.

Now that you've defined your contract, you need to actually implement these operations. Open the `CustomerService` class, which implements the ICustomerService interface. VB implements the methods automatically (you may need to press Enter after the `Implements ICustomerService` for these to actually be implemented), and in C# you can use the smart tag (Ctrl+.) to have the methods automatically implemented. The service contract is now complete and ready for the operations to be implemented (that is, write the code that performs each operation). However, before you do so you still need to define the properties of the data class, and at the same time you should also define the data contract.

Creating the Data Contract

You are returning objects containing data from some of the operations you expose in your service and accepting objects as parameters. Therefore, you should specify the structure of these data objects being transferred by decorating their classes with data contract attributes.

> **NOTE** *From the .NET Framework 3.5 SP1 onward, it is no longer essential that you explicitly define a contract for your data classes if the classes are public and each has a default constructor. (This is referred to as having an inferred data contract instead of a formal data contract.) However, it is useful (and recommended) to create a formal contract anyway — especially if you need to conform to a specific message format in your communication, have non-.NET clients access your service, or want to explicitly define what properties in the data class are included in the message. Because explicitly specifying the data contract is generally recommended, this is the approach you will be taking in the example.*

This example requires only one data class — the `CustomerData` class that you already created (although no properties have been defined on it as yet), which you can now decorate with the data contract attributes. Whereas the service contract attributes were found in the `System.ServiceModel` namespace, data contract attributes are found in the `System.Runtime.Serialization` namespace, so C# developers need to start by adding a using statement for this namespace in their classes:

```
using System.Runtime.Serialization;
```

Each data class first needs to be decorated with the `DataContract` attribute, and then you can decorate each property to be serialized with the `DataMember` attribute:

VB

```
<DataContract([Namespace]:="http://www.professionalvisualstudio.com")>
Public Class CustomerData
    <DataMember()> Public Property CustomerID As Integer
    <DataMember()> Public Property Title As String
    <DataMember()> Public Property FirstName As String
    <DataMember()> Public Property MiddleName As String
    <DataMember()> Public Property LastName As String
    <DataMember()> Public Property Suffix As String
    <DataMember()> Public Property CompanyName As String
    <DataMember()> Public Property EmailAddress As String
    <DataMember()> Public Property Phone As String
End Class
```

C#

```
[DataContract(Namespace="http://www.professionalvisualstudio.com")]
public class CustomerData
{
    [DataMember] public int CustomerID { get; set; }
    [DataMember] public string Title { get; set; }
    [DataMember] public string FirstName { get; set; }
    [DataMember] public string MiddleName { get; set; }
    [DataMember] public string LastName { get; set; }
    [DataMember] public string Suffix { get; set; }
    [DataMember] public string CompanyName { get; set; }
    [DataMember] public string EmailAddress { get; set; }
    [DataMember] public string Phone { get; set; }
}
```

If you don't want a property to be serialized, simply don't apply the `DataMember` attribute to it. Like the service contract attributes you can also set the value of each of the various properties each attribute has. For example, the `DataContract` attribute enables you to set properties such as the namespace for the class's data contract (the `Namespace` property) and an alternative name for the class's data contract (the `Name` property). The `DataMember` attribute also has a number of properties that you can set, such as the member's name (the `Name` property) and whether or not the member must have a value specified (`IsRequired`).

> **NOTE** *When defining your data contract, you might ask why you are decorating the data classes directly and aren't defining the contract on an interface as you did with the service contract (which was considered good practice). This is because only concrete types can be serialized — interfaces cannot (and thus cannot be specified as parameter or return types in WCF calls). When an object with only an interface specifying its type is to be deserialized, the serializer would not know which type of concrete object it should create the object as. There is a way around this, but it's beyond the scope of this chapter. If you try to create an interface and decorate it with the* `DataContract` *attribute, this generates a compile error.*

You must be aware of some caveats when designing your data contracts. If your data class inherits from another class that isn't decorated with the `DataContract` attribute, you receive an error when you attempt to run the service. Therefore, you must either also decorate the inherited class with the data contract attributes or remove the data contract attributes from the data class (although this is not recommended) so the data contract is inferred instead.

If you choose to have inferred data contracts and not decorate the data classes with the data contract attributes, all public properties will be serialized. You can, however, exclude properties from being serialized if you need to by decorating them with the `IgnoreDataMember` attribute. A caveat of inferred data contracts is that the data classes must have a default constructor (that is, one with no parameters) or have no constructors at all (in which case a default constructor will be created for it by the compiler). If you do not have a default constructor in a data class with an inferred contract, you'll receive an error when you attempt to run the service. When an object of that type is passed in as an operation's parameter, the default constructor will be called when the object is created, and any code in that constructor will be executed.

> **NOTE** *Although it's not strictly required, it's best that you keep your data contract classes separate from your other application classes, and that you use them only for passing data in and out of services (as data transfer objects, aka DTOs). This way you minimize the dependencies between your application and the services that it exposes or calls.*

CONFIGURING WCF SERVICE ENDPOINTS

A WCF service has three main components: the Address, the Binding, and the Contract (easily remembered by the mnemonic ABC):

- The address specifies the location where the service can be found (the where) in the form of a URL.
- The binding specifies the protocol and encoding used for the communication (the how).
- The contract details the capabilities and features of the service (the what).

The configurations of each of these components combine to form an *endpoint*. Each combination of these components forms a separate endpoint; although it may be easier to consider it as each service having multiple endpoints (that is, address/binding combinations). What makes WCF so powerful is that it abstracts these components away from the implementation of the service, enabling them to be configured according to the technologies the service supports.

With this power, however, comes complexity, and the configuration of endpoints can become rather complex. In particular, many different types of bindings are supported, each having a huge number of options. However, recent versions of WCF have had the goal of simplifying the configuration process. The result is that there are default endpoints, standard endpoints, default protocol mappings, default binding configurations, and default behavior configurations. You need to configure only the "exceptions," not the "norm." Because endpoint configuration can become complex, this chapter focuses on just the most common requirements.

Endpoints for the service are defined in the `App.config` file. Though you can open the `App.config` file and edit it directly, Visual Studio comes with a configuration editor tool to simplify the configuration process. Right-click the `App.config` file in the Solution Explorer, and select Edit WCF Configuration from the context menu. This opens the Microsoft Service Configuration Editor, as shown in Figure 32-2.

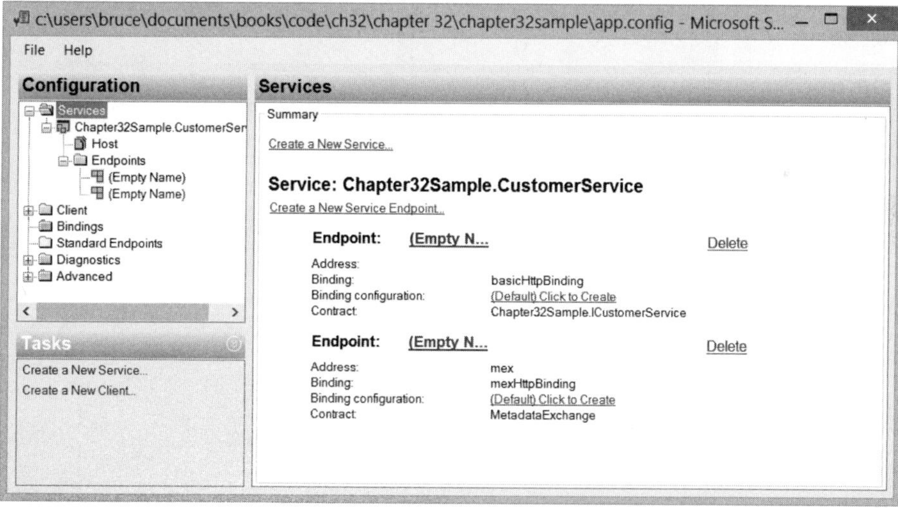

FIGURE 32-2

The node you are most interested in is the Services node. Selecting this node displays a summary in the Services pane of all the services that have been configured and their corresponding endpoints. A service is already listed here; although it is the configuration for the default service that was created by the project template (Service1), which no longer exists. Therefore, you can delete this service from the configuration and start anew. (Click the service and press Delete.)

> **NOTE** *If you try running the service (detailed in the next section) without properly configuring an endpoint for it (or have an incorrect name for the service in the configuration), you'll receive an error stating that the WCF Service Host cannot find any service meta data. If you receive this error, ensure that the service name (including its namespace) in the configuration matches its name in the actual service implementation.*

The first step is to define your service in the configuration. From the Tasks pane, click the Create a New Service hyperlink. This starts the New Service Element Wizard. In the service type field, you can directly type the qualified name of your service (that is, include its namespace), or click the Browse button to discover the services available. (It's best to use the Browse function because this automatically fills in the next step for you.) If you use this option, you must have compiled your project first, and then you can navigate down into the bin\Debug folder to find the assembly, and drill through it to display the services within that assembly (as shown in Figure 32-3). Now you have specified the service implementation, but next you need to specify the contract, binding, and address for the endpoint.

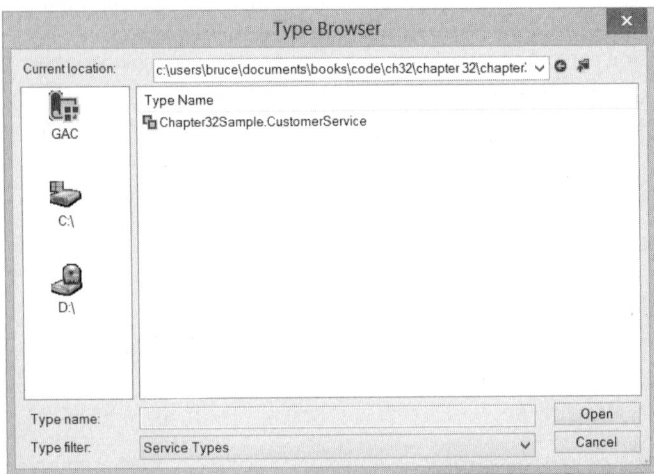

FIGURE 32-3

If you used the Browse button in the previous step (recommended), this next step (specifying the service contract) will have already been filled in for you (as shown in Figure 32-4). Otherwise, fill this in now.

The next step prompts you to select the communication mode that your service will use (see Figure 32-5). There are several choices offered: TCP, HTTP, Named Pipes, MSMQ, and Peer to Peer. This is, in an indirect manner, how you specify the binding for the service (the "B" in the ABC mentioned at the beginning of this chapter). Each binding has a default/standard binding configuration; although additional configurations can be created for a binding (under the Bindings node in the Configuration tree) that enable you to configure exactly how a binding behaves. The custom bindings

FIGURE 32-4

configuration can become rather complex, with a myriad of options available. However, in many cases you'll find that you just need default binding attributes. In this chapter, assume that the default bindings are satisfactory for your needs.

Choosing which binding you should use depends on your usage scenario for the service. The wizard includes a description under each option detailing the purpose for the option, the goal being to help you make your choice. You must remember, however, that not all clients may support the binding you choose — therefore, you must also consider what clients will be using your service and choose the binding accordingly. Of course, WCF supports multiple endpoints for a single service, so creating additional endpoints with different bindings is well within its capabilities.

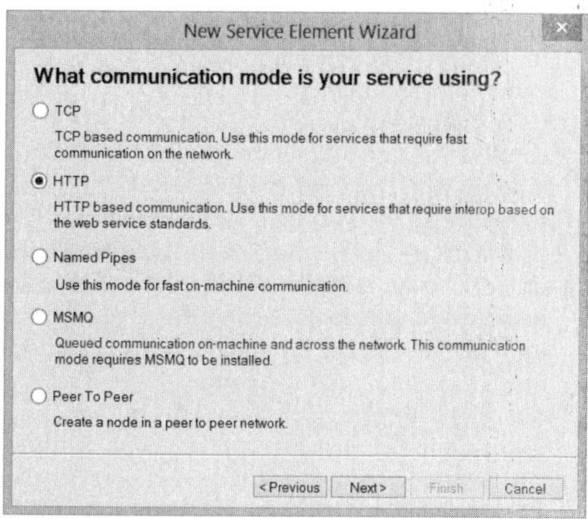

FIGURE 32-5

If you select HTTP as the communications protocol, you are prompted with an additional screen. This screen allows you to select whether or not you want to use basic or advanced web services interoperability. These choices correspond to two frequently used bindings: basicHttpBinding and wsHttpBinding. The basicHttpBinding binding is used to communicate in the same manner as the ASMX web services (which conform to the WS-I Basic Profile 1.1). The wsHttpBinding binding implements a number of additional specifications other than the basicHttpBinding binding (including reliability and security specifications), and additional capabilities such as supporting transactions. However, older .NET clients (pre-.NET Framework 3.0), non-.NET clients, mobile clients, and Silverlight clients cannot access the service using this binding. For this example, select the HTTP protocol and the Advanced Web Services interoperability option. This combination of selections is how you can choose wsHttpBinding to be the binding for the service.

The final step is to specify the address for the endpoint. You can specify the entire address to be used by starting the address with a protocol (such as `http://`), or specify a relative address to the base address (discussed shortly) by just entering a name. In this case, delete the default entry and leave it blank — this endpoint simply uses the base address that you are about to set up. A warning displays when moving on from this step, but it can be safely ignored.

A summary is shown of the endpoint configuration, and you can finish the wizard. This wizard has allowed you to create a single endpoint for the service, but chances are you need to implement multiple endpoints. You can do this easily by using the New Service Endpoint Element Wizard to create additional endpoints. Underneath the service node that was created will be an Endpoints node. Select this, and then click the Create a New Service Endpoint hyperlink in the Tasks pane. This opens the wizard that can help you to create a new endpoint.

As mentioned earlier you now need to configure a base address for the endpoint. The URL that is used as the base address depends on the type of protocol that the service will use for communication. With the wsHttpBinding binding, a standard http URL is specified to make the service accessible. Under the newly created service node is a Host node. Select this, and from the Host pane that appears, click the New button to add a new base address to the list (which is currently empty). A dialog appears asking for the base address, and it contains a default entry. The address you enter here will largely depend on the binding that was selected earlier. Because you chose one of the HTTP bindings, use `http://localhost:8733/Chapter32Sample` as the base address (port 8733 was chosen at random) for this example.

Your service is now configured with the endpoints that it will support. There is another topic related to service configuration that is worth mentioning — that of behaviors. In essence, WCF behaviors modify the execution of a service or an endpoint. You will find that a service behavior containing two element extensions has already been configured for the service by the project template. If you expand the Advanced node and select the Service Behaviors node under it, you'll find a behavior has been defined containing the `serviceMetadata` and `serviceDebug` element extensions. The `serviceMetadata` behavior element extension enables meta data for the service to be published. Your service must publish meta data for it to be discoverable and to be added as a service reference for a client project (that is, create a proxy). You could set this up as a separate endpoint with the mexHttpBinding binding, but this behavior merges this binding with the service without requiring it to be explicitly configured on the service. This makes it easy to ensure all your services are discoverable. Clicking the serviceMetadata node in the tree shows all its properties — ensure that the `HttpGetEnabled` and the `HttpsGetEnabled` properties are set to True. The other behavior element is the `serviceDebug` behavior extension. When debugging your service it can be useful for a help page to be displayed in the browser when you navigate to it (essentially publishing its WSDL at the HTTP get URL). You can do this by setting both the `HttpHelpPageEnabled` and `HttpsHelpPageEnabled` properties to True. Another useful property to set to true while debugging is the `IncludeExceptionDetailsInFaults` property, enabling you to view a stack trace of what exception occurred in the service from the client. Although this behavior is useful in debugging, it's recommended that you remove it before deploying your service (for security purposes).

> **NOTE** *The mexHttpBinding serves two purposes. First, it indicates that the binding will be used to expose the meta data for the service using the Metadata Exchange standard. Second, it indicates that the meta data information is retrievable through the HTTP protocol. There are other bindings that can expose meta data information through, for example, TCP or named pipes. These bindings are typically used in conjunction with a service that processes requests using the corresponding network protocol.*

HOSTING WCF SERVICES

With these changes made you can now build and run the WCF Service Library. Unlike a standard class library, a WCF Service Library can be "run" because Visual Studio 2012 ships with the WCF Service Host utility. This is an application that can be used to host WCF services for the purpose of debugging them. Figure 32-6 shows this utility appearing in the taskbar.

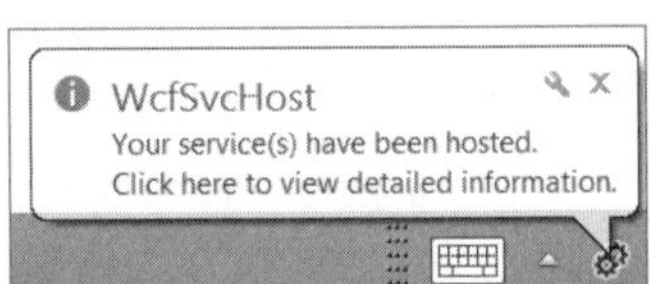

FIGURE 32-6

As the balloon in Figure 32-6 indicates, clicking the balloon or the taskbar icon brings up a dialog showing more information about the service that is running. If the service doesn't start correctly, this dialog can help you work out what is going wrong.

> **NOTE** *If you aren't running under elevated privileges, you may end up with an error from the WCF Service Host relating to the registration of the URL you specified in the configuration file. The issue is a result of security policies on the computer that are preventing the WCF Service Host from registering the URL you have specified. If you receive this error, you can resolve it by executing the following command using an elevated permissions command prompt (that is, while running as administrator), replacing the parameters according to the address of the service and your Windows username:*
>
> ```
> netsh http add urlacl url=http://+:8733/Chapter32Sample user=<username>
> ```

> *This command allows the specified user to register URLs that match the URL prefix. Now when you try to run your WCF Service Library again, it should start successfully.*
>
> *In some situations, you may receive an InvalidOperationException with a message indicating that the X.509 certificate could not be loaded. If you do, add the following XML segment to the endpoint element in your config file:*
>
> ```
> <identity>
>    <dns value="localhost" />
> </identity>
> ```

In addition to hosting your WCF service, Visual Studio 2012 also launches the WCF Test Client utility, as shown in Figure 32-7. This utility automatically detects the running services and provides a simple tree representation of the services and their corresponding operations.

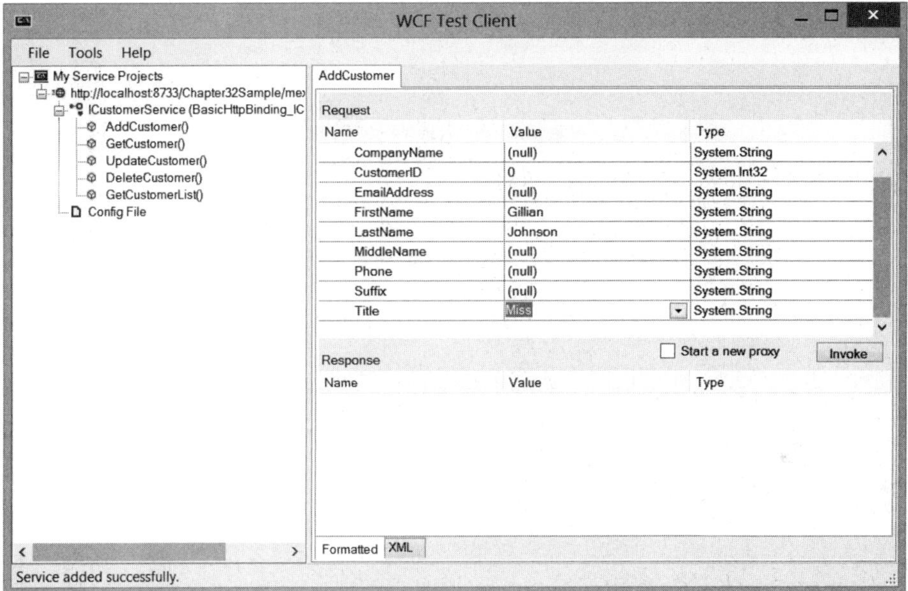

FIGURE 32-7

When you double-click a service operation, you'll see the tab on the right side of the dialog change to display the request and response values. Unlike the basic test page for ASP.NET Web Services, the WCF Test Client can help you simulate calls to WCF services that contain complex types. In Figure 32-7, you can see that in the Request section each parameter is displayed, and the `customer` object parameter of the `AddCustomer` operation has been broken down with data entry fields for each of its properties (those that were marked with the `DataMember` attribute). After setting values for each of these properties, you can then invoke the operation by clicking the Invoke button. Figure 32-8 also shows that any return value displays in a similar layout in the Response section of the tab.

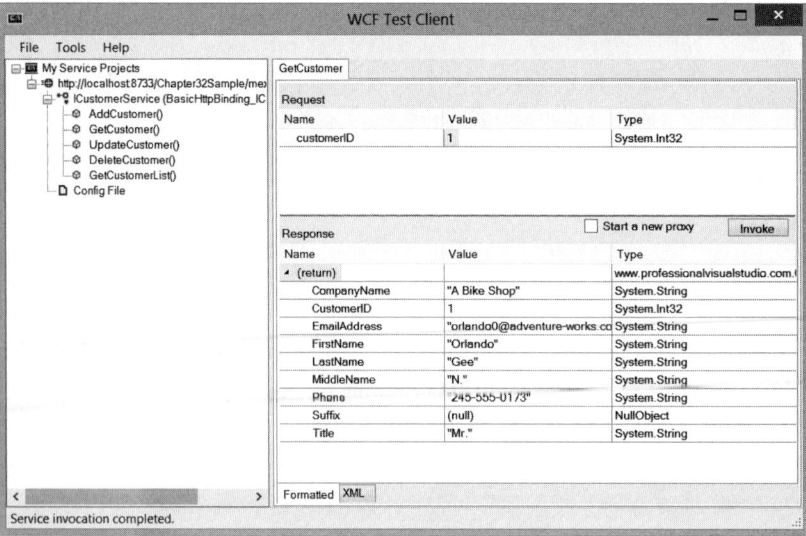

FIGURE 32-8

If you try to isolate an issue, it can be useful to see exactly what information travels down the wire for each service request. You can do this using third-party tools such as Fiddler, but for a simple XML representation of what was sent and received, you can simply click the XML tab. Figure 32-9 shows the body XML for both the request and the response. There is additional XML due to the request and response, each being wrapped in a SOAP envelope.

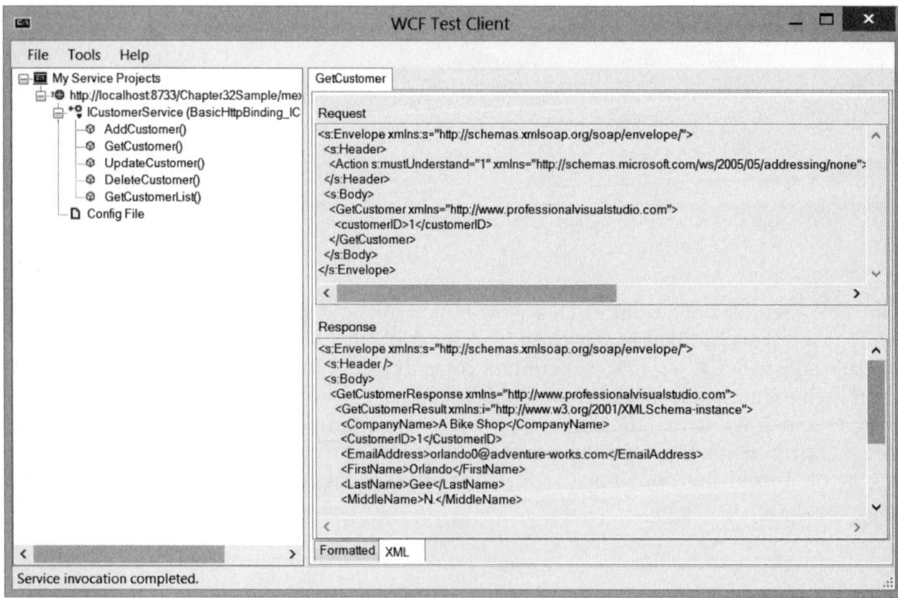

FIGURE 32-9

This is fine while you debug the service, but in production you need to properly host your service. You have a lot of ways to host your service, and how you choose to do so depends on your scenario. If it's a situation in which the service acts as a server (which clients communicate with) and communicates via HTTP, then Internet Information Services (IIS) is probably your best choice. If your service is used to communicate between two applications, your application can be used to host the service. Other options you may want to consider are hosting the service in a Windows Service, or (if the host machine runs Windows Vista/7 or Windows Server 2008) under Windows Process Activation Services (WAS). Now take a look at the two most common scenarios: hosting your service in IIS and hosting it in a .NET application (which will be a console application).

The first example shows how to host your WCF service in IIS. The first step is to set up the folder and files required. Create a new folder (under your IIS wwwroot folder, or anywhere you choose) with a name of your own choosing, and create another folder under this called bin. Copy the compiled service assembly (that is, the `.dll` file) into this folder. Also take the `App.config` file and copy it into the folder one level higher (that is, the first folder you created), and rename it to `web.config`.

Now you need to create a simple text file (in the Visual Studio IDE, Notepad, or a text editor of your choice) and call it `CustomerService.svc`. (It can be any name, but it does require the `.svc` extension.) Put this line as the contents of the file:

```
<%@ServiceHost Service="Chapter32Sample.CustomerService"%>
```

Essentially, this specifies that IIS should host the service called Chapter32Sample.CustomerService (which it expects to find in one of the assemblies in the bin folder).

In summary, you should have a `CustomerService.svc` file and a `web.config` file in a folder, and the service assembly (`dll`) in the bin folder below it. Ensure (in the folder permissions) that the IIS process has read access to this folder.

Now you need to configure the service in IIS. Open IIS, and under the default website add a new application. Give it a name (such as CustomerService), and specify the folder created earlier as its physical path. Also make sure you select to use the ASP.NET v4.5 application pool (so it uses V4.5 of the .NET Framework), and that should be it!

You can then navigate to the service's URL in a browser to see if it works, and use the WCF Test Client to actually test the operations.

> **NOTE** *If you create the project using the WCF Service Application project template, the correct structure and required files are already created for you and ready to host under IIS.*

The other example goes through hosting the WCF service in a .NET application (known as a self-hosted service). You can either put the service code (created previously) directly in this project, or reference the service project you created earlier. For this example, just create a simple console application to act as the host, and reference the existing service project. Create a new console application project in Visual Studio called CustomerServiceHost, and add a reference to the service project. You also need to add a reference to the System.ServiceModel assembly. Copy the `App.config` file from the service project into this project (so you can use the service configuration previously set up).

Use the following code to host the service:

VB

```
Imports System.ServiceModel
Imports Chapter32SampleVB
```

```
Module CustomerServiceHost
    Sub Main()
        Using svcHost As New ServiceHost(GetType(CustomerService))
            Try
                'Open the service, and close it again when the user presses a key
                svcHost.Open()

                Console.WriteLine("The service is running...")
                Console.ReadLine()

                'Close the ServiceHost.
                svcHost.Close()

            Catch ex As Exception
                Console.WriteLine(ex.Message)
                Console.ReadLine()
            End Try
        End Using
    End Sub
End Module
```

C#

```
using System;
using System.ServiceModel;
using Chapter32SampleCS;

namespace CustomerServiceHost
{
    class Program
    {
        static void Main(string[] args)
        {
            using (ServiceHost serviceHost =
                                    new ServiceHost(typeof(CustomerService)))
            {
                try
                {
                    // Open the service, and close it again when the user
                    // presses a key
                    serviceHost.Open();

                    Console.WriteLine("The service is running...");
                    Console.ReadLine();

                    serviceHost.Close();
                }
                catch (Exception ex)
                {
                    Console.WriteLine(ex.Message);
                    Console.ReadLine();
                }
            }
        }
    }
}
```

In summary, the configuration for the service is read from the `.config` file (although it could also be specified programmatically), so you just need to create a service host object (passing in the type of the service to be hosted), and open the host. When you are done you just need to close the host and clean up!

Now you can run the project and access the service using the URL specified in the `.config` file. As you can see, little code is required to host a WCF service.

CONSUMING A WCF SERVICE

Now that you have successfully created your WCF service it's time to access it within an application. To do so add a Windows Forms project to your solution called CustomerServiceClient.

The next thing is to add a reference to the WCF service to the Windows Forms application. Right-click the project node in the Solution Explorer tool window, and select Add Service Reference. This opens the dialog shown in Figure 32-10, in which you can specify the WCF service you want to add a reference to. As you can see, there is a convenient Discover button that you can use to quickly locate services contained within the current solution.

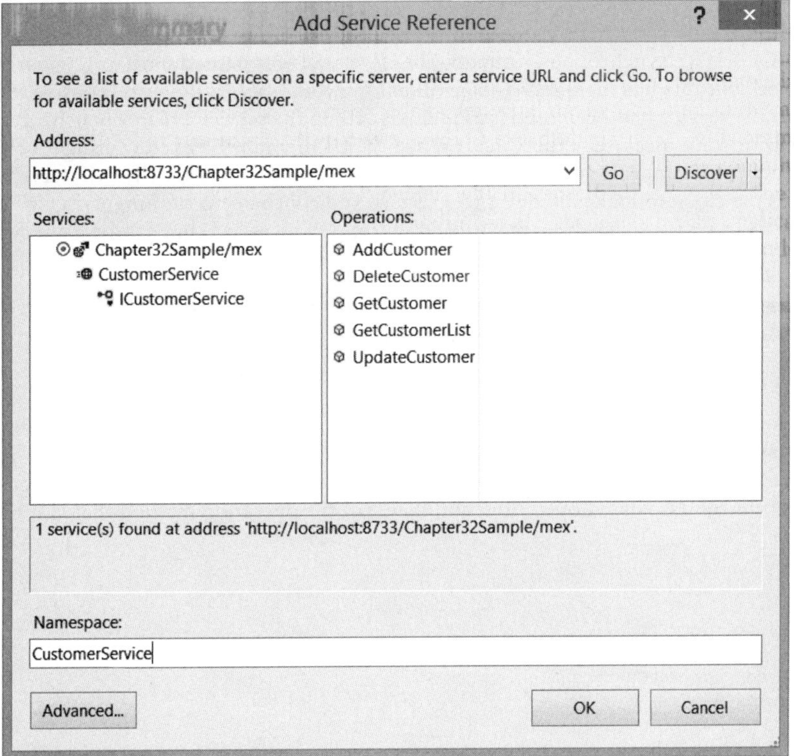

FIGURE 32-10

Select the ICustomerService node in the Services tree, change the namespace to CustomerServices, and click the OK button to complete the process. The next step is to create a form that displays or edits data from the service. Put the code to communicate with the service in the code behind for this form. Start by adding a using/Imports statement to the top of the code for the namespace of the service:

VB

```
Imports CustomerServiceClient.CustomerServices
```

C#

```
using CustomerServiceClient.CustomerServices;
```

Say you have a BindingSource control on your form called customerDataBindingSource, whose DataSource property you want to set to the list of customers to be retrieved from the service. All you need to do is create an instance of the service proxy and call the operation, and the data will be returned:

VB

```
Dim service As New CustomerService
customerDataBindingSource.DataSource = service.GetCustomerList()
```

C#

```
CustomerService service = new CustomerService();
customerDataBindingSource.DataSource = service.GetCustomerList();
```

You can now run this application and it communicates with the WCF service. This example demonstrated communicating with the WCF service synchronously (that is, the UI thread was paused until a response had been received from the server), but this has the disadvantage of making your application unresponsive to the user until the response from the service had been received. Though calling the service synchronously is easy code to write, it doesn't provide for a nice user experience. (When the UI thread is blocked waiting for the service call to return, the application appears to be "frozen.") Fortunately, you can also call WCF services asynchronously. This allows the client to make a request to a service and continue on running without waiting for the response. When a response has been received, an event will be raised that can be handled by the application from which it can act upon that response.

> **NOTE** *Silverlight clients support only asynchronous service calls.*

To enable the asynchronous methods to be created on the service proxy, you must specifically request them by selecting the Generate Asynchronous Operations check box in the Configure Service Reference dialog (detailed later in this section). To call the WCF service asynchronously, create an instance of the service, handle the `Completed` event for the associated operation, and then call the operation method that is suffixed with `Async`:

VB

```
Dim service As New CustomerService
AddHandler service.GetCustomerListCompleted, _
            AddressOf service_GetCustomerListCompleted
service.GetCustomerListAsync()
```

C#

```
CustomerService service = new CustomerService();
service.GetCustomerListCompleted += service_GetCustomerListCompleted;
service.GetCustomerListAsync();
```

The operation call returns immediately, and the event handler specified will be called when the operation is complete. The data that has been returned from the service will be passed into the event handler via `e.Results`:

VB

```
Private Sub service_GetCustomerListCompleted(ByVal sender As Object, _
                                             ByVal e As
GetCustomerListCompletedEventArgs)
    customerDataBindingSource.DataSource = e.Result
End Sub
```

C#

```
private void service_GetCustomerListCompleted(object sender,
GetCustomerListCompletedEventArgs e)
{
    customerDataBindingSource.DataSource = e.Result;
}
```

As of .NET 4.5, the mechanics of making asynchronous WCF service calls is easier on the client side, but it requires some additional effort on the server side. WCF services supports the use of the async/await pattern for asynchronous calls. On the server side, the interface and implementation need to be modified to return a generic task object. For example, the following changes would be made to the ICustomerService and CustomerService files:

VB

```
Public Interface ICustomerService

    <OperationContract()>
    Function GetCustomer(ByVal customerID As Integer) As Task(Of CustomerData)

End Interface

Public Class CustomerService
    Implements ICustomerService

    Public Async Function GetCustomer(ByVal customerID As Integer) As Task(Of CustomerData)

        Return Await Task.Factory.StartNew(Function() reallyGetCustomerData())

    End Function
End Class
```

C#

```
public interface ICustomerService
{
    [OperationContract]
    Task<CustomerData> GetCustomer(int customerID);
}

public class CustomerService : ICustomerService
{
    public async Task<CustomerData> GetCustomer(int customerID)
    {
       return await Task.Factory.StartNew(() => reallyGetCustomerData());
    }
}
```

With this configuration on the server side, the client application making this call is simplified to the following:

VB

```
Dim service As New CustomerService
Await customerDataBindingSource.DataSource = service.GetCustomerListAsync()
```

C#

```
CustomerService service = new CustomerService();
await customerDataBindingSource.DataSource = service.GetCustomerListAsync();
```

When you add a reference to the WCF service to your rich client application, you can notice that an `App.config` file was added to the project (if it didn't already exist). In either case, if you take a look at this file, you'll see that it now contains a `system.serviceModel` element that contains bindings and client elements. Within the bindings element you can see that there is a `wsHttpBinding` element (this is the default WCF binding), which defines how to communicate with the WCF service. Here you can see that the subelements override some of the default values. The `Client` element contains an endpoint element. This element defines the `Address` (which in this case is a URL), a `Binding` (which references the customized `wsHttpBinding` defined in the bindings element), and a `Contract` (which is the CustomerServices.ICustomerService interface of the WCF service that is to be called). Because this information is all defined in the configuration file, if any of these elements changes (for example, the URL of the endpoint) you can just modify the configuration file instead of recompiling the entire application.

When you make changes to the service, you need to update the service proxy that was created by Visual Studio when you added the service reference to your project. (Otherwise it remains out of date and does not show new operations added to it, and so on.) You can do this by simply right-clicking the service reference (under the Service References node in your project) and selecting the Update Service Reference item from the context menu.

If you right-click a service reference (under the Service References node in your project) you'll also find a Configure Service Reference option. This brings up the dialog shown in Figure 32-11 (which can also be accessed from the Add Service Reference dialog by clicking the Advanced button).

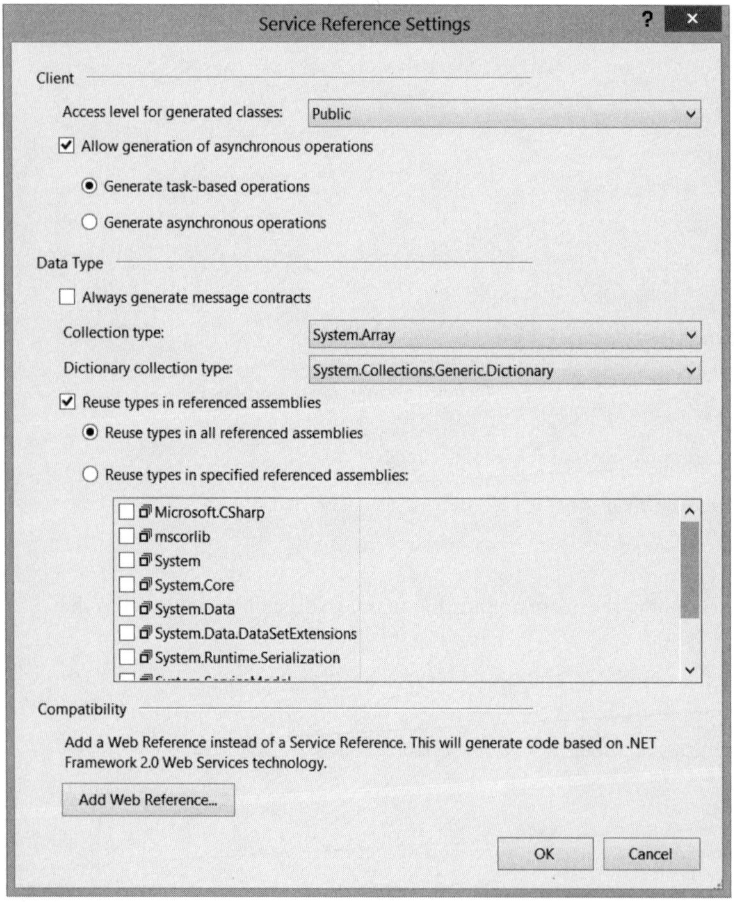

FIGURE 32-11

This dialog allows you to configure how the service proxy is generated, with a variety of options available. Of particular interest is the Reuse Types in Referenced Assemblies option. This option (when enabled) means that if the service reference generator finds that a type (that is, class/object) consumed/returned by the service is defined in an assembly referenced by the client, the proxy code generated will return/accept objects of that type instead of creating a proxy class for it. The big benefit of this is where you manage both ends of the system (both server and client) and want to pass objects between them that have associated business logic (such as validation logic, business rules, and so on). The usual process is to (on the client side) copy the property values from a proxy object into a business object (when requesting data), and then copy property values from a business object into a proxy object (to pass data back to the server). However, this option means that you can have both the server and the client reference an assembly that contains the types to be passed between them (with corresponding business logic code for both ends), and simply pass the objects backward and forward between the server and the client without requiring a proxy class as an intermediary (on the client side). This saves you from having to write a lot of property mapping code, which becomes a maintenance burden and has a high potential to contain incorrect mappings.

SUMMARY

In this chapter you learned how to create a WCF service, host it, consume it, and configure it for different purposes/uses. However, WCF isn't the end of the story for communication layers — a number of technologies are built on top of WCF to enhance its capabilities. These include WCF Data Services and WCF RIA Services, with the latter detailed in Chapter 36., "WCF RIA Services."

33

Windows Workflow Foundation (WF)

WHAT'S IN THIS CHAPTER?

- Understanding Windows Workflow Foundation
- Creating a basic workflow
- Hosting and executing a workflow
- Hosting the workflow designer in your application

Windows Workflow Foundation (WF) is a powerful platform for designing and running workflows — a central tenet in many business applications. WF was introduced with the .NET Framework 3.0 and was completely redesigned and rewritten for its .NET Framework 4.0 version to overcome some of the problems it had in its previous incarnations. This has the unfortunate side-effect of rendering .NET 4.0 workflows incompatible with workflows created in earlier versions, but leaving it a much more robust technology as a result. The version of WF included with .NET 4.5 includes a number of small, incremental changes in the designer and available templates, but nothing that rivals the difference between .NET 3.5 and 4.0. This chapter takes you through using the WF designer, and the process of creating and running workflows using WF.

WHAT IS WINDOWS WORKFLOW FOUNDATION?

Before discussing Windows Workflow, you should first examine exactly what workflow is. A workflow is essentially a model of the steps that form a business process. For example, this may incorporate document approvals, job status tracking, and so on.

A well-designed workflow requires a clear separation between the steps in the business process (the work to be done) and the business rules/logic that binds them (the *flow*).

Windows Workflow is a complete workflow solution, including both the design and the run-time components required to design or create and run workflows. These workflows can then be hosted in an application or exposed publicly as a service.

> **NOTE** *One of the powerful features of WF is that you can host both the WF run time and the WF designer in your application, enabling end users to reconfigure workflows through the WF designer hosted in your application.*

Using WF requires you to break your business process into discrete tasks (known as activities), which can then be declaratively connected and controlled in a configurable workflow using the WF designer.

You can use WF in your own products, but you can also find it embedded in various Microsoft products, including SharePoint and Windows Server AppFabric.

WHY USE WINDOWS WORKFLOW?

A common question raised by those who investigate WF is regarding why should they use it, rather than embed business logic directly in the code. It's a valid question, and whether or not you should use it comes down to the business problem that you want to solve and the business process you need to model. This chapter covers some of the scenarios in which it might be appropriate to use WF, but you'll first look at some of the benefits you would gain with using it.

One of the primary scenarios in which you would achieve the most benefits from using WF is where you have a business process that frequently changes (or the rules within the business process frequently change). Alternatively, you may have an application deployed to different customers, each of whom has different business processes. The business logic or rules that form workflows in WF are defined declaratively rather than being embedded in code, which has the advantage of enabling the workflow to be reconfigured without requiring the application to be recompiled. This, combined with the ability to host the WF designer in your own application, enables you to design highly configurable applications.

Another scenario in which using WF provides a lot of advantages is when you model long-running processes. Some workflows can run from seconds, to minutes, hours, days, and even years. WF provides a framework for managing these long-running processes, enabling a workflow to be persisted while waiting for an event (rather than remaining memory resident) and continued after a machine restart.

An advantage of designing and visualizing your workflows in the WF designer is that the workflow diagram can be used as a form of documentation of the business process or logic. This diagram can be exported from the WF designer as an image and used in documentation or presentations. This helps provide a high degree of transparency for the business process you model.

Ultimately, it's not appropriate to use WF in all applications that incorporate a business process that requires modeling. If any of the benefits listed previously are core requirements in your application, you should seriously consider designing your workflows and activities using WF. However, if none of the listed benefits are necessary (nor likely to be in the future), it's a decision you need to make based on whether or not you think it can improve the development practices of your team, and whether or not you believe that the imposition of such a framework can still provide more benefits through its use and outweigh the potential problems that it may create (which are not unheard of).

WORKFLOW CONCEPTS

Before considering the practical aspects of designing and executing workflows, first run through some of the important concepts around workflows and the terminology that is involved.

Activities

An activity is a discrete unit of work; that is, it performs a task. An activity doesn't have to just perform a single task — an activity can contain other activities (known as a composite activity), which can each contain activities themselves, and so on. A workflow is an activity itself, and so are control flow activities (discussed shortly). You can think of an activity as the fundamental building block of workflows.

Activities can have input and output arguments, which enable the flow of data in and out of the activity, and return a value. An activity can also have variables, which (like in code) store a value that any activities can also get or set. The activity in which a variable is defined designates its scope.

> **NOTE** *You can think of activities as being much like a method in regular code.*

WF includes a base library of predefined activities that cover a wide variety of tasks, which you can use in your workflow. These include activities that:

- Control execution flow (If, DoWhile, ForEach, Switch, and so on)
- Provide messaging functionality (for communicating with services)
- Persist the current workflow instance to a database
- Provide transaction support
- Enable collection management (add/remove items in a collection, clear a collection, and determine whether or not an item exists in the collection)
- Provide error handling (try, catch, throw, and rethrow)
- Provide some primitive functionality (delays, variable assigning, write to console, and so on)

Of course, despite this wide range of available predefined activities, you no doubt want to create custom activities to suit your own requirements, especially when you have complex logic to implement. These are written in code and appear in the Toolbox in the WF designer, and you can drag and drop them into your workflow.

When creating your own custom activities, you have a number of custom activity types to choose from: `Activity`, `CodeActivity`, `NativeActivity`, and `DynamicActivity`. (The custom activity inherits from one of these base classes.)

Activities based on the `Activity` class are composed of other activities and are designed visually in the WF designer. As previously stated, workflows are activities themselves, so your workflow is actually based on the `Activity` class. Activities composed in this manner can be used in other activities, too.

An activity based on `CodeActivity`, as its name suggests, is an activity whose action(s) or logic is defined in code. This code is actually a class that inherits from `CodeActivity` and overrides the `Execute` method in which the code to be executed should be placed.

Activities don't necessarily have to be executed synchronously, blocking the continuing execution of the workflow while performing a long-running task, or waiting for an operation to complete, a response or input to be received, or an event to be raised. You can create asynchronous activities by inheriting from the `AsyncCodeActivity` class. This is much like the `CodeActivity` class, except rather than having a single `Execute` method to be overridden, it has a `BeginExecute` and an `EndExecute` method instead. When an asynchronous activity is executed, it will do so on a separate thread from the scheduler and return immediately. It can then continue to execute without blocking the execution of the main workflow. The scheduler that invoked it will be notified when it has completed executing.

> **NOTE** *A workflow cannot be persisted or be unloaded while an asynchronous activity is executing.*

An activity based on the `NativeActivity` class is much like one that inherits from `CodeActivity`, but whereas `CodeActivity` is limited to interacting with arguments and variables, `NativeActivity` has full access to all the functionality exposed by the workflow run time (which passes it a `NativeActivityContext` object that provides it with this access). This includes the ability to schedule and cancel child activity execution, aborting activity execution, access to activity bookmarks, and scheduling and tracking functions.

Control Flow Activities

Control flow activities are used to control the flow of activities. This essentially provides the binding between them that organizes them into a workflow and forms the logic or rules of the process being modeled. A control flow activity is just a standard activity but is designed to control the execution or flow of the activities it contains (by scheduling the execution of those activities).

There are two primary types of control flow activities (essentially workflow types): Sequence and Flowchart. A Sequence executes the activities that it contains (as its name suggests) in sequence. It's not possible to go backward and return to a previous step in a sequence; execution can move only forward through the sequence. A Flowchart, however, enables the execution to return to a previous step, making it more suited to decision-making (that is, business) processes than sequences.

You are not limited to using a single control flow activity in a workflow — because they are activities, you can mix and match them as required in the same workflow.

Expressions

Expressions are VB code (only) that return a value and are used in the designer to control the values of variables and arguments. You can think of them much like formulas in, say, Excel. Expressions are generally bound to an activity's input arguments, used to set the value of variables, or used to define conditions on activities (such as the If activity).

Workflow Run Time/Scheduler

The workflow run time (also known as the scheduler) is the engine that takes a workflow definition file and executes it in the context of a host application. The host application starts a given workflow in the workflow run time using the `WorkflowInvoker`, the `WorkflowApplication`, or the `WorkflowServiceHost` classes.

The `WorkflowInvoker` class is used in a hands-off approach to execute the workflow, leaving the workflow run time to handle the entire execution of the workflow. The `WorkflowApplication` class is used when requiring a hands-on approach to executing the workflow (such as resuming a persisted instance), enabling the execution to be controlled by the host. The `WorkflowServiceHost` class is used when hosting the workflow as a service to be used by client applications.

Bookmarks

A bookmark marks a place in the workflow from which its execution can be resumed at a later point in time. Bookmarks enable a workflow instance to be "paused" while it's waiting for input to be received, specifying a point from which it will be resumed when that input has been received. A bookmark is given a name and specifies a callback function, pinpointing the activity that is currently executing, and specifying the method in the activity that should be called when the workflow is resumed.

Creating a bookmark stops the workflow from executing and releases the workflow thread (although the workflow isn't complete, but simply paused), enabling the workflow to be persisted and unloaded. The host is then tasked with capturing the input that the workflow is waiting on and resuming that workflow's instance execution again from the bookmark position (passing in any data to the callback method received from the awaited input).

Bookmarks are particularly useful in long-running processes where the workflow is waiting for an input to be received, that potentially may not be received for quite some time. In the meantime, it releases the resources that it's using (freeing them up for use by other workflows), and its state can be persisted to disk (if required).

Persistence

Persistence enables the current state of a workflow instance and its meta data (including the values of in-scope variables, arguments, bookmark data, and so on) to be serialized and saved to a data store (known as an *instance store*) by a *persistence provider*, to be retrieved and resumed at a later point in time. To persist a workflow instance, the workflow execution must be idle (such as if it's waiting for input), and a bookmark must be defined to mark the current execution point in the workflow.

Persistence is particularly important in several circumstances:

- When you have long-running workflows
- When you want to unload workflows that are idle and waiting for input
- If the machine or server may restart in the times that the workflow is idle
- If the execution may even continue on a different server (such as in a server farm)

> **NOTE** *The workflow is not persisted to the instance, only its state. You need to be aware of the consequences of modifying the workflow while instances are still alive and persisted, and cater accordingly.*

WF comes with a default persistence provider called `SqlWorkflowInstanceStore` that handles persisting a workflow instance to a SQL Server database. You can also create your own custom persistence provider by inheriting from the `InstanceStore` class.

You have two ways to persist a workflow instance. One is to use the predefined Persist activity from the Toolbox in your workflow, which persists the workflow instance when executed by the run time. The other option is for the host to register an event handler for the `PersistableIdle` event, which is raised by the run time when the workflow instance is idle (but not yet complete). The host can then choose whether or not to persist the workflow instance, returning a value from the `PersistIdleAction` enumeration that tells the run time what it should do.

Tracking

WF enables you to implement tracking in your workflows, where various aspects of the execution of a workflow can be logged for analysis. Tracking provides transparency over your workflow, enabling you to see what it has done in the past and its current execution state by the workflow run time emitting *tracking records*.

You can specify the granularity at which the tracking records will be emitted by configuring a *tracking profile*, which can be defined either in the `App.config` file or through code. This enables you to specify which tracking records you want the workflow run time to emit. The types of tracking records that can be emitted include workflow life cycle records (such as when a workflow starts or finishes), activity life cycle records (such as when an activity is scheduled or completes, or when an error occurs), bookmark resumption records, and custom tracking records (which you can emit from your custom activities). These tracking records can include associated data, such as the current values of variables and arguments.

Where tracking records are written is determined by specifying a *tracking participant*. By default, the WF run time emits tracking records to the Windows Event Log. You can create your own tracking participants if you, for example, want to write tracking records to a different source, such as a database.

You can also trace the execution of a workflow for troubleshooting and diagnostic purposes, which makes use of the standard .NET trace listeners. Tracing can be configured in the `App.config` file.

GETTING STARTED

Start by opening the New Project dialog and navigating to the Workflow category under your favorite language (as shown in Figure 33-1).

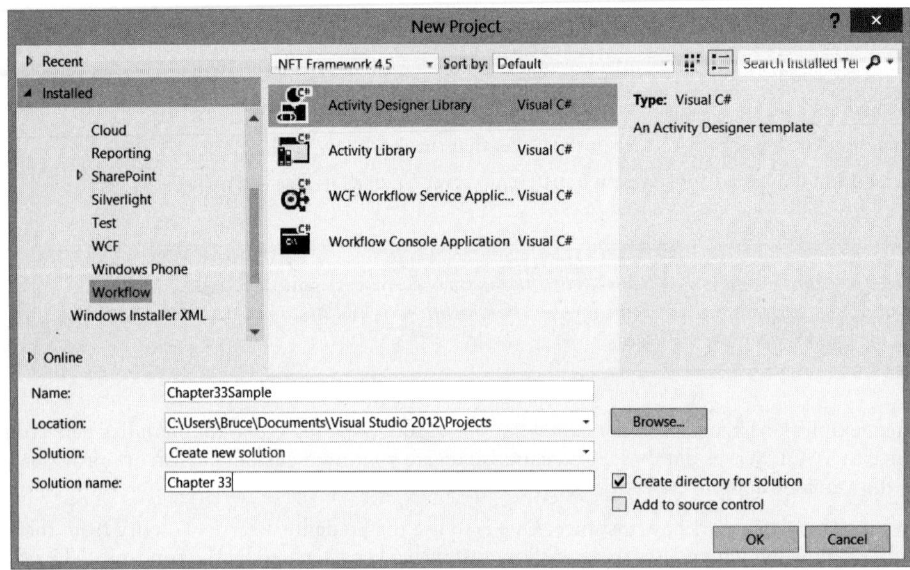

FIGURE 33-1

As you can see, you have four project types to choose from as follows:

- **Activity Designer Library:** Enables you to create and maintain a reusable library of activity designers to customize how their corresponding activities look and behave in the WF designer.
- **Activity Library:** Creates a project that enables you to create and maintain a reusable library of activities (consisting of other activities) that you can then use in your workflows. Think of it much like a class library but for workflows.
- **WCF Workflow Service Application:** Creates a workflow hosted and publicly exposed as a WCF service.
- **Workflow Console Application:** Creates an empty workflow hosted in a console application.

> **NOTE** *You aren't limited to hosting workflows in a console application or WCF service — you can also host them in other platforms such as Windows Forms, WPF, or ASP.NET applications. Add a workflow to an existing project using the Add New Item dialog and selecting Activity from the Workflow category. (There is no Workflow item because a workflow is essentially an activity itself, containing other activities.)*

For the sample project, you'll use the simplest option to get up and running by using the Workflow Console Application project template. As you can see from Figure 33-2, the project it generates is simple, containing `Program.cs`/`Module1.vb` and `Workflow1.xaml`. The `Program` class (for C# developers), or `Module1` module (for VB developers), as found in any console application, contains the entry point for the application (that is, the static/shared `Main` method), which is automatically configured to instantiate and execute the workflow. The `Workflow1.xaml` file is the file where you define your workflow.

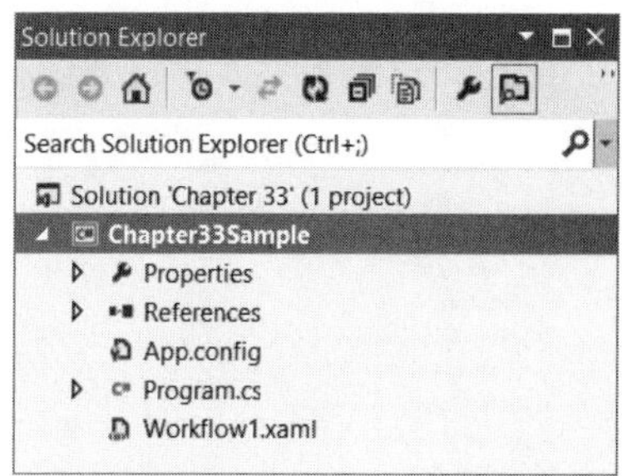

FIGURE 33-2

> **NOTE** *The workflow file is a XAML file — a file format you may recognize because it is used to define user interfaces in WPF and Silverlight. However, in this case it is used to declaratively define a workflow. You can view and edit the underlying XAML for a workflow by right-clicking the file and selecting View Code from the context menu.*

Before you do anything else, compile and run the application as is to see the result. You should find that a console window briefly appears before the application automatically ends (because it is not currently configured to actually do anything).

The name `Workflow1.xaml` isn't meaningful, so you no doubt want to change that to something more appropriate. Unfortunately, Visual Studio doesn't help you much in this respect (unlike with forms and classes) because changing the filename does not automatically change the class created behind the scenes for the workflow, nor does it change any references to the class when you change its name in the designer. For example, to rename the workflow and its corresponding class to `SimpleProcessWorkflow`, you need to:

- Change the name of the file (in the Solution Explorer).
- Change the name of the corresponding class (by clicking the design surface, and assigning the name to the `Name` property in the Properties tool window).
- Change all existing references to the workflow class. In this case where you haven't done anything with your project yet, the only reference will be in the `Program` class (for C# developers) or `Module1` module (for VB developers), which needs to be updated accordingly. The class name does not appear in IntelliSense and indicates an error when you enter it, if you have not compiled the project after changing the class name (because it's only then that the compiler regenerates the class).

THE WORKFLOW FOUNDATION DESIGNER

The WF designer enables you to drop control flow activities and standard activities from the Toolbox onto a workflow design surface. Once on the design surface, you can connect them to form the workflow. When you first create the project, the empty workflow displays in the designer, as shown in Figure 33-3.

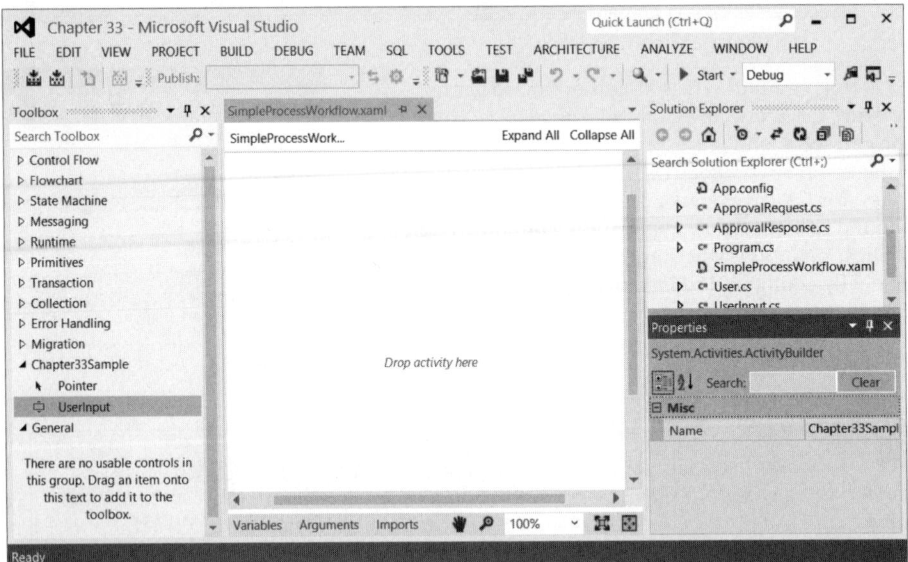

FIGURE 33-3

At the bottom of the designer are the three hyperlink buttons: Variables, Arguments, and Imports. Clicking one of these buttons pops up a pane at the bottom of the designer that enables you to modify their respective configurations.

Variables can be defined for use by activities within a given scope (which is defined by a parent activity to which the variables are attached). Add a variable by selecting the activity, clicking on the Variables tab (as shown in Figure 33-4), clicking in the area that says Create Variable, and entering a name for it. You can set the type for the variable by clicking in the Variable Type column and selecting the type from the drop-down list. If the type that you need doesn't appear in the list, you can click the Browse for Types item, which pops up a dialog enabling you to type in the qualified name of the type, or navigate through the referenced assemblies tree to find it. Clicking in the Scope column displays a drop-down list that enables you to modify the scope of the variable (by selecting the activity it belongs to). This activity and its child activities will therefore have access to the variable. Clicking in the Default column enables you to enter an expression (in the language of your project) that sets the default value of the variable.

> **NOTE** *The default value column accepts expressions rather than values. If you want to assign a value to the variable rather than an expression, you need to enter the literal value, not simply the value itself. The literal values for numeric values are identical, but if the variable is a string, you need to enclose it in double quotes. This also applies when setting the default value of arguments.*

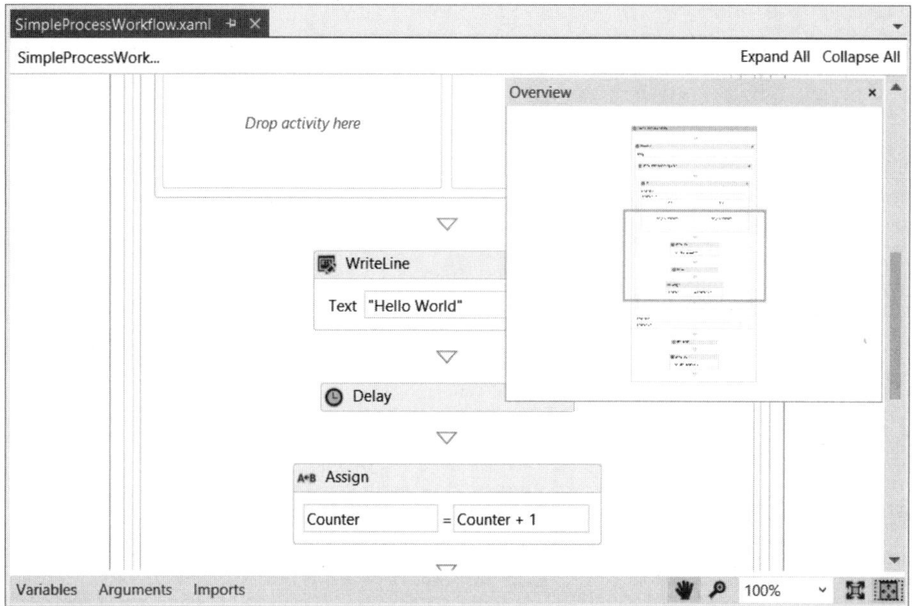

FIGURE 33-7

As previously discussed, one of the advantages of using WF is that the diagram of the workflow can be used as a form of documentation for your business process/logic/rules. It can often be useful to place this diagram in documentation or presentations, and the way to do this is quite easy. Right-click anywhere on the design surface. Two items appear in the context menu that you can use for this purpose: Save as Image and Copy as Image. Selecting the Copy as Image menu item copies a picture of the entire diagram to the clipboard, whereas the Save as Image menu item shows a dialog box enabling you to save the diagram to your choice of a JPEG, PNG, GIF, or XPS document. You can then paste the diagram into your document or presentation (if you copied it to the clipboard) or import it if you had saved it to disk.

CREATING A WORKFLOW

This section walks through the process of creating a simple workflow that demonstrates a number of the features of WF. For this example, you simply write output to the console window and receive input from the user, but do so in a workflow rather than regular code.

Designing a Workflow

The first thing you want to do is drop a control flow activity onto the designer that schedules the execution of the activities that it contains. For this example, use a Sequence activity for this purpose. You can find the Sequence activity under the Control Flow category in the Toolbox. Drag and drop it into your SimpleProcessWorkflow workflow, as demonstrated in Figure 33-8.

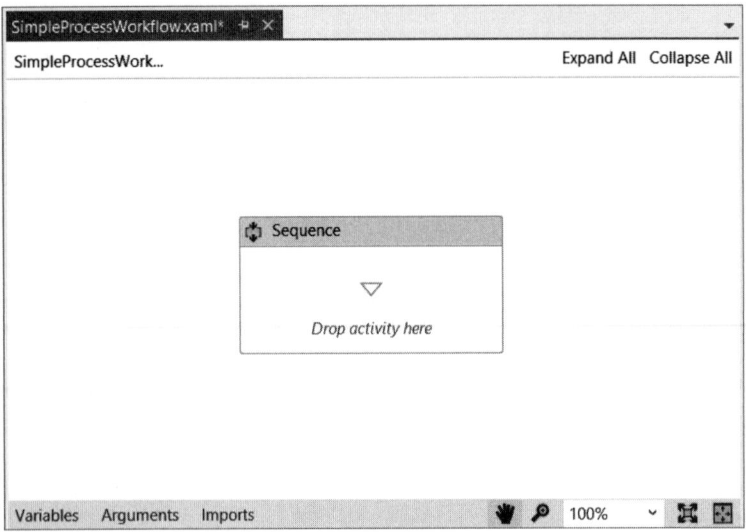

FIGURE 33-8

At this point, it would be useful to give it a meaningful name; click in its header and change it to SimpleProcessSequence. You can also simply select the activity and set its `DisplayName` property in the Properties tool window.

For this initial example, you'll get the workflow to execute a do/while loop that writes a message to the console five times. To do this, you'll then need to drop a DoWhile activity into the Sequence activity from the Control Flow category in the Toolbox. After you do that, both the new activity and the Sequence activity display as invalid. (An icon with an exclamation mark appears on the right side of the headers of both activities.) This is because an expression needs to be assigned to the condition of the DoWhile activity before it can be considered valid.

> **NOTE** *If you attempt to compile the application that has an invalid activity, it still compiles, but when you try to run it, you'll receive a run-time error. You can, however, see a list of all the validation errors in a workflow as errors in the Error List tool window.*

Because you want to place more than one activity in the DoWhile activity, add a Sequence activity as its child. Call this sequence WriteHelloWorldSequence.

Now find the WriteLine activity in the Toolbox (under the Primitives category), and drag and drop that into the WriteHelloWorldSequence activity. To make it write Hello World to the output each time it's executed, set its Text argument to `"Hello World"`. (With the argument accepting an expression and being a string value that you are assigning, you need to assign it as a literal value by enclosing it in quotes.)

So that the output can be seen more easily, drop a Delay activity (from the Primitives category in the Toolbox) into the WriteHelloWorldSequence activity, following the WriteLine activity. The `Delay` activity's `Duration` argument accepts a `TimeSpan` type — you'll use an expression to specify its value as 200 milliseconds because it's more readable than the literal value:

```
TimeSpan.FromMilliseconds(200)
```

To control the number of times this loop executes, add a variable called `Counter` to the SimpleProcessSequence activity (which is available to all the activities in the sequence). Select the SimpleProcessSequence activity and pop up the Variables pane. Click where it says Create Variable, enter `Counter` as its name, a type of `Int32`, and a default value of `0`.

Back in the DoWhile activity, you can now specify the following expression as its condition:

```
Counter < 5
```

The final step is to actually increment the `Counter` variable. Add an Assign activity (from the Primitives category in the Toolbox) to the sequence (following the Delay activity), setting its `To` argument to `Counter`, and its `Value` argument to `Counter + 1`.

Your simple workflow is now complete and should look like Figure 33-9.

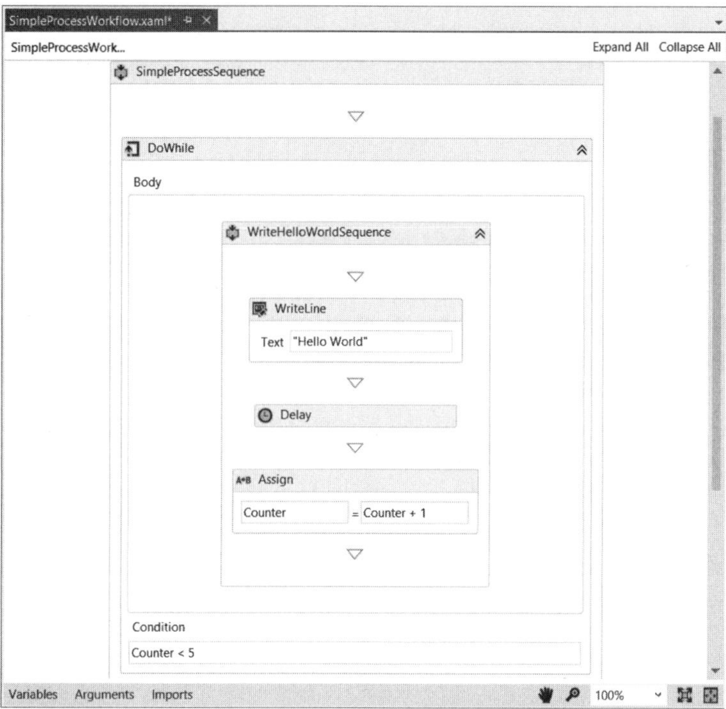

FIGURE 33-9

Now you can run your application, which executes the workflow with the results shown in Figure 33-10.

FIGURE 33-10

Writing Code Activities

Now create a custom activity whose work is defined in code to get input from the user. Add a new item to your project, select the Code Activity item template from the Workflow category in the Add New Item dialog (as shown in Figure 33-11), and call it UserInput.

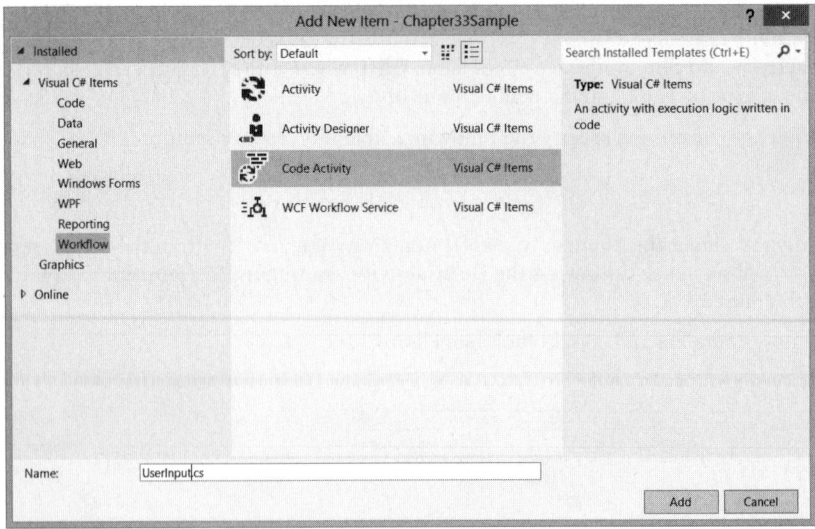

FIGURE 33-11

This creates a class that inherits from `System.Activities.CodeActivity` and overrides the `Execute` method into which you can write the code that this activity will execute. It also includes a sample input argument called `Text` (defined as a property on the class), which you can delete because this activity won't require any inputs. (Also delete the line of code in the `Execute` method that retrieves its value.)

This activity obtains input from the user that other activities in the workflow can use. You can return the value either as an output argument or as a return value. Either way is acceptable, so for this example return the value.

To return a value, inherit from its generic version (into which you pass the type that the activity returns) instead of inheriting from the CodeActivity class. Change the class to inherit from the generic `CodeActivity` class, passing in the type of the return value. Change the `Execute` method to return a type instead of void (C# developers), or to a function that returns a type (VB developers). Then it's simply a case of returning the value returned from the `Console.ReadLine()` function in the `Execute` method:

VB

```
Public NotInheritable Class UserInput
    Inherits CodeActivity(Of String)

    Protected Overrides Function Execute(ByVal context As CodeActivityContext) _
                                                                      As String
        Return Console.ReadLine()
    End Function
End Class
```

C#

```
public sealed class UserInput : CodeActivity<string>
{
    protected override string Execute(CodeActivityContext context)
    {
        return Console.ReadLine();
    }
}
```

If you switch back now to the workflow in the designer, you'll find that the activity is nowhere to be found in the Toolbox. However, after you compile your project, it appears in the Toolbox, under the category with the same name as your project, as shown in Figure 33-12.

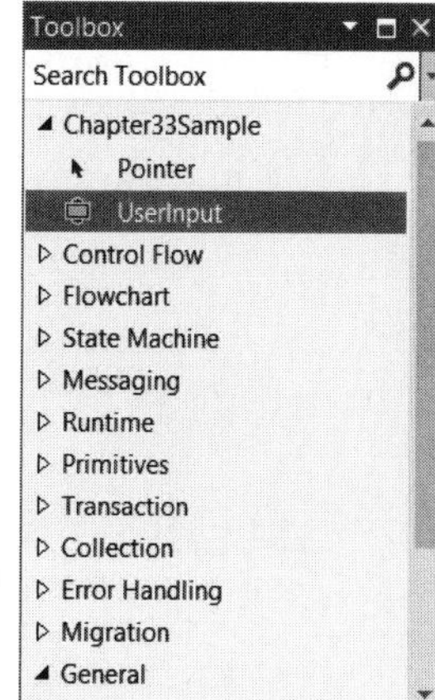

FIGURE 33-12

Drop the activity from the Toolbox into your workflow, in the main SimpleProcessSequence sequence activity after the DoWhile activity. There is no nice designer user interface for the activity (just a simple block), but you could design one by creating an activity designer for it. However, a discussion of this is beyond the scope of this chapter.

When you select it, the Properties tool window has a property called `Result` in which an expression to work with the return value of the `Execute` method in the activity can be specified. Assign the return value to a variable, which activities following it in the sequence can use. Create a new variable in the Variables pane called `UserInputValue` with a type of `String`. In the Properties tool window, you can now simply set `UserInputValue` as the expression for the `Result` property, which assigns the return value from the activity to the `UserInputValue` variable. You can prove this works by adding a WriteLine activity following the UserInput activity that then writes the value of this variable back out to the console.

Executing a Workflow

If you inspect the `Main` method (the entry point of the application) in the `Program.cs` file (for C# developers) or `Module1.vb` (for VB developers) you can find the code used to execute the workflow:

VB

```
WorkflowInvoker.Invoke(New SimpleProcessWorkflow())
```

C#

```
WorkflowInvoker.Invoke(new SimpleProcessWorkflow());
```

This makes use of the `WorkflowInvoker` class to invoke the workflow, which, as described earlier, has no control over the actual execution of the workflow other than simply initiating its execution.

If you want more control over the execution of a workflow (such as if you need to resume execution from a bookmark, or persist/unload a workflow), you need to turn to the `WorkflowApplication` class to invoke your workflow instead. Basic use of the `WorkflowApplication` class to invoke a workflow and handle its `Complete` event is as follows:

VB

```
Dim syncEvent As New AutoResetEvent(False)

Dim app As New WorkflowApplication(New SimpleProcessWorkflow())

app.Completed = Function(args)
                    Console.WriteLine("Workflow instance has completed!")
                    Thread.Sleep(1000)
                    syncEvent.Set()
                    Return Nothing
                End Function

app.Run()
syncEvent.WaitOne()
```

C#

```
AutoResetEvent syncEvent = new AutoResetEvent(false);

WorkflowApplication app = new WorkflowApplication(new SimpleProcessWorkflow());

app.Completed = (e) =>
{
    Console.WriteLine("Workflow instance has completed!");
    Thread.Sleep(1000);
    syncEvent.Set();
};

app.Run();
syncEvent.WaitOne();
```

> **NOTE** *You need to add an Imports/using statement to the* `System.Threading` *namespace at the top of the file for the code snippets above to work.*

This code assigns a delegate that runs when the workflow has completed executing. Because the `Run` method returns immediately, wait for the workflow to complete executing before continuing (and exiting the application) using the `WaitOne` method on a `AutoResetEvent`, which is notified in the `Completed` handler that it can enable the thread execution to continue.

> **NOTE** *Although we are referring to "events" here, you'll note from the code snippets that they aren't events at all. Instead, they are properties to which you can assign delegates. However, for the purposes of simplifying their description, they continue to be referred to as events.*

Executing a workflow via the `WorkflowApplication` class actually invokes it on a background thread, with the `Run` method returning immediately. The host can attach event handlers to various events raised by the `WorkflowApplication` class (such as when a workflow instance has completed, is idle, thrown an unhandled exception, and so on), and also gains the ability to abort/cancel/terminate a workflow instance, load one from a instance store, persist it, unload it, and resume from a bookmark.

You can pass input arguments into a workflow and obtain output argument values from it. Input arguments are exposed as properties from your workflow class, so assign values to these before invoking the workflow. Output arguments are returned in a dictionary (which is the return value of the `WorkflowInvoker.Invoke` method), each having a string key with the name of the argument and a corresponding object value that you can cast to the appropriate type.

As previously noted, workflows/activities are XAML files. By default, the XAML file is compiled into the application (as a resource), but what if you want to take advantage of the fact that you can reconfigure a workflow without recompiling the application? In that case, you must have the XAML file as a content file in your project instead, and dynamically load it into your application from file. This is where the `ActivityXamlServices` class is useful. Load the XAML file as an activity using the `ActivityXamlServices` class, and then invoke (that is, execute) the activity that it returns with the `WorkflowInvoker` or `WorkflowApplication` class:

VB

```
Dim activity As Activity = ActivityXamlServices.Load("SimpleProcessWorkflow.xaml")
WorkflowInvoker.Invoke(activity)
```

C#

```
Activity activity = ActivityXamlServices.Load("SimpleProcessWorkflow.xaml");
WorkflowInvoker.Invoke(activity);
```

> **NOTE** *Loading and executing a workflow from a file becomes more complicated when it uses custom activities (such as the UserInput activity), because the run time needs a reference to the assemblies containing those custom activities so it can use them. However, going into this further is beyond the scope of this chapter.*

Debugging Workflows

In addition to having a rich designer support for building workflows, WF also includes debugging capabilities. To define a breakpoint in a workflow, simply select the activity and press F9, or select Breakpoint ➢ Insert Breakpoint from the right-click context menu. Figure 33-13 demonstrates what an activity looks like when it has a breakpoint set on it (on the left), and how the activity is highlighted when stepping through the workflow and it is the current execution item (on the right).

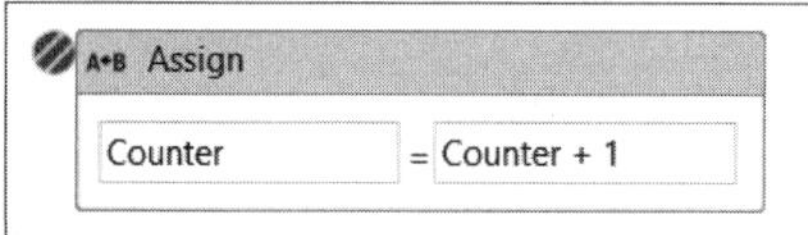

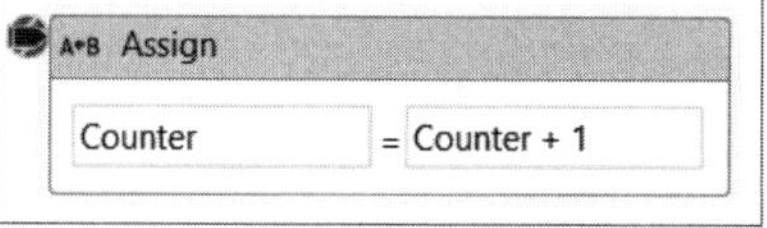

FIGURE 33-13

As in a normal debugging session, step through code using shortcut keys when in a workflow. Pressing F10 steps through the workflow, and pressing F11 steps into the current activity. You can view the values of variables currently in scope in the Locals tool window.

Of course, your custom code activities can be debugged as normal by setting breakpoints in the code editor and stepping through the code.

Testing Workflows

Having a well-defined testing framework is extremely important in business applications, with it especially vital that the underlying business logic for the application is well covered with tests. Therefore, it is essential, with your workflow being at the core of your business logic, that it be testable, too. Luckily, this is indeed possible, and you can use your favorite unit testing framework — going so far as to use Test Driven Development (TDD) practices if you want. As discussed in the "Executing a Workflow" section, use the `WorkflowInvoker.Invoke` method to execute your workflow. You can pass input argument values into the workflow and obtain the resulting output argument values (in a dictionary). Therefore, testing your workflow is as easy as supplying input argument values and asserting that the corresponding output argument values are as expected.

HOSTING THE WORKFLOW DESIGNER

One of the benefits of having a declarative configurable workflow is that it can be reconfigured at will to support changing business requirements without the application needing to be recompiled. This means (in theory) that an end user given the right tools (that is, the WF designer) should modify the workflow without requiring a developer. (Creating custom activities is a different story, however.) Of course, it's probably asking too much to have a casual end user use the WF designer and modify a workflow without training — it actually is a tool designed to be used by developers. That said, with a little training, IT-savvy users (such as business analysts and so on) could successfully take on this task.

If this is the case, it is easy to host the WF designer in your own application and expose it to the end user for modification. The WF designer is a WPF component that you can host in your own WPF applications, making it available to the users to modify a workflow as required. You can also host the WF designer in Windows Forms using the WPF interoperability described in Chapter 18, "Windows Presentation Foundation (WPF)." This chapter, however, focuses on hosting it natively in a WPF application.

> **NOTE** *The coverage of this topic assumes you have some experience working with WPF and XAML. See Chapter 18 for more information on these topics.*

Create a new WPF project called WFDesignerHost. Add the following assembly references to the project:

- System.Activities.dll
- System.Activities.Core.Presentation.dll
- System.Activities.Presentation.dll

You also need to add a reference to any assemblies that contain custom activities that you want to be used in the workflows through your application.

The designer has three main (separate) components: the Toolbox, the Properties window, and the designer surface. Now create a user interface that instantiates and displays the three of these.

Open up the `MainWindow.xaml` file and set the name of the Grid control to WFLayoutGrid. Also add three columns to this Grid. (You will no doubt want to define some appropriate widths for these columns later.) Host the Toolbox in the first column, the designer surface in the second, and the Properties window in the third. The Toolbox can be created either declaratively in XAML or in code, but the designer surface and Properties window can be created only in code. For the purpose of this example, create all three of these controls in code.

Open up the code behind the `MainWindow.xaml` file. Import the following namespaces:

VB

```
Imports System.Activities
Imports System.Activities.Core.Presentation
Imports System.Activities.Presentation
Imports System.Activities.Presentation.Toolbox
Imports System.Activities.Statements
Imports System.Linq
Imports System.Reflection
Imports System.Windows
Imports System.Windows.Controls
```

C#

```
using System;
using System.Activities;
using System.Activities.Core.Presentation;
using System.Activities.Presentation;
using System.Activities.Presentation.Toolbox;
using System.Activities.Statements;
using System.Linq;
using System.Reflection;
using System.Windows;
using System.Windows.Controls;
```

First, you need to register the designer meta data:

VB

```
Private Sub RegisterMetadata()
    Dim metaData As New DesignerMetadata()
    metaData.Register()
End Sub
```

C#

```
private void RegisterMetadata()
{
    DesignerMetadata metaData = new DesignerMetadata();
    metaData.Register();
}
```

Now add the Toolbox to the page. The Toolbox is not automatically populated with activities — instead you need to populate it with the activities you want to make available to the user. The following code handles this by creating an instance of the Toolbox and adding all the activities in the same assembly as the Sequence activity to it.

VB

```
Private Sub AddToolboxControl(ByVal parent As Grid, ByVal row As Integer,
                              ByVal column As Integer)
    Dim toolbox As New ToolboxControl()

    Dim category As New ToolboxCategory("Activities")
    toolbox.Categories.Add(category)

    Dim query = From type In Assembly.GetAssembly(GetType(Sequence)).GetTypes()
                Where type.IsPublic AndAlso
                Not type.IsNested AndAlso
                Not type.IsAbstract AndAlso
                Not type.ContainsGenericParameters AndAlso
                (GetType(Activity).IsAssignableFrom(type) OrElse
                    GetType(IActivityTemplateFactory).IsAssignableFrom(type))
                Order By type.Name
                Select New ToolboxItemWrapper(type)

    query.ToList().ForEach(Function(item)
                               category.Add(item)
                               Return Nothing
                           End Function)
```

```
        Grid.SetRow(toolbox, row)
        Grid.SetColumn(toolbox, column)
        parent.Children.Add(toolbox)
    End Sub
```

C#

```
    private void AddToolboxControl(Grid parent, int row, int column)
    {
        ToolboxControl toolbox = new ToolboxControl();

        ToolboxCategory category = new ToolboxCategory("Activities");
        toolbox.Categories.Add(category);

        var query = from type in Assembly.GetAssembly(typeof(Sequence)).GetTypes()
                    where type.IsPublic &&

                    !type.IsNested &&
                    !type.IsAbstract &&
                    !type.ContainsGenericParameters &&
                    (typeof(Activity).IsAssignableFrom(type) ||
                    typeof(IActivityTemplateFactory).IsAssignableFrom(type))
                    orderby type.Name
                    select new ToolboxItemWrapper(type);

        query.ToList().ForEach(item => category.Add(item));

        Grid.SetRow(toolbox, row);
        Grid.SetColumn(toolbox, column);
        parent.Children.Add(toolbox);
    }
```

Now you add the designer and the Properties window (both are controls returned from instantiating the `WorkflowDesigner` class):

VB

```
    Private Sub AddDesigner(ByVal parent As Grid,
                            ByVal designerRow As Integer,
                            ByVal designerColumn As Integer,
                            ByVal propertiesRow As Integer,
                            ByVal propertiesColumn As Integer)
        Dim designer As New WorkflowDesigner()
        designer.Load(New Sequence())

        Grid.SetRow(designer.View, designerRow)
        Grid.SetColumn(designer.View, designerColumn)
        parent.Children.Add(designer.View)

        Grid.SetRow(designer.PropertyInspectorView, propertiesRow)
        Grid.SetColumn(designer.PropertyInspectorView, propertiesColumn)
        parent.Children.Add(designer.PropertyInspectorView)
    End Sub
```

C#

```
    private void AddDesigner(Grid parent, int designerRow, int designerColumn,
                                          int propertiesRow, int propertiesColumn)
    {
        WorkflowDesigner designer = new WorkflowDesigner();
        designer.Load(new Sequence());

        Grid.SetRow(designer.View, designerRow);
```

```
        Grid.SetColumn(designer.View, designerColumn);
        parent.Children.Add(designer.View);

        Grid.SetRow(designer.PropertyInspectorView, propertiesRow);
        Grid.SetColumn(designer.PropertyInspectorView, propertiesColumn);
        parent.Children.Add(designer.PropertyInspectorView);
    }
```

Now call these three functions from the window's `New` method/constructor, like so:

VB

```
Public Sub New()
    InitializeComponent()

    RegisterMetadata()
    AddToolboxControl(WFLayoutGrid, 0, 0)
    AddDesigner(WFLayoutGrid, 0, 1, 0, 2)
End Sub
```

C#

```
public MainWindow()
{
    InitializeComponent();

    RegisterMetadata();
    AddToolboxControl(WFLayoutGrid, 0, 0);
    AddDesigner(WFLayoutGrid, 0, 1, 0, 2);
}
```

Now you can run the project and test it. Your final user interface should look something like Figure 33-14 (which can, of course, be improved upon by spending some time styling the page).

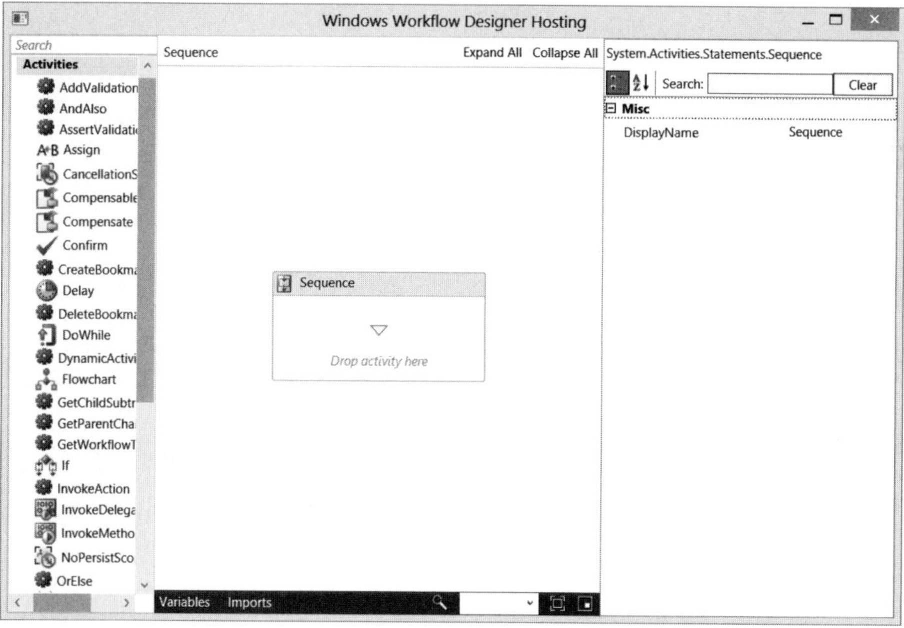

FIGURE 33-14

SUMMARY

In this chapter, you learned that Windows Workflow is a means of defining a business process, which is useful to use when you have a business process that changes frequently or is a long-running process. You also learned how to create and run a basic workflow, and how to host the workflow designer in your own application. Windows Workflow is quickly becoming the standard for implementing workflows on the Microsoft platform, enabling you to reuse the skills you have gained here to also build workflows in the various products that support it.

34

Client Application Services

WHAT'S IN THIS CHAPTER?

- Accessing client application services
- Managing application roles
- Persisting user settings
- Specifying a custom login dialog

A generation of applications built around services and the separation of user experience from back-end data stores has seen the requirements for occasionally connected applications emerge. Occasionally connected applications are those that continue to operate regardless of network availability. In Chapter 35, "Synchronization Services," you'll learn how data can be synchronized to a local store to allow the user to continue to work when the application is offline. However, this scenario leads to discussions (often heated) about security. Because security (that is, user authentication and role authorization) is often managed centrally, it is difficult to extend so that it incorporates occasionally connected applications.

In this chapter you'll become familiar with the client application services that extend ASP.NET Application Services for use in client applications. ASP.NET Application Services is a provider-based model for performing user authentication, role authorization, and profile management. In Visual Studio 2012, you can configure your rich client application, either Windows Forms or WPF, to make use of these services throughout your application to validate users, limit functionality based on what roles users have been assigned, and save personal settings to a central location.

CLIENT SERVICES

This chapter introduces you to the different application services via a simple WPF application. In this case it is an application called ClientServices, which you can create by selecting the (C# or VB) WPF Application template from the FileNew ➪ Project ➪ menu item.

To begin using the client application services, you need to enable the check box on the Services tab of the project properties designer, as shown in Figure 34-1. The default authentication mode is to use Windows authentication. This is ideal if you are building your application to work within the confines of a single organization and you can assume that everyone has domain credentials. Selecting this option ensures that those domain credentials are used to access the roles and settings services.

Alternatively, you can elect to use Forms authentication, in which case you have full control over the mechanism used to authenticate users. We return to this topic later in the chapter.

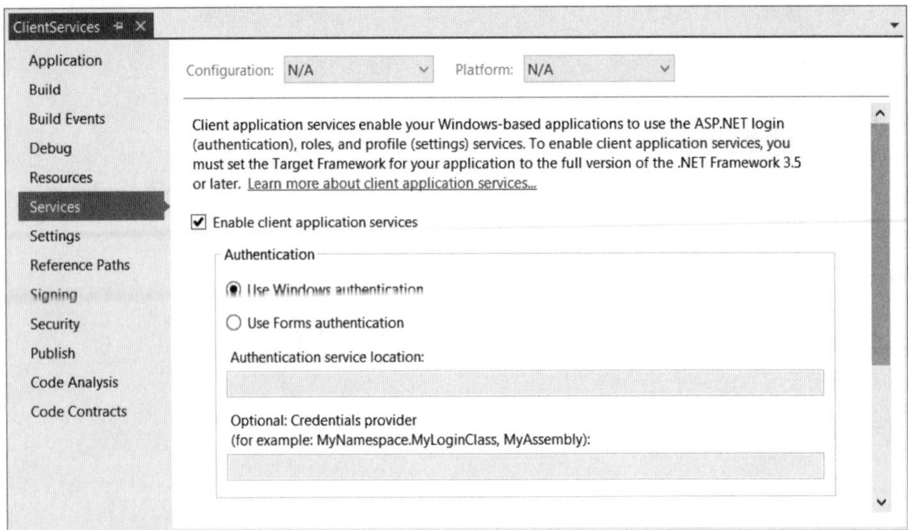

FIGURE 34-1

> **NOTE** *You can also add the client application services to existing applications via the Visual Studio 2012 Project Properties Designer in the same way as for a new application.*

When you enabled the client application services, an `app.config` file was added to your application if one did not already exist. Of particular interest is the `<system.web>` section, which should look similar to the following snippet:

```
<system.web>
    <membership defaultProvider="ClientAuthenticationMembershipProvider">
        <providers>
            <add name="ClientAuthenticationMembershipProvider" type=
            "System.Web.ClientServices.Providers.ClientWindowsAuthentication
MembershipProvider, System.Web.Extensions, Version=4.0.0.0, Culture=neutral,
PublicKeyToken=31bf3856ad364e35" serviceUri="" connectionStringName="Default
Connection" credentialsProvider=""/>
        </providers>
    </membership>
    <roleManager defaultProvider="ClientRoleProvider" enabled="true">
        <providers>
            <add name="ClientRoleProvider"
type="System.Web.ClientServices.Providers.ClientRoleProvider, System.Web.Ext
ensions, Version=4.0.0.0, Culture=neutral, PublicKeyToken=31bf3856ad364e35"
serviceUri="" cacheTimeout="86400" connectionStringName="DefaultConnection"/>
        </providers>
    </roleManager>
 </system.web>
```

Here you can see that providers have been defined for membership and role management. You can extend the client application services framework by building your own providers that can talk directly to a database or to some other remote credential store such as Active Directory. Essentially, all the project properties designer does is modify the `app.config` file to use the providers that ship with the .NET Framework and define associated properties. To implement your own providers, you need to create concrete classes that implement the abstract methods defined in the `System.Web.Security.RoleProvider`, `System.Web.Security.MembershipProvider`, or `System.Configuration.SettingsProvider` classes (depending on which provider you implement).

After you define the default role and membership providers, use the client application services to validate the application user. To do this, you need to invoke the `ValidateUser` method on the `System.Web.Security.Membership` class, as shown in the following snippet:

C#

```
using System.Web.Security;
public partial class MainWindow : Window{
    public MainWindow(){
        InitializeComponent();
    }
    private void Window_Loaded(object sender, RoutedEventArgs e){
        if (Membership.ValidateUser(null, null)){
            MessageBox.Show("User is valid");
        }
        else{
            MessageBox.Show("Unable to verify user, application exiting");
            this.Close();
            return;
        }
    }
}
```

VB

```
Imports System.Web.Security
Class MainWindow
    Private Sub Window_Loaded(ByVal sender As System.Object,
                    yVal e As System.Windows.RoutedEventArgs) Handles Me.Loaded
        If Membership.ValidateUser(Nothing, Nothing) Then
            MessageBox.Show("User is valid")
        Else
            MessageBox.Show("Unable to verify user, application exiting")
            Me.Close()
            Return
        End If
    End Sub
End Class
```

Interestingly, there is no overload of the `ValidateUser` method that accepts no arguments; instead, when using Windows authentication, you should use `Nothing` (VB) or `null` (C#) for the username and password arguments. In this case, `ValidateUser` does little more than prime the `CurrentPrincipal` of the application to use the client application services to determine which roles the user belongs to, and by default returns true. Using this method is the equivalent of logging the user in to the application.

> **NOTE** *The preceding code snippet, and others throughout this chapter, may require you to import the* `System.Web.Security` *namespace into this class file. You may also need to manually add a reference to* `System.Web.dll` *to resolve type references.*

The client application services include an application framework for handling security. For a long time VB has had its own application framework for Windows Forms Applications enabled and disabled via the Application tab on the project properties designer. This framework already includes limited support for handling user authentication, but it conflicts with the client application services. Figure 34-2 shows how you can elect to use an application-defined authentication mode so that you can use both the Windows application framework and the client application services in your application.

This setting is available only if you develop a Windows Forms Application in VB.

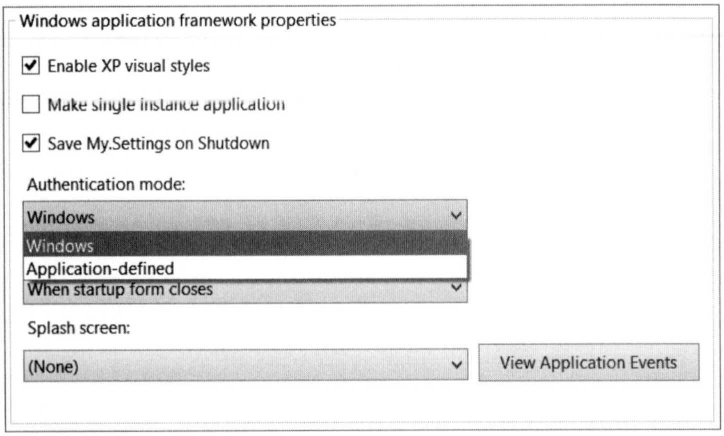

FIGURE 34-2

ROLE AUTHORIZATION

So far, you have seen how to enable the client application services, but they haven't started to add value because the user was already authenticated by the operating system when you were using Windows authentication for the client application. What isn't handled by the operating system is specifying which roles a user belongs to and thus what parts or functions within an application the user can access. Although this could be handled by the client application, it would be difficult to account for all permutations of users, and the system would be impractical to manage because every time a user was added or changed roles, a new version of the application would have to be deployed. Instead, it is preferable to have the correlations between users and roles managed on the server, allowing the application to work with a much smaller set of roles through which to control access to functionality.

The true power of the client application services becomes apparent when you combine the client-side application framework with the ASP.NET Application Services. To see this, you should add a new project to your solution using the (VB or C#) ASP.NET Empty Web Application template (under the Web node in the New Project dialog), calling it ApplicationServices.

Right-click the newly created project in Solution Explorer and select Properties to bring up the project properties designer. Because you reference this web application from other parts of the solution, it is preferable to use a predefined port and virtual directory with the Visual Studio Development Server. On the Web tab, set the specific port to `12345` and the virtual path to `/ApplicationServices`.

ASP.NET Application Services is a provider-based model for authenticating users, managing roles, and storing profile (aka settings) information. To enable the role management service for access via client application services, add the following snippet before the `<system.web>` element in the `web.config` file in the ApplicationServices project:

```
<system.web.extensions>
    <scripting>
        <webServices>
            <roleService enabled="true"/>
        </webServices>
    </scripting>
</system.web.extensions>
```

Because you want to perform some custom logic to determine which roles a user belongs to, you need to create a custom role provider, called `CustomRoles`, to take the place of the default role provider. This is done by adding a new class to your project and implementing the `RoleProvider` abstract class. For this role provider, you are interested only in returning a value for the `GetRolesForUser` method; all other methods can be left as method stubs.

C#

```
public class CustomRoles: RoleProvider{
    public override string[] GetRolesForUser(string username){
        if (username.ToLower().Contains("nick")){
            return new string[] { "All Nicks" };

        }
        else{
            return new string[] { };
        }
    }

    // The rest of the implementation has been omitted for brevity
}
```

VB

```
Public Class CustomRoles
    Inherits RoleProvider

    Public Overrides Function GetRolesForUser(ByVal username As String) As String()
        If username.ToLower.Contains("nick") Then
            Return New String() {"All Nicks"}
        Else
            Return New String() {}
        End If
    End Function

    ' The rest of the implementation has been omitted for brevity
End Class
```

You now have a custom role provider and have enabled role management. The only thing missing is the glue that lets the role management service know to use your role provider. You provide this by adding the following `roleManager` node to the `<system.web>` element in the `web.config` file:

```
<roleManager enabled="true" defaultProvider="CustomRoles">
    <providers>
        <add name=" CustomRoles" type="ApplicationServices.CustomRoles"/>
    </providers>
</roleManager>
```

The last thing to do is to make use of this role information in your application. You do this by first configuring your application with the URI to use for loading role information. On the Services tab of the ClientServices project properties (refer to Figure 34-1), enter `http://localhost:12345/ApplicationServices` in the Authentication service location TextBox. Next, you need to add a call to `IsUserInRole` to the `Window_Loaded` method:

C#

```
private void Window_Loaded(object sender, RoutedEventArgs e){
    if (Membership.ValidateUser(null, null))
    { // Commented out for brevity.
    }
    if (Roles.IsUserInRole("All Nicks")){
        MessageBox.Show("User is a Nick, so should have Admin rights.");
    }
}
```

VB

```
Private Sub Window_Loaded(ByVal sender As System.Object,
                          ByVal e As System.Windows.RoutedEventArgs) Handles Me.Loaded
    If Membership.ValidateUser(Nothing, Nothing) Then
        '. Commented out for brevity .
    End If
    If Roles.IsUserInRole("All Nicks") Then
        MessageBox.Show("User is a Nick, so should have Admin rights.")
    End If
End Sub
```

To see your custom role provider in action, set a breakpoint in the `GetRolesForUser` method. For this breakpoint to be hit, you must have both the client application and the web application running in debug mode. To do this, right-click the Solution node in the Solution Explorer window and select Properties. From the Startup Project node, select Multiple Startup Projects, and set the action of both projects to start. Now when you run the solution, you'll see that the `GetRolesForUser` method is called with the Windows credentials of the current user as part of the validation of the user.

> **NOTE** *Depending on the type of client services application you create, you might need to wire up the* `Window_Loaded` *method for your breakpoint to be hit. For example, with a WPF application, a* `Loaded="Window_Loaded"` *attribute needs to be added to the* `Window` *element in MainWindow.xaml.*

USER AUTHENTICATION

In some organizations it would be possible to use Windows authentication for all user validation. Unfortunately, in many cases this is not possible, and application developers must create their own solutions to determine which users should access a system. This process is loosely referred to as *forms-based authentication* because it typically requires the provision of a username and password combination via a login form of some description. Both ASP.NET Application Services and the client application services support forms-based authentication as an alternative to Windows authentication.

To begin with, you need to enable the membership management service for access by the client application services. Adding the `<authenticationService>` element to the `<system.web.extensions>` element in the `web.config` file does this. You disabled the SSL requirement, which is clearly against all security best practices and not recommended for production systems.

```
<system.web.extensions>
        <scripting>
              <webServices>
                      <authenticationService enabled="true" requireSSL="false"/>
                      <roleService enabled="true"/>
```

The next step is to create a custom membership provider that determines whether or not a specific username and password combination is valid for the application. To do this, add a new class, `CustomAuthentication`, to the ApplicationServices application, and set it to inherit from the `MembershipProvider` class. As with the role provider you created earlier, you'll provide a minimal implementation that validates credentials by ensuring the password is the reverse of the supplied username and that the username is in a predefined list.

C#

```
public class CustomAuthentication : MembershipProvider{
    private string[] mValidUsers = { "Nick" };

    public override bool ValidateUser(string username, string password)
    {
        var reversed = new string(password.Reverse().ToArray());
        return (from user in mValidUsers
                where string.Compare(user, username, true) == 0 &&
                      user == reversed
                select user).Count() > 0;
    }
    // The rest of the implementation has been omitted for brevity
}
```

VB

```
Public Class CustomAuthentication
    Inherits MembershipProvider
    Private mValidUsers As String() = {"Nick"}

    Public Overrides Function ValidateUser(ByVal username As String,
                                        ByVal password As String) As Boolean
        Dim reversed As String = New String(password.Reverse.ToArray)
        Return (From user In mValidUsers
                Where String.Compare(user, username, True) = 0 And
                        user = reversed).Count > 0
    End

   'The rest of the implementation has been omitted for brevity
End Class
```

As with the role provider you created, you also need to inform the membership management system that it should use the membership provider you have created. You do this by adding the following snippet to the <system.web> element in the `web.config` file:

```
<membership defaultProvider="CustomAuthentication">
    <providers>
        <add name="CustomAuthentication"
  type="ApplicationServices.CustomAuthentication"/>
    </providers>
</membership>
<authentication mode="Forms"/>
```

On the client application, only minimal changes are required to take advantage of the changes to the authentication system. On the Services tab of the project properties designer, select Use Forms Authentication. This enables both the Authentication Service Location textbox and the Optional: Credentials Provider textbox. For now just specify the authentication service location as `http://localhost:12345/ApplicationServices`.

Previously, using Windows authentication, you performed the call to `ValidateUser` to initiate the client application services by supplying `Nothing` as each of the two arguments. You did this because the user credentials could be automatically determined from the current user context in which the application was running. Unfortunately, this is not possible for Forms authentication, so you need to supply a username and password:

C#

```
private void Window_Loaded(object sender, RoutedEventArgs e){
    if (Membership.ValidateUser("Nick", "kciN")){
        MessageBox.Show("User is valid");
    }
}
```

VB

```
Private Sub Window_Loaded(ByVal sender As System.Object,
                          ByVal e As System.Windows.RoutedEventArgs) _
                          Handles Me.Loaded
    If Membership.ValidateUser("Nick", "kciN") Then
        MessageBox.Show("User is valid")
    End IF
End Sub
```

If you specify a breakpoint in the `ValidateUser` method in the ApplicationServices project, you can see that when you run this solution the server is contacted to validate the user. You'll see later that this information can then be cached locally to facilitate offline user validation.

SETTINGS

In the .NET Framework v2.0, the concept of settings with a User scope was introduced to allow per-user information to be stored between application sessions. For example, window positioning or theme information might have been stored as a user setting. Unfortunately, there was no way to centrally manage this information. Meanwhile, ASP.NET Application Services had the notion of profile information, which was essentially per-user information, tracked on a server, which could be used by web applications. Naturally, with the introduction of the client application services, it made sense to combine these ideas to allow settings to be saved via the web. These settings have a scope of User (Web).

As with the membership and role services, you need to enable the profile service for access by the client application services. You do this by adding the `<profileService>` element to the `<system.web.extensions>` element in the `web.config` file:

```
<system.web.extensions>
    <scripting>
        <webServices>
            <profileService enabled="true"
                            readAccessProperties="Nickname"
                            writeAccessProperties="Nickname" />
            <authenticationService enabled="true" requireSSL="false"/>
```

Following the previous examples, you can build a custom profile provider that uses an in-memory dictionary to store user nicknames. This isn't a good way to track profile information because it would be lost every time the web server recycled and would not scale out to multiple web servers. Nevertheless, you need to add a new class, `CustomProfile`, to the ApplicationServices project and set it to inherit from `ProfileProvider`.

C#

```
using System.Web.Profile;
using System.Configuration;
public class CustomProfile : ProfileProvider{
    private Dictionary<string, string> nicknames =
```

```
                                         new Dictionary<string, string>();

        public override System.Configuration.SettingsPropertyValueCollection
            GetPropertyValues(System.Configuration.SettingsContext context,
                  System.Configuration.SettingsPropertyCollection collection){
            var vals = new SettingsPropertyValueCollection();
            foreach (SettingsProperty setting in collection){
                var value = new SettingsPropertyValue(setting);
                if (nicknames.ContainsKey(setting.Name)) {
                    value.PropertyValue = nicknames[setting.Name];
                }
                vals.Add(value);
            }
            return vals;
        }

        public override void SetPropertyValues(SettingsContext context,
                              SettingsPropertyValueCollection collection){
            foreach (SettingsPropertyValue setting in collection){
                nicknames[setting.Name] = setting.PropertyValue.ToString();
            }
        }

        // The rest of the implementation has been omitted for brevity
    }
```

VB

```
Imports System.Configuration

Public Class CustomProfile
    Inherits ProfileProvider
    Private nicknames As New Dictionary(Of String, String)

    Public Overrides Function GetPropertyValues(ByVal context As SettingsContext,
                       ByVal collection As SettingsPropertyCollection) _
                                           As SettingsPropertyValueCollection
        Dim vals As New SettingsPropertyValueCollection
        For Each setting As SettingsProperty In collection
            Dim value As New SettingsPropertyValue(setting)
            If nicknames.ContainsKey(setting.Name) Then
                value.PropertyValue = nicknames.Item(setting.Name)
            End If
            vals.Add(value)
        Next
        Return vals
    End Function

    Public Overrides Sub SetPropertyValues(ByVal context As SettingsContext,
                              ByVal collection As SettingsPropertyValueCollection)
        For Each setting As SettingsPropertyValue In collection
            nicknames.Item(setting.Name) = setting.PropertyValue.ToString
        Next
    End Sub

    'The rest of the implementation has been omitted for brevity
End Class
```

The difference with the profile service is that when you specify the provider to use in the `<system.web>` element in the `web.config` file, you also need to declare what properties can be saved via the profile service (see the following snippet). For these properties to be accessible via the client application services, they must have a corresponding entry in the `readAccessProperties` and `writeAccessProperties` attributes of the `<profileService>` element, as shown earlier.:

```
<profile enabled="true" defaultProvider="CustomProfile">
    <providers>
        <add name="CustomProfile" type="ApplicationServices.CustomProfile"/>
    </providers>
    <properties>
        <add name="Nickname" type="string"
             readOnly="false" defaultValue="{nickname}"
             serializeAs="String" allowAnonymous="false" />
    </properties>
</profile>
```

As an aside, the easiest way to build a full profile service is to use the utility `aspnet_regsql.exe` (typically found at `c:\Windows\Microsoft.NET\Framework\v4.0.30319\aspnet_regsql.exe`) to populate an existing SQL Server database with the appropriate table structure. The command to do this (executed from a command line prompt) is:

```
aspnet_regsql -S server -U userId -P password -A p
```

The `server`, `userid`, and `password` tokens in the command line correspond to the name of the database server, and the user ID and password of a SQL user with sufficient rights to be able to create a database on the server. Since no database is specified in the command line, the default database name of `aspnetdb` is used. If you want to have the schema added to an existing database, use the `-d databasename` option in the command line.

You can then use the built-in `SqlProfileProvider` (`SqlMembershipProvider` and `SqlRoleProvider` for membership and role providers, respectively) to store and retrieve profile information. To use this provider, change the profile element you added earlier to the following:

```
<profile enabled="true" defaultProvider="CustomProfile">
    <providers>
        <add name="SqlProvider"
             type="System.Web.Profile.SqlProfileProvider"
             connectionStringName="SqlServices"
             applicationName="SampleApplication"
             description="SqlProfileProvider for SampleApplication" />
```

The `connectionStringName` attribute needs to correspond to the name of a SQL Server connection string located in the `connectionStrings` section of the `web.config` file.

To use the custom profile provider you have created, in the client application, you need to specify the web settings service location on the Services tab of the project properties designer. This location should be the same as for both the role and authentication services: `http://localhost:12345/ApplicationServices`.

This is where the Visual Studio 2012 support for application settings is particularly useful. If you now go to the Settings tab of the project properties designer and click the Load Web Settings button, you are initially prompted for credential information because you need to be a validated user to access the profile service. Figure 34-3 shows this dialog with the appropriate credentials supplied.

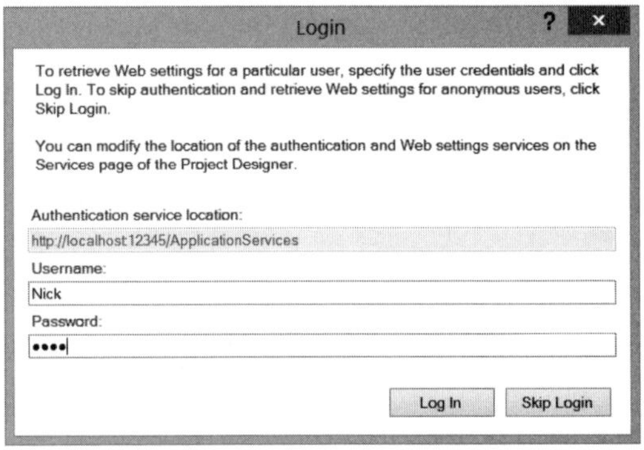

FIGURE 34-3

After a valid set of credentials is entered, the profile service is interrogated, and a new row is added to the settings design surface, as shown in Figure 34-4. Here you can see that the scope of this setting is indeed User (Web) and that the default value, specified in the `web.config` file, has been retrieved.

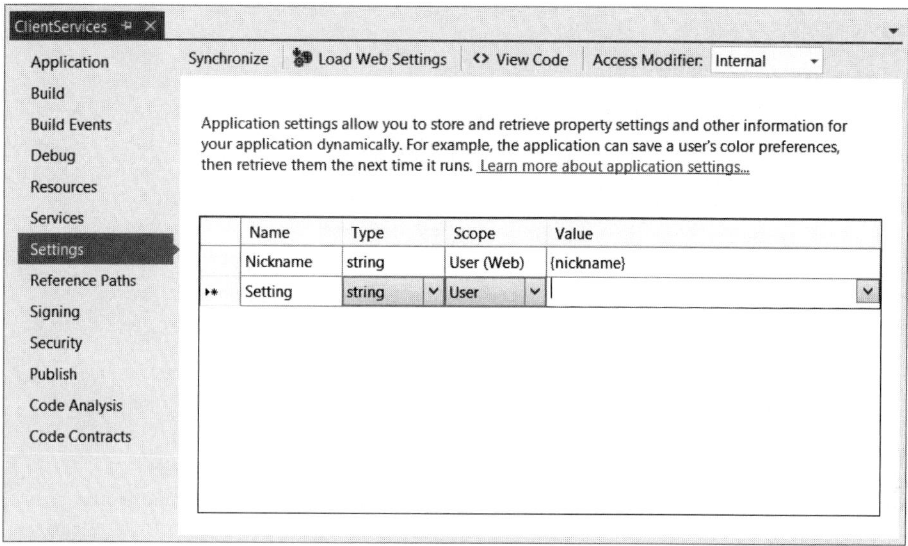

FIGURE 34-4

If you take a look at the `app.config` file for the client application, you can notice that a new `sectionGroup` has been added to the `configSections` element. This simply declares the class that will be used to process the custom section that has been added to support the new user settings.:

```
<configSections>
    <sectionGroup name="userSettings"
                  type="System.Configuration.UserSettingsGroup, System,
                        Version=4.0.0.0, Culture=neutral,
                        PublicKeyToken=b77a5c561934e089" >
      <section name="ClientServices.Properties.Settings"
               type="System.Configuration.ClientSettingsSection, System,
                     Version=4.0.0.0, Culture=neutral,
                     PublicKeyToken=b77a5c561934e089" allowExeDefinition=
                     "MachineToLocalUser" requirePermission="false" />
    </sectionGroup>
  </configSections>
```

Toward the end of the `app.config` file, you'll see the custom section that has been created. As you would expect, the name of the setting is `Nickname`, and the value corresponds to the default value specified in the `web.config` file in the ApplicationServices project.

```
<userSettings>
    <ClientAppServicesVB.MySettings>
        <setting name="Nickname" serializeAs="String">
            <value>{nickname}</value>
        </setting>
    </ClientAppServicesVB.MySettings>
</userSettings>
```

To make use of this in code you can use the same syntax as for any other setting. Here you simply retrieve the current value, request a new value, and then save this new value:

C#

```
private void Window_Loaded(object sender, RoutedEventArgs e){
    // Commented out for brevity
    MessageBox.Show(My.Settings.Nickname)
    Properties.Settings.Default.Nickname = "Not the default Name";
    My.Settings.Save()
```

VB

```
Private Sub Window_Loaded(ByVal sender As System.Object,
                          ByVal e As System.Windows.RoutedEventArgs) _
                                                  Handles Me.Loaded
    ' Commented out for brevity
    MessageBox.Show(My.Settings.Nickname)
    My.Settings.Nickname = InputBox("Please specify a nickname:", "Nickname")
    My.Settings.Save()
```

If you run this application again, the nickname you supplied the first time will be returned.

LOGIN FORM

Earlier, when you were introduced to Forms authentication, you used a hard-coded username and password to validate the user. Although it would be possible for the application to prompt the user for credentials before calling `ValidateUser` with the supplied values, there is a better way that uses the client application services framework. Instead of calling `ValidateUser` with a username/password combination, you go back to supplying `Null/Nothing` as the argument values and define a credential provider; then the client application services can call the provider to determine the set of credentials to use.

C#

```
private void Window_Loaded(object sender, RoutedEventArgs e){
    if (Membership.ValidateUser(null, null)){
        MessageBox.Show("User is valid");
    }
}
```

VB

```
Private Sub Window_Loaded(ByVal sender As System.Object,
                          ByVal e As System.Windows.RoutedEventArgs) _
                                                  Handles Me.Loaded
    If Membership.ValidateUser(Nothing, Nothing) Then
        MessageBox.Show("User is valid")
    End If
End Sub
```

This probably sounds more complex than it is because it is relatively easy to create a credentials provider. Start by adding a login form to the client application. Do this by selecting the Login Form template from the Add New Item dialog and calling it LoginForm. Unfortunately, this template is only available for VB developers as a Windows Forms form. If you want to create a WPF version or are working in C#, you need to add a new Window to the ClientServices project and add a TextBox (name it UsernameTextBox), a PasswordBox (name it PasswordTextBox), and two Buttons (name them OK and Cancel). While you have the designer open, click the OK button and change the `DialogResult` property to `OK`.

To use this login form as a credential provider, modify it to implement the IClientFormsAuthenticationCredentialsProvider interface. An alternative strategy would be to have a separate class that implements this interface, and then displays the login form when the GetCredentials method is called. The following code snippet contains the code-behind file for the LoginForm class, showing the implementation of the IClientFormsAuthenticationCredentialsProvider interface:

C#

```
using System.Web.ClientServices.Providers;
public partial class LoginForm : Window,
                                IClientFormsAuthenticationCredentialsProvider {
    public LoginForm(){

        InitializeComponent();
    }

    private void OK_Click(object sender, RoutedEventArgs e){
        this.DialogResult = true;
        this.Close();
    }

    private void Cancel_Click(object sender, RoutedEventArgs e){
        this.DialogResult = false;
        this.Close();
    }

    public ClientFormsAuthenticationCredentials GetCredentials(){
        if (this.ShowDialog() ?? false) {
            return new ClientFormsAuthenticationCredentials(
                                   UsernameTextBox.Text,
                                   PasswordTextBox.
                                   Password,
                                   false);
        }
        else{
            return null;
        }
    }
}
```

VB

```
Imports System.Web.ClientServices.Providers

Public Class LoginForm
    Implements IClientFormsAuthenticationCredentialsProvider

    Public Function GetCredentials() As ClientFormsAuthenticationCredentials _
            Implements IClientFormsAuthenticationCredentialsProvider.GetCredentials
        If Me.ShowDialog() = Forms.DialogResult.OK Then
            Return New ClientFormsAuthenticationCredentials(UsernameTextBox.Text,
                                                            PasswordTextBox.Text,
                                                            False)
        Else
            Return Nothing
        End If
    End Function
End Class
```

> **NOTE** *The C# and VB code snippets are quite different. This is because the C# snippet uses a WPF window, whereas the VB snippet uses the Windows Form Login Form template.*

As you can see from this snippet, the `GetCredentials` method returns `ClientFormsAuthenticationCredentials` if credentials are supplied, or `Nothing` (VB)/`null` (C#) if Cancel is clicked. Clearly this is only one way to collect credentials information, and there is no requirement that you prompt the user for this information. (The use of dongles or employee identification cards are common alternatives.)

With the credentials provider created, it is just a matter of informing the client application services that they should use it. You do this via the Optional: Credentials Provider field on the Services tab of the project properties designer, as shown in Figure 34-5.

Now when you run the application, you are prompted to enter a username and password to access the application. This information is then passed to the membership provider on the server to validate the user.

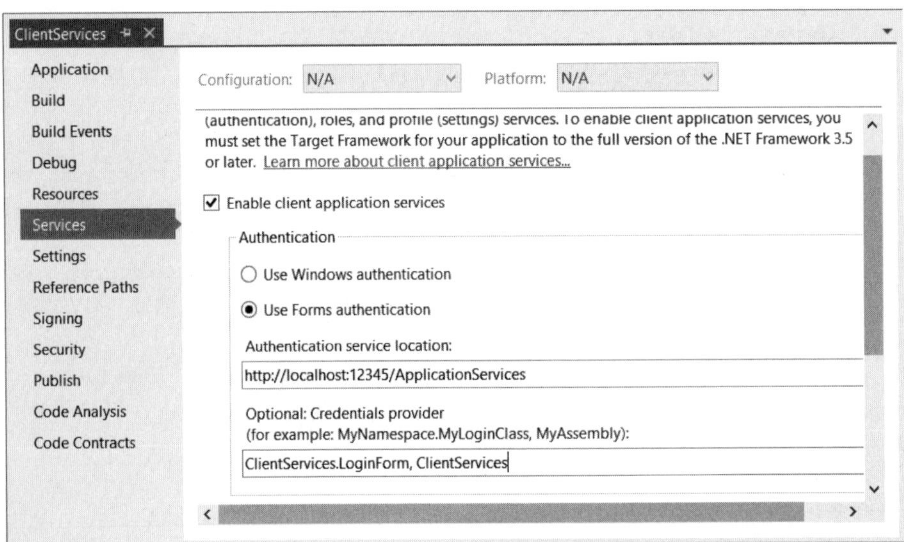

FIGURE 34-5

OFFLINE SUPPORT

In the previous steps, if you had a breakpoint in the role provider code on the server, you may have noticed that it hit the breakpoint only the first time you ran the application. The reason for this is that it is caching the role information offline. If you click the Advanced button on the Services tab of the project properties designer, you'll see a number of properties that can be adjusted to control this offline behavior, as shown in Figure 34-6.

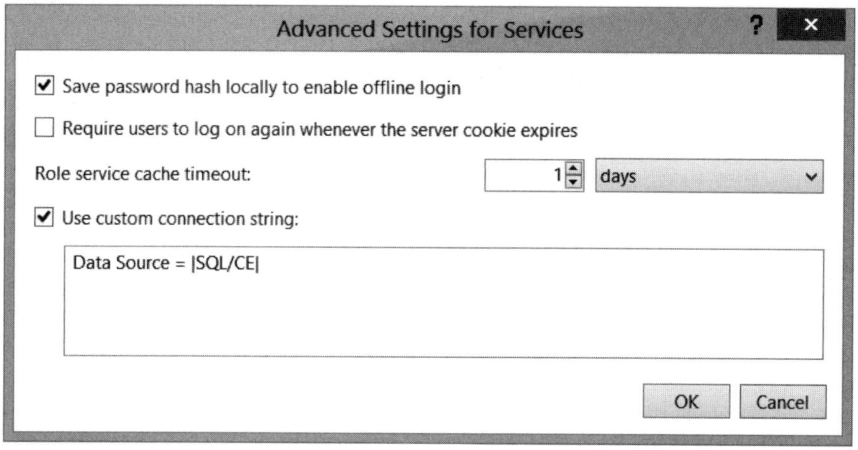

Advanced Settings for Services

Save password hash locally to enable offline login

Require users to log on again whenever the server cookie expires

Role service cache timeout: 1 days

Use custom connection string:

Data Source = |SQL/CE|

OK Cancel

FIGURE 34-6

It's the role service cache timeout that determines how frequently the server is queried for role information. Because this timeout determines the maximum period it takes for role changes to be propagated to a connected client, you must set this property according to how frequently you expect role information to change. Clearly, if the application is running offline, the changes will be retrieved the next time the application goes online (assuming the cache timeout has been exceeded while the application is offline).

Clicking the Save Password Hash check box means that the application doesn't have to be online for the user to log in. The stored password hash is used only when the application is running in offline mode, in contrast to the role information, for which the cache is queried unless the timeout has been exceeded.

Whether the application is online or offline is a property maintained by the client application services because it is completely independent of actual network or server availability. Depending on your application, it might be appropriate to link the two as shown in the following example, where offline status is set during application startup or when the network status changes. From the project properties designer, click the View Application Events button on the Application tab (VB), or open `App.xaml` and add an event handler for the `Startup` event. This displays a code file in which the following code can be inserted:

C#

```
using System.Net.NetworkInformation;
public partial class App : Application{
    private void Application_Startup(object sender, StartupEventArgs e){
        NetworkChange.NetworkAvailabilityChanged +=
        new NetworkAvailabilityChangedEventHandler
                               (NetworkChange_NetworkAvailabilityChanged);
        this.UpdateConnectivity();
    }

    private void NetworkChange_NetworkAvailabilityChanged(object sender,
                                   NetworkAvailabilityEventArgs e){
        this.UpdateConnectivity();
    }

    private void UpdateConnectivity(){
        System.Web.ClientServices.ConnectivityStatus.IsOffline =
 !System.Net.NetworkInformation.NetworkInterface.GetIsNetworkAvailable();
    }
}
```

VB

```
Class Application
    Private Sub MyApplication_Startup(ByVal sender As Object,
           ByVal e As System.Windows.StartupEventArgs) Handles Me.Startup
        AddHandler System.Net.NetworkInformation.NetworkChange.
        NetworkAvailabilityChanged, _
                      AddressOf MyApplication_NetworkAvailabilityChanged
        UpdateConnectivity()
    End Sub
    Private Sub MyApplication_NetworkAvailabilityChanged(
          ByVal sender As Object,
          ByVal e As System.Net.NetworkInformation.NetworkAvailabilityEventArgs)
        UpdateConnectivity()
    End Sub

    Private Sub UpdateConnectivity()
        System.Web.ClientServices.ConnectivityStatus.IsOffline = Not _
        My.Computer.Network.IsAvailable()
    End Sub
End Class
```

This is a rudimentary way to detect whether or not an application is online, and most applications require more complex logic to determine if they are connected. The other thing to consider is that when the application comes back online, you may want to confirm that the user information is still up to date using the `RevalidateUser` method on the `ClientFormsIdentity` object (only relevant to Forms authentication):

C#

```
(System.Threading.Thread.CurrentPrincipal.Identity as
             System.Web.ClientServices.ClientFormsIdentity).RevalidateUser()
```

VB

```
CType(System.Threading.Thread.CurrentPrincipal.Identity,
             System.Web.ClientServices.ClientFormsIdentity).RevalidateUser()
```

The last property in the Advanced dialog determines where the cached credential and role information is stored. This check box has been enabled because you chose to use Windows authentication earlier in the example. If you use Forms authentication, you can clear this check box. The client application services use `.clientdata` files to store per-user data under the `Application.UserAppDataPath`, which is usually something like `C:\Users\Nick\AppData\Roaming\ClientServices\1.0.0.0`. (This differs on Windows XP.) Using a custom connection string enables you to use a SQL Server Compact Edition (SSCE) database file to store the credentials information. This is required for offline support of Windows authentication.

> **NOTE** *Unfortunately, the designer is limited in that it doesn't enable you to specify any existing connections you may have. If you modify the* `app.config` *file, you can tweak the application to use the same connection.*
>
> *This might be a blessing in disguise because the* `|SQL/CE|` *datasource property (which is the default) actually lets the client application services manage the creation and setup of the SSCE database file. (Otherwise you have to ensure that the appropriate tables exist.)*
>
> *The files created are* `.spf` *instead of the usual* `.sdf` *file extension; they are still SSCE database files that you can explore with Visual Studio 2012.*

SUMMARY

This chapter showed you how the ASP.NET Application Services can be extended for use with client applications. With built-in support for offline functionality, the client application services enable you to build applications that can seamlessly move between online and offline modes. Combined with the Microsoft ADO.NET Synchronization Services, they provide the necessary infrastructure to build sophisticated, occasionally connected applications.

35

Synchronization Services

WHAT'S IN THIS CHAPTER?

- What an occasionally connected application is and why you would build an application that way
- Wiring up Synchronization Services to build an occasionally connected application
- Separating Synchronization Services across multiple tiers
- Performing both single and bidirectional synchronization

Application design has gone through many extremes, ranging from standalone applications that don't share data, to public web applications in which everyone connects to the same data store. Recently, a flurry of peer-to-peer applications have appeared in which information is shared between nodes but no central data store exists. In the enterprise space, key buzzwords such as Software as a Service (SaaS) and Software and Services (S+S) highlight the transition from centralized data stores, through an era of outsourced data and application services, toward a hybrid model where data and services are combined within a rich application.

One of the reasons organizations have leaned toward web applications in the past has been the need to rationalize their data into a single central repository. Although rich client applications can work well across a low-latency network using the same data repository, they quickly become unusable if every action requires data to be communicated between the client and server over a slow public network. To reduce this latency, an alternative strategy is to synchronize a portion of the data repository to the client machine and to make local data requests. This not only improves performance (because all the data requests happen locally), but it also reduces the load on the server. In this chapter, you discover how building applications that are occasionally connected can help you deliver rich and responsive applications using the Microsoft Synchronization Services for ADO.NET.

OCCASIONALLY CONNECTED APPLICATIONS

An occasionally connected application is one that can continue to operate regardless of connectivity status. You have a number of different ways to access data when the application is offline. Passive systems simply cache data that is accessed from the server so that when the connection is lost at least a subset of the information is available. Unfortunately, this strategy means that a limited set of data is available and is only suitable for scenarios in which there is an unstable or unreliable connection, rather than completely disconnected applications. In the latter case, an active system that synchronizes data to the local system is required. The Microsoft Synchronization Services for ADO.NET (Sync Services) is a synchronization framework that dramatically simplifies the problem of synchronizing data from any server to the local system.

SERVER DIRECT

To become familiar with the Sync Services, you can use a simple database that consists of a single table that tracks customers. You can create this using the Server Explorer within Visual Studio 2012. Right-click the Data Connections node, and from the shortcut menu, select Create New SQL Server Database. Figure 35-1 shows the Create New SQL Server Database dialog in which you can specify a server and a name for the new database.

When you click OK, a database with the name CRM is added to the SQL Server Express instance, and a data connection is added to the Data Connections node in the Server Explorer. From the Tables node, under the newly created data connection, select Add New Table from the right-click shortcut menu, and create columns for CustomerId (primary key), Name, Email, and Phone so that the table matches what is shown in Figure 35-2.

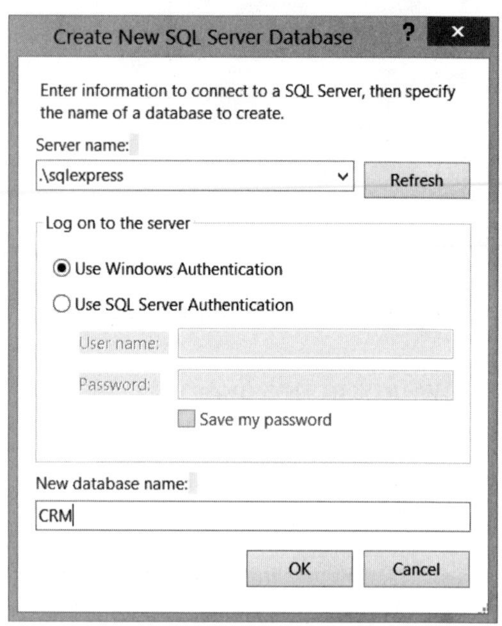

FIGURE 35-1

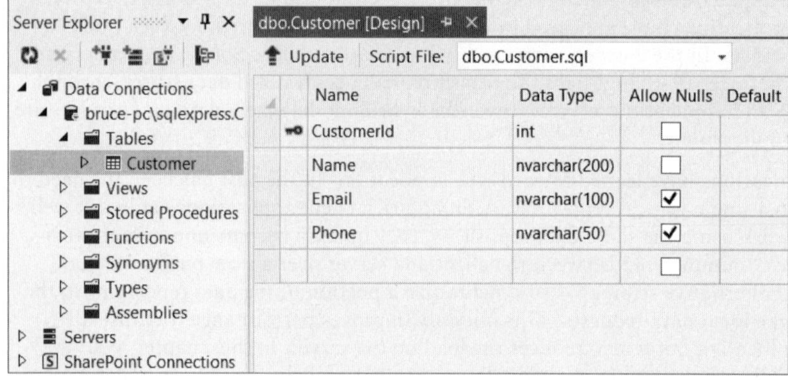

FIGURE 35-2

Now that you have a simple database to work with, it's time to create a new Windows Forms Application. In this case the application is titled QuickCRM, and in the Solution Explorer tool window of Figure 35-3, you can see that Form1 is renamed to MainForm and two additional forms, ServerForm and LocalForm, are added.

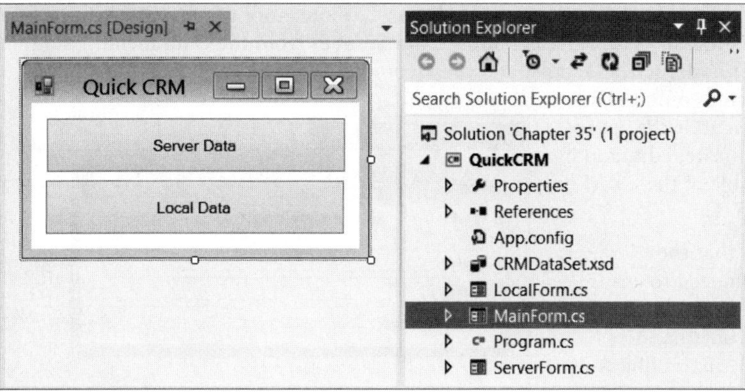

FIGURE 35-3

MainForm has two buttons (refer to the editor area of Figure 35-3) and has the following code to launch the appropriate forms:

VB

```
Public Class MainForm
    Private Sub ServerButton_Click(ByVal sender As System.Object,
                                   ByVal e As System.EventArgs) _
                          Handles ServerButton.Click
        My.Forms.ServerForm.Show()
    End Sub

    Private Sub LocalButton_Click(ByVal sender As System.Object,
                                  ByVal e As System.EventArgs) _
                          Handles LocalButton.Click
        My.Forms.LocalForm.Show()
    End Sub
End Class
```

C#

```
public partial class MainForm : Form {
    public MainForm(){
        InitializeComponent();
    }

    private void ServerButton_Click(object sender, EventArgs e){
        (new ServerForm()).ShowDialog();
    }
    private void LocalButton_Click(object sender, EventArgs e){
        (new LocalForm()).ShowDialog();
    }
}
```

Before looking at how you can use Sync Services to work with local data, take a look at how you might have built an always-connected, or server-bound, version. From the Data menu, select Add New Data Source, and step through the Data Source Configuration Wizard, selecting the DataSet option, followed by the CRM database created earlier, saving the connection string to the application configuration file, and adding the Customer table to the CRMDataSet.

Open the ServerForm designer by double-clicking it in the Solution Explorer tool window. If the Data Sources tool window is not already visible, select Show Data Sources from the Data menu. Using the drop-down on the Customer node, select Details, and then from the CustomerId node, select None. Dragging the Customer node across onto the design surface of the ServerForm adds the appropriate controls so that you can locate, edit, and save records to the Customer table of the CRM database, as shown in Figure 35-4.

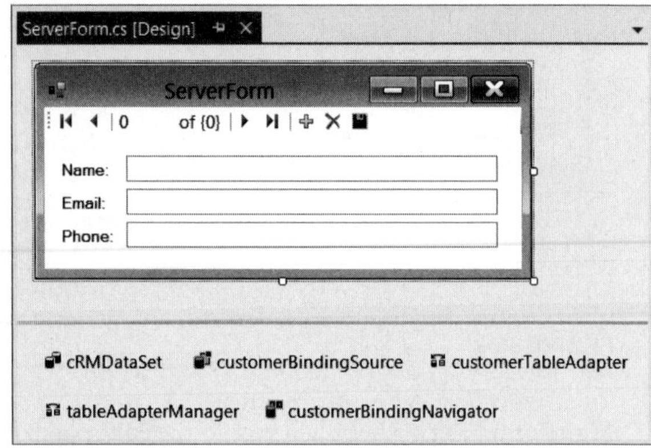

FIGURE 35-4

Recall from the table definition that the CustomerId can't be null, so you need to ensure that any new records are created with a new ID. To do this tap into the `CurrentChanged` event on the `CustomerBindingSource` object. You can access this either directly in the code-behind of the ServerForm or by selecting `CustomerBindingSource` and finding the `CurrentChanged` event in the Properties tool window.

VB

```
Private Sub CustomerBindingSource_CurrentChanged _
                    (ByVal sender As System.Object, ByVal e As System.EventArgs) _
                                    Handles CustomerBindingSource.CurrentChanged
    If Me.CustomerBindingSource.Current Is Nothing Then
        Return
    End If

    Dim c As CRMDataSet.CustomerRow = CType(CType(Me.CustomerBindingSource.Current,
                                        DataRowView).Row,CRMDataSet.CustomerRow)
    If c.RowState = DataRowState.Detached Then
        c.CustomerId = Guid.NewGuid
    End If
End Sub
```

C#

```
private void customerBindingSource_CurrentChanged(object sender, EventArgs e){
    if (this.customerBindingSource.Current == null){
        return;
    }

    var c = (this.customerBindingSource.Current as DataRowView)
                .Row as CRMDataSet.CustomerRow;

    if (c.RowState == DataRowState.Detached){
        c.CustomerId = Guid.NewGuid();
    }
}
```

This completes the part of the application that connects directly to the database to access the data. You can run the application and verify that you can access data while the database is online. If the database goes offline or the connection is lost, an exception is raised by the application when you attempt to retrieve from the database or save changes.

GETTING STARTED WITH SYNCHRONIZATION SERVICES

Underlying the ability to synchronize data between a local and remote database is the Sync Framework. For Visual Studio 2012, version 2.1 of the Sync Framework is the one to work with, and to use the synchronization functionality that we're discussing in this chapter, you need to make sure that it has been installed.

To start, add a LocalDB to your project. Use the Add New Item dialog (right-click the project in Solution Explorer, and select Add ➪ New Item). In the dialog, navigate to the `Data` folder, and select the Service-Based Database template. For this example, give it the name `LocalCRM.mdf`. In the Data Source Configuration Wizard, select a Dataset, accept the default connection string (which should be called LocalCRMConnectionString), and save the string in the configuration file. On the final screen of the wizard, a message indicates that the database doesn't contain any objects. Have no fear...you'll be adding objects soon enough.

For this example, you need to add two forms: one that allows the server data to be displayed and modified and another that displays the data that is stored on the client. At the moment, there are two data sources: one pointing to the SQL Server database and another pointing to the `LocalCRM.mdf` file. While the LocalForm form is in design mode, drag the Customer node from the CRMDataSet data source onto the form. This action creates a connection to the server database, which is addressed momentarily.

Part of the process of a synchronized application is to get the data in sync. To do this, the databases need to be provisioned with a number of different elements. These elements enable change tracking to be managed on the tables, making it easier to keep the data on the two sides synchronized. This provisioning is done programmatically. And conveniently, it enables the database schemas to be kept in sync as well. Start by opening the MainForm and adding a Load event handler to the form. In the Load event, you need to perform three steps. First, provision the server. Second, provision the client. And finally synchronize the data.

One of the key concepts with the Sync Framework is scope. By adding one or more tables to the scope, you can arrange for all the updates for the tables to be included in a single transaction. This sounds simple and straightforward, but there is a bit of a wrinkle. If you are performing a large number of updates, keeping them all in one transaction can have a negative impact on performance. So there is a setting (`BatchSize` on the synchronization provider object) that controls how many updates are kept in each transaction. If you want to batch your updates, set the `BatchSize` property to a nonzero value.

Start by provisioning the server. Add the following code to the Load event handler for the MainForm form.

VB

```
Dim scopeName = "CRMScope"
Dim serverConn = New SqlConnection(Settings.Default.CRMConnectionString)
Dim clientConn = New SqlConnection(Settings.Default.LocalCRMConnectionString)

Dim serverProvision = New SqlSyncScopeProvisioning(serverConn)
If Not serverProvision.ScopeExists(scopeName) Then
   Dim serverScopeDesc = New DbSyncScopeDescription(scopeName)

   Dim serverTableDesc = SqlSyncDescriptionBuilder.GetDescriptionForTable("Customer", _
      serverConn)

   serverScopeDesc.Tables.Add(serverTableDesc)
   serverProvision.PopulateFromScopeDescription(serverScopeDesc)

   serverProvision.Apply()
End If
```

C#

```
var scopeName = "CRMScope";
var serverConn = new SqlConnection(Settings.Default.CRMConnectionString);
```

```
var clientConn = new SqlConnection(Settings.Default.LocalCRMConnectionString);

var serverProvision = new SqlSyncScopeProvisioning(serverConn);
if (!serverProvision.ScopeExists(scopeName))
{
   var serverScopeDesc = new DbSyncScopeDescription(scopeName);

   var serverTableDesc = SqlSyncDescriptionBuilder.GetDescriptionForTable("Customer",
      serverConn);

   serverScopeDesc.Tables.Add(serverTableDesc);
   serverProvision.PopulateFromScopeDescription(serverScopeDesc);

   serverProvision.Apply();
}
```

In this code, you can see the basic provisioning steps. The first step is to create the scope-provisioning object using a connection to the server database. Then, if the named scope has not already been added, create a new instance of the scope, add the wanted tables to the scope, and then apply the provisioning functionality.

The scope information is maintained beyond the running of the application. In other words, if you create a scope the first time the application runs, that scope still exists the next time the application runs. This has two side effects. First, it means that you should uniquely name your scopes so that there is no inadvertent collision with other applications. Second, you can't add a new table to a scope and have that table be provisioned properly (at least not without performing additional configuration).

For the second step, do the same thing with the client provisioning:

VB

```
Dim clientProvision = New SqlSyncScopeProvisioning(clientConn)
If Not clientProvision.ScopeExists(scopeName) Then
   Dim serverScopeDesc = New DbSyncScopeDescription(scopeName)

   Dim serverTableDesc = SqlSyncDescriptionBuilder.GetDescriptionForTable("Customer", _
      clientConn)

   clientScopeDesc.Tables.Add(clientTableDesc)
   clientProvision.PopulateFromScopeDescription(slientScopeDesc)

   clientProvision.Apply()
End If
```

C#

```
var clientProvision = new SqlSyncScopeProvisioning(clientConn);
if (!clientProvision.ScopeExists(scopeName))
{
   var clientScopeDesc = new DbSyncScopeDescription(scopeName);

   var clientTableDesc = SqlSyncDescriptionBuilder.GetDescriptionForTable("Customer",
      clientConn);

   clientScopeDesc.Tables.Add(clientTableDesc);
   clientProvision.PopulateFromScopeDescription(clientScopeDesc);

   clientProvision.Apply();
}
```

The third step is to perform the synchronization. The Sync Framework 2.1 includes a `SyncOrchestrator` (as opposed to the `SyncAgent` in the previous versions) to manage the synchronization process. Add the following code below the two provisioning blocks:

VB

```
Dim syncOrchestrator = New SyncOrchestrator()

Dim localProvider = New SqlSyncProvider(scopeName, clientConn)
Dim remoteProvider = New SqlSyncProvider(scopeName, serverConn)

syncOrchestrator.LocalProvider = localProvider
syncOrchestrator.RemoteProvider = remoteProvider

syncOrchestrator.Direction = SyncDirectionOrder.Download

Dim syncStats = syncOrchestrator.Synchronize()
```

C#

```
var syncOrchestrator = new SyncOrchestrator();

var localProvider = new SqlSyncProvider(scopeName, clientConn);
var remoteProvider = new SqlSyncProvider(scopeName, serverConn);

syncOrchestrator.LocalProvider = localProvider;
syncOrchestrator.RemoteProvider = remoteProvider;

syncOrchestrator.Direction = SyncDirectionOrder.Download;

var syncStats = syncOrchestrator.Synchronize();
```

This is the data and schema synchronization step. There is a provider object created for each end of the synchronization. One of the additions with Sync Framework 2.1 is support for SQL Azure as being one of the endpoints.

The final step in the example is to configure the synchronization process. Fortunately, the code to do this has already been shown. With some minor changes, it's the previous code. To put this code in the proper place, open the LocalForm in design mode. On the toolstrip at the top of the page, add a new toolstrip button to the right of the Save button (right-click to the right of the Save button and select Insert ➪ Button). Then, double-click the just added button to create and navigate to the Click event handler. When there, add the following code:

VB

```
Dim scopeName = "CRMScope"
Dim serverConn = New SqlConnection(Settings.Default.CRMConnectionString)
Dim clientConn = New SqlConnection(Settings.Default.LocalCRMConnectionString)

Dim syncOrchestrator = New SyncOrchestrator()

Dim localProvider = New SqlSyncProvider(scopeName, clientConn)
Dim remoteProvider = New SqlSyncProvider(scopeName, serverConn)

syncOrchestrator.LocalProvider = localProvider
syncOrchestrator.RemoteProvider = remoteProvider

syncOrchestrator.Direction = SyncDirectionOrder.Download

Dim syncStats = syncOrchestrator.Synchronize()

Me.customerTableAdapter.Fill(this.cRMDataSet.Customer)
```

C#

```
var scopeName = "CRMScope";
var serverConn = new SqlConnection(Settings.Default.CRMConnectionString);
var clientConn = new SqlConnection(Settings.Default.LocalCRMConnectionString);

var syncOrchestrator = new SyncOrchestrator();

var localProvider = new SqlSyncProvider(scopeName, clientConn);
var remoteProvider = new SqlSyncProvider(scopeName, serverConn);

syncOrchestrator.LocalProvider = localProvider;
syncOrchestrator.RemoteProvider = remoteProvider;

syncOrchestrator.Direction = SyncDirectionOrder.Download;

var syncStats = syncOrchestrator.Synchronize();

this.customerTableAdapter.Fill(this.cRMDataSet.Customer);
```

The differences between this code snippet and the previous one is that this one must define the scope name and connections. And the find statement (the Fill method) is used to refresh the data that displays on the form.

The final addition is a single line of code added to the Load method for the LocalForm. If you recall, you dragged the Customer node from the CRMDataSet data source, which is linked to the CRM database. You need to change that to link to the local CRM storage. So in the Load method, prior to the fill, the connection string for the table adaptor is changed to point to the local CRM. When finished, the Load method should look like the following:

VB

```
Private Sub LocalForm_Load(ByVal sender As System.Object, _
                           ByVal e As System.EventArgs) _
                           Handles LocalForm.Load

   Me.customerTableAdapter.Connection.ConnectionString = _
      QuickCRM.Properties.Settings.Default.LocalCRMConnectionString
   Me.customerTableAdapter.Fill(this.cRMDataSet.Customer)

End Sub
```

C#

```
private void LocalForm_Load(object sender, EventArgs e)
{
   this.customerTableAdapter.Connection.ConnectionString =
      QuickCRM.Properties.Settings.Default.LocalCRMConnectionString;
   this.customerTableAdapter.Fill(this.cRMDataSet.Customer);
}
```

At this point, you can run the application. After a brief pause (while the provisioning is taking place), the MainForm displays. Click the Server Data button to display the Server form. Add a number of records to the database, making sure you save them. Close the form and click the Local Data button. The data is visible.

Close the Local form and click the Server Data button again. In the Server form, either add new records or change the existing ones. (Or go completely wild and do both.) When you finish, close the form and reopen the Local form. Your changes are not there; however, when you click the button that you added to the toolbar (which basically performs a refresh), the new and changed data becomes visible.

> **NOTE** *If you receive a SyncException indicating that a COM class was not registered when the Synchronize method is executed, there can be a couple of causes. First, if you're running on a 64-bit platform, make sure that the 64-bit version of the Sync Framework has been installed. Also, if you attempt to create an application for a 32-bit machine while running on a 64-bit platform, make sure that the 32-bit version of the Sync Framework has been installed.*

SYNCHRONIZATION SERVICES OVER N-TIERS

So far, the entire synchronization process is conducted within the client application with a direct connection to the server. One of the objectives of an occasionally connected application is to synchronize data over any connection, regardless of whether it is a corporate intranet or the public Internet. Unfortunately, with the current application you need to expose your SQL Server so that the application can connect to it. This is clearly a security vulnerability, which you can solve by taking a more distributed approach. Sync Services has been designed with this in mind, enabling the server components to be isolated into a service that can be called during synchronization.

Sync Services supports separating the synchronization process so that the communication to either of the endpoints can be implemented in a custom provider. From the perspective of an N-Tier application, the actual implementation of the provider could be done through a WCF service (for example) instead of a direct database connection. To do this, you need to create a WCF service that implements the four methods that makes up Sync Service, as shown in the following `IServiceCRMCacheSyncContract` interface:

VB

```
<ServiceContractAttribute()> _
Public Interface IServiceCRMCacheSyncContract
    <OperationContract()> _
    Function ApplyChanges(ByVal groupMetadata As SyncKnowledge, _
                          ByVal dataSet As DataSet, _
                          ByVal syncSession As SyncSession) As SyncContext
    <OperationContract()> _
    Function GetChanges(ByVal groupMetadata As SyncKnowledge, _
                        ByVal syncSession As SyncSession) As SyncContext
    <OperationContract()> _
    Function GetSchema(ByVal tableNames As Collection(Of String), _
                       ByVal syncSession As SyncSession) As SyncSchema
    <OperationContract()> _
    Function GetServerInfo(ByVal syncSession As SyncSession) As SyncServerInfo
End Interface
```

Now, create a custom provider class derived from the `SyncProvider` base class. In your custom class, you override some of the methods from the base class and call the corresponding methods through the WCF service proxy.

After the class has been constructed, you can set the Remote Provider on the Sync Orchestrator to be a new instance of the custom `SyncProvider` class. Now, when you call `Synchronize`, Sync Services uses the Remote Provider to call the methods on the WCF Service. The WCF Service in turn communicates with the server database carrying out the synchronization logic.

SUMMARY

In this chapter you have seen how to use the Microsoft Sync Framework to build an occasionally connected application. Although you have other considerations when building such an application, such as how to detect network connectivity, you have seen how to perform synchronization of both the data and the schema, and how to separate the client and server components into different application tiers. With this knowledge, you can begin to work with this technology to build richer applications that can continue to work regardless of where they are used.

36

WCF RIA Services

WHAT'S IN THIS CHAPTER?

- Understanding WCF RIA Services
- Creating a domain service
- Exposing data
- Consuming WCF RIA Services in Silverlight

In Chapter 32, "Windows Communication Foundation (WCF)," you saw how WCF provided a standardized means of communication in a technology-agnostic manner. WCF RIA Services (commonly referred to as RIA Services) is a layer on top of WCF that provides a prescriptive pattern and framework for designing data-driven applications that consume data from a server. WCF RIA Services currently target Silverlight applications, but with a view to support additional presentation technologies. This chapter looks at how to use RIA Services to create an end-to-end Silverlight application.

GETTING STARTED

RIA Services is currently most closely associated with and focused toward Silverlight for the client platform, so you start by creating a Silverlight project. You can find a Business Application template (as shown in Figure 36-1 under the Silverlight category), which can create all the solution structure required to start with RIA Services (a Silverlight project, an ASP.NET web application, and the RIA Services link between the two).

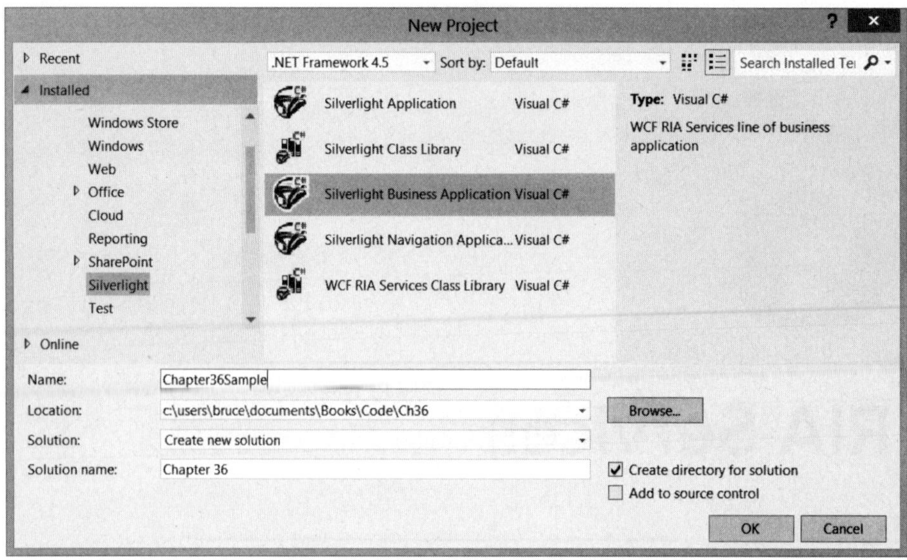

FIGURE 36-1

This creates a Silverlight project and an ASP.NET project — with the structure of the ASP.NET project shown in Figure 36-2.

The ASP.NET project already supports and implements some basic functionality using the RIA Services pattern. There is a `Services` folder and a `Models` folder in the project (refer to Figure 36-2). The `Services` folder already contains two domain services (AuthenticationService and UserRegistrationService) for providing authentication and user registration operations to the client. The `Models` folder contains two data classes (`User` and `RegistrationData`) that are passed between the server and the client. You can also find a `Shared` folder under the `Models` folder, which has a file called `User.shared.vb` or `User.shared.cs` that contains code to be shared between the server and the client projects.

As demonstrated in Chapter 23, "Silverlight," the Silverlight and ASP.NET projects are linked together such that the Silverlight application is copied to somewhere in the ASP.NET project when either project is compiled. However, by introducing RIA Services into the picture, you now have another link between the projects. This link is configured in the project properties of the Silverlight project (as shown in Figure 36-3). In the Silverlight project, you select the ASP.NET project that is the other half of the RIA Services link. Now the build process is modified somewhat. When the Silverlight project is built, it looks at the files in the ASP.NET project to find classes which are marked as participating in RIA Services. Then, using attributes which are found in those classes, client-side classes are generated and included in the Silverlight project. Only then is the output from the Silverlight project copied back to the ASP.NET project.

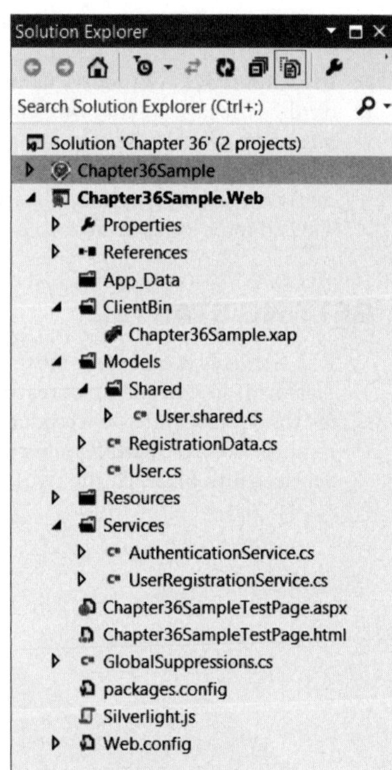

FIGURE 36-2

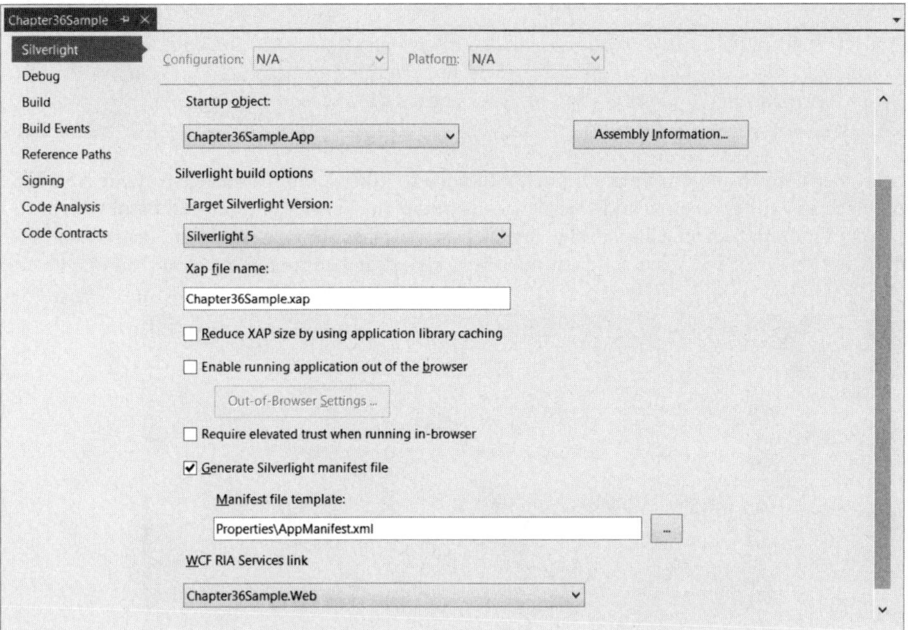

FIGURE 36-3

This link is set up by using the Business Application project template; however, if you have an existing Silverlight project or web application that you want to use RIA Services with, you can manually link the projects together by linking the Silverlight project to an ASP.NET project with this option.

Now you are ready to start writing some code. The example you work through demonstrates some of the key concepts of the RIA Services pattern. Your aim is to expose customer data and operations from the server and make the data and operations accessible from the client.

You use your Entity Framework model of the AdventureWorksLT2008R2 database that you created in Chapter 30, "The ADO.NET Entity Framework." It's not necessary to pass entities from your model back and forth between the server and the client, and in many cases it's considered bad practice. The entities are essentially a model of your data layer, which conceptually is not something that the presentation layer should be exposed to. Regardless of whether you pass entities or Plain Old CLR Objects (POCO) objects of your own design (referred to as *presentation model types* in RIA Services) back and forth is a decision you must make, dependent on many factors. Using entities makes development much faster but also less flexible than using presentation model types. RIA Services works just as well using presentation model types as it does with entities, despite more work being involved in initially creating the Domain Services. Therefore, the best practice would be to use presentation model types as the data transfer mechanism; however, we will focus on using entities in this chapter because they provide the easiest means to get started.

DOMAIN SERVICES

Now that you have your server and client projects connected via RIA Services, it's time to expose some data and operations from the server, which you consume from your client at a later point.

Start by assuming that the Entity Framework model of the AdventureWorksLT2008R2 database from Chapter 30 has been added to your ASP.NET project (including adding the connection string that it uses to the `web.config` file). If not, do so now.

> **WARNING** *Ensure that you compile the ASP.NET project before continuing on to the next step; otherwise the Domain Service Class Wizard does not display your entity model in the available DataContexts/ObjectContexts drop-down list.*

To expose the customer data from your entity model, you need to add a domain service to your ASP.NET project. The best place in your project to add this service is under the Services folder. Add a new item to this folder, and select Domain Service Class under the Web category as the item template (as shown in Figure 36-4). You use this service to serve up customer data, so call it `CustomerService` (`.cs` or `.vb`).

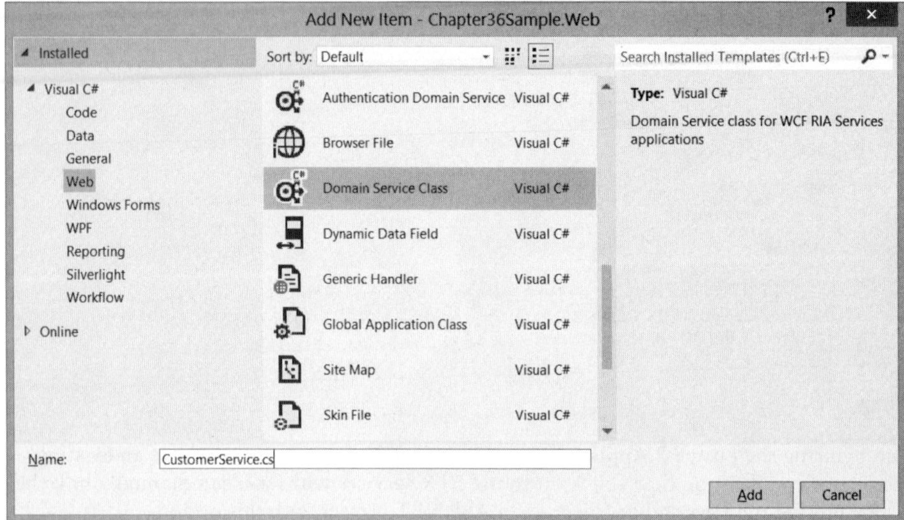

FIGURE 36-4

Clicking OK initiates the Add New Domain Service Class window, as shown in Figure 36-5.

If it hasn't automatically selected your Entity Framework model for the AdventureWorksLT2008R2 database in the Available DataContexts/ObjectContexts drop-down list, select it now. All the entities from your entity model display in the list. Here, you can select one or more entities that you want to expose from your domain service. When you select an entity, the wizard creates a domain operation to return a collection of that entity from the domain service. If you select the Enable Editing option for an entity, the wizard also creates Insert, Update, and Delete domain operations for that entity on the domain service.

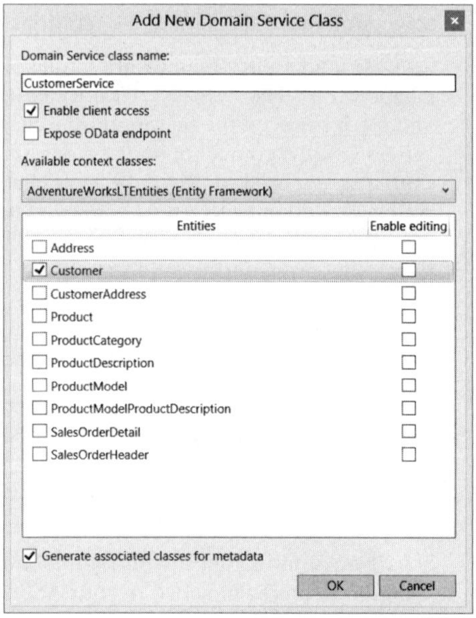

FIGURE 36-5

> **NOTE** *If you use POCO/presentation model types instead of Entity Framework or LINQ-to-SQL types, you can select the <empty domain service class> option from the Available DataContexts/ObjectContexts drop-down list and implement the domain operations.*

You should ensure that the Enable client access check box is checked. This ensures that the `EnableClientAccess` attribute is applied to the service when it is created, which means that code will be generated on the client by the RIA Services code generator to enable it to access the domain service.

There is also a check box used to enable an OData endpoint. OData (or Open Data) is an AtomPub-based format for retrieving and updating data using a REST interface. If you enable an OData endpoint, the client application communicates with the domain service using this format. Although its usefulness in a Silverlight scenario is questionable, if the client is built using another technology (such as JavaScript) OData capability can be quite handy. For this particular example, the check box can be left unchecked.

There is also a Generate Associated Classes for Meta Data check box on the wizard. Meta data classes enable you to add special attributes to properties on the data class being transferred (such as how the entity should be created on the client and data validation rules) without the need to modify the source object (which is important when, for example, you regenerate your object's code with a code generator or an ORM). Instead, you can apply attributes to the properties in a meta data class that correlate with the properties on the actual class, and these attributes control how the associated entity is created on the client and apply other attributes (such as validation rules) to the entity it creates on the client. You can find a thorough explanation of meta data classes in Chapter 24, "Dynamic Data."

It's not essential to generate meta data classes for your entities; although it does provide a degree of control over the data passed between the server and the client, so it is recommended that you create them.

Select the Customer entity, select the Enable Editing check box for it, and ensure both the Enable client access and Generate associated classes for meta data check boxes are selected. Clicking OK creates the domain service and meta data classes for you.

DOMAIN OPERATIONS

Domain operations are operations on a domain service that can be called from the client. The types of domain operations that exist in a domain service can each be considered to be a CRUD (Create, Read, Update, Delete) operation, an invoke operation, or a custom operation.

The names and the method signature of these operations are convention-based, so RIA Services can implicitly determine what type of operation it is and generate the correct corresponding operation in the client project. If for some reason you don't want to use the given conventions, you can decorate the operation (that is, the method) with an attribute to specify what type of operation is represented.

> **NOTE** *Some people prefer to decorate their operations even when they follow the naming/signature convention to explicitly define what type of operation is represented.*

Now take a look at what domain operations have been generated for you in your domain service by the wizard and what other types of operations you can create.

Query Operations

When you open the `CustomersService` (`.cs` or `.vb`) file you see that the basic CRUD operations have been implemented for your Customer entity. The default `Read` (aka `Get` or `Query`) operation returns a collection of entities with the following method signature:

VB

```
Public Function GetCustomers() As IQueryable(Of Customer)
```

C#

```
public IQueryable<Customer> GetCustomers()
```

Note how the `GetCustomers` operation returns an IQueryable collection of the Customer entity. This is one of the most powerful features of RIA Services, in that this feature enables you to write a LINQ query on the client that can be used to filter and shape the entities that it wants returned. This LINQ query is actually serialized and sent to the server before being executed. Where you see the power of this feature is when you try to implement filtering/paging/grouping/sorting on the client. Instead of requiring a raft of complex operations on the server to implement these behaviors, you need only the one simple operation that returns an IQueryable collection, and then a LINQ query can be provided by the client to filter/shape the results on the server before returning them. Alternatively, you can modify the `Get` operation and add your own parameters to it, which the operation can use to filter and shape the results to return to the client.

Insert/Update/Delete Operations

The insert (also known as create), update, and delete operations are automatically called when you submit a change set to the server (based on the actions taken upon the results of a query operation on the client) and cannot be called explicitly from the client. These actions are covered later in the chapter, but for now take a look at the operations that have been implemented for you automatically by the Domain Service Class Wizard and how they are implemented. The operations that were created for you have the following method signatures:

VB

```
Public Sub InsertCustomer(ByVal customer As Customer)
Public Sub UpdateCustomer(ByVal currentCustomer As Customer)
Public Sub DeleteCustomer(ByVal customer As Customer)
```

C#

```
public void InsertCustomer(Customer customer)
public void UpdateCustomer(Customer currentCustomer)
public void DeleteCustomer(Customer customer)
```

Each of these accepts an entity of the given type and performs the appropriate server-side action on that entity. They each have a convention for its naming; they must not return a value; and their method signature must accept an entity as the only parameter. The naming convention and alternative attribute is as follows:

- The method name of insert operations must start with Insert, Create, or Add. Otherwise, apply the `Insert` attribute to the method.
- The method name of update operations must start with Update, Change, or Modify. Otherwise, apply the `Update` attribute to the method.
- The method name of delete operations must start with Delete or Remove. Otherwise, apply the `Delete` attribute to the method.

Other Operation Types

Other types of operations supported by RIA Services (but not fully detailed here) follow:

- An invoke operation is essentially the same as a service operation in a standard WCF Service (that is, a method exposed by the service). Invoke operations are created as methods on the domain context on the client and are called immediately. (That is, they aren't queued until changes are submitted to the server.)
- A custom operation is one that is called at any time on the client but whose execution is deferred on the server until a changeset is submitted. Custom operations act upon entities and are actually created as methods on their associated entities on the client in addition to being created as methods on the domain context that is generated for the domain service.

CONSUMING A DOMAIN SERVICE IN SILVERLIGHT

Before you look at actually consuming a domain service in the Silverlight project, take a look at what RIA Services has generated for you. As mentioned earlier in the chapter, RIA Services automatically generates code in the Silverlight project to communicate with the server. This code is generated in a folder called `Generated_Code`, which is not added to the project but can be seen if you select the Silverlight project in the Solution Explorer and click the Show All Files button. Code is generated by RIA Services in files under this folder (as shown in Figure 36-6), with the primary code generated file being `<web project name>.g.cs` (or `.vb`). For example, for the sample project, the primary code gen file is `Chapter36Sample.Web.g.cs` (or `.vb`).

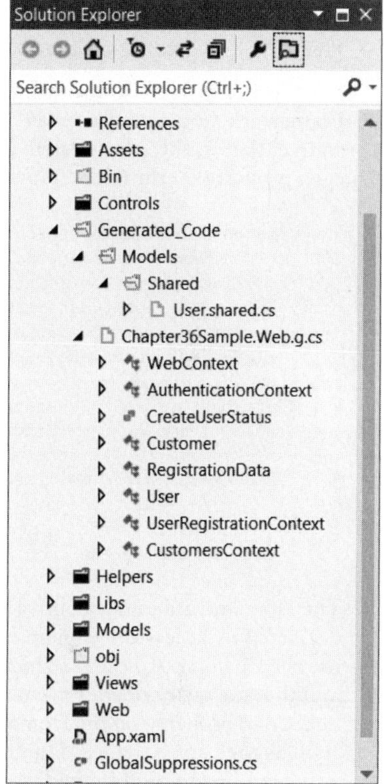

FIGURE 36-6

You can open this file to inspect its contents to see what the code generator has created for you. Of particular interest, note that the entities (or presentation model classes) exposed by domain services in the web project have a corresponding class generated in this file (decorated with attributes from the meta data classes or the classes themselves). You can also find that for each domain service on the client there will be a corresponding *domain context class* created, which handles communicating with the domain service from the client. The operations exposed by a domain service will be created on the corresponding domain context, and you call the operations on the domain context instead of attempting to reference the domain service.

> **NOTE** *Corresponding operations for the Insert/Update/Delete operations on the domain service are not created on the domain context because these operations are managed by the changeset. Changes made to a collection of entities retrieved from the server via a query operation are handled by the RIA Services framework in a changeset, and when* `SubmitChanges` *is called on the domain context, the framework handles calling the Insert/Update/Delete operations on the domain service as required.*

If you follow standard RIA Services naming conventions, a domain service called CustomersService in the web project results in a corresponding domain context in the Silverlight project called CustomersContext.

Now, attempt to populate a data grid with a list of customers retrieved from the server. You have two primary means to do so: Either use a declarative XAML-based approach or a code-based approach. The XAML-based approach is the easiest way to start, so this section uses that approach.

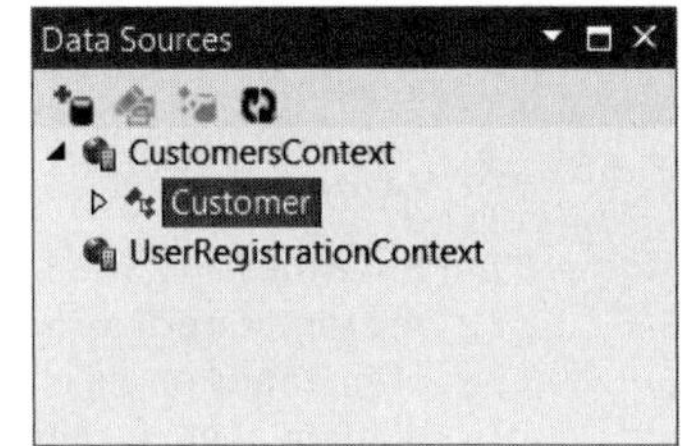

FIGURE 36-7

The easiest way to start with the XAML-based approach is to simply use the Data Sources window — as detailed in Chapter 18, "Windows Presentation Foundation (WPF)" — and drag and drop an entity exposed by a domain context from this window and onto your page. A data source has already been created in your project for each data context created by the RIA Services code generator (as shown in Figure 36-7), so you don't need to worry about creating the data sources.

For this example you consume the CustomersService that exposes the Customer entities from the Entity Framework model on the server, so drag and drop the Customer entity (from the CustomersContext data source, that is, the selected item in Figure 36-7) onto the page. This creates a data grid with a column for each property on the entity. Now if you look at the XAML, you can see how it ties together:

```
<riaControls:DomainDataSource AutoLoad="True" QueryName="GetCustomersQuery"
        Name="customerDomainDataSource" Height="0" Width="0">
    <riaControls:DomainDataSource.DomainContext>
        <Services:CustomersContext />
    </riaControls:DomainDataSource.DomainContext>
</riaControls:DomainDataSource>

<data:DataGrid AutoGenerateColumns="False" Height="250"
        ItemsSource="{Binding ElementName=customerDomainDataSource, Path=Data}"
        Name="CustomerDataGrid" RowDetailsVisibilityMode="VisibleWhenSelected">
    <data:DataGrid.Columns>
        <!--This code has been removed for purposes of brevity-->
    </data:DataGrid.Columns>
</data:DataGrid>
```

The DomainDataSource control used is a part of the RIA Services framework and provides the bridge to declaratively access the domain context in XAML. The DomainDataSource control specifies that it should use the CustomersContext (which corresponds to the CustomersService on the server) as its domain context, and that the query operation that should be called on this domain context is `GetCustomersQuery`. The `AutoLoad` property on the DomainDataSource control is set to True, meaning this query will be called as soon as the page is loaded. Finally, the `ItemsSource` property is set on the data grid where it uses element name binding to bind to the DomainDataSource control and use that as its source of data.

Now you can run your project, and you will find that the data grid is automatically populated with the results of the query from the server (as shown in Figure 36-8).

AdventureWorks   Customers   About

login

Customers

Company Name	Customer ID	Email Address	First Name	Last Name	Middle Name	Modified Date	Na
A Bike Store	1	orlando0@adver	Orlando	Gee	N.	13/10/2004 15	
Progressive Sport:	2	keith0@adventu	Keith	Harris		13/10/2004 15	
Advanced Bike Co	3	donna0@advent	Donna	Carreras	F.	13/10/2004 15	
Modular Cycle Sys	4	janet1@adventu	Janet	Gates	M.	13/10/2004 15	
Metropolitan Spor	5	lucy0@adventur	Lucy	Harrington		13/10/2004 15	
Aerobic Exercise C	6	rosmarie0@adve	Rosmarie	Carroll	J.	13/10/2004 15	
Associated Bikes	7	dominic0@adver	Dominic	Gash	P.	13/10/2004 15	
Rural Cycle Empo	10	kathleen0@adve	Kathleen	Garza	M.	13/10/2004 15	

FIGURE 36-8

As discussed previously, the advantage of returning an IQueryable from a domain service operation is that RIA Services enables you to specify filtering, sorting, grouping, and paging options — all of which are performed on the server. This is also easy to do in XAML by specifying descriptors on the DomainDataSource. Now, take a look at performing each of these in turn.

Add a textbox to the page that automatically filters the customers by the company name, and call it `searchTextBox`. Now you can add a filter descriptor to the DomainDataSource that specifies the name of the property to filter (`PropertyPath`) and the operator specifying how the matching will be done (`Operator`). You can then add a `ControlParameter` to the filter descriptor, which links to the textbox (by providing the name of the textbox), uses the text in the textbox as the search criteria (by providing the name of the property on the textbox to get the value from), and runs the filter each time the text is changed (by providing the name of the event on the textbox that invokes the filtering when raised).

```
<riaControls:DomainDataSource AutoLoad="True" QueryName="GetCustomersQuery"
                              Name="CustomerDomainDataSource" Height="0" Width="0">
    <riaControls:DomainDataSource.DomainContext>
        <my:CustomersContext />
    </riaControls:DomainDataSource.DomainContext>

    <riaControls:DomainDataSource.FilterDescriptors>
        <riaControls:FilterDescriptor PropertyPath="CompanyName"
                        Operator="Contains"
                        Value="{Binding ElementName=searchTextBox, Path=Text}" />
    </riaControls:DomainDataSource.FilterDescriptors>
</riaControls:DomainDataSource>
```

Sorting is automatically handled by the data grid (click the column headers to sort by that column), and if the results are paged, it automatically goes back to the server to get the new page of results according to the current page and sort criteria. You can, however, specify the initial sorting using sort descriptors on the DomainDataSource by providing the name of the property to sort on and the sort direction:

```
<riaControls:DomainDataSource AutoLoad="True" QueryName="GetCustomersQuery"
                              Name="CustomerDomainDataSource" Height="0" Width="0">
    <riaControls:DomainDataSource.DomainContext>
        <my:CustomersContext />
    </riaControls:DomainDataSource.DomainContext>

    <riaControls:DomainDataSource.SortDescriptors>
        <riaControls:SortDescriptor PropertyPath="CompanyName" Direction="Ascending" />
    </riaControls:DomainDataSource.SortDescriptors>
</riaControls:DomainDataSource>
```

Grouping again is handled in a similar manner by providing group descriptors and simply providing the name of the property to group on:

```
<riaControls:DomainDataSource AutoLoad="True" QueryName="GetCustomersQuery"
                              Name="CustomerDomainDataSource" Height="0" Width="0">
    <riaControls:DomainDataSource.DomainContext>
        <my:CustomersContext />
    </riaControls:DomainDataSource.DomainContext>

    <riaControls:DomainDataSource.GroupDescriptors>
        <riaControls:GroupDescriptor PropertyPath="SalesPerson" />
    </riaControls:DomainDataSource.GroupDescriptors>
</riaControls:DomainDataSource>
```

Paging the data in the grid (to display, for example, 20 customers at a time) is easy with the DataPager control. Add the control to your page, bind its `Source` property to the DomainDataSource control, and provide its `PageSize` property with the number of items to be displayed in the data grid:

```
<data:DataPager PageSize="20"
                Source="{Binding Data, ElementName=CustomerDomainDataSource}"/>
```

The page size specifies how many items should be displayed in the grid, not how many items should be retrieved from the server. If you just set the `PageSize` property, the entire collection will still be retrieved from the server and paged on the client instead. To retrieve a single page of items at a time and go back to the server to retrieve more items when navigating between pages, you need to set the `LoadSize` property on the DomainDataSource control. Generally, you want to set both properties to the same value. Now, it can retrieve and display a single page of items and request and display a new page of items from the server each time you navigate to a new page with the DataPager control.

In the background, any changes you make to the data in the data grid (such as adding rows, deleting rows, and updating values) will be tracked in a changeset by the RIA Services framework. Submitting these changes back to the server is a case of calling the `SubmitChanges()` method on the domain context. Add a button to the page called `SubmitButton`. In its `Click` event handler (in the code behind), add the following line of code:

VB

```
CustomerDomainDataSource.SubmitChanges()
```

C#

```
CustomerDomainDataSource.SubmitChanges();
```

Clicking the button now submits any changes you've made back to the server.

> **NOTE** *You can also reject any changes made using the* `RejectChanges()` *method on the DomainDataSource control.*

The final page that implements loading, filtering, sorting, grouping, paging, and saving the data is shown in Figure 36-9.

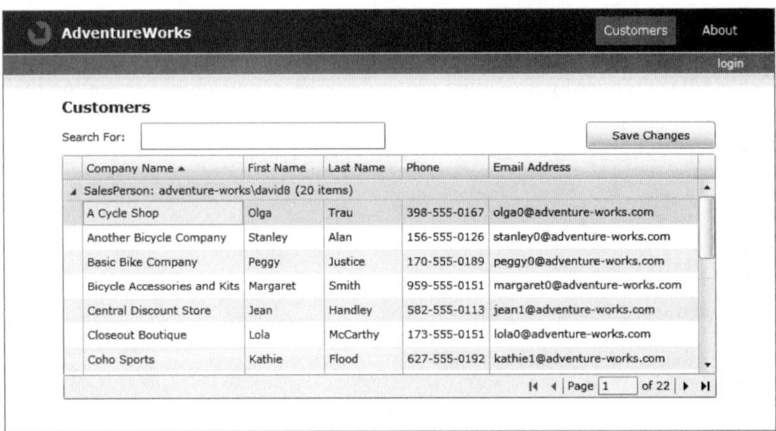

FIGURE 36-9

As you can see, RIA Services is an extremely powerful framework for managing data, simplifying otherwise hard-to-implement functionality, and quickly and easily creating functional business applications.

> **NOTE** *The DomainDataSource control makes it easy to consume data from RIA Services in a Silverlight application; however, at times you may want to interact with the domain service in code instead. This is possible by creating an instance of the corresponding domain context and using the methods on it. However, communication with the domain service is performed asynchronously, requiring your code to be structured accordingly.*

SUMMARY

In this chapter you learned how WCF RIA Services can vastly simplify architecting and developing an end-to-end, data-driven Silverlight application, through its combination of prescriptive design patterns, code generation, and feature-rich framework. RIA Services provides many more features than described here, including decorating classes and their properties with attributes (such as validation rules that RIA Services enforces); using meta data classes (that is, classes associated with the entities being passed between the server and the client that attributes can be applied to and projected onto the associated entities such that the original entities don't need to be modified); sharing code between the server and the client; built-in authentication and security functionality; and much more. However, this chapter should help you start using RIA Services to provide a means for communicating between your Silverlight application and the server.

PART VIII
Configuration and Resources

37

Configuration Files

WHAT'S IN THIS CHAPTER?

- Understanding the .NET configuration system
- Using configuration files within your application
- Storing custom types in configuration files

One of the challenges to build applications is adjusting the way the application functions on-the-fly without having to rebuild it. There's a long history of applications using configuration files to control the way an application runs. .NET applications use a series of XML configuration files that can be adjusted to determine application behavior. This chapter explores the structure of these configuration files and demonstrates how you can store custom information using a configuration section handler.

.CONFIG FILES

The .NET Framework configuration system consists of several configuration files (discussed in the following sections) that can be used to adjust one or more applications on a computer system. Part of this system is an inheritance model that ensures that configurations can be applied at the appropriate level. This model is such that sections defined in a configuration file at a lower level override the same sections specified in a file higher up the chain. If no configuration file defines a value or section, the default values are taken from the schema files to which the configuration files must adhere.

Machine.Config

At the root of the inheritance model is the `machine.config` file (located in the systemroot\Microsoft .NET\Framework\versionNumber\CONFIG\ folder, or systemroot\Microsoft .NET\Framework64\versionNumber\CONFIG\ for 64-bit machines), which defines configuration settings for the entire system. All configuration files inherit from this file and can override these settings.

Web.Config

Web applications are configured via the `web.config` file. This file can be located in a number of locations, depending on the scope to which the settings need to be applied. To apply a configuration to all web applications on a machine, place the `web.config` file in the same directory as the machine.config file. In most cases the settings need to be applied at a much finer granularity. As such, the web.config file can also be placed in any virtual directory or subdirectory to control web applications at that level. If it is placed in the root folder for a website, the configuration will be applied to all ASP.NET applications in that website.

A word of caution: When you work with virtual directories that do not align with the directory structure on the computer, it's possible to have an application that has different configurations depending on how it is referenced. For example, consider C:\inetpub\wwwroot\MainApplication\Contacts\Contact.aspx, which has been set up with both MainApplication and Contacts as virtual directories. You can reference the contact page as either:

```
http://localhost/MainApplication/Contacts/Contact.aspx
```

or:

```
http://localhost/Contacts/Contact.aspx
```

In the first case, the configuration settings that are applied are inherited from the MainApplication folder and may be overridden by a configuration file in the Contacts folder. However, in the second case, settings are applied only from the configuration file within the Contacts folder.

> **NOTE** *Making changes to a* web.config *file causes the ASP.NET application to restart. This is quite an effective way to force a web application to flush its cache and behave as if it were accessed for the first time, without having to restart the entire server.*

App.Config

Windows applications can be configured via an application configuration file, which also inherits from machine.config. Because the output assembly name is known only when an application is compiled, this file starts off as app.config and is renamed to *application*.exe.config as part of the build process. For example, an application with AccountingApplication.exe as the main executable would have a configuration file entitled AccountingApplication.exe.config. This configuration file is automatically loaded based on its name when the application is loaded. If an app.config file is added to a dll, it will be renamed to assembly.dll.config during the build process.

Security.Config

In conjunction with the application configuration files are a number of security configuration files. These also follow an inheritance path but across a different dimension. Instead of being application-focused, the security configuration files are broken down into enterprise (Enterprisesec.config), machine (Security.config), and user (Security.config). The enterprise- and machine-level files are both stored in the same location as the machine.config file, whereas the user-level file is stored under the user-specific application data folder.

ApplicationHost.Config

IIS7 changes the way configuration information is stored to use a set of configuration files that work in parallel with those for ASP.NET and the .NET Framework. Because IIS and the .NET Framework are versioned independently, configuration information specific to the individual technologies are held in the machine.config/web.config and the applicationHost.config files, respectively. However, because there is an interrelationship between IIS and ASP.NET, the applicationHost.config file does fit into the configuration file inheritance hierarchy. Because the `applicationHost.config` file is specific to an instance of IIS, it fits into the inheritance hierarchy after both the `machine.config` and `web.config` files located at the machine level (that is, located in the *systemroot*\Microsoft .NET\Framework*versionNumber*\CONFIG\ folder).

The `applicationHost.config` file can be found in the *systemroot*\System32\InetSrv\Config folder, and the corresponding schema files can be found in the `Schema` subdirectory. There are also `administration.config` and `redirection.config` files in this folder that are responsible for IIS feature delegation and configuration file redirection, respectively.

CONFIGURATION SCHEMA

A configuration file, regardless of whether it is a `machine.config`, a `web.config`, or an application configuration file, needs to adhere to the same configuration schema that determines which elements should be included. The schema is located at `C:\Program Files\Microsoft Visual Studio 11.0\Xml\Schemas\DotNetConfignn.xsd` (`C:\Program Files (x86)\Microsoft Visual Studio 11.0\Xml\Schemas\DotNetConfignn.xsd` on 64-bit machines) where the value of *nn* is 20, 30, 35, and 40, depending on the version of .NET. The schema is broken down into a number of sections.

Section: configurationSections

Configuration files can be customized to contain any structured XML data. To do this, you must define a custom section in the `configurationSections` block within the configuration file. This defines both the name of the configuration section and the class that is to be called in order to process the section.

The `configurationSections` section in the `machine.config` file defines the handlers for each of the standard configuration sections discussed here. You can define your own configuration sections in your application configuration file so long as you specify which class will be used to validate and process that section. For example, the following code snippet defines the section handler for the `ConfigurationApplication.My.MySettings` configuration section, along with the corresponding section. The schema of this section must correspond to what the `System.Configuration.ClientSettingsSection` class expects, rather than the normal configuration file schema:

```
<configuration>
  <configSections>
    <section name="ConfigurationApplication.My.MySettings"
                 type="System.Configuration.ClientSettingsSection,
System, Version=2.0.0.0, Culture=neutral, PublicKeyToken=b77a5c561934e089"
                 requirePermission="false" />
  </configSections>
  .
  <ConfigurationApplication.My.MySettings>
    <setting name="PrimaryServer" serializeAs="String">
      <value>www.builttoroam.com</value>
    </setting>
  </ConfigurationApplication.My.MySettings>
</configuration>
```

You can include `configSections` in a `sectionGroup` element that can be used to help lay out configuration information. The preceding example can be extended as follows:

```
<configuration>
  <configSections>
    <sectionGroup name="applicationSettings"
                      type="System.Configuration.ApplicationSettingsGroup,
System, Version=2.0.0.0, Culture=neutral, PublicKeyToken= b77a5c561934e089" >
    <section name="ConfigurationApplication.My.MySettings"
```

```
                     type="System.Configuration.ClientSettingsSection,
System, Version=2.0.0.0, Culture=neutral, PublicKeyToken=b77a5c561934e089"
                     requirePermission="false" />
    <section name="ReferencedAssembly.My.MySettings"
                     type="System.Configuration.ClientSettingsSection,
System, Version=2.0.0.0, Culture=neutral, PublicKeyToken=b77a5c561934e089"
                     requirePermission="false" />
    </sectionGroup>
  </configSections>

  <applicationSettings>
    <ConfigurationApplication.My.MySettings>
      <setting name="PrimaryServer" serializeAs="String">
        <value>www.builttoroam.com</value>
      </setting>
    </ConfigurationApplication.My.MySettings>
    <ReferencedAssembly.My.MySettings>
      <setting name="SecondaryServer" serializeAs="String">
        <value>www.peaksite.com</value>
      </setting>
    </ReferencedAssembly.My.MySettings>
  </applicationSettings>
</configuration>
```

Where used, the configSections element must appear as the first child of the configuration element.

Section: startup

The startup configuration section determines the version of the framework that is either required (requiredRuntime) or supported (supportedRuntime) by the framework. By default, a .NET application will attempt to execute using the same version of the framework on which it was built. Any application being built with support for multiple versions of the framework should indicate this with the supportedRuntime element, defining the most preferred framework version first:

```
<configuration>
  <startup>
    <supportedRuntime version="v4.0.20409"/>
    <supportedRuntime version="v2.0.50727"/>
    <supportedRuntime version="v1.1.4322"/>
  </startup>
</configuration>
```

This configuration section would be used by an application that has been tested for versions 4.0, 2.0, and 1.1 of the .NET Framework. Anomalies were detected in the testing for version 1.0 of the .NET Framework, so it has been omitted from the supportedRuntime list. The version number must correspond exactly to the installation directory for that framework version (for example, version 4.0 of the .NET Framework typically installs to C:\WINDOWS\Microsoft.NET\Framework\v4.0.20409\).

Section: runtime

Garbage collection is a feature of the .NET Framework that distinguishes it from nonmanaged environments. The process of collecting and disposing of unreferenced objects is usually done in parallel with the main application on a separate thread. This means that the user should not see any performance issues as a result of this process being run. However, there may be circumstances when this process should be run inline with the main application. The runtime section of the configuration file can be used to provide limited control over how the .NET run-time engine operates. Among other things, you can specify whether or not the garbage collection should be done concurrently with the main application.

This section can also be used to specify a location in which to search for assemblies that may be required by an application. This attribute can be useful if an application references assemblies that are in a nonstandard location. The following code illustrates the use of the `codeBase` attribute to locate the `ImportantAssembly.dll`, as well as to dictate that garbage collection be done inline with the main application thread:

```
<configuration>
  <runtime>
    <assemblyBinding xmlns="urn:schemas-microsoft-com:asm.v1">
      <dependentAssembly>
        <assemblyIdentity name="ImportantAssembly"
                          publicKeyToken="32ab4ba45e0a69a1"
                          culture="neutral" />
        <codeBase version="2.0.0.0" href="./ImportantAssembly.dll"/>
      </dependentAssembly>
    </assemblyBinding>
    <gcConcurrent enabled="false"/>
  </runtime>
</configuration>
```

Section: system.runtime.remoting

The `remoting` section of the configuration file can be used to specify information about remote objects and channels required by the application. For example, the default HTTP channel can be directed to listen to port 8080 by means of the following configuration snippet:

```
<configuration>
  <system.runtime.remoting>
    <application>
      <channels>
        <channel port="8080" ref="http"/>
      </channels>
    </application>
  </system.runtime.remoting>
</configuration>
```

Section: system.net

Because of the current demand for more secure operating environments, organizations often use proxies to monitor and protect traffic on their networks. This can often result in applications not functioning correctly unless they have been configured to use the appropriate proxies. The networking section of the configuration files can be used to adjust the proxy that an application uses when making HTTP requests.

The .NET Framework ships with an `SmtpClient` class that can be used to send mail from within an application. Obviously, doing this requires information such as the server and the credentials to use when sending mail. Although such information can be hard-coded within an application, a more flexible approach would be to specify it in a configuration file that can be adjusted when the application is deployed. The following configuration snippet illustrates the use of the default proxy (although it bypasses the proxy for local addresses and the DeveloperNews website) and specifies the default SMTP settings to be used by the SMTP client:

```
<configuration>
  <system.net>
    <defaultProxy>
      <proxy usesystemdefaults="true"
             proxyaddress="http://192.168.200.222:3030"
             bypassonlocal="true" />
      <bypasslist>
        <add address="[a-z]+\.developernews\.com" />
```

```
        </bypasslist>
      </defaultProxy>
      <mailSettings>
        <smtp deliveryMethod="network">
          <network host="smtp.developernews.com"
             port="25" defaultCredentials="true" />
        </smtp>
      </mailSettings>
  </system.net>
</configuration>
```

Section: cryptographySettings

Although the .NET Framework contains base implementations for a number of cryptographic algorithms, such as the hashing function, sometimes it is necessary to override these algorithms. When this is required, the `cryptographySettings` section of the configuration file can be included to remap existing algorithm names, or map new names, to another implementation class.

Section: system.diagnostics

Debugging is always the hardest part of writing an application. It is made even more difficult when the application is in production and the error cannot be replicated in the debugging environment. One technique that is particularly important for debugging this type of error is to use trace statements:

```
Trace.WriteLine("The application made it this far before crashing.")
```

Both trace and debug statements work similarly to events and event handlers. For the preceding `WriteLine` statement to have any effect, an object must be listening for this `WriteLine`. This is typically done by a `TraceListener` class. The framework supports a number of default trace listeners that can be wired up to the application via the `diagnostics` section of the configuration file, as shown in the following section in which an `EventLog` trace listener has been attached to the application:

```
<configuration>
  <system.diagnostics>
    <trace autoflush="true" indentsize="0">
      <listeners>
        <add name="MyEventListener"
type="System.Diagnostics.EventLogTraceListener, system,
version=1.0.3300.0, Culture=neutral, PublicKeyToken=b77a5c561934e089"
initializeData="DeveloperApplicationEventLog"/>
      </listeners>
    </trace>
</system.diagnostics>
</configuration>
```

The `initializeData` attribute specifies a text string to be passed into the constructor for the trace listener. In the case of the event-log listener, this text corresponds to the name of the event log into which trace statements will be inserted.

Other elements can also be added to the `diagnostics` section of the configuration file — for example, to determine the level of trace logging to perform, which determines how verbose the trace messages are; or to control whether or not the debug assertion dialog displays for an application.

Section: system.web

The `system.web` section of the configuration file is used to control how web applications behave. This is the section that can have quite a deep hierarchy because configuration settings can be specified on a machine, web server, website, web application, or even subfolder basis. Because this section controls the security requirements for a web application, it is often used to restrict access to certain areas of the web application.

webServices

Although web service applications use several configuration settings, such as `authentication` and `impersonation` sections, the `system.web` section of the configuration file contains some settings that are particular to the way that web services operate. For example, the following code snippet enables the use of `SOAP` and `Documentation` protocols but removes the `POST` and `GET` protocols for the application:

```
<configuration>
  <system.web>
    <webServices>
      <protocols>
        <add name="HttpSoap"/>
        <remove name="HttpPost"/>
        <remove name="HttpGet"/>
        <add name="Documentation"/>
      </protocols>
    </webServices>
  </system.web>
</configuration>
```

By default, only `SOAP` and `Documentation` are enabled for web services. Quite often, for debugging purposes, it is convenient to allow the `POST` protocol so that the web service can be tested via a web browser. You should do this on an application basis by including the appropriate section in the configuration file within the application folder.

Section: compiler

The `compiler` section of the configuration file is used to list the compilers installed on a computer. The following snippet shows how the VB.NET compiler is referenced in the `machine.config` file. Within an application, this information can be accessed via the `CodeDomProvider` framework class:

```
<configuration>
  <system.codedom>
    <compilers>
      <compiler language="vb;vbs;visualbasic;vbscript" extension=".vb"
type="Microsoft.VisualBasic.VBCodeProvider, System, Version=2.0.0.0,
Culture=neutral, PublicKeyToken=b77a5c561934e089" />
    </compilers>
  </system.codedom>
</configuration>
```

Configuration Attributes

All configuration elements can specify a `configSource`, which is simply a redirection to a separate file. This can be useful if a configuration file becomes unwieldy in length. The following code snippet illustrates how a section of a configuration file can be extracted and subsequently referenced by means of this attribute:

```
<!—Original Configuration File—>
<configuration>
.
  <WindowsApplication1.My.MySettings>
    <setting name="Button1_Text" serializeAs="String">
      <value>Press Me!</value>
    </setting>
  </WindowsApplication1.My.MySettings>
</configuration>
```

```
<!—Reduced Configuration File using configSource—>
<configuration>
.
  <WindowsApplication1.My.MySettings configSource="MySettings.Config" />
</configuration>

<!—Code from MySettings.Config—>
<WindowsApplication1.My.MySettings>
  <setting name="Button1_Text" serializeAs="String">
    <value>Press Me!</value>
  </setting>
</WindowsApplication1.My.MySettings>
```

The following are a few limitations for using a `configSource`:

- There is no merging of configuration sections between the referenced file and the original configuration file. If you include the section in both files, a configuration error will be generated when you attempt to run the application.
- This attribute cannot be applied to configuration section groups. This can be a significant limitation because the purpose of a section group is to group items that relate similar configuration sections. A logical separation could see all items in a particular section group in a separate configuration file.
- If the attribute is used within a `web.config` file, changing the referenced configuration file will not restart the ASP.NET application. For the configuration information to be reread, you need to either manually restart the ASP.NET application or modify the `web.config` file.

Each element within the configuration file inherits a number of attributes that can be set to control whether or not that element can be overridden. To prevent an element, or even an entire section, from being overridden, you can lock it. Five different locking attributes (outlined in Table 37-1) can be used to specify any number of configuration attributes and elements that are to be locked.

Locking configuration items is particularly relevant when you deal with web applications, which might contain a deep hierarchy of configuration inheritance. Windows applications inherit only from the `machine.config` file, so it is unlikely that you need to lock items.

TABLE 37-1: Locking Attributes

CONFIGURATION ELEMENT	DESCRIPTION
`LockItem`	Locks the element to which this attribute is applied, including all other attributes provided on that element and all child elements
`LockAttributes`	Locks the comma-delimited list of attributes provided
`LockAllAttributesExcept`	Locks all attributes except those provided in the comma-delimited list
`LockElements`	Locks the comma-delimited list of child elements provided
`LockAllElementsExcept`	Locks all child elements except those provided in the comma-delimited list

APPLICATION SETTINGS

Applications frequently have settings that do not fit into the default configuration schema. The four mechanisms for storing this information are discussed in the following sections.

Using appSettings

The first technique is to use the predefined `appSettings` section of the configuration file. This section can be used to store simple name-value pairs of application settings, which might be useful for storing the name of the server, as in the following example:

```
<configuration>
  <appSettings>
    <add key="Server" value="http://www.builttoroam.com"/>
  </appSettings>
</configuration>
```

This value can easily be accessed within code by means of the `AppSettings` property of the `ConfigurationManager` class (which requires a reference to the `System.Configuration` assembly):

VB

```
Dim server As String = ConfigurationManager.AppSettings("Server")
```

C#

```
var server = ConfigurationManager.AppSettings["Server"];
```

One of the weaknesses of this approach is that the name of the setting is specified as a string, rather than as a strongly typed property. It also assumes that the value will be a string, which is often not the case.

> **NOTE** *In the case of web applications, you should use the* `WebConfigurationManager` *class instead of the* `ConfigurationManager` *class because it provides access to additional configuration information specific to ASP.NET applications.*

Project Settings

Using the Settings tab of the project properties designer, you can define application settings of a variety of types. Figure 37-1 illustrates how the `PrimaryServer` setting would appear in this designer.

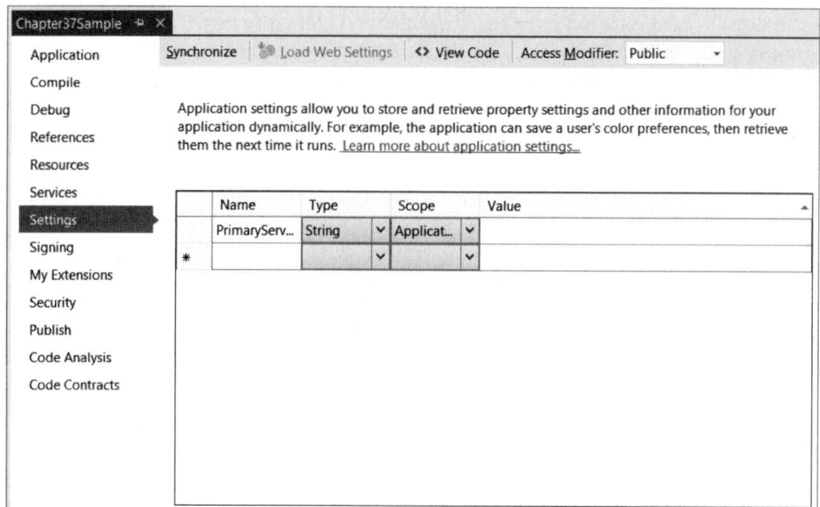

FIGURE 37-1

Adding application settings via this designer does not use the `appSettings` section as you might expect. Instead, it defines a new section in the configuration, as discussed earlier in the section on the `configSection` element and shown in the following snippet:

```
<configuration>
...
  <ConfigurationApplication.My.MySettings>
```

```
      <setting name="PrimaryServer" serializeAs="String">
        <value>www.builttoroam.com</value>
      </setting>
    </ConfigurationApplication.My.MySettings>
  </configuration>
```

To access this setting in code, you can make use of the generated strongly typed access properties:

VB

```
Dim primaryServer as String = My.Settings.PrimaryServer
```

C#

```
string primaryServer = Properties.Settings.Default.PrimaryServer;
```

Dynamic Properties

The third mechanism for storing application-specific information is the use of dynamic properties. These are typically used to dynamically set designer properties. For example, you could set the text on a Button1 using the following configuration block:

```
<configuration>
...
  <applicationSettings>
    <ConfigurationApplication.My.MySettings>
      <setting name="Button1_Text" serializeAs="String">
        <value>Press Me Now!</value>
      </setting>
    </ConfigurationApplication.My.MySettings>
  </applicationSettings>
</configuration>
```

The preceding code uses the same syntax as application settings defined using the project properties designer. Actually, they are one and the same; the only difference is that in the `InitializeComponent` method of the form, a line of code sets the button text:

VB

```
Me.Button1.Text =
             Global.ConfigurationApplication.My.MySettings.Default.Button1_Text
```

C#

```
this.button1.Text =
             global::ConfigurationApplication.
Properties.Settings.
             Default.Button1_Text;
```

When this application is deployed, the text displayed on Button1 is dynamically loaded from the configuration file. In the following steps, for example, you set the size of a control, Button1, to be dynamically loaded from the configuration file:

1. Select Button1 on the designer surface and press F4 to display the Properties window. Locate the `ApplicationSettings` item within the Data category or in the alphabetic list, as shown in Figure 37-2.

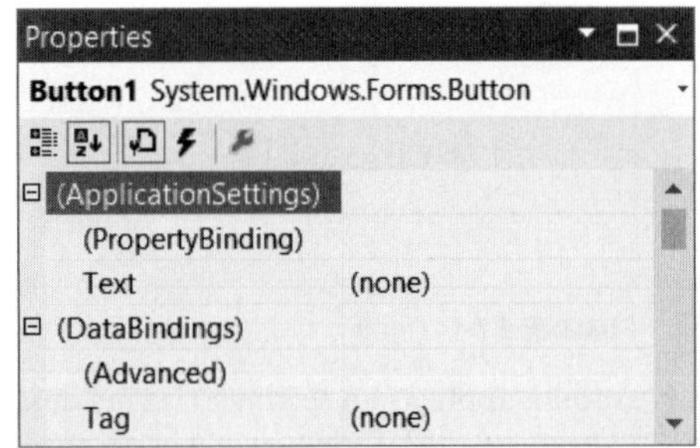

FIGURE 37-2

2. Click the ellipsis button (. . .) next to the `PropertyBinding` row. This opens a dialog that lists the available properties for Button1, along with any application settings that have been assigned, as shown in Figure 37-3.
3. Select the drop-down next to the `Size` property and select New. This opens a dialog in which you can specify a default value, a name for the application setting, and the scope of the setting.
4. Specify a name for the application setting — for example, Button1_Size, and set the scope to Application. You can modify the default value or simply accept the value that has been extracted from the current properties of Button1, as shown in Figure 37-4.
5. Click OK on both dialogs. If you open the `app.config` file that is available from the Solution Explorer window, you'll see a section that defines the Button1_Size setting.

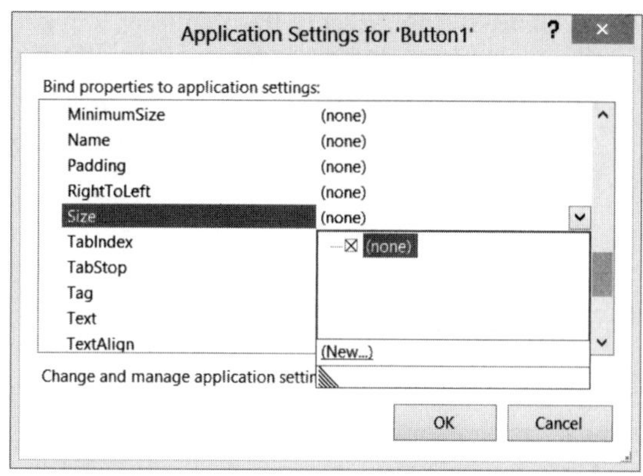

FIGURE 37-3

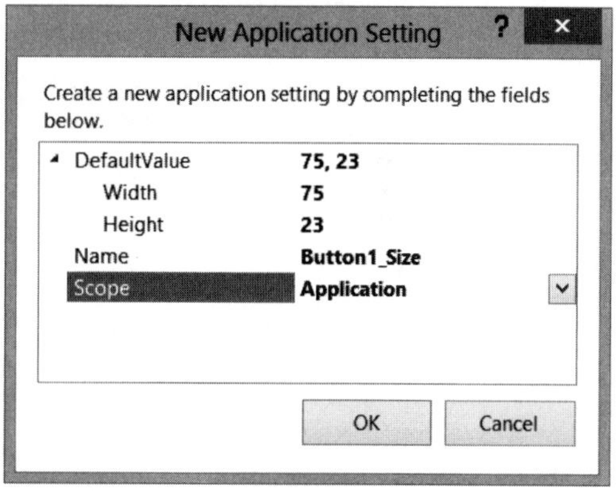

FIGURE 37-4

Custom Configuration Sections

Developers often want to include more structured information in the configuration file than can be stored in the `appSettings` section. To solve this problem and eliminate any need for additional configuration files, you can create a custom configuration section. The new configuration section must be defined at the top of the configuration file via the `configSection` element, complete with a reference to a class that should be used to process that portion of the configuration file.

In the past this process was fairly complex because the class needed to implement the IConfigurationSectionHandler interface. This exposed a simple method, `Create`, which was called the first time that section was referenced in code. There was little support from the framework to process the section, and a class implementing this interface often resorted to parsing the XML block to determine settings.

Visual Studio 2012 provides robust support for creating custom configuration sections via the `ConfigurationSection` and `ConfigurationElement` classes. These provide the basis for creating classes that map to the structure of the data being stored in the configuration files. Instead of mapping a class that processes the configuration section, you can create a much simpler class that maps to the section. When the section is referenced in code, an instance of this class is returned with the appropriate data elements set. All the XML processing that would have otherwise been necessary is handled by the .NET Framework.

Although this mapping makes the process of writing a custom configuration section much easier, you may sometimes want more control over how the section is read. Two options can be used to give you this control:

- The first option is to go back to using a configuration section handler and manually process the XML file. This can be useful if the original XML representation is required. However, it still requires that the XML file be processed.
- The second strategy is to create an appropriate mapping class as an in-between measure. Instead of referencing this class directly, another class can be generated that exposes the configuration information in the right way.

If you need to use either of these options, it might be worth taking a step back to determine whether or not the configuration section structure is actually in a format suited to the data being stored.

In the following example your application requires a list of registered entities with which to work. One type of entity is a company, and you need to be provided with both the company name and the date on which it was registered. The XML snippet that you would like to have in the configuration file might look like the following:

```
<RegisteredEntities>
  <Companies>
    <add CompanyName="Random Inc" RegisteredDate="31/1/2005" />
    add CompanyName="Developer Experience Inc" RegisteredDate="1/8/2004" />
  </Companies>
</RegisteredEntities>
```

When generated, the corresponding classes that would map to the preceding snippet might look like the following: (Again, this requires a reference to the System.Configuration assembly.)

VB

```
Public Class RegisteredEntities
    Inherits ConfigurationSection

<ConfigurationProperty("Companies")> _
    Public ReadOnly Property Companies() As Companies
        Get
            Return CType(MyBase.Item("Companies"),Companies)
        End Get
    End Property
End Class

<ConfigurationCollectionAttribute(GetType(Company))> _
Public Class Companies
    Inherits ConfigurationElementCollection

    Protected Overrides Function CreateNewElement() As ConfigurationElement
        Return New Company
    End Function

    Protected Overrides Function GetElementKey _
                        (ByVal element As ConfigurationElement) As Object
        Return CType(element, Company).CompanyName
    End Function

    Public Sub Add(ByVal element As Company)
        Me.BaseAdd(element)
    End Sub

End Class

Public Class Company
    Inherits ConfigurationElement

<ConfigurationProperty("CompanyName",DefaultValue:="Random Inc",
IsKey:=true, IsRequired:=true)> _
    Public Property CompanyName() As String
        Get
            Return CType(MyBase.Item("CompanyName"),String)
        End Get
        Set
            MyBase.Item("CompanyName") = value
        End Set
    End Property

<ConfigurationProperty("RegisteredDate",DefaultValue:="31/1/2005",
```

```
IsKey:=false, IsRequired:=false)> _
    Public Property RegisteredDate() As String
        Get
            Return CType(MyBase.Item("RegisteredDate"),String)
        End Get
        Set
            MyBase.Item("RegisteredDate") = value
        End Set
    End Property
End Class
```

C#

```
class RegisteredEntities : ConfigurationSection{
    [ConfigurationProperty("Companies")]
    public Companies Companies{
        get{
            return base["Companies"] as Companies;
        }
    }
}

[ConfigurationCollection(typeof(Company))]
class Companies : ConfigurationElementCollection{
    protected override ConfigurationElement CreateNewElement(){
        return new Company();
    }

    protected override object GetElementKey
           (ConfigurationElement element){
        return (element as Company).CompanyName;
    }

    public void Add(Company element){
        BaseAdd(element);
    }
}

class Company : ConfigurationElement{
    [ConfigurationProperty("CompanyName", DefaultValue = "Random Inc",
                           IsKey = true, IsRequired = true)]
    public string CompanyName{
        get{
            return base["CompanyName"] as string;
        }
        set{
            base["CompanyName"] = value;
        }
    }

    [ConfigurationProperty("RegisteredDate", DefaultValue = "31/1/2005",
                           IsKey = false, IsRequired = true)]
    public string RegisteredDate{
        get{
            return base["RegisteredDate"] as string;
        }
        set{
            base["RegisteredDate"] = value;
        }
    }
}
```

The code contains three classes required to correctly map the functionality of this section. The registered entities section corresponds to the `RegisteredEntities` class, which contains a single property that returns a company collection. A collection is required here because you want to support the addition of multiple companies. This functionality could be extended to clear and remove companies, which might be useful if you had a web application to control which companies are available to different portions of the application. Lastly, there is the `Company` class that maps to the individual company information being added.

To access this section from within the code, you can simply call the appropriate section using the `configurationManager` framework class:

VB

```
Dim registered as RegisteredEntities= _
    ctype(configurationmanager.GetSection("RegisteredEntities"),RegisteredEntities)
```

C#

```
var registered =
      ConfigurationManager.GetSection("RegisteredEntities") as RegisteredEntities;
```

> **NOTE** *For the .NET configuration system to correctly load the RegisteredEntities section, you also need to register this section in the configSections of your configuration file. You can do this by adding* `<section name="RegisteredEntities" type="ConfigurationApplication.RegisteredEntities, Configuration Application, Version=1.0.0.0, Culture=neutral, PublicKeyToken=null"/>` *to the configSections immediately before the* `</configSections>` *tag.*

Automation Using SCDL

You just saw how custom configuration sections can be written and mapped to classes. Although this is a huge improvement over writing section handlers, it is still a fairly laborious process that is prone to error. Furthermore, debugging the configuration sections is nearly impossible because it's difficult to track what's going wrong.

As part of another project to support ASP.NET developers, a development manager for the ASP.NET team at Microsoft recognized that the process of creating these mapping classes was mundane and could easily be automated. To this end, he created a small application entitled SCDL (`http://blogs.msdn.com/dmitryr/archive/2005/12/07/501365.aspx`) that could take a snippet of configuration data, such as the `RegisteredEntities` section discussed previously, and output both the mapping classes and a schema file that represented the section supplied. When generated, this code can be included in the application. Furthermore, if the snippet of configuration data is to be included as a noncompiled file within the solution, it is possible to automate the generation of the mapping classes via a prebuild `batch` command. If changes need to be made to the structure of the section, they can be made in the snippet. That way, the next time the solution is built, the mapping classes update automatically.

IntelliSense

Even after you get the custom configuration sections correctly mapped, there is still no support provided by Visual Studio 2012 for adding the custom section to the configuration file. Unlike the rest of the configuration file, which has support for IntelliSense and reports validation issues, your custom section cannot be validated.

To get IntelliSense and validation for your custom configuration section, you need to indicate the structure of the configuration section to Visual Studio 2012. You can do this by placing an appropriate schema (as generated by the SCDL tool) in the XML Schemas folder, which is usually located at `C:\Program Files\Microsoft Visual Studio 11.0\Xml\Schemas\`. Unfortunately, this is where it gets a little bit more complex because it is not enough to place the file in that folder; you also need to tell it that the schema should be included in the catalog used for parsing configuration files. To register your schema, follow these steps:

1. Generate your schema file from your configuration snippet:

```
Scdl.exe snippet.scdl snippet.vb snippet.xsd
```

2. Copy the schema file (in this case, `snippet.xsd`) to the schema folder.
3. Create a new text file called `Config.xsd` and include the following lines. If your schema is called something different, you should update these lines appropriately. You may also add additional lines to include more than one schema. Do not remove the `DotNetConfig.xsd` line because that removes validation for the standard configuration sections:

```
<?xml version="1.0" encoding="utf-8" ?>
<xs:schema xmlns:xs="http://www.w3.org/2001/XMLSchema">
  <xs:include schemaLocation="DotNetConfig.xsd"/>
  <xs:include schemaLocation="snippet.xsd"/>
</xs:schema>
```

4. Open `Catalog.xml` in a text editor and replace `DotNetConfig.xsd` with `Config.xsd`. This effectively remaps the validation, and IntelliSense, for configuration files to use `Config.xsd` instead of `DotNetConfig.xsd`. However, because this file sources both `DotNetConfig.xsd` and your schema information, you get validation for both your configuration section and the standard configuration sections.

USER SETTINGS

Because configuration files are commonly used to store settings that control how an application runs, you often need to dynamically change these to suit the way an individual uses the application. Rather than having to build an entirely different framework for accessing and saving these settings, you can simply change the scope of your settings. Figure 37-5 illustrates the Settings tab of the Project Properties page where you can indicate whether or not you want a setting to have Application or User scope.

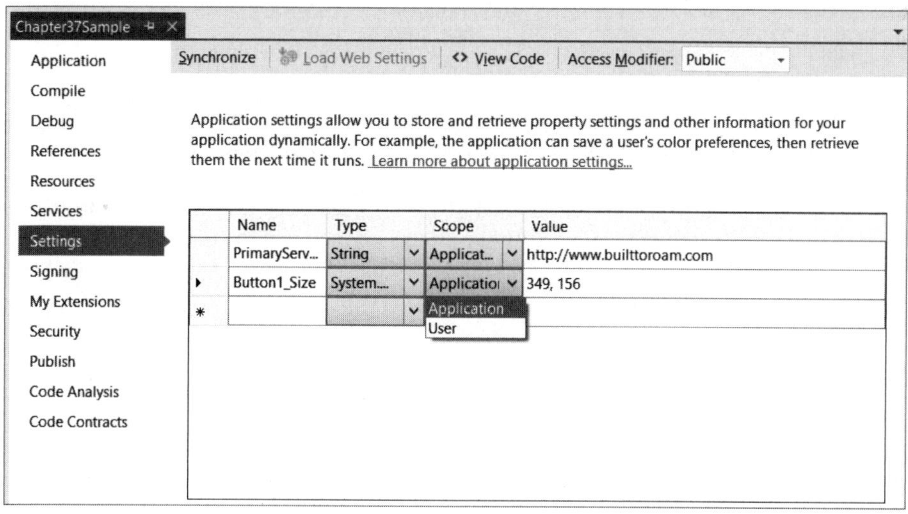

FIGURE 37-5

In essence, by changing the scope of a setting you make the choice as to whether you want the setting to be read-only — in other words, it applies to the application regardless of which user uses the application — or read-write. When you access a project setting from code, if you try to assign a value to an Application setting, you get a compile error, whereas with a User setting, you can assign a new value. Assigning a new value to the User setting changes only the value for that setting for the duration of that application session. If you want to persist the new value between sessions, you should call the `Save` method on the designer-generated `Settings` object, as shown in the following code snippet:

VB

```
Properties.Settings.Default.BackgroundColor = Color.Blue;
Properties.Settings.Default.Save();
```

Table 37-2 lists the other methods defined on the `Settings` object that may be useful when manipulating User settings.

TABLE 37-2: Settings Objects Methods

METHOD NAME	FUNCTIONALITY
`Save`	Persists the current value of the setting.
`Reload`	Restores the persisted value of the setting.
`Reset`	Returns the persisted, and in-memory, value of a setting to the default value. (This is the value you define during development in the Settings tab of the Project Properties page.) You do not need to call `Save` after calling `Reset`.
`Upgrade`	When versioning your application you can call `Upgrade` to upgrade user settings to new values associated with your application. You may want to be cautious about when you call this method because you may inadvertently clear user settings.
`(event) SettingChanging`	Event raised when a setting is about to change.
`(event) PropertyChanged`	Event raised when a setting has changed.
`(event) SettingsLoaded`	Event raised when settings are loaded from persisted values.
`(event) SettingsSaving`	Event raised prior to current values being persisted.

When building an application that makes use of User-scoped settings, it is important to test the application as if you were using it for the first time. The first time you run your application there will be no user-specific settings, which means your application will either use the values in the application configuration file or the default values that are coded in the designer-generated file. If you have been testing your application, the Synchronize button on the Settings tab of the Project Properties page (shown in the top-left corner of Figure 37-5) removes any user-specific settings that may have been persisted during earlier executions of your application.

REFERENCED PROJECTS WITH SETTINGS

As applications grow, you need to break up the logic into assemblies that are referenced by the main application. With Visual Studio 2012, it is possible to share application settings among assemblies using the project properties designer. Figure 37-6 shows the Settings tab of the project properties designer for a reference assembly. In this case the Access Modifier drop-down has been set to Public to allow access to these settings from the main application.

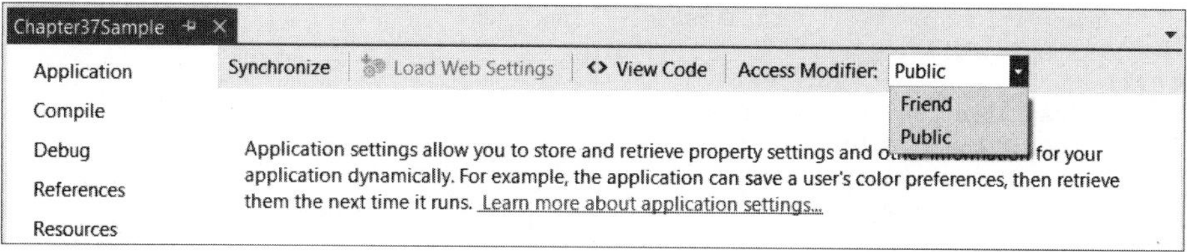

FIGURE 37-6

To access this property from the main application, you can again use the generated strongly typed access properties:

VB

```
ReferencedAssembly.My.MySettings.Default.SecondaryServer
```

C#

```
ReferencedAssembly.Properties.Settings.Default.SecondaryServer
```

A word of caution about using the project properties designer and referenced application settings: If you examine the code behind file for the settings designer, for each of the settings you have defined, there is a strongly typed access property, as previously discussed. What is important is the `DefaultSettingValueAttribute` that is applied. This is significant because it determines the value that will be returned by this property if the configuration file does not have any value specified. In the following snippet, the default value of www.peaksite.com will be returned if there is no `SecondaryServer` element defined in the configuration file:

VB

```
Namespace My
    Partial Friend NotInheritable Class MySettings
        Inherits Global.System.Configuration.ApplicationSettingsBase
.
<Global.System.Configuration.ApplicationScopedSettingAttribute(),  _
Global.System.Diagnostics.DebuggerNonUserCodeAttribute(),  _
Global.System.Configuration.DefaultSettingValueAttribute("www.peaksite.com")>  _
        Public ReadOnly Property SecondaryServer() As String
            Get
                Return CType(Me("SecondaryServer "),String)
            End Get
        End Property
    End Class
End Namespace
```

Now, you might ask why this is important when you deal with referenced application settings. It is because although the project properties designer enables you to specify that you want to allow access to settings from another assembly, it doesn't enable you to indicate that an application does reference settings from another assembly. The upshot is that when it compiles the application it takes only the `app.config` file in the application project folder, rather than combining the elements from the `app.config` files in the referenced assembly folder.

Unfortunately, because of the default value attribute, you are unlikely to notice this until the application is deployed and you realize that some of the settings are missing from the `app.config` file. Because of this, you should make sure you manually combine these files. In this case the result would be this:

```
<configuration>
.
  <applicationSettings>
    <ConfigurationApplication.My.MySettings>
```

```
      <setting name="PrimaryServer" serializeAs="String">
        <value>www.softteq.com</value>
      </setting>
    </ConfigurationApplication.My.MySettings>
    <ReferencedAssembly.My.MySettings>
      <setting name="SecondaryServer" serializeAs="String">
        <value>www.peaksite.com</value>
      </setting>
    </ReferencedAssembly.My.MySettings>
  </applicationSettings>
</configuration>
```

SUMMARY

In this chapter you learned how to use configuration files not only to control how your application runs, but also to store settings that may need to be adjusted at run time. You can also store simple name-value information, as well as more structured information, within the configuration file.

38

Connection Strings

WHAT'S IN THIS CHAPTER?

- Creating connection strings for use in your application
- Working with the Visual Studio 2012 Connection dialogs to specify how to connect to a data source
- Accessing connection strings from within code

A large proportion of applications need to persist data, and the obvious candidate for enterprise software is a relational database. The .NET Framework provides support for working with SQL Server, SQL Server Compact Edition, Oracle, ODBC, and OLE DB databases. Many other databases are also supported through third-party providers. To connect to any of these databases, you need to specify a connection string that determines the location of the server or database engine, the name of the database, authentication information, and other connection parameters. This chapter explains how to create and store connection strings. In addition, you'll learn about encrypting and working with connection strings in code.

CONNECTION STRING WIZARD

Connection strings are similar to XML in that although they can be read it is neither an enjoyable experience nor recommended to work with them directly. Because connection strings are strings, it is easy to introduce errors, misspell words, or even omit a parameter. Unlike XML, which can easily be validated against a schema, connection strings are harder to validate. The Connection String Wizard built into Visual Studio 2012 enables you to specify database connections without manually editing the connection string.

You can invoke the Connection String Wizard in a number of ways, which you can experience when you start to work with any of the data controls in either the Windows Form or Web Form designers. To illustrate the wizard, follow these steps to add a new data source to an existing Windows Forms application. Connect to the sample Adventure WorksLT2008R2 database, which you need to download from the Codeplex website (`www.codeplex.com` and search for AdventureWorksLT2008R2).

1. From the Data menu within Visual Studio 2012, select Add New Data Source, which opens the Data Source Configuration Wizard.
2. Select Database followed by either DataSet or Entity Data Model. If you select Entity Data Model, you have an additional prompt to create an Empty Model or to generate the model from a database. Selecting the database option here (or just selecting DataSet a step earlier), prompts you to specify a database connection to use. If a connection already exists, you can select it from the drop-down and the associated connection string appears in the lower portion of the window, as shown in Figure 38-1.

   The connection string connects to the AdventureWorksLT2008R2 database using LocalDB's capability to attach a database file. Later you'll look at the properties of a SQL Server connection string in more detail.

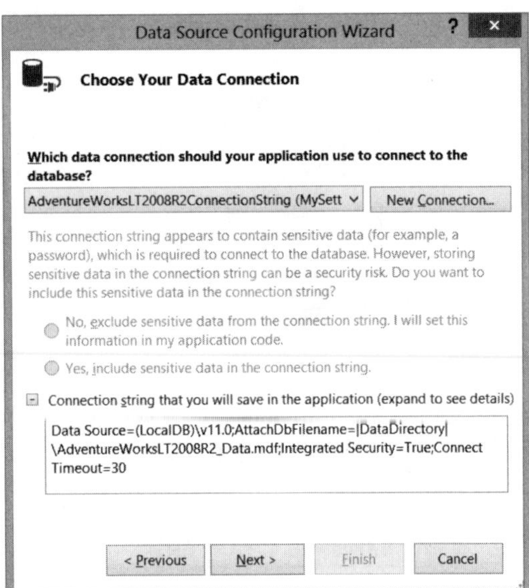

FIGURE 38-1

> **NOTE** *If you used local databases in earlier versions of .NET, you might wonder what the LocalDB portion of the connection string is. This refers to a version of SQL Express created specifically for developers. It is no longer necessary to install a full version of SQL Express to create data-driven applications. LocalDB provides a low-footprint, low-configuration, and low administration alternative that can be used instead. You can find a brief discussion about the capabilities of LocalDB at the end of this chapter.*

3. To create a new connection, click the New Connection button to open the Add Connection dialog, in which you can specify the properties of the connection string. Figure 38-2 shows the dialog as it would appear for a SQL Server Database File connection. This dialog is specific to the database source being configured.

   Notice in Figure 38-2 that only the basic connection properties (such as the database filename and authentication information) are presented.
4. Click the Advanced button to open the Advanced Properties window, as shown in Figure 38-3, where you can configure all properties for a SQL Server connection. At the bottom of this window is the connection string being constructed. The default values are omitted from the connection string. When a value is set, it appears in the connection string and in bold in the Properties window. The list of available properties is again based on the data source being used.
5. Click OK to return to the Add Connection window where you can change the type of data source by clicking the Change button. This opens the Change Data Source dialog, as shown in Figure 38-4.

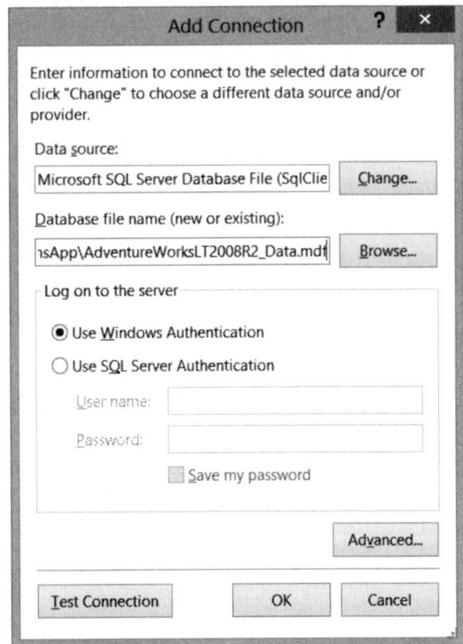

FIGURE 38-2

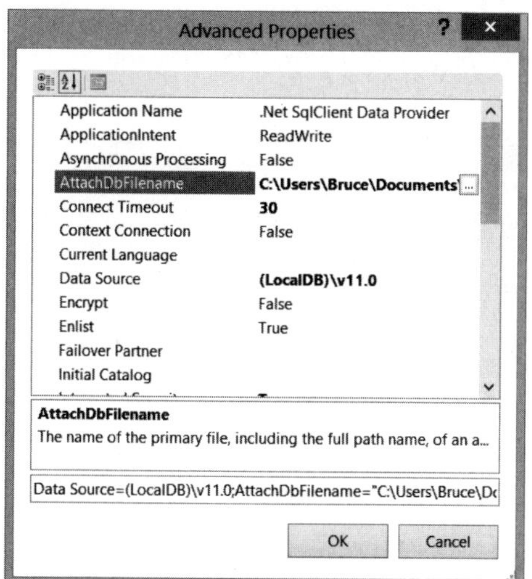

FIGURE 38-3

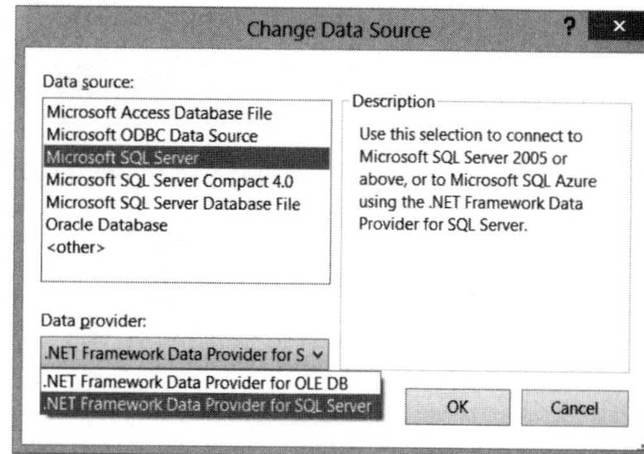

FIGURE 38-4

The list on the left contains all the data sources currently registered in the `machine.config` file. For a given data source, such as Microsoft SQL Server, there may be multiple data providers — in this case, the SQL Server and OLE DB providers.

> **NOTE** *Selecting an alternative data source-data provider combination results in a different Add Connection dialog, displaying parameters relevant to that database connection. In most cases you need to open the Advanced Properties window to configure the connection.*

6. After specifying the data source and connection settings using the Add Connection dialog, return to the Data Source Configuration Wizard. If you are creating a new connection, you are given the option to save the connection string in the application configuration file, as shown in Figure 38-5. Unless you can guarantee that the location of the database, the authentication mode, or any other connection property will not change at a later stage, it is a good idea to store the connection string in the configuration file. Saving the connection string to the configuration file has the added benefit that you can reuse the same configuration string throughout the application.

   If you don't save the connection string to the configuration file, it is explicitly assigned to the connection object you are creating, which makes reuse difficult. Alternatively, saving the connection string in the configuration file means that other connection objects can access the same string. If the database connection changes at a later stage, you can easily update it in a single location.

FIGURE 38-5

7. The Data Source Configuration Wizard continues to step you through selecting which database objects you want to add to your data source. This is covered in more detail in Chapter 28, "Datasets and Data Binding."

> **NOTE** *If you use LocalDB as your database engine, after you specify the database objects, you will be asked if the database file should be included with your project. You can find the details on what that entails in the "LocalDB" section.*

When you save a connection string to an application configuration file, it is added to the `connectionStrings` configuration section, as shown in the following snippet from an `app.config` file: (The same section can exist in a `web.config` file for a web application.)

```
<?xml version="1.0" encoding="utf-8" ?>
<configuration>
<appSettings />
<connectionStrings>
<add
      name="Connection_Strings.Properties.Settings.
      AdventureWorksLTConnectionString"
      connectionString="Data Source=(LocalDB)\v11.0;
         AttachDbFilename=|DataDirectory|\AdventureWorksLT2008R2_Data.mdf;
         Integrated Security=True;Connect Timeout=30"
      providerName="System.Data.SqlClient" />
</connectionStrings>
</configuration>
```

The `connectionStrings` section of a configuration file uses the standard element collection pattern, which enables multiple connection strings to be specified, and then referenced in code. For example, the preceding connection string can be accessed in code as follows: (This assumes your project has a reference to the System.Configuration assembly.)

C#

```
private void OpenConnectionClick(object sender, EventArgs e){
    var sqlCon = new System.Data.SqlClient.SqlConnection();
    sqlCon.ConnectionString = ConfigurationManager.
    ConnectionStrings["AdventureWorksLTConnectionString"].ConnectionString;
    sqlCon.Open();
}
```

VB

```
Private Sub OpenConnectionClick(ByVal sender As System.Object,
                                ByVal e As System.EventArgs) _
                                                  Handles BtnOpenConnection.Click
    Dim sqlCon As New SqlClient.SqlConnection
    sqlCon.ConnectionString = ConfigurationManager.ConnectionStrings _
               ("AdventureWorksLTConnectionString").ConnectionString
    sqlCon.Open()
End Sub
```

A nice artifact of working with the Connection String Wizard is that it also adds strongly typed support for accessing the connection string from within your code. This means that you can access the connection string using the following strongly typed methods, rather than call them using a string constant:

C#

```
Properties.Settings.Default.AdventureWorksLTConnectionString;
```

VB

```
My.Settings.AdventureWorksLTConnectionString
```

The other advantage of saving the connection string in the configuration file is that when you edit the project settings, the connection strings are listed alongside other settings for the project, as shown in Figure 38-6. Not only can you modify the connection string directly, but you also have a shortcut to the Connection String Wizard via the ellipsis button to the right of the connection string value, which enables you to adjust the connection properties without fear of corrupting the connection string. Note that the ellipsis button is not visible until you click in the cell containing the connection string value.

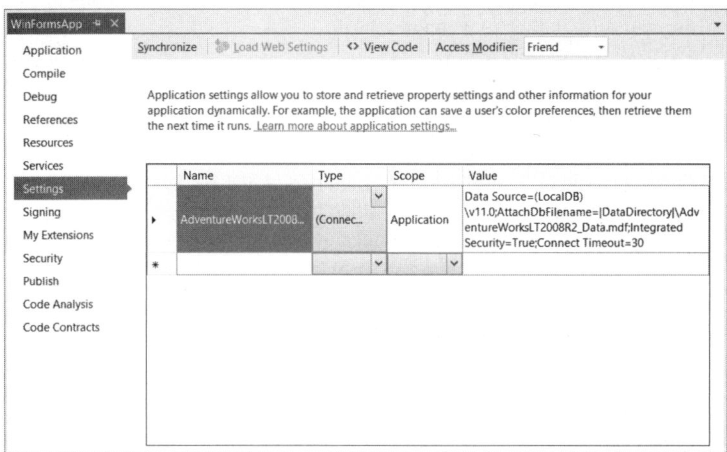

FIGURE 38-6

Figure 38-6 shows that the name of the connection string excludes the rather lengthy prefix, `Connection_Strings.Properties.Settings`, which is in the application configuration file. This prefix determines which connection strings should be included in both the project properties designer and for providing strongly typed support.

> **NOTE** *Given the inherent danger of getting data source properties wrong when manually editing the connection strings in the configuration file versus the benefits of using either the Add Data Source Wizard or the project properties designer, it is highly recommended that you avoid the manual approach wherever possible.*

SQL SERVER FORMAT

Probably the most familiar data provider is the SQL Server database provider. Table 38-1 details some of the common connection properties you may need to specify to connect to your database server.

TABLE 38-1: Some Common Connection Properties

CONNECTION PROPERTY	DESCRIPTION
`Asynchronous Processing`	Determines whether or not the connection supports asynchronous database calls. Most applications try to deliver a responsive user interface, so it is important for it not to freeze when retrieving data. In the past this could be achieved only by doing the data processing in a separate thread from the user interface. The data access methods, such as `ExecuteNonQuery`, support calls using the `Begin` and `End` asynchronous pattern. For example, `BeginExecuteNonQuery` returns immediately so that the user interface does not block while the data access is performed.

(continues)

TABLE 38-1 *(continued)*

CONNECTION PROPERTY	DESCRIPTION
`AttachDBFilename`	Introduced in SQL Server 2005, this property means you can work with databases that aren't permanently attached to a SQL Server instance. This property is a path reference to the primary database file that contains the database. Specifying `AttachDBFilename` effectively attaches and detaches the database when required.
`Connect Timeout`	Determines the maximum length of time that the `Open` method blocks when attempting to connect to the database. This should not be confused with the `Timeout` property on the `SQLCommand` class, which determines the timeout for a given command to execute.
`Data Source`	The hostname or IP address of the instance of SQL Server that the connection accesses. In cases in which multiple instances exist on a given machine, or in which SQL Server has been assigned an instance name other than the default instance, this needs to be specified as part of the Data Source field, for example, `192.168.205.223\InstanceName`.
`Initial Catalog`	Specifies the name of the database to connect to.
`Integrated Security`	If `IntegratedSecurity` is used, the Windows credentials of the current user will be used to connect to the database server. To provide user ID and password, this property must be set to `false`. Also be aware that when working with ASP.NET using Windows authentication without impersonation, if `IntegratedSecurity` is enabled, the authenticated web user's credentials will be used to access the database server.
`MultipleActiveResultSets`	Enables multiple result sets to be returned across a given connection. For example, a single database command might contain two `SELECT` statements. If the `MultipleActiveResultSets` property is enabled, the results of both `SELECT` statements will be returned and can be used to populate a DataSet. This property is compatible only with SQL Server 2005 and above.
`Password`	Used for the SQL Server user account used to access the database server.
`User ID`	Specifies the SQL Server account used to access the database server. Mixed-mode authentication for the SQL Server must be enabled, and the `IntegratedSecurity` property must be set to `false`.

Each connection string property must be specified as it appears in the preceding table, but they can be in any order in the connection string. A semicolon is used to separate each property. An example connection string might be as follows:

```
Data Source=.;Initial Catalog=AdventureWorksLT;Integrated Security=True;
MultipleActiveResultSets=True
```

IN-CODE CONSTRUCTION

Although the Connection String Wizard in Visual Studio 2012 provides a convenient tool for writing connection strings, it is often necessary to build one dynamically — a feat easily done with the `SqlConnectionStringBuilder` class. String builder classes also exist for Oracle, ODBC, and OLE DB, and they all derive from the generic `DBConnectionStringBuilder` class, which exposes the `ConnectionString` property.

This example demonstrates creating a connection builder object based on an existing connection string and changing the authentication mode to use the user ID and password provided by the user before assigning the new connection string to the connection object. In addition, the example demonstrates the use of the

`MultipleActiveResultSets` property to retrieve multiple tables from the database using a single command object:

C#

```
private void LoadDataClick(object sender, EventArgs e){
    //Update the connection string based on user settings
    var sqlbuilder = new System.Data.SqlClient.SqlConnectionStringBuilder
(Properties.Settings.Default.AdventureWorksLTConnectionString);
    if (!string.IsNullOrEmpty(this.TxtUserId.Text)){
        sqlbuilder.IntegratedSecurity = false;
        sqlbuilder.UserID = this.TxtUserId.Text;
        sqlbuilder.Password = this.TxtPassword.Text;
    }
    sqlbuilder.MultipleActiveResultSets = true;
    //Create the connection based on the updated connection string
    var sqlCon = new System.Data.SqlClient.SqlConnection();
    sqlCon.ConnectionString = sqlbuilder.ConnectionString;
    //Set the command and create the dataset to load the data into
    var sqlcmd = new System.Data.SqlClient.SqlCommand(
                                  "SELECT * FROM Person.Contact;" +
                                  "SELECT * FROM Person.ContactType", sqlCon);
    var ds = new DataSet();
    var rds = new System.Data.SqlClient.SqlDataAdapter(sqlcmd);
    //Open connection, retrieve data, and close connection
    sqlCon.Open();
    rds.Fill(ds);
    sqlCon.Close();
}
```

VB

```
Private Sub LoadDataClick (ByVal sender As System.Object, _
                          ByVal e As System.EventArgs) Handles Button1.Click
    'Update the connection string based on user settings
    Dim sqlbuilder As New SqlClient.SqlConnectionStringBuilder _
                          (My.Settings.AdventureWorksLTConnectionString)
    If Not Me.TxtUserId.Text = "" Then
        sqlbuilder.IntegratedSecurity = False
        sqlbuilder.UserID = Me.TxtUserId.Text
        sqlbuilder.Password = Me.TxtPassword.Text
    End If
    sqlbuilder.MultipleActiveResultSets = True
    'Create the connection based on the updated connection string
    Dim sqlCon As New SqlClient.SqlConnection
    sqlCon.ConnectionString = sqlbuilder.ConnectionString
    'Set the command and create the dataset to load the data into
    Dim sqlcmd As New SqlClient.SqlCommand("SELECT * FROM Person.Contact;" & _
                                           "SELECT * FROM Person.ContactType", _
                                           sqlCon)
    Dim ds As New DataSet
    Dim rds As New SqlClient.SqlDataAdapter(sqlcmd)
    'Open connection, retrieve data, and close connection
    sqlCon.Open()
    rds.Fill(ds)
    sqlCon.Close()
End Sub
```

The important thing to note about this code sample is that the `MultipleActiveResultSets` property is enabled, which means that multiple `SELECT` statements can be specified in the `SqlCommand` object. The `SqlCommand` object is then used by the `SqlDataAdapter` object to fill the DataSet. The `DataSet` object contains two data tables, each populated by one of the `SELECT` statements.

ENCRYPTING CONNECTION STRINGS

Although using Windows authentication and integrated security is an easy-to-configure and secure option for implementing authentication in a database connection it is not always possible to do so; sometimes you must resort to specifying a user ID and password in a connection string. It is recommended that this information not be hard-coded into your application because it can easily be extracted from the assembly. As such, this information needs to be either specified by the users each time they use the system or added to the connection string in the configuration file. The upshot of this is that you need a mechanism for encrypting configuration sections. This walk-through shows you how to encrypt a section of a configuration file for a web application, StagingWebsite, which has a `web.config` file as follows:

```
<?xml version="1.0"?>
<configuration>
<connectionStrings>
<add name="AdventureWorksLTConnectionString"
     connectionString="Data Source=(LocalDB)\v11.0;
       AttachDbFilename=|DataDirectory|\AdventureWorksLT2008R2_Data.mdf;
       Integrated Security=True;Connect Timeout=30"
     providerName="System.Data.SqlClient" />
</connectionStrings>
<!-
.
->
</configuration>
```

Using the command prompt, execute the following commands in sequence, replacing `UserName` with the name of the account that the web application will run as (for example, the AspNet account). And keep in mind that if the account that you're using to run the web application is a domain account, you need to use the `domain\UserName` as the user name. Also, notice that the third command in the list references an app named `StagingWebsite`. This is actually a virtual directory that contains the web application whose configuration file you're encrypting. You'll need to change that application name to match the virtual directory for your own web application:

1. `cd\WINDOWS\Microsoft.NET\Framework\v4.0.30319`
2. `aspnet_regiis -pa "NetFrameworkConfigurationKey" "UserName"`
3. `aspnet_regiis -pe "connectionStrings" -app "/StagingWebsite" -prov "DataProtectionConfigurationProvider"`

Executing these commands modifies the `web.config` file as follows: (If you get an error saying that the RSA key container was not found, you may need to execute `aspnet_regiis -pc "NetFrameworkConfigurationKey" -exp` to create the key container.)

```
<?xml version="1.0"?>
<configuration>
<connectionStrings configProtectionProvider="RsaProtectedConfigurationProvider">
<EncryptedData Type="http://www.w3.org/2001/04/xmlenc#Element"
   xmlns="http://www.w3.org/2001/04/xmlenc#">
<EncryptionMethod Algorithm="http://www.w3.org/2001/04/xmlenc#tripledes-cbc" />
<KeyInfo xmlns="http://www.w3.org/2000/09/xmldsig#">
<EncryptedKey xmlns="http://www.w3.org/2001/04/xmlenc#">
<EncryptionMethod Algorithm="http://www.w3.org/2001/04/xmlenc#rsa-1_5" />
<KeyInfo xmlns="http://www.w3.org/2000/09/xmldsig#">
<KeyName>Rsa Key</KeyName>
</KeyInfo>
<CipherData>
<CipherValue>Y4Be/ND8fXTKl3r0CASBK0oaOSvbyijYCVUudf1AuQl
pU2HRsTyEpR2sVpxrOukiBhvcGyWlv4EM0AB9p3Ms8FgIA3Ou6mGORhxfO9eIUGD+M5tJSe6wn/
9op8mFV4W7YQZ4WIqLaAAu7MKVI6KKK/ANIKpV8l2NdMBT3uPOPi8=</CipherValue>
</CipherData>
</EncryptedKey>
```

```
</KeyInfo>
<CipherData>
<CipherValue>BeKnN/kQIMw9rFbck6IwX9NZA6WyOCSQlziWzCLA8Ff/JdA0W/dWIidnjae1
vgpS8ghouYn7BQocjvc0uGsGgX1PfvsLq18//1ArZDgiHVLAXjW6b+eKbE5vaf5ss6psJdCRRB0ab5xao
NAPHH/Db9UKMycWVqP0badN+qCQzYyU2cQFvK1S7Rum8VwgZ85Qt+FGExYpG06YqVR9tfWwqZmYwtW8iz
r7fijvspm/oRK4Yd+DGBRKuXxD6EN4kFgJUil7ktzOJAwWly4bVpmwzwJT9N6yig54lobhOahZDP05gtk
Lor/HwD9IKmRvO1jv</
   CipherValue>
</CipherData>
</EncryptedData>
</connectionStrings>
<!–
.
–>
</configuration>
```

As you can see from this example, the connection string is no longer readable in the configuration file. The commands you executed did two things. Ignoring the first command (because it simply changes the directory so that you can access the `asp_regiis` executable), the second command permits access to the key container NetFrameworkConfigurationKey for the user Nick. This key container is the default container for the RSAProtectedConfigurationProvider, which is specified in the `machine.config` file. For your application to decrypt data from the configuration file, the user that the application is running as must access the key container. To determine the identity of this user, execute the following command:

```
System.Security.Principal.WindowsIdentity.GetCurrent( ).Name
```

The third command encrypts the `connectionStrings` section of the configuration file for the web application StagingWebsite. Other sections of the configuration file can also be encrypted using the same command. If at some later stage you need to decrypt the configuration section, execute the same command, but with `-pd` instead of `-pe`, for example:

```
aspnet_regiis -pd "connectionStrings" -app "/StagingWebsite"
```

> **WARNING** *After a configuration file has been encrypted using the technique just described, it can no longer be moved to another machine without some additional effort. The encryption process uses the machine key setting for the computer on which it is executed. If the configuration file is moved to another machine with a different machine key, the value can no longer be decrypted. For this reason, the encryption process is typically performed on the target machine for your application, or as would be the case in an application running on a server farm, each machine would be configured with the same machine key.*

LOCALDB

Developers who create database applications don't always have access to a fully installed instance of SQL Server. For this reason, Microsoft has provided a free but scaled down version of SQL Server that could be used as a development platform and that is compatible with the "real" SQL Server products so that deployment is not a worry. Since SQL Server 2005, this free edition was known as SQL Server Express. LocalDB is actually an execution mode of SQL Server Express. The difference is that the installation process includes only the minimal collection of files necessary to start the database engine. Installation of LocalDB is optionally part of the Visual Studio 2012 process, through an .msi (Microsoft Installer), or as part of a SQL Server Express setup.

There are two types of instances for LocalDB: Named and Automatic. Automatic instances are public in that they are created and managed automatically. When establishing a connection to an automatic instance, the infrastructure necessary to run the database is created with no additional effort required by the developer. To put this in the common vernacular, "it just works." The only caveat is that the naming of the automatic instance is convention-based to avoid conflicts with named instances. The instance name is a single "v" character followed by the release number. For example, the LocalDB instance for SQL Server 2012 is named v11.0.

Named instances are private. Instead of being available to any application, they are owned by a single application. The creation of the infrastructure and the starting of the engine is done either manually through the LocalDB management API or through the configuration file.

If you are starting the named instance manually, there is a SQLLocalDB.exe command-line utility available in the Tools/Binn directory of your SQL Server version (for example, c:\Program Files\Microsoft SQL Server\110). The following commands create and start a LocalDB instance named SampleDB:

```
"C:\Program Files\Microsoft SQL Server\110\Tools\Binn\SqlLocalDB.exe" create SampleDB
"C:\Program Files\Microsoft SQL Server\110\Tools\Binn\SqlLocalDB.exe" start SampleDB
```

Alternatively, the LocalDB API includes `LocalDBCreateInstance` and `LocalDBStartInstance` methods. As a word of caution, the API is based on a COM object and, at least as of this writing, there are no managed classes to act as a wrapper.

SUMMARY

This chapter showed you how to use Visual Studio 2012 to take charge of your application and configure it to connect to a database using a connection string. With the built-in support of the data classes in the .NET Framework, connection strings can be dynamically created and modified, so you never need to handcraft a connection string again.

39

Resource Files

WHAT'S IN THIS CHAPTER?

- Understanding what an application resource is
- Defining and using resources within your application
- Defining culture-specific resources
- Extending the default resource types

Developers often overlook the humble XML resource file, because it is often hidden by Visual Studio 2012 so as not to clutter the solution. Because its most common use is as a backing file for forms or web pages, you can write large applications without interacting directly with resource files. However, resource files are an important tool that you need to use in order to write applications that can be easily maintained and translated into other languages.

The first part of this chapter explains why resource files are important and describes the features that enable developers to work with them. The remainder of the chapter explains how you can use resource files to localize an application for different languages and cultures.

WHAT ARE RESOURCES?

A resource is any data required by an application, whether it is a string, an icon, an image, or even an audio clip. Resources are nonexecutable and support the running of the application through the provision of data such as location, size, and other physical properties of controls. Though most resources are strings, images, audio clips, or icons, there is no reason why a resource could not be a more complex object that supports serialization.

Three types of resource files can be compiled into an application: text, resx (XML resource file), and resources (binary resource file) file formats. Whole files can also be embedded as application resources where needed. Most developers who use Visual Studio 2012 use resx files and embedded file resources.

Text File Resources

Text files are the most basic sort of resource because they are limited to providing string values. In applications for which a large number of string literals need to be managed, using a simple text file can be the easiest way to do it because that way they are not cluttered among the other resources of the application.

The format of strings defined in a text resource file is a name-value pair, where the name is used to reference the resource in code, as shown in the following example:

```
Error_Unable_To_Connect = Unable to connect to specified server
```

Because each name-value pair is delimited by a new line, this character cannot be added to the string. However, C-style escape characters can be used to insert new lines (`\n`) or tabs (`\t`) into the text.

You can add comments to the resource file by prefixing a line with a semicolon, as shown here:

```
;Error message to be displayed when a connection could not be made to the server
Error_Unable_To_Connect = Unable to connect to specified server
```

Text resource files should be saved with the file extension of `.txt` or `.restext`. The latter is useful when you want to distinguish text resource files from regular text files.

Although text resource files are easy to edit and update, it is harder to integrate them into your application. As text files, they cannot be directly compiled into an application; they must instead be converted into either resx or resources files. Do this using the Resource Generator utility, `resgen.exe`, located in the `\bin\NETFX 4.0 Tools` folder of the Windows SDK (located at `C:\Program Files\Microsoft SDKs\Windows\v8.0A\bin`):

```
resgen StringResources.txt StringResources.resources
```

Include the output file — in this case, `StringResources.resources` — in your application to access those resources.

A prebuild event can be used to convert text resource files into a resources file that can be compiled into the main application build. This ensures that the resources files contained in the application are always up to date. To do this, include the text resource file in the application and set the build action property to `None`. Navigate to the Project Properties window for the project that contains the text resource file, and on the Compile tab, select Build Events (VB) or the Build Events tab (C#). In the prebuild events, enter the `resgen` command required to compile your text resource file:

```
"C:\Program Files\Microsoft SDKs\Windows\v8.0A\bin\NETFX 4.0 Tools\resgen.exe"
   "$(ProjectDir)StringResources.txt" "$(ProjectDir)StringResources.resources"
```

> **NOTE** *If you run on a 64-bit platform, the path to resgen includes* `C:\Program Files (x86)` *instead of* `C:\Program Files`.

Building the application generates the resources file that needs to be included within your application with the build action property set to `Embedded Resource`. Figure 39-1 illustrates how both the text file and the resources file are included within an application with appropriate build action properties.

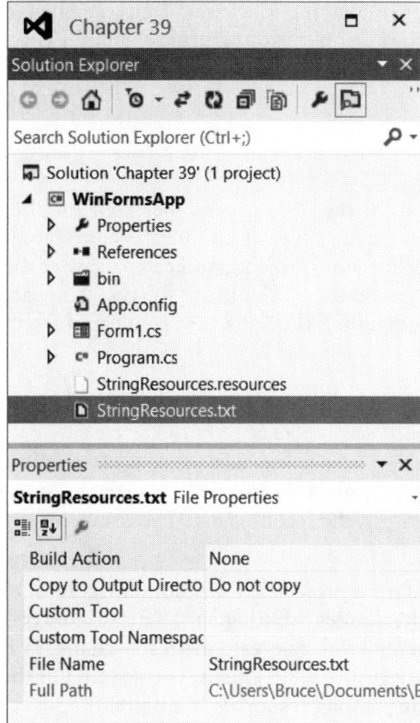

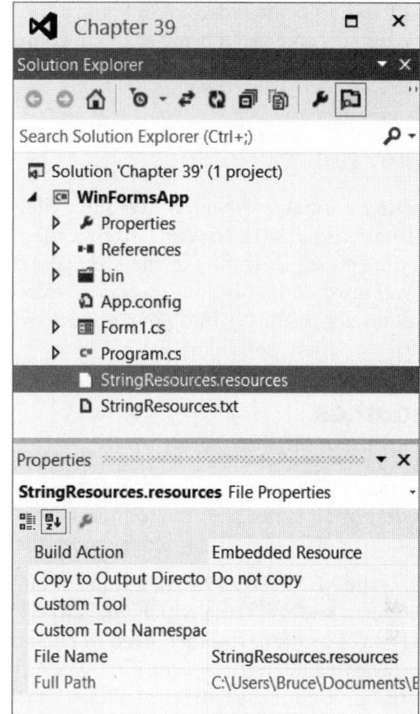

FIGURE 39-1

Resx Resource Files

A more user-friendly format for resources is the XML resource file, commonly referred to as a resx file. This is a simple XML data file that contains name-value pairs of XML nodes. The advantage of this format is that the value is not restricted to just a string; it can be of any type that is serializable or that can be represented as a string.

The following XML snippet shows a resource named `HelloWorld` with an associated value and comment. As you can see from the code, no information is available about the type of data contained within the resource because it is a string resource:

```
<data name="HelloWorld">
  <value>Say Hello</value>
  <comment>This is how we say hello</comment>
</data>
```

The next snippet illustrates how a more complex data type can be stored in a resource file as a string representation. It also shows how an assembly alias can be used to reference an external assembly that contains type information. When this resource is accessed, the type information will be used to convert the string value to an object of this type:

```
<assembly alias="System.Drawing" name="System.Drawing, Version=4.0.0.0,
  Culture=neutral, PublicKeyToken=b03f5f7f11d50a3a" />
<data name="Button1.Location" type="System.Drawing.Point, System.Drawing">
  <value>71, 43</value>
</data>
```

Although resx files can be included in an application without you having to use the Resource File Generator (Resgen), they are still converted prior to being compiled into the application. During the build process, resources files are generated for each resx file in the application. These are subsequently linked into the application.

Binary Resources

The third resource format is the binary resource file, indicated by the `.resources` file extension. Behind the scenes, Visual Studio 2012 converts all resx files into `.resources` files as an intermediate step during compilation (you can see these files in the `\obj\debug` folder for your project), and as you saw earlier in this chapter, you must manually convert text resources into `.resources` files using Resgen. You can also integrate other binary resources into your project by simply including the `.resources` file and setting the build action to `Embedded Resource`.

Adding Resources

Visual Studio 2012 supports a rich user interface for adding and modifying resource files. It is still possible to view the contents of a resource file within the IDE. However, unless the resource is a string, or has a string representation, it is not possible to modify the value within the resource file. The resource editor provides support for strings, images, icons, audio files, and more.

Double-clicking the My Project (VB) or Properties (C#) node for a project in the Solution Explorer opens the project properties editor, from which you can select the Resources tab to open the default, or project, resource file. For C# projects you then need to click the presented link to create the resource file. (VB projects already have a default resource file.) When the default resource file opens, you see that in the top-left corner of the resource editor is a drop-down list that navigates among resources of different types, as shown in Figure 39-2. Double-clicking any resx file within the Solution Explorer also brings up this resource editor.

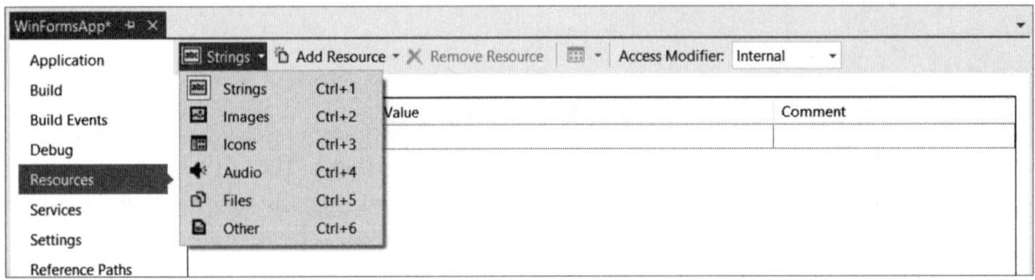

FIGURE 39-2

The editor displays the resource in an appropriate format, according to its type. For example, strings are presented in an editable textbox, whereas images are presented as thumbnails that can be opened and edited. Adding new resources is as simple as selecting the Add Resource drop-down, choosing the appropriate resource type, and adding the necessary information. After you add a resource, it appears in the resource editor, as shown in Figure 39-3.

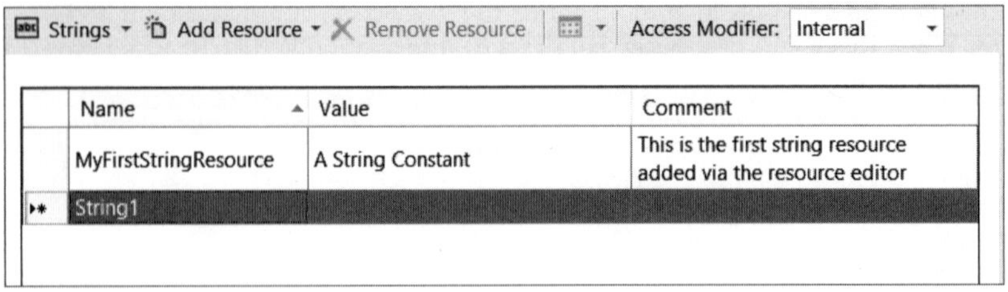

FIGURE 39-3

Figure 39-3 shows an additional column that gives you the option to specify a comment alongside your resource. Unfortunately, the resource editor is the only place in Visual Studio 2012 where this comment displays.

Embedding Files as Resources

It is often necessary to embed an entire file in an application. You can do this by including the file in the application and modifying the build action. Depending on the file type, when the item is included in the application, the build action (click the file and open the Properties window) is normally set to either `Compile` or `None`. If this is changed to `Embedded Resource`, the entire file is added to the application as an embedded resource.

Alternatively, you can use the resource editor to add a file resource (refer to Figure 39-2). When images, icons, and other files are added to an existing resource file by means of the resource editor, they are added as a `resxfileref` item. The file appears in the resources directory, but the build action will be `None`. When the application is built, these files are compiled into the resources file prior to being linked into the application. In the past, the data from these files was pulled out and added to the resx file as a binary block. This meant that, when added, the data couldn't be easily modified. With the File reference item, the data remains in an associated file and can easily be updated.

Naming Resources

Resources are named for the resource file to which they belong and the root namespace. For example, if you have a resource file called `Sample.resources` in a project called MyProject, the full resource name is `MyProject.Sample`.

This is particularly important to remember when you make a file an embedded resource by changing the build action. You can access any file by prefixing the filename with the project name. Unlike with resource files, the name of the file retains the extension. For example, if you have a file called `ASimpleDataDocument.doc` in a project called MyProject, it needs to be referenced as `MyProject.ASimpleDataDocument.doc`.

> **NOTE** *Any directory structure will be ignored for the purpose of naming embedded resources. Pay attention to this...it can save you hours of debugging as you attempt to figure out why your resource is not found by your application at run time.*

Accessing Resources

The method that you use to access resources depends on how they are embedded in the application. You have already seen that you have two ways to embed resources: The first is to add a file to the project and set the build action to `Embedded Resource`; the second is via the resource editor. To access resources added by a change to the build action, you need to use the `GetManifestResourceNames` and `GetManifestResourceStream` methods. The following code retrieves the names of all the resources in the assembly by querying the manifest. It then creates a stream for accessing the relevant resource file. As discussed in the previous section, the name of the embedded resource file returned by the `GetManifestResourceNames` method and accepted by the `GetManifestResourceStream` method is in the form *`Rootnamespace.Filename.File_extension`* (for example, `MyProject.ASimpleDataDocument.doc`).

VB

```
Dim names = Reflection.Assembly.GetExecutingAssembly.GetManifestResourceNames
Dim resources = From n In names
                Select Assembly.GetExecutingAssembly.GetManifestResourceStream(n)
For Each r In resources
```

```
        Using strm As New IO.StreamReader(r)
            MsgBox(strm.ReadToEnd)
        End Using
    Next
```

C#

```
var names = Assembly.GetExecutingAssembly().GetManifestResourceNames();
var resources = from n in names
                select Assembly.GetExecutingAssembly().GetManifestResourceStream(n);
foreach (var r in resources){
    using (var strm = new StreamReader(r)){
        MessageBox.Show(strm.ReadToEnd());
    }
}
```

Resources added via the resource editor can be accessed in code by means of a resource manager, which you can easily create from the name of the resource file to which they belong and a reference to the assembly from which the resource should be extracted:

VB

```
Dim res As New ResourceManager("WorkingWithResources.Resources",
                               Assembly.GetExecutingAssembly)
```

C#

```
var res = new ResourceManager("WorkingWithResources.Properties.Resources",
                               Assembly.GetExecutingAssembly());
```

When created, resources can be extracted by means of either the `GetObject` or `GetString` function:

```
res.GetObject("StringResource")
```

For more complex resources, such as files, you may also want to use the `GetStream` function. All three functions take the name of the resource as the only parameter.

Designer Files

The Resource Generator utility, Resgen, has a number of features that enable you to build strongly typed wrapper classes for your resource files. When you add a resx file to your application, Visual Studio 2012 automatically creates a designer file that wraps the process of creating a resource manager and accessing the resources by name. The accessor properties are all strongly typed and are generated by the designer to reduce the chance of invalid type conversions and references. For example, if you have a string resource, `StringResource`, contained in a resource file, `MyResources`, you can use the following code to access the string:

VB

```
My.Resources.MyResources.MyStringResource
```

C#

```
MyResources.StringResource
```

The designer-generated code is different for VB and C#. This is because C# uses the generic ResXFileCodeGenerator custom tool, whereas VB uses the VbMyResourcesResXFileCodeGenerator custom tool to integrate the resource file into the `My` namespace.

Unfortunately, Visual Studio 2012 does not automatically generate the designer file for text resource files because text resource files cannot be explicitly added to the application. The process of generating a resource file from the text file can be extended to include the generation of the designer file.

An argument is available in Resgen that facilitates the generation of this designer file:

```
resgen sample.txt sample.resources /str:vb
```

Both of the output files need to be added to the application so that the resources are accessible. To ensure that the resources can be correctly accessed, you must ensure that the naming used within the designer file matches the naming of the compiled resources. You can provide additional parameters to control the namespace, class name, and output filename:

```
resgen sample.txt defaultnamespace.sample.resources
    /str:vb,defaultnamespace,sample,sample.vb
```

In this case, the fully qualified output class would be `defaultnamespace.sample`, and the use of this file would allow access to resources without an exception being raised. When the correct command has been determined, you can update your prebuild event to include the generation of the designer file. This way, every time the file is modified and saved and the application is compiled, the designer file is re-created.

RESOURCING YOUR APPLICATION

Writing an application often requires data such as images, icons, or sounds (collectively known as *resources*) to enhance the appearance of the application. Furthermore, best coding practices suggest that the use of constant strings throughout your application be avoided. In either case, you can put together a custom solution that stores these resources in files that need to be shipped with the application.

An alternative is to include them in a resource file that can be compiled into your application. This way, you not only have the resources in a format that you can work with, but they are also automatically available within your application.

In Visual Studio 2012, forms are initially represented by two files: the generated designer file (for example, `Form1.Designer.vb`) and the code-beside file (for example, `Form1.vb`). When a control, such as a button, is first added to the form, a resource file (for example, `Form1.resx`) is automatically created for the form. By default, this resource file contains little data because most properties are hard-coded into the designer file. This file becomes important when localization is turned on for the form. When this is done, via the properties grid as shown in Figure 39-4, the designer properties for the controls on the form are persisted to the resource file.

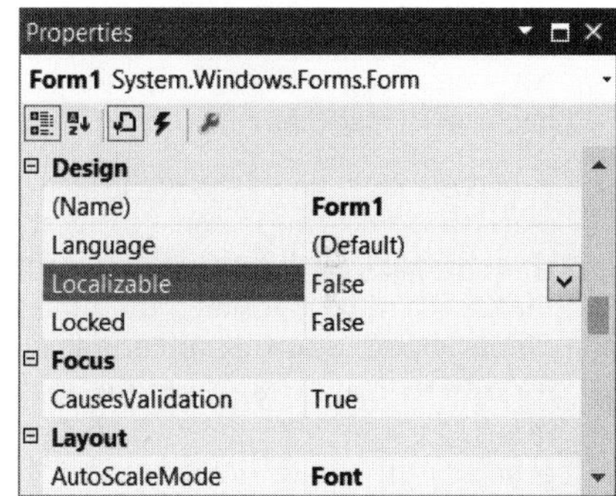

FIGURE 39-4

The following code snippet shows the designer-generated method `InitializeComponent`, which creates and sets properties on Button1. This is how the code would appear with the `Localizable` property on the form set to `False`:

```
Private Sub InitializeComponent()
    Me.Button1 = New Button
    '
    'Button1
```

```
        '
        Me.Button1.Location = New Point(71, 43)
        Me.Button1.Size = New Size(185, 166)
        Me.Button1.Text = "Button1"
        Me.Button1.TabIndex = 0
        Me.Button1.Name = "Button1"
        Me.Button1.UseVisualStyleBackColor = True
        '
        'Form1
        '
        Me.Controls.Add(Me.Button1)
    End Sub
```

After the `Localizable` property of the form has been set to `True`, the form uses the `ComponentResourceManager` class to load and apply properties found in the associated resource file. (This framework class is covered in more detail in the "ComponentResourceManager" section later in this chapter.)

```
    Private Sub InitializeComponent()
        Dim resources As New ComponentResourceManager(GetType(Form1))
        Me.Button1 = New Button
        '
        'Button1
        '
        resources.ApplyResources(Me.Button1, "Button1")
        Me.Button1.Name = "Button1"
        Me.Button1.UseVisualStyleBackColor = True
        '
        'Form1
        '
        Me.Controls.Add(Me.Button1)
    End Sub
```

Although the resource files generated by the forms designer can be manually edited, this is not encouraged because changes may be overwritten the next time the file is regenerated by the designer.

When resource files are used properly, they can provide a number of benefits because they are a convenient place to store strings, icons, images, and other data that might be referenced by an application. The use of resource files, both for tracking form properties and for application data, is a must for any application that needs to be translated for a foreign culture. (*Culture* is used here because more than language can differ among countries and ethnic groups.) Resource files enable developers to provide alternative data for different cultures. When the application is run, the .NET Framework uses the current culture information to determine which data to load, based upon the resource fallback process. (The fallback process is discussed in the section "Loading Culture Resource Files.") Common examples of information that might need to be varied among cultures are prompts, titles, error messages, and button images. In some cases, even the position and size of the controls might need to be localized.

Control Images

A number of Windows Forms controls have images as properties. For example, the PictureBox control has `Image`, `ErrorImage`, and `InitialImage` properties. If you click the ellipsis in the value column of the Properties window for any of these properties, you see the dialog shown in Figure 39-5, which enables you to select an image for the specified property.

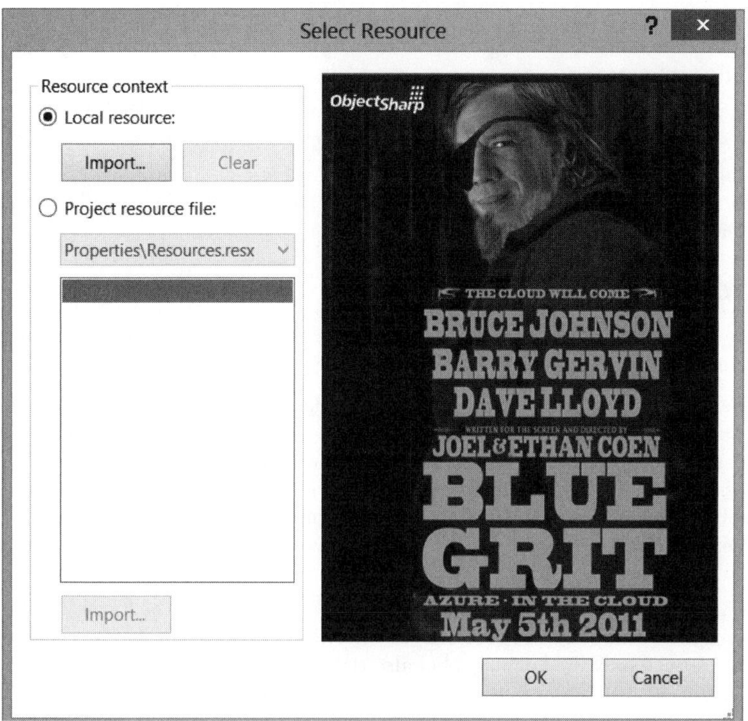

FIGURE 39-5

Before selecting an image, you have to decide whether you want to store it in the resource file associated with the current form (that is, a Local resource) or in a project-level resource file. The former option stores the image in a Base64-encoded block within the actual resource file, whereas the latter adds the image to the project and adds an appropriate reference to the selected resource file. Clearly, the latter is normally preferable because it means that you can change the image without having to import it again.

SATELLITE RESOURCES

One of the big advantages of placing data in a resource file is the resulting capability to translate the data for foreign cultures. Instead of all the languages being included in a single resource file, each culture's data is stored in a resource file that has a suffix defined by that culture.

Cultures

Cultures are defined by a combination of two lowercase letters, which represent the language, and two uppercase letters, which represent the country or region of the culture. These two pairs of letters are separated by a hyphen. For example, U.S. English and Australian English are represented as `en-US` and `en-AU`, respectively. The corresponding resource files for these cultures would be `MyResource.en-US.resx` and `MyResource.en-AU.resx`. You can find a full list of culture identifiers for a specific operating system at `http://msdn.microsoft.com/en-us/goglobal/bb896001.aspx`. If you are curious, you can look over all the available cultures, which are returned by `CultureInfo.GetCultures(CultureTypes.AllCultures)`. Approximately 220 cultures are available in Windows 8; although different service packs or language packs can add new cultures. As well, you can create a custom culture for use in an application. The cultures can be classified as follows:

- **Invariant culture:** No language or country identifier (for example, `Form1.resx`). Data is not dependent upon culture — for example, this might be the company logo, which will not vary and is not dependent upon culture information.
- **Neutral culture:** Language identifier (for example, `Form1.en.resx`). Data is dependent upon language alone — for example, a simple warning message that merely needs to be translated.
- **Specific culture:** Language and country identifier (for example, `Form1.en-US.resx`). Data is dependent upon both language and country/region — for example, form layout, color, and prompts should all be translated and adjusted for specific regions.

Creating Culture Resources

If you create additional resource files for a form, you must ensure that the `Localizable` property is set to `True`. You have three ways to create culture-specific resource files:

- If you know the identifier of the culture for which you want to generate a resource file, you can simply save the resx file to *`filename.culture_identifier`*`.resx`. For example, if you were converting the resource file `Form1.resx` to Australian English, you would save it as `Form1.en-AU.resx`. When you do this, Visual Studio removes the original resx file from the solution and adds the new culture-specific resx file. To get both files to show up nested under the Form1 node, you actually need to exclude the new resx file, refresh the solution view (by closing and reopening the solution), and then put both files back into the project.
- Visual Studio supports a much better way to create culture-specific resource files for forms. From the Properties window for the form, you can select `Language`. The name of this property is slightly misleading because it adjusts not only the language, but also the country/region of the form in designer mode. This property is initially set to `(Default)` and should always be returned to this setting after you finish generating or modifying resource files for specific cultures. To generate the resource file for Australian English, select `English (Australia)` from the Language drop-down, and make the appropriate changes to the form. When you are comfortable with the new layout, save it and reset the `Language` property to `(Default)`.
- The last way to generate culture-dependent resource files is to use `WinRes.exe`. Although it's not added to the Start menu, it is available under the Windows SDK folder (located at `C:\Program Files\Microsoft SDKs\Windows\v8.0A\bin\NETFX 4.0 Tools` or at `C:\Program Files (x86)\Microsoft SDKs\Windows\v8.0A\bin\NETFX 4.0 Tools` on a 64-bit platform) and is a graphical utility for generating resource files for forms. This utility can load an existing resource file, allow properties of all controls on the form to be modified, and then save the changes to a particular culture resource file. Before opening a form's resource file using this utility, make sure that the `Localizable` property is set to `True;` otherwise the file will not load properly.

Loading Culture Resource Files

At this point you might wonder how resource files interact, and whether culture-specific resource files have to be created and compiled at the same time as the main application. The answer to both of these questions lies in the resource fallback process, which is the mechanism by which the `ResourceManager` class loads resources.

The fallback process has three levels based upon the current user interface culture (UI culture) of the executing thread. This can be accessed in code via the `CultureInfo.CurrentUICulture` property. Be aware that this is different from `CultureInfo.CurrentCulture`, which is the current culture used in string comparisons, date formats, and so on. Unlike the current culture, which is based upon the regional settings of the computer (which you can adjust using Control Panel ➪ Regional Settings), the default UI culture is dependent upon the Windows user interface language pack that is currently selected. Unless you have a Windows Multilingual User Interface Pack installed, you cannot modify the default UI culture for your applications.

Although you can't change the default user interface culture, you can adjust this property in code. A word of caution here, however: Without the interface pack installed, some cultures may not display correctly.

```
Thread.CurrentThread.CurrentUICulture = New CultureInfo("en-US")
```

Using the current user interface culture, the fallback process tries to locate resources based on a culture match. For example, if the UI culture is `en-US`, the process would start off by looking for specific culture resources that match both language (English) and country (U.S.). When no resource can be located, the process falls back to neutral culture resources that match just the language (English). If the fallback process still can't locate a resource, the process falls back to *invariant culture*, indicating there is no match for language or country.

Satellite Culture Resources

So far this chapter has mentioned only how a resource can be converted into a new culture and added to an application. Although this method gives you control over which cultures are deployed with your application, it would be better if you didn't have to rebuild your entire application whenever a culture resource needed to be modified, or when you decided to add support for a new culture.

When Visual Studio 2012 compiles culture resources, it splits the resource files into a hub-and-spoke arrangement, using satellite assemblies to contain culture resources. At the hub is the main assembly that would contain the invariant resources. Satellite assemblies are then created for each culture for which a resource has been created. The naming of the satellite assembly is of the form `MyApp.resources.dll` and is located in a subdirectory named according to the culture under the main output path. Although there is an implicit relationship between specific cultures and neutral cultures (for example, between `en-US` and `en`), satellite assemblies for both types should reside in a subdirectory under the main output path.

Another alternative is for the main assembly and satellite assemblies to be installed into the Global Assembly Cache (GAC). In this case, each assembly must be strongly named so that it is unique within the cache.

Clearly, the resource fallback process needs to accommodate assemblies both in the GAC and subdirectories. Hence, for each culture level (specific, neutral, and invariant) the GAC is checked first, followed by the culture subdirectory. Finally, if no resource is found, an exception is raised.

Note that culture resource files do not have to contain all the resources defined in the default resource file. The resource fallback process loads the resource from the default resource file if it is not located in a more specific resource file, so it makes sense to save in the specified culture only those resources that are different.

ACCESSING SPECIFICS

Numerous shortcuts have been built into the .NET Framework to support the most common tasks related to accessing resources. These shortcuts include single-line image loading, cross-assembly referencing, and the use of the `ComponentResourceManager` class.

Bitmap and Icon Loading

Images and icons are two of the most common data types held in resource files. Therefore, both the `Bitmap` and `Icon` classes in the framework support a constructor that can create an instance directly from a resource without the need for a resource manager. For example, if you have an image, `MyImage.bmp`, that you included in your project by setting the build action to `Embedded Resource`, you can access the image directly using the following code:

```
Dim img As New Bitmap(GetType(ThisClass), "MyImage.bmp")
```

Here, the class, `ThisClass`, can be any class in the root namespace of the project that contains the embedded resource.

Cross-Assembly Referencing

In Visual Studio 2012, you can control the accessibility level for resource files. With the Access Modifier option in the resource editor, as shown in Figure 39-6, you can choose between keeping a resource internal to the assembly it is defined in (Friend [VB] or Internal [C#]) or making it publicly accessible (Public).

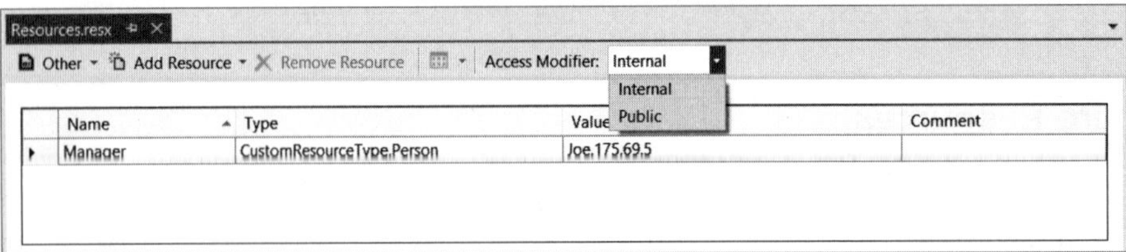

FIGURE 39-6

If you set the Access Modifier to Public, you can then access this resource from another assembly by prefixing the resource name with the assembly name. For example, in the following code the `MyPerson` resource is located in the `CustomResourceType` assembly:

```
Dim p As Person = CustomResourceType.My.Resources.MyPerson
```

ComponentResourceManager

In the first example in this chapter, after localization was turned on, a `ComponentResourceManager` object was used to retrieve resources associated with the form. The `ComponentResourceManager` extends the base `ResourceManager` by providing additional functionality for retrieving and applying component properties. Here are the original four lines required to set the properties defined for Button1:

```
Me.Button1.Location = New Point(71, 43)
Me.Button1.Size = New Size(185, 166)
Me.Button1.Text = "Button1"
Me.Button1.TabIndex = 0
```

Using the `ComponentResourceManager`, they can be condensed into just one line:

```
resources.ApplyResources(Me.Button1, "Button1")
```

In earlier versions of Visual Studio (that is, prior to 2010), the code generated when localization was turned on was more verbose. For each property, a separate call was made to the `ResourceManager` to retrieve it by name, as shown in this code snippet:

```
Me.Button1.Location = CType(resources.GetObject("Button1.Location"), Point)
Me.Button1.Size = CType(resources.GetObject("Button1.Size"), Size)
Me.Button1.TabIndex = CType(resources.GetObject("Button1.TabIndex"), Integer)
Me.Button1.Text = resources.GetString("Button1.Text")
```

You can still write this code because the `GetObject` method is still available on the `ComponentResourceManager`. The issue with writing this code is that each property that is going to be localized needs to be known at compile time. Because of this, every property on every control was added to the resource file. This added excess properties (even when they were no different from the default values) to the resource file. It also added huge overhead during the loading up of a form because each property was set via a resource property.

The ApplyResources method in the ComponentResourceManager class works in reverse. When you specify a control name, which must be unique on a form, all resources that start with that prefix are extracted. The full resource name is then used to determine the property to set on the control. For example, a resource with the name Button1.Location would be extracted for the control called Button1, and the value used to set the Location property on that control.

This process eliminates the need to have all properties specified in a resource file. It also allows culture resource files to specify additional properties that might not have been defined in the default resource file.

You might wonder whether any additional penalties exist in using the ComponentResourceManager. To set a property on a control using the name of the property, the ComponentResourceManager uses *reflection* to find the appropriate property. After it has been retrieved, it can be invoked. Each search done to set the property is relatively expensive. However, given the reduced number of properties to be set, the trade-off is definitely worthwhile because the application can easily be localized without recompilation of the main application.

CODING RESOURCE FILES

In addition to the rich visual tools that Visual Studio 2012 provides for editing resource files, you can use code to create resource files. The .NET Framework provides support for reading and writing resource files using two interfaces: IResourceReader and IResourceWriter. After the resource files have been created, they need to be added to the application or manually linked so that they can be referenced within the application.

- **IResource Reader:** The reader interface ensures that resource readers have the following methods:
  - **GetEnumerator:** The GetEnumerator method retrieves an IDictionaryEnumerator object that permits the developer to iterate over each of the resources in the resource file.
  - **Close:** The Close method is used to close the resource reader and release any associated resources.
- **IResource Writer:** The writer interface ensures that resource writers have the following methods:
  - **AddResource:** Three overloads to the AddResource method support adding resources to the resource file. Both of the framework implementations of this interface have either an additional overload of this method or an alternative method for adding resources. The overloads that are part of this interface support adding resources in a name-value pair. Each method has the resource name as the first parameter and a value, such as a string, byte array, or object, as the second parameter. The final implementation that takes an object as a parameter may need to be serializable or converted to a string via a type converter.
  - **Close:** The Close method writes resources out to the stream before closing it.
  - **Generate:** Unlike the Close method, the Generate method simply writes the resources out to the stream without closing it. When this method is called, any other method causes an exception to be raised.

ResourceReader and ResourceWriter

ResourceReader and ResourceWriter are an implementation of the IResource interfaces to support reading and writing directly to resources files. Although reading and writing to this format is the most direct approach because it reduces the need to use Resgen to generate the resources file, it does limit the quality of information that can be retrieved in reading from the file. Each resource is treated as a series of bytes where the type is unknown.

ResxResourceReader and ResxResourceWriter

ResxResourceReader and ResxResourceWriter are more versatile implementations of the IResource interfaces. In addition to supporting the IResource interface, ResxResourceWriter supports an additional overload of the `AddResource` method, whereby a ResxDataNode can be added. A ResxDataNode is similar to a dictionary entry because it has a key (in this case, the `Name` property) and a value (which you must set when the node is created). However, the difference is that this node can support additional properties such as a comment and, as an alternative to a value, a File reference (for example, one that indicates where an image needs to be added to a resource file).

As mentioned previously, you can add a File reference to a resx file so that the file is still editable, yet has the benefit of being compiled into the resource file by `resgen.exe`. The supporting class in the framework is `ResxFileRef`. This can be instantiated and added as a resource via the ResxResourceWriter. This inserts an XML node similar to the following snippet:

```
<data name="Figure_11_2" type="ResXFileRef, System.Windows.Forms">
<value>.\Resources\CompanyLogo.tif;System.Drawing.Bitmap, System.Drawing,
Version=4.0.0.0, Culture=neutral, PublicKeyToken=b03f5f7f11d50a3a</value>
</data>
```

> **WARNING** *Resource files are the best means to store static application data. Although they are linked in to the application as part of the compilation process, their contents can easily be extracted and made human-readable. Because of this, however, resource files are not suitable for storing secure data such as passwords and credit card information.*

CUSTOM RESOURCES

Although Visual Studio provides good support for international application development using resource files, at times it is not possible to get the level of control required using the default behavior. This section delves a little deeper into how you can serialize custom objects to the resource file and how you can generate designer files, which give you strongly typed accessor methods for resource files you have created.

Visual Studio 2012 enables you to store strings, images, icons, audio files, and other files within a resource file. You can do all this using the rich user interface provided. To store a more complex data type within a resource file, you need to serialize it into a string representation that can be included within the resource file.

The first step in adding any data type to a resource file is to make that data type serializable. You can do this easily by marking the class with the `Serializable` attribute. After it is marked as serializable, you can add the object to a resource file using an implementation of the IResourceWriter interface — for example, ResXResourceWriter:

VB

```
<Serializable()> _
Public Class Person
    Public Property Name As String
    Public Property Height As Integer
    Public Property Weight As Double
End Class
Dim p As New Person
p.Name = "Bob"
p.Height = 167
p.Weight = 69.5
```

```
Dim rWriter As New ResXResourceWriter("foo.resx")
rWriter.AddResource("DefaultPerson", p)
rWriter.Close()
```

C#

```
[Serializable()]
public class Person{
    public string Name { get; set; }
    public int Height { get; set; }
    public double Weight { get; set; }
}
var p = new Person(){
                Name = "Bob",
                Height = 167,
                Weight = 69.5};
var rWriter = new ResXResourceWriter("foo.resx");
rWriter.AddResource("DefaultPerson", p);
rWriter.Close();
```

However, serializing an object this way has a couple of drawbacks:

- You need to use code to write out this resource file before the build process so that the resource file can be included in the application. Clearly this is an administrative nightmare because it is an additional stage in the build process.
- Furthermore, the serialized representation of the class is a binary blob and is not human-readable. The assumption here is that what is written in the generating code is correct. Unfortunately, this is seldom the case, and it would be easier if the content could be human-readable within Visual Studio 2012.

A workaround for both of these issues is to define a TypeConverter for the class and use that to represent the class as a string. This way, the resource can be edited within the Visual Studio resource editor. TypeConverters provide a mechanism through which the framework can determine whether it is possible to represent a class (in this case a `Person` class) as a different type (in this case as a string). The first step is to create a TypeConverter using the ExpandableObjectConverter, as follows:

VB

```
Imports System.ComponentModel
Imports System.ComponentModel.Design.Serialization
Imports System.Globalization
Public Class PersonConverter
    Inherits ExpandableObjectConverter
    Public Overrides Function CanConvertFrom(ByVal context As _
                                            ITypeDescriptorContext, _
                                            ByVal t As Type) As Boolean
        If t Is GetType(String) Then Return True
        Return MyBase.CanConvertFrom(context, t)
    End Function
    Public Overrides Function ConvertFrom( _
                                ByVal context As ITypeDescriptorContext, _
                                ByVal info As CultureInfo, _
                                ByVal value As Object) As Object
        If (TypeOf (value) Is String) Then
            Try
                If value Is Nothing Then Return New Person()
                Dim vals = CStr(value).Split(","c)
                If vals.Length <> 3 Then Return New Person()
                Return New Person With {.Name = vals(0), _
                                        .Height = Integer.Parse(vals(1)), _
                                        .Weight = Double.Parse(vals(2))}
```

```
            Catch
                Throw New ArgumentException("Can not convert '" & _
                                                value.ToString & _
                                                "' to type Person")
            End Try
        End If
        Return MyBase.ConvertFrom(context, info, value)
    End Function
    Public Overrides Function ConvertTo(ByVal context As ITypeDescriptorContext, _
                                        ByVal culture As CultureInfo, _
                                        ByVal value As Object, _
                                        ByVal destType As Type) As Object
        If (destType Is GetType(String) And TypeOf (value) Is Person) Then
            Dim c = TryCast(value, Person)
            Return c.Name & "," & c.Height.ToString & "," & c.Weight.ToString
        End If
        Return MyBase.ConvertTo(context, culture, value, destType)
    End Function
End Class
```

C#

```
public class PersonConverter : ExpandableObjectConverter{
    public override bool CanConvertFrom(ITypeDescriptorContext context,
                                        Type t){
        if (typeof(string) == t) return true;
        return base.CanConvertFrom(context, t);
    }
    public override object ConvertFrom(ITypeDescriptorContext context,
                                       CultureInfo culture, object value){
        if (value is string){
            try{
                if (value == null) return new Person();
                var vals = (value as string).Split(',');
                if (vals.Length != 3) return new Person();
                return new Person{
                            Name = vals[0],
                            Height = int.Parse(vals[1]),
                            Weight = double.Parse(vals[2])
                        };
            }
            catch (Exception){
                throw new ArgumentException("Can not convert '" +
                                    value.ToString() + "' to type Person");
            }
        }

        return null;
    }

    public override object ConvertTo(ITypeDescriptorContext context,
                            CultureInfo culture, object value, Type destType){
        if (typeof(string) == destType && value is Person){
            var c = value as Person;
            return c.Name + "," + c.Height.ToString() + "," + c.Weight.ToString();
        }
        return base.ConvertTo(context, culture, value, destType);
    }
}
```

The class represented also needs to be attributed with the `TypeConverter` attribute:

VB

```
<System.ComponentModel.TypeConverter(GetType(PersonConverter))> _
<Serializable()> _
Public Class Person
    Public Property Name As String
    Public Property Height As Integer
    Public Property Weight As Double
End Class
```

C#

```
[System.ComponentModel.TypeConverter(typeof(PersonConverter))]
[Serializable()]
public class Person{
    public string Name { get; set; }
    public int Height { get; set; }
    public double Weight { get; set; }
}
```

Now you can add this item to a resource file using the string representation of the class. For example, an entry in the resx file might look like this:

```
<assembly alias="CustomResourceType" name="CustomResourceType, Version=1.0.0.0,
Culture=neutral, PublicKeyToken=null" />
<data name="Manager" type="CustomResourceType.Person, CustomResourceType">
<value>Joe,175,69.5</value>
</data>
```

> **NOTE** *Creating custom resource types is a difficult process because Visual Studio 2012 doesn't refresh your* `TypeConverter` *after it has been loaded the first time. You can either strongly name the assembly in which the* `TypeConverter` *is located and increment the version number each time you change it, or you must restart Visual Studio for the changes to take effect.*

SUMMARY

This chapter demonstrated how important XML resource files are in building an application that can both access static data and be readily localized into foreign languages and cultures. The rich user interface provided by Visual Studio 2012 enables you to easily add resources such as images, icons, strings, audio files, and other files to an application.

The built-in support for localizing forms and generating satellite assemblies empowers developers to write applications that can target a global market. You have also seen that the user interface provided within Visual Studio 2012 is extensible, meaning that you can modify it to interact with your own custom resource types.

PART IX
Debugging

Using the Debugging Windows

WHAT'S IN THIS CHAPTER?

- Learning basic debugging concepts in Visual Studio, including breakpoints and DataTips
- Understanding the debugging windows in Visual Studio
- Using and unwinding exceptions during a debug session

Debugging an application is one of the more challenging tasks developers must tackle, but correct use of the Visual Studio 2012 debugging windows can help you analyze the state of the application and determine the cause of any bugs. This chapter examines the numerous windows available in Visual Studio 2012 to support you in building and debugging applications.

THE CODE WINDOW

The most important window for debugging purposes is the code window. With the capability to set breakpoints and step through code, this window is the starting point for almost all debugging activities. Figure 40-1 shows a simple snippet of code with both a breakpoint and the current execution point visible.

Customer.cs
DebugApp.Customer | CustomerName

```
        private string mCustomerName;

        public string CustomerName
        {
            get
            {
                return mCustomerName;
            }                        mCustomerName - "Dante Hicks"
            set
            {
                mCustomerName = value;
            }
        }
```

100 %

FIGURE 40-1

Breakpoints

The first stage in debugging an application is usually to identify the area causing the error by setting a breakpoint and gradually stepping through the code. The next chapter covers in detail setting breakpoints and working with the current execution point. Breakpoints are marked in the code window with a red dot in the margin of the page and a colored highlighting of the code itself.

When a breakpoint is encountered, the current execution point is marked with a yellow arrow in the margin, and the actual code is also highlighted in yellow. As discussed in the next chapter, this marker can be dragged forward and backward to control the order of execution. However, you should do this judiciously because it modifies the behavior of the application.

DataTips

After hitting a breakpoint, the application is paused, or is in Debug Mode. In this mode, you can retrieve information about current variables simply by hovering your mouse over the variable name. Figure 40-1 shows that the value of the `mCustomerName` variable is currently "Dante Hicks." This debugging tooltip is commonly referred to as a Data Tip and you can use it to view not only the values of simple types, such as strings and integers, but also to drill down and inspect more complex object types, such as those made up of multiple nested classes.

> **NOTE** *DataTips are used to both query and edit the value of a variable.*

In Chapter 42, "DataTips, Debug Proxies, and Visualizers," you'll learn how the layout of this DataTip can be customized using type proxies and type visualizers.

THE BREAKPOINTS WINDOW

When debugging a complex issue, you can set numerous breakpoints to isolate the problem. Unfortunately, this has two side effects. One, the execution of the application is hampered because you have to continually press F5 to resume execution. Two, and more significantly, the execution of the application is slowed considerably by the presence of conditional breakpoints, which enable you to specify an expression that is executed to determine if the application should be paused. The more complex the breakpoint conditions are, the slower the application will run. Because these breakpoints can be scattered through multiple source files, it becomes difficult to locate and remove breakpoints that are no longer required.

The Breakpoints window, as shown in Figure 40-2, is accessible via Debug ⇨ Windows ⇨ Breakpoints and provides a useful summary of all the breakpoints currently set within the application. Using this window, breakpoints can easily be navigated to, disabled, and removed.

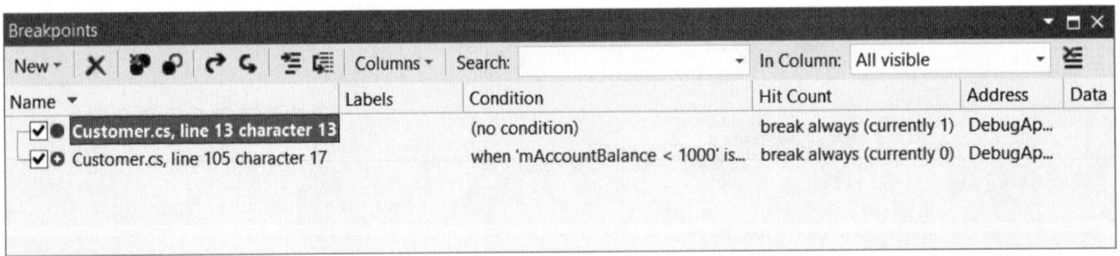

FIGURE 40-2

Two currently active breakpoints are in the `Customer.cs` file (refer to Figure 40-2). The first is a regular breakpoint with no conditions. This condition is in bold because the application is currently in Break mode at that breakpoint. The second breakpoint has a condition whereby the application will break only if the `mAccountBalance` variable has a value less than 1000.

The Breakpoints window, like most other debugging windows, is made up of two regions: the toolbar and the breakpoint list. Several functions are available on the toolbar in Visual Studio 2012, including search, import, and export of breakpoints. These functions are explained further in Chapter 41.

Each item in the breakpoint list is represented by a check box that indicates whether or not the breakpoint is enabled, an icon and breakpoint descriptor, and any number of columns that show properties of the breakpoint. The columns can be adjusted using the Columns drop-down from the toolbar. You can set additional breakpoint properties by right-clicking the appropriate breakpoint and choosing the desired option from the context menu.

THE OUTPUT WINDOW

One of the first debugging windows you encounter when you run your application is the Output window. By default, the Output window appears every time you build your application and shows the build progress. Figure 40-3 shows the successful build of a sample solution. The final line of the Output window indicates a summary of the build, which in this case indicates three successfully built projects. In the output there is also a summary of the warnings and errors encountered during the build. In this case there were no errors or warnings. Although the Output window can be useful if for some reason the build fails unexpectedly, most of the time the errors and warnings are reported in the Error List.

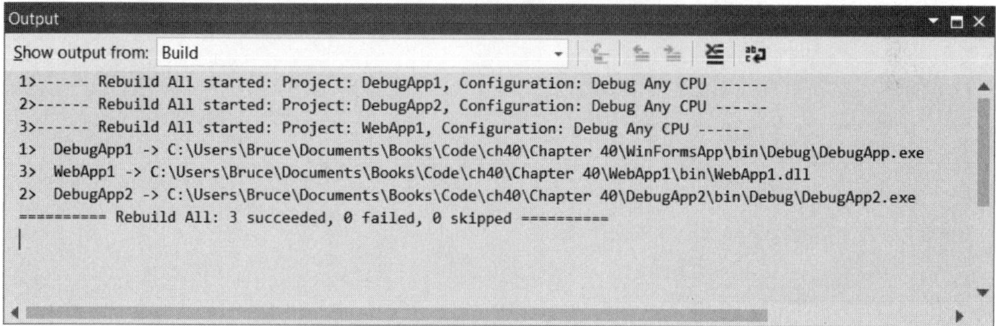

FIGURE 40-3

> **NOTE** *Observant readers might notice a subtle change between the output in Visual Studio 2012 as compared to earlier versions. Specifically, the build for each of the projects is performed in parallel instead of in sequence. That's the reason why you see three Build Started messages followed by three completion messages.*

The Output window has a secondary role as the standard output while the application runs. You can use the drop-down on the left of the toolbar to toggle between output sources. Figure 40-3 shows the output of the build, but as you perform other activities in Visual Studio, additional entries are created in the drop-down list. For example, when you run your application in Debug mode, Visual Studio creates an entry called Debug, which displays any messages that either the run time or your code has emitted using `Debug.Write` or `Debug.WriteLine`. Likewise, a Refactor entry is created to show the results of any recent refactoring operation that was performed.

> **NOTE** *The output from external tools such as* `.bat` *and* `.com` *files that are executed through Visual Studio (as External Tools) is normally displayed in the Command window. The output from these tools can also be displayed in the Output window by setting the Use Output Window option in the Tools ➪ External Tools dialog box.*

The other icons on the toolbar, in order from left to right, enable you to navigate to the source of a build message, go to the previous message, go to the next message, clear the window contents, and toggle word wrapping for the Output window.

THE IMMEDIATE WINDOW

Often when you write code or debug your application, you want to evaluate a simple expression either to test a bit of functionality or to remind yourself of how something works. This is where the Immediate window (Debug ➪ Windows ➪ Immediate) comes in handy. This window enables you to run expressions as you type them. Figure 40-4 shows a number of statements — from basic assignment and print operations to more advanced object creation and manipulation.

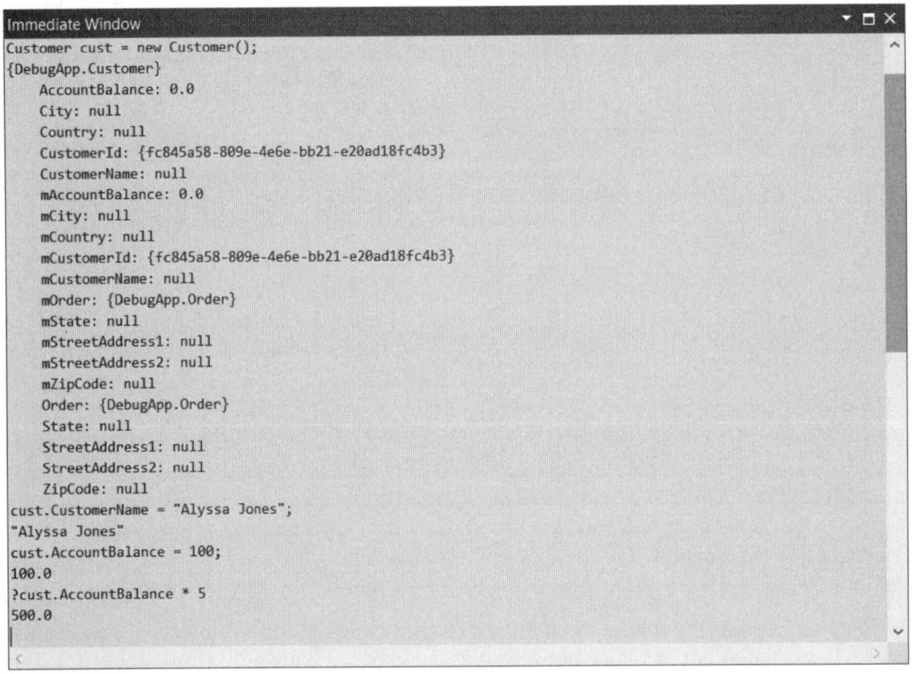

```
Immediate Window
Customer cust = new Customer();
{DebugApp.Customer}
    AccountBalance: 0.0
    City: null
    Country: null
    CustomerId: {fc845a58-809e-4e6e-bb21-e20ad18fc4b3}
    CustomerName: null
    mAccountBalance: 0.0
    mCity: null
    mCountry: null
    mCustomerId: {fc845a58-809e-4e6e-bb21-e20ad18fc4b3}
    mCustomerName: null
    mOrder: {DebugApp.Order}
    mState: null
    mStreetAddress1: null
    mStreetAddress2: null
    mZipCode: null
    Order: {DebugApp.Order}
    State: null
    StreetAddress1: null
    StreetAddress2: null
    ZipCode: null
cust.CustomerName = "Alyssa Jones";
"Alyssa Jones"
cust.AccountBalance = 100;
100.0
?cust.AccountBalance * 5
500.0
```

FIGURE 40-4

A `Customer` object is created in a C# project within the Immediate window (refer to Figure 40-4). Within a Visual Basic project, you can't do explicit variable declaration (for example, Dim x as Integer). Instead it is done implicitly using the assignment operator.

One of the more useful features of the Immediate window is that you can use it while you write code. When you create objects in the Immediate window at design time, it invokes the constructor and creates an instance of that object without running the rest of your application.

If you invoke a method or property that contains an active breakpoint, Visual Studio changes to Debug mode and breaks at the breakpoint. This is especially useful if you work on a particular method that you want to test without running the entire application.

The Immediate window supports a limited form of IntelliSense, and you can use the arrow keys to track back through the history of previous commands executed.

> **NOTE** *IntelliSense is supported only in the Immediate window when running in Debug mode, not during design-time debugging.*

The Immediate window also enables you to execute Visual Studio commands. To submit a command, you must enter a greater than symbol (>) at the start of the line. There is an extremely large set of commands available; almost any action that can be performed within Visual Studio is accessible as a command. Fortunately, IntelliSense makes navigating this list of available commands more manageable.

There is also a set of approximately 100 predefined aliases for commands. One of the more well-known aliases is `?`, which is a shortcut for the `Debug.Print` command that prints out the value of a variable. You can see the full list of predefined aliases by entering `>alias`, as shown in Figure 40-5.

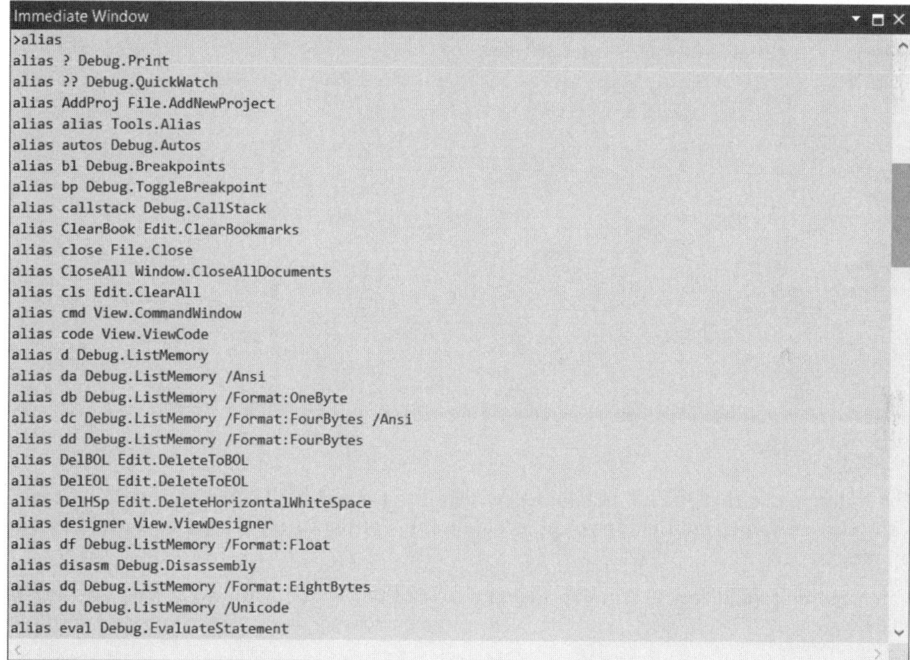

FIGURE 40-5

THE WATCH WINDOWS

Earlier in this chapter you saw how to use DataTips in the code window to examine the content of a variable by hovering the mouse over a variable name. When the structure of the object is more complex, it becomes difficult to navigate the values using just the DataTip. Visual Studio 2012 has a series of Watch windows that display variables, providing an easy-to-use interface for drilling down into the structure.

QuickWatch

The QuickWatch window (Debug ➪ QuickWatch) is a modal dialog that you can launch by right-clicking the code window. Whatever you select in the code window is inserted into the Expression field of the dialog, as shown in Figure 40-6, where a `Customer` object is visible. Previous expressions you have evaluated appear in the drop-down associated with the Expression field.

FIGURE 40-6

The layout of the Value tree in the QuickWatch window is similar to the DataTip. Each row shows the variable name, the current value, and the type of object. The value of the variable can be adjusted by typing in the Value column.

Use the Add Watch button to add the current expression to one of the Watch windows. These are variables to be continuously watched.

Watch Windows 1–4

Unlike the QuickWatch window, which is modal and shows a variable value at a particular execution point, you can use the Watch windows to monitor a variable value as you step through your code. Although there are four Watch windows, a single window is sufficient in most cases. Having four separate windows means that you can have different sets of variables in the different windows, which might be useful if you work through a more complex issue that involves multiple classes.

Figure 40-7 shows an `Order` and `Customer` class in a Watch window (Debug ➪ Windows ➪ Watch 1 to Watch 4). Similar to both the QuickWatch window and the DataTips discussed previously, you can use the user interface to drill down into more complex data types.

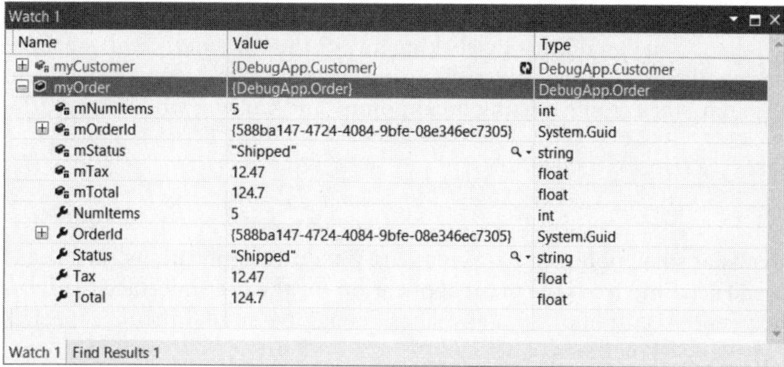

Watch 1

Name	Value	Type
myCustomer	{DebugApp.Customer}	DebugApp.Customer
myOrder	{DebugApp.Order}	DebugApp.Order
mNumItems	5	int
mOrderId	{588ba147-4724-4084-9bfe-08e346ec7305}	System.Guid
mStatus	"Shipped"	string
mTax	12.47	float
mTotal	124.7	float
NumItems	5	int
OrderId	{588ba147-4724-4084-9bfe-08e346ec7305}	System.Guid
Status	"Shipped"	string
Tax	12.47	float
Total	124.7	float

Watch 1 | Find Results 1

FIGURE 40-7

Additional variables to be watched can be added either by typing into the Name column on an empty line or by right-clicking the variable in the code window and selecting Add Watch from the context menu.

Autos and Locals

The Autos and Locals windows are two special Watch windows in which the variables are automatically added by the debugger. The Autos window (Debug ➪ Windows ➪ Autos) contains variables that are used in the current, preceding, and future lines of code. Similarly, the Locals window (Debug ➪ Windows ➪ Locals) shows all variables used in the current method. Other than being automatically generated, these windows behave the same as the Watch windows.

THE CODE EXECUTION WINDOWS

In addition to inspecting the contents of variables during a debugging session, it is essential that you carefully evaluate the logic of your code to ensure that everything executes in the order that you expect. Visual Studio 2012 has a group of debugger windows that show exactly what was loaded and being executed at the time you paused the program execution. This allows you to better understand the run-time behavior of your source code and quickly track down logic errors.

Call Stack

As applications grow in complexity, it is quite common for the execution path to become difficult to follow. The use of deep inheritance trees and interfaces can often obscure the execution path. This is where the call stack is useful. Each path of execution must have a finite number of entries on the stack (unless a cyclic pattern emerges, in which case a stack overflow is inevitable). The stack can be viewed using the Call Stack window (Debug ➪ Windows ➪ Call Stack), as shown in Figure 40-8.

Call Stack

Name	Language
DebugApp.exe!DebugApp.Order.Order() Line 12	C#
DebugApp.exe!DebugApp.Customer.createOrder() Line 19 + 0x15 bytes	C#
DebugApp.exe!DebugApp.Customer.Customer() Line 14 + 0xe bytes	C#
DebugApp.exe!DebugApp.Form1.button1_Click(object sender, System.EventArgs e) Line 41 + 0x15 bytes	C#
[External Code]	
DebugApp.exe!DebugApp.Program.Main() Line 19 + 0x1d bytes	C#
[External Code]	

FIGURE 40-8

Using the Call Stack window, it is easy to navigate up the execution path to determine from where the current executing method is being called. You can do this by clicking any of the rows in the call stack, which are known as frames. Other options available from the call stack, using the right-click context menu, enable viewing the disassembler for a particular stack frame, setting breakpoints, and varying what information displays.

Threads

Most applications use multiple threads at some point. In particular for Windows applications, you need to run time-consuming tasks on a thread separate from the main application for the user interface to always appear responsive. Of course, concurrent execution of threads makes debugging more difficult, especially when the threads access the same classes and methods.

Figure 40-9 shows the Threads window (Debug ➪ Windows ➪ Threads), which lists all the active threads for a particular application. Notice that in addition to the threads created in the code, the debugger has created additional background threads. For simplicity, the threads used by this application, including the main user interface thread, have been given names so that they can easily be distinguished.

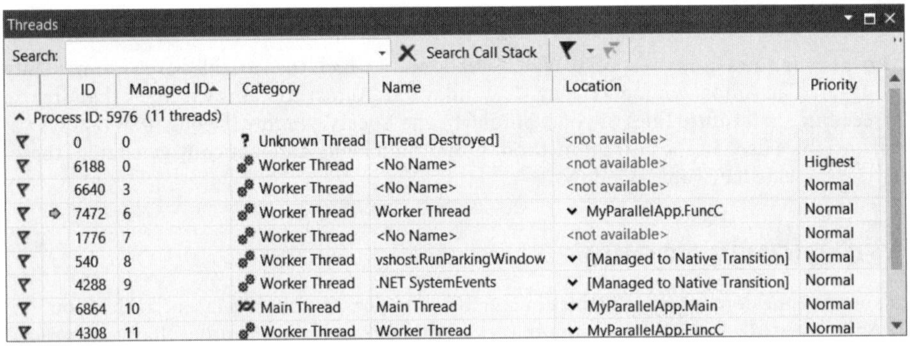

Threads

Search: | Search Call Stack

ID	Managed ID	Category	Name	Location	Priority
Process ID: 5976 (11 threads)					
0	0	Unknown Thread	[Thread Destroyed]	<not available>	
6188	0	Worker Thread	<No Name>	<not available>	Highest
6640	3	Worker Thread	<No Name>	<not available>	Normal
7472	6	Worker Thread	Worker Thread	MyParallelApp.FuncC	Normal
1776	7	Worker Thread	<No Name>	<not available>	Normal
540	8	Worker Thread	vshost.RunParkingWindow	[Managed to Native Transition]	Normal
4288	9	Worker Thread	.NET SystemEvents	[Managed to Native Transition]	Normal
6864	10	Main Thread	Main Thread	MyParallelApp.Main	Normal
4308	11	Worker Thread	Worker Thread	MyParallelApp.FuncC	Normal

FIGURE 40-9

The Threads window shows an arrow next to the thread currently viewed in the code window. To navigate to another thread, simply double-click that thread to bring the current location of that thread into view in the code window and update the call stack to reflect the new thread.

In Break mode, all threads of an application are paused. However, when you step through your code with the debugger, the next statement to be executed may or may not be on the same thread you are interested in. If you are interested only in the execution path of a single thread, and the execution of other threads can be suspended, right-click the thread in the Threads window, and select Freeze from the context menu. To resume the suspended thread, select Thaw from the same menu.

Debugging multithreaded applications is explained further in Chapter 44, "Advanced Debugging Techniques."

Modules

The Modules window (Debug ➪ Windows ➪ Modules), as shown in Figure 40-10, displays a list of assemblies referenced by the running application. Those assemblies that make up the application can also have debugging symbols loaded, which means that they can be debugged without dropping into the disassembler. This window is particularly useful if you want to find the version of an assembly currently loaded and where it has been loaded from.

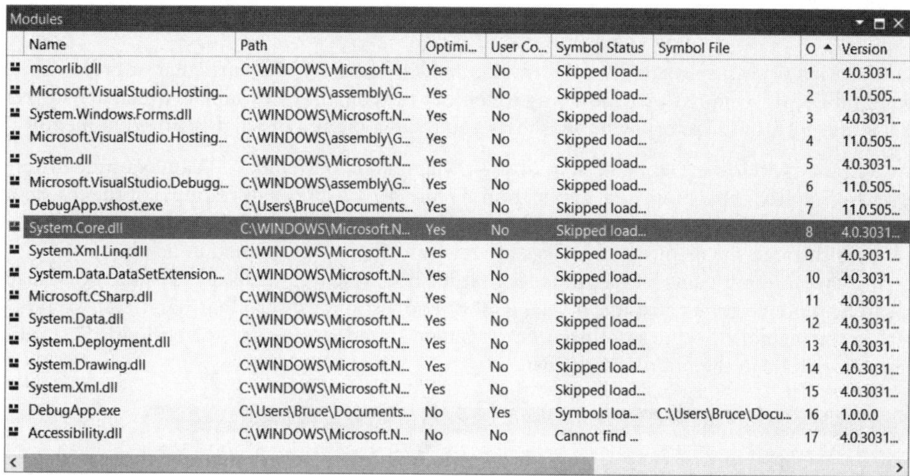

Name	Path	Optimi...	User Co...	Symbol Status	Symbol File	O	Version
mscorlib.dll	C:\WINDOWS\Microsoft.N...	Yes	No	Skipped load...		1	4.0.3031...
Microsoft.VisualStudio.Hosting...	C:\WINDOWS\assembly\G...	Yes	No	Skipped load...		2	11.0.505...
System.Windows.Forms.dll	C:\WINDOWS\Microsoft.N...	Yes	No	Skipped load...		3	4.0.3031...
Microsoft.VisualStudio.Hosting...	C:\WINDOWS\assembly\G...	Yes	No	Skipped load...		4	11.0.505...
System.dll	C:\WINDOWS\Microsoft.N...	Yes	No	Skipped load...		5	4.0.3031...
Microsoft.VisualStudio.Debugg...	C:\WINDOWS\assembly\G...	Yes	No	Skipped load...		6	11.0.505...
DebugApp.vshost.exe	C:\Users\Bruce\Documents...	Yes	No	Skipped load...		7	11.0.505...
System.Core.dll	C:\WINDOWS\Microsoft.N...	Yes	No	Skipped load...		8	4.0.3031...
System.Xml.Linq.dll	C:\WINDOWS\Microsoft.N...	Yes	No	Skipped load...		9	4.0.3031...
System.Data.DataSetExtension...	C:\WINDOWS\Microsoft.N...	Yes	No	Skipped load...		10	4.0.3031...
Microsoft.CSharp.dll	C:\WINDOWS\Microsoft.N...	Yes	No	Skipped load...		11	4.0.3031...
System.Data.dll	C:\WINDOWS\Microsoft.N...	Yes	No	Skipped load...		12	4.0.3031...
System.Deployment.dll	C:\WINDOWS\Microsoft.N...	Yes	No	Skipped load...		13	4.0.3031...
System.Drawing.dll	C:\WINDOWS\Microsoft.N...	Yes	No	Skipped load...		14	4.0.3031...
System.Xml.dll	C:\WINDOWS\Microsoft.N...	Yes	No	Skipped load...		15	4.0.3031...
DebugApp.exe	C:\Users\Bruce\Documents...	No	Yes	Symbols loa...	C:\Users\Bruce\Docu...	16	1.0.0.0
Accessibility.dll	C:\WINDOWS\Microsoft.N...	No	No	Cannot find ...		17	4.0.3031...

FIGURE 40-10

The symbols have been loaded for the `DebugApp.exe` application (refer to Figure 40-10). All the other assemblies have been skipped because they contain no user code and are optimized. If an appropriate symbol file is available, you can load it for an assembly via the Load Symbols option from the right-click context menu.

Processes

Building multitier applications can be quite complex, and you often need to have all the tiers running. To do this, Visual Studio 2012 can start multiple projects at the same stage, enabling true end-to-end debugging. Alternatively, you can attach to other processes to debug running applications. Each time Visual Studio attaches to a process, that process is added to the list in the Processes window (Debug ➪ Windows ➪ Processes). Figure 40-11 shows a solution containing two Windows applications and a web application.

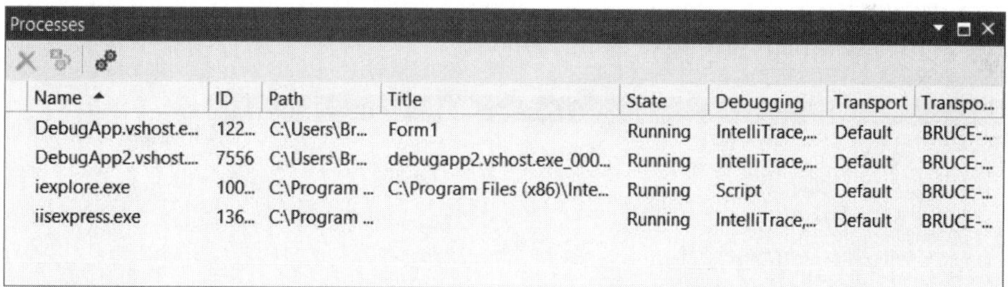

Name	ID	Path	Title	State	Debugging	Transport	Transpo...
DebugApp.vshost.e...	122...	C:\Users\Br...	Form1	Running	IntelliTrace,...	Default	BRUCE-...
DebugApp2.vshost....	7556	C:\Users\Br...	debugapp2.vshost.exe_000...	Running	IntelliTrace,...	Default	BRUCE-...
iexplore.exe	100...	C:\Program ...	C:\Program Files (x86)\Inte...	Running	Script	Default	BRUCE-...
iisexpress.exe	136...	C:\Program ...		Running	IntelliTrace,...	Default	BRUCE-...

FIGURE 40-11

The toolbar at the top of the Processes window enables you to detach or terminate a process that is currently attached or attach to another process.

THE MEMORY WINDOWS

The next three windows are typically used for low-level debugging when all other alternatives have been exhausted. Stepping into memory locations, using a disassembler, or looking at Registry values requires a lot of background knowledge and patience to analyze and make use of the information presented. Only in rare cases while developing managed code would you be required to perform debugging at such a low level.

Memory Windows 1–4

You can use the four Memory windows to view the raw contents of memory at a particular address. Whereas the Watch, Autos, and Locals windows provide a way to look at the content of variables, which are stored at specific locations in memory, the Memory window shows you the big picture of what is stored in memory.

Each of the four Memory windows (Debug ➪ Windows ➪ Memory 1 to Memory 4) can examine different memory addresses to simplify debugging your application. Figure 40-12 shows an example of the information that displays when using this window. You can use the scrollbar on the right of the window to navigate forward or backward through the memory addresses to view information contained in neighboring addresses. The only caveat about using the scrollbar is that it's not typical in its usage. The memory space for a computer can be quite large. As a result, if the memory had a standard scrollbar handle, it would be easy to get "lost" in the memory. So the scrollbar in the Memory windows uses a "spring-loaded" scrollbar that always keeps the handle in the middle of the list.

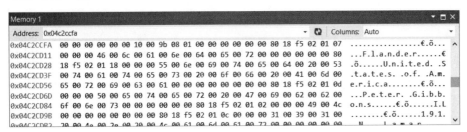

```
Memory 1
Address: 0x04c2ccfa                                    Columns: Auto
0x04C2CCFA  00 00 00 00 00 00 10 00 9b 08 01 00 00 00 00 00 00 80 18 f5 02 01 07  .................€.õ...
0x04C2CD11  00 00 00 46 00 6c 00 61 00 6e 00 64 00 65 00 72 00 00 00 00 00 00 80  ...F.l.a.n.d.e.r......€
0x04C2CD28  18 f5 02 01 18 00 00 00 55 00 6e 00 69 00 74 00 65 00 64 00 20 00 53  .õ......U.n.i.t.e.d. .S
0x04C2CD3F  00 74 00 61 00 74 00 65 00 73 00 20 00 6f 00 66 00 20 00 41 00 6d 00  .t.a.t.e.s. .o.f. .A.m.
0x04C2CD56  65 00 72 00 69 00 63 00 61 00 00 00 00 00 00 00 00 80 18 f5 02 01 0d  e.r.i.c.a........€.õ...
0x04C2CD6D  00 00 00 50 00 65 00 74 00 65 00 72 00 20 00 47 00 69 00 62 00 62 00  ...P.e.t.e.r. .G.i.b.b.
0x04C2CD84  6f 00 6e 00 73 00 00 00 00 00 00 80 18 f5 02 01 02 00 00 00 49 00 4c  o.n.s......€.õ......I.L
0x04C2CD9B  00 00 00 00 00 00 00 00 80 18 f5 02 01 0c 00 00 00 31 00 39 00 31 00  ........€.õ......1.9.1.
```

FIGURE 40-12

Disassembly

Interesting debates arise periodically over the relative performance of two different code blocks. Occasionally this discussion devolves to talking about which MSIL instructions are used, and why one code block is faster because it generates one fewer instruction. Clearly, if you call that code block millions of times, disassembly might give your application a significant benefit. However, more often than not, a bit of high-level refactoring saves more time and involves less arguing. Figure 40-13 shows the Disassembly window (Debug ➪ Windows ➪ Disassembly) where a variable is written to the console from within a Button click. You can see MSIL instructions that make up this action.

```
Disassembly
Address: DebugApp.Form1.button1_Click(object, System.EventArgs)
Viewing Options
00000209  call     dword ptr ds:[089BC574h]
0000020f  mov      dword ptr [ebp-44h],eax
00000212  mov      eax,dword ptr [ebp-44h]
00000215  mov      dword ptr [ebp-24h],eax

            MessageBox.Show(myCustomer.CustomerName);
00000218  mov      eax,dword ptr [ebp-1Ch]
0000021b  mov      eax,dword ptr [eax+0000013Ch]
00000221  mov      dword ptr [ebp-48h],eax
00000224  push     5
00000226  push     48h
00000228  mov      ecx,3Eh
0000022d  mov      edx,74h
00000232  call     FE9D8170
00000237  mov      ecx,dword ptr [ebp-48h]
0000023a  cmp      dword ptr [ecx],ecx
0000023c  call     dword ptr ds:[089BC49Ch]
00000242  mov      dword ptr [ebp-4Ch],eax
00000245  push     5
00000247  push     3Fh
00000249  mov      ecx,3Eh
0000024e  mov      edx,79h
```

FIGURE 40-13

A breakpoint has been set on the call to the constructor, and the execution point is at this breakpoint (refer to Figure 40-13). While still in this window, you can step through the lines of MSIL and review what instructions are executed.

Registers

Using the Disassembly window to step through MSIL instructions can become difficult to follow as different information is loaded, moved, and compared using a series of registers. The Registers window (Debug ⇨ Windows ⇨ Registers), as shown in Figure 40-14, enables the contents of the various registers to be monitored. Changes in a register value are highlighted in red, making it easy to see what happens as each line steps through in the Disassembly window.

```
Registers
EAX = 04C2CE3C EBX = 04C2ADC4 ECX = 7E9C9000 EDX = 09513960 ESI = 04C1FCDC EDI = 0AAEE6D0
EIP = 09FF6548 ESP = 0AAEE68C EBP = 0AAEE6D8 EFL = 00000246

0AAEE6BC = 04C1FCDC
```

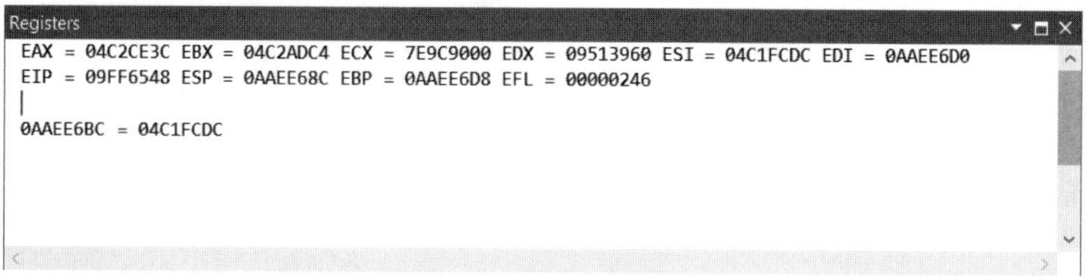

FIGURE 40-14

INTELLITRACE (ULTIMATE EDITION ONLY)

One of the more interesting features in the Ultimate edition of Visual Studio is IntelliTrace. One of the limitations of traditional debuggers is that they show only a snapshot of the state of the application at a single point in time. The IntelliTrace feature of Visual Studio collects information during the debugging session, thereby allowing you to go back to an earlier point and view the application state at that time. And with Visual Studio 2012, Microsoft introduces a standalone data collector for IntelliTrace. This collector enables the data used by IntelliTrace to be gathered on machines where Visual Studio is not installed (such as a production machine). Even better, the installation of the data collector can be done by simply copying a file onto the machine. However, data collected in this manner must be moved back to a system with Visual Studio (and the source code and PDB files) before it can be read.

> **NOTE** *You can think of IntelliTrace as your black box flight recorder for debugging.*

IntelliTrace has two data collection levels. By default it collects information about diagnostic events only, such as entering Break mode, stepping through code in the debugger, or when an exception is thrown. You can also configure IntelliTrace to collect detailed information, such as the details of every function call, including the parameters passed to that function and the values that were returned.

The IntelliTrace Events window (Debug ⇨ Windows ⇨ IntelliTrace Events) as shown in Figure 40-15, enables you to navigate to past diagnostic events. When you click a past event, the execution point in the code window changes from a yellow arrow to a red arrow with a stopwatch icon. The call stack is also updated to reflect the historical state of the application.

IntelliTrace
Switch to IntelliTrace Calls View
All Categories | All Threads
Search
Exception: Thrown: "The message filter indicated that the application is busy.
Exception: Caught: "The message filter indicated that the application is busy.
Debugger: Beginning of Application: Main, Program.cs line 16
Gesture: Clicked "button1" (Button)
Debugger: Breakpoint Hit: createOrder, Customer.cs line 27
User Prompt: Displayed "" (MessageBox)
User Prompt: Clicked "OK"
Live Event: Breakpoint Hit: button1_Click, Form1.cs line 57

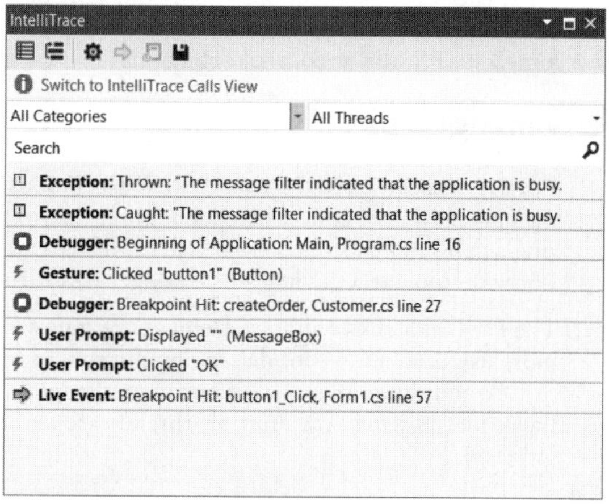

FIGURE 40-15

If you have enabled the detailed data collection level, you can use the Autos and Locals windows to inspect the contents of variables that have been collected.

You can change the data collection level or disable it completely from the IntelliTrace tab in the options menu (Tools ➪ Options). You can also configure IntelliTrace to exclude certain assemblies from the data collection.

> **WARNING** *You can expect a reasonable performance impact if you enable the detailed data collection level. You must also ensure that you have enough free disk space to collect this data. The Edit and Continue functionality is also disabled for the detailed level.*

THE PARALLEL DEBUGGING WINDOWS

Nowadays it is almost impossible to purchase a new computer that has a single processor. The trend to include multiple CPUs, which has been necessary due to physical limitations that have been reached in CPU architecture, will certainly continue into the future as the primary way for hardware vendors to release faster computers.

Unfortunately, software that has not been written to explicitly run on multiple CPUs does not run faster on a many-core machine. This is a problem for many users who have been conditioned over the past couple of decades to expect their applications to run faster when they upgrade to newer hardware.

The solution is to ensure that your applications can execute different code paths concurrently on multiple CPUs. The traditional approach is to develop software using multiple threads or processes. Unfortunately, writing and debugging multithreaded applications is difficult and error-prone, even for an experienced developer.

Visual Studio 2012 and .NET Framework version 4.5 include a number of features aimed to simplify the act of writing such software. The Task Parallel Library (TPL) is a set of extensions to the .NET Framework to provide this functionality. The TPL includes language constructs, such as the `Parallel.For` and `Parallel.ForEach` loops, and collections specifically designed for concurrent access, including `ConcurrentDictionary` and `ConcurrentQueue`.

In the `System.Threading.Tasks` namespace are several classes that greatly simplify the effort involved in writing multithreaded and asynchronous code. The `Task` class is similar to a thread; however, it is more lightweight and therefore performs much better at run time.

Writing parallel applications is only one part of the overall development life cycle — you also need effective tools for debugging parallel applications. To that end Visual Studio 2012 includes two debugging windows aimed specifically at parallel debugging — the Parallel Stacks window and the Parallel Tasks window.

Parallel Stacks

Recall from earlier in the chapter that you can use the Call Stacks window to view the execution path of the current line of code when debugging. One of the limitations of this window is that you can see only a single call stack at a time. To see the call stack of other threads, you must use the Threads window or Debug Location toolbar to switch the debugger to a different thread.

The Parallel Stacks window (Debug ➪ Windows ➪ Parallel Stacks), as shown in Figure 40-16, is one of the more useful windows for debugging multithreaded and parallelized applications. It provides not just a way to view multiple call stacks at once but also provides a graphical visualization of the code execution, including showing how multiple threads are tied together and the execution paths that they share.

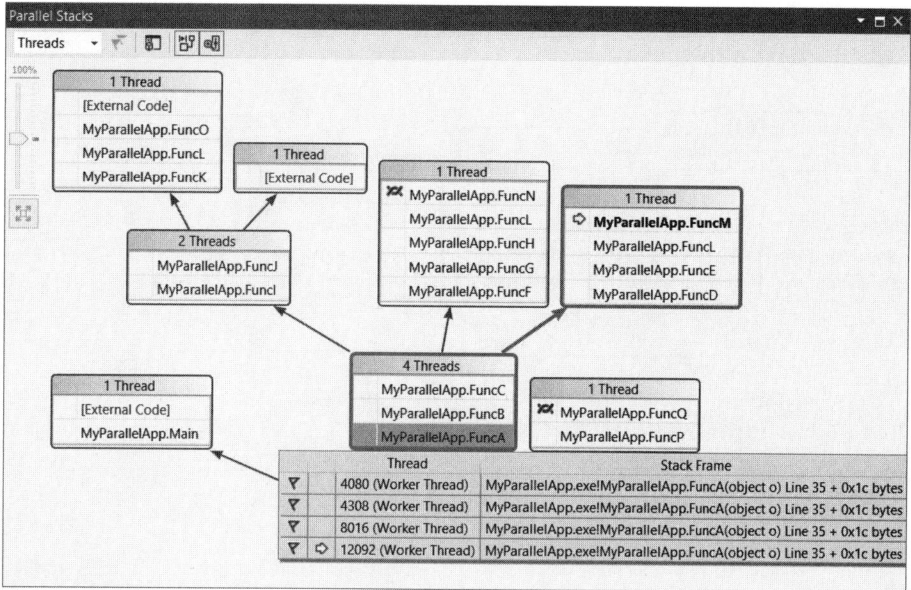

FIGURE 40-16

The Parallel Stacks window in Figure 40-16 shows an application currently executing multiple threads. The call graph is read from bottom to top. The Main thread appears in one box, and the other threads are grouped together in different boxes. The reason for these threads being grouped is because they share the same call stack (that is, each thread called `FuncA`, which then called `FuncB`, which in turn called `FuncC`). After these threads execute `FuncC`, their code paths diverge. One thread executes `FuncD`, which then calls `FuncE`, `FuncL`, and `FuncM`. A different thread executes `FuncF`, `FuncG`, `FuncH`, `FuncL`, and `FuncN`. The other two threads execute `FuncI`, which call `FuncJ`, and so on. You can see how visualizing all the call stacks at once provides a much better understanding on the state of the application as a whole and what has led to this state, rather than just the history of an individual thread.

A number of other icons are used on this screen. The execution point of the current thread is shown with a yellow arrow. This is against `FuncM` in a box on the right side of the diagram (refer to Figure 40-16). Each box that the current thread has progressed through as part of its execution path is highlighted in blue. The wavy lines (also known as the cloth thread icon) shown against the call to an anonymous method in `FuncQ` in the bottom-right box indicates that this is the current execution point of a noncurrent thread.

You can hover over the thread count label at the top of each box to see the Thread IDs of the applicable threads. You can also right-click any entry in a call stack to access various functions such as navigating to the applicable line of source code in the code editor or switching the visualization to a different thread.

If you work with an application that uses numerous threads or tasks, or has a deep call stack, you may find that the Parallel Stacks call graph visualization does not fit in the one window. In this case you can click the icon in the bottom-right corner of the window to display a thumbnail view, which enables you to easily pan around the visualization. You can see this in Figure 40-17.

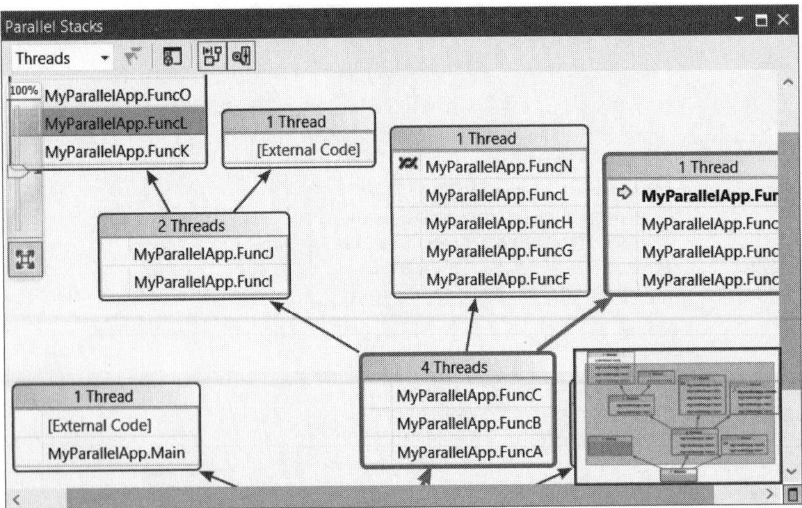

FIGURE 40-17

Parallel Tasks

At the beginning of this section the Task Parallel Library was introduced, which includes the `Task` class found in `System.Threading.Tasks` and the `Parallel.For` loops. The Parallel Tasks window (Debug ➪ Windows ➪ Parallel Tasks), as shown in Figure 40-18, assists you in debugging applications that use these features by displaying a list with the state of all the current tasks.

Parallel Tasks

		ID	Status	Location	Task	Thread Assignment	AppDomain	Process
⚑		1	Blocked	MyParallelApp.FuncM	FuncA	12092 (Worker Thre	1 (MyParallel	7576
⚑	➪	2	Active	MyParallelApp.FuncR	FuncA	4080 (Worker Threa	1 (MyParallel	7576
⚑		3	Blocked	MyParallelApp.FuncJ	FuncA	8016 (Worker Threa	1 (MyParallel	7576
⚑		4	Active	MyParallelApp.FuncR	FuncA	4308 (Worker Threa	1 (MyParallel	7576
⚑		6	Active	MyParallelApp.FuncR.A	FuncR.Ar	11044 (Worker Thre	1 (MyParallel	7576
⚑		7	Active	MyParallelApp.FuncR.A	FuncR.Ar	5076 (Worker Threa	1 (MyParallel	7576
⚑		8	Scheduled		<FuncR>		1 (MyParallel	7576
⚑		9	Scheduled		<FuncR>		1 (MyParallel	7576
⚑		10	Scheduled		FuncT		1 (MyParallel	7576
⚑		11	Scheduled		FuncT		1 (MyParallel	7576
⚑		12	Scheduled		FuncT		1 (MyParallel	7576
⚑		13	Scheduled		FuncT		1 (MyParallel	7576
⚑		14	Scheduled		FuncT		1 (MyParallel	7576

FIGURE 40-18

The application that has been paused has created 14 tasks, 5 of which are running, 2 of which are deadlocked, and 7 of which are in a waiting state (refer to Figure 40-18). You can click the flag icon to flag one or more tasks for easier tracking.

> **NOTE** `Parallel.For`, `Parallel.ForEach`, *and the Parallel LINQ library (PLINQ) use the* `System.Threading.Tasks.Task` *class as part of their underlying implementation.*

EXCEPTIONS

Visual Studio 2012 has a sophisticated exception handler that provides you with a lot of useful information. Figure 40-19 shows the Exception Assistant dialog that appears when an exception is raised. In addition to providing more information, it also displays a series of actions. The Actions list varies depending on the type of exception being thrown. Common options include the ability to view details of the exception, to copy it to the clipboard, and to open exception settings.

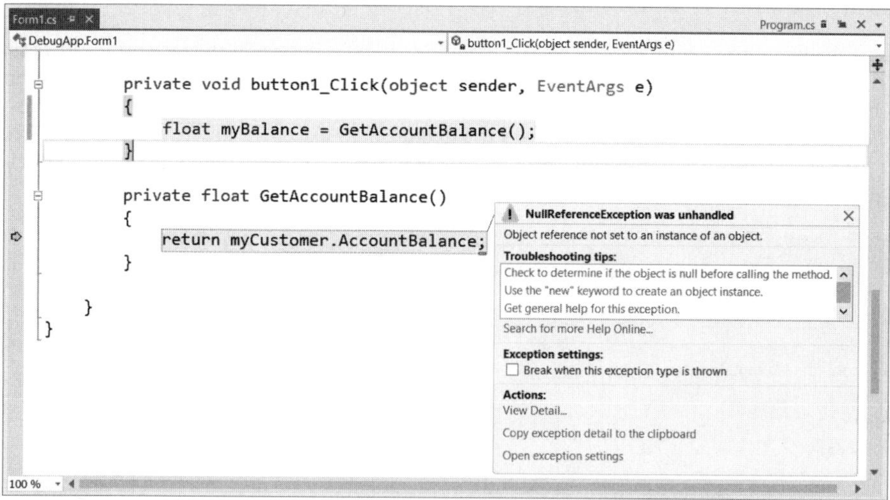

FIGURE 40-19

If you select the View Detail action item from the exception, you are presented with a modal dialog that provides a breakdown of the exception that was raised. Figure 40-20 shows the attributes of the exception, including the Stack Trace, which can be viewed in full by clicking the down arrow to the right of the screen.

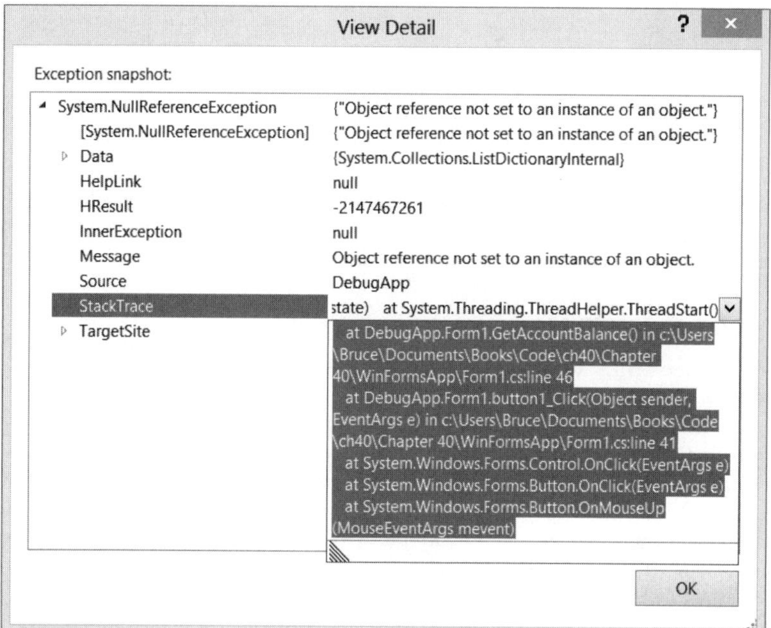

FIGURE 40-20

Of course, at times exceptions are used to control the execution path in an application. For example, some user input may not adhere to a particular formatting constraint, and instead of using a Regular Expression to determine whether or not it matches, a parse operation has been attempted on the string. When this fails, it raises an exception, which can easily be trapped without stopping the entire application.

By default, all exceptions are trapped by the debugger because they are assumed to be exceptions to the norm that shouldn't have happened. In special cases, such as invalid user input, it may be important to ignore specific types of exceptions. This can be done via the Exceptions window, accessible from the Debug menu.

Figure 40-21 shows the Exceptions window (Debug ⇨ Exceptions), which lists all the exception types that exist in the .NET Framework. Each exception has two debugging options. The debugger can be set to break when an exception is thrown, regardless of whether or not it is handled. If the Just My Code option has been enabled, checking the User-unhandled box causes the debugger to break for any exception that is not handled within a user code region. More information on Just My Code is provided in Chapter 42, which examines debugging attributes.

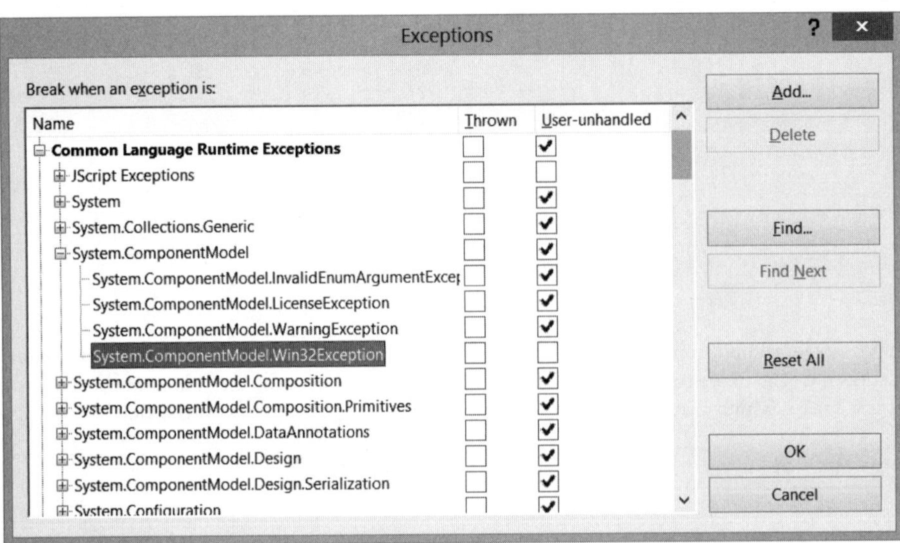

FIGURE 40-21

Unfortunately, the Exceptions window doesn't pick up any custom exception types that you may have created, but you can add them manually using the Add button. You need to provide the full class name, including the namespace; otherwise, the debugger cannot break on handled exceptions. Clearly, unhandled exceptions can still cause the application to crash.

Customizing the Exception Assistant

As with a lot of the configurable parts within Visual Studio 2012, the information displayed by the Exception Assistant is stored in an XML file (`C:\Program Files\Microsoft Visual Studio 11.0\Common7\IDE\ExceptionAssistantContent\1033\DefaultContent.xml`). This file can be modified either to alter the assistant information for existing exception types or to add your own custom exception types. If you have your own exception types, it is better practice to create your own XML document. Simply placing it in the same directory as the `DefaultContent.xml` is sufficient to register it with Visual Studio for the next time your application is debugged. An example XML file is provided in the following code listing:

```
<?xml version="1.0" encoding="utf-8" ?>
<AssistantContent Version="1.0" xmlns="urn:schemas-microsoft-com:xml-msdata:
  exception-assistant-content">
  <ContentInfo>
    <ContentName>Additional Content</ContentName>
    <ContentID>urn:exception-content-microsoft-com:visual-studio-7-default-
    content</ContentID>
    <ContentFileVersion>1.0</ContentFileVersion>
    <ContentAuthor>David Gardner</ContentAuthor>
    <ContentComment>My Exception Assistant Content for Visual Studio
    </ContentComment>
  </ContentInfo>
  <Exception>
    <Type>DebugApp1.MyException</Type>
    <Tip HelpID="http://www.professionalvisualstudio.com/MyExceptionHelp.htm">
      <Description>Silly error, you should know better...</Description>
    </Tip>
  </Exception>
</AssistantContent>
```

This example registers help information for the exception type `MyException`. The `HelpID` attribute can provide a hyperlink for more information about the exception. When this exception is raised, the debugger displays the window shown in Figure 40-22.

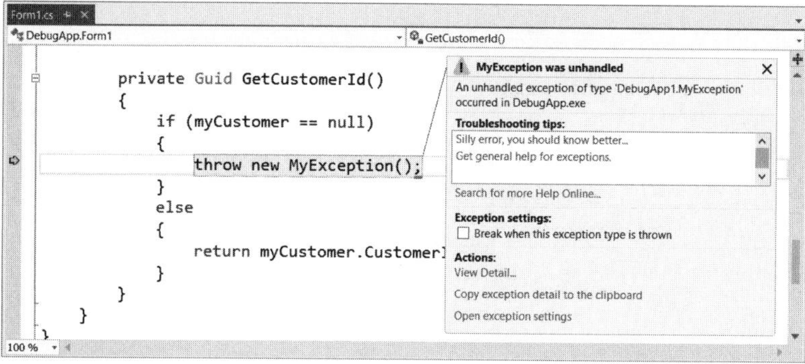

FIGURE 40-22

Unwinding an Exception

In Figure 40-23, there is a useful item in the Actions list of an exception helper window, which is to enable editing. This is effectively the capability to unwind the execution of the application to just before the exception was raised. In other words, you can effectively debug your application without restarting your debugging session.

The Enable Editing option appears only if you have configured Visual Studio to break when an exception is thrown, as discussed earlier in this chapter. As with many of the debugging features, both the Exception Assistant and the capability to unwind exceptions can also be disabled via the Debugging tab of the Options window.

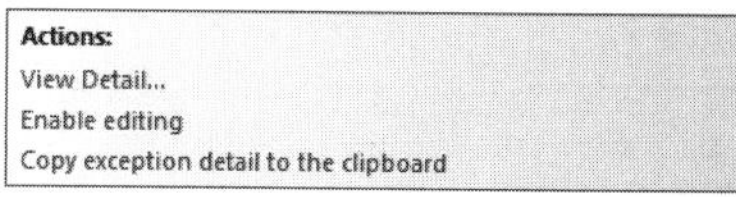

FIGURE 40-23

> **NOTE** *An alternative way to unwind the exception is to select the Unwind to This Frame item from the right-click context menu off the Call Stack window after an exception has been raised. This can be useful to check what the state of the application was just before the exception was thrown. You can unwind an exception only if it is handled (that is, contained within a try . . . catch block). You should also ensure that the debugger is set to break when the exception is thrown. You can do this via the Debug ➪ Exceptions window.*

SUMMARY

This chapter has described each of the debugging windows in detail so that you can optimize your debugging experience. Although the number of windows can seem somewhat overwhelming at first, they each perform an isolated task or provide access to a specific piece of information about the running application. As such, you can easily learn to navigate between them, returning to those that provide the most relevant information for you.

The following chapter provides more detail about how you can customize the debugging information. This includes changing the information displayed in the DataTip and visualizing more complex variable information.

Debugging with Breakpoints

WHAT'S IN THIS CHAPTER?

- Using breakpoints, conditional breakpoints, and tracepoints to pause code execution
- Controlling the program execution during debug by stepping through code
- Modifying your code while it runs using the Edit and Continue feature

Long gone are the days in which debugging an application involved adding superfluous output statements to track down where an application was failing. Visual Studio 2012 provides a rich, interactive debugging experience that includes breakpoints, tracepoints, and the Edit and Continue feature. This chapter covers how you can use these features to debug your application.

BREAKPOINTS

A *breakpoint* is used to pause, or break, an application at a particular point of execution. An application that has been paused is in Break mode, causing a number of the Visual Studio 2012 windows to become active. For example, you can use the Watch window to view variable values. Figure 41-1 shows a breakpoint added to the constructor of the `Customer` class. The application breaks on this line if the `Customer` class constructor is called.

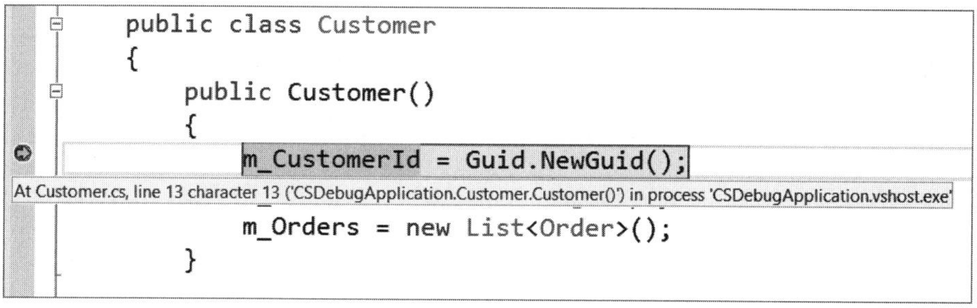

```
public class Customer
{
    public Customer()
    {
        m_CustomerId = Guid.NewGuid();
At Customer.cs, line 13 character 13 ('CSDebugApplication.Customer.Customer()') in process 'CSDebugApplication.vshost.exe'
        m_Orders = new List<Order>();
    }
```

FIGURE 41-1

Setting a Breakpoint

You can set breakpoints either through the Debug menu, using the Breakpoint item from the right-click context menu, or by using the keyboard shortcut, F9. The Visual Studio 2012 code editor also provides a shortcut for setting a breakpoint using a single mouse click in the margin.

An application can be paused only on a line of executing code. This means that a breakpoint set on either a comment or a variable declaration is repositioned to the next line of executable code when the application is run.

Simple Breakpoints

You can set a breakpoint on a line of code by placing the cursor on that line and enabling a breakpoint using any of the following methods:

- Selecting Toggle Breakpoint from the Debug menu
- Selecting Insert Breakpoint from the Breakpoint item on the right-click context menu
- Pressing F9
- Clicking once in the margin of the code window with the mouse

Selecting Location from the Breakpoint item on the right-click context menu for the line of code with the breakpoint set displays the File Breakpoint dialog, as shown in Figure 41-2. Here, you can see that the breakpoint is set at line 13 of the `Customer.cs` file. There is also a Character number, which provides for the case in which multiple statements appear on a single line.

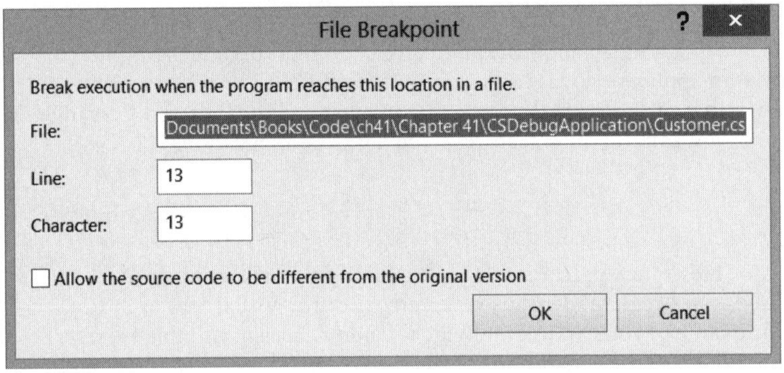

FIGURE 41-2

Function Breakpoints

Another type of breakpoint that you can set is a function breakpoint. The usual way to set a breakpoint on a function is to select the function signature and either press F9 or use the mouse to create a breakpoint. In the case of multiple overloads, this requires you to locate all the overloads and add the appropriate breakpoints. Setting a function breakpoint enables you to set a breakpoint on one or more functions by specifying the function name.

To set a function breakpoint, from the New Breakpoint item on the Debug menu, select Break At Function. This loads the New Breakpoint dialog, as shown in Figure 41-3, in which you can specify the name of the function on which to break. There is a toggle to enable IntelliSense checking for the function name. The recommendation is to leave this checked because it becomes almost impossible to set a valid breakpoint without this support.

New Breakpoint

Break execution when the program reaches this location in a function.

Function: AddOrder(Guid)

Use IntelliSense to verify the function name

Line: 1

Character: 1

Language: C#

OK Cancel

FIGURE 41-3

Unfortunately, the IntelliSense option doesn't give you true IntelliSense as you type, unlike other debugging windows. However, if you select the name of the function in the code window before creating the breakpoint, the name of the function is automatically inserted into the dialog.

When setting a function breakpoint, you can specify either the exact overload you want to set the breakpoint on or just the function name. In Figure 41-3, the overload with a single Guid parameter has been selected. Unlike a full method signature, which requires a parameter name, to select a particular function overload, you should provide only the parameter type. If you omit the parameter information and there are multiple overloads, you are prompted to select the overloads on which to place the breakpoint, as illustrated in Figure 41-4.

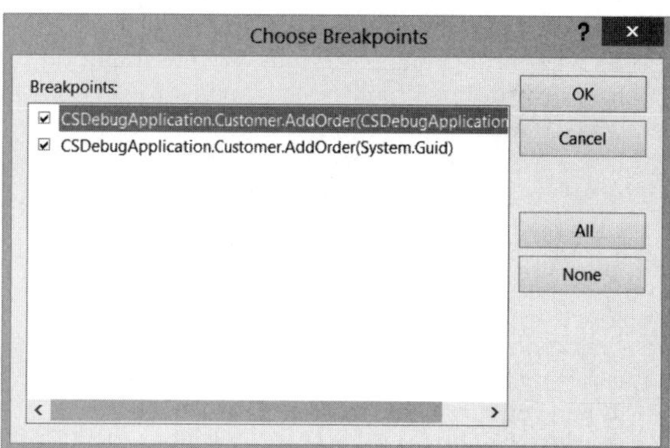

FIGURE 41-4

Address Breakpoint

Another way to set a breakpoint is via the Call Stack window. When the application is in Break mode, the call stack shows the current list of function calls. After selecting any line in the call stack, you can set a breakpoint in the same way as a file breakpoint, as described earlier. (Toggle Breakpoint from the Debug menu, use the F9 keyboard shortcut, or use Insert Breakpoint from the context menu.) Figure 41-5 shows a short call stack with a new breakpoint set on a control event on `Form1`.

Call Stack

Name	Language
CSDebugApplication.exe!CSDebugApplication.Customer.AddOrder(CSDebugApplication.Order order) Lin	C#
CSDebugApplication.exe!CSDebugApplication.Form1.AddOrderToCustomer(CSDebugApplication.Custon	C#
CSDebugApplication.exe!CSDebugApplication.Form1.linkLabel1_LinkClicked(object sender, System.Windc	C#
[External Code]	
CSDebugApplication.exe!CSDebugApplication.Program.Main() Line 19 + 0x1d bytes	C#
[External Code]	

FIGURE 41-5

The call stack is generated using function addresses. As such, the breakpoint that is set is an address breakpoint. This type of breakpoint is only useful within a single debugging session because function addresses are likely to change when an application is modified and rebuilt.

Adding Break Conditions

Though breakpoints are useful for pausing an application at a given point to review variables and watch application flow, if you are looking for a particular scenario, it may be necessary to break only when certain conditions are valid. Breakpoints can be tailored to search for particular conditions, to break after a number of iterations, or even to be filtered based on process or machine name.

Condition

A breakpoint condition can be specified by selecting Condition from the Breakpoint item on the right-click context menu for the breakpoint. This brings up the Breakpoint Condition dialog, as shown in Figure 41-6, which accepts a boolean expression that determines whether the breakpoint will be hit. If the expression evaluates to `false`, the application continues past the breakpoint without breaking.

In Figure 41-6, which is for a breakpoint set within the `Order` class, the condition specifies that the order total must be greater than 1000. As with most debugging windows, the Condition field provides rich IntelliSense support to aid writing valid conditions. If an invalid condition is specified, the debugger throws an appropriate error message and the application breaks the first time the breakpoint is reached.

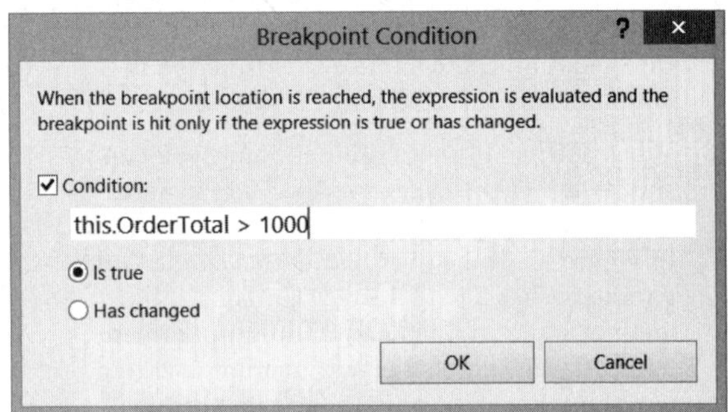

FIGURE 41-6

When a condition, or a hit count, as shown in the next section, is placed on a breakpoint, the breakpoint changes appearance. The solid red dot is replaced with a red dot with a white cross. When you move your mouse across this dot, the tooltip provides useful information about the breakpoint condition, as shown in Figure 41-7.

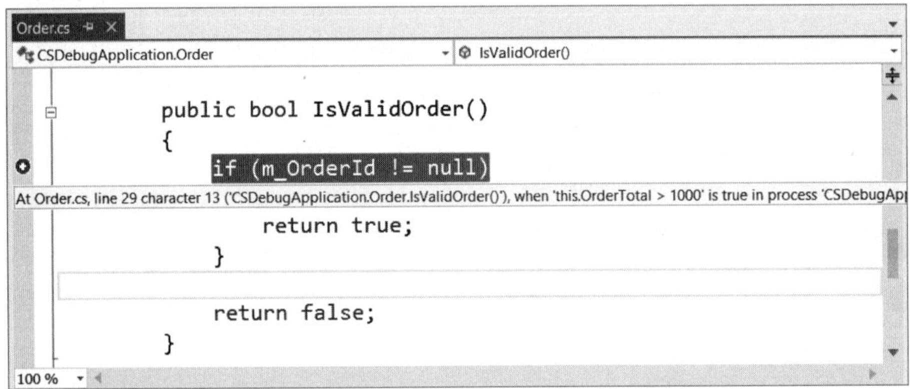

FIGURE 41-7

Sometimes it is more relevant to know when this condition changes status, rather than when it is true. The Has Changed option breaks the application when the status of the condition changes. If this option is selected, the application does not break the first time the breakpoint is hit because there is no previous status to compare against.

> **NOTE** *Using multiple breakpoints with complex conditions can significantly slow down the execution of your application, so it is recommended that you remove breakpoints that are no longer relevant in order to speed up the running of your application.*

Hit Count

Though it's perhaps not as useful as breakpoint conditions, it is also possible to break after a particular number of iterations through a breakpoint. To do this, select Hit Count from the Breakpoint item on the right-click context menu. Figure 41-8 shows the Breakpoint Hit Count dialog, which you can use to specify when the breakpoint should be hit.

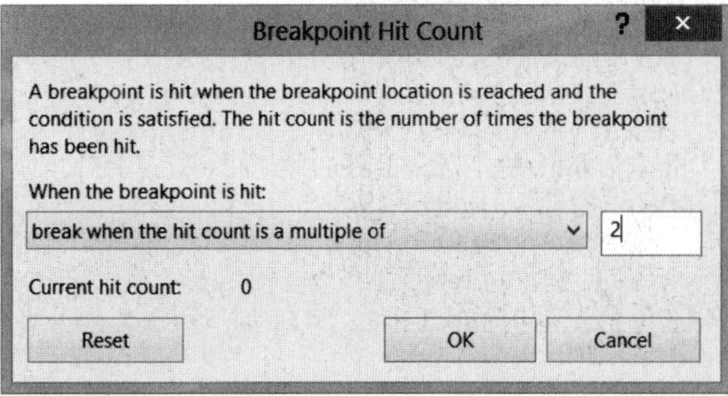

FIGURE 41-8

Every time the application runs, the hit count is reset to zero and can be manually reset using the Reset button. The hit count is also unique to each breakpoint. The hit count condition is one of four options:

- **Always**—Disregard the hit count.
- **Is Equal To**—Break if the hit count is equal to the value specified.
- **Multiple Of**—Break if the hit count is a multiple of the value specified (refer to Figure 41-8).
- **Is Greater Than or Equal To**—Break if the hit count is greater than or equal to the value specified.

Figure 41-9 shows the Breakpoints window, which provides additional information about the status of each of the breakpoints.

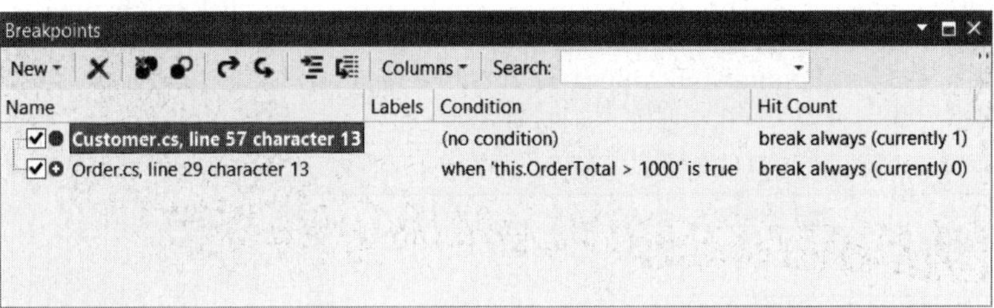

FIGURE 41-9

Filter

A single solution may contain multiple applications that need to be run at the same time. This is a common scenario when building a multitier application. When the application runs, the debugger can attach to all these processes, enabling them to be debugged. By default, when a breakpoint is reached, all the processes break. You can control this behavior from the Debugging (General) node in the Options window, accessible from the Options item on the Tools menu. Unchecking the Break All Processes When One Process Breaks check box enables processes to be debugged individually.

If a breakpoint is set in a class library used by more than one process, each process breaks when it reaches that breakpoint. Because you might be interested in debugging only one of these processes, you can place a filter on the breakpoint that limits it to the process you are interested in. If you debug applications on multiple machines, you also can specify a machine name filter.

Filtering can be useful for a multithreaded application for which you want to limit the breakpoints to a particular thread. Although the breakpoint is triggered only when a thread matches the filter criteria, all threads still pause. Figure 41-10 shows the Breakpoint Filter dialog and the possible filter conditions.

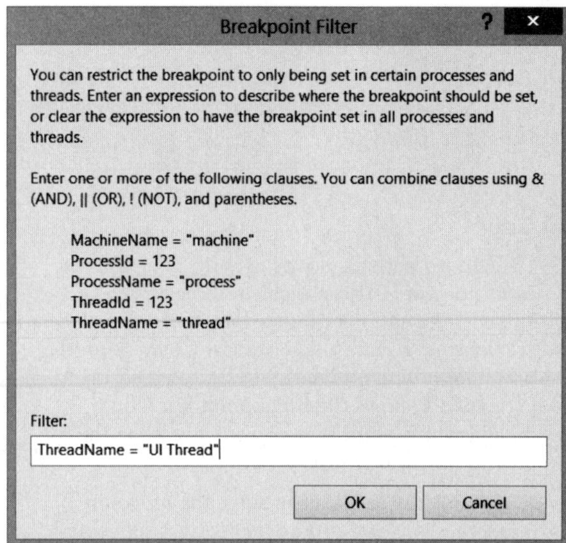

FIGURE 41-10

Working with Breakpoints

You often need to adjust a breakpoint because it might be in the wrong location or no longer relevant. In most cases it is easiest to remove the breakpoint, but in some cases — for example, when you have a complex breakpoint condition — it might be preferable to adjust the existing breakpoint.

Deleting Breakpoints

To remove a breakpoint that is no longer required, select it, either in the code editor or in the Breakpoints window, and remove it using the Toggle Breakpoint item from the Debug menu. Alternatively, the Delete Breakpoint item from the right-click context menu or the Delete Breakpoint icon from the Breakpoints window toolbar can remove the breakpoint. As you might expect, any configuration regarding the deleted breakpoint (such as conditions, filters, and so on) is lost.

Disabling Breakpoints

Instead of deleting a breakpoint, simply disabling the breakpoint can be useful when you have a breakpoint condition set or you track a hit count. To disable a breakpoint, select it either in the code editor or in the Breakpoints window, and disable it using the Disable Breakpoint item from the right-click context menu. Alternatively, you can uncheck the check box against the breakpoint in the Breakpoints window. Figure 41-11 shows how a disabled breakpoint would appear in the code window.

Customer.cs CSDebugApplication.Customer Shipping

```
public Customer()
{
    m_CustomerId = Guid.NewGuid();
    m_CustomerName = String.Empty;
    m_Orders = new List<Order>();
}
```

100 %

FIGURE 41-11

Changing Breakpoint Locations

You can modify the location of a breakpoint by selecting Location from the Breakpoint item on the right-click context menu. Depending on what type of breakpoint has been set, the dialog shows the location of the breakpoint as either a line and character position in a file or function, or as an address within an assembly. If the location is either a file or function position, the breakpoint can be adjusted so that it is in the correct location. Address breakpoints are harder to relocate because you need to ensure that the new address is a valid location for a breakpoint.

Labeling Breakpoints

Visual Studio 2012 includes the capability to assign a label to a breakpoint. This is particularly useful if you want to group a set of related breakpoints together. When labeled, you can search for and perform a bulk action on all breakpoints with a specific label.

To assign a label to a breakpoint, right-click the breakpoint, and choose Edit Labels. This displays the Edit Breakpoint Labels dialog, as shown in Figure 41-12, where you can attach one or more labels to the breakpoint.

After you have labeled your breakpoints, you can perform bulk actions on them by opening the Breakpoints window (Debug ➪ Windows ➪ Breakpoints). This window, as shown in Figure 41-13, enables you to filter the list by typing a label in the Search box and pressing Enter. You can then select one of the actions from the toolbar, such as Enable or Disable All Breakpoints Matching the Current Search Criteria.

FIGURE 41-12

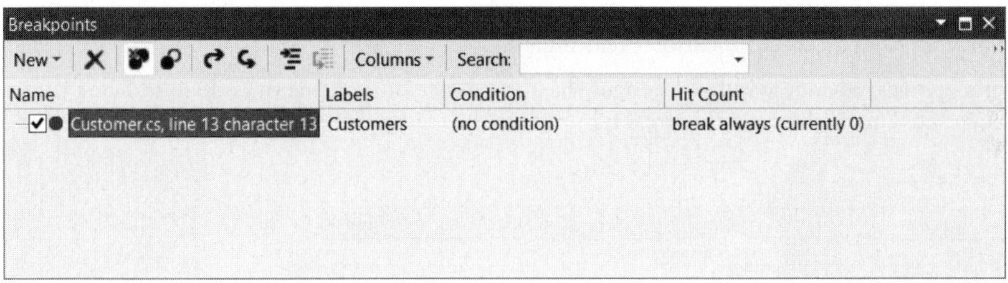

FIGURE 41-13

> **NOTE** *By default, the search will be performed across all columns shown in the Breakpoints window. You can limit the search to specific columns by changing the Columns drop-down from All Visible to a specific column.*

Import and Export of Breakpoints

Another debugging feature provided by Visual Studio 2012 is the import and export of breakpoints. This feature enables you to back up and restore breakpoints, and share them among developers.

Export of breakpoints is performed from the Breakpoints window (Debug ➪ Windows ➪ Breakpoints). If you want to export only a subset of your breakpoints, first filter the list by entering a search criterion. When the list of breakpoints that you want to export displays, click the Export All Breakpoints Matching the Current Search Criteria button from the toolbar.

Import of breakpoints can also be performed from the Breakpoints window by clicking the appropriate button on the toolbar.

TRACEPOINTS

A *tracepoint* differs from a breakpoint in that it triggers an additional action when it is hit. For purposes such as applying filters, conditions, and hit counts, a tracepoint can be thought of as a breakpoint.

Tracepoints can be compared to using either `Debug` or `Trace` statements in your code, but tracepoints can be dynamically set as the application is being debugged and will not affect your code.

Creating a Tracepoint

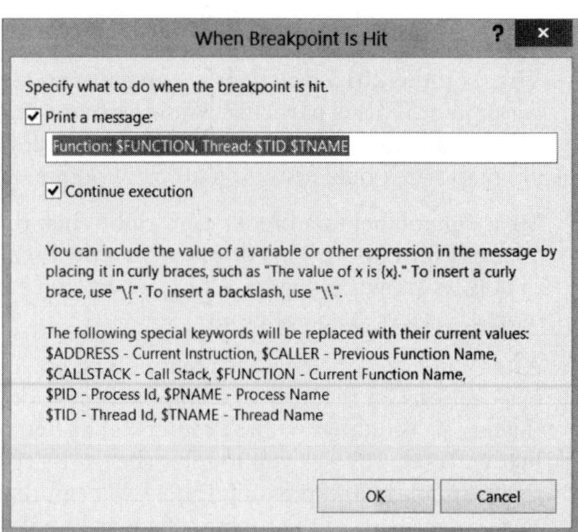

FIGURE 41-14

You can create tracepoints from either an existing breakpoint or the Breakpoint right-click context menu. To create a tracepoint from an existing breakpoint, select When Hit from the Breakpoint right-click context menu. The resulting dialog, as shown in Figure 41-14, allows you to specify the message that should be printed to the console window. Alternatively, to create a tracepoint at a new location, select Insert Tracepoint from the Breakpoint item on the right-click context menu. This again loads the dialog shown in Figure 41-14, so you can customize the tracepoint action.

By default, after a tracepoint action has been defined, the Continue Execution check box will be checked, so the application will not break at this point. Unchecking this option causes the application to break at the tracepoint as if it were a breakpoint. The message will be printed prior to the application breaking.

After you set a tracepoint, the code window changes the appearance of that line of code to indicate that a tracepoint has been set. This is shown in Figure 41-15, where the tracepoint appears with a red diamond in the margin.

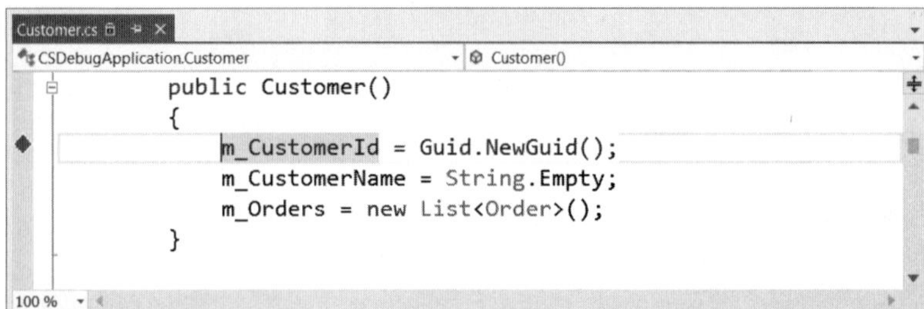

FIGURE 41-15

If the Continue Execution check box is unchecked, the visual appearance of the tracepoint becomes the same as that of a breakpoint. The rationale for this behavior is that the diamond-shaped visual cue indicates that the debugger will not stop at the tracepoint, rather than indicating that there are actions associated with the tracepoint.

Output Messages

As the dialog in Figure 41-14 suggests, you can use a number of keywords with your trace message. However, a couple of keywords are not listed by the dialog: `$FILEPOS`, which gives the location of the current file, and `$TICKS`, which can be used as a relative time indicator.

EXECUTION CONTROL

After reaching a breakpoint, it is often useful to step through code and review both variable values and program execution. Visual Studio 2012 not only enables you to step through your code, but it also permits you to adjust the execution point to backtrack or even repeat operations. The line of code about to be executed is highlighted, and an arrow displays on the left, as shown in Figure 41-16.

```
Customer.cs
CSDebugApplication.Customer    AddOrder(Order order)

        public void AddOrder(Order order)
        {
            if (order.IsValidOrder())
                m_Orders.Add(order);
            else
                throw new ApplicationException("Order is not valid");
        }
100 %
```

FIGURE 41-16

Stepping Through Code

The first step to manipulate the execution point is simply to step through code in the expected order of execution. You can use three sizes of increments to step the debugger forward. It is important to remember that when stepping through code it is actually being run, so variable values may change as you progress through the application.

Stepping Over (F10)

Stepping Over is fully executing the line that currently has focus and progressing to the next line in the current code block. If the end of the code block has been reached, Stepping Over returns to the calling code block.

Stepping Into (F11)

Stepping Into behaves the same as Stepping Over when the line is a simple operator, such as a numeric operation or a cast. When the line is more complex, Stepping Into steps through all user code. For example, in the following code snippet, pressing F10 through the `TestMethod` steps through only the lines of code within `TestMethod`. Pressing F11 steps through `TestMethod` until the `MethodA` call is made, and then the debugger steps through `MethodA` before returning to `TestMethod`:

C#

```
public void TestMethod()
{
    int x = 5 + 5;
    MethodA();
}

private void MethodA()
{
    Console.WriteLine("Method A being executed");
}
```

Stepping Out (Shift+F11)

If you step into a long method by accident, it is quite often convenient to step back out of that method without having to either step over every line in that method or setting a breakpoint at the end of the method. Stepping Out moves the cursor out of the current method to where it was called. Considering the previous snippet, if you entered `MethodA`, pressing Shift+F11 would immediately return the cursor to the end of `TestMethod`.

Step Filtering

One useful feature is the ability to automatically step over properties and operators. In many cases, public properties are simply wrappers for a private member variable, and as a result there is little to be gained from stepping into them while debugging. This debugger option is especially useful if you call a method that passes a number of properties as parameters, such as the method call listed here:

C#

```
printShippingLabel(cust.name, shipTo.street, shipTo.city, shipTo.state,
shipTo.zipCode);
```

With the Step Over Properties and Operators option enabled, the debugger steps directly into the first line of the `printShippingLabel` method if you press F11. If you need to, you can manually step into a specific property by right-clicking the code editor window and selecting Step Into Specific. This displays a submenu with each of the available properties listed, as shown in Figure 41-17.

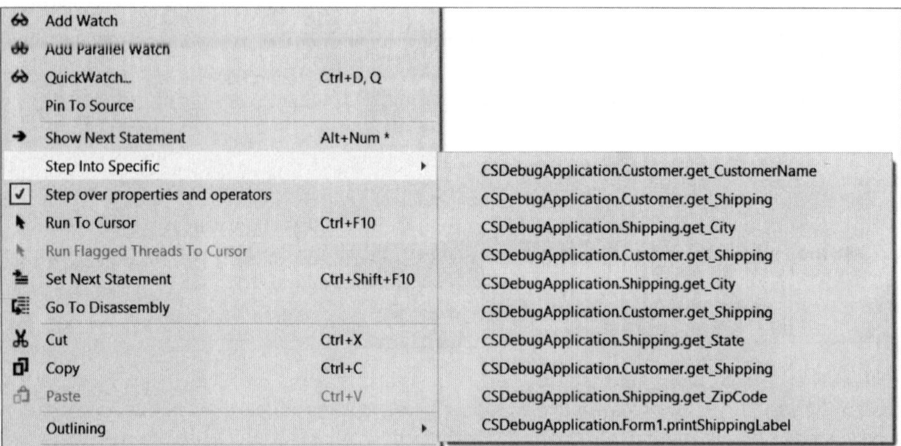

FIGURE 41-17

The Step Over Properties and Operators option is enabled by default. You can enable or disable it during debugging by right-clicking anywhere in the code editor window and selecting it from the context menu, or from the Options dialog window. (Select Tools ⇨ Options, and then from the tree view on the left side, select Debugging).

Moving the Execution Point

As you become familiar with stepping in and out of functions, you will find that you are occasionally overzealous and accidentally step over the method call you are interested in. In this case, what you need to do is go back and review the last action. Though you can't actually unwind the code and change the application back to its previous state, you can move the execution point so that the method is reevaluated.

To move the current execution point, select and drag the yellow arrow next to the current line of execution (refer to Figure 41-16) forward or backward in the current method. Use this functionality with care because it can result in unintended behavior and variable values.

EDIT AND CONTINUE

One of the most useful features of Visual Studio 2012 debugging is Edit and Continue. Both C# and Visual Basic have support for Edit and Continue, enabling you to make changes to your application on-the-fly. Whenever your application is paused, you can make changes to your code and then resume execution. The new or modified code is dynamically added to your application with the changes taking immediate effect.

Rude Edits

At this point, you are likely wondering whether any limitations exist on the changes that you can make. The answer is yes, and there are quite a few types of *rude edits*, which refer to any code change that requires the application to be stopped and rebuilt. A full list of rude edits is available from the Visual Studio 2012 help resource under the Edit and Continue topic, and they include the following:

- Making changes to the current, or active, statement
- Making changes to the list of global symbols — such as new types or methods — or changing the signatures of methods, events, or properties
- Making changes to attributes

Stop Applying Changes

When changes are made to the source code while the application is paused, Visual Studio must integrate, or apply, the changes into the running application. Depending on the type or complexity of the changes made, this could take some time. If you want to cancel this action, you can select Stop Applying Code Changes from the Debug menu.

SUMMARY

Most developers who use Visual Studio 2012 use breakpoints to track down issues with their application. In this chapter, you learned how to optimize the use of breakpoints to reduce the amount of time spent locating the issue.

The following chapter examines data tips and explains how to create debugging proxy types and visualizers. This enables you to customize the debugging experience and reduce the time spent wading through unnecessary lines of code.

42

DataTips, Debug Proxies, and Visualizers

WHAT'S IN THIS CHAPTER?

- Inspecting the contents of your variables using DataTips
- Applying attributes to your classes and member variables to customize the debugger behavior
- Creating type proxies and visualizers to represent complex variables and data types in a useful way within the debugger

Other than writing code, debugging is likely the most time-consuming activity when writing an application. If you consider all the time you spend stepping through code, looking at the Watch window to see the value of a variable, or even just running the application looking for any exceptions being raised, you realize that this is one of the most time-consuming parts of writing software.

Previous chapters have focused on how you can use the various debugging windows to retrieve information about the current status of your application, and how you can set breakpoints and tracepoints to generate debugging information. This chapter goes beyond what is provided out-of-the-box, and looks at how you can customize the debugging experience to reduce the time spent wading through unnecessary lines of code.

Using debugging proxy types and visualizers, you can represent complex variables and data types in a useful way within the debugger. This allows you to filter out unnecessary information and zero in on the most relevant properties of an object, thereby making it easier to determine when your application is not functioning correctly and to trace the source of the issue.

DATATIPS

You have many ways to inspect the value of variables within Visual Studio while debugging. For many types, the easiest way to inspect a variable is simply to hover the mouse over it, which displays the value of the variable in a *DataTip*. Figure 42-1 shows a DataTip for a string property.

In addition to viewing the value of the variable, you can right-click the DataTip to perform a number of actions. These include copying the value that displays, adding the variable to the Watch window, or even editing the current value of the variable for simple types such as strings or integers.

FIGURE 42-1

The DataTip-based features of Visual Studio 2012 include both pinned and floating DataTips. You can think of these as the electronic equivalents of Post-it Notes for Visual Studio. To create a pinned DataTip, click the pin icon on the right side of the DataTip. The DataTip now stays pinned to that line of code in the source file of the code editor and becomes visible anytime a debugging session is underway.

Figure 42-2 shows a Visual Studio workspace with pinned DataTips for the variables `c.CustomerName` and `o1.Total`. A menu appears when you hover over a pinned DataTip. Clicking the icon with double arrows displays a text input field below the DataTip where you can enter some text. You can also click the pin icon in the menu to convert the pinned DataTip to a floating DataTip. The DataTip for the `c` variable in Figure 42-2 is a floating DataTip.

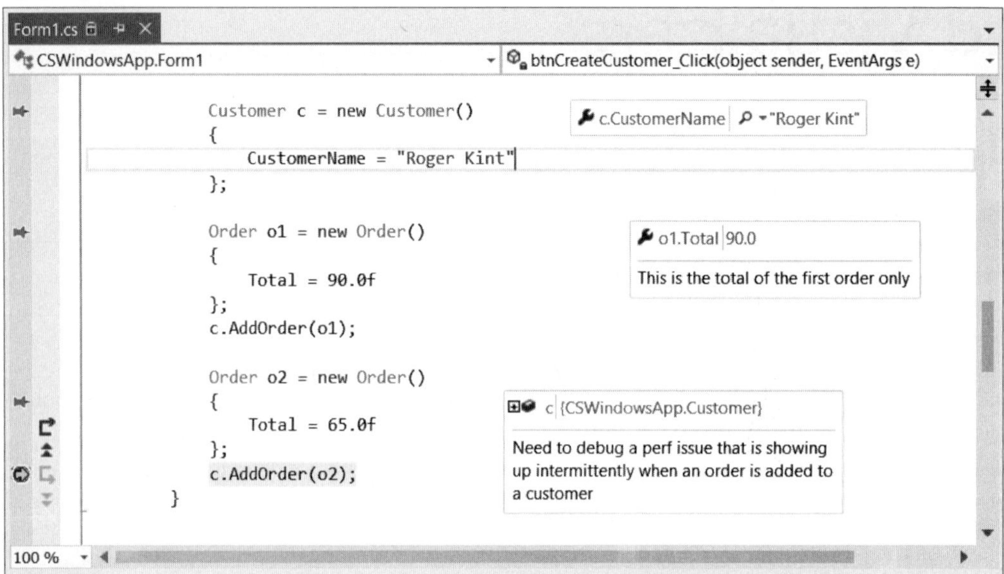

FIGURE 42-2

You can drag a pinned DataTip to any line of code in the source file to which it has been pinned but not anywhere outside of the code editor window. Pinned DataTips also disappear if you switch to a different source code file. Floating DataTips, on the other hand, are always visible during a debugging session and you can drag them to any location on your monitor.

A pin icon appears in the margin of the code editor for each pinned DataTip. This icon is still visible after the debug session finishes; you can hover the mouse over it and the DataTip appears with the value during the last debug session.

You can close an individual pinned or floating DataTip by clicking the x icon, or close all of them by selecting Debug ➪ Clear All DataTips from the menu. You also see a menu option to clear all DataTips pinned to the current source file in the code editor if it contains any.

Finally, DataTips can be imported and exported to an external XML file, which can be useful for backup purposes, or sharing them among developers. This is done by selecting Import DataTips or Export DataTips from the Debug menu.

DEBUGGER ATTRIBUTES

This section outlines a number of debugging attributes that can be applied to code to affect the way the debugger steps through it. Some of the debugging attributes can also be used to customize the appearance of your types when you hover over them in Break mode.

> **NOTE** *The debugging attribute classes are contained within the* `System.Diagnostics` *namespace. Rather than specify the full namespace for each attribute, the source code examples in this chapter assume that it has been added as an import.*

DebuggerBrowsable

The first attribute you can apply to fields and properties is the `DebuggerBrowsable` attribute. The `DebuggerBrowsable` attribute takes a single parameter that determines how the member displays in the variable tree. In the following code snippet, the field `Orders` is set to `Collapsed`:

C#

```
public class Customer
{
    [DebuggerBrowsable(DebuggerBrowsableState.Collapsed)]
    public List<Order> Orders;
}
```

VB

```
Public Class Customer
   <DebuggerBrowsable(DebuggerBrowsableState.Collapsed)> _
   Public Orders As List(Of Order)
End Class
```

> **NOTE** *In .NET Framework 2.0, the* `DebuggerBrowsable` *attribute was interpreted only by the C# debugger and had no effect when applied to Visual Basic code. This limitation has been removed in newer versions of the .NET Framework.*

Figure 42-3 (right) shows the same snippet of code with `DebuggerBrowsable` initially set to `Collapsed` (or not specified). Figure 42-3 (below, left) shows the same snippet with `DebuggerBrowsable` set to the `RootHidden` value, where the actual `Orders` item does not appear, just the contents of the collection. Finally, in Figure 42-3 (below, right) the `Never` value is used for `DebuggerBrowsable`, in which case the `Orders` member does not appear.

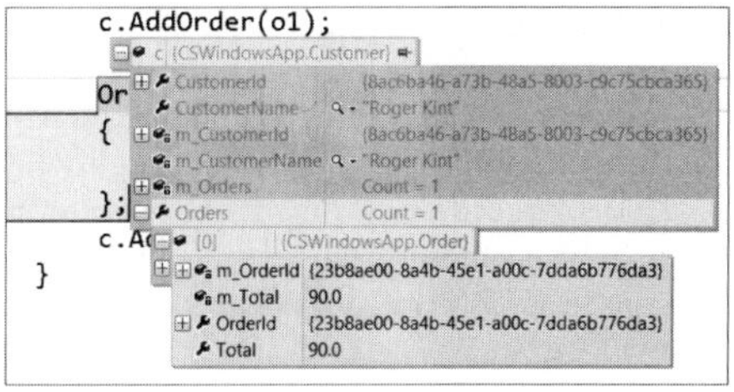

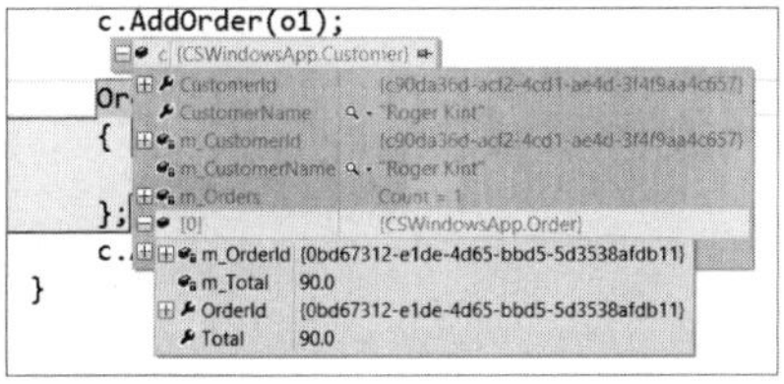

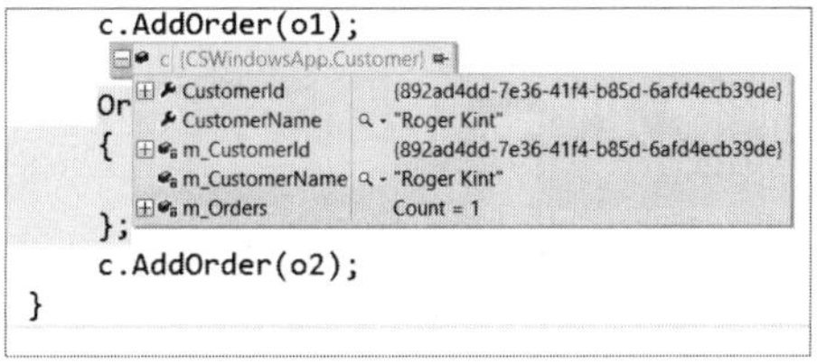

FIGURE 42-3

DebuggerDisplay

When you hover your mouse over a variable while you are in Break mode, the first thing you see in the tooltip is the type of object you are hovering over. In Figure 42-3, a mouse was initially hovering over the `Customer` class, followed by the `Order` class. This information is not particularly useful because most of the time you have a good idea about the type of object you are dealing with. It would be better for this single line to contain more useful information about the object. This is the case for well-known types, such as strings and integers, where the actual value displays.

You can use the `DebuggerDisplay` attribute to change the single-line representation of the object from the default full class name. This attribute takes a single parameter, which is a string. The format of this string can accept member injections using the `String.Format` breakout syntax. For example, the attributes applied to the `Customer` and `Order` classes might be as follows:

C#

```
[DebuggerDisplay("Customer {CustomerName} has {Orders.Count} orders")]
public class Customer

[DebuggerDisplay("Order made on {DateOrdered} which is worth ${Total}")]
public class Order
```

VB

```
<DebuggerDisplay("Customer {CustomerName} has {Orders.Count} orders")> _
Public Class Customer

<DebuggerDisplay("Order made on {DateOrdered} which is worth ${Total}")> _
Public Class Order
```

This gives you the debugger output, as shown in Figure 42-4, which indicates that customer Roger Kint has one order, which, as you can see from the description, includes the amount of the order and the date on which it was made.

Looking at the syntax for the `DebuggerDisplay` attribute, you can see that the output string consists of both static text and field and property information from the object. For example, the `CustomerName` property for the `Customer` object is referenced using the `{CustomerName}` syntax within the static text.

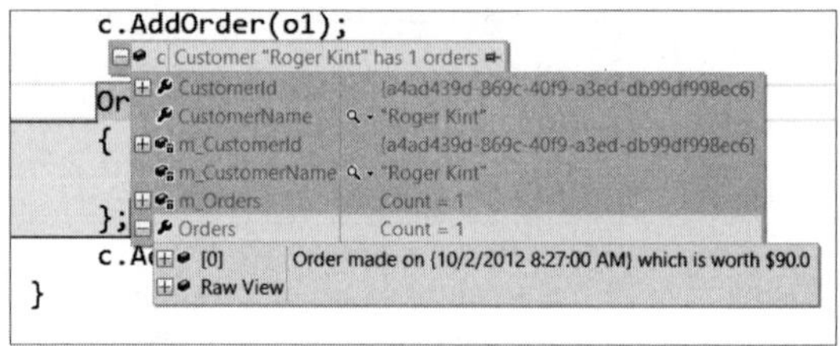

FIGURE 42-4

DebuggerHidden

You can add the `DebuggerHidden` attribute to code that you don't want to step through when debugging. Code marked with this attribute is stepped over and does not support breakpoints. If this code makes a call to another method, the debugger steps into that method. Taking the following code snippet, a breakpoint can be set in both `ClickHandler` and `NotSoHiddenMethod`:

C#

```
private void ClickHandler(object sender, EventArgs e)
{
   HiddenMethod();
}

[DebuggerHidden()]
```

```
public void HiddenMethod()
{
    Console.WriteLine("Can't set a breakpoint here");
    NotSoHiddenMethod();
}

public void NotSoHiddenMethod()
{
    Console.WriteLine("Can set a breakpoint here!");
}
```

VB

```
Private Sub ClickHandler(ByVal sender As Object, ByVal e As EventArgs)
   HiddenMethod()
End Sub

<DebuggerHidden()> _
Public Sub HiddenMethod()
   Console.WriteLine("Can't set a breakpoint here")
   NotSoHiddenMethod()
End Sub

Public Sub NotSoHiddenMethod()
   Console.WriteLine("Can set a breakpoint here!")
End Sub
```

If you step through this code, the debugger goes from the call to `HiddenMethod` in the `ClickHandler` method straight to `NotSoHiddenMethod`. The call stack at this point is shown in Figure 42-5, and you can see that `HiddenMethod` does not appear in the stack.

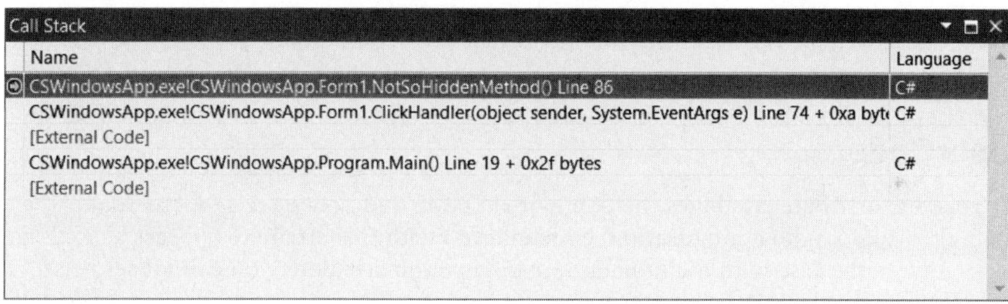

FIGURE 42-5

As with all the `System.Diagnostic` attributes, the CLR ignores this, so you can still see the method call in the stack trace of any exceptions thrown at run time.

DebuggerStepThrough

Like the `DebuggerHidden` attribute, when the `DebuggerStepThrough` attribute is applied to a piece of code, that code is stepped over when debugging, regardless of whether this code calls other methods.

Similar to the `DebuggerHidden` attribute, breakpoints cannot be set within a block of code marked with the `DebuggerStepThrough` attribute. However, if a breakpoint is set within a section of code that is called by that code, the attributed code will be marked as *external code* in the call stack. This is illustrated in Figure 42-6, which shows the code that was listed in the previous section. However, in this case `DebuggerStepThrough` has been set on `HiddenMethod` instead of `DebuggerHidden`.

Visual Studio 2012 supports the Just My Code option, configurable from the Debugging node in the Options dialog (select Tools ➪ Options). Unchecking this option makes all code contained within your application appear in the call stack, as shown in Figure 42-7. This includes designer and other generated code that you might not want to debug. When this option is unchecked, breakpoints can also be set in blocks of code marked with this attribute.

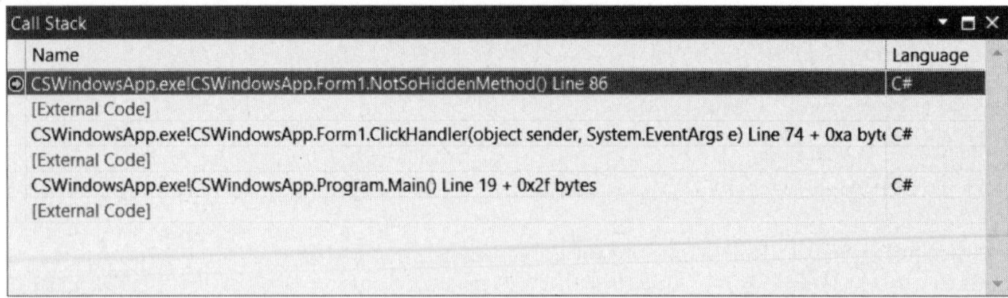

FIGURE 42-6

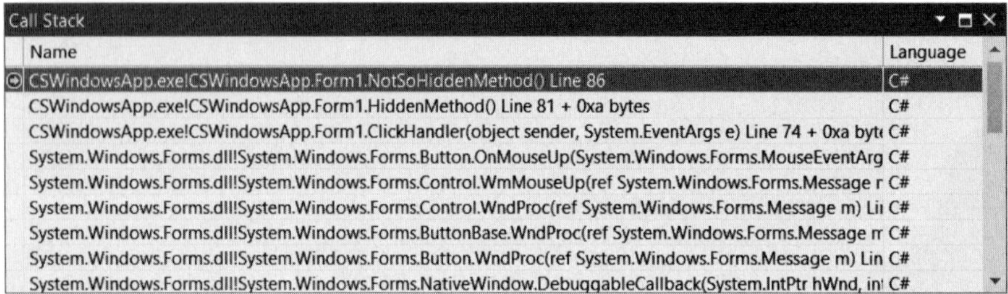

FIGURE 42-7

> **NOTE** *You can also right-click the call stack and select Show External Code to reveal any hidden or designer code.*

DebuggerNonUserCode

The `DebuggerNonUserCode` attribute combines the `DebuggerHidden` and `DebuggerStepThrough` attributes. In the default Visual Studio configuration, code marked with this attribute appears as external code in the call stack. As was the case with the `DebuggerStepThrough` attribute, you cannot set breakpoints in blocks of code marked with this attribute. Stepping through code steps into any code called by that block of code in the same way it does for the `DebuggerHidden` attribute.

DebuggerStepperBoundary

`DebuggerStepperBoundary` is the most obscure of all the `Debugger` attributes because it comes into effect only under specific conditions. It is used to avoid a misleading debugging experience that can occur when a context switch is made on a thread within the boundaries of the `DebuggerNonUserCode` attribute. It is entirely possible in this scenario that the next user-supplied code module stepped into may not actually relate to the code that was in the process of being debugged. To avoid this invalid debugging behavior, the `DebuggerStepperBoundary` attribute, when encountered under this scenario, escapes from stepping through code and instead resumes normal execution of the code.

TYPE PROXIES

So far, you have seen how you can modify the tooltip to show information that is more relevant to debugging your application. However, the attributes discussed so far have been limited in how they control what information is presented in the expanded tree. The `DebuggerBrowsable` attribute enables you to hide particular members, but there is no way to add more fields. This is where the `DebuggerTypeProxy` attribute can be used to provide you with complete control over the layout of the tooltip.

The other scenario where a type proxy is useful is where a property of a class changes values within the class. For example, the following snippet from the `Customer` class tracks the number of times the `OrderCount` property has been accessed. Whenever the tooltip is accessed, the `CountAccessed` property is incremented by one:

C#

```
public class Customer
{
    private int m_CountAccessed;
    public int OrderCount
    {
        get
        {
            m_CountAccessed++;
            return this.Orders.Count;
        }
    }

    public int CountAccessed
    {
        get
        {
            return this.m_CountAccessed;
        }
    }
}
```

Figure 42-8 illustrates the tooltip you want to be shown for the `Customer` class. Instead of showing the full list of orders to navigate through, it provides a summary about the number of orders, the maximum and minimum order quantities, and a list of the items on order.

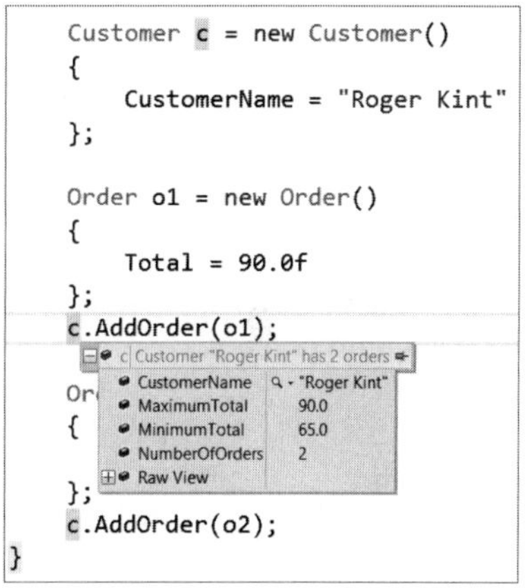

```
Customer c = new Customer()
{
    CustomerName = "Roger Kint"
};

Order o1 = new Order()
{
    Total = 90.0f
};
c.AddOrder(o1);
Or   c  Customer "Roger Kint" has 2 orders
{      CustomerName    "Roger Kint"
       MaximumTotal    90.0
       MinimumTotal    65.0
       NumberOfOrders  2
};     Raw View
c.AddOrder(o2);
}
```

FIGURE 42-8

The first line in the tooltip is the same as what you created using the `DebuggerDisplay` attribute. To generate the rest of the tooltip, you need to create an additional class that can act as a substitute for presenting this information. You then need to attribute the `Customer` class with the `DebuggerTypeProxy` attribute so that the debugger knows to use that class instead of the `Customer` class when displaying the tooltip. The following code snippet shows the `CustomerProxy` class that has been nested within the `Customer` class:

C#

```
[DebuggerDisplay("Customer {CustomerName} has {Orders.Count} orders")]
[DebuggerTypeProxy(typeof(Customer.CustomerProxy))]
public class Customer
{
    private int m_CountAccessed;
    public int OrderCount
    {
        get
        {
            m_CountAccessed++;
```

```
                return this.Orders.Count;
            }
        }

        public int CountAccessed
        {
            get
            {
                return this.m_CountAccessed;
            }
        }

        public class CustomerProxy
        {
            public string CustomerName;
            public int NumberOfOrders;
            public decimal MaximumTotal = decimal.MinValue;
            public decimal MinimumTotal = decimal.MaxValue;

            public CustomerProxy(Customer c)
            {
                this.CustomerName = c.m_CustomerName;
                this.NumberOfOrders = c.m_Orders.Count;
                foreach (Order o in c.m_Orders)
                {
                    this.MaximumTotal = Math.Max(o.Total, this.MaximumTotal);
                    this.MinimumTotal = Math.Min(o.Total, this.MinimumTotal);
                }
            }
        }
    }
```

There are few reasons why you should create public nested classes, but a type proxy is a good example because it needs to be public so that it can be specified in the `DebuggerTypeProxy` attribute. It should be nested so that it can access private members from the `Customer` class without using the public accessors.

Raw View

On occasion, you might want to ignore the proxy type. For example, this might be true if you are consuming a third-party component that has a proxy type defined for it that disguises the underlying data structure. If something is going wrong with the way the component behaves, you might need to review the internal contents of the component to trace the source of the issue.

In Figure 42-8, you may have noticed at the bottom of the tooltip is a Raw View node. Expanding this node displays the debugger tooltip as it is normally shown, without any proxy types or debugger display values.

In addition, you can turn off all type proxies in Visual Studio through the Tools ➪ Options menu. Under the Debugging node, check the box that says Show Raw Structure of Objects in Variables Windows. Doing this prevents all type proxies and debugger displays from being shown.

VISUALIZERS

This section of the chapter looks at a feature in Visual Studio 2012 that you can use to help debug more complex data structures. Two of the most common data types programmers work with are `Strings` and `DataTables`. `Strings` are often much larger than the area that can display within a tooltip, and the structure of the `DataTable` object is not suitable for displaying in a tooltip, even using a type proxy. In both of these cases, a visualizer has been created that enables the data to be viewed in a sensible format.

After a visualizer has been created for a particular type, a magnifying glass icon appears in the first line of the debugger tooltip. Clicking this icon displays the visualizer. Figure 42-9 shows the Text Visualizer dialog that appears.

Before you can start writing a visualizer, you need to add a reference to the `Microsoft.VisualStudio.DebuggerVisualizers` namespace. To do this, right-click the project in the Solution Explorer, and select Add Reference from the context menu. You should also add this namespace as an import to any classes for which you plan to create debugger visualizers.

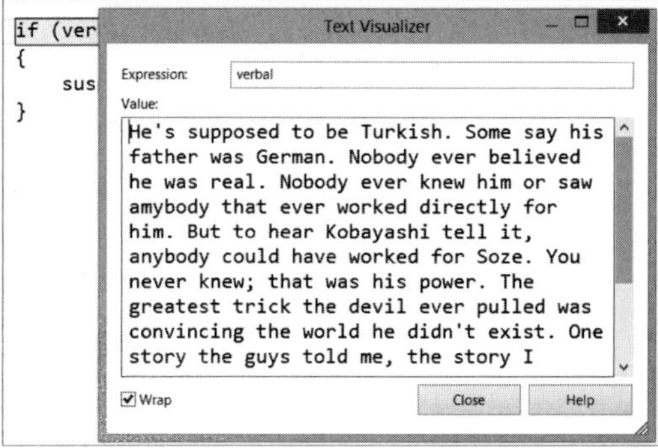

FIGURE 42-9

A visualizer typically consists of two parts: the class that acts as a host for the visualizer and is referenced by the `DebuggerVisualizer` attribute applied to the class being visualized, and the form that is then used to display, or visualize, the class. Figure 42-10 shows a simple form, `CustomerForm`, which can be used to represent the customer information. This is just an ordinary Windows Form with a couple of `TextBox` controls, a `DataGridView` control, and a button. The only unique aspect to this form is that it has been marked as `Serializable`, and its constructor has been changed to accept a `Customer` object, from which the customer information is extracted and displayed, as shown in the following code:

C#

```
[Serializable()]
public partial class CustomerForm : Form
{
    public CustomerForm(Customer c)
    {
        InitializeComponent();

        this.txtCustomerId.Text = c.CustomerId.ToString();
        this.txtCustomerName.Text = c.CustomerName;
        this.dgOrders.DataSource = c.Orders;
    }

    private void btnOk_Click(object sender, EventArgs e)
    {
        this.DialogResult = DialogResult.OK;
        this.Close();
    }
}
```

The next stage is to wire this form up to be used as the visualizer for the `Customer` class. You do this by creating the nested `CustomerVisualizer` class, which inherits from the `DialogDebuggerVisualizer` abstract class, as shown in the following code:

Customer Information

Customer ID: d6e1ccb5-a6fb-48d9-95b3-fbd42e0e73b4

Customer Name: Roger Kint

OrderId	Total	DateOrdered	Status	DateShipped
a96dc1e0-7a08-4f...	90	10/2/2012 8:50 ...	New	
6a749d26-7d45-4...	65	10/2/2012 8:50 ...	New	

Ok

FIGURE 42-10

C#

```
[Serializable()]
[DebuggerDisplay("Customer {CustomerName} has {Orders.Count} orders")]
[DebuggerTypeProxy(typeof(Customer.CustomerProxy))]
[DebuggerVisualizer(typeof(Customer.CustomerVisualizer))]
public class Customer
{
    //...
    public class CustomerVisualizer : DialogDebuggerVisualizer
    {
        protected override void Show(
                         IDialogVisualizerService windowService,
                         IVisualizerObjectProvider objectProvider)
        {
            Customer c = (Customer)objectProvider.GetObject();
            CustomerForm cf = new CustomerForm(c);
            windowService.ShowDialog(cf);
        }
    }
}
```

Unlike the type proxy, which interacts with the actual `Customer` object being debugged, visualizers need to serialize the class being debugged so that the class can be moved from the process being debugged to the process that is doing the debugging, and will subsequently be shown in the visualizer. As such, both the `Customer` and `Order` classes need to be marked with the `Serializable` attribute.

The `Show` method of the `CustomerVisualizer` class does three things. To display the `Customer` object being debugged, first you need to get a reference to this object. You do this via the `GetObject` method on the `ObjectProvider` object. Because the communication between the two processes is done via a stream, this method does the heavy lifting associated with deserializing the object so that you can work with it.

Next, you need to pass the `Customer` object to a new instance of the `CustomerForm`. Finally, use the `ShowDialog` method on the `windowService` object to display the form. It is important that you display the form using this object because it ensures that the form displays on the appropriate UI thread.

Lastly, note that the `CustomerVisualizer` class is referenced in the `DebuggerVisualizer` attribute, ensuring that the debugger uses this class to load the visualizer for `Customer` objects.

If you write components and want to ship visualizers separately from the components themselves, visualizers can be installed by placing the appropriate assembly into either the `C:\Program Files\Microsoft Visual Studio 11.0\Common7\Packages\Debugger\Visualizers` directory (`Program Files (x86)` on 64-bit Windows), or the `Documents\Visual Studio 2012\Visualizers` directory.

ADVANCED TECHNIQUES

Thus far, this chapter has covered how to display and visualize objects you debug. In earlier chapters, you learned how to modify field and property values on the object being debugged via the DataTip. The missing link is being able to edit more complex data objects. The final section in this chapter looks at how to extend your visualizer so that you can save changes to the `Customer` object.

Saving Changes to Your Object

When you created the `CustomerVisualizer`, you had to retrieve the `Customer` object from the communication stream using the `GetObject` method. This essentially gave you a clone of the `Customer` object being debugged to use with the visualizer. To save any changes you make in the `CustomerVisualizer`, you need to send the new `Customer` object back to the process being debugged. You can do this using the `ReplaceObject` method on the `ObjectProvider`, which gives you a `CustomerVisualizer`.

Before you can call the `ReplaceObject` method you need to make some changes to pass the modified `Customer` object back to the visualizer. You can do this by saving the `Customer` object to an internal variable when it is initially passed into the class and exposing this variable via a read-only property. This is shown in the following code:

C#

```
[Serializable()]
public partial class CustomerForm : Form
{
    public CustomerForm(Customer c)
    {
        InitializeComponent();

        this.txtCustomerId.Text = c.CustomerId.ToString();
        this.txtCustomerName.Text = c.CustomerName;
        this.dgOrders.DataSource = c.Orders;

        m_ModifiedCustomer = c;
    }

    private Customer m_ModifiedCustomer;
    public Customer ModifiedCustomer
    {
        get
        {
            m_ModifiedCustomer.CustomerId = new Guid(txtCustomerId.Text);
            m_ModifiedCustomer.CustomerName = txtCustomerName.Text;
            m_ModifiedCustomer.Orders = (List<Order>)dgOrders.DataSource;
            return m_ModifiedCustomer;
        }
    }
    private void btnOk_Click(object sender, EventArgs e)
    {
        this.DialogResult = DialogResult.OK;
        this.Close();
    }
}
```

You can now easily access the modified `Customer` object and save the changes back by calling the `ReplaceObject` method as shown here:

C#

```
[Serializable()]
[DebuggerDisplay("Customer {CustomerName} has {Orders.Count} orders")]
[DebuggerTypeProxy(GetType(Customer.CustomerProxy))]
[DebuggerVisualizer(GetType(Customer.CustomerVisualizer))]
public class Customer
{
    ...

    public class CustomerVisualizer : DialogDebuggerVisualizer
    {
        protected override void Show(
                        IDialogVisualizerService windowService,
                        IVisualizerObjectProvider objectProvider)
        {
            Customer c = (Customer)objectProvider.GetObject();
            CustomerForm cf = new CustomerForm(c);
            if (windowService.ShowDialog(cf) ==
                                System.Windows.Forms.DialogResult.OK)
                objectProvider.ReplaceObject(cf.ModifiedCustomer);
        }
    }
}
```

> **NOTE** *An alternative method is to use data binding for all the* `Customer` *fields on the form with a* `BindingSource` *object. This* `BindingSource` *object can be exposed with a public modifier, thereby making it accessible from the visualizer class. All that is needed then is to set the* `Customer` *object as the* `DataSource` *of this* `BindingSource` *object by the visualizer class.*

SUMMARY

Debugging applications is one of the most time-consuming and frustrating activities in the development cycle. In this chapter, you learned how you can take charge of Visual Studio 2012 by customizing the debugging experience.

Using debugging proxy types and visualizers, you can control how information is presented to you while you debug your application. This means that you can easily determine when your application is not functioning correctly and trace the source of the issue.

Debugging Web Applications

WHAT'S IN THIS CHAPTER?

- Using Visual Studio to debug both server-side ASP.NET code and client-side JavaScript running in a web browser
- Enabling and viewing ASP.NET trace logs for an individual web page or the entire application
- Configuring Health Monitoring so that you are notified as soon as a problem occurs in an ASP.NET application

With Visual Studio 2012, debugging solutions for the web is just as straightforward as doing the same for Windows-based applications. You can use most of the same debugging windows already discussed in previous chapters, as well as deal with errors through the Exception Assistant. However, you can use some differences and additional features specific to web applications to target your debugging practices more closely to the web paradigm.

In addition to the standard debugging techniques, ASP.NET also provides you with a comprehensive tracing capability, and even the capability to perform health monitoring on your system to ensure it runs in the manner you expect, and exposing problematic scenarios when it doesn't.

> **NOTE** *If you use Windows 7 with UAC, and you use the full version of IIS rather than the built-in web development server or IIS Express for debugging, then you must launch Visual Studio with administrator rights. Right-click the Visual Studio 2012 shortcut, and select Run as Administrator. To always launch as the administrator, right-click the shortcut and select Properties; then select the Compatibility tab, and check the Run This Program as an Administrator check box.*

DEBUGGING SERVER-SIDE ASP.NET CODE

Before you can perform any debugging in a web application, you first need to ensure that ASP.NET debugging is enabled in your web application or website project. For web application projects, enable debugging options by right-clicking the project entry in the Solution Explorer and selecting Properties. Select the Web tab option page and ensure that the ASP.NET debugger option is checked, as illustrated in Figure 43-1.

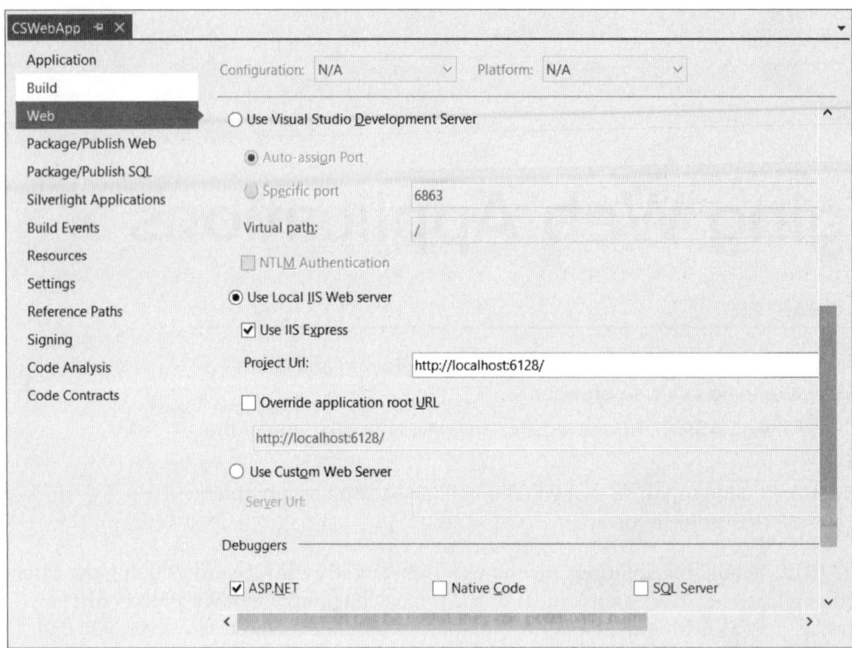

FIGURE 43-1

If you want to include unmanaged code, stored procedures, or Silverlight in your debugging of the web applications, you can activate the Native Code, SQL Server, and Silverlight debuggers here. Native code and SQL Server debugging are explained in the next chapter, and Silverlight debugging is discussed in the "Debugging Silverlight" section later in this chapter.

> **NOTE** *Enabling debugging in other web application projects, such as ASP.NET Web Service or ASP.NET MVC applications, is exactly the same as for standard ASP.NET web applications. From a debugging perspective, there are no differences between any of these project types.*

Because website projects do not have a project file, you must use a slightly different procedure to enable debugging. Enable debugging in website projects by right-clicking the project entry in the Solution Explorer and selecting Property Pages from the context menu. When the Property Pages dialog displays, navigate to the Start Options page, and ensure that the ASP.NET debugger option is checked, as shown in Figure 43-2.

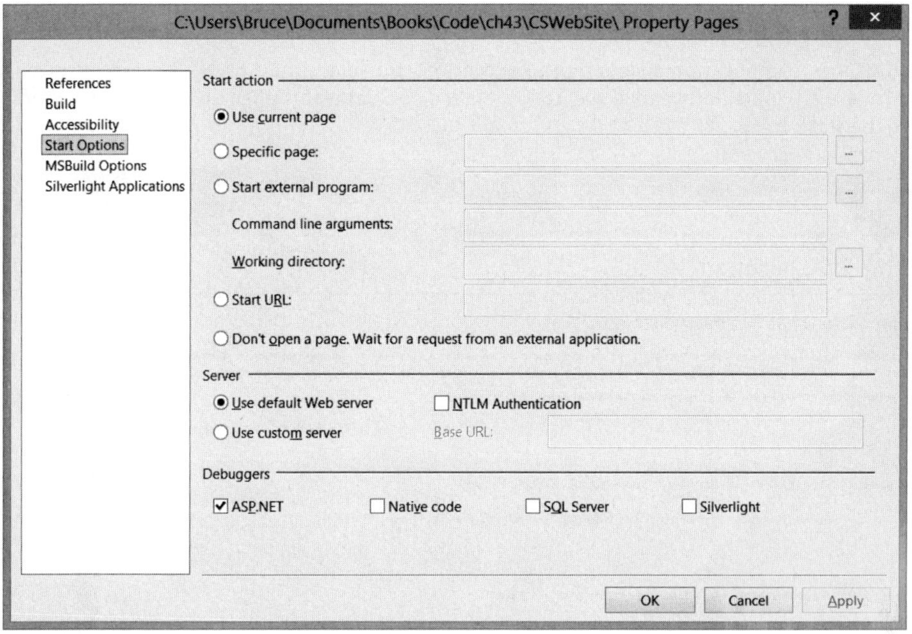

FIGURE 43-2

As with web application projects, you can also customize how a website project is to be started, including not opening any specific page, but running the server so it listens for a request from another application.

In addition to enabling the ASP.NET debugger in the property pages, you must enable the compiler debug option in the `web.config` file. Locate the compilation node within `system.web` and set the `debug` attribute to `true`. The following code shows a minimal `web.config` file with the debug option enabled, ready for hooking the debugger to the application:

```
<?xml version="1.0"?>
<configuration>
    <system.web>
        <compilation debug="true" targetFramework="4.5" />
    </system.web>
    <system.webServer>
        <modules runAllManagedModulesForAllRequests="true" />
    </system.webServer>
</configuration>
```

Note that even when you activate the ASP.NET debugger in the Start Options, without setting the `debug` attribute to `true`, you cannot debug the application. However, Visual Studio can detect this discrepancy and present you with a dialog informing you that to debug you need to change the `web.config` file. It also provides an option for Visual Studio to automatically change this attribute for you.

> **NOTE** *You should never deploy an ASP.NET application into production with the* `debug="true"` *option set within the* `web.config` *file. Doing so causes your application to run slower, use more memory, and prevent some items from being cached.*

Web Application Exceptions

By default, when your web application encounters an exception, it displays the ASP.NET server error page, as shown in Figure 43-3. Colloquially called the Yellow Screen of Death, this page displays the exception details including the stack trace.

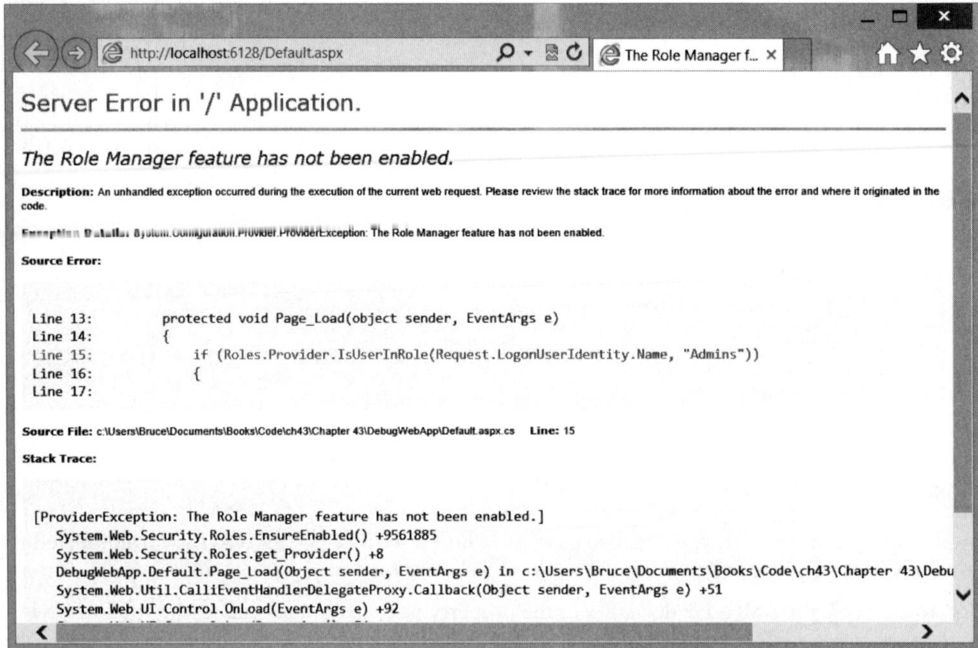

http://localhost:6128/Default.aspx
The Role Manager f...
Server Error in '/' Application.
The Role Manager feature has not been enabled.
Description: An unhandled exception occurred during the execution of the current web request. Please review the stack trace for more information about the error and where it originated in the code.
ProviderException: The Role Manager feature has not been enabled.
Source Error:
Line 13: protected void Page_Load(object sender, EventArgs e)
Line 14: {
Line 15: if (Roles.Provider.IsUserInRole(Request.LogonUserIdentity.Name, "Admins"))
Line 16: {
Line 17:
Source File: c:\Users\Bruce\Documents\Books\Code\ch43\Chapter 43\DebugWebApp\Default.aspx.cs Line: 15
Stack Trace:
[ProviderException: The Role Manager feature has not been enabled.]
System.Web.Security.Roles.EnsureEnabled() +9561885
System.Web.Security.Roles.get_Provider() +8
DebugWebApp.Default.Page_Load(Object sender, EventArgs e) in c:\Users\Bruce\Documents\Books\Code\ch43\Chapter 43\Debu
System.Web.Util.CalliEventHandlerDelegateProxy.Callback(Object sender, EventArgs e) +51
System.Web.UI.Control.OnLoad(EventArgs e) +92

FIGURE 43-3

The server error page is generated under both debug and normal execution. Although it is useful to have this information during development, it is not something that you should display to your end users. Fortunately, there is an easy way to configure redirections for exceptions, including standard HTTP errors, by editing the `customErrors` section in the `web.config` file.

Modifying the previous `web.config` file to include these redirection options for 403 (access denied) and 404 (page not found) can result in a configuration similar to the following:

```
<?xml version="1.0"?>
<configuration>
    <system.web>
        <compilation debug="true" targetFramework="4.5" />
        <customErrors mode="RemoteOnly" defaultRedirect="GenericErrorPage.htm">
            <error statusCode="403" redirect="AccessDenied.html" />
            <error statusCode="404" redirect="PageNotFound.html" />
        </customErrors>
    </system.web>
    <system.webServer>
        <modules runAllManagedModulesForAllRequests="true" />
    </system.webServer>
</configuration>
```

The `mode` attribute of the `customErrors` section defines three options for displaying a custom error page instead of the default server error page:

- **On:** The custom error page always displays.
- **Off:** The server error page always displays.
- **RemoteOnly:** The server error page displays if the browser request comes from the local computer; otherwise, the custom error page displays.

The server error page is useful in production scenarios in which you cannot run the application in Debug mode. However, when debugging, it is useful to break execution as soon as an exception occurs. You can do this by enabling the Break When an Exception Is Thrown option for the Common Language Runtime. Figure 43-4 shows how this option is set in the Exceptions dialog under the Debug ➪ Exceptions menu item.

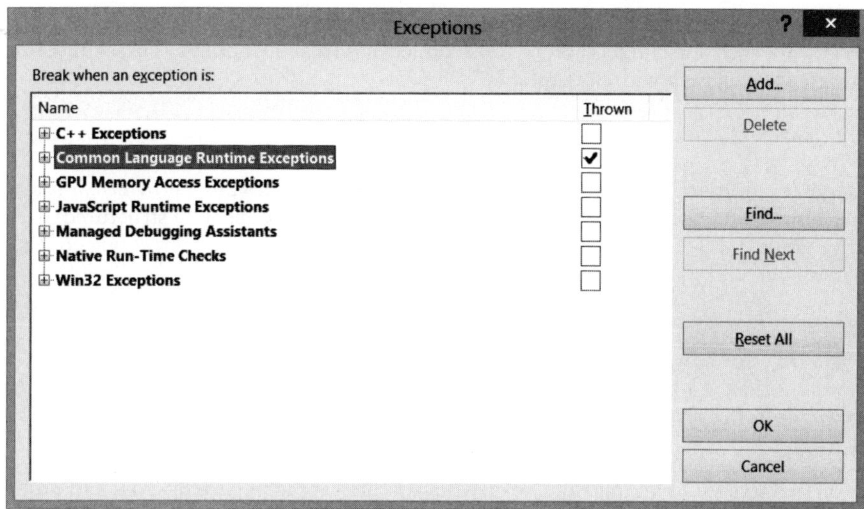

FIGURE 43-4

After you enable this option, when an exception occurs, Visual Studio drops back into the IDE and positions the workspace so that the statement at issue is visible. Just like Windows-based applications, Visual Studio can aid you by displaying the Exception Assistant when errors occur. As shown in Figure 43-5, web errors are fully detailed and include information about which part of the statement is in error.

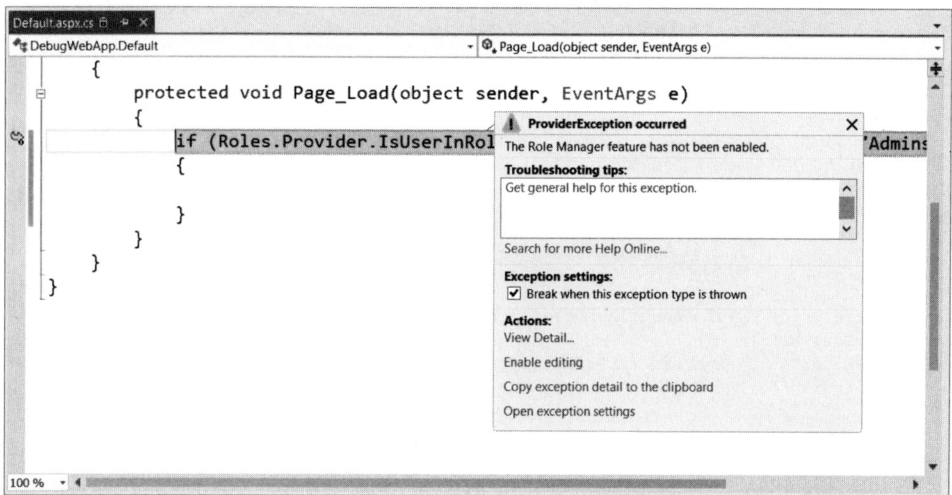

FIGURE 43-5

You can gather additional information on the error by clicking the View Detail link, which provides you with a comprehensive exception object visualizer that you can navigate to determine the content of the error at hand.

Edit and Continue

Edit and Continue, which enables you to modify code when the application is paused in a debug session, is disabled by default in ASP.NET web applications. This useful feature can be enabled by right-clicking the project entry in the Solution Explorer and selecting Properties. Under the Web tab option page, check the Enable Edit and Continue option. This is supported only for the built-in Visual Studio development web server.

Website projects do not support Edit and Continue; however, because they naturally support an iterative style of development, it is not such a useful feature for those projects. Edit and Continue is explained in more detail in Chapter 41, "Debugging with Breakpoints."

Error Handling

Although debugging your applications is indeed easy with the tools Visual Studio 2012 provides, it is always best to try to avoid error situations proactively. You can do this in web applications with structured Try-Catch exception handling, but you also want to make your solutions more solid by including code to handle any errors that fall outside any Catch conditions.

> **NOTE** *The term* error handling *and not* exception handling *is used here because it is broader than trapping program exceptions and also covers HTML errors, such as Page Not Found and Authentication Required.*

You can catch errors on two levels: On an individual page you can intercept unexpected errors and produce a custom-built error, or you can catch errors on an application-wide level through the implementation of a routine to handle errors in the `global.asax` file.

Page-Level Errors

To handle an error on an individual page, you need to implement an event handler routine that intercepts the `Error` event that is implemented in the Page's base class. When this event is raised, you can then perform whatever actions you need to take place when unexpected errors occur. A typical routine might look like this:

C#

```
void Page_Error(object sender, EventArgs e)
{
    Response.Write("An unexpected error has occurred.");
    Server.ClearError();
}
```

VB

```
Private Sub Page_Error(ByVal sender As Object, ByVal e As System.EventArgs) _
    Handles MyBase.Error
    Response.Write("An unexpected error has occurred.")
    Server.ClearError()
End Sub
```

As discussed previously, you can also set custom redirections for standard HTTP error codes in the `web.config` file, so you should use this method only for errors that are not already handled and are specific to the individual page.

Application-Level Errors

At the web application level, you can also trap a series of errors through the `global.asax` file. By default, Visual Studio 2012 web projects do not include this file, so you first need to add it to the project through the Add New Item dialog. Select the Global Application Class item, leave the name as `global.asax`, and click Add to add the file to your project.

When this class is added to the project, the template includes stubs for the commonly encountered application events, including the error event. To handle any errors that are not catered to elsewhere in the project, add your processing code to this `Application_Error` routine, like so:

C#

```
protected void Application_Error(object sender, EventArgs e)
{
    Server.Transfer("UnexpectedError.aspx");
}
```

VB

```
Sub Application_Error(ByVal sender As Object, ByVal e As EventArgs)
    Server.Transfer("UnexpectedError.aspx")
End Sub
```

This sample routine simply transfers the user to an errors page that determines what to do by interrogating the `Server.GetLastError` property.

DEBUGGING CLIENT-SIDE JAVASCRIPT

One of the most useful features of Visual Studio 2012 for front-end web developers is the excellent support for debugging client-side JavaScript code. Combined with the IntelliSense support for JavaScript, this significantly eases the difficulty of developing JavaScript code.

> **NOTE** *JavaScript debugging works only if you use Internet Explorer as your web browser during the debug session.*

Setting Breakpoints in JavaScript Code

Setting breakpoints for JavaScript code is no different from setting any other breakpoint. Within the editor window, any breakpoints in JavaScript code display with a white circle in the center, as shown in Figure 43-6.

> **WARNING** *JavaScript debugging will be disabled if the Silverlight debugger is enabled.*

```
<script type="text/javascript">
    function showOption(selectCtl) {
        var optionSelected = selectCtl.value;
        optionDisplay = document.getElementById("divOptionSelected");
        optionDisplay.innerHTML = optionSelected + " was selected.";
    }
</script>
```

FIGURE 43-6

> **NOTE** *JavaScript breakpoints have the same functionality as standard breakpoints. This includes setting conditions, hit counts, or even running a macro as part of a tracepoint.*

When the debugger hits a breakpoint, it pauses execution and displays the HTML code that has been rendered on the client, as shown in Figure 43-7. This provides a true debug experience because it includes all client-side elements such as the ViewState and server controls rendered in HTML.

```
Default.aspx [dynamic]
<body>
    <script type="text/javascript">
        function showOption(selectCtl) {
            var optionSelected = selectCtl.value;
            optionDisplay = document.getElementById("divOptionSelected");
            optionDisplay.innerH[document {...}]Selected + " was selected.";
        }
    </script>

    <form method="post" action="De
    <div>
        <select id="selOptions" or                                 );">
            <option value="Option                                  Option 1</option>
            <option value="Option
        </select>
    </div>
    <div id="divOptionSelected">Op                                 v>
    </form>
</body>
</html>

[Methods]           {...}
activeElement       {...}
alinkColor          "#0000ff"
all                 {...}
anchors             {...}
applets             {...}
ATTRIBUTE_NODE      2
attributes          null
bgColor             "#ffffff"
body                {...}
CDATA_SECTION_NODE  4
characterSet        "utf-8"
charset             "utf-8"
childNodes          {...}
COMMENT_NODE        8
```

FIGURE 43-7

Visual Studio 2012 also has comprehensive watch visualizers for client-side elements. Figure 43-7 demonstrates this with a tooltip that shows the properties and methods of the document object.

You can also set both client-side JavaScript breakpoints and Visual Basic or C# server-side breakpoints at the same time on the same page. This enables you to step through both server-side and client-side code in a single debug session.

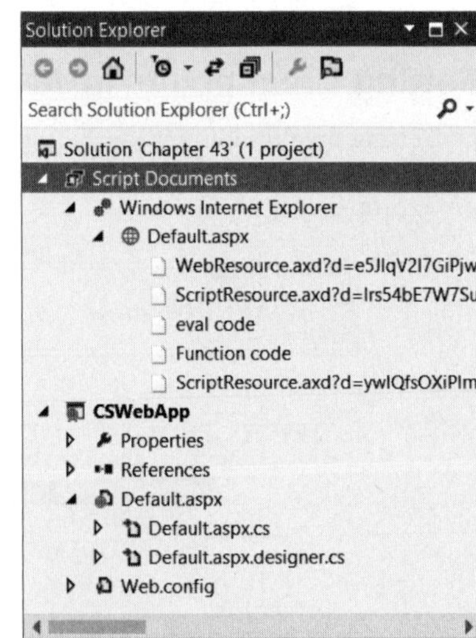

FIGURE 43-8

Debugging Dynamically Generated JavaScript

Several scenarios exist in which ASP.NET sends down to the client JavaScript that has been dynamically generated on the server. For example, the ASP.NET AJAX controls such as the Update Panel generates client-side JavaScript files that are actually stored as resources in the ScriptManager control.

When you run a web application in Debug mode, the Visual Studio Solution Explorer shows a list of all the script references that the page you debug has loaded, as shown in Figure 43-8. Double-clicking any of the links under the Script Documents node displays the JavaScript code and enables you to set breakpoints within those scripts.

Debugging ASP.NET AJAX JavaScript

ASP.NET AJAX provides both Debug and Release versions of its client JavaScript libraries. The Release version is optimized for performance and minimizes the size of the JavaScript that must be downloaded to the client. The Debug version is more verbose and provides additional debugging features at run time, such as type and argument checking.

If debugging is enabled in the `web .config` file, ASP.NET AJAX uses a debug version of the client libraries. You can also enable the debug version on a per-page basis by setting `ScriptMode="Debug"` on the ScriptManager control.

ASP.NET AJAX also includes the `Sys.Debug` class, which you can use to add debug statements to your client JavaScript. You can use this class to display the properties of objects at run time, generate trace messages, or use assertions.

The Page Inspector

One of the major improvements over the last few years of browser enhancements is the introduction of tools that enable developers to more easily explore the HTML, CSS, and JavaScript that go into a specific page. Internet Explorer, Firefox, and Chrome have a set of developer tools specifically designed to assist in this process. With Visual Studio 2012, the Page Inspector tool enables developers to inspect the elements that display in the browser and integrates that experience with the originating source code. As well, you can make changes to the HTML and CSS dynamically *and* have those changes persisted in the source.

To start the process, right-click a project or page in Solution Explorer, and select the View in Inspector option. Alternatively, you can use the Ctrl+K, Ctrl+G keyboard chord to launch the Page Inspector for the current page. Launching the Page Inspector builds the project and launches it through the Page Inspector window (see Figure 43-9).

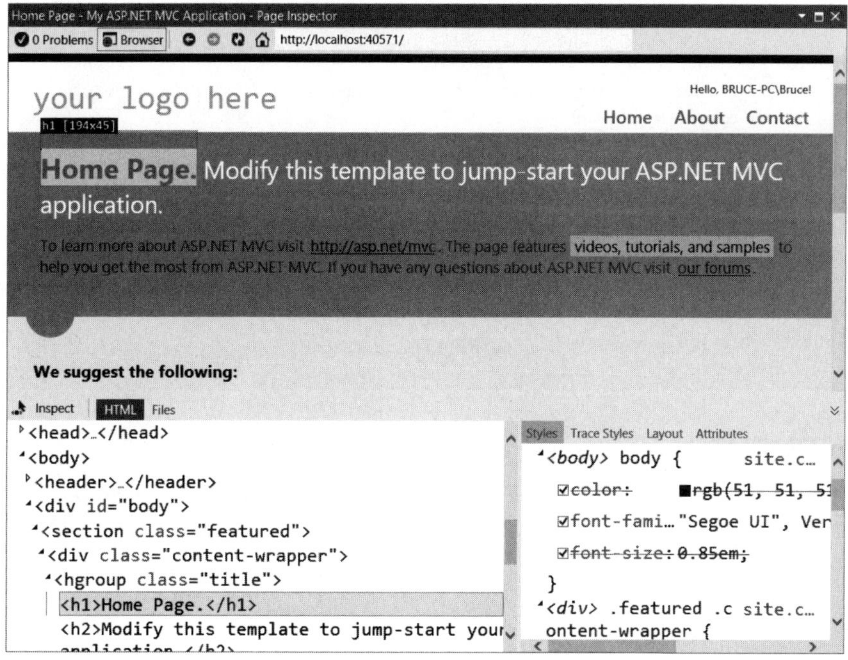

FIGURE 43-9

The Page Inspector requires an app setting in the `web.config` file to be present, so if this is the first time running it for the project, you'll be prompted to add it.

As you can see in Figure 43-9, the Page Inspector has a number of regions that operate with one another. The top half contains the page as it would appear in a browser. In the lower-left portion is the HTML that is used to render that page. Selecting an element in the HTML portion causes the corresponding visual element in the top half to be highlighted (refer to Figure 43-9).

The region to the bottom right is also related to the selected HTML element. Specifically, it contains the CSS rules that have been applied to the element. You can use the check box to the left of the rule to enable or disable the style to see its effect. And by selecting the value of the style to the right of the rule, it can be modified with the change immediately reflected in the top half.

But the Page Inspector doesn't stop at enabling you to modify the value of the CSS rules. You can also easily find the file where the rule is defined through the Trace Styles tab (see Figure 43-10).

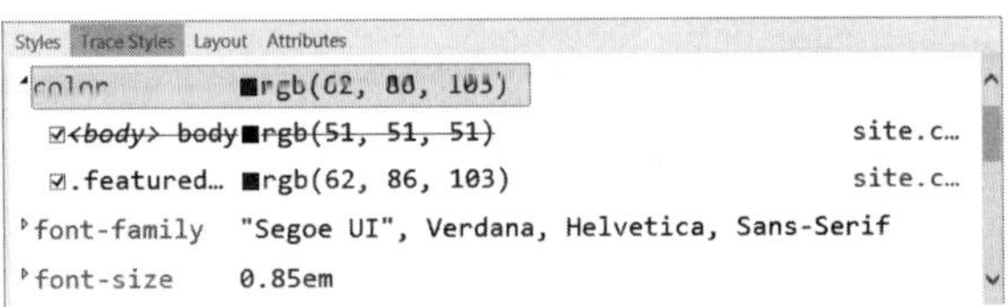

FIGURE 43-10

Locate the style you want to trace in the list and expand to identify the HTML element about which you are concerned. Click the name of the element (or the link to the file on the right) to go to the location where the style is defined, making it easy to update the value permanently.

The contents of an HTML page can be the result of processing a number of different files. It can be difficult to keep track of all these files for a given page. To address this need, the Page Inspector includes a Files tab that lists the contributing files (see Figure 43-11).

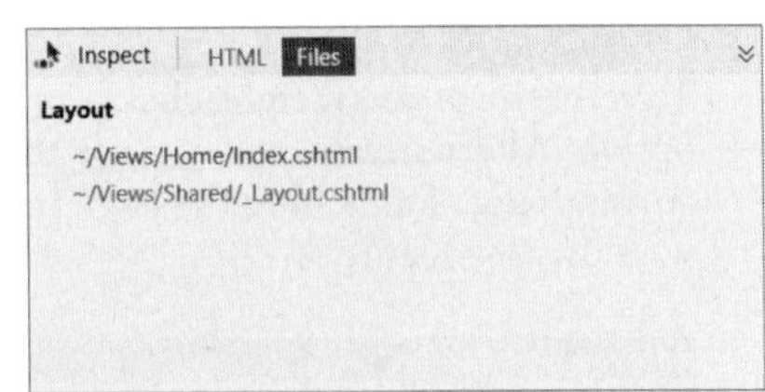

FIGURE 43-11

One other area in which the Page Inspector can come in handy is when working with the attributes associated with the HTML elements. In the Attributes section of the Inspector (see Figure 43-12), a list of the attributes that are defined on the currently selected element is visible. The current value for each attribute displays, but by clicking the value, you can place it into edit mode where it can be changed. And the change is reflected in the browser view. You can also add or remove attributes from the elements using the Add attribute and Remove attribute buttons.

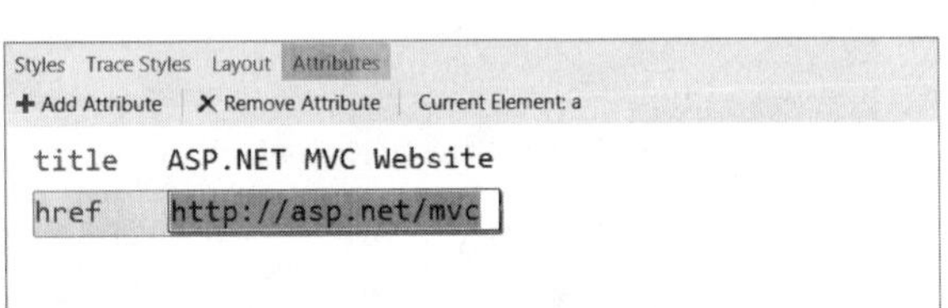

FIGURE 43-12

DEBUGGING SILVERLIGHT

Visual Studio 2012 includes a native debugger that makes it easy to debug Silverlight applications. When you create a new Silverlight application, Visual Studio prompts you either to generate an HTML test page to host the Silverlight application, or to utilize an existing or new web project, as shown in Figure 43-13.

Figure 43-13 displays a test page that hosts the Silverlight application in the web application project that is part of the existing solution, which enables Silverlight debugging in this web application. If you select either of the other two options, you do not need to perform any additional steps to enable Silverlight debugging.

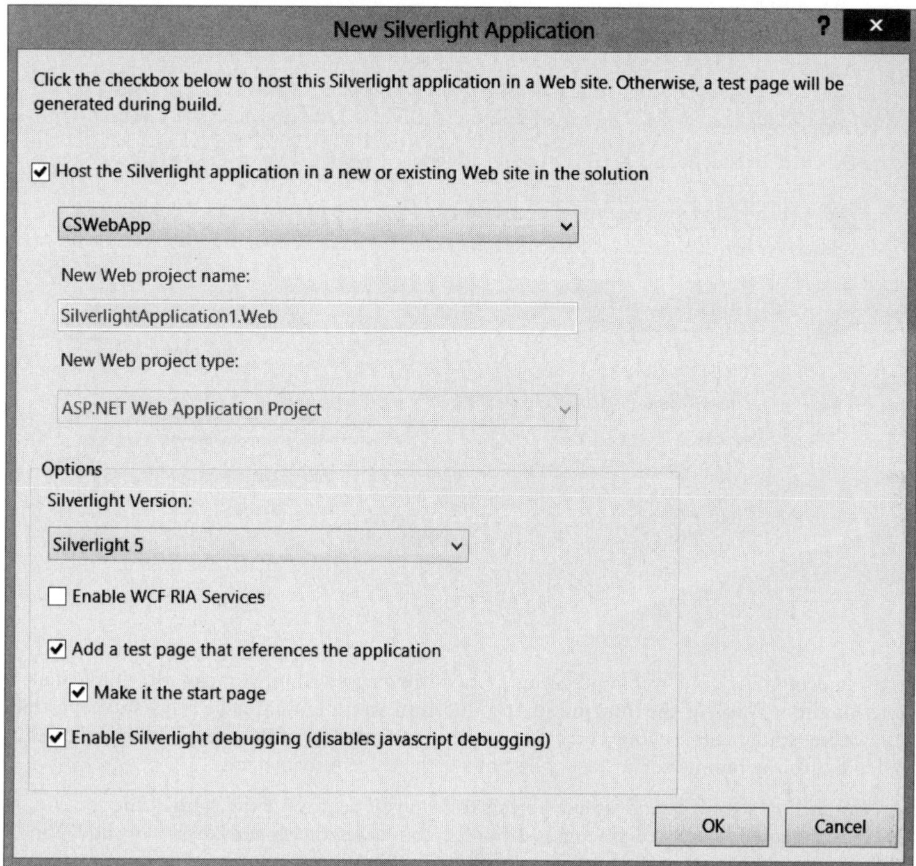

FIGURE 43-13

You can always enable or display support for Silverlight debugging in an existing web application project under the Web option page of the project properties.

After the Silverlight debugger is enabled, you can set breakpoints in the code-behind class files of the XAML pages. When the breakpoint is encountered during debugging, the session pauses and displays the current line of code, as shown in Figure 43-14. You can step through the code, view the call stack, and interrogate the properties of objects, just as you would with any Web or Windows Forms application.

The only major limitations with Silverlight debugging are that Edit and Continue are not supported, and JavaScript debugging is disabled.

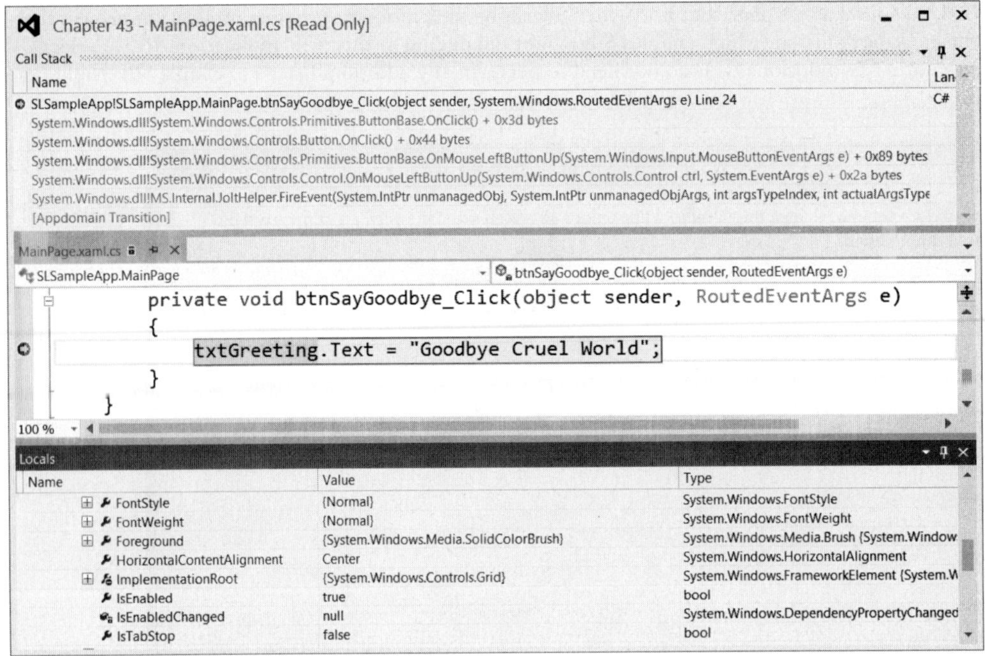

FIGURE 43-14

TRACING

In addition to actively debugging your web applications when things go wrong, you can also implement ASP .NET tracing functionality to look at the information produced in an individual page request. Using tracing enables you to add debug statements to your code that are only viewable when viewing locally; when the web application deploys to the remote server, users do not see the trace information.

Trace information can include variables and simple objects to help you determine the state of the specific request and how it was executed. ASP.NET tracing is different from using the `Trace` class in normal Windows applications in that its output is produced on the actual ASP.NET web page or in a standalone trace viewer, rather than the output windows that `Trace` commands use.

Page-Level Tracing

To implement page-level tracing, you simply need to include a `trace` attribute in the `@Page` directive at the top of the page you want to trace. A simple ASPX page with tracing activated might look like the following:

```
<%@ Page Language="C#" AutoEventWireup="true" Trace="true"
TraceMode="SortByCategory" CodeBehind="ShowTrace.aspx.cs"
Inherits="CSWebApp.ShowTrace" %>

<!DOCTYPE html PUBLIC "-//W3C//DTD XHTML 1.0 Transitional//EN"
"http://www.w3.org/TR/xhtml1/DTD/xhtml1-transitional.dtd">

<html xmlns="http://www.w3.org/1999/xhtml" >
<head runat="server">
    <title>Trace Example Page</title>
</head>
<body>
    <form runat="server">
```

```
        <div>Hello!</div>
        </form>
    </body>
    </html>
```

In addition, you can specify how the tracing messages associated with the page request should appear by using the `TraceMode` attribute. Set this to `SortByTime` to output the tracing messages in the order that they were produced, or `SortByCategory` to categorize them into different message types. Figure 43-15 shows the trace output for the sample page defined in the previous code when sorted by category.

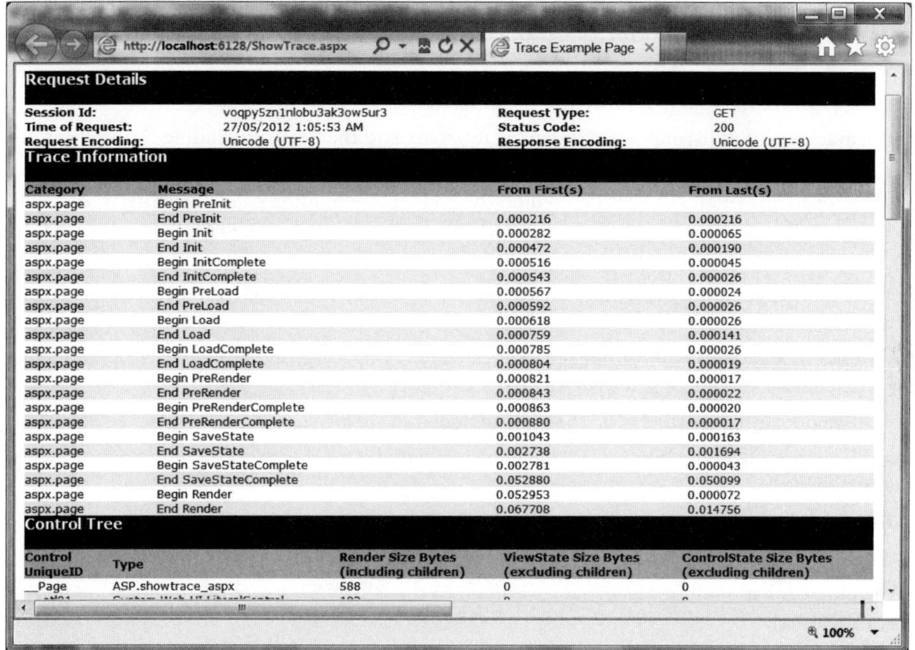

Request Details

Session Id:	voqpy5zn1nlobu3ak3ow5ur3	Request Type:	GET
Time of Request:	27/05/2012 1:05:53 AM	Status Code:	200
Request Encoding:	Unicode (UTF-8)	Response Encoding:	Unicode (UTF-8)

Trace Information

Category	Message	From First(s)	From Last(s)
aspx.page	Begin PreInit		
aspx.page	End PreInit	0.000216	0.000216
aspx.page	Begin Init	0.000282	0.000065
aspx.page	End Init	0.000472	0.000190
aspx.page	Begin InitComplete	0.000516	0.000045
aspx.page	End InitComplete	0.000543	0.000026
aspx.page	Begin PreLoad	0.000567	0.000024
aspx.page	End PreLoad	0.000592	0.000026
aspx.page	Begin Load	0.000618	0.000026
aspx.page	End Load	0.000759	0.000141
aspx.page	Begin LoadComplete	0.000785	0.000026
aspx.page	End LoadComplete	0.000804	0.000019
aspx.page	Begin PreRender	0.000821	0.000017
aspx.page	End PreRender	0.000843	0.000022
aspx.page	Begin PreRenderComplete	0.000863	0.000020
aspx.page	End PreRenderComplete	0.000880	0.000017
aspx.page	Begin SaveState	0.001043	0.000163
aspx.page	End SaveState	0.002738	0.001694
aspx.page	Begin SaveStateComplete	0.002781	0.000043
aspx.page	End SaveStateComplete	0.052880	0.050099
aspx.page	Begin Render	0.052953	0.000072
aspx.page	End Render	0.067708	0.014756

Control Tree

Control UniqueID	Type	Render Size Bytes (including children)	ViewState Size Bytes (excluding children)	ControlState Size Bytes (excluding children)
__Page	ASP.showtrace_aspx	588	0	0

FIGURE 43-15

Application-Level Tracing

You can enable application-level tracing through the `web.config` file. Within the `system.web` node, you need to include a trace node that contains the attribute enabled with a value of `true`. When using application-level tracing, you can control how the tracing is produced through the `pageOutput` attribute. When set to `true`, you receive the tracing information at the bottom of every page (refer to Figure 43-15), whereas a value of `false` ensures that the tracing information never appears on the page and is instead only accessible through the Trace Viewer (covered in "The Trace Viewer" section later in this chapter). You can also restrict the amount of information to trace with the `requestLimit` attribute. Including a trace node for the `web.config` file you saw earlier in this chapter results in a configuration like the following:

```
<?xml version="1.0"?>
<configuration>
    <system.web>
        <compilation debug="true" targetFramework="4.5" />
        <customErrors mode="RemoteOnly" defaultRedirect="GenericErrorPage.htm">
            <error statusCode="403" redirect="AccessDenied.html" />
            <error statusCode="404" redirect="PageNotFound.html" />
        </customErrors>
        <trace enabled="true" pageOutput="false" traceMode="SortByCategory"/>
```

```
        </system.web>
        <system.webServer>
            <modules runAllManagedModulesForAllRequests="true" />
        </system.webServer>
    </configuration>
        </system.web>
    </configuration>
```

Trace Output

Tracing output is voluminous. The simple Hello page defined earlier produces almost three full printed pages of information, including the following categories of data:

- **Request Details:** The specific details of the current session, time of the request, what type of request it was, and the HTTP code that is returned to the browser.
- **Trace Information:** A full listing of each event as it begins and then ends, including the amount of time taken to process each event.
- **Control Tree:** A listing of all controls defined on the page, including the page object itself, as well as HTML elements. Each object also has a size listed, so you can determine whether any abnormal object sizes are affecting your application's performance.
- **Session State and Application State:** These two lists show the keys and their values for the individual session and the application overall.
- **Request Cookies Collection and Response Cookies Collection:** A list of any known ASP.NET request and response cookies on the system that your application can access.
- **Headers Collection:** A list of the HTTP headers included in the page.
- **Response Headers Collection:** The HTTP headers associated with the response, indicating what type of object is returned.
- **Form Collection:** A list of any forms defined in the page.
- **Querystring Collection:** A list of any query strings used in the page request.
- **Server Variables:** A list of all server variables known to the ASP.NET server and application you're currently executing.

As you can see, when tracing is implemented for a web page or application, you gain access to an enormous amount of information that you can then use to determine how your application performs. You can see whether problems exist in the various collections in the way of missing or extraneous data, as well as analyze the Trace Information list to determine whether there are any abnormally long processing times for any specific events.

The Trace Viewer

The Trace Viewer is a custom handler included in your web application when you have application tracing activated. When tracing is reported at the application level, you can navigate to this page and view all page tracing output as it occurs. To view the Trace Viewer, browse to the `trace.axd` page in the root directory of your website.

The Trace Viewer provides a summary table of all requests made in the application, along with the time the request was made and the HTTP status code returned in the response. It also provides a link to detailed information for each request (which is the same information that you can see on a page trace discussed earlier), as shown in Figure 43-16.

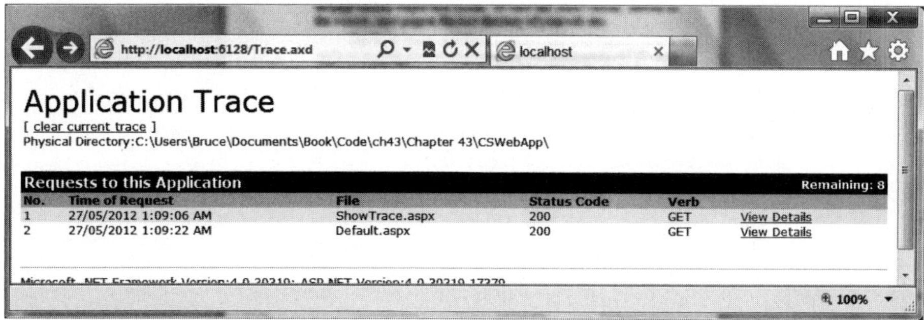

FIGURE 43-16

Custom Trace Output

You can supplement the default trace information with your own custom-built trace messages, using the `Trace.Warn` and `Trace.Write` methods. Both have the same set of syntactical overloads, and the only real difference is that messages outputted using the `Warn` method display in red text.

The simplest form for these commands is to include a message string like so:

```
Trace.Warn("Encountered a potential issue")
```

However, you can categorize your warnings and messages by using the second and third forms of the methods, including a category and optionally an error object as well:

```
Trace.Warn("MyApp Error Category", "Encountered a potential issue", myAppException)
```

HEALTH MONITORING

ASP.NET includes a built-in framework for generating and capturing events to monitor a web application. This feature, Health Monitoring, enables you to become more proactive in managing your production web applications, enabling you to be notified as soon as a problem occurs.

> **NOTE** *The Health Monitoring provides much more than just alerting you that an exception has occurred. You can also instrument your code and generate alerts for custom events, for example, if a user fails to log on or attempts to access a restricted area.*

Health Monitoring is enabled through the `web.config` file. Within the `system.web` node you need to include a `healthMonitoring` node that contains the attribute `enabled` with a value of `true`. This node also contains the details of which provider to use and rules for handling different events. Extending the `web.config` file from earlier, you can create an SMTP provider and a rule that e-mails the details of any unhandled exceptions to the webmaster. You can also modify the `web.config` file to include a reference to an SMTP server so that the provider can send the e-mail notifications.

```
<?xml version="1.0"?>
<configuration>
    <system.web>
        <compilation debug="true" targetFramework="4.5" />
        <customErrors mode="RemoteOnly" defaultRedirect="GenericErrorPage.htm">
            <error statusCode="403" redirect="AccessDenied.html" />
            <error statusCode="404" redirect="PageNotFound.html" />
        </customErrors>
        <trace enabled="true" pageOutput="false" traceMode="SortByCategory"/>
        <healthMonitoring enabled="true">
```

```
            <providers>
                <add name="SMTPProvider"
                     type="System.Web.Management.SimpleMailWebEventProvider"
                     from="server@yourdomain.com"
                     to="webmaster@yourdomain.com"
                     subjectPrefix="Exception on WebApp:"
                     bufferMode="Critical Notification"/>
            </providers>
            <rules>
                <clear />
                <add name="All Errors Default"
                     eventName="All Errors"
                     provider="SMTPProvider" />
            </rules>
        </healthMonitoring>
    </system.web>
    <system.net>
        <mailSettings>
            <smtp><network host="mail.yourdomain.com"/></smtp>
        </mailSettings>
    </system.net>
    <system.webServer>
        <modules runAllManagedModulesForAllRequests="true" />
    </system.webServer>
</configuration>
```

When this is in place, anytime an exception is generated and not handled, an e-mail is sent to the specified address. This e-mail message contains a large amount of useful troubleshooting information, including the exception details and stack trace. Figure 43-17 shows an example message.

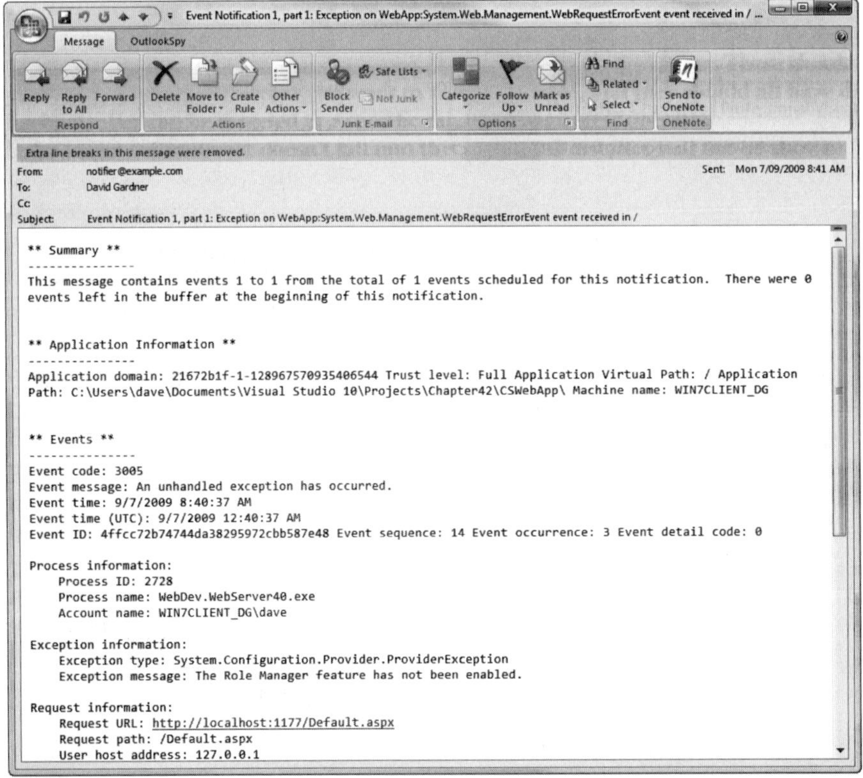

FIGURE 43-17

In addition to the SMTP provider, there is also an Event Log, WMI, and SQL Server provider. Quite complex rules can be enabled to direct the notifications to one of more of these providers. If none of these meet your needs, you can even write your own custom provider.

SUMMARY

With the combination of Visual Studio 2012 and ASP.NET server-side capabilities, you have a wide array of tools to help you look after your web solutions. These features enhance the already impressive feature set available with normal Windows application debugging, with web-specific features such as JavaScript and Silverlight debugging, page- and application-level error handling, and the capability to trace code, which you can use to monitor the way pages are executed in your web applications without interrupting your end users.

In addition, the ASP.NET Health Monitoring framework enables you to proactively manage your production web applications by notifying you as soon as a problem occurs.

44

Advanced Debugging Techniques

WHAT'S IN THIS CHAPTER?

- Adding debugging actions to your code with the `Debug` and `Trace` classes
- Learning techniques for debugging applications already running on the local or remote computer
- Debugging multithreaded applications, SQL Server stored procedures, and mixed-mode applications

As you've seen throughout the last several chapters, Visual Studio 2012 comes with a great variety of ways to debug and run through your applications, including catching errors and displaying them to you for action before the code executes too far; a number of techniques for effectively debugging web applications; and other features, such as breakpoints and visualizing errors.

However, there is still more functionality in Visual Studio that you can use to customize your experience with debugging projects, databases, unmanaged code, and even the .NET Framework. In this chapter you find advanced techniques for debugging your projects regardless of language or technology.

START ACTIONS

Visual Studio provides several ways to launch applications at the start of a debugging session. For most projects the default start option will be sufficient, which in the case of a Windows executable launches the program directly. In the case of a web application, Visual Studio opens the default web browser and loads the current page or navigates to the root path of the web application if there is no active page.

In some scenarios you may want a different action to occur during a debugging session. For example, you may need to always open a specific web page when the web application is started. In these scenarios you can change the start options on the Debug or Web project property page. Figure 44-1 shows the start actions for a Windows Forms project.

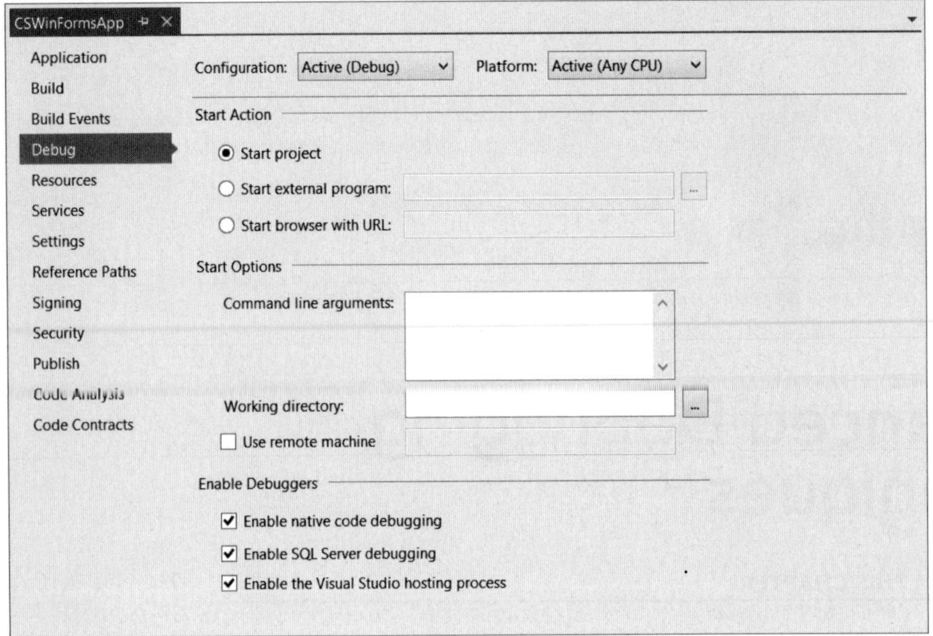

FIGURE 44-1

In addition to starting the project directly, you can also choose to start an external program that presumably subsequently calls your project into the execution process. Alternatively, you can choose to launch the default web browser on your system with a specific URL, again with the assumption that the URL ultimately invokes your project.

Often, applications are built with the capability to exhibit different behavior depending on command-line arguments. If your project is of this variety and you need to test the different configurations, you can use the Command Line Arguments textbox to specify which set of arguments is to be included in the execution of the project. You should enter the command-line arguments in exactly the same way you expect the end user to do so when that user invokes your application after it deploys.

You can override the default directory from which the application should be executed by setting the Working Directory option. This equates to the same setting when you edit a Windows shortcut. In addition, you can also specify a different machine to control the debugging process of the application by activating the Use Remote Machine option. You must explicitly specify the remote computer path because it does not have an associated browse option.

The final section of the Debug page pertains to the different kinds of debugging that will be performed during the execution of your application. By default, the only debugging process active is the debugging of managed code inside the Visual Studio environment, but you can optionally include native unmanaged code or SQL Server stored procedures. These debuggers are discussed later in the chapter.

> **NOTE** *The configuration and platform settings are available only when you have the Show Advanced Build Configurations setting activated. You can find this in the Tools ➪ Options ➪ Projects and Solutions ➪ General options page, and it is on by default for all environment configurations except for Visual Basic programmers.*

You can find the start actions for ASP.NET web applications on the Web property page for the project, as shown in Figure 44-2. The default is to launch the website with whichever page is currently open in the code editor or web designer. You can change this to always use a specific page or URL. The other option is to start an external program or wait for a request from an external application. This is particularly useful when debugging a web service invoked by another application.

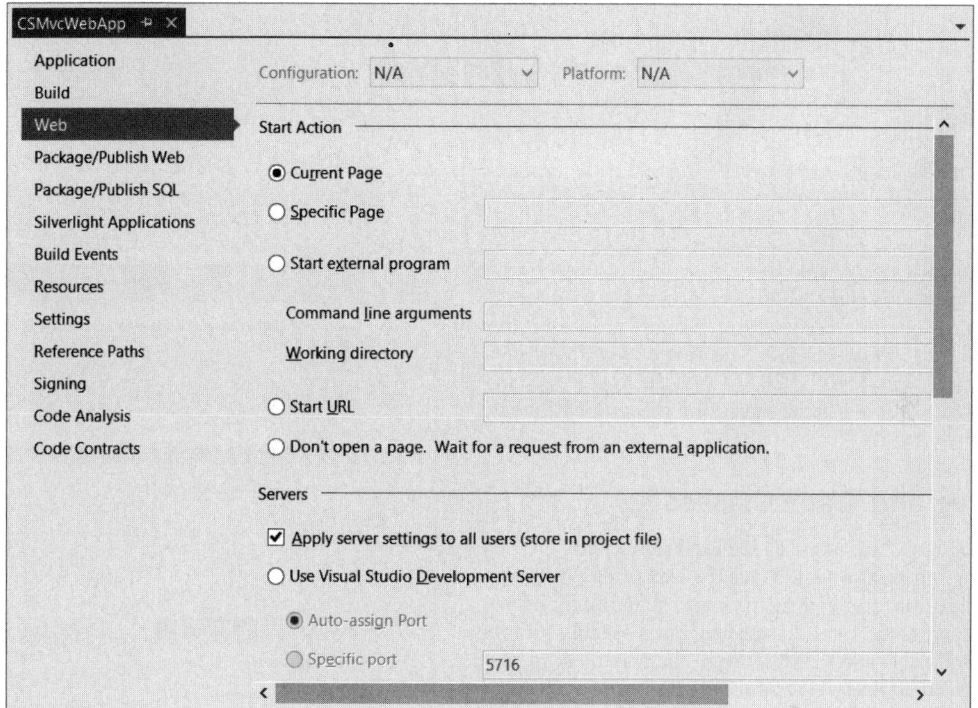

FIGURE 44-2

ASP.NET web application projects can also choose from one of three web server options. The built-in Visual Studio Development Server is the most convenient because it does not require installation or configuration. Unlike IIS, the Visual Studio Development Server supports Edit and Continue. The Custom Web Server option enables you to specify a remote web server to debug against.

DEBUGGING WITH CODE

Three classes ship with the .NET Framework under the `System.Diagnostics` namespace that you can use to build debugging support directly into your code: the `Debug`, `Debugger`, and `Trace` classes. When used properly, these classes provide a powerful way for you to interact with the debugger.

The functionality provided by all three of these classes is exposed through static/shared methods and properties, which makes it easy to add them to your code.

The Debugger Class

The `Debugger` class provides programmatic access to certain debugger functions within Visual Studio. For example, the following code snippet checks whether the application is running under a debugger and, if not, launches one and attaches it to the process:

C#

```
if (!Debugger.IsAttached)
{
    Debugger.Launch();
}
```

VB

```
If Not Debugger.IsAttached() Then
    Debugger.Launch()
End If
```

When this code is executed while the application is running normally outside Visual Studio, the program execution pauses, and you are presented with a dialog box similar to the one shown in Figure 44-3. Selecting a New Instance of Microsoft Visual Studio 2012 loads the application in Visual Studio and continues executing the application in Debug mode.

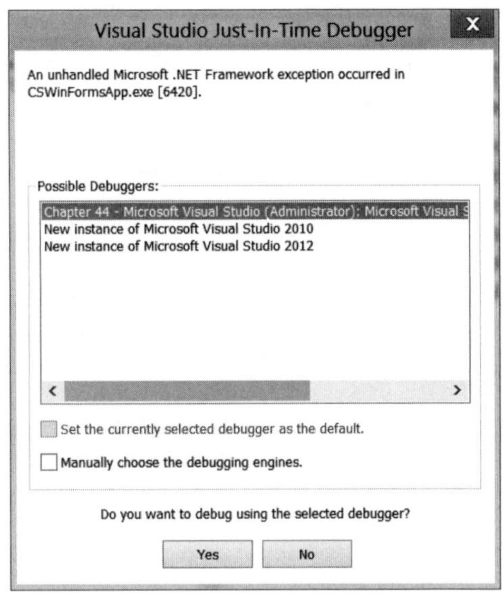

FIGURE 44-3

The Debug and Trace Classes

The `Debug` and `Trace` classes are used to output debugging information and trace the execution path of your application. Most of the properties and methods are common across the two classes, which may seem redundant. However, there is a key difference in the way these methods are implemented and the results are presented to you.

The `Debug` class should be used if you need to output information only while running in Debug mode. The `Trace` class can be used if you want output in both the Debug and Release versions. While you debug an application during development, both your tracing and debugging output go to the Output window in Visual Studio. However, in Release mode, any `Debug` statements are suppressed by the compiler and not invoked during execution. This ensures that you can include a large amount of debug code in your application without increasing the size or decreasing the performance of your release code.

> **NOTE** *The ability to use* `Trace` *and* `Debug` *statements in different build configurations is specified through compiler directives. Within Visual Studio, you can enable or disable these directives from the project properties pages. You can find these settings on the Build property page for C# projects and under the Advanced Compiler Options button on the Compile property page for Visual Basic projects.*

The methods available to output debug messages in the `Debug` and `Trace` classes are listed in Table 44-1.

TABLE 44-1: Methods for Outputting Debug Messages

METHOD	OUTPUTS
`Write`	The text or string representation and an optional category.
`WriteIf`	The text and an optional category, if the condition specified as an argument evaluates to true.
`WriteLine`	The text followed by a carriage return and an optional category.
`WriteLineIf`	The text followed by a carriage return and an optional category, if the condition specified as an argument evaluates to true.

You can also offset the output by increasing or decreasing the indenting through the `Indent` and `Unindent` methods.

You can use the `Assert` method on the `Debug` and `Trace` classes to create an assertion, which tests a condition that was specified as an argument. If the condition evaluates to true, no action occurs. If the condition evaluates to false, the assertion fails. If you run in Debug mode, your program pauses execution, and a dialog box displays, as shown in Figure 44-4.

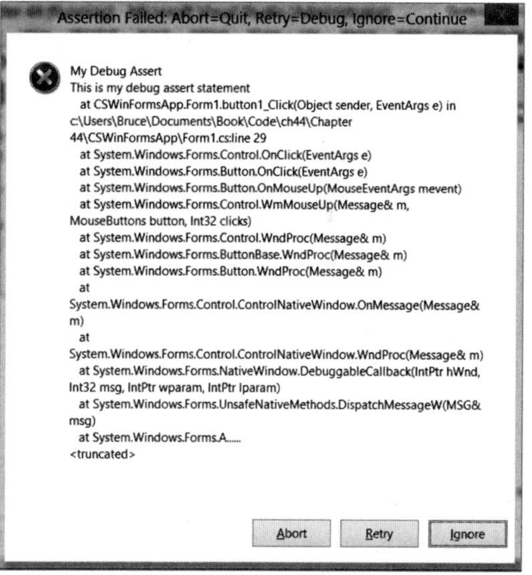

FIGURE 44-4

Selecting Abort terminates the application execution. Retry breaks at the statement, and Ignore continues execution.

While running in Debug mode, all output from the `Debug` and `Trace` classes displays in the Output window. However, with a Release build all trace output is collected by a listener. A listener is simply an object that receives trace output and writes it to an output device. An output device could be a text file, Windows event log, or some other custom logging repository.

Finally, Trace Switches are available, which allow you to enable, disable, and filter tracing output. Trace Switches can be declaratively enabled within the `app.config` file for an application.

DEBUGGING RUNNING APPLICATIONS

Sometimes you need to debug an application that runs outside Visual Studio. Many reasons exist for why you would want to do this, such as if a defect appears only when an application executes in production. Fortunately, Visual Studio provides a simple method to attach and debug a Windows executable or web application actively running.

Attaching to a Windows Process

Attaching to a running Windows process is a fairly straightforward task in Visual Studio. Ideally, you have the original source code open in Visual Studio; in which case you can debug the process as if you had launched it in Debug mode from Visual Studio.

> **NOTE** *If you debug an executable without access to the source code, the available debugging features are limited. If the executable were built without debug information or symbols, available features are further limited, and it is unlikely that you can gain much useful information by debugging it in this way. Therefore, it is recommended that when you perform a release build you should perform two builds: one with and one without debug symbols. The symbols should be archived in a safe location so that they can be accessed if you ever need to attach to a running process or debug a memory dump.*

From the Debug menu, use the Attach to Process command. This displays the Attach to Process dialog window (see Figure 44-5), from which you can browse all active processes. Locate the application that you want to debug from the Available Processes list and click the Attach button.

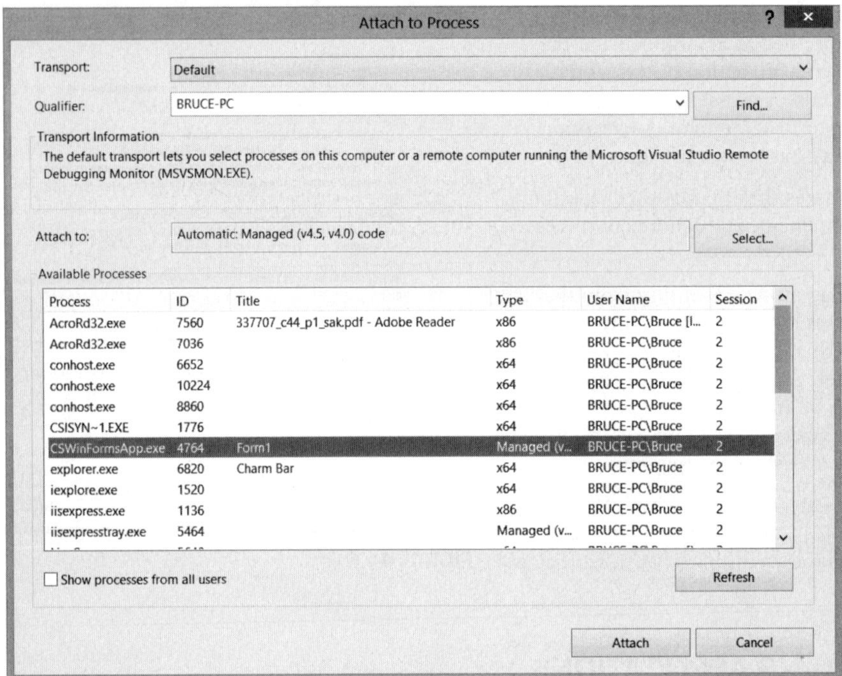

FIGURE 44-5

Because attaching to an application requires these manual steps, it is not well suited if you want to debug a problem that occurs during startup. Also, if you debug an application that does not require any user input and finishes quickly, you may not have time to attach to it. In both these scenarios it would be better to either launch the application in Debug mode from within Visual Studio, or create a custom build with a `Debugger.Break()` statement in the startup code of the application.

When you finish debugging an attached process, you should always cleanly detach from the process by selecting Debug ➪ Detach All. You can also choose to end the application by selecting Debug ➪ Terminate All.

Attaching to a Web Application

Attaching to an ASP.NET web application is almost as easy as attaching to a Windows application. However, before you attach to a web application, you must ensure that it has debugging enabled by editing the `web.config` file for the application. Locate the Compilation node within `system.web` and set the `debug` attribute to `true`. The following listing shows a minimal `web.config` file with the Debug option set, ready for attaching the debugger to the application:

```
<configuration>
    <appSettings/>
    <connectionStrings/>
    <system.web>
        <compilation debug="true" />
    </system.web>
</configuration>
```

ASP.NET automatically detects any changes to `web.config` settings and applies them immediately. Therefore, you don't need to restart the computer or the IIS service for this change to take effect. As discussed in Chapter 43, "Debugging Web Applications," this change can have an adverse effect on performance, so you should never leave it enabled in production.

After you have enabled debugging, you can attach to the web application. The process you need to attach to is the ASP.NET worker process, which is either the native process within IIS (called `w3wp.exe` for IIS 6.0 or higher, or `aspnet_wp.exe` on older versions of IIS) or the built-in Visual Studio 2012 development server `WebDev.WebServer.exe`.

> **NOTE** *Because the IIS process normally runs under the* `ASPNET` *or* `NETWORK SERVICE` *account, you need to run Visual Studio with Administrator rights to attach the debugger to it.*

To begin debugging, from the Debug menu in Visual Studio 2012, select Attach to Process. Select the Show Processes in All Sessions check box if you are attaching to ASP.NET under IIS. Locate the ASP.NET worker process from the Available Processes list, and click the Attach button. As shown in Figure 44-6, you may be prompted to restart Visual Studio with elevated rights.

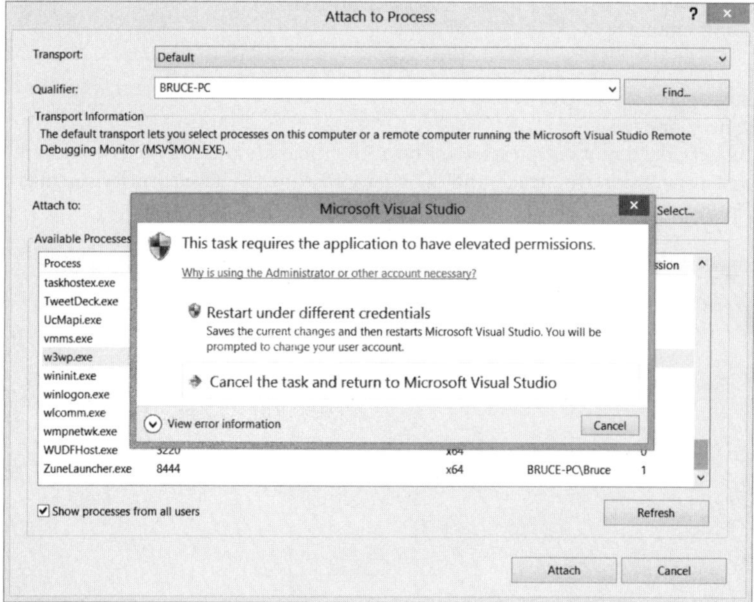

FIGURE 44-6

Remote Debugging

Remote debugging enables you to attach to an application executing on another machine. This can be useful for those cases in which a bug manifests only on a nonprogrammer's computer, or if you need to debug a Windows Service or ASP.NET web application running on a production server.

Debugging a remote application is no different from debugging a local application. After you attach to the remote application, you can set breakpoints, watch variables, and step through code. However, before you can attach to a remote process, you must ensure that the Remote Debugging Monitor is running on the machine to be debugged.

The Remote Debugging Monitor, `msvsmon.exe`, is a small executable shipped with Visual Studio 2012. By default, you can find the 32-bit version installed in the directory `C:\Program Files\Microsoft Visual Studio 11.0\Common7\IDE\Remote Debugger\x86`.

> **NOTE** *The x64 version of* `msvsmon.exe` *is not installed by default with Visual Studio 2012 unless you run a 64-bit version of Windows. The IA-64 version of* `msvsmon.exe` *is available only with the Visual Studio Team System.*

You can simply copy this folder over to the remote machine and run it locally, or create a share and run it from a UNC path. You can also choose to install the Remote Debugging Monitor on the remote machine by running the setup MSI file on the Visual Studio installation DVD media under the `Remote Debugger` directory.

When you launch `msvsmon.exe` on a remote computer for the first time, it attempts to configure the Windows Firewall to open the network ports necessary to enable remote debugging. In some environments, such as on a Windows Server 2003, it prompts you to make the necessary changes, as shown in Figure 44-7. On the Developer's machine, Visual Studio makes the necessary changes to the Windows Firewall to enable it to connect to a remote machine.

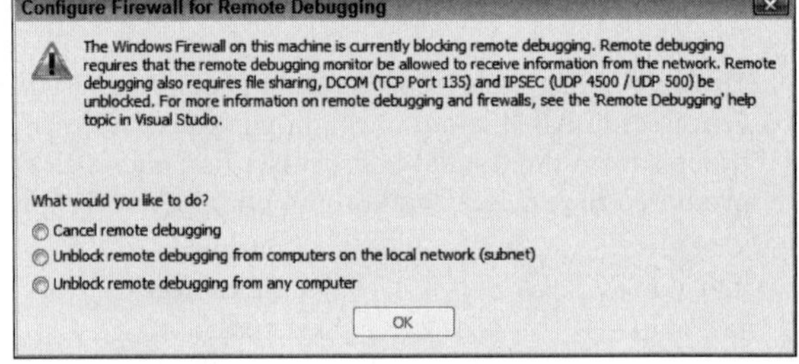

FIGURE 44-7

After you start the Remote Debugging Monitor, it simply listens on the network for incoming debugging requests. By default, remote requests must be authenticated, and only users who are Administrators have the necessary permissions to attach and debug applications. These security settings can be changed from the Tools ➪ Options menu, as shown in Figure 44-8.

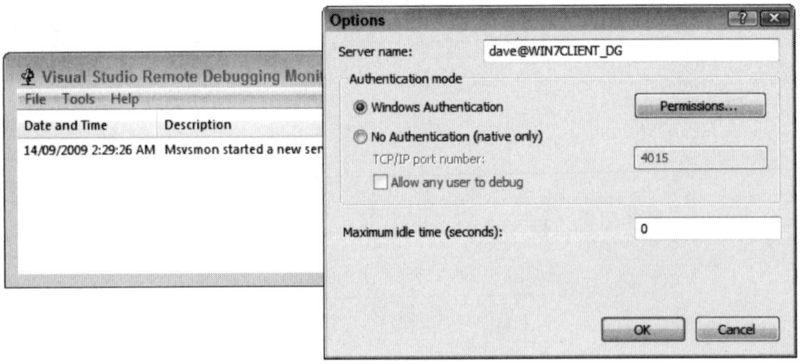

FIGURE 44-8

> **WARNING** *If you enable the No Authentication mode in the Options, your machine will be vulnerable to any user on the network. A remote user could launch applications on your computer, access data, or perform untold mischievous or destructive actions by using a debugger. You have been warned!*

When you have the Remote Debugging Monitor running on the remote machine, you can attach to an application on that machine through the Debug ➪ Attach to Process menu. Enter the computer name or IP address of the remote machine in the field marked Qualifier. Visual Studio connects to the Remote Debugging Monitor, authenticates you, and finally displays the list of processes running on the remote machine. Simply select a process to attach to, and you can debug as if you had attached to a local process.

IntelliTrace

One of the banes of a professional developer's existence is the "no repro" bug. This is a bug that a tester has found while exploring the application. Yet when the bug description is passed back to the development team, it cannot reproduce it. Now the bug goes back and forth with neither side able to identify the difference between the two systems that would seem to be the root of the issue.

With IntelliTrace, the tester can capture a detailed view of exactly what was happening in the application when the bug occurred. This information is then provided to the developer, who can actually step through the application seeing the value of the variables as if they had attached to the running process. From the perspective of one who has dealt with this situation many times, there is little question that IntelliTrace is a valuable tool to add to the developer's toolbox.

The default configuration for IntelliTrace is to collect information at specific, predefined points within the .NET Framework. The actual points depend on the type of application or library involved. Windows Forms apps would be focused on user interface events such as key presses and button clicks. ADO.NET gathers events on command executions. If the defaults are not to your liking, use the IntelliTrace Events options page (IntelliTrace ➪ IntelliTrace Events page from the Tools ➪ Options menu option).

When one of these points of interest is hit, the debugger stops and collects the wanted values for the event. It also gathers generally useful information such as the call stack and the current active threads. The information is saved to an IntelliTrace log.

Now see what this looks like in practice. Figure 44-9 illustrates a typical IntelliTrace window. The window is available through the Debug ➪ Windows ➪ IntelliTrace Events menu option.

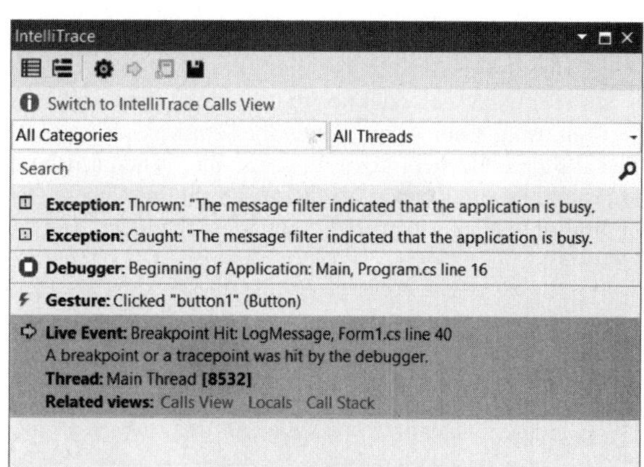

FIGURE 44-9

Each of the events tracked by IntelliTrace gets its own line in the window. You can see that after the application started, a button was clicked and then the execution hit a breakpoint. But IntelliTrace tracks more information than just the events. If you click one of the lines, details about the event appear. This includes a link to other windows of interest, such as the Locals and Call Stack windows, as shown in Figure 44-10.

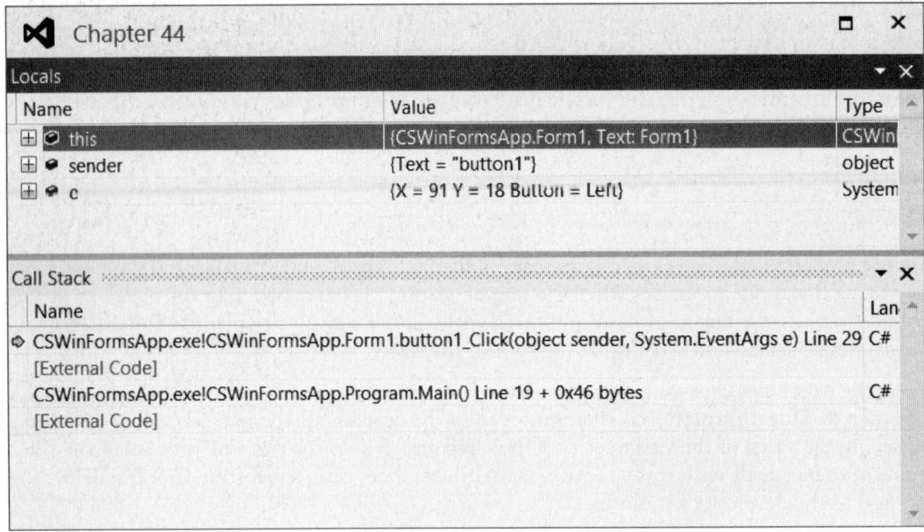

FIGURE 44-10

Visual Studio 2012 takes IntelliTrace a step further. It enables the IntelliTrace log files to be captured on a production server that does not have Visual Studio installed on it. A CAB file named `IntelliTrace Collection.cab` contains the necessary assemblies. The CAB file is unpacked on the production machine, and then using a number of PowerShell commands, the IntelliTrace collector can be turned on. Now the events and calls are collected into an `.iTrace` file. When finished, the file can be sent to a development machine. Using Visual Studio to open the file causes the IntelliTrace window to appear. But more useful is that you have the ability to click a captured event, view the locals and call stack windows, and even step through the application.

> **WARNING** *The files generated by IntelliTrace can get large. And if IntelliTrace capturing is turned on, the files are created each time you run a debugging session. In that situation, you can have multiple GBs of tracing information that accumulate on your development machine. So it's a good idea to keep IntelliTrace turned off until you need it.*

.NET FRAMEWORK SOURCE

One of the more interesting trends that has emerged from Microsoft in recent years is an increased openness and even willingness to embrace open source. The ASP.NET MVC Framework, covered in Chapter 22, "ASP.NET MVC," is a good example of this because the source code for this has been released as a buildable Visual Studio project solution.

However, arguably more significant than this has been the release of the source code for a large number of base class libraries in the .NET Framework. Available under the read-only Microsoft Reference License, it enables you to step into and debug the .NET Framework code as part of a debugging session. Though you could always infer the programmer's intent by using Reflector, there is no comparison to browsing the actual source code, *including the inline documentation*. The good news is that this documentation is quite comprehensive.

> **NOTE** *The source code is not available for every assembly that ships as part of the .NET Framework, nor is it available for every version that has been released. For the assemblies available, there has often been a delay between when the framework was publicly released and when the source code became available. You can find the list of currently available assemblies at* `http://referencesource.microsoft.com/netframework.aspx`.

The first step to enabling access to the source code is to configure some Debugger settings. Open the Tools ➪ Options menu item, and select the Debugging category. If you use the Visual Basic Profile, you need to select the Show All Settings option to see all these options. Ensure that the Enable .NET Framework Source Stepping option is checked, as shown in Figure 44-11. When you check this option you may be presented with two prompts; the first indicates that the Enable Just My Code option has been disabled, and the second advises that a symbol cache location default has been set.

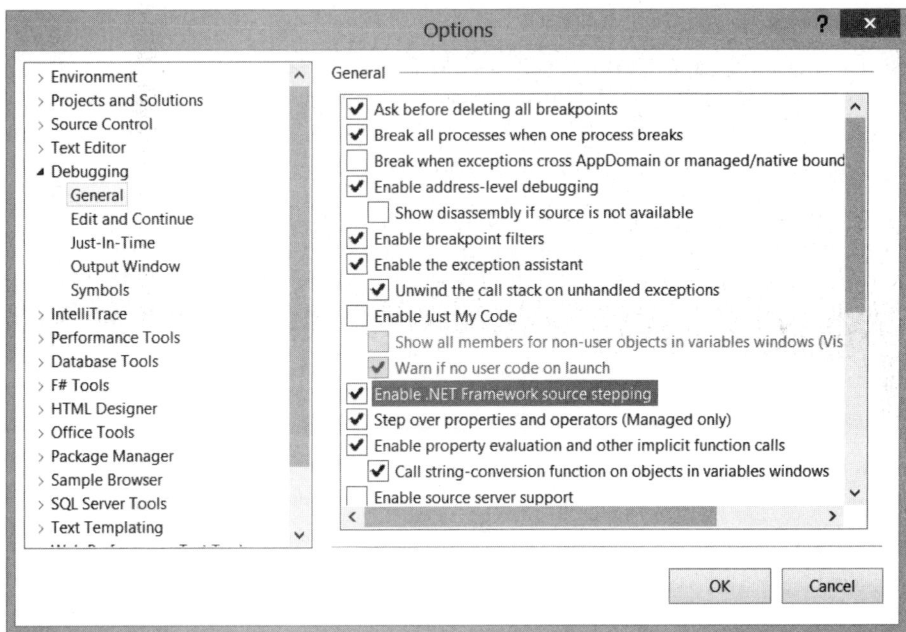

FIGURE 44-11

Secondly, navigate to the Symbols category in the Options dialog (see Figure 44-12) and check the symbol cache location that was automatically added. You can modify the cache location if required, but ensure that you have full read/write access to the target directory. If you configure these options while running in Debug mode, you also have the option to download the symbols immediately by clicking the Load All Symbols button. Otherwise, if you are not running a debug session, the symbols applicable to the current project are downloaded as soon as you click OK.

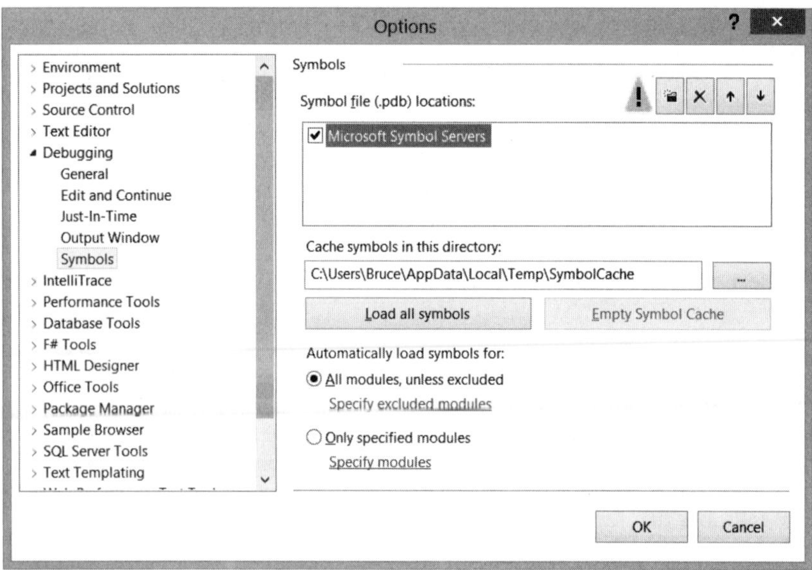

FIGURE 44-12

You also need to identify the location of the Symbol Server. This is the place from which the symbols will be downloaded. The URL for the Microsoft Symbol Server is already known to Visual Studio, but you can also specify third-party servers (to assist with debugging third-party components) or local servers that have been appropriately configured.

You can now step into and browse the .NET Framework base class libraries during a debugging session. Set a breakpoint in your application code and run in Debug mode. When the breakpoint is hit, open the Call Stack window (Debug ➪ Windows ➪ Call Stack) to display the execution path. If the symbols have been loaded, the code available for debugging will not be grayed out, and you can double-click the entry in the Call Stack, or step into the source code during your debug session, as shown in Figure 44-13. If this is the first time you view the code, you are prompted to accept the Microsoft Reference Library license.

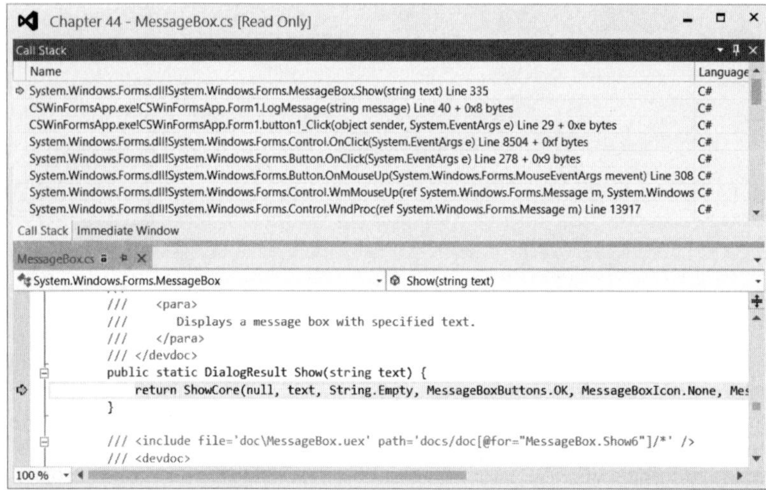

FIGURE 44-13

MULTITHREADED AND PARALLELIZED APPLICATION DEBUGGING

Multithreaded applications have traditionally been notoriously difficult to debug properly. Seemingly fundamental tasks, such as keeping track of which thread you are currently inspecting and what other threads are currently executing, are some of the reasons why this task is so hard. Fortunately, Visual Studio 2012 provides support for debugging multithreaded applications.

Chapter 40, "Using the Debugging Windows," discussed the Threads debug window, which lists all the active threads for a particular application. Functionality accessed through this window includes the ability to set a friendly name for a thread. You can also set flags on individual threads, which means that you don't have to spend as much time trying to keep track of thread IDs.

To further improve debugging, you can identify each thread within the source code editor window. This is enabled from the Threads window by right-clicking any entry and selecting Show Threads in Source. The result of this is shown in Figure 44-14, where a cloth thread icon (consisting of two interlocking wavy lines) displays in the gutter. The thread icon indicates that a thread, or several threads, is stopped at this location. When you hover over the thread icon, a tooltip is displayed that identifies which threads are stopped here. The thread names listed are the friendly names that have been entered in the Threads window.

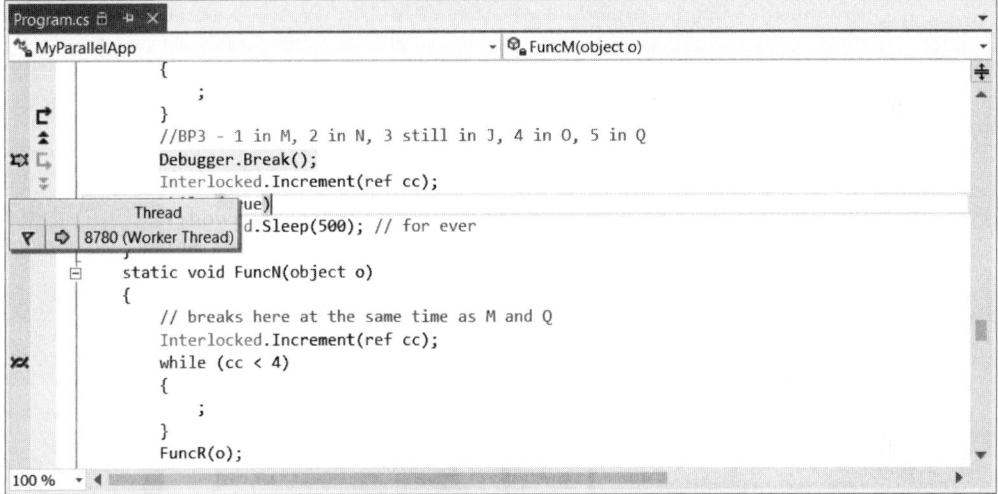

FIGURE 44-14

Within the Debug Location toolbar, as shown in Figure 44-15, you can navigate between threads. When you select a different thread from the Thread drop-down list, the Call Stack updates with the selected thread's execution path, and the execution point moves to the current location in the source code. The call graph in the Parallel Stacks window also updates to reflect the newly selected current thread.

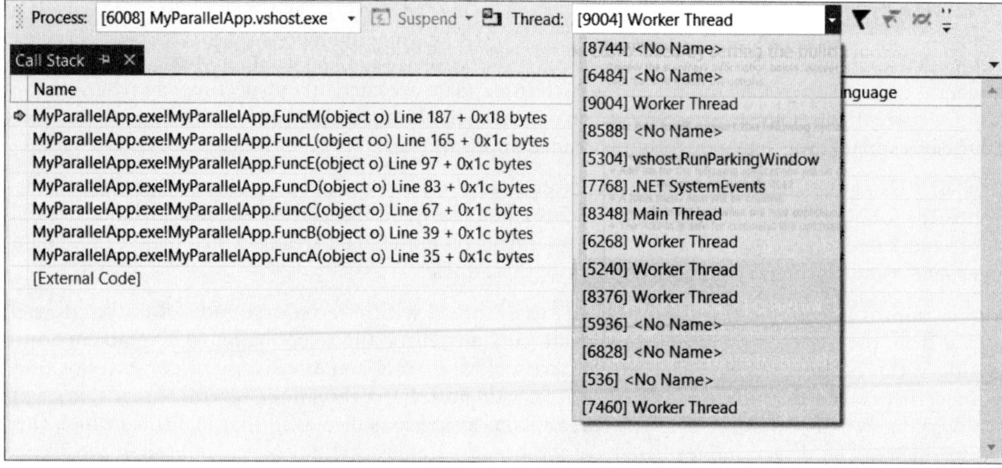

FIGURE 44-15

You can also flag both threads and tasks from the Threads and Parallel Tasks windows. Flagging enables you to keep track of a thread or task within a debugging session, and filter out some of the tasks or threads you are not interested in. In Figure 44-16, the first two tasks are flagged in the Parallel Tasks window. By selecting the Show Only Flagged option on the toolbar of the Parallel Stacks window, you can filter the call graph to hide the tasks that you are not interested in.

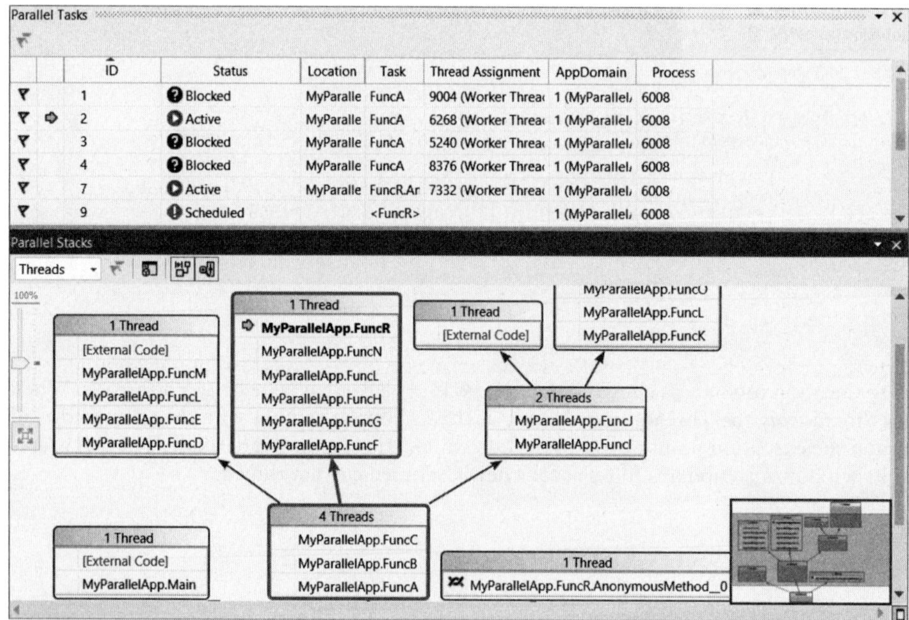

FIGURE 44-16

Though debugging multithreaded and parallelized applications is still not a trivial task, these features do make it much easier to drill down on specific threads and tasks, and filter out the unimportant information from the Visual Studio debugger windows.

DEBUGGING SQL SERVER STORED PROCEDURES

Another useful feature of the debugging model found in Visual Studio 2012 is the capability to debug stored procedures in SQL Server databases. You need to first check the Enable SQL Server Debugging setting in the Debug property page of your project, as shown in Figure 44-17. When activated, whenever your code encounters a stored procedure, you can debug the procedure code inline with your own code.

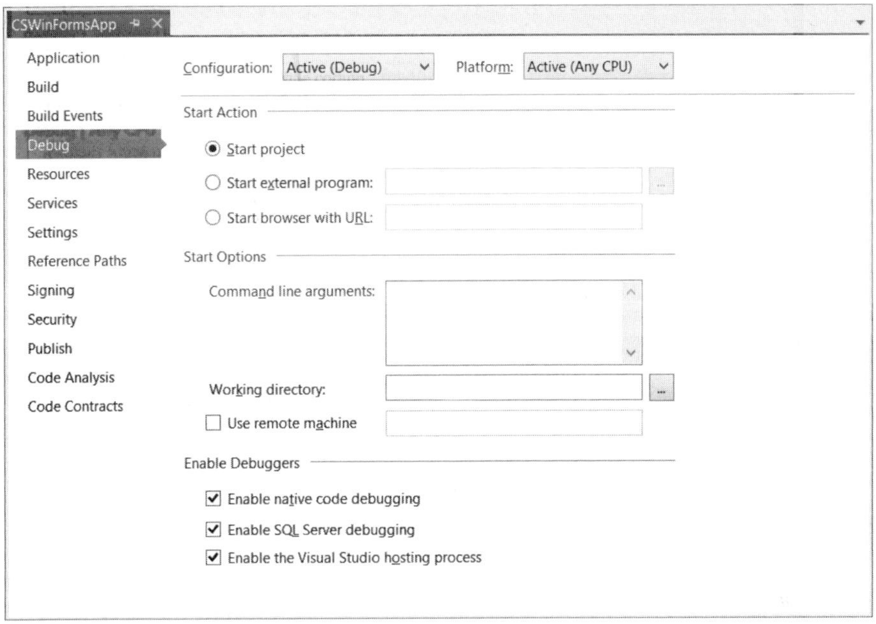

FIGURE 44-17

You can even include breakpoints within a stored procedure so that you can trace through the SQL Server code without halting the application code execution.

Your Windows account must be a member of the sysadmin group on SQL Server to debug stored procedures.

MIXED-MODE DEBUGGING

A mixed-mode application is any application that combines managed code (Visual Basic, C#, Managed C++, and so on) with native code (typically C++). Debugging a mixed-mode application is not all that different from debugging a pure managed-code application; however, you must first configure the application to support native code debugging. Refer to Figure 44-17 in the previous section, which shows the native unmanaged code debugger enabled, along with the SQL Server debugger.

Mixed-mode debugging has a limitation that you should be aware of. When debugging a mixed-mode application, you may find that some operations, such as stepping through code, run slowly. This can be improved by unchecking the option to Enable Property Evaluation and Other Implicit Function Calls on the Debugger Options page.

> **NOTE** *Because native call stacks and managed call stacks are different, the debugger cannot always provide a single, complete call stack for mixed code. Though rare, it is possible that there might be some discrepancies in the call stack. You can find more information on this in the MSDN library.*

POST-MORTEM DEBUGGING

Even with well-tested applications, it is inevitable that there will be latent bugs within your code that show up after the software has been released. Fortunately, you can debug many of the errors on user computers after they occur.

Post-mortem debugging involves inspecting a dump of the application's memory that was taken when the error or unexpected behavior occurred. This could be when an unhandled exception is thrown, or if the application enters a hung state, or simply if the application exhibits behavior that indicates it may have a memory leak.

In the past you would use tools such as WinDbg with the Son of Strike (SOS) extension to debug memory dumps of .NET applications. However, WinDbg was designed for native code debugging, and even with the additional support provided by SOS it was still difficult to perform tasks such as matching the MSIL back to the source code.

> **NOTE** *Post-mortem debugging, as described here, works only for .NET 4.0 and 4.5 applications and websites. It is also better if your application is compiled in a debug configuration. If not, you do not have access to a lot of useful information.*

Generating Dump Files

You have several ways to generate dump files, including the Windows Task Manager, WinDbg, and Visual Studio. On Windows Vista or later operating systems, the simplest method is to right-click the process in the Windows Task Manager and select Create Dump File.

One of the more functional tools for generating dumps is the `adplus.vbs` script, which is a command-line interface to WinDbg. The adplus script and WinDbg are installed with the Debugging Tools for Windows, which is available from `http://www.microsoft.com/whdc/DevTools/Debugging/`. You must install the version that matches the processor architecture on the target machine (x86, x64, Itanium).

To generate the dump file, open a command prompt, change the directory to the install location of the Debugging Tools, and enter the following command:

```
adplus -hang -pn processname.exe
```

This command attaches to the application called *processname.exe* in noninvasive mode, generates the dump, and then detaches. The application continues to run after this.

If you debug a hung application, an application using an excessive amount of memory, or an application exhibiting unexpected behavior, you should take one or more memory dumps at the appropriate times. It may involve a degree of trial and error to ensure that you generate a dump that contains useful information.

If you debug a specific exception thrown in an application, you need to use the -c switch to pass in a file that configures adplus to generate a dump file when that exception is thrown.

You can also use Visual Studio 2012 to generate a dump file during a debug session. To do so, pause execution and select Debug ➪ Save Dump As.

Debugging Dump Files

To get the most out of post-mortem debugging you need to configure Visual Studio to load your symbol files. Symbol files have a PDB extension and are generated as part of a debug build. You can find them in the debug output build directory; there is one for each assembly that was built.

Under Visual Studio select Tools ➪ Options and then select the Symbols category under Debugging. You can specify either a URL or a local directory as the location of your symbol files. The public Microsoft Symbol Servers will already be included; add your own local symbol directories, as shown in Figure 44-18.

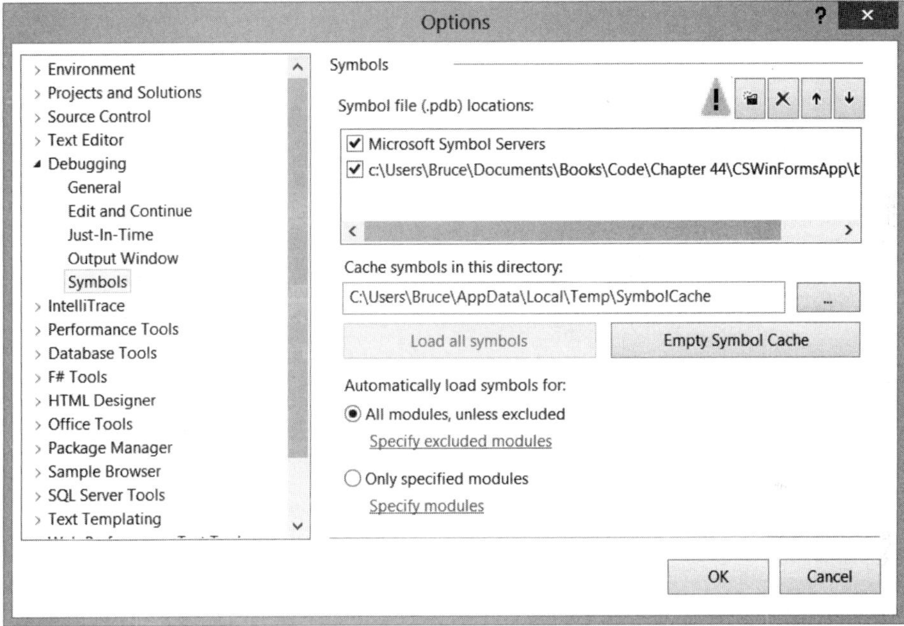

FIGURE 44-18

Now that you have generated your dump file and set up the symbols, use Visual Studio to begin post-mortem debugging. Select File ➪ Open ➪ File and locate the dump file. When opened, Visual Studio displays the Dump Summary page, as shown in Figure 44-19.

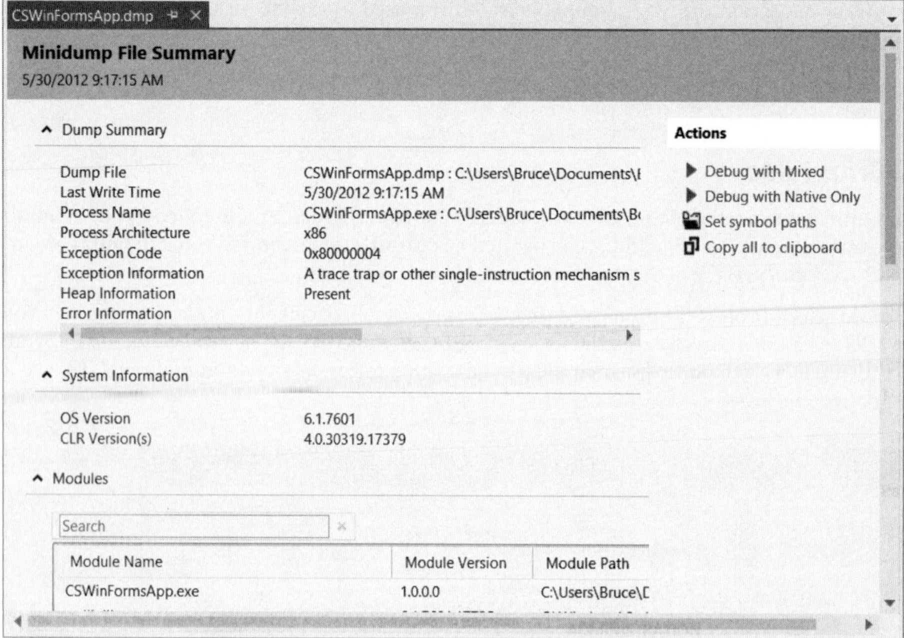

FIGURE 44-19

Click the Debug with Mixed link to load the dump and all symbols and begin debugging. This link displays only if the dump is from a managed application that targets the .NET Framework 4.0 or 4.5; otherwise you can use only the Debug with Native Only option.

Debugging a dump file is much the same as any other debugging session; you can display the call stack, inspect the contents of variables, and view the threads. The one main limitation is that because you are looking at a snapshot, and not a live application, you cannot step through the source code.

SUMMARY

This chapter completes the discussion on debugging your projects and applications, offering details about advanced debugging techniques. Visual Studio 2012 can meet a wide spectrum of debugging scenarios, such as multithreaded applications, stored procedures, unmanaged code, and even the .NET Framework. These techniques provide you with a set of effective debugging options for tracking down the issues in your projects regardless of language or technology.

PART X
Build and Deployment

45

Upgrading with Visual Studio 2012

WHAT'S IN THIS CHAPTER?

- Taking advantage of the IDE when working on older projects
- Updating projects to use the latest run time and libraries

Each time a new version of Visual Studio is released, there is always a delay before developers start to use it. There have been a number of reasons for this in the past. A frequent reason, the need to upgrade existing applications to a new version of the .NET Framework at the same time, is no longer relevant due to multitargeting. However, the incompatibility of solution and project files have continued to cause problems. That changes as of Visual Studio 2012.

In this chapter, you see how easy it is to migrate existing .NET applications into Visual Studio 2012. This is done in two parts: upgrading to Visual Studio 2012 and then upgrading the .NET Framework version the application makes use of to 4.5.

UPGRADING FROM VISUAL STUDIO 2010

One of the design goals with Visual Studio 2012 was to avoid what had become a constant with previous versions: the need to upgrade your project files. And with a few exceptions, Microsoft has succeeded.

When a project from Visual Studio 2010 is opened in Visual Studio 2012, it is placed into one of three categories:

- **Changes required**—Some modifications of the project and assets are required to open the project in Visual Studio 2012. After the changes have been made, the project can still be opened in Visual Studio 2010.
- **Update required**—Some modifications of the projects and assets are required. After the changes have been made, the project may not be opened from Visual Studio 2010.
- **Unsupported projects**—Projects that fall into this category cannot be opened from Visual Studio 2012.

For many experienced developers, the fact that the first category exists is a big deal. Previously, if you have worked on a team of developers and wanted to take advantage of the latest in Visual Studio goodies, you needed to wait until *all* the team members could upgrade because the project files were not backward compatible.

With most projects (Table 45-1 outlines the exceptions), round-trip compatibility is now a reality. You can create a project in Visual Studio 2010 SP1, open the projects in Visual Studio 2012, and then open them again in Visual Studio 2010 SP1. Of course, there are some limitations to this process. For example, the changes that you make to your project can't use features specific to Visual Studio 2012, for example, changing your project to target .NET 4.5. But beyond that fairly reasonable sort of restriction, backward compatibility is now here.

To start with, let's go through the various project types that are backward compatible. This would be projects that fit into the first two categories previously listed. One of the assumptions made with this compatibility is that Visual Studio is allowed to automatically upgrade the project. The automatic upgrade process is initiated by simply opening the project in Visual Studio.

TABLE 45-1: Compatible Project Types

PROJECT TYPE	COMPATIBILITY ISSUES
ASP.NET MVC 3 or 4	None.
ASP.NET MVC 2	Visual Studio 2012 doesn't support ASP.NET MVC 2. To open the project in Visual Studio 2012, you need to convert your project to ASP.NET MVC 3.
ASP.NET Web Forms	None.
Blend	None.
Coded UI Test	None.
F#	None.
LightSwitch	None.
Modeling	None.
MPI/Cluster Debugging	None, so long as the same version of the run time and tools have been installed into Visual Studio.
Office 2010 VSTO	None, as long as the project targets .NET Framework 4.
Rich Internet Applications	Upgraded projects can be opened only in Visual Studio 2012. In other words, there is no backward compatibility.
SharePoint 2010	None.
Silverlight 4 or 5	None.
Silverlight 3	As part of the upgrade process, Visual Studio asks to convert the project to Silverlight 5. If you allow this to happen, then it is backward compatible. Otherwise, it is not.
SQL Server CE 3.5	The project must be upgraded to support SQL Server CE 4 to open the project in both Visual Studio 2010 SP1 and Visual Studio 2012.
SQL Server Express LocalDB	The upgraded project can be opened only in Visual Studio 2012. In other words, there is no backward compatibility. As well, the database file must be upgraded to SQL Server 2012. Database files that are not upgraded cannot be accessed through the LocalDB functionality but are still available through SQL Server Express.
SQL Server 2008 R2 Express	None.
SQL Server Report Project	None, but if you run in local mode, you won't get the designer-time experience for controls related to the Visual Studio 2010 viewer.

PROJECT TYPE	COMPATIBILITY ISSUES
Visual C++	None, if Visual Studio 2012 and Visual Studio 2010 SP1 are installed on the same computer.
Visual Studio 2010 Web	None.
Visual Studio 2010 Database	Certain artifacts are not supported in Visual Studio 2012, includeing unit tests, data comparison files, data generation plans, custom rules for static code analysis, custom deployment extension, and partial projects.
Visual Studio 2010 SQL Server Data Tools	None.
Visual Studio Lab Management	Microsoft Test Manager can open environments created in either version. However, the Microsoft Test Manager version must match the Team Foundation Server version in your environment.
WCF	None.
Windows Forms	None.
Windows Workflow	None.
WPF	None.

Naturally, you're left with a list of project types that are no longer (or, at least, not as of this writing) supported by Visual Studio 2012. This includes the following project types:

- BizTalk 2010 R2
- Cloud Tools
- MSI/Setup Projects
- SharePoint 2007
- Windows Mobile
- Windows Phone

The project types in this list fall into two distinct categories. The first are projects that are no longer supported. The second are projects that depend on a separately shipped set of tools. Those tools (and this relates to BizTalk, Cloud tools, and Windows Phone) are controlled by different teams within Microsoft than Visual Studio. As such, the tools are upgraded on a different schedule than .NET and Visual Studio. Because support for the project types is dependent on these tools, the timing for support is in the hands of those product teams. For most such tools that are not currently supported, it is likely that that their teams will provide support in the future.

> **NOTE** *If you're a Visual Studio 2008 user, the news is not as good. The backward compatibility feature applies only to Visual Studio 2010 SP1 projects. So you will not be able to open your projects in Visual Studio 2008 once they have been converted to Visual Studio 2012. You can open your projects and solutions in Visual Studio 2012, but the files will be converted to the new format, rendering them incapable of being opened in Visual Studio 2008.*

UPGRADING TO .NET FRAMEWORK 4.5

After you migrate your application across to Visual Studio 2012 and tidy up your build environment, you should consider the upgrade path to .NET Framework 4.5. With the last few upgrades (actually, since the base of .NET stabilized at version 2.0), there have not been many breaking changes. The same is true for .NET 4.5, which means that the upgrade from version 4.0 should be relatively painless.

In most cases, upgrading your application is just a matter of changing the Target Framework project property. Figure 45-1 shows the project properties dialog for a C# Class Library project. On the Application tab there is a drop-down that lists the different target frameworks available for you to select.

> **NOTE** *For VB projects, this drop-down list is in the Advanced Compile Options dialog box, which you can access from the Compile tab in the project properties designer.*

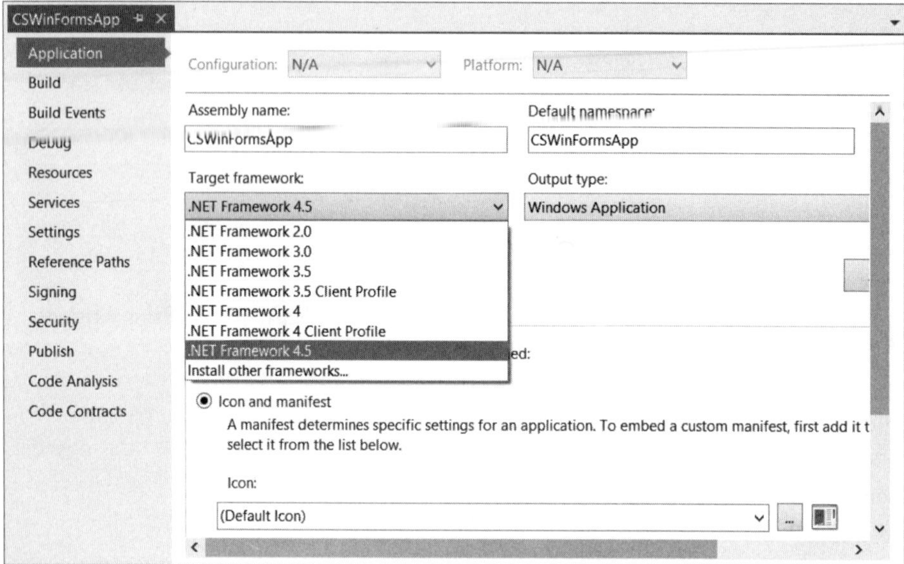

FIGURE 45-1

One of the additions to .NET with versions 3.5 and 4.0 was the concept of a Client Profile. If you have had the joy of downloading and installing the full version of the .NET Framework, you can appreciate the size of the code base. However, not all of the code base is valuable to every single type of project. For example, .NET includes classes related to the processing of incoming requests to generate HTML in a website. This type of class is not likely to be used if you create an application that runs on a standalone client computer. For this reason, Visual Studio 2012 enables you to target your applications to a subset of the .NET Framework, known as the Client Profile. Refer to Figure 45-1 to see options for that.

The Client Profile has been discontinued for .NET Framework 4.5. The optimization of the download package for .NET along with additional deployment alternatives has led to the decision that there is no need to provide both the full package and the client profile. If you upgrade automatically from .NET Framework 4.0 Client Profile, the project will be set to target .NET Framework 4.5.

As soon as you select a new framework version, the dialog in Figure 45-2 appears. If you select Yes, all pending changes to the project will be saved and the project will be closed, updated, and reopened with the new target framework version. It is recommended that you immediately attempt a rebuild to ensure that the application still compiles.

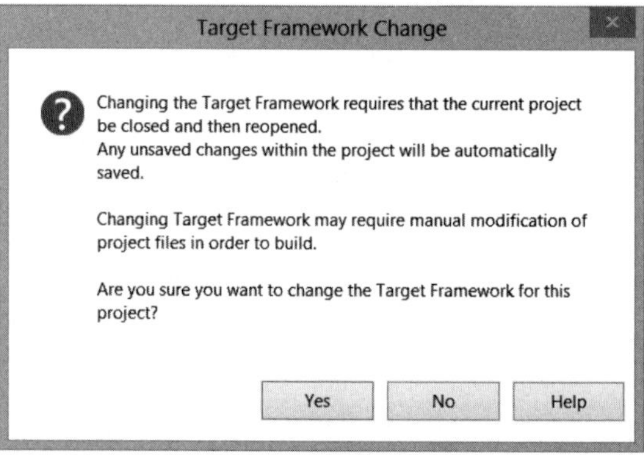

FIGURE 45-2

SUMMARY

In this chapter, you have seen how you can upgrade existing .NET applications to Visual Studio 2012 and version 4.5 of the framework. Using the latest toolset and framework version clearly has some advantages in performance, functionality, and usability. However, don't overlook the limitations that using the latest .NET Framework might impose. If your target market still uses old operating systems, such as Windows 2000, you may want to stay on version 2.0 of the framework because this is supported on these platforms. Visual Studio 2012 enables you to have the best of both worlds, only upgrading when you want to.

46

Build Customization

WHAT'S IN THIS CHAPTER?

- Customizing the build environment
- Performing actions at the beginning and the end of the build
- Creating custom MSBuild scripts

Although you can build most of your projects using the default compilation options set up by Visual Studio 2012, occasionally you need to modify some aspect of the build process to achieve what you want. This chapter looks at the various build options available to you in both Visual Basic and C#, outlining what the different settings do so that you can customize them to suit your requirements.

In addition, you learn how Visual Studio 2012 uses the MSBuild engine to perform its compilations and how you can get under the hood of the configuration files that control the compilation of your projects.

GENERAL BUILD OPTIONS

Before you start on a project, you can modify some settings in the Options pages for Visual Studio 2012. These options apply to every project and solution that you open in the IDE and as such can be used to customize your general experience for compiling your projects.

The first port of call for professional Visual Basic developers should be the General page of the Projects and Solutions group. By default, the Visual Basic development settings of the IDE hide some of the build options from view, so the only way to show them is to activate the Show Advanced Build Configurations option.

When this is active, the IDE displays the Build Configuration options in the My Project pages, and the Build ➪ Configuration Manager menu command also becomes accessible. Other language environments don't need to do this because these options are activated on startup. (Although you can certainly turn them off if you don't want them cluttering your menus and pages.)

Two other options on this page relate to building your projects. One enables Visual Studio to automatically show the Output window when you start a build, and the other enables Visual Studio to automatically show the Error window if compilation errors occur during the build process. By default, all language configurations have both of these options turned on.

The Build and Run options page (as shown in Figure 46-1) in the Projects and Solutions group has more options available to you to customize the way your builds take place.

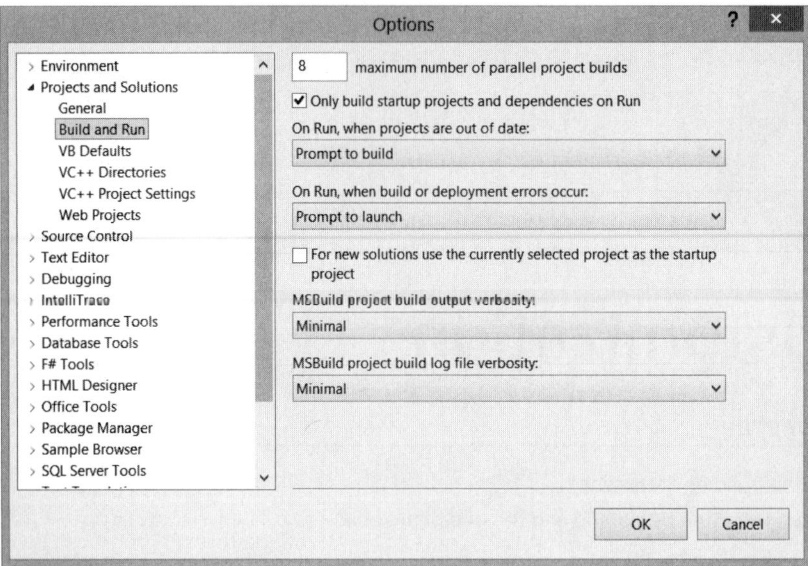

FIGURE 46-1

It's unclear from this page, but some of these options affect only C# projects, so it's worth running through each option, what it does, and what languages it affects:

- **Maximum Number of Parallel Project Builds:** This controls how many simultaneous build processes can be active at any one time (assuming the solution being compiled has multiple projects). One of the changes with Visual Studio 2012 is that the default value for this setting changed. So if you upgrade from Visual Studio 2010, make sure that this value is modified (if it hasn't already been) to fit the number of processors on your build machine.
- **Only Build Startup Projects and Dependencies on Run:** This option builds only the part of the solution directly connected to the startup projects. This means that any projects that are not dependencies for the startup projects are excluded from the default build process. This option is active by default, so if you have a solution that has multiple projects called by the startup projects through late-bound calls or other similar means, they will not be built automatically. You can either deactivate this option or manually build those projects separately.
- **On Run, When Projects Are Out of Date:** This option is used for C++ projects only and gives you three options for out-of-date projects (projects that have changed since the last build). The default is Prompt to Build, which forces the build process to occur whenever you run the application. The Never Build option always uses the previous build of out-of-date projects, and the Prompt to Build gives you an option to build for each out-of-date project. Note that this applies only to the Run command, and if you force a build through the Build menu, projects are rebuilt according to the other settings in the build configuration and on this Options page.
- **On Run, When Build or Deployment Errors Occur:** This controls the action to take when errors occur during the build process. Despite official documentation to the contrary, this option does indeed affect the behavior of builds in Visual Basic and C#. Your options here are the default Prompt to Launch, which displays a dialog prompting you for which action to take; Do Not Launch, which does not start the solution and returns to design time; and Launch Old Version, which ignores compilation errors and runs the last successful build of the project.

The option to launch an old version enables you to ignore errors in subordinate projects and still run your application; but because it doesn't warn you that errors occurred, you run the risk of getting confused about what version of the project is active.

When you use the Prompt to Launch option, if you subsequently check the Do Not Show This Dialog Again option in the prompt dialog, this setting is updated to either Do Not Launch or Launch Old Version, depending on whether you choose to continue.

> **NOTE** *It is recommended that you set this property to Do Not Launch because this can improve the efficiency with which you write and debug code — one fewer window to dismiss!*

- **For New Solutions Use the Currently Selected Project as the Startup Project:** This option is useful when you build a solution with multiple projects. When the solution is being built, the Visual Studio build process assumes that the currently selected project is the startup project and determines all dependencies and the starting point for execution from there.
- **MSBuild Project Build Output Verbosity:** Visual Studio 2012 uses the MSBuild engine for its compilation. MSBuild produces its own set of compilation outputs, reporting on the state of each project as it's built. You have the option to control how much of this output is reported to you:
  - By default, the MSBuild verbosity is set to Minimal, which produces only a small amount of information about each project, but you can turn it off completely by setting this option to Quiet, or expand on the information you get by choosing one of the more detailed verbosity settings.
  - MSBuild output is sent to the Output window, which is accessible via View ➪ Other Windows ➪ Output (under some environmental setups this will be View ➪ Output). If you can't see your build output, make sure you have set the Show Output From option to Build (see Figure 46-2).

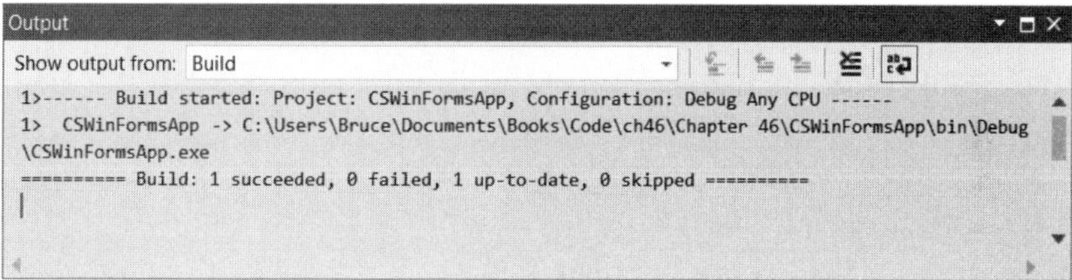

FIGURE 46-2

- **MSBuild Project Build Log File Verbosity:** When Visual Studio builds a C++ project, it generates a text-based log file of MSBuild activities as well as the normal information that goes to the Output window. The amount of information that goes into this text file can be controlled independently using this option. One way to take advantage of this is to have more detailed information go into the log file and leave the Output window set to Minimal, which streamlines the normal development experience but gives you access to more detailed information when things go wrong. If you do not want Visual Studio to produce this separate log file, you can turn it off using the Projects and Solutions ➪ VC++ Project Settings ➪ Build Logging setting.

It's also worth taking a look at the other Options pages in the Projects and Solutions category because they control the default Visual Basic compilation options (Option Explicit, Option Strict, Option Compare, and Option Infer), and other C++-specific options relating to build. Of note for C++ developers is the capability to specify PATH variables for the different component types of their projects, such as executables and include files, for different platform builds, and whether to log the build output (see the preceding list).

MANUAL DEPENDENCIES

Visual Studio 2012 can detect interproject dependencies between projects that reference each other. This is then used to determine the order in which projects are built. Unfortunately, in some circumstances Visual Studio can't determine these dependencies, such as when you have custom steps in the build process. Luckily, you can manually define project dependencies to indicate how projects are related to each other. You can access the dialog shown in Figure 46-3 by selecting either the Project ➪ Project Dependencies or Project ➪ Build Order menu commands.

> **NOTE** *These menu commands are available only when you have a solution with multiple projects in the IDE.*

You first select the project that is dependent on others from the drop-down, and then check the projects it depends on in the bottom list. Any dependencies that are automatically detected by Visual Studio 2012 will already be marked in this list. You can use the Build Order tab to confirm the order in which the projects will be built.

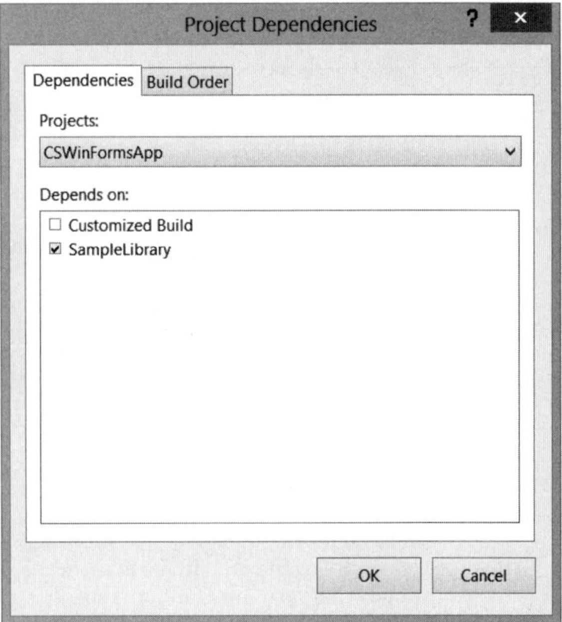

FIGURE 46-3

THE VISUAL BASIC COMPILE PAGE

Visual Basic projects have an additional set of options that control how the build process occurs. To access the compile options for a specific project, open My Project by double-clicking its entry in the Solution Explorer. When the project Options page displays, navigate to the Compile page from the list on the left side (see Figure 46-4).

The Build Output Path option controls where the executable version (application or DLL) of your project is stored. For Visual Basic, the default setting is the `bin\Debug\` or `bin\Release\` directory (depending on the current configuration), but you can change this by browsing to the wanted location.

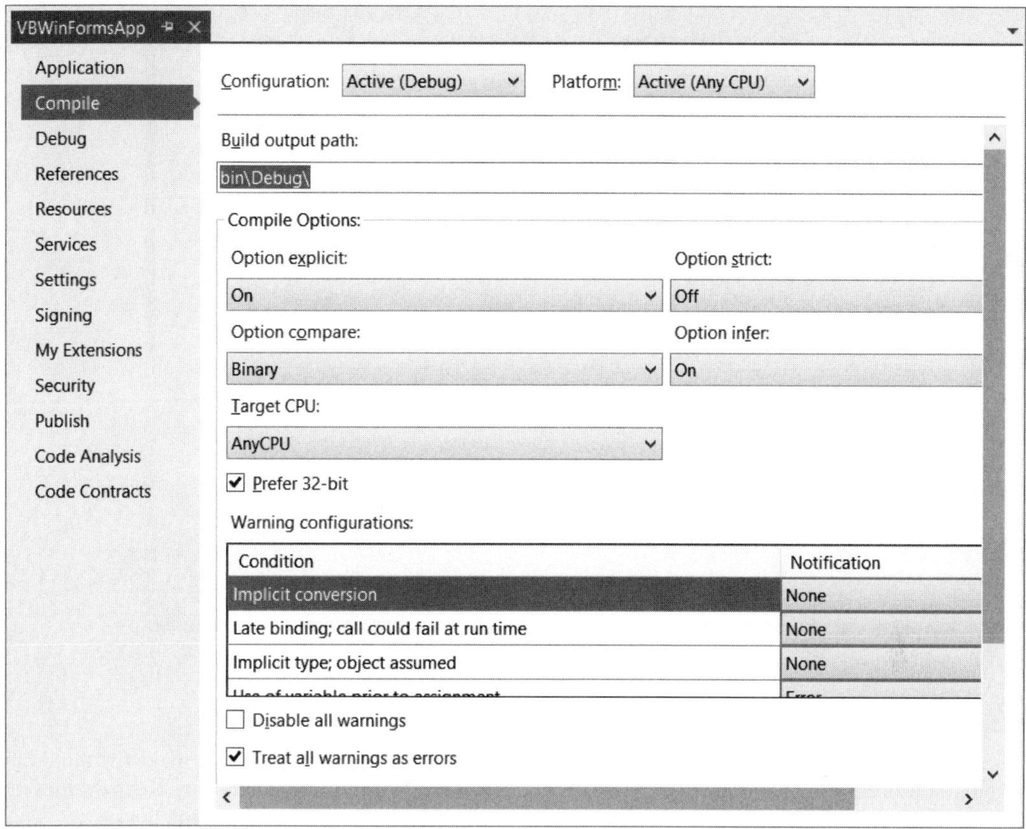

FIGURE 46-4

> **NOTE** *You should enable the Treat All Warnings as Errors option because this can, in most cases, encourage you to write better, less error-prone code.*

You should be aware of two additional sets of hidden options. The Build Events button at the bottom of the Compile page is available to Visual Basic developers who want to run actions or scripts before or after the build has been performed. They are discussed in a moment. The other button is labeled Advanced Compile Options.

Advanced Compiler Settings

Clicking the Advanced Compile Options button displays the Advanced Compiler Settings dialog (see Figure 46-5) in which you can fine-tune the build process for the selected project, with settings divided into two broad groups: Optimizations and Compilation Constants.

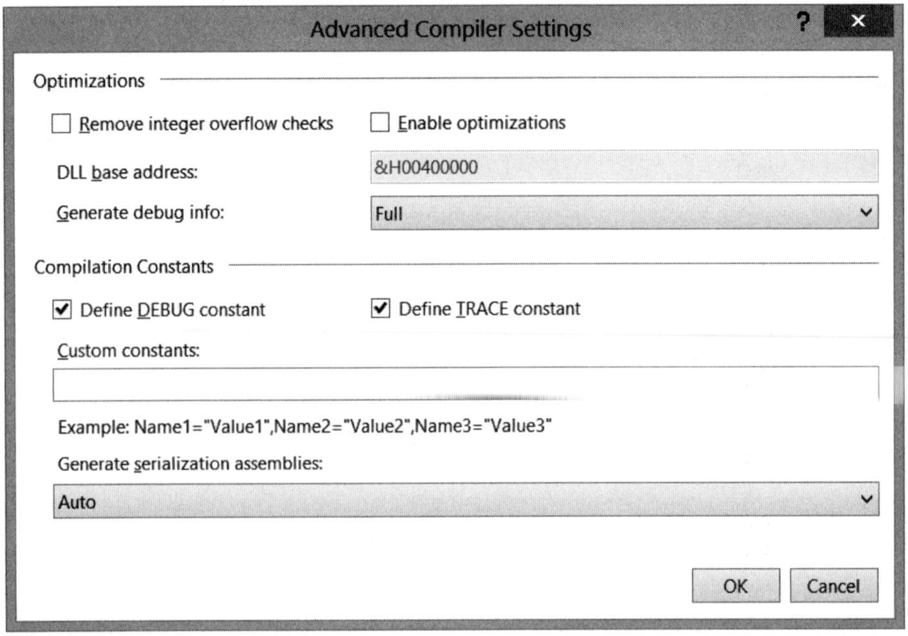

FIGURE 46-5

Optimizations

The settings in the Optimizations group control how the compilation is performed to make the build output or the build process itself faster or to minimize the output size. Normally, you can leave these options alone, but if you do require tweaks to your compilation, here's a summary of what each option does:

- **Remove Integer Overflow Checks:** By default, your code is checked for any instance of a possible integer overflow, which can be a potential cause for memory leaks. Deactivating this option removes those checks, resulting in a faster-running executable at the expense of safety.
- **Enable Optimizations:** Optimizing the build may result in faster execution with the penalty being that it takes marginally longer to build.
- **DLL Base Address:** This option enables you to specify the base address of the DLL in hexadecimal format. This option is disabled when the project type will not produce a DLL.
- **Generate Debug Info:** This controls when debug information will be generated into your application output. By default, this option is set to full (for Debug configurations), which enables you to attach a debugger to a running application. You can also turn debugging information off completely or set the option to pdb-only (the default for Release configurations) to generate only the PDB debugging information. The latter means that you can still debug the application when it is started from within Visual Studio 2012 but you can see only the disassembler if you try to attach to a running application.

Compilation Constants

You can use compilation constants to control what information is included in the build output and even what code is compiled. The Compilation Constants options control the following:

- **Define `DEBUG` Constant and Define `TRACE` Constant:** Enable debug and trace information to be included in the compiled application based on the `DEBUG` and `TRACE` flags, respectively. From a functional perspective, if the `DEBUG` constant is not present, then the compiler excludes calls to any of the methods on the Debug class from the finished application. Similarly, if the `TRACE` constant is not present, then calls to methods on the Trace class are not included in the compiled application.

- **Custom Constants:** If your application build process requires custom constants, you can specify them here in the form `ConstantName="Value"`. If you have multiple constants, they should be delimited by commas.

The last option doesn't fall under compilation constants, but it does enable you to further customize the way the project builds.

- **Generate Serialization Assemblies:** By default, this option is set to Auto, which enables the build process to determine whether serialization assemblies are needed, but you can change it to On or Off if you want to hard-code the behavior.

> **NOTE** *Serialization assemblies are created using the* `Sgen.exe` *command-line tool. This tool generates an assembly that contains an* `XmlSerializer` *for serializing (and deserializing) a specific type. Normally these assemblies are generated at run time the first time an* `XmlSerializer` *is used. Pre-generating them at compile time can improve the performance of the first use. Serialization assemblies are named* `TypeName.XmlSerializers.dll`. *See the documentation of* `Sgen.exe` *for more info.*

Build Events

You can perform additional actions before or after the build process by adding them to an events list. Click the Build Events button on the My Project Compile page to display the Build Events dialog. Figure 46-6 shows a post-build event that executes the project output after every successful build.

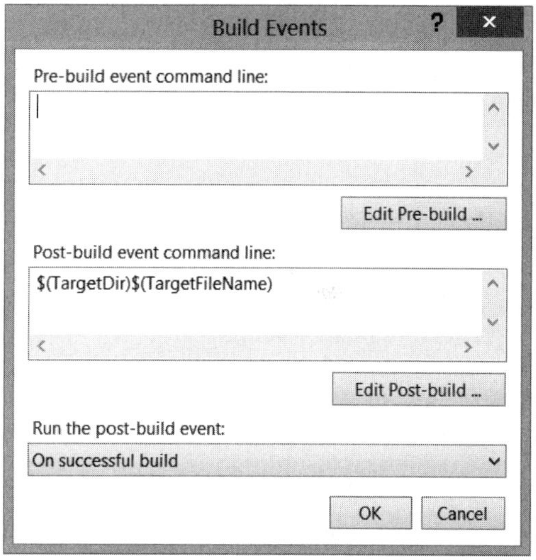

Each action you want to perform should be on a separate line, and can be added directly into either the Pre-Build Event Command Line text area or the Post-Build Event Command Line text area, or you can use the Edit Pre-Build and Edit Post-Build buttons to access the known predefined aliases that you can use in the actions.

FIGURE 46-6

> **NOTE** *If your pre- or post-build event actions are batch files, you must prefix them with a call statement. For example, if you want to call* `archive_previous_build.bat` *before every build, you need to enter* `call archive_previous_build.bat` *into the Pre-Build Event Command Line text box. In addition to this, encase any paths that contain spaces in double-quotes. This applies even if the path with spaces comes from one of the built-in macros.*

As shown in Figure 46-7, the Event Command Line dialog includes a list of macros you can use in the creation of your actions. The current value displays for each macro so that you know what text will be included if you use it.

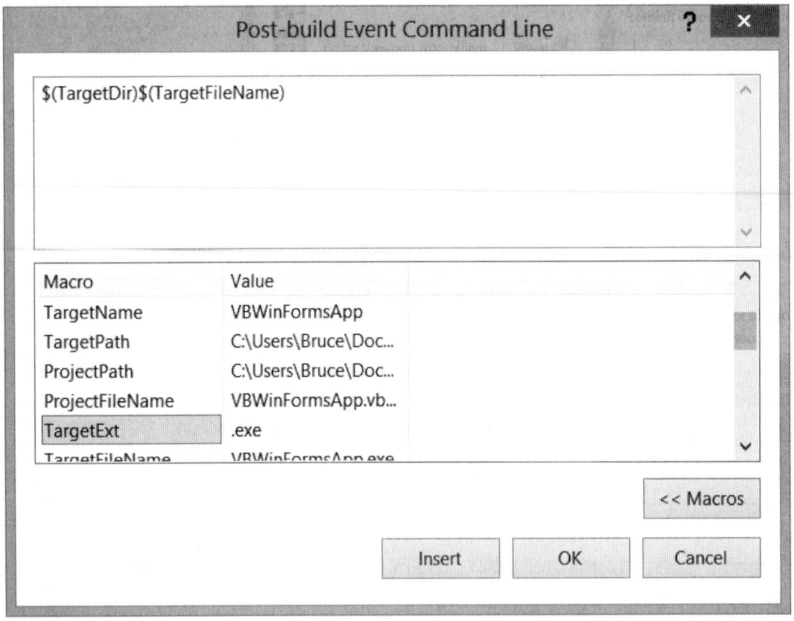

FIGURE 46-7

In this sample, the developer has created a command line of `$(TargetDir)$(TargetFileName)$(TargetExt)`, assuming that it would execute the built application when finished. However, analyzing the values of each of the macros, it's easy to see that the extension will be included twice, which can be amended quickly by either simply removing the `$(TargetExt)` macro or replacing the entire expression with the `$(TargetPath)` macro.

At the bottom of the Build Events dialog (see Figure 46-6), there is an option to specify the conditions under which the Post-Build Event will be executed. The valid options follow:

- **Always:** This option runs the Post-Build Event script even if the build fails. Remember that there is no guarantee when this event fires that Visual Studio has produced any files, so your post-build script should handle this scenario.
- **On Successful Build:** This is the default option. It causes the Post-Build Event script to be run whenever the build is considered to be successful. Note that this means that it will run even if your project is up to date (and therefore is not rebuilt).
- **When the Build Updates the Project Output:** This option is similar to On Successful Build, except that it fires only the Post-Build Event script when the project output files have changed. This is a great option for keeping a local cache of archived builds of your projects because it means you copy only a file into the archive if it has changed since the last build.

There are no filter options for determining if the Pre-Build Event will be executed.

C# BUILD PAGES

C# provides its own set of build options. In general, the options are the same as those available to a Visual Basic project, but in a different location because C# programmers are more likely to tweak the output than Visual Basic developers, who are typically more interested in rapid development than in fine-tuning performance.

Instead of a single Compile page in the project property pages, C# has a Build page and a Build Events page. The Build Events page acts in exactly the same way as the Build Events dialog in Visual Basic, so refer to the previous discussion for information on that page.

As you can see in Figure 46-8, many of the options on the Build page have direct correlations to settings found in the Compile page or in the Advanced Compiler Settings area of Visual Basic. Some settings, such as Define `DEBUG` Constant and Define `TRACE` Constant, are identical to their Visual Basic counterparts.

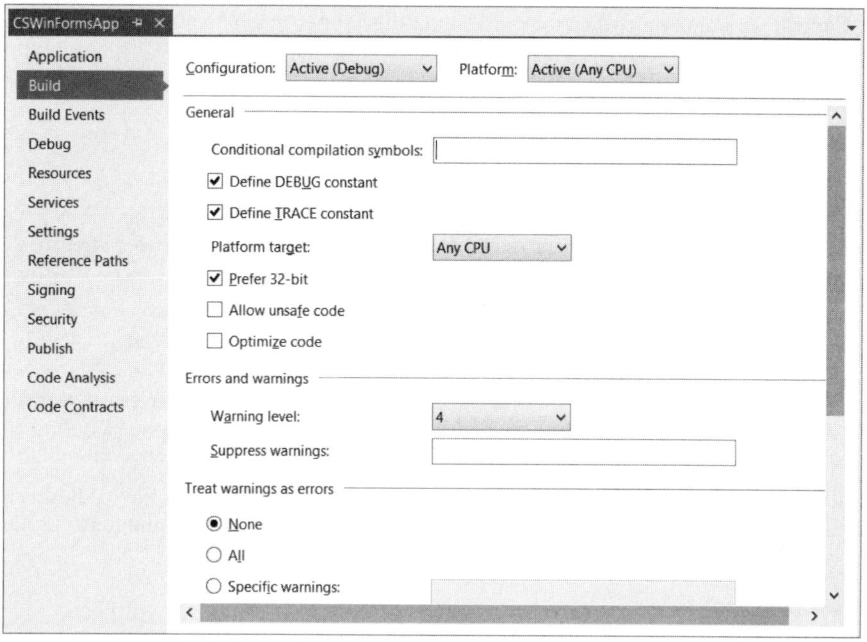

FIGURE 46-8

However, some are renamed to fit in with a C++-based vocabulary; for example, Optimize Code is equivalent to Enable Optimizations. As with the Visual Basic compile settings, you can determine how warnings are treated, and you can specify a warning level.

Clicking the Advanced button on the Build page invokes the Advanced Build Settings dialog, as shown in Figure 46-9, which includes settings that are not accessible to Visual Basic developers. These settings give you tight control over how the build will be performed, including information on the internal errors that occur during the compilation process and what debug information is to be generated.

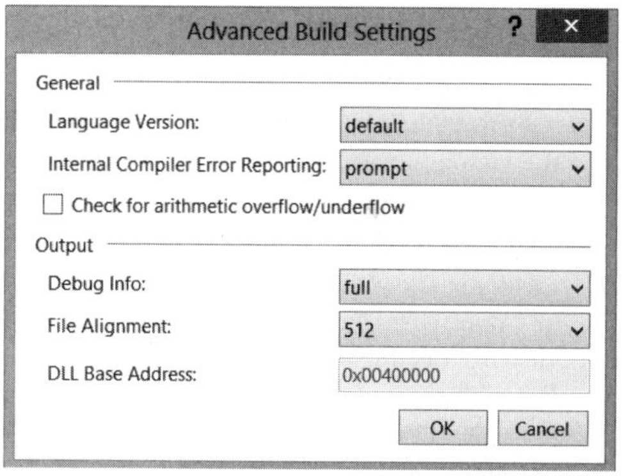

FIGURE 46-9

These settings are mostly self-explanatory, so the following list is a quick summary of what effect each one has on the build:

- **Language Version:** Specifies which version of the C# language to use. The default is to use the current version. In Visual Studio 2012, along with two earlier versions of C#, the other options are ISO-1 and ISO-2, which restricts the language features to those defined in the corresponding ISO standard.
- **Internal Compiler Error Reporting:** If errors occur during the compilation (not compilation errors, but errors with the compilation process itself), you can have information sent to Microsoft so that it can add it to its revision of the compiler code. The default setting is Prompt, which asks you whether you want to send the information to Microsoft. Other values include None, which won't send the information; Send, to automatically send the error information; and Queue, which adds the details to a queue to be sent later.
- **Check for Arithmetic Overflow/Underflow:** Checks for overflow errors that can cause unsafe execution. Underflow errors occur when the precision of the number is too fine for the system.
- **Debug Info:** Identical to the Visual Basic Generate debug info setting.
- **File Alignment:** Used to set the section boundaries in the output file, and enables you to control the internal layout of the compiled output. The values are measured in bytes.
- **DLL Base Address:** Identical to the Visual Basic setting of the same name.

Using these settings for your projects enables you to closely control how the build process performs. However, you have another option with Visual Studio 2012, which is to edit the build scripts directly. This is made possible because Visual Studio 2012 uses MSBuild for its compilations.

MSBUILD

Visual Studio 2012 uses MSBuild, which is the compilation engine Microsoft originally released with Visual Studio 2005. It uses XML-based configuration files to identify the layout of a build project, including all the settings discussed earlier in this chapter, as well as what files should be included in the actual compilation.

Visual Studio uses MSBuild configuration files as its project definition files. This enables the MSBuild engine to be used automatically when compiling your applications within the IDE because the same settings file is used for both your project definition in the IDE and the build process.

How Visual Studio Uses MSBuild

As mentioned, the contents of Visual Studio 2012 project files are based on the MSBuild XML Schema and can be edited directly in Visual Studio, so you can customize how the project is loaded and compiled.

However, to edit the project file you need to effectively remove the project's active status from the Solution Explorer. Right-click the project you want to edit in the Solution Explorer, and choose the Unload Project command from the bottom of the context menu that displays.

The project will be collapsed in the Solution Explorer and marked as unavailable. In addition, any open files that belong to the project will be closed while it is unloaded from the solution. Right-click the project entry again, and an additional menu command will be available to edit the project file (see Figure 46-10).

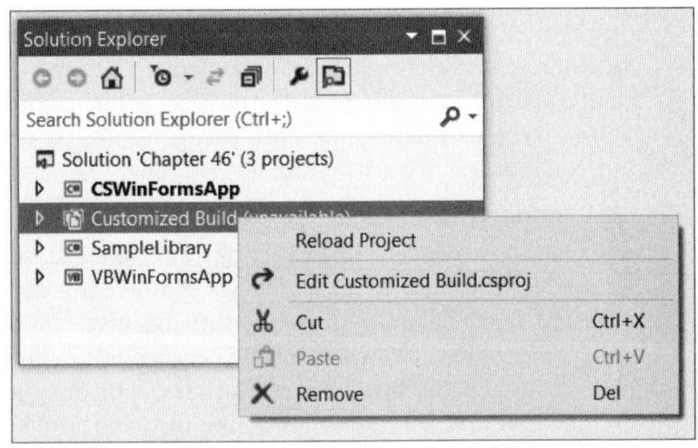

FIGURE 46-10

The XML-based project file will be correspondingly opened in the XML editor of Visual Studio 2012, enabling you to collapse and expand nodes. The following listing is a sample MSBuild project file for an empty C# project:

```
<?xml version="1.0" encoding="utf-8"?>
<Project
  ToolsVersion="4.0"
  DefaultTargets="Build"
  xmlns="http://schemas.microsoft.com/developer/msbuild/2003">
  <PropertyGroup>
    <Configuration Condition=" '$(Configuration)' == '' ">Debug</Configuration>
    <Platform Condition=" '$(Platform)' == '' ">x86</Platform>
    <ProductVersion>8.0.30703</ProductVersion>
    <SchemaVersion>2.0</SchemaVersion>
    <ProjectGuid>{04ABE6E2-5500-467B-BB01-0BBF0258E94A}</ProjectGuid>
    <OutputType>Exe</OutputType>
    <AppDesignerFolder>Properties</AppDesignerFolder>
    <RootNamespace>ConsoleApplication</RootNamespace>
    <AssemblyName>ConsoleApplication</AssemblyName>
    <TargetFrameworkVersion>v4.5</TargetFrameworkVersion>
    <FileAlignment>512</FileAlignment>
  </PropertyGroup>
  <PropertyGroup Condition=" '$(Configuration)|$(Platform)' == 'Debug|x86' ">
    <PlatformTarget>x86</PlatformTarget>
    <DebugSymbols>true</DebugSymbols>
    <DebugType>full</DebugType>
    <Optimize>false</Optimize>
    <OutputPath>bin\Debug\</OutputPath>
    <DefineConstants>DEBUG;TRACE</DefineConstants>
    <ErrorReport>prompt</ErrorReport>
    <WarningLevel>4</WarningLevel>
  </PropertyGroup>
  <PropertyGroup Condition=" '$(Configuration)|$(Platform)' == 'Release|x86' ">
    <PlatformTarget>x86</PlatformTarget>
    <DebugType>pdbonly</DebugType>
    <Optimize>true</Optimize>
    <OutputPath>bin\Release\</OutputPath>
    <DefineConstants>TRACE</DefineConstants>
    <ErrorReport>prompt</ErrorReport>
    <WarningLevel>4</WarningLevel>
  </PropertyGroup>
  <ItemGroup>
    <Reference Include="System" />
    <Reference Include="System.Core" />
    <Reference Include="System.Xml.Linq" />
    <Reference Include="System.Data.DataSetExtensions" />
    <Reference Include="Microsoft.CSharp" />
    <Reference Include="System.Data" />
    <Reference Include="System.Xml" />
  </ItemGroup>
  <ItemGroup>
    <Compile Include="Program.cs" />
    <Compile Include="Properties\AssemblyInfo.cs" />
  </ItemGroup>
  <Import Project="$(MSBuildToolsPath)\Microsoft.CSharp.targets" />
  <!-- To modify your build process, add your task inside one of the targets
       below and uncomment it. Other similar extension points exist, see
     Microsoft.Common.targets.
  <Target Name="BeforeBuild">
```

```
  </Target>
  <Target Name="AfterBuild">
  </Target>
  -->
</Project>
```

The XML contains the information about the build. Most of these nodes directly relate to settings you saw earlier in the Compile and Build pages but also include any Framework namespaces that are required. The first `PropertyGroup` element contains project properties that apply to all build configurations. This is followed by two conditional elements that define properties for each of the two build configurations, Debug and Release. The remaining elements are for project references and projectwide namespace imports.

When the project includes additional files, such as forms and user controls, each one is defined in the project file with its own set of nodes. For example, the following listing shows the additional XML that is included in a standard Windows Application project, identifying the Form, its designer code file, and the additional application files required for a Windows-based application:

```
<ItemGroup>
  <Compile Include="Form1.cs">
    <SubType>Form</SubType>
  </Compile>
  <Compile Include="Form1.Designer.cs">
    <DependentUpon>Form1.cs</DependentUpon>
  </Compile>
  <Compile Include="Program.cs" />
  <Compile Include="Properties\AssemblyInfo.cs" />
  <EmbeddedResource Include="Properties\Resources.resx">
    <Generator>ResXFileCodeGenerator</Generator>
    <LastGenOutput>Resources.Designer.cs</LastGenOutput>
    <SubType>Designer</SubType>
  </EmbeddedResource>
  <Compile Include="Properties\Resources.Designer.cs">
    <AutoGen>True</AutoGen>
    <DependentUpon>Resources.resx</DependentUpon>
  </Compile>
  <None Include="Properties\Settings.settings">
    <Generator>SettingsSingleFileGenerator</Generator>
    <LastGenOutput>Settings.Designer.cs</LastGenOutput>
  </None>
  <Compile Include="Properties\Settings.Designer.cs">
    <AutoGen>True</AutoGen>
    <DependentUpon>Settings.settings</DependentUpon>
    <DesignTimeSharedInput>True</DesignTimeSharedInput>
  </Compile>
</ItemGroup>
```

You can also include additional tasks in the build process in the included Target nodes for `BeforeBuild` and `AfterBuild` events. However, these actions will not appear in the Visual Studio 2012 Build Events dialog discussed earlier. The alternative is to use a `PropertyGroup` node that includes `PreBuildEvent` and `PostBuildEvent` entries. For instance, if you wanted to execute the application after it was successfully built, you could include the following XML block immediately before the closing `</Project>` tag:

```
<PropertyGroup>
  <PostBuildEvent>"$(TargetDir)$(TargetFileName)"</PostBuildEvent>
</PropertyGroup>
```

When you finish editing the project file's XML, you need to re-enable it in the solution by right-clicking the project's entry in the Solution Explorer and selecting the Reload Project command. If you still have the project file open, Visual Studio asks if you want to close it to proceed.

The MSBuild Schema

An extended discussion on the MSBuild engine is beyond the scope of this book. However, it's useful to understand the different components that make up the MSBuild project file so that you can look at and update your own projects.

Four major elements form the basis of the project file: *items*, *properties*, *targets*, and *tasks*. Brought together, you can use these four node types to create a configuration file that describes a project in full, as shown in the previous sample C# project file.

Items

`Items` are those elements that define inputs to the build system and project. They are defined as children of an `ItemGroup` node, and the most common item is the `Compile` node used to inform MSBuild that the specified file is to be included in the compilation. The following snippet from a project file shows an `Item` element defined for the `Form1.cs` file of a Windows Application project:

```
<ItemGroup>
  <Compile Include="Form1.cs">
    <SubType>Form</SubType>
  </Compile>
</ItemGroup>
```

Properties

`PropertyGroup` nodes are used to contain any properties defined to the project. Properties are typically key/value pairings. They can contain only a single value and are used to store the project settings you can access in the Build and Compile pages in the IDE.

`PropertyGroup` nodes can be optionally included by specifying a `Condition` attribute, as shown in the following sample listing:

```
<PropertyGroup Condition=" '$(Configuration)|$(Platform)' == 'Release|x86' ">
  <DebugType>pdbonly</DebugType>
  <Optimize>true</Optimize>
  <OutputPath>bin\Release\</OutputPath>
  <DefineConstants>TRACE</DefineConstants>
  <ErrorReport>prompt</ErrorReport>
  <WarningLevel>4</WarningLevel>
</PropertyGroup>
```

This XML defines a `PropertyGroup` that will be included only in the build if the project is being built as a Release for the x86 platform. Each of the six property nodes within the `PropertyGroup` uses the name of the property as the name of the node.

Targets

`Target` elements enable you to arrange tasks (discussed more in the "Assembly Versioning via MSBuild Tasks" section) into a sequence. Each `Target` element should have a `Name` attribute to identify it, and it can be called directly, thus enabling you to provide multiple entry points into the build process. The following snippet defines a `Target` with a name of `BeforeBuild`:

```
<Target Name="BeforeBuild">
</Target>
```

Tasks

Tasks define actions that MSBuild can execute under certain conditions. You can define your own tasks or take advantage of the many built-in tasks, such as Copy. Shown in the following snippet, Copy can copy one or more files from one location to another:

```
<Target Name="CopyFiles">
    <Copy
        SourceFiles="@(MySourceFiles)"
        DestinationFolder="\\PDSERVER01\SourceBackup\"
    />
</Target>
```

Assembly Versioning via MSBuild Tasks

One aspect of most automated build systems is planning application versioning. In this section, you see how you can customize the build process for your project so that it can accept an external version number. This version number will be used to update the AssemblyInfo file, which will subsequently affect the assembly version. Start by looking at the AssemblyInfo.cs file, which typically contains assembly version information such as the following:

```
[Assembly: AssemblyVersion("1.0.0.0")]
```

What the build customization needs to do is replace the default version number with a number supplied as part of the build process. To do this, use a third-party MSBuild library entitled MSBuildTasks, which is a project on Tigris (http://msbuildtasks.tigris.org/). This includes a FileUpdate task that you can use to match on a regular expression. Before you can use this task, you need to import the MSBuildTasks Targets file. This file is installed into the default MSBuild extensions path by the MSBuildTasks MSI.

```
<Project ToolsVersion="4.0" DefaultTargets="Build"
xmlsn="http://schemas.microsoft.com/developer/msbuild/2003">
  <!-- Required Import to use MSBuild Community Tasks -->
<Import Project="$(MSBuildExtensionsPath)\MSBuildCommunityTasks\
MSBuild.Community.Tasks.Targets"/>
  <PropertyGroup>
    . . .
```

Because you want to update the AssemblyInfo file before the build, you could add a call to the FileUpdate task in the BeforeBuild target. This would make it harder to maintain and debug later. A much better approach is to create a new target for the FileUpdate task and then make the BeforeBuild target depend upon it, as follows:

```
<Import Project="$(MSBuildToolsPath)\Microsoft.CSharp.targets" />
<Target Name="BeforeBuild" DependsOnTargets="UpdateAssemblyInfo">
</Target>
<Target Name="UpdateAssemblyInfo">
  <Message Text="Build Version: $(BuildVersion)" />
  <FileUpdate Files="Properties\AssemblyInfo.cs"
              Regex="\d+\.\d+\.\d+\.\d+"
              ReplacementText="$(BuildVersion)" />
</Target>
```

Here you can use a property called $(BuildVersion), which doesn't yet exist. If you run MSBuild against this project now, it can replace the version numbers in your AssemblyInfo file with a blank string. Unfortunately, this does not compile. You could simply define this property with some default value like this:

```
<PropertyGroup>
    <BuildVersion>0.0.0.0</BuildVersion>
    <Configuration Condition=" '$(Configuration)' == '' ">Debug</Configuration>
```

This works, but it means that when building your project in Visual Studio 2012 it will always have the same version. Luckily, the MSBuildTasks library has another task called `Version`, which can generate a version number for you. Here is the code:

```
<Target Name="BeforeBuild" DependsOnTargets="GetVersion;UpdateAssemblyInfo">
</Target>
. . .
<Target Name="GetVersion" Condition=" $(BuildVersion) == ''">
  <Version BuildType="Automatic" RevisionType="Automatic" Major="1" Minor="3" >
    <Output TaskParameter="Major" PropertyName="Major" />
    <Output TaskParameter="Minor" PropertyName="Minor" />
    <Output TaskParameter="Build" PropertyName="Build" />
    <Output TaskParameter="Revision" PropertyName="Revision" />
  </Version>
  <CreateProperty Value="$(Major).$(Minor).$(Build).$(Revision)">
    <Output TaskParameter="Value" PropertyName="BuildVersion" />
  </CreateProperty>
</Target>
```

The new `GetVersion` target will be executed only if `$(BuildVersion)` is not specified. It calls into the `Version` task from MSBuildTasks, which sets the major version number to 1 and the minor version number to 3. (You could, of course, configure these instead of hard-coding them.) The Build and Revision numbers are automatically generated according to a simple algorithm. These components of the version are then put together in a `CreateProperty` task, which comes with MSBuild, to create the full `$(BuildVersion)` that you need. Finally, this task has been added to the list of targets that `BeforeBuild` depends on.

Now when you build the project in Visual Studio 2012, you will get an automatically generated version number as per usual. In your automated build process, you can specify the version number as an argument to the MSBuild call, for example:

```
MSBuild CustomizedBuild.csproj /p:BuildVersion=2.4.3154.9001
```

SUMMARY

You can customize the default build behavior with an enormous range of options in Visual Studio 2012 because of the power and flexibility of the MSBuild engine. Within the project file you can include additional actions to perform both before and after the build has taken place, as well as include additional files in the compilation.

47 Assembly Versioning and Signing

WHAT'S IN THIS CHAPTER?

- Versioning assemblies
- Signing an assembly to give it a strong name
- Managing strongly named assemblies in the Global Assembly Cache

When you create a .NET assembly, you can optionally sign it to provide it with a strong name. An assembly without a strong name is identified by its filename, which often is not enough to uniquely identify it. This means that other projects that depend on your assembly cannot be guaranteed to consume the correct version. A strongly named assembly can be uniquely identified by dependent projects and even system administrators, who can apply a security policy to your assembly.

In this chapter, you learn how to use Visual Studio 2012 to set the assembly version number, and how you can use a digital signature to sign your assembly so that it can't be tampered with. This also results in a strongly named assembly, which can be added to the Global Assembly Cache.

ASSEMBLY NAMING

Every .NET assembly, whether it is an executable or a class library, contains a manifest that has information about the assembly's identity. Primarily this includes the name and version number of the assembly but also includes culture and public key if it is a strongly named assembly. This information can be easily viewed by opening an assembly in Telerik's JustDecompile, as shown in Figure 47-1.

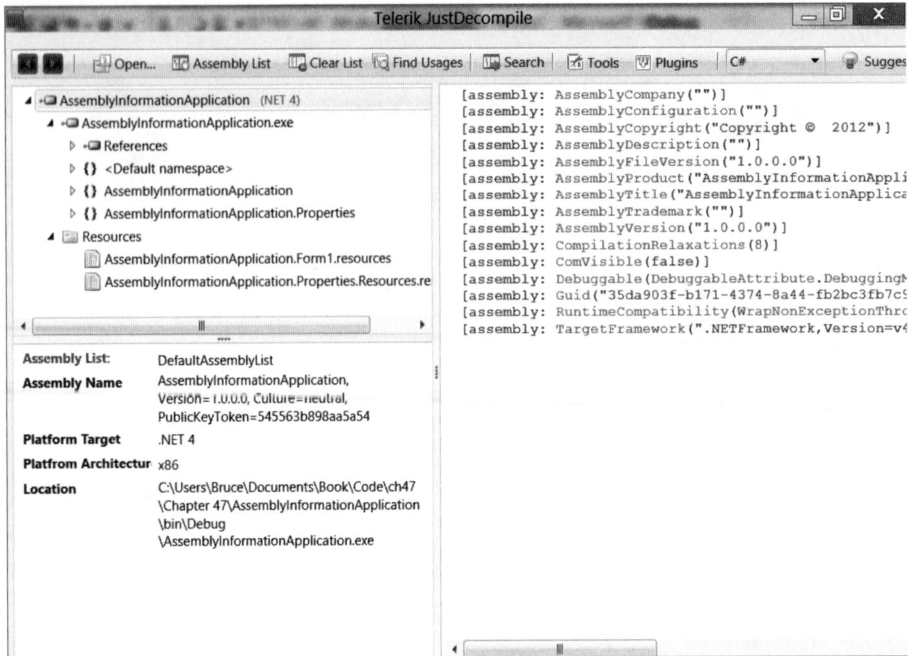

FIGURE 47-1

The assembly `AssemblyInformationApplication.exe` does not have a public key (refer to Figure 47-1). Other assemblies, such as `System.Data`, have a full name such as:

```
System.Data, Version=2.0.0.0, Culture=neutral, PublicKeytoken=b77a5c561934e089
```

Although it is useful to be able to see these details, it is difficult to get this information directly. It can be discovered, but the individual values are not found in one place. The `sn.exe` program (discussed later in this chapter in the section "Signing an Assembly") has an option to retrieve the public key token. You can use the IL Disassembler (`ILDASM.exe`) to view the version and culture. And programmatically you get this information from the `FullName` property on the appropriate `Assembly` object. For this reason, not to mention the utility of being able to decompile a .NET assembly, a free tool like Just Decompile is well worth the time spent downloading it.

You specify the name of your assembly in Visual Studio 2012 via the project properties editor, as shown in Figure 47-2. In this figure you can see the Assembly Name field on the main Application tab and the Assembly Version in the inset, which is accessible via the Assembly Information button.

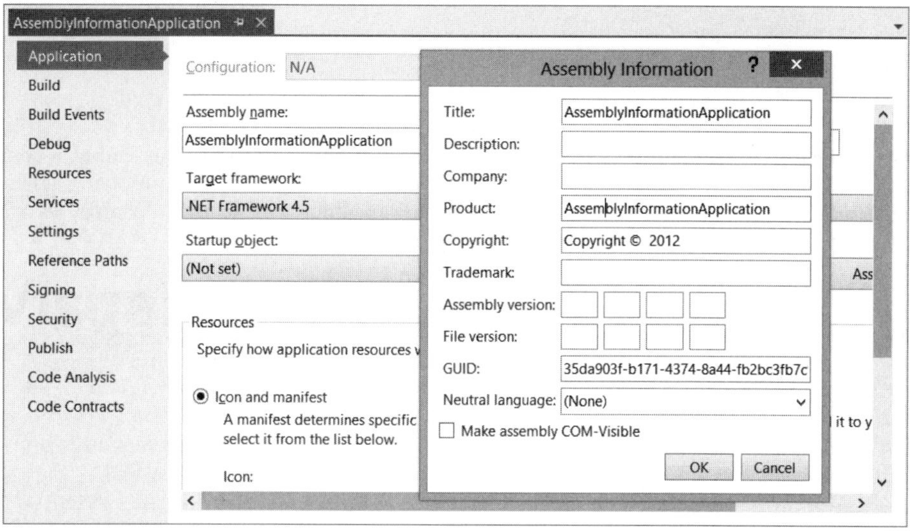

FIGURE 47-2

The assembly properties presented in the inset dialog (refer to Figure 47-2) appear in the `AssemblyInfo` file added to your project by default.

> **NOTE** *If you use a C# project, you can find the* `AssemblyInfo.cs` *file by expanding the Properties item found underneath the project in Solution Explorer. If you use VB, you can find the* `AssemblyInfo.vb` *file under My Project but only after Show All Files has been checked for the project.*

The following snippet illustrates the `AssemblyVersion` and `AssemblyFileVersion` assembly attributes used to define the version and file version of the assembly:

VB

```
' Version information for an assembly consists of the following four values:
'
'      Major Version
'      Minor Version
'      Build Number
'      Revision
'
' You can specify all the values or you can default the Build and Revision Numbers
' by using the '*' as shown below:
' <Assembly: AssemblyVersion("1.0.*")>
<Assembly: AssemblyVersion("1.0.0.0")>
<Assembly: AssemblyFileVersion("1.0.0.0")>
```

C#

```
// Explanatory comments removed
[assembly: AssemblyVersion("1.0.0.0")]
[assembly: AssemblyFileVersion("1.0.0.0")]
```

If you wonder what the difference is between the assembly version and file version of an assembly, it comes down to usage. The assembly version information is used by the .NET Framework when resolving assembly and type information. On the other hand, the file version displays in Windows Explorer when you look at the file properties.

> **NOTE** *There is much debate over whether the assembly version and file version number should be in sync, but essentially it is up to you. Some developers prefer keeping them in sync because it means that they can determine the assembly version via Windows Explorer. Alternatively, other organizations use the file version to represent changes to an assembly (for example, a hotfix or service pack), whereas the assembly version is used for new versions of the application.*

As the comments in the VB snippet explain, assembly version numbers have four components — Major, Minor, Build, and Revision. Again, how you increment these is completely up to you. You can even elect for Visual Studio 2012 to increment them for you by specifying an * for the build and/or revision numbers. One fairly common strategy is to use the Major and Minor numbers to represent the actual version of the product being worked on. Incrementing just the Minor number would perhaps represent minor fixes and minimal new functionality (similar to a service pack), whereas the Major number would represent new core functionality.

This leaves the Build and Revision numbers that you can use to perhaps tie into the build process. For example, the Build number might represent the week number into development for a particular release, whereas the Revision number might represent the most recent revision number in the source repository. This last value then becomes important because you can use it in isolation to access the exact source code from the repository used to build a particular version.

VERSION CONSISTENCY

The default project configuration doesn't lend itself easily to having a consistent version number across all projects within a solution. However, using the ability to include linked files in a project, you can coerce Visual Studio 2012 into giving you version consistency. This is particularly important if you have an automated build system that automatically increments the version number. Instead of updating any number of `AssemblyInfo` files, it can simply modify a single file and have all projects updated.

You need to start by creating an additional `AssemblyInfo` file, say `GlobalAssemblyInfo.vb`, in the solution folder. To do this, right-click the Solution node and select Add New Item. The new item will be added to a Solution Items folder in your solution. Into this file you need to move the `AssemblyVersion` and `AssemblyFileVersion` attributes from the `AssemblyInfo` file in your projects. (You also need to import the `System.Reflection` namespace unless you fully qualify the attribute names.)

After you do this, you then need to add this file into each of your projects. You do this via the Add Existing Item right-click menu item for the projects in the Solution Explorer tool window. When you locate the `GlobalAssemblyInfo.vb` or `GlobalAssemblyInfo.cs` file, make sure you select the Add As Link item from the Add drop-down that is shown in Figure 47-3.

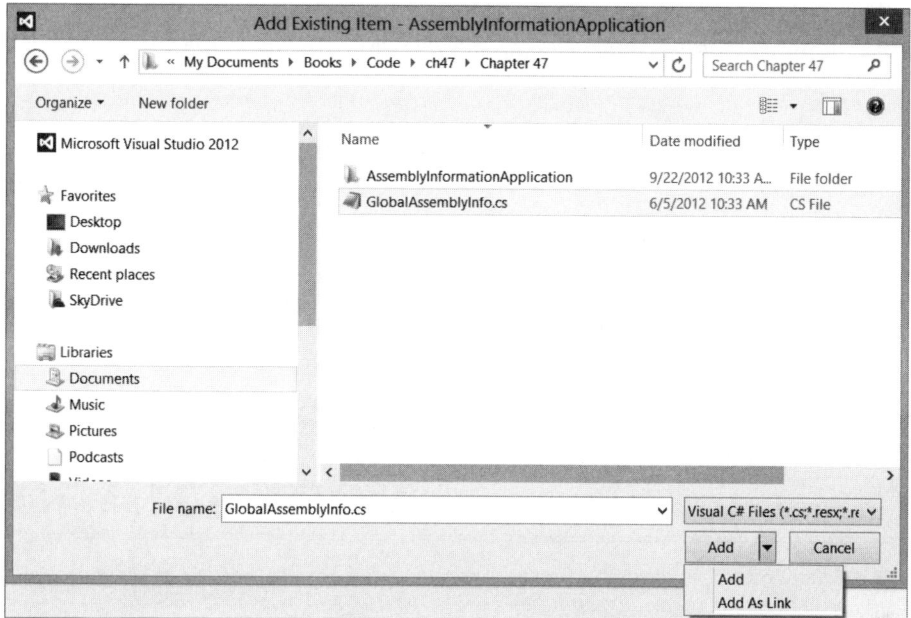

FIGURE 47-3

You can use this one `GlobalAssemblyInfo` file in any number of projects; the one limitation is that it is specific to VB or C#. If you have a solution that uses a mix of VB and C# projects, you must have a central `GlobalAssemblyInfo` file for each language — this is still better than maintaining the version information in a separate file for each project. Note that you can include other assembly attributes in these central files, such as `AssemblyCopyright`, `AssemblyCompany`, and `AssemblyTrademark`, if appropriate.

STRONGLY NAMED ASSEMBLIES

A strong name consists of the parts that uniquely identify an assembly's identity. This includes the plain-text name and a version number. Added to these elements are a public key and a digital signature. These are generated with a corresponding private key. Because of this private/public key system coupled with a digital signature, strong names can be relied on to be completely unique. Further, by signing your assembly you can prevent someone from maliciously tampering with your code. .NET assemblies are relatively easy to reverse engineer, modify, and compile as a modified assembly. The hash created as part of the signing process changes as the assembly is modified — in effect providing a security mechanism against unauthorized modifications.

Using a strong name can also ensure that the version of your assembly is the one that has been shipped. No modification can be made to it without affecting its signature and thus breaking its compatibility with the generated strong name.

As mentioned previously, using strong names also gives administrators the ability to explicitly set security policy against your solutions by referring to their unique names. This can give a corporation confidence that when deployed the software runs as expected because it cannot be tampered with without affecting the signing of the strong name.

> **NOTE** *After you start using strong-named assemblies in your solution, you must use strong-named files down the chain of references because allowing an unsigned assembly as part of the chain would break the security that strong-naming your assembly was intended to implement.*

THE GLOBAL ASSEMBLY CACHE

Every computer that has the .NET Framework installed has a systemwide cache, called the Global Assembly Cache (GAC), which can be used to store assemblies to be shared by multiple applications. Assemblies added to the GAC are accessible from any .NET application on the same system. This can be a huge saving for organizations where you have common functionality that you want to share between applications.

In this cache (usually stored in a folder within the `Windows` directory) you can find the common language run-time components as well as other globally registered binary files that you, and anyone else, can consume. If an assembly is going to be used only by a single application, it should be deployed in that application's folder.

> **NOTE** *Adding assemblies to the GAC is not recommended unless you need to share assemblies between applications, and they are too large to redistribute alongside each application. And for most applications written by companies that don't have "Microsoft" in its name, this is a high bar that is rarely exceeded.*

If you do decide to share the assembly between applications, you must store it in the GAC. Your assembly must also be strong-named. You don't have a choice in the matter because the cache interrogates all files to ensure that their integrity is valid; hence, it needs the strong-name versioning to compare against. Instructions on how to strongly name your assemblies appear in the "Signing an Assembly" section.

When you have a strongly named assembly, you can add it to the GAC by using the `gacutil.exe` command-line tool like this:

```
gacutil.exe /i AssemblyInformationApplication.dll
```

If an assembly with the same strong name already exists, you can force a reinstall with the `/f` option. To uninstall the assembly, use this command:

```
gacutil.exe /u AssemblyInformationApplication
```

> **NOTE** `Gacutil.exe` *is a part of the Microsoft .NET Framework Software Developer Kit (SDK) and not a part of the standard redistributable. This means that you can rely on it being present only in development environments. For deployment to the GAC on client machines, you should use an MSI file.*

SIGNING AN ASSEMBLY

Signing an assembly in Visual Studio involves the generation of a strong-name key (`.snk`) file via the `sn.exe` utility. And the assembly attributes of your application's configuration file need to be modified to reference this file. Visual Studio has built-in support for signing all managed code projects using the Signing tab in the project properties editor, as shown in Figure 47-4.

The Signing tab enables you to sign the assembly in the lower half of the page. You first should select the Sign the Assembly check box to indicate that you will be generating a strong name. You then need to select the strong-name key file to use when signing the assembly.

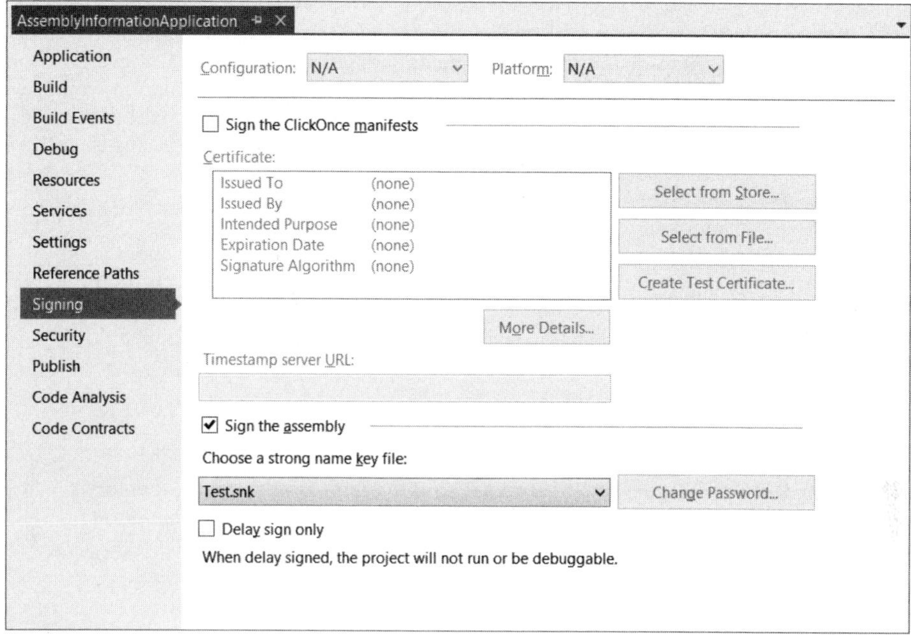

FIGURE 47-4

Existing key files can be in either the older `.snk` paired key file format or the more recent `.pfx` format. From the drop-down list, select the Browse option to locate the file in your file system, and click OK in the dialog to save the key file to the Signing page settings.

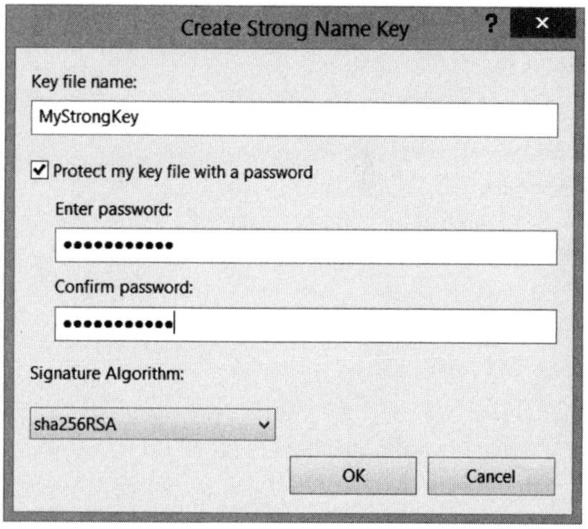

Alternatively, you can create a new strong-named key by selecting the New option from the drop-down list. When you choose New, you can create a new `.pfx` formatted strong-named file. Figure 47-5 shows the Create Strong Name Key dialog. You can simply choose a filename to use for the key, or you can additionally protect the key file with a password. If you do decide to add a password, you will be prompted to enter the password if you build your application on any other computer the first time. Thereafter, Visual Studio can remember the password.

FIGURE 47-5

Either way, after you create and select the key file, it will be added to your project in the Solution Explorer, enabling you to easily include it for deployment projects.

One of the main reasons you might want to sign your assemblies is to ensure that they cannot be modified. There is little cost associated with signing assemblies, and along with protection against unauthorized modification, you gain the ability to version your assemblies. And due to the mechanism used to sign assemblies, the key (pun intended) to the signing process is the strong-name key file. Most organizations place a high level of security around the strong-name key file used to sign their assemblies. They not only don't want to lose the file (it would prevent assemblies from being upgradable in the future), but they also don't want to allow a large number of people to be able to access it. Possession of the key file is all that is required to create assemblies associated with a particular company

As such, it is likely that you won't have access to the private key to successfully sign the assembly. When you're in this situation, you still need to dictate that the application be digitally signed. However, instead of providing the full strong-name key file, which contains the public and private key information, you provide only a file containing the public key information and select the Delay Sign Only check box. Later, typically as part of your build process for the released assemblies, you need to sign the assemblies using the full key:

```
sn -R AssemblyInformationApplication MyOrganizationsStrongkey.snk
```

If you choose to delay the signing of your assemblies, you cannot debug or even run the application because it will fail the assembly verification process that is part of the pre-execution checks that the .NET Framework does on assemblies. Actually, this is a little inaccurate because you can register your assembly (or any assembly signed with the same public key) so that the verification step will be skipped:

```
sn -Vr AssemblyInformationApplication.exe
```

> **NOTE** *You should only ever register assemblies to skip verification on development machines. Further, you can unregister an assembly (or all assemblies signed with the same public key) using the* `sn` *command with the* `-Vu` *parameter.*

SUMMARY

Strongly naming your assembly and thus safeguarding it from improper use is straightforward to implement and can be done completely from within the Visual Studio 2012 IDE. The Signing page gives you the ability to both create and set the key file without having to edit the application's assembly attributes directly.

48

Obfuscation, Application Monitoring, and Management

WHAT'S IN THIS CHAPTER?

- Exploring the features of Dotfuscator and Analytics–Community Edition, a free post-build hardening and application monitoring tool that ships with Visual Studio
- Understanding how obfuscation can be used to prevent your assemblies from being easily decompiled
- Using tamper defense to protect your application assemblies from unauthorized modification
- Configuring application expiry to encode a specific date after which your application can't be executed
- Setting up usage tracking to determine what applications and features are used

If you've peeked under the covers at the details of how .NET assemblies are executed, you will have picked up on the fact that instead of compiling to machine language (and regardless of the programming language used), all .NET source code is compiled into the Microsoft Intermediary Language (MSIL, or just IL, for short). The IL is then *just-in-time* compiled when it is required for execution. This two-stage approach has a number of significant advantages, such as enabling you to dynamically query an assembly for type and method information, using reflection. However, this is a double-edged sword because this same flexibility means that once-hidden algorithms and business logic can easily be reverse-engineered and modified, legally or otherwise. This chapter introduces tools and techniques that help to protect your source code from prying eyes and monitor the execution of your applications.

THE MSIL DISASSEMBLER

Before looking at how you can protect your code from other people and monitor its behavior "in the wild," this section describes a couple of tools that can help you build better applications. The first tool is the Microsoft .NET Framework IL Disassembler, or ILDasm. This is included as part of the

Microsoft Windows SDK, which is installed by default with Visual Studio 2012. If you are running Windows 7, you can find it under Start ➪ All Programs ➪ Microsoft Windows SDK v7.1 ➪ Microsoft Windows SDK Tools ➪ IL Disassembler. If you are running Windows 8, use the Search charm and enter **IL** into the search text box. The IL Disassembler will appear as one of the Apps. In Figure 48-1, a small class library has been opened using this tool, and you can immediately see the namespace and class information contained within this assembly.

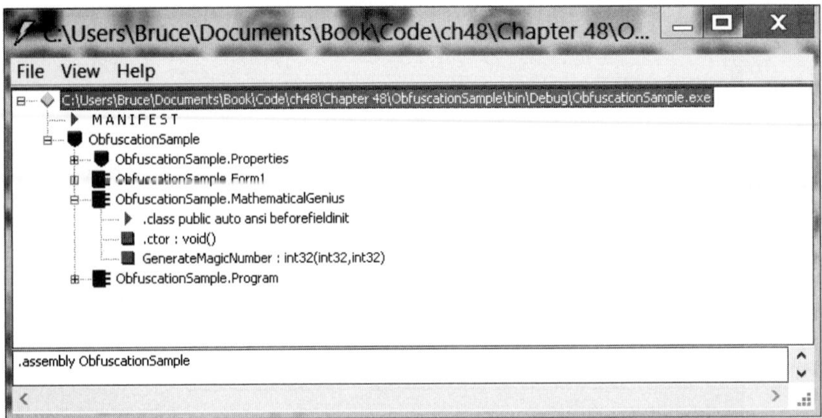

FIGURE 48-1

To compare the IL that is generated, the original source code for the `MathematicalGenius` class is as follows:

C#

```
namespace ObfuscationSample
{
    public class MathematicalGenius
    {
        public static Int32 GenerateMagicNumber(Int32 age, Int32 height)
        {
            return (age * height) + DateTime.Now.DayOfYear;
        }
    }
}
```

VB

```
Namespace ObfuscationSample
    Public Class MathematicalGenius
        Public Shared Function GenerateMagicNumber(ByVal age As Integer, _
                                              ByVal height As Integer) As Integer
            Return (age * height) + Today.DayOfWeek
        End Function
    End Class
End Namespace
```

Double-clicking the `GenerateMagicNumber` method in ILDasm opens up an additional window that shows the IL for that method. Figure 48-2 shows the IL for the `GenerateMagicNumber` method, which represents your super-secret, patent-pending algorithm. In actual fact, anyone who is prepared to spend a couple of hours learning how to interpret MSIL could quickly work out that the method simply multiplies the two `int32` parameters, `age` and `height`, and then adds the current day of the year to the result.

```
ObfuscationSample.MathematicalGenius::GenerateMagicNumber : int32(int...
Find  Find Next
.method public hidebysig instance int32  GenerateMagicNumber(int32 age,
                                                             int32 height) cil managed
{
  // Code size       23 (0x17)
  .maxstack  2
  .locals init ([0] int32 CS$1$0000,
           [1] valuetype [mscorlib]System.DateTime CS$0$0001)
  IL_0000:  nop
  IL_0001:  ldarg.1
  IL_0002:  ldarg.2
  IL_0003:  mul
  IL_0004:  call       valuetype [mscorlib]System.DateTime [mscorlib]System.DateTime::get_Now()
  IL_0009:  stloc.1
  IL_000a:  ldloca.s   CS$0$0001
  IL_000c:  call       instance int32 [mscorlib]System.DateTime::get_DayOfYear()
  IL_0011:  add
  IL_0012:  stloc.0
  IL_0013:  br.s       IL_0015
  IL_0015:  ldloc.0
  IL_0016:  ret
} // end of method MathematicalGenius::GenerateMagicNumber
```

FIGURE 48-2

If you haven't spent any time understanding how to read MSIL, a decompiler can convert this IL back into one or more .NET languages.

DECOMPILERS

One of the most widely used decompilers is .NET Reflector from Red Gate Software (available for download at `http://www.red-gate.com/products/reflector/`). Reflector can be used to decompile any .NET assembly into C#, Visual Basic, Managed C11, and even Delphi. In Figure 48-3, the same assembly you just accessed is opened using ILDasm, in Reflector.

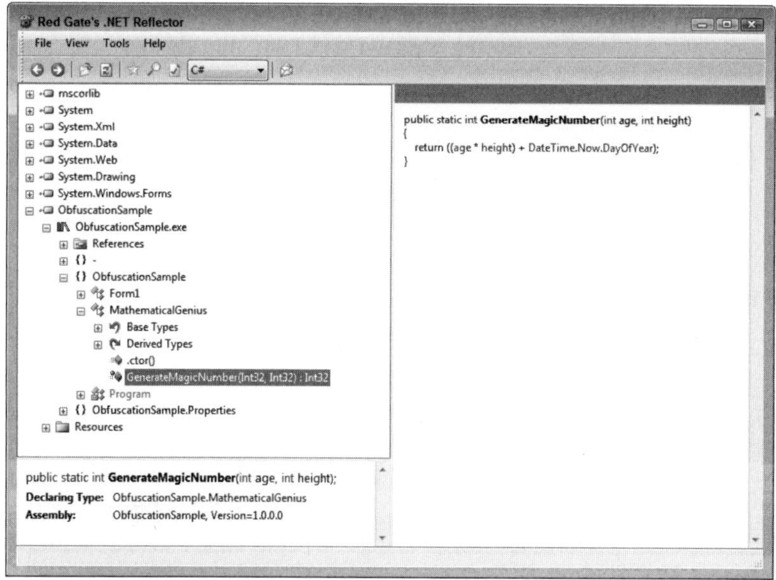

FIGURE 48-3

In the pane on the left of Figure 48-3, you can see the namespaces, type, and method information in a layout similar to ILDasm. Double-clicking a method should open the Disassembler pane on the right, which displays the contents of that method in the language specified in the toolbar. In this case, you can see the C# code that generates the magic number, which is almost identical to the original code.

NOTE *You may have noticed in Figure 48-3 that some of the .NET Framework base class library assemblies are listed, including System, System.Data, and System.Web. Because obfuscation has not been applied to these assemblies, they can be decompiled just as easily using Reflector. However, Microsoft has made large portions of the actual .NET Framework source code publicly available, which means you can browse the original source code of these assemblies including the inline comments (see Chapter 44, "Advanced Debugging Techniques").*

If the generation of the magic number were a real secret on which your organization made money, the ability to decompile this application would pose a significant risk. This is made worse when you add the `Reflector.FileDisassembler` add-in, written by Denis Bauer (available at `http://www.denisbauer.com/NETTools/FileDisassembler.aspx`). With this add-in, an entire assembly can be decompiled into source files, complete with a project file.

OBFUSCATING YOUR CODE

So far, this chapter has highlighted the need for better protection for the logic embedded in your applications. Obfuscation is the art of renaming symbols and modifying code paths in an assembly so that the logic is unintelligible and can't be easily understood if decompiled. Numerous products can obfuscate your code, each using its own tricks to make the output less likely to be understood. Visual Studio 2012 ships with the Community Edition of Dotfuscator and Analytics from PreEmptive Solutions, which this chapter uses as an example of how you can apply obfuscation to your code.

NOTE *Obfuscation does not prevent your code from being decompiled; it simply makes it more difficult for a programmer to understand the source code if it is decompiled. Using obfuscation also has some consequences that need to be considered if you need to use reflection or strong-name your application.*

Dotfuscator and Analytics

Although Dotfuscator can be launched from the Tools menu within Visual Studio 2012, it is a separate product with its own licensing. The Community Edition (CE) contains only a subset of the functionality of the commercial edition of the product, the Dotfuscator Suite. If you are serious about trying to hide the functionality embedded in your application, you should consider upgrading. You can find more information on the commercial version of Dotfuscator at `http://www.preemptive.com/products/dotfuscator/compare-editions`.

Dotfuscator CE uses its own project format to keep track of which assemblies you are obfuscating and any options that you specify. After starting Dotfuscator from the Tools menu, it opens with a new unsaved project. Select the Inputs node in the navigation tree, and then click the button with the plus sign under the Inputs listing to add the .NET assemblies that you want to obfuscate. Figure 48-4 shows a new Dotfuscator project into which has been added the assembly for the application from earlier in this chapter.

NOTE *Unlike other build activities that are typically executed based on source files, obfuscation is a post-build activity that works with an already compiled set of assemblies. Dotfuscator takes an existing set of assemblies, applies the obfuscation algorithms to the IL, and generates a set of new assemblies.*

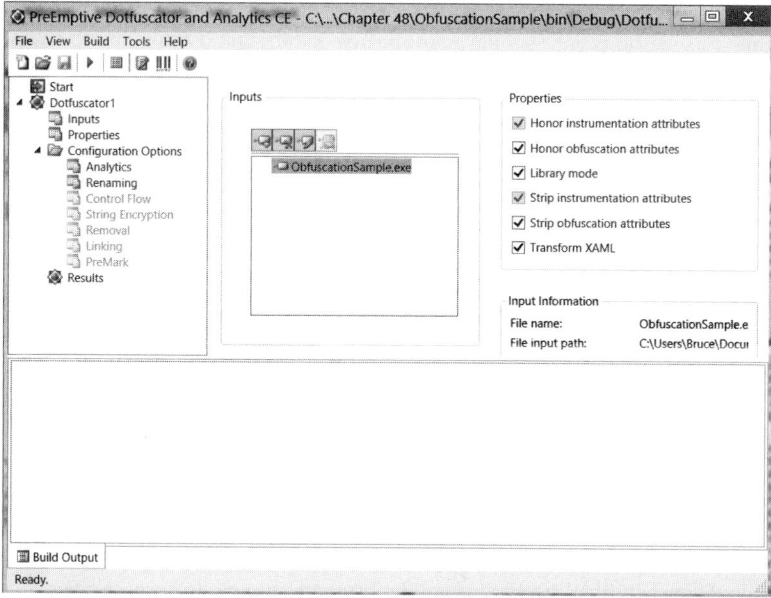

FIGURE 48-4

On the right side of the interface, make sure that Library mode is unchecked. Then you can select Build Project from the Build menu, or click the Play button (fourth from the left) on the toolbar, to obfuscate this application. If you have saved the Dotfuscator project, the obfuscated assemblies will be added to a Dotfuscated folder under the folder where the project was saved. If the project has not been saved, the output is written to `c:\Dotfuscated`.

If you open the generated assembly using Reflector, as shown in Figure 48-5, you can see that the `GenerateMagicNumber` method has been renamed, along with the input parameters. In addition, the

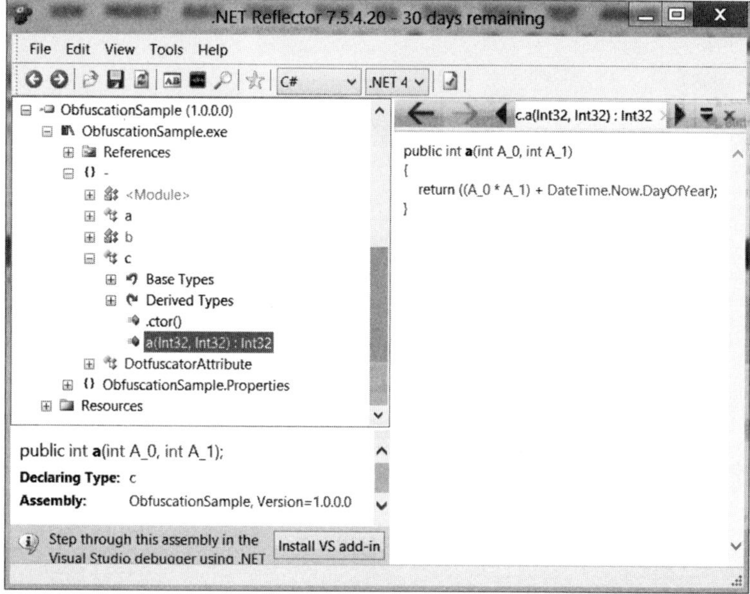

FIGURE 48-5

namespace hierarchy has been removed, and classes have been renamed. Although this is a rather simple example, you can see how numerous methods with similar, nonintuitive names could cause confusion and make the source code difficult to understand when decompiled.

> **NOTE** *The free version of Dotfuscator obfuscates assemblies by only renaming classes, variables, and functions. The commercial version employs several additional methods to obfuscate assemblies, such as modifying the control flow of the assembly and performing string encryption. In some cases, control flow actually triggers an unrecoverable exception inside decompilers, effectively preventing automated decompilation.*

The previous example obfuscated the public method of a class, which is fine if the method will be called only from assemblies obfuscated along with the one containing the class definition. However, if this were a class library or API that will be referenced by other unobfuscated applications, you would see a list of classes that have no apparent structure, relationship, or even naming convention. This would make working with this assembly difficult. Luckily, Dotfuscator enables you to control what is renamed during obfuscation. Before going ahead, you need to refactor the code slightly to pull the functionality out of the public method. If you didn't do this and you excluded this method from being renamed, your secret algorithm would not be obfuscated. By separating the logic into another method, you can obfuscate that while keeping the public interface unchanged. The refactored code would look like the following:

C#

```
namespace ObfuscationSample
{
    public class MathematicalGenius
    {
        public static Int32 GenerateMagicNumber(Int32 age, Int32 height)
        {
            return SecretGenerateMagicNumber(age, height);
        }

        private static Int32 SecretGenerateMagicNumber(Int32 age, Int32 height)
        {
            return (age * height) + DateTime.Now.DayOfYear;
        }
    }
}
```

VB

```
Namespace ObfuscationSample
    Public Class MathematicalGenius
        Public Shared Function GenerateMagicNumber(ByVal age As Integer, _
                                        ByVal height As Integer) As Integer
            Return SecretGenerateMagicNumber(age, height)
        End Function

        Private Shared Function SecretGenerateMagicNumber(ByVal age As Integer, _

                                        ByVal height As Integer) As Integer
            Return (age * height) + Today.DayOfWeek
        End Function
    End Class
End Namespace
```

After rebuilding the application, you need to reopen the Dotfuscator project by selecting it from the Recent Projects list. You have several different ways to selectively apply obfuscation to an assembly. First, you can enable Library mode on specific assemblies by selecting the appropriate check box on the Inputs screen (see Figure 48-4). This has the effect of keeping the namespace, class name, and all public properties and methods intact, while renaming all private methods and variables. Second, you can manually select which elements should not be renamed from within Dotfuscator. To do this, open the Renaming item from the navigation tree, as shown in Figure 48-6.

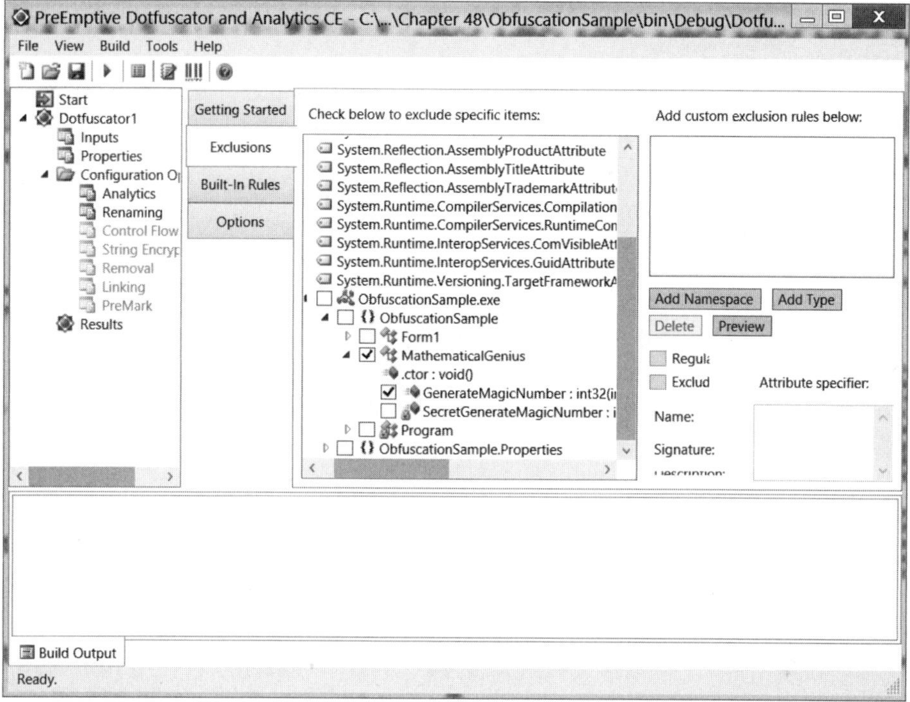

FIGURE 48-6

The Renaming dialog opens on the Exclusions tab where you can see the familiar tree view of your assembly with the attributes, namespaces, types, and methods listed. As the name of the tab suggests, this tree enables you to exclude certain elements from being renamed. The `GenerateMagicNumber` method (refer to Figure 48-6), as well as the class that it is contained in, is excluded. (Otherwise, you would have ended up with something like `b.GenerateMagicNumber`, where `b` is the renamed class.) In addition to explicitly choosing which elements will be excluded, you can also define custom rules that can include regular expressions.

After you build the Dotfuscator project, click the Results item in the navigation tree. This screen shows the actions that Dotfuscator performed during obfuscation. The new name of each class, property, and method displays as a subnode under each renamed element in the tree. You can see that the `MathematicalGenius` class and the `GenerateMagicNumber` method have not been renamed, as shown in Figure 48-7.

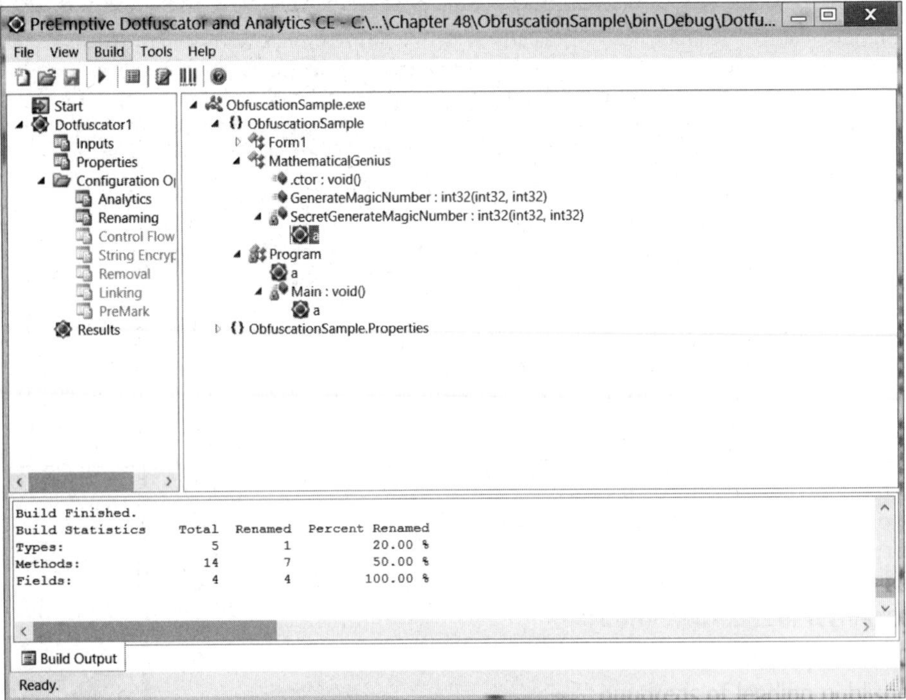

FIGURE 48-7

The `SecretGenerateMagicNumber` method has been renamed to `a`, as indicated by the subnode with the Dotfuscator icon.

Obfuscation Attributes

In the previous example you saw how to choose which types and methods to obfuscate within Dotfuscator. Of course, if you were to start using a different obfuscating product, you must configure it to exclude the public members. It would be more convenient to annotate your code with attributes indicating whether a symbol should be obfuscated. You can do this by using the `Obfuscation` and `ObfuscationAssemblyAttribute` attributes from the `System.Reflection` namespace.

The default behavior in Dotfuscator is to override exclusions specified in the project with the settings specified by any obfuscation attributes. Refer to Figure 48-4 to see a series of check boxes for each assembly added to the project, of which one is Honor Obfuscation Attributes. You can change the default behavior so that any exclusions set within the project take precedence by unchecking the Honor Obfuscation Attributes option on a per-assembly basis.

ObfuscationAssemblyAttribute

The `ObfuscationAssemblyAttribute` attribute can be applied to an assembly to control whether it should be treated as a class library or as a private assembly. The distinction is that with a class library it is expected that other assemblies will be referencing the public types and methods it exposes. As such, the obfuscation tool needs to ensure that these symbols are not renamed. Alternatively, as a private assembly, every symbol can be potentially renamed. The following is the syntax for `ObfuscationAssemblyAttribute`:

C#

```
[assembly: ObfuscateAssemblyAttribute(false, StripAfterObfuscation=true)]
```

VB

```
<Assembly: ObfuscateAssemblyAttribute(False, StripAfterObfuscation:=True)>
```

The two arguments that this attribute takes indicate whether it is a private assembly and whether to strip the attribute off after obfuscation. The preceding snippet indicates that this is not a private assembly and that public symbols should not be renamed. In addition, the snippet indicates that the obfuscation attribute should be stripped off after obfuscation — after all, the less information available to anyone wanting to decompile the assembly, the better.

Adding this attribute to the `AssemblyInfo.cs` or `AssemblyInfo.vb` file automatically preserves the names of all public symbols in the ObfuscationSample application. This means that you can remove the exclusion you created earlier for the `GenerateMagicNumber` method.

ObfuscationAttribute

The downside of the `ObfuscationAssemblyAttribute` attribute is that it exposes all the public types and methods regardless of whether they existed for internal use only. On the other hand, the `ObfuscationAttribute` attribute can be applied to individual types and methods, so it provides a much finer level of control over what is obfuscated. To illustrate the use of this attribute, refactor the example to include an additional public method, `EvaluatePerson`, and place the logic into another class, `HiddenGenius`:

C#

```
namespace ObfuscationSample
{

    [System.Reflection.ObfuscationAttribute(ApplyToMembers=true, Exclude=true)]
    public class MathematicalGenius
    {
        public static Int32 GenerateMagicNumber(Int32 age, Int32 height)
        {
            return HiddenGenius.GenerateMagicNumber(age, height);
        }

        public static Boolean EvaluatePerson(Int32 age, Int32 height)
        {
            return HiddenGenius.EvaluatePerson(age, height);
        }
    }

    [System.Reflection.ObfuscationAttribute(ApplyToMembers=false, Exclude=true)]
    public class HiddenGenius
    {
        public static Int32 GenerateMagicNumber(Int32 age, Int32 height)
        {

            return (age * height) + DateTime.Now.DayOfYear;
        }

        [System.Reflection.ObfuscationAttribute(Exclude=true)]
        public static Boolean EvaluatePerson(Int32 age, Int32 height)
        {
            return GenerateMagicNumber(age, height) > 6000;
        }
    }
}
```

VB

```
Namespace ObfuscationSample
    <System.Reflection.ObfuscationAttribute(ApplyToMembers:=True,Exclude:=True)> _
    Public Class MathematicalGenius
        Public Shared Function GenerateMagicNumber(ByVal age As Integer, _
                                                   ByVal height As Integer) As Integer
            Return HiddenGenius.GenerateMagicNumber(age, height)
        End Function

        Public Shared Function EvaluatePerson(ByVal age As Integer, _
                                              ByVal height As Integer) As Boolean
            Return HiddenGenius.EvaluatePerson(age, height)
        End Function
    End Class

    <System.Reflection.ObfuscationAttribute(ApplyToMembers:=False,Exclude:=True)> _
    Public Class HiddenGenius
        Public Shared Function GenerateMagicNumber(ByVal age As Integer, _
                                                   ByVal height As Integer) As Integer
            Return (age * height) + Today.DayOfWeek
        End Function

        <System.Reflection.ObfuscationAttribute(Exclude:=True)> _
        Public Shared Function EvaluatePerson(ByVal age As Integer, _
                                              ByVal height As Integer) As Boolean
            Return GenerateMagicNumber(age, height) > 6000
        End Function
    End Class
End Namespace
```

In this example, the `MathematicalGenius` class is the class that you want to expose outside of this library. As such, you want to exclude this class and all its methods from being obfuscated. You do this by applying the `ObfuscationAttribute` attribute with both the `Exclude` and `ApplyToMembers` parameters set to `True`.

The second class, `HiddenGenius`, has mixed obfuscation. As a result of some squabbling among the developers who wrote this class, the `EvaluatePerson` method needs to be exposed, but all other methods in this class should be obfuscated. Again, the `ObfuscationAttribute` attribute is applied to the class so that the class does not get obfuscated. However, this time you want the default behavior to be such that symbols contained in the class are obfuscated, so the `ApplyToMembers` parameter is set to `False`. In addition, the `Obfuscation` attribute is applied to the `EvaluatePerson` method so that it will still be accessible.

Words of Caution

In a couple of places it is worth considering what can happen when obfuscation — or more precisely, renaming — occurs, and how it can affect the workings of the application.

Reflection

The .NET Framework provides a rich reflection model through which types can be queried and instantiated dynamically. Unfortunately, some of the reflection methods use string lookups for type and member names. Clearly, the use of renaming obfuscation prevents these lookups from working, and the only solution is not to mangle any symbols that may be invoked using reflection. Note that control flow obfuscation does not have this particular undesirable side-effect. Dotfuscator's *smart obfuscation* feature attempts to automatically determine a limited set of symbols to exclude based on how the application uses reflection.

For example, say that you use the field names of an enum type. Smart obfuscation can detect the reflection call used to retrieve the enum's field name and then automatically exclude the enum fields from renaming.

Strongly Named Assemblies

One of the purposes behind giving an assembly a strong name is that it prevents the assembly from being tampered with. Unfortunately, obfuscating relies on taking an existing assembly and modifying the names and code flow before generating a new assembly. This would mean that the assembly no longer has a valid strong name. To allow obfuscation to occur, you need to delay signing of your assembly by checking the Delay Sign Only check box on the Signing tab of the Project Properties window, as shown in Figure 48-8.

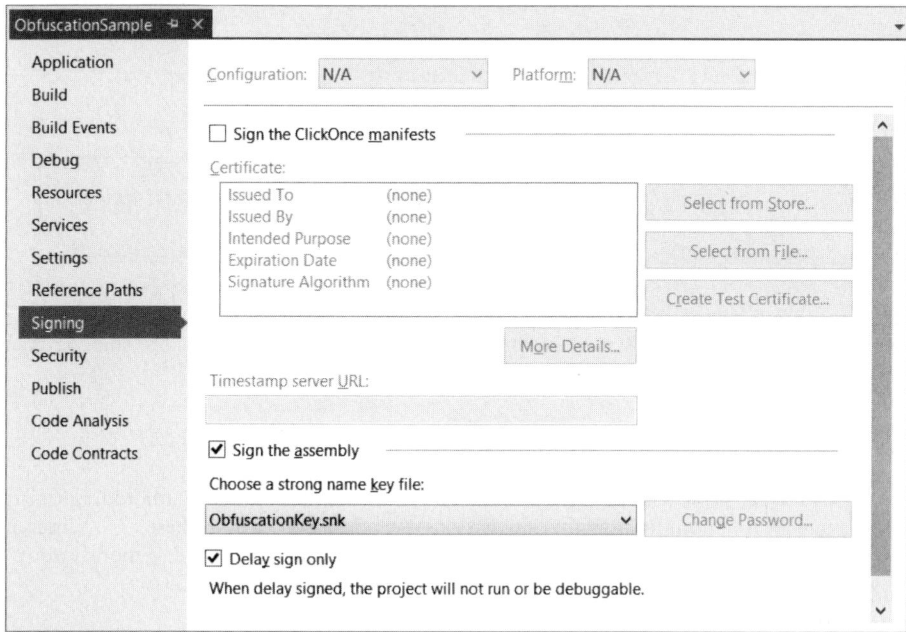

FIGURE 48-8

After building the assembly, you can then obfuscate it in the normal way. The only difference is that after obfuscating you need to sign the obfuscated assembly, which you can do manually using the Strong Name utility, as shown in this example:

```
sn -R ObfuscationSample.exe ObfuscationKey.snk
```

> **NOTE** *The Strong Name utility is not included in the default path, so you either need to run this from a Visual Studio Command Prompt (Start ➪ All Programs ➪ Microsoft Visual Studio 2012 ➪ Visual Studio Tools) or enter the full path to* `sn.exe`.

Debugging with Delayed Signing

As displayed on the Project Properties window, checking the Delay Sign Only box prevents the application from being able to be run or debugged. This is because the assembly will fail the strong-name verification process. To enable debugging for an application with delayed signing, you can register the appropriate assemblies for verification skipping. This is also done using the Strong Name utility. For example, the following code skips verification for the `ObfuscationSample.exe` application:

```
sn -Vr ObfuscationSample.exe
```

Similarly, the following reactivates verification for this application:

```
sn -Vu ObfuscationSample.exe
```

This is a pain for you to do every time you build an application, so you can add the following lines to the post-build events for the application:

```
"$(DevEnvDir)..\..\..\Microsoft SDKs\Windows\v8.0A\bin\NETFX 4.0 Tools\sn.exe" -Vr
"$(TargetPath)"
"$(DevEnvDir)..\..\..\Microsoft SDKs\Windows\v8.0A\bin\NETFX 4.0 Tools\sn.exe" -Vr
"$(TargetDir)$(TargetName).vshost$(TargetExt)"
```

> **WARNING** *Depending on your environment, you may need to modify the post-build event to ensure that the correct path to* `sn.exe` *is specified.*

The first line skips verification for the compiled application. However, Visual Studio uses an additional `vshost` file to bootstrap the application when it executes. This also needs to be registered to skip verification when launching a debugging session.

APPLICATION MONITORING AND MANAGEMENT

The version of Dotfuscator that ships with Visual Studio 2012 has a lot of functionality for adding run-time monitoring and management functionality to your applications. As with obfuscation, these capabilities are injected into your application as a post-build step, which means you typically don't need to modify your source code in any way to take advantage of them.

The application monitoring and management capabilities include

- **Tamper Defense:** Exits your application and optionally notifies you if it has been modified in an unauthorized manner.
- **Application Expiry:** Configure an expiration date for your application, after which it will no longer run.
- **Application Usage Tracking:** Instrument your code to track usage, including specific features within your application.

Although you can use the Honor Instrumentation Attributes check box to turn on and off the injection of the instrumentation code (as shown in Figure 48-9), the default behavior is to have instrumentation enabled.

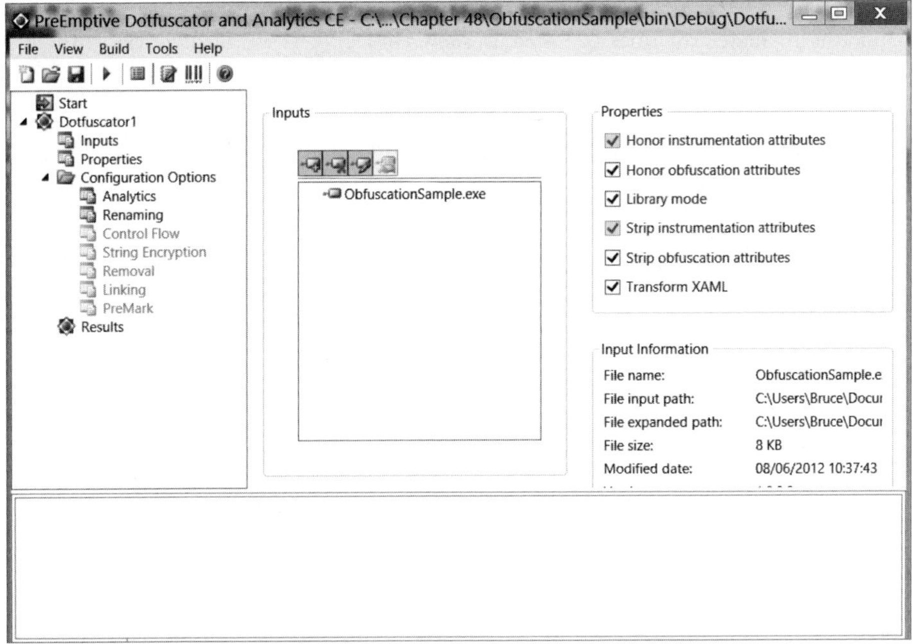

FIGURE 48-9

Specifying the functionality to be injected into your application is accomplished by adding Dotfuscator attributes — either as a custom attribute within your source code or through the Dotfuscator UI.

Tamper Defense

Tamper defense provides a way for you to detect when your applications have been modified in an unauthorized manner. Whereas obfuscation is a *preventative control* designed to reduce the risks that stem from unauthorized reverse engineering, tamper defense is a *detective control* designed to reduce the risks that stem from unauthorized modification of your managed assemblies. The pairing of preventative and detective controls is a widely accepted risk management pattern, for example, fire prevention and detection.

Tamper defense is applied on a per-method basis, and tamper detection is performed at run time when a protected method is invoked.

To add tamper defense to your application, select the Analytics node under the Configuration Options portion of the navigation menu and then select the Attributes tab. You see a tree that contains the assemblies you have added to the Dotfuscator project with a hierarchy of the classes and methods that each assembly contains. Navigate to the `HiddenGenius.GenerateMagicNumber` function, right-click it, and select Add Attribute. This displays the list of available Dotfuscator attributes, as shown in Figure 48-10.

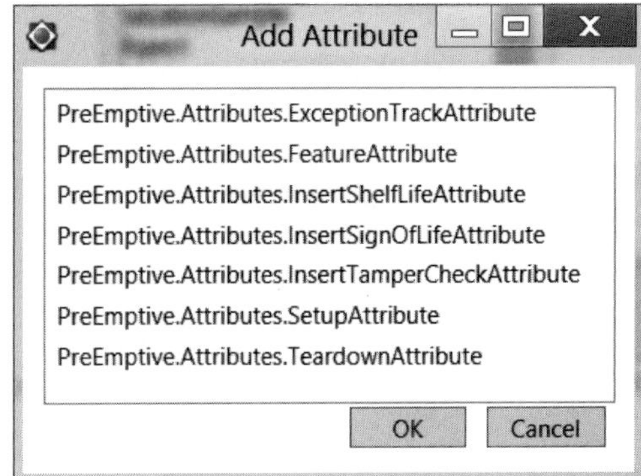

FIGURE 48-10

Select the `InsertTamperCheckAttribute` attribute, and click OK. The attribute is added to the selected method, and the attribute properties are listed, as shown in Figure 48-11. Finally, select the `ApplicationNotificationSinkElement` property, and change the value to `DefaultAction`.

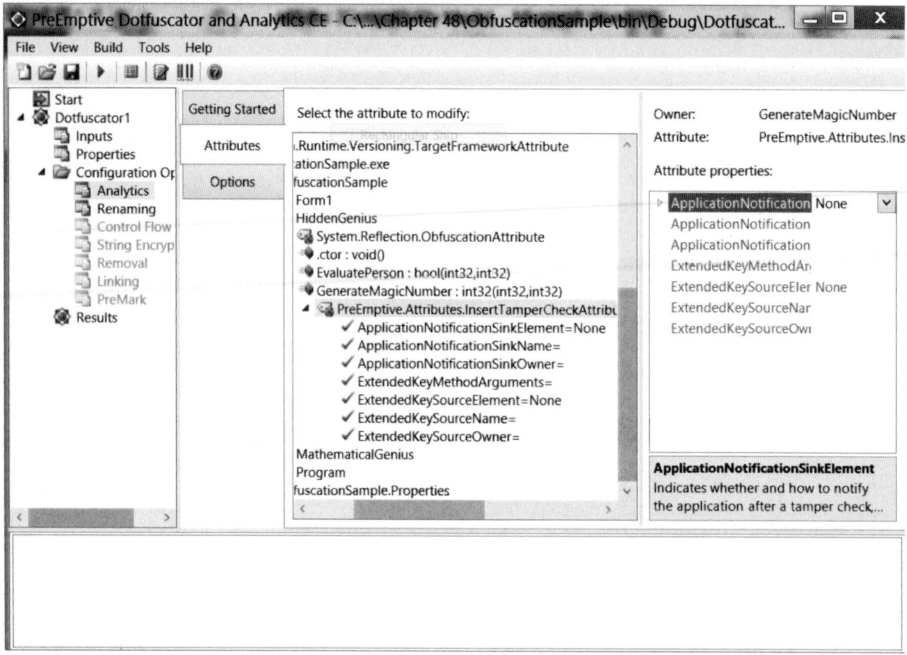

FIGURE 48-11

You can now build the Dotfuscator project to inject the tamper defense functionality into your application.

To help you test the tamper defense functionality, Dotfuscator ships with a simple utility that simulates tampering of an assembly. Called TamperTester, you can find this utility in the same directory in which Dotfuscator is installed (by default at `C:\Program Files\Microsoft Visual Studio 11.0\PreEmptive Solutions\Dotfuscator and Analytics Community Edition`). This should be run from the command line with the name of the assembly and the output folder as arguments:

```
tampertester ObfuscationSample.exe c:\tamperedapps
```

> **WARNING** *Make sure you run the TamperTester utility against the assemblies that were generated by Dotfuscator and not the original assemblies built by Visual Studio.*

By default, your application immediately exits if the method has been tampered with. You can optionally configure Dotfuscator to generate a notification message to an endpoint of your choosing. The commercial edition of Dotfuscator includes two primary extensions to the CE version; it enables you to add a custom handler to be executed when tampering is detected, supporting a custom real-time tamper defense in lieu of the default exit behavior; and PreEmptive Solutions offers a notification service that accepts tamper alerts and automatically notifies your organization as an incident response.

Runtime Intelligence Instrumentation and Analytics

The term *Runtime Intelligence* (*RI*) refers to technologies and managed services for the collection, integration, analysis, and presentation of application usage patterns and practices. In Visual Studio 2012, Dotfuscator and Analytics CE can inject RI instrumentation into your assemblies to stream session and feature usage data to an arbitrary endpoint. The following sections describe how to use Dotfuscator's Runtime Intelligence instrumentation and some of the free and for-fee Runtime Intelligence analytics options that are available.

To use Dotfuscator and Analytics CE instrumentation, you must first enable it within your Dotfuscator project. Click the Analytics item in the navigation tree and select the Options tab. Ensure that all the options under Analytics Configuration are enabled, as shown in Figure 48-12.

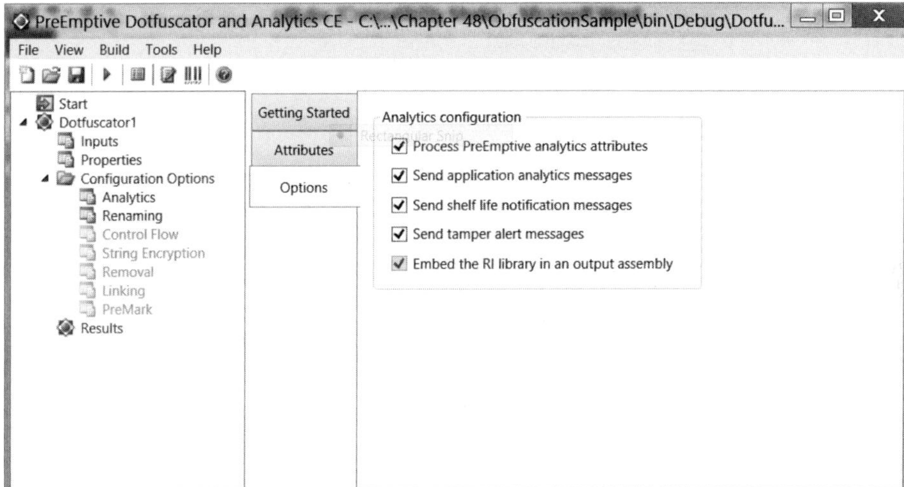

FIGURE 48-12

Next you must add some attributes to your assemblies to ensure that they can be uniquely identified and any instrumentation data can be accessed. Under the Attributes tab of the Analytics node is the class hierarchy of any assemblies you have added to Dotfuscator. Right-click each of the top-level nodes (the node that contains the full path to your assembly), select Add Attribute, and add a new `BusinessAttribute` attribute.

Select `CompanyKey` from the attribute properties listing. This attribute provides a unique identifier for your company and should be the same across all your assemblies. You can click the button labeled with the ellipsis to generate a new `CompanyKey`. However, if you plan on using the PreEmptive's free Runtime Intelligence Portal, leave the company key as the default value. Regardless of whether you use the free portal or another one, make sure that you enter a value for the `CompanyName` property. That value displays in the portal and any reports.

Repeat this to add a new `ApplicationAttribute` attribute to your assemblies. The `GUID` property of this attribute should contain a unique identifier that is the same across all assemblies within this application. As with the `CompanyKey` property, you can generate a new value for the `GUID` property by clicking the button labeled with the ellipsis. You should also enter values for the `Name` and `Version` properties, but the `ApplicationType` property can be left blank.

After you add these attributes, your project should look similar to Figure 48-13.

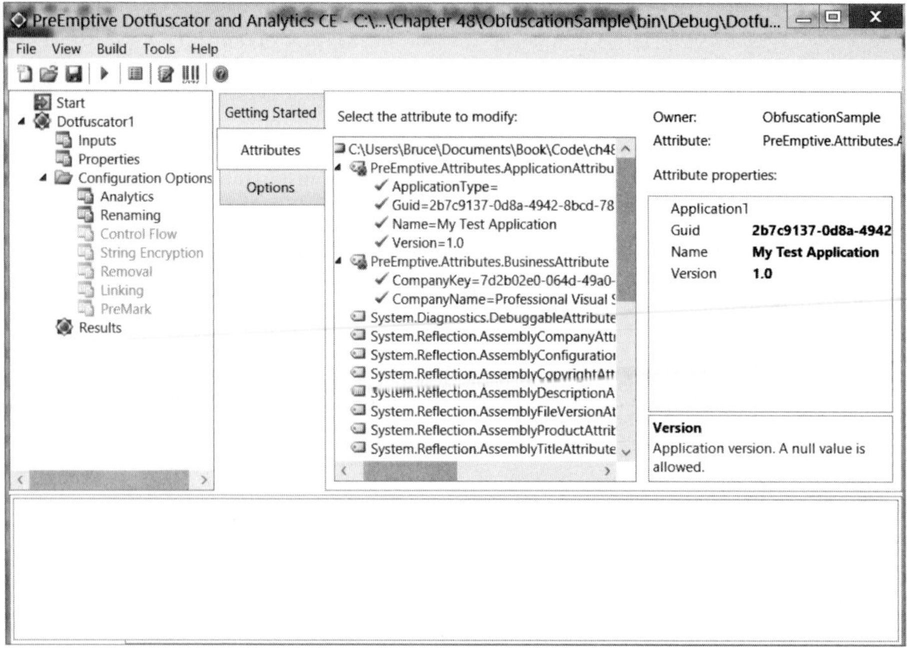

FIGURE 48-13

The final step is to add `SetupAttribute` and `TeardownAttribute` attributes to your application. These attributes can be added to any method and are usually defined once each per application; though that is not strictly necessary if your application has multiple entry and exit points. `SetupAttribute` should be placed on a method called soon after application startup. Likewise, the `TeardownAttribute` attribute must be added to a method called just before the application exits. It is sometimes a good idea to create methods specifically for these attributes.

For a C# Windows Forms application, you can place the attributes on the `Main` method; alternatively, you can modify the `Program.cs` class by adding the `AppStart` and `AppEnd` methods, as shown in the following listing:

C#

```
static class Program
{
    static void Main()
    {
        Application.EnableVisualStyles();
        Application.SetCompatibleTextRenderingDefault(false);
        AppStart();
        Application.Run(new Form1());
        AppEnd();
    }

    static void AppStart()
    {
    }

     static void AppEnd()
    {
    }
    }
```

For a VB Windows Forms application, you can use the Application Events functionality provided with the Windows application framework to specify `Startup` and `Shutdown` methods, as shown in the following listing:

VB

```
Imports Microsoft.VisualBasic.ApplicationServices
Namespace My
    Partial Friend Class MyApplication
        Private Sub MyApp_Startup(ByVal sender As Object, _
                                  ByVal e As StartupEventArgs) _
                                  Handles Me.Startup

        End Sub

        Private Sub MyApp_Shutdown(ByVal sender As Object, _
                                   ByVal e As System.EventArgs) _
                                   Handles Me.Shutdown
        End Sub
    End Class
End Namespace
```

After you have a `startup` and `shutdown` method defined in your application, you can add the `SetupAttribute` and `TeardownAttribute` attributes. Locate your startup method in the tree; then right-click it and select Add Attribute. Select `SetupAttribute` and click OK. In the attribute properties you need to specify a value for the `CustomEndpoint` property, which instructs Dotfuscator where to send any instrumentation messages. Click the ellipsis button, and select PreEmptive's Free Runtime Intelligence Services from the list.

> **NOTE** *You shouldn't collect information about application usage without asking permission from your users; otherwise, your application could be flagged as spyware. The* `SetupAttribute` *provides three properties to help configure this —* `OptInSourceElement`, `OptInSourceName`, *and* `OptInSourceOwner`.

The Runtime Intelligence Service is a managed service provided by PreEmptive Solutions that aggregates and manages Runtime Intelligence data generated by your application and a web portal that includes run-time analytics. PreEmptive Solutions offers a commercial version of its Runtime Intelligence Service, along with a toolkit that enables developers to create their own endpoint that captures the run-time notifications. The toolkit has been published to Codeplex (`http://riendpointkit.codeplex.com`) and provides libraries and examples that you can use to craft your own endpoint. Alternatively, if you run Team Foundation Server 2012 in your environment, you can configure TFS to accept incoming instrumentation messages and convert them to work items. PreEmptive also includes a workload that enables the aggregation service to be easily deployed into Windows Azure.

Finally, add the `TeardownAttribute` attribute to the appropriate method and then build the Dotfuscator project. Run the application a couple of times to generate some instrumentation messages. You can also use the TamperTester utility described in the previous "Tamper Defense" section to create a "tampered" version of the application that generates Tamper notifications.

Later in the "Application Usage Tracking" section of this chapter you see how the usage tracking can be extended to cover usage of specific features within your application.

Application Expiry

The application expiry feature, also known as *Shelf Life*, enables you to specify an expiration date for your application, after which it will no longer run. This can be useful in a number of scenarios, such as when releasing beta or trial versions of software.

Application expiry requires a Shelf Life Activation Key (SLAK). In the past, this key has been issued by PreEmptive. As of this writing, there is no indication whether this will continue with the version included with Visual Studio 2012, but a visit to the PreEmptive website (`http://www.preemptive.com`) should make that clear.

Two attributes are available to help implement application expiry. The `InsertShelfLifeAttribute` attribute enforces the expiration dates, ensuring that the application will not run after the specified date. It can also send a notification to an arbitrary endpoint when an expired application is executed. The `InsertSignOfLifeAttribute` attribute sends a notification to the Runtime Intelligence service every time your application is executed. This enables you to find out how often an application was executed.

Before adding the application expiry attributes, you should set up your assembly with the `BusinessAttribute`, `ApplicationAttribute`, `SetupAttribute`, and `TeardownAttribute` attributes, as described in the previous section on Runtime Intelligence.

It's a good idea to add the application expiry attributes to a method called shortly after the application is started. You may also want to add a method that is called regularly, just in case your users leave your application running after the expiry date. In Figure 48-14, the `InsertShelfLifeAttribute` and `InsertSignOfLifeAttribute` attributes have been added to the `Form1.InitializeComponent` method. This ensures that the application expiry date is checked every time Form1 is invoked.

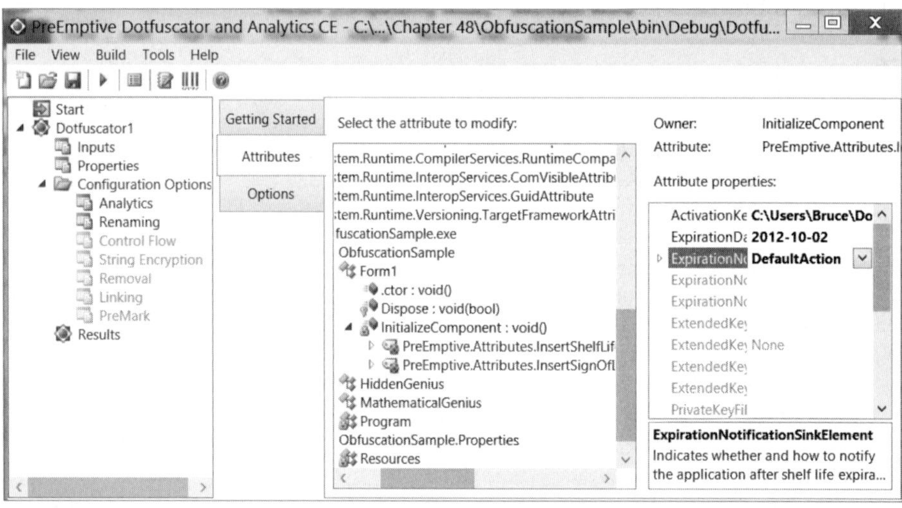

FIGURE 48-14

Both attributes require a Shelf Life Activation Key. After you have obtained this key from PreEmptive, save it to your local disk, and set the path to this file in the `ActivationKeyFile` property. Setting the `ExpirationDate` property to a date in the past is a good way to test this feature.

When an application expires, the behavior is determined by two settings. First, if you have Send Shelf Life Notification Messages checked on the Instrumentation Options tab, it sends a notification message to the endpoint you have specified. Second, if you have set the `ExpirationNotificationSinkElement` property to `DefaultAction`, the application immediately exits.

The commercial edition of Dotfuscator enables you to specify a warning date and add custom handlers that are executed when the warning date or expiration date are reached. You could use this to deactivate specific features or display a friendly message to the users advising them that the application has expired.

The commercial version of Dotfuscator also enables your application to obtain the shelf life information from an external location, such as a web service or configuration file. This enables you to support other expiration scenarios such as expiring 30 days from installation or renewing annual subscriptions.

Application Usage Tracking

Earlier in this chapter you saw how to add the `SetupAttribute` and `TeardownAttribute` attributes to your application. By adding these attributes your application can send notification messages, and thereby allow you to track usage data and system environment statistics for your applications. These attributes are also used to determine application stability because a missing Teardown notification indicates that the application may have crashed or a user may have gotten frustrated and simply forced an exit.

In addition to tracking application startup and shutdown, Dotfuscator enables you to further instrument your code to track usage of specific features within your application. With Dotfuscator CE, you can add up to 10 `FeatureAttribute` attributes to your methods, each one specifying the same or a different feature. This enables you to aggregate your application's methods into a logical, high-level "feature" grouping that is independent of the actual class hierarchy of your code.

In Figure 48-15, you can see that a `FeatureAttribute` attribute has been added to the `EvaluatePerson` and the `GenerateMagicNumber` methods of the `MathematicalGenius` class. These features have been given a descriptive name, which displays when viewing the usage reports. These attributes also have the `FeatureEventType` property set to `Tick`, which simply tracks that the feature has been used.

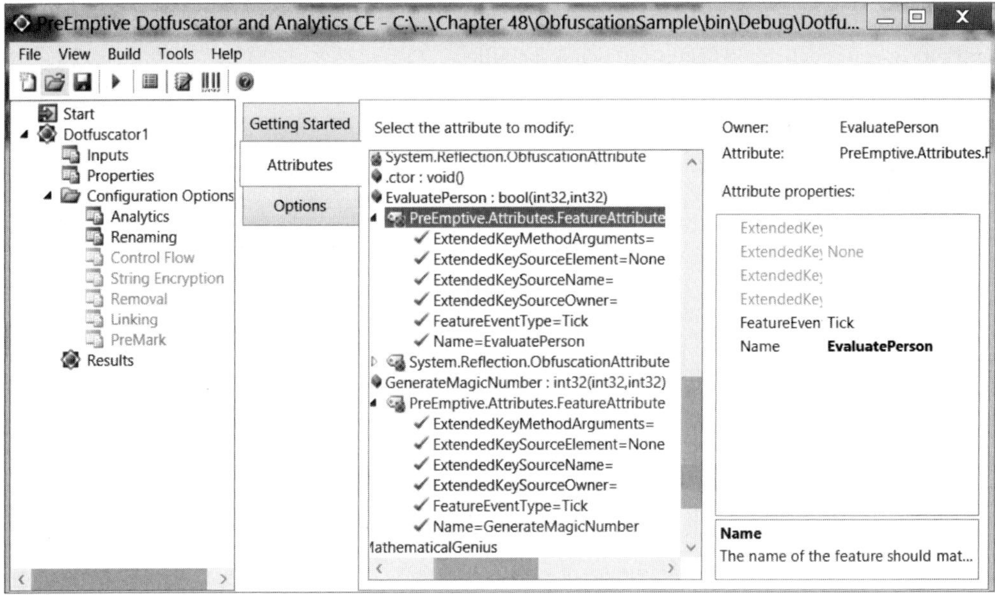

FIGURE 48-15

In addition to Tick feature tracking, you can also track the amount of time a feature was used. In this case you need to add two `FeatureAttribute` attributes: one with the `FeatureEventType` property set to `Start` and the other set to `Stop`. This generates two instrumentation messages and allows the Runtime Intelligence analytics service to calculate feature usage duration.

The commercial edition of Dotfuscator includes

- Unlimited feature tracking
- Injection of the Microsoft WMI SDK for hardware and software stack detection
- Extensible data capture to include custom data values
- An SSL run-time data transmission option

You can use Runtime Intelligence data to improve the development process, provide greater visibility into application usage for IT operations, and serve as an additional data source for business activity and performance monitoring. Microsoft's own Customer Experience Improvement Program (CEIP) relies on this kind of usage data. (For a description of its program, visit `http://www.microsoft.com/products/ceip/`.)

As managed code moves beyond the desktop and the in-house server to the web client (Silverlight), the cloud (Azure), and your mobile devices, Runtime Intelligence will likely become an increasingly important part of your application life-cycle management toolkit.

SUMMARY

This chapter introduced two tools, ILDasm and Reflector, which demonstrated how easy it is to reverse-engineer .NET assemblies and learn their inner-workings. You also learned how to use Dotfuscator and Analytics to

- Protect your intellectual property using obfuscation.
- Harden your applications against modification using tamper defense.
- Monitor and measure application usage with Runtime Intelligence instrumentation.
- Enforce your application's end-of-life with shelf life.

49 Packaging and Deployment

WHAT'S IN THIS CHAPTER?

- Creating installers for your projects
- Customizing the installation process
- Installing Windows Services
- Deploying projects over the web with ClickOnce
- Updating ClickOnce projects

One area of software development that is often overlooked is how to deploy the application. Building an installer is a simple process and can transform your application from an amateur utility to a professional tool. This chapter looks at how you can build a Windows Installer for any type of .NET application.

One of the more controversial choices that Microsoft made for Visual Studio was the decision to retire Visual Studio Installer Projects. Although this announcement was made more than two years prior to the release of Visual Studio 2012, that doesn't mean that the impact of the decision won't be felt by many developers.

With Visual Studio 2012, there are basically two choices available to deploy your application. Included with Visual Studio 2012 is the InstallShield Limited Edition project template. Actually, what is included is a link that points you to a download InstallShield Limited Edition. When it is installed (and Visual Studio restarted), you see the template appear in the New Project dialog.

The second alternative, and the one that will be discussed in this chapter, is to utilize the Windows Installer XML (WiX) Toolset. This toolset, which is available through the Extensions and Updates dialog, enables you to specify the contents and functionality of the installation package through XML files. And although the idea of using XML files might initially sound daunting, it provides all the functionality that had been part of Visual Studio setup projects in Visual Studio 2010. In fact, it provides even more functionality. And although the toolset is tightly integrated into Visual Studio, it is also available through a command-line interface, making it quite suitable to use in a build process.

If you are concerned about using an external tool such as WiX, there are a number of points in its favor. First, it was actually developed internally at Microsoft before being released as an open-source toolkit under the Common Public License. It has been used to create the deployment package for a number of Microsoft products, including SQL Server and Office.

WINDOWS INSTALLER XML TOOLSET

WiX is a toolkit that consists of a number of different components, each with its own purpose. And because geeks like to find humor in naming, the components are named after elements related to candles. (WiX is pronounced "wicks" as in "the candle has four wicks.") The components are:

- **Candle**—The compiler that converts XML documents to object files that contain symbols and/or references to symbols.
- **Light**—The linker that takes one or more object files and resolves the symbols references. The output for Light also typically includes the packaged MSI or MSM file.
- **Lit**—A tool that can combine multiple object files (such as are produced by Candle) into a new object file that can then be processed by Light.
- **Dark**—A decompiler that examines existing MSI and MSM files and generates the XML documents that represent the installation package.
- **Tallow/Heat**—Tallow generates a WiX file list code by walking a directory tree. The fragment of XML produced is suitable for incorporation with other WiX source files by Candle. Heat is a more recent tool that performs a similar task, albeit in a more general manner.
- **Pyro**—A tool used to create Patch files (`.msp` files) without the need for the Windows Installer SDK.
- **Burn**—A recently added tool that acts as a bootstrapper/installer chainer. The basic idea is to allow packages to specify dependencies, and the Burn coordinates the installation of the prerequisites prior to the installation of the main package.

To start creating a WiX package, you need to get the toolkit installed into your development environment. You do this using the Extensions and Updates menu option from the Tools menu. The Extensions and Updates dialog is used to search for and install tools that have been published to the Visual Studio community. If you search the Online gallery using a keyword of **Installer**, you see the Windows Installer XML Toolset appear, as shown in Figure 49-1.

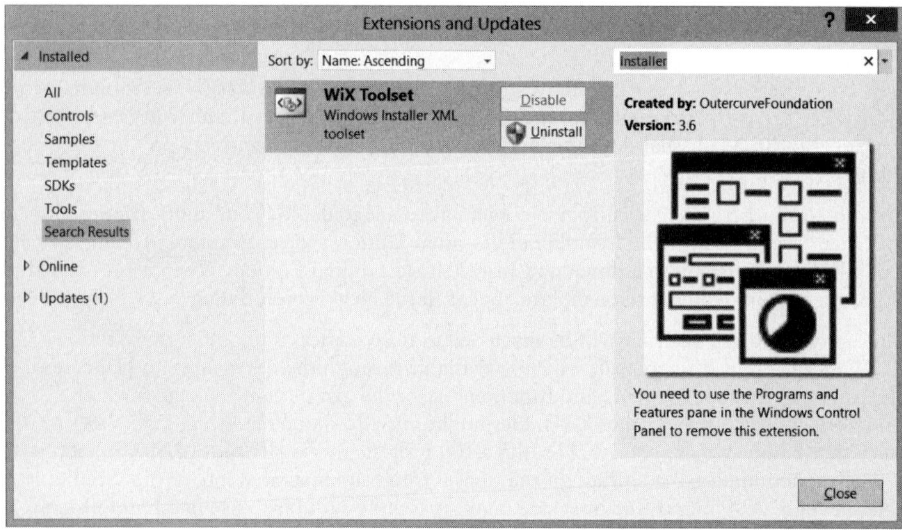

FIGURE 49-1

Building an Installer

To build an installer with Visual Studio 2012, you need to add an additional project to the application that you want to deploy. Figure 49-2 shows the available setup and deployment project templates included with WiX. The Setup Project should be used for Windows Forms applications. There is a separate template available for Windows service applications. The same Setup Project can be used for `ASP.NET` websites or web services. If you want to build an installer that will be integrated into a larger installer, you may want to build a merge module. Alternatively, you can use the Setup Library project to create an installer component — a piece of installation functionality that you might use in multiple installation packages, in a manner similar to how you use assemblies in multiple applications.

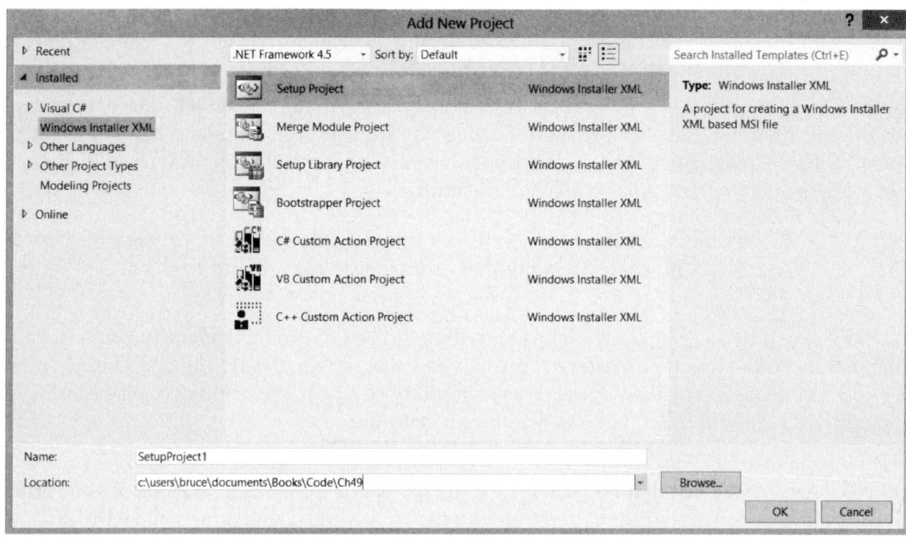

FIGURE 49-2

Upon creation of the project, a single file appears in the designer. To be fair, the setup project does contain other files, but the `Product.wxs` file is the starting point and the heart of the installation package. So begin by taking a look at the contents. Figure 49-3 shows the default file.

```
Product.wxs
<?xml version="1.0" encoding="UTF-8"?>
<Wix xmlns="http://schemas.microsoft.com/wix/2006/wi">
  <Product Id="04BBD56E-8B00-4AA2-B92D-4F814FF39FDE" Name="BaseSetup" Language="1033" Version="1.0.0.0"
           Manufacturer="" UpgradeCode="3213479F-A512-4961-BB80-38294F8D6C91">
    <Package InstallerVersion="200" Compressed="yes" InstallScope="perMachine" />

    <MajorUpgrade DowngradeErrorMessage="A newer version of [ProductName] is already installed." />
    <MediaTemplate />

    <Feature Id="ProductFeature" Title="BaseSetup" Level="1">
      <ComponentGroupRef Id="ProductComponents" />
    </Feature>
  </Product>

  <Fragment>
    <Directory Id="TARGETDIR" Name="SourceDir">
      <Directory Id="ProgramFilesFolder">
        <Directory Id="INSTALLFOLDER" Name="BaseSetup" />
      </Directory>
    </Directory>
  </Fragment>

  <Fragment>
    <ComponentGroup Id="ProductComponents" Directory="INSTALLFOLDER">
      <!-- TODO: Remove the comments around this Component element and the ComponentRef below in order to -->
      <!-- <Component Id="ProductComponent"> -->
        <!-- TODO: Insert files, registry keys, and other resources here -->
      <!-- </Component> -->
    </ComponentGroup>
  </Fragment>
100 %
```

FIGURE 49-3

You can notice that the file is divided into three main elements:

- **Product** — This section describes the fundamental information about the installation. This includes the manufacturer, the components that are to be included, the media that is to be used, and other details used to create the MSI or MSM file.
- **Directory Fragment** — This section describes the layout of the folders placed onto the target machine. You might notice that the default appears to be organized in a hierarchical manner. This is not a coincidence but a function of the declarative nature of WiX. The hierarchy in this fragment represents the hierarchy of the directory created on the target file system.
- **Component Group Fragment** — This section describes the features to be installed. The component group defines the files that make up a feature. Through a yet-to-be-seen fragment, the files in the component group are mapped onto the directory structure. And in the Product fragment, the component groups that make up the product are identified.

To start, consider the `Product` element. As already mentioned, this element describes the piece of software being installed. In the `Product` element, there are a number of attributes that should be defined — or at least modified from the default.

There are two GUIDs related to the `Products`. The `Id` attribute is used to uniquely identify your package. The WiX product enables you to specify an asterisk as a GUID value, in which case the GUID is generated as part of the compilation process. For the `Product`, you should take advantage of this because each installation will be different and therefore will need a unique identifier.

The second GUID is the `UpgradeCode`. This value is used if you create an upgrade installation package, — in other words, for the installation package for the second or subsequent versions of your product. Every upgrade needs to reference the upgrade code, so unlike the `Id` attribute, this value will be the same for every version of your product. As such, you should set the attribute value to a GUID that you generate.

The other four attributes that should be set relate more to the user interface and experience of the installation process. The Name attribute is the name of the product. This is the value that appears when you look at the Program and Features portion of Control Panel. The `Language` attribute is the culture identifier for this installation. The default value of 1033 is U.S. English. The `Version` attribute is the version of the product that is installed and is in the typical format for a version number. Finally, the `Manufacturer` attribute defines the organization producing the product.

The `Product` element has a number of subelements that provide additional details about the installation. The `MajorUpgrade` element can determine the action that should be taken when an application is upgraded to a more recent version. Possible actions include uninstalling the old version and installing the new one, replacing the files or a custom action.

The purpose of the `MediaTemplate` element has been going out of style as of late. It indicates the size and format of the media onto which the installation package will be placed. In fact, through WiX you can specify into which media component (such as a DVD disc) that a particular file will be placed. The default `MediaTemplate`, however, is usually sufficient because it includes the values that create a single file.

The remaining element in the `Product` describes the feature (or features) included in the installation package. A *feature* in WiX parlance is a collection of deployment items intended to be installed as an atomic unit. It could be as simple as one file per feature, or there could be multiple files in a single feature. But regardless, from the user's perspective, the feature is the level at which the user has the choice to install or not to install. As such, there can be one or more `Feature` elements in the `Product`.

The example shown in Figure 49-3 only has a single feature. The attributes are, for the most part, fairly typical. The `Id` is a unique textual identifier for the feature. The `Title` is the name given to the feature. It appears in the installation user interface, so it should be user-friendly. The `Level` is used to nest `Features` one within the other.

For a given feature, you specify the `ComponentGroups` that are related to it. The `ComponentGroup` indicates a particular block of installation elements. It can be a single assembly or a configuration file; it can be a collection of files of different type. But the important aspect to the declaration is that the Id for the `ComponentGroup` must match a `ComponentGroup` defined in one of the subsequent fragments.

The next major component to a WiX file is the `Directory` fragment. First, notice that it's not actually a second-level XML element (that is, at the same level as the `Product`). Instead, it's a subelement of a fragment. This arrangement is done to allow `Directory` fragments to be placed in different packages and still be easily combined by the linker when the installation file is constructed.

The contents of the `Directory` fragment are intended to mimic the file system that will exist on the target system after the installation is complete. Referring to Figure 49-3, you can see that there is a three-level nesting that has been defined. Each level has an `Id` associated with it. The `Id` can be meaningful, as is the case here. But ultimately, you have the ability to map the placement of individual files into specific directories by referencing the `Id`. The `Name` attribute is optional; however if you plan to create directories where none already exist, as is the case with the `INSTALLFOLDER` element, it should be included. In the example, the default value for the directory created under Program Files is the name of the project.

The final fragment (refer to Figure 49-3) is a `ComponentGroup`, which contains a reference to the individual files that make up the group. The `Id` for the group is important because it must match an `Id` specified in the `ComponentGroupRef` back when the `Features` were being listed. The `ComponentGroup` element has a `Directory` attribute; the value of this attribute specifies the directory where the files in the group will be placed. The value must match one of the `Ids` of a `Directory` element in the `Directory` fragment.

Using Heat to Create Fragments

Visual Studio 2010 and earlier versions had a Setup Wizard that would be used to initialize a setup project with the appropriate values. WiX does not currently have such functionality. To work around this issue, WiX provides a tool that examines various types of artifacts and creates WiX fragments based on which it finds. The tool is known as Heat. And fortunately, one of the artifact types that it understands is Visual Studio project files.

> **NOTE** *Although the equivalent functionality to a Setup Wizard is not present, that does not mean that people are not working on addressing that issue. Although not currently available, there is a WiX component named Votive that aims at filling this gap. It is not production-ready as of this writing, but the timing is such that it may be downloadable by or shortly after the publication date of this book.*

Heat is a useful tool. However, it is a command-line utility and, as such, you need to take a simple step to integrate it into Visual Studio. Specifically, it needs to be placed into your External Tools collection. To access the collection, select Tools ➪ External Tools from the menu. The dialog shown in Figure 49-4 appears.

To add a new comment, click the Add button. For the new tool, specify a name of **Harvest Project**. The command (which, not surprisingly, is implemented in `heat.exe`) is found in the WiX Toolset v3.6 directory underneath Program Files, or Program Files (x86) if you're running on a 64-bit machine. The Arguments value is where the magic takes place. There are a number of parameters that need to be defined. And you can use the project tokens as well. Set the Argument value to the following.

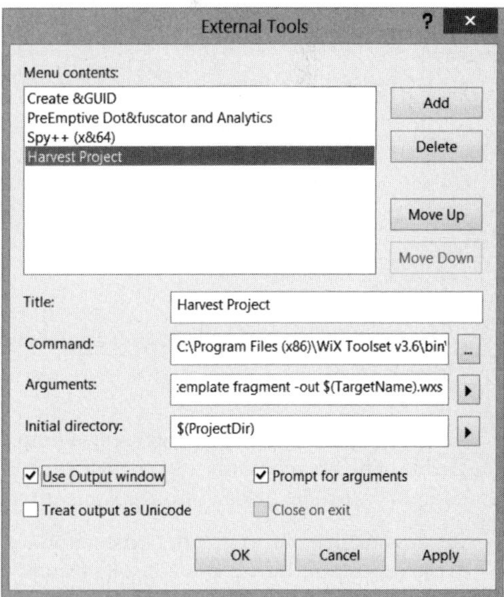

FIGURE 49-4

```
project $(ProjectFileName) -pog Binaries -ag -template fragment -out $(TargetName).wxs
```

Finally, set the Initial Directory value to `$(ProjectDir)`. This enables the utility to find the needed files starting at the project's root. Make sure that Use Output Window is checked; then a final click on the OK button completes the creation process.

Now that the Heat command is available, you can put it to use. First, in Solution Explorer, make sure that the file within the project being harvested is selected. Then use the Tools ➪ Harvest Project menu option to scan the current project. If all goes well, the Output window should look something like Figure 49-5.

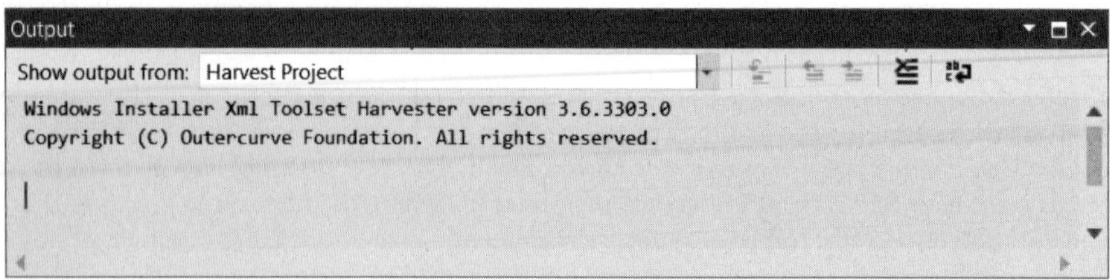

FIGURE 49-5

The results from harvesting your project in this manner is a `.wxs` file. More precisely, it is a `.wxs` file that has the same name as your project. You can locate it in the same directory as your project file. To view that file in Visual Studio, use the Show All Files button in the Solution Explorer. You'll notice that a `.wxs` file is now visible. Double-click it to open the file. The results should appear similar to Figure 49-6, which is generated from a simple "Hello World" style WPF application named WpfSampleApp.

```
WpfSampleApp.wxs
<?xml version="1.0" encoding="utf-8"?>
<Wix xmlns="http://schemas.microsoft.com/wix/2006/wi">
    <Fragment>
        <DirectoryRef Id="WpfSampleApp.Binaries">
            <Component Id="cmpE147175526C6B5E6DEB3414E7F16AF44" Guid="*">
                <File Id="fil3115C32E4A3C0D0F2264EEF969A31F37"
                      Source="$(var.WpfSampleApp.TargetDir)\WpfSampleApp.exe" />
            </Component>
            <Component Id="cmpEAA8CDBECF07B377E269818F81751D4F" Guid="*">
                <File Id="fil7026F1B06577DF3DF56257DDD7C00ED1"
                      Source="$(var.WpfSampleApp.TargetDir)\WpfSampleApp.exe.config" />
            </Component>
        </DirectoryRef>
    </Fragment>
    <Fragment>
        <ComponentGroup Id="WpfSampleApp.Binaries">
            <ComponentRef Id="cmpE147175526C6B5E6DEB3414E7F16AF44" />
            <ComponentRef Id="cmpEAA8CDBECF07B377E269818F81751D4F" />
        </ComponentGroup>
    </Fragment>
</Wix>
100 %
```

FIGURE 49-6

The contents of these WiX fragments complete the installation packaging story. There are two fragments visible. The first contains a `DirectoryRef` element. The purpose of this element is to enable multiple components to be placed into the same directory in the target machine.

Inside the `DirectoryRef` are two `Component` elements. Each component represents a file. The first component is the executable for the project. The second component is the configuration file. The `Source` attribute indicates the components.

The second fragment is the `ComponentGroup` previously discussed. The difference is that the `ComponentGroup` in Figure 49-3 had no files. This one does. In particular, the files contained in this `ComponentGroup` (as represented by the `ComponentRef` elements) refer to the files' identity in the `DirectoryRef`. The `Id` attribute in the `ComponentRef` matches the `Id` in the `Component` in the `DirectoryRef`.

This constant indirection might seem quite convoluted. And to a certain extent it is, but it enables a great deal of flexibility. By defining a directory reference and including components within it, you can place files from different components into the same physical directory with a minimum of effort.

The Heat-generated fragments need to be incorporated into the setup project to be included in the installation package. To accomplish this, copy the two fragments and paste them into the `Product.wxs` file from the setup project. In doing so, delete the existing `ComponentGroup` fragment.

Now the two components need to be referenced in the `Product.wxs` file. This is done in two steps. First, in the Feature element in the `Product`, set the `ComponentGroupRef Id` to be the `Id` of the `ComponentGroup` in the Heat-generated fragments. In the example, that would be `WpfSampleApp.Binaries`. This includes the components as part of the feature being installed.

Second, in the `DirectoryRef` element in the Heat-generated fragment, set the `Id` to `INSTALLFOLDER`. This links the components (and the files) into the target directory when the installation is performed. The result of these changes should result in a `Product.wxs` file that looks like Figure 49-7.

```
Product.wxs
<?xml version="1.0" encoding="UTF-8"?>
<Wix xmlns="http://schemas.microsoft.com/wix/2006/wi">
  <Product Id="04BBD56E-8B00-4AA2-B92D-4F814FF39FDE" Name="Chapter29Setup" Language="1033" Version="1.0.0.0"
           Manufacturer="VS 2012" UpgradeCode="3213479F-A512-4961-BB80-38294F8D6C91">
    <Package InstallerVersion="200" Compressed="yes" InstallScope="perMachine" />

    <MajorUpgrade DowngradeErrorMessage="A newer version of Chapter 49 is already installed." />
    <MediaTemplate />

    <Feature Id="ProductFeature" Title="Chapter49Setup" Level="1">
      <ComponentGroupRef Id="WpfSampleApp.Binaries" />
    </Feature>
  </Product>

  <Fragment>
    <Directory Id="TARGETDIR" Name="SourceDir">
      <Directory Id="ProgramFilesFolder">
        <Directory Id="INSTALLFOLDER" Name="Chapter49Setup" />
      </Directory>
    </Directory>
  </Fragment>

  <Fragment>
    <DirectoryRef Id="INSTALLFOLDER">
      <Component Id="cmpE147175526C6B5E6DEB3414E7F16AF44" Guid="*">
        <File Id="fil3115C32E4A3C0D0F2264EEF969A31F37"
              Source="$(var.WpfSampleApp.TargetDir)\WpfSampleApp.exe" />
      </Component>
      <Component Id="cmpEAA8CDBECF07B377E269818F81751D4F" Guid="*">
        <File Id="fil7026F1B06577DF3DF56257DDD7C00ED1"
              Source="$(var.WpfSampleApp.TargetDir)\WpfSampleApp.exe.config" />
      </Component>
    </DirectoryRef>
  </Fragment>
  <Fragment>
    <ComponentGroup Id="WpfSampleApp.Binaries">
      <ComponentRef Id="cmpE147175526C6B5E6DEB3414E7F16AF44" />
      <ComponentRef Id="cmpEAA8CDBECF07B377E269818F81751D4F" />
    </ComponentGroup>
  </Fragment>
</Wix>
70 %
```

FIGURE 49-7

There is one more step that needs to be done before the setup project can be built. You might notice that in the fragment generated by Heat, there were two references to `$(var.WpfSampleApp.TargetDir)`. This is a preprocessor variable that will be resolved when the setup project is built. However, at it currently stands, the variable is unrecognized. To change that, you need to add a reference to the WpfSampleApp project to the WiX project. Right-click on the WiX project in Solution Explorer and select Add Reference. In the Add Reference dialog that appears, select the Project tab and double-click on the WpfSampleApp. Then click OK to complete the process.

Now the project can be built. The output from the build process (that is, the .`MSI` file) can be found in the `bin\Debug` directory. If you execute this file (by double-clicking on it in Windows Explorer, for example), you'll see a standard set of installation screens. And the result will be a file placed into your Program Files directory named Chapter 49. To remove this, you need to use the Programs And Features application within Control Panel to uninstall the application. In other words, you have created a full-fledged installation of your application.

As you might expect, a large number of customizations can be done to the installation, both in terms of its functionality and its appearance. If you are interested in the details and capabilities, visit the WiX home page at `http://wix.sourceforge.net`. There, you can not only find the full documentation, but also links to tutorials and even the complete source code.

The Service Installer

You can create an installer for a Windows Service the same way you would create an installer for a Windows application. However, a Windows Service installer not only needs to install the files into the appropriate location, but it also needs to register the service so it appears in the services list.

The WiX Toolset provides a mechanism for doing this. It is the `ServiceInstall` and `ServiceControl` elements that describe what you want to happen when the service is installed. The XML related to these components can be seen next:

```
<Component Id='ServiceExeComponent'
  Guid='YOURGUID-D752-4C4F-942A-657B02AE8325'
  SharedDllRefCount='no' KeyPath='no'
  NeverOverwrite='no' Permanent='no' Transitive='no'
  Win64='no' Location='either'>

  <File Id='ServiceExeFile' Name='ServiceExe.exe' Source='ServiceExe.exe'
    ReadOnly='no' Compressed='yes' KeyPath='yes' Vital='yes'
    Hidden='no' System='no'
    Checksum='no' PatchAdded='no' />

  <ServiceInstall Id='MyServiceInstall' DisplayName='My Test Service'
    Name='MyServiceExeName' ErrorControl='normal' Start='auto'
    Account='Local System' Type='ownProcess'
    Vital='yes' Interactive='no' />

  <ServiceControl Id='MyServiceControl' Name='MyServiceExeName'
    Start='install' Stop='uninstall' Remove='uninstall' />

</Component>
```

The `File` element is similar in purpose to the WiX fragments illustrated in Figure 49-7. In this case, it identifies that file that implements the service that is being installed. The most important element is `KeyPath`. It needs to be set to yes, whereas the `KeyPath` in the `Component` needs to be set to no.

The `ServiceInstall` element contains information about the service. This includes the name that appears in the service control applet (`DisplayName`) and the "real" name of the service (the `Name` attribute). If you have created installers for services in earlier versions of Visual Studio, you might be recosting the `Account` and `Interactive` attributes as being related to the account under which the service will run and whether the service will interact with the desktop.

The `ServiceControl` element describes what should happen to the service when it is installed. The three attributes in `ServiceControl` that matter are `Start`, `Stop`, and `Remove`. The values of these attributes determine what should happen when the service in installed or removed. The values previously shown would have the service start when it is installed, and both stopped and removed when the service is uninstalled.

CLICKONCE

Using a Windows installer is a sensible approach for any application development. However, deploying an installer to thousands of machines, and then potentially having to update them, is a daunting task. Although management products help reduce the burden associated with application deployment, web applications often replace rich Windows applications because they can be dynamically updated, affecting all users of the system. *ClickOnce* enables you to build self-updating Windows applications. This section shows you how to use Visual Studio 2012 to build applications that can be deployed and updated using ClickOnce.

One Click to Deploy

To demonstrate the functionality of ClickOnce deployment, this section uses the same application used to build the Windows Installer, WpfSampleApp, which simply displays an empty form. To deploy this application using ClickOnce, select the Publish option from the right-click context menu of the project. This opens the Publish Wizard, which guides you through the initial configuration of ClickOnce for your project.

The first step in the Publish Wizard enables you to select a location to deploy to. You can choose to deploy to a local website, an FTP location, a file share, or even a local folder on your machine. Clicking Browse opens the Open Web Site dialog, which assists you in specifying the publishing location.

The next step asks you to specify where the users are expecting to install the application from. The default option is for users to install from a CD or DVD-ROM disc. More commonly, you want to install from a file share on a corporate intranet or a website on the Internet. Note that the location you publish to and the location the users install from can be different. This can be useful while testing new releases.

The contents of the final step change depending on the installation option selected. If your application is installed from a CD or DVD-ROM, this step asks if the application should automatically check for updates. If this option is enabled, you must provide a location for the application to check. In the case that your users will be installing from a file share or website, it is assumed that the application will update from the location that it was originally installed from. Instead, the final question relates to whether the application will be available offline. If the offline option is selected, an application shortcut is added to the Start menu, and the application can be removed in the Add/Remove Programs dialog in the operating system. The user can run the application even if the original installation location is no longer available. If the application is only available online, no shortcut is created, and the users must visit the install location every time they want to run the application.

The last screen in the wizard enables you to verify the configuration before publishing the application. After the application has been published, you can run the `Setup.exe` bootstrap file that is produced to install the application. If you install from a website, you get a `default.htm` file generated as well. This file, shown in Figure 49-8, uses some JavaScript to detect a few dependencies and provides an Install button that launches the `Setup.exe`.

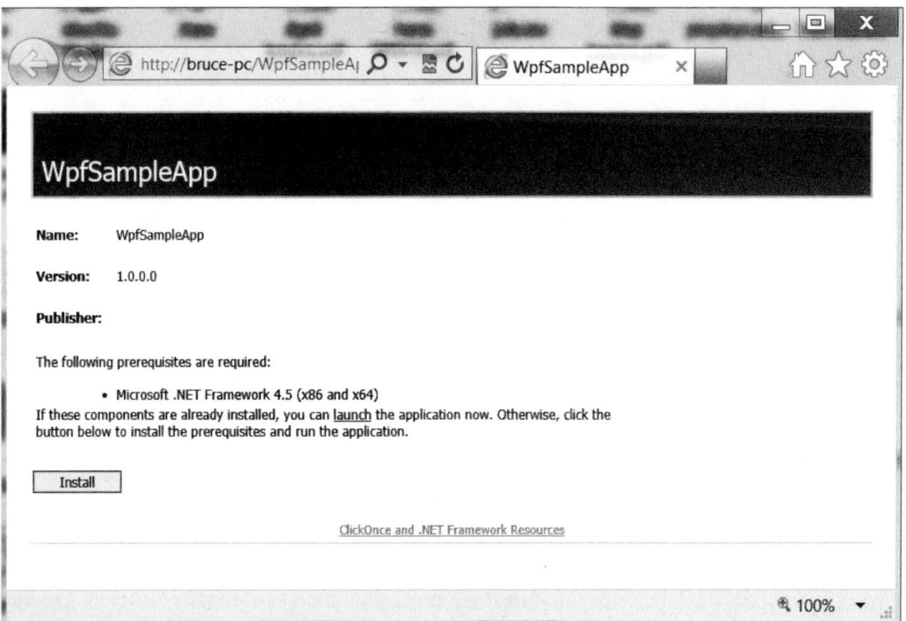

FIGURE 49-8

Clicking the Install button at this location displays a dialog prompting you to run or save `Setup.exe`. Selecting Run (or running `Setup.exe` from a different kind of install) shows the Launching Application dialog, as shown in Figure 49-9, while components of your application are retrieved from the installation location.

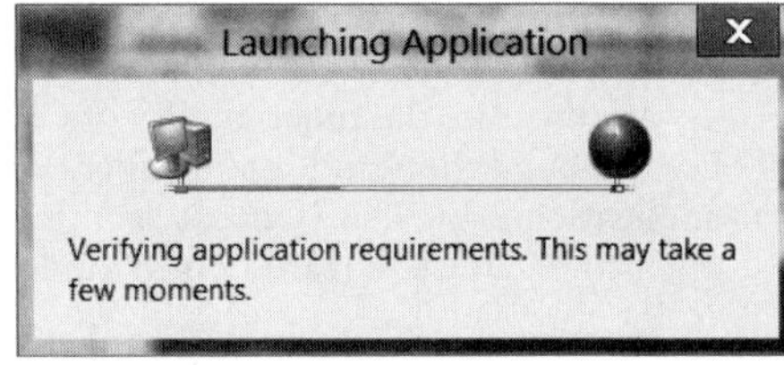

FIGURE 49-9

After information about the application has been downloaded, a security warning launches, as shown in Figure 49-10. In this case, the security warning is raised because although the deployment manifest has been signed, it has been signed with a certificate that is not known on the machine on which it is installed.

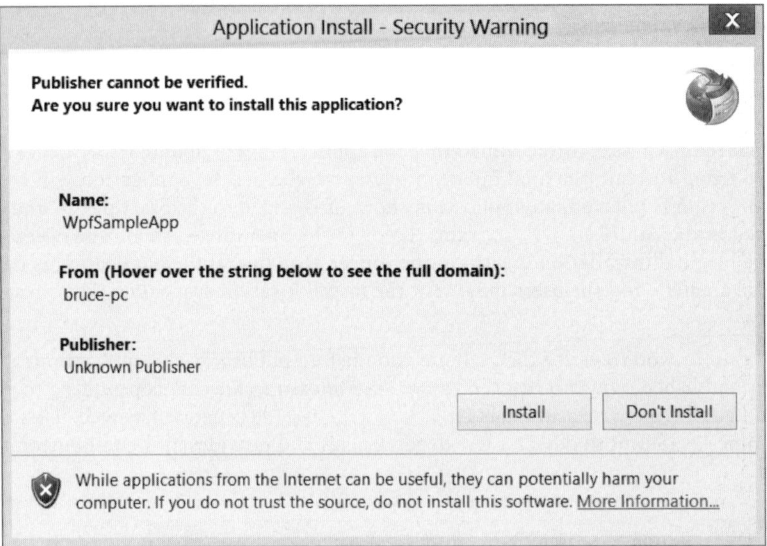

FIGURE 49-10

> **NOTE** *The deployment manifest of a ClickOnce application is an XML file that describes the application to be deployed along with a reference to the current version. Although it is not required, each deployment manifest can be signed by the publisher to provide the manifest with a strong name. This prevents the manifest from being tampered with after it is deployed.*

Three options are available for signing the deployment manifest. By default, Visual Studio 2012 creates a test certificate to sign the manifest, which has the format `application name_TemporaryKey.pfx` and is automatically added to the solution. (This happens when the application is first published using the Publish Now button.) Though this certificate can be used during development, it is not recommended for deployment. The other alternatives are to purchase a third-party certificate, from a company such as VeriSign, or to use the certificate server within Windows Server to create an internal certificate.

The advantage of getting a certificate from a well-known certificate authority is that it can automatically be verified by any machine. Using either the test certificate or an internal certificate requires installation of that certificate in the appropriate certificate store. Figure 49-11 shows the Signing tab of the Project Properties window, where you can see that the ClickOnce manifest is signed with a certificate that has been generated on the local computer. An existing certificate can be used by selecting it from the store or from a file. Alternatively, another test certificate can be created.

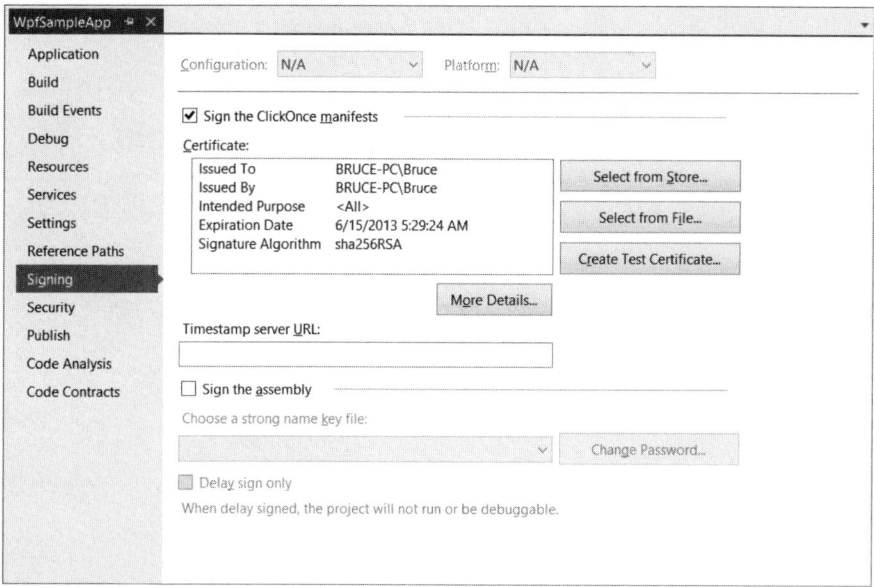

FIGURE 49-11

If you want your application to install with a known publisher, you need to add the test certificate into the root certificate store on the machine on which you install the product. Because this also happens to be the deployment machine, you can do this by clicking More Details. This opens a dialog that outlines the certificate details, including the fact that it can't be authenticated. (If you use the certificate created by default by Visual Studio 2012, you need to use the Select from File button to reselect the generated certificate and then use the More Details button. There seems to be an issue here, in that the details window does not show the Install Certificate button without this additional step.) Clicking Install Certificate enables you to specify that the certificate should be installed into the Trusted Root Certification Authorities store. This is not the default certificate store, so you need to browse for it. Because this is a test certificate, you can ignore the warning that is given, but remember that you should not use this certificate in production. Now when you publish your application and try to install it, you see that the dialog has changed, looking similar to the one shown in Figure 49-12.

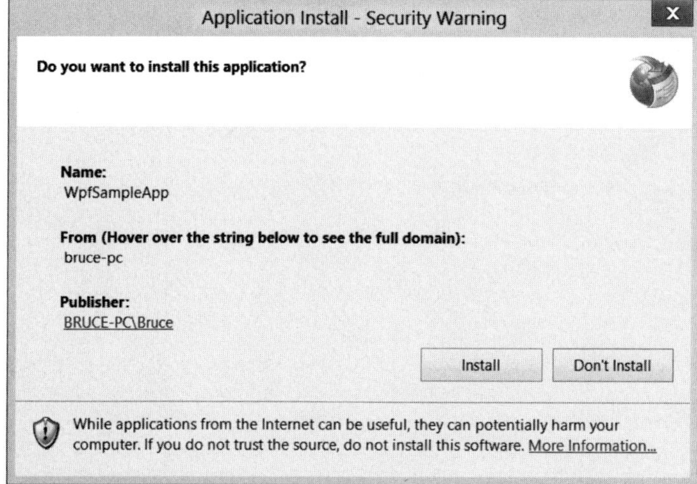

FIGURE 49-12

Although you have a known publisher, you are still warned that additional security permissions need to be granted to this application for it to execute. Clicking the rather minimalist More Information hyperlink opens a more informative dialog, as shown in Figure 49-13. As with the security coding within Windows Server 2008 and Windows 7, there are three types of icons: green for positive security, red for potential security weaknesses, and yellow for informative or best practice guidance.

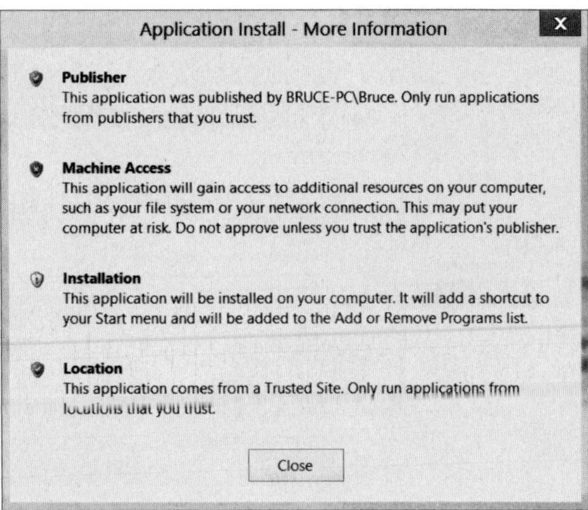

FIGURE 49-13

ClickOnce deployment manifests are rated on four security dimensions. You've just seen how you can specify a well-known publisher, critical for safe installation of an application. By default, ClickOnce publishes applications as full trust applications, giving them maximum control over the local computer. This is unusual because in most other cases Microsoft has adopted a security-first approach. To run with full trust, the application requires additional security permissions, which might be exploited. The Sample Application will be available online and offline; and though this isn't a major security risk, it does modify the local file system. Lastly, the location from which the application is installed is almost as important as the publisher in determining how dangerous the application might be. In this case, the application was published within the local network, so it is unlikely to be a security threat.

Because this application doesn't actually do anything, you can decrease the trust level that the application requires. As shown in Figure 49-14, this application is configured to be a partial-trust application based on the Local Intranet zone. This changes the Machine Access icon to green, leaving only the Installation icon yellow. Unfortunately, the only way you can get this to be green would be to not install the application, which means that it would not be available offline.

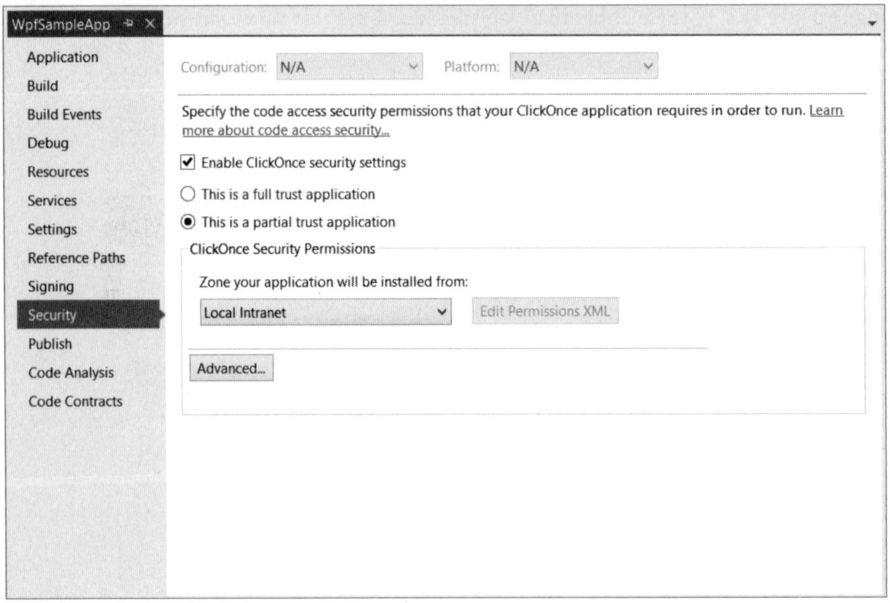

FIGURE 49-14

Ideally, you would like to bypass the Application Install dialog and have the application automatically be granted appropriate permissions. You can do this by adding the certificate to the Trusted Publishers store. Even for well-known certificate authorities, for the application to install automatically, the certificate needs to be added to this store. With this completed, you see only the progress dialog as the application is downloaded, rather than the security prompt.

When installed, the application can be launched either by returning to the installation URL (refer to Figure 49-8) or by selecting the shortcut from the newly created Start Menu folder with the same name as the application.

One Click to Update

At some point in the future, you might make a change to your application — for example, you might add a button to the simple form you created previously. ClickOnce supports a powerful update process that enables you to publish the new version of your application in the same way you did previously, and existing versions can be upgraded the next time they are online. As long as you are content with the current set of options, the update process is just the Publish process. When using the Publish Wizard to update an existing application, all the values previously used to publish the application are preconfigured for you.

You can check the settings in the Publish tab of the Project Properties designer (Figure 49-15). The designer shows the publish location, the installation location, and the install mode of the application. There is also a setting for the Publish Version. This value is not shown in the Publish Wizard, but by default this version starts at 1.0.0.0 and increments the right-most number every time the application is published.

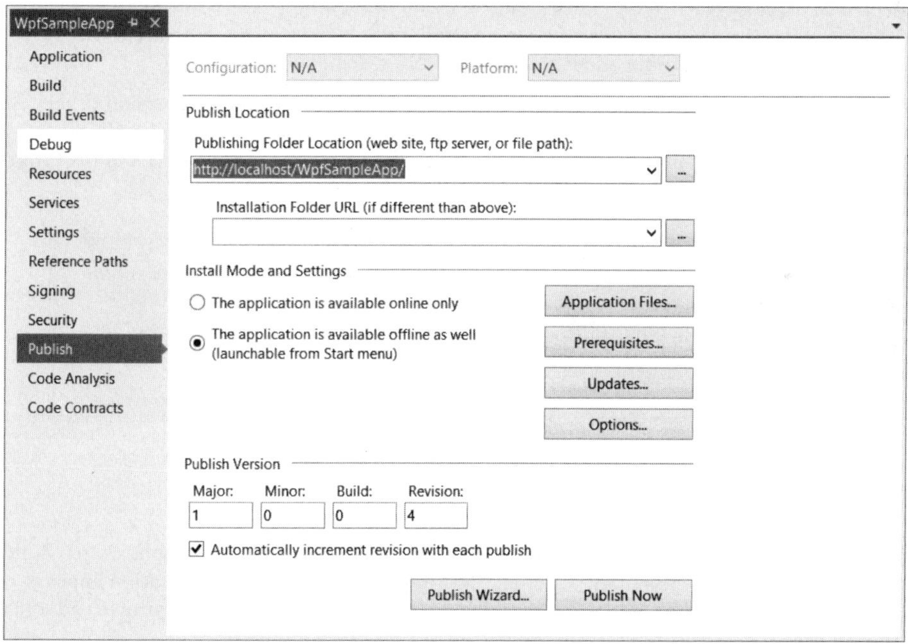

FIGURE 49-15

Along the right are a number of buttons that bring up more advanced options, most of which are not exposed by the wizard. The Application Updates dialog (Figure 49-16) enables you to configure how the application updates itself. In Figure 49-16, the application updates once every four weeks after it has started. You can also specify a minimum required version, which can prevent older clients from executing until they are updated.

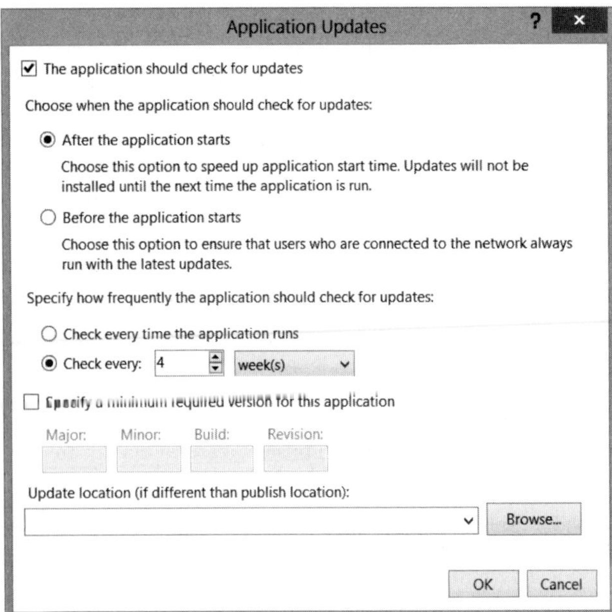

FIGURE 49-16

With this change, now when you publish a new version of your application, any existing users will be prompted to update their application to the most recent version.

One of the most powerful features of ClickOnce deployment is that it tracks a previous version of the application that was installed. This means that at any stage, not only can it do a clean uninstall, but it can also roll back to the earlier version. The application can be rolled back or uninstalled from the Programs and Features list from the Control Panel.

> **NOTE** *For users to receive an update, they do need to contact the original deployment URL when the application performs the check for a new version (for example, when the application starts). You can also force all users to upgrade to a particular version (that is, they won't get prompted) by specifying the minimum required version in the Application Updates dialog (Figure 49-16).*

SUMMARY

This chapter walked you through the details of building installers for various types of applications. Building a good-quality installer can make a significant difference in how professional your application appears. ClickOnce also offers an important alternative for those who want to deploy their application to a large audience.

50

Web Application Deployment

WHAT'S IN THIS CHAPTER?

- Publishing website and web projects
- Publishing database scripts with web applications
- Copying website changes to a remote server
- Creating web application packages for deployment with the Web Deployment tool
- Keeping machines up to date with the Web Platform Installer
- Extending the Web Platform Installer to include your own applications

In the previous chapter you saw how to deploy your Windows application using either an installer or ClickOnce. But how do you deploy web applications? This chapter walks you through deploying website and Web application projects. It also covers packaging web applications for remote deployment with the Web Deployment tool and integrating with the Web Platform Installer.

One of the most important aspects of building your application is to think about how you will package it so that it can be deployed. Though a large proportion of web applications are only for internal release, where a simple copy script might be sufficient, if you do want to make your web application available for others to purchase and use, you need to focus on making the deployment process as simple as possible.

WEBSITE DEPLOYMENT

Web projects created with Visual Studio 2012 fall into two broad categories: Web application projects and Web site projects. This section demonstrates tools that are specifically for deploying and maintaining Web site projects.

Publish Web Site

The simplest way to deploy a website from Visual Studio 2012 is to publish it via the Publish Web Site item on the Build menu. Selecting this option presents you with the dialog shown in Figure 50-1. It has only a few basic options that enable you to publish debugging information, enable in-place updating of your website, and enforce different naming policies and security requirements.

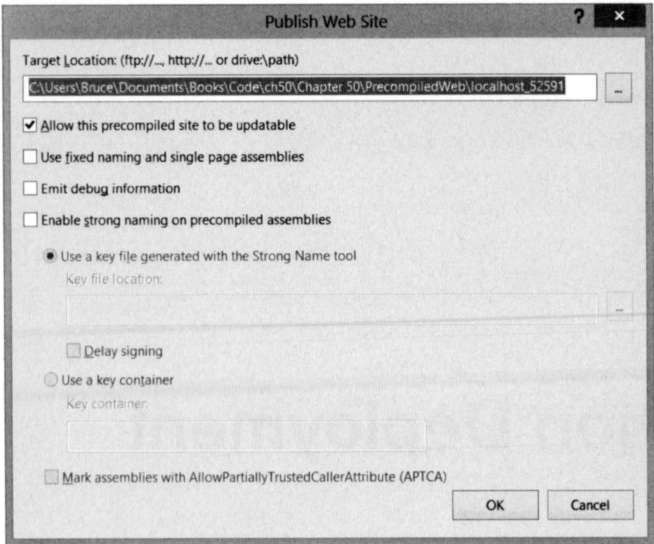

FIGURE 50-1

Usually you simply use the Target Location box to specify the location that you want to publish to. This location can be a local instance of IIS, an FTP site, elsewhere on the filesystem, or a remote instance of IIS. Clicking the ellipsis button next to the Target Location textbox (refer to Figure 50-1) brings up a dialog to specify the details of where you want to publish to, as shown in Figure 50-2.

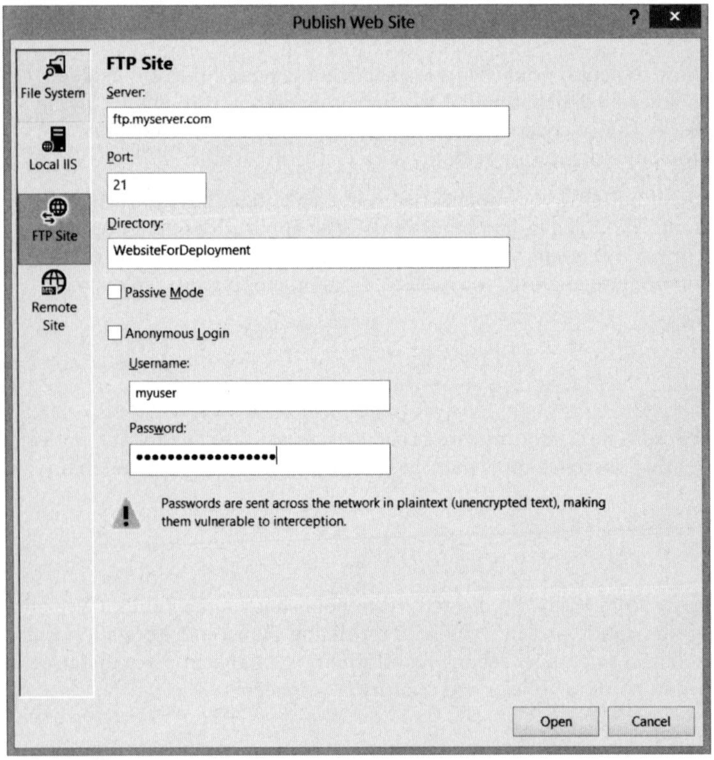

FIGURE 50-2

> **NOTE** *In Figure 50-2 you can publish to a private FTP account, and if this is the first time you publish this site, you may need to define this folder as an IIS application for the website to function.*

Copy Web Site

After a website has been published, it is important that you have some way to update it. One option is to go through the process of publishing your website again. However, this publishes the entire website, even if only a single file needs to be updated. An alternative is to use the Copy Web Site tool, as shown in Figure 50-3, to synchronize files between your development project and the website. You can access this tool from the right-click context menu in the Solution Explorer or via the website menu.

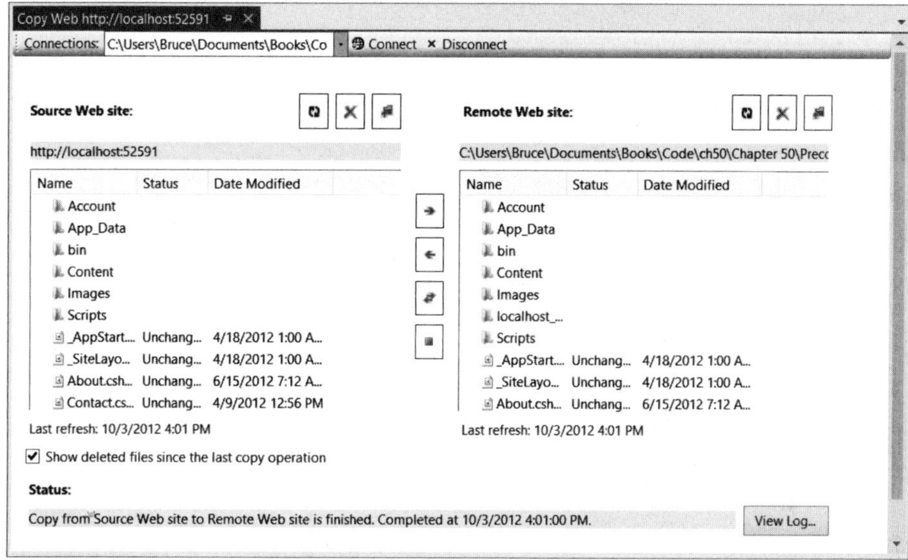

FIGURE 50-3

To view the existing files on the remote website, you need to either select a recent connection from the drop-down list or click the Connect button. This opens a dialog (refer to Figure 50-2), where you can specify how to connect to the remote website. After you connect you can see which files are out of sync. You can then use the right and left arrows to move files between your local project and the remote website.

WEB APPLICATION DEPLOYMENT

Web application projects are quite different from Web Site projects and come with a different set of tools for deployment. Visual Studio 2012 introduces the capability to deploy with the Web Deployment tool, which is used to easily import and export IIS applications along with their dependencies — such as IIS meta data and databases — from the command line, IIS 7.0 management console, PowerShell cmdlets, or directly from Visual Studio. It also provides the ability to manage several versions of configuration data for different environments in a clean manner without duplication.

Publishing a Web Application

The quickest way to deploy a Web application project is to simply publish it directly from Visual Studio. Select the Publish item from the right-click context menu in Solution Explorer to display the Publish Web dialog. Each time you do a deployment you do so against a particular profile, which encapsulates the target environment settings. A Web Application project maintains a collection of profiles, which enable you to deploy the one web application to a number of target environments and keep the settings for each separate. If this is the first time you have run the Publish Web dialog, you need to create the profile (which consists of giving it a name to start) before you can continue with the next steps. You can do this by selecting <New...> from the drop-down. You will be prompted for the name of your profile and when provided, you can then move to the Connection tab (shown in Figure 50-4).

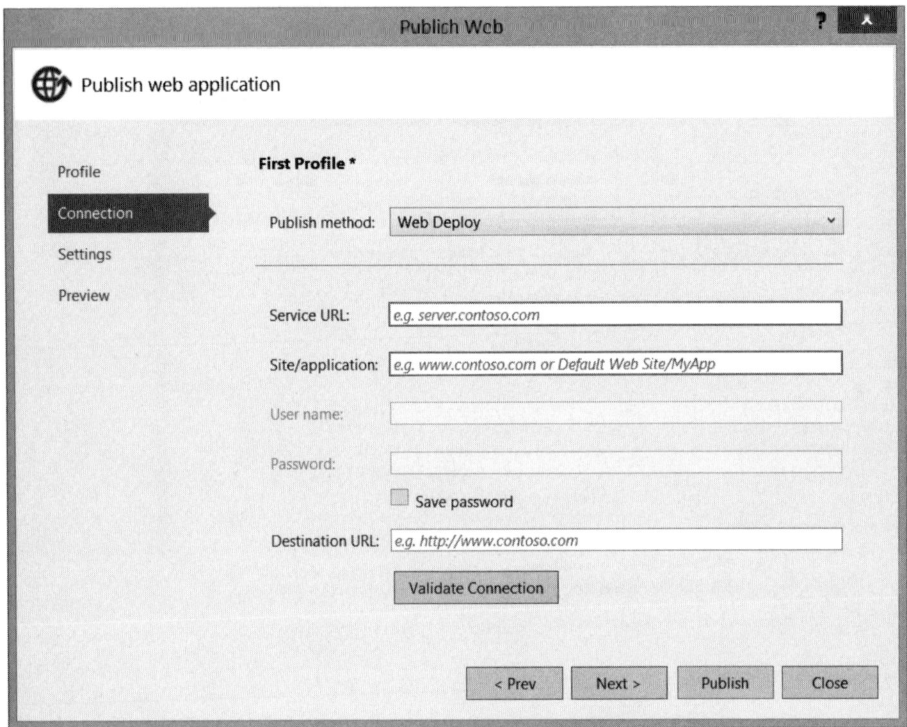

FIGURE 50-4

The Connection tab in this wizard enables you to define the connection. Several options for Publish Method determine what you see in the lower part of the dialog window: Web Deploy, Web Deploy Package, FTP, Filesystem, and Front-Page Server Extensions (FPSE). The Filesystem and Front-Page Server Extensions options both enable you to enter the target location for the web application to be published. The FTP option offers the same but also enables you to enter FTP credentials. The Web Deploy option enables you to specify the service URL and the destination URL as well as the site/application combination that is the target of the publication. If necessary, credentials can be provided. The Web Deploy Package option takes what would normally be deployed through a Web Deploy and instead packages it into a Zip file. So instead of needing to identify the target system, you can just specify the path to the file that will be created.

The Settings tab enables you to configure some additional settings for the deployment. Again, the publish methods break the contents of this step into two categories. Both categories enable you to specify the configuration (by default, Debug and Release) that will be deployed. As well, there is a check box that can remove all the files from the target that are not deployed. However, the Web Deploy and Web Deploy Package include a section that enables a database to be deployed with the web application (Figure 50-5).

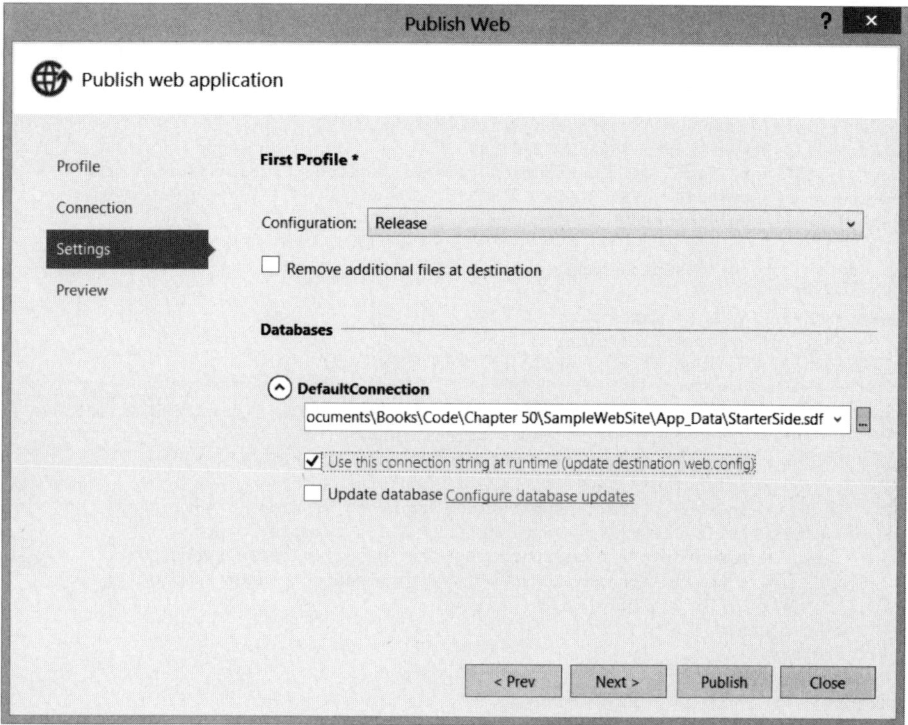

FIGURE 50-5

When you deploy a database, the Publish Wizard examines the application and identifies any databases that are part of the application. These become choices that you can make in the drop-down list. Alternatively, you can specify the database connection manually. Also, there are check boxes that enable you to update the `web.config` file with the new connection information and to update the schema of an existing database with the deploying database.

If you use the Web Deploy Package option, it packages all the necessary files, along with all the meta data required to install and configure your application package, into a single Zip file. This Zip file can then be installed via the IIS 7.0 interface, the command line, PowerShell cmdlets, or directly from Visual Studio.

The fourth tab in this dialog is called Preview. While it is not a requirement that you visit this tab in order to publish your Web application, it can be useful as a last check to ensure the publication of the application is what your expect. The tab displays a list of the files that are different between the application which is already published and the one that you're about to publish. To see this list, there is a Start Preview button that needs to be clicked, and the process of comparison can take a few minutes. But once the list is present, the files that are being updated and the last date they were modified is shown. Next to each file is a check box that provides you with the opportunity to remove some files from the update, if you prefer.

WEB PROJECT INSTALLERS

In addition to using the Web Deployment tool, you can create a standard Windows Installer package to manage a web application or website deployment. This is done using the same Windows Installer Toolkit (WiX) component covered in Chapter 49, "Packaging and Deployment." But moving files onto the target machine is not sufficient for a web project. The installation needs to create a virtual directory as well. Fortunately, WiX supports this functionality. Consider the `.wxs` file shown here:

```
<?xml version="1.0" encoding="UTF-8"?>
<Wix xmlns="http://schemas.microsoft.com/wix/2006/wi"
     xmlns:iis="http://schemas.microsoft.com/wix/IIsExtension">
  <Product Id="381ED4A8-90AA-49F5-9F63-CD128B33895C" Name="Sample Web App"
     Language="1033" Version="1.0.0.0" Manufacturer="Professional Visual Studio 2012"
     UpgradeCode="A8E5F094-C6B0-46E5-91A1-CC5A8C65079D">
     <Package InstallerVersion="200" Compressed="yes" />

     <Media Id="1" Cabinet="SampleWebApp.cab" EmbedCab="yes" />

     <Directory Id="TARGETDIR" Name="SourceDir">
        <Directory Id="ProgramFilesFolder">
           <Directory Id="WebApplicationFolder" Name="MyWebApp">

              <Component Id="ProductComponent" Guid="80b0ee2a-a102-46ec-a456-33a23eb0588e">
                 <File Id="Default.aspx" Name="Default.aspx"
                       Source="..\SampleWebApp\Default.aspx" DiskId="1" />
                 <File Id="Default.aspx.cs" Name="Default.aspx.cs"
                       Source="..\SampleApp\Default.aspx.cs" DiskId="1"/>
                 <iis:WebVirtualDir Id="SampleWebApp" Alias="SampleWebApp"
                       Directory="WebApplicationFolder" WebSite="DefaultWebSite">
                    <iis:WebApplication Id="SampleWebApplication" Name="Sample" />
                 </iis:WebVirtualDir>
              </Component>
           </Directory>
        </Directory>
     </Directory>

     <iis:WebSite Id='DefaultWebSite' Description='Default Web Site'
        Directory='WebApplicationFolder'>
        <iis:WebAddress Id="AllUnassigned" Port="80" />
     </iis:WebSite>

     <Feature Id="ProductFeature" Title="Sample Web Application" Level="1">
        <ComponentRef Id="ProductComponent" />
     </Feature>
  </Product>
</Wix>
```

There are a number of elements unique to web installation. First, notice that the WiX element contains a namespace with a prefix of `iis`. This namespace contains the elements processed to create the virtual directory. You also need to add a reference in your setup project to the `WixIIsExtension` assembly in the WiX Toolkit directory.

The second difference is in the Component placed inside the Directory hierarchy. The `WebVirtualDir` element is used to create a virtual directory. Specifically, the directory named `WebApplicationFolder` is created, with the directory added to the default website for the server. In the `WebVirtualDir` element, the WebApplication directs the installer to make the just created virtual directory as a web application.

Finally, notice the `WebSite` element. This tells the installer to utilize (or create, if necessary) the default website when accessing the `WebApplicationFolder` directory. And the `WebAddress` element sets the application to listen on port 80 on all unassigned endpoints.

THE WEB PLATFORM INSTALLER

Web applications tend to rely on a large number of technologies and tools to function correctly both during development and in production. Even after your environment is correctly set up for a single application, relationships and dependencies between applications need to be understood and managed. Finally, there are always new tools, libraries, and applications available on the Internet, which you can build on when creating your own projects. As your environment becomes more complex, it can be quite a challenge to keep everything working correctly and up to date.

The Microsoft Web Platform Installer, as shown in Figure 50-6, is a simple tool designed to manage the software that you have installed on your web servers and development machine.

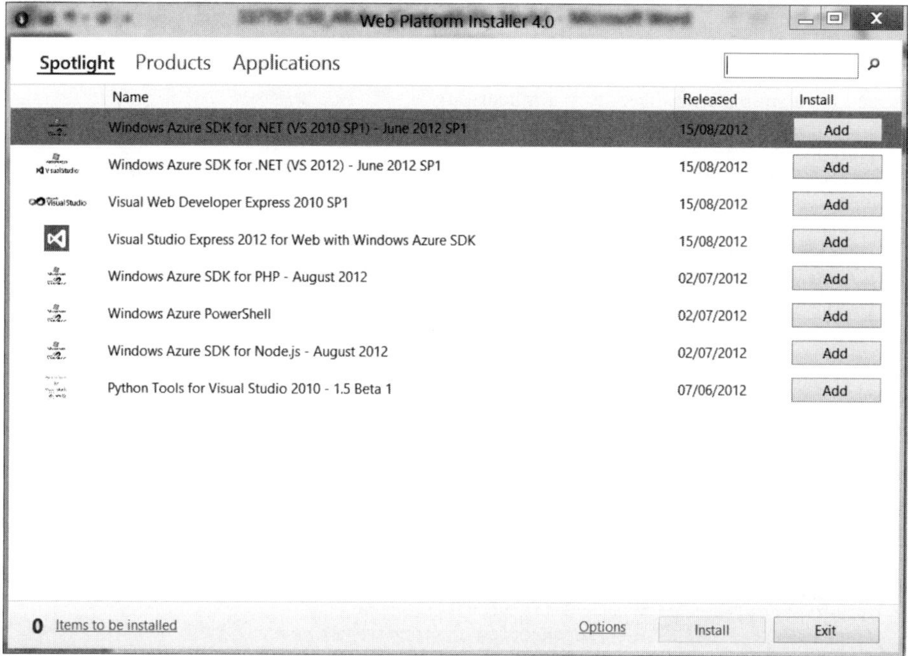

FIGURE 50-6

After you download the Web Platform Installer from `http://www.microsoft.com/web`, you can run it as many times as you like. It can detect which components you already have on your machine, and you can add and remove components with the click of a button. It can even take care of dependencies between components and install everything you need.

The Web Platform Installer can manage components beyond just the Web Platform. Also available is a collection of applications from the Microsoft Web Application Gallery at `http://www.microsoft.com/web/gallery`. These applications are filed under various categories under the Web Applications tab. Just like the components in the Web Platform, these applications can have their own prerequisites and the Web Platform Installer can ensure they are installed.

If you are already packaging your web application for deployment with the Web Deploy Package option from the Publish dialog, it is ready to be distributed using the Web Platform Installer. You can get your application added to the Web Application Gallery by filling in a simple form on the Microsoft Web portal. After your application is approved, it shows up ready to be installed on any machine with the Web Platform Installer on it.

Extending the Web Platform Installer

As mentioned in the previous section, it is quite easy to have your application included in the Web Application Gallery to make it available to a large audience. There are some scenarios in which you would like to take advantage of the Web Platform Installer but do not want to make your application publicly available. This might be because your application is used privately within your company or because your application is not yet ready for release and you want to test the deployment procedure.

The Web Platform Installer relies on atom feeds to ensure that the list of components and products that it installs are always kept up to date. Each entry in these feeds corresponds to an application or component in the user interface of the Web Platform Installer. The Web Platform and Web Application tabs each come from different feeds at `http://www.microsoft.com/web/webpi/2.0/WebProductList.xml` and `http://www.microsoft.com/web/webpi/2.0/WebApplicationList.xml`, respectively. In addition to these two feeds, each installation of the Web Platform Installer can specify additional feeds that reference more components.

Here is a sample feed for a simple timesheets web application:

```
<?xml version="1.0" encoding="utf-8"?>
<feed xmlns="http://www.w3.org/2005/Atom">
  <version>1.0.0</version>
  <title>Adventure Works Product WebPI Feed</title>
  <link href="http://www.professionalvisualstudio.com/SampleProductFeed.xml" />
  <updated>2012-08-15T08:29:14Z</updated>
  <author>
    <name>Adventure Works</name>
    <uri>http://www.professionalvisualstudio.com</uri>
 </author>
 <id>http://www.professionalvisualstudio.com/SampleProductFeed.xml</id>

 <entry>

    <productId>TimeSheets</productId>
    <title resourceName="Entry_AppGallerySIR_Title">Adventure Works Timesheets</title>

    <summary resourceName="Entry_AppGallerySIR_Summary">
       The Adventure Works corporate Timesheeting system</summary>
    <longSummary resourceName="Entry_AppGallerySIR_LongSummary">
       The Adventure Works corporate Timesheeting system</longSummary>
    <productFamily resourceName="TestTools">Human Resources</productFamily>

    <version>1.0.0</version>
    <images>
      <icon>c:\AdventureWorksIcon.png</icon>
    </images>
    <author>
      <name>Adventure Works IT</name>
      <uri>http://www.professionalvisualstudio.com</uri>
    </author>
    <published>2012-08-19T23:30:48Z</published>

    <discoveryHint>
      <or>
        <discoveryHint>
          <registry>
            <keyPath>HKEY_LOCAL_MACHINE\SOFTWARE\AdventureWorks\Timesheets</keyPath>
            <valueName>Version</valueName>
            <valueValue>1.0.0</valueValue>
          </registry>
        </discoveryHint>
```

```
        <discoveryHint>
          <file>
            <filePath>%ProgramFiles%\AdventureWorks\Timesheets.exe</filePath>
          </file>
        </discoveryHint>
      </or>
    </discoveryHint>

    <dependency>
      <productId>IISManagementConsole</productId>
    </dependency>

    <installers>
      <installer>
        <id>1</id>
        <languageId>en</languageId>
        <architectures>
          <x86 />
        </architectures>
        <osList>
          <os>
            <!-- the product is supported on Vista/Windows Server SP1 + -->
            <minimumVersion>
              <osMajorVersion>6</osMajorVersion>
              <osMinorVersion>0</osMinorVersion>
              <spMajorVersion>0</spMajorVersion>
            </minimumVersion>
            <osTypes>
              <Server />
              <HomePremium />
              <Ultimate />
              <Enterprise />
              <Business />
            </osTypes>
          </os>
        </osList>
        <eulaURL>http://www.professionalvisualstudio.com/eula.html</eulaURL>

        <installerFile>
          <!-- size in KBs -->
          <fileSize>1024</fileSize>
          <installerURL>http://www.professionalvisualstudio.com/Timesheets_x86.msi
          </installerURL>
          <sha1>111222FFF000BBB444555EEEAAA777888999DDDD</sha1>
        </installerFile>

        <installCommands>
          <msiInstall>
            <msi>%InstallerFile%</msi>
          </msiInstall>
        </installCommands>
      </installer>
    </installers>
  </entry>

  <tabs>
    <tab>
    <groupTab>
    <id>AdventureWorksHRTab</id>
    <name>Adventure Works Human Resources</name>
    <description>Adventure Works HR Apps</description>
    <groupingId>HRProductFamilyGrouping</groupingId>
```

```
      </groupTab>
      </tab>
    </tabs>

    <groupings>
      <grouping>
        <id>HRProductFamilyGrouping</id>
        <attribute>productFamily</attribute>
        <include>
          <item>Human Resources</item>
        </include>
      </grouping>
    </groupings>
  </feed>
```

The first part specifies some standard information about the feed, including the date it was last updated and author information. This is all useful if the feed is consumed using a normal feed reader. Following this is a single `entry` node containing information about the application. The Web Platform Installer can use the value of `productId` to refer to the application in other places, including being listed as a dependency for other components.

The `discoveryHint` node determines if this application is already installed. The sample application can be detected by looking for a specific Registry key value or by looking for a specific application by name. If either one of these items is found, the Web Platform Installer considers this application to be already installed. In addition to these two kinds of hints, you can use an `msiProductCode` hint to detect applications installed via MSI.

The sample timesheets application has a dependency on the IIS Management Console. Each component that your application relies upon can be specified by its `productId`. If it is not already installed on the target machine, the Web Platform Installer installs it for you. In addition to dependencies, you can specify `incompatibilities` for your application, which can prevent both applications from installing at once.

The last component of the application entry is the `installers` element. There should be one `installer` element for each installer that you want to make available, and they should all have different identifiers. Each installer can be targeted at a specific range of languages, operating systems, and CPU architectures. If the target environment doesn't fall into this range, the installer will not be shown. Each installer should specify an installer file, which will be downloaded to a local cache before the specified `installCommands` are executed against it.

> **NOTE** *An installer file requires a size and a SHA1 hash so that the Web Platform Installer can verify that the file has been downloaded correctly. Microsoft provides a tool called File Checksum Integrity Verifier (*`fciv.exe`*), which can be used to generate the hash. You can download this tool from* `http://download.microsoft.com`.

The final two elements relate to what displays in the Web Platform Installer user interface. Each `tab` element adds to the list of tabs on the left. In the example, you add a tab based on a `grouping` of products, which is defined in the `groupings` element based on the `productFamily` attribute.

To add this feed to a Web Platform Installer instance, click the Options link to bring up the Options page. Enter the URL to the atom feed into the textbox, and click the Add Feed button. When you click OK the Web Platform Installer refreshes all the feeds and reloads all the applications including the Adventure Works timesheets application, as shown in Figure 50-7.

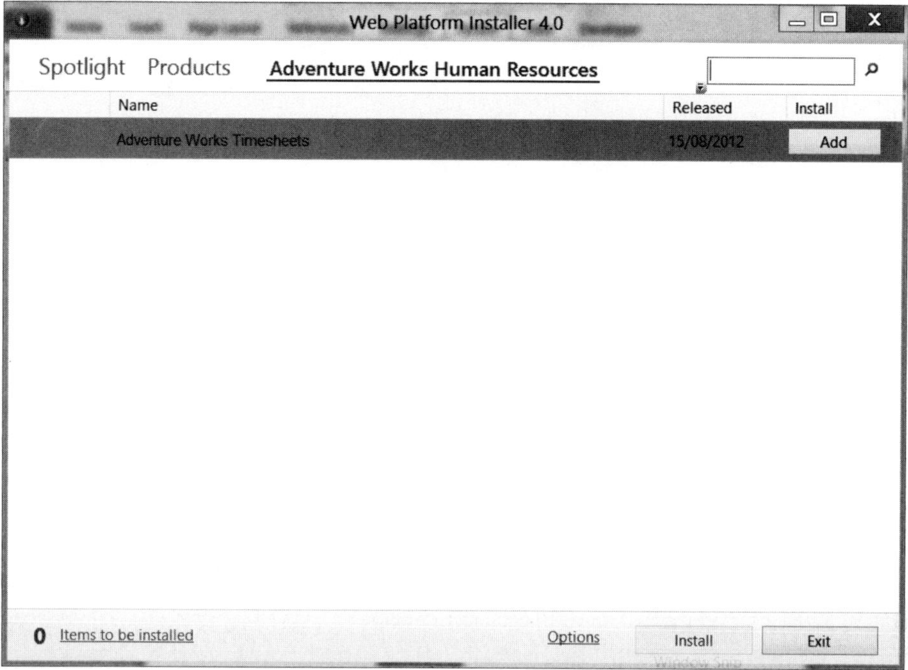

FIGURE 50-7

SUMMARY

This chapter showed you how to use a number of the features of Visual Studio 2012 to package your web applications and get them ready for deployment. The Web Deployment tool makes deployment to a number of environments and machines quick and painless. The Windows Installer Toolkit provides a mechanism to perform a typical installation of a web application. Finally, the Web Platform Installer provides you with an easy way to reach a large number of potential customers or to manage your own suite of enterprise applications.

PART XI
Customizing and Extending Visual Studio

51

The Automation Model

WHAT'S IN THIS CHAPTER?

- Understanding the Visual Studio extensibility options
- Working with the Visual Studio automation model

Often you will find yourself performing repetitive tasks when working in Visual Studio, and wish you could bundle all those tasks into a single automated task, streamlining your workflow, decreasing your frustration at doing the same thing repeatedly, and consequently increasing your productivity. Alternatively, perhaps you want to add functionality to Visual Studio to share with other developers in your company (or even around the world). Fortunately, Visual Studio has been designed to be very extensible — in fact, many features that you may have thought were built into Visual Studio are actually extensions themselves! This extensibility is exposed to make it very easy to add the functionality to Visual Studio that suits your requirements. Extensibility points include automating tasks, adding new tool windows, adding features to the code editor, adding your own menu items (including items to the code editor's context menu), creating debug visualizers, creating your own wizards, extending existing dialogs, and even adding your own editors/designers and programming languages. This chapter looks at the options available for extending Visual Studio and takes a look at the automation model used by add-ins.

VISUAL STUDIO EXTENSIBILITY OPTIONS

Unfortunately, the extensibility story in Visual Studio is a bit murky because a number of different means exist to extend Visual Studio, and it can be hard to determine which method you should use for what you want to achieve. Here are the various extensibility options available for Visual Studio, and the context in which it is most appropriate to use each:

- **Add-ins** work using the Visual Studio automation model, enabling you to create tool windows and wizards, and integrate other features seamlessly within the IDE. Add-ins are compiled projects (in your favorite .NET language or Visual C++), enabling you to ship a binary to other developers rather than the code itself. Chapter 52, "Add-Ins," covers how to develop add-ins for Visual Studio 2012.
- **VSPackages** are a part of the Visual Studio SDK (a separate download and install) and provide even more power than add-ins. VSPackages enable you to access the core internal interfaces in Visual Studio, and thus are ideally suited to integrating your own editors, designers, and

programming languages into Visual Studio. Coverage of VSPackages, however, is beyond the scope of this book. More information of VSPackages can be found in the book *Professional Visual Studio Extensibility* by Keyvan Nayyeri.

- **Managed Extensibility Framework (MEF) component parts** enable you to extend the WPF-based code editor in Visual Studio 2012 to change its appearance and behavior. If you want to add features to the code editor, this is the best option for your needs. Chapter 53, "Managed Extensibility Framework (MEF)," covers how to develop code editor extensions for Visual Studio 2012.

The next couple of chapters take you through some of the various ways in which you can extend Visual Studio, including using add-ins and the Managed Extensibility Framework (MEF). However, this chapter continues by looking at the core Visual Studio 2012 automation model that these extensibility components rely upon to interact with Visual Studio.

THE VISUAL STUDIO AUTOMATION MODEL

The Visual Studio automation model, also known as Development Tools Extensibility (abbreviated as DTE, which you see used in the automation model), is an object model exposed by Visual Studio that you can program against to interact with the IDE. This object model enables you to perform many actions in Visual Studio to achieve a required behavior, handle events raised by Visual Studio (such as when a command has been activated), and various other functions such as displaying a custom dockable tool window within the Visual Studio IDE.

This object model is the means by which many components interact with the Visual Studio IDE, so this section takes a deeper look at its structure and the functionality that it exposes.

An Overview of the Automation Model

The Visual Studio automation model (DTE) is a COM-based object model that has been added to with each new version of Visual Studio. As you can imagine, the evolution over time can make it somewhat confusing and messy.

DTE consists of various COM interfaces and their associated implementations covering the facets of functionality in Visual Studio. Because the concrete classes mostly implement a corresponding interface, you can expect to see lots of pair classes: an interface and its implementation. For example, the root object is the DTE class, which implements the `_DTE` interface.

By their very nature, interfaces don't support extensibility and should never be changed because any change in their structure breaks the structure of any class that implements the original interface. As Visual Studio matured and new versions were released (each requiring new functionality to be added to the existing classes in the object model), this created a problem. Microsoft couldn't update the existing interfaces or it would cause problems with existing add-ins, so instead it decided to create new versions of the interfaces with each new Visual Studio version by deriving from the previous version and adding the new requirements to it. These new interfaces were suffixed with a revision number, so they didn't have the same name as their predecessor, thus creating the messy and unfriendly model existing today where multiple interfaces/classes represent the same part of the object model.

For example, you can check out the `Debugger`, `Debugger2`, `Debugger3`, `Debugger4`, and `Debugger5` interfaces. The `Debugger` interface was a part of Visual Studio 2003 and was the original interface. `Debugger2` is an updated version of `Debugger` for Visual Studio 2005; `Debugger3` came with Visual Studio 2008; `Debugger4` came with Visual Studio 2008 SP1; and `Debugger5` came with Visual Studio 2010. The root DTE interface also has a revision called DTE2, and you can normally use this rather than its predecessor.

What this means in practical terms is that navigating the object model hierarchy isn't straightforward. The model can expose the methods on the classes in the early manifestation of the model, but you need to cast the object to a more recent interface to access the functions it exposes. For example, the first iteration of the `Solution` object didn't provide the ability to create a solution folder — this didn't come until later where the `AddSolutionFolder` method was exposed on the object by the `Solution2` interface. So the following code will *not* work:

C#

```
DTE.Solution.AddSolutionFolder("TestFolder"); // Will not work
```

VB

```
DTE.Solution.AddSolutionFolder("TestFolder") 'Will not work
```

but this code will work:

C#

```
Solution2 solution = (Solution2)DTE.Solution;
Solution.AddSolutionFolder("TestFolder");
```

VB

```
Dim solution As Solution2 = DirectCast(DTE.Solution, Solution2)
solution.AddSolutionFolder("TestFolder")
```

As you can see, this makes using the automation model difficult to work with. It is frequently necessary to cast objects as interfaces to access the wanted methods and properties, also creating that "code smell" that is often associated with less-than-desirable implementations.

Because the underlying automation model is COM-based and you use managed code to interact with it, you need to use interop assemblies to provide the bridge between your managed code and the COM object model. Unfortunately, like the object model, these are somewhat messy, too. An additional interop assembly has been added with each version of Visual Studio, so your project needs to reference each interop assembly, from the base interop assembly up to the one released with the lowest version of Visual Studio that your add-in can support. For example, if you create add-ins that support Visual Studio 2010, you need to have references to your project to `EnvDTE.dll` (from Visual Studio 2003), `EnvDTE80.dll` (from Visual Studio 2005), `EnvDTE90.dll` (from Visual Studio 2008), `EnvDTE90a.dll` (from Visual Studio 2008 SP1), and `EnvDTE100.dll` (from Visual Studio 2010). This chain of references is just as required, even if you are creating your add-in in Visual Studio 2012.

> **NOTE** *In Visual Studio 2010 and Visual Studio 2012, the Visual Studio SDK somewhat takes the place of the Visual Studio automation model, with fewer new features in Visual Studio added to the automation model and more focus and emphasis placed on using VSPackages instead (in the Visual Studio SDK). This means that Visual Studio 2012 doesn't have a Debugger6 interface. But, despite its flaws, the Visual Studio automation model is still functional and can perform many of the common tasks when integrating with Visual Studio.*

Now take a look at some of the various functional areas of Visual Studio that the automation model exposes, including solutions and projects, documents and windows, commands, debuggers, and events. All these exist under the root `DTE` object (which should be cast to `DTE2` to expose the more recent revision of this object).

> **NOTE** *The code examples are simply code snippets. They are not intended to be standalone solutions but to be integrated into existing projects.*

Solutions and Projects

The `DTE.Solutions` object enables you to automate the currently open solution, such as enumerate the projects that it contains, create a new project in the solution (or remove a project), add a solution folder, get/update solution configuration and properties, get/update its build configuration, or even open a new solution in the Visual Studio IDE and work with that. The following code demonstrates enumerating the projects in a solution and printing the project names and the number of project items in each project to the Output window:

C#

```
foreach (Project project in DTE.Solution.Projects)
    Debug.WriteLine(project.Name + " contains " +
                    project.ProjectItems.Count.ToString() + " project items");
```

VB

```
For Each project As Project In DTE.Solution.Projects
    Debug.WriteLine(project.Name & " contains " & _
                project.ProjectItems.Count.ToString() & " project items")
Next project
```

> **NOTE** *You can also enumerate the projects in the active solution using the* `DTE.ActiveSolutionProjects` *collection.*

You can also program against the projects in the solution. This includes enumerating the project items in a project and the files it contains. You can also get/update the project's configuration and properties, and add or remove items from the project:

C#

```
Project project = DTE.Solution.Projects.Item[0];
foreach (ProjectItem projectItem in project.ProjectItems)
{
    Debug.WriteLine(projectItem.Name);
}
```

VB

```
Dim project As Project = DTE.Solution.Projects.Item(1) 'Get first project
   For Each projectItem As ProjectItem In project.ProjectItems
    Debug.WriteLine(projectItem.Name)
Next projectItem
```

Windows and Documents

Windows in Visual Studio are either tool windows (such as the Solution Explorer, Tasks window, and so on) or document windows (files open in the code editor or a designer). Working with all types of windows is relatively simple.

You can enumerate through all the open windows and get details of each window as follows:

C#

```
' This includes both tool windows and document windows
foreach (Window2 window in DTE.Windows)
{
    Debug.WriteLine(window.Caption + " | State = " + window.WindowState.ToString());
}
```

VB

```
' This includes both tool windows and document windows
For Each window As Window2 In DTE.Windows
    Debug.WriteLine(window.Caption & " | State = " & window.WindowState.ToString())
Next window
```

Next, take a look at how to work with tool windows. Use the following code to get a reference to a window (regardless of whether it's open) and interact with the window (activating it, showing it, hiding it, collapsing it, pinning it, and so on):

C#

```
Window2 window = DTE.Windows.Item(Constants.vsWindowKindTaskList);
window.Visible = true;     // Show it
window.IsFloating = false; // Dock it
window.AutoHides = false;  // Pin it
window.Activate();
```

VB

```
Dim window As Window2 = DTE.Windows.Item(Constants.vsWindowKindTaskList)
window.Visible = True 'Show it
window.IsFloating = False 'Dock it
window.AutoHides = False 'Pin it
window.Activate()
```

You can get a reference to a specific tool window (such as the Task List), and interact with its functionality (such as adding tasks to the Task List):

C#

```
TaskList tasksWindow = DTE.ToolWindows.TaskList;
tasksWindow.TaskITems.Add("", "", "Created by a program");
```

VB

```
Dim tasksWindow As TaskList = DTE.ToolWindows.TaskList
tasksWindow.TaskItems.Add("", "", "Created by a program")
```

As you can see, working with the tool windows is fairly straightforward. Now look at how to work with document windows. You can get a reference to the active window in the IDE like so:

C#

```
Window2 window = DTE.ActiveWindow;
```

VB

```
Dim window As Window2 = DTE.ActiveWindow
```

You can even obtain a reference to the Visual Studio IDE window itself to manipulate:

C#

```
Window2 window = DTE.MainWindow;
```

VB

```
Dim window As Window2 = DTE.MainWindow
```

You can automate the document windows in Visual Studio, including opening or closing a document window, activating it, and getting the project item object opened in the document window. The following example enumerates through the open document windows, printing the filename and its path to the output window:

C#

```
foreach (Document document in DTE.Documents)
{
    Debug.WriteLine(document.Name + ", Path=" + document.Path);
}
```

VB

```
For Each document As Document In DTE.Documents
    Debug.WriteLine(document.Name & ", Path=" & document.Path)
Next document
```

To get a reference to the active document window, use

C#

```
Document document = DTE.ActiveDocument;
```

VB

```
Dim document As Document = DTE.ActiveDocument
```

You can use the `DTE.WindowConfigurations` collection to manipulate the configuration of windows in the IDE.

Commands

Every executable action in Visual Studio is represented by a command. For example, all menu items execute a command when selected. Every command has a unique name, numeric ID (within its grouping), and GUID designating its grouping. Visual Studio has thousands of commands, as you can see by enumerating the `DTE.Commands` collection like so:

C#

```
foreach (Command command in DTE.Commands)
{
    Debug.WriteLine(command.Name + ", ID=" + command.ID + ", GUID=" + command.Guid);
}
```

VB

```
For Each command As Command In DTE.Commands
    Debug.WriteLine(command.Name & ", ID=" & command.ID & ", GUID=" & command.Guid)
Next command
```

To perform an action in Visual Studio through your add-in, you need to get a reference to the appropriate command and execute it. For example, say you want to comment out the selected code in the code editor. This command is called `Edit.CommentSelection`, and you can execute it using the following code:

C#

```
DTE.ExecuteCommand("Edit.CommentSelection");
```

VB

```
DTE.ExecuteCommand("Edit.CommentSelection")
```

You can also listen for commands being executed, which are raised by Visual Studio as events that you can handle. An event will be raised before the command is executed, and another event will be raised after the command has completed. For example, you may want to do something particular when text is pasted into the code editor (that is, respond to the `Edit.Paste` command). Handling events is discussed briefly at the end of this chapter and is discussed further in Chapter 52, "Add-Ins."

Debugger

You can control the various functions of the Visual Studio debugger using the `DTE.Debugger` automation object. This enables you to work with breakpoints, control code execution, and examine various aspects of the application being debugged (including processes and threads).

The following code demonstrates enumerating through all the breakpoints in the current solution:

C#

```
foreach (Breakpoint2 breakpoint in DTE.Debugger.Breakpoints)
{
    Debug.WriteLine(breakpoint.Name + " | File: " & breakpoint.File +
                    " | Function: " + breakpoint.FunctionName +
                    " | Line: " + breakpoint.FileLine);
}
```

VB

```
For Each breakpoint As Breakpoint2 In DTE.Debugger.Breakpoints
    Debug.WriteLine(breakpoint.Name & " | File: " & breakpoint.File & _
                    " | Function: " & breakpoint.FunctionName & _
                    " | Line: " & breakpoint.FileLine)
Next breakpoint
```

You can also control the execution of code when debugging an application, such as starting debugging, terminating debugging, stepping over a line of code, running to the current cursor position, and so on. The following code demonstrates starting the current solution in the debugger:

C#

```
DTE.Debugger.Go();
```

VB

```
DTE.Debugger.Go()
```

Events

The automation model enables you to listen for various actions in Visual Studio and respond to them by raising events that you can handle. The events are categorized into a number of objects according to their functional area under the `DTE.Events` object, including `DocumentEvents`, `WindowEvents`, `BuildEvents`, `SolutionEvents`, `ProjectsEvents`, `DebuggerEvents`, and many others. Chapter 52 demonstrates handling events in add-ins.

SUMMARY

In this chapter you were introduced to the various means of extending the functionality of Visual Studio 2012. You then took a look at the structure and capabilities of the Visual Studio automation model, which components use to extend Visual Studio. The following chapter looks at how add-ins use this means of extending Visual Studio using this object model.

52

Add-Ins

WHAT'S IN THIS CHAPTER?

- Understanding the structure of add-ins
- Creating add-ins
- Testing and debugging add-ins
- Deploying add-ins

As detailed in Chapter 51, "The Automation Model," Visual Studio add-ins are components that run within Visual Studio and extend its functionality via the Visual Studio automation model.

This chapter takes you through the process of creating a Visual Studio add-in that integrates with the Visual Studio IDE to display a tool window (that enables you to store some notes), perform actions in Visual Studio (copy selected text from the code editor), and handle Visual Studio events (capture the cut and copy command events from the code editor).

DEVELOPING AN ADD-IN

When you create a Visual Studio add-in project, the Add-in Wizard appears and helps you to create the appropriate structure and base functionality in your add-in based on your input to its questions. From there you are on your own to implement the functionality from this base framework. You start from the base that it gives you and gradually add functionality to make it a useful tool.

The Add-in Wizard

Start by creating a new project, using the Visual Studio Add-in project template in the Extensibility project category (under the Other Project Types category), as shown in Figure 52-1.

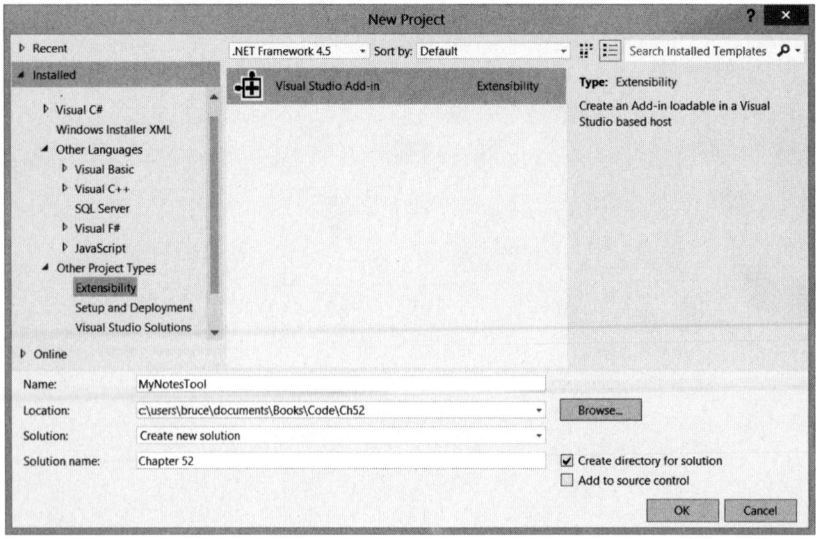

FIGURE 52-1

Clicking OK starts the Add-In Wizard. This section goes through each of the wizard's steps and the options that each step provides.

There is a welcome page at the start, which gives a short description of the wizard (as shown in Figure 52-2).

In the next step of the Add-In Wizard (as shown in Figure 52-3) you need to choose a development language for your add-in (because the Visual Studio Add-In project template was not under a particular language category in the New Project dialog). You have four options — Visual C#, Visual Basic, Visual C++/CLR, and Visual C++/ATL. Visual Studio generates the project in the language that you choose here.

Now you need to choose an application host for your add-in (as shown in Figure 52-4). A single application host is available for your add-ins: the Visual Studio 2012 IDE. You can check or uncheck each host to select or deselect it. Your add-in will be available to the application hosts that you select here.

FIGURE 52-2

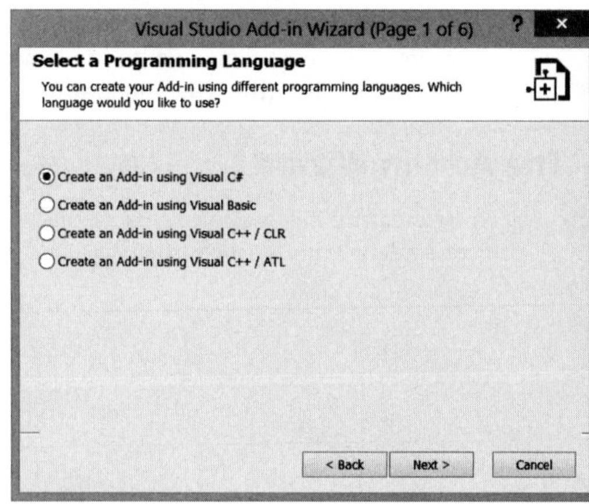

FIGURE 52-3

Now you can enter a name and description for your add-in (as shown in Figure 52-5). This information is what end users see in the Add-in Manager dialog in Visual Studio for your add-in.

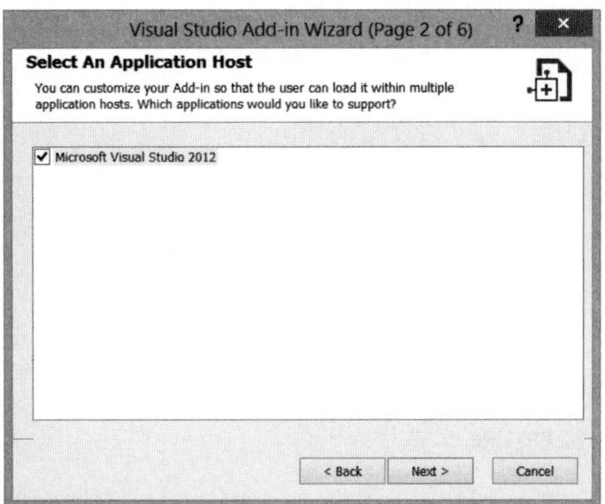

FIGURE 52-4

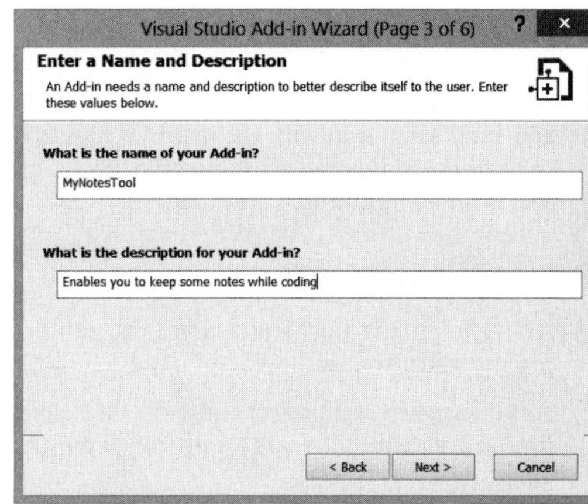

FIGURE 52-5

The next step contains the options for how your add-in will load and interact with Visual Studio. You can check three options to include in your add-in (as shown in Figure 52-6). The first option specifies that your add-in will have a menu item in the Tools menu that can be used to activate it. The second option indicates that you would like to load your add-in when the Visual Studio IDE starts, and the third option is used to specify that your add-in doesn't show any modal user interfaces, and thus can be used with command-line builds.

The next step (as shown in Figure 52-7) enables you to display some information in the Visual Studio About box for your add-in. Doing so is especially useful if you are releasing your add-in as a product.

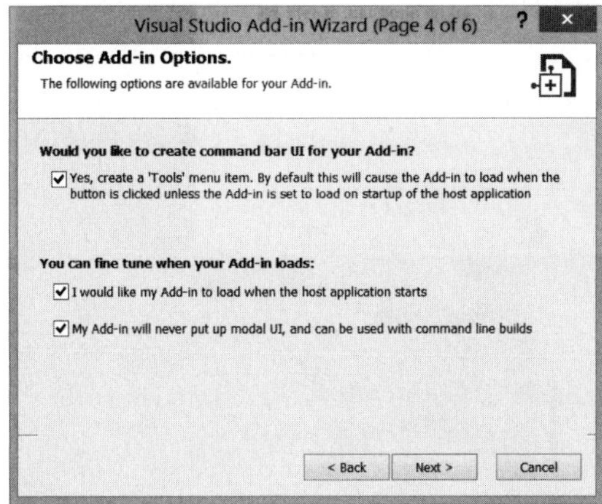

FIGURE 52-6

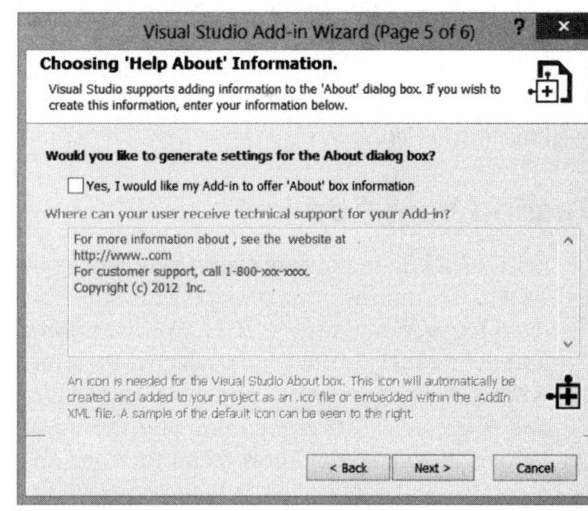

FIGURE 52-7

In the final step you see a summary of what you have chosen in your wizard (as shown in Figure 52-8). At this stage, you can go back and change your options or click the Finish button to go ahead and generate the solution and initial code for your add-in.

After you click the Finish button, Visual Studio generates a solution with the required files to create the add-in, configured according to the options you selected for the add-in.

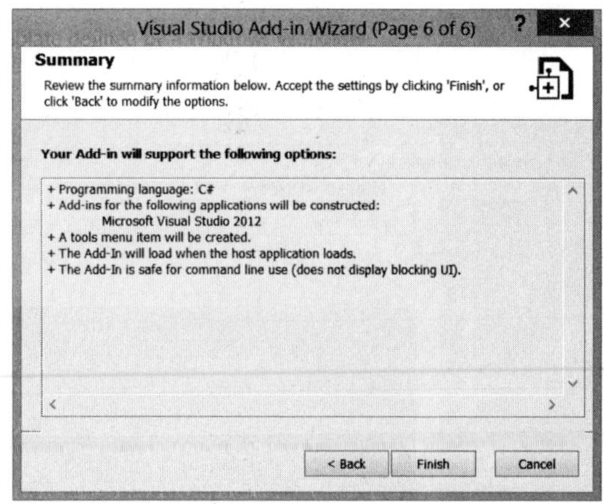

FIGURE 52-8

Project Structure

After the project has been created, you can find the project structure, as shown in Figure 52-9.

As you can see, the project consists of a `Connect.cs` (or `Connect.vb`) file and two files with the `.AddIn` extension.

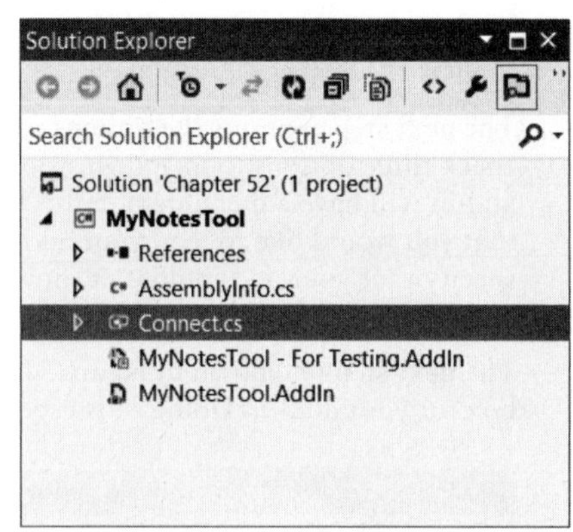

FIGURE 52-9

The `Connect.cs`/`Connect.vb` file contains the core class that controls the add-in. The `.AddIn` files are used to enable Visual Studio to discover the add-in so it can load it. One is located in your project folder, but the other is a linked file (`MyNotesTool - For Testing.AddIn`) located in the `My Documents\Visual Studio 2012\Addins` folder of your Windows user profile. As its name suggests, this file is used so that Visual Studio can discover your add-in during its testing and debugging. The reason the file is in this folder is that it is one of the paths that Visual Studio looks in to discover add-in files. If you open both files, you can find that they are identical with one exception — the Assembly node of the linked file includes the full path to the compiled add-in assembly, whereas the other includes only the name of the assembly (expecting it to be in the same folder as the `.AddIn` file). We take a closer look at `.AddIn` files later in this chapter.

Testing Your Add-in

First, check to make sure everything works OK by simply running your project. This starts a new instance of Visual Studio 2012 in which you can test and debug the add-in. If you selected the options in the wizard to start automatically when the IDE is started and to create a Tool menu item, you should see a menu item at the top of the Tools menu for your add-in, with a default smiley face icon (which you can change to your own icon), as shown in Figure 52-10.

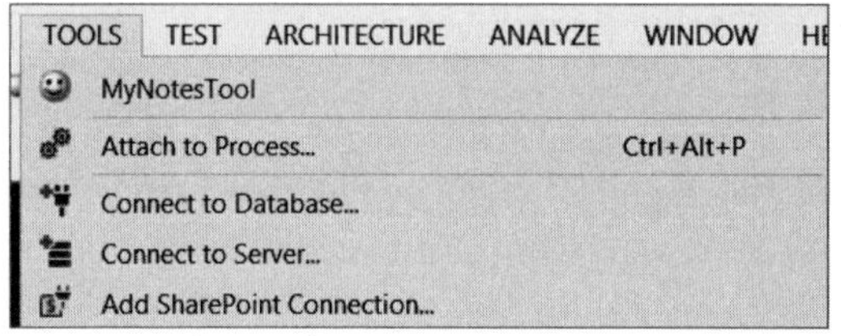

FIGURE 52-10

If you haven't selected the add-in to load automatically with the IDE, you can start it from the Add-In Manager (Tools ➪ Add-In Manager) and put a check mark in the check box next to its name, as shown in Figure 52-11.

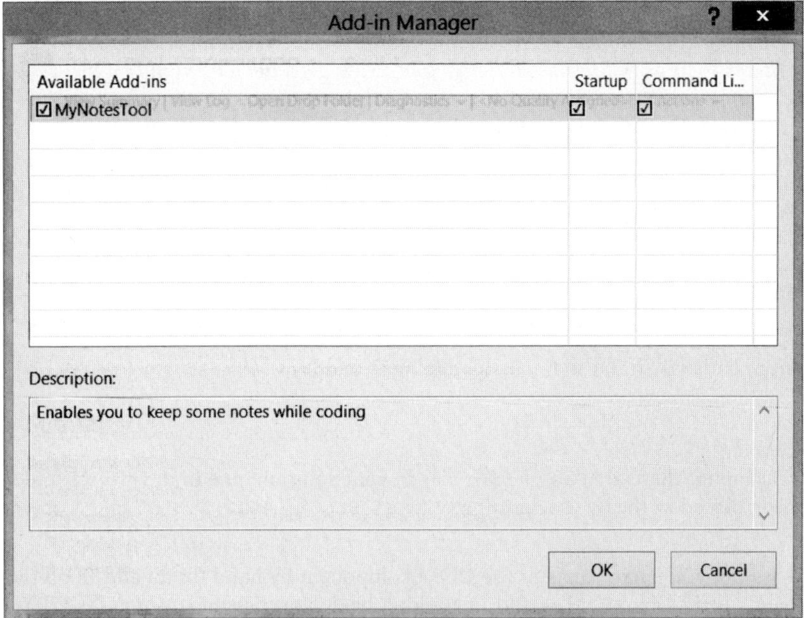

FIGURE 52-11

If your add-in does not appear in the Add-In Manager, Visual Studio cannot find the `.AddIn` file. Go to Tools ➪ Options, and select the Add-In Security category (under the Environment category, as shown in Figure 52-12). Make sure that the path where the testing `.AddIn` file is located is listed in the Add-In File Paths list. It's also possible that the environment variables used in this dialog are not declared in your system, so check these, too.

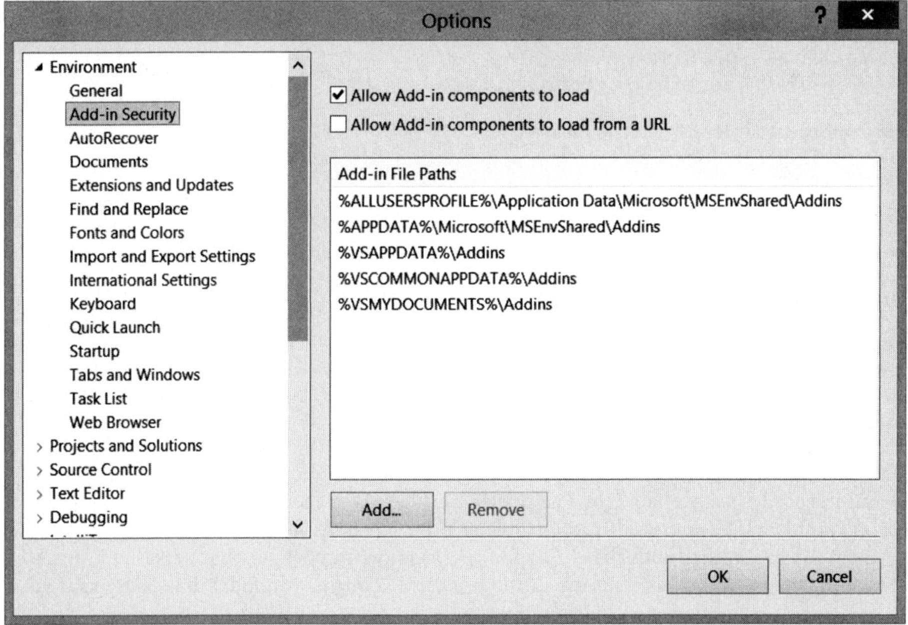

FIGURE 52-12

WARNING *Not having your environment variables defined is a common problem with getting your Add-Ins to appear. Specifically, the* `VSMYDOCUMENTS` *(which should point to the location where Visual Studio 2012 creates the* `.AddIn` *file) environment variable is not always defined properly after you upgrade from Visual Studio 2010. To determine if you are having problem, add the path to where the* `.AddIn` *file is located explicitly to the Add-In Security screen as described in the "Testing Your Add-in" section. If after doing so your add-in appears when you run the Extensibility project, then the problem is that* `VSMYDOCUMENTS` *is not defined. A more permanent fix would then be to create an environment variable called* `VSMYDOCUMENTS` *that references* `C:\Users\<your user name>\Documents\Visual Studio 2012`.

Close the debugging instance of Visual Studio to finish debugging the add-in.

The .AddIn File

As mentioned earlier in this chapter, there are two `.AddIn` files in your solution: one in the project folder and a linked file that has been placed in the `My Documents\Visual Studio 2012\Addins` folder on your machine.

In early versions of Visual Studio, you had to register the COM component by hand for an add-in on the machine, making deployment a little difficult. (The add-in couldn't be deployed using a simple XCOPY.) `.AddIn` files were designed to make the process of deploying add-ins easier. By placing the `.AddIn` file in a folder that Visual Studio is configured to look in, Visual Studio can discover your add-in and load it (without worrying about the need to register the add-in). Essentially, `.AddIn` files point Visual Studio to where your add-in is (which is usually in the same path as the `.AddIn` file).

`.AddIn` files are XML files that point Visual Studio to the location of your add-in. They also contain configuration information such as the hosts the add-in should be accessible to (including different versions of Visual Studio), the description that appears in the Add-in Manager, and the add-in's startup options.

If you open an `.AddIn` file, you can find XML similar to the following:

```
<?xml version="1.0" encoding="UTF-16" standalone="no"?>
<Extensibility xmlns="http://schemas.microsoft.com/AutomationExtensibility">
    <HostApplication>
        <Name>Microsoft Visual Studio</Name>
        <Version>11.0</Version>
    </HostApplication>
    <Addin>
        <FriendlyName>My Notes</FriendlyName>
        <Description>Enables you to keep some notes while coding</Description>
        <Assembly>MyNotesTool.dll</Assembly>
        <FullClassName>MyNotesTool.Connect</FullClassName>
        <LoadBehavior>5</LoadBehavior>
        <CommandPreload>1</CommandPreload>
        <CommandLineSafe>1</CommandLineSafe>
    </Addin>
</Extensibility>
```

Of particular note are the `HostApplication` nodes, listing each host application name and its specific version that the add-in should be accessible to. The preceding file makes the add-in available to Visual Studio 2012. If you want to make your add-in accessible to other versions of Visual Studio, simply add additional `HostApplication` nodes, with the corresponding version number for that version of Visual Studio (Visual Studio 2010 = 10.0, Visual Studio 2008 = 9.0). Of course, you must make sure that you don't use features specific to Visual Studio 2012, and remove references to the higher EnvDTE dlls than the lowest version you are supporting.

> **NOTE** *If you upgrade an add-in from a previous version of Visual Studio, you need to add another* `HostApplication` *node to the existing* `.AddIn` *file, with a value of 11.0 in the* `Version` *node so that it runs under Visual Studio 2012.*

The Connect Class

This section looks at the structure of the core class that manages the add-in. The `Connect.cs` class (or `Connect.vb`) manages the life cycle of the add-in, and you can find a number of methods that handle the event notifications from the IDTExtensibility2 and IDTCommandTarget interfaces that are implemented by the class.

The IDTExtensibility2 interface exposes handlers for the events raised by Visual Studio that notifies the add-in at each point in its life cycle. The following methods form the IDTExtensibility2 interface:

- **`OnConnection`** — Called when the add-in is loaded by Visual Studio
- **`OnStartupComplete`** — Called when Visual Studio has finished loading
- **`OnAddInsUpdate`** — Called when the collection of add-ins in Visual Studio has changed
- **`OnBeginShutdown`** — Called when Visual Studio is shutting down
- **`OnDisconnection`** — Called when the add-in is being unloaded by Visual Studio

The IDTCommandTarget interface exposes handlers for the events of named commands used by the add-in. The following methods form the IDTCommandTarget interface:

- **`Exec`** — Called when a command used by the add-in is called from Visual Studio (such as when the menu item created under the Tools menu is selected). Visual Studio can pass this method the name of the command, so you can respond accordingly.
- **`QueryStatus`** — Called when the status of a command (such as whether it is available) is requested by Visual Studio.

Creating a Tool Window

Now that you have looked at the structure and life cycle of an add-in, it's time to add some functionality to interact with the Visual Studio IDE and implement some useful behavior. The sample you work through in this chapter creates a dockable tool window in Visual Studio that enables you to place some notes while working in Visual Studio. Unfortunately, the Add-In Wizard doesn't provide options to help in creating your own tool window (which is one of the more common requirements when writing add-ins), so you must do this yourself. This section takes you through the steps to do so.

> **NOTE** *Despite Visual Studio 2012 having its entire user interface written using WPF, you still have to use Windows Forms for your tool windows when creating add-ins. To use WPF for your tool windows, you need to use VSPackages in the Visual Studio 2012 SDK when extending Visual Studio instead.*

Add a new Windows Forms User Control item to your project, and call it `NotesUserControl` (`.cs` or `.vb`). Add a RichTextBox control to the user control, name it `rtbNotes`, set the `BorderStyle` property to `None`, and dock it to fill the area of the control.

Now return to the `Connect.cs` (or `.vb`) file, and add the following method to it to simplify the process of creating the tool window:

VB

```
Private toolWindow As Window2 = Nothing

Private Function CreateToolWindow(ByVal guid As String,
                                  ByVal windowTitle As String,
                                  ByVal classPath As String) As Object
    Dim windowObject As Object = Nothing

    Dim windows As Windows2 = DirectCast(_applicationObject.Windows, Windows2)
    Dim assemblyLocation As String = Assembly.GetCallingAssembly().Location

    toolWindow = DirectCast(windows.CreateToolWindow2(_addInInstance,
                                                      assemblyLocation, classPath,
                                                      windowTitle, guid,
                                                      windowObject), Window2)

    Return windowObject
End Function
```

C#

```
private Window2 toolWindow = null;

private object CreateToolWindow(string guid, string windowTitle, string classPath)
{
    object windowObject = null;

    Windows2 windows = (Windows2)_applicationObject.Windows;
    string assemblyLocation = Assembly.GetCallingAssembly().Location;

    toolWindow = (Window2)windows.CreateToolWindow2(_addInInstance,
        assemblyLocation, classPath, windowTitle, guid, ref windowObject);

    return windowObject;
}
```

> **NOTE** *A reference needs to be maintained to the user control at the class level because windows of add-ins are not destroyed/cleaned up during the life cycle of the add-in — instead they are merely hidden.*

You can create the tool window when the menu item in the Tools menu is selected. You are notified of this in the `Exec` method, and you can notice that the wizard already created the code to respond to this. (Although it currently does nothing.) Use the following code to create the tool window and have it displayed in Visual Studio. (The code to be added to the method has been bolded.)

VB

```
Private notesUserControl As NotesUserControl

Public Sub Exec(ByVal commandName As String,
                ByVal executeOption As vsCommandExecOption,
```

```
                ByRef varIn As Object, ByRef varOut As Object,
                ByRef handled As Boolean) Implements IDTCommandTarget.Exec
    handled = False
    If executeOption = vsCommandExecOption.vsCommandExecOptionDoDefault Then
        If commandName = "MyNotesTool.Connect.MyNotesTool" Then
            ' An ID that uniquely identifies this tool window
            Dim windowID As String = "{fb9e4681-681d-4216-9a28-0f09f3528360}"

            ' Create the tool window if it hasn't already been created
            If toolWindow Is Nothing Then
                notesUserControl = DirectCast(CreateToolWindow(windowID,
                    "My Notes" , "MyNotesTool.NotesUserControl" ), NotesUserControl )
            End If

            ' Make the tool window visible if it's currently hidden
            toolWindow.Visible = True

            handled = True
            Return
        End If
    End If
End Sub
```

C#

```
private NotesUserControl notesUserControl;

public void Exec(string commandName, vsCommandExecOption executeOption,
                 ref object varIn, ref object varOut, ref bool handled)
{
    handled = false;
    if (executeOption == vsCommandExecOption.vsCommandExecOptionDoDefault)
    {
        if (commandName == "MyNotesTool.Connect.MyNotesTool")
        {
            // An ID that uniquely identifies this tool window
            string windowID = "{fb9e4681-681d-4216-9a28-0f09f3528360}" ;

            // Create the tool window if it hasn't already been created
            if (toolWindow == null)
            {
                notesUserControl = ( NotesUserControl)
                    CreateToolWindow(windowID, "My Notes" ,
                                     "MyNotesTool.NotesUserControl" );
            }

            // Make the tool window visible if it's currently hidden
            toolWindow.Visible = true;

            handled = true;
            return;
        }
    }
}
```

As you can see from the code, it's now a relatively easy process to create the window. You pass an ID that uniquely identifies this tool window, a window title, and the qualified name of the user control class to the `CreateToolWindow` method you created earlier, and it handles calling the extensibility model to create the tool window in Visual Studio.

Now, run your project and select the menu item for the add-in under the Tools menu. The user control displays as a tool window (as shown in Figure 52-13), which you can then move around and dock to the IDE as if it were any other tool window.

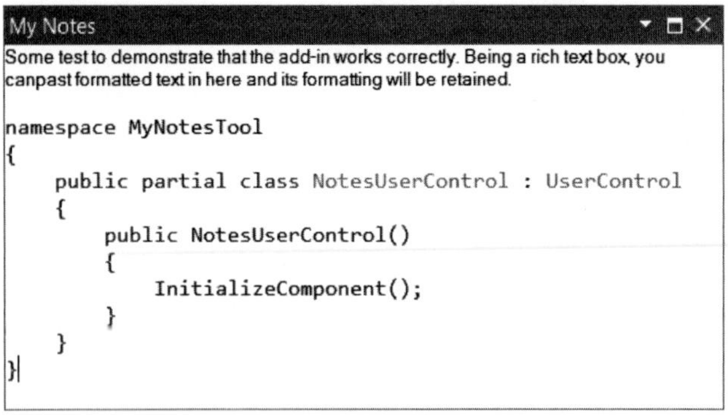

My Notes

Some test to demonstrate that the add-in works correctly. Being a rich text box, you canpast formatted text in here and its formatting will be retained.

```
namespace MyNotesTool
{
    public partial class NotesUserControl : UserControl
    {
        public NotesUserControl()
        {
            InitializeComponent();
        }
    }
}
```

FIGURE 52-13

> **NOTE** *Visual Studio remembers the location of the window (using its unique ID to store and retrieve these details), so the next time you load Visual Studio, the window appears where you last placed it. (Although this works only when the add-in is not being debugged.) However, for it to display when Visual Studio starts, you must create the tool window when the add-in starts (rather than when its menu item is selected).*

Accessing the Visual Studio Automation Model

You can now add your own additional functionality to the tool window (in the user control) such as loading and saving the text to a text file (if you want) as if you were programming a standard application. However, this example doesn't currently demonstrate integrating with the functionality of Visual Studio and the events it raises, so add a feature to demonstrate this by creating a button to take selected code from the code editor and insert it into the notes at the current caret position.

To get to the Visual Studio object model from the user control, you must make the class-level variable `_applicationObject` in the `Connect` class static and expose it publicly by wrapping it in a property, as shown in the following code:

VB

```
Private Shared _applicationObject As DTE2

Public ReadOnly Property ApplicationObject() As DTE2
    Get
        Return _applicationObject
    End Get
End Property
```

C#

```
private static DTE2 _applicationObject;

public static DTE2 ApplicationObject
{
    get { return Connect._applicationObject; }
}
```

Add a ToolStrip control to the user control with a button that copies the selected text in the code editor and inserts it into the textbox when clicked. In the event handler for this button, add the following code:

VB

```
Private Sub btnCopy_Click(ByVal sender As System.Object,
                          ByVal e As System.EventArgs) Handles btnCopy.Click
    If Not Connect.ApplicationObject.ActiveDocument Is Nothing Then
        Dim selection As TextSelection = DirectCast(
            Connect.ApplicationObject.ActiveDocument.Selection, TextSelection)

        rtbNotes.SelectedText = selection.Text
    End If
End Sub
```

C#

```
private void btnCopy_Click(object sender, EventArgs e)
{
    if (Connect.ApplicationObject.ActiveDocument != null)
    {
        TextSelection selection =
            Connect.ApplicationObject.ActiveDocument.Selection as TextSelection;

        rtbNotes.SelectedText = selection.Text;
    }
}
```

This takes the selected text from the active code editor document and inserts it at the current caret position in the RichTextBox in the user control. Note that the code will be unformatted (that is, no syntax coloring) when it's put into the RichTextBox. Alternatively, you can use the following code to copy the text out of the code editor and paste it into the RichTextBox, which would retain the syntax coloring but lose the existing contents of the clipboard:

VB

```
Private Sub btnCopy_Click(ByVal sender As System.Object,
                          ByVal e As System.EventArgs) Handles btnCopy.Click
    If Not Connect.ApplicationObject.ActiveDocument Is Nothing Then

        Connect.ApplicationObject.ActiveDocument.Selection.Copy()
        rtbNotes.Paste()
    End If
End Sub
```

C#

```
private void btnCopy_Click(object sender, EventArgs e)
{
    if (Connect.ApplicationObject.ActiveDocument != null)
    {
        Connect.ApplicationObject.ActiveDocument.Selection.Copy();
        rtbNotes.Paste();
    }
}
```

Handling Visual Studio Events

As a final example, handle an event raised by Visual Studio. Handle the Cut and the Copy command events (before the command is actually executed), get the selected text from the code editor, and automatically insert it into the RichTextBox.

First, you need to get a reference to the commands whose events you want to capture (the Cut and Copy commands), and then the command events objects themselves. C# developers also add an event handler for the `BeforeExecute` event for each command:

VB

```
Private WithEvents cutEvent As CommandEvents = Nothing
Private WithEvents copyEvent As CommandEvents = Nothing

Private Sub EnableAutoCopy()
    ' Enable the event listening for the Cut and Copy commands
    Dim cmdCut As Command = Connect.ApplicationObject.Commands.Item("Edit.Cut", 0)
    Dim cmdCopy As Command = Connect.ApplicationObject.Commands.Item("Edit.Copy",
                                                                             0)

    cutEvent = Connect.ApplicationObject.Events.CommandEvents(cmdCut.Guid,
                                                              cmdCut.ID)
    copyEvent = Connect.ApplicationObject.Events.CommandEvents(cmdCopy.Guid,
                                                               cmdCopy.ID)
End Sub
```

C#

```
private CommandEvents cutEvent = null;
private CommandEvents copyEvent = null;

private void EnableAutoCopy()
{
    // Enable the event listening for the Cut and Copy commands
    Command cmdCut = Connect.ApplicationObject.Commands.Item("Edit.Cut", 0);


    cutEvent = Connect.ApplicationObject.Events.get_CommandEvents(cmdCut.Guid,
                                                                  cmdCut.ID);
    cutEvent.BeforeExecute += new
        _dispCommandEvents_BeforeExecuteEventHandler(OnBeforeCutCopy);

    Command cmdCopy = Connect.ApplicationObject.Commands.Item("Edit.Copy", 0);

    copyEvent = Connect.ApplicationObject.Events.get_CommandEvents(cmdCopy.Guid,
                                                                   cmdCopy.ID);
    copyEvent.BeforeExecute += new
        _dispCommandEvents_BeforeExecuteEventHandler(OnBeforeCutCopy);
}
```

Now you can define the event handler method that will handle the `BeforeExecute` event for both commands, extracting the selected text from the code editor and inserting it into the RichTextBox:

VB

```
Private Sub OnBeforeCutCopy(ByVal guid As String, ByVal id As Integer,
                            ByVal customIn As Object, ByVal customOut As Object,
                            ByRef cancel As Boolean) _
                            Handles cutEvent.BeforeExecute, copyEvent.BeforeExecute
    Dim codeWindow As TextWindow = TryCast(
        Connect.ApplicationObject.ActiveWindow.Object, EnvDTE.TextWindow)

    If Not codeWindow Is Nothing Then
        rtbNotes.SelectedText = codeWindow.Selection.Text &
            Environment.NewLine & Environment.NewLine
    End If
End Sub
```

C#

```
private void OnBeforeCutCopy(string guid, int id, object customIn,
                             object customOut, ref bool cancel)
{
    TextWindow codeWindow = Connect.ApplicationObject.ActiveWindow.Object
                                                       as EnvDTE.TextWindow;

    if (codeWindow != null)
    {
        rtbNotes.SelectedText = codeWindow.Selection.Text +
            Environment.NewLine + Environment.NewLine;
    }
}
```

Finally, you need to clean things up when the add-in is unloaded and release any event handlers you have active. (The `CloseToolWindow` method will be called from the `Connect` class in the `OnDisconnection` method.)

VB

```
private void DisableAutoCopy()
{
    if (cutEvent != null)

        Marshal.ReleaseComObject(cutEvent);

    if (copyEvent != null)
        Marshal.ReleaseComObject(copyEvent);

    cutEvent = null;
    copyEvent = null;
}

public void CloseToolWindow()
{
    DisableAutoCopy();
}
```

C#

```
private void DisableAutoCopy()
{
    if (cutEvent != null)
        Marshal.ReleaseComObject(cutEvent);

    if (copyEvent != null)
        Marshal.ReleaseComObject(copyEvent);

    cutEvent = null;
    copyEvent = null;
}

public void CloseToolWindow()
{
    DisableAutoCopy();
}
```

DEPLOYING ADD-INS

Despite being a COM component (which typically require registration in Windows), Visual Studio add-ins are easy to deploy because of the `.AddIn` file, which enables Visual Studio to discover your add-in and use it.

As discussed earlier in the chapter, Visual Studio can look in each of the paths listed in the Options dialog (see Figure 52-12) for files with an `.AddIn` extension. Therefore, when deploying your add-in, you need to place the `.AddIn` file and the add-in assembly (that is, the `.dll` file) into one of these paths (typically a user profile's `My Documents\Visual Studio 2012\Addins` folder), enabling Visual Studio to discover and load your add-in when it starts up.

You can use a simple XCOPY operation to deploy your add-in to another user's machine, but the best way would be to create a setup program to do this for you. You could use a standard Windows installer package (`.msi`), but in this instance it's probably better to use a Visual Studio Content Installer package. Unfortunately, it's a manual process to create a Visual Studio Content Installer package, but it's easy to create. It essentially consist of your files packed into a zip file, but with a `.vsi` extension, and a specially formatted XML file (also included in the zip file) with a `.vscontent` extension that contains the details of the files to be installed (from the zip file) and where they are to be installed to.

Start by creating an XML file in your project with the name `MyNotesTool.vscontent`, and add the following content:

```
<VSContent xmlns="http://schemas.microsoft.com/developer/vscontent/2005">
  <Content>
    <FileName>MyNotesTool.Addin</FileName>
    <FileName>MyNotesTool.dll</FileName>
    <DisplayName>My Notes</DisplayName>
    <Description>
      Enables you to keep notes in a tool window in
      Visual Studio while you code.
    </Description>
    <FileContentType>Addin</FileContentType>
    <ContentVersion>2.0</ContentVersion>
  </Content>
</VSContent>
```

Now, in Windows Explorer (or your favorite zip tool), combine the `MyNotesTool.AddIn` file, the `MyNotesTool.dll` file, and the `MyNotesTool.vscontent` file into a zip file, and name it `MyNotesTool.vsi` (do not include the `.zip` extension). Now when people double-click this `.vsi` file, the add-in automatically installs and is ready for them to use when they next open Visual Studio.

SUMMARY

In this chapter, you were introduced to Visual Studio add-ins and went through the process of creating one that displayed a dockable tool window, retrieved text from the code editor, and responded to some code editor events. Finally, you looked at the best way to deploy your add-in to other developers.

53

Managed Extensibility Framework (MEF)

WHAT'S IN THIS CHAPTER?

- Architecting extensible applications
- Hosting the Managed Extensibility Framework in your applications
- Understanding the Visual Studio 2012 Editor components
- Extending the Visual Studio 2012 Editor
- Importing Visual Studio Services

Creating loosely coupled applications that can be extended after deployment can be a difficult process. You have many design decisions to make, including identifying and loading extensions that have been deployed, and making application services available to loaded extensions. The Managed Extensibility Framework (MEF) is an open source library created by Microsoft designed to reduce the complexity of creating extensible applications. It enables you to expose reusable parts of your application to plug-ins or extensions that are discovered and loaded at run time and design your application in a loosely coupled fashion.

Visual Studio 2012 uses the MEF library to provide extension points for the main editor control. It is expected that in future versions of Visual Studio, more areas will be exposed for this kind of extension.

This chapter is split into three sections. The first section is an introduction to how MEF works and how to use it in your own applications. The middle section describes the components of the Visual Studio 2012 Editor control and how they interact. The final section describes the process of extending the editor with MEF and provides a complete sample that emphasizes certain types of comment in your code.

> **NOTE** *The MEF library is revised on a regular basis. For the latest information about MEF, check* `http://mef.codeplex.com`.

GETTING STARTED WITH MEF

In this section, you create a simple application that demonstrates the manner in which most applications use the capabilities offered by MEF. How you include MEF in your project depends on which version of the .NET Framework you target. For .NET Framework 4.0, the MEF library is contained within the `System.ComponentModel.Composition` assembly, which is installed in the GAC as a part of the .NET Framework installation. If you target .NET 4.5, there is a version of MEF (appropriately named MEF 2) that is currently under development as of this writing. At the moment, you can download MEF 2 Previews from the same CodePlex project. If you plan to target Windows Store applications, you can use NuGet to include the `Microsoft.Composition` package in your project.

The key component of MEF is the `CompositionContainer`, which is found in the `System.ComponentModel.Composition.Hosting` namespace. A *composition container* is responsible for creating *composable parts* of your application, which in the default MEF implementation are just normal .NET objects. These parts might be a core aspect of your application or might come from externally deployed extension assemblies loaded dynamically at run time.

Each part can provide one or more *exports* that other composable parts need and may require one or more externally provided *imports* that other parts provide. Imports and exports can be simple properties or fields, or they can be entire classes. When you request a part from the composition container, it attempts to locate the part and satisfy any import dependencies it might have. Each of these imports must be provided (exported) by other parts that the container is aware of and may have import requirements of their own, which in turn must also be satisfied.

To build a bare-bones MEF application, create a new command-line project, add a reference to the `System.ComponentModel.Composition` assembly, and replace the contents of `Program.cs` (C#) or `Module1.vb` (VB) with the following:

C#

```
using System.ComponentModel.Composition;
using System.ComponentModel.Composition.Hosting;

namespace GettingStartedCS
{
    class Program
    {
        static void Main(string[] args)
        {
            var app = new ApplicationRoot();
            app.Run();
        }
    }

    class ApplicationRoot
    {
        public void Run()
        {
            Compose();
        }

        private void Compose()
        {
            var compositionContainer = new CompositionContainer();
            compositionContainer.ComposeParts(this);
        }
    }
}
```

VB

```
Imports System.ComponentModel.Composition
Imports System.ComponentModel.Composition.Hosting

Module Module1

    Sub Main()
        Dim app As New ApplicationRoot
        app.Run()
    End Sub

End Module

Class ApplicationRoot
    Sub Run()
        Compose()
        Console.WriteLine("OK")
    End Sub

    Private Sub Compose()
        Dim compositionContainer As New CompositionContainer
        compositionContainer.ComposeParts(Me)
    End Sub
End Class
```

> **NOTE** *The* `ComposeParts` *method is an extension method in the* `System.Component Model.Composition` *namespace, so if you do not have this namespace included, this code will not compile.*

All the sample does is create a `CompositionContainer` and then ask it to *compose* the `Application Root` class. The `ComposeParts` method satisfies the import requirements of the parts that you provide it. If it cannot satisfy these requirements, it throws a `System.ComponentModel.Composition .CompositionException`. Because the `ApplicationRoot` class has no import requirements, the application simply writes OK to the console and ends. This is not exciting but does provide a base on which you can add functionality.

Imports and Exports

The previous code sample asks the container to satisfy the import requirements of the `ApplicationRoot` class. Before you add an import requirement to that class, you need an exported class to satisfy the dependency. The `ApplicationRoot` class prints a status message when composition is complete. You can delegate this responsibility to another class and then ask the composition container to provide an instance of that class during composition.

To make a part available to the rest of your program, you can export it by applying an `ExportAttribute` to it. This code snippet creates a simple class and exports it:

C#

```
[System.ComponentModel.Composition.Export]
class StatusNotificationService
{
  public void ShowStatus(string statusText)
  {
    System.Console.WriteLine(statusText);
  }
}
```

VB

```
<System.ComponentModel.Composition.Export()>
Public Class StatusNotificationService
    Public Sub ShowStatus(ByVal statusText As String)
        System.Console.WriteLine(statusText)
    End Sub
End Class
```

By adding an `ExportAttribute` onto the `StatusNotificationService` class, MEF can treat it as a composable part. However, the `Export` attribute is just meta data, and MEF is still not aware of this part and does not use it. The simplest way to make the part available to MEF during part composition is to provide an instance of the exported class to the `ComposeParts` method. Change the `Compose` method of the `ApplicationRoot` class to instantiate an instance of the `StatusNotificationService` class, and pass it into the `ComposeParts` method call as a second parameter.

Finally, to specify that the `ApplicationRoot` class requires an instance of this part, add a property to the `ApplicationRoot` class, and mark it up with an `ImportAttribute`. Following is the full listing for the `ApplicationRoot` class. There is some code added after the call to `Compose` in the `Run` method that uses the newly imported part:

C#

```
class ApplicationRoot
{
  public void Run()
  {
    Compose();
    NotifcationService.ShowStatus("Composition Complete");
  }

  public void Compose()
  {
    var compositionContainer = new CompositionContainer();
    var statusNotificationService = new StatusNotificationService();
    compositionContainer.ComposeParts(this, statusNotificationService);
  }

  [System.ComponentModel.Composition.Import]
  public StatusNotificationService NotificationService { get; set; }
}
```

VB

```
Class ApplicationRoot
    Sub Run()
        Compose()
        NotificationService.ShowStatus("Composition Complete")
    End Sub

    Private Sub Compose()
        Dim compositionContainer As New CompositionContainer
        Dim statusNotificationService As New StatusNotificationService
        compositionContainer.ComposeParts(Me, statusNotificationService)
    End Sub

    <System.ComponentModel.Composition.Import()>
    Property NotificationService() As StatusNotificationService

End Class
```

Contracts

When the composition container attempts to resolve dependencies during a composition, it uses a string called a *contract* to match imports up to exports. By default, if no contract is supplied, MEF uses the fully qualified type name of the exported item as the contract. You can override this contract by supplying either a string or a type to the constructor of either the `ImportAttribute` or the `ExportAttribute`. The following code snippet shows three exports that all have the same contract:

C#

```
class Settings
{
  [Export]
  public string Username;

  [Export(typeof(string))]
  public string Password;

  [Export("System.String")]
  public string Server;
}
```

VB

```
Public Class Settings
    <Export()>
    Dim Username As String

    <Export(GetType(String))>
    Dim Password As String

    <Export("System.String")>
    Dim Server As String
End Class
```

> **NOTE** *It is recommended to use a type for the contract because a fully qualified type name is more likely to be unique. If you need to use string contracts, you should come up with a way to ensure they are all unique.*

You can specify a contract that is different than the type of the export, if required. The best reason to do this is if the type implements an interface or inherits from an abstract base class. In the following sample, the `SaveOperation` class is not aware of the concrete message sender it will use and instead imports an abstraction: `IMessageService`. The `CommandLineMessageService` exports itself under the contract of the `IMessageService` interface. In this way, the `SaveOperation` class can take advantage of message sending without worrying about the details of how these messages are sent. If you want to change the way the application works later, you could implement a new `IMessageService` and then change which concrete type exported the contract.

C#

```
public interface IMessageService
{
  void SendMessage(string message);
}

[Export(typeof(IMessageService))]
public class CommandLineMessageService : IMessageService
{
```

```
    public void SendMessage(string message)
    {
      Console.WriteLine(message);
    }
  }

  public class SaveOperation
  {
    [Import]
    public IMessageService MessageService { get; set; }

    public void DoSave()
    {
      MessageService.SendMessage("Saving...");
      // Perform the save operation
      MessageService.SendMessage("Saved");
    }
  }
```

VB

```
Public Interface IMessageService
    Sub SendMessage(ByVal message As String)
End Interface

<Export(GetType(IMessageService))>
Public Class CommandLineMessageService
    Implements IMessageService

    Public Sub SendMessage(ByVal message As String) _
      Implements IMessageService.SendMessage
        Console.WriteLine(message)
    End Sub
End Class

Public Class SaveOperation
    <Import()>
    Public Property MessageService As IMessageService

    Public Sub DoSave()
        MessageService.SendMessage("Saving...")
        ' Perform the save operation
        MessageService.SendMessage("Saved")
    End Sub
End Class
```

> **NOTE** *Exporting abstractions and strings raises a potential issue. If there are many exports with the same contract, MEF does not know which one to use to satisfy any given import. If this is the case, you can import an enumerable collection for a contract instead of a single instance using the* `ImportMany` *attribute. You can also attach more meta data to an export, which you can use to refine the imports. See* `http://mef.codeplex.com` *for more information on this technique.*

Catalogs

In the sample code so far, the only way that the `CompositionContainer` is made aware of parts is by passing instances into the `ComposeParts` method. This means that your application needs to know about each part added to the container, which does not work for extensions that need to be deployed after release. It also gets a little tedious after a while.

Locating parts is the job of a *catalog*, which can be provided to the `CompositionContainer` constructor. If a composition container is constructed with a catalog, it consults the catalog whenever it needs to locate an export. MEF ships with four catalogs:

- A `TypeCatalog` is created with a list of part types. The parts will be instantiated as required by the composition container to fulfill the import requirements during part composition.
- An `AssemblyCatalog` is similar to the `TypeCatalog` except that it scans an entire assembly looking for part types.
- A `DirectoryCatalog` scans a folder structure looking for assemblies, which can be examined for part types.
- An `AggregateCatalog` collects the parts from a number of other catalogs. This is useful because the composition container constructor can accept only a single catalog.

The following code sample demonstrates creating a composition container that looks for parts in the currently executing assembly and in all the assemblies in the `/Extensions` folder:

C#

```
var assemblyCatalog = new AssemblyCatalog(Assembly.GetExecutingAssembly());
var directoryCatalog = new DirectoryCatalog(@".\Extensions\");
var aggregateCatalog = new AggregateCatalog(assemblyCatalog, directoryCatalog);

var compositionContainer = new CompositionContainer(aggregateCatalog);
```

VB

```
Dim assemblyCatalog As New AssemblyCatalog(Assembly.GetExecutingAssembly())
Dim directoryCatalog As New DirectoryCatalog(".\Extensions\")
Dim aggregateCatalog As New AggregateCatalog(assemblyCatalog, directoryCatalog)

Dim compositionContainer As New CompositionContainer(AggregateCatalog)
```

> **NOTE** *You can create your own catalog by creating a new class that inherits from* `ComposablePartCatalog` *and overriding the* `Parts` *property.*

Advanced MEF

MEF supports a number of advanced scenarios that can be useful to you when you create host applications, or when you create add-ons or extensions for another host application. These include:

- Exporting properties, fields, and methods
- Importing fields, methods, and constructor arguments
- Importing collections
- Composition batches and recomposition
- Lazy imports
- Catalog filtering
- Part lifetimes
- Importing and exporting custom meta data

See the MEF Programming Guide on `http://mef.codeplex.com` for more information about these topics.

THE VISUAL STUDIO EDITOR

The Visual Studio 2012 Editor (like the Visual Studio 2010 Editor) is written completely in managed code, using MEF to manage its structure. From an extensibility perspective, it imports many predefined contracts as part of its normal operations. Each one of these predefined contracts is a potential point of extensibility. In addition, it exports a number of services, also using predefined contracts. With the exportation of these services, third-party tools and custom add-ins can gain access to the presentation layer and the underlying model of the editor.

The editor consists of four main subsystems: Text Model, Text View, Classification, and Operations.

The Text Model Subsystem

The Text Model subsystem is used to represent text and enable its modification. It is a logical model only, which doesn't have any responsibility for displaying pixels on the screen.

The chief component of this subsystem is the `ITextBuffer`, which represents a sequence of characters that should be displayed by the editor. The `ITextBuffer` can be persisted to the file system as an `ITextDocument`, but it doesn't need to be. It can be an entirely in-memory representation. To create new `ITextBuffer` instances, you can use an `ITextBufferFactoryService`. Any number of threads can make changes to an `ITextBuffer` until one of them calls the `TakeThreadOwnership` method.

Whenever an `ITextBuffer` is changed, a new version is created. Each version is represented as an immutable `ITextSnapshot`. Because these snapshots cannot change, any number of threads can refer to them safely, even if the `ITextBuffer` that they refer to is still changing.

To make a change to an `ITextBuffer`, you can use the `CreateEdit` method to create an instance of the `ITextEdit` interface. `ITextEdit` enables you to replace a span of text in the buffer with a new set of characters. The `ITextEdit` instance can be applied to the `ITextBuffer` by calling its `Apply` method. It can be abandoned by calling either the `Cancel` or `Dispose` method. Only one `ITextEdit` can be instantiated for an `ITextBuffer` at any given time, and if the buffer is owned by a particular thread, only that thread can create the edits.

> **NOTE** *The* `ITextBuffer` *interface contains* `Insert`, `Replace`, *and* `Delete` *convenience methods, which just wrap up the creation and application of an* `ITextEdit` *instance.*

All operations within a single `ITextEdit` occur relative to the initial state of the `ITextBuffer` at the time when the edit was created. Because of this you cannot insert some text and then remove it again within a single edit.

When an `ITextEdit` is applied, new instances of `ITextVersion` and `ITextSnapshot` are created and a `Changed` event is raised. The `ITextVersion` represents the changes between the current state of the `ITextBuffer` and the previous state, whereas the `ITextSnapshot` is a read-only view of the `ITextBuffer` after the edit has been applied. The changes in an `ITextVersion` are represented as a list of `ITextChange` instances which, if they are applied to a snapshot, would produce the subsequent snapshot. This collection is always `null` (`Nothing`) for the most recent version.

The Text View Subsystem

The Text View subsystem is responsible for managing the display of text on the screen. This includes which lines should be displayed and how text should be formatted. It is also responsible for enhancing the text with visual adornments such as the squiggly line, which notifies you of compilation errors. Finally, this subsystem manages the borders around the edges of the editor, which can be enhanced with additional information.

The main part of this subsystem is the `ITextView` interface. Instances of this interface are used to represent text visually on the screen. This is used for the main editor window but also for things like tooltip text. The `ITextView` keeps track of three different text buffers through its `TextViewModel` property:

- The data buffer, which is the actual text
- The edit buffer in which text edits occur
- The visual buffer, which actually displays

Text is formatted based on *classifiers* (see "The Classification Subsystem" section next) and decorated with adornments, which come from adornment providers attached to the text view.

The part of the text displayed on the screen is the *view port*. The view port relies on a logical coordinate system that has (0,0) as the top left of the text. If the editor is not zoomed or transformed in any way, each unit of distance in the view is the equivalent of a single pixel. Each line of text displayed on the screen is an instance of the `ITextViewLine` interface. This interface can be used to map from pixel points to characters.

Finally, the entire editor and all adornments and margins are contained within an `IWpfTextViewHost`.

> **NOTE** *The Text View subsystem comes in two parts. One part is technology-agnostic and is found in the* `Microsoft.VisualStudio.Text.UI` *assembly. The other part is the WPF implementation; you can find it in the* `Microsoft.VisualStudio.Text.UI.WPF` *assembly. In most cases, the WPF-specific items contain the text* **WPF** *in the name.*

The Classification Subsystem

The Classification subsystem manages the recognition and formatting of different types of text. It is also responsible for tagging text with additional meta data, which the Text View subsystem uses to attach glyphs and adornments as well as to highlight and outline text (such as collapsed regions of code).

The Operations Subsystem

The Operations subsystem defines editor behavior and commands. It also provides the Undo capability.

EXTENDING THE EDITOR

Editor extensions are `.vsix` packages, which export contracts that Visual Studio components import. When Visual Studio loads these packages, it adds their contents to a MEF catalog, which is then used to compose parts of the editor control. The Visual Studio Integration SDK comes with a number of templates so that you can start to create editor controls. These appear under the Extensibility page of the New Project dialog, as shown in Figure 53-1.

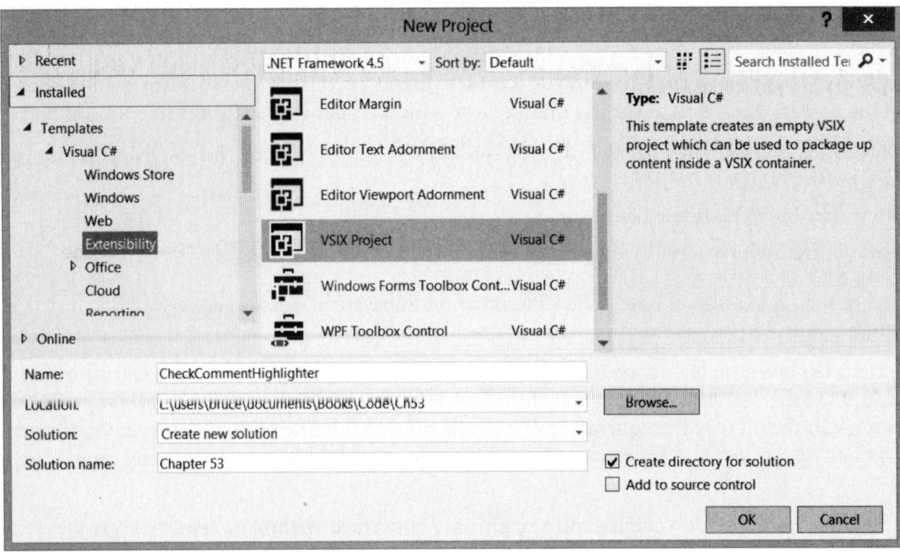

FIGURE 53-1

> **NOTE** *The Visual Studio 2012 SDK is not installed with Visual Studio 2012. You can download a copy from* `http://www.microsoft.com/en-us/download/details.aspx?id=29930`.

If you want to start with a clean slate, you need to use the VSIX Project template. To expose editor extensions via this package, start by editing the `source.extension.vsixmanifest` file. Then click the Assets tab, and use the New button to add the current project as an MEF Component, as shown in Figure 53-2.

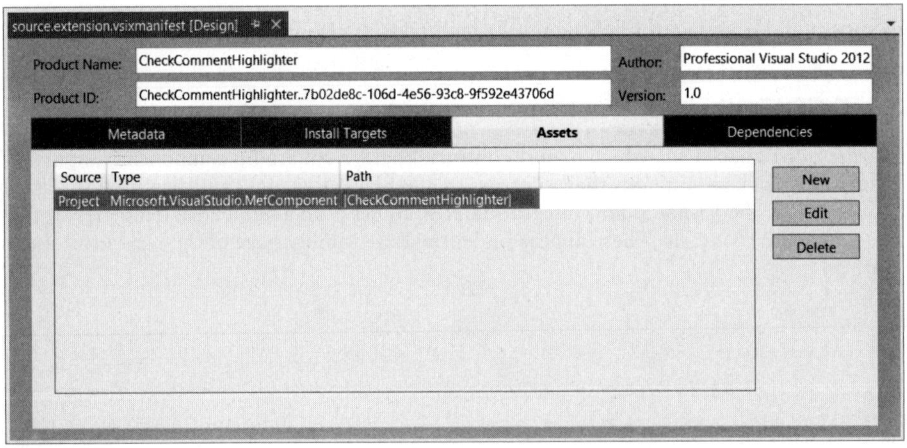

FIGURE 53-2

When your project is set up to contain MEF content, all you need to do is to create classes that export known extension contracts, and Visual Studio picks them up. In addition to this, you can import service contracts from Visual Studio that can provide you with access to the full capabilities of the editor.

During development, editor extensions can be run and debugged in the Experimental Instance of Visual Studio. The Experimental Instance behaves like a separate installation of Visual Studio with its own settings and Registry. It also manages a separate set of extensions. When you are ready to deploy your extension to the normal instance of Visual Studio, you can double-click the `.vsix` package, which is created as a part of the build process. This package is entirely self-contained, so you can use it to deploy your extension to other machines as well.

Editor Extension Points

The Visual Studio 2012 Editor looks for a number of contracts, which it uses to extend the editor behavior at run time. Usually, you need to create at least two classes for each type of extension that you are exposing. One class will perform the work of the extension and the other will typically be imported by Visual Studio and asked to provide instances of your main extension class when required.

Content Types

Each `ITextBuffer` is assigned a *content type* when it is created that identifies the type of text it contains. Examples of content types include Text, Code, CSharp, or Basic. Content types are used as filters for the various editor extensions that you can create by adding a `ContentTypeAttribute` to the exported extension. An example would be an IntelliSense provider that is valid only for XML content.

> **NOTE** *Even though content type is assigned to an* `ITextBuffer` *when it is created, it can be changed by calling the* `ChangeContentType` *method.*

You can create your own content types by exporting a property or field with the `ContentTypeDefinition` contract. Each content type can have multiple parent content types, which are defined by adding a `BaseDefinitionAttribute` to the exported content type for each parent type. To get a full list of content types, you can import the `IContentTypeRegistryService`, which maintains a list of registered content types.

> **NOTE** *A content type can be associated with a file extension using a* `FileExtensionAttribute`*. The file extension must be one that has been registered with Visual Studio already. Search for* **ProvideLanguageExtension Attribute Class** *on MSDN for more information on how to do this.*

Classification Types and Formats

A *classification type* is meta data that can be applied to any span of text. Some examples of classification types include "keyword" or "comment," both of which inherit from the classification type "code." You can create your own classification types by exporting a property or field of the `ClassificationTypeDefinition` class. This allows you to attach custom behavior to the text.

> **NOTE** *Classification types are not the same thing as content types. Each* `ITextBuffer` *has a single content type but may contain spans of text that have many different classifications.*

Classification types are attached to spans of text using an `IClassifier` instance. A *classifier aggregator* collects the classifications from a number of different classifiers for a text buffer and creates a unique, non-overlapping set of classifications from that buffer. In effect, a classifier aggregator is a classifier itself because it also provides classifications for a span of text. To get the classifier aggregator for a particular `ITextBuffer` instance of text you can import the `IClassificationAggregatorService` and call its `GetClassifier` method, passing in the text buffer.

You can define a format for a specific classification type by deriving a new class from `ClassificationFormatDefinition` and exporting it with an `EditorFormatDefinition` contract. The base class contains a number of properties that you can use to change the way text is rendered. You associate the format definition with the classification type by using the `ClassificationTypeAttribute` on the exported class. This attribute accepts a string that is a comma-separated list of classification types that the format applies to. You can also use `DisplayNameAttribute` and `UserVisibleAttribute` to show this classification format in the Fonts and Settings page of the Options dialog. You can also specify a `PriorityAttribute`, which can help to determine when the format is applied.

Margins

A *margin* is a piece of UI around the edges of the main editor window. There are four predefined margins names: Top, Bottom, Left, and Right, which act as containers for other margins that you can define. You could define a margin that turns red when a generated file is opened to warn users that they should not edit the file.

To create a margin, you need to make a new class that implements `IWpfTextViewMargin`, which contains properties for the margin size as well as for the actual `UIElement` that draws the margin on the screen. To register your margin with Visual Studio, you need to export a class with the `IWpfTextViewMarginProvider` contract. This interface contains a single method that should return an instance of your `IWpfTextViewMargin`. In addition to the MEF export, the margin provider can also provide the following:

- A `NameAttribute`, which is used to give the provider a human-readable name.
- A `ContentTypeAttribute`, which identifies the content type that the margin should be made available for.
- An `OrderAttribute` and a `MarginContainerAttribute`, which are both used to determine where the margin should be drawn. The order is specified by supplying the string name of another margin to run either `Before` or `After`. The container identifies which border the margin should be displayed against (top, bottom, left, or right).

Tags

A *tag* is a piece of meta data applied to a specific span of text. Examples of tags include `SquiggleTag`, `TextMarkerTag`, and `OutliningRegionTag`. Tags are associated with spans of text using instances of the `ITagger` interface. To register an `ITagger`, you need to create a class that implements the `ITaggerProvider` interface, override the `CreateTagger` method, and then export the new class with the `ITaggerProvider` contract. Your tagger provider should also be marked up with the `TagTypeAttribute`, which identifies the type of tag its taggers produce.

> **NOTE** *Classification is a special case of tagging provided by a* `ClassifactionTag`.

Adornments

An *adornment* is a special effect that can be applied to a span of text or to the editor surface. You can define your own adornments, which are just standard WPF `UIElements`. Each type of adornment is rendered in a separate layer so that different adornment types don't interfere with each other. To specify a layer on which your adornment belongs, your adornment class should export an `AdornmentLayerDefinition` along with a

NameAttribute and an OrderAttribute. The Order can be defined as Before or After one of four built-in adornment layers: Selection, Outlining, Caret, and Text. When the adornment wants to display itself, it can request an instance of the IAdornmentLayer from the IWpfTextView by name. This interface exposes methods to add UIElements to the layer and clear all adornments out of the layer.

To create your adornment, you need to export a class with the IWpfTextViewCreationListener contract. This class should simply instantiate a new adornment whenever a text view is created. It is up to the adornment to wire itself up to the events that it uses to redraw its contents. This class can be marked up with a standard ContentTypeAttribute to filter the content types on which it will appear. It can also include a TextViewRoleAttribute that defines for which kind of text view it should appear. The PredefinedTextViewRoles contains a list of valid values.

Mouse Processors

Mouse processors can capture events from the mouse. Each mouse processor should derive from MouseProcessorBase and override the event handlers that they want to handle. To expose your mouse processor to Visual Studio, you must export a class under the IMouseProcessorProvider contract. You also need to apply a ContentTypeAttribute to identify the types of content for which the mouse processor is available.

Drop Handlers

Drop handlers customize the behavior of the Visual Studio editor when content is dropped into it. Each drop handler should implement IDropHandler. You need an IDropHandlerProvider to provide your drop handler to Visual Studio. This provider class should export the IDropHandlerProvider contract along with the following meta data:

- A NameAttribute to identify your drop handler.
- A DropFormatAttribute, which specifies the format of text for which this handler is valid. Twenty-three built-in formats are supported, which are all handled in a specific order. Check the MSDN documentation for the full list.
- An OrderAttribute, which identifies where in the order of drop handlers this handler should execute. You do this by providing Before and After components of the Order. Each component is just a text name for the handler. The default drop handler provided by Visual Studio is called DefaultFileDropHandler.

Editor Options

Editor options enable your extensions to expose settings. These settings can be imported into other components of the system and used to alter their behavior. This type of export is used to expose the value of your option to other components, but Visual Studio does nothing to expose these options to the user. If you want the user to manage these options, you need to create your own UI.

To create a new editor option, you must derive from one of the three abstract base classes EditorOptionDefinition<T>, ViewOptionDefinition<T>, or WpfViewOptionDefintion<T> and specify the type of the option value being created (that is, boolean or string). These base classes provide abstract properties for you to implement containing information about the option, including its current value and its default value. To make the editor option available to Visual Studio, you should export it with the EditorOptionDefinition contract.

IntelliSense

IntelliSense is a term used to describe a set of features that provide contextual information and statement completion services. No matter what type of IntelliSense extension you provide, the components and the process are always the same:

- A *broker* controls the overall process.
- A *session* represents the sequence of events, which typically starts with a user gesture triggering the presenter and ends with the committal or cancellation of the selection.

- A *controller* determines when a session should begin and end. It also decides the manner in which the session ends.
- A *source* provides content for the IntelliSense session and determines the best match for display.
- A *presenter* is responsible for displaying the content of a session.

It is recommended that you provide at least a source and a controller when defining IntelliSense extensions. You should provide a presenter only if you want to customize the display of your feature.

To provide an IntelliSense source, you need to create a class that implements one (or more) of these interfaces: `ICompletionSource`, `IQuickInfoSource`, `ISignatureHelpSource`, or `ISmartTagSource`. Each of these interfaces defines methods that provide you with the context for the session and allow you to return the information that will be displayed.

For each of the interfaces implemented, you need another class that implements the corresponding provider interface: `ICompletionSourceProvider`, `IQuickInfoSourceProvider`, `ISignatureHelpSource Provider`, or `ISmartTagSourceProvider`. This provider class must be exported using its provider interface as a contract. In addition to the export, you can specify a `NameAttribute`, an `OrderAttribute`, and a `ContentTypeAttribute`.

To provide an IntelliSense controller, you need a class that implements `IIntellisenseController`. This interface provides methods for the controller to attach and detach `ITextBuffers`. When the controller senses an event that should begin an IntelliSense session, it requests one from the correct type of broker: `ICompletionBroker`, `IQuickInfoBroker`, `ISignatureHelpBroker`, or `ISmartTagBroker`. The easiest way to get access to a broker is to import one into the controller provider (defined next) and pass it into the constructor of the IntelliSense controller.

Finally, you need an `IIntellisenseControllerProvider` that is exported along with a `NameAttribute`, an `OrderAttribute`, and a `ContentTypeAttribute`.

Editor Services

Visual Studio exposes a large number of editor services under well-known contracts that you can import into your extension classes. Here are a few common ones (see the MSDN documentation for a complete list):

- `IContentTypeRegistryService` manages the collection of content types available to be assigned to `ITextBuffers`. This service enables you to add and remove content types, as well as query the currently registered content types.
- `ITextDocumentFactoryService` provides the ability to create new documents and load existing documents from the file system. It also has events for when `ITextDocuments` are created and disposed.
- `IClassifierAggregatorService` contains only a single method, `GetClassifier`, that returns a classifier for a given `ITextBuffer`. It creates and caches classifiers if they don't already exist.
- `ITextSearchService` is responsible for locating specific text within a defined region of text. It has methods to find all instances or just find the next instance.
- `IWpfKeyboardTrackingService` enables you to switch the keyboard tracking over to WPF in the editor. Normally, Visual Studio performs its own keyboard tracking, so if you use WPF controls that listen for keyboard events, they will never be detected. This service enables you to toggle the capability for WPF to have the first shot at handling keyboard events. Keyboard events that are left unhandled by WPF will be passed to Visual Studio and handled as normal.

The Check Comment Highlighter Extension

This section shows the complete source code for a sample extension with explanations along the way. In our office, whenever we come across something that doesn't seem to be quite right, we attach a comment asking for an explanation using the special token `check:` followed by a few sentences describing what aspect we think is wrong. Normally, if we encounter a piece of code with a check comment and we can answer the query, we try to find a way to refactor the code so that the answer is obvious or supply a comment explaining why the code is the way it is. (On the rare occasion that the check comment exposes an error, we fix it.) Using this technique, our code becomes more maintainable over time as it gets easier to read and understand. We have tools that enable us to extract a list of these comments from the code base, but it would be handy if we could highlight them within the code editor itself. The Check Comment Margin Highlighter does just that by adding a glyph in the margin on the left (where breakpoints normally appear) for any line that contains a comment that contains the token `check:`.

The code comes in two parts: a tagger and a glyph factory. Here is the complete code listing for the tagger:

C#

```
using System;
using System.Collections.Generic;

using System.ComponentModel.Composition;

using Microsoft.VisualStudio.Text;
using Microsoft.VisualStudio.Text.Classification;
using Microsoft.VisualStudio.Text.Editor;
using Microsoft.VisualStudio.Text.Tagging;
using Microsoft.VisualStudio.Utilities;

namespace CheckCommentHighlighter
{
    class CheckCommentTag : IGlyphTag { }

    class CheckCommentTagger : ITagger<CheckCommentTag>
    {
        private readonly IClassifier _classifier;

        public CheckCommentTagger(IClassifier classifier)
        {
            _classifier = classifier;
        }

        public IEnumerable<ITagSpan<CheckCommentTag>> GetTags(
             NormalizedSnapshotSpanCollection spans)
        {
            foreach (var span in spans)
            {
                foreach (var classification in
                         _classifier.GetClassificationSpans(span))
                {
                    var isComment = classification.ClassificationType
                                                  .Classification
                                                  .ToLower()
                                                  .Contains("comment");

                    if (isComment)
                    {
                        var index = classification.Span.GetText()
                                                  .ToLower().IndexOf("check:");
                        if (index != -1)
                        {
                            var tag = new CheckCommentTag();
                            var snapshotSpan = new SnapshotSpan(
                                        classification.Span.Start + index, 6);
                            yield return new TagSpan<CheckCommentTag>(
                                                     snapshotSpan,
```

```
                                                        tag);
                        }
                    }
                }
            }
        }

        public event EventHandler<SnapshotSpanEventArgs> TagsChanged;
    }


    [Export(typeof(ITaggerProvider))]
    [TagType(typeof(CheckCommentTag))]
    [ContentType("code")]
    class CheckCommentTaggerProvider : ITaggerProvider
    {
        [Import]
        private IClassifierAggregatorService AggregatorService;

        public ITagger<T> CreateTagger<T>(ITextBuffer buffer) where T : ITag
        {
            if( buffer == null )
                throw new ArgumentNullException("buffer");

            var classifier = AggregatorService.GetClassifier(buffer);

            return new CheckCommentTagger(classifier) as ITagger<T>;
        }
    }

}
```

VB

```
Imports System.ComponentModel.Composition
Imports Microsoft.VisualStudio.Text
Imports Microsoft.VisualStudio.Text.Tagging
Imports Microsoft.VisualStudio.Text.Editor
Imports Microsoft.VisualStudio.Text.Classification
Imports Microsoft.VisualStudio.Utilities

Friend Class CheckCommentTag
  Inherits IGlyphTag

End Class


Friend Class CheckCommentTagger
  Implements ITagger(Of CheckCommentTag)

  Private m_classifier As IClassifier

  Friend Sub New(ByVal classifier As IClassifier)
    m_classifier = classifier
  End Sub

  Private Function GetTags(ByVal spans As NormalizedSnapshotSpanCollection)
    As IEnumerable(Of ITagSpan(Of CheckCommentTag))
    Implements ITagger(Of CheckCommentTag).GetTags

    Dim Tags As New List(Of ITagSpan(Of CheckCommentTag))
    For Each span As SnapshotSpan In spans
      For Each classification As ClassificationSpan In
```

```
          m_classifier.GetClassificationSpans(span)

          If classification.ClassificationType.Classification.ToLower()
            .Contains("comment") Then

            Dim index As Integer = classification.Span.GetText().ToLower()
              .IndexOf("check:")

            If index <> -1 Then
              Dim snapshotSpan As New SnapshotSpan(classification.Span.Start
                  + index, 6)

              Dim tag As New CheckCommentTag
                Tags.Add(New TagSpan(Of CheckCommentTag)(snapshotSpan, tag))
            End If
          End If
        Next classification
      Next span
      Return Tags
    End Function

    Public Event TagsChanged As EventHandler(Of SnapshotSpanEventArgs)
      Implements ITagger(Of CheckCommentTag).TagsChanged

  End Class

  <Export(GetType(ITaggerProvider)), ContentType("code"),
    TagType(GetType(CheckCommentTag))>
  Friend Class CheckCommentTaggerProvider
    Implements ITaggerProvider

    <Import()>
    Friend AggregatorService As IClassifierAggregatorService

    Public Function CreateTagger(Of T As ITag)(ByVal buffer As ITextBuffer)
      As ITagger(Of T) Implements ITaggerProvider.CreateTagger

      If buffer Is Nothing Then
        Throw New ArgumentNullException("buffer")
      End If

      Dim Classifier = AggregatorService.GetClassifier(buffer)
      Dim tagger As New CheckCommentTagger(Classifier)

      Return TryCast(tagger, ITagger(Of T))

    End Function
  End Class
```

Three classes are defined here. The first is the `CheckCommentTag` class. It inherits from `IGlyphTag` but has no implementation on its own. It is purely a marker that identifies when a particular span of text should have this glyph applied. We could have supplied some properties on the tag class to pass information to the glyph factory later that could be used to affect the type of `UIElement` displayed.

The second class is the `CheckCommentTagger` class. This class is responsible for identifying spans of text that should have the `CheckCommentTag` applied. It does this by implementing the `ITagger<CheckCommentTag>` interface. This interface consists of a method called `GetTags` and a `TagsChanged` event. `GetTags` takes a collection of spans and returns a collection of `ITagSpans`. In this implementation, it finds all the comments with the help of a classifier, and searches for the string `check:`. If it finds this string, it creates a new `TagSpan<CheckCommentTag>` item, which it applies to just the span of text that covers the `check:` string.

The final class is `CheckCommentTaggerProvider`, which contains the MEF export meta data that Visual Studio looks for in the extension. This class is exported using the `ITaggerProvider` contract, which means that Visual Studio adds it to an internal list of tagger providers to be called upon whenever taggers are required. Two other pieces of meta data are also attached to this class. The `TagTypeAttribute` specifies the type of tags that will be produced by any taggers that this provider creates. The `ContentTypeAttribute` supplies a filter on the kinds of content on which this tagger provider should be used. In this case, the attribute specifies that this tagger provider should be called upon only when the editor contains code, which is a common base content-type provided by the editor.

The tagger provider class also has an import requirement for an `IClassifierAggregatorService`. This service is used in the construction of taggers, which occurs in the `CreateTagger<T>` method. This method is passed an `ITextbuffer` for which it is to provide a tagger. It uses the `AggregatorService` to retrieve a classifier and then uses the classifier to construct the `CheckCommentTagger` defined in the previous code snippet.

This code is enough to allow Visual Studio to mark up check comments as requiring a glyph, but if you deploy the extension as it is now, you won't see anything because there are no components offering to draw a `CheckCommentTag`. For that you need a *glyph factory*, which is the other half of the extension. Here is the code:

C#

```
using System.ComponentModel.Composition;
using System.Windows;
using System.Windows.Media;
using System.Windows.Shapes;

using Microsoft.VisualStudio.Text.Editor;
using Microsoft.VisualStudio.Text.Formatting;
using Microsoft.VisualStudio.Text.Tagging;
using Microsoft.VisualStudio.Utilities;

namespace CheckCommentHighlighter
{
    class CheckCommentGlyphFactory : IGlyphFactory
    {
        public UIElement GenerateGlyph(IWpfTextViewLine line, IGlyphTag tag)
        {
            var validTag = tag as CheckCommentTag != null;
            if (!validTag)
                return null;

            return new Polygon
            {
                Fill = Brushes.LightBlue,
                Stroke = Brushes.DarkBlue,
                StrokeThickness = 2,
                Points = new PointCollection
                {
                    new Point(0, 0),
                    new Point(16, 8),
                    new Point(0, 16)
                }
            };

        }
    }

    [Export(typeof(IGlyphFactoryProvider))]
    [TagType(typeof(CheckCommentTag))]
    [Name("CheckCommentGlyph")]
```

```
    [ContentType("code")]
    [Order(After="VSTextMarker")]
    class CheckCommentGlyphFactoryProvider : IGlyphFactoryProvider
    {
        public IGlyphFactory GetGlyphFactory(IWpfTextView view,
                                             IWpfTextViewMargin margin)
        {
            return new CheckCommentGlyphFactory();
        }
    }
}
```

VB

```
Imports System.ComponentModel.Composition
Imports System.Windows
Imports System.Windows.Media
Imports System.Windows.Shapes

Imports Microsoft.VisualStudio.Text.Editor
Imports Microsoft.VisualStudio.Text.Formatting
Imports Microsoft.VisualStudio.Text.Tagging
Imports Microsoft.VisualStudio.Utilities

Friend Class CheckCommentGlyphFactory
    Implements IGlyphFactory


    Public Function GenerateGlyph(ByVal line As IWpfTextViewLine,
ByVal tag As IGlyphTag) As UIElement Implements IGlyphFactory.GenerateGlyph
        If tag Is Nothing OrElse Not (TypeOf tag Is CheckCommentTag) Then
            Return Nothing
        End If

        Dim triangle As New System.Windows.Shapes.Polygon()

        With triangle
            .Fill = Brushes.LightBlue
            .Stroke = Brushes.DarkBlue
            .StrokeThickness = 2
            .Points = New PointCollection()
            With .Points
                .Add(New Point(0, 0))
                .Add(New Point(16, 8))
                .Add(New Point(0, 16))
            End With
        End With

        Return triangle
    End Function

End Class

<Export(GetType(IGlyphFactoryProvider)), Name("CheckCommentGlyph"),
Order(After:="VsTextMarker"), ContentType("code"),
TagType(GetType(CheckCommentTag))>
Friend NotInheritable Class TodoGlyphFactoryProvider
    Implements IGlyphFactoryProvider


    Public Function GetGlyphFactory(
ByVal view As Microsoft.VisualStudio.Text.Editor.IWpfTextView,
ByVal margin As Microsoft.VisualStudio.Text.Editor.IWpfTextViewMargin)
```

```
As Microsoft.VisualStudio.Text.Editor.IGlyphFactory
Implements Microsoft.VisualStudio.Text.Editor.IGlyphFactoryProvider.GetGlyphFactory
        Return New CheckCommentGlyphFactory()

    End Function
End Class
```

Just as with the code to expose the check comment tagger to Visual Studio, two classes are at work here: One class actually creates glyphs, and another class provides instances of this glyph factory to Visual Studio on demand. The `CheckCommentGlyphFactory` is simple. It just checks to ensure that the tag is of the correct type and then creates the visual element that is to be displayed. This can be any WPF `UIElement`. In this implementation, it is a light blue triangle pointing to the right with a dark blue border.

The second class is the actual gateway into Visual Studio. It is exported using the `IGlyphFactoryProvider` contract, associated with a specific tag and content type. It also specifies a name that makes it easier to identify. Finally, it specifies that it should be drawn after items in the `VSTextMarker` layer, which means it will appear to be on top of items in this layer. The actual implementation of this class is a simple factory method for instances of the `CheckCommentGlyphFactory` class.

If you run this extension, it starts in the Experimental Instance of Visual Studio. Load a code file and add a comment that starts with `Check:` and a blue triangle appears in the margin to the left, as shown in Figure 53-3.

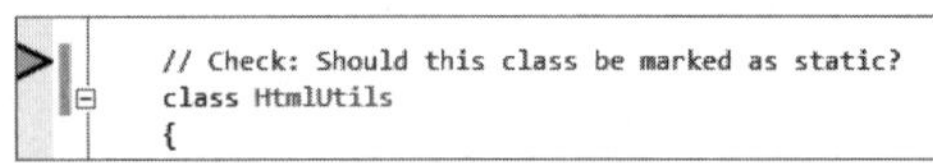

FIGURE 53-3

SUMMARY

The Managed Extensibility Framework simplifies the process of creating extensible applications by enabling you to think of your application as a collection of composable parts, each of which exposes exports and requires imports. You can add extensions to your application by creating appropriate catalogs of parts and providing them to your composition container. MEF can cover a much wider range of capabilities than those covered in this chapter. Be sure to check out the MEF Programming Guide on `http://mef.codeplex.com` for more information.

Visual Studio 2012 can create a highly extensible run time by taking advantage of MEF. It watches extensions for known exported contracts, which it uses when composing the WPF Editor control, enabling you to easily extend its behavior. In addition to this, Visual Studio exports a number of services on well-known contracts that you can import for use in your extensions. For more information about the Visual Studio Editor and how to extend it using MEF, consult the Visual Studio 2012 Editor topic on MSDN, which contains many examples of extensions.

PART XII
Visual Studio Ultimate

54

Visual Studio Ultimate for Architects

WHAT'S IN THIS CHAPTER?

- Creating models of your solution
- Enforcing application architecture
- Exploring existing architectures

The last few versions of Visual Studio have seen wide swings in functionality for architectural features. To a certain extent, these changes were driven by corresponding changes of opinion in how Visual Studio should deal with application architecture. The result is that features related to architectural concepts now fall into one of two broad categories: modeling and exploration.

On the modeling side is the ability to create UML Diagrams that you can use to build up an application model. And you can use one of the diagrams to determine and enforce certain relationships between code elements in your projects.

The other category includes a number of features that revolve around navigating and understanding existing code bases. This includes the ability to generate Sequence Diagrams from C# and VB methods, as well as Dependency Graphs of various components in your solution. And Visual Studio 2012 includes the Architecture Explorer, which is used to quickly navigate your solution.

MODELING PROJECTS

A *model* in software terms is an abstract representation of some process or object. You create models to better understand and communicate to others the way different parts of the application are intended to work. In Visual Studio 2012, you keep all your models together in a Modeling Project. You can find Modeling Projects on their own page in the Add New Project dialog. You can also create a new Modeling Project by adding a diagram to your solution with the Architecture ➪ New Diagram menu option. This brings up the Add New Diagram dialog, as shown in Figure 54-1. At the bottom of this dialog is a drop-down list enabling you to select an existing Modeling Project or offering to create a new one for you.

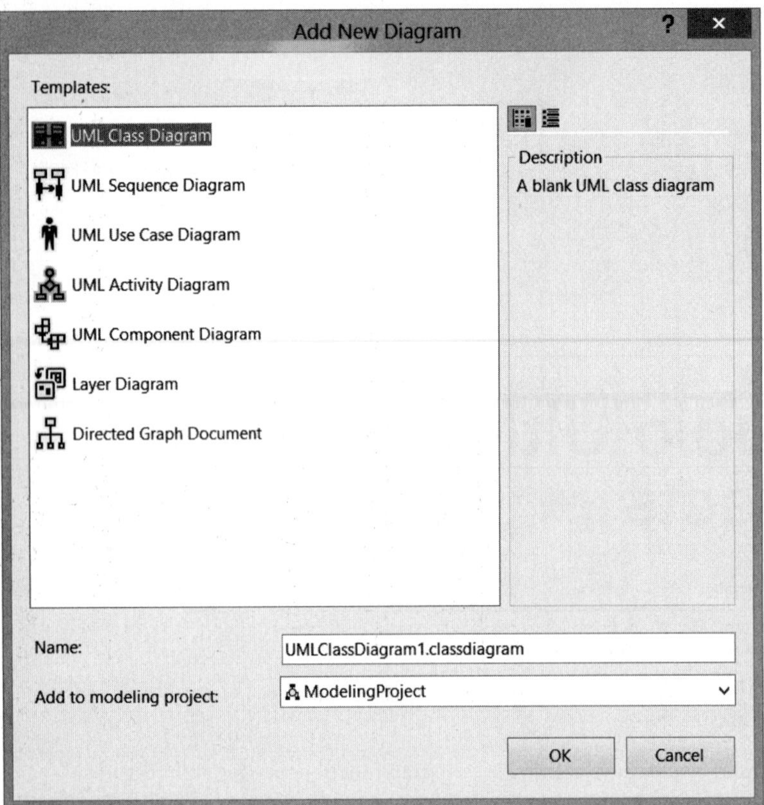

FIGURE 54-1

Many of the diagrams in a Modeling Project can easily be attached to Work Items in Team Foundation Server, which makes them a great tool for communicating with the rest of the team.

> **NOTE** *The capability to create Modeling Projects and their associated diagrams is limited to the Ultimate edition of Visual Studio 2012. The Premium edition includes the capability to view Modeling Projects and diagrams already created by someone else.*

UML Diagrams

The Unified Modeling Language (UML) is an industry standard for creating diagrammatic models. Visual Studio 2012 has the capability to create the most common UML Diagrams, including Activity Diagrams, Component Diagrams, Class Diagrams, Sequence Diagrams, and Use Case Diagrams.

> **NOTE** *The Visual Studio 2012 UML Diagrams adhere to the UML 2.0 standard.*

Use Case Diagrams

A Use Case Diagram (Figure 54-2) defines the users of a system (Actors) and the tasks they need to achieve with the system (Use Cases). Each use case can consist of subordinate use cases. Use Case Diagrams are typically high level.

Modeling Use Cases helps you to focus on the objectives of the end users and ensure that their needs are met by the application that you provide. In addition, it helps to identify the boundaries of your application for the user's needs, which is good for understanding the scope of what you need to build. Use Cases are typically associated with User Story and Test Case work items within Team Foundation Server (TFS).

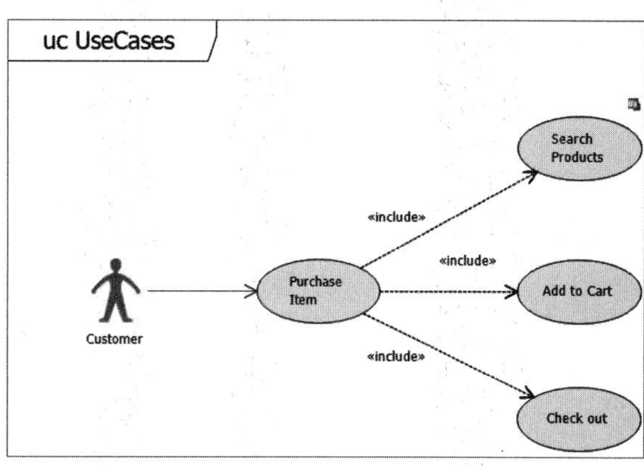

FIGURE 54-2

Activity Diagrams

An Activity Diagram (Figure 54-3) describes the actions and decisions that go into performing a single task. You can use Activity Diagrams and Use Case Diagrams to show different views of the same information. Use Cases are often better at showing the hierarchical nature of tasks that a user performs, whereas Activity Diagrams show how each of the subtasks are used.

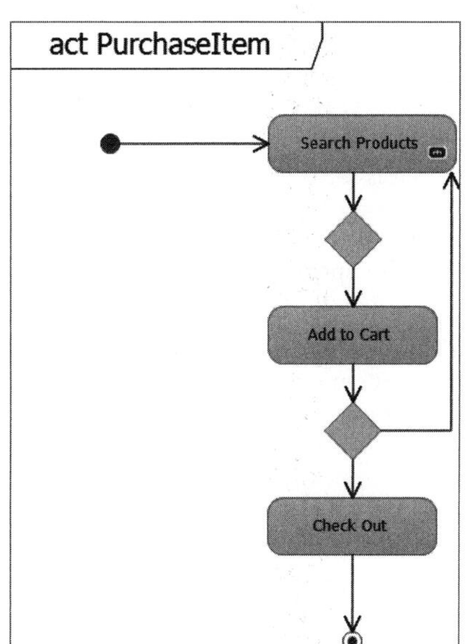

FIGURE 54-3

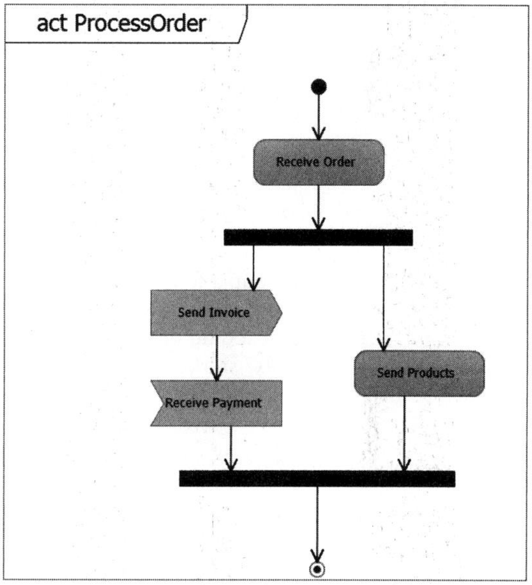

FIGURE 54-4

Activity begins with the small black circle and follows the arrows until they reach the circle with the ring around it. Each rounded box is an activity, and each diamond shape represents a decision about which activity to move to next. The small fork icon in the bottom-right corner of the Search Products activities identifies it as calling another activity.

Activity Diagrams can also run activity streams in parallel, as shown in Figure 54-4. This figure also shows sending and receiving events asynchronously.

> **NOTE** *It is common to represent algorithms as Activity Diagrams.*

Sequence Diagrams

A Sequence Diagram (Figure 54-5) shows the messages passed between different components in a system or between systems during some larger activity. You use a Sequence Diagram when you want to show the flow of activities from one actor to another within a system.

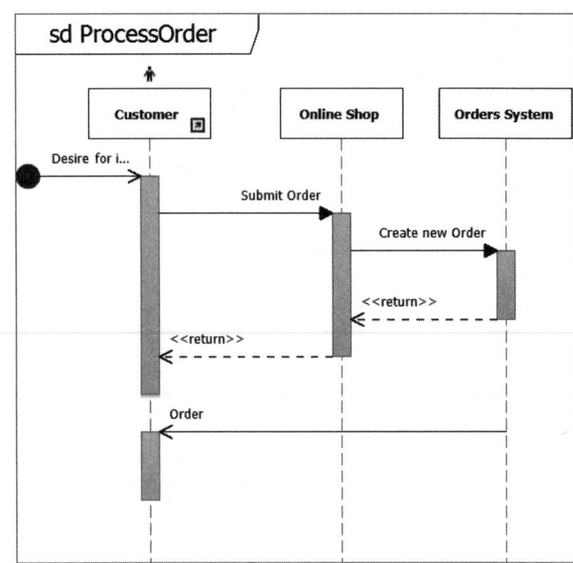

FIGURE 54-5

Running along the top of the diagram are boxes representing the different actors involved. Running down from each actor is a dashed lifeline. The dashed lifeline becomes a thicker block to indicate where in the process the actor is performing some operation. As you read a Sequence Diagram, moving down a lifeline equates to moving forward in time. Running between the lifelines are messages passed back and forth between the different actors. Messages can be synchronous (closed arrow) or asynchronous (open arrow). Messages can be found, which means that you don't know where they come from, or lost, which means that you don't know where they go. These commonly appear at the boundaries of the activity being modeled.

An Interaction Use (Figure 54-6) is a piece of a Sequence Diagram that is separated out and can be reused. To create an Interaction Use, select it from the Toolbox, and then drag a rectangle over the lifelines that should be involved. After an Interaction Use has been created, you can use it to generate another Sequence Diagram or link it to an existing one. Double-clicking an Interaction Use opens its diagram.

Sometimes you need to group a few execution contexts and messages together. For example, you might want to repeat an interaction in a loop. To do this, you need to create a Combined Fragment (Figure 54-7) by selecting the elements that should be involved and selecting one of the Surround With options. For instance, the right-side of Figure 54-7 shows the results from selecting the Loop option. Other possibilities include parallel, sequential and optional.

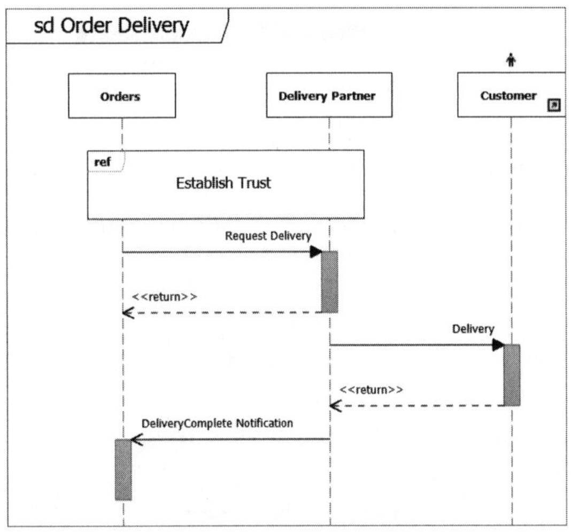

FIGURE 54-6

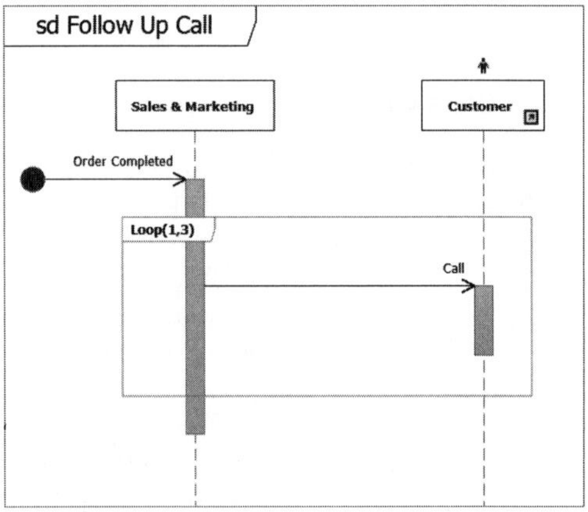

FIGURE 54-7

> **NOTE** *Although they both use the same notation, UML Sequence Diagrams should not be confused with .NET Sequence Diagrams. UML Sequence Diagrams can be created only within Modeling Projects and can include elements from other parts of the model. .NET Sequence Diagrams are generated from existing .NET code and are not a part of the model.*

Component Diagrams

A component is a single unit of functionality that can be replaced within its environment. Each component hides its internal structure but publishes provided interfaces that other components can use to access its features. In addition, each component can publish a set of required interfaces that it needs to perform its tasks. A Component Diagram (Figure 54-8) shows the components in a system along with their published and required interfaces. It also shows how published interfaces match up with required interfaces.

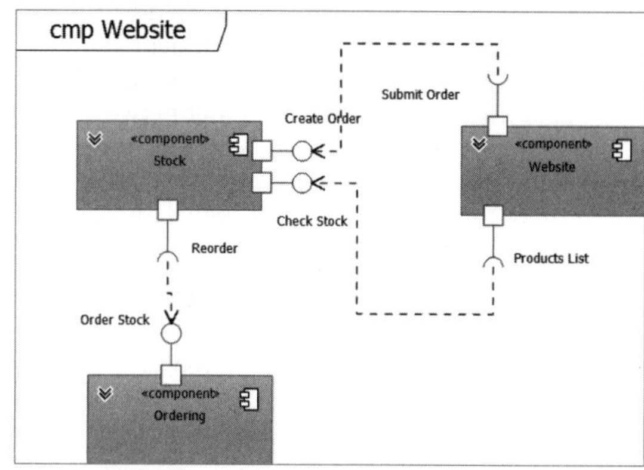

FIGURE 54-8

Modeling components helps you to think about the parts of your application as discrete units. This in turn reduces the coupling in your design, making your application easier to maintain and evolve going forward. You typically model interactions between systems components (or between the parts inside a component) with a Sequence Diagram. You can use a Class Diagram to model the interfaces of a component along with the data that travels between the interfaces (parameters).

You can also use a Class Diagram to describe the classes that make up components' parts. Finally, you use an Activity Diagram to model the internal processing of a component.

Class Diagrams

A Class Diagram (Figure 54-9) enables you to model the types in your system and the relationships between them. These are probably the most widely used of the UML Diagram types in the industry. You can define classes, interfaces, and enumerations. Each of these items can be related to each other by inheritance, composition, aggregation, or just association. Each item can have attributes and operations defined on them. Finally, these items can be grouped into packages.

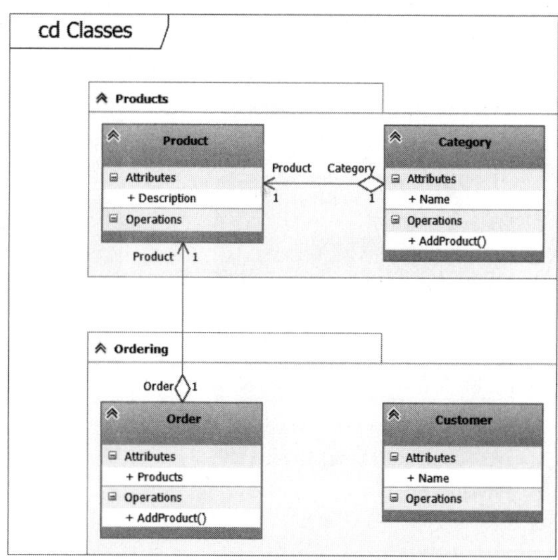

FIGURE 54-9

> **NOTE** *Although based on the same notation, UML Class Diagrams should not be confused with .NET Class Diagrams. A UML Class Diagram is used to define and organize elements of the model. A .NET Class Diagram performs a similar role for .NET code. Changing a .NET Class Diagram alters the underlying .NET code.*

UML Model Explorer

Each of the UML Diagrams actually present different views of the same underlying model. To see the entire model, you can use the UML Model Explorer tool window (Figure 54-10). As you add content to your model using the various diagrams, each element also appears in the UML Model Explorer.

You can add items directly to the model using the context menu on many of the nodes in the UML Model Explorer. You can also drag elements from the Model Explorer directly onto the surface of many diagrams. Doing this creates a link between the original element and its appearance on the diagram. When you try to delete any element from a UML Diagram, you have the option to simply remove it from the diagram or to remove it from the model altogether.

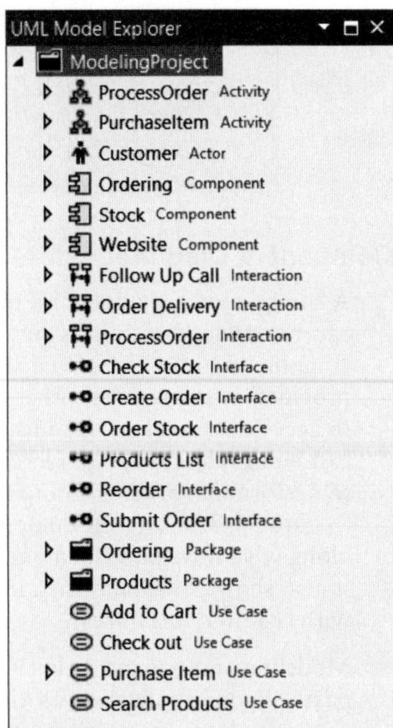

FIGURE 54-10

Using Layer Diagrams to Verify Application Architecture

A Layer Diagram (Figure 54-11) is a tool that helps you specify the high-level structure of a software solution. It consists of different areas or layers of your application and defines the relationships between them.

Each layer is a logical group of classes that commonly share a technical responsibility, such as being used for data access or presentation.

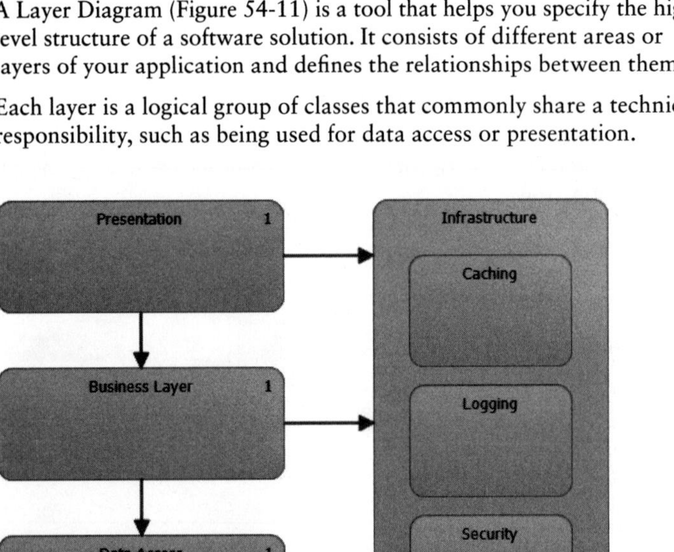

FIGURE 54-11

After you create a new Layer Diagram, you can drag each layer onto the design surface and configure it with a name. You can draw directed or bidirectional dependency links between layers. A layer depends on another layer if any of its components have a direct reference to any of the components in the layer it depends on. If there is not an explicit dependency, it is assumed that no components match this description.

> **NOTE** *Layers can be nested inside one another (refer to Figure 54-11). Specifically, the layers on the right side of the figure have been nested in that manner. The reason for doing this is to make changes to the diagram easier. You can associate projects with these inner layers. Then, if you need to make changes in the future, the associations "follow" as you move the layers around.*

After you create a Layer Diagram, you can use it to discover communications between layers in your compiled application and to verify that these links match the design. Before you do this, you need to associate projects with each layer by dragging them from the Solution Explorer onto the layer. As you do this, entries are added to the Layer Explorer tool window (Figure 54-12) and a number inside each layer is updated to reflect the number of artifacts associated with it.

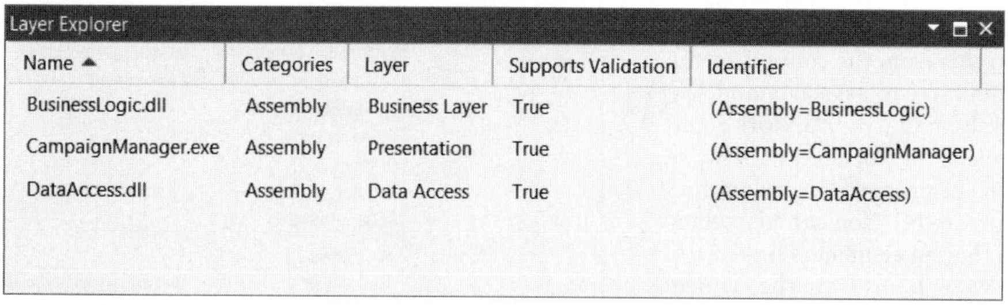

Layer Explorer

Name ▲	Categories	Layer	Supports Validation	Identifier
BusinessLogic.dll	Assembly	Business Layer	True	(Assembly=BusinessLogic)
CampaignManager.exe	Assembly	Presentation	True	(Assembly=CampaignManager)
DataAccess.dll	Assembly	Data Access	True	(Assembly=DataAccess)

FIGURE 54-12

> **NOTE** *You can create new layers by dragging projects from the Solution Explorer directly onto the Layer Diagram surface.*

After the Layer Diagram has assemblies associated with it, you can fill in any missing dependencies by selecting Generate Dependencies from the design surface context menu. This analyzes the associated assemblies, builds the project if necessary, and fills in any missing dependencies. Note that the tool won't ever delete unused dependencies.

When your Layer Diagram contains all the layers and only the dependencies that you would expect, you can verify that your application matches the design specified by the Layer Diagram. To do this, you can select Validate Architecture from the design surface context menu. The tool analyzes your solution structure and any violations found appear as build errors, as shown in Figure 54-13. Double-clicking one of these errors opens a Directed Graph showing the relationships between the various projects.

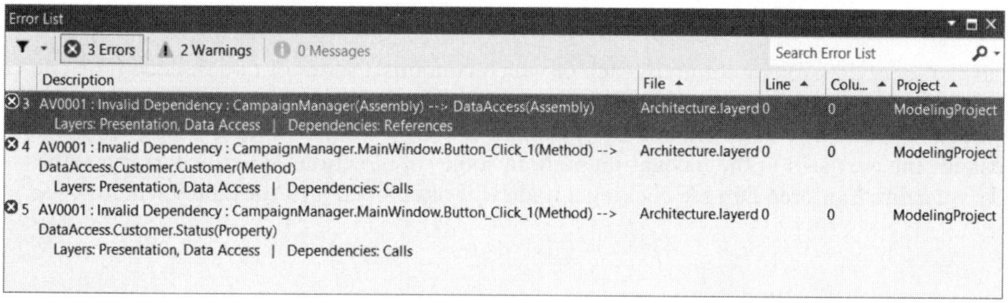

Error List

3 Errors | 2 Warnings | 0 Messages | Search Error List

	Description	File ▲	Line ▲	Colu... ▲	Project ▲
3	AV0001 : Invalid Dependency : CampaignManager(Assembly) --> DataAccess(Assembly) Layers: Presentation, Data Access | Dependencies: References	Architecture.layerd	0	0	ModelingProject
4	AV0001 : Invalid Dependency : CampaignManager.MainWindow.Button_Click_1(Method) --> DataAccess.Customer.Customer(Method) Layers: Presentation, Data Access | Dependencies: Calls	Architecture.layerd	0	0	ModelingProject
5	AV0001 : Invalid Dependency : CampaignManager.MainWindow.Button_Click_1(Method) --> DataAccess.Customer.Status(Property) Layers: Presentation, Data Access | Dependencies: Calls	Architecture.layerd	0	0	ModelingProject

FIGURE 54-13

> **NOTE** *Not all artifacts that can be linked to a Layer Diagram support validation. The Layer Explorer window has a Supports Validation column, which can help you determine if you have linked artifacts for which this is true.*

Modeling projects have a boolean property called `ValidateArchitecture`, which is used to determine if all Layer Diagrams should be validated whenever the project is built. You can also request that Team Foundation Build validates your architecture by adding a property called `ValidateArchitectureOnBuild` to your `TfsBuild.proj` file or Process Template and setting it to true.

Linking to Team Foundation Server

Each of the elements of a diagram in a Modeling Project, as well as the diagrams themselves, can be linked to Work Items in Team Foundation Server. You can do this from the context menu of the item you would like to associate and select either Create Work Item or Link to Work Item. When a model element is associated with Work Items, it displays in the properties window for that element (Figure 54-14). You can also get a list of Work Items that an element is linked to by selecting View Work Items from the element's context menu. You can even remove them by selecting Remove Work Items from the same context menu.

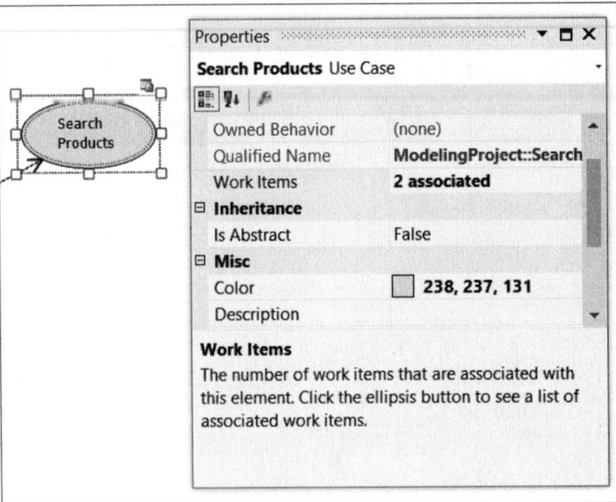

FIGURE 54-14

EXPLORING CODE

Many advanced features in Visual Studio are designed to help you understand and navigate the structure of an existing code base. Directed Graphs give you a high-level view of the relationships between various types of components within your project. The Architecture Explorer enables you to deep dive into different areas while still leaving a trail of breadcrumbs to help you understand where you are. The capability to generate Sequence Diagrams enables you to quickly understand how a particular method behaves, especially as it relates to other methods and classes.

The Architecture Explorer

One of the hardest aspects of navigating a new code base is understanding where you are in relation to everything else. The Architecture Explorer window (Figure 54-15) enables you to move quickly through the code structure with single clicks, leaving a trail that always makes it easy to figure out how you got to wherever you end up. You can drag some elements from the Architecture Explorer directly onto the design surfaces of many of the other diagrams in this chapter.

Figure 54-15 shows the progression of columns, each of which contains a series of nodes. Each time you click a node in a column, a new column opens up based on the node selected. Between each of the columns is a collapsed Action column, which you can expand by clicking it (Figure 54-16). Selecting a different action allows you to change the next step in the navigation path. In some cases, actions actually perform some task outside of the Architecture Explorer. Double-clicking a node will often open it in the editor window.

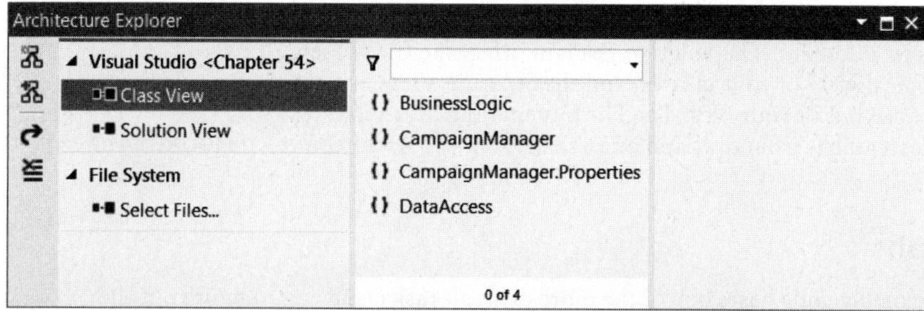

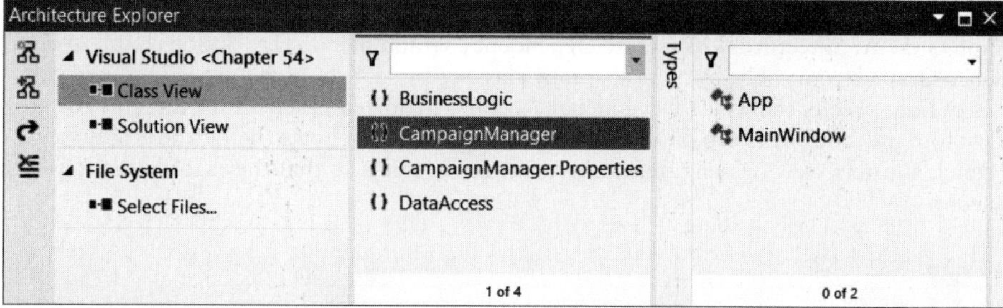

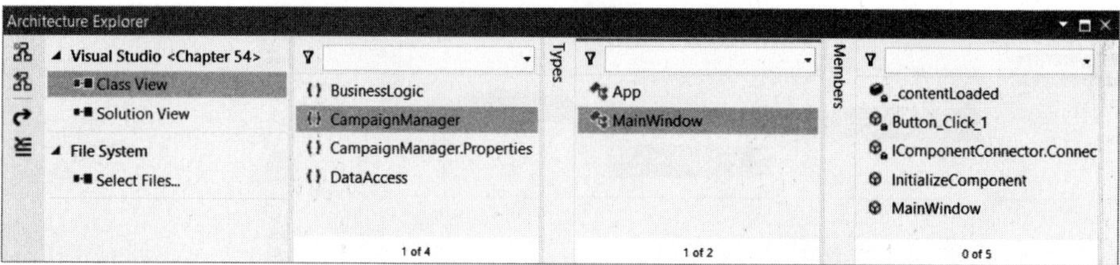

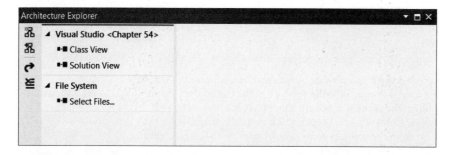

FIGURE 54-15

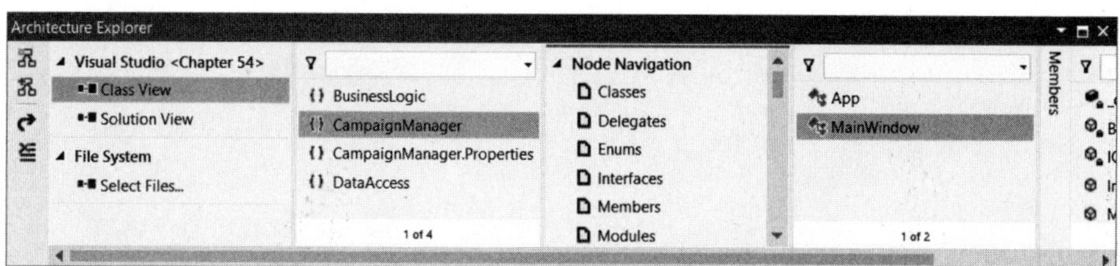

FIGURE 54-16

> **NOTE** *You can select multiple nodes in a column to see a union of the results in the next column.*

Each column in the Architecture Explorer can be independently filtered in one of two ways. The simplest way is to type into the textbox at the top of the column and press Enter. This filters the content based on the information you entered. The other way is to use the Category and Property Filter box (Figure 54-17) by clicking the small filter icon in the top-left corner of the column. When a column is filtered, it has a large filter icon in its background.

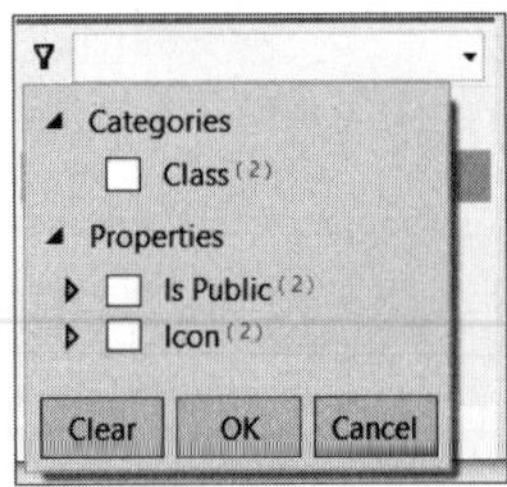

FIGURE 54-17

The first column is Architecture, which is a special column that contains views, each of which belongs to a domain. The Solution domain offers the Class View, which is based on a logical view of your classes, and the Solution View, which is based on the physical layout of your files. The File System domain enables you to load compiled assemblies from disk and analyze them in the Architecture Explorer.

Dependency Graphs

When you inherit an existing code base, one of the more difficult tasks is trying to figure out the dependencies between the different assemblies, namespaces, and classes. A Dependency Graph enables you to visualize the dependencies between items at different levels of focus. The easiest way to create a Dependency Graph is the Architecture ➪ Generate Dependency Graph menu. This option enables you to create a Dependency Graph by assembly, by namespace, by class, or by some custom criteria that you can define. Four basic options specify the way a Dependency Graph is arranged based on the direction of arrows: top to bottom, left to right, bottom to top, and right to left. Figure 54-18 shows the Left to Right view. There is also a Quick Clusters view, which attempts to arrange the items so that they are closest to the things they connect to.

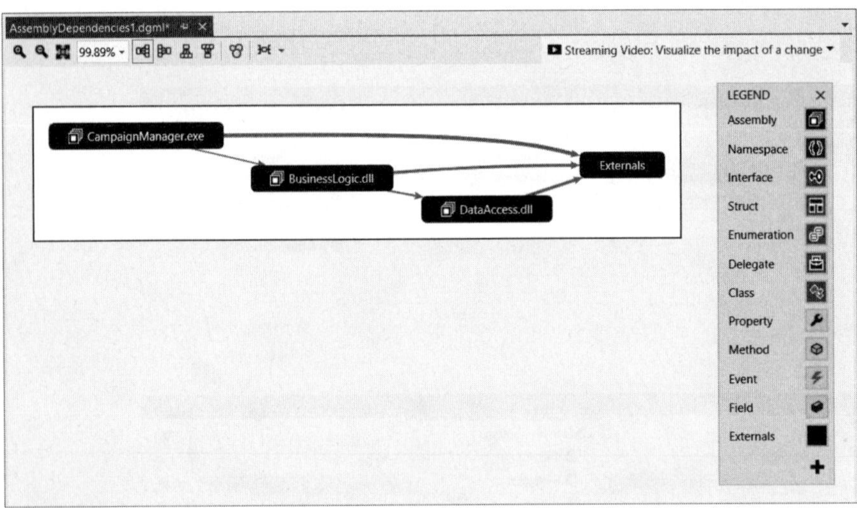

FIGURE 54-18

Generate Sequence Diagram

A .NET Sequence Diagram enables you to model the implementation of a C# or VB method. The best way to create a .NET Sequence Diagram is to right-click a method signature in the editor window and select Generate Sequence Diagram to display the Generate Sequence Diagram dialog, as shown in Figure 54-19.

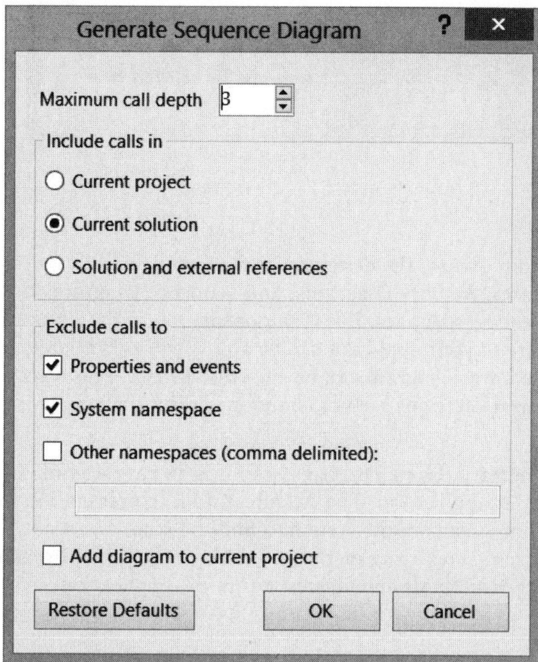

FIGURE 54-19

After you click OK, Visual Studio analyzes your project and produces a .NET Sequence Diagram, as shown in Figure 54-20. You can make changes to this Sequence Diagram without affecting the underlying code, so you can use this diagram to rapidly try out different ideas to see how the code should work.

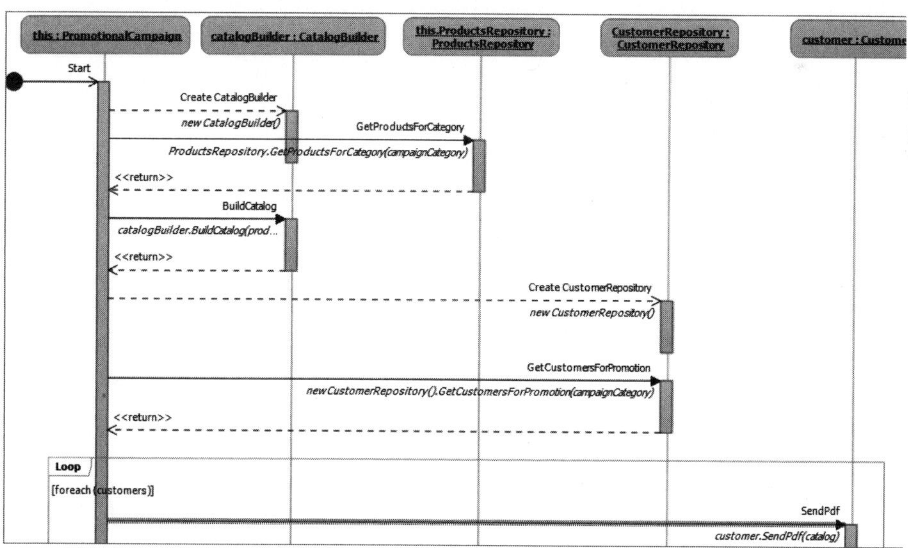

FIGURE 54-20

NOTE *You can add a .NET Sequence Diagram to any .NET project by using the Add New Item dialog. If you add a Sequence Diagram this way, it will not be related to a specific .NET method.*

SUMMARY

Modeling Projects provide a great way for you to communicate the design of your project clearly, unambiguously, and effectively. Use Use Case Diagrams, Activity Diagrams, and Sequence Diagrams to model user requirements from a number of different perspectives. Use Component Diagrams, Class Diagrams, and Layer Diagrams to model the structure of your application. The ability to verify that your application meets the architecture as designed by the Layer Diagram can be a useful sanity check to ensure project quality standards remain high and architectural decisions are not abandoned after the project is underway.

Getting up to speed with an existing code base can be hard. Using Directed Graphs is an easy way to identify the relationships between various parts of your application. The Architecture Explorer enables you to rapidly move through the connections between components in the system to find the items you want. Finally, the ability to generate a Sequence Diagram from an existing method enables you to quickly grasp the fundamentals of how a method interacts with other methods and classes within the application.

55

Visual Studio Ultimate for Developers

WHAT'S IN THIS CHAPTER?

- Analyzing code for potential problems
- Profiling applications to find bottlenecks
- Developing database projects

The Premium and Ultimate editions of Visual Studio 2012 have many advanced features for developers, mainly designed to improve quality and facilitate database development. The quality tools include code metrics, static analysis, and profiling tools. It's not that you can't develop quality software with other editions or that using these tools ensures that your software performs well. Obviously, there's more to it than using a few tools, but these can be of great help to reduce the time invested in other tasks such as code review and debugging. The most interesting debugging tool is IntelliTrace, which enables you to capture environment information associated with failed test cases.

Chapter 27, "Visual Database Tools," examines some of the tools available for working with databases in Visual Studio 2012. This chapter looks at two main areas: SQL-CLR development and tools to help teams working with databases. The first aids in developing and deploying .NET code hosted inside SQL Server. The second enables you to version schema changes, isolating developers and allowing them to compare changes, auto-generate data, and share their modifications easily with other developers or DBAs.

CODE METRICS

Code metrics serve as a reference to know how maintainable your code is. Visual Studio 2012 provides five metrics for your source code, which are all shown in the Code Metrics window (Figure 55-1). To open this window, use the Analyze ➪ Calculate Code Metrics or the Analyze ➪ Windows ➪ Code Metric Results menu. When the window displays, you can use the toolbar button in the top left to recalculate the metrics.

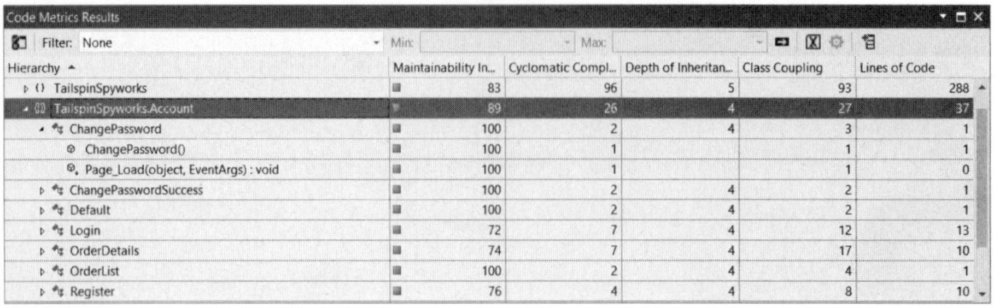

Code Metrics Results

Filter: None Min: Max:

Hierarchy	Maintainability In...	Cyclomatic Compl...	Depth of Inheritan...	Class Coupling	Lines of Code
TailspinSpyworks	83	96	5	93	288
TailspinSpyworks.Account	89	26	4	27	37
ChangePassword	100	2	4	3	1
ChangePassword()	100	1		1	1
Page_Load(object, EventArgs) : void	100	1		1	0
ChangePasswordSuccess	100	2	4	2	1
Default	100	2	4	2	1
Login	72	7	4	12	13
OrderDetails	74	7	4	17	10
OrderList	100	2	4	4	1
Register	76	4	4	8	10

FIGURE 55-1

Directly from the list, you can filter any of the metrics to show methods that fall within a specified range, export to Excel, configure columns to remove metrics, or create a Team Foundation Server work item. Export to Excel is particularly useful to generate reports using pivot tables or to work with a flat view of the information using filters and sorts. For example, if you want to look for methods with more than 15 lines of code, filtering directly in the Code Metrics window can get you a lot of namespaces and types, but you must expand each to see whether or not there are any methods, whereas in Excel you can easily filter out namespaces and types and look at only methods.

As you use the metrics to make decisions about your code, remember that the actual values are not as important as relative values. Having a rule that states "All methods must have less than 25 lines of code" is not as useful as one that makes relative statements such as "prefer shorter methods." You should also consider the changing values as important, so if your average Maintainability Index is going down, it might be a sign you need to focus on making code easier to maintain.

> **NOTE** *For each metric except for Maintainability Index, lower numbers are considered to be better.*

Lines of Code

The name is self-explanatory; however, it's worth mentioning that the purpose of this metric should be to get only a clue of the complexity of the code, and must *not* be used to measure progress. Clearly, a method with five lines of code that calls other methods is simpler than if you inline all 25 lines of code in that method:

```
public class OrdersGenerator
{
  public void GenerateOrder(Order order)
  {
    IsUnderCreditLimit(order);
    IsCustomerBlocked(order.Customer);
    AreProductsInStock(order);
    IsCustomerBlocked(order);
    SaveOrder(order);
  }
  // remaining methods are omitted.
}
```

If you compare a class with six methods, as shown in the preceding code, with a class having the same functionality but with all the code inlined in one method, the latter will have 25 lines. Assuming the remaining methods have five lines each, the former will be 30 lines long, although it is simpler. You must be careful about how to consider this metric; a longer class might be better than a short one.

> **NOTE** *Use the Extract Method refactoring discussed in Chapter 8, "Code Snippets and Refactoring," to reduce this metric. Be sure to keep an eye on extracted methods to see if they might be better in a new class.*

Depth of Inheritance

This metric counts the base classes; some recommendations are to have a value lower than 6. But this, like other metrics, must be looked at with special care. It's hard to give a recommended value, and it's relative to which classes you inherit from. If you inherit from `LinkLabel`, you have a depth of 4, but your base classes are less likely to change than if you inherit from a third-party provided class and have a depth of 1. For most third-party classes there is a higher likelihood that, at some point in the future, the third-party will change its component and break yours. On the other hand, it is a relatively rare occurrence when Microsoft introduces a breaking change in an existing class. However, there is also a consideration that you won't be forced to upgrade to a new third-party class, but it is much more difficult to avoid upgrading .NET classes. The point is that this metric is relative to the source for the base classes you use.

Class Coupling

This counts the dependencies an item has on other types except for primitives and built-in types such as Int32, Object, and String. The more dependencies you have, the harder it's supposed to be to maintain because it would be more probable that changes on other types cause a break in your code. Similarly to depth of inheritance, the importance you give is relative to the dependencies you have. A class referencing System libraries is less likely to have a break than classes referencing other types that are still being actively developed. You can see a value for this metric at each level of the hierarchy (project, namespace, type, and member).

Cyclomatic Complexity

Cyclomatic Complexity is a measure of how many paths of execution there are through your code. A method with higher cyclomatic complexity is harder to understand and maintain than one with a lower value. It is hard to find a recommended value for this metric because it depends on the level of your team and on the team that maintains the product. Far more important is trending information — a steadily increasing cyclomatic complexity indicates that your code is getting harder to understand and follow. Having said that, sometimes a complex solution is warranted.

Maintainability Index

This metric is calculated using a formula that considers cyclomatic complexity, lines of code, and the Halstead volume, which is a metric that considers the total and distinct number of operators and operands. It gives you a range between 0 and 100, with the higher being easier to maintain than the lower.

Excluded Code

Code marked with the `CompilerGenerated` and `GeneratedCode` attributes won't be considered in the metrics. Datasets and Web Service Proxies are examples of code marked with the `GeneratedCode` attribute, but other generated code (like Windows Forms) isn't marked and will be considered in the metric's results.

MANAGED CODE ANALYSIS TOOL

This is a tool based on FxCop that is part of the IDE. It enables you to perform static code analysis using a set of rules that define the quality decisions that you want to apply to your code. You can configure which set of rules to apply to each project from the project property page, as shown in Figure 55-2.

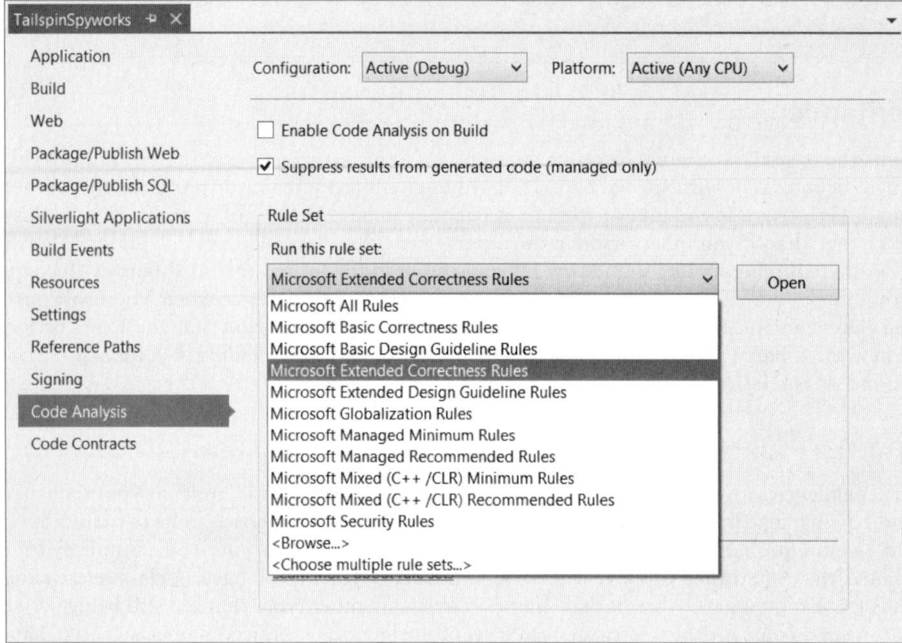

FIGURE 55-2

You can right-click a project and select Run Code Analysis, or if you select Enable Code Analysis on Build in the project's property window, you can simply compile it. The rules will be evaluated, and if there is any violation (and there will be sooner or later) you'll receive a set of warnings in the Error List window.

> **NOTE** *By default each violation appears as a warning, but you can change this behavior.*

If you right-click a warning and select Show Error Help, you have a description of the rule, the cause, the steps on how to fix violations, and suggestions on when to suppress warnings. Suppressing warnings is done with the `System.Diagnostics.CodeAnalysis.SuppressMessageAttribute`, which can be applied to the offending member or to the assembly as a whole. You can quickly and easily generate these attributes by selecting one of the Suppress Message menu options from the right-click menu in the Errors window.

More than 200 rules are conveniently organized into 11 categories, and you can add custom rules if needed. Depending on your project, you might want to exclude some categories or some particular rules. For example, if you don't need globalization and don't have plans in the future to support it, you might exclude that category. You can even create your own sets of rules (Add New Item ⇨ Code Analysis Rule Set) if the ones provided by Microsoft don't meet your needs.

When you first start with Code Analysis tools, you should turn on all the rules and either exclude or suppress the warnings as needed. This is an excellent way to learn best practices. After a couple of iterations, new code written will be less prone to violating a rule. If you start a new project, you might want to add a check-in policy, which prevents code with Analysis warnings from being checked in.

> **NOTE** *Never suppress a warning unless you have a good reason. Finding these violations again can be quite difficult.*

C/C++ CODE ANALYSIS TOOL

This tool is similar to the Managed Code Analysis Tool but works for unmanaged code. To activate it simply go to your C++ project's properties window, look for the Code Analysis node inside the Configuration Properties, and select Yes for Enable Code Analysis for C/C++ on Build. Every time you compile your project, the tool intercepts the process and attempts to analyze each execution path.

It can help you detect crashes that are otherwise hard to find with other techniques such as debugging that are time-consuming. It can detect memory leaks, uninitialized variables, pointer management problems, and buffer over/under runs.

PROFILING TOOLS

Profiling tools enables you to detect and correct performance and memory issues in your projects. You can start a profiling session by selecting the Launch Performance Wizard from the Analyze menu. The first step of the wizard asks you to select one of four profiling methods:

- CPU Sampling reports the CPU utilization at regular intervals while your application runs. This type of profiling is good for initial analysis or to identify issues specifically related to CPU usage.
- Instrumentation actually inserts additional lines of code into your assembly to report on the length of time each method call takes. You can use this sort of profiling to get a detailed look at where your application spends most of its time.
- The .NET Memory profiler collects data about objects as they are created and as they are cleared up by the garbage collector.
- Concurrency profiling collects information about multithreaded applications and provides some visualizations that you can use to explore several concurrency-related issues.

Next you need to select a project, executable, DLL, or website to profile. With that information, the Performance Wizard creates a performance session and opens the Performance Explorer window. You could also create a blank session from the Performance Explorer or from a test in the Test Results window.

In the Performance Explorer (Figure 55-3), you can see the different components that make up this performance session. And although you can instrument or sample a DLL, you need a point of entry for your application to run when you start the session, so be sure to include an executable, website, or test project as a target.

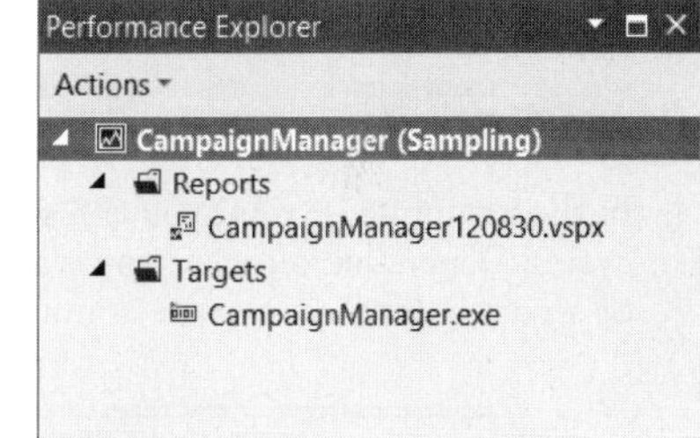

FIGURE 55-3

> **NOTE** *If you have high code coverage, profiling unit test projects can give you a good insight into which methods take the longest to execute or use the most memory. Be wary of reacting to this information, though, because long-running methods may be called infrequently, and improving an already fast method that is called many times will have a greater impact on overall application performance.*

Configuring Profiler Sessions

To configure your session, simply right-click and select Properties. In the General section you can change between Sampling, Instrumentation, and Concurrency (Figure 55-4), and choose if you want to activate .NET memory profiling collection, the output for the reports, and the report names.

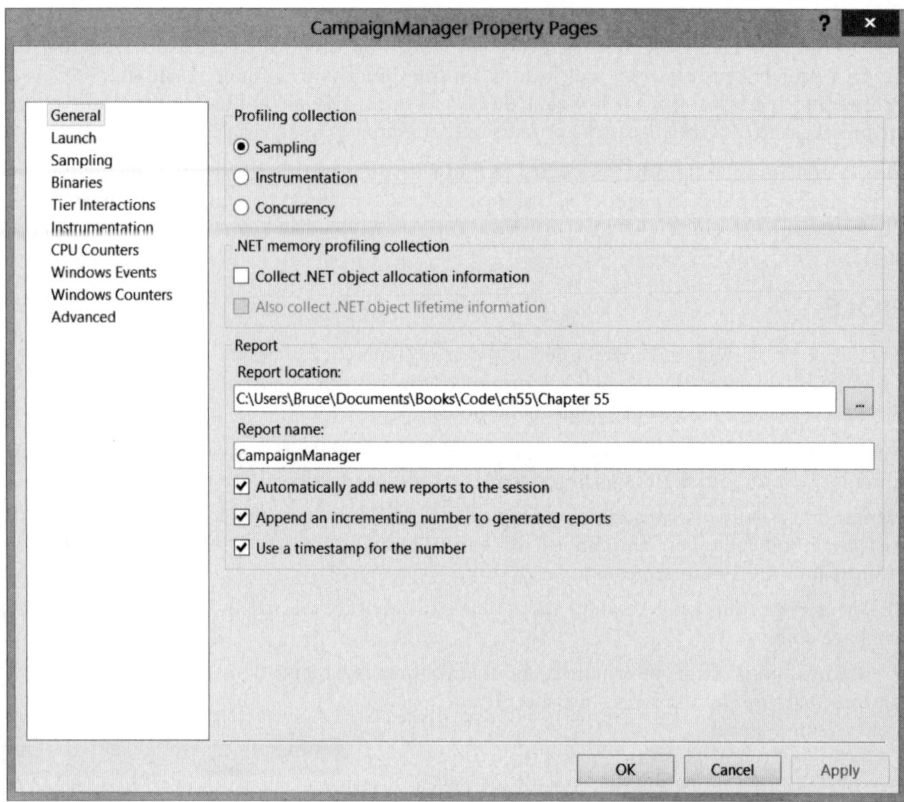

FIGURE 55-4

In the Sampling section, you can select when to take samples; by default this is set to 10,000,000 clock cycles. Depending on what you want to track, you can change the sample event to page faults, system calls, or a particular performance counter.

> **NOTE** *For some versions of operating systems, you might not be able to change the Sampling variables. For instance, as of this writing, Windows 8 64-bit showed a message These Settings Are Not Supported for CPU Samplings on This Version of Windows. Your mileage may vary.*

Enabling Tier Interaction Profiling (TIP) enables you to collect information about synchronous ADO.NET calls between your application and SQL Server. This includes the number of times each query is made and how long each one took. If you are profiling an ASP.NET WebForms application, TIP can also provide data about page request counts and generation times.

The Instrumentation section is used to specify pre- and post-instrument events; for example, signing an assembly with a strong name. These settings are set on a per-target basis. The last section in the property page, Advanced, is also used when instrumentation is selected, and there you can specify additional command arguments. To see a list of available options, search for VSInstr on MSDN. VSInstr is the tool used to instrument binaries.

The remaining sections are used to specify the collection of different counters or events. CPU Counters enable you to capture additional low-level information and displays as extra columns in the different report views, which are only available for instrumentation. The Windows Counters are system performance counters, and you can see the results in the Marks report view.

The Windows Events section enables you to specify event trace providers. To see the information on Windows events, you need to manually get a text report using the following command:

```
Vsperfreport c:\<path>ReportName.vsp /calltrace /output:c:\<path>
```

Reports

After you are set, you can start the application, test, or website from the Performance Explorer. It runs as usual but collects data. After your application terminates, a report generates. Table 55-1 shows a description of some of the report views, and Figure 55-5 shows the Summary view.

TABLE 55-1: Some Report Views

VIEW NAME	DESCRIPTION
Summary	Shows function information. Sampling it shows functions causing the most work and functions with the most individual work. With instrumentation it shows the most called functions with the most individual work and functions taking the longest. From here you can navigate to the Functions view. If Collect .NET Object Allocation Information is selected (refer to Figure 55-4), it shows functions allocating the most memory and types with the most memory allocated and most instances.
Call Tree	Contains a hierarchy of the functions called. The Call Tree has a feature called Hot Spot that can point you to child functions taking the most time.
Modules	Shows information about the module sampled or instrumented.
Caller/Callee	Shows you which functions a particular function called and which functions called it.
Functions	Presents a list of all the functions sampled or instrumented. Double-clicking each function enables you to navigate to the caller/callee window.
Object Lifetime	To improve the performance of garbage collection, the managed heap is divided into different generations. Objects are placed into the different generations based on their lifetime (that is, how long they continue to be referenced). The object lifetime report displays the number and size of the objects that are created in the profiled application and the generation they were in when reclaimed.
Allocations	Shows the number of instances and bytes allocated of a particular type.

Additional reports can be generated using the command-line tool VSPerfReport. For more information, consult the MSDN documentation.

Allocations and Object Lifetime are only available if you select Collect .NET Object Allocation Information and Also Collect .NET Object Lifetime Information, respectively, in the session's property page. Some of the report views are different depending on the configuration. To see a description of a particular column, simply hover over its title. You should go through the documentation on MSDN to get a thorough description on each report.

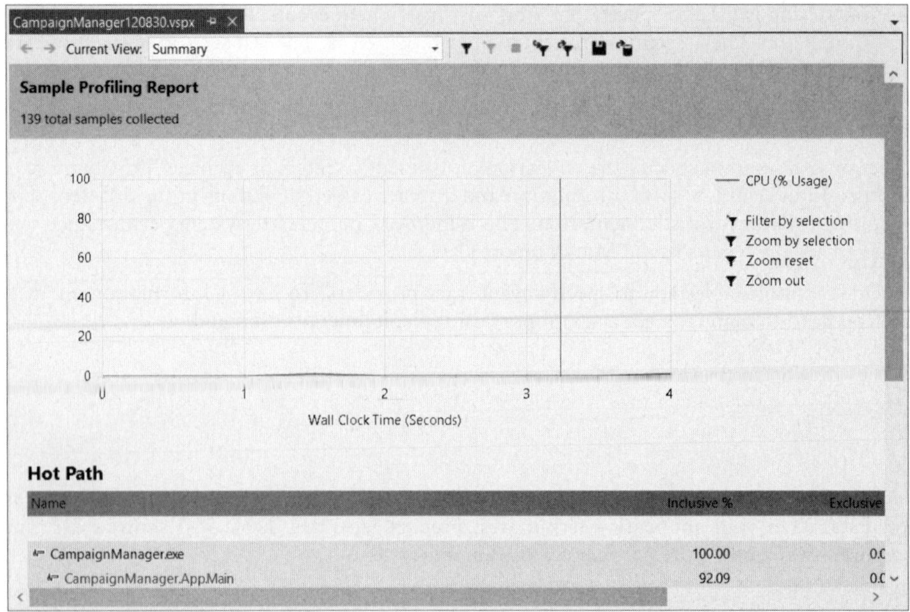

FIGURE 55-5

In all the views, you can use the filter from the toolbar to get to specific information. You can add or remove columns by right-clicking a header and sort using a particular column. Reports can be exported to either XML or CSV, and successive reports can be compared against one another, enabling you to spot changes in your application's performance.

STANDALONE PROFILER

This is a command-line tool that is useful when you need to profile an application without installing Visual Studio on the machine — for example, in a production environment. Depending on the edition of Visual Studio 2012, this tool may or may not already be installed. For the Ultimate edition, the command is ready for use with no additional effort. For Premium or Professional, the tool needs to be installed separately. To install this tool, you need to execute `vs_profiler.exe` from the Visual Studio installation media located in the Standalone Profiler folder. It installs the tools in the directory `%ProgramFiles%\Microsoft Visual Studio 11.0\Team Tools\Performance Tools`. If you use the command-line profiler often, you can add this path to the system path.

The following commands profile an application using sampling with the default settings. The first line enables the trace. The next command switches the profiler to use CPU Sampling and to output a report. In this case the report will be saved in the ApplicationToProfile directory on a file named `Report.vsp`. Then you launch the application and interact with it as usual; when finished, you'll finally shut down the Profiler. You can then open and inspect the generated report in Visual Studio:

```
C:\ApplicationToProfile>vsperfclrenv /traceon
Enabling VSPerf Trace Profiling of managed applications (excluding allocation
profiling).
...
C:\ApplicationToProfile>vsperfcmd -start:sample -output:Report
Microsoft (R) VSPerf Command Version 11.0.50522 x86
...
```

```
C:\ApplicationToProfile>vsperfcmd -launch:Application.exe
Microsoft (R) VSPerf Command Version 11.0.50522 x86
...
Successfully launched process ID:4144 Application.exe
C:\ApplicationToProfile>vsperfcmd -shutdown
Microsoft (R) VSPerf Command Version 11.0.50522 x86
...
Shutting down the Profile Monitor
```

INTELLITRACE

IntelliTrace is a tool that makes the process of debugging your application much easier. It operates like a flight recorder while you are in a debug session and enables you to look at historical values and state. In addition to this, you can save IntelliTrace sessions and load them back up at a later time. Testers who use Microsoft Test Manager can also collect IntelliTrace information while they run through test cases, providing you with the exact state of the system when a bug is reported.

> **NOTE** *IntelliTrace currently supports C# and VB projects with experimental support for F#. And Windows Store applications are supported for events only. You cannot use IntelliTrace by using the Attach to Process command or in remote debugging scenarios.*

When a debugging session is started and IntelliTrace is enabled (Tools ➪ Options ➪ IntelliTrace) the IntelliTrace window (Figure 55-6) displays. This window maintains a list of diagnostic events that IntelliSense can detect.

As each new diagnostic event occurs, Visual Studio adds it to the end of the list. If you pause the execution or hit a breakpoint, the IntelliTrace window becomes active. If you click any of the diagnostic events, it expands to show a little more information. This expanded view contains a list of Related Views, which have been updated by IntelliTrace to reflect the state of the application at the time of the event. You can check the call-stack, add watches, check locals, and generally perform any of the tasks that you would normally do during a normal debugging session. When you are ready to resume execution of the application you can click the Return to Live Debugging button.

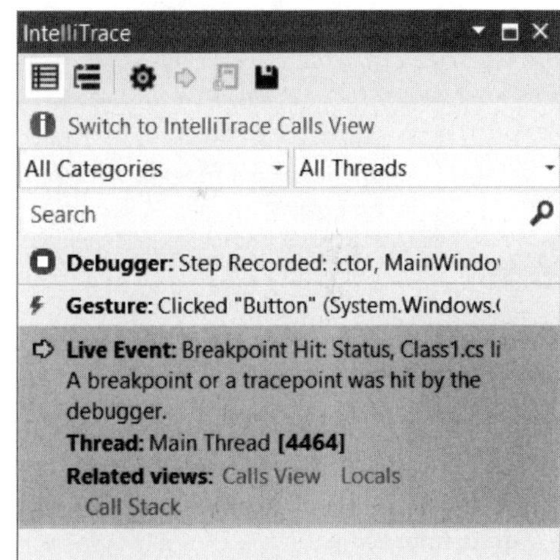

FIGURE 55-6

IntelliTrace can capture two types of information during a debugging session. IntelliTrace Events are enabled by default and include Visual Studio debugger events such as application start and hitting breakpoints. Throwing and catching exceptions are also IntelliTrace events. When a tester collects IntelliTrace information, the beginning and end of a test along with any failures form contextual events covered under the label of IntelliTrace Events. Finally, the Framework can raise some diagnostic events. You can find a list of these in the IntelliTrace options.

The other type of information that IntelliTrace can track is method calls along with parameter information. To use this information, you need to turn it on before starting the debugging session (Tools ➪ Options ➪ IntelliTrace). After Call Information is activated, you can switch the IntelliTrace window over to the Show Calls View (Figure 55-7), which shows each method call entry and exit along with a sublist of events that occurred during their execution. Referring to Figure 55-7, you can see that for any point in the call view you can navigate into the code (via the Switch to Entry of Call option) or a view of the local variable values (through the Go to Locals Window option).

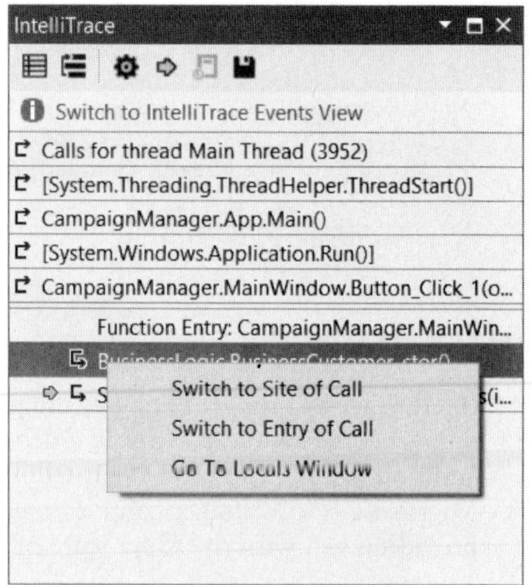

FIGURE 55-7

When you are in an IntelliTrace session with Call Information enabled, a new border is added to the editor window, which contains IntelliTrace navigational markers (Figure 55-8). You can use these to navigate the IntelliSense information from inside the editor.

IntelliTrace files (`.tdlog` files) are stored in a default location on your hard drive and can be archived and re-opened later. When you open a `.tdlog` file, you'll see the IntelliTrace Summary view. By double-clicking a thread or an exception, you can open the IntelliTrace session at the appropriate point and begin debugging again.

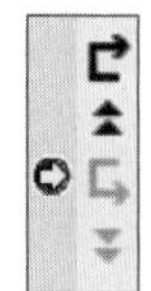

FIGURE 55-8

> **NOTE** *By default, IntelliTrace files are stored in the* `C:\ProgramData\Microsoft Visual Studio\11.0\TraceDebugging` *folder. You can always check where the files are stored from Tools ➪ Options ➪ IntelliTrace ➪ Advanced. Also, be warned that if you have enabled IntelliTrace, then every debugging session creates these files. There are not small files, so over time you may find a large amount of disk space being used up by the log files.*

DATABASE TOOLS

Most applications require some kind of database to store data when it is not being used. In Visual Studio 2012 the number of projects used for database has been reduced. The SQL-CLR Database project has been deprecated; although its functionality is still available. As well, there is only one database project. (The wizard is no longer present in Visual Studio 2012.) But the capability of the remaining project is still quite impressive.

Database Schemas

You can find the Database Project available in Visual Studio 2012 in the SQL Server node under Other Languages, as shown in Figure 55-9. There is only one project available out of the box. This project enables you to create an offline representation of your DB schema so that you can version it along with your code. It creates a file for each schema object and deploys the changes to a database.

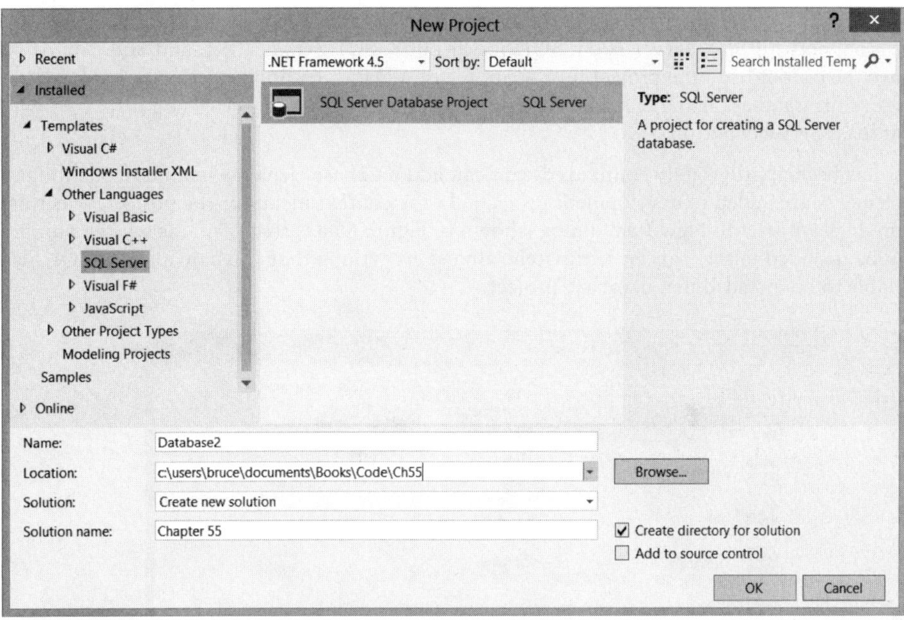

FIGURE 55-9

Because the Visual Studio 2010 wizard is no longer present in Visual Studio 2012, the result of adding a database project is a bare project within the Solution Explorer. It is incumbent upon you to add the functionality that you require. As a starting point, Figure 55-10 includes the initial properties screen for the project (accessed by right-clicking the project in the Solution Explorer and selecting Properties from the context menu).

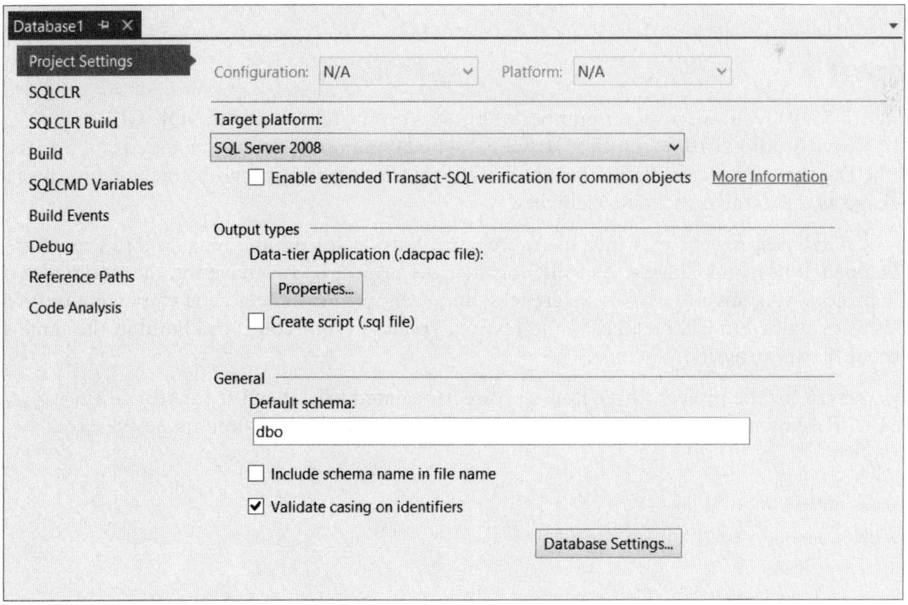

Database1
Project Settings
SQLCLR
SQLCLR Build
Build
SQLCMD Variables
Build Events
Debug
Reference Paths
Code Analysis
Configuration: N/A
Platform: N/A
Target platform:
SQL Server 2008
Enable extended Transact-SQL verification for common objects
More Information
Output types
Data-tier Application (.dacpac file):
Properties...
Create script (.sql file)
General
Default schema:
dbo
Include schema name in file name
Validate casing on identifiers
Database Settings...

FIGURE 55-10

The Target platform property indicates the database onto which the output from this project will be deployed. There is support for SQL Server 2005, SQL Server 2008, SQL Server 2012, and SQL Azure. As well, you can have the output from the project be a script file or a Data Tier application. And you can use options to configure the database being created through the default schema and the dialog displayed when you click the Database Settings button.

After the project has been appropriately configured, you can add database elements in a manner similar to how coding elements are added to development projects. In the context menu for the project, selecting Add ➪ New Item displays an Add New Item dialog (shown in Figure 55-11) that contains a large number of items that can be included in the project. Ultimately, almost everything that you can add to a SQL Server database is available to be included in a database project.

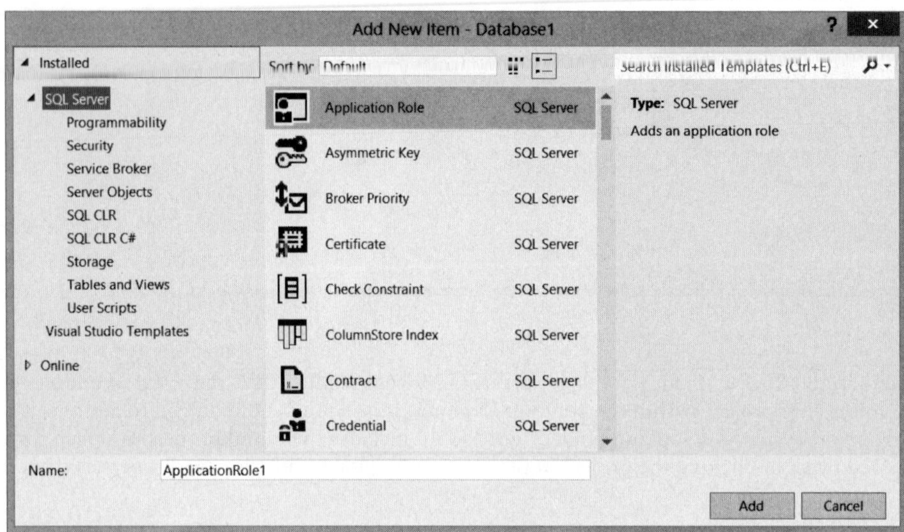

FIGURE 55-11

SQL-CLR Support

If you refer to Figure 55-10, you can notice a number of options on the left related to SQL-CLR configuration. In Visual Studio 2010, creating SQL-CLR-related components required a separate project. However, with the Database Project in Visual Studio 2012, SQL-CLR elements can be included in the same deployment package as the database schema elements.

You can add to the database project types such as Aggregates, User-Defined Functions, Stored Procedures, Triggers, User-Defined Types, and Classes. As well, consider the project to also have the characteristics of a normal VB/C# project; you can add classes, references, and even web references. You can create unit tests for your methods as explained in Chapter 11, "Unit Testing," refactor your code, and build in the same way you would for other library projects.

In the Properties section for the project, three tabs are directly related to SQL-CLR functionality. The first tab SQLCLR (shown in Figure 55-12) is used to configure the assembly and namespace to be deployed.

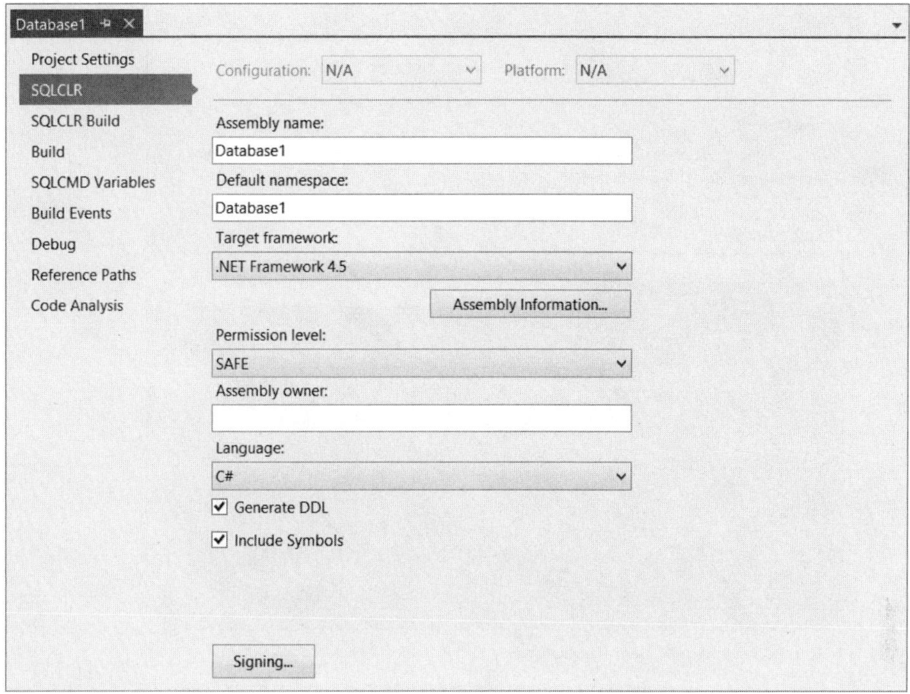

FIGURE 55-12

Most of the properties in this tab are similar to those found in typical projects in that they set the name of the assembly, the default namespace, the target .NET Framework version, and additional attributes related to the assembly. The value that is most useful in a SQL-CLR environment is the Permission Level. This property specifies the properties that must be granted to the assembly by the host process in SQL Server. The values for the property are as follows:

- **SAFE:** The only functionality allowed within the assembly is local data access and computational code. No external access to files, the network, or the Registry is available.
- **EXTERNAL_ACCESS:** The same access as SAFE, except the restrictions on network access, files, or the Registry are removed. However, there are still limitations, such as not being able to invoke unmanaged code.
- **UNSAFE:** This is basically the anything-goes mode. All resources, both inside and outside SQL Server, can be accessed.

The SQLCLR Build tab contains information related to building the assembly. How this information affects the build process is covered in Chapter 6, "Solutions, Projects, and Items."

The SQLCMD Variables tab provides configurable values to your assembly. Conceptually, this is similar to the AppSettings portion of a configuration file. As you can see in Figure 55-13, three values are associated with each variable: the variable name, the default value, and the local value. For each variable that you require in your assembly, add a row to the grid that is visible.

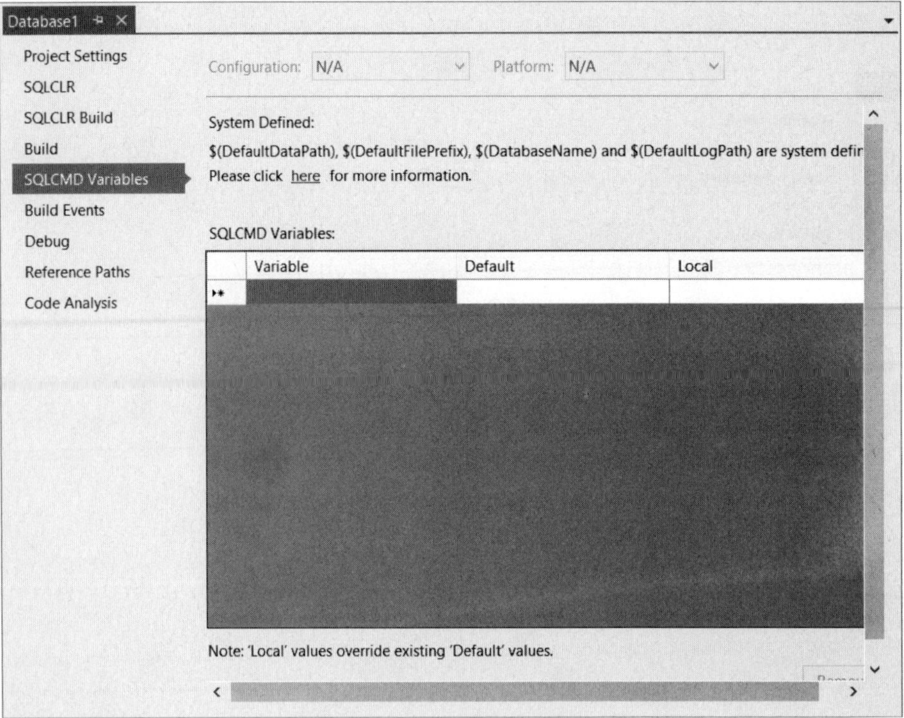

FIGURE 55-13

When the project is published, there is an opportunity to provide the specific values for these variables. If a value is not provided, then the default value is used.

Debugging a project that utilizes SQL-CLR components is a bit different because your code runs in an SQL Server context. First, you need to allow Visual Studio to remotely debug the code. This is needed only the first time you debug your project. However, the point of entry for your code is through a script that uses any of your managed objects.

Database Refactoring

Chapter 8 introduces the topic of refactoring for normal .NET code. For databases you have only a few refactoring tasks: Rename, Move Schema, Expand Wildcards, and Fully Qualify Names. You can rename tables, columns, stored procedures, constraints, and indexes, as well as other database objects. You can also rename the references to other servers or databases if a cross-database reference is used in the scripts.

To rename an object (such as a table or a column) from the Schema View (the designer view for a script element), right-click it, and select Rename from the Refactor submenu. Alternatively, you can select the object in the Schema View and select the SQL ➪ Refactor ➪ Rename menu item. When renaming an object, there is a Preview changes check box on the Rename dialog that allows you to see a preview of the changes. An example is shown in Figure 55-14. In the upper pane you'll see the old version, and in the lower pane you'll see the new one for all the dependencies.

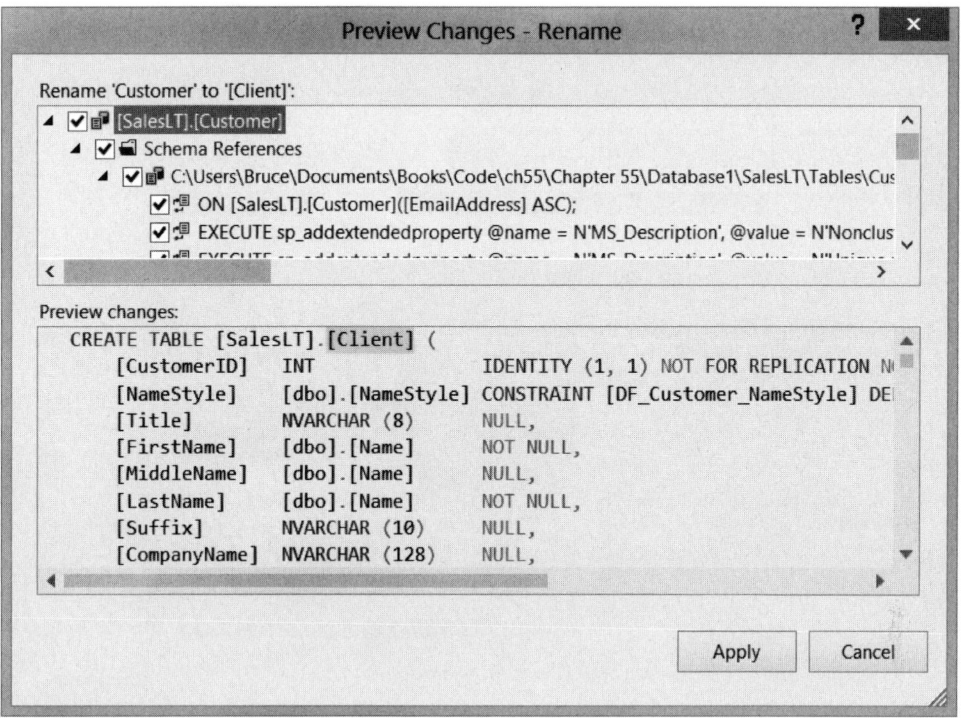

FIGURE 55-14

Renaming is easily done when the schema is offline, such as prior to initial deployment into production. But for tables and columns (which are online), it can be hard to deploy to the database. Many changes require the old object to be dropped and re-created, which can result in data loss. If you need to preserve your data, you should either modify the deployment script or apply the refactoring manually. See "Protecting Data During a Renaming Operation" on MSDN for more information.

Schema Compare

The Schema Compare tool enables you to compare schemas between databases or Database Projects. To use it, from the SQL ⇨ Schema Compare menu, select New Schema Comparison. You must select a project or database as Source and a project or database as Target. After the source and target have been selected, click the Compare button. When you do that, a window similar to the one shown in Figure 55-15 displays. The lower pane shows both versions of the selected object with the changes highlighted. It's handy to use the filters from the toolbar; by default all objects display. You should select Non Skip Objects to see only the differences.

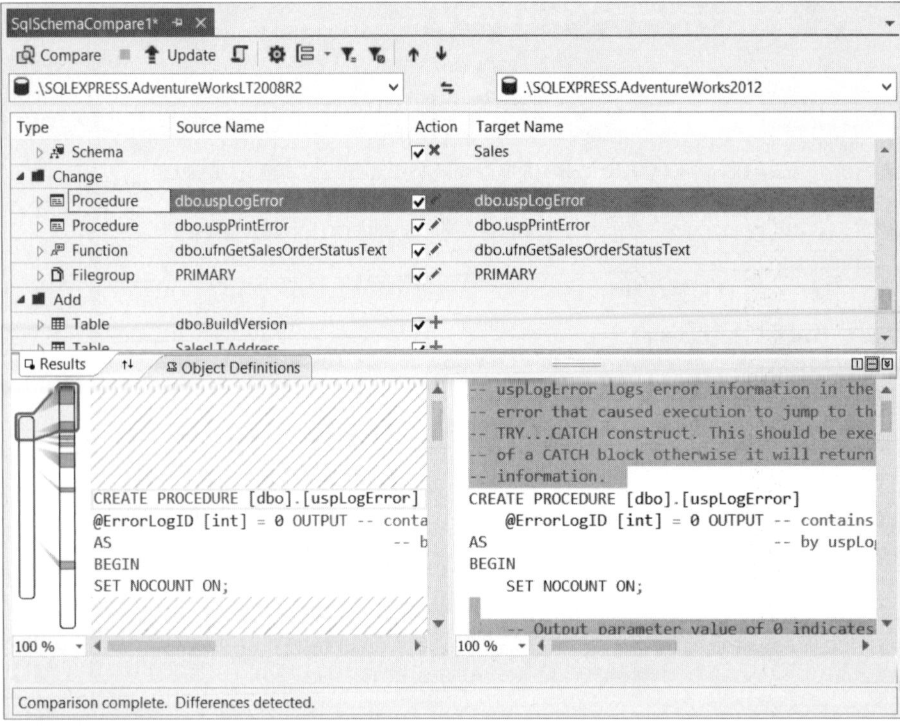

FIGURE 55-15

For each DB object, you can see the applied action. Then from the toolbar you can either select Write Updates to apply all the changes or Export to Editor to get the SQL statements used for the update if you need to do manual changes or hand it out to your DBA.

To customize the options for Schema Comparisons, click the Options button (the gear icon in Figure 55-15). By default, Block on Possible Data Loss is selected; this is recommended but can cause some updates to fail. You can uncheck this option, but be sure you're running on a test database and that you can regenerate the data. Other options such as Ignore White Space can be useful to reduce unnecessary changes.

Remember that if you use a Database Project as the target, clicking the Update button writes the changes from the source to the target.

Static Analysis

Visual Studio 2012 Premium and Ultimate include static analysis tools for databases as well as for code. To run the static analysis tools, select SQL ➪ Static Analysis ➪ Run. Currently, there are more than a dozen rules spread across three categories to help you develop databases: Design, Naming, and Performance.

Transact-SQL Editor

This editor enables you to work with Transact-SQL (T-SQL) code directly in Visual Studio. To open it, you can double-click a `.sql` file in Solution Explorer or from the Schema View of a Database Project. Another option is to start with a blank editor; to do this go to SQL ➪ Transact-SQL Editor, and select New Query Connection. Now you can start to write your T-SQL, with nice coloring and most of Visual Studio's shortcuts and features like bookmarks and search and replace. From the toolbar or the T-SQL Editor menu, you can validate syntax, execute your code, include client statistics, disconnect to work offline, and reconnect when you need to run a query. When you run the queries, the results can display on a grid or text format or be exported to a file. You can also change this behavior from the menu or toolbar.

Best Practices

The following is a list of best practices compiled through work with Database Professionals that work on small- and medium-sized projects:

- Each developer works with his own local SQL database instance, one for development and another for testing. This is necessary to isolate uncommitted and untested changes to avoid affecting other developers working on the database at the same time. It is strictly necessary for managed-code debugging purposes because starting a debugging session can cause all managed threads to stop. From the project properties for Database Projects, you can specify the database to target for each Solution Configuration, but SQL-CLR projects can target only one database.
- Each developer works with two databases, one for development and one for unit testing because different data will be used for each.
- Use (local) or 127.0.0.1 for the hostname instead of, say, MikesComputer or 192.168.2.6, which would work only on one machine.
- If you use database instances, be sure all your developers have an instance with the same name.
- All developers should have the same SQL Server version. Although SQL Server Express can be used for design-time validation and testing purposes, some features, such as Text Indexing, are not supported.
- Clear the Block Incremental Deployment if Data Loss Might Occur check box in the project properties window for the Solution Configuration used for Test Databases. Because you will have a Data Generation Plan, data will be easy to re-create after changes have been made to the schema.
- When deploying to a production database, build the Database Project; then modify the build script to manually deploy it to the server. You can lean on the Schema Comparison tool to have a more granular view of the changes made.

SUMMARY

In this chapter, you saw a couple of advanced features that are part of Visual Studio 2012 Premium. All these target quality improvement. Code Metrics and the Analysis Tool can analyze your code or binaries statically, collecting metrics and evaluating rules. The metrics are useful to see how maintainable your code is. For the analysis, you have rules for different categories to help you ensure that your code performs well before it runs. On the other hand, the Profiling Tools evaluate your code at run time, and IntelliTrace enables you to explore the execution of your application during a debugging session.

This chapter covered some of the most important features for database developers. You saw how easy it is to develop code for SQL-CLR and how the SQL Server Database Projects can help you work on a team, versioning and merging your changes. Advanced features such as refactoring and unit testing can change the way you develop databases, and tools such as Schema Compare, Data Compare, Data Generation, and the T-SQL Editor support the process as well.

56

Visual Studio Ultimate for Testers

WHAT'S IN THIS CHAPTER?

- Testing web and windows applications
- Identifying relationships between code and tests
- Planning, executing, and coordinating testing tasks
- Managing test environments

You can test an application in many ways. Chapter 11, "Unit Testing," introduced the concept of unit tests, which are small executable pieces of code that verify a particular aspect of behavior for a single method or class. The first part of this chapter examines the advanced tools built into Visual Studio that are available for other testing tasks, including testing web applications. You'll also learn how to track the relationships between tests and code.

Visual Studio also contains a product called Test Manager. This tool is designed for testers to interact directly with Team Foundation Servers and manage test plans, suites, and cases. Test Manager is available with the Ultimate edition of Visual Studio and as a part of a separate pack called Test Elements. If you are a tester, or spend a great deal of time working on the testing aspect of development projects, then Test Manager is worth a look. Although beyond the scope of this book, a number of tools can make your life not only easier, but it can make capturing and conveying exception conditions to the development team seamless.

AUTOMATED TESTS

An automated test is a piece of code that verifies the behavior of your application without any user input or control. After the system has been asked to run an automated test, it can be left unattended until it completes.

The starting point for creating a new automated test is a testing project. The mechanics of creating a test project was covered in Chapter 11, but for the upcoming examples it's useful to create a Web Performance and Load Test project. To add a new test to an existing project, use the Add ➪ New Item option from the Solution's context menu. There is a Test node in the Add New Item dialog with the different test templates displayed on the right side. Alternatively (and probably more convenient), the context menu also includes options to add a Unit Test, a Load Test, a Web Performance Test, a Coded UI Test, an Ordered Test, or a Generic Test (see Figure 56-1).

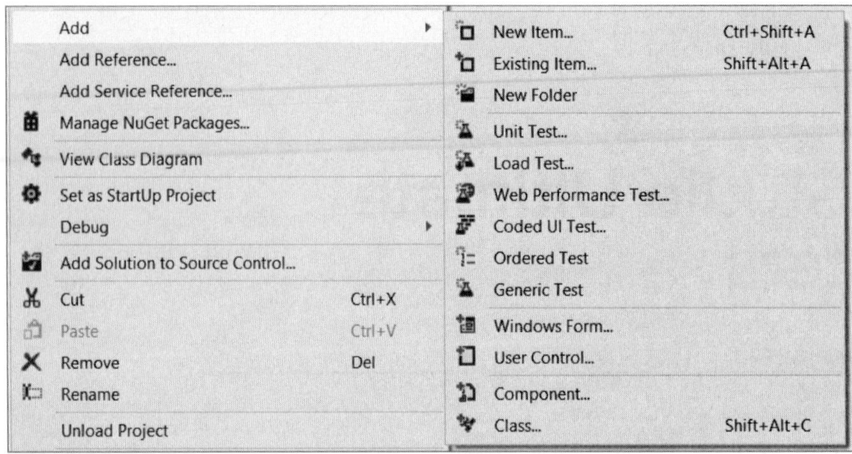

FIGURE 56-1

> **NOTE** *Depending on which edition of Visual Studio you use, you might not have all the tests shown in Figure 56-1. Coded UI Tests are only available in the Premium and Ultimate editions. Web Performance Tests and Load Tests are only available in the Ultimate edition. The rest of the automated tests are available in all three editions.*

Web Performance Tests

This type of automated test simulates web requests, enables you to inspect the responses, and evaluate different conditions to determine if the test passes. When you create a new Web Performance Test, Internet Explorer opens with the Web Test Recorder enabled, as shown in Figure 56-2. Navigate to and around your site as if you were a normal user. When done, simply click Stop. This opens the Web Test Designer, as shown in Figure 56-3. From there you can customize your test, adding validation and extraction rules, context parameters, comments, data sources, calls to other Web Performance Tests, or insert transactions. You can also specify response time goals for requests.

FIGURE 56-2

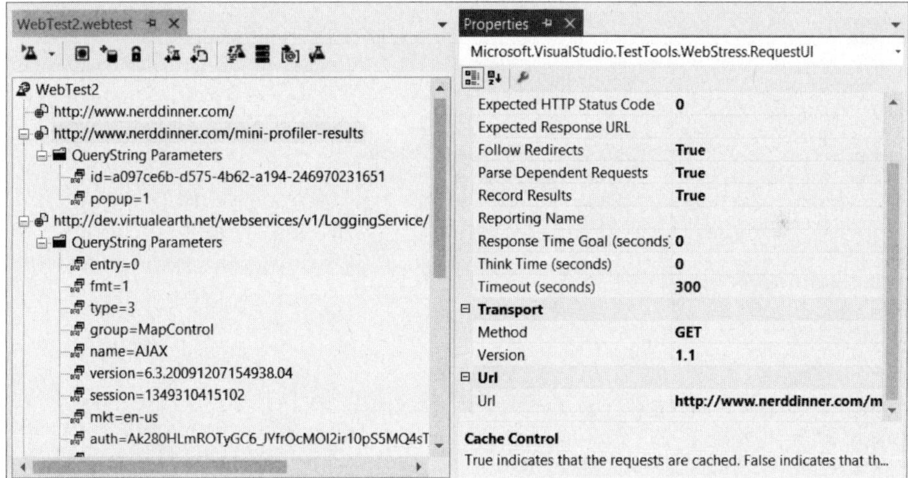

FIGURE 56-3

You often need to run the same set of tests against different web servers; to do this, configure which server the test runs against as a context parameter. From the Web Test Designer, you can right-click the main node and select Parameterize Web Servers. Visual Studio inspects the URLs in each request and determines the context parameters it needs to create.

You can link your requests using the output from one of them as input for the next; to do this, add extraction rules to a specific request. You can extract from fields, attributes, HTTP headers, hidden fields, and text, or even use regular expressions. The result of an extraction sets a context parameter, which you can then use, for example, as a form or query string parameter in further requests. You can add a product and then search for it using the ID in another request.

You can add form and query string parameters from the context menu of a request. By selecting a form or query string parameter from the properties window, you can set its value to a context parameter or bind it to a data source.

No test framework would be complete without validations. When you record a test, a Response URL Validation Rule is added asserting that the response URL is the same as the recorded response URL. This is not enough for most scenarios. From the context menu at the Web Performance Test or for an individual request, you can add validation rules. You can check that a form field or attribute has a certain value or that a particular tag is included, find some text, or ascertain that the request doesn't take more than a specified length of time.

Double-clicking the `.testconfig` file in Solution Explorer allows you to further customize how Web Performance Tests run. There you can choose the number of iterations, the browser and network type, and whether or not the test engine should simulate think times. You can have many Test Run Configurations and from the Test menu select the active one.

You can run a Web Performance Test directly from the Web Test Designer. After a test is run, you can see its details by double-clicking it in the Test Results window. To open this window, from the Test Windows menu, select Test Results. There you can see each request's status, total time, and bytes. When you select a request, you'll see the details of the selected request and received response, values of the context parameters, validations and extraction rules, and a web-browser-like view displaying the web page. An example is shown in Figure 56-4.

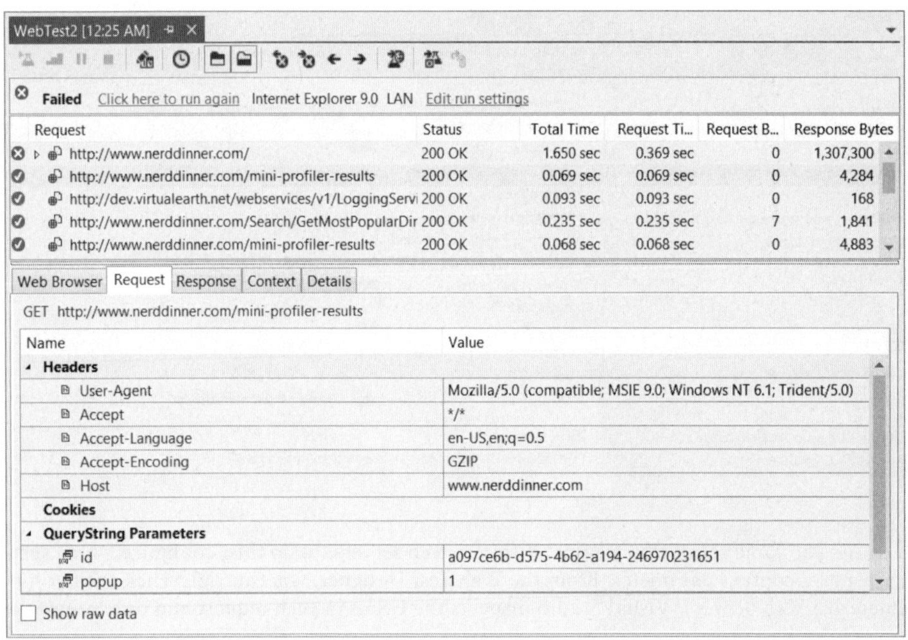

FIGURE 56-4

If you need additional flexibility, you can code the Web Performance Tests using .NET and the Web Testing Framework. The best way to learn how to use the framework and start coding your test is by generating code for a recorded Web Performance Test. You have this option (Generate Code) in the Web Test context menu.

> **NOTE** *Although Visual Studio provides support for some ASP.NET-specific features, you can use Web Performance Tests for sites built using other technologies.*

Load Tests

Whereas web and load testing are meant to test functional requirements, Load Tests can run a set of tests repeatedly, so you can see how your application performs. When you create a new Load Test, you are presented with a wizard that guides you through the necessary steps. First, you need to create a scenario; here you define if you want to use think times. When you recorded the Web Performance Tests, the time you took between each request was also recorded and can be used as the think time. It can be edited for each Web request in the properties window.

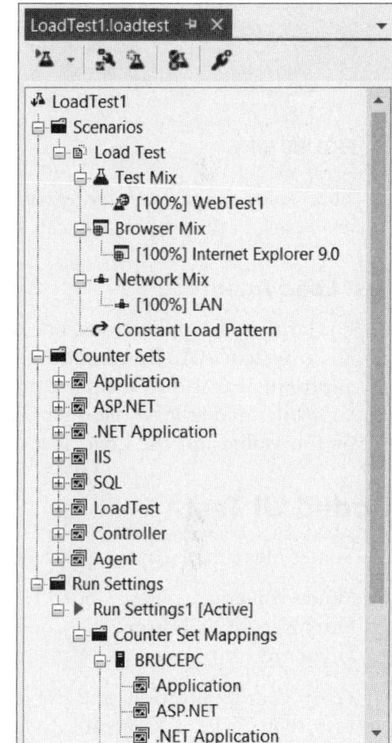

FIGURE 56-5

As part of the scenario, you'll define the load pattern; for example, a constant load of 100 users or a load incrementing by 10 every 10 seconds until you get to 200 users. The next steps, Test, Browser, and Network Mix, define how tests will be run by virtual users, specify which browsers will be used to run the tests, and determine the kinds of network that will be simulated. In the Test Mix step you can add Generic, Ordered, and Web Performance Tests.

In the Counter Sets step, you'll add the computers that you want to monitor and the performance counters you are interested in. For example, you can monitor your Database Server and IIS. In the last step, Run Settings, you can specify the test duration or test iterations, how often samples will be taken for performance counters, a test description, how many identical errors will be recorded, and the validation level. We defined a validation level for each Validation Rule in our Web Performance Tests. Because evaluation of these rules can be expensive, in Load Tests only rules with a level equal to or below the specified validation level will be evaluated.

When you click Finish, you are presented with the Load Test Designer, as shown in Figure 56-5. There you can add additional scenarios, counter sets, or new run settings.

When you run the tests, you'll see the Load Test Monitor; by default it shows the Graphs view. In the left-side pane you have a tree view of the counters that are collected. You can select items there to add them to the graphics. From the toolbar, you can change to Summary or Tables view, export to Excel or CSV, and add analysis notes. In the Graphs view at the bottom, you have a legends pane, as shown in Figure 56-6. There you can select/deselect the counters that you want to include in the graphs. While the test runs, the monitor is updated on each sample interval. In the Tables view, you can see the Requests, Errors, Pages, SQL Trace, Tests, Thresholds, and Transactions.

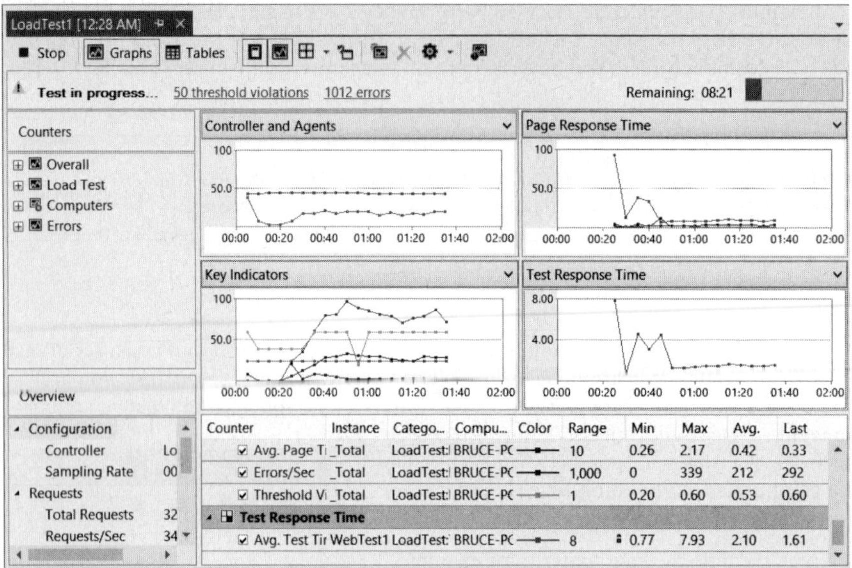

FIGURE 56-6

Thresholds are particularly important. These are values for each performance counter that enable you to spot problems. In the graphs, you can see points where violations occurred marked with a warning or error icon.

Test Load Agent

For large-scale applications, one computer might not be enough to simulate the wanted load. Visual Studio Team System 2012 Test Load Agent can distribute the work across different machines. It can simulate approximately 1,000 users per processor. This product requires a separate installation and requires one controller and at least one agent. To configure the environment, select the Manage Test Controllers button on the toolbar for the Load Test designer. There you can select a controller and add agents.

Coded UI Test

Sometimes the best way to test an application is to drive it from the outside as a user would.

When you create a new Coded UI Test, it starts the Coded UI Test Builder (Figure 56-7). When you click the Start Recording button, the Coded UI Test Builder tracks all the actions that you take with the mouse and keyboard.

Open your application, and use it to get into the state that you'd like to test; then click the Generate Code button. This prompts you to name your recorded method, which will be saved in the test project as a part of the UI Map. This map is a description of actions and assertions that you can use to automate and test your application.

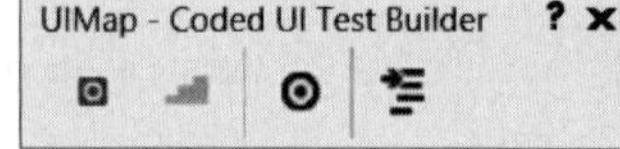

FIGURE 56-7

> **NOTE** *Each test project contains a single UI Map, which all the Coded UI Tests share.*

When your application is in the wanted state, you can create assertions about different parts of the user interface. To do this, drag the crosshair icon from the Coded UI Test Builder over the part of the UI that you want to make an assertion about. When you release the mouse button, the Add Assertions dialog displays, as in Figure 56-8.

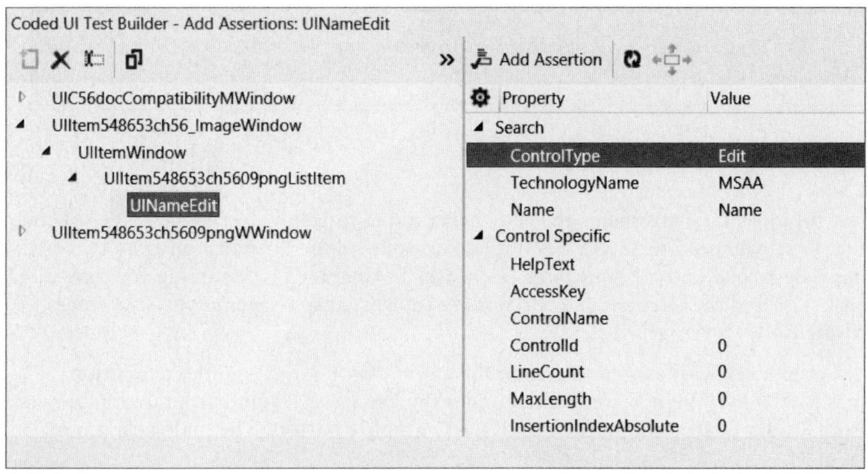

FIGURE 56-8

On the left is a collapsible panel showing the UI control map, which displays the hierarchy of all controls that have been identified so far. On the right is a list of properties that the Coded UI Test Builder has identified along with their values. To make an assertion about one of these properties, you can right-click it and select Add Assertion. Each assertion has a comparator and a comparison value to be tested against.

Generic Tests

Not every kind of test is covered in Team System. This is why Microsoft included the concept of Generic Tests, so you can easily use custom tests and also the rest of the features such as Test Results, Assign Work Items, and Publish Test Results.

To configure a Generic Test, you need to specify an existing program and optionally specify its command-line arguments, additional files to deploy, and environment variables. The external application can communicate the test result back to Team System in two ways. One is with the Error Level, where a value of 0 indicates success and anything else is considered a failure. The other is to return an XML file that conforms to the `SummaryResult.xsd` schema located in Visual Studio's installation path. In MSDN you can find information about this schema and how to report detailed errors using XML.

Ordered Test

Use Ordered Tests when you need to group tests and run them as a whole, or if tests have dependencies on each other and need to be run in a particular order. It's a good practice to create atomic Unit Tests in order to run them in isolation with repeatable results. It isn't recommended to use Ordered Tests just to deal with dependencies between Unit Tests. A good reason for creating Ordered Tests is to create a performance session for more than one test.

In the Ordered Test Editor, you have a list of the available tests that you can add to the Ordered Test; the same test can be added more than once. You can also choose to continue after a failure. When the test is run, it executes each of the selected tests in the specified order.

RELATING CODE AND TESTS

Tests and code are heavily interconnected. Tests have no reason to exist without the code that they verify, and code that is not verified by tests is potentially incorrect. Visual Studio contains a tool designed to make the link between tests and code more explicit. Code Coverage can determine which areas of your code are executed during a test run, which tells you if you need to add more tests to your solution.

> **NOTE** *Code Coverage is available only for the Premium and Ultimate editions of Visual Studio 2012.*

Code Coverage

Code Coverage is a useful tool that instruments the code being tested to help you see which lines of code are actually executing. First, you need to have a Test Project on your solution. To demonstrate this, you can refer to the example described under "Your First Test Case" in Chapter 11. Assuming you have already created the `UnitTest1` class and the `CurrentStatus_NullPaidUpToDate_TemporaryStatus` test is passing, you can activate Code Coverage.

To open the Test Run properties window, double-click the `Local.testsettings` file in Solution Explorer. The settings for Code Coverage are located under the Data and Diagnostics tab. Enable the Code Coverage (Visual Studio 2010) option; then click the Configure button. The dialog shown in Figure 56-9 displays.

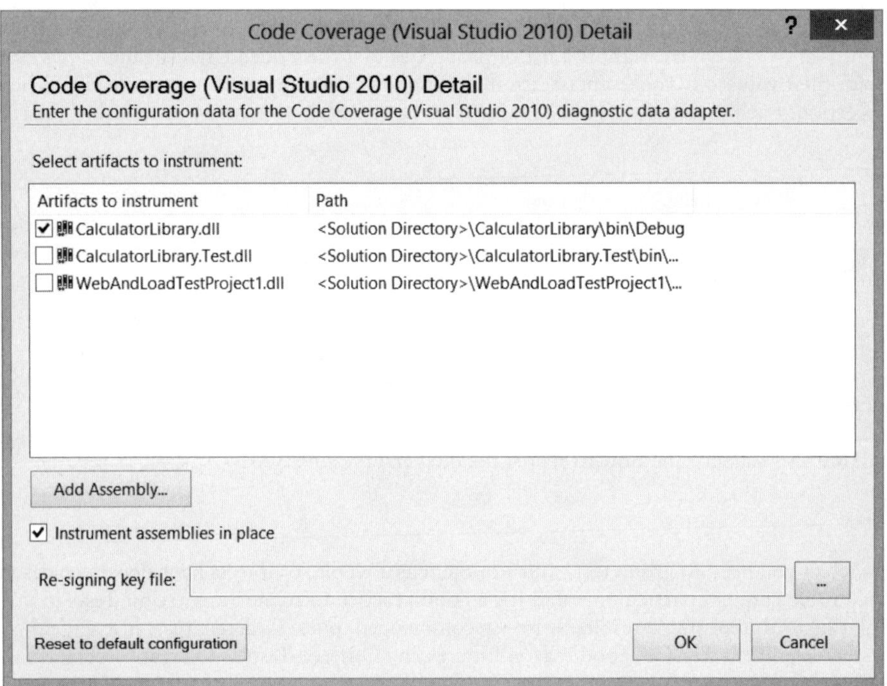

FIGURE 56-9

Through this dialog, select the assemblies to instrument. If you sign your assemblies, similar to the procedure when you profile using instrumentation, you need to re-sign them.

Now, simply run your test, and from the Test Results window, right-click it and select Code Coverage. Figure 56-10 shows the Code Coverage window, indicating the not-covered and covered blocks for each assembly, namespace, type, and member. Double-clicking a member opens the code file with the executed lines highlighted in blue (most of the highlighted lines in Figure 56-11) and untouched lines in red (the `return 0;` line in Figure 56-11).

Hierarchy	Not Covered (Blocks)	Not Covered (% Blocks)	Covered (Blocks)	Covered (% Blocks)
Bruce_BRUCE-PC 2012-10-04 0...	335	93.06 %	25	6.94 %
calculatorlibrary.dll	1	10.00 %	9	90.00 %
CalculatorLibrary	1	10.00 %	9	90.00 %
Calculator	1	10.00 %	9	90.00 %
Add(int, int)	0	0.00 %	2	100.00 %
Divide(int, int)	1	25.00 %	3	75.00 %
Multiply(int, int)	0	0.00 %	2	100.00 %
Subtract(int, int)	0	0.00 %	2	100.00 %
calculatorlibrary.test.dll	334	95.43 %	16	4.57 %

FIGURE 56-10

```
public int Multiply(int x, int y)
{
    return x * y;
}

public double Divide(int x, int y)
{
    if (y == 0)
        return 0;
    else
        return x / y;
}
```

FIGURE 56-11

Referring to Figure 56-11, the `Divide` method has 33 percent in not-covered statements. The `if` statement is evaluated, as is the the second branch of the `if` statement (that is, when `y` does not equal `0`). The remaining branch is never touched. So two of the three statements are considered to be covered. The non-covered statement is an indication that you need additional test cases. One way additional tests cases could be created was described in the "Data" section in Chapter 11, where you specify a DataSource with the additional input.

When you have code that is never touched, this can lead you to think three things:

- It is code that actually isn't used and is getting in your way, decreasing your project's maintainability. Solution: Simply delete it.
- That code isn't tested. Solution: Create a new test.
- The code is so simple that there's probably no need to test it. Think twice about this, even for simple properties or methods. The code is likely referenced elsewhere in your application, in which case any errors in the code may cause issues in your application. This is a good reason to write a new test case. Right-clicking the member being tested and selecting Find All References can help you see if this is unused code, but it won't find references from data-bound properties or projects not in the solution.

It's not necessary to take this practice to an extreme and look for 100 percent Code Coverage. In many projects it's not worth it, especially if you have legacy code or you didn't start using unit testing. Don't let your code coverage go down. Iteration after iteration, or better yet (if you use continuous integration), check-in after check-in, your percentage should increase, or at least remain constant. Most important, rather than looking at the numbers at a test suite level, it's useful to look at them at the code level to see if you're missing critical test cases.

VISUAL STUDIO TEST MANAGEMENT

The way to manage your tests in Visual Studio is through the Test View window. When you run a set of tests, you are presented with the Test Results window. If it doesn't appear automatically, you can open it from the Test ⇨ Windows menu. There you can sort the tests and results to see error messages. You can select what tests to rerun; by default failing, inconclusive and not-executed tests will be checked, and passed tests will be unchecked. Because the list of results can be big, you can use sorting, filtering, and grouping, or even change the view to display a left pane with the Test Lists.

From the Test Results window, you can export the Test Result to save a `.trx` file containing all the details and a folder with the test output. You can simply send the files to someone else who can import them from the Test Results window by selecting the `.trx` file. This person can see the same results the tester saw and even rerun the tests to reproduce the error on his machine. The latter is possible because the binaries are included with every test output.

Instead of passing Test Result files from one computer to another, it would be better to publish them to the Team Foundation Server. This option is available in the Test Results window's toolbar. You will be prompted to select a team project. The team project must have a build configured, as you can see in Chapter 57, "Team Foundation Server," in the section "Team Foundation Build." The benefit of publishing, besides making the data available to other people, is that the data can also be used for reports.

MICROSOFT TEST MANAGER

Microsoft Test Manager 2012 is a tool that helps you to plan, execute, and track your testing activities. It integrates directly with a Team Foundation Server and enables you to create, update, and query work items directly. It is launched directly from the Start menu and connects immediately to your Team Foundation Server and the associated project. Figure 56-12 shows the screen that initially appears when the Test Manager is launched. This screen is used to select the test plan that you would like to open.

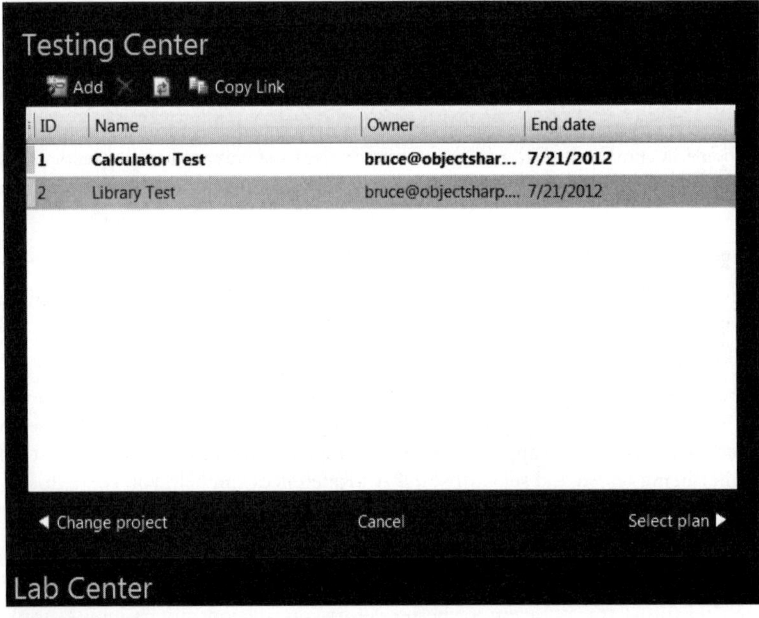

FIGURE 56-12

There are two different UIs for Test Manager. After you select a plan (or create a new one) using the dialog shown in Figure 56-12, you'll see the Testing Center (Figure 56-13). It has four tabs along the top that relate to the basic types of activities that the Testing Center provides to create and run suites of tests.

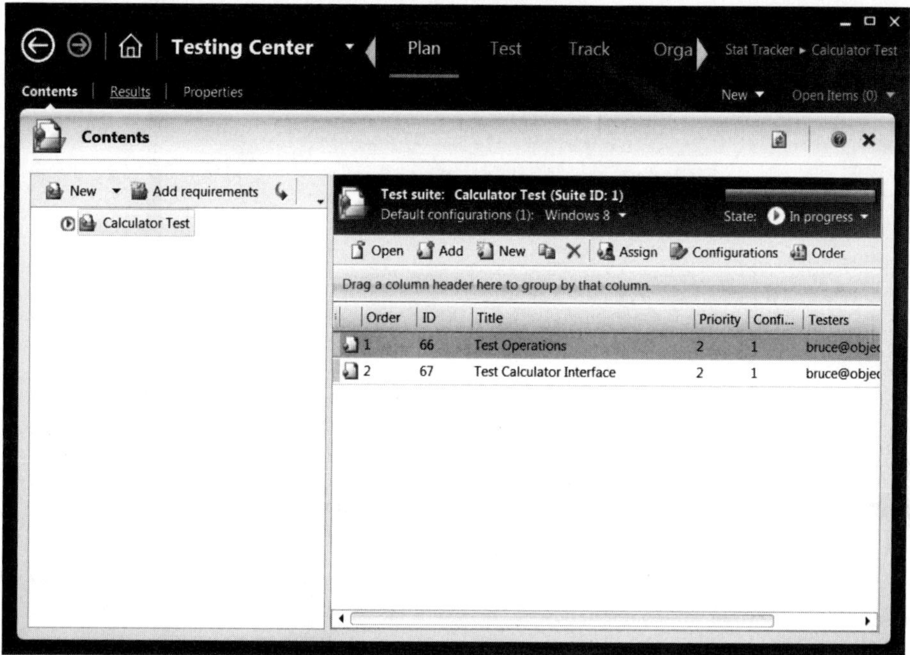

FIGURE 56-13

Testing Center

All tests in the Testing Center are organized into test plans. It is recommended that you create a test plan for each releasable version of your application. The screen that appears when the Testing Center is opened and is shown in Figure 56-13, is named the Contents View. From here you can create new tests, add existing tests, and assign testers and configurations to your tests.

> **NOTE** *Each plan has a state, which can be In Planning, In Progress, or Complete. This information is stored in the Team Foundation Server and can be surfaced in reports. When a plan is in progress, a percentage of how many of the planned test cases are complete is also available.*

If you open an existing test case or create a new one, you see the Test Case window, as shown in Figure 56-14. Each test case is made up of a number of actions. Each action comes with a description of what the tester should do, along with a description of how to verify that the action has completed successfully.

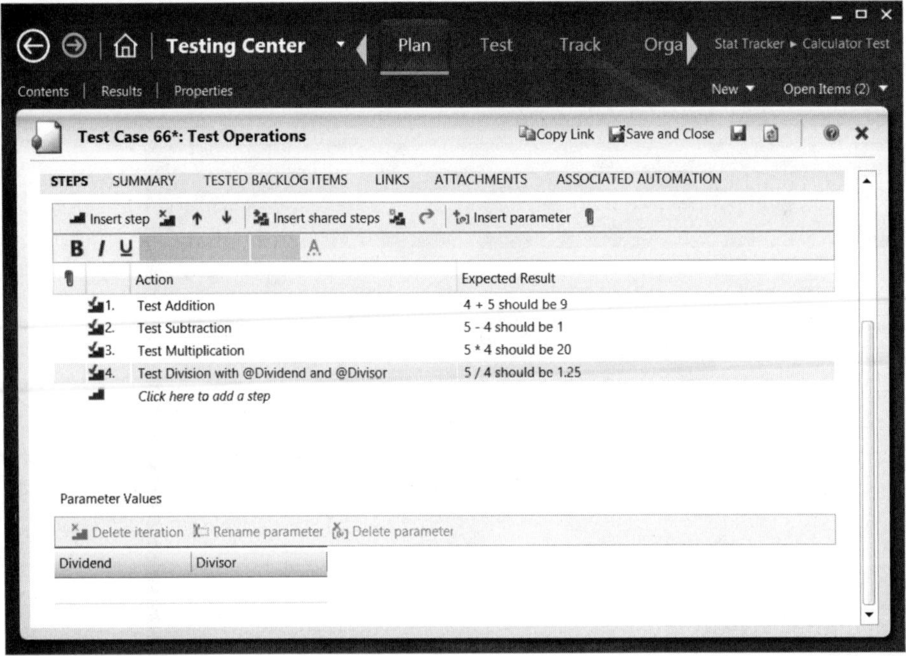

FIGURE 56-14

Actions can have parameters like the ones shown in Figure 56-14. Each parameter can have multiple values defined, and there will be one iteration of the test for each value.

To run a test case, select it on the Test tab, and click the Run button. This opens the Test Runner window (Figure 56-15). This window shows a list of steps and marks the progress of the tester. As you complete each step, you can mark it as passed or failed.

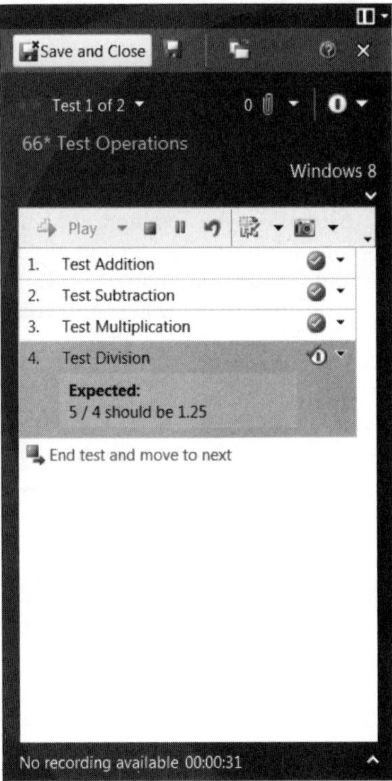

FIGURE 56-15

> **NOTE** *You can record the steps of a manual test as you go through, which allows you to automate the process when you want to rerun the test later.*

On the toolbar of the Test Runner window are buttons that enable you to attach items to the results of this test run, including comments, screenshots, files, and even a whole snapshot of the system that developers can use later to help in debugging issues. You can create bugs directly from this toolbar as well.

Lab Center

If you click the Testing Center heading, you can switch to the Lab Center (Figure 56-16). The Lab Center manages the environments that you run tests on. This can include information on physical and virtual environments.

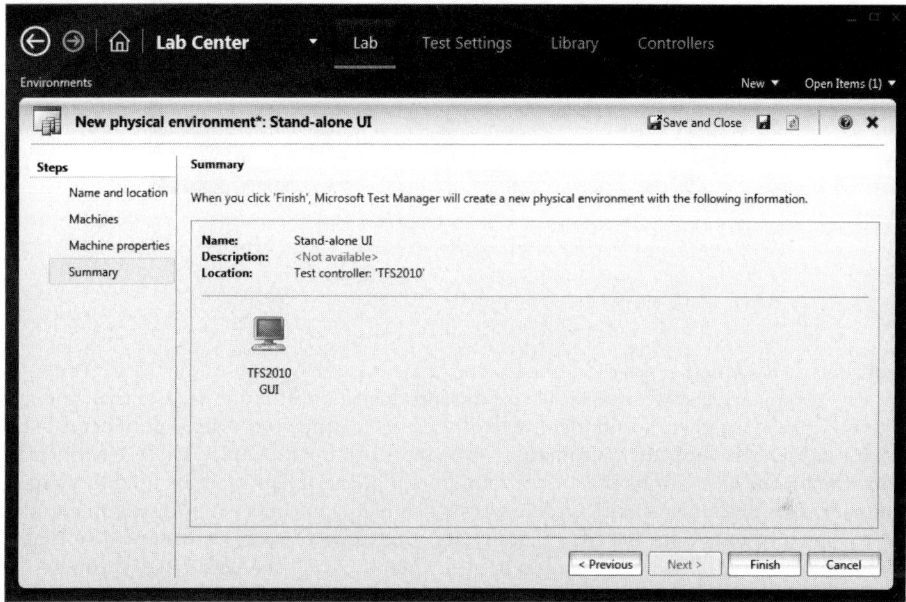

FIGURE 56-16

To use the features of Lab Center, you need to install a Test Controller and associate it with a project collection in your Team Foundation Server. When your Test Controller is available, you can use the Lab Center to maintain a collection of Physical Machines, Virtual Machines, and Virtual Machine Templates. When a tester starts a test, she will be connected to one of these machines, and if she spots an error, she can take a system snapshot, which will be attached to the bug report. When a developer retrieves the bug, she can reconnect to the test machine and have it put back into this state by the Test Controller.

To configure the data that is collected on each machine in the environment, use the Data and Diagnostics page on the Test Settings tab (Figure 56-17). You can collect many different kinds of data, from mouse clicks and keyboard strokes to full video of the desktop during the test.

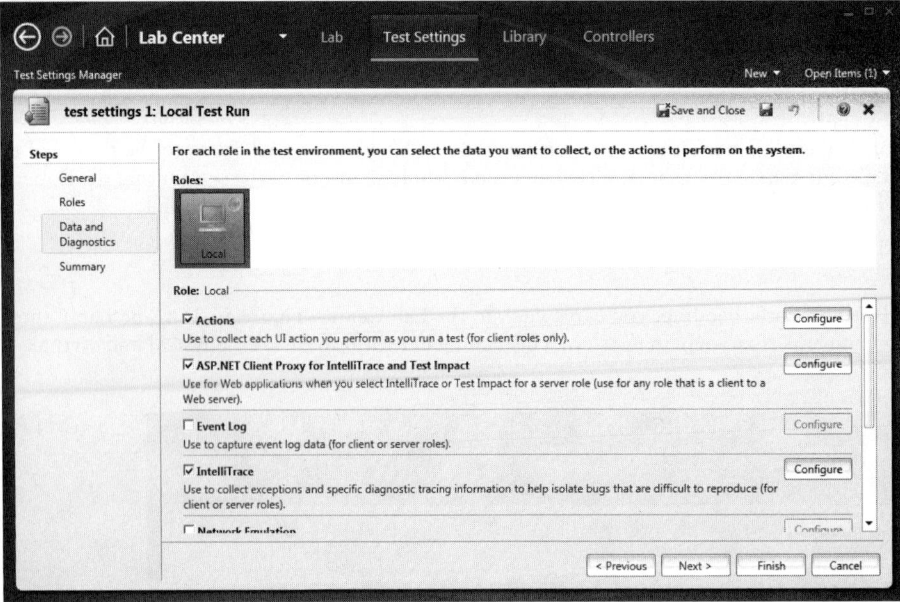

FIGURE 56-17

SUMMARY

In this chapter you saw the different types of automated tests included in Visual Studio 2012. You started with Web Performance Tests, which enable you to reproduce a set of requests, and then you continued with Load Tests, which help to simulate several users executing your tests simultaneously to stress your application. You also looked at automating your application with Coded UI Tests, which helps to test the ways in which your user can interact with your system. Generic Tests can be used to wrap existing tests that use other mechanisms, and Ordered Tests can help you run a set of tests sequentially. You learned how to map unit tests onto the code that it tests with Code Coverage tools and how that information is used to determine which tests need to be run when the code changes. Finally, you looked at options to manage your tests, like grouping them in lists and publishing the results to Team Foundation Server.

The Microsoft Test Manager is a tool targeted at helping testers do their jobs. By creating test cases and organizing them into plans, you can more easily manage testing tasks, and integration with Team Foundation Server makes it easy to track progress and communicate results with the rest of the team.

57

Team Foundation Server

WHAT'S IN THIS CHAPTER?

- Managing project tasks
- Visualizing source code repository changes
- Creating build configurations
- Reporting progress

Software projects are notoriously complex; few are delivered successfully on time, within budget, and up to the wanted quality levels. As software projects increase and require larger teams, the processes involved to manage them are more complicated, and not just for the manager, but also for the developers, the testers, the architects, and the customer. Over time there have been many approaches to solving software project management problems, including quality models such as CMMI, methodologies such as RUP, or Agile Practices, Scrum, and Continuous Integration. Clearly a tool that helps support all the pieces necessary to ensure more successful software projects is (or should be) on the wish list of every development manager.

The most basic requirement for a software project, even for the smallest one-person project, is to have a source control repository. For bigger projects, more sophisticated features are needed, such as labeling, shelving, branching, and merging. Project activities need to be created, prioritized, assigned, and tracked, and at the end of the day (or better yet even before every change is checked in to your repository) you need to ensure that everything builds and all tests pass. To make this process smoother and improve team communication, a way to report to project managers or peer developers is also required.

Team Foundation Server (TFS) 2012 enables you to do all this. In this chapter you'll see how version control works, how it integrates with work item tracking, and how each change can be verified to ensure it works before it is checked in. you'll also learn how project managers can see reports to get a better understanding of the project status and how they can work using Excel and Project to manage work items. The team can interact using the project's portal in SharePoint, and different stakeholders can get the information they need through the report server or configure it to get their reports directly by e-mail.

> **NOTE** *TFS 2012 has a few features that make it easy to get up and running, including reduced requirements and streamlined installation. You can even install it on a client operating system such as Windows 7 or Windows 8.*

TEAM PROJECT

To begin working with TFS, you need to create a team project. A *team project* contains all the information about your project, including source code, tasks that need to be performed, instructions for building your application, documentation, quality metrics, and planning information. Each team project can also have its own SharePoint collaboration portal.

In Visual Studio 2012, team projects are grouped together under *team project collections*. All the projects with a team project collection share basic infrastructure such as a data warehouse, a work item schema, and a pool of IDs (for work items and changeset numbers). If you have logical groups of projects within your enterprise, it is a good idea to create a team project collection for each one.

> **NOTE** *You cannot back up and restore individual projects. This can be done only at the project collection level.*

PROCESS TEMPLATES

When you create a new team project, you need to select the *process template*, which defines the way in which you intend to use the tool. Select the one that better suits your organization's process or methodology. Out of the box, Team Foundation Server comes with a number of different templates. The specific list depends on the version of TFS to which you connect. For TFS 2010, there are two templates, one for Agile Development and the other for CMMI. If you connect to TFS 2012, the out of the box templates are Visual Studio Scrum 2.0, MSF for Agile 6.0, and MSF for CMMI 6.0. Any of these options are great as a starting point. If your company already has a defined process, it can be incorporated into these existing templates; you can use a third-party process template or create your own from scratch.

The rest of this chapter uses Visual Studio Scrum 2.0 and refers to the other templates when necessary. As well, the chapter uses the version of TFS at `http://www.tfspreview.com`. The reason is that this site provides a trial version of TFS with no need to install software.

To create a new team project, start with the Team Explorer window, as shown in Figure 57-1. The drop-down for the Home field expands to show a Projects and My Teams option, followed by New Team Project. This causes the web page for your team project to display in the browser. Clicking the Create a Team Project link displays the dialog shown in Figure 57-2.

Team Explorer - Home
Search Work Items (Ctrl+')
Home | OnSports
Home
My Work
Pending Changes
Work Items
Builds
Web Access
Projects and My Teams
Settings
OnSports
Stat Tracker
Connect to Team Projects...
New Team Project...
Settings

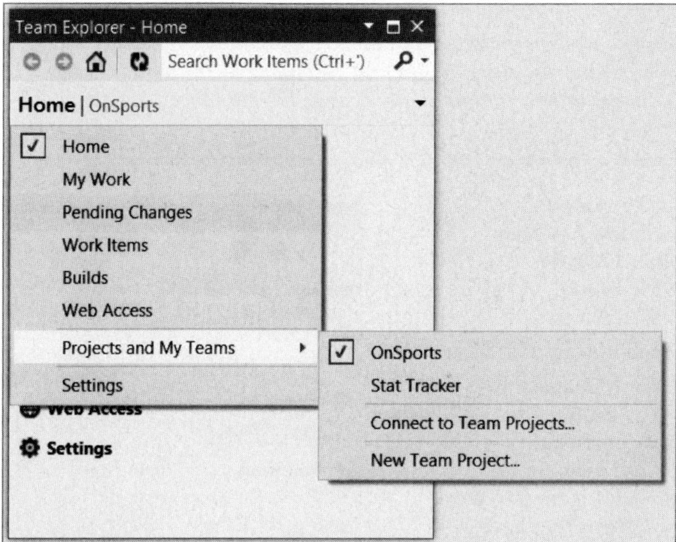

FIGURE 57-1

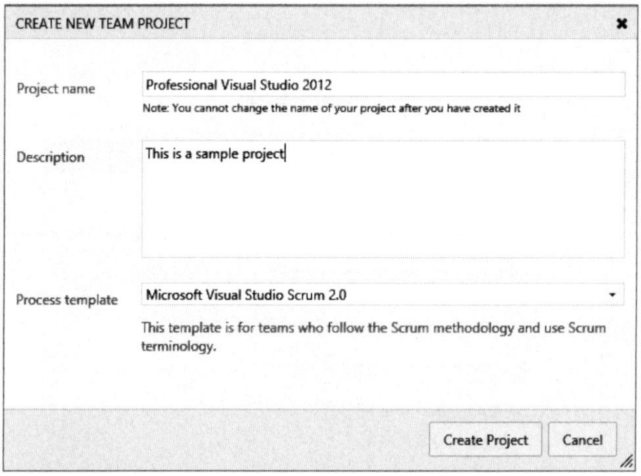

CREATE NEW TEAM PROJECT
Project name
Professional Visual Studio 2012
Note: You cannot change the name of your project after you have created it
Description
This is a sample project
Process template
Microsoft Visual Studio Scrum 2.0
This template is for teams who follow the Scrum methodology and use Scrum terminology.
Create Project
Cancel

FIGURE 57-2

A process template creates the environment for the team project. This usually consists of defining work item types (as you'll see in the section titled "Work Item Tracking"), setting up default groups and permissions, preparing a version control repository, configuring reports, and creating a custom SharePoint portal with the appropriate document structure and process guidance. A different process could omit some of these or add custom tasks.

If you connect to a TFS server (as opposed to `tfspreview.com`), when the wizard finishes it opens the Guidance page, which details the process used, defines the responsibilities of the roles involved, explains the different types of work items, and provides step-by-step guidance about specific tasks such as How to Create a Vision Statement.

> **NOTE** *If you customize your process template, the guidance pages are not automatically generated. In other words, any changes that you make to the template are not reflected in the guidance pages unless you manually change the guidance pages in the template.*

You navigate to the different features of TFS through the Team Explorer tool window. This window has been completely redesigned for Visual Studio 2012. It has six different sections (see Figure 57-3): My Work, Pending Changes, Work Items, Builds, Web Access, and Settings.

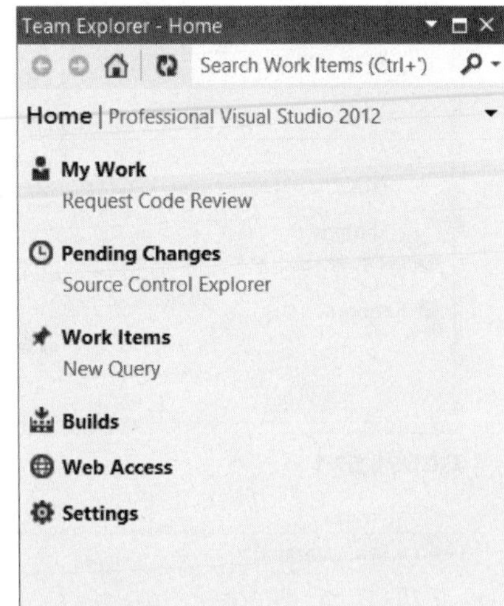

FIGURE 57-3

The idea behind the redesign was to not only enable the developer to focus on the most common tasks, but also drill into these tasks to quickly get to the functionality required. Figure 57-4 illustrates the detailed view for two of the sections. On the left side of Figure 57-4 is the My Work view, where you have easy access to work items that have been assigned to you and that you're already working on. As well, your shelved or suspended work is visible, along with any requests for code reviews (both made by and made to you).

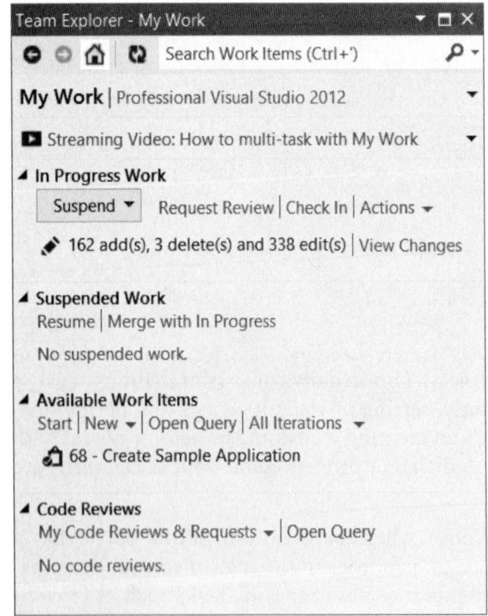

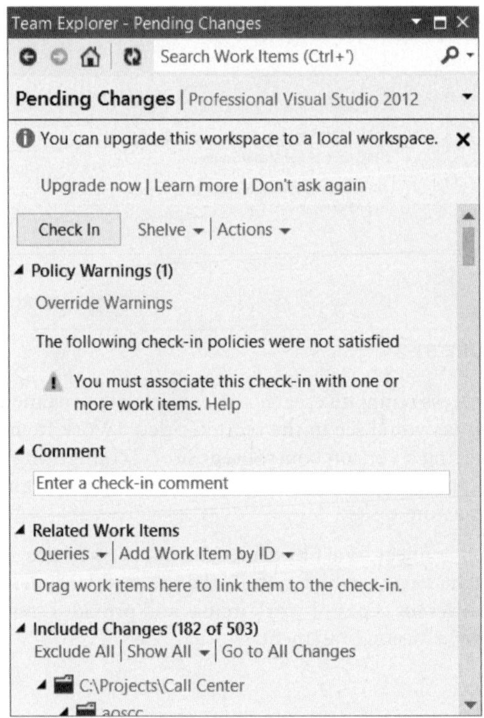

FIGURE 57-4

On the right side of Figure 57-4 is the Pending Changes view, where you can quickly check in the code that has been modified. As well, you can associate a comment with the check-in, along with specifying any related work items.

WORK ITEM TRACKING

Team Foundation Server enables you to manage activities using *work items*. As you see in the following sections, you can search for work items using *work item queries* and manage them using Visual Studio, Excel, Project, or Web Access. Different types of work items are defined by your process template.

> **NOTE** *Both TFS 2010 and TFS 2012 support hierarchical work items. As a result, you can create subtasks and parent tasks. You can also create predecessor and successor links between work items, which enables you to manage task dependencies. These work item links even synchronize with Microsoft Excel and Microsoft Project providing even greater flexibility for managing work items.*

Work Item Queries

As you can see from the list of queries shown in Figure 57-5 you can look for different work items using the work item queries from Team Explorer. The Scrum process template includes eight team queries. As you might expect, the number of queries available out of the box are different for the other process templates.

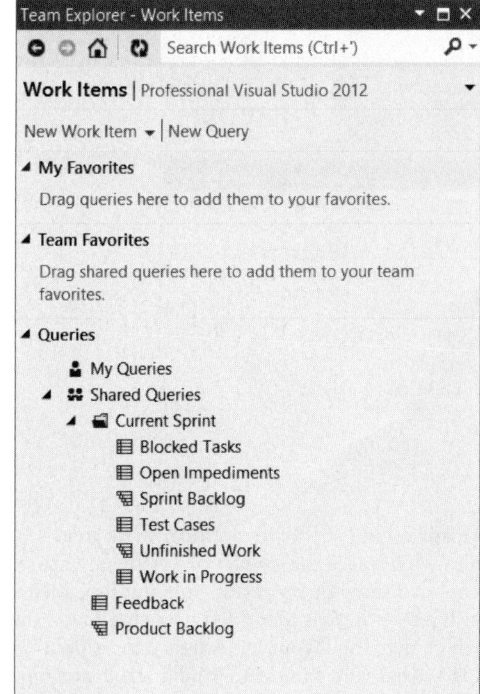

FIGURE 57-5

NOTE *There is a folder of queries called Workbook Queries in the SharePoint portal created when a new team project is added to a local TFS server. These are used to support some of the Excel workbook reports found in the Documents area.*

Most of the time the standard queries are sufficient, but you have the option to create new ones. If you have sufficient permissions (such as, if you're a project administrator) you can add new team queries to make them available to everyone with access to this project. If you have permission to modify the process template, you can add new team queries, so projects created with the edited templates include them. Changes in the templates don't apply to team projects already created. If you don't have permission to publish a publicly available query, you still have the ability to create a personal query that will be visible to just you.

NOTE *When you create the same queries over and over from one project to another, you should add those to your process templates. Over time, there will be less need to create custom queries.*

To create a new query, click the New Query link (refer to Figure 57-5). Alternatively, you can right-click the My Queries node and select New Query.

Now you can visually design your query. In this case (as shown in Figure 57-6) you care only about the work items of the selected project, assigned to the current user and under Iteration 1. You specify this using the `@me` and `@Project` variables. You can also specify which columns you want visible in the grid and sorting options by using the Column Options link just above the query results section. After all the criteria and columns have been set up, run the new query to see a sublist of the work items.

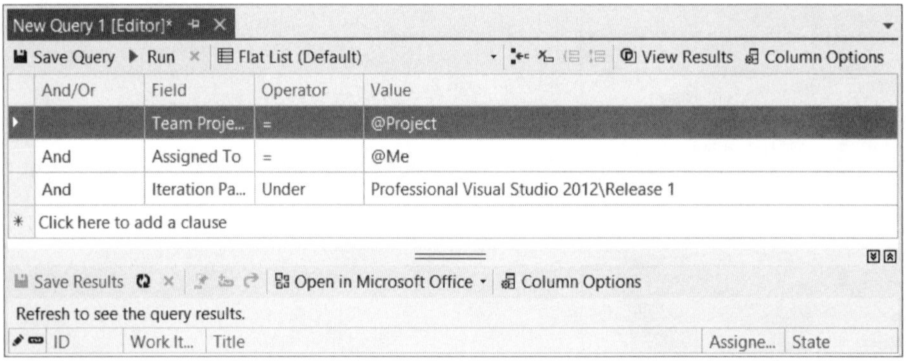

FIGURE 57-6

In Team Foundation Server 2010 and 2012, queries can take advantage of the hierarchical work item structure to show work items that are directly related, enabling you to see the impact of cutting a feature or the required tasks necessary to complete a feature. You can also show query results in a flat list, a list of work items and their direct links, or a tree of work items. Each of these is identified by a small icon that appears next to the query in the Team Explorer. And you can change the layout by using a drop-down control (refer to Figure 57-6 with the default value of Flat List). Also, you can create folder structures for your work item queries, and each query or folder can be secured separately.

> **NOTE** *Although a folder of work item queries can be secured, there is nothing stopping unauthorized users from duplicating the queries.*

Work Item Types

In Visual Studio Scrum 2.0 you have five types of work items: bugs, tasks, product backlog items, impediments, and test cases. Each work item has different fields depending on its type. For example, a bug will have test information and a system info field, whereas a task contains effort information about estimated, remaining, and completed hours. Both MSF for Agile Development and CMMI have similar lists. All these fields are customizable either at a template or team-project level.

Adding Work Items

The basic way to add work items is via the Team ➪ New Work Item menu option and selecting the work item type you want to add, or with the New Work Item link in the Team Explorer (refer to Figure 57-5). Regardless of how it is created, you get the Work Item entry screen (Figure 57-7). Through this screen, all the information related to the work item can be entered or modified. Along with basic description information, each work item can be related to many other TFS artifacts through links. Team Foundation Server 2010 and 2012 understand several different types of links, including Parent, Child, Predecessor, and Successor. To add a link, click the Links tab, and click the Link To button.

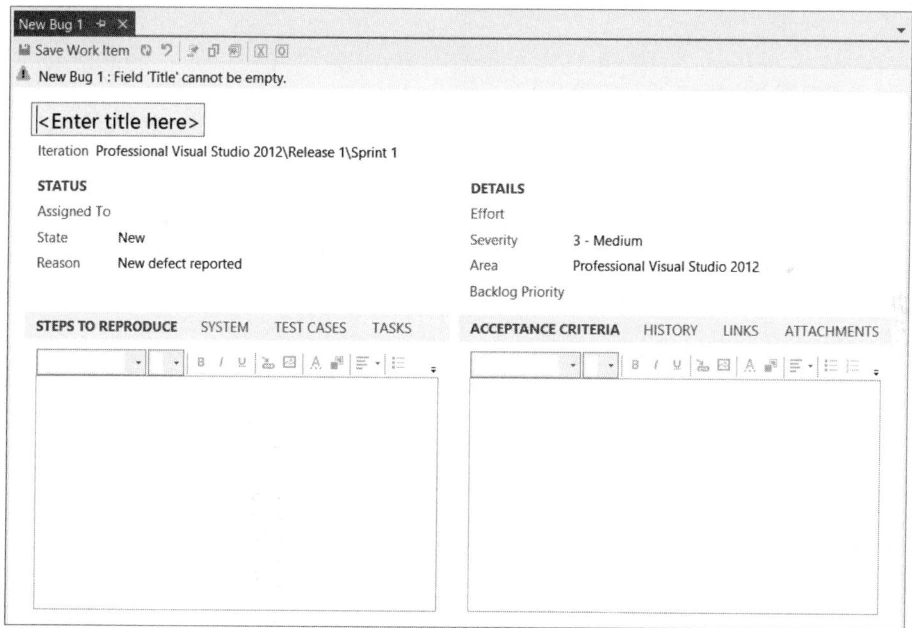

FIGURE 57-7

Work Item State

During your normal daily activity, you'll work on tasks described by work items assigned to you. Each work item is described by a simple state machine that determines the allowed next states for any given state. This state machine is a part of the work item definition and is determined by the process template. Whenever a new state is selected, you can provide a reason for the state transition. The reason field enables you to differentiate between the bugs that are active because they are new and those that are active because they have reoccured.

EXCEL AND PROJECT INTEGRATION

Looking at, adding, or editing work items can get a bit complicated and won't scale well when you have hundreds of tasks. This can be problematic especially for project managers who are not used to working inside Visual Studio. They usually prefer to work from Excel or Project. This integration is easy using the provided add-ins.

Excel

From the Ribbon, simply click New List, and choose a Team Project and Work Item Query. This retrieves all the information from a web service and displays it in Excel. After it's there you can sort, filter, edit, and publish changes back to the server, refresh the changes made by others, add links or attachments, and choose columns to be displayed. Another way to do this is from a work item query. From a work item query's context menu, select Open in Microsoft Excel. This creates a new Excel worksheet with the information. Figure 57-8 shows both options, and Figure 57-9 shows the results in Excel.

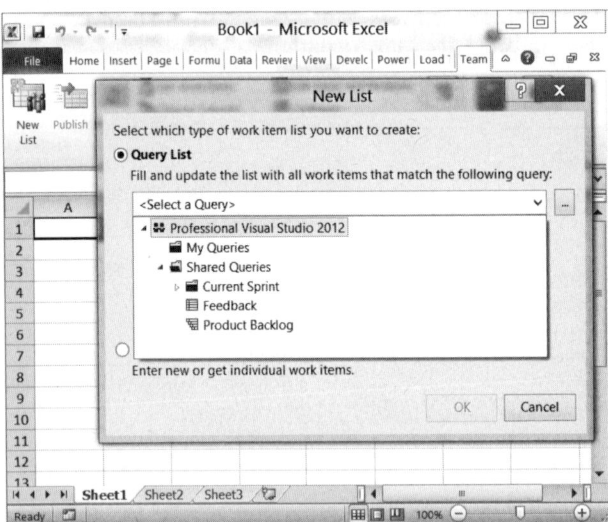

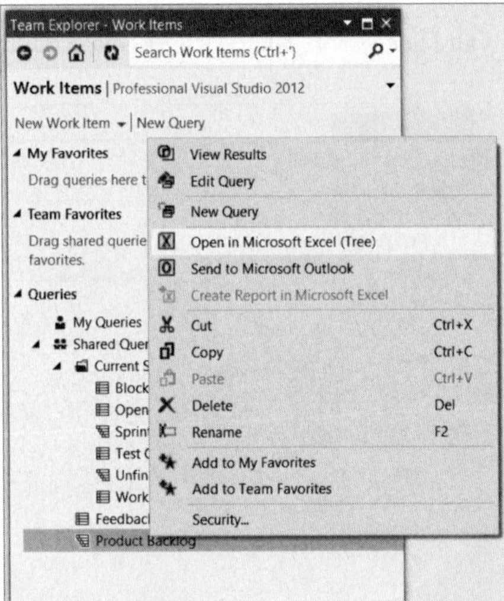

FIGURE 57-8

	A	B	C	D	E	F
1	**Project:** Agile **Server:** localhost\DefaultCollection **Query:** Open Work Items **List type:** Flat					
2	ID	Stack Rank	Priority	Work Item Type	Assigned To	State
3	70		2	Bug	Administrator	Active
4	61		2	Task	April Stewart (Dev Lead)	Active
5	62		2	Task	Abu Obeida Bakhach (Dev)	Active
6	63		2	Task	Michael Affronti (PM)	Active
7	64		2	Task	April Stewart (Dev Lead)	Active
8	65		2	Task	Doris Krieger (Dev)	Active
9	66		2	Task	Michael Affronti (PM)	Active
10	67		2	Task	Michael Affronti (PM)	Active
11	68		2	Task	Michael Affronti (PM)	Active
12	69		2	Task	Christine Koch (Tester)	Active

FIGURE 57-9

The out-of-the-box templates create a number of standard work item-based Excel workbooks, which are hosted on the SharePoint Portal. These are found in the Documents node under Excel Reports.

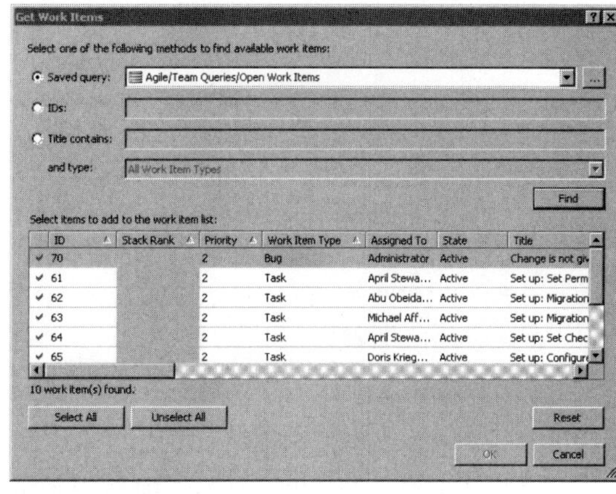

FIGURE 57-10

Project

TFS also provides an add-in for Project. Similar to when you use Excel, you can connect to a server, choose a team project, and select a work item query, but instead of using the entire list, you have to choose each of the work items you want to import to your project, as shown in Figure 57-10.

After your work items are imported, you can edit each of their fields directly in Project. This is possible because of the column mappings between TFS fields and MS Project Columns. For example, Resource Names in Project can map to the Assigned To field in TFS. Fields that exist only in Team System will be mapped to Text Fields in Project; for example, Work Item Type is mapped to Text 24. This is preconfigured in the process template.

You can add new work items, nest them in iterations or areas, assign them to people, choose a work item type, balance workloads between resources, see project reports, and refresh the progress from the server after each developer changes the work remaining or work item state.

TFS 2012 and 2010 both understand the notion of hierarchical work items and successor and predecessor tasks. When the work items are loaded into Project, it can take advantage of these links to create a normal Project experience. As new associations are created and updated, Project can even return the updated data to TFS in a form it can understand.

> **NOTE** *If you use Project with TFS, you should look at the article "Quick Tips and Operational Differences When Tracking Tasks Using Office Project and Team Foundation" on MSDN at* `http://msdn.microsoft.com/en-us/library/dd380701(VS.100).aspx`.

VERSION CONTROL

Version Control (sometimes called *Source Control*) is a tool that enables you to manage, share, and retain a history of changes to your source code. To interact with the TFS version control system, use the Source Control Explorer window, as shown in Figure 57-11. You can open this window from the Team Explorer window or View ➪ Other Windows ➪ Source Control Explorer.

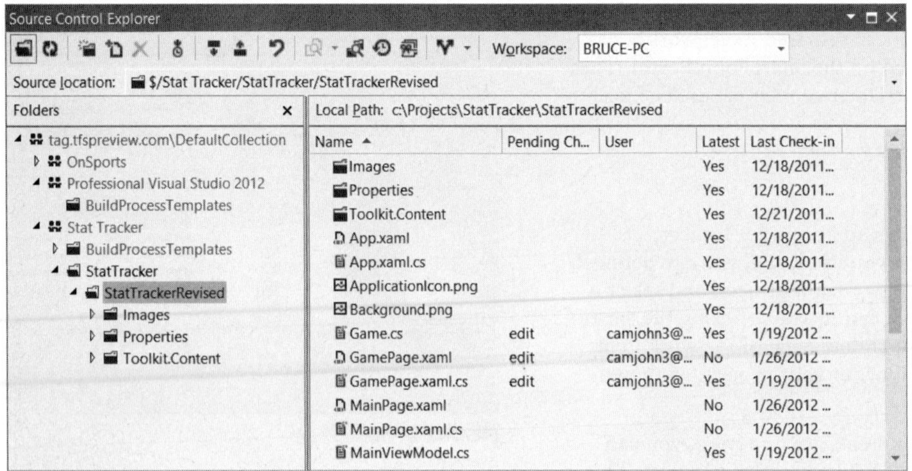

FIGURE 57-11

To work with files on your machine, you need a *workspace* that defines a set of mappings between paths on your local file system and the remote system. You can define a different local folder for each path, but a good practice is to have only one mapping for a team project; this helps keep all the solutions and projects relative to each other. You can make a good case for doing this even across different team projects. To define this mapping, click the Local Path link that reads Not Mapped, and create the workspace mapping.

After your workspace is set up, you can get the latest version of the source code and start working with it, add files, check out files (mark as edit) or check in (upload/persist) changes, view change history, and compare folders.

Working from Solution Explorer

When you create a new project through Visual Studio, you have the option to add it to Source Control. This option is available on the New Project dialog. Visual Studio attempts to automatically bind it and adds it according to any previously defined mapping. For example, if you have a TFS team project named Northwind mapped to location `c:\Projects\Northwind` and you add a new project at `c:\Projects\Northwind\MyProject`, Visual Studio adds the new project to the Northwind team project. That's why you need to set the location to a folder inside your workspace (the local path you mapped to).

The Solution Explorer you are used to working with in Visual Studio will be the main place to interact with your source control system. Every time you add a new file to the solution, it will be added to source control; when you open a file and VS detects you're editing it, it will be automatically checked out for you. After you finish working, you can simply right-click the solution and choose Check In to persist your changes in the server. See the section "Source Control" in Chapter 13, "Code Consistency Tools," for more information on the common tasks; this chapter explains the specifics of Source Control as it relates to Team Foundation Server 2012.

> **NOTE** *Though it is common to work directly with TFS source control via the Solution Explorer, this can have some disadvantages because it means that Visual Studio can manipulate only the files referenced by your solution. If you have other items in source control that are not part of your solution, you need to manage these from the Source Control Explorer window.*

Check Out

Files under source control are by default read-only; in TFS terms you would say the file is *checked in*. To start editing a file, you need to check it out. This is done for you automatically when you modify it from VS. When the file is a text file (that is, a C#, VB, or XML file), the IDE will do a *shared check-out*; if it's a binary file (that is, a Word document, SQL Server Compact Edition Database, or another resource) an *exclusive check-out* will be made.

Shared check-outs enable two or more developers to modify a file at the same time, whereas an exclusive check-out prevents a second developer from checking out the file. You can choose to do an exclusive check-out on a text file if you need to prevent anyone from modifying it. This is not a recommended practice, and you should use it only when you actually need it. A good example of this is when you are about to update the data for a WCF reference. This sort of information is textual but not easy to merge because many files are all updated at once. By using exclusive check-outs you can ensure that no one else is modifying the reference at the same time as you.

> **NOTE** *If you install the TFS 2012 Power Tools, you can check files in and out directly from Windows Explorer.*

Check In

To preserve your changes in the server, you need to check in the edited files. You can select which files to include in this *changeset*, add comments to it, associate it with work items, and add check-in notes (Figure 57-12).

Depending on the policies defined for the team project, you might need to associate your check-in with a work item, run code analysis, have it pass tests, or at least successfully build the solution. To modify a team project's policies, open the Source Control Settings window (Team ➪ Team Project Settings ➪ Source Control) and go to the Check-In Policy tab. After the policies are defined, you'll get Policy Warnings (Figure 57-13); these can be overridden.

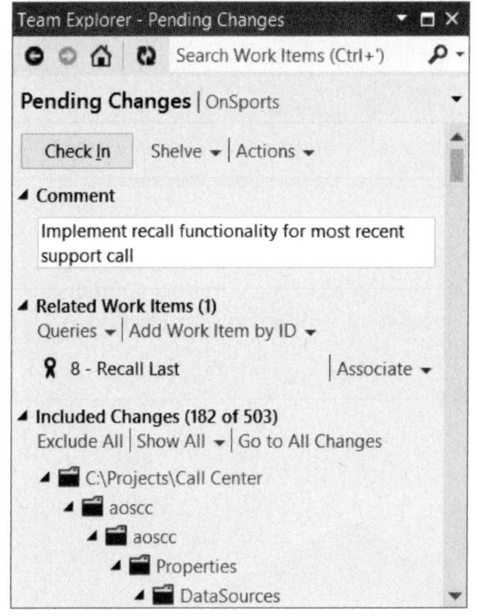

FIGURE 57-12

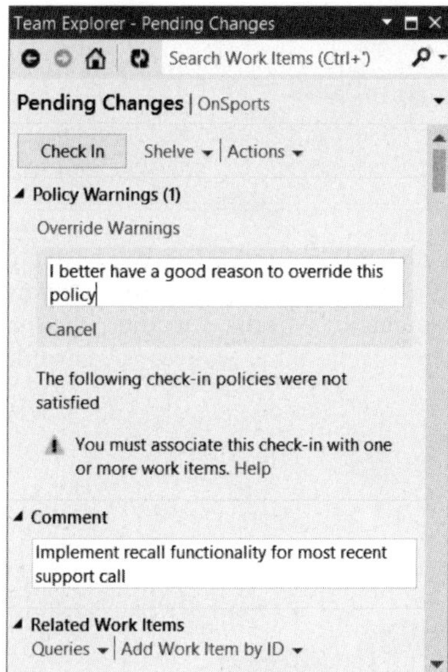

FIGURE 57-13

> **NOTE** *You should check in a group of files related to a logical change at the same time rather than one at a time. The set of files associated with a check-in along with any notes and work item associations become a changeset. Changesets make managing project history and merging much easier.*

Resolve Conflicts

Although shared check-outs enable multiple developers to work on the same file, this can lead to conflicts. These can easily be resolved with the help of Visual Studio. If conflicts are detected, the Pending Changes - Conflicts window (Figure 57-14) appears. Through this interface, you can compare versions and look at all the changes to that file. To resolve it, you can use Auto Merge and let Visual Studio merge the changes for you, undo your local changes, discard server changes, or merge changes manually in the merge tool.

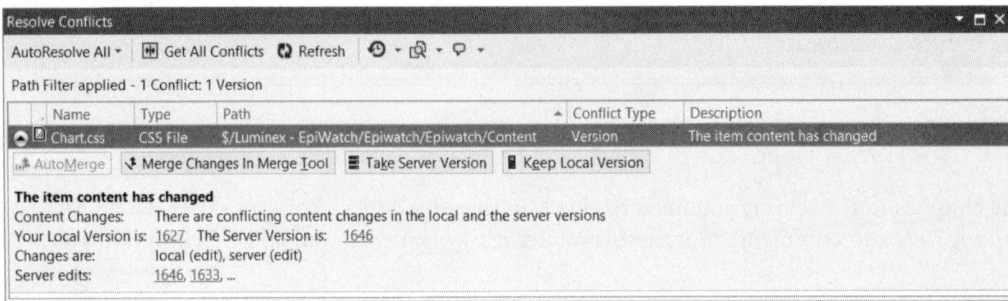

FIGURE 57-14

When the changes are made in different parts of the file (for example, two different methods), VS can automatically resolve changes, but if changes are made in the same line, you must either choose a version or manually merge both files using the Merge Changes tool.

> **NOTE** *Visual Studio can compare text to determine if changes overlap, but this does not guarantee the resulting file can compile or behave as expected. This option is useful but you must use it with caution. Over time, you will have more confidence in choosing which files to auto-merge to save time and which are worth a quick look just to be sure.*

With the Merge Changes tool (Figure 57-15), you have a view of "their" version (that is, the server version), your version, and a merged version. You can navigate easily between changes and conflicts. For conflicts, you can manually edit the offending lines or select a version to keep. When all conflicts are resolved, you can accept the changes, keep the new file as your current version, and proceed to check in.

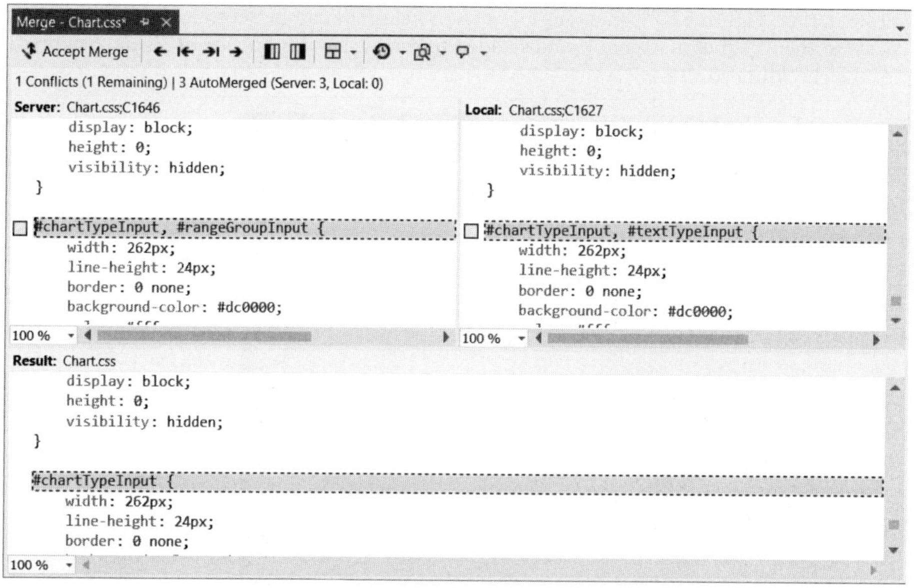

Merge - Chart.css*

Accept Merge

1 Conflicts (1 Remaining) | 3 AutoMerged (Server: 3, Local: 0)

Server: Chart.css;C1646

```
    display: block;
    height: 0;
    visibility: hidden;
}

#chartTypeInput, #rangeGroupInput {
    width: 262px;
    line-height: 24px;
    border: 0 none;
    background-color: #dc0000;
```

Local: Chart.css;C1627

```
    display: block;
    height: 0;
    visibility: hidden;
}

#chartTypeInput, #textTypeInput {
    width: 262px;
    line-height: 24px;
    border: 0 none;
    background-color: #dc0000;
```

Result: Chart.css

```
    display: block;
    height: 0;
    visibility: hidden;
}

#chartTypeInput {
    width: 262px;
    line-height: 24px;
    border: 0 none;
```

FIGURE 57-15

> **NOTE** *After resolving conflicts, you should run the automated tests again to ensure there are no breaking changes. As you can see in the "Team Foundation Build" section, this test can be run automatically in the server before each check-in, but it's best to get the feedback as early as possible.*

Working Offline

Team Foundation Server uses HTTP and web services and can work perfectly through the Internet to allow for collaboration of distributed teams. However, if you don't have an available connection, VS enables you to work offline when you try to open a bound project.

All files under Source Control are read-only. When you save a file, you will be warned and should simply choose Overwrite. When the connection with TFS can be reestablished, you can select to go online from Solution Explorer or by right-clicking the solution. VS looks for files in the solution without the read-only attribute; if those are not in Source Control, it adds them, and if they exist it checks them out.

Alternatively (and supported only in TFS 2012), you can convert your workspaces to be a local one. This addresses a common complaint leveled at the server focus of TFS 2010.Specifically, all the TFS 2010 operations require a connection to the server. There are times when this can cause your local and server versions of the source code to be out of sync — not to mention performance issues if you frequently work with large changesets.

In TFS 2012, you can create local workspaces. If you refer back to the right side of Figure 57-4, you'll notice an option to convert your workspace to a local version. For an existing workspace, you'll can also change the location from Server to Local. The dialog to do this is buried deep in the menu hierarchy of File ➪ Source Control ➪ Advanced ➪ Workspaces. Then edit your current workspace and click the Advanced button. The resulting dialog (Figure 57-16) includes a Location field that can be set to Local. This not only enables offline access to the files, but also enables files added to the file system outside of Visual Studio to be detected as part of the check-in process.

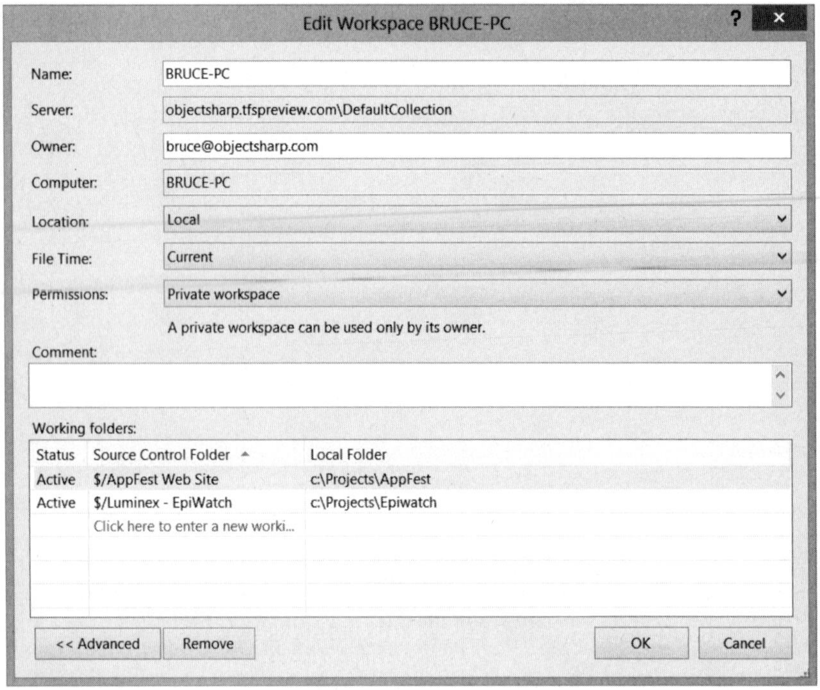

FIGURE 57-16

Label

Labeling a specific version allows you to refer to it easily. To create a label simply right-click a folder in Source Control Explorer that you want to mark, select Advanced ➪ Apply Label, and write a Name and optionally a Comment (Figure 57-17). Similarly, you can get to a specific version using the label. The perfect use for this is to release a version.

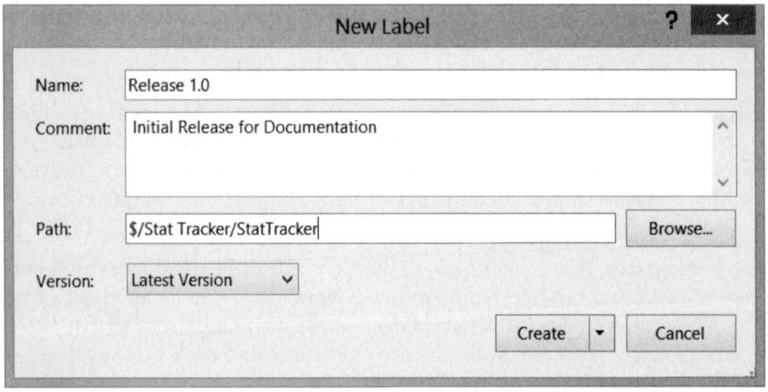

FIGURE 57-17

To get a labeled version, right-click a file or folder in Source Control Explorer, and select Advanced ➪ Get Specific Version from the context menu. On the Type combo box in the Get window (Figure 57-18) select Label. You can search for labels by name, team project, and owner. When you find the label, to be sure you get the exact labeled version, you will probably choose to overwrite writable files.

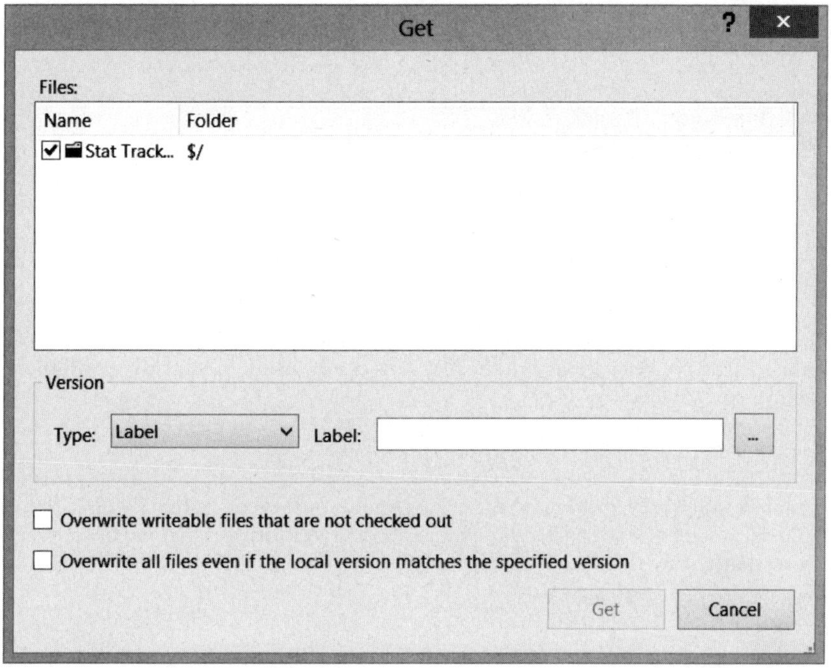

FIGURE 57-18

> **NOTE** *You should undo, shelve, or check in any pending changes before getting a specific version to separate the latest changes in your workspace from the labeled version.*

If you want to get the version in a different location, you can create a branch. You'll see this in the "Branch" section later in the chapter.

History

Every change you make is persisted in the server (or locally) and you can get to any specific version of a file; a great way to do it is through the History window. Simply right-click a file in Source Control or Solution Explorer, and select View History. From there you can see how a file has evolved over time (Figure 57-19). When you right-click any version, you can compare it to your version, open it, and view details of the changeset (including the comments and related work items).

History - LinesForm.cs

Source location: C:\Projects\Call Center\CallCenterModule\LinesForm.cs

Changesets   Labels

Changeset	Change	User	Date	Path	Comment
48	edit	bruce@objectsharp.com	8/12/2012 1:13:21 PM	$/OnSp...	
47	edit	bruce@objectsharp.com	8/4/2012 10:17:02 AM	$/OnSp...	Implement recall functionalit
43	edit	bruce@objectsharp.com	6/30/2012 11:55:16 AM	$/OnSp...	Updated the Action stored p
41	edit	bruce@objectsharp.com	6/9/2012 11:14:03 PM	$/OnSp...	
40	edit	bruce@objectsharp.com	5/12/2012 3:13:51 PM	$/OnSp...	Corrected the posting of the
37	edit	bruce@objectsharp.com	4/14/2012 2:40:34 PM	$/OnSp...	Arranged for the On This Cal

FIGURE 57-19

Toward the top of Figure 57-19 is a tab to switch between Changesets and Labels. Switching to Labels view displays a list of all the labels that have been applied to the file. This can be useful to quickly see all the changes made between two versions.

Annotate

The *annotate* command enables you to see who edited each line of code and when (Figure 57-20). From each of the changes made, you can get to each particular changeset to see details, get that particular version, compare it to its previous version, locate the file in the History window, or annotate from that version.

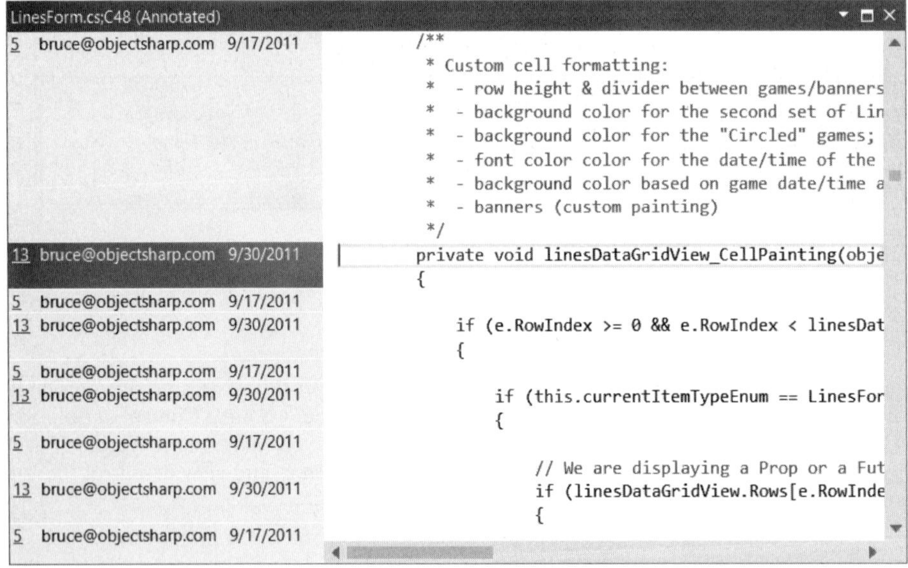

FIGURE 57-20

Shelve

When you check in a file, that change is automatically available to others. Sometimes you need to persist your changes without affecting everyone — a scenario that can happen when you need to work from another computer and want to upload your changes and send them somewhere else, or when you are in the middle of something and are assigned a new task.

Shelving persists your changes in the server. You can associate a *shelveset* to work items and add comments and check-in notes, much as you would when checking in. You can optionally evaluate check-in policies before shelving and choose to undo local changes after the shelve is done. The latter is useful when you need to work on some other work item without the shelved changes interfering with what you are doing. Shelving changes is also useful if you move to another machine and don't want to make the same change in both places. To get to the changes, you can *unshelve* your shelveset, and your files will be checked out again.

Each shelveset is a read-only snapshot of the files at the time when it was created. Because of this, each shelveset is not versioned, and if you save a new shelveset with the same name as an existing one, it simply overwrites it. This can be extremely handy for common tasks such as Work in Progress or For Review.

> **NOTE** *Shelvesets are uniquely identified by a combination of their name and the name of the user who created them, so even if you use the same naming scheme for your shelvesets as another team member, you cannot overwrite each other's work.*

Although the default behavior is for you to see the shelvesets that you have created, you can see the shelvesets that other people have created and even retrieve them, which can be useful if you need a colleague to review some code before it is checked in or to hand a task off to someone when it is not in a state that is ready to be checked in.

There is an option hidden behind the Details when unshelving a shelveset to Preserve Shelveset on Server. If you uncheck this option the shelveset is deleted from the server as you retrieve it. You can also delete shelvesets without retrieving them from the Unshelve dialog. It is a good idea to clean out shelvesets regularly that you don't need anymore to make it easier for you to find the ones you actually use.

Branch

A *branch*, in source control terms, is a parallel version of your code. This is useful for different purposes. Here are a couple of examples:

- **Hot fixes or bugs for stable versions while working on new ones:** When you release 1.0 you label all your source code and start working on 2.0. Then a critical bug is found but version 2.0 is months away from being ready. You can branch from version 1.0. (You can get to this version using the label.) Then you can fix the bug in the new branch and release version 1.1. Later you can merge the change made and integrate it with the main branch.
- **Creating a branch from the latest version to do a big refactoring or a change you are not sure will work and thus don't want to affect the main branch:** If it works you can merge it with the main branch, and if it doesn't you can simply delete it.

You must choose wisely what branching strategy is better for your organization, type of product, and process, or when you could substitute by simply labeling a version or shelving a change. Abuse of branching can exponentially complicate source-code management. Codeplex hosts branching guidance that provides additional scenarios (`http://www.codeplex.com/TFSBranchingGuideII`).

To create a new branch, right-click the folder you want to branch from, and select Branching and Merging ➪ Branch. You will be asked which version you want to branch from and where the branch should be saved in the source control repository.

> **NOTE** *Branches have become first-class features in TFS, so the tools can take full advantage of them. You can mark an existing folder as a branch by supplying the required meta data, which enables branches from previous versions to take advantage of this as well.*

After you have a few branches, you can use the Branch Visualization (Figure 57-21) tool to see the hierarchy of your branches by selecting View Hierarchy from the Branching and Merging drop-down in the Source Control Explorer. You can initiate merges from this tool by dragging from one branch to a valid target branch.

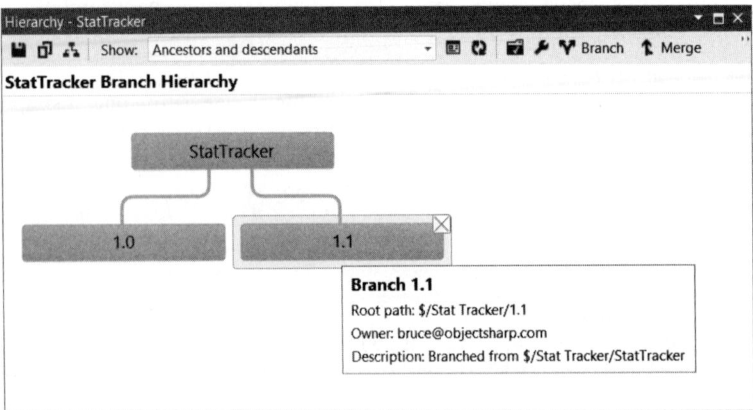

FIGURE 57-21

Another useful tool in TFS is Changeset Tracking, which enables you to see where the changes in a particular changeset have come from. It has two views: Timeline Tracking (which is shown in Figure 57-22) and Hierarchy Tracking, which shows the hierarchy between the branches in a clearer fashion. Just as with the Branch Visualization view, you can initiate a merge by dragging a changeset from one branch to another.

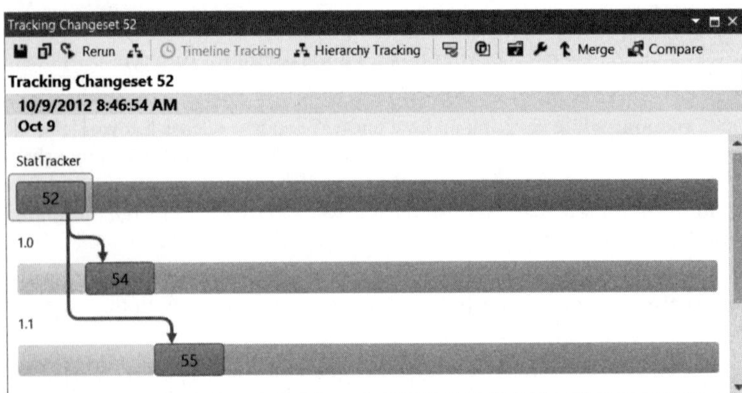

FIGURE 57-22

Merge

If you fix a bug or implement a feature in one branch, it would be advantageous to apply that same changeset to other branches. This is what the *merge* operation does. To begin a merge, right-click the folder or file you want to merge, and select Branching and Merging ➪ Merge. After you select a source and destination for the merge, you are presented with a list of changesets that can be applied. Select the changesets that you want, and click Finish. If there are any conflicts, you have the opportunity to fix them.

TEAM FOUNDATION BUILD

Team Foundation Build is a tool, part of TFS, and its responsibility is to get the latest version from source control to a local workspace, build the projects as configured, run tests, do other tasks, and finally report the results and leave the output in a shared folder. Each machine that can build a project for you is called a *build agent*. TFS 2012, like TFS 2010, also includes the concept of a *build controller*, which is responsible for coordinating the activities of several build agents. The information that each build agent needs to do its job is called a *build definition*.

To create a new build definition, click the Builds link in Team Explorer, and select New Build Definition. In the General tab you need to write the build name and optionally a description.

By default the build must be manually queued, but in the Trigger tab you can modify this behavior. You have five options, as shown in Figure 57-23. An important option to note is the Gated Check-In option. When you have build definitions triggered this way, check-ins do not necessarily go straight into source control. Instead they are shelved (you will be prompted about this) and built by a build agent first. If the build succeeds, the shelveset is saved into the source control repository. If it does not, you are notified, and it is up to you to retrieve the shelveset, make any required changes, and check it in again. Using this type of build definition prevents the situation in which the contents of the source control repository do not compile, which can significantly impact the rest of the team.

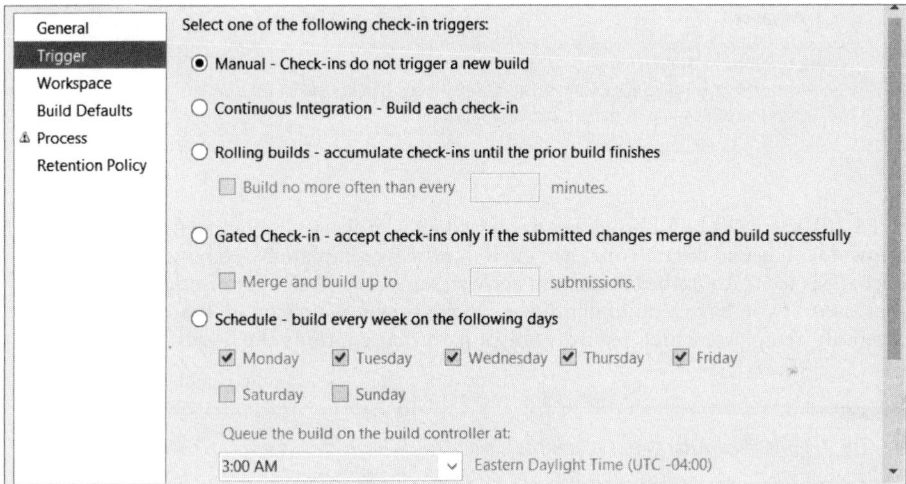

FIGURE 57-23

Depending on how big your project is, how long it takes to build and run the tests, and how often the team checks in, this option may cause some overhead. The third option, Rolling Builds, can definitely help alleviate the workload, but it's better to wait until you find you need it.

Configuring the workspace will be used in complex scenarios in which you have dependencies between team projects, so the defaults in that tab might be enough. In the build defaults page, you can choose a build controller and a shared folder to drop the output into. These will be used for triggered builds, but for manual builds this can be overridden.

The Process tab, shown in Figure 57-24, enables you to configure the build process. Here you must select at least one project or solution and a configuration (such as `x86|Debug` or `AnyCPU|Release`). The rest of the values are optional. You can use them to specify the location of any automated test assemblies, whether or not to perform code analysis, whether or not the build agent should publish the project symbols anywhere, how to format the build number, and more.

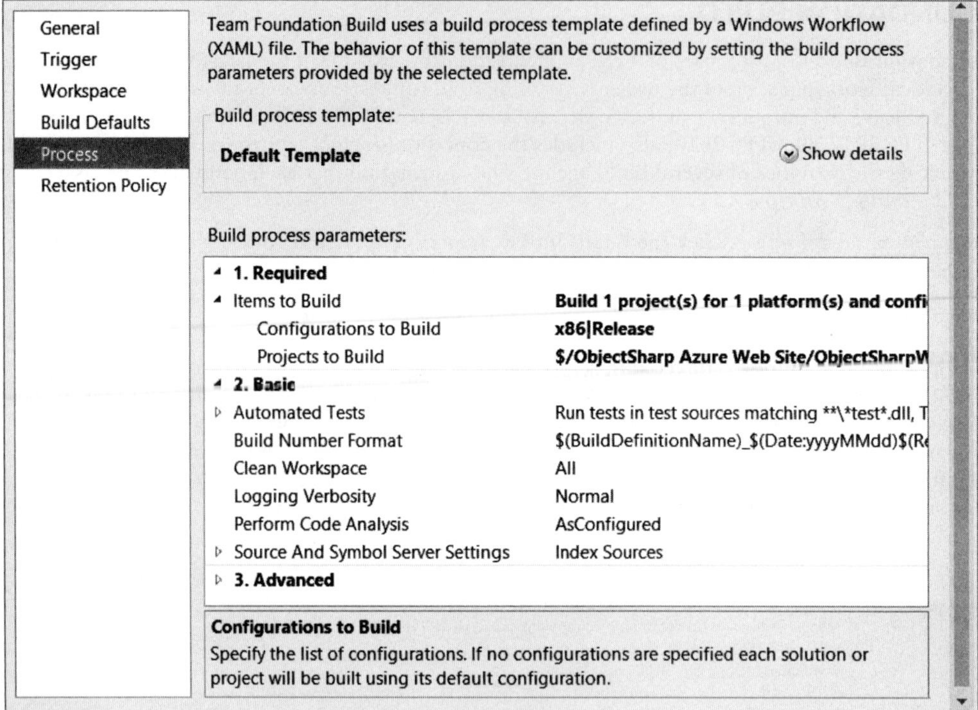

FIGURE 57-24

TFS 2012 (and TFS 2010 as well) build processes are based on a process template defined with Windows Workflow 4.0. You can create your own custom process template by copying the default one and making changes to it. A number of custom activities are related to Team Build, and you can always create your own. If you have a build definition from a previous version of Team Build, you should use the Upgrade Template, which requires only a path that contains the legacy `TfsBuild.proj` file.

> **NOTE** *By default the build process templates are located in the* `$/TeamProjectName/BuildProcessTemplates` *folder in the source control repository.*

The retention policy enables you to choose how many of the builds left in the shared folder are kept before some are deleted. It is recommended to use the Keep 10 Latest option, at least for successful builds, until you need to reduce the number of files kept. There are two sets of settings. The ones under Private relate to builds that form a part of a gated check-in and are not as important to keep.

To start a build manually, you can click the Builds node in the Team Explorer, and select Actions ➪ Queue New Build. After the build is queued, you can open it by double-clicking it in the My Builds list. This opens the Build Report (shown in Figure 57-25), which includes information on current activity, previous build statuses and durations, and provides links to a number of other areas and activities related to this build.

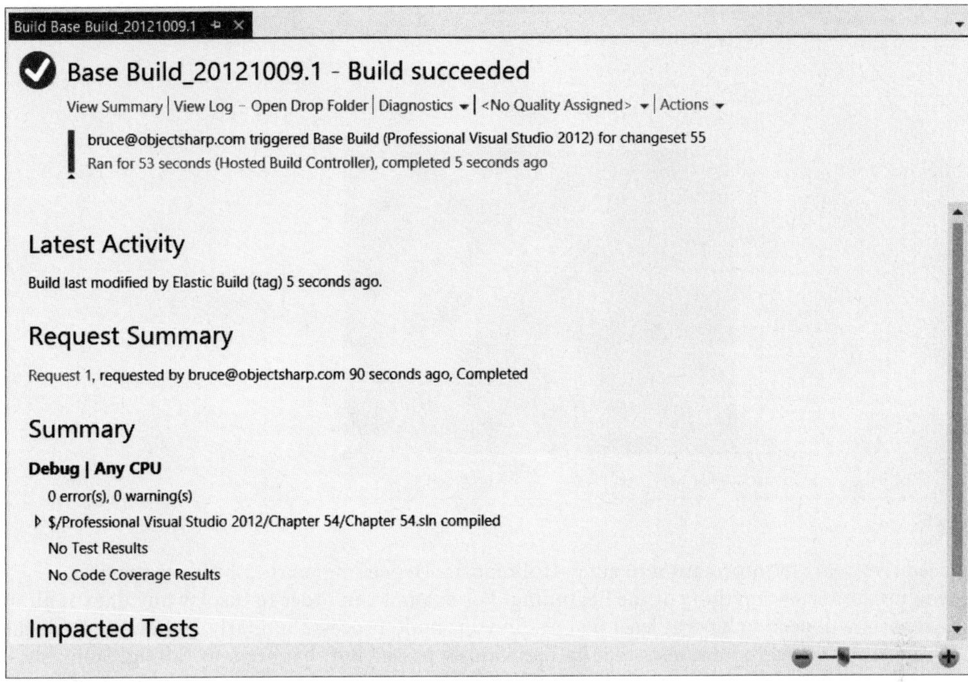

FIGURE 57-25

> **NOTE** *If you want to be notified of build events while you work, a Build Notifications system tray application is installed with Team Explorer. When configured, this application adjusts its icon to indicate that the builds are broken, building, or successfully built.*

REPORTING AND BUSINESS INTELLIGENCE

TFS uses Report Server, which is part of Microsoft SQL Server, to provide useful information for project managers, customers, and developers. Reports can be accessed directly from Team Explorer, the reports site (`http://mytfs/reports/`), SharePoint, or Web Access, or they can be configured as a subscription from the Reports site to be left in a Windows file share or sent through e-mail.

The great benefit these have is that developers can focus on their work instead of manually filling out reports. All the information is collected during their daily work, checking out and checking in code, fixing bugs, and relating what they do to work items. This way project managers and stakeholders can get to the information they need from the reports TFS provides.

Each process template provides its own set of reports. The CMMI version provides three additional reports and templates, such as Scrum for Team System from Conchango, and has reports appropriate for the Scrum methodology, such as Delta Report and Burndown Charts. Here, we will focus on MSF for Agile Development.

Some of the reports included are Burndown and Burn Rate, Stories Progress, Build Success over Time, Build Quality Indicators, Test Case Readiness, Test Plan Progress, Bug Status, Bug Trends, and Reactivations. Figure 57-26 shows how the work has been resolved over a couple of years and how much work is left. In the report you can filter by dates, work item type, iteration, and area. You can export to XML, CSV, TIFF, PDFW, the web, and Excel.

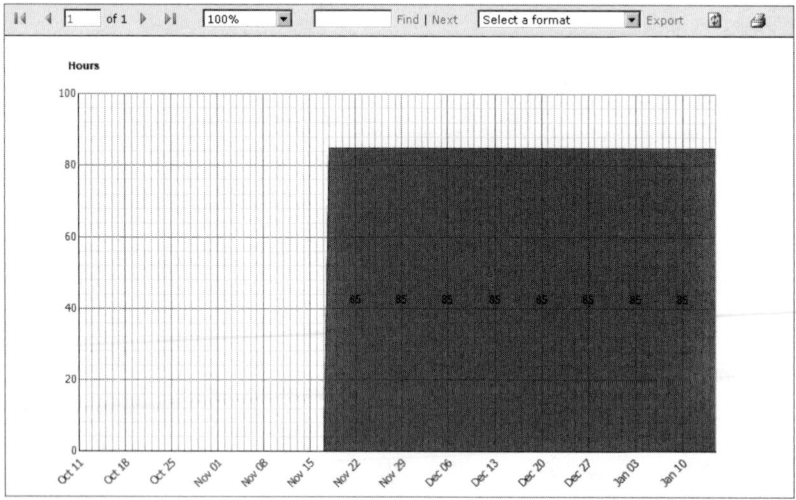

FIGURE 57-26

You don't need two years of information to get useful reports. Depending on the nature of the data displayed, you might not see anything at the beginning. For example, in order to display any data at all, the Test Failing reports will need to have at least one test in your build process. Similarly, to have data for the Regressions report, you need to have tests that had previously passed but that are now failing. Similarly, the Scenarios Details report needs you to register at least a Scenario Work Item. After a couple iterations of working with TFS, you will have a lot of useful metrics for free.

> **NOTE** *Microsoft has been clear that you should not access the data in the TFS databases directly but should instead use the reports and tools provided. In TFS 2012 (and in TFS 2010), there are Data Warehouse Views, which have been added over the tables in each TFS database. There is some guarantee that these views will not change moving forward, and they have been designed so that you can create your own reports.*

TEAM PORTAL

Team Foundation uses SharePoint to create a portal for each team project. It has all the benefits of SharePoint but is customized for each process template. The home in each team portal includes the most important reports, latest announcements, and useful links. TFS also includes the ability to create custom dashboards, which can be for specific users or for everyone on the project. To navigate to the project portal, select Web Access in the Team Explorer.

Documents

Depending on the process template, certain documents will be included as templates. For example, MSF for Agile Software Development includes Word documents to create personas and scenarios.

Process Guidance

Inside SharePoint are documents that define the process that your project adheres to. This guidance is available to all developers on the team.

SharePoint Lists

You can have picture libraries, discussion boards, surveys, announcements, links, events, contacts, and custom lists. This can help improve team collaboration.

Dashboards

Dashboards are SharePoint Web Part pages that have been preconfigured with useful Web Parts to give you an overview of a project's status. The MSF for Agile process template defines two dashboards out of the box, including My Dashboard (Figure 57-27), which contains lists of Tasks, Bugs, and Test Cases that are assigned to you; and Project Dashboard, which contains metrics and information about the progress of the entire team. If you are using Visual Studio Scrum 2.0, there are also to out-of-the-box dashboards. And they are also for an individual (My Dashboard) and a project (Project Dashboard). The difference is the information that is provided. The Scrum project dashboard includes burn-down rates and velocity charts. The individual dashboard includes lists of the work items that are assigned to you (Tasks, Bugs, Impediments). For both project templates, using the SharePoint UI, you can copy an existing dashboard and make changes to the web parts displayed.

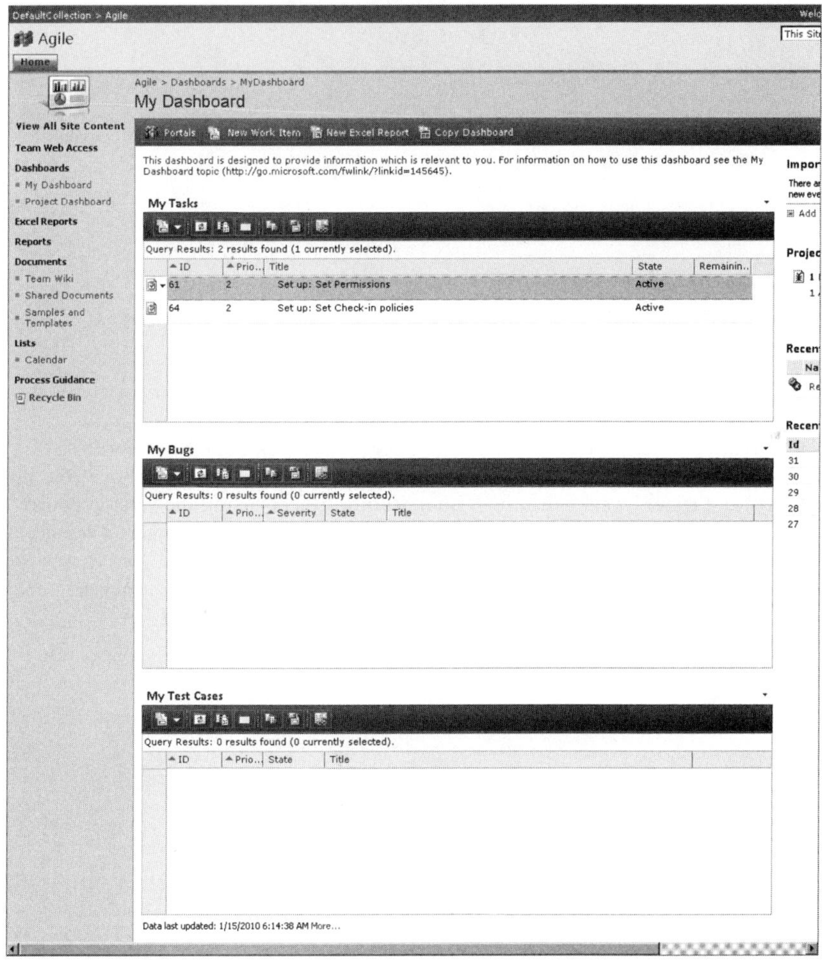

FIGURE 57-27

WEB ACCESS

The Web Access tool (previously known as Team System Web Access in Visual Studio 2010) provides a web interface to TFS that enables you to do everything you can do from VS but in a web interface (Figure 57-28). You can create and modify work items as well as work item queries, see the reports and documents, and initiate and monitor builds. The only area with limited functionality is Source Control. You can see history and changeset details, but you can't check out/check in documents due to the web client nature.

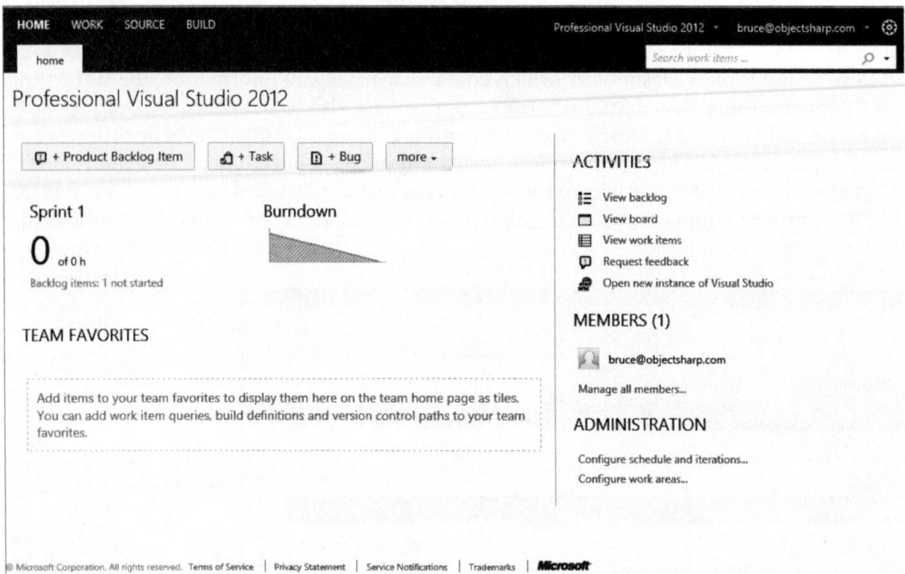

FIGURE 57-28

SUMMARY

In this chapter, you saw how Team Foundation Server can help you get the work done by integrating the different roles involved. The project managers file and monitor work items in either Excel or Project, whereas architects, developers, and testers work with the Visual Studio Projects using the version control features, easily relating changes to their assigned work items. Optionally, each change triggers a team build that ensures the quality standards are met. TFS monitors everything and generates metrics for reports that can be viewed through the different interfaces such as Visual Studio, Team Portal, and Web Access.

INDEX

A

E

F

M

N

O

P

S

T

U

V

W

X

Z